D0388556

EDUCATION

"Anyone who would attempt the task of felling a virgin forest with a pen knife would probably feel the same paralysis of despair that the reformer feels when confronted with existing school systems." —Ellen Key,
The Century of the Child, 1909

SEXISM

"When my public activities are reported it is very annoying to read how I looked, if I smiled, if a particular reporter liked my hairstyle."
—Vijaya Lakshmi Pandit,
former President of the UN General Assembly,
The Glasgow Scotsman, 1955

LOVE

"Do you want me to tell you something really subversive? Love *is* everything it's cracked up to be. That's why people are so cynical about it." —Erica Jong,
How to Save Your Own Life, 1977

GOSSIP

"Gossip, like poetry and fiction, penetrates to the truth of things." —Patricia Meyer Spacks,
Hudson Review, 1982

ELAINE PARTNOW is the author of *The Quotable Woman: From Eve to 1799* and *The Quotable Woman: 1800-1981*. In addition to her work on this series, she is a performing artist and playwright with more than twenty-five years' experience on stage and in film. She is the founder of the Living History Institute, which brings "performing scholars" to schools. Her one-woman show, "Hear Us Roar: A Woman's Connection," has been performed across the United States, as well as in Guadalajara, Mexico, and Wuxi, China. Ms. Partnow lives in Seattle, Washington.

Also by Elaine Partnow

The Quotable Woman, 1800–1981
The Quotable Woman, Eve–1799
Breaking the Age Barrier
Photographic Artists and Innovators, with Turner Browne

Plays

Hear Us Roar, A Woman's Connection
Hispanic Women Speak

THE NEW QUOTABLE WOMAN

*The Definitive Treasury of
Notable Words by Women
from Eve to the Present*

Compiled and Edited by
Elaine Partnow

A MERIDIAN BOOK

MERIDIAN
Published by the Penguin Group
Penguin Books USA Inc., 375 Hudson Street, New York, New York 10014, U.S.A.
Penguin Books Ltd, 27 Wrights Lane, London W8 5TZ, England
Penguin Books Australia Ltd, Ringwood, Victoria, Australia
Penguin Books Canada Ltd, 10 Alcorn Avenue, Toronto, Ontario, Canada M4V 3B2
Penguin Books (N.Z.) Ltd, 182–190 Wairau Road, Auckland 10, New Zealand

Penguin Books Ltd, Registered Offices: Harmondsworth, Middlesex, England

Published by Meridian, an imprint of New American Library,
a division of Penguin Books USA Inc. This is an authorized reprint
of a hardcover edition published by Facts on File, Inc.

First Meridian Printing, September, 1993
10 9 8 7 6 5 4 3

This is a completely revised edition of *The Quotable Woman: From Eve to 1799* and
The Quotable Woman 1800–1981.

Ⓜ REGISTERED TRADEMARK—MARCA REGISTRADA

LIBRARY OF CONGRESS CATALOGING-IN-PUBLICATION DATA
The New quotable woman / compiled and edited by Elaine Partnow—
  The Definitive Treasury of Notable Words by Women from Eve to the Present.
      p.   cm.
  Rev. combined ed. of: The quotable woman, from Eve to 1799 and The
quotable woman, 1880–1981.
  Originally published: New York: Facts on File, 1992.
  Includes index.
  ISBN 0-452-01099-3
  1. Women—Quotations.   2. Quotations, English.   I. Partnow,
Elaine.   II. Quotable woman, from Eve to 1799.   III. Quotable woman,
1880–1981.
PN6081.5.N49   1993
082′.082—dc20   93–17685
                                                    CIP

Printed in the United States of America

to my sister,
Judith Partnow Hyman,
whose constant faith and support
have buoyed and bolstered me.
Thanks, Sis.

I feel we are like the children of Israel who,
having wandered in the wilderness of prejudice
and ridicule for forty years, feel a peculiar
tenderness for the young women on whose shoulders
we are about to leave our burdens.
The true woman is as yet a dream of the future.
                    —Elizabeth Cady Stanton

                    I would venture to guess that Anon,
                    who wrote so many poems without
                    signing them, was often a woman.
                              —Virginia Woolf

CONTENTS

PREFACE

The Quotable Woman first popped into my head like a holographic image one dark and dreary night: I saw the book in its entirety—the cover, the title, the indexes, even the layout of the pages. It was a flash of inspiration that altered the course of my life.

I didn't know how to begin. The longest paper I'd ever written was a dissertation for English Lit at UCLA. So I bought some 5x8 index cards, pulled out Volume A of the 1956 *World Book Encyclopedia* that my parents had purchased for me and my sisters the year I graduated junior high, and began looking for entries on women, little knowing it was to become my main occupation during the next sixteen years.

The *World Book* proved neither very deep nor very wide in the world of women, but I'd gotten my feet wet. I rolled up my trouser legs and trudged on downstream. It was a lonely journey. Having been an actor for seventeen years, I was used to swimming in schools, not wading alone. But within a year I'd amassed a manuscript of five hundred pages: enough, I figured, for an audition.

When I stumbled across a Los Angeles publishing house called Wollstonecraft, I knew I'd found an angel. My research had taught me that Mary Wollstonecraft,[1] author of *A Vindication of the Rights of Women,* was the great grandmother of modern-day feminism. The angel's name was Annette Welles, and before I could finish my song-and-dance the publishing house executive and the actor had a book contract.

During the next three years I often felt I was drowning in a sea of women's words. As fate would have it, it wasn't me that drowned, but Wollstonecraft, sunk by financial problems. Within two weeks I found Stan Corwin, who took on *TQW* under his own imprint. Later he hired Georgia Griggs, who'd been editor-in-chief at Wollstonecraft, to work side-by-side with me for six months preparatory to typesetting *TQW* for Corwin; she was a true mentor to me. These three helped me find my sea legs and saved me from going under.

In the last year of pre-production there was so much to do I couldn't handle it all. Suddenly I found myself with a part-time staff, all women, all personal friends— Janine Watson, actors Hazel Medina and Krista Michaels, artist Paula Gray. On Fridays I'd serve us lunch in the living room, as my big Jacobean dining table had been commandeered by *TQW*. What a time we had!

How different were the following years when I created the prequel in a shed in

---

[1] All women quoted can be found in the Biography Index and each quotation cited can be found under the contributor's entry in the Quotations Section. Therefore, I have deliberately chosen to forsake footnotes of contributor quotations in the Preface and Introduction.

the woods in the swamps of Louisiana. The 8x22 travel trailer my husband and I had moved into on our five acres of wooded land wasn't big enough to house my research, so we put together a metal shed frame of 10,000 screws (without aid of electricity!), closeted it in plywood and a corrugated plastic pitched roof ("it shed a lovely light") and moved in "baby." Summertime humidity was so great, my books had to be wiped down with Lysol every other week to save them from mildew; winters were so cold, I had to wear army surplus gloves with the fingers cut off so my hands would be supple enough to type (I was still using 5x8 index cards). There were stories about us at IBM service repair headquarters in Baton Rouge: we were known as that odd couple who typed in a tent. It was quite a sight to see the crewcut service man drive down our bumpy dirt road, hand carved out of the woods, and pop out with his briefcase, business suit and blue tie.

> The exigencies of country life consumed huge quantities of time. My work slowed; deadlines were extended. My paperwork was soiled by the hens, walked on by the cats, drooled on by the dogs and eaten by the cockroaches. I thought of our [American] foremothers, who had to tolerate and overcome greater hardships than I was facing, and how they'd managed, despite their overwhelming load of tasks, to write journals, letters, books and poems. How strong the impulse to communicate one's own experience of the world with others.[2]

After two years in the woods, the cockroaches and earwigs won: we moved to New Orleans. There I completed preparation of the manuscript and—*after* it was all done— I got my first computer!

My one colleague during this time was Claudia Alexander, a professor of English at Southeastern Louisiana University, who agreed to work as assistant editor. She made the initial selection of contributors and quotations from the Renaissance, her specialty, and did a tremendous amount of research on the Biographical Index. Fluent in Italian, Claudia chose to translate several poems and passages that otherwise could not have been included. What a godsend!

Upon completion of that second volume I began a brand-new career in the field of arts-in-education. For years I'd dreamed of a way to connect the world of women in history to the world I knew—acting. The women I was discovering inspired me to speak in my own voice. I began to create portraits, living-history portraits, of those who had especially moved me and to put them together as interactive theater pieces: *Hispanic Women Speak, Great American Women, A Visit With Emily Dickinson*. I brought the performances to classrooms and children's organizations in New Hampshire, Louisiana, California, Texas, Oregon, Washington—even Wuxi, China! I wrote a full-length work, *Hear Us Roar: A Woman's Connection*, in which *I* was one of

---

[2] From the Preface of *The Quotable Woman: Eve–1799*.

the major characters, too. These works changed me—who and what I am and what I do.

There came a time in my early years as a researcher when I thought this new river I was rowing, this Woman's River, meant that the other—the Theater River—had run dry. I have now come to understand the old African proverb "No matter how full it is, the river must grow."

***

As I labor over this major revision and expansion of *TQW*, I again ask myself, "What's the point of all this? Why am I doing this work?" Poet Leonora Speyer says when she gives talks she likes to call upon her "radiant cloud of witnesses to back [her] up, saying the thing [she] would say, and saying it so much more eloquently."

The feminist anthologist Robin Morgan has written that "only she who attempts the absurd can achieve the impossible." I have known almost from the beginning that this work could never be finished. Yet I kept reading, looking, searching, sifting, classifying. I learned to grow new arms and eyes and hands, new receptors. My office filled up with boxes of magazine clippings and notes, my shelves spilled over with found second-hand books; I ravaged the libraries of friends and relatives. I upgraded my computer to a hard disk. The collection kept growing and the unwieldiness of the 3,000+-page manuscript demanded some creative storage. So my "baby" lay cradled, page after reworked page, in the five pull-out storage bins of the old yellow changing table my sister Susan had used to clean, clothe and caress her two babies, Jessica and Tyler.

The absurdity of my goal was unquestionable—but I like to think that I have at least approached the impossible with the material I've gathered here. This time around, special effort went into seeking out women from other cultures around the world, as well as subcultures in my own country: the Native American, the Mexican-American, the African-American. It was rewarding to be able to include a number of contemporary world leaders. Indira Gandhi and Golda Meir are now joined by Benizir Bhutto, Corazon Aquino, Margaret Thatcher, Gro Bruntland, Violeta Chamorro and others.

In the years since I first became the author of *TQW* many fingers have been pointed at me for creating a sexist work. "Why the separatism? Aren't you being just as sexist as you accuse others of having been in the introduction to your book?"

In that first introduction I created a chart illustrating the paucity of women represented in the classic books of quotations. Of the 2,000 contributors in the fourteenth edition of Bartlett's *Familiar Quotations*, only 7.5% of the contributors were women, and only one-half of one percent of all the quotations cited were penned by them. The Oxford *Book of Quotations* bettered those percentages—barely: 8.5% women, 1% quotations by women. And so it was with many others. There have been some dramatic changes in newer editions, but the representation is still shameful. And, although two or three other collections of women's quotations have appeared since *TQW* first came out, none have approached it for sheer volume or detail of resources.

I don't think the attempt to balance the scales is sexist. When the indispensable classic reference works of our society have evolved to an egalitarian status, I will gladly go coed in my own work. As Shulamith Firestone remarks in *The Dialectic of Sex:* "Perhaps it is true that a presence of only the female side of things . . . is limited. But . . . is it any more limited than the prevailing male view of things, which—when not taken as absolute truth—is at least seen as 'serious,' relevant and important."

It is deplorable that, just as so many superior women poets and authors were considered inferior by the patriarchy of 17th-century literary criticism, there still exists an "unconscious bias in favor of men in their writings. . . . We must challenge the critics—including some of the female critics—to examine [that] bias."[3] Yet it is still men who control the worlds of publishing and media, still men who comprise the bulk of academe. The possibility for the disregard, if not disappearance, of so many talented women of our own day remains uncomfortably distinct. When we reach across the centuries to unearth these women, when we experience the connections between all of us, they live again—and our lives are renewed.

***

My husband heard me singing "I've Got You Under My Skin" while working at my computer one morning. I was classifying a quotation under "heart, loving." "Hey, you can't be singing while you're working," he chided. But sing I did. And laughed, and cried, and lit up, and became enraged. Always it was the connections to my own life that energized me, pushed me through the thirty months of often tedious research and organization of this completely revised and expanded edition of *TQW*. "This eagerness to seek hidden but necessary connections," Victoria Ocampo intoned, "connections that revealed a close relationship between the world where I was born in the flesh and the other worlds where I was reborn, has been the enterprise of my whole life."

Quotation-plucking may be an odd and narrow avocation, but it is one to which I have become addicted. The flush of inspiration that washes over me each time a connection is made is electric. I want more. So I've kept on searching, plucking— and singing—over sixteen years.

I am keenly mindful of the many inaccuracies, oversights and exclusions that are inevitable in a work of this size. And while I will continue to hone and expand the work for future editions (target: 2000), I can only beg the reader's indulgence if she or he finds someone or some work overlooked.

---

[3] Betsko, Kathleen and Koenig, Rachel, *Interviews with Contemporary Women Playwrights*, 1987.

Ironically, with this present work, I have had less assistance than with each prior edition of *TQW*. Perhaps it is a mark of my growing expertise; as likely it reflects the tightening of the economy. However, my heart still warms with gratitude toward those who lent their support, both moral and financial, and those who labored on the earlier editions and whose input lives on in these pages. Annette Welles, whom I spoke of earlier, died last year, but her spirit lives on in these pages. In addition to others I already mentioned: my sisters Susan Partnow and Judith Hyman; my folks, Al and Sylvia Partnow; my friends Pat Jolly, the late Arthur Charbonnet, Bob Chieger; past editors Marcy Posner, Beth Sue Rose, Eleanor Wedge, Gerard Helferich, Robert B. Hutchins; Catherine Plantego, Carlo de Maio, Michael Fanning and Anna Balakian; and current editor Gary Krebs.

I received encouragement, advice and some labor on the current volume from Maureen Kearns, Amanda Weintraub, Shannon Harvey, Susan Talbot, Tamu Gray, Lisa Lynch, my niece Lesley Hyman, Michele Kort, Helene Lopez and Deb Brody, my first editor at Facts On File. My agent, Faith Hamlin of Sanford Greenberger, has been a marvel of humor, understanding and generosity of spirit. Most of all I thank my husband, Turner Browne. Not only has his faith in me and the work that I do been constant over the years, but his willingness to take over my share of domestic chores as deadline pressures began to sap my time and strength has, in very practical terms, made it possible for me to produce this work.

As I continue to paddle my way down this mighty Woman's River I realize, at last, what it is I am trying to do. I am trying to make a wave. A wave filled with particles. The particles of our history. Women's history. Each is as unique as it is common. Each is the same, but different. Together they make a wave. Just one. But one that invites the diver to swim beyond.

—Elaine Partnow
Seattle

INTRODUCTION

The first *Quotable Woman,* published in 1977, covered women born from 1800 on. It was painful to leave out such of my "sheroes" as Jane Austen (1799) and Sojourner Truth (1797). I was less frustrated after I'd completed the prequel, published in 1985, having now reached all the way back to Eve. Still, I longed to see the entire breadth of work in a single volume. Eighteen years after having begun what has become a life's work I can at last enjoy the fruit of that dream. This new edition covers over 4,000 years of women in history, with more than 2500 women, 15,000 quotations and four indexes.[4] (Perhaps in the year 2000 I will create yet another edition with 5,000 women and 25,000 quotations!)

The first order of the day in compiling this major revision was to edit the earlier editions. I cut out about one-third of those quotations, updated material on 150 or so of the more contemporary women, and added 450 new contributors. More importantly, I supplemented the Quotations Section with about 2,000 new quotations. In a review of the Quotations Section I inserted numerous new footnotes. The Biographical Index was brought up-to-date and the Subject Index underwent major changes and refinements. Two new indexes—the Occupation Index and the Ethnicity and Nationality Index—were created.

Criteria

On what basis did I cut out previous material? I've attempted to jettison the less relevant stuff of the sixties and seventies, timely in its day, but have added the stuff of the eighties and nineties. While each new edition has improved the scope, depth and accuracy of the book, the attempt to keep current cannot help but leave some jetsam. No matter how conscientious the attempt at objectivity, the present moment does influence the compiler—in both the larger world and the very personal. On the heels of my discovery that my dear brother-in-law had cancer, each quotation that bespoke of an orphan's cry left me weeping over my own young niece and nephew and so remained in the book. (I am glad to report he is in complete remission.) But the two central criteria were: (1) Does the quotation still have an emotional, spiritual or intellectual impact? and (2) does it possess either a timelessness or pertinent timeliness?

[4] *The Quotable Woman: 1800–1975* (New York: Corwin Books, 1977); 1,334 contributors, approximately 10,000 quotations. *The Quotable Woman: Eve–1799* (New York: Facts On File, 1985); 805 contributors, approximately 6,000 quotations.

How to keep a book "timeless," "ageless"? Some topics of the day that seem to be of monumental import will, inevitably, vitiate with the passage of time and will seem irrelevant, even trivial years later. When I reread Oriana Fallaci's tender and moving *Letter to a Child Never Born* in which she says to the embryo just beginning to flourish inside her: "Equality, Child, like freedom, exists only where you are now. Only as an egg in the womb are we all equal," my mind was bombarded with current headlines and articles documenting the thousands of babies born with addictions to cocaine and heroin who might never attain full physical or mental growth, babies born with AIDS who will die. So, despite their topicality, the exclusion of subjects like crack and AIDS would, I think, leave a gaping hole for researchers. Let's hope they will become the jetsam of the next edition.

Although I like to believe I have developed a keener sensibility for what constitutes a good quote, the criteria used in selecting new material have been much the same as stated in the Preface to the first edition:

> My ground rules for choosing the contributors were based on reputation, remarkableness, quotability, and availability of their work. The attempt was made to be as representative of as many professions and nations as possible, though writers and poets, American and English, do predominate. . . .

The quotations were chosen for various reasons—some for their lyricism, some for their uniqueness and piquancy, some because they were revelatory of the author's [or another's] character, some because they were memorable and pertinent. Considered were infamous quotations, celebrated quotations, inventive quotations, and always, always, usable quotations. A conscious effort was maintained to be as objective and eclectic as possible (although, as I mention elsewhere, using oneself as a sieve makes that quite impossible, really).

As always, there are scores of notable women who were left out for a variety of reasons: there are no extant writings or documentation of their words, they worked in collaboration with men, they were translators,[5] or, outstanding achievers though they may have been, I could find nothing quotable to include.

Reflecting the Chinese respect for age, the authors in *Seven Contemporary Chinese Women Writers*,[6] are presented by year of birth, the oldest appearing first. I too have maintained a chronological order of the contributors in the Quotations Section. It offers a sweeping flight through the timeline of women's history and an awareness of the parallel times in which women from different nations and continents lived. Even the waxing and waning popularity of first names prove at least amusing.

Biblical women can all be found in a separate section at the head of the Quotations Section: since much of the Bible was written centuries after the history it documents,

---

[5] An exception is Mary Sidney Herbert, whose translations of the psalms are so far removed from any I've seen in several English versions of the Bible that, in my opinion, they comprise original works.
[6] Edited by Gladys Yang, contributor 2076.

these quotations may be considered attributions rather than actual. It seemed more practical to present biblical women "in order of appearance," if you will, rather than chronologically, since there is often great disparity among experts' findings with respect to lifespan. But I have attempted to identify that information as well as to find out the approximate years in which the various books of the Bible were written. All biblical passages are from the King James version, with the exception of those books that do not appear in that translation: Judith, Tobit, Esther (lettered verses only), 2 Maccabees, and Daniel (chapter 13 only): these are from the Jerusalem version.

Footnotes flourish in the Quotations Section. Most often they indicate that the woman cited is a contributor in *TQW*, but also they annotate persons of note and, infrequently, obscure terminology (wherever it was not confusing I have maintained original spellings and syntax). There may be occasions when the reader questions the need for references that seem obvious. But distribution may take the work to readers of vastly diverse cultures and to young people who may not even know, for example, who Walt Whitman was.

The Indexes

How often I have been asked, "How many scientists, musicians, athletes are in your book?" An Occupation Index seemed a natural. In the past one had to peruse the Biographical Index with care and notepad to accumulate that information. Now, it's all done for you. It is amazing how many women have had multiple professions. It would seem that *one* was quite enough. If Hsaio Hung's observation is accurate— that "each of the 360 trades in this world of ours has its share of miseries"—a lot of women in this text had an awful lot of miseries! The lively women in these pages, most of whom were also mothers and householders, must have been in sync with dancer Ruth St. Denis' mind-set when she wrote: "I used to say that if a person wanted to keep alive, in distinction to merely existing, he should change his occupation every ten years."

I tried to organize professions in related groups as an aid to the researcher: an outline of those groups and the specific professions that fall under them can be found in the Notes to the Occupation Index. The span of time I was dealing with caused many consternations and spurred imaginative solutions, and so a contributor listed in the Biographical Index as a healer falls under the occupation of medical practitioner in the Occupation Index; a witch comes under occultist, and so on.

The Ethnicity and Nationality Index helps the scholar seeking out the thoughts of, for instance, Asian women, or Native Americans or Scandinavians. Both these new indexes provide useful and time-saving information and work synergistically with the other sections of the book.

The Subject Index furnishes those "clouds of witnesses" Leonora Speyer writes of. Here you can find the key witness, the one that will unlock the puzzle. What is the author trying to say? Is it embodied in a word in the quotation, or need it be abstracted? More often than not the latter was so. I often pondered long and hard over a single quotation, examining its content and trying to foretell what word or words would most likely bring it to the searcher's attention. Many quotations are classified in three, four, even five categories. For example, Françoise Parturier's acrimonious observation "And the more deodorants there are in the drugstores, the worse [woman] smells in literature" is classified under "literature, representation of women in," "commercialism," and "women, image of"; so, whether the reader is doing a study of the image of women or of women in literature or of commercialism, she or he may still be led to the same quotation.

This is a *subjective* subject index, unlike the more typical keyword or phrase index, which can, in my opinion, throw one off track (unless you already know the quotation and its context). For example, Hildegarde von Bingen's lovely salutation, "Greetings, greenest branch" in a keyword index would probably go under "greetings" or "branch"; but, as it is a welcome to the Virgin Mary, that would not be very elucidating, particularly for the religious historian. In this Subject Index it is categorized under "plant life," "spring" and "Virgin Mary."

Abundant cross-referencing aids the researcher. But, despite the myriad guideposts provided, the search may still prove taxing: while you needn't find a needle in a haystack, you may have to search in several for a camel.

The entry of a subclassification does not exclude the possibility that there might be a more appropriate quotation for your purposes under the general classification. For example, the subcategory "student, woman," does not necessarily imply that the general entries under student do not pertain to women, but that the subclassification pertains *exclusively* to women.

Where two terms have the same meaning, I have sometimes classified both so the researcher might find quotes with the term of choice; *e.g.,* "old age" and "the elderly" are both classified, with cross-references to each other.

I approximate there are 4,000 classifications and subclassifications.

Synergy

After all these years I have only just discovered several new uses of the Subject Index. The uniting of the two volumes provides a sweeping view of women over the millennia, and the emergence of the two new indexes and how they can work with the other two have shed a light not available before.

Here are some "handy hints," if you will, shortcuts that can save a lot of scouring time.

If one acquires a loose knowledge of the decades associated with contributor numbers, a look through the Subject Index reveals when certain topics became major issues of the day.

• When looking for quotations on a certain subject by specific women, scan for their contributor numbers under appropriate classifications. Similarly, if you're trying to find a quote you only vaguely recall, but know it was written by Colette, look for her contributor number under possible classifications.

• If you're looking for humorous quotations on a certain topic, check out the Occupation Index for humorists and comedians, make note of their contributor numbers, then look in the Subject Index under the topic of your choice and search for those contributor numbers.

• If you're searching for remarks about the environment by Native American women, find them in the Nationality Index, get contributors numbers from the Biographical Index, and look for their contributor numbers under environment and ecology in the Subject Index.

Each section of the book is preceded by its own "Notes to . . . ," which reveals the nuts and bolts of abbreviations, format, etc. Each section is useful on its own as well as in concert with the others.

Semantics

The Subject Index offers a fascinating view of fashion in semantics—what's in, what's out, what comes, what goes. "Technology" is referred to by Helen Keller in an *American Magazine* article in 1912. "Avarice" is used up until 1900, then greed takes over. "Diligence" is hardly used at all after 1900. The word "lesbian" first appears in 1928, though allusions to love between women begin almost at the beginning. "Racism" first appears in Annie Wood Besant's 1913 essay "Wake Up, India: A Plea for Social Reform." "Parenting" is first cited in Mauve Brennan's article "The Eldest Child" in *The New Yorker* in 1968. "Freeway" is seen first here in 1976. "Empowerment" does not appear until 1986. We think of some topics as so contemporary, but "air pollution" is mentioned in an article written in 1861 by Rebecca Davies. The first two mentions of "lawyer" I came across were from the 17th century—and both refer to them as being "mercenary."

The subject of "sin" is practically abandoned from 1920 on. Eleanor Roosevelt wrote: "Television has completely revised what should go at a political convention." In 1952! And in 1890 Laura Howe penned:

Once there was an elephant
Who tried to use the telephant
No, no, I mean an elephone
Who tried to use the telephone.

Using *The Handbook of Non-Sexist Writing*[7] as a guide, I have tried to use sex neutral terms throughout the work. "Poet" refers to all poets, male and female. If a

---

[7]   Miller, Casey and Swift, Kate (New York: Lippincott & Crowell, 1980).

quotation is specifically about one gender or the other, it will be found under "poet, ~ male" or "poet, ~ woman".[8] The same applies to actor, comedian, adventurer, host, hero, ballet dancer, etc. Only when the feminine form is clearly of ancient derivation—priestess, goddess, princess, empress, etc.—and has not been imposed as a diminutive and therefore deprecatory term, as in suffragette, authoress, hostess, is it differentiated in major classifications.

In my struggle to remove sexist language from the indexes, I have faced several conundrums. For "common man" do I use "common person" or "commoner"? Neither seemed entirely satisfactory (I used "commoner" with a cross-reference to "people, ordinary~"). If we have a god and a goddess, does that imply that god is male? Solution. God, with a capital G, is the Judeo-Christian god, which, in my psyche, not being human, has no gender; in your frame of reference, well . . . you decide. But god and goddess, lower case, refer to mythological and historical religious figures that are gender specific.

In rare cases I have chosen terms not in common use as a way of getting away from sexist terminology. Although there are references under "brotherhood" and under "sisterhood," these refer quite particularly to men and to women. Where the former commonly refers to "the brotherhood of man," I have used *"esprit de corps"* and "solidarity": thorough cross-referencing takes the guess work out of finding those terms.

In the Biographical Index, rather than refer to a woman as so-and-so's mistress, I have changed the term to lover; rather than call a woman a hostess, she is dubbed a society leader, or, if she is French, a salonist; these changes were applied to the Occupation Index as well.

Each mini-battle posed its own dilemmas, and each was a good fight—nonviolent, productive, progressive. "Finding language that will allow people to act together while cherishing each other's individuality is probably the most feminist and therefore truly revolutionary function of writers"—Gloria Steinem.

What has been attempted here is a flight through women's history—a bird's eye-view of the world of women that offers a convenient and comprehensive source of women of the world and their issues.

---

[8] I have conceded to using "woman" as an adjective, the accepted practice today, but have retained the prerogative of some exceptions when it just didn't sound right. For example, under "orgasm" the subclassification "female~" remains.

HOW TO USE THIS BOOK

The women quoted are presented in chronological order according to the year of their birth, then alphabetically within each year. Each contributor has been given a number; guides to these contributor numbers appear in the running heads throughout the Quotations Section and are used in lieu of page numbers in the Biographical and Subject Indexes.

Where firm birth and/or death dates were not known, but it was possible to make a reasonable guess, dates are followed by a question mark; when guesses were more broadly based, dates are preceded by a "c.," for circa. Dates shown with a slash (e.g., 1734/35) indicate that birth or death was definitely in one of those two years. If neither year of birth nor of death can be surmised, flourished dates are given, indicated by "fl." In all instances it is the first year appearing that dictates the contributor's place in the chronology; thus (?–1301) places that contributor among women born or flourishing in 1301, even though she may have been born much earlier.

The quotations for each woman are presented chronologically according to the copyright or publication date of the source. If only an approximate year of publication is known, a circa date is given. Parenthetical dates within a source indicate the time at which the quotation was *originally* spoken or written or, when contained in a contemporary anthology, originally published. In some cases, no date of publication could be ascertained; these quotations follow the dated sources and, where the year should appear, are indicated by "n.d." (no date).

When possible, the location of a quotation within the source is given—that is, the part, chapter, stanza, act or scene. If, however, a quote was taken from something other than its original source—for example, from a critical review—and the precise location is not known, it precedes those quotations that are more specifically designated. Of course, many books have no chapter or part numbers or subheadings, and many poems are not separated into stanzas, and so locations cannot always be specified.

Abbreviations used in source citations are: Vol.—volume; Pt.—part; Bk.—book; Ch.—chapter; St.—stanza; Sec.—section; No.—number; Sc.—scene; l.—line; l.l.—last line(s); c.—circa; ed.—editor; tr.—translator.

When a quotation is taken from a book, an article, or any work by a writer other than the contributor, it is indicated by the words "Quoted in" followed by the source and its author. In the case of anthological works "Quoted in" is not used, but editors are indicated.

Quotation marks around a quotation indicate that it is dialogue spoken by a character in a work of fiction or that it appeared in quotations in the original work. Except for exchanges of dialogue, original paragraphing is not indicated in prose selections, whereas in poetry the integrity of form has been maintained.

For information concerning the use of the Biographical, Subject, Career and Nationality Indexes, see notes preceding each index.

Quotations from the Bible

1. Eve (pre-4000 B.C.)

1 The serpent beguiled me, and I did eat.
Genesis, 3:13
c.9th century B.C.

2. Hagar (c.2300–c.1850 B.C.)

1 Thou God seest me: . . . Have I also here looked after him that seeth me?
Genesis, 16:13
c.9th century B.C.

3. Sarah (c.1987–c.1860 B.C.)

1 After I am waxed old shall I have pleasure, my lord being old also? Genesis, 18:12
c.9th century B.C.

2 God hath made me to laugh, so that all that hear will laugh with me. Ibid., 21:6

4. Lot's daughter (the elder) (fl. c.18th century B.C.)

1 Our father is old, and there is not a man in the earth to come in unto us after the manner of all the earth:
Come, let us make our father drink wine, and we will lie with him, that we may preserve seed of our father. Genesis, 19:31, 32
c.9th century B.C.

5. Leah (18th century B.C.)

1 Is there yet any portion or inheritance for us [Leah and Rachel] in our father's house?
Are we not counted of him strangers? For he hath sold us, and hath quite devoured also our money.

For all the riches which God hath taken from our father, that is ours, and our children's. . . . Genesis, 31:14–16,*
c.9th century B.C. with Rachel

*See contr. 6.

6. Rachel (d. 1732 B.C.?)

1 Give me children, or else I die.
Genesis, 30:1
c.9th century B.C.

Coauthor with Leah. See 5:1.

7. Pharaoh's daughter (fl. c.1250 B.C.)

1 Because I drew him [Moses] out of the water. Exodus, 2:10
c.9th century B.C.

8. Zipporah (fl. c.1230 B.C.)

1 Surely a bloody husband art thou to me. . . .
A bloody husband thou art, because of the circumcision. Exodus, 4:25,26
c.9th century B.C.

9. Miriam (fl. c.1250–1230 B.C.)

1 Sing ye to the Lord, for he hath triumphed gloriously; the horse and his rider hath he thrown into the sea. Exodus, 15:21
c.9th century B.C.

10. Five Daughters of Zelophehad: Mahlah, Noah, Hoglah, Milcah and Tirzah (fl. 1240–1200 B.C.)

1 Our father died in the wilderness, and he was not in the company of them that hath gathered themselves together against the Lord in the company of Kôf-ăh; but died in his own sin, and had no sons.

Why should the name of our father be done away from among his family, because he hath no son? Give unto us therefore a possession among the brethren of our father.

Numbers, 27:3, 4
c.9th century B.C.

11. Deborah (fl. c.1070 B.C.)

1 Speak, ye that ride on white asses, ye that sit in judgment, and walk by the way.

Judges, 5:10, with Barak*
c.550 B.C.

2 So let all thine enemies perish, O Lord: but let them that love him be as the sun when he goeth forth in his might. And the land had rest forty years.

Ibid., 5:31

*Leader who, with Deborah, delivered Israel from the Canaanites.

12. Jael (fl. 1070 B.C.)

1 Turn in, my Lord, turn in to me; fear not.

Judges, 4:18
c.550 B.C.

13. Daughter of Jephthah the Gileadite (fl. 1140 B.C.)

1 Let this thing be done for me: let me alone two months, that I may go up and down upon the mountains, and bewail my virginity.

Judges, 11:37
c.550 B.C.

4. First wife of Samson (fl. c.1080 B.C.)

1 Thou dost but hate me, and lovest me not; thou hast put forth a riddle unto the children of my people, and hast not told it me.

Judges, 14:16
c.550 B.C.

15. Delilah (fl. 1080 B.C.)

1 How canst thou say, I love thee, when thine heart is not with me? thou hast mocked me these three times, and hast not told me wherein thy great strength lieth.

Judges, 16:15
c.550 B.C.

16. Naomi (fl. c.1100 B.C.)

1 Go, return each to her mother's house. . . .*

Ruth, **1:8
late 5th or 4th century B.C.

*Spoken to her daughters-in-law, Ruth and Orpah. See 17.

17. Ruth (fl. c.1100 B.C.)

1 Intreat me not to leave thee,* or to return from following after thee: for whither thou goest, I will go; and where thou lodgest, I will lodge: thy people shall be my people, and thy God my God:

Where thou diest, will I die, and there will I be buried: the Lord do so to me, and more also, if ougt but death part thee and me.

Ruth, 1:16,17
late 5th or 4th century B.C.

*Her mother-in-law, Naomi: see 16.

18. Hannah (c.1040 B.C.)

1 My heart rejoiceth in the Lord, mine horn is exalted in the Lord: my mouth is enlarged over mine enemies; because I rejoice in thy salvation.

There is none holy as the Lord: for there is none beside thee: neither is there any rock like our God.

Talk no more so exceeding proudly; let not arrogancy come out of your mouth: for the Lord is a God of knowledge, and by him actions are weighed.

The bows of the mighty men are broken, and they that stumbled are girded with strength.

They that were full have hired out themselves for bread; and they that were hungry ceased: so that the barren hath born seven; and she that hath many children is waxed feeble.

The Lord killeth, and maketh alive: he bringeth down to the grave, and bringeth up.

The Lord maketh poor, and maketh rich: he bringeth low, and lifteth up.

He raiseth up the poor out of the dust, and lifteth up the beggar from the dunghill, to set them among princes, and to make them inherit the throne of glory: for the pillars of the earth are the Lord's, and he hath set the world upon them.

He will keep the feet of his saints, and the wicked shall be silent in darkness; for by strength shall no man prevail.

The adversaries of the Lord shall be broken to pieces; out of heaven shall he thunder upon them: the Lord shall judge the ends of the earth;

and he shall give strength unto his king, and exalt the horn of his anointed.
1 Samuel, 2:1–10
c.550 B.C.

19. Wife of Phinehas (c.1040–970 B.C.)

1 The glory is departed from Israel: for the ark of God is taken.
1 Samuel, 4:22
c.550 B.C.

20. Abigail (fl. 990 B.C.)

1 Behold, let thine handmaid be a servant to wash the feet of the servants of my lord.
1 Samuel, 25:41
c.550 B.C.

21. Michal (fl. c.1010–970 B.C.)

1 If thou save not thy life tonight, tomorrow thou shalt be slain.
1 Samuel, 19:11
c.550 B.C.

22. Tamar (fl. c.990 B.C.)

1 Nay, my brother, do not force me; for no such thing ought to be done in Israel: do not thou this folly.
2 Samuel, 13:12
c.550 B.C.

23. Woman of Tekoa (fl. c.940 B.C.)

1 For we must needs die, and are as water spilt on the ground, which cannot be gathered up again. . . .
2 Samuel, 14:14
c.550 B.C.

24. Woman of Abel of Bethmaacah (fl. c.1040–970 B.C.)

1 why wilt thou swallow up the inheritance of the Lord?
2 Samuel, 20:19
c.550 B.C.

25. Bathsheba (fl. c.1000–970 B.C.)

1 And thou, my lord, O king, the eyes of all Israel are upon thee, that thou shouldest tell them who shall sit on the throne of my lord the king after him.
1 Kings, 1:20
c.550 B.C.

26. Prostitute of Jerusalem (mother of the living child) (fl. c.950 B.C.)

1 O my lord, give her the living child, and in no wise slay it: she is the mother thereof.
1 Kings, 3:26
c.550 B.C.

27. Prostitute of Jerusalem (mother of the dead child) (fl. c.950 B.C.)

1 Let it be neither mine nor thine, but divide it.
1 Kings, 3:26
c.550 B.C.

28. Queen of Sheba (fl. c.950 B.C.)

1 Howbeit I believed not the words, until I came, and mine eyes had seen it: and, behold, the half was not told me: thy wisdom and prosperity exceedeth the fame which I heard.
1 Kings, 10:7
c.550 B.C.

29. Jezebel (fl. c.874–853 B.C.)

1 . . . arise, and eat bread, and let thine heart be merry. . . .
1 Kings, 21:7
c.550 B.C.

30. Huldah (fl. c.586 B.C.)

1 Behold therefore, I will gather thee unto thy fathers, and thou shalt be gathered into thy grave in peace; and thine eyes shall not see all the evil which I will bring upon this place.
2 Kings, 22:20
c.550 B.C.

31. Judith (fl. c.600–495 B.C.)

1 If you cannot sound the depths of the heart of man or unravel the arguments of his mind, how can you fathom the God who made all things, or sound his mind or unravel his purposes?
Judith, 8:12–14
c.150 B.C.

2 But you have no right to demand guarantees where the designs of the Lord our God are concerned. For God is not to be coerced as man is, nor is he, like mere man, to be cajoled.
Ibid., 8:16

3 Her sandal ravished his eyes,
  her beauty took his soul prisoner . . .
  and the scimitar cut through his neck!
  Ibid., 16:9

4 May your whole creation serve you!
  For you spoke and things came into being,
  you sent your breath and they were put together,
  and no one can resist your voice.
  Ibid., 16:14

5 A little thing indeed
  is a sweetly smelling sacrifice, . . .
  Ibid., 16:16

6 Woe to the nations
  who rise against my race!
  Ibid., 16:17

32. Sarah (fl. c.724–722 B.C.)

1 I cannot cause my father a sorrow which would
  bring down his old age to the dwelling of the
  dead.
  Tobit, 3:10
  c.175–164 B.C.

33. Anna (fl. c.724–722 B.C.)

1 Alas! I let you leave me, my child, you, the
  light of my eyes.
  Tobit, 10:5
  c.175–164 B.C.

34. Esther (fl. c.519–465 B.C.)

1 . . . if I perish, I perish.
  Esther, 4:16
  c.199–150 B.C.

2 . . . you, lord, chose
  Israel out of all the nations
  and our ancestors out of all the people of old
  times
  to be your heritage for ever;
  Ibid., 4:17

3 Never let men mock at our ruin.
  Ibid.

35. Mother of the Seven Brothers (fl. c.164–161 B.C.)

1 I do not know how you appeared in my womb;
  it was not I who endowed you with breath and
  life, I had not the shaping of your every part.
    It is the creator of the world, ordaining the
  process of man's birth and presiding over the
  origin of all things . . .
  2 Maccabees, 7:22, 23
  c.A.D. 41–44

2 I implore you, my child, observe heaven and
  earth, consider all that is in them, and acknowledge that God made them out of what did not
  exist, and that mankind comes into being the
  same way.
  Ibid., 7:28

36. Wife of Job (c.8th century B.C.)

1 Dost thou still retain thine integrity? curse God,
  and die.
  Job, 2:9
  c. early 5th century B.C.

37. Susanna (fl. c.587–538 B.C.)

1 But I prefer to fall innocent into your power
  than to sin in the eyes of the Lord.
  Daniel 13:23
  c.167–164 B.C.

38. Salome (fl. c.A.D. 20)

1 I will that thou give me by and by in a charger
  the head of John the Baptist.
  Mark, 6:25
  A.D. 68

39. Mary (fl. c.7 B.C.–A.D. 25)

1 My soul doth magnify the Lord, And my spirit
  hath rejoiced in God my Savior.
    For he hath regarded the low estate of his
  handmaiden; for, behold, from henceforth all
  generations shall call me blessed.
    For he that is mighty hath done to me great
  things; and holy is his name.
    And his mercy is on them that fear him from
  generation to generation.
    He hath shewed strength with his arm; he
  hath scattered the proud in the imagination of
  their hearts.
    He hath put down the mighty from their seats,
  and exalted them of low degree.
    He hath filled the hungry with good things;
  and the rich he hath sent empty away.
    He hath helped his servant Israel, in remem-
  brance of his mercy;
    As he spake to our fathers, to Abraham, and
  to his seed for ever.
  Luke, 1:46–55
  c.A.D. 65–80

40. Elisabeth (fl. c.20 B.C.–A.D. 1)

1 Blessed art thou [Mary]* among women, and
  blessed is the fruit of thy womb.

And whence is this to me, that the mother of my Lord should come to me?

For, lo, as soon as the voice of thy salutation sounded in mine ears, the babe [John the Baptist] leaped in my womb for joy.

And blessed is she that believed: for there shall be a performance of those things which were told her from the Lord.   Luke, 1:42–45
c.A.D. 65–80

*See 39.

41. Samaritan Woman (fl. c.A.D. 25)

1 How is it that thou [Christ], being a Jew, askest drink of me, which am a woman of Samaria? . . . .   John, 4:9
A.D. 100

2 Come, see a man, which told me all things that ever I did: is not this the Christ?   Ibid., 4:29

42. Mary Magdalene (fl. c.A.D. 25)

1 They have taken away the Lord out of the sepulchre, and we know not where they have laid him.   John, 20:2
A.D. 100

Quotations from 2300 B.C.–A.D. 1990

43. Enheduanna (b. c.2300 B.C.?)

1 O lady of all truths. . . . "Inanna* and An,"
adapted by Anne Draffkorn Kilmer;
The Exaltation of Inanna by
William W. Hallo and
J. J. A. van Dijk   *1968*

*Sumerian goddess of love.

2 You are in all our great rites.
Who can understand you?
adaped by Aliki and Willis
Barnstone,
Ibid.

3 With cries of labor I gave birth to this
hymn. . . .   adapted by Anne
Draffkorn Kilmer,
op. cit.

4 My honeyed tongue is tied with confusion
Untitled,
adapted by Anne Draffkorn
Kilmer, op. cit.

44. Kubatum (fl. c.2032 B.C.)

1 my sweet and darling one,
with whom I would speak honey—
youth, I am in love with you!
"Love Song to King Shu-Suen,"
St. 6, Thorkild Jacobsen, tr.;
Most Ancient Verse, Thorkild
Jacobsen and John A. Wilson, eds.
n.d.

45. Eristi-Aya (c.1790–1745 B.C.)

1 even warriors seized as booty in war are
treated humanely.
At least, treat me like them!
"A Letter to Her Mother,"
Willis Barnstone, tr.; *A Book of
Women Poets,* Aliki and Willis
Barnstone, eds.   *1980*

46. Hatshepsut (fl. 1503–1482 B.C.)

1 My command stands firm like the mountains
and the sun's disk shines and spreads rays over
the titulary of my august person, and my falcon
rises high above the kingly banner unto all
eternity.   Quoted in *The
Remarkable Women of Ancient
Egypt*
by Barbara Lesko
1978

47. Ankhesenpaton (fl. 1390s B.C.)

1 My husband, Nib-khuruia,* has recently died,
and I have no son. But thy sons, they say, are
many. If thou wilt send me a son of thine, he
shall become my husband.
Letter to Shuppiluliuma,
the Hittite king (62 B.C.),
Quoted in *When Egypt Ruled the East,*
Ch. 15, by George Steindorff and
Keith C. Seele   *1942*

*Official name of Tutankhamen, who ruled c.1379–1362
B.C.

48. Penelope (c.1214 B.C.–?)

1 Careless to please, with insolence ye woo!
Quoted in *The Odyssey* by
Homer   *c.800 B.C.*

2 When have I not been dreading dangers more
grievous than the reality? Love is a thing replete
with anxious fears.
Quoted in *Epistulae Heroidum*
[*Letters from Heroines*] by Ovid
c.20 B.C.

49. Semiramis (8th century B.C.)

1 Nature gave me the form of a woman; my
actions have raised me to the level of the most
valiant of men.   Quoted in *Women of
Beauty and Heroism*
by Frank B. Goodrich   *1858*

(6)

50. Sappho (fl. c.610–635 B.C.)

1 When anger spreads through the breast, guard
thy tongue from barking idly.
Untitled fragment, Quoted
in *Women in the Golden Ages,*
by Amelia Gere Mason   *1901*

2 . . . death is an evil; the gods have so judged;
had it been good, they would die.
Untitled fragment, op. cit.

3 I do not expect to touch the heavens with my
two arms. . . .   Untitled fragment,
Quoted in *Distinguished Women
Writers*
by Virginia Moore   *1934*

4 Gentle ladies, you will remember till old age
what we did together in our brilliant youth!
Untitled fragment, op. cit.

5 Now Eros has shaken my thoughts, like a wind
among highland oaks.
Untitled fragment, op. cit.

6 Love, fatal creature. . . .   Untitled
fragment, op. cit.

7 Now love the limb-loosener sweeps me
away. . . .   Untitled fragment, op. cit.

8 Some say an army of horsemen
is the fairest sight
on this sluggish black earth,
others an army of foot-soldiers, and others a
navy of ships,
but I say it is the one you love.
Untitled fragment, op. cit.

9 Like a mountain whirlwind
punishing the oak trees,
love shattered my heart.   Untitled
fragment, *Greek Lyric Poetry,*
Willis Barnstone, ed. and
tr.   *1962*

10 all my flesh is wrinkled with age,
my black hair has faded to white,

my legs can no longer carry me,
once nimble like a fawn's,

but what can I do?
It cannot be undone,

no more than can pink-armed Dawn
not end in darkness on earth.
Untitled, Sts. 2–5, op. cit.

11   If I meet
you suddenly, I can't

speak—my tongue is broken;
a thin flame runs under
my skin; seeing nothing,

hearing only my own ears
drumming, I drip with sweat;
trembling shakes my body

and I turn paler than
dry grass. At such times
death isn't far from me.   Untitled, *The
Penguin Book of Women Poets,*
Carol Cosman, Joan Keefe and
Kathleen Weaver, eds.   *1978*

12 The angel of spring, the mellow-throated
nightingale.   No. 39, *Fragments
n.d.*

13 Art thou the topmost apple
The gatherers could not reach,
Reddening on the bough?
Shall I not take thee?   Op. cit., No. 53

51. Erinna (fl. 610–595 B.C.)

1 Little trails through my heart that are
Still warm—my remembrances of you.
"The Distaff," Marylin Bentley
Arthur, tr.; *Women Poets of the
World,* Joanna Bankier and
Deirdre Lashgari, eds.   *1983*

52. Corinna (ca.520–420 B.C.)

1 When he sailed into the harbor
his ship became a snorting horse.
Untitled, St. 1,
Greek Lyric Poetry,
Willis Barnstone, ed. and
tr.   *1962*

2 will you sleep forever?
you were not like that, Corinna,
in the old days.
Untitled, John Dillon, tr.; *The
Penguin Book of Women Poets,*
Carol Cosman, Joan Keefe and
Kathleen Weaver, eds.   *1978*

53. Telesilla (5th century B.C.)

1 Run swiftly to escape
the rape of the hunter Alpheus.
Untitled, *Greek Lyric Poetry,*
Willis Barnstone, ed. and tr.   *1962*

54. Artemisia (fl. 480 B.C.)

1 Spare your ships, and do not risk a battle; for
these people [the Greeks] are as much superior

to your people in seamanship, as men to women.   Remark to King Xerxes,* Quoted in *The Persian Wars*, Bk. VIII, by Herodotus   *c.450 B.C.*

2 This, too, you should remember, O king; good masters are apt to have bad servants, and bad masters good ones.   Ibid.

*519?–465 B.C., King of Persia (486–465 B.C.)

55. Praxilla (fl. c.451 B.C.)

1 You gaze at me teasingly through the window: a virgin—and below—a woman's thighs.
     Untitled, *Greek Lyric Poetry*, Willis Barnstone, ed. and tr.   *1962*

2 Loveliest of what I leave
     is the sun himself
Next to that the bright stars
     and the face of mother moon
Oh yes, and cucumbers in season,
     and apples, and pears.
     "Adonis, Dying," John Dillon, tr.; *The Penguin Book of Women Poets*, Carol Cosman, Joan Keefe and Kathleen Weaver, eds.   *1978*

3 Watch out, my dear,
     there's a scorpion under every stone.
     Untitled fragment, op. cit.

56. Aspasia (fl. c.420s B.C.)

1 . . . if you don't endeavor that there be not a better husband and wife in the world than yourselves, you will always be wishing for that which you shall think best.
     Quoted by Socrates in *Dialogue of Aeschines* by Plato   *c.A.D. 360–386*

2 Your great glory is not to be inferior to what God has made you, and the greatest glory of a woman is to be least talked about by men, whether they are praising you or criticizing you.   Quoted in *History of the Peloponnesian War* by Thucydides   *c.A.D. 413*

57. Theano (fl. c.420s B.C.)

1 Put off your shame with your clothes when you go in to your husband, and put it on again when you come out.
     Quoted in *Lives, Teachings, and Sayings of Famous Philosophers; Pythagoras*, Bk. VIII, Sec. 43, by Diogenes Laertius   *c.300 B.C.*

2 The gods could not be honored by lies.
     Quoted in *Biography of Distinguished Women*, by Sarah Josepha Hale* rev. ed.   *1879*

*See 703.

58. Ambapali (4th century B.C.)

1 Such was my body once. Now it is weary and tottering,
the home of many ills, an old house with flaking plaster.
Not otherwise is the world of the truthful.
     Untitled, St. 9, *The Wonder That Was India*, A. L. Basham, ed. and tr.   *1959*

59. Phyrne (4th century B.C.)

1 He* is not a man but a statue.
     Quoted in *Lives, Teachings, and Sayings of Famous Philsophers*, by Diogenes Laertius   *c.300 B.C.*

*The Greek philosopher Xenocrates.

60. Lady Ho (fl. 300 B.C.)

1 When a pair of magpies fly together
They do not envy the pair of phoenixes.
     "A Song of Magpies," *The Orchid Boat, Women Poets of China*, Kenneth Rexroth and Ling Chung, eds. and trs. *1972*

61. Mother of Sumangala (c.3rd–1st century B.C.)

1 A free woman. At last free!
Free from slavery in the kitchen
where I walked back and forth stained
and squalid among cooking pots.
     Untitled, Willis Barnstone, tr.; *A Book of Women Poets*, Aliki and Willis Barnstone, eds.   *1980*

62. Sibyl, the Jewish (fl. c.199–c.165 B.C.)

1 . . . here is a city, Chaldean Ur,
Whence come the race of most upright men,
Who are ever right-minded and their works good.

They are neither concerned for the sun's
course,
Nor the moon's, nor for monstrosities on
earth,
Nor for satisfaction from ocean's depths,
Nor for signs of sneezing and the augury from
birds;
Nor for soothsaying, nor sorcery, nor incanta-
tions;
Nor for deceitful follies of ventriloquists.
They do not, Chaldean fashion, astrologize,
Nor watch the stars. . . .
But they are concerned about rightness and
virtue. *The Fourth Book of Sibylline
Oracles
c.100 B.C.*

63. Chuo Wên-chün (179?–117 B.C.)

1 Why should marriage bring only tears?
All I wanted was a man
With a single heart,
And we would stay together
As our hair turned white,
Not somebody always after wriggling fish
With his big bamboo rod.
"A Song of White Hair," *The
Orchid Boat, Women Poets of
China,* Kenneth Rexroth and
Ling Chung,
eds. and trs. *1972*

64. Cornelia (fl. 160–140 B.C.)

1 These* are all the jewels of which I can
boast. Quoted in *Biography of
Distinguished Women*
by Sarah Josepha Hale** *1876*

*Her sons, Tiberius and Caius Gracchi.
**See 703.

65. Hsi-chün (fl. c.105 B.C.)

1 Would I were a yellow stork
And could fly to my old home!
"Lament of Hsi-Chün,"
Translations from the Chinese,
Arthur Waley, tr. *1919*

66. Wife of Ch'in Chia (1st century B.C.)

1 I stood on tiptoe gazing into the distance,
Interminably gazing at the road that had taken
you. "Chi'in Chia's Wife's Reply,"
Translations from the Chinese,
Arthur Waley, tr. *1919*

67. Hortensia (85 B.C.–?)

1 . . . you assume the glorious title of reformers
of the state, a title which will turn to your eternal
infamy, if, without the least regard to the laws
of equity, you persist in your wicked resolution
of plundering those [women] of their lives and
fortunes, who have given you no just cause of
offence. (c.45 B.C.), Quoted in
Civil Wars,
Vol. IV, by Appian of
Alexandria *A.D. 32–34*

68. Cleopatra VII (69 B.C.–A.D. 30)

1 Leave the fishing-rod, Great General, to us sov-
ereigns of Pharos and Canopus. Your game is
cities and kings and continents.
Remark to Marc Antony,*
Quoted in
Cleopatra of Egypt, Ch. 9, by
Philip W. Sergeant *1909*

*83?–30 B.C. Roman general.

2 As surely as one day I shall administer justice
on the Capitol. . . .* Ibid., Ch. XIII

*Her favorite oath, referring to the capital of the Roman
Empire

3 Fool! Don't you see now that I could have
poisoned you a hundred times had I been able
to live without you! Remark to Marc
Antony, Quoted in
*Cleopatra's Daughter, The Queen
of Mauretania,* Ch. 5, by
Beatrice Chanler *1934*

4 Nothing could part us while we lived, but death
seems to threaten to divide us. You, a Roman
born, have found a grave in Egypt. I, an Egyptian, am to seek that favour, and none but that,
in your country.
Spoken over Marc Anthony's
tombstone, Quoted in *The Life and Times of
Cleopatra,*
Ch. 20, by Arthur
Weigall *1968*

*The source for all her remarks can be found in the work
of Plutarch, who probably derived this last speech from the
diary of her doctor, Olympus.

69. Sulpicia (fl. 63 B.C.–A.D. 14)

1 Drat my hateful birthday
to be spent in the boring old country.
Untitled, John Dillon, tr.; *The
Penguin Book of Women Poets,*
Carol Cosman,
Joan Keefe and Kathleen
Weaver, eds. *1978*

2 At last love has come. I would be more
  ashamed
to hide it in cloth than leave it naked
                                    Untitled,
              A Book of Women Poets,
          Aliki and Willis Barnstone, eds.
                      and trs.   *1980*

3 Friends worry about me and are upset that
  somehow
I might tumble into bed with a nobody
                          Untitled, op. cit.

4 Trips are often poorly timed.
                          Untitled, op. cit.

70. Porcia (?–42 B.C.)

1 Brutus,* I am Cato's** daughter, and I was
brought into thy house, not, like a mere con-
cubine, to share thy bed and board merely, but
to be a partner in thy troubles. Thou, indeed,
art faultless as a husband; but how can I show
thee any grateful service if I am to share neither
thy secret suffering nor the anxiety which craves
a loyal confidant? I know that woman's nature
is thought too weak to endure a secret; but good
rearing and excellent companionship go far
towards strengthening the character, and it is
my happy lot to be both the daughter of Cato
and the wife of Brutus. Before this I put less
confidence in these advantages, but now I know
that I am superior even to pain.***
                      from *Parallel Lives* by
          Plutarch (c.A.D. 100), Quoted in
                  Plutarch's Lives, Vol. VI,
          B. Perrin, tr.   *1914–1926*

*85?–42 B.C. Roman political and military leader.
**95–46 B.C. Roman statesman.
***Spoken shortly before Caesar's murder, when she sensed
Brutus' troubled mind; she wounded her thigh with a small
knife just before making the above speech.

71. Okkur Macatti (c.1st–3rd century)

1 In Jasmine country, it is evening
for the hovering bees,
but look, he hasn't come back.

He left me and went in search
of wealth.   "What She Said,"
                            Speaking of Siva,
              A. K. Ramanujan, ed. and
                            tr.   *1973*

72. Venmanipputi (c.1st–3rd century)

1 my arms grow beautiful
in the coupling

and grow lean
as they come away
What shall I make of this?
              "What She Said to her Girl-
                  friend," St. 2, *Interior
          Landscape: Love Poems from a
          Classical Tamil Anthology,* A. K.
          Ramanujan, ed. and tr.   *1967*

73. Agrippina the Younger (c.14–59)

1 No philosophy, my son [Nero]; it is of no use
to an emperor.   Quoted in
                  The Great Empress, A Portrait,
                  Ch. 8, by Maximilian Schele
                            de Vere   *1870*

2 Strike the womb that bore a monster!
                            Ibid., Ch. 11

74. Boadicea (fl. c.40–65)

1 It will not be the first time, Britons, that you
have been victorious under the conduct of your
queen. For my part, I come not here as one
descended of royal blood, not to fight for empire
or riches, but as one of the common people, to
avenge the loss of their liberty, the wrongs of
myself and children.
              Speech, Quoted in *Biography of
                      Distinguished Women*
          by Sarah Josepha Hale*   *1876*

*See 703.

2 Roman lust has gone so far that not even our
own persons remain unpolluted. If you weigh
well the strengths of our armies, you will see
that in this battle we must conquer or die. This
is a woman's resolve. As for the men, they may
live or be slaves.
              Quoted in *The Dinner Party, A
              Symbol of Our Heritage* by Judy
                      Chicago*   *1979*

*See 2259.

75. Arria, the Elder (d.42)

1 It does not hurt, my Paetus.*
              Quoted in *Epistles,* Bk. III,
              epistle 16, by Pliny the Younger
                            c.100–109

*Remark to her husband, who had been ordered to commit
suicide, after she had stabbed herself.

76. Pan Chao (c.45–c.115)

1 The virtues of women are not brilliant talent,
nor distinction and elegance. The virtues of

women are reserve, quiet, chastity, orderliness, governing herself to maintain a sense of shame, and conducting herself according to the rules of Confucian etiquette. from *Nü Chieh* [*Precepts for Women*], quoted in *Chinese Women: Yesterday and Today* by Florence Ayscough *1936*

2 Only needle-and-thread's delicate footsteps are truly broad-ranging yet without beginning! "Needle and Thread," St. 3, Richard Mather and Rob Swigart, trs.; *Women Poets of the World,* Joanna Bankier and Deirdre Lashgari, eds. *1983*

3 How can those who count pennies calculate their worth?
They may carve monuments yet lack all understanding Ibid., St. 5

77. Poppæa Sabina (fl. 50–60)

1 Rather die than see my beauty pass away! Quoted in *The Great Empress, A Portrait,* Ch. 9, by Maximilian Schele de Vere *1870*

78. Pompeia Plotina (c.80–122)

1 May the gods send me forth from this august palace, whenever I may be destined to leave it, even as I now enter it; and may the high destiny to which fortune now raises me leave me in possession of the same qualities with which I this day assume it. Speech (99), Quoted in *Biography of Distinguished Women* by Sarah Josepha Hale* *1876*

*See 703.

79. Sulpicia (fl. 80–99)

1 . . . Priscus Cato* held it of such deep import to determine whether the Roman stock would better be upheld by prosperity or adversity.— By adversity, doubtless; for when the love of country urges them to defend themselves by arms, and their wife held prisoner together with their household goods, they combine just like wasps, (a bristling band, with weapons all unsheathed along their yellow bodies,). . . .
Satire c.90

*Probably the same as Publius Valerius Cato, the 1st-century A.D. Roman poet and grammarian.

2 . . . when care-dispelling peace has returned, forgetful of labour, commons and fathers together lie buried in lethargic sleep. Ibid.

80. Ts'ai Yen (162?–239?)

1 Heaven was pitiless.
It sent down confusion and separation.
Earth was pitiless.
It brought me to birth in such a time.
War was everywhere.
Every road was dangerous.
Soldiers and civilians everywhere
Fleeing death and suffering.
"Eighteen Verses Sung to A Tatar Reed Whistle," I:2, *The Orchid Boat, Women Poets of China,* Kenneth Rexroth and Ling Chung, eds. and trs. *1972*

2 Men here are as savage as giant vipers,
And strut about in armour, snapping their bows. Ibid., II:1

81. Vivia Perpetua (183?–205)

1 Continue firm in the faith, love one another, and be not offended at our sufferings.
Quoted in *Biography of Distinguished Women* by Sarah Josepha Hale* *1876*

*See 703.

82. Auvaiyar (3rd century?)

1 This is the womb that carried him, like a stone cave lived in by a tiger and now abandoned.
Untitled, George Hart, tr.; *Women Poets of the World,* Joanna Bankier and Deirdre Lashgari, eds. *1983*

83. Kaccipēṭṭu Nannākaiyār (3rd century?)

1 I grow lean in loneliness, like a water lily gnawed by a beetle.
"What She Said," St. 3, *Interior Landscape: Love Poems from a Classical Tamil Anthology,* A. K. Ramanujan, ed. and tr. *1967*

84. Tzǔ Yeh (c.3rd–4th century)

1 I let down my silken hair
Over my shoulders
And open my thighs
Over my lover.
"Tell me, is there any part of me
That is not lovable?"   "Song," II,
                                         The Orchid Boat,
                                    Women Poets of China,
                                   Kenneth Rexroth and Ling
                                   Chung, eds. and trs.   *1972*

85. Zenobia of Palmyra (240–300)

1 By valor alone, by the force of arms only, can
wars be brought to a close.
                      Letter to Aurelian Augustus* (272),
                           Quoted in *Women of Beauty
                                          and Heroism*
                        by Frank B. Goodrich   *1858*

*212?–75, Roman emperor (270–75)

86. Iwa no Hime (?–347)

1 In the autumn field,
Over the rice ears,
The morning mist trails,
Vanishing somewhere. . . .
Can my love fade too?   "Longing for the
           Emperor," *The Penguin Book of
   Japanese Verse*, Geoffrey Bownas
           and Anthony Thwaite, eds. and
                                trs.   *1964*

87. Hypatia (c.370–d. 415)

1 Life is an unfoldment, and the further we travel
the more truth we can comprehend. To understand the things that are at our door is the best
preparation for understanding those that lie
beyond.   Quoted in *Little Journeys
          to the Homes of Great Teachers,*
             "Hypatia," by Elbert
                      Hubbard   *1908*

2 Men will fight for a superstition quite as quickly
as for a living truth—often more so, since a
superstition is so intangible you cannot get at it
to refute it, but truth is a point of view, and so
is changeable.   Ibid.

3. He who influences the thought of his times,
influences all the times that follow. He has made
his impress on eternity.   Ibid.

4 It does not make much difference what a person
studies—all knowledge is related, and the man
who studies anything, if he keeps at it, will
become learned.   Ibid.

5 To rule by fettering the mind through fear of
punishment is another world, is just as base as
to use force.   Ibid.

88. Egeria (fl. 381–384)

1 I saw many holy monks from those parts when
they came to Jerusalem on pilgrimage to the
holy places, and all they told me about Uz*
made me eager to take the trouble to make a
further journey to visit it—if one can really
speak of trouble when one sees one's wishes
fulfilled.   from *Travels,* Quoted in *Egeria:
                    Diary of a Pilgrimage,*
          George E. Gingras, ed. and
                           tr.   *1970*

*The Land of Uz was probably near Damascus, although
there is little evidence of its actual location.

89. Aelia Pulcheria (399–454)

1 The more princes abstain from touching the
wealth of their people, the greater will be their
resources in the wants of the state.
                    Quoted in *Biography of
                       Distinguished Women*
          by Sarah Josepha Hale*   *1876*

*See 703.

90. Brigid of Kildare (453–523)

1 I should like a great lake of ale
For the King of kings
           "The Feast of St. Brigid of Kildare,"
                                       n.d.

91. Maximilla (fl. c.465)

1 I am pursued like a wolf out of the sheep fold;
I am no wolf: I am word and spirit and
power.   Quoted in "Word, Spirit and
                             Power:
          Women in Early Christian
                       Communities"
          by Elisabeth Schüssler Fiorenza,
             Women of Spirit, Rosemary
                      Reuther and Eleanor
             McLaughlin, eds.   *1979*

92. Baudonivia (6th century)

1 I am but the least among the least, small is my understanding and timid my heart.
                    Letter to her abbess, Dedimia,
                    Quoted in
                    *Women and Their Letters in the
                    Early Middle Ages*
                    by Eleanor Shipley
                    Duckett   *1965*

93. Caesaria (c.6th century)

1 . . . you cannot fight lust if you do not flee from the presence of men.
                    Quoted in *Women in Frankish
                    Society, Marriage and the
                    Cloister, 500–900*, Ch. 6,
                    by Suzanne Fonay
                    Wemple   *1981*

2 . . . read and hear assiduously the divine lessons . . . to gather from them precious daisies for your ears and make from them rings and bracelets.   Ibid., Ch. 8

94. Theodora (c.508–d. 547/48)

1 For a King, death is better than dethronement and exile.   Attributed   *n.d.*

95. Radegunda (c.518–587)

1 If you do not understand what is read, it is because you do not ask solicitously for a mirror of the soul.
                    Quoted in *Vita Radegundis* [*Life of
                    Radegunda*] by Fortunatus   *c.580–600*

96. Bertegund (fl. 530s)

1 Go home and govern our children. I will not return to you [her husband], for the married will not see the kingdom of heaven.
                    Quoted in *Histoire Française,*
                    Ch. 6,
                    by Gregory of Tours*
                    c.538

*French bishop and writer (538/39–594/95).

97. Al-Khansa (575–646)

1 He is dead, who was the buckler of our tribe   "For Her Brother," St. 3,
                    E. Powys Mathers, tr.; *The Penguin
                    Book of Women Poets,*
                    Carol Cosman,
                    Joan Keefe and Kathleen
                    Weaver, eds.
                    1978

2 . . . every tribe is a journey to ruin

and every treaty is erased by time.
                    "In Death's Field," Sts. 12, 13,
                    Willis Barnstone, tr.,
                    A Book of Women Poets, Aliki
                    and Willis Barnstone, eds.
                    1980

98. Liadan (7th century)

1 Not vain,
it seemed, our choice,
to seek Paradise through pain.
                    "Liadan Laments Cuirithir," * St.
                    3,
                    *The Penguin Book of Women
                    Poets,* Carol Cosman,
                    Joan Keefe and Kathleen
                    Weaver, eds.   *1978*

*Her lover who, after she became a nun, unknown to Liadan became a monk.

2 Gain without gladness
Is in the bargain I have struck
                    Untitled, St. 1, Frank O'Connor, tr.;
                    The Penguin Book of Irish Verse,
                    Brendan Kennelly, ed.
                    1981

99. Hind bint Utba (fl. 600–635)

1 Rrrrrrrraaarghr
We have paid you back
Battle feeds battle
and war that follows war is always violent.
                    "Fury Against the Moslems at
                    Uhud,"
                    St. 1, Bridget Connelly and
                    Deirdre Lashgari, trs.; *Women
                    Poets of the World,* Joanna
                    Bankier and Deirdre Lashgari,
                    eds.   *1983*

100. Laila Akhyaliyya (fl. 665–699)

1 No life is favored,
nor corpse reborn.

Every youth passes through destruction
   to Allah.   "Lamenting Tauba,"
              St. 3, Willis Barnstone, tr.;
              A Book of Women Poets,
              Aliki and Willis Barnstone,
                       eds.   *1980*

2 Our lungs are strong
  when we wail with the first knives
    of dawn.   "Laila Boasting,"
          Willis Barnstone, tr., op. cit.

101. Nukada (fl. 665–699)

1 When, loosened from the winter's bond,
  The spring appears,
  The birds that were silent
  Come out and sing,
  The flowers that were prisoned
  Come out and bloom;
  But the hills are so rank with trees
  We cannot seek the flowers,
  And the flowers are so tangled with weeds
  We cannot take them in our hands.
           Untitled, from *Manyō-Shū*
           *[Collection of Ten Thousand
           Leaves]*   mid-8th century

102. Yamatohime (fl. 671)

1 Others may forget you, but not I.
  I am haunted by your beautiful ghost.
          Untitled, *One Hundred Poems
                from the Japanese,*
         Kenneth Rexroth, tr.   *1964*

103. Safiya bint Musafir (fl. 674)

1 Emptied with weeping
  my eyes are
  two buckets of the waterman
  as he walks among the orchard trees
            "At the Badr Trench," *
           St. 1, Bridget Connelly and
               Deirdre Lashgari, trs.;
         Women Poets of the World,
         Joanna Bankier and Deirdre
             Lashgari, eds.   *1983*

*Burial place for 14 Muslim martyrs killed at Battle of
Badr at Medina (now in Saudi Arabia) in 674

104. Chao Luan-luan (fl. 8th century)

1 Small cherries sip delicately
  At the edge of the wine cup.
          "Red Sandalwood Mouth,"
             *The Orchid Boat,
         Women Poets of China,*
         Kenneth Rexroth and Ling
        Chung, eds. and trs.   *1972*

2 Slender, delicate, soft jade,
  Fresh peeled spring onions—
  They are always hidden in emerald
  Sleeves of perfumed silk.   "Slender
                Fingers," op. cit.

105. Egburg (fl. 8th century)

1 No sailor tossed by the tempest hopes so keenly
  for the harbour, not thus does the thirsty field
  wait for the rain, not so eagerly does the anxious
  mother look from the curving shore for the
  coming of her son, as, My Father, I long for
  the sight of you.
        Letter to St. Boniface (c. 716–726),
          Quoted in *Women and Letters in
             the Early Middle Ages*
              by Eleanor Shipley
               Duckett   *1965*

106. Kasa no Iratsume (8th century)

1 To love someone
  Who does not return that love
  Is like offering prayers
  Back behind a starving god
  Within a Buddhist temple.
          Untitled, from *Manyō-Shū*
          *[Collection of Ten Thousand
              Leaves]*,
            Harold P. Wright,
        tr.   *c. mid-8th century*

107. Lady Kii (fl. 8th century)

1 . . . the idle ways
  of the beach.   Untitled, *The Burning
        Heart: Women Poets of Japan,*
         Kenneth Rexroth and Ikuko
       Atsumi, eds. and trs.   *1977*

108. Li Yeh (fl. 8th century)

1 It is good to get drunk once in a while.
  What else is there to do?   "A Greeting to
               Lu Hung-Chien,"
       *The Orchid Boat, Women Poets
               of China,*
         Kenneth Rexroth and Ling
       Chung, eds. and trs.   *1972*

109. Mahodahi (fl. c.700–1050)

1 The sun's charioteer is lost. . . .
        Untitled, Willis Barnstone, tr.;
            A Book of Women Poets,
         Aliki and Willis Barnstone, eds.
                      1980

110. Ōtomo no Sakano-e no Iratsume (c.700–750)

1 Ah! I have handed over
The jewel to its owner;
So from henceforth, my dear pillow,
Let us two sleep together.
"On the Marriage of a
Daughter," in toto,
from *Manyō-Shū*, Vol. IV,
An Anthology of Japanese Poems,
Miyamori Asatarō, ed. and tr.
1938

2 Do not smile to yourself
Like a green mountain
With a cloud drifting across it.
People will know we are in love.
Untitled, *One Hundred Poems
from the Japanese*,
Kenneth Rexroth, ed. and
tr. *1964*

3 My heart, thinking
"How beautiful he is"
Is like a swift river
Which though one dams it and dams it
Will still break through. Untitled, from
*Manyō-Shū, Japanese Poetry:
The Uta*,
Arthur Waley, ed. and tr.
1976

111. Sila (c.700–1050)

1 We knew long evenings wet with the moon.
Untitled, Willis Barnstone, tr.;
The Book of Women Poets,
Aliki and Willis Barnstone, eds.
1980

112. Śilabhlaṭṭarikā (fl. c.700–1050)

1 I too am still the same;
and yet with all my heart I yearn for the
reedbeds by the stream
which knew our happy, graceful
unending bouts of love.   "The Wanton,"
from *Treasury of Well-Turned Verse*
comp. by Vidya Kara (c.1100),
Quoted in *Sanskrit Poetry*,
Daniel H. H. Ingalls, ed. and
tr. *1955*

113. Vidya (fl. c.700–1050)

1 I praise the disc of the rising sun
red as a parrot's beak, sharp-rayed,

friend of the lotus grove,
an earring for the goddess of the east.
"The Sun," from *Treasury of
Well-Turned Verse*
comp. by Vidya Kara (c.1100),
Quoted in *Sanskrit Poetry*,
Daniel H. H. Ingalls, ed. and
tr. *1955*

2 Friends,
you are lucky you can talk
about what you did as lovers:
the tricks, laughter, the words,
the ecstasy.
After my darling put his hand on the knot
of my dress,
I swear I remember nothing.
Untitled, in toto,
Willis Barnstone, tr.;
A Book of Women Poets,
Aliki and Willis Barnstone,
eds. *1980*

114. Rabi'a the Mystic (712–801)

1 My Lord
if I worship Thee from fear of Hell
burn me in Hell

and if I worship Thee from hope of Paradise
exclude me thence

but if I worship Thee
for Thine own sake alone
do not withhold from me Thine Eternal
Beauty   "A Prayer,"
Sts. 1–3.
Quoted in *Rabi'a the Mystic and
Her Fellow Saints in Islam*,
Margaret Smith   *1928*

115. Young Woman of Harima (fl. c.715–719)

1 If you go away,
why should I adorn myself?
Untitled, from the Manyōshū,
Quoted in *Land of the Reed Plains*,
Kenneth Yashuda, ed. & tr.
1972

116. Khosrovidoukht Koghtnatsi (?–737)

1 More astonishing to me
than the lyrics made for you,

more amazing than the music composed
for your death,
is the sound of the sobbing mourning
                    "More Astonishing,"
                    St. 1 (737), *Anthology of*
                        Armenian Poetry,
                    Diana Der Hovanessian and
                    Marzbed Margossian, eds. and
                            trs.   *1978*

117. Rabi'a bint Isma'il of Syria (?–755)

1 But if You consume me in fire, goal of my
    longing,
    where then lies my hope of You, and where
        my fear?   "Sufi Quatrain,"
                    St. 2, Deirdre Lashgari, tr.;
                    Women Poets of the World,
                    Joanna Bankier and Deirdre
                    Lashgari, eds.   *1983*

118. Hsüeh T'ao (768–831)

1 Blossoms crowd the branches: too beautiful to
    endure.
    Thinking of you, I break into bloom again.
                    "Spring-Gazing Song,"
                        Carolyn Kizer, tr.;
                    A Book of Women Poets,
                    Aliki and Willis Barnstone,
                            eds.   *1980*

2 He is gone, who knew the music of my
    soul.   "Weaving Love Knots" 2,
                            op. cit.

119. Lady Ishikawa (fl. 780–800)

1 You were soaked, my lord,
    with the drops of mountain dew:
    how I wish that I were they!
                    Untitled, from the *Manyōshū,*
                    Quoted in *Land of the Reed Plains,*
                    Kenneth Yashuda, ed. and tr.
                            1972

120. Ono no Komachi (834–880)

1 So lonely am I
    My body is a floating weed
    Severed at the roots.
    Were there water to entice me,
    I would follow it, I think.   Untitled, in toto,
                        from *Kokinshū* (905),
                    Anthology of Japanese Literature,
                    Donald Keene, ed. and tr.
                            1955

2 A thing which fades
    With no outward sign—
    Is the flower
    Of the heart of man
    In this world!   Untitled,
                    Japanese Poetry: The Uta,
                    Arthur Waley, ed. and tr.
                            1976

121. Kassia (fl. c.840)

1 You meet your friend, your face
    brightens—you have struck gold.
                    Untitled, Patrick Diehl, tr.; *The*
                        Penguin Book of Women Poets,
                    Carol Cosman, Joan Keefe and
                        Kathleen Weaver   *1978*

2 Poverty? wealth? seek neither—
    One causes swollen heads,
    The other, swollen bellies.
                    Untitled, Patrick Diehl, tr.,
                            op. cit.

3 Better unborn than fool.
    If born, spare earth your tread.
    Don't wait. Go straight to hell.
                    Untitled, Patrick Diehl, tr.,
                            op. cit.

4 No remedy for fools,
    No helping them, but death.
    In office? puffed and strutting.
    Acclaimed? beyond endurance.
    Columns of stone will kneel
    Before you change a fool.
                    Untitled, Patrick Diehl, tr.,
                            op. cit.

5 A nun—a door unopened.
                    Untitled, Patrick Diehl, tr.,
                            op. cit.

122. The Empress of Nijo (842–910)

1 Spring has already come round
        While on the ground lies snow;
    The frozen tears of *uguisu**
        Soon in the soft warm breeze will
        thaw.   "The Tears of *Uguisu*,"
                    in toto, from *Kokin Shū*, Vol. I,
                    An Anthology of Japanese Poems,
                    Miyamori Asatarō, ed. and
                            tr.   *1938*

* A bird similar to a nightingale.

123. Yü Hsüan-chi (c.843–868)

1 I lift my head and read their names
In powerless envy.   "On A Visit to
Ch'ung Chên Taoist Temple
I see In the South Hall the List
of Successful Candidates in the
Imperial Examinations,"
The Orchid Boat,
Women Poets of China,
Kenneth Rexroth and Ling
Chung, eds. and trs.   *1972*

2 To find a rare jewel is easy.
To get a good man is harder.
"For a Neighbor Girl," *
A Book of Women Poets,
Aliki and Willis Barnstone, eds.
1980

*Quotations 2–5 tr. by Geoffrey Waters.

3 How do we get the life we want?
I am a loosed boat floating a thousand
miles.   "At the End of Spring,"
St. 2, op. cit.

4 Evening, page by page, I hum beneath my
quilt.   "Rhyming a Friend's Poem,"
St. 3, op. cit.

5 Thinking hard, hunting rhymes, humming by
my lamp,
Awake all night, I fear the cold quilt.
"Sent to Wen T'ing
on a Winter Night,"
St. 1, op. cit.

124. Han Ts'ui-p'in (fl. 850s)

1 Red leaf, I order you—
Go find someone
In the world of men.   "A Poem Written
On A Floating Red Leaf,"
The Orchid Boat,
Women Poets of China,
Kenneth Rexroth and Ling
Chung, eds. and trs.   *1972*

125. Lady Ise (875?–938?)

1 Not even in dreams
Can I meet him anymore. . . .   Untitled,
Japanese Literature: An
Introduction for
Western Readers,
Donald Keene, ed. and
tr.   *1955*

2 . . . my reputation
reaches to the skies
like a dust storm.   Untitled,
The Burning Heart: Women
Poets of Japan,
Kenneth Rexroth and Ikuko
Atsumi, eds. and trs.   *1977*

3 And like the maple leaves
of autumn, when members
of the household
have scattered
in their own ways,
uncertainty
fills the air.   "Elegy: Ise Lamenting the
Death of Empress Onshi,"
Etsuko Terasaki with Irma
Brandeis, tr.,
A Book of Women Poets,
Aliki and Willis Barnstone, eds.
1980

126. Andal (fl. c.10th century)

1 Sing,
but not too loudly, so he will come.
Untitled,
Willis Barnstone, tr.;
A Book of Women Poets,
Aliki and Willis Barnstone, eds.
1980

2 we will do good things,
use good words,
give away our possessions and live for him.
Untitled,
Willis Barnstone, tr., op. cit.

127. Gormley (fl. 10th century)

1 though I have loved twenty men
this is not what women seek.
"Gormley's Laments,"
St. 1, Joan Keefe, tr.; *The*
Penguin Book of Women Poets,
Carol Cosman, Joan Keefe and
Kathleen Weaver, eds.   *1978*

2 I paid poets for their words
before God took my riches.   Ibid., St. 14

128. Rabi'a of Balkh (fl. 10th century)

1 My wish for you
that God should make your love
fall on a heart as cold and stony as
your own   Untitled,
Deirdre Lashgari, tr.;
Women Poets of the World,
Joanna Bankier and Deirdre
Lashgari, eds.   *1983*

129. Qernertoq (fl. c.900–1400)

1 It seems as if
I'll never get beyond
the foot-prints that I made
"The Widow's Song," St. 2,
*Eskimo Poets of Canada and
Greenland,*
Tom Lowenstein, ed. and tr.
1973

130. Vallana (fl. c.900–1100)

1 who could save me from plunging into a sea
of shame
but the love god
who teaches us how to faint?   Untitled,
Willis Barnstone, tr.;
A Book of Women Poets,
Aliki and Willis Barnstone, eds.
1980

131. Hroswitha of Gandersheim (c.935–1000)

1 I know that it is as wrong to deny a divine gift
as to pretend falsely that we have received
it.   "Epistle of the Same to Certain
Learned Patrons of this Book,"
The Plays of Roswitha,
Christopher St. John, tr.
1923

2 GALLICANUS. It is said that the face is the mirror
of the soul.   *Gallicanus,*
Pt. I, Sc. 3, op. cit.

3 IRENA. A God who can be bought cheap in the
market-place, what is he but a slave?
Dulcitius,
Sc. 1, op. cit.

4 IRENA. Better far that my body should suffer
outrage than my soul.   Ibid., Sc. 12

5 ANDRONICUS. . . . . it is not in our power to
attain a precise knowledge of the causes of
things.   *Callimachus,*
Sc. 9, op. cit.

6 EPHREM. Out of the mouths of babes and
sucklings!   *Abraham,*
Sc. 1, op. cit.

7 ABRAHAM. It is human to sin, but it is devilish
to remain in sin.   Ibid., Sc. 7

8 DISCIPLES. It is better to know nothing than to
be bewildered.   *Paphnutius,*
Sc. 1, op. cit.

9 THAIS. Remorse has killed everything.
Ibid., Sc. 3

10 THAIS. Rumour never delays.   Ibid., Sc. 6

11 ANTONY. What pleasures God sends us, when
we resign ourselves to have none!
Ibid., Sc. 10

12 PAPHNUTIUS. Grace is the free gift of God and
does not depend on our merits. If it did, it could
not be called grace.   Ibid., Sc. 12

132. Daughter of Ki no Tsurayuki (fl. 947–967)

1 But if the *uguisu* * inquire
For their home, oh! what shall I say?
"The *Uguisu*'s Home," **
from *Go Shūi Shū,* Vol. IX,
An Anthology of Japanese Poems,
Miyamori Asatarō, ed. and tr.
1938

* A bird similar to a nightingale.
** Poem in response to Emperor Murakami's order to
transplant a plum tree from the poet's garden to his own.

133. Mother of Michitsuna (fl. 954–974)

1 Every day he promises that it shall be tomorrow.
And when tomorrow comes, it is to be the day
after. Of course I do not believe him; yet each
time that this happens I begin imagining that he
has repented,—that all has come right again. So
day after day goes by.
Diary entry (970), *Kagero
Nikki [Gossamer Diary]
954–974*

2 Have you any idea
How long a night can last, spent
Lying alone and sobbing?
Untitled, *One Hundred Poems
from the Japanese,*
Kenneth Rexroth, tr.   *1964*

134. 'Aisha bint Ahmad al-Qurtubiyya (fl. 965–999)

1 I am a lioness
and will never allow my body
to be anyone's resting place.   Untitled,
Elene Margot Kolb, tr.;
Women Poets of the World,
Joanna Bankier and Deirdre
Lashgari, eds.   *1983*

135. Sei Shonagon (966/67–1013?)

1 One writes a letter, taking particular trouble to
get it up as prettily as possible; then waits for

the answer, making sure every moment that it cannot be much longer before something comes. At last, frightfully late, is brought in—one's own note, still folded or tied exactly as one sent it, but so fingermarked and smudged that even the address is barely legible. "The family is not in residence," the messenger says, giving one back the note. *Makura no Soshi [The Pillow-Book of Sei Shonagon],* (991–1100), Arthur Waley, tr. *1928*

2 Among five thousand arrogants, you too will surely find a place. Ibid.

3. There is nothing in the whole world so painful as feeling that one is not liked. It always seems to me that people who hate me must be suffering from some strange form of lunacy. Ibid.

4 Writing is an ordinary enough thing; yet how precious it is! When someone is in a far corner of the world and one is terribly anxious about him, suddenly there comes a letter, and one feels as though the person were actually in the room. It is really very amazing. Ibid.

136. Nakatsukasa (fl. c.970)

1 Before they bloomed I longed for them;
After they bloomed, I mourned that they
must fade;
The mountain cherry-flowers
Sorrow alone for my poor heart have
made. "Pining for a Dead Child,"
in toto,
from *Go Shūi Shū,* Vol. I,
An Anthology of Japanese Poems,
Miyamori Asatarō, ed. and tr.
1938

137. Izumi Shikibu (974?–c.1030)

1 Ah, when I count the years still left,
I find them quickly told;
In all the world is nought so sad
As growing old.
"At the Close of the Year,"
in toto, from *Shin Kokin Shū,*
Vol. VI,
An Anthology of Japanese Poems,
Miyamori Asatarō, ed. and tr.
1938

2 Perhaps
A heart in love
Becomes a deep ravine? Untitled,
Edwin A. Cranston, tr.;
*The Penguin Book
of Women Poets,*
Carol Cosman, Joan Keefe and
Kathleen Weaver, eds. *1978*

3 When you broke from me
I thought I let the thread
of my life break Untitled,
Willis Barnstone, tr.,
A Book of Woman Poets,
Aliki and Willis Barnstone,
eds. *1980*

4 I wore out the darkness
until lazy dawn. Untitled,
Willis Barnstone, tr., op. cit.

138. Murasaki Shikibu (974–1031?)

1 . . . so quick was I at picking up the language [Chinese] that I was soon able to prompt my brother whenever he got stuck. At this my father used to sigh and say to me: "If only you were a boy how proud and happy I should be." But it was not long before I repented of having thus distinguished myself; for person after person assured me that even boys generally become very unpopular if it is discovered that they are fond of their books. For a girl, of course, it would be even worse. . . .
Murasaki Shikibu Nikki [The Diary of Murasaki Shikibu],
Hakubunkwan text
c.994–1010

2 Who has told you that the fruit belies the flower? For the fruit you have not tasted, and the flower you know but by report.* Ibid.

*Addressing Michinaga, the prime minister, and implying that he has neither read her book, *The Tale of Genji,* nor won her love.

3 "We are told," answered Genji, "that everything which happens to us in this life is the result of our conduct in some previous existence. If this is to be taken literally I suppose I must now accept the fact that in a previous incarnation I must have misbehaved myself in some way." *Genji Monogatari [The Tale of Genji],* (1001–1015) Vol. II, "The Sacred Tree," Ch. 3, Arthur Waley, tr. *1925–1933*

4 "What is all this about criminals?" he growled. "Surely you know that some of the most distinguished men in history both here and in China have been forced at one time or another to retire from Court. There is nothing disgraceful about it." Ibid.

5 "It is only as a background to music that the sound of the sea is tolerable." Ibid., Ch. 4

6 "A night of endless dreams, inconsequent and wild, is this my life; none more worth telling than the rest." Ibid.

7 "You had best be quick, if you are ever going to forgive me at all; life does not last forever."   Ibid., Ch. 5

8 Princes are the lamps that alight this world. . . .   Ibid., Ch. 9

9 "Though the snow-drifts of Yoshino were heaped across his path, doubt not that whither his heart is set, his footsteps shall tread out their way."   Ibid., Vol. III, "A Wreath of Cloud," Ch. 1

10 Indeed, she had seen enough of the world to know that in few people is discretion stronger than the desire to tell a good story. . . . Ibid., Ch. 2

11 "Beauty without colour seems somehow to belong to another world."   Ibid.

12 "I have noticed that children of good families, assured of such titles and emoluments as they desire, and used to receive the homage of the world however little they do to deserve it, see no advantage in fatiguing themselves by arduous and exacting studies."   Ibid., Ch. 3

13 "You cannot simply disappear while people are talking to you."   Ibid., Ch. 7

14 "But I have a theory of my own about what this art of the novel is, and how it came into being. . . . it happens because the storyteller's own experience of men and things, whether for good or ill . . . has moved him to an emotion so passionate that he can no longer keep it shut up in his heart."   Ibid.

15 "Some people have taken exception on moral grounds to an art [storytelling] in which the perfect and imperfect are set side by side. But even in the discourses which Buddha in his bounty allowed to be recorded, certain passages contain what the learned call Upāya or 'Adapted Truth'. . . ."   Ibid.

16 "I have never thought there was much to be said in favour of dragging on long after all one's friends were dead. . . ."
                          Ibid., Vol. IV, "Blue Trousers," Ch. 1

17 "It would be fatal, for example, if this situation were suddenly sprung upon the world in all its details. But allowed to leak out piecemeal, it will do very little harm. What matters is that people should have plenty of time to get used to one part of a scandal before the next is allowed to leak out."   Ibid.

18 "Now faithlessness, that once was held a crime, rules all the world, and he a half-wit is accounted whose heart is steadfast for an hour."   Ibid., Ch. 4

19 But unfortunately, Genji reflected, people who do not get into scrapes are a great deal less interesting than those who do.   Ibid., Ch. 6

20 "Though the body moves, the soul may stay behind."   Ibid., Ch. 7

21 "Think not that I have come in quest of common flowers; but rather to bemoan the loss of one whose scent has vanished from the air."
                          Ibid., Ch. 12

139. Akazome Emon (fl. c.11th century)

1 Why do I still long
  for the floating world?   Untitled,
                          The Burning Heart:
                          Women Poets of Japan,
                          Kenneth Rexroth and Ikuko
                          Atsumi, eds. and trs.   1977

140. Maryam bint Abi Ya'qub al-Ansari (fl. 1000–1035)

1 What can you expect
  from a woman with seventy-seven years,
  frail as the web of a spider?   Untitled,
                          Elene Margot Kolb, tr.;
                          Women Poets of the World,
                          Joanna Bankier and Deirdre
                          Lashgari, eds.   1983

141. Wallada (fl. 1000–1035)

1 Expect my visit when the darkness comes.
  The night I think is best for hiding all.
  If the full moon felt like me she wouldn't rise;
  if the star, it wouldn't move;
  if the night, it wouldn't fall.   Untitled,
                          Quoted in *The Troubadours and*
                          Their World of the Twelfth and
                          Thirteenth Centuries,
                          by Jack Lindsay   1976

2 Time passes, yet I see no end to your long
    absence,
  Nor does patience free me from the bondage
    of yearning!   "A Correspondence to
                          Ibn Zaidun:* #4,"
                          A. R. Nykl, tr.;
                          The Penguin Book
                          of Women Poets,
                          Carol Cosman, Joan Keefe and
                          Kathleen Weaver, eds.   1978

*Her lover, an Andalusian writer of classical Arabic poetry.

142. Lady Sarashina (1008–1060?)

1 They will come back next Spring—those
    cherry blooms
    that scatter from the tree.
  But how I yearn for her who left
  And never will return!
                          As I Crossed a Bridge of
                      Dreams: Recollections of Woman
                          in Eleventh Century Japan,
                          Ivan Morris, tr.   *1971*

2 There is no difference in their sounds—
  This wind that blows across the Barrier now
  And the one I heard so many years ago.
                                            Ibid.

143. Suo (fl. 1035–1065)

1 That spring night I spent
  Pillowed on your arm
  Never really happened
  Except in a dream.
  Unfortunately I am
  Talked about anyway.   Untitled,
                          One Hundred Poems
                          from the Japanese,
                      Kenneth Rexroth, ed. and tr.
                                            1964

144. Li Ch'ing-chao (1084–1151)

1 My body is a prisoner
  In this room above the misty
  River, the jade green river,
  That is the only companion
  of my endless days.   Untitled, St. 2,
                      Love and the Turning Year:
                      One Hundred More Poems
                          from the Chinese,
                      Kenneth Rexroth, ed. and tr.
                                            1970

2 Who can
  Take a letter beyond the clouds?
                              Untitled, op. cit.

3 Search. Search. Seek. Seek.
  Cold. Cold. Clear. Clear.
  Sorrow. Sorrow. Pain. Pain.
  Hot flashes. Sudden chills.
  Stabbing pains. Slow agonies.
                          "A Weary Song
                      to a Slow Sad Tune,"
                                  op. cit.

4 But I am startled by the breaking cup of
  Spring.   to the tune "A Hilly Garden,"
                          The Orchid Boat,
                      Women Poets of China,
                  Kenneth Rexroth and Ling
                  Chung, eds. and trs.   *1972*

5 Nothing is left of Spring but fragrant dust.
                          "Spring Ends," op. cit.

6 The jade
  burner
  is cold,
  a companion
  to
  my
  feelings,
  which
  are
  water.   Untitled,
                          St. 3, Willis Barnstone
                          and Sun Chu-chin, trs.;
                      A Book of Women Poets,
                  Aliki and Willis Barnstone, eds.
                                            1980

7 Dense
  sleep
  doesn't
  fade
  a wine
  hangover.   Untitled,
                              St. 2, op. cit.

8 There is no way to banish this feeling.
  As it leaves the eyebrows,
  it enters the heart.   to the tune "Yi chian
                                          mei,"
                          St. 3, Marsha Wagner, tr.;
                      Women Poets of the World,
                      Joanna Bankier and Deirdre
                      Lashgari, eds.   *1983*

145. Hildegarde von Bingen (1098–1179)

1 Greetings, greenest branch
                  Song 71, "About the Blessed
                              Virgin Mary,"
                  St. 1, *Symphony of the Harmony of*
                          Heavenly Relations
                              1151–1158

2 I am that supreme and fiery force that sends
  forth all living sparks. Death hath no part in
  me, yet I bestow death, wherefore I am girt
  about with wisdom as with wings. I am that
  living and fiery essence of the divine substance
  that glows in the beauty of the fields, and in the
  shining water, and in the burning sun and the
  moon and the stars, and in the force of the
  invisible wind, the breath of all living things, I
  breathe in the green grass and in the flowers,
  and in the living waters. . . . All these live and
  do not die because I am in them . . . I am the
  source of the thundered word by which all creatures were made, I permeate all things that they
  may not die. I am life.   *Book of Divine Works*
                                          c.1167

3 . . . man . . . rushes to woman like the stag to the spring, and the woman to him like the threshing floor of the barn, shaken and heated by the many blows of the flail when the grain is threshed.   Quoted in *Women in the Middle Ages* by Sibylle Harksen   *1975*

4 The prophetic spirit orders that God be praised with cymbals of jubilation and with the rest of the musical instruments which the wise and studious have created, since all of the arts (whose purpose is to fill uses and needs of man) are brought to life by that breath of life which God breathed into the body of man: and therefore it is just that God be praised in all things.
> Letter to the Prelates
> of Mainz (c.1178),
> Quoted in *Women in Music,*
> Carol Neuls-Bates   *1982*

146. Héloise (c.1098–1164)

1 Can it be said, in fact, that one is truly penitent, whatever be the bodily penances submitted to, when the soul still harbors the thought of sin and burns with the same passions as of old?
> Letter to Peter Abelard,*
> Quoted in
> *Women of Medieval France*
> by Pierce Butler   *1907*

*1079–1142. French theologian and philosopher.

2 The blessings promised us by Christ were not promised to those alone who were priests; woe unto the world, indeed, if all that deserved the name of virtue were shut up in a cloister.
> Ibid.

3 Riches and power are but gifts of blind fate, whereas goodness is the result of one's own merits.   Letter to Peter Abelard, #2,
> *The Letters of Abelard and Heloise,*
> C. K. Scott Moncrieff,
> tr.   *1925*

4 Prosperity seldom chooses the side of the virtuous. . . .   First letter to Abelard
> (c.1122),
> *The World's Great Letters,*
> M. Lincoln Schuster,
> ed.   *1940*

5 . . . I was more pleased with possessing your heart than with any other happiness . . . the man was the thing I least valued in you.
> Ibid.

6 We fluctuate long between love and hatred before we can arrive at tranquillity.   Ibid.

7 To my lord / no / my father
my husband / no / my brother
his servant / no / his daughter

his wife / no / his sister
To my Abelard his Heloise.   Untitled,
> Quoted in
> *Women in the Middle Ages*
> by Sibylle Harksen
> *1975*

8 When my self is not with you, it is nowhere
. . .   Letter to Peter Abelard,
> op. cit.

147. Alais (fl. c.12th century)

1 . . . shall I stay unwed? that would please me,
for making babies doesn't seem so good,
and it's too anguishing to be a wife.
> Untitled,
> St. 1, with Iselda and Carenza,*
> *The Women Troubadours,*
> Meg Bodin   *1976*

*See 148 and 150.

148. Carenza (fl. c.12th century)

Co-author with Alais. See 147:1

149. Domna H. (fl. c.12th century)

1 for when a man is in love's grip
it's wrong for him to knowingly
ignore his lady's orders.   Untitled, St. 2,
> *The Women Troubadours,*
> Meg Bodin   *1976*

150. Iselda (fl. c.12th century)

Co-author with Alais. See 147:1.

151. Kasmuneh (fl. c.12th–13th century)

1 A vine I see, and though 'tis time to glean,
No hand is yet stretched forth to cull the
fruit.   "Overripe Fruit,"
> *A Treasury of Jewish Poetry,*
> Nathan and Maryann Ausubel,
> eds.   *1957*

152. Mahādēviyakka (fl. 12th century)

1 husband, inside,
lover outside.
I can't manage them both.   Untitled,
> *Speaking of Siva,*
> A. K. Ramanujan, ed. and tr.
> *1973*

2 When all the world is the eye of the lord,
onlooking everywhere, what can you
cover and conceal? Untitled,
op. cit.

3 Till you know and lose this knowing
you've no way
of knowing
my lord white as jasmine.* Untitled,
op. cit.

*Another name for the god Siva.

153. Mahsati (fl. 12th century)

1 Better to live as a rogue and a bum,
a lover all treat as a joke
to hang out with a crowd of comfortable
drunks,
than crouch in a hypocrite's cloak.
Selected Quatrains, #1,
Deirdre Lashgari, tr.;
Women Poets of the World,
Joanna Bankier and Deirdre Lashgari,
eds. *1983*

2 Gone are the games we played all night,
gone the pearls my lashes strung.
You were my comfort and my friend.
You've left, with all the songs I'd sung.
Ibid., #4

154. Stewardess of the Empress Kōka
(fl. 12th century)

1 For the sake of a night
Short as the nodes
Of the reeds of Naniwa
Must I live on,
My flesh wasted with longing? Untitled,
*One Hundred Poems
from the Japanese*,
Kenneth Rexroth, tr. *1964*

155. T'ang Wan (fl. c.12th century)

1 The worlds love runs thin.
to the tune "The Phoenix
Hairpin,"
The Orchid Boat,
Women Poets of China,
Kenneth Rexroth and Ling
Chung, eds. and trs. *1972*

2 My troubled mind sways
Like the rope of a swing. Ibid.

156. Eleanor of Aquitaine (c.1122–1204)

1 Trees are not known by their leaves, nor even
by their blossoms, but by their fruits. In this
wise we have known your cardinals.
Letter to Pope Celestine III (1192),
Quoted in *Eleanor of Aquitaine*
by Amy Kelly *1950*

2 I have lost the staff of my age, the light of my
eyes. Comment on the death of
her son, Richard I (1199),
op. cit.

157. Frau Ava (?–1127)

1 I am yours,
you are mine.
Of this we are certain.
You are lodged
in my heart,
the small key
is lost.
You must stay there
forever. Attributed, attached to a letter
to a cleric (c.1160),
Willis Barnstone, tr.;
A Book of Women Poets,
Willis and Aliki Barnstone,
eds. *1980*

158. Tibors (c.1130–1182)

1 nor did it ever come to pass, if you went off
angry,
that I felt joy until you had come back
Untitled,
from *Die Provenzalischen
Dichterinnen*
by Oscar Schultz-Gora (1888),
Quoted in *The Women
Troubadours*,
Meg Bodin, tr. *1976*

159. Horikawa (fl. 1135–1165)

1 Will he always love me?
I cannot read his heart.
This morning my thoughts
Are as disordered
As my black hair. Untitled,
*One Hundred Poems
from the Japanese*,
Kenneth Rexroth and
Ikuko Atsumi, eds. and
trs. *1964*

160. Azalais de Porcairages (c.1140–?)

1 Now we are come to the cold time
                    Untitled, St. 1,
                    Quoted in
          The Women Troubadours,
          Meg Bodin, tr.   *1976*

2 Handsome friend, I'll gladly stay
forever in your service—
such noble mien and such fine looks—
so long as you don't ask too much
                    Ibid., St. 5

161. Beatritz de Dia (c.1140–post-1189?)

1 For times to come, I tell the plight
I've earned through loving in excess.
                    Untitled,
          *The Troubadours and Their
          World of the Twelfth and
          Thirteenth Centuries,*
          Jack Lindsay   *1976*

2 If all the pangs are mine, I say
unequal parts in love we play.   Untitled,
                    op. cit.

3 Those bad-talking gossips
No one who counts
Pays any attention to them.
They are a fog that rises
Against the sunlight.   Untitled,
                    St. 2, Doris Earnshaw, tr.;
          Women Poets of the World,
          Joanna Bankier and Deirdre
          Lashgari, eds.   *1983*

162. Marula (fl. c.1156)

1 She was troubled with indescribable love.
                    "Meeting after Separation,"
                    Tambimuttu and
                    G. V. Vaidya, trs.;
          Indian Love Poems,
          Tambimuttu, ed.   *n.d.*

163. Marie de France (1160?–1215?)

1 Whoever has received knowledge
and eloquence in speech from God
should not be silent or secretive
but demonstrate it willingly.
When a great good is widely heard of,
then, and only then, does it bloom,
and when that good is praised by man,
it has spread its blossoms.
                    Prologue, 11. 1–8,
          The Lais of Marie de France,
          Robert Hannings and Joan
          Ferrante. trs.   *1978*

2 Whoever deals with good material
feels pain if it's treated improperly.
                    "Guigemar,"
                    11. 1, 2, op. cit.

3 you have to endure what you can't change.
                    Ibid., 1. 410

4 But he who hides his sickness
can hardly be brought back to health;
love is a wound in the body,
and yet nothing appears on the outside.
                    Ibid., 11. 481–484

5 But Fortune, who never forgets her duty, turns
her wheel suddenly.   Ibid., 11. 538, 539

6 indeed, I condemned myself
when I slandered all womankind.
                    "Le Fresne [The Ash Tree],"
                    11. 79, 80, op. cit.

7 whether it makes you weep or sing
justice must be carried out.
                    "Lanval," 11. 435, 436
                    op. cit.

8 Whoever wants to tell a variety of stories ought
to have a variety of beginnings   "Milun,"
                    11. 1, 2, op. cit.

9 With the two of them it was just
as it is with the honeysuckle
that attaches itself to the hazel tree:
when it has wound and attached
and worked itself around the trunk,
the two can survive together;
but if someone tries to separate them,
the hazel dies quickly
and the honeysuckle with it.
"Sweet love, so it is with us:
You cannot live without me, nor I without
    you."   "Chevrefoil [The Honeysuckle],"
                    11. 68–78, op. cit.

10 "Whoever believes in a man is very
foolish."   "Eliduc," 1. 1084,
                    op. cit.

164. Alamanda (fl. 1165–1199)

1 I'm so angry that my body's
all but bursting into flame.   Untitled, St. 1,
                    Quoted in
          The Women Troubadours,
          Meg Bodin, tr.   *1976*

165. Marie de Ventadorn (c.1165–?)

1 . . . the lady
ought to do exactly for her lover
as he does for her, without regard to rank;

for between two friends neither one should
rule.   Untitled, St. 2,
                                         Quoted in
                   The Women Troubadours,
                   Meg Bodin, tr.   *1976*

2 . . . to me it's nothing short of treason
if a man says he's her equal *and* her
servant.   Ibid., St. 5

166. Garsenda de Forcalquier
(c.1170–?)

1 . . . it's you who stands to lose
if you're not brave enough to state your case
                                    Untitled, St. 1,
                                         Quoted in
                   The Women Troubadours,
                   Meg Bodin, tr.   *1976*

167. Aldrude (fl. 1170s)

1 It is by those only who are truly great, that
virtue is esteemed more than riches or honours,
or that virtuous actions can be duly
appreciated.   (1172) Quoted in *Biography
                       of Distinguished Women*
                   by Sarah Josepha Hale,* ed.
                                              1876

*See 703.

2 Courage is relaxed by delay.   Ibid.

168. Isabella (c.1180–?)

1 . . . if I sang your praises
it wasn't out of love
but for the profit I might get from it
                                    Untitled, St. 2,
                                         Quoted in
                   The Women Troubadours,
                   Meg Bodin, tr.   *1976*

169. Chu Shu-chên (fl. c.1182–1200)

1 I write poems, change and correct them,
And finally throw them away.   "Sorrow,"
                   *Love and the Turning Year:
                   One Hundred More Poems
                       from the Chinese,*
                   Kenneth Rexroth, ed. and tr.
                                              1970

2 Like a flight of arrows the wind
Pierces my curtain.
                   "Stormy Night in Autumn,"
                   *One Hundred Poems
                       from the Chinese,*
                   Kenneth Rexroth, ed. and tr.
                                              1971

3 Alone in the dark, I am
Going mad, counting my sorrow.   Ibid.

4 It is easier to see Heaven
Than to see you.   "Spring Joy,"
                   (1182), *The Orchid Boat,
                   Women Poets of China,*
                   Kenneth Rexroth and Ling
                   Chung, eds. and trs.   *1972*

170. Lombarda (c.1190–?)

1 but then when I remember what my name records,
all my thoughts unite in one accord.
                                    Untitled, St. 3,
                                         Quoted in
                   The Women Troubadours,
                   Meg Bodin, tr.   *1976*

171. Clare of Assisi (1193/94–1253)

1 . . . sisters beware of all pride, vain ambition,
envy, greed, and of taking part in the cares and
busy ways of the world . . .
                   Rule and Testament
                                              1253

172. Mistress of Albrecht of Johanns-dorf (fl. 13th century)

1 How can you combine two unlike things, to
cross the sea and bide with me? You leave the
tenderness of my heart, then how can you cherish it also?   Quoted in
                   Saint Elizabeth
                   By Elisabeth von Schmidt-Pauli;
                   Olga Marx, tr.   *1932*

173. Mukta Bai (fl. 13th century)

1 What is beyond the mind,
has no boundary,
In it our senses end.   Untitled,
                   Willis Barnstone, tr.;
                   A Book of Women Poets,
                   Aliki and Willis Barnstone, eds.
                                              1980

2 Mukta says: Words cannot contain him,
yet in him all words are.   Ibid.

174. La Compiuta Donzella (fl. 13th cen-tury)

1 To leave the world serve God
make my escape from all pretension . . .
That is my wish

For what I see flourish and ascend
the stalk is only
insanity, low acts and lies of men.
> Untitled, Sts. 1 and 2,
> Laura Stortoni, tr.;
> *Women Poets of the World,*
> Joanna Bankier
> and Deirdre Lashgari, eds.
> *1983*

2 . . . all men find evil
a proper ornament   Ibid., St. 3

175. Duchess of Lorraine (fl. 13th century)

1 Churl Death, who wars on all mankind,
you have taken from me what I most loved.
Now I am the Phoenix, alas! alone and bereft,
the single bird of which they tell.
> "Elegy," St. 3
> Quoted in
> *Medieval Lyrics of Europe*
> by Willard R. Trask, tr.   *1969*

176. Wang Ch'ing-hui (fl. c.13th century)

1 Suddenly, one day, war drums on horseback
Came like thunder, tearing off the sky,
And all glorious flowery days were gone
forever.   Untitled,
> *The Orchid Boat,*
> *Women Poets of China,*
> Kenneth Rexroth and Ling
> Chung, eds. and trs.   *1972*

177. Castelloza (c.1200–?)

1 . . . at any moment I might
rediscover reason to rejoice   Untitled, St. 4
> Quoted in
> *The Women Troubadours,*
> Meg Bodin, tr.   *1976*

2 the more I sing
the worse I fare in love   Untitled, St. 1,
op. cit.

3 And if you left me now,
I wouldn't feel a thing,
for since no joy sustains me
a little pain won't drive me mad.   Ibid., St. 4

178. Shikishi (?–1201)

1 The blossoms have fallen.
I stare blankly at a world
Bereft of color.   Untitled,
> *Anthology of Japanese Literature,*
> Donald Keene, ed. and tr.
> *1955*

179. Elizabeth of Thuringia (1206/07–1231)

1 We must not sadden God with sullen looks.
> Quoted in *Saint Elizabeth*
> by Elisabeth von Schmidt-Pauli;
> Olga Marx, tr.   *1932*

2 We are made loveless by our possessions.
> Ibid.

3 We women were allowed to stand at the Cross.
We saw His wounds bleed and His eyes grow
dim. As He was dying Jesus put His faith in us,
we were to carry His love through the whole
world and here we sit and have forgotten
Him.   Ibid.

180. Beruriah (fl. 1210–1280)

1 How do you make out [that such a prayer should
be permitted]? Because it is written "Let *hattaim* [sins] cease"? Is it written *hottim* [sinners]?
It is written *hattaim!* Further, look to the end of
the verse "and let the wicked men be no more."
Since the sins will cease, there will be no more
wicked men! Rather pray for them that they
should repent, and there will be no more
wicked.   Quoted in *The Jewish Woman:*
> *New Perspectives,*
> Elizabeth Koltun, ed.   *1976*

181. Mechtild von Magdeburg (c.1212–1283)

1 I come to my Beloved
Like dew upon the flowers.
> Introduction, *Das fliessende Licht
> der Gottheit [The Flowering Light of God]*
> *1344*

2 The fish cannot drown in the water, the bird
cannot sink in the air, gold cannot perish in the
fire, where it gains its clear and shining worth.
God has granted to each creature to cherish its
own nature. How can I withstand my
nature?   Ibid.

3 . . . a hungry man can do no deep study, and
thus must God, through such default, lose the
best prayers.   Ibid.

4 Those who would know much, and love little,
will ever remain at but the beginning of a godly
life.   Ibid.

5 I cannot dance, Oh, Lord, unless Thou lead
me.   Ibid.

6 Of the heavenly things God has shown me, I
can speak but a little word, not more than a
honey bee can carry away on its feet from an
overflowing jar.   Ibid.

182. Guillelma de Rosers (fl. 1235–1265)

1 a man who keeps his word is worth much
more
than one whose plans are constantly revised.
Untitled, St. 2,
Quoted in
The Women Troubadours,
Meg Bodin, tr.   *1976*

2 . . . there's no such thing
as chivalry that doesn't spring from love
Ibid., St. 3

183. Hadewijch (fl. 1235–1265)

1 All things
Crowd me in!
I am so wide!   "All things Confine,"
St. 1, Frans van Rosevelt, tr.;
*The Penguin Book
of Women Poets,*
Carol Cosman, Joan Keefe and
Kathleen Weaver, eds.   *1978*

2 Love appears every day
for one who offers love,
That wisdom is enough.   "Poem on the
Seven Names of Love,"
St. 2, Willis Barnstone
and Elene Kolb, trs.;
A Book of Women Poets,
Aliki and Willis Barnstone, eds.
1980

3 Take care, you who wish
to deal with names
for love. Behind their sweetness
and wrath, nothing endures.
Nothing but wounds and kisses.   Ibid., St. 10

184. Gertrude the Great (fl. 1256–1302)

1 . . . growing in the knowledge of virtue like
unto these trees, I flower in the greenness of
good deeds . . .
from *Legacy of Divine Piety,*
Quoted in *Women in the Middle
Ages: Religion, Marriage, and
Letters*
by Angela M. Lucas   *1983*

2 . . . looking down on things earthly in free
flight like these doves, I approach heaven, and
with my bodily senses removed from external
turmoil, apprehend thee with my whole mind
. . .   Ibid.

185. Lady Nijo (1258–1306?)

1 "Even consolation brings pain."
(1284), *The Confessions of Lady
Nijo,* Karen Brazell, tr.
1973

2 Its blossoms detaining travelers
The cherry tree guards the pass
On Osaka Mountain.   Ibid.   (1289)

3 A roof of cedar branches,
Pine pillows, bamboo blinds,
If only these could screen me
From this world of sorrow.   Ibid.

186. Kuan Tao-shêng (1262–1319)

1 I am your clay.
You are my clay.
In life we share a single quilt.
In death we will share one coffin.
"Married Love,"
*The Orchid Boat,
Women Poets of China,*
Kenneth Rexroth and Ling
Chung, eds. and trs.   *1972*

187. Empress Eifuku (1271–1342)

1 we
Were caught in bed by the dawn   Untitled,
*One Hundred More Poems
from the Japanese,*
Kenneth Rexroth, ed. and tr.
1974

188. Jeanne of Navarre (1271–1307/9?)

1 When you kill these Flemish boars, do not spare
the sows; them I would have spitted.
Attributed comment about
revolt of Flanders (1302),
Quoted in *Women
of Medieval France*
by Pierce Butler   *1907*

189. Padeshah Khatun (fl. 14th century)

1 Two yards of veil won't make any woman a
lady
nor a hat make any head worthy of command
"Sovereign Queen,"
Deirdre Lashgari, tr.;
Women Poets of the World,
Joanna Bankier and Deirdre
Lashgari, eds.   *1983*

190. Bridget of Sweden (1303–1373)

1 Mary is the lily in God's garden.
Revelations, Vol. III
1344–1349

2 Pride alienates man from heaven; humility
leads to heaven.   Ibid., Vol. V,
                           "Book of Questions"

3 The source of justice is not vengeance but
charity.   Ibid.

4 JUDGE. If the nobleman is superior to the commoner, the nobleman should fear that his ultimate Judgment will be the more severe, because
God has given him more.   Ibid.

5 To write well and speak well is mere vanity if
one does not live well.   Ibid.

6 Man, the author of evil, must bear it.   Ibid.

7 I beheld a Virgin of extreme beauty wrapped in
a white mantle and a delicate tunic . . . with
her beautiful golden hair falling loosely down
her shoulders. . . . She stood with uplifted
hands, her eyes fixed on heaven, rapt, as it
were, in an ecstasy of contemplation, in a rapture of divine sweetness. And while she stood
in prayer, I beheld her Child move in her womb
and . . . she brought forth her Son, from Whom
such ineffable light and splendor radiated that
the sun could not be compared to it. . . . And
then I heard the wonderful singing of many
angels.*   Ibid., Vol. VII

*Her vision of the nativity has become the standard, "in-
fluencing Western art, music, literature and even the decisions at the Council of Trent." (Anthony Butkovich,
Revelations, 1972).

8 Woe is me, I have become like a newborn whelp
that cannot see, and cannot find the paps of its
mother. Woe is me, for in my blindness I see
that I shall never see God.   Ibid., Vol. VIII,
                             "Written of the Devil"

9 The world would have peace if the men of
politics would only follow the Gospel.
                         Prayer, "In Honor of our Lord
                                   Jesus Christ,"
                         Quoted in Revelations
                         by Anthony Butkovich   1972

191. Juliana of Norwich (c.1342–1417?)

1 He shewed me a little thing, the quantity of a
hazel nut, lying in the palm of my hand. . . .
I looked thereupon and thought: "What may
this be?" And I was answered . . . thus: "It is
all that is made. . . . It lasts and ever shall last
because God loves it, and hath all-things its
being through the love of God."
                         Revelations of Divine Love,
                         Ch. 4   1373

2 And then our good Lord opened my ghostly
eye, and shewed me my soul in the midst of
my heart. I saw the soul so large as it were an
endless world, and also as it were a blessed
kingdom. And by the conditions that I saw

therein, I understood that it is a worshipful
city.   Ibid., Ch. 68

3 He said not, "thou shalt not be troubled, thou
shalt not be travailed, thou shalt not be dis-
eased;" but He said, "Thou shalt not be
overcome."   Ibid.

192. Catherine of Siena (1347–1380)

1 Every evil, harm, and suffering in this life or in
the next comes from the love of riches.
                         The Dialogue of the Seraphic
                         Virgin Catherine of Siena,
                         Algar Thorold, ed. and tr.
                                           1896

2 . . . the Devil invites men to the water of death
. . . and blinding them with the pleasures and
conditions of the world, he catches them with
the hook of pleasure . . .   Ibid., Ch. 44

3 The Devil often places himself upon the tongues
of creatures, causing them to chatter non-
sensically . . .   Ibid., Ch. 66

4 Thy miseries are not hid from thee now, for the
worm of conscience sleeps no longer . . .
                                   Ibid., Ch. 132

5 . . . if thou wish to reach the perfection of
love, it befits thee to set thy life in order.
                                   Letter to
                         Monna Alessa dei Saracini,
                         Saint Catherine of Siena
                         as Seen in her Letters,
                         Vida D. Scudder, ed. and tr.
                                           1906

6 Make two homes for thyself, my daughter.
One actual home . . . and another spiritual
home, which thou art to carry with thee
always. . . .   Ibid.

7 . . . perfection does not consist in macerating
or killing the body, but in killing our perverse
self-will.   Letter to Daniella of
                             Orvieto, op. cit.

8 . . . sometimes God works through rascally
men, in order that they may execute justice on
His enemy.   Letter to Giovanna,
                             Queen of Naples,
                             op. cit.

9 Vidi arcana Dei [I have seen the hidden things
of God].   Quoted in Catherine of Siena:
                                   Fire and Blood
                             by Igino Girodani;
                             Thomas J. Tobin, tr.
                                           1959

10 My soul . . . can see no other remedy pleasing
to God than peace. Peace, peace, therefore, for
the love of Christ crucified!
                         Letter to Pope Gregory XI,
                                   op. cit.

193. Jefimija (c.1348–c.1405)

1 The sorrow for him is burning steadily in
   my heart
  And I am overcome by my motherly ways.
         "The Lament Over the Dead Son
  Overcome by Her Motherly Ways," St. 3
              *An Anthology of Medieval
              Serbian Literature in English,*
              Mateja Matejic and Dragan
              Milivojevic, eds.   *1978*

194. Jevgenija (c.1353–1405)

1 Who is this one?
  Whisper into my ears!
  Is this the one for whom I used to
      long . . . ?   "Who Is This One?,"
              St. 1, *An Anthology of Medieval
              Serbian Literature in English,*
              Mateja Matejic and Dragan
              Milivojevic, eds.   *1978*

195. Margherita Datini (1360–1423)

1 You say, always sermonizing, that we will have
  a fine life, and every month and every week
  will be the one. You have told me this for ten
  years, and today it seems more timely than ever
  to reply: it is your fault. . . .
    If you delay so much, you will never seize
  this "fine life," and if you say, "Look at the
  hardships that I undergo every day, never can
  one live in this world without them:" that is no
  excuse for not living a fine life for the soul and
  the body.   Letter to [her husband]
              Francesco di Marco Datini
                    (January 1386),
              Quoted in *Women
              in the Middle Ages,*
              by Frances and Joseph Gies
                    1978

196. Christine de Pisan (1363/64–1430/ 31)

1 If it were customary to send little girls to school
  and to teach them the same subjects as are taught
  to boys, they would learn just as fully and would
  understand the subtleties of all arts and sciences.
  Indeed, maybe they would understand them better . . . for just as women's bodies are softer
  than men's, so their understanding is
  sharper.   Prologue,
              La Cité des Dames
              [The City of Women]   *1404*

2 Honour to Womankind! It needs must be
  That God loves Woman, since He fashioned
      Thee.*   Untitled,
                    St. 2 (1429),
                    Quoted in
              Of Six Medieval Women
              by Alice Kemp-Welch,
                    tr.   *1913*

3 She* seemeth fed by that same armour's
      touch,
  Nurtured on iron—   Untitled poem,
                    St. 1 (1429), op. cit.

*All references to Joan of Arc.

4 Learn to know what people are,
  And so, by seeing what they're like,
  Protect yourself from gross mistake.
              "Christine to Her Son,"
              St. 2, Barbara Howes, tr.;
                    Poems from France,
              William Jay Smith, ed.   *1967*

5 Where true love is, it showeth; it will not
      feign.   "The Epistel of Othea to
                    Hector,"
                    St. 27,
                    *The Penguin Book
                    of Women Poets,*
              Carol Cosman, Joan Keefe and
              Kathleen Weaver, eds.   *1978*

6 He is too unwise that, for default of one,
  will therefore despise woman everyone.
                    Ibid., St. 45

7 Trust not on fortune, called the great goddess;
  . . . .
  Before men's eyes she casteth a great mist.
  When they find her favourable, they think
      they be well;
  And yet is it feeble hold on a slipper eel.
                    Ibid., St. 74

8 I will not stay when you behave
  harshly, insult me like a cur,
  for things have changed. I won't concur
  and won't reveal my sorrow, save
  I'll always dress in black and rave.
                    Untitled, St. 3,
                    Willis Barnstone, tr.;
              A Book of Women Poets,
              Aliki and Willis Barnstone, eds.
                    1980

9 Alone am I, menaced by mourning,
  Alone am I, dyed deeper than dark brown,
  Alone am I, my love no longer living.
                    Untitled, St. 4,
              Julie Allen, tr., op. cit.

10 Marriage is a lovely thing   Untitled, St. 1,
                    Joanna Bankier, tr.;
              Women Poets of the World,
              Joanna Bankier and Deirdre
              Lashgari, eds.   *1983*

197. Lalleswari (fl. 1365–1399)

1 I set forth hopeful—cotton-blossom Lal.
Untitled,
George Grierson, tr., adapted by
Deirdre Lashgari;
Women Poets of the World,
Joanna Bankier and Deirdre
Lashgari, eds.   *1983*

2 Good repute is water carried in a sieve.
Untitled,
George Grierson, tr., op. cit.

198. Margaret of Nassau (fl. 1367)

1 Know, my love, that I should like to call
you a thief, because you have stolen my
heart. . . .   Letter to Matilda of Cleves
(1367),
Quoted in
Women in the Middle Ages
by Sibylle Harksen   *1975*

199. Chao Li-hua (fl. c.1368–1644)

1 my boat goes west, yours east
heaven's a wind for both journeys
"Farewell,"
J. P. Seaton, tr.;
A Book of Women Poets,
Aliki and Willis Barnstone, eds.
1980

200. Margery Kempe (1373–1438?)

1 She thought that she loved God more than He
did her. She was smitten with the deadly wound
of vainglory, and felt it not, for she many times
desired that the crucifix should loosen His hands
from the Cross, and embrace her in token of
love.   *The Book of Margery Kempe*
c.1435

2 "I have oftentimes told thee, daughter, that
thinking, weeping, and high contemplation is
the best life on earth, and thou shalt have more
merit in Heaven for one year of thinking in thy
mind than for a hundred years of praying with
thy mouth. . . ."   Ibid.

3 And sometimes those that men think were revelations, are deceits and illusions, and therefore
it is not expedient to give readily credence to
every stirring, but soberly abide . . .
Ibid., Ch. 89

201. Juliana Berners (1388?–?)

1 A faythfulle frende wold I fayne finde,
to fynde hym where he myghte be founde.
But now is the worlde wext so unkynde,
Yet frenship is fall to the grounde;
(Now a Frende I have Founde)
That I woll nother banne ne curse,
But of all frendes in felde or towne
Ever, gramercy, myn own purse.
"Song," St. 1,
Boke of Saint Albans   *1486*

202. A Northern Mother* (fl. 1350s)

*This is the only name this author is known by. We *assume*
she lived about the time of the date of her book but it may
well have been earlier.

1 Laugh not to scorne nodir [neither] olde ne
young,
Be of good bering and have a good tongue
The Good Wife Taught her
Daughter, St. 2   *1350*

2 . . . good name is worth gold. . .
Ibid., St. 13

3 . . . their thrift wexis thin
That spend more than they win   Ibid., St. 17

4 . . . better it is a childe to be unborne,
Than for unteaching to be forlorne.
Ibid., St. 24

203. Nahabed Kouchak (fl. 15th century)

1 My heart is turned into a wailing child,
In vain with sweets I seek to still its cries;
Sweet love, it calls for thee in sobbings wild
All day and night, with longing and with
sighs.
What solace can I give it?
"My Heart Is Turned into a
Wailing Child,"
St. 1,
Armenian Legends and Poems,
Zabelle C. Boyajian, ed.   *1916*

2 On the morning of thy birth
We were glad but thou wert wailing,
See that when thou leav'st the earth
Thou art glad and we bewailing.
"Birthday Song,"
St. 1, op. cit.

204. Mehri (c.1404–1447)

1 Each subtlety hard for the pedant to solve
I found a drop of wine would dissolve.
"Coming Across,"
Deirdre Lashgari, tr.,
Women Poets of the World,
Joanna Bankier and Deirdre
Lashgari, eds.   *1983*

205. Alessandra de' Machingi Strozzi (1406–1471)

1 One has nothing to do now but to pay taxes.
. . . It is miraculous how much money they
extort from us, and yet we seem to gain no
advantage.   Letter to her son,
Lorenzo (1452),
Quoted in
Famous Women of Florence
by Edgecumbe Staley, tr.
1909

2 Those who have no money are bound to go
down . . .   Letter to her son, Filippo
(1464),
op. cit.

3 A man, when he is a man indeed, makes woman
a woman.   Letter (c.1466),
op. cit.

206. Joan of Arc (c.1412–1431)

1 Messire, I am but a poor village girl; I cannot
ride on horseback nor lead men to battle.
Attributed response to vision of St.
Michael (c.1425),
Quoted in
Women of Beauty and Heroism,
by Frank B. Goodrich   *1858*

2 My brothers in Paradise tell me what to do.
Remark, op. cit.

3 I know neither A nor B; but I come from God
to deliver Orleans and consecrate the king.
Ibid.

4 Children say that people are hung sometimes for
speaking the truth.   Defense at her tribunal
(23 February 1431),
op. cit.

5 If I am not [in a state of grace], God bring me
there; if I am, God keep me there!   Ibid.

207. Isotta Nogarola (1418–1466)

1 There are already so many women in the world!
Why then . . . was I born a woman, to be
scorned by men in words and deeds?
Letter to Guarino Veronese,
Quoted in "Book-Lined Cells"
by Margaret King, tr.;
Beyond Their Sex,
Patricia Labalme, ed.   *1980*

208. Lucrezia de' Medici (1425–1482)

1 Here is the mighty king
He has conquered the evil
Which has lasted many years,
And makes the earth tremble
Removing sorrows from it
Thus filling the seats of paradise
To restore his court.
"Here is the Mighty King,"
Claudia Alexander with
Carlo Di Maio, trs.;
from *Laude,* Quoted in *Poesia
italiana: Il quatrocento,*
Giulio Ferroni, ed.   *1978*

209. Costanza Varano Sforza (1426–1447)

1 Even the wisest and most famous men would
fear to attempt to praise you adequately. What
then can I, an ignorant, unlettered, and inexperienced girl hope to do?   "Oration to
Bianca Maria Visconti,*
Quoted in "Book-Lined Cells"
by Margaret King, tr.;
Beyond Their Sex,
Patricia Labalme, ed.   *1980*

*Last surviving member of the Visconti family of Milan,
who dominated the history of northern Italy in the 14th and
15th centuries.

210. Sister Bertken (c.1427–c.1514)

1 I must sow lilies by the light of the dawn,
And start my work early as the new day is
born.   "A Ditty,"
St. 8 (1518), Jonathan Crewe, tr.;
Women Poets of the World,
Joanne Bankier and Deirdre
Lashgari, eds.   *1983*

211. Margaret of Anjou (1430–1482)

1 The world is always disposed to consider what
is done by a great and powerful monarch as of

course right, and even when it would seem to them wrong they believe that its having that appearance is only because they are not in a position to form a just judgment on the question, not being fully acquainted with the facts, or not seeing all the bearings of them.

> Remark to Henry VI,
> her husband,
> Quoted in *The History of*
> *Marguerite d'Anjou,*
> Ch. 9, by Jacob Abbott   *1861*

212. Macuilxochitl (1435–1499?)

1 Will my songs
be borne to his house
where he dwells in mystery?
Or do thy flowers bloom
here only?
Let the dance begin!   "Battle Song,"

> St. 2, Miguel León-Portilla and
> Catherine Rodriguez-Nieto, trs.;
> *Trece poetas del mundo azteca*
> *[Thirteen Poets of the Aztec World],*
> Miguel León-Portilla, ed.
> *1967*

213. Elizabeth Woodville Grey (1437?–1492)

1 . . . desire of kingdom knoweth no kindred . . .

> Speech to the Archbishop of
> Canterbury (1483),
> Quoted in *Chronicles*
> by Raphael Holinshed   *1577*

2 . . . for as ye think I fear too much, be you well ware that you fear not as far too little.

> Ibid.

214. Margaret Mautby Paston (1441–1484)

1 I would that ye should not be too hasty to be married till ye were more sure of your livelode, for ye must remember what charge ye shall have; and if ye have not [the means] to maintain it it will be a great rebuke. And therefore labour that ye . . . be more in surety of your land ere than ye be married.

> Letter to her son, John Paston II
> (1469),
> *The Paston Letters and Papers of*
> *the Fifteenth Century,*
> Pt. II, Norman Davis, ed.
> *1976*

215. Catherine of Genoa (1447–1510)

1 I am so washed in the tide of His measureless love that I seem to be below the surface of a sea and cannot touch or see or feel anything around me except its water.

> *La Vita della B. Caterina Fiesca*
> *Adorna Dama Genouese*
> *1681*

2 My Me is God, nor do I recognize any other Me except my God himself.   Quoted in

> *The Perennial Philosophy*
> by Aldous Huxley   *1945*

216. Isabella I (1451–1504)

1 Whosoever hath a good presence and a good fashion, carries continual letters of recommendation.   Quoted in

> *Apophthagmes New and Old,*
> #99, Francis Bacon, ed.
> *1625*

2 . . . kings who wish to reign have to labor. . . .

> Remark (1476), Quoted in *Isabella of Spain*
> by William Thomas Walsh
> *1930*

3 . . . in all human affairs there are things both certain and doubtful, and both are equally in the hands of God.   Ibid.

4 Since . . . kings, like other men, are exposed to mortal accidents . . . they should be prepared for death. . . .   Letter* to

> Archbishop of Granada,
> (1492/93),
> op. cit.

*Occasioned by the attempted assassination of her husband, King Ferdinand V of Aragon.

5 Although I have never doubted it . . . the distance is great from the firm belief to the realization from concrete experience.   Ibid.

217. Gwerfyl Mechain (c.1460–1500)

1 Before the men who drink here, I offer
a perfect world.
I want nothing more.
I walk among men, faultlessly,
sing intimate songs
and pour the mead.   "Lady of the Ferry Inn,"

> St. 2, Willis Barnstone, tr.;
> *A Book of Women Poets,*
> Aliki and Willis Barnstone, eds.
> *1980*

2 Tiny snow of the stunningly cold black day
  is white flour,
  is flesh of the earth,
  cold lamb fleece on the mountain
                          "In the Snowfall,"
                  St. 1, Willis Barnstone, tr.,
                                       op. cit.

218. Caterina Sforza (1462–1509)

1 Could I write all, the world would turn to
  stone.   Letter to her Dominican confessor
                              (c.1501–1509),*
                      Quoted in *The Medici*
                  by G. F. Young   *1930*

*From her prison in the Castel Sant'Angelo, Rome.

2 War is not for ladies and children like mine.
                      Letter to her uncle,
                  Ludovico Sforza il Moro
                      (27 August 1498),
                  Quoted in *Caterina Sforza*
                  by Ernst Breisach   *1967*

219. Clemence Isaure (1464–1515/16)

1 . . . I, alas, plaintive and solitary,
  I who have known only that I love, and that
  I suffer,
  I must—a stranger to the world, to happi-
      ness—
  Weep . . . and die.   Untitled,
                  St. 2, Michael Fanning, tr.;
                  *Dictats de Dona Clamenza
                          Isaure   1505*

220. Elizabeth of York (1465/66–1503)

1 Delivered from sorrow, annexed to pleas-
      ance,
  Of all comfort having abundance.
  This joy and I, I trust, shall never twin—
  My heart is set upon a lusty pin.
                  "My Heart Is Set
  Upon a Lusty Pin," St. 1, *The Women Poets
                              in English*,
              Ann Stanford, ed.   *1972*

221. Cassandra Fedele (1465–1558)

1 Do that for which nature has suited
  you. . . .   "Letter to Alessandra Scala,"
                  from *Clarissimae feminae
                  Cassandrae Fidelis benetae
              epistolae et orationes posthumae*
                              (1536),
                  Quoted in "Book-Lined Cells"
                      by Margaret King, tr.;
                          Beyond Their Sex,
              Patricia Labalme, ed.   *1980*

2 . . . many of you no doubt will see it as
  audacious, that I, a maiden . . . have come
  forth to speak in this radiance of learned
  men. . . .   "Oration delivered in Padua,"
                                       op. cit.

222. Florencia del Pinar (fl. 1465–1499)

1 These birds were born
  singing for joy;
  such softness imprisoned
  gives me much sorrow—
  yet no one weeps for me.   "To Some
                  Partridges, Sent to Her Alive"
                      (c.1511), Julie Allen, tr.;
                      A Book of Women Poets,
                  Aliki and Willis Barnstone, eds.
                                       1980

223. Laura Cereta (1469–1499)

1 Burning with the fires of hatred, the more they
  gnaw others, spewing forth words, the more are
  they wordless, gnawed within.
                          From *Epistolae*,
                  Quoted in "Book-Lined Cells"
                      by Margaret King, tr.;
                          Beyond Their Sex,
              Patricia Labalme, ed.   *1980*

2 The free mind, not afraid to labor, presses on
  to attain the good.   Ibid.

224. Elisabetta Gonzaga (1471–1526)

1 Who is there among us whose conduct is so
  perfect as to close the mouth of slanderers? . . .
  trouble yourself no more on the subject, but
  . . . allow the wrong to recoil on the heads of
  those who invent these slanders, and who, in
  my judgment, are sufficiently punished by seeing
  how hateful they become in the eyes of all
  virtuous and honest persons.
                  Letter to Isabella d'Este*
                              (1513),
                  Quoted in *Isabella d'Este*,
                  Vol. II, by Julia Cartwright
                                       1903

*See 225.

225. Isabella d'Este (1474–1530)

1 This [Milan] is the school of the Master and
  of those who know, the home of art and
  understanding.
              (1492), Quoted in *Beatrice d'Este*
                  by Julia Cartwright   *1899*

*See 226.

2 . . . the discontent of the people is more dangerous to a monarch than all the might of his enemies on the battlefield.
Letter to her husband (February 1495), from Milan, op. cit.

3 I am here in Mantua, but all my heart is in Rome.   Letter to Cardinal Bibbiena (1515),
Quoted in *Isabella d'Este*,
Vol. II, by Juliana Cartwright
1903

4 Neither hope nor fear. *(Nec spe nec metu.)*
Personal motto,
Quoted in *Great Ages of Man: The Renaissance*
by John R. Hale   *1964*

5 . . . resolve to think of nothing but . . . health in the first place and . . . honor and comfort in the second, because in this fickle world we can do nothing else, and those who do not know how to spend their time profitably allow their lives to slip away with much sorrow and little praise.   Letter to Elisabetta of Urbino (1492),
Quoted in *Lucrezia Borgia**
by Rachel Erlanger   *1978*

*See 230.

226. Beatrice d'Este (1475–1497)

1 I cannot say much of the perils of the chase, since game is so plentiful here that hares are to be seen jumping out at every corner—so much so, that often we hardly know which way to turn to find the best sport.
Letter to Isabella d'Este* (1491),
Quoted in *Beatrice d'Este*
by Julia Cartwright   *1899*

*See 225.

2 Wherever I turn, in the house or out-of-doors, I seem to see your face before my eyes, and when I find myself deceived, and realize that you are really gone, you will understand how sore my distress has been—nay, how great it still is.   Letter to Isabella d'Este, her sister (1495), op. cit.

227. Barbara Torelli (1475–1533)

1 Would that my fire might warm this frigid ice
And turn with tears, this dust to living flesh
Poem on the death of her husband* (1508),
Quoted in *Lucrezia Borgia***
by Rachel Erlanger   *1978*

*Her second husband was murdered by the Bentivoglio, the family of her first husband.
**See 230.

228. Elizabeth Brews (fl. 1477)

1 Cousin, it is but a simple oak that [is] cut down at the first stroke.   Letter to John Paston III, her son-in-law (February 1477),
Paston Letters, 1422–1509,
James Gairdner, ed.   *1904*

229. Agnes Paston (?–1479)

1 This world is but a thoroughfare, and full of woe; and when we depart therefrom, right nought bear with us but our good deeds and ill.
Letter to her son John (c.1444),
The Paston Letters and Papers of the Fifteenth Century,
Pt. II, Norman Davis, ed.   *1976*

2 There knoweth no man how soon God will call him; and therefore it is good for every creature to be ready. Whom God visiteth, he loveth.
Ibid.

230. Lucrezia Borgia (1480–1519)

1 . . . my husbands have been very unlucky.
Remark to her father after the murder of her second husband,
Quoted in *Lucrezia Borgia*,
Rachel Erlanger   *1978*

2 The more I try to do God's will the more he visits me with misfortune.
Remark upon hearing of the death of her brother, op. cit.

231. Margaret of Austria (1480–1530)

1 The time is troubled, but time will clear;
After the rain one awaits fair weather.
Untitled roundelay, St. 1,
Quoted in *Margaret of Austria: Regent of the Netherlands*
by Jane de Iongh: M. D. Herter-Norton, tr.   *1953*

2 All goes awry and lawless in the land,
Where power takes the place of justice.
Untitled roundelay, St. 1, op. cit.

3 *Fortune. Infortune. Fort. Une.* (Fortune persecutes one harshly.)   Motto (1506), op. cit.

232. Catherine of Aragon (1485–1536)

1 . . . I am in debt in London. . . . So that, my lord, I am in the greatest trouble and anguish in

the world. . . . I have now sold some bracelets to get a dress of black velvet, for I was all but naked; . . . certainly I shall not be able to live in this manner.　Letter to King Ferdinand of
Spain (1505),
Quoted in *Letters of Royal and
Illustrious Ladies
of Great Britain,*
Vol. I, Mary Anne Everett
Wood Green, ed.　*1846*

2 Our time is ever passed in continual feasts.
Letter to King Ferdinand of
Spain (1509),
op. cit.

3 They tell me nothing but lies here, and they think they can break my spirit. But I believe what I choose and say nothing. I am not so simple as I seem.　Letter to King
Ferdinand of Spain (1508),
Quoted in *Catherine of Aragon*
by Garrett Mattingly　*1941*

4 I came not into this realm as merchandise, nor yet to be married to any merchant.
Letter replying to request she
acquiesce to the marriage of
Henry VIII and Anne Boleyn*
(1533),
op. cit.

*See 249.

233. Elisabeth of Brandenburg (1485–1545)

1 I believe in Him who made the sun and the moon and all the stars. . . . May he not tarry to fetch me. . . . I am so weary of life.
Last words (1545),
Quoted in
Women of the Reformation,
Vol. I: *Germany and Italy,*
by Roland H. Bainton　*1971*

234. Veronica Gambara (1485–1550)

1 . . . we . . . lack all hope,
Sure of nothing but our dying.　Untitled,
Brenda Webster, tr.,
from *Rime* (1759);
The Penguin Book of Women Poets,
Carol Cosman, Joan Keefe and Kathleen
Weaver, eds.　*1978*

2 . . . blissful in heaven you see dawn appear
And under your feet you see the stars. . . .
Sonnet on the death of an
unidentified poet,
Claudia Alexander with Carlo
DiMaio, trs.;
from *Rime* (1759),
Poesia italiana: il cinquecento,
Giulio Ferroni, ed.　*1978*

235. Vittoria da Colonna (1492–1547/49)

1 Your virtue may raise you above the glory of being king. The sort of honour that goes down to our children with real lustre is derived from our deeds and qualities, not from power or titles.　Letter to Francesco,
Marquis of Pescara, her
husband,
Quoted in *Biography of
Distinguished Women*
by Sarah Josepha Hale*　*1876*

*See 703.

2 Thou knowest, Love, I never sought to flee
From thy sweet prison, nor impatient threw
Thy dear yoke from my neck; nor e'er
withdrew
What, that first day, my soul bestowed on
thee. . . .　Untitled sonnet (c.1525–1529),
Letter to Francesco, Marquis of
Pescara (1509),
Quoted in *A Princess of the
Italian Reformation:
Giulia Gonzaga**
by Christopher Hare**　*1912*

*See 253.
**Pseudonym of Marian Andrews.

3 . . . the swaggering knights prepare to ride.
The war begins. They gloat and cannot
wait.
They think they are masters of their fate
Untitled sonnet (c.1529–1549),
Quoted in
Women of the Reformation,
Vol. I: *Germany and Italy,*
by Roland H. Bainton,
tr.　*1971*

4 By true humility we reach the light
And know the sacred writings to be true.
Read little, then, and believe the more.
Untitled sonnet (c.1529–1549),
op. cit.

5 One cannot have a lively faith, I trow,
Of God's eternal promises if fear
Has left the warm heart chilled and sear
And placed a veil between the I and Thou.
Untitled sonnet (c.1529–1549),
op. cit.

6 That which dims other eyes, brightens
mine,
for, closing them, the door is opened
to sleep which brings me to my sun.
"When the Orient is lit,"
St. 4 (c.1525–1549),
tr. Brenda Webster;
Women Poets of the World,
Johanna Bankier and Deirdre
Lashgari, eds.　*1983*

236. Argula von Grumbach (1492–post-1563)

1 Where do you read in the Bible that Christ, the apostles, and the prophets imprisoned, banished, burned or murdered anyone?
Letter of protest to the faculty of the University of Ingolstadt (1523),
Quoted in *Women of the Reformation,* Vol. I: *Germany and Italy,* by Roland H. Bainton   *1971*

2 To obey my man indeed is fitting,
But if he drives me from God's Word
In Matthew ten it is declared
Home and child we must forsake
When God's honor is at stake.   *Untitled, op. cit.*

3 I am distressed that our princes take the Word of God no more seriously than a cow does a game of chess.
Letter to her cousin, Adam von Torring, op. cit.

4 I have even heard some say, "if my father and mother were in hell, I wouldn't want to be in heaven." Not me, not if all my friends were down there.   *Ibid.*

237. Marguerite of Navarre (1492–1549)

1 A father will have compassion on his son. A mother will never forget her child. A brother will cover the sin of his sister. But what husband ever forgave the faithlessness of his wife?
Mirror of the Sinful Soul 1531

2 . . . spite will make a woman do more than love. . . .   "Novel III, the first day,"
The Heptameron, or Novels of the Queen of Navarre 1558

3 I have heard much of these languishing lovers, but I never yet saw one of them die for love.   *Ibid.,* "Novel VIII, the first day"

4 To me it seems much better to love a woman as a woman, than to make her one's idol, as many do. For my part, I am convinced that it is better to use than to abuse.   *Ibid.,* "Novel XIII, the Second Day"

5 . . . all the lovers I have had have invariably begun by talking of my interests, and telling me that they loved my life, my welfare, and my honor, and the upshot of it all has no less invariably been their own interest, their own pleasure, and their own vanity.   *Ibid.,* "Novel XIV, the Second Day"

6 . . . no one ever perfectly loved God who did not perfectly love some of His creatures in this world.   *Ibid.,* "Novel XIX, the Second Day"

7 . . . there is no greater ninny than a man who thinks himself cunning, nor any one wiser than he who knows that he is not so.   *Ibid.,* "Novel XXIX, the Third Day"

8 He who knows his own incapacity, knows something, after all. . . .   *Ibid.*

9 . . . the first step man takes in self-confidence, removes him so far from the confidence he ought to have in God.   *Ibid.,* "Novel XXX, the Third Day"

10 Man is wise . . . when he recognizes no greater enemy than himself. . . .   *Ibid.*

11 . . . God always helps madmen, lovers, and drunkards. . . .   *Ibid.,* "Novel XXXVIII, the Fourth Day"

12 . . . fools live longer than the wise, unless someone kills them . . . for . . . fools do not dissemble their passions. If they are angry they strike; if they are merry they laugh; but those who deem themselves wise hide their defects with so much care that their hearts are all poisoned with them.   *Ibid.*

13 When one has one good day in the year, one is not wholly unfortunate.   *Ibid.,* "Novel XL, the Fourth Day"

14 A prison is never narrow when the imagination can range in it as it will.   *Ibid.*

15 Blessed . . . is he who has it in his power to do evil, yet does it not.   *Ibid.,* "Novel XLIII, the Fifth Day"

16 Though jealousy be produced by love, as ashes are by fire, yet jealousy extinguishes love as ashes smother the flame.
Ibid., "Novel XLVIII, the Fifth Day"

17 There is no hunter who does not take pleasure in blowing his horn over his quarry, or lover who is not very glad to proclaim the glory of his victory.   *Ibid.,* "Novel XLIX, the Fifth Day"

18 I never knew a mocker who was not mocked . . . a deceiver who was not deceived, or a proud man who was not humbled.   *Ibid.,* "Novel LI, the Sixth Day"

19 People pretend . . . not to like grapes when they are too high for them to reach.   *Ibid.,* "Novel LIII, the Sixth Day"

20 . . . some there are who are much more ashamed
of confessing a sin than of committing it.
Ibid.,
"Novel LX, the Sixth Day"

21 I did not know that love could grow through
death. But now I know.
Dialogue on the death of her
brother, King Francis I (c.1547/48),
Quoted in
Women of the Reformation,
Vol. II: France and England,
by Roland H. Bainton   1973
op. cit.

238. Mary of France (1496–1533)

1 God's will sufficeth me. (La Volonté de Dieu
me suffit.)   Personal motto (1514),
Quoted in Mary Tudor: The
White Queen
by Walter C. Richardson
1970

2 Sir, your Grace knoweth well that I did marry
for your pleasure . . . and now I trust you will
suffer me to marry as me liketh for to do.
Letter to her brother, Henry VIII
(c.1514/15),
op. cit.

239. Katherine Zell (1497/98–1562)

1 You remind me that the Apostle Paul told women
to be silent in church. I would remind you of
the word of this same apostle that in Christ there
is no longer male nor female.
"Entschuldigung [Apology of]
Katharina Schutzinn" (1524),
Quoted in
Women of the Reformation,
Vol. I: Germany and Italy,
by Roland H. Bainton   1971

2 Faith is not faith which is not tried.
"Den Leydenden
Christgläubigen" [To Suffering
Believers in Christ] (1524),
op. cit.

3 Save us from murmuring against any cross laid
upon us.   "Den Psalmen Misere"
(1558),
op. cit.

4 Lead us not into the temptation of believing
that we have truly forgiven, while rancor
lingers. . . .   Ibid.

240. Mira Bai (1498–1547)

1 She drinks the honey of her vision.   Untitled,
St. 4, Willis Barnstone
and Usha Nilsson, trs.;
A Book of Women Poets,
Aliki and Willis Barnstone, eds.
1980

2 Hari is an ocean,
my eyes touch him.
Mira is an ocean of joy.
She takes him inside.   Untitled, op. cit.

3 The energy that holds up mountains is the one
Mirabai bows down to, He lives century after
century, and the test I set for him he has
passed.   "The Clouds,"
News of the Universe,
Robert Bly, ed. and adapter
1980

4 I have felt the swaying of the elephant's
shoulders . . .
and now you want me to climb on a
jackass? Try to be serious!
"Why Mira Can't Go Back to her
Old House,"
op. cit.

5 Get up, dear child, the dawn has come,
outside the door wait gods and men.
Untitled,
Usha Nilsson, tr.;
Women Poets of the World,
Joanna Bankier and Deirdre
Lashgari, eds.   1983

241. Huang O (1498–1569)

1   Once more I will shyly
Let you undress me and gently
Unlock my sealed jewel.   "A Farewell to
A Southern Melody,"
The Orchid Boat,
Women Poets of China,
Kenneth Rexroth and Ling
Chung, eds. and trs.   1972

2   I will allow only
My lord to possess my sacred
Lotus pond, and every night
You can make blossom in me
Flowers of fire.   To the tune "Soaring
Clouds,"
op. cit.

3 Maybe you can fool some girls,
But you can't fool Heaven.
To the tune "Red Embroidered
Shoes,"
op. cit.

4 Go and make somebody else
Unsatisfied.   Ibid.

242. Diane de Poitiers (1499–1566)

1 Farewell sweet kisses, pigeon-wise,
  With lip and tongue, farewell again
  The secret sports betwixt us twain
            "To Henry II Upon His Leaving
                      for a Trip" (c.1552),
            Quoted in *The Life and Times of
                Catherine de Medici**
            by Francis Watson   *1935*

*See 258.

2 The years that a woman subtracts for her
    age are not lost. They are added to the
    ages of other women.   Attributed,   *n.d.*

243. Lal Ded (fl. 16th century?)

1 Like water in goblets of unbaked clay
  I drip out slowly,
  and dry.   Untitled,
            Willis Barnstone, tr.;
            A Book of Women Poets,
            Aliki and Willis Barnstone,
                      eds.   *1980*

2 I came by the way
  but didn't go back by the way.   Untitled,
            Willis Barnstone, tr., op. cit.

244. Honor Lisle (c.1500–1550)

1 Good my lord, whereas in my former letters I
  have written to you that you should write to me
  with your own hand, whereof two lines should
  be more comfort to me than a hundred of another
  man's hand. . . .
            Letter to Arthur Plantagenet
                              (1539),
            Quoted in *Letters of Royal and
            Illustrious Ladies of Great Britain,*
            Vol. III, Mary Everett Wood
                Green, ed.   *1846*

245. Caterina Cibo (1501–1557)

1 . . . all creatures are flames of love.
            Quoted in *Seven Dialogues*
            by Bernardino Orchino (n.d.);
                              cited in
            Women of the Reformation,
            Vol. I: *Germany and Italy,*
            by Roland H. Bainton   *1971*

2 We have but a little knowledge of God. . . .
    We are like bats who cannot look upon the light
    of the sun. God is infinite, immense, uncircum-
    scribed, but our intellect is finite, limited, im-
    prisoned in this body of darkness, stained with
    primal sin.   Ibid.

246. Maria of Hungary and Bohemia (1505–1558)

1 Full well I know
  God is my sword,
  And of my Lord
  None is me relieving.   Untitled,
                      St. 1 (1529),
            Women of the Reformation,
            Vol. III: *From Spain to
                      Scandinavia,*
            by Roland H. Bainton   *1977*

247. Mihri Hatun (?–1506)

1 At one glance
  I love you
  With a thousand hearts   Untitled,
            St. 1, Tâlat S. Halman, tr.;
                      *The Penguin Book
                      of Women Poets,*
            Carol Cosman, Joan Keefe and
            Kathleen Weaver, eds.   *1978*

2 Let the zealots think
  Loving is sinful
  Never mind
  Let me burn in the hellfire
  Of that sin   Ibid., St. 3

248. Hwang Chin-i (c.1506–1544)

1 I cut in two
  A long November night   Untitled,
                      Peter H. Lee, tr.;
                      *The Penguin Book
                      of Women Poets,*
            Carol Cosman, Joan Keefe and
            Kathleen Weaver, eds.   *1978*

2 Mountains are steadfast but the mountain
                      streams
  Go by, go by
  And yesterdays are like the rushing
                      streams,
  They fly, they fly,
  And the great heroes, famous for a day,
  They die, they die.   Untitled,
                Peter H. Lee, tr., op. cit.

249. Anne Boleyn (1507–1536)

1 Commend me to the king, and tell him he is
  constant in his course of advancing me; from a
  private gentlewoman he made me a marquise,
  and from a marquise a queen; and now, as he
  had left no higher degree of earthly honour, he
  hath made me a martyr.   (19 May 1536),
                      Quoted in
            Apophthagmes New and Old,
            No. 9, Francis Bacon   *1625*

2 I will rather lose my life than my virtue, which will be the greatest and best part of the dowry I shall bring my husband.
Letter to Henry VIII,
Quoted in
Women of Beauty and Heroism
by Frank B. Goodrich 1858

3 I have heard say the executioner is very good, and I have a little neck. Remark shortly before
execution (19 May 1536),
op. cit.

4 Alas! poor head, in a very brief space thou wilt roll in the dust upon the scaffold; and as in life thou didst not merit to wear the crown of a queen, so in death thou deservest not better doom than this.* Spoken at her execution
(19 May 1536),
op. cit.

*The linen cap she placed over her head before submitting to the executioner.

5 What will be, will be, grumble who may. *(Ainsi sera, groigne qui groigne.)*
Motto embroidered on servants'
livery (c.1530/31),
Quoted in *Anne Boleyn*
by Marie Louise Bruce 1972

6 I am her death, as she is mine.
Said of Catherine of Aragon's*
death (January 1536),
op. cit.
*See 232.

7 The people will have no difficulty in finding a nickname for me, I shall be Queen Anne Lack-Head. Spoken at her execution
(19 May 1536),
op. cit.

250. Elisabeth of Braunschweig (1510–1558)

1 Obey God, the emperor, and your mother.
Treatise on government written
for her son, Erich II,
Quoted in
Women of the Reformation,
Vol. I: *Germany and Italy,*
by Roland H. Bainton 1971

2 Woe, woe, woe and again woe to you if you do not change. Letter to her son,
op. cit.

3 Better be hurt than to hurt. Hymn,
op. cit.

4 No one without the experience knows the anguish which children can cause and yet be loved. From *Book of Consolation for Widows,*
op. cit.

251. Marina de Guevara (c.1510–1559)

1 Better than the castigation of the flesh is the overcoming of pride and anger.
Testimony before the Inquisition
(1558/59),
Women of the Reformation,
Vol. III: *From Spain to Scandinavia,*
by Roland H. Bainton 1977

2 To bring the heart into tune with God is better than audible prayer. Ibid.

252. Renée de France (1510–1575)

1 . . . Satan is the father of lies and God of the truth. . . . Letter to John Calvin*
(1564),
Quoted in *Queen of Navarre:
Jeanne d'Albret**
by Nancy Lyman
Roelker 1968

*1509–64. French religious reformer.
**See 271.

2 Had I had a beard I would have been the King of France. I have been defrauded by that confounded Salic law.* Quoted in *Women of the
Reformation,*
Vol. I: *Germany and Italy,*
by Roland H. Bainton 1971

*European law of succession (derived from a 5th-century Frankish code) preventing women from succeeding to a throne.

253. Giulia Gonzaga (1513–1566)

1 What mad credulity is ours! How infinite is the cupidity of mortals! Letter to Livia
Negra,
Quoted in *A Princess of the
Italian Reformation:
Giulia Gonzaga*
by Christopher Hare* 1912
*Pseudonym of Marian Andrews.

2 . . . what should we do if we had to remain in this world perpetually? We cannot inhabit a house for three days in this miserable world without being dissatisfied. Ibid.

3 The promises of the alchemist are like those of the astrologers, who boast that they can foretell future things, and do not even know the present or the past. . . . I do not know whether their fraud is more shameful, or our folly in believing, as we do. . . . Ibid.

254. Catherine Parr (1513–1548)

1 A goodly example and lesson for us to follow at all times and seasons, as well in prosperity as in adversity, to have no will but God's will. . . . But we be yet so carnal and fleshly, that we run headlong like unbridled colts, without snaffle or bit.

If we had the love of God printed in our hearts, it would keep us back from running astray. And until such time as it pleases God to send us this bit to hold us in, we shall never run the right way, although we speak and talk never so much of God and His word.
"The Lamentation on or Complaint of a Sinner," *The Lamentation of a Sinner* 1545

2 We be so busy and glad to find and spy out other men's doings that we forget and can have no time to weigh and ponder our own. Ibid.

255. Chiara Cantarini Matraini (1514–post-1597)

1 Return soul of the sky, candid moon
To the first sphere, shining and beautiful,
And with your customary brilliance restore
The crown of silver to the darkened sky
Untitled sonnet,
Claudia Alexander with Carlo DiMaio, trs.;
from *Poemas* (1560),
Poesia italiana: il cinquecento,
Giulio Ferroni, ed. 1978

2 . . . that weak and tired vessel finding
Itself with broken mast and sail
Bereft of helmsman, tossed by monstrous waves,
Seems like my soul deprived of light, bereft of every hope. Untitled sonnet, op. cit.

256. Teresa of Avila (1515–1582)

1 The hour I have long wished for is now come. Last words (1582)
Quoted in
Distinguished Women Writers by Virginia Moore 1934

2 How is it that there are not many who are led by sermons to forsake open sin? Do you know what I think? That is because preachers have too much worldly wisdom. They are not like the Apostles, flinging it all aside and catching fire with love of God; and so their flame gives little heat. "Life" (1562),
The Complete Works of Saint Teresa of Jesus,
Vol. I, E. Allison Peers, ed. and tr. 1946

3 I only wish I could write with both hands, so as not to forget one thing while I am saying another. "Way of Perfection," Ch. 20 (1579),
op. cit., Vol. II

4 . . . I believe that honour and money nearly always go together . . . seldom or *never* is a poor man honoured by the world; however worthy of honour he may be, he is apt rather to be despised by it. Ibid., Ch. 22

5 How is it, Lord, that we are cowards in everything save in opposing Thee?
"Exclamations of Soul to God" (1569),
Selected Writings of St. Teresa of Avila,
E. Allison Peers, tr.; William J. Doheny, ed. 1950

6 O incomprehensible Wisdom! In truth Thou needest all the love which Thou hast for Thy creatures to enable Thee to endure such folly and to await our recovery. . . . Ibid.

7 It is true that we cannot be free from sin, but at least let our sins not be always the same. . . . "Conception of Love of God" (1571),
op. cit.

8 If we plant a flower or a shrub and water it daily it will grow so tall that in time we shall need a spade and a hoe to uproot it. It is just so, I think, when we commit a fault, however small, each day, and do not cure ourselves of it. Ibid.

9 Humility must always be doing its work like a bee making its honey in the hive: without humility all will be lost. "Interior Castle" (1577),
op. cit.

10 Untilled soil, however fertile it may be, will bear thistles and thorns; and so it is with man's mind. "Maxims for Her Nuns," op. cit.

11 Accustom yourself continually to make many acts of love, for they enkindle and melt the soul. Ibid.

12 Be gentle to all and stern with yourself. Ibid.

13 Remember that you have only one soul; that you have only one death to die; that you have only one life, which is short and has to be lived by you alone; and there is only one glory, which is eternal. If you do this, there will be many things about which you care nothing. Ibid.

14 . . . about the injunction of the Apostle Paul
that women should keep silent in church? Don't
go by one text only.   Letter,
Quoted in *Women of the
Reformation,*
Vol. III: *From Spain to
Scandinavia,*
by Roland H. Bainton   *1977*

15 Let nothing disturb thee,
Nothing affright thee;
All things are passing;
God never changeth.
Patient endurance
Attaineth to all things;
Who God possesseth
In nothing is wanting;
Alone God sufficeth.   "Nada te turbe"
("Nothing disturbs thee"; aka
"Saint Teresa's Bookmark"),
in toto, Henry Wadsworth
Longfellow, tr.;
An Anthology of Spanish Poetry,
John A. Crow, ed.   *1979*

16 God walks among the pots and pipkins.
Attributed   *n.d.*

257. Mary I of England (1516–1558)

1 When I am dead and opened, you shall find
"Calais" lying in my heart.
Quoted in *Chronicles,*
Vol. III, by Raphael
Holinshed   *1585*

2 . . . there are two things only, soul and body.
My soul I offer to God, and my body to your
Majesty's service.
Letter to Edward VI (c.1552),
Quoted in *Catherine of Aragon*
by Garrett Mattingly   *1942*

3 May it please you to take away my life rather
than the old religion.   Ibid.

258. Catherine de' Medici (1519–1589)

1 Ah, sentiments of mercy are in unison with a
woman's heart.   Quoted in *The
Huguenots in France and
America,*
Vol. I, Ch. 3, by Hannah
Farnham Lee*   *1843*

*See 682.

2 . . . suppress this violence of emotion. I have
always found it best *to appear to yield.* Assume
a seeming conformity to your husband's will,
even attend mass, and you will more easily get
the reins into your own hands.   Ibid., Ch. 7,
Remark to Queen of Navarre,*

*See 237.

3 *Lachrymae hinc, hinc dolor.* (Tears henceforth,
henceforth sadness.)   Motto (1559),
Quoted in *The Medici*
by G. F. Young   *1930*

4 When I see these poor people burnt, beaten, and
tormented, not for thieving or marauding, but
simply for upholding their religious opinions,
when I see some of them suffer cheerfully, with
a glad heart, I am forced to believe that there is
something in this which transcendeth human
understanding.
Letter regarding persecution of
Protestants (1559/60),
op. cit.

5 If things were even worse than they are after all
this war they might have laid the blame upon
the rule of a woman; but if such persons are
honest they should blame only the rule of men
who desire to play the part of kings. In future,
if I am not any more hampered, I hope to show
that women have a more sincere determination
to preserve the country than those who have
plunged it into the miserable condition to which
it has been brought.   Letter to Ambassador of
Spain (1570),
op. cit.

6 . . . never did woman who loved her husband
succeed in loving his whore. One must call a
spade a spade, though the term is an ugly one
on the lips.   Letter (1583),
Quoted in *Women of Power*
by Mark Strage   *1976*

259. Laura Terracina (c.1519–1577?)

1 . . . alas, who has taken you from me?
Who has torn you from my breast so bra-
zenly
And locked such beauty in a little grave?
Untitled sonnet,
Claudia Alexander with Carlo
DiMaio, trs.;
Poesia italiana: il cinquecento,
Giulio Ferroni, ed.   *1978*

2 . . . I see virtue abandoned
and the Muses enslaved by such baseness
that my brain is nearly overwhelmed.
"Sonnett to Marcantonio
Passero,"
Claudia Alexander, tr., op. cit.

260. Catherine Willoughby (1519/20–1580)

1 Undoubtedly the greatest wisdom is not to be
too wise. . . .
Letter to William Cecil (1559),
Quoted in
Women of the Tudor Age
by Cecilie Gaff   *1930*

2 . . . though God wink . . . He sleepeth
not. . . . Ibid.

3 Christ's plain coat without a seam is fairer
to the older eyes than all the jaggs* of
Germany. Ibid.

*A slash made in a garment to show a different color
beneath.

4 God is a marvellous man.
Quoted by Catherine Parr* in a
letter to Thomas Seymour
(c.1548),
Cited in *Tudor Women*
by Alison Plowdon 1979

*See 254.

261. Anne Askew (1520–1546)

1 . . . unadvised hasty judgment is a token apparent of a very slender wit.
Testimony at inquisition (1545),
Quoted in *Actes and monuments
of these latter and perillous dayes*
(aka *The Book of Martyrs*)
by John Foxe 1563

2 God has given me the bread of adversity and
the water of trouble. Letter to King
Henry VIII (1546),
op. cit.

3 . . . what God hath charged me with his mouth,
that have I shut up in my heart. Ibid.

4 Like as the armed knight
Appointed to the field,
With this world will I fight,
And faith shall be my shield.
"The Ballad Which Anne Askew
Made and Sang When She Was
in Newgate,"
St. 1 (1547),
The Women Poets in English,
Ann Stanford, ed. 1972

262. Madeleine Fradonnet (c.1520–1587)

1 Distaff, my pride and care, I vow to thee
That I shall love thee ever nor exchange
Thy homely virtue for a pleasure strange
"To My Distaff,"
with Catherine Fradonnet,
*Anthology of European Poetry,
13th to 17th century,*
William Stirling, tr.; Mervyn
Savill, ed. 1947

263. Pernette du Guillet (c.1520–1545?)

1 True love, to whom my heart is prey,
How dost thou hold me in thy sway,
That in each day I find no fault
But daily wait for love's assault "Song,"
St. 1, William Stirling, tr. (1947);
*Rymes de Gentille et Vertueuse
Dame de Pernette due Guillet,
Lyonaisse* (1545)

2 As the body denies the means to look
Into the spirit or know its force,
Likewise Error for me drew
Around my eyes the blindfold of ignorance
"Epigram,"
Joan Keefe with Richard
Terdiman, trs. (1978), op. cit.

3 I no longer need be concerned
whether daylight goes or night comes,
. . . because my Day,* with tender brilliance,
enlightens me through and through.
"Epigram 8,"
Ann Rosalind Jones, tr. (1981),
op. cit.

*Allusion to the poet Maurice Scève, with whom she had
a liaison.

264. Isabella da Morra (1520–1546)

1 Once more, O arid valley
O wild river, O wretched, barbarous stones
You shall hear my eternal pain and weep-
ing. Untitled sonnet,
Claudia Alexander with Carlo
DiMaio, trs.;
Poesia italiana: il cinquecento,
Giulio Ferroni, ed. 1978

2 Turbid Siri,* now that my bitter end is here,
proclaim my sorrow. . . .
Tumultuously incite your waves
And say, "Not merely tears, but the copi-
ous weeping
Of Isabella increased me while she lived."
Untitled poem,
Claudia Alexander with Carlo
DiMaio, trs., op. cit.

*A river running between Calabria and Basilicata in south-
ern Italy.

265. Ippolita Castiglione (?–1521)

1 My dear Lord,—I have got a little daughter, of
which I think you will not be sorry. I have been
much worse than I was last time, and have had
three attacks of high fever, but to-day I feel
better, and hope to have no more trouble. I will

not try to write more, lest I overdo myself, but commend myself to you with all my heart— Your wife who is a little tired out with pain, your Ippolita.

> Letter to Baldassare Castiglione, her husband (24 August 1521; four days before her death), Quoted in *Isabella D'Este** by Julia Cartwright *1903*

*See 225.

266. Lucrezia Gonzaga (1522–pre-1552)

1 . . . a poor man's life is like sailing near the coast, whereas that of a rich man resembles the condition of those who are in the main sea. The former can easily throw a cable on the shore, and bring their ship safe into a harbour; whereas the latter cannot do it without much danger and difficulty.

> Letter to Hortensio Lando, Quoted in *Women's Record* by Sarah Josepha Hale* *1855*

*See 703.

2 . . . all things are good which are according to nature, and what is there more natural to all men than death?

> Letter to Ippolita Gonzaga (c.1552), Quoted in *A Princess of the Italian Reformation: Giulia Gonzaga* by Christopher Hare* *1912*

*Pseudonym of Marian Andrews.

3 . . . he alone acts wisely who, being mortal, expects nothing from this life of ours but mortal things.

> Ibid.

267. Luisa Sigea (1522–1560)

1 You have written me a letter which . . . exudes the fragrance of a life unspotted, which I would inhale were I not so spoiled by the stench of the human as to be incapable of the divine. . . .

> Letter to a friend (n.d.), *Women of the Reformation, Vol. III: From Spain to Scandinavia,* by Roland H. Bainton *1977*

2 Blaze with the fire that is never extinguished.

> "Dialogue of Blesilla and Flaminia," op. cit.

268. Gaspara Stampa (1523–1554)

1 Love made me such that I live in fire like a new salamander on earth

or like that other rare creature, the Phoenix,
who expires and rises at the same time.

> Untitled sonnet, Lynne Lawner, tr.; *The Penguin Book of Women Poets,* Carol Cosman, Joan Keefe and Kathleen Weaver, eds. *1978*

2 I hate who loves me, love who scorns me.

> Untitled sonnet, Lynne Lawner, tr., op. cit.

3 O love, what strange and wonderful fits:
one sole thing, one beauty alone,
can give me life and deprive me of wits.

> Untitled sonnet, J. Vitiello, tr., *A Book of Women Poets,* Aliki and Willis Barnstone, eds. *1980*

4 Deeply repentant of my sinful ways
And of my trivial, manifold desires,
Of squandering, alas, these few brief days
Of fugitive life in tending love's vain fires

> Untitled sonnet, Lorna de'Lucchi, tr., *Women Poets of the World,* Joanna Bankier and Deirdre Lashgari, eds. *1983*

269. Louise Labé (1524/25–1566)

1 O terrible fate! Suffering the scorpion to feast
on me, I seek protection from the pain
of poison by appealing to the beast
that stings me.

> Sonnet I, *Oeuvres* (1555), Willis Barnstone, tr.; *A Book of Women Poets,* Aliki and Willis Barnstone, eds. *1980*

2 A woman's heart always has a burned mark.

> Sonnet II, Wilis Barnstone, tr., op. cit.

3 However much Love tries to batter us
our force congeals at every impetus,
becoming fresh with each attacking prong.

> Sonnet IV, Willis Barnstone, tr., op. cit.

4 I live, I die, I burn myself and drown.

> Sonnet VIII, Willis Barnstone, tr., op. cit.

5 Only outside my body can I live
or else in exile like a fugitive.

> Sonnet XVII,* op. cit.

*Quotations 5–9 tr. by Willis Barnstone.

6 Kiss me again, rekiss me, kiss me more,
give me your most consuming, tasty one,
give me your sensual kiss, a savory one,
I'll give you back four burning at the core.
Sonnet XVIII,
op. cit.

7 What grandeur makes a man seem venerable?
What hair? What color of his skin? What size?
What kind of glance is best? What honeyed eyes?
Sonnet XXI,
op. cit.

8 Your brutal goal was to make *me* a slave
beneath the ruse of being served by you.
Pardon me, friend, and for once hear me through:
I am outraged with anger and I rave.
Sonnet XXIII,
op. cit.

9 Don't blame me, ladies, if I've loved. No sneers
if I have felt a thousand torches burn
Sonnet XXIV,
op. cit.

270. Olimpia Morata (1526–1555)

1 Never does the same desire enlist us all.
Tastes are not conferred by Zeus on all alike.
Untitled (c.1542),
Jules Bonnet and Roland H.
Bainton, trs.;
Women of the Reformation,
Vol. I: *Germany and Italy*,
by Roland H. Bainton   *1971*

2 I, a woman, have dropped the symbols of my sex,
Yarn, shuttle, basket, thread   Ibid.

3 Remembering that the span of our life is but
toil and trouble and we soon fly away, may I
give myself to the contemplation of things
eternal.   Letter to her sister, Vittoria
(c.1553),
op. cit.

4 God is a light to our feet. Let us not be troubled
by men, for what is man if not a fleeting shadow,
a windblown leaf, a fading flower, and vanishing smoke!   Last letter, to Lavinia della
Rovere (1555),
op. cit.

271. Jeanne d'Albret (1528–1572)

1 . . . arms once taken up should never be laid
down, but upon one of three conditions—a safe

peace, a complete victory, or an honourable
death.   Quoted in *Biography
of Distinguished Women*
by Sarah Josepha Hale*   *1876*

*See 703.

2 . . . the task of women and men who do not
bear arms . . . is to fight for peace . . . do
your part, for God's sake. As for me I will
spare nothing.   Letter to Cardinal de
Bourbon (1568),
Quoted in *Queen of Navarre:
Jeanne d'Albret*
by Nancy Lyman
Roelker   *1968*

3 . . . if religion separates us, does our common
blood then separate? do friendship and natural
duty cease to exist? *Non, mon frère.*   Ibid.

4 . . . in this world . . . I see nothing but
vanity.   Spoken during her last illness,
op. cit.

5 Nothing is impossible to a valiant heart. *(À
coeur vaillant rien d'impossible.)*
Motto (adopted by her son,
Henry IV)   *n.d.*

272. Anne Cooke Bacon (c.1528–1610?)

1 Ignorance, especially of the heavenly things, is
the greatest lack that can be seen in man.
*Sermons . . . concerning the
predestination and election of
God: very expedient to the setting
forth of his glory among
creatures,*
15th sermon   *c.1570*

2 Simple ignorance hath not so much confused
. . . wisdom, as Philosophie, which maketh
men bold, unshamefaced, hot, lyers, proud,
contentious, frenticke, foolysh, and wicked.
Ibid., 17th sermon

273. Elizabeth Hoby Russell (1528–post-1603)

1 No one need honor me with tears, or lament my
burial! This is why! I go through the stars to
God! *(Nemo me lachrymis decoret, neque funera
fletio! Faxit cur! Vado perastra deo!)*
Composed for and inscribed on
her monument in Bisham
Church near Great Marlow,
England, John Williams, tr.;
Quoted in *Society Women of
Shakespeare's Time*
by Violet A. Wilson   *1924*

2 I beseech your Majesty, let me have Justice, and I will then trust the law.
> Spoken to King James I (1603),
> Quoted in *Diary of Lady
> Margaret Hoby,* *
> Dorothy M. Meads, ed.   *1930*

*See 315.

3 Though I be not so bad a bird as to defile mine own nest, yet I know my children. . . .
> Letter to [William Cecil, Lord]
> Burghley (n.d.),
> op. cit.

274. Maria Cazalla (fl. 1530s)

1 You do this to a woman? I dread more the affront than the pain.
> Testimony before the Inquisition
> (c.1531–1534),
> *Women of the Reformation,*
> Vol. III: *From Spain to
> Scandinavia,*
> by Roland H. Bainton   *1977*

275. Catherine Killigrew (1530?–1583)

1 In thee my soul shall own combined
The sister and the friend.

If from my eyes by thee detained
The wanderer cross the seas,
No more thy love shall soothe, as friend,
No more as sister please.
> Untitled, Sts. 2, 3,
> *Women of the Reformation,*
> Vol. III: *From Spain to
> Scandinavia,*
> By Roland H. Bainton   *1977*

276. Anne d'Este (1531–post-1563)

1 My sweet god, so much blood, surely some of it will fall upon our house.
> Comment on the mass execution
> of conspirators
> (March 22, 1560),
> Quoted in *Women of Power*
> by Mark Strage   *1976*

277. Elizabeth I of England (1533–1603)

1 Much suspected of me,
Nothing proved can be,
Quoth Elizabeth, prisoner.
> Scratched with a Diamond on
> her Window at Woodstock
> Prison (c. 1554–1555),
> *Actes and monuments of these
> later and perillous dayes* (aka
> *The Book of Martyrs*)
> by John Foxe   *1563*

2 The [use of the] sea and air is common to all; neither can a title to the ocean belong to any people or private persons, for as much as neither nature nor public use and custom permit any possession thereof.
> Letter to the Spanish
> Ambassador   *1580*

3 I know I have the body of a weak and feeble woman, but I have the heart and stomach of a king, and of a king of England too. . . .
> Speech to the Troops at Tilbury
> on the Approach of the Armada
> *1588*

4 . . . I know they are most deceived that trusteth most in themselves. . . .
> Letter to Edward Seymour, Lord
> Protector (February 21, 1549),
> *The Sayings of Queen Elizabeth,*
> Frederick Chamberlain,
> ed.   *1923*

5 For, what is a family without a steward, a ship without a pilot, a flock without a shepherd, a body without a head, the same, I think, is a kingdom without the health and safety of a good monarch.
> Letter to King Edward VI
> (c.1551), op. cit.

6 I am more afraid of making a fault in my Latin, than of the Kings of Spain, France, Scotland, the whole House of Guise, and all of their confederates.
> To the Archbishop
> of St. Andrews (n.d.),
> op. cit.

7 For the face, I grant, I might well blush to offer, but the mind I shall never be ashamed to present. For though from the grace of the picture the colours may fade by time, may give by weather, may be spotted by chance; yet the other nor time with her swift wings shall overtake, nor the misty clouds with their lowerings may darken, nor chance with her slippery foot may overthrow.
> Letter to King Edward VI
> (15 May 1549–1553?),
> *The Letters of Queen Elizabeth
> the First,*
> G. B. Harrison, ed.   *1935*

8 The king's word is more than another man's oath.
> Letter (1554),
> op. cit.

9 . . . I cannot but muse for my part, and blush for theirs, to see the rebellious hearts and devilish intents of Christians in name, but Jews in deed. . . .
> Letter to Mary,
> Queen of Scots* (August 22, 1556,)
> op. cit.

*See 285.

10 And among earthly things I chiefly wish this one, that there were as good surgeons for making anatomies of hearts that might show my thoughts to your Majesty, as there are expert physicians

of the bodies, able to express the inward griefs of their maladies to their patients. Ibid.

11 You know a kingdom knows no kindred. . . . Letter to Sir Henry Sidney (1565), op. cit.

12 A strength to harm is perilous in the hand of an ambitious head. Ibid.

13 Where might is mixed with wit, there is too good an accord. Ibid.

14 . . . when I make collection of sundry kinds of discontentments, all tied in a bundle, I suppose the faggot will be harder altogether to be broken. Letter to Sir Edward Stafford (c.August 1580), op. cit.

15 Let him never procure her harm whose love he seeks to win. Ibid.

16 Brass shines as fair to the ignorant as gold to the goldsmith. Letter to "the Monk" (c.1581), op. cit.

17 I hope you will remember that who seeketh two strings to one bow, he may shoot strong but never straight. Letter to James VI [of Scotland] (1585), op. cit.

18 Eyes of youth have sharp sight, but commonly not so deep as those of elder age. . . .
Letter to Robert Devereux, Earl of Essex (8 July 1597), op. cit.

19 To trust this traitor upon oath is to trust a devil upon his religion. Letter to Robert Devereux, Earl of Essex (17 September 1599), op. cit.

20 My care is like a shadow in the sun—
Follows me flying, flies when I pursue it.
"On the Departure of the Duke d'Alençon" (1582), The Poems of Queen Elizabeth I, Leicester Bradner, ed. 1964

21 Never think you fortune can bear the sway Where virtue's force can cause her to obey.
"On Fortune," op. cit.

22 No crooked leg, no bleared eye,
No part deformed out of kind,
Nor yet so ugly half can be
As in the inward suspicious mind.
Written in her French psalter, op. cit.

23 'Twas God the word that spake it,
He took the Bread and brake it;
And what the word did make it;
That I believe, and take it.
Answer on being asked her opinion of Christ's presence in the Sacrament, op. cit.

24 Semper eadem [Ever the same].
Motto n.d.

25 All my possessions for a moment of time.
Attributed n.d.

26 I am no lover of pompous title, but only desire that my name be recorded in a line or two, which shall briefly express my name, my virginity, the years of my reign, the reformation of religion under it, and my preservation of peace. To her ladies, discussing her epitaph n.d.

278. Sofonisba Anguissola (c.1535-1540– 1625)

1 It will be a great pleasure to me if I have gratified your Holiness's wish, but I must add that, if the brush could represent the beauties of the queen's [Isabel of Valois] soul to your eyes, they would be marvelous. However, I have used the utmost diligence to present what art can show, to tell your Holiness the truth.
Letter to Pope Pius IV (16 September 1561), Quoted in The Lives of the Painters, Sculptors, and Architects, Vol. III, by Giorgio Vasari; A. B. Hinds, tr. 1927

279. Jane Grey (1537–1554)

1 Think not, O mortal, vainly gay,
That thou from human woes art free;
The bitter cup I drink today,
Tomorrow may be drunk by thee.
Lines written on prison wall at the Tower of London (1554), Quoted in Woman's Record by Sarah Josepha Hale* 1855

*See 703.

2 One of the greatest benefits that ever God gave me is, that he sent me so sharp and severe parents and so gentle a schoolmaster.
"The Scholemaster" (1569), The English Works of Roger Ascham, William Aldis Wright, ed. 1904

280. Margaret Bryan (fl. c.1539)

1 The minstrels played, and his grace [Edward VI] danced . . . so wantonly that he could not

stand still, and was as full of pretty toys as ever I saw child in my life.
Letter to [Thomas] Cromwell (1539),
Letter of Royal and Illustrious Ladies,
Vol. III, Mary Anne Everett Wood Green, ed. *1846*

281. Anna Maria of Braunschweig (fl. 1540s)

1 I'd rather marry a wise old man than a young fool.
Quoted in *Women of the Reformation,*
Vol. I: *Germany and Italy,*
by Roland H. Bainton *1971*

282. Lettice Knollys (1540–1634)

1 . . . country life is fittest for disgraced persons.
Letter to her son, the Earl of Essex (c. 1595–1598),
Quoted in *Queen Elizabeth's Maids of Honour*
by Violet A. Wilson *n.d.*

283. Countess de Marcelle (fl. c.1540s)

1 By compelling us to return to the world, it is not liberty the Calvinists offer us, but bondage.*
Quoted in *The Huguenots in France and America,*
Vol. II, Ch. 26, by Hannah Farnham Lee** *1843*

*The Calvinists attempted to abolish monasteries and convents in France.
**See 682.

284. Isabella de' Medici Orsini (1542–1576)

1 Make yourself happy where you are adored, and on no account seek another abode.
Letter to her sister-in-law, Bianca Capello (24 September 1572),
Quoted in *Famous Women of Florence*
by Edgecumbe Staley *1909*

285. Mary, Queen of Scots (1542–1587)

1 Farewell, France! farewell beloved country, which I shall never more behold!
(August 1559), Quoted in *Women of Beauty and Heroism*
by Frank B. Goodrich *1858*

2 Here the sun can never penetrate, neither does any pure air ever visit this habitation, on which descend drizzling damps and eternal fogs, to such excess that not an article of furniture can be placed beneath the roof, but in four days it becomes covered with green mould.
Remark (1586/87) from her prison cell, op. cit.

3 I will that you do nothing by which any spot may be laid on my honor or conscience; but wait till God of His goodness shall put a remedy to it.
Last words (8 February 1587), op. cit.

4 No more tears now; I will think upon revenge.
Remarking on the murder of her servant, David Riccio (1566),
Quoted in *Memorials of Mary Stewart,*
J. Stevenson, ed. *1883*

5 Look to your consciences and remember that the theater of the world is wider than the realm of England.
Remark at her trial (1586),
Quoted in *The Tragedy of Fotheringhay*
by Mrs. Maxwell-Scot *1905*

6 Ah! here are many counsellors, but not one for me.
Ibid.

7 As a sinner I am truly conscious of having often offended my Creator and I beg him to forgive me, but as a Queen and Sovereign, I am aware of no fault or offence for which I have to render account to anyone here below.
To Sir Amyas Paulet (October 1586),
Quoted in *Mary, Queen of Scots*
by Antonia Fraser* *1969*

*See 2101.

8 I do not desire vengeance. . . . I would rather pray with Esther* than take the sword with Judith.**
Remark at her trial (October 1586), op. cit.

*See 34.
**See 31.

9 In my end is my beginning. *(En ma fin est mon commencement.)*
Motto, op. cit.

10 Constancy does become all folks well, but none better than princes, and such as have rule over realms.
Quoted in *Women of the Reformation,*
Vol. III: *From Spain to Scandinavia,*
by Roland H. Bainton *1977*

11 I mean to constrain none of my subjects; and I trust they should have no support to constrain me.
Ibid.

286. Mary Grey (1543/44–1578)

1 . . . the princes favor is not so soon gotten
agayn, and . . . to be without it is such a
greff to any true subjectes harte, as no tur-
ment can be greater. . . .   Letter to
William Cecil, Lord Burghley,
written from prison (1566),
*Original Letters Illustrative of
English History,*
Vol. II, Henry Ellis, ed.
1824–1846

287. Veronica Franco (1546–1591)

1 Now that my mind is bent upon revenge,
my disrespectful, my rebellious lover,
step up and arm yourself with what you
will.

What battlefield do you prefer? this place?
this secret hideaway where I have/sam-
pled—
unwarily—so many bitter sweets?
Untitled, Sts. 10, 11,
Lynne Lawner, tr.;
*The Penguin Book
of Women Poets,*
Carol Cosman, Joan Keefe and
Kathleen Weaver, eds.   *1978*

2 Alas! I say now and always will say
That to live without you is cruel death to
me
And pleasures to me are cruel torments.
"Lontana dall'Amante e da
Venezia" ["Far from My Lover
and from Venice"],
Claudia Alexander with Carlo
DiMaio, trs.;
Poesia italiana: il cinquecento,
Giulio Ferroni, ed.   *1978*

288. Catherine Fradonnet (1547–1587)

*Co-author with Madeline Fradonnet. See 262.

289. Idelette de Bure Calvin (?–1549)

1 O glorious resurrection! God of Abraham and
of all our fathers! The faithful have in so many
ages hoped in Thee, and not one has been
disappointed! I will also hope!
Dying words (1549),
Quoted in *The Huguenots in
France and America,*
Vol. I, Ch. 3, by Hannah
Farnham Lee*   *1843*

*See 682.

290. Elizabeth Bowes (fl. 1550)

1 Alas, wretched woman that I am, for the self-
same sins that reigned in Sodom and Gomorrah
reign in me!   Letter to John
Knox (c.1550),
Women of the Reformation,
Vol. III: *From Spain to
Scandinavia,*
by Roland H. Bainton   *1977*

291. Renée de Chateauneuf Rieux (1550–1587)

1 Marriage is a lottery in which men stake their
liberty and women their happiness.
Attributed   *n.d.*

292. Grace Sherrington (c.1552–1620)

1 She [her governess] scoffed at all dalliance, idle
talk, and wanton behaviour appertayning thereto.
. . . She counselled us when we were alone so
to behave ourselves as if all the worlde did
looke upon us, and to doe nothing in secret
whereof our conscience might accus
us. . . .   Quoted in *Diary of
Lady Margaret Hoby* *
Dorothy M. Meads, ed.   *1930*

*See 315.

2 If all fathers and mothers were . . . provident
and careful, and governors and governesses put
in trust by them were diligent and faithfull in
performing their trust, so many parents should
not be discomfited as they are in their age by
the wickedness and misfortunes of their
children.   Ibid.

293. Marguerite of Valois (1553–1615)

1 Joy takes far away from us the thoughts of our
actions; sorrow it is that awakens the soul.
Memoirs (1594–1600)   *1628*

2 . . . mistrust is the sure forerunner of
hatred.   Ibid., Letter IX

3 Adversity is solitary, while prosperity dwells in
a crowd.   Ibid., Letter XII

4 Science conducts us, step by step, through the
whole range of creation, until we arrive, at
length, at God.   Ibid.

5 In my sadness and solitude, I rediscovered the
great gifts of study and devotion—gifts which,

among the vanities and magnificence of my former good fortune, I had never truly tasted.   Ibid.

6 . . . the sight of you . . . is as necessary for me as is the sun for the spring flowers.
Letter to Jacques de Harlay,
Marquess of Chanvallon (1582),
Quoted in *A Daughter
of the Medicis*
by Jean H. Mariejol; John Peile,
tr.   *1929*

7 . . . let no one ever say that marriages are made in Heaven; the gods would not commit so great an injustice!   Letter to Jacques
de Harlay (1582),
Quoted in *Queen of Hearts*
by Charlotte Haldane   *1968*

294. Margaret Clitherow (1556?–1586)

1 They that think much and are not willing to do such base things [as housework], have little regard of well-doing or knowledge of themselves.   Quoted in *A True Report of
the Life and Martyrdom of Mrs.
Margaret Clitherow*
by Fr. John Mush   *1586*

2 God forbid that I should will any to do that in my house which I would not willingly do myself. . . .   Ibid.

3 . . . bear me company this night, not for any fear of death, for it is my comfort, but the flesh is frail.   Remark to a friend
before her execution,
op. cit.

295. Zofia Olesnicka (fl. 1556)

1 Better to safeguard Thy treasure,
Which neither moth nor rust can corrupt
Than enmeshed in the ways of the world
To forfeit Thy favor forever.
Hymn, St. 5 (1556),
Quoted in *Women of the
Reformation,*
Vol. III: *From Spain to
Scandinavia,*
by Roland H. Bainton   *1977*

296. Anne Dacre Howard (1557–1630)

1 In sad and ashy weeds I sigh. . . .
Elegy on the Death of Her
Husband, 1.1 (1595),
The Women Poets in English,
Ann Stanford, ed.   *1972*

2 I envy aire because it dare
Still breathe, and he not so;
Hate earthe, that doth entomb his youth,
And who can blame my woe?   Ibid., St. 3

297. Joyce Lewes (?–1557)

1 I thank my God that he will make me worthy to adventure my life in his quarrel.
At her execution (1557),
Quoted in *Actes and monuments
of these latter and perillous dayes*
(aka *The Book of Martyrs*),
Vol. VIII, by John
Foxe   *1563*

298. Mother Benet (fl. 1558)

1 O man! be content, and let us be thankful; for God hath given us enough, if we can see it.
Quoted in *Actes and monuments of
these latter and perillous dayes*
(aka *The Book of Martyrs*)
by John Foxe   *1563*

2 I cannot firkin [store] up my butter, and keep my cheese in the chamber and wait a great price, and let the poor want, and so displease God.
Ibid.

299. Wife of Prest (?–1558)

1 How save you souls, when you preach nothing but damnable lies. . . .
Testimony to examining bishop,
Quoted in *Actes and monuments
of these latter and perillous dayes*
(aka *The Book of Martyrs*)
by John Foxe   *1563*

2 Farewell you with your salvation.   Ibid.

3 God forbid that I should lose the life eternal, for this carnal and short life.
At her execution (1558),
op. cit.

300. Elizabeth Young (fl. 1558)

1 . . . I had rather all the world should accuse me, than mine own conscience.
Testimony at her first
examination,
Quoted in *Actes and monuments
of these latter and perillous dayes*
(aka *The Book of Martyrs*)
by John Foxe   *1563*

2 If ye take away my meat, I trust God will take my hunger.   Ibid., Second
examination

3 Here is my carcase: do with it what you will
. . . ye can have no more but my blood.
Ibid.

4 No man can be the head of Christ's church; for
Christ himself is the head, and his word is the
governor of all. Ibid., Seventh
examination

301. Catherine de Bourbon (1559–1604)

1 . . . [King Henry of] Navarre can ill brook
words when *deeds* are so much wanted.
Remark to Count de Soissons,
Quoted in *The Huguenots in
France and America,*
Vol. I, Ch. 15, by Hannah
Farnham Lee* *1843*

*See 682.

2 Command me, my King, to make you a little
page, for I fear that unless you command it
yourself, he will not consent to lodge in my
body. Letter to her brother, Henry IV
of France
(18 August 1599)
Quoted in *Queen of Navarre:
Jeanne d'Albret**
by Nancy Lyman Roelker,
tr. *1968*

*See 271.

302. Anne Locke (fl. 1560s)

1 . . . why (casting off all impediments that pres-
seth down) do we not run on our course with
cheerfulness and Hope, having Christ so mighty
a King, for our captain and Guide?
Preface to her translation of
The Markes of the Children of God
by J. Taffin *1590*

303. Blanche Parry (fl. 1560s)

1 . . . madam . . . if you ever marry without
the Queen's [Elizabeth I]* writing, you and your
husband will be undone, and your fate worse
than that of my Lady Jane.**
Letter to Lady Catherine Grey
(c.1560),
Quoted in *Queen Elizabeth's
Maids of Honour*
by Violet A. Wilson *n.d.*

*See 277.
*Sister of Lady Catherine, see 279; subsequently, Cather-
ine was imprisoned after her secret marriage to the Earl of
Hertford.

304. Frances Walsingham (c.1560–post-
1603)

1 I will have more care of my self for your little
one's sake. Letter to her husband, the
Earl of Essex (c.1599),
Quoted in *Society Women of
Shakespeare's Time*
by Violet A. Wilson *1924*

2 Simple thankes is a slender
recompens. . . . Letter to Robert Cecil
(December 1599),
op. cit.

305. Mary Sidney Herbert (1561–1621)

1 My fellow, my companion, held most dear,
My soul, my other self, my inward friend
The Psalmes of David (c.1593),
Psalm LV, "Exaudi, Deus,"
St. 4, C. Whittingham,
ed. *1823*

2 There is a God that carves to each his own.
Psalm LVIII,
"Si Vere Utique," St. 4, op. cit.

3 How thou hast been the target of my head
Psalm LXIII, St. 3,
op. cit.

4 O Sun, whom light nor flight can match,
Suppose thy lightful flightful wings
*Thou lend to me,
And I could flee
As far as thee the ev'ning brings*
Psalm CXXXIX,
"Domine, Probasti,"
St. 5, op. cit.

5 If ever hapless woman had a cause
To breathe her plaints into the open air,
And never suffer inward grief to pause,
Or seek her sorrow-shaken soul's repair:
Then I, for I have lost my only brother,*
Whose like this age can scarcely yield
another.
"If Ever Hapless Woman Had a Cause,"
St. 1 (c.1599),
The Woman Poets in English,
Ann Stanford, ed. *1972*
*The poet Sir Philip Sidney (1554–1586), who, in their
joint translation of the Psalms, translated the first 43.

306. Penelope Devereaux Rich (1562/63–
post-1605)

1 . . . they will seem . . . such crafty workmen
as will not only pull downe all the obstacles of
theyr greatnes, but when they are in theyr full

strengths (like gyants) make warr agaynst Heaven.　　　Letter to Queen Elizabeth I*
(1599),
Quoted in *Society Women of Shakespeare's Time*
by Violet A. Wilson　*1924*

*See 277.
**Requesting permission to visit her brother, the Earl of Essex, during his imprisonment.

2 Faction . . . careth not upon whose neck they buyld the walles of theyr owne fortunes. . . .　　　Ibid.

307. Elizabeth Grymeston (1563?–1603)

1 I resolved to break the barren soil of my fruitless brain.　　Dedicatory letter to her son, Bernye Grymeston,
Miscelanea: Prayer, Meditations, Memoratives　1604

2 I have prayed for thee, that thou mightest be fortunate in two hours of thy life time: in the hour of thy marriage, and at the hour of thy death.　　　Ibid.

3 Defer not thy marriage till thou comest to be saluted with a "God speed you, Sir," as a man going out of the world after forty; neither yet to the time of "God keep you, Sir," whilst thou are in thy best strength after thirty; but marry in the time of "You are welcome, Sir," when thou are coming into the world: for seldom shalt thou see a woman out of her own love to pull a rose that is full blown, deeming them always sweetest at the first opening of the bud.　　Ibid.

4 Crush the serpent in the head,
Break ill eggs ere they be hatched.
Kill bad chickens in the tread,
Fledged they hardly can be catched.
In the rising stifle ill,
Lest it grow against thy will.　　Ibid.

5 Our best life is to die well: for living here we enjoy nothing: things past are dead and gone: things present are always ending: things future always beginning: while we live we die; and we leave dying when we leave living.
Ibid., Ch. 4

6 Epicurism is the fuel of lust; the more thou addest, the more she is enflamed.
Ibid., Ch. 20,
"Memoratives"

7 If thou givest a benefit, keep it close; but if thou receivest one, publish it, for that invites another.　　　Ibid.

8 On the anvil of upbraiding is forged the office of unthankfulness.　　　Ibid.

9 Be not at any time idle. Alexander's soldiers

should scale molehills rather than rest unoccupied; it is the woman that sitteth still that imagineth mischief; it is the rolling stone that riseth clean, and the running water that remaineth clear.　　　Ibid.

10 There be four good mothers have four bad daughters: Truth hath Hatred; Prosperity hath Pride; Security hath Peril, and Familiarity hath Contempt.　　　Ibid.

11 A fair woman is a paradise to the eye, a purgatory to the purse, and a hell to the soul.
Ibid.

308. Hŏ Nansŏrhŏn (1563–1589)

1 Yesterday I fancied I was young;
But already, alas, I am aging.
"A Woman's Sorrow,"
Peter H. Lee, tr.;
The Penguin Book of Woman Poets,
Carol Cosman, Joan Keefe and Kathleen Weaver, eds.　*1978*

2 Numberless are the sorrowful.
Untitled, Peter H. Lee, tr.,
op. cit.

309. Marie de Jars (1565–1645)

1 . . . even if a woman has only the name of being educated she will be evilly spoken of.
Proumenoir (1594),
Quoted in *A Daughter of the Renaissance*
by Marjorie Henry Ilsley　*1963*

2 I am on the side of those who believe that vice comes from stupidity and consequently that the nearer one draws to wisdom the farther one gets from vice.　　Preface to *Essais* by Montaigne
(1595), op. cit.

3 Pierre, your life is condemned
By the crime of a single moment:
While you believe that you are just for a whole year
Because you are good for a single day.
"Illusions Bigottes"
(1626), op. cit.

4 Knowledge not based on ethics cannot . . . bring real honor nor profit to its master. . . .　　　"Advis"
(1634), op. cit.

5 Since language and speech are the cement of human society whoever falsifies them should be punished for counterfeit or for poisoning the public water well.　　　Ibid.

6 What are our efforts but a flood-gate of reeds against the roaring torrent of fortune? Ibid.

7 Society is a cage of idiots "A Lenten" (1634), op. cit.

310. Elizabeth Joceline (1566–1622)

1 . . . all the delight a Parent may take in a child is honey mingled with gall. Introduction
The Mothers Legacie to her Unborne Childe 1624

2 Drunkennesse . . . is the highway to hell. . . . Ibid., Ch. 9

3 . . . there is nothing more contrary to our wicked nature then this loving our neibour as our selves. Wee can with ease envie him if hee be rich, or scorne him if he be poore; but love him? Ibid., Ch. 10

311. Isabella Whitney (fl. 1567–1573)

1 Gold savours well, though it be got with occupations vile:
If thou hast gold, thou welcome art,
though virtue thou exile. "The 103. Flower,"
A Sweet Nosegay or Pleasant Posye Containing a Hundred and Ten Phylosophicall Flowers 1573

2 Such poor folk as to law do go are driven oft to curse:
But in mean while, the Lawyer thrives,
the money in his purse. "The 104. Flower," op. cit.

312. Emilia Lanier (1569/70–c.1640–45)

1 If Eve did err, it was for knowledge sake,
No subtle Serpent's falsehood did betray him,
If he would eat it, who had power to stay him?
Not Eve, whose fault was only too much love,
Which made her give this present to her Dear,
That what she tasted, he likewise might prove,
Whereby his knowledge might become more clear Eve's Apology,"
Salve Deus Rex Judeorum 1611

2 Then let us [women] have our Liberty again,
And challenge to your selves no Sovereignty;
You came not in the world without our pain,
Make that a bar against your cruelty;

Your fault being greater, why should you disdain
Our being your equals, free from tyranny? Ibid.

313. Mairi MacLeod (1569–1674?)

1 To Ullinish
with its white-hoofed herds,
Where once in childhood
I was nourished
On breast-milk
of smooth-skinned women
"A Complaint About Exile,"
ll. 11–16, Joan Keefe, tr.,
The Penguin Book of Women Poets,
Carol Cosman, Joan Keefe and Kathleen Weaver, eds. *1978*

314. Antoinette de Pons Guercheville (1570–1632)

1 If I am not noble enough to be your wife, I am too much so to be your mistress.
Remark to Henry IV,
Quoted in *Biography of Distinguished Women*
by Sarah Josepha Hale* *1876*

*See 703.

2 A king, wherever he is, should always be master. As to myself, I also choose to be free.
Message to Henry IV, op. cit.

315. Margaret Hoby (1570–1633)

1 . . . it is not sufficient only to have faith . . . but I must likewise pray especially for that virtue which is opposed to that vice whereunto I am then tempted.
Diary Entry (10 December 1599),
Diary of Lady Margaret Hoby,
Dorothy M. Meads, ed. *1930*

2 They are unworthy of God's benefits and special favors that can find no time to make a thankful record of them.
Diary Entry (1 April 1605), op. cit.

316. Katherine Stubbes (1571–1591/92)

1 I would rather be a door keeper in the house of
my God, than to dwell in the tents of the
wicked.   Spoken during her final illness
(1591/92),
Quoted in *Women of the*
Reformation,
Vol. III: *From Spain to*
Scandinavia,
by Roland H. Bainton   *1977*

317. Elizabeth Clinton (1574–1630?)

1 Now who shall deny the own mother's suckling
of their own children to be their duty, since
every godly matron hath walked in these steps
before them: Eve, the mother of all the living;
Sarah, the mother of all the faithful; Hannah,
so graciously heard of God; Mary, blessed among
women, and called blessed of all ages.
The Countess of Lincoln's
Nurserie   1622

2 Whatsoever things are true, whatsoever things
are honest . . . whatsoever things are just,
whatsoever things are pure, whatsoever things
are of good report . . . think on these things;
these things do, and the God of peace shall be
with you.   Ibid.

3 Trust not other women whom wages hire . . .
better than yourselves whom God and nature
tie. . . .   Ibid.

318. Beatrice Cenci (1577–1599)

1 I am no Turk and no dog that I should wish to
shed my own blood.
Testimony at her trial (1599),
Quoted in *Beatrice Cenci*
by Morris Bishop and Henry
Longan Stuart, Corrado Ricci. tr.   *1925*

2 I no longer know what to do in order not to fall
from one evil into another, and even though I
slew myself, I would fall under the curse of the
Holy Father.   Letter to her defense lawyer,
Prospero Farinaccio (1599),
op. cit.

3 Alas! Alas! O Madonna *santissima*, aid me!
. . . Let me down! I will tell the truth.
Remark during torture on the
rack (1599),
op. cit.

319. Frances Abergavenny (fl. 1580s)

1 No thought let there arise in me
Contrarie to thy precepts ten.
"The Precious Perles of perfect
Godliness" (c.1581),
The Monument of Matrones
conteining seven severall Lamps
of Virginitie, or Distinct
Treatises. . . ,
Vol. I, Thomas Bentley, ed.
1582

320. Alice Harvey (fl. 1580–1600)

1 All the speed is in the morning.
Quoted in *Commonplace Book*
by Gabriel Harvey   *c.1580*

321. Elizabeth Vernon (c.1580–post-1647)

1 . . . ever you like best I should be, that place
shall be most pleasing to me. . . .
Letter to her husband, Henry
Wriothesley, 3rd Earl of
Southampton (July 8, 1599),
Quoted in *Society Women of*
Shakespeare's Time
by Violet A. Wilson   *1924*

322. Lucy Harington (1581–1627)

1 Death be not proud, thy hand gave not this
blow. . . .   "Elegy," 1.1,
Women Poets in English,
Ann Stanford, ed.   *1972*

2 And teach this hymn of her with joy, and sing,
The grave no conquest gets, Death hath no
sting.   Ibid., last ll.

323. Mistress Bradford (fl. 1582)

1 As Hanna* did applie, dedicate, and give her
first child and sonne Samuel unto thee: even so
doo I deere Father; beseeching thee, for Christ's
sake, to accept this my gift.
"The praier that maister
Bradford's mother said and
offered unto God in his** behalfe,
a little before his martyrdome,"
The Monument of Matrones
conteining seven severall Lamps
of Virginitie, or Distinct
Treatises. . . ,
Thomas Bentley, ed.   *1582*

*See 18.
**Her son, John Bradford, executed c.1582 for heresy.

324. Elizabeth Tyrwhit (fl. 1582)

1 . . . from Sathan deliver me, with the bread of Angels feede me, from fleshlie lusts purge me, from sudden death and deadlie sinne, O Lord take me.   "Another praier at our uprising,"
Morning and Evening praiers, with divers Psalmes, Hymnes, and Meditations, made and set forth by the Ladie Elizabeth Tyrwhit   1582

2 Sweets dews from heven to earth God grant, of peace & quiet mind,
That we may serve the living God, as his statutes doo bind.   "The Hymne or praier to the sonne of God," op. cit.

325. Ann Wheathill (fl. 1584)

1 . . . humilitie . . . the beautiful flowre of vertue that groweth in the garden of man's soule. . . .
Prayer 9, A Handfull of holesome (though homelie) Hearbs, gathered out of the Godlie Garden of Gods most Holie Word: for the common Benefit and comfortable Exercise of all such as are Devoutlie disposed   1584

2 The yong chickens, when the kite striketh at them, have no other refuge but to run dickering under the wings of the hen: no more hath mankind any other defense against his enemies, but onelie the covering of Thy grace, and the shaddowe of Thy most precious passion. . . .
Prayer 28, op. cit.

326. Elizabeth Carew (1585?–1639)

1 Tis not enough for one that is a wife
   To keep her spotless from an act of ill:
But from suspicion she should free her life,
   And bare herself of power as well as will   *The Tragedie of Mariam the Faire Queene of Jewry, Act III   1613*

2 For in a wife it is no worse to find
A common body, than a common mind.
Ibid.

3 CHORUS. The fairest action of our human life,
   Is scorning to revenge an injury;
For who forgives without a further strife,
   His adversary's heart to him doth tie:
And 't is a firmer conquest, truly said,
To win the heart, and overthrow the head.
Ibid., Act IV, Sc. 1

4 When she hath spacious ground to walk upon,
   Why on the ridge should she desire to go?
Ibid.

5 . . . benefit upbraided, forfeits thanks.
Ibid., Act V, Sc. 1

327. Catalina de Erauso (1585–post-1624)

1 I went out of the convent; I found myself in the street, without knowing where to go; that was no matter; all I wanted was liberty.
Quoted in Biography of Distinguished Women by Sarah Josepha Hale *   1876*

* See 703.

2 In this attempt [to cross the deserts of the Andes] I *may* find death; by remaining here [in this sanctuary] I shall certainly find it.   *Ibid.*

328. Mary Ward (1585–1645)

1 Fervour is not placed in feelings but in will to do well, which women may have as well as men. There is no such difference between men and women that women may not do great things as we have seen by example of many saints who have done great things.   Quoted in *The Life of Mary Ward by Mary Catherine Elizabeth Chambers   1884*

329. Mary Sidney Wroth (1586?–1640?)

1 . . . wounds still cureless, must my rulers be.   "Morea's Sonnet," St. 2, *The Countess of Montgomeries Urania   c.1615*

2 Had I not happy been, I had not known
So great a loss; a king deposed feels most
The torment of a throne-like-want when lost. . . .   "Pamphilia's Sonnet," St. 3, op. cit.

3 O Memory, could I but loose thee now . . .   "Lindamira's Complaint," 1. 1, op. cit.

330. Anna of Saxony (fl. c.1587)

1 . . . many pregnant women in confinement and small children of noble as well as of common rank are often miserably neglected, injured, harmed and crippled at the time of the birth or

in the following six weeks, all through the clumsiness, arrogance, and rashness of the mid-wives and assisting women; few sensible mid-wives are to be found in this country [Germany]. (c.1587),
Quoted in
Women in the Middle Ages
by Sibylle Harksen *1975*

331. Francesca Caccini (1587–1640?)

1 I would rather lose my life before the desire to study and the affection I have always had for virtue, because this is worth more than all trea-sure and all grandeur.
Letter to Michaelangelo
Buonarroti the Younger, from
Genoa (May 26, 1617),
Quoted in *Women in Music*
by Carol Neuls-Bates *1982*

332. Margaret Lambrun (fl. 1587).

1 I confess to you, that I suffered many struggles within my breast, and have made all possible efforts to divert my resolution from so perni-cious a design, but all in vain; I found myself necessitated to prove by experience the certain truth of that maxim, that neither reason nor force can hinder a woman from vengeance, when she is impelled thereto by love.
Remark to Queen
Elizabeth I* when caught
attempting to assassinate her
(1587),
Quoted in *Biography of
Distinguished Women*
by Sarah Josepha Hale** *1876*
* See 277.
** See 703.

2 Your majesty ought to grant me a pardon [with-out assurances from me]. . . . A favour given under . . . restraint is no more a favour; and, in so doing, your majesty would act against me as a judge. *Ibid.*

333. Jane Anger (fl. 1589)

1 We are the grief of man, in that we take all the grief from man: we languish when they laugh, we lie sighing when they sit singing, and sit sobbing when they lie slugging and sleeping. *Protection for Women 1589*

2 The lion rages when he is hungry, but man rails when he is glutted. *Ibid.*

334. Anne Dowriche (fl. 1589)

1 As winde disperse the wavring chaffe, and toss it quite away,
All worldly pompe shall so consume, and pass without delay. "Dedicatory poem
to her brother,"
The French Historie 1589

2 Who thinke they swim in wealth (blinded by guile):
Yet wanting Truth; are wretched, poore & vile. Epilogue: "Veritie purtraied by the
French Pilgrime,"
St. 1, op. cit.

3 . . . malicious Men devise
Torments for Truth. . . . Ibid., St. 2

335. Anne Clifford (1590–1676)

1 I am like an owl in the desert.
Diary entry (May 1616),
*The Diary of
the Lady Anne Clifford,*
Vita Sackville-West,* ed. *1923*
* See 1440.

2 I . . . strived to sit as merry a face as I could upon a discontented heart . . . knowing that God often brings things to pass by contrary means. Ibid. (March 1617)

336. Mary Harding (fl. c.1591)

1 . . . how weary my lady of the courte, and what littel gayne there is gotten in this tyme. Letter to Countess of Rutland
(1594),
Quoted in *Queen Elizabeth's*
Maids of Honour*
by Violet A. Wilson *n.d.*
* See 277.

337. Anne Hutchinson (1591–1643)

1 An oath, sir, is an end of all strife, and it is God's ordinance.
Spoken at her trial in Boston
(1 November 1637),
in *Antinomianism in the Colony
of Massachusetts Bay, 1636–1638,*
Charles Francis Adams, ed.
1894

2 I thinke the soule to be nothing but Light. *Ibid.*

3 What from the Church at Boston? I know no such church, neither will I own it. Call it the whore and strumpet of Boston, no Church of Christ! Remark (c.1638), op. cit.

338. Margaret Winthrop (c.1591–1647)

1 I have many reasons to make me love thee, whereof I will name two, first because thou lovest God, and secondly because that thou lovest me. Letter to John Winthrop, *The Winthrop Papers,* Samuel E. Morison et al., eds. *1929*

339. Sarah Copia Sullam (1592–1641)

1 The lying tongue's deceit with silence blight, Protect me from its venom, you, my Rock, And show the spiteful sland'rer by this sign That you will shield me with your endless might. "My Inmost Hope," *A Treasury of Jewish Poetry,* Nathan and Marynn Ausubel, eds. *1957*

340. Artemisia Gentileschi (1593–1652/ 53)

1 I have the greatest sympathy for your lordship, because the name of a woman makes one doubtful until one has seen the work. Letter to Don Antonio Ruffo, a patron (30 January 1649), Quoted in *Women Artists: 1550–1950* by Ann Sutherland Harris and Linda Nochlin *1976*

2 As long as I live, I will have control over my being. . . . Letter to Ruffo (March 1649), op. cit.

3 You will find the spirit of Caesar in the soul of this woman. Letter to Ruffo (November 1649), op. cit.

341. Gabrielle de Coignard (?–d.1594)

1 I'm dust and ashes, Lord; remember this.

You are the wind and I am straw, or less, For you can sweep me into nothingness. Ah, do not let me fall in the abyss! "Prayer," Sts. 3, 4, Raymond Oliver, tr.; *Women Poets of the World,* Joanna Bankier and Deirdre Lashgari, eds. *1983*

342. Elizabeth Compton (fl. 1595)

1 I would have two gentlewomen, lest one should be sick. . . . It is an indecent thing for a gentlewoman to stand mumping alone when God hath blessed their Lord and Lady with a great estate. Letter to her husband [William, Earl of Northampton], Quoted in *Court of King James* by Goodman *n.d.*

343. Pocahontas (1595/96–1616/17)

1 You promised my father [Chief Powhatan] that whatever was yours should be his, and that you and he would be all one. Being a stranger in our country, you called Powhatan father; and I for the same reason will now call you so. Remark to Captain John Smith (c.1616), Quoted in *Women of Beauty and Heroism* by Frank B. Goodrich *1858*

344. Rachel Speght (1597–?)

1 Some dogs barke more upon custome then curstnesse; and some speake evill of others, not that the defamed deserve it, but because through custom and corruption of their hearts they cannot speak well of any. "Epistle Dedicatorie," *A Mouzell for Melastomus, the Cynicall Bayter of, and foule mouthed Barker against Evahs Sex. Or an apologeticall Answere to that Irreligious and Illiterate Pamphlet made by Jo[seph] Sw[etnam] and by him intituled, The Arraignement of Women 1617*

2 . . . man was created of the dust of the earth, but woman was made of a part of man, after that he was a living soule: yet was shee not produced from Adam's foote, to be his too low inferiour; nor from his head to be his superiour, but from his side, neare his heart, to be his equall. . . . "Essay," op. cit.

3 . . . then are those husbands to be blamed, which lay the whole burthen of domesticall affaires and maintenance on the shoulder of their wives. For, as yoake-fellowes they are to sustayne part of each others cares, griefs, and calamities. . . . Ibid.

4 For as Christ turned water into wine, a farre more excellent liquor . . . So the single man is by marriage changed from a Batchelour to a Husband, a farre more excellent title: from a solitarie life unto a joyfull union. . . . Ibid.

5 Marriage is a merri-age, and this world's Paradise, where there is mutuall love.   Ibid.

6 And from the soul three faculties arise,
The mind, the will, the power; then wherefore shall
A woman have her intellect in vain,
Or not endeavor Knowledge to attain.
"A Dream,"
St. 14,
Mortalitie's Memorandum, with a Dreame Prefixed, imaginarie in manner, reall in matter   1621

7 All parts and faculties were made for use; The God of Knowledge nothing gave in vain.
Ibid., St. 15

345. Lucy Hay (1599–1660)

1 Spell well, if you can.   *Thoughts*   n.d.

346. Marie de L'Incarnation (1599–1672)

1 The air is excellent and in consequence this [Quebec] is an earthly paradise where crosses and thorns grow so lovingly that the more one is pricked by them, the more filled with tenderness is the heart.
Letter to Mother Marie-Gillette Roland (1640),
Quoted in
Word from New France
by Joyce Marshall   *1967*

2 We see nothing, we walk gropingly, and . . . ordinary things do not come about as they have been foreseen and advised. One falls and, just when one thinks oneself at the bottom of an abyss, one finds oneself on one's feet.
Letter to her son (1652),
op. cit.

3 Everything is savage here [Quebec], the flowers as well as the men.
Letter to her sister (1653), op. cit.

4 . . . if God strikes us with one hand, he consoles us with another.   Letter to her son (1665), op. cit.

5 If practical affairs . . . cause some objects to pass through my imagination, these are but little clouds, like those that pass across the sun and remove it from our sight for a brief moment, leaving it bright as before.
Letter to Father Poncet, S.J. (1670),
op. cit.

6 Writing teaches us our mysteries. . . .
Letter to her son (1670),
op. cit.

347. Kshetrayya (fl. 17th century)

1 He* set my heart floating on the honey stream of his words,
With his amorous kiss he burnt my lips,
And left me utterly alone, and unfulfilled.
"Dancing-Girl's Song,"
St. 2,
Indian Love Poems,
Tambimuttu and R. Appalaswamy, eds. and trs.
n.d.

*The god Krishna.

348. Marchioness de Tibergeau (fl. 17th century)

1 No, it isn't the point of poetry to write of the tenderness of love:
To pick away at it, finding just the right words,
Arranging all in perfect measure and rhyme,
Stripping the heart to feed the mind.
Untitled,
Elaine Partnow,* tr.,
Quoted in *Biography of Distinguished Women*
by Sarah Josepha Hale*   *1876*

*Author.
*See 703.

349. Wang Wei (fl. 17th century)

1 A traveller's thoughts in the night
Wander in a thousand miles of dreams.
"Seeking A Mooring,"
The Orchid Boat,
Women Poets of China,
Kenneth Rexroth and Ling Chung, eds. and trs.   *1972*

350. Brilliana Harley (1600–1643)

1 . . . that is the evil in [those who are] melancholy; it acts most, inwardly; full of thoughts they are, but not active in expressions. Many times they are so long in studying what is fit for them to do, that the opportunity is past.
Letter to her son,
Edward (4 January 1638),
Letters of the Lady Brilliana Harley,
Thomas Taylor Lewis, ed.
1854

2 . . . man is so forgetful of his God, that all, and most of all great men, live in prosperity as

if they were lords of what they had, forgetting that they are but tenants at will.
Letter to her son (29 November 1639),
op. cit.

3 . . . keep your heart above the world, and then you will not be troubled at the changes in it.
Letter to her son (15 July 1642),
op. cit.

351. Lucrezia Marinella (fl. 1600)

1 It is an amazing thing to see in our city [Venice] the wife of a shoemaker, or a butcher, or a porter dressed in silk with chains of gold at the throat, with pearls and a ring of good value . . . and then in contrast to see her husband cutting the meat, all smeared with cow's blood, poorly dressed, or burdened like an ass, clothed with the stuff from which sacks are made . . . but whoever considers this carefully will find it reasonable, because it is necessary that the lady, even if low-born and humble, be draped with such clothes for her natural excellence and dignity, and that the man less adorned as if a slave, or a little ass, born to her service.
The Nobility and Excellence of
Women together with the Defects
and Deficiences of Men   1600

352. Ann Sutcliffe (fl. 1600–1630)

1 . . . remember thy dayes of Darknes, for they are many.   Meditations of Man's Mortalitie. Or, a Way to true Blessednesse, 2nd ed.   1634

2 . . . the Glory of this World, is but the singing of Syrens, sweet but a deadly poison.   Ibid.

3 Pride, in it selfe doth beare a poyson'd breath. . . .   Ibid.

353. Anne of Austria (1601–1666)

1 God does not pay at the end of every week, but He pays.   Letter to Cardinal Mazarin,
Letters   n.d.

354. Elizabeth Raleigh (fl. 1601)

1 I wish she would be as ambitious to do good as she is apt to the contrary.
Letter to Sir Robert Cecil
(c.1601),
Quoted in Society Women of
Shakespeare's Time
by Violet A. Wilson   1924

355. Priscilla Alden (1602?–pre-1687)

1 John, why do you not speak for yourself?*
Quoted in Collections of
American Epitaphs and
Inscriptions with Original Notes,
Vol. III, Rev. Timothy Alden,
ed.   1814

*Reply to John Alden's (1559?–1687; American Pilgrim colonist) intervention for Miles Standish. (1584?–1656; English colonial settler in America).

356. María de Agreda (1602–1664/65)

1 Earth has 2,502 leagues, and up to the half of it, which is the place or seat of Hell, there are 1,251 leagues of profundity. In this center or middle of the Earth are the Purgatory and the Limbo. Hell has many caverns and mansions of punishment, and everything in there forms a big infernal cavern with a mouth in it, and is a proven fact that there is a big stone, bigger than the mouth, to cover it, when Hell will be sealed with all the sinners inside of it, where they have to suffer for all the eternities to come.
Quoted in
Women in Myth and History
by Violeta Miqueli   1962

357. Violante do Céu (1602?–1693)

1 You fool yourself and live a crazy day or year, dizzy with adventures, and bent solely on pleasures! Know the argument or rigid doom and find a wiser way.
"Voice of a Dissipated Woman
Inside a Tomb, Talking to
Another Woman Who Presumed
to Enter a Church with the
Purpose of Being Seen and
Praised by Everyone, Who Sat
Down Near a Sepulchar
Containing This Epitaph, Which
Curiously Reads,"
Rimas Varias   1646

2 . . . the end which ends with no way out.
Ibid.

358. Anna Maria Marchocka (1603–1652)

1 Humbly I beseech Thee, my Father. Cover me with Thy pinions, enlighten mine eyes that I wander not in a haze, knowing not what to write nor where.
Prayer found in her
Autobiography,
Quoted in Women of the
Reformation,
Vol. III: From Spain to
Scandinavia,
by Roland H. Bainton   1977

359. Elizabeth Melvill (fl. 1603)

1 The brain of man most surely did invent
That purging place, he answer'd me again:
For greediness together they consent
To say that souls in torment may remain,
Till gold and goods relieve them of their
pain.   *Ane Godlie Dreame Complit in*
Scottish Meter be M.M.,
Gentilwoman in Cul Ross, at the
Request of her Freindes,
St. 1   *1606*

2 The fire was great, the heat did pierce me
sore;
My faith was weak, my grip was wondrous
small,
I trembled fast, my fear grew more and
more. . . .   Ibid., St. 8

360. Marcela de Carpio de San Feliz (1605–1688)

1 Love giving gifts
Is suspicious and cold;
I have all, my Belovèd,
When thee I hold.   "Amor Mysticus,"
St. 3,
The Catholic Anthology,
Thomas Walsh, ed.   *1927*

2 But in Thy chastising
Is joy and peace.
O Master and Love,
Let Thy blows not cease.   Ibid., St. 8

361. A. M. Bigot de Cornuel (c.1605-14–1694)

1 Turenne's small change. *(La monnaie de M.*
*Turenne.)**   Remark,
Quoted in *Nouvelle Biographie*
Universelle   *1853–1866*

*I.e., the eight generals appointed to take the place of the
great French marshall Henri de La Tour d'Auvergne, vicomte de Turenne (1611–1675).

2 No man is a hero to his valet. *(Il n'y a point de*
héros pour son valet de chambre.)
Letter (13 August 1628),
*Lettres de Mlle. Aissé,**   n.d.

*See 463.

362. Anna van Schurman (1607–1678)

1 Woman has the same erect countenance* as
man, the same ideals, the same love of beauty,
honor, truth, the same wish for self-development, the same longing after righteousness, and
yet she is to be imprisoned in an empty soul of
which the very windows are shuttered.
Quoted in *The Dinner*
Party, A Symbol of our Heritage
by Judy Chicago**   *1979*

*Probably a faulty translation; more likely, "stance" or
"posture."
**See 2259.

363. Madeleine de Scudéry (1607–1701)

1 In order to represent the heroic spirit it is undoubtedly necessary to have the hero do something extraordinary, as in a moment of heroic
rapture, but this should not continue too long or
it will degenerate into something ridiculous and
will not have any good effect on the reader.
Preface,
Ibrahim or the Illustrious Bassa,
an Excellent New
Romance   *1652*

2 Since the body and the mind are so closely
linked that one cannot suffer without the other,
I fell ill.   Ibid., Vol. I

3 It is certain that I am inconstant, but at the same
time I am not troublesome. I never contradict
anyone's opinions or stand in the way of his
pleasures. I give to others the freedom that I
would have them accord me. I do not find fault
with constancy, although I myself am happier
with change, and my soul is so passionate that
I could never condemn anything connected with
love.   Ibid., Vol. II

4 Any road that can take us where we want to go
is the right one. Don't trouble yourself in asking
if what you do is just, but only if it is
advantageous.   Ibid.

5 . . . among private citizens it is prudent not to
rise above the average.   Ibid., Vol. III

6 He who imposes unnecessary problems upon
himself cannot complain because he is the sole
cause of whatever ills befall him.
Ibid., Vol. IV

7 When we know the truth in our own consciences
it is unnecessary to be troubled about anything
else.   *Artamenes, or The*
Grand Cyrus, an Excellent New
Romance,
Vol. I   *1653–1655*

8 I find nothing more extravagant than to see a
husband who is still in love with his wife.
Ibid., Vol. VI

9 I do not think that she has ever been indisposed
on a day when there was a party to attend.
Ibid., Vol. VII

10 . . . by staying in Babylon during the autumn and winter, in Susa during the spring, and in Ecbatana during the summer, he was able to live in an eternal springtime, feeling neither the great discomfort of the cold nor that of the heat.   *Ibid.,* Vol. X

11 I would, without a doubt, rather be a simple soldier than be a woman, because to be truthful, a soldier can become king, but a woman can never become free.   *Clelia, An Excellent New Romance,* Vol. I   *1656–1661*

12 It is better to find glory in one's own merit. In fact it is more important to have self-respect than to gain respect from others, and it is better to earn glory than to publicize it.
        Ibid., Vol. III

13 In losing a husband one loses a master who is often an obstacle to the enjoyment of many things.   *Ibid.,* Vol. IV

14 . . . the familiarity of married life does not encourage love to grow.   *Ibid.,* Vol. VI

15 . . . one always admires her at first but inevitably comes to the point of despising her.
        Ibid., Vol. IX

16 In fashioning a good portrait of an evil man one can sometimes instill a loathing for vice.
        Ibid.

17 Victory follows me, and all things follow victory. *(La victoire me suit, et tout suit la victoire.)*   "Tyrannic Love"   *n.d.*

364. Henrietta Maria (1609–1666)

1 Queens of England are never drowned.
   Written during storm at sea (February 1642), *Letters of Queen Henrietta Maria,* Mary Anne Everett Wood Green,* ed.   *1857*

*See 826.

365. Jane Owen (fl. 1610–d. 1633?)

1 Among all the Passions of the mind, there is not any, which hath so great a sovereignty, and command over man, as the Passion of Feare.   *An Antidote against Purgatory. Or Discourse, wherein is shewed that Good Workes, and Almes-Deeds, are a meanes for the preventing, or mitigating the Torments of Purgatory*   *1634*

366. Anne Bradstreet (1612?–1672)

1 That there is a God my Reason would soon tell me by the wondrous workes that I see, the vast frame of the Heaven and the Earth, the order of all things, night and day, Summer and Winter, Spring and Autumn, the dayly providing for this great household upon the Earth, the preserving and directing of All to its proper end.
   "To My Dear Children: Religious Experience and Occasional Pieces," Dedication to *The Tenth Muse Lately Sprung Up in America*   *1650*

2 I am obnoxious to each carping tongue
Who says my hand a needle better fits,
A Poet's pen all scorn I should thus wrong,
For such despite they cast on Female wits:
If what I do prove well, it won't advance,
They'll say it's stoln, or else it was by chance.   Prologue, St. 5, *Several Poems Compiled with Great Variety of Wit and Learning*   *1678*

3 Ye Cooks, your Kitchen implements I frame
Your Spits, Pots, Jacks, what else I need not name
Your dayly food I wholsome make, I warm
Your shrinking Limbs, which winter's cold doth harm.   "The Four Elements; Fire," op. cit.

4 But thou art bound to me, above the rest
Who am thy drink, thy blood, thy sap and best. . . .   *Ibid.,* "Water,"

5 Man at his best estate is vanity.
   "Of the Four Ages of Man: Middle Age," op. cit.

6 Let such as say our Sex is void of Reason,
Know 'tis a Slander now, but once was Treason.   "In Honour of that High and Mighty Princess, Queen Elizabeth,"* op. cit.

*See 277.

7 And he that knowes the most, doth still bemoan
He knows not all that here is to be known.
   "The Vanity of All Worldly Things," op. cit.

8 Thou ill-form'd offspring of my feeble brain. . . .   "From the Author to her Book," op. cit.

9 If ever two were one, than surely we.
If ever man were lov'd by wife, than thee.
   "To my Dear and loving Husband," op. cit.

10 I had eight birds hatcht in one nest,
Four Cocks there were, and Hens the rest,

I nurst them up with pain and care,
Nor cost nor labour did I spare
    "In reference to her Children"
        (23 June 1656?), op. cit.

11 More fool than I to look on that was lent,
As if mine own, when thus impermanent.
    "In Memory of my dear Child,
        Anne Bradstreet"
        (20 June 1669), op. cit.

12 There is no object that we see; no action that
we do; no good that we enjoy; no evill that we
feel, or fear, but we may make some spiritual
advantage of all: and he that makes such improvement is wise, as well as pious.
    "Meditations Devine and Moral,"
    *The Works of Anne Bradstreet in
        Prose and Verse,*
    John Harvard Ellis, ed.   *1867*

13 A prosperous state makes a secure Christian,
but adversity makes him Consider.
        Ibid., VIII

14 . . . those parents are wise that can fit their
nurture according to their Nature.   Ibid., X

15 Authority without wisdom is like a heavy axe
without an edg[e], fitter to bruise than
polish.   Ibid., XII

367. Bathsua Makin (1612?–1674?)

1 . . . these men of Law and their confederates
. . . the caterpillars of this Kingdom, who with
their uncontrolled exactions and extortions, eat
up the free-born people of this Nation. . . .
    *The Malady . . . and Remedy of
    Vexations and Unjust Arrests and
        Actions   1646*

2 A learned woman is thought to be a comet, that
bodes mischeif whenever it appears.
    *An Essay to Revive the Ancient
    Education of Gentlewomen
        1673*

3 To ask too much is the way to be denied
all.   Ibid.

4 One generation passeth away and another com-
eth, but the earth, the theatre on which we act,
abideth forever.   Ibid.

5 Merely to teach gentlewomen to frisk and dance,
to paint their faces, to curl their hair, to put on
a whisk,* to wear gay clothes, is not truly to
adorn, but to adulterate their bodies; yea, (what
is worse) to defile their souls.   Ibid.

*A woman's scarf, worn around the neck.

6 Had God intended women only as a finer sort
of cattle, He would not have made them reasonable. Brutes, a few degrees higher than . . .
monkeys . . . might have better fitted some

men's lust, pride, and pleasure; especially those
that desire to keep them ignorant to be tyran-
nized over.   Ibid.

7 . . . a little philosophy, carries a man from
God, but a great deal brings him back
again.   Ibid.

8 . . . a little knowledge, like windy bladders,
puffs up, but a good measure of true knowledge,
like ballast in a ship, settles down and makes a
person move more even in his station; 'tis not
knowing too much, but too little that causes
irregularity.   Ibid.

9 Objection: Women do not desire learning.
    Answer: Neither do many boys . . . yet I
suppose you do not intend to lay fallow all
children that will not bring forth fruit of
themselves.   Ibid.

368. Henriette de Coligny (1613?–1673)

1 His cleverness in the art of love is unequaled.

He knows how to draw the soul out by the
    ear.   Untitled sonnet (c.1725),
        Quoted in *Precious Women*
        by Dorothy Backer   *1974*

369. Dorothy Leigh (?–c.1616)

1 . . . gather hony of each flowre,
    as doth the labrous Bee.
Shee lookes not who did place the Plant,
    nor how the flowre did grow;
Whether so stately up aloft,
    or neere the ground below.
But where she finds it, there she workes,
    and gets the wholsome food,
And beares it home, and layes it up,
    to doe her Countrey good.
        "Counsell to my Children,"
            prefatory poem,
        The Mother's Blessing   1616

2 . . . Feare not to be poore with Lazarus, but
feare a thousand times to be rich with
Dives.*   Ibid., Ch. 6

*Latin for rich; traditionally used as the name for the
unnamed rich man in Luke 16:19 ff.

3 . . . have your Children brought up with much
gentlenesse and patience . . . for forwardnes
and curstnesse doth harden the heart of a child,
and maketh him weary of vertue.
        Ibid., Ch. 11

4 . . . a woman fit to be a man's wife is too good
to be his servant.   Ibid., Ch. 13

370. Costantia Munda (fl. 1617)

1 . . . things simply good
Keep still their essence, though they be with-
stood
By all the compices of hell. . . .
Prefatory poem,
The Worming of a Mad Dogge
1617

2 . . . printing that was invented to be the storehouse of famous wits, the treasure of Divine
literature . . . is become . . . the nursery and
hospitall of every spurious and pernicious brat,
which proceeds from base phreneticall braine-
sicke bablers.   Ibid. [Text]

3 . . . you lay open your imperfections . . . by
heaping together the . . . fragments . . . of
diverse english phrases . . . by scraping together the glaunder and . . . the refuse of idle-
headed Authors and making a mingle-mangle
gallimauphrie of them . . . let every bird take
his owne feathers, and you would be as naked
as Aesop's jay.   Answer to Joseph Swetnam's
"The Arraignment of Lewd, Idle,
Forward and Unconstant
Women"
(1617), op. cit.

371. Joane Sharp (fl. 1617)

1 Any answere may serve an impudent lyar,
    Any mangie scab'd horse doth fit a scab'd
Squire   "Epilogue: A Defence of Women,
against the Author of the
Arraignment of Women,"
Quoted in *Ester Hath Hang'd*
Haman: or An Answere to a lewd
Pamphlet, entituled, The
*Arraignment of Women** by*
Ester Sowernam**   *1617*

*Written by Joseph Swetnam in 1617.
**See 372.

2 To make a poore Maden or woman a whore,
They care not how much they spend of their
store.
But where is there a man that will any thing
give
That woman or maide may with honestie
live?   Ibid.

372. Ester Sowernam (fl. 1617)

1 The world is a large field, and it is full of
brambles, bryers, and weedes.
"To the Reader,"
Ester Hath Hang'd Haman: or*
An Answere to a lewd Pamphlet,
entituled, The Arraignment of
*Women**   1617*

*See 34.
**Written by Joseph Swetnam in 1617.

2 In all dangers, troubles, and extremities, which
fell to our Saviour, when all men fled from
Him, living or dead, women never forsook
Him.   Ibid., Ch. 3

3 . . . forbeare to charge women with faults which
come from the contagion of Masculine
serpents.   Ibid., Ch. 7

373. Charlotte Bregy (1619?–1693)

1 I never oppose the opinions of any; but I must
own that I never adopt them to the prejudice of
my own.   Letters (1688),
Quoted in *Biography of*
Distinguished Women
by Sarah Josepha Hale*   *1876*

*See 703.

2 I am indolent; I never seek pleasure and diver-
sions, but when my friends take more pains than
I do to procure them for me, I feel myself
obliged to appear very gay at them, though I
am not so in fact.   Ibid.

374. Lucy Hutchinson (1620–1671)

1 The greatest excellency she had was the power
of apprehending and the virtue of loving him;
so, as his shadow, she waited on him everywhere, till he was taken into that region of light
which admits of none, and then she vanished
into nothing.   Journal entry,
Quoted in
Leading Women of the
Restoration
by Grace Johnstone   *1891*

2 'Twas not her face he loved, her honour and
her virtue were his mistresses. . . .   Ibid.

375. Ninon de Lenclos (1620–1705)

1 Old age is woman's hell. (*La vieillesse est*
l'enfer des femmes.) La Coquette vengée   *1659*

2 We should take care to lay in a stock of provisions, but not of pleasures: these should be gathered day by day.
Correspondence authentique de Ninon de Lenclos,
Émile Colombey, ed. *1886*

3 The joy of the mind is the measure of its strength.
(La joie de l'esprit est marque de sa force.)
Ibid.

4 What you priests tell us is sheer nonsense. I don't believe a single word of it.
Quoted in *The Immortal Ninon* by Cecil Austin *1927*

5 I put your consolations by,
And care not for the hopes you give:
Since I am old enough to die,
Why should I longer wish to live?
Untitled, op. cit.

6 Love never dies of starvation, but often of indigestion. *L'Esprit des autres,* Ch. 3 *n.d.*

376. Jane Cavendish (1621–1669)

1 LUCENAY. My distruction is that when I marry Courtly I shall bee condemn'd to looke upon my Nose, whenever I walke and when I sitt at meate confin'd by his grave winke to looke upon the Salt, and if it bee but the paireing of his Nales to admire him.
The Concealed Fansyes, with Elizabeth Brackley* c.1644–1646

*See 379.

377. Leonora Christina (1621–1685)

1 Who can have any care for a child when one does not love its father? "A Record of the Sufferings of the Imprisoned Countess Leonora Christina" (1674–1685),
Memoirs of Leonora Christina, F. E. Bunnet, tr. *1929*

2 . . . in the twinkling of an eye much may change; the hand of God, in whom are the hearts of kings, can change everything.
Preface, op. cit.

3 The past is rarely remembered without sorrow, for it has been either better or worse than the present. Ibid.

4 What is all our labour here,
The servitude and yoke we bear?
Are they aught but vanity?
Art and learning what are ye?
Like a vapour all we see Spiritual song,
St. 1 (1682), op. cit.

5 The vanished hours can ne'er come back again,
Still may the old their youthful joys retain;
The past may yet within our memory live,
And courage vigor to the old may give.
"Contemplation on Memory and Courage, recorded to the honour of God by the suffering Christian woman in the sixty-third year of her life, and the almost completed 21st year of her captivity" (1684), op. cit.

6 I am but dust and ashes,
Yet one request I crave:
Let me not go unawares
Into the silent grave. "A Morning Hymn," St. 6, op. cit.

378. Margareta Ruarowna (fl. 1621)

1 O King . . . The nations in Thy sight are as nothing and are esteemed as vain and empty. The world before Thee is as the quivering of the balance, as the drop of the morning dew when it lights upon the earth.
From *Prayer Book* (1621),
Quoted in *Women of the Reformation,*
Vol. III: *From Spain to Scandinavia,*
by Roland H. Bainton *1977*

379. Elizabeth Brackley (c.1623–1663)

*Co-author with Jane Cavendish. See 376.

380. Margaret Cavendish (1623/24–1673/74)

Mirth laughing came, and running to me, flung
Her fat white arms about my neck. . . .
"Mirth and Melancholy,"
Mirth, *Poems & Fancies* *1653*

2 My music is the buzzing of a fly. Ibid.,
Her Dwelling

3 Since all heroic actions, public employments, powerful governments, and eloquent pleadings are denied our sex in this age, or at least would be condemned for want of custom . . . I write. "An Epistle to My Readers,"
Nature's Pictures, Drawn by Fancies Pencil to the Life *1656*

4 A man awalking did a lady spy;
To her he went, and when he came hard by,

Fair Lady, said he, why walk you alone?
Because, said she, my thoughts are then my
own   "The Effeminate Description,"
op. cit.

5 For had my brain fancies in 't
To fill the world, I'd put them all *in print:*
No matter whether they be well or ill exprest,
My *will* is done, and that please woman
best.   *The True Relation of my Birth,*
Breeding, and Life   1656

6 Many times married women desire children, as
maids do husbands, more for honour than for
comfort or happiness, thinking it a disgrace to
live old maids, and so likewise to be barren.
Sociable Letters   1664

7 Women's minds are like shops of small-wares,
wherein some have pretty toys, but nothing of
any great value.   Ibid.

8 . . . one may be my very good friend, and yet
not of my opinion.   Ibid., Letter XVI

9 Everyone's conscience in religion is between
God and themselves, and it belongs to none
other.   Ibid.

10 But nature be thanked, she has been so bountiful
to us as we oftener enslave men than men
enslave us. They seem to govern the world, but
we really govern the world in that we govern
men. For what man is he that is not governed
by a woman, more or less?   Ibid.

11 . . . I think a bad husband is far worse than no
husband, and to have unnatural children is more
unhappy than to have no children.
Ibid., Letter XCIII

12 I had rather die in the adventure of noble
achievements, than live in obscure and sluggish
security.   *The Description of a New*
World Called the Blazing
World   1666

13 The shortest-lived Fame lasts longer than the
longest life of Man.   Ibid.

14 Women make poems? burn them, burn them,
Let them make bone-lace, let them make bone-
lace   (1662), Quoted in
*Reconstructing Aphra,**
by Angeline Goreau   *1980*

*Aphra Behn. See 406.

15 . . . for all the Brothers were Valiant, and all
the Sisters virtuous.   Epitaph,
Westminster Abbey   n.d.

16 Whereas in nature we have as clear an understanding as men, if we were bred in schools to
mature our brains and to manure our understand-
ings, that we might bring forth the fruits of
knowledge.   "The Preface to the Reader,"
The World's Olio   n.d.

381. Hannah Woolley (1623–c.1675)

1 . . . blows are fitter for beasts than for rational
creatures.   *The Gentlewoman's*
Companion   1675

2 . . . a woman in this age is considered learned
enough if she can distinguish her husband's bed
from that of another.   (c.1675), Quoted in
The Stuarts in Love
by Maurice Ashely   *1964*

382. Mary of Warwick (1624–1678)

1 O Lord, from my soul I bless Thee for making
me again remember the wormwood and the gall
I had met with from all my worldly enjoyments,
to which I had too much let out my heart, and
from which I did foolishly expect too much
comfort.   Diary (December 2, 1672),
Quoted in
Leading Women of the
Restoration
by Grace Johnstone   *1891*

2 I will begin my first rule of advice to your
lordship, with desiring you not to turn the day
into night . . . by sleeping so long in the
morning. . . .   Letter to George, Earl of
Berkeley,
"Rules for a Holy Life,"
op. cit.

383. Eleanor Audeley (fl. 1625–1651)

1 POPE. Kings I Depose, and all their Race, to
Raigne.
DIVELL. And Popes to Friers I can turne
againe.   *A Warning to the*
Dragon and all his
Angels   1625

2 No man so well knowes his owne frailtie, as the
Lord your God knowes how prone Devotion is
to Superstition.   Ibid.

384. Bessie Clarkstone (?–1625)

1 O for absolution! O for a drop to coole my
tormented soule.   Quoted in *The Conflict*
in Conscience of a deare
Christian, named Bessie
Clarkstone, in the Parish of
Lanark, which she lay under
three yeare & an half
by John Wreittoun   *1631*

2 Alas, I have long to live, and a wretched life
. . . sighs helpe not, sobs helpe not, groanes
helpe not, and prayer is faint.   Ibid.

385. Ann Fanshawe (1625–1680)

1 Endeavour to be innocent as a dove, but as wise as a serpent.   *Memoirs of Ann, Lady Fanshawe   c.1670*

2 . . . it was never seen that a vicious youth terminated in a contented, cheerful old age. . . .   Ibid.

3 . . . reserve some hours daily to examine yourself and fortune; for if you embark yourself in perpetual conversation or recreation, you will certainly shipwreck your mind and fortune.   Ibid.

4 My glory and my guide, all my comfort in this life, is taken from me.* See me staggering in my path, because I expected a temporal blessing as a reward for the great innocence and integrity of his whole life.   Ibid.

*Referring to the death of her husband, Sir Richard Fanshawe (1608–1666), diplomat and author.

386. Christina of Sweden (1626–1689)

1 There is a star above us which unites souls of the first order, though worlds and ages separate them.   *Maxims (1660–1680), cited in toto in Pensées de Christine, reine de Suède   1825*

2 Life becomes useless and insipid when we have no longer either friends or enemies.   Ibid.

3 Fools are more to be feared than the wicked.   Ibid.

4 We grow old more through indolence, than through age.   Ibid.

5 I love men, not because they are men, but because they are not women.   Ibid.

6 Confessors of princes are like men engaged in taming tigers and lions: they can induce the beasts to perform hundreds of movements and thousands of actions, so that on seeing them one might believe they were completely tamed; but when the confessor least expects it, he is knocked over by one blow of the animal's paw, which shows that such beasts can never be completely tamed.   Ibid.

7 Nuns and married women are equally unhappy, if in different ways.   Ibid.

8 As you know, no one over thirty years of age is afraid of tittle-tattle. I myself find it much less difficult to strangle a man than to fear him.   *Letter (1657), Quoted in Christina of Sweden by Sven Stolpe   1960*

9 God has neither form nor shape under which we can know Him; when he speaks of Himself in metaphors and similes, He is adapting Himself to our foolishness, our limited capacity.   *Marginal notes (c.1684), op. cit.*

387. Marie de Sévigné (1626–1696)

1 I love you so passionately that I hide a great part of my love not to oppress you with it.   *Letter to Françoise Marguerite, the Comtesse de Grignan,* her daughter, *Letters of Madame de Sévigné to Her Daughter and Friends   1811*

*See 410.

2 . . . the most astonishing, the most surprising, the most marvelous, the most miraculous, the most magnificent, the most confounding, the most unheard of, the most singular, the most extraordinary, the most incredible, the most unforeseen, the greatest, the least, the rarest, the most common, the most public, the most private till today . . . I cannot bring myself to tell you: guess what it is.   *Letter to M. de Coulanges, op. cit.*

3 If I inflict wounds, I heal them.   *From letters to her daughter, op. cit.*

4 There is no real evil in life, except great pain; all the rest is imaginary, and depends on the light in which we view things.   Ibid.

5 There is no person who is not dangerous for someone. *(Il n'y a personne qui ne soit dangereux pour quelqu'un.)*   Ibid.

6 . . . lonely as a violet, easy to be hid. . . .   Ibid.

7 When I step into this library, I cannot understand why I ever step out of it.   Ibid.

8 Ah, how easy it really is to live with me! A little gentleness, a little social impulse, a little confidence, even superficial, will lead me such a long way.   Ibid.

9 We like so much to hear people talk of us and of our motives, that we are charmed even when they abuse us.   Ibid.

10 The desire to be singular and to astonish by ways out of the common seems to me to be the source of many virtues.   Ibid.

11 There is nothing so lovely as to be beautiful. Beauty is a gift of God and we should cherish it as such.   Ibid.

12 I have seen the Abbé de la Vergne; we talked about my soul; he says that unless he can lock me up, not stir a step from me, take me to and from church himself, and neither let me read, speak, nor hear a single thing, he will have nothing to do with me whatever.   Ibid.

13 It is sometimes best to slip over thoughts and not go to the bottom of them. *(Il faut glisser sur les pensées et ne pas les approfondir.)*
Ibid.

14 The mind should be at peace but the heart debauches it perpetually.   Ibid.

15 . . . long journeys are strange things: if we were always to continue in the same mind we are in at the end of a journey, we should never stir from the place we were then in; but Providence in kindness to us causes us to forget it. It is much the same with lying-in women. Heaven permits the forgetfulness that the world may be peopled, and that folks may take journeys to Provence.   Ibid. (31 May 1671)

16 True friendship is never serene.
Ibid. (10 September 1671)

17 Luck is always on the side of the big battalions. *(La fortune est toujours pour les gros bataillons.)*   Ibid. (22 December 1673)

18 . . . it seldom happens, I think, that a man has the civility to die when all the world wishes it.   Ibid. (1 March 1680)

19 . . . a lucky marriage pays for all.
Ibid. (11 September 1680)

20 . . . this life is a perpetual chequer-work of good and evil, pleasure and pain. When in possession of what we desire, we are only so much the nearer losing it; and when at a distance from it, we live in expectation of enjoying it again. It is our business, therefore, to take things as God is pleased to send them.
Ibid. (22 September 1680)

388. Ann-Marie-Louise d'Orléans (1627–1693)

1 . . . self-love is scarcely conducive to piety.   "Self-Portrait,"
Mademoiselle's Portrait Gallery   1657

2 . . . fate has been more lacking in judgment than I, for had it had more sense it would doubtless have treated me better.   Ibid.

3 Children who are the object of great respect . . . usually become horribly puffed up.
From *Memoirs* (1652–1688),
Quoted in *The Grand Mademoiselle*,
Francis Steegmuller, tr.   *1956*

4 Nothing so disfigures a person, to my taste, as the inability to *talk*. . . .   Ibid.

5 . . . there is no doubt that Cupid is French. . . .   Ibid.

6 The sight of a person of my quality exposing himself to danger always does wonders for a population.   Ibid.

7 There is nothing so tiresome as other people's business.   Ibid.

389. Dorothy Osborne (1627–1695)

1 . . . there are certain things that custom has made almost of absolute necessity, and reputation I take to be one of those. . .
Letter (c.1653), *Letters,*
E. A. Parry, ed.   *1914*

2 All letters, methinks, should be as free and easy as one's discourse, not studied as an oration, nor made up of hard words like a charm.
Letter to Sir William Temple
(October 1653),
op. cit.

390. Alice Thornton (1627–1707)

1 Therefore it highly concerned me to enter into this greatest change of my life [marriage] with abundance of fear and caution, not lightly, nor unadvisedly, nor, as I may take my God to witness that knows the secrets of hearts, I did it not to fulfill the lusts of the flesh, but in chastity and singleness of heart, as marrying in the Lord.   *The Autobiography of Mrs. Alice Thornton, of East Newton, Co. York   1875*

391. Dorothy Berry (fl. 1630s)

1   Whose Noble Praise
Deserves a Quill pluckt from an Angels wing,
And none to write it but a Crowned King.
Dedicatory poem, Quoted in
A Chaine of Pearle. Or A Memoriall of the peerless Graces, and Heroick Vertues of Queene Elizabeth, * of Glorious Memory*
by Diana Primrose   *1630*

2 Shee, Shee* it was, that gave us Golden Daies   Ibid.

*Queen Elizabeth I. See 277.

392. Diana Primrose (fl. 1630)

1 . . . Great Eliza,* Englands brightest Sun,
"The Induction,"
*A Chaine of Pearle. Or a
Memoriall of the peerless Graces,
and Heroick Vertues of Queene
Elizabeth, of Glorious
Memory   1630*

*Queen Elizabeth I. See 277.

2 . . . that Vestall Fire
Still flaming, never would Shee condescend
To Hymen's* Rightes. . . .
"The Second Pearle. Chastity,"
op. cit.

*Eponymous god of fruitfulness; also, in Attic legend, representative of happy married life.

3 O Golden Age! O blest and happy years!
O music sweeter than that of the Spheres!
When Prince and People mutually agree
In sacred concord and sweet symphony!
"The Fourth Pearle. Temperance,"
op. cit.

393. R. M. (?–1630?)

1 Women that are chaste when they are trusted, prove often wantons when they are causelesse
suspected.   "Live Within
Compasse in Chastitie,"
*The Mothers Counsell or, Live
within Compasse. Being the last
Will and Testament to her
dearest Daughter.   1630*

2 There cannot be a greater clog to man than to be troubled with a wanton woman.
"Out of Compasse in Chastitie is
Wantonesse," op. cit.

3 Heaven made Beauty like itselfe to view,
Not to be lockt up in a smokie mew:
A rosie vertuous cheeke is heavens gold,
Which all men joy to touch, all to behold.
"Live Within Compasse in
Beautie,"
op. cit.

4 To frivolous questions silence is ever the best answer.
"Live Within Compasse in Humilitie,"
op. cit.

5 When Dogs fall on snarling, Serpents on hissing, and Women on weeping, the first meanes to bite, the second to sting, and the last to deceive.   "Out of Compasse in
Humilitie is Pride,"
op. cit.

394. Katherine Fowler Philips (1631–1664)

1 Who to another does his heart submit,
Makes his own idol, and then worships it
"Against Love,"
St. 2,
*Poems, By the Incomparable
Mrs. K. P.   1664*

2 How soon we curse what erst we did adore.
"A Sea-Voyage From Tenby to
Bristol, Begun September 5,
1652. Sent From Bristol to
Lucasia, September 8, 1652,"
op. cit.

3 He who commands himself is more a prince,
Than he who nations keep in awe   Untitled,
op. cit.

4 *Christ* will be King, but I ne'er understood
His Subjects built his Kingdom up with
Blood   "Upon the Double Murther of
King Charles I in Answer to a
Libellous Copy of Rimes by
Vavasor Powell," *Poems.
By the most deservedly Admired
Mrs. Katherine Philips, the
Matchless Orinda* . . .   1678*

*Pseudonym of Katherine Philips.

5 Slander must follow Treason. . . .   Ibid.

6 They are, and yet they are not, two.
"Friendship in Embleme, or the
Seal. To my Dearest Lucasia,"
St. 6, op. cit.

7 Honour's to th' mind as Beauty to the sense,
The fair result of mixed Excellence.
"To the truly competent Judge
of Honour, Lucasia, upon a
scandalous Libel
made by J. J.,"*
op. cit.

*Colonel John Jones, signer of the death warrant of Charles I.

8 Such horrid Ignorance benights the Times,
That Wit and Honour are become our
Crimes.   "The Prince of Phancy,"*
op. cit.

*William Cartwright (1611–1643), poet, playwright, wit, scholar.

9 A Chosen Privacy, a cheap Content,
And all the Peace a Friendship ever lent,
A Rock which civil Nature made a Seat,
A Willow that repulses all the heat
"A Revery,"
op. cit.

10 He only dies untimely who dies late.
For if 'twere told to Children in the Womb,

To what a Stage of Mischiefs they must come
....
what we call their Birth would count their
    Death.   "2 Cor. 5, 19. God was in
        Christ Reconciling the World to
                      himself,"
                      op. cit.

11 I did but see him, and he dis-appear'd,
    I did but pluck the Rose-bud and it fell
               "Orinda upon little Hector
                    Philips,"*
                    St. 2,
                    op. cit.

*Her son.

12 I'm so entangl'd and so lost a thing
    By all the shocks my daily sorrow bring
          "Orinda to Lucasia parting
          October, 1661, at London,"
                    op. cit.

13 But I can love, and love at such a pitch,
    As I dare boast it will ev'n you enrich
          Ibid., "To my Lady M[argaret]
          Cavendish,* chusing the Name of
                  Polycrite,"
                    op. cit.

*See 380

14 For kindness is a Mine, when great and true,
    Of Nobler Ore than even *Indians* knew;
    'Tis all that Mortals can on Heav'n bestow,
    And all that Heav'n can value here below.
                    Ibid.

15 For my sake talk of Graves no more
          Ibid., "To my Atenor,*
          March 16, 1661/2,"
                    op. cit.

*Her friend, Philip James.

16 Death is as coy a thing as Love.   Ibid.

17 And when our Fortune's most severe,
    The less we have, the less we fear.   Ibid.

18 Woes have their Ebb as well as Flood   Ibid.

19 Friendship's an abstract of this noble flame,
    'Tis love refin'd, and purged from all its
        dross,
    'Tis next to angel's love, if not the same,
    As strong in passion is, though not so gross.
                  "Friendship,"
                    op. cit.

20 Poets and friends are born to what they are.
                    Ibid.

21 I find too there are few Friendships in the World
    Marriage-proof. . . .   *Letters from Orinda to
                Poliarchus*   1705

*Name used by her husband, James Philips.

22 . . . we may generally conclude the Marriage
    of a Friend to be the Funeral of a
    Friendship. . . .   Ibid.

23 Waste not in vain the crystal Day,
    But gather your Rose-buds while you may.
                    Ibid.

24 I now see by Experience that one may love too
    much, and offend more by a too fond Sincerity,
    than by a careless Indifferency, provided it be
    but handsomely varnish'd over with civil
    Respect.   Letter to Sir
          Charles, No. XII, *Letters from
          Orinda to Poliarchus. The Second
          Edition, with Additions*   1729

395. Marie-Catherine Desjardins (1632–1683)

1 Beautiful lovers, hold your tongues, you err to
    the extreme;
    Taking turns a hundred times to say: I love
    you.
    In love, one must speak with elegance.
                    "Madrigal,"
                Elaine Partnow, tr.*
          Quoted in *Biography of
             Distinguished Women*
    by Sarah Josepha Hale**   1876

*Author.
**See 703.

2 A sweet languor takes me from my senses,
    I die away in the arms of my faithful lover,
    and in this death I rediscover life.
    *(Une douce langueur m'ôte le sentiment;
    Je Meurs entre les bras de mon fidèle amant,
    Et c'est dans cette mort que je trouve la vie.)*
    Untitled sonnet, Quoted in *Precious Women*
             by Dorothy Backer   1974

396. Kawai Chigetsu-Ni (1632–1736)

1 Grasshoppers
    Chirping in the sleeves
    Of a scarecrow.   Untitled haiku,
          *The Burning Heart: Women
                  Poets of Japan,*
          Kenneth Rexroth and Ikuko
          Atsumi, eds. and trs.   1977

397. Anne Wharton (1632?–1685)

1 May yours* excel the matchless Sappho's**
    name;

May you have all her wit, without her
shame.   "The Temple of Death"   *1695*

*The English writer Aphra Behn. See 406.
**See 50.

2 Sorrow may make a silent moan,
But joy will be revealed.   Untitled, St. 2,
Tooke's Collection of
Miscellaneous Poems,
n.d.

*Probably John Horne Tooke (1736–1812), English politician and philologist.

398. Mary Dyer (fl. 1633–d. 1660)

1 In obedience to the will of the Lord I came and
in His will I abide faithful to the death.
Last words on the gallows
(1 June 1660), Boston,
Quoted in
Notable American Women,
Edward T. James, ed.   *1971*

2 My life not availeth me in comparison of the
liberty of the truth.   Carved on
monument to Mary Dyer at the
Boston Statehouse   *n.d.*

399. Catharina Regina von Greiffenberg
(1633–1694)

1 You empress of the stars, the heaven's worthy
crown,

The world's great eye, and soul of all spreading earth   "Spring-Joy Praising God.
Praise of the Sun,"
St. 1, George C. Schoolfield, tr.;
*Anthology of German Poetry
through the Nineteenth Century,*
Alexander Gode and Frederick
Ungar, eds.   *1963*

2 You mirror-spectrum-glance, you many-colored gleam!
You glitter to and fro, are incomprehensibly
clear   "On the Ineffable
Inspiration of the Holy Spirit,"
St. 3,
Geistliche Sonnette, 1662,
Michael Hamburger, tr.;
*The Penguin Book
of Women Poets,*
Carol Cosman, Joan Keefe and
Kathleen Weaver, eds.   *1978*

400. Marie Madeleine de La Fayette
(1634–1692/93)

1 Most mothers think that to keep young people
away from love-making it is enough never to
speak of it in their presence.
The Princess of Clèves,
First Part   *1678*

2 Ambition and love-making were the soul of this
Court,* and obsessed the minds of men and
women alike.   *Ibid.*

*The court of Henry II of France.

3 "If you judge by appearances in this place,"
replied Madame de Chartres, "you will often
be deceived; what appears on the surface is
almost never the truth."   *Ibid.*

4 "I have enjoyed all the pleasures that revenge
can give. . . ."   *Ibid.,* Second Part

5 "I was wrong in believing there was a man
capable of hiding what pleases his vanity."
Ibid. Third Part

6 ". . . all who marry Mistresses who love them
tremble when they marry them, and have fears
with regard to other men when they remember their wives' conduct with themselves. . . ."   *Ibid.,* Fourth Part

7 "One reproaches a lover, but can one reproach
a husband, when his only fault is that he no
longer loves?"   *Ibid.*

8 The necessity of dying, which she saw close at
hand, accustomed her to detaching herself from
everything. . . .   *Ibid.*

401. Françoise de Maintenon (1635–1719)

1 Nothing is more adroit than irreproachable
conduct.   Motto, *Maximes de Mme de
Maintenon*   *1686*

2 Delicacy is to love what grace is to beauty.
Ibid.

3 Frankness does not consist in saying a great
deal, but in saying everything, and this everything is soon said when one is sincere, because
there is no need of a great flourish and because
one does not need many words to open the
heart.   Letter to Madame de
Saint-Périer (21 October 1708),
*Lettres sur l'éducation des
filles*   *1854*

4 . . . thanks to the goodness of God, I have no
passions, that is to say, I love no one to the

point of being willing to do anything that God would not approve.

> Remark to Madame Glapion
> (October 1708),
> *Lettres historiques et
> édifantes*, Vol. II   *1856*

5 Behold the fine appointment he makes with me! That man never did love anyone but himself.*
(Voyez le beau rende vous qu'il me donne! Cet homme là n'a jamais aimé que lui-même.)

> Remark (1 September 1715),
> op. cit.

*Reference to Louis XIV's remark to her, while on his deathbed, "We shall meet again soon."

6 [I wish] to remain an enigma to posterity.

> *Correspondance générale de Mme
> de Maintenon,*
> Vol. I, Théophile Lavallée, ed.
> *1865–1866*

7 The longer I live, the more I grow in the opinion that it is useless to pile up wealth.

> Letter to Madame de Brinon
> (April 1683),
> op. cit., Vol. II

8 I am determined to aid those who aid themselves, and to let the good-for-nothing suffer.

> *Lettres,*
> Vol. I, Marcel Langlois, ed.
> *1935–1939*

9 [Marriage is] a state that causes the misery of three quarters of the human race.

> Letter to Gobelin (1 August
> 1674),
> op. cit.

10 You know that my mania is to make people hear reason.

> Letter to Madame de
> Ventadour (February 1692),
> op. cit.

402. Mary Rowlandson (c.1635–post-1678)

1 I had often before this said, that if the Indians should come, I should chuse rather to be killed by them then taken alive but when it came to the tryal my mind changed; their glittering weapons so daunted my spirit, that I chose rather to go along with those (as I may say) ravenous Bears, then that moment to end my dayes.

> *The Sovereignty & Goodness of
> God, Together, with the
> Faithfulness of His Promises
> Displayed; Being a Narrative of
> the Captivity and Restauration of
> Mrs. Mary Rowlandson   1682*

403. Rachel Russell (1636–1723)

1 . . . so little we distinguish how, and why we love, to me it argues a prodigious fondness of one's self. . . .

> Letter to Dr.
> Fitzwilliam,
> *Letters*   *c.1793*

2 I was too rich in possessions whilst I possessed him*. . . .

> Ibid.

*Her husband, Lord William Russell, first Duke of Bedford.

3 . . . that biggest blessing of loving and being loved by those I loved and respected; on earth no enjoyment certainly to be put in the balance with it.

> Letter to the Earl of
> Galway,
> op. cit.

4 . . . the conversation of friends . . . is the nearest approach we can make to heaven while we live in these tabernacles of clay; so it is in a temporal sense also, the most pleasant and the most profitable improvement we can make of the time we are to spend on earth.

> Letter to Lady Sunderland,
> op. cit.

5 . . . who would live and not love?   Ibid.

404. Antoinette Deshoulières (1638–1694)

1   It isn't easy for one who thinks
To be honest, and yet play the game;
The desire for gain, a day and night occupation,
   Is a dangerous spur
That goads one towards jeopardy.

> Untitled poem,
> Elaine Partnow,* tr.,
> Quoted in *Biography of
> Distinguished Women*
> by Sarah Josepha Hale**   *1876*

*Author.
**See 703.

2 Alas! little sheep, you are blessed!
You pass through our fields without care, without alarm.

> From *Les Moutons*
> (1695),
> "Idylle,"
> Elaine Partnow,* tr., op. cit.

*Author.

3 No one is satisfied with his fortune, nor dissatisfied with his intellect. *(Nul n'est content de sa fortune; Ni mécontent de son esprit.)*

> "Epigram"   *n.d.*

405. Makhfi (1639–1703)

1 I want to go to the desert
but modesty is chains on my feet.　　Untitled,
Willis Barnstone, tr.;
A Book of Women Poets,
Aliki and Willis Barnstone, eds.
1980

2 My tears break forth, my will is overridden,
Reason retreats and resolutions wane;
The stormy bursts of weeping come unbidden,
Wayward and fitful as the April rain.
Untitled,
St. 2, Paul Whalley, tr.;
Women Poets of the World,
Joanna Bankier and Deirdre
Lashgari, eds.　　*1983*

406. Aphra Behn (1640–1689)

1 Who is't that to women's beauty would submit,
And yet refuse the fetters of their wit?
Prologue,
The Forced Marriage　　*1670/71*

2 AMINTA. While to inconstancy I bid adieu, I
find variety enough in you.　　Ibid.

3 This humour is not à-la-mode. . . .
Prologue,
The Amorous Prince　　*1671*

4 . . . I have heard the most of that which bears
the name of learning, and which has abused
such quantities of ink and paper, and continually
employs so many ignorant, unhappy souls, for
ten, twelve, twenty years in a university (who
yet poor wretches think they are doing some
thing all the while) as logic, etc. and several
other things (that shall be nameless lest I mis-
spell them) are much more absolutely nothing
than the errantist play that e'er was writ.
"An Epistle to the
Reader,"
The Dutch Lover　　*1673*

5 ALONZO. . . . the natural itch of talking and
lying. . . .　　Ibid., Act II, Sc. 6

6 SILVIO. . . . he loves most that gives a loose to
love.　　Ibid., Act III, Sc. 4

7 OLINDA. . . . this marrying I do not like: 'tis
like going on a long voyage to sea, where after
a while even the calms are distasteful, and the
storms dangerous: one seldom sees a new object,
'tis still a deal of sea, sea; husband, husband,
every day,—till one's quite cloyed with it.
Ibid., Act. IV, Sc. 1

8 SIR TIMOTHY. The Devil's in her tongue, and so
'tis in most women's of her age; for when it has
quitted the tail, it repairs to the upper tier.
The Town Fop　　*1676*

9 Come away! Poverty's catching.
Ibid., *The Rover*
Act I, Sc. 1　　*1677*

10 Variety is the soul of pleasure.
Ibid., Act II, Sc. 1, 1.1.

11 Money speaks sense in a language all nations
understand.　　Ibid., Act III, Sc. 1

12 One hour of right-down love
Is worth an hour of dully living on.
Ibid., Act V, Sc. 1

13 Conscience: a chief pretence to cozen fools
withal. . . .　　Ibid., Epilogue

14 Constancy, that current coin for fools.　　Ibid.

15 Sure he's too much a gentleman to be a
scholar.　　*Sir Patient Fancy*　　*1678*

16 He has been on the point of going off these
twenty years.　　Ibid.

17 LADY KNOWELL. Can anything that's great or
moving be expressed in filthy English?　　Ibid.

18 She's a chick of the old cock.
Ibid., Act IV, Sc. 4

19 The Devil takes this curset plotting age,
'T has ruin'd all our plots upon the stage;
Suspicions, new elections, jealousies,
Fresh informations, new discoveries,
Do so employ the busy fearful town,
Our honest calling here is useless grown:
Each fool turns politician now, and wears
A formal face, and talks of state-affairs.
Prologue,
The Feigned Curtezans
1679

20 Patience is a flatterer, sir—and an ass, sir.
Ibid., Act III, Sc. 1

21 'Tis not your saying that you love,
Can ease me of my smart;
Your actions must your words approve,
Or else you break my heart.　　"Song,"
*Poems upon Several
Occasions*　　*1684*

22 Since Man with that inconstancy was born,
To love the absent, and the present scorn,
Why do we deck, why do we dress
For a short-liv'd happiness?　　"To Alexis,"
op. cit.

23 Take back your gold, and give me current
love,
The treasure of your heart, not of your
purse　　"On Desire,"
op. cit.

24 All I ask, is the privilege for my masculine part, the poet in me . . . if I must not, because of my sex, have this freedom, I lay down my quill and you shall hear no more of me. . . .
Preface,
The Lucky Chance
1686

25 Too much curiosity lost Paradise.
Ibid., Act III, Sc. 3

26 Faith, Sir, we are here to-day, and gone tomorrow. Ibid., Act IV

27 Madam, 'twas a pious fraud, if it were one.
Ibid., Act V, Sc. 7

28 Oh, what a dear ravishing thing is the beginning of an Amour! *The Emperor of the Moon,*
Act I, Sc. 1 *1687*

29 Of all that writ, he was the wisest bard, who spoke this mighty truth—
He that knew all that ever learning writ,
Knew only this—that he knew nothing yet.
Ibid., Sc. 3

30 Advantages are lawful in love and war. Ibid.

31 How many idiots has it [love] made wise! how many fools eloquent! how many homebred squires accomplished! how many cowards brave!
The Fair Jilt *1688*

32 "These people represented to me," she said, "an absolute idea of the first state of innocence, before man knew how to sin: and 'tis most evident and plain that simple nature is the most harmless, inoffensive and virtuous mistress. 'Tis she alone, if she were permitted, that better instructs the world than all the inventions of man: religion would here but destroy that tranquility they possess by ignorance; and laws would tech 'em to know offences of which now they have no notion." *Oroonoko, The Royal Slave* *1688*

33 . . . in that country . . . where the only crime and sin against a woman, is, to turn her off, to abandon her to want, shame, and misery; such ill morals are only practised in Christian countries, where they prefer the bare name of religion. . . . Ibid.

34 For when the mind so cruel is grown
As neither love nor hate to own,
The life but dully lingers on.
"To Damon" *1689*

35 Love, like Reputation, once fled, never returns more. *History of the Nun* *1689*

36 . . . that perfect tranquillity of life, which is nowhere to be found but in retreat, a faithful friend, and a good library. . . .
The Lucky Mistake *1689*

37 This money certainly is a most devilish thing! *The Court of the King Bantam* *1696*

38 That Love, the great instructor of the mind,
That forms anew, and fashions every soul,
Refines the gross defects of humankind.
"Iris to Damon," *The Lover's Watch* *1696*

39 Though love, while soft and flattering, promises nothing but pleasures; yet its consequences are often sad and fatal.
The History of Agnes De Castro, n.d.

40 Nothing is more capable of troubling our reason, and consuming our health, than secret notions of jealousy in solitude. Ibid.

407. Joane Hit-him-home (fl. 1640)

Co-author with Mary Tattlewell. See 408.

408. Mary Tattlewell (fl. 1640)

1 . . . what have we women done,
That any one who was a mother's sonne
Should thus affront our sex? Hath he forgot
From whence he came? or doth hee seek to blot
His own conception? "Epistle to the Reader: Long Megge of Westminster, hearing the abuse, offeres to women to riseth out of her grave and thus speaketh," *The Women's Sharpe Revenge: or an Answer to Sir Seldome Sober that writ those railing Pamphelets called The Juniper and The Crab-Tree Lectures, etc. Being a sound Reply and a full Confutation of those Bookes: with an Apology in this case for the Defence of us Women,* with Joane Hit-him-home* *1640*

*See 407.

2 . . . the corrupt heart discovereth itself by the lewd tongue. Essay, op. cit.

3 Nature hath bestowed upon us two eares, and two eyes, yet but one tongue; which is an Embleme unto us that though we heare and see much, yet ought wee to speak but little. . . . Ibid.

4 . . . even fooles being silent have passed for wise men. . . . Ibid.

5 . . . hee never came to me empty mouth'd or handed; for hee was never unprovided of stew'd Anagrams, bak'd Epigrams, sous'd Madrigalls, pickled Round delayes, broyld Sonnets, parboild Elegies, perfum'd poesies for Rings, and a thousand other such foolish flatteries, and knavish devices. . . .   Ibid.

409. Anna Hume (fl. 1644)

1 Reader, I have oft been told,
Verses that speak not Love are cold.
                    "To the Reader,"
        The Triumphs of Love, Chastity,
                Death: translated out of
                    Petrarch*   1644

*1304–74. Italian poet.

2 The fatal hour of her short life drew near,
That doubtful passage which the world
    doth fear   "The Triumph of Death,"
                        op. cit., Ch. 1

410. Françoise de Grignan (c.1646-1648–1705)

1 We [women] have not enough reason to use all our strength. [Nous n'avons pas assez de raison pour employer toute notre force.]
                    Letter to her mother
                [Mme. de Sévigné],*
        Quoted in Letters of Madame de
        Sévigné to Her Daughter and Her
                        Friends   1811

*See 387.

411. Nur Jahan (?–1646)

1 My eyes have one job: to cry.   Untitled,
                    Willis Barnstone, tr.;
                A Book of Women Poets,
        Aliki and Willis Barnstone, eds.
                                1980

2 The key to my locked spirit is your laughing mouth.   Untitled,
            Willis Barnstone, tr., op. cit.

412. Maria Sibylla Merian (1647–1717)

1 From my youth I have been interested in insects. First I started with the silkworms in my native Frankfurt am Main. After that . . . I started to collect all the caterpillars I could find in order to observe their changes . . . and I painted them very carefully on parchment.   Quoted in
                    "A Surinam Portfolio,"
        Natural History   December
                                1962

413. Jeanne-Marie de la Motte Guyon (1648–1717)

1 But though my wing is closely bound,
My heart's at liberty;
My prison walls cannot control
The flight, the freedom of the soul.
                    "A Prisoner's Song,"
                written while imprisoned at the
                    Castle of Vincennes
                        c. 1695–1702

2 There is nothing great, there is nothing holy, there is nothing wise, there is nothing fair, but to depend wholly upon God, like a child who does and can do only what is bidden.
            Lettres chrétiennes et spirituelles,
                    Vol. III   1717–1718

3 I know but one path, but one way, but one road, which is that of continual renouncement, of death, of nothingness. Everybody flies this way and seeks with passion all that makes us live; nobody is willing to be nothing, yet how shall we find what we are all seeking by a road which leads precisely wrong?   Ibid.

4 The soul is no longer either confined or possessed, nor does it possess or even enjoy; it perceives no difference between God and itself, sees nothing, possesses nothing, distinguishes nothing, even in God. God is the soul and the soul is God.   Ibid., Vol. V

5 My condition in marriage was rather that of a slave than that of a free woman.
            La Vie de Mme J.-M. B. de La
            Mothe Guion, écrite par elle-même
            [Autobiography], Vol. I   1720

6 Let us love without reasoning about it, and we shall find ourselves filled with love before others have found out the reasons that lead to loving.   Ibid.

414. Anna Tompson Hayden (1648?–1720?)

1 For none Can tell who shall be next,
Yet all may it expect;
Then surely it Concerneth all,
Their time not to neglect.
                "Upon the Death of yt desireable
                    young virgin, Elizabeth
            Tompson, Daughter of Joseph &
            Mary Tompson of Bilerika, who
            Deceased in Boston out of the
                hous of Mr legg, 24 August,
                1712, aged 22 years,"
            Handkerchiefs from Paul: Being
            Pious and Consolatory Verses of
                    Puritan Massachusetts,
                Kenneth B. Murdock, ed.
                                1927

415. Maria Anna Mancini (1649–1714)

1 You weep, and you are the master! *(Vous pleu-
rez, et vous êtes le maître!)*
Remark to Louis XIV (c. 1658),
in response to being sent away
from Paris,
Memoires, n.d.

416. Nell Gwyn (1650–1687)

1 Here is a sad slaughter at Windsor, the young
mens taking your Leaves and going to France,
and, although they are none of my Lovers, yet
I am loathe to part with the men.
Letter to Madam Jennings
(April 14, 1684),
Quoted in
The Story of Nell Gwynn
by Peter Cunningham   *1892*

417. Juana Inés de la Cruz (1651–1695)

1 Nothing could be funnier
Than the tale of him befouling
His own mirror, and then scowling
When the image was a blur. "Redondillas,"
St. 5, Garrett Strange, tr.,
The Catholic Anthology,
Thomas Walsh, ed.   *1927*

2 The greater evil who is in—
When both in wayward paths are
straying—
The poor sinner for the pain,
Or he that pays for the sin?   Ibid., St. 9

3 This evening when I spake with thee,
beloved,
as in thy face and in thy mien I saw
that I could not persuade thee with my
words,
the longing came for thee to see my heart
"This evening when I spake with
thee, beloved . . . ,"   St. 1,
Anthology of Mexican Poetry,
Octavio Paz, ed.; Samuel
Beckett, tr.   *1958*

4 Oh dreaded destiny and yet pursued!
"Crimson lute that comest in the
dawn. . . ,"
St. 4, op. cit.

5 I do not value wealth or riches,
Wherefore I shall be ever more content

To bring more richness to my mind
And not to keep my mind on riches.
"En perseguirme, mundo, ¿ qué
interesas?" ["Oh World, Why do
you thus pursue me?"],
St. 2, Muriel Kittel, tr.;
*An Anthology of Spanish Poetry,
from Garcilaso to García Lorca,*
Angel Flores, ed.   *1961*

6 In my opinion, better far it be
To destroy vanity within my life
Than to destroy my life in vanity.
Ibid., St. 4

7 "Diuturna enfermedad de la Esperanza . . ."
("Perpetual Infirmity of Hope . . .")
Title of poem,
Muriel Kittel, tr., op. cit.

8 Lure of the world, senescent lushness,
Imagination's decrepit verdure,
Today expected by the happy,
And by the hapless not before tomorrow.
"Esperanza" ["Hope"],
St. 2, Kate Flores, tr., op. cit.

9 my hope, although its greenness cost me
dear,
is watered by mine eyes.
"Que expresan sentimientos de
ausente" ("Verses expressing the
feelings of a lover"),
St. 15, Samuel Beckett, tr., op. cit.

10 What magical infusions, brewed
from herbals of the Indians
of my own country, spilled their old
enchantment over all my lines?
"En reconocimiento a las
inimitables plumas de la Europa"
("In acknowledgment of the
praises of European writers"),
St. 14, Constance Urdang, tr.,
op. cit.

11 You have brought disgrace on me
in making me so famous, for
the light you shed reveals my faults
more clearly, making them stand out.
Ibid., St. 20

12 Everything that you receive
is not measured according to
its actual size, but, rather, that
of the receiving vessel.   Ibid., St. 27

13 I believed, when I entered this convent, I was
escaping from myself, but alas, poor me, I
brought myself with me!   Quoted in
Women in Myth and History
by Violeta Miqueli   *1962*

14 this in which flattery has undertaken
to extenuate the hideousness of years,
and, vanquishing the outrages of time,

to triumph o'er oblivion and old age,
is an empty artifice of care.   Untitled,
Samuel Beckett, tr.;
*The Penguin Book
of Women Poets,*
Carol Cosman, Joan Keefe and
Kathleen Weaver, eds.   *1978*

15 Critics: in your sight
no woman can win:
keep you out, and she's too tight;
she's too loose if you get in.
Verses from "A Satirical Romance,"
St. 3, Samuel Beckett, tr., op. cit.

16 . . . sorting the reasons to leave you or hold
you,
I find an intangible one to love you,
and many tangible ones to forego you.
Untitled, Judith Thurman, tr.,
op. cit.

17 . . . as love is union, it knows no extremes of
distance.   "Repuesta a
Sor Filotea" (Reply to Sister
Philotea: 1691), Quoted in *A Woman
of Genius: The Intellectual
Autobiography of Sor Juana Ines de
la Cruz* by Margaret Sayers
Peden   *1982*

18 One will abide, and will confess that another is
nobler than he, that another is richer, more
handsome, and even that he is more learned,
but that another is richer in reason scarcely any
will confess: *Rare is he who will concede
genius.*   Ibid.

19 But, lady, as women, what wisdom may be ours
if not the philosophies of the kitchen? Lupercio
Leonardo spoke well when he said: how well
one may philosophize when preparing dinner.
And I often say, when observing these trivial
details: had Aristotle* prepared victuals, he would
have written more.   Ibid.

*Greek philosopher, logician and scientist (384 B.C.–322).

20 And I would add that a fool may reach perfection
(if ignorance may tolerate perfection) by having
studied his little of philosophy and theology and
by having some learning of tongues, by which
he may be a fool in many sciences and languages: a great fool cannot be contained solely
in his mother tongue.   Ibid.

21 For misuse is not the blame of art, but rather of
the evil teacher who perverts the arts, making
of them the snare of the devil; and this occurs
in all the arts and sciences.   Ibid.

22 . . . in the formal and theoretical arts . . .
each may illuminate and open the way to others,
by nature of their variations and their hidden
links, which were placed in this universal chain
by the wisdom of their Author in such a way

that they conform and are joined together with
admirable unity and harmony.   Ibid.

418. Anne Dacier (1651–1720)

1 Silence is the ornament of women.
Quoted in *Biography of
Distinguished Women*
by Sarah Josepha Hale*   *1876*

*See 703.

2 . . . let her [her granddaughter] conceal her
learning with as much care as she might crook-
edness or lameness.   Letter to her
daughter,
Quoted in *The Life of Lady
Mary Wortley Montagu*
by Robert Halsband   *1956*

*See 458.

419. Margaret Godolphin (1652–1678)

1 If you speake anything they like, say 'tis
borrowed. . . .   Quoted in
The Life of Mrs. Godolphin
by John Evelyn; H. Sampson,
ed.   *1939*

2 . . . may the Clock, the Candle, may everything I see, teach and instruct me some
thing.   Ibid.

3 . . . children servants master father mouther,
things that though they are blessings yet often
they prove otherwis, and the best of them have
days in which one thinkes one could live without
them. . . .   Letter to John Evelyn
(July 1675),
Quoted in *John Evelyn and
Mrs. Godolphin,*
Ch. 8, by W. G. Hiscock
1951

4 . . . god knows a litle pain maks one forget a
long health, and the unkindes of one frind maks
one forget the frindship of many for a time, for
we by nateur are apter to grine then laugh, the
first sound we make is crying, our childhood is
scarce any thing els but frowardnes, and so but
in a litle more reasonable maner we proceed till
we dye, so that unles we had hops of a beter
world we wear of all things most
miserable, . . .   Ibid.

5 . . . our wholl life is, in my opinion, a search
after remedys, which doe often, if not always,
exchange rather than cuer a deseas. . . .
Last letter to John Evelyn,
op. cit., Ch. 11

420. Anne Collins (fl. 1653)

1 As in a cabinet or chest
One jewel may exceed the rest.
                    Untitled, St. 2,
        Divine Songs and Meditacions
                              1653

2 Cheerfulness
Doth express
A settled pious mind;
Which is not prone to grudging,
From murmuring refin'd.
                        "Song,"
                  St. 5, op. cit.

421. Francisca Gregoria (1653–1736)

1 Fair plaything of the breeze tonight
        "Envying a Little Bird,"
          The Catholic Anthology,
        Thomas Walsh, ed.   *1927*

422. Mary Lee (1656–1710)

1 MALE VOICE. Then blame us not if we our
        interest mind,
And would have knowledge to ourselves
        confined,
Since that alone pre-eminence does give,
And robbed of it we should unvalued live.
While you are ignorant, we are secure,
A little pain will your esteem procure.
            The Ladies' Defence: Or, the
            Bride-Woman's Counsellor
            Answered: A Poem in a Dialogue
            between Sir John Brute, Sir
            William Loveall, Melissa, and a
            Parson   1701

2   The restless atoms play. . . .
Of them, composed with wonderous art,
    We are our selves a part,
And on us still they nutriment bestow;
To us they kindly come, from us they
        swiftly go,
And through our veins in purple torrents
        flow.
    Vacuity is nowhere found,
Each place is full, with bodies we're encom-
        passed round:
    In sounds they're to our ears conveyed,
In fragrant odors they our smell delight,
And in ten thousand curious forms dis-
        played
    They entertain our sight   "The Offering,"
                        Part One, op. cit.

3 Wife and servant are the same
But only differ in the name,
For when that fatal knot is tied,

Which nothing, nothing can divide,
When she the word *obey* has said,
And man by law supreme has made,
Then all that's kind is laid aside,
And nothing left but state and pride.
                "To the Ladies,"
                        op. cit.

423. Mary Morpeth (fl. 1656)

1 Perfection in a woman's work is rare;
From an untroubled mind should verses
        flow;
My discontent makes mine too muddy
        show;
And hoarse encumbrances of household
        care,
Where these remain, the Muses ne'er re-
        pair.   "Til William Drummond, of
                        Hawthornden,"
                Quoted as Prefix to *Poems*
        by William Drummond   *1656*

424. Anne Killigrew (1660–1685)

1 More rich, more noble I will ever hold
The Muse's laurel, than a crown of gold.
        "Upon the Saying That My
        Verses Were Made by Another,"
                St. 2, *Poems*   *1686*

2 I willingly accept Cassandra's fate,
To speak the truth, although believed too
        late.   Ibid., St. 6

3 But O, the laurel'd fool that doats on fame,
Whose hope's applause, whose
        fear's to want a name:
Who can accept for pay
Of what he does, what others say
                "The Discontent,"
                St. 2, op. cit.

4 Too loud, O Fame! thy trumpet is too shrill
                        Ibid., St. 3

5 Farewel to Unsubstantial Joyes,
Ye Gilded Nothings, Gaudy Toyes
        "A Farewel to Worldly Joyes,"
                        op. cit.

425. Anne Finch (1661–c.1720-1722)

1 Give me, O indulgent fate!
Give me yet before I die
A sweet, yet absolute retreat,
'Mongst the paths so lost and trees so high
That the world may ne'er invade

Through such windings and such shade
My unshaken liberty.
                "The Petition for an Absolute Retreat,"
                Miscellany Poems, Written by a Lady
                1713; reprint 1928

2 . . . I have applied
Sweet mirth, and music, and have tried
A thousand other arts beside,
To drive thee from my darkened breast,
Thou, who has banished all my rest.
                        "To Melancholy,"
                        op. cit.

3 Trail all your pikes, dispirit every drum,
March in a slow procession from afar,
Ye silent, ye dejected, men of war.
Be still the hautboys, and the flute be dumb!
Display no more, in vain, the lofty banner;
For see where on the bier before ye lies
The pale, the fall'n, the untimely sacrifice
To your mistaken shrine, to your false idol
Honour.   "Trail All Your Pikes,"
                        in toto, op. cit.

4 How gaily is at first begun
Our life's uncertain race!   "Life's Progress,"
                                St. 1, op. cit.

5 To-morrow and to-morrow cheat our
     youth.
In riper age, to-morrow still we cry,
Not thinking that the present age we die,
Unpractis'd all the good we have design'd:
There's no to-morrow to a willing mind.
                        "No To-Morrow,"
                        op. cit.

6 Now the Jonquille o'ercomes the feeble
     brain;
We faint beneath the aromatic pain.
                        "The Spleen,"
                        op. cit.

7 He lamented for Behn,* o'er that
     place of her birth,
And said amongst women there was none
     on earth
Her superior in fancy, in language, or wit,
Yet owned that a little too loosely she writ.
                        The Introduction
                        "Aristomenes,"
                        op. cit.

* Aphra Behn. See 406.

8 How are we fal'n, fal'n, by mistaken rules?
                        Ibid.

426. Mary II of England (1662–1694)

1 There is but one command which I wish him*
to obey; and that is, *"Husbands, love your
wives."* For myself, I shall follow the injunction, *"Wives, be obedient to your husbands in
all things."*   Quoted in *Biography
                        of Distinguished Women*
                by Sarah Josepha Hale**   *1876*

* Her husband, William III (1650–1702), king of England
(1689–1702).
** See 703.

427. Kata Szidónia Petröczi (1662–1708)

1 Hourly I howl the change in my fate.
                        "Swift Floods,"
                        St. 1, Laura Schiff, tr.;
                        Women Poets of the World,
                        Joanna Bankier and Deirdre
                        Lashgari, eds.   *1983*

428. Mary de la Rivière Manley (1663– 1724)

1 Orinda,* and the Fair Astrea* gone,
Not one was found to fill the Vacant
     Throne:
Aspiring Man had quite regain'd the Sway,
Again had Taught us humble to Obey;
till you** (Nature's third state, in favour of
     our Kind)
With stronger Arms, their Empire have dis-
joyn'd   Commendatory verses quoted in
              Foreword to *Agnes de Castro*
                        by Catherine
                        Cockburn**   *1695*

* Orinda is Katherine Philips; see 394. Astrea refers to
Aphra Behn; see 406.
** See 448.

2 No time like the present.   *The Lost Lover,*
                        Act IV, Sc. 1   *1696*

3 What can pay love but love?
                        Ibid., Act V, Sc. 3

4 . . . he fell martyr to her tongue. A landmark
for husbands, how they suffer the growth of
authority in that tyrannical unruly member!
                        "Corinna,"
                        *Secret Memoirs and Manners of
                        Several Persons of Quality of
                        Both Sexes. From the New
                        Atalantis, an Island in the
                        Mediterranean*   *1709*

5 Whatever false notion the world or you may
have of virtue, I must confess I should be very
loathe to bind my self to a man for ever, before
I was sure I should like him for a
night. . . .   Ibid.

6 . . .the truly covetous have never enough!
                        Ibid.

7 . . . she still went on in her own Way . . . till Experience gave her enough of her indiscretion.
>*The Adventures of Rivella: or, The History of the Author of the Atalantis* 1714

8 As long as we have Eyes, or Hands, or Breath,
We'll Look, or Write, or Talk you all to Death
>Prologue, *Lucius, the First Christian King of Britain* 1717

429. Marie Jeanne L'Heritier de Villandon (1664–1734)

1 You care for nothing but loving and joking.
>"Rondeau, to a Young Girl," Elaine Partnow,* tr.; Quoted in *Biography of Distinguished Women* by Sarah Josepha Hale** 1876

* Author.
** See 703.

430. Anne of England (1665–1714)

1 O, my dear brother, how I pity thee!
>Remark to her brother, the future King William III, on her deathbed (20 July 1714), Quoted in *Biography of Distinguished Women* by Sarah Josepha Hale* 1876

* See 703.

431. Grisell Home (1665–1746)

1 When bonny young Johnnie cam' o'er the sea,
He said he saw naething sae lovely as me. . . . "Warena My Heart Licht I Wad Dee,"
>*Scottish Song,* Mary Carlyle Aitken, ed. 1874

432. Honnamma (fl. 1665–1699)

1 Wasn't your mother a woman?
>Untitled, Willis Barnstone, tr.; *A Book of Woman Poets,* Aliki and Willis Barnstone, eds. 1980

2 Here and in the other world happiness
comes to a person, not a gender.
>Ibid.

433. Henrietta Johnston (c. 1665–1728/29)

1 . . . reason and conscience startle not.
>Letter to her husband (August 1713), Quoted in *Henrietta Johnston, America's First Pastellist* by Margaret Simons Middleton 1966

434. Mary Astell (1666?–1731)

1 Women are from their very Infancy debarr'd those advantages [of education] with the want of which they are afterwards reproached, and nursed up in those vices with which will hereafter be upbraided them. So partial are Men as to expect Bricks when they afford no straw.
>*A Serious Proposal to the Ladies for the Advancement of their True and Greatest Interest* 1694

2 They only who have felt it know the Misery of being forc'd to marry where they do not love; of being yok'd for life to a disagreeable Person and imperious Temper, where Ignorance and Folly (the ingredients of a Cockscomb, who is the most unsufferable Fool) tyrannizes over wit and Sense.
>*Reflections Upon Marriage* 1700

3 . . . Beauty with all the Helps of Art, is of no long Date; the more it is help'd, the sooner it decays. . . .
>Ibid.

4 . . . he who only or chiefly chose for Beauty, will in a little Time find the same Reason for another Choice.
>Ibid.

5 There is not anything so excellent, but some will carp at it. . . .
>Quoted in Preface (December 18, 1724), *Letters of the Right Honourable Lady Mary Wortley Montagu** 1766

* See 458.

435. Sarah Kemble Knight (1666–1727)

1 May all that dread the cruel fiend of night Keep on, and not at this curs't mansion light.
>Untitled (c. 1704), *The Journal of Madame Knight,* Theodore Dwight, Jr., ed. 1825

2 I ask thy Aid, O Potent Rum!
To charm these wrangling Topers Dum.
Thou hast their Giddy Brains possest—

The man confounded with the Beast—
And I, poor I, can get no rest.
Intoxicate them with thy fumes;
O still their Tongues till morning comes!
        "Resentments Composed because
        of the Clamor of Town Topers
        Outside My Apartment,''
        in toto, op. cit.

436. Mary Griffith Pix (1666–1720?)

1 The First Time she was grave, as well she
  might,
For Women will be damn'd sullen the first
  Night;
But faith, they'll quickly mend, so be n't
  uneasie:
To Night she's brisk, and trys New Tricks
  to please ye.   Prologue,
                  The Spanish Wives
                  1696

2 . . . instead of making his life easie with jolly
Bona-robas [courtesans], [he] dotes on a Pla-
tonick Mistress, who never allows him greater
favours than to read Plays to her, kiss her hand,
and fetch Heart-breaking Sighs at her Feet.
                    The Innocent
              Mistress   *1697*

437. Sophia Dorothea of Celle (1666–1726)

1 . . . my illness only comes from loving you,
and I do not want to be cured of it.
                  Letter to George I
                  (c. 1689–1694),
            Quoted in *Lives of the*
  Hanoverian Queens of England
               by Alice Drayton
             Greenwood   *1909*

438. Susannah Centlivre (c.1667–1723)

1 LUDOVICHO. I never strike Bargains in the
Dark.   *The Perjur'd Husband,*
           Act I, Sc. 1   *1700*

2 COUNT BASSINO. Why must his generous Passion
thus be starv'd, And be confin'd to one alone?
The Woman, whom Heaven sent as a Relief,
To ease the Burden of a tedious Life, And be
enjoy'd when summon'd by Desire, Is now
become the Tyrant of our Fates.   Ibid., Sc. 2

3 ARMANDO. . . . there's more Glory in subduing
Our wild Desires, than an embattl'd Foe.
                Ibid., Act IV, Sc. 1

4 AMELIA. I have the best Proof in the World of
it, ocular Demonstration.   Act III, Sc. 1,
                    The Beau's Duel,
                        1702

5 TOPER. Yesterday I carried to wait on a Relation
of ours that has a Parrot, and whilst I was
discoursing about some private Business, she
converted the Bird, and now it talks of nothing
but the Light of the Spirit, and the Inward
man.   Ibid.

6 You see gallants 'it has been our Poets'
  care,
To shew what Beaus in their Perfection are,
By Nature *Cowards, foolish, useless Tools,*
Made *Men* by *Taylors* and by *Women,*
  Fools.   Ibid., Epilogue

7 He surest strikes that smiling gives the
blow.   Ibid.

8 Friendship's a noble name, 'tis love refined.
                The Stolen Heiress,
        Act II, Sc. 2   *1702*

9 Writing is a kind of Lottery in this fickle
Age. . . .   Preface,
             Love's Contrivance
                    1703

10 OCTAVIO. . . . for I find by the beating of my
Pulse, the Motion of my Brain, and the Heav-
ings of my Heart, I am very far gone in that
dangerous Distemper call'd Love, and you are
the only Physician can save my life.
             Ibid., Act III, Sc. 1

11 LUCINDA. Once a week! I wou'd not for the
World bed with you oftener; why 'tis not the
Fashion, Sir Toby; and I assure you when I
marry I hope to be my own Mistress, and follow
my own Inclination, which will carry me to the
utmost Pinnacle of the Fashion.
             Ibid., Act IV, Sc. 1

12 'Tis the defect of age to rail at the pleasures of
youth.   *The Basset-Table,*
                  Act I   *1705*

13 LADY LUCY. . . . nothing melts a Woman's
Heart like gold.   Ibid., Act IV

14 HECTOR. Love's Fever is always highest when
the Cash is at an Ebb.   *The Gamester,*
                Act I   *1705*

15 VALERE. . . . there's nothing like ready Money
to nick Fortune.   Ibid., Act III

16 HECTOR. Lying is a thriving Vocation. Ibid.

17 HECTOR. What Business had you to get Children, without you had Cabbage enough to maintain 'em?   Ibid.

18 All policy's allowed in war and love.
                 Love At A Venture,
                Act I   *1706*

19 SIR GEORGE AIRY. . . . a Man that wants Money thinks none can be unhappy that has it. . . .   *The Busy Body,*
                                    Act I   *1709*

20 CHARLES. . . . Want, the Mistress of Invention, still tempts me on. . . .   Ibid.

21 ISABINDA. Let me tell you, Sir, Confinement sharpens the Invention, as Want of Sight strengthens the other Senses, and is often more pernicious, than the Recreation innocent Liberty allows.   Ibid., Act II

22 MANAGE. . . . my present Profession is Physick—Now, when my Pockets are full, I cure a Patient in three Days; when they are empty, I keep him three months.   Act II,
                    *The Man's Bewitched; or, The
                    Devil to Do About Her   1709*

23 DON PERRIERA. . . . sure Cuckoldom is so rank a Scent, that tho' I lived in *England,* where they scarce breathe any other Air, I cou'd distinguish it.   *Mar Plot, or, The
                    Second Part of the Busy Body,*
                                    Act I, Sc. 1   *1711*

24 MARPLOT. I had rather fathom the Depth of Man's Thoughts, than his Pocket. . . .
                                    Ibid., Act III, Sc. 1

25 FLORELLA. . . . nobody can boast of Honesty till they are try'd. . . .
                                    The Perplex'd Lovers,
                                    Act III, Sc. 1   *1712*

26 DON LOPEZ. There is no Condition of Life without its Cares, and it is the Perfection of a Man to wear 'em as easy as he can. . . .
                                    *The Wonder: A Woman Keeps a
                                    Secret,*
                                    Act I, Sc. 1   *1714*

27 'Tis my opinion every man cheats in his way, and he is only honest who is not discovered.
                                    The Artifice,
                                    Act V   *1724*

28 When the glowing of passion's over, and pinching winter comes, will amorous sighs supply the want of fire, or kind looks and kisses keep off hunger?   Ibid.

439. Susanna Wesley (1668?–1742)

1 Let every one enjoy the present hour.
                    Quoted in *The Women of
                    Methodism: Its Three Foundresses . . .*
                    by Abel Stevens   *1866*

2 [To subdue the will of the child] is the only strong and rational foundation of a religious education, without which both precept and example will be ineffectual. But when this is

thoroughly done, then a child is capable of being governed by the reason and piety of its parents till its own understanding comes to maturity, and the principles of religion have taken root in the mind.   Letter to her son, John Wesley,
                                    op. cit.

3 God's prescience is no more the effective cause of the loss of the wicked than our foreknowledge of the rising of to-morrow's sun is the cause of its rising.   Ibid.

440. Frances Boothby (fl. 1669)

1 I'm hither come, but what d'ye think to
   say?
   A Womans Pen present you with a Play:
   Who smiling told me I'd be sure to see,
   That once confirm'd, the House would
   empty be.
   Not one yet gone!   Prologue,
                    *Marcelia; or, The Treacherous
                    Friend   1669*

2 You powerful Gods! if I must be
   An injur'd offering to Love's deity,
   Grant my revenge, this plague on men,
   That woman ne'er may love again.   "Song,"
                                    St. 1, op. cit.

441. Marie Thérèse Rodet Geoffrin (1669–1757)

1 Give and forgive.   Quoted in *Biography of
                    Distinguished Women*
                    by Sarah Josepha Hale*   *1876*

*See 703.

2 We should not let the grass grow on the path of friendship.   Ibid.

3 Among those advantages which attract for us the most consideration are good manners, an erect bearing, a dignified demeanour, and to be able to enter a room gracefully; we dare not speak ill of a person who has all these advantages, for they presuppose thoughtfulness, order, and judgment.   Ibid.

442. Anne Baynard (1672–1697)

1 . . . it is a sin to be content with a little knowledge.   Quoted in *Biography of
                    Distinguished Women*
                    by Sarah Josepha Hale*   *1876*

*See 703.

2 I could wish that all young persons might be exhorted to . . . read the great book of nature,

wherein they may see the wisdom and power of the Creator, in the order of the universe, and in the production and preservation of all things.　　　　From her deathbed, op. cit.

443. Mary Davys (1674–1732)

1 As a Child born of a common Woman, has many Fathers, so my poor Offspring has been laid at a great many Doors. . . . I am proud they think it deserves a better Author.
Preface,
*The Northern Heiress; or,
The Humours of York　　1716*

2 The Pedant despises the most elaborate Undertaking, unless it appears in the World with *Greek* and *Latin* Motto's; a Man that would please him, must pore an Age over musty Authors, till his Brains are as worm-eaten as the Books he reads, and his Conversation fit for nobody else. . . .　　*The Reform'd Coquet; or, the Memoirs of Amoranda　　1724*

3 . . . the busy part of our Species, who are so very intent upon getting Money, that they lose the pleasure of spending it.　　Ibid.

4 It is the way of the Damn'd, Madam, to desire all Mankind should be in their own miserable State. . . .　　Ibid.

5 I have often told myself, it is much better never to know a Satisfaction, than lose it as soon as acquainted; since nothing can give a Man a greater Damp than a Reflection upon past Pleasures, when he has no View to their return.
"To Berina, November 1,"
*Familiar Letters, Betwixt a
Gentleman and a Lady　　1725*

6 How many brave Men, courageous Women, and innocent Children did I see butcher'd, to do God good Service? . . . I went to the *Irish* Rebellion, where I saw more than three hundred thousand Souls muder'd in cold Blood . . . crying, *Nits will become Lice, destroy Root and Branch:* with a thousand other Barbarities, too tedious as well as too dreadful to repeat, beside what has been transacted abroad.　　Ibid.,
"To Artander, November 10"

7 . . . we Women as naturally love Scandal, as you Men do Debauchery; and we can no more keep up Conversation without one, than you can live an Age without t'other.
Ibid., "To Artander, December 10"

8 I cannot say I was ever so glutted with Pleasure in my Life, as to be weary of it, nor properly speaking, can any body say so; because, when

once a Man is tir'd of a thing, it is no longer a Pleasure, but retiring from it is; so that a Person who has power to follow his own Inclinations, is always in Pleasure. . . .　　Ibid.,
"To Berina, December 26"

9 . . . Love, like Edg'd-Tools, shou'd never be play'd with.　　Ibid.,
"To Artander, January 12"

10 When Women write, the Criticks, now-a-days,
Are ready, e'er they see, to damn their Plays;
Wit, as the Men's Prerogative, they claim,
And with one Voice, the bold Invader blame.　　Prologue,
*The Self-Rival; A Comedy
1725*

444. Elizabeth Rowe (1674–1736/37)

1 Thy numerous Works exalt Thee thus,
　And shall I silent be?
No; rather let me cease to breathe,
　Than cease from praising Thee!
"Hymn," St. 8,
*Poems on Several Occasions by
Philomela　　1696*

2 . . . the studious follies of the great,
The tiresome farce of ceremonious state.
"Despair,"
op. cit.

3 By this thy glorious lineage thou dost prove
Thy high descent; for GOD himself is Love.
"Ode to Love,"
St. 11,
*Miscellaneous Works in Prose
and Verse　　1739*

445. Rosalba Carriera (1675–1757)

1 . . . I think that pleasures should be enjoyed with great sobriety and moderation.
Quoted in *Portraits and
Backgrounds,*
Ch. 6, by Evangeline Wilbour
Blashfield　　1917

2 You may be sure that I know that there is a world, men, and bread beyond the lagoons [of Venice], but I submit to the will of heaven which has decreed that my journeys shall be only to my easel. I am contented with but little bread, while as to men, believe me there is nothing in the world that I think less of. . . .　　Ibid.

3 . . . for three years I have been deprived of my sight. I wish you to learn from my own hand

that thanks to the Divine Goodness I have recovered it. I see but as one sees after an operation, that is to say very dimly. Even this is a blessing for one who has had the misfortune to become blind. When I was sightless I cared for nothing, now I want to see everything. . . .   Letter (23 August 1749),
                                          from Venice,
                                       op. cit., Ch. 7

446. Elizabeth Thomas (c.1675-1677– 1730/31)

1 Ah! strive no more to know what fate
   Is pre-ordain'd for thee:
'Tis vain in this my mortal state,
   For Heaven's inscrutable decree
Will only be reveal'd in vast Eternity.
                              "Predestination;
                            or the Resolution,"
                      *Miscellany Poems on Several
                              Subjects   1722*

447. Penelope Aubin (1679–1731)

1 Love and Honour had a sharp contest, but at last Love got the Victory, and the rose.
                        The Life of the Lady Lucy,
                              Ch. 2   *1726*

2 This is the vast difference betwixt doing well and ill; that in Vice the Pleasure is always momentary and of no duration, and the Remorse for having done it, sure and lasting; but in doing virtuous Deeds, tho' we may suffer Loss and Pain for some short time, yet we have always a secret Satisfaction within, that supports us under them, and the End brings us Honour and generally Reward, even in this world. . . .
                                    Ibid., Ch. 10

448. Catherine Cockburn (1679–1749)

1 . . . when a Woman appears in the World under any distinguishing Character, she must expect to be the mark of ill Nature.
                        Dedication to Princess Anne,
                        Fatal Friendship   1698

2 . . . We tax our Judgment, when we cease to love.   *Love at a Loss; or,*
                      Most Votes Carry It   1700

3 LESBIA. Hands, and Seals, and Oaths cannot secure
A mind like Man's unfaithful and impure.
                              Ibid., Epilogue

4 But who the useful art can teach,
When sliding down a steepy way,
   To stop, before the end we reach?
                              "The Caution,"
                                    St. 3,
                              The Female Wits,
                        Lucyle Hook, ed.   *1704*

5 A heart whose safety but in flight does lie,
Is too far lost to have the power to fly.
                              "The Vain Advice,"
                                    St. 2,
                      The Works of Mrs. Catharine
                      Cockburn, Theological, Moral,
                      Dramatic, and Poetical,
                      Thomas Birch, ed.   *1751*

6 Being married in 1708, I bid adieu to the muses, and so wholly gave myself up to the cares of a family, and the education of my children, that I scarce knew, whether there was any such thing as books, plays, or poems stirring in Great Britain. "Account of the Life of the Author,"
                                    op. cit., Vol. I

7 . . . when anything is written by a woman, that [men] cannot deny their approbation to, [they] are sure to rob us of the glory of it, by concluding 'tis not her own; or at least, that she had some assistance, which has been said in many instances to my knowledge unjustly.
                                    Ibid., Vol. II

8 You* were our Champion, and the Glory ours.
Well you've maintain'd our equal right in Fame,
To which vain Man had quite engrost the
   claim   Commendatory verses quoted
                        in *The Royal Mischief*
                  by Mary de la Rivière Manley*
                                          1796

*See 428.

449. Joan Philips (fl. 1679–1682)

1 Thou dull companion of our active years,
   That chill'st our warm blood with thy
      frozen fears,
How is it likely thou shouldst long endure,
When thought itself thy ruin may procure?
                              "Maidenhead,"
                      Female Poems on Several
                              Occasions   1679

2 Think me all man: my soul is masculine,
And capable of as great things as thine.
                  "To Phylocles, Inviting Him to
                              Friendship,"
                              St. 3, op. cit.

450. Elizabeth Haddon Estaugh (1680–1762)

1 I'll venture to say, few, if any, in a married State, ever lived in sweeter Harmony than we did.   Quoted in Introduction to *A Call to the Unfaithful Professors of Truth* by John Estaugh   *1744*

2 I have received from the lord a charge to love thee, John Estaugh.   Attributed, Quoted in *Tales of a Wayside Inn* by Henry Wadsworth Longfellow*   *1863*

*American poet (1807–1882).

451. Elizabeth Elstob (1683–1756)

1 . . . I shou'd think it as Glorious an Employment to instruct Poor Children as to teach the Children of the Greatest Monarch.
Letter to George Ballard (c. 1740), Quoted in *A Galaxy of Governesses* by Bea Howe   *1954*

2 . . . you can come into no company of Ladies and or Gentlemen, where you shall not hear an open and Vehement exclamation against Learned Women.   Letter to George Ballard (c. 1753), op. cit.

452. Eleonora von dem Knesebeck (fl. 1684–1713)

1 The [British] government must have done a deed of great injustice since they stop my mouth, for if they can answer to all the world for what they have done . . . why am I not [allowed to] speak? If their judgements are righteous, how should I dare to speak wrongfully?   (c. 1697), Quoted in *Lives of the Hanoverian Queens of England* by Alice Drayton Greenwood   *1891*

453. Jane Brereton (1685–1740)

1 Pope* is the emblem of true wit,
The sunshine of the mind.
"On Mr. Nash's** Picture at Full Length, Between the Busts of Sir Isaac Newton*** and Mr. Pope," St. 4, *Mrs. Jane Brereton's Poems* *1744*

*British poet and satirist Alexander Pope (1688–1744).
**British satirist and pamphleteer Thomas Nash (1567–1601).
***British physicist and mathematician (1643–1727).

2 I scorn this mean fallacious art
By which you'd steal, not win, my heart
"To Damon,"
St. 1, op. cit.

3 . . . Cupid's empire won't admit
Nor own, a Salic law.*   "To Philotinus,"
St. 2, op. cit.

*European law of succession (derived from a 5th-century Frankish code), prohibiting daughters from inheriting land and women from succeeding to a throne.

454. Mrs. Taylor (fl. 1685)

1   . . . tears,
Those springs that water Love.   "Song,"
St. 2,
Miscellany, Being a Collection of Poems by several Hands,
Aphra Behn,* ed.   *1685*

*See 406.

2 Alas! it does my soul perplex,
When I his charms recall,
To think he should despise the sex,
Or what's worse, love them all.   "Song,"
St. 3, op. cit.

455. Claudine Alexandrine de Tencin (1685–1749)

1 Unless God visibly interferes, it is physically impossible that the state [France] should not fall to pieces.   Quoted in *Biography of Distinguished Women* by Sarah Josepha Hale*   *1876*

*See 703.

456. Mary Chandler (1687–1745)

1 Fatal effects of luxury and ease!
We drink our poison and we eat disease
"Temperance,"
The Female Poets of Great Britain,
Frederic Rowton, ed.   *1853*

457. Jane Barker (fl. 1688–1715)

1   Happy life . . .
Fearless of twenty-five and all its train,
Of slights and scorns, or being called old maid. . . .
Ah lovely state how strange it is to see,
What mad conceptions some have made of thee,
As though thy being was all wretchedness,
Or foul deformity in the ugliest dress.
"A Virgin Life,"
Poetical Recreations   *1688*

2 Poverty's the certain fate
Which attends a poet's state.
"Poetical Recreations,"
op. cit.

3 . . . thus we see that Human Projects are mere
Vapours, carried about with every Blast of cross
Accidents. . . .   *Love Intrigues*   *1713*

4 . . . Love is apt to interpret things in its own
Favour. . . .   Ibid.

458. Mary Wortley Montagu (1689–1762)

1 I will not be cheated—nor will I employ long
years of repentance for moments of joy.
Comment to [Alexander] Pope,
Quoted in *History of English Literature*
by Jeremy Collier   *c. 1720*

2 And we meet with champagne and a chicken at
last.   "The Lover: A Ballad," St. 4,
Six Town Ecologues   *1747*

3 In crowded courts I find myself alone,
And pay my worship to a nobler throne.
"In Answer to a Lady who
advised Retirement,"
St. 1,
The London Magazine
May 1750

4 Nature is seldom in the wrong, custom
always.   Letter to Miss Anne Wortley
(August 8, 1709),
Letters of the Right Honourable
Lady Mary Wortley Montagu
1767

5 . . . I hate the noise and hurry inseparable from
great estates and titles, and look upon both as
blessings that ought only to be given to fools,
for 'tis only to them that they are blessings.
Letter to Wortley Montagu,
her husband (28 March 1710),
op. cit.

6 General notions are generally wrong.   Ibid.

7 A woman, till five-and-thirty, is only looked
upon as a raw girl, and can possibly make no
noise in the world till about forty.
Letter to Lady R[ich], from Vienna
(20 September 1716),
op. cit.

8 . . . if it were the fashion to go naked, the face
would be hardly observed.
Letter to Lady Rich from
Sophia, Turkey (1717),
op. cit.

9 I am patriot enough to take pains to bring this
useful invention [smallpox innoculation] into
fashion in England; and I should not fail to write
to some of our doctors very particularly about

it, if I knew any one of them that I thought had
virtue enough to destroy such a considerable
branch of revenue for the good of mankind.
Letter to Lady Mar [her sister],
from Belgrade (1 April 1717),
op. cit.

10 . . . to be ever beloved, one must be ever
agreeable.   Letter to Mr. Wortley Montagu
(c. 1720),
op. cit.

11 The last pleasure that fell in my way was Madame de Sévigné's* letters; very pretty they are,
but I assert without the least vanity, mine will
be full as entertaining forty years hence. I advise
you, therefore, to put none of them to the use
of waste-paper.   Letter to Lady Mar (1724),
op. cit.

*See 387.

12 I give myself sometimes admirable advice, but
I am incapable of taking it.
Letter to Lady Mar (1725),
op. cit.

13 Nobody can deny but religion is a comfort to
the distressed, a cordial to the sick, and sometimes a restraint on the wicked; therefore,
whoever* would laugh or argue it out of the
world, without giving some equivalent for it,
ought to be treated as a common enemy.
Letter to Countess of Bute
[her daughter]
(1752),
op. cit.

*Refers to the Irish satirist Jonathan Swift (1667–1745).

14 . . . the knowledge of numbers is one of the
chief distinctions between us and the brutes.
Letter to Countess of Bute
(28 January 1753),
op. cit.

15 True knowledge consists in knowing things, not
words.   Ibid.

16 People are never so near playing the fool as
when they think themselves wise.
Letter to Countess of Bute
(1 March 1755),
op. cit.

17 Civility costs nothing and buys everything.
Letter to Countess of Bute
(30 May 1756),
op. cit.

18 . . . it is now eleven years since I have seen
my figure in a glass, and the last reflection I
saw there was so disagreeable, that I resolved
to spare myself the mortification in the
future.   Letter, from Venice
(c. 1758–1761),
op. cit.

19 It [her health] is so often impaired that I begin to be as weary of it as mending old lace; when it is patched in one place, it breaks out in another.   Ibid.

20 I enjoy vast delight in the folly of mankind; and, God be praised, that is an inexhaustible source of entertainment.
                        Letter to Countess of Mar (n.d.),
                                            op. cit.

21 Life is too short for any distant aim;
   And cold the dull reward of future fame.
                "Epistle to the Earl of Burlington,"
                        Poetical Works   1768

22 Satire should, like a polished razor keen,
   Wound with a touch that's scarcely felt or
   seen.   "To the Imitator [Alexander Pope]*
             of the First Satire of Horace,"**
                                            op. cit.

*English poet and satirist (1688–1744).
**Roman poet (65–8 B.C.).

23 Be plain in dress, and sober in your diet;
   In short, my dreary, kiss me! and be quiet.
                        "In Summary of Lord
                        Lyttleton's Advice to a Lady,"
                                            op. cit.

24 But the fruit that will fall without shaking,
   Indeed is too mellow for me.
                        "To a Lady Making Love; or,
                        Answered, for Lord Hamilton,"
                                            op. cit.

25 A real marriage bears no resemblance to these marriages of interest or ambition. It is two lovers who live together. A priest may well say certain words, a notary may well sign certain papers— I regard these preparations in the same way that a lover regards the rope ladder that he ties to his mistress's window.   Essay,
                                              n.d.

459. Mary Barber (1690?–1757)

1 A richer present I design,
   A finished form, of work divine,
   Surpassing all the power of art;
   A thinking head, a grateful heart.
                        "On Sending my Son as a
                        Present to Dr. [Jonathan] Swift,
                        Dean of St. Patrick's,
                        on his Birthday,"
                        Poems on Several Occasions
                                              1734

460. Francisca Josefa del Castillo y Guevara (1691?–1743)

1 The land grew bright in a single flower—
   One great carnation rare. . . .
                        "Christmas Carol,"
                                            St. 1,
                        The Catholic Anthology,
                        Thomas Walsh, ed.   1927

2 "My sin has led me far
   As some wild thirsting bee
   Beneath Thy meadow star,
   Idly forgetting Thee;
   But Thou dost call me home; I hear
   Thy voice whose sweetness charms mine
   ear.   "The Holy Ecologue,"
                                       St. 6, op. cit.

461. Martha Corey (?–1692)

1 Ye are all against me and I cannot help it.*
                        Remark (1692),
                        Quoted in Notable American Women,
                        Edward T. James, ed.   1971

*Remark at her trial in Salem, Massachusetts, for witchcraft.

462. Eliza Haywood (1693?–1756)

1 Flattery is a Vice so much in Fashion, and, I am sorry to say, so much encouraged, that there is nothing more difficult than to find a Patron who not expects, nor would be pleased with it. . . .   Dedication,
                        The Rash Resolve   1724

2 How little are the ill judging Multitude capable of chusing for themselves! How far are Wealth and Beauty, the two great Idols of the admiring World, from being real Blessings to the Possessors of them!   The Mercenary Lover; or, the
                        Unfortunate Heiresses   1726

3 The base are always Cowards, the same Meaness of Spirit which makes them the one, inclines them to the other also; they are ever in Fear, and while there remains even the smallest Probability of Danger, Peace is a Stranger to their Minds.   Ibid.

4 The natural Propensity which all People have to listen to any Arguments which may serve to excuse the Errors they commit. . . .   Ibid.

5 "I am not without some share of that too common Foible of Humanity, which makes us place

less Value on the things we are in possession of, than those above our reach. . . .''
The Secret History of the Present Intrigues of the Court of Caramania,
Pt. I   *1727*

6 He represented to her, that the greatest Glory of a Monarch was the Liberty of the People, his most valuable Treasures in *their* crowded Coffers, and his securest Guard in their *sincere Affection.*
Adventures of Eovaii, Princess of Ijaveo 1736

7 . . . nothing but Liberty was denied her.
"The History of Yximilla,"
op. cit.

8. To endure all the toils and hardships of the field with patience and intrepidity, to be fearless of danger when the duties of his post commanded, is highly laudable and emulative; but to run into them without a call, and when bravery can be of no service, is altogether idle; and courage like all other virtues, degenerates into a vice by being carried to an extreme.
"Effeminacy in the Army,"
The Female Spectator 1744–1746

9 Nature is in itself abhorrent of vice. . . .
"Masquerades, How Prejudicial,"
op. cit.

10 All that can justly be objected against any arguments made use of to prove the reasonableness of a belief in a plurality of worlds is, that to us, that live in this, it is no manner of concern, since there is not a possibility of travelling to them, or of ever becoming acquainted with the inhabitants.   "Flying-Machines, The Impossibility of Their Use,"
op. cit.

11 Philosophy is the toil which can never tire the persons engaged in it; all its ways are strewed with roses, and the farther you go, the more enchanting objects appear before you and invite you on.
"Study of Philosophy Recommended,"
op. cit.

12 I desire no other Revenge for my abused Sincerity, than that you may, some time or other, find a Woman fair enough to create a real Passion in you; and as insensible of it, as you are of mine.   "The History of Graciana,"
Memoirs of a Certain Island Adjacent to the Kingdom of Utopia   1775

13 She was so exact an Economist, and made so good use of her Time, that she had always an Opportunity of being happy with the Man she

lik'd, and never miss'd one with the Man whose Purse was at her devotion.
"The History of Hortensia,"
op. cit.

14 That Generosity and open Candor, which is almost inseparable from good Sense, renders the Person possess'd of it, at once incapable of a base Action himself, or of suspecting it in others.   "The History of Count Orainos, and Madame Del Millmonde,"
op. cit.

463. Charlotte Elizabeth Aissé (1694/95–1733)

1 We sup wretchedly, we have neither good fish nor good friends.   Letter,
Quoted in *Portraits and Backgrounds,* Ch. 5,
by Evangeline Wilbour Blashfield *1917*

2 It seems to be a natural human impulse to profit by the weakness of others. I do not know how to use such arts; I know only one: to make life so sweet to him I love that he will find nothing preferable to it.   Letter,
op. cit., Ch. 6

3 . . .I could never love where I could not respect.   Ibid.

464. Elizabeth Tollet (1694–1754)

1 The conscious moon and stars above
Shall guide me with my wandering love.
"Winter Song,"
Poems on Several Occasions. With Anne Boleyn to King Henry VIII, an Epistle   1755*
*See 249.

2 'Tis vanished all! remains alone
The eyeless scalp of naked bone;
The vacant orbits sunk within;
The jaw that offers at a grin.
Is this the object, then, that claims
The tribute of our youthful flames?
"On a Death's Head,"
op. cit.

465. Ariadne (fl. 1695)

1 [I] could not conquer the Inclination I had for Scribling from my Childhood. And when our Island enjoyed the Blessing of the incomparable Mrs. [Aphra] Behn,* even then I had much ado to keep my Muse from shewing her Imperti-

nence; but, since her death, has claim'd a kind of Privilege; and, in spite of me, broke from her Confinement. *Preface, She Ventures and He Wins 1695*

*See 406

2 Our Author hopes indeed,
You will not think, though charming
Aphra's* dead,
All Wit with her, and with Orinda's** fled.
Ibid., Prologue

*The playwright Aphra Behn. See 406.
**Pseudonym of the poet Katherine Philips. See 394.

466. Cornelia Bradford (1695?–1755)

1 The Punsters are of Opinion, that though we could not Cope with the Rebellion at first, we shall make shift to Wade thro' it at last.*
From article in *American Weekly Mercury,*
Quoted in *Andrew Bradford,*
Colonial Journalist
by A. J. DeArmond 1949

*Neither Sir John *Cope* nor Field Marshal George *Wade* was successful in stemming the Jacobite invasion of 1745.

467. Marie Anne du Deffand (1697–1780)

1 What more can you ask? He [Voltaire] has invented history! *(Que voulez-vous de plus? Il a inventé l'histoire!).*
Quoted in *L'Esprit dans histoire*
by Fournier 1857

2 The distance is nothing: it is only the first step that is difficult.* Letter to Jean Le Rond d'Alembert (7 July 1763), *Correspondance inédite* 1859

*Refers to the legend that St. Denis, carrying his head in his hands, walked two leagues.

3 I do not know why Diogenes* went looking for a man: nothing could happen to him worse than finding one. *Ibid.*

*Greek philosopher (412?–323 B.C.).

4 . . . everything seems insupportable to me. This may very well be because I am insupportable myself. *Ibid.*

5 I hear nothings, I speak nothings, I take interest in nothing and from nothing to nothing I travel gently down the dull way which leads to becoming nothing. *Ibid.*

6 I remember thinking in my youth that no one was happy but madmen, drunkards, and lovers. *Ibid.*

7 Faith is a devout belief in what one does not understand. *Ibid.*

8. I love nothing and that is the true cause of my ennui. *Ibid.*

9. God is not more incomprehensible than you; but if he is not more just, it is hardly worth while believing in him. *Ibid.*

10 Vanity ruins more women than love.
Quoted in *Lettres à Voltaire,*
Joseph Trabucco, ed. 1922

11 Women are never stronger than when they arm themselves with their weaknesses. *Ibid.*

468. Friederika Karoline Neuber (1697–1760)

1 Dear reader, here is something for you to read. To be sure, it is not written by a great, scholarly man. Oh, no! It is by a mere woman whose name you scarcely know and for whose station in life you have to look among the most humble of people, for she is nothing but a comedian. She cannot be responsible for anything but her own art, though she does know enough to understand another artist when he talks about his work. If you should ask her why she writes at all, her answer will be the customary feminine "Because." If any one asks you who helped her, you had better answer, "I don't know"— for it may very well be that she did it all herself. Preface to the play *Vorspiel,*
Quoted in *Enter the Actress*
by Rosamond Gilder 1931

469. Susanna Wright (1697–1784)

1 Flowers on thy breast, and round thy head,
With thee their sweets resign,
Nipp'd from their tender stalks, and dead,
Their fate resembles thine
"On the Death of a Young Girl,"
St. 11 (1737),
*Women Poets in Pre-
Revolutionary America,*
Pattie Cowell, ed. 1981

2 And what are they—a vision all the past,
A bubble on the water's shining face,
What yet remain, till the first transient blast,
Shall leave no more remembrance of their place. "My Own Birth-Day,"
St. 2 (1 August 1761),
op. cit.

470. Mary Delany (1700–1788)

1 Hail to the happy times when fancy led
My pensive mind the flow'ry path to tread,
And gave me emulation to presume,
With timid art, to trace fair nature's bloom
    Preface, *Flora, or, Herbal*   *n.d.*

471. Sarah Updike Goddard (c.1700–1770)

1 . . . [the] mystick art of printing. . . .
    Untitled poem,
    from *Providence Gazette*
    (16 March 1765),
    Quoted in *William Goddard,*
    Newspaperman, Ch. 4,
    by Ward L. Miner   *1962*

2 Ye learned physicians, whose excellent
  skill,
Can save, or demolish, can cure, or can kill;
To a poor forlorn damsel contribute your
  aid,
Who is sick, very sick of remaining a maid.
    "The Distressed Maid"
    (30 August 1766),
    op. cit.

3 . . . every one who takes delight in publicly or
privately taking away any person's *good name,*
or striving to render him ridiculous, are in the
gall of bitterness, and in the bonds of iniquity,
whatever their pretences may be for it.
    Letter to her son,
    William Goddard (1765),
    Ch. 5, op. cit.

472. Fukuzoyo Chiyo (c.1701-1703–1775)

1   The dew of the rouge-flower
When it is spilled
  Is simply water.
    Untitled haiku,
    R. H. Blyth, tr.;
    The Penguin Book
    of Women Poets,
    Carol Cosman, Joan Keefe and
    Kathleen Weaver, eds.   *1978*

2 After a long winter
giving
each other nothing, we collide
with blossoms in our hands.   Untitled,
    in toto, David Ray, tr.;
    A Book of Women Poets,
    Aliki and Willis Barnstone, eds.
    1980

473. Jane Wiseman (fl. 1701)

1 The Reception it [her play] met with in the
World, was not kind enough to make me Vain,
nor yet so ill, to discourage my Proceeding.
    Dedication,
    Antiochus the Great; or, The
    Fatal Relapse   *1701*

474. Constantia Grierson (1706?–1733)

1 And if to wit, our courtship they pretend,
'Tis the same way that they a cause defend;
In which they give of lungs a vast expence,
But little passion, thought, or eloquence
    "To Miss Laetitia Van Lewen
    (Afterwards Mrs. Pilkington),* at
    a Country Assize,"
    Poems on Several Occasions,
    Mary Barber, ed.**   *1734*

*See 485.
**See 459.

475. Mercy Wheeler (1706–c. 1733)

1 Poor, wretched and vile sinners all
Rank'd with the heathen nation,
Who unto God ne'er pray nor call,
For pardon and salvation.   Untitled,
    St. 1 (1732),
    Women Poets in Pre-
    Revolutionary America,
    Pattie Cowell, ed.   *1981*

476. Anna Williams (1706–1783)

1 When Delia strikes the trembling string,
  She charms our list'ning ears;
But when she joins her voice to sing,
  She emulates the spheres.
    "On A Lady Singing,"
    St. 1,
    Quoted in *Biography of*
    Distinguished Women
    by Sarah Josepha Hale*   *1876*

*See 703.

477. Selina Hastings (1707–1791)

1 I am well; all is well—well for ever. I see,
wherever I turn my eyes, whether I live or die,
nothing but victory.*
    Quoted in *The Women of*
    Methodism: Its Three Foundresses . . .
    by Abel Stevens   *1866*

*Remark after a stroke that presaged her death.

2 My work is done; I have nothing to do but to
   go to my Father*   Ibid.

*Some of her last words.

478. Jane Colman Turell (1708-1735)

1 My good fat Bacon, and our homely Bread,
   With which my healthful Family is fed.
   Milk from the Cow, and Butter newly
       churn'd,
   And new fresh Cheese, with Curds and
       Cream just turn'd.   "An Invitation Into
                         the Country, In Imitation of
                                      Horace,"
                                         St. 4
              Reliquiae Turellae et Lachrymae Paternae
                  [Relics of Turell and Paternal
                               Tears]   1735

2 Dauntless you undertake th' unequal strife,
   And raise dead virtue by your verse to life.
   A woman's pen strikes the curs'd serpent's
       head,
   And lays the monster gasping, if not dead.
                   "On Reading the Warning by
             Mrs. Singer,"* Women Poets in Pre-
                          Revolutionary America,
                  Pattie Cowell, ed.   1981

*Elizabeth Singer Rowe. See 444.

3 . . .no pain is like a bleeding heart.
                   "Part of the Fifth Chapter of
                   Canticles Paraphras'd From the
                               8th Verse,"
                   St. 1 (14 September 1725),
                                     op. cit.

4   Thrice in my womb I've found the
        pleasing strife,
   In the first struggles of my infant's life:
   But O how soon by Heaven I'm call'd to
       mourn,
   While from my womb a lifeless babe is torn?
   Born to the grave ere it has seen the light,
   Or with one smile had cheer'd my longing
       sight.   "Lines On Childbirth,"
                                 St. 2, op. cit.

479. Mary Washington (1708-1789)

1 I am not surprised at what George has done, for
   he was always a very good boy.
                   Recollections and Private
              Memoirs of Washington by his
              adopted son, George Washington
              Parke Curtis, with a Memoir of
                     the Author, by his
                   daughter . . .   1860

480. Lydia Fish Willis (1709-1767)

1 The gate is straight,—the way is narrow,—my
   heart is hard,—my sins are great,—my strength
   is weak,—my faith is so benighted with doubts,
   that I am ready to cast all offered good
   away. . . .

   Such languid, faint desires I feel,
   Within this wicked, stupid heart,
   I should, I would, but that, I will,
   I hardly dare (with truth) assert.
                   "Lines from an Undated Letter
                                  to her Niece,"
                     Rachel's Sepulchre; Or, a
                   Memorial of Mrs. Lydia Willis,
                   taken Chiefly, from her Letters to
                       Friends . . .   1767?

481. Sarah Fielding (1710-1768)

1 ". . . the height of my distress lies in not
   knowing my own mind; if I could once find that
   out, I should be easy enough. I am so divided
   by the desire of riches on the one hand, and by
   my honour and the man I like on the other, that
   there is such a struggle in my mind I am almost
   distracted."   David Simple   c. 1750

2 "I hope to be excused by those gentlemen who
   are quite sure they have found one woman who
   is a perfect angel, and that all the rest are perfect
   devils. . . ."   Ibid.

3 "I think there is nothing so pleasant as revenge;
   I would pursue a man who had injured me to
   the very brink of life. I know it would be
   impossible for me ever to forgive him; and I
   would have him live only that I might have the
   pleasure of seeing him miserable."   Ibid.

482. Marie de Beauveau (1711-1786)

1 Say what you will in two
   Words and get through.
                   "Air: Sentir avec ardeur,"
                   St. 1, Ezra Pound,* tr.;
                   Confucius to Cummings;
                       An Anthology of Poetry,
              Ezra Pound and Marcella Spann, eds.
                                         1964

*American poet and critic (1885-1972).

2 An idiot
   Will always
   Talk a lot.   Ibid., St. 2

483. Catherine Clive (1711–1785)

1 WILLING. But don't your heart ache when you think of the first night, hey?
The Rehearsal: or, Boys in Petticoats 1753

2 MRS. HAZARD. Oh fie, Miss! that will never do: you speak your words as plain as a parish girl: the audience will never endure you in this kind of singing; if they understand what you say. You must give your words the Italian accent. Ibid.

3 Necessity or inclination brings every one to the stage. Quoted in
The Life of Mrs. Catherine Clive
by Percy Fitzgerald 1888

4 I am at present in such health and such spirits, that when I recollect I am an old woman, I am astonished. Letter to Mr.
[David] Garrick,* London
(14 April 1769),
Ibid.

*English actor and theater manager (1717–1779).

5 I have seen your lamb turned into a lion: by this your great labour was entertained; they thought they all acted very fine—they did not see you pull the wires. Letter to Mr. Garrick, from Twickenham
(23 June 1776),
op. cit.

484. Ho Shuang-ch'ing (1712–?)

1 The hardest thing in the world
Is to reveal a hidden love. To the tune
"A Watered Silk Dress,"
The Orchid Boat,
Women Poets of China,
Kenneth Rexroth and Ling
Chung, eds. and trs. 1972

485. Laetitia Pilkington (1712–1750/51)

1 Lying is an occupation
Used by all who mean to rise;
Politicians owe their station
But to well-concerted lies.

These to lovers give assistance
To ensnare the fair one's heart;
And the virgin's best resistance
Yields to this commanding art.

Study this superior science,
Would you rise in church or state;

Bid to truth a bold defiance,
'Tis the practice of the great. "Song,"
in toto,
Memoirs of Mrs. Laetitia
Pilkington, written by herself,
Wherein are occasionaly
interspersed all her Poems, with
Anecdotes of several eminent
persons living and dead 1748

486. Alicia Cockburn (1713–1794)

1 I've seen the smiling of fortune beguiling,
I've felt all its favours and found its decay;
Sweet was its blessing and kind its caressing,
But now it is fled—it is fled far away.
"The Flowers of the Forest,"*—
Scottish Song,
Mary Carlyle Aitken, ed.
1874

*This is a reworking of a much older, anonymous song. (Cf. Jean Elliot, 509:1.) The reference is to the thousands of men led by James IV who were slain at the Battle of Flodden Field (9 September 1513).

2 The flowers of the forest are withered away.
Ibid., refrain

487. Abigail Colman Dennie (1715–1745)

1 Yet still my fate permits me this relief,
To write to lovely Delia* all my grief.
To you alone I venture to complain;
From others hourly strive to hide my pain.
Lines From a Letter to Her
Sister, Jane Colman
(23 March 1733),
Quoted in *New England*
Historical and Genealogical
Register, No. 14
1860

*Her sister, the poet Jane Colman Turell. See 478.

488. Mary Monk (?–1715)

1 O'er this marble drop a tear,
Here lies fair Rosalind;
All mankind were pleased with her,
And she with all mankind.
"Lady of Pleasure,"
Marinda: Poems and Translations
on Several Occasions 1716

2 A just applause and an immortal name
Is the true object of the Poet's aim
"Epistle to Marinda,"
op. cit.

3 Say, shouldst thou grieve to see my sorrows end?

Thou know'st a painful pilgrimage I've
    past;
And shouldst thou grieve that rest is come
    at last?
Rather rejoice to see me shake off life,
And die as I have liv'd, thy faithful wife.
                "Verses written on her deathbed
                    at Bath, to her husband in
                    London,"
                    op. cit.

489. Elizabeth Carter (1717–1806)

1 For Wealth, the smiles of glad content,
  For Power, its amplest, best extent,
      An empire o'er the mind.
                    "Ode to Wisdom,"
                    St. 7,
          Poems Upon Particular Occasions
                    1738

2 Beneath her clear discerning eye,
  The visionary shadows fly
      Of Folly's painted show:
  She sees, through every fair disguise,
  That all but Virtue's solid joys
      Is vanity and woe.   Ibid., St. 16

3 I have nothing to assist me but industry; genius
  I have none, and I want mightily to know
  whether one can make any progress without
  it.   Quoted in *A Woman of
                    Wit and Wisdom*
          by Alice C. C. Gaussen   1906

4 I am sick of people of sense because they can
  act like fools, and of fools because they cannot
  talk like people of sense, and of myself for
  being so absurd as to trouble my head about
  them.   Letter to a friend
                    (1745),
                    op. cit.

5 Do you want employment? Choose it well before
  you begin, and then pursue it. Do you want
  amusement? Take the first you meet with that
  is harmless, and never be attached to any. Are
  you in a moderate station? Be content, though
  not affectedly so; be philosophical, but for the
  most part keep your thoughts to yourself. Are
  you sleepy? Go to bed.   Ibid.

490. Maria Theresa (1717–1780)

1 My son,* as you are the heir to all my worldly
  possessions, I cannot dispose of them; but my
  children are still, as they have ever been, my

own. I bequeath them to you; be to them a
father.   Last words
                    (29 November 1780),
                    Quoted in *Biography of
                    Distinguished Women*
          by Sarah Josepha Hale**   1876

*Joseph II (1741–1790), Holy Roman Emperor, 1765–
1790.
**See 703.

2 I want to meet my God awake.
                Remark on her deathbed
                (November 1780), refusing drugs;
                attributed by Thomas Carlyle,
                    n.d.

491. Anne Steele (1717–1778/79)

1 Little monitor, by thee
  Let me learn what I should be;
  Learn the round of life to fill,
  Useful and progressive still. "To My Watch,"
                    *Poems on Subjects Chiefly
                    Devotional*   1760

492. Mary Draper (c. 1718–1810)

1 He [her son] is wanted and must go. You [her
  daughter] and I, Kate, have also service to do.
  Food must be prepared for the hungry; for before
  to-morrow night, hundreds, I hope thousands,
  will be on their way to join the continental
  forces.   Response to a call to arms (1776),
                    Quoted in *The Women of the
                    American Revolution*
          by Elizabeth F. Ellet   1848

493. Mary Hearne (fl. c.1719)

1 Love . . . generally hurries us on without
  Consideration. . . .   "The Third Day,"
                    The Lover's Week   1718

2 . . . Love and Reason, like a Fever and Ague,
  took their alternate Turns in my
  Breast. . . .   "The Amours of Calista and
                    Torismond,"
          The Female Deserters   1719

3 . . . therefore You should not by the vulgar
  Notion of Marriage make yourself uneasy, since
  that Ceremony is nothing but a piece of Formality, introduced on purpose to bring Profit to
  the Church; and I think that Love is much more
  to be Esteem'd, which has no other Motive but
  mutual Affection.   Ibid.

494. Frances Fulke Greville (1720–1789)

1 No peace nor ease the heart can know,
　Which, like the needle true,
Turns at the touch of joy or woe,
　But, turning, trembles too.
　　　　　　　"Prayers for Indifference," *
　　　　　　　　　St. 6 (1753),
　　　　Maxims and Characters　1756

*See Isabella Howard, 500:1, for reply poem.

2 And what of life remains for me
　I'll pass in sober ease;
Half pleased, contented will I be,
　Content but half to please.
　　　　　　　　Ibid., last stanza

495. Charlotte Lennox (1720–1804)

1 I am not cruel enough to wish his Death; say
that I command him to live, if he can live
without Hope.
　　　Arabella; or, The Female Quixote,
　　　　　　　Vol. I　1752

2 "Oh! Sir," cried Sir George, "I have Stock
enough by me, to set up an Author Tomorrow,
if I please: I have no less than Five Tragedies,
some quite, others almost finished; Three or
Four Essays on Virtue, Happiness, etc., Three
thousand Lines of an Epic Poem; half a Dozen
Epitaphs; a few Acrostics; and a long String of
Puns, that would serve to embellish a Daily
Paper, if I was disposed to write one."
　　　　　　　　Ibid., Vol. II

3 The only Excellence of Falshood . . . is its
Resemblance to Truth. . . .　　　Ibid.

4 It is the Fault of the best Fictions, that they
teach young Minds to expect strange Adventures
and sudden Vicissitudes, and therefore encourage them often to trust to Chance. A long Life
may be passed without a single Occurrence that
can cause much Surprize, or produce any unexpected Consequence of great Importance.
　　　　　　　　Ibid.

5 Oh couldst thou teach the tortur'd Soul to
　know,
With Patience, each Extream of human
　Woe　　"On reading [Francis] Hutcheson*
　　　　　　　on the Passions,"
　　　　　Poems on Several Occasions
　　　　　　　4 November 1752

*British philosopher and moralist (1694–1746) and author
of "An Essay on the Nature and Conduct of the Passions
and Affections . . ." (1728).

6 ". . . I believe there is an intelligent cause
which governs the world by physical rules. As

for moral attributes, there is no such thing; it is
impious and absurd to suppose it."
　　　　　　　　Henrietta,
　　　　　　　Vol. II　1758

7 "Whatever is, is best. The law of nature is
sufficiently clear; and there is no need of super-
natural revelation."　　　　　Ibid.

8 MISS AUTUMN. I protest I tremble at the idea, of
being one day, what my stepmother is at present.
Oh heavens! in the midst of wrinkles and grey
hairs, to dream of gentle languishment, vows,
ardors!—but there is some comfort yet, fifty and
I are at an immense distance.
　　　　　　　The Sister　1759

9 In a word, the savage is subject to none but
natural evils. . . .　　　Euphemia,
　　　　　　　Vol. III　1790

10 The life of a good man is a continual
prayer.　　　　　Ibid., Vol. IV

496. Elizabeth Montagu (1720–1800)

1 Will an intelligent spectator not admire the pro-
digeous structures of Stone-Henge because he
does not know by what law of mechanics they
were raised?　　An Essay on the Writing and
　　　　Genius of Shakespeare Compared
　　　　with Greek and French Dramatic
　　　　　　Poets (1769)　1785

2 To judge therefore of Shakespeare by Aristotle's
rule is like trying a man by the Laws of one
Country who acted under those of another.
　　　　　　　　Ibid.

3 Shakespeare seemed to have had the art of the
Dervish in the Arabian tales who could throw
his soul into the body of another man and be at
once possessed of his sentiments, adopt his
passions and rise to all the functions and feelings
of his situation.　　　　　Ibid.

4 Gold is the chief ingredient in the composition
of worldly happiness. Living in a cottage on
love is certainly the worst diet and the worst
habitation one can find out.
　　　　　　The Letters of Mrs.
　　　　　　Elizabeth Montagu
　　　　　　　1810–1813

5 If she [Catherine the Great]* is not a good
woman, she is a great Prince.
　　　　　　Letter to Lord Lyttleton,
　　　　　　　　op. cit.

*See 514.

6 . . . there is a much higher character from that
of a wit or a poet or a savant, which is that of
a rational sociable being, willing to carry on the
commerce of life with all the sweetness and

condescension, decency and virtue will permit.
Letter to Mrs. William Robinson, her sister-in-law, op. cit.

7 Minds ripen at very different ages. Ibid.

8 I endeavor . . . to be wise when I cannot be merry, easy when I cannot be glad, content with what cannot be mended and patient when there is no redress.
Letter (c. 1739), op. cit.

9 There are but two kinds of people I think myself at liberty to hate and despise, the first is of the class of *soi disant* philosophers who by sophistry would cheat the less accute out of their principles, the only firm basis of moral virtue; the second are witts who ridicule whatsoever things are lovely, whatsoever things are of good report.
Letter (1768), op. cit.

10 It is surprizing what money I have spent out of a principle of economy; because they are cheap I have bought more shoes than a millipede could wear in VII years. By my caps you would think I had more heads than Hydra.
Letter to her brother (1776), op. cit.

11 But where there has not subsisted a good form of government and a regular system of Laws and mode of manners the people in general never are of a good character.
Letter to Mrs. Carter (1777), op. cit.

12 We are become a scoundrel nation worthy to be scorned and fit to be cudgel'd.
Letter (1779), op. cit.

13 Wit in women is apt to have bad consequences; like a sword without a scabbard, it wounds the wearer and provokes assailants. I am sorry to say the generality of women who have excelled in wit have failed in chastity. . . .
(1750), Quoted in
Reconstructing Aphra
by Angeline Goreau 1980

497. Peg Woffington (1720–1760)

1 I count time by your absence; I have not seen you all morning, and is it not an age since then?
Remark to David Garrick* (1776),
Quoted in *Days of the Dandies*, Ch. 6,
by J. Fitzgerald Molloy, n.d.

*English actor and theater manager (1717–1779).

498. Jeanne-Antoinette Poisson de Pompadour (1721–1764)

1 The King and I have such implicit confidence in you* that we look upon you as a cat, or a dog, and go on talking as if you were not there.
Quoted in
The Memoirs of Louis XV and of Madame de Pompadour
by Mme du Hausset 1802

*Mme du Hausset, her bed-chamber attendant. See 568.

2 It is a wolf who makes the sheep reflect.
Ibid.

3 After us the deluge! *(Après nous le déluge!)*
Her motto, op. cit.

4 Wait a moment, monsieur, and we will set forth together. *(Attendez-moi, monsieur le curé, nous partirons ensemble.)*
Last words, spoken to the priest, op. cit.

499. Anna Dorothea Lisiewska-Therbusch (1721–1782)

1 I would not have dared suggest it to you, but you have done well, and I thank you.*
Quoted by Denis Diderot in
Diderot Salons,
Vol. III, 1767, Jean Adhémar and Jean Seznec, eds. 1963

*In response to Diderot's voluntary disrobing for his portrait bust by her.

500. Isabella Howard (c.1722–c.1793-1795)

1 "I dare not change a first decree:
She's doomed to please, nor can be free:
Such is the lot of Beauty!"
"Reply by the Countess of C—,"*
St. 11 (c. 1753),
The Female Poets of Great Britain,
Frederic Rowton, ed. 1853

*Reply poem to Frances Greville's "Prayers for Indifference." See 494:1–2.

501. Mary Leapor (1722–1746)

1 Our servile Tongues are taught to cry for Pardon
Ere the weak Senses know the Use of Words:
Our little Souls are tortur'd by Advice;

And moral Lectures stun our Infant Years:
Thro' check'd Desires, Threatnings, and
  Restraint
The Virgin runs; but ne'er outgrows her
  Shackles
They still will fit her, even to hoary Age.
                              Untitled,
              Poems Upon Several Occasions,
                        Vol. II   *1751*

2 And all the arts that ruin while they please.
                        "The Temple of Love—a
                                   Dream,"
                              St. 3, op. cit.

502. Eliza Pinckney (1722?–1793)

1 Be particularly watchful against heat of temper;
it makes constant work for repentance and
chagrine.   Letter to Charles
                        Pinckney* (1761),
            *Journal and Letters of Eliza
                        Lucas Pinckney,*
                    Harriet R. Holbrook, ed.
                                   1850

* Her husband, a politician and judge.

503. Janet Graham (1723/24–1805)

1 Alas! my son, you little know
The sorrows that from wedlock flow,
Farewell to every day of ease,
When you have got a wife to please.
                        "The Wayward Wife,"
                              Scottish Song,
                    Mary Carlyle Aitken, ed.
                                   1874

2 Great Hercules and Samson too,
Were stronger men than I or you,
Yet they were baffled by their dears,
And felt the distaff and the shears.   Ibid.

504. Frances Brooke (1724–1789)

1 To be happy in this world, it is necessary not
to raise one's ideas too high. . . .
            The History of Emily Montague,
                        Vol. I, Letter XV,
                                   1769

2 I have said married women are, on my principles, forbidden fruit: I should have explained
myself; I mean in England, for my ideas on this
head change as soon as I land at Calais.
                        Ibid., Letter XXXVI

3 We have been saying, Lucy, that 'tis the strang-
est thing in the world people should quarrel
about religion, since we undoubtedly all mean
the same thing; all good minds in every religion

aim at pleasing the Supreme Being; the means
we take differ according to where we are born,
and the prejudices we imbibe from education; a
consideration which ought to inspire us with
kindness and indulgence to each other.
                              Ibid., Letter L

4 Parents should chuse our company, but never
even pretend to direct our choice. . . .
                        Ibid., Letter LXV

5 . . . this love is the finest cosmetik in the
world.   Ibid., Letter XCIII

6 . . . happiness is not to be found in a life of
intrigue. . . .   Ibid., Letter XCIX

7 In my opinion, the man who conveys, and
causes to grow, in any country, a grain, a fruit,
or even a flower, it never possessed before,
deserves more praise than a thousand heroes: he
is a benefactor, he is in some degree a
creator.   Ibid., Letter CXXI

8 It is a painful consideration, my dear, that the
happiness or misery of our lives are generally
determined before we are proper judges of
either.   Ibid., Letter CLII

9 Restrained by custom, and the ridiculous prejudices of the world, we go with the crowd, and
it is late in life before we dare to think.   Ibid.

10 A marriage where not only esteem, but passion
is kept awake, is, I am convinced, the most
perfect state of sublunary happiness: but it requires great care to keep this tender plant
alive. . . .   Ibid., Letter LXXIII

11 If the Supreme Creator had meant us to be
gloomy, he would, it seems to me, have clothed
the earth in black, not in that lively green, which
is the livery of chearfulness and joy.
                    Ibid., Vol. IV, Letter CXCIV

12 ROSINA. Why should I repine? Heaven, which
deprived me of my parents and my fortune, left
me health, content, and innocence. Nor is it
certain that riches lead to happiness. Do you
think the nightingale sings the sweeter for being
in a gilded cage?   *Rosina: A Comic Opera,*
                        Act I, Sc. 1   *1783*

13 RUSTIC. . . . I hate money when it is not my
own.   Ibid., Act II, Sc. 1

14 ROSINA. Whoever offends the object of his love
is unworthy of obtaining her.   Ibid.

505. Frances Sheridan (1724–1766)

1 I must take her down a peg or so.   *The Dupe,*
                        Act IV, Sc. 4   *1760*

2 As quick as lightning.   *The Discovery,*
                        Act I, Sc. 2   *1763*

3 What taught me silently to bear,
To curb the sigh, to check the tear,
When sorrow weigh'd me down?

'T was Patience!   "Ode to Patience,"
                                    Sts. 3, 4,
                    *The Female Poets of Great
                                    Britain,*
                    Frederic Rowton, ed.   *1853*

506. Eva Maria Garrick (1725–1822)

1 Groans and complaints are very well for those
who are to mourn but a little while; but a sorrow
that is to last for life will not be violent or
romantic.   Quoted by Hannah
                                More* in *Biography of
                                Distinguished Women*
                    by Sarah Josepha Hale**   *1876*

*See 557.
**See 703.

507. Bridget Fletcher (1726–1770)

1 God's only son by woman came,
To take away our shame;
And so thereby, to dignify,
Also to raise our fame.
                    Hymn XXXVI: St. 1,
                    "The Greatest Dignity of a
                Woman, Christ Being Born of One,"
                    Hymns and Spiritual Songs
                                    1773

508. Hester Chapone (1727–1801)

1 "Love worketh no ill to his neighbour;" there
fore, if you have true benevolence; you will
never do any thing injurious to individuals, or
to society. Now, all crimes whatever are (in
their remoter consequences at least, if not immediately and apparently) injurious to the society in which we live.
                    "The Two Commandements,"
                    *Letters on the Improvement of
                        the Mind*   *1773*

2 Affectation is so universally acknowledged to
be disgusting, that it is among the faults which
the most intimate friends cannot venture gravely
to reprove in each other; for to tell your friends
that they are habitually affected, is to tell them
they they are habitually disagreeable; which nobody can bear to hear.   "Affectation,"
                    Miscellanies in Prose and Verse
                                    1775

3 Thrice welcome, friendly Solitude,
O let no busy foot intrude,

Nor listening ear be nigh!
                                "Ode to Solitude,"
                    St. 1, *A Volume of Miscellanies*
                                    1775

4 I make no scruple to call romances the worst of
all species of writing; unnatural representation
of the passions, false sentiment, false precepts,
false wit, false honour, and false modesty, with
a strange heap of improbable, unnatural incidents mixed up with true history. . . .
                    Letter to Elizabeth
                    Carter (31 July 1750),
                    The Works of Mrs. Chapone,
                    Vol. I   *1818*

509. Jean Elliot (1727–1805)

1 I've heard them lilting, at the ewes milking.
Lasses a' lilting, before dawn of day;
But now they are moaning, on ilka green
loaning;
The Flowers of the Forest* are a' wede
away.   "The Flowers of the Forest,"
                                    Scottish Song,
                    Mary Carlyle Aitken, ed.
                                    1874

*The forces of James IV who were slain at Flodden Field
(9 September 1513). See note on Alicia Cockburn, 486:1.

2 The prime of our land, lie cauld in the clay.
                                    Ibid.

510. Hannah Griffitts (1727–1817)

1 Then for the sake of Freedom's name,
(Since British wisdom scorns repealing)
Come sacrifice to Patriot fame,
And give up tea by way of healing.
                    " 'Beware of the Ides of March,'
                    Said the Roman Augur To Julius
                                    Caesar,"
                                    St. 3 (1775),
                    *Women Poets in Pre-
                    Revolutionary America,*
                    Pattie Cowell, ed.   *1981*

2 Like a Newton,* sublimely he soar'd,
To a summit before unattain'd,
New regions of science explor'd,
And the palm of philosophy gain'd.
                    "Inscription On A Curious
                    Chamberstove In the Form of an
                    Urn, Contriv'd in Such A
                    Manner as to Make the Flame
                    Descend Instead of Rising,
                    Invented By The Celebrated B.F.,"**
                                    St. 1 (1776),
                                    op. cit.

*British physicist and mathematician (1642–1727).
**Benjamin Franklin, American printer and publisher, au-

thor, inventor and scientist, and diplomat (1706–1790); poem also attributed to Jonathan Odell.

511. Sarah Prince Gill (1728–1771)

1 —Thou, thou art all!
My soul flies up and down in thoughts of thee,
And finds herself but at the center still!
I AM, thy name! Existence, all thine own!
Creation's nothing to Thee, the great
    Original!   Untitled, St. 1,
    Dying Exercises of Mrs. Deborah
    Prince and Devout Meditations of
    Mrs. Sarah Gill . . .   *1784*

512. Margaret Klopstock (1728–1758)

1 I could not speak, I could not play; I thought I saw nothing but Klopstock.*
    Letter to Samuel Richardson**
    (14 March 1758), from
    Hamburg,
    Letters from the Dead to the
    Living   *post 1758*

*Her husband, the poet Friedrich Gottlieb Klopstock (1724–1803).
**The English novelist (1689–1761).

2 It is long since I made the remark that the children of geniuses are not geniuses.
    Letter to Samuel Richardson
    (26 August 1758),
    op. cit.

513. Mercy Otis Warren (1728–1814)

1 BRUTUS. . . . hoodwink'd justice
Drops her scales, and totters from her basis.
    The Adulateur, Act I, Sc. 1   *1773*

2 E———R. [sic] Honors, places, pensions—
'Tis all a cheat, a damn'd, a cruel cheat.
    Ibid., Act V, Sc. 2

3 CRUSTY CROWBAR. I too am almost sick of the parade
Of honours purchas'd at the price of peace.
    The Group,
    Act I, Sc. 1   *1775*

4 MONSIEUR. So great the itch I feel for titl'd place
Some honorary post, some small distinction,
To save my name from dark oblivious jaws,
I'll Hazard all, but ne'er give up my place.
    Ibid., Act II, Sc. 1

5 HATEALL. I broke her spirits when I'd won her purse*
    Ibid., Sc. 3

*His wife's dowry.

6 HATEALL. Then the green Hick'ry, or the willow twig,

Will prove a curse for each rebellious dame
Who dare oppose her lord's superior will.
    Ibid.

7 SECRETARY. What shifts, evasions, what delusive tales,
What poor prevarication for rash oaths,
What nightly watchings, and what daily cares
To dress up falshood in some fair disguise
    Ibid.

8 VALENTINIAN. I fear no storms but from an injur'd wife
    The Sack of Rome, Act II, Sc. I
    1790

9 VALENTINIAN. Where are his friends?—his num'rous train of clients?
Where the admiring crowds fed by his hand,
And basking in his wealth?
HERACLIUS. Just as the world in ev'ry age have done,
Playing their court where better fortune smiles   Ibid., Sc. 4

10 MAXIMUS. The bird of death that nightly pecks the roof   Ibid., Act III, Sc. 1

11 GAUDENTIUS. Ambition, in a noble, virtuous mind,
Is the first passion that the gods implant,
And soars to glory till it meets the skies
    Ibid., Sc. 2

12 GAUDENTIUS. Fate may do much before we meet again;
She has a busy hand, and swiftly rides
On revolution's wheel. . . .
    Ibid., Act IV, Sc. 5

13 EDOXIA. Enough of life and all life's idle pomp—
Nor by a tyrant's fiat will I live—
I leave the busy, vain, ambitious world
To cheat itself anew, and o'er and o'er
Tread the same ground their ancestors have trod,
In chace of thrones, of sceptres, or of crowns,
'Till all these bubbles break in empty air,
Nor leave a trace of happiness behind.
    Ibid., Act V, Sc. 3

14 DON JUAN DE PADILLA. Let freedom be the mistress of thy heart   *The Ladies of Castile,*
    Act I, Sc. 1   *1790*

15 DE HARO. But in the hero ne'er forget the man.   Ibid., Sc. 2

16 FRANCIS. Mistaken man!   Ibid., Sc. 5

17 MARIA. Today the cap of liberty's toss'd up—
Tomorrow torn and given to the winds,
And all their leaders, by the fickle throng
Are sacrific'd by violence, or fraud.
    Ibid., Act II, Sc. 4

18 DON JUAN. Most men are brave till courage
has been try'd,
And boast of virtue till their price is
known. . . . Ibid., Sc. 5

19 DON PEDRO. . . . the bubble freedom—empty
name!—
'Tis all a puff—a visionary dream—
That kindles up this patriotic flame;
'Tis rank self love, conceal'd beneath a mask
Of public good. The hero's brain inflates—
He cheats himself by the false medium,
Held in virtue's guise, till he believes it just
Ibid.

20 DE HARO. Great souls—form'd in the same
etherial mould,
Are ne'er at war—they, different paths
Of glory may pursue, with equal zeal;
Yet not a cruel, or malignant thought,
Or rancorous design, deform the mind.
Ibid., Act III, Sc. 1

21 DON JUAN. To learn to die is an heroic work
Ibid., Act IV, Sc. 2

22 MARIA. Maternal softness weakens my resolve,
And wakes new fears—thou dearest, best of
men,
Torn from my side, I'm levell'd with my sex.
The wife—the mother—make me less than
woman. Ibid., Sc. 5

23 'Tis social converse, animates the soul.
"To Fidelio,* Long Absent on
the Great Public Cause, Which
Agitates All America" (1776),
St. 1, *Miscellaneous Poems*   n.d.

*Pseudonym of James Warren, her husband, who fought
in the Revolutionary War.

24 The balm of life, a kind and faithful friend.
Ibid.

25 Each humbler muse at distance may admire,
But none to Shakespeare's fame e'er dare
aspire. "To Mrs. Montague,* Author
of 'Observation, On the Genius
and Writings of Shakespeare,' "
St. 2 (10 July 1790), Plymouth,
op. cit.

*Elizabeth Robinson Montague. See 496.

514. Catherine II of Russia (1729–1796)

1 For to tempt and to be tempted are things very
nearly allied, and in spite of the finest maxims
of morality impressed upon the mind, whenever
feeling has anything to do in the matter, no
sooner is it excited than we have already gone
vastly farther than we are aware of.
Memoirs,
A. Herzen, ed. and tr.
1857

2 I may be kindly, I am ordinarily gentle, but in
my line of business I am obliged to will terribly
what I will at all. Letter (30 August 1774),
Correspondance avec le Baron F.
M. Grimm (1774–1796)   1878

3 A great wind is blowing, and that gives you
either imagination or a headache.
Letter (29 April 1775),
op. cit.

4 I am one of the people who love the why of
things. Letter (20 January 1776),
op. cit.

5 In my position you have to read when you want
to write and to talk when you would like to
read; you have to laugh when you feel like
crying; twenty things interfere with twenty others; you have not time for a moment's thought,
and nevertheless you have to be constantly ready
to act without allowing yourself to feel lassitude,
either of body or spirit; ill or well, it makes no
difference, everthing at once demands that you
should attend to it on the spot.
Letter (23 August 1794),
op. cit.

6 Your wit makes others witty. (*Votre esprit en
donne aux autres.*) Letter to Voltaire,
The Complete Works of
Catherine II,
Evdokimov, ed.   *1893.*

7 I praise loudly, I blame softly. Letter,
op. cit.

8 If Fate had given me in youth a husband whom
I could have loved, I should have remained
always true to him. The trouble is that my heart
would not willingly remain one hour without
love. Letter to Prince
Potemkin (1774),
Quoted in *Memoirs,*
Katharine Anthony, ed. and tr.
1925

9 At the age of fourteen she made the three-fold
resolution, to please her Consort, [Empress]
Elizabeth, and the Nation.
Epitaph, written by herself
(1789),
op. cit.

10 To govern you have to have eyes and hands,
and a woman has only ears.
Quoted in *Daughters of Eve*
by Gamaliel Bradford   *1928*

515. Sarah Crosby (1729–1804)

1 The day after, at church, the Lord showed me
that many things which I had thought were sins
were only temptations, and also what a little
thing it was for him to take the root of sin out
of my heart.

Quoted in *Women of Methodism:
Its Three Foundresses . . .*
By Abel Stevens   *1866*

516. Marguerite Brunet (1730–1820)

1 Will I then really have no company here, and
does the King absolutely insist that I sleep
alone?   Remark upon entering her prison cell,
Quoted in *Enter the Actress*
by Rosamond Gilder   *1931*

2 . . . these special gala performances are always
good for trade.   Remark, op. cit.

517. Elizabeth Cooper (fl. 1730s)

1 BELLAIR. . . . Money is of no Value till 'tis
used.   *The Rival Widows; or, Fair Libertine*
1735

2 BELLAIR. We can talk of Murder, Theft, and
Treason, without blushing: and surely there's
nothing a-kin to Love that's half so wicked.
Ibid.

518. Caterina Gabrielli (1730–1796)

1 In this case, your majesty has only to engage
one of your field-marshals to sing.
Reply to Catherine the Great's
response ("None of my field-
marshals receive so enormous a sum!") to
Gabrielli's fee of 5,000
ducats to sing,
Quoted in *Biography of
Distinguished Women*
by Sarah Josepha Hale*   *1876*

*See 703.

519. Sophie de la Briche Houdetot (1730–1813)

1 Youth, I loved you; those loveliest years,
Brief as they were, when love was my only
occupation.   "Imitation de Marot,"
Elaine Partnow,* tr.
Quoted in *Biography of
Distinguished Women*
by Sarah Josepha Hale**   *1876*

*Author.
**See 703.

520. Mrs. Weddell (fl. 1730s–1740s)

1 [I cannot] admit of making the People's Taste
the Rule of Writing, [for] it is known to all who

consider the Intention of a Theatre, That its
peculiar Business is to correct a wrong Taste,
instead of complying with it.
Preface, *The City Farce*   *1737*

2 . . . [they are] a wise People, and fond of
Liberty, who consider all Men as Denizens of
the Earth's plenteous Blessings, nor think the
casual Tincture of the Skin, differing from the
European Hue alienates any from the indubitable
Right they are naturally entitled to, as Fellow
Creatures.   Preface, *Incle and Yarico*
1742

3 [Africa] . . .
Where the Remembrance of the Multitudes
Borne hence, to Slav'ry, by our Countrymen,
Must make each Man we meet an Enemy.
Ibid.

521. Lucy Terry (c.1731–c.1822)

1 Eunice Allen see the Indians comeing
And hoped to save herself by running
And had not her petticoats stopt her
The awful creatures had not cotched her
And tommyhawked her on the head
And left her on the ground for dead.
"Bars Fight,"*
*The Poetry of the Negro,
1746–1970,*
Langston Hughes and Arna
Bontemps, eds.   *1949*

*Refers to an Indian raid on Deerfield, Massachusetts (25
August, 1746).

522. Martha Washington (1731–1802)

1 . . . the greater part of our happiness or misery
depends on our dispositions, and not on our
circumstances. We carry the seeds of the one or
the other about with us in our minds wherever
we go.   Letter to Mrs. Warren*
(26 December 1789),
Quoted in
Lives of Celebrated Women
by Samuel Griswold
Goodrich   *1844*

*Probably Mercy Otis Warren; see 513.

2 It is all over now. I shall soon follow him. I
have no more trials to pass through.*
Remark (1799),
op. cit.

*Referring to the death of her husband, George Washington
(1732–99), 1st president of the United States (1789–97).

3 I live a very dull life here . . . indeed I think
I am more like a state prisoner than anything

else. . . . Letter to a relative,
Quoted in *Martha Washington*
by Anne Hollingsworth
Wharton   *1897*

4 . . . steady as a clock, busy as a bee, and cheerful as a cricket. . . . Letter to a
friend,
op. cit.

523. Julie-Jeanne-Eléonore de Lespinasse (1732–1776)

1 There is a certain hour in the day when I wind up my moral machine as I wind my watch. And then, the movement once given, it goes more or less well. . . . What is curious is that no one suspects the effort required to appear what I am thought really to be.
Letter to Condorcet*
(4 May 1771),
Lettres inédites   *1887*

*Marquis de Condorcet (1743–1794), French philosopher and politician.

2 . . . people observe very little, and it is fortunate, for there is not much to be gained by seeing more than others do.   Ibid.

3 If you can attain repose and calm, believe that you have seized happiness. Alas! Is there any other! And can there be any when one has made one's existence dependent upon another? Were he a god, the sacrifice would be too great.
Letter (23 August 1772),
op. cit.

4 I do nothing but love, I know nothing but love.   Letter to Guibert* (30 May 1773),
Lettres   *1906*

*François-Apollini Guibert, French military reformer (1744–1790).

5 I cannot read with interest: I am always reading what I feel and not what I see.
Letter (8 August 1773),
op. cit.

6 Ah! how the mind weakens when one loves.
Ibid.

7 The logic of the heart is absurd.
Letter (27 August 1774),
op. cit.

8 You know that when I hate you, it is because I love you to a point of passion that unhinges my soul.   Letter (1774),
op. cit.

524. Mary Knowles (1733–1807)

1 He [Dr. Johnson] gets at the substance of a book directly; he tears out the heart of it.

Letter (15 April 1778),
Quoted in *The Life of Samuel Johnson,*
LL. D.* by James Boswell
1791

*English author and lexicographer (1709–84).

525. Mary Masters (fl. 1733–1755)

1 What if the charms in him I see
Only exist in thought
"To Lucinda," St. 2,
*Poems on Several
Occasions*   *1733*

2 Love is a mighty god, you know,
That rules with potent sway;
And when he draws his awful bow,
We mortals must obey.   Ibid., St. 6

526. Louise Honorine de Choiseul (1734–1801)

1 You know you love me, but you do not feel it.   Letter to Marie du Deffand,*
*Correspondance complète de
Mme Du Deffand avec la
duchesse de Choiseul, l'abbé
Barthélemy et M.
Craufurt*   *1866*

*See 467.

2 It is well to love even a dog when you have the opportunity, for fear you should find nothing else worth loving.   Quoted in
Portraits of Women
by Gamaliel Bradford   *1916*

3 If I have learned anything, I owe it neither to precepts nor to books, but to a few opportune misfortunes. Perhaps the school of misfortunes is the very best.   Ibid.

4 He [Jean-Jacques Rousseau] has always seemed to me to be a charlatan of virtue.   Ibid.

5 He [Voltaire] tells us he is faithful to his enthusiasms; he should have said, to his weaknesses. He has always been cowardly where there was no danger, insolent where there was no motive, and mean where there was no object in being so. All which does not prevent his being the most brilliant mind of the century. We should admire his talent, study his works, profit by his philosophy, and be broadened by his teaching. We should adore him and despise him, as is indeed the case with a good many objects of worship.   Ibid.

6 My scepticism has grown so great that it falls over backward and from doubting everything I have become ready to believe everything.
Ibid.

7 We grow old as soon as we cease to love and trust.   Ibid.

8 Good-by, dear child, I wish you good sleep and a good digestion. I don't know anything better to desire for those I love.   Ibid.

527. Mrs. Pennington (1734–1759)

1 On glories greater glories rise.
Ode to Morning," St. 1,
The Female Poets of Great Britain,
Frederic Rowton, ed.   *1853*

528. Nancy Hart (1735?–1830)

1 Surrender your damned Tory carcasses to a Whig woman.
On her capture of five Loyalists,
Quoted in *The Women of the
American Revolution,*
Vol. II, by Elizabeth F. Ellet
1848

529. Caroline Keppel (1735–?)

1 What's this dull town to me?
Robin's not near—
He whom I wished to see,
Wished for to hear;
Where's all the joy and mirth
Made life a heaven on earth?
O! they're all fled with thee,
Robin Adair   "Robin Adair"   *n.d.*

530. Theodosia De Visme Burr (1736–1794)

1 Piety teaches resignation. . . . The better I am acquainted with it, the more charms I find.
Letter to her husband, Aaron Burr*
(6 March 1781),
Memoirs of Aaron Burr,
Vol. I, Matthew L. Davis, ed.
1836–1837

*American vice president (1801–1805) and politician (1756–1836).

2 I am impatient for the evening; for the receipt of your dear letter; for those delightful sensations which your expression of tenderness alone can excite. Dejected, distracted without them, elated, giddy even to folly with them, my mind, never at medium, claims everything from your partiality.   Letter to Aaron Burr
(August 1786),
op. cit.

531. Mary Katherine Goddard (c.1736–1738–1816)

1 . . . [it is] their duty to inquire into everything that has a tendency to restrain the liberty of the Press. . . .   Letter to the
Baltimore Committee of Safety
(May/June 1776),
Quoted in *William Goddard,
Newspaperman,*
Ch. 8, by Ward L.
Miner   *1962*

2 The Stoppage of the *Paper-Mill,* near this Town, for the Want of a Supply of Rags, and the enormous Prices demanded at the Stores here for PAPER, constrains us to print the *Maryland Journal* on this dark and poor Sort, which our Readers will, we are persuaded excuse, for one Week at least, when they are assured, that rather than deprive them of *the important Intelligence of the Times,* by the Discontinuance of our *Journal,* we have given from *Forty* to *Fifty Pounds* a Week for the Article of Paper *alone,* an equal Quantity of which, might, formerly, have been purchased for *Eight Dollars!*
Notice in *Maryland Journal*
(26 May 1778),
op. cit.

532. Ann Lee (1736–1784)

1 It is not I that speak, it is Christ who dwells in me.   Quoted in *The Testimony of
Christ's Second Appearing*
by Benjamin S. Youngs   *1808*

2 I converse with Christ; I feel him present with me, as sensibly as I feel my hands together.
Ibid.

533. Annis Stockton (1736–1801)

1 . . . future ages shall enroll thy name
In sacred annals of immortal fame.
"Addressed to General Washington
in the Year 1777 After the
Battles of Trenton and Princeton,"
*Columbian Magazine
January 1787*

2 For, oh! I find on earth no charms for me
But what's connected with the thought of thee!   "Epistle to Mr. S[tockton],"
*Women Poets in Pre-
Revolutionary America,*
Pattie Cowell, ed.   *1981*

3 Thousands of heroes from his dust shall rise
"On Hearing That General [Dr. Joseph] Warren Was Killed on Bunker Hill, the 17th of June, 1775,"
op. cit.

534. Elizabeth Graeme Ferguson (1737–1801)

1 A transient, rich, and balmy sweet
   Is in thy fragrance found;
   But soon the flow'r and scent retreat—
   Thorns left alone to wound.
                    "On a Beautiful Damask Rose,
                    Emblematical of Love and
                    Wedlock," St. 3,
                    Columbian Magazine
                    May 1789

2 Thus over all, self-love presides supreme
                    "On the Mind's Being Engrossed
                    By One Subject,"
                    Columbian Magazine
                    July 1789

3 Birth day odes to lords and kings,
   Oft are strain'd and stupid things!
   Poet laureate's golden lays,
   Fulsome hireling's hackney'd praise!
                    "An Ode Written on the
                    Birthday of Mr. Henry Ferguson
                    By His Wife When They Had
                    Been Married Two Years, He
                    Aged 26 Years,"
                    St. 1 (12 March 1774),
                    *Women Poets in Pre-
                    Revolutionary America,*
                    Pattie Cowell, ed.   *1981*

4 . . . angel-like he spake, and God-like
      died.   "On the Death of Leopold,
                    Hereditary Prince of Brunswick,
                    Who was Drowned in the Oder,
                    April 17, 1785, in Attempting to
                    Save Some Children Whose
                    Mother had Left Them on the
                    Banks of that River"
                    (5 July 1785), Montgomery County,
                    op. cit.

535. Margaret Morris (1737?–1816)

1 A loud knocking at my door brought me to it.
   . . . I opened it, and a half a dozen men, all
   armed, demanded the key of the empty house.
   . . . I put on a very simple look and exclaimed—"Bless me! I hope you are not Hessians!"*

   "Do we look like Hessians?" asked one rudely.
   "Indeed, I don't know."
   "Did you ever see a Hessian?"
   'No—never in my life; but they are *men;* and
   you are men; and may be Hessians for aught I
   know!"   From her Journal
                    (16 December 1776),
                    Quoted in *The Women of the
                    American Revolution,*
                    Vol. II, by Elizabeth F.
                    Ellet   *1848*

*German mercenaries hired by the British.

2 . . . there is a god of battle as well as a God
   of peace. . . .   Ibid. (27 December 1776)

536. Suzanne Chardon Necker (1737–1794)

1 . . . I cannot help thinking that the vows most
   women are made to take are very foolhardy. I
   doubt whether they would willingly go to the
   altar to swear that they will allow themselves to
   be broken on the wheel every nine months.
                    Quoted in *Mistress to
                    an Age: A Life of Madame de Staël**
                    by J. Christopher Herold
                    1958

*See 637.

2 Governesses have always one great disadvan-
   tage; if they are qualified for their calling, they
   intercept the child's affection for its mother.
                    Ibid.

537. Mary Fletcher (1739–1815)

1 I was deeply conscious it [religion] is one of the
   most delicate subjects in the world, and requires
   both much wisdom and much love, to extinguish
   false fire, and yet keep up the true.
                    Quoted in
                    *The Women of Methodism:
                    Its Three Foundresses . . .*
                    by Abel Stevens   *1866*

2 I feel at this moment a more tender affection
   toward him* than I did at that time [of her
   marriage], and by faith I now join my hand
   afresh with his.   Journal entry
                    (12 November 1809),
                    op. cit.

*Her husband, Jean Guillaume de la Flechère; written
during her widowhood, on the anniversary of her marriage.

538. Madame de Charrière (1740–?)

1 I would prefer being my lover's laundress and
   living in a garret to the arid freedom and the
   good manners of our great families.
                    Quoted in *Mistress to An Age: A
                    Life of Madame de Staël**
                    by J. Christopher Herold
                    1958

*See 637.

539. Mrs. Hoper (fl. 1740s)

1 The Stage shall flourish, Tragedy shall
   thrive,

And Shakespear's Scenes ne'er die whilst
They* survive   Prologue, *Queen Tragedy
                        Restores   1749*

*Othello, Hamlet, Falstaff and Richard II.

540. Clementina Rind (c. 1740–1774)

1 Open to ALL PARTIES, but Influenced by
NONE   Motto,
                    Quoted in *Virginia Gazette*
                    (first issue) *16 May 1766*

541. Martha Brewster (fl. 1741–1757)

1 Oh!———he———is———gone.
              "To the Memory of that worthy
                Man Liet. NATHANAEL
              BURT of *Springfield* . . . [who
                died] in the Battle of Lake-
                George in the Retreat, September
                8th, 1753,"
                        *Poems on Divers
                        Subjects   1757*

2 There is a wheel within a wheel
              "A Farewell to Some of My
                Christian Friends at Goshen, in
                Lebanon,"
                St. 4 (5 April 1745), op. cit.

3 Dear friends, the life is more than meat,
    The soul excels the clay;
O labor then for gospel food,
    Which never shall decay.   Ibid., St. 14

4 O absence! absence! sharper than a thorn
              "A Letter to My Daughter Ruby
                        Bliss,"
                        op. cit.

542. Sarah Parsons Moorhead (fl. 1741/42)

1 Despise the blest instructions of their
    tongue,
Conversion is become the drunkard's song;
God's glorious work, which sweetly did
    arise,
By this unguarded sad imprudence dies;
Contention spreads her harpy claws
    around,
In every church her hateful stings are
    found.   "To the Reverend Mr. James
                        Davenport on His Departure
                        from Boston, By Way of a
                        Dream," St. 1
                        1742

543. Hester Lynch Piozzi (1741–1821)

1 It is a maxim here [at Venice], handed down
from generation to generation, that change breeds

more mischief from its novelty than advantage
from its utility.   "Observations on a Journey
                        through Italy,"
                    *Autobiography, Letters and
                        Literary Remains,*
                Abraham Hayward, ed.   *1861*

2 The tree of deepest root is found
Least willing still to quit the ground:
'Twas therefore said by ancient sages,
That love of life increased with years
So much, that in our later stages,
When pain grows sharp and sickness rages,
The greatest love of life appears.
                        "Three Warnings,"
                        op. cit.

3 Ah! he was a wise man who said Hope is a
good breakfast but a bad dinner. It shall be my
supper, however, when all's said and done.
                    From *Autobiography* . . . .,
                        Vol. II

4 A physician can sometimes parry the scythe of
death, but has no power over the sand in the
hourglass.   Letter to Fanny Burney*
                        (12 November 1781),
                        op. cit.

*See 577.

544. Dorcas Richardson (1741?–1834)

1 I do not doubt that men who can outrage the
feelings of a woman by such threats, are capable
of perpetrating any act of treachery and inhumanity towards a brave but unfortunate enemy.
But conquer or capture my husband [Captain
Richard Richardson], if you can do so, before
you boast the cruelty you mean to mark your
savage triumph! And let me tell you, mean-
while, that some of you, it is likely, will be in
a condition to implore *his* mercy, before he will
have need to supplicate, or deign to accept
yours.   Remark to the British,
                    Quoted by Dr. Joseph Johnson in
                    The Women of the American Revolution
                        by Elizabeth F. Ellet   *1848*

545. Sarah Kirby Trimmer (1741–1810)

1 Happy would it be for the animal creation, if
every human being . . . consulted the welfare
of inferior creatures, and neither spoiled them
by indulgence, nor injured them by tyranny!
Happy would mankind be . . . by cultivating
in their own minds and those of their own
children, the divine principle of general
benevolence.   *Fabulous Histories: or, The
                    History of the Robins. Designed
                    for the Instruction of Children,
                    Respecting Their Treatment of
                        Animals,* 13th ed., 1821

2 Every living creature that comes into the world has something allotted him to perform, therefore he should not stand an idle spectator of what others are doing. Ibid.

546. Isabella Graham (1742–1814)

1 Hail! thou state of widowhood,
State of those that mourn to God;
Who from earthly comforts torn,
Only live to pray and mourn.
"Widowhood" (1774),
Life and Writings n.d.

547. Anne Home (1742–1821)

1 'Tis hard to smile when one would weep,
To speak when one would silent be;
To wake when one would wish to sleep,
And wake to agony.
"The Lot of Thousands,"
Poems by Mrs. John Hunter
1802

2 My mother bids me bind my hair
With bands of rosy hue,
Tie up my sleeves with ribbons rare,
And lace my bodice blue.
"For why," she cries, "sit still and weep,
While others dance and play?"
Alas! I scarce can go or creep
While Lubin is away.
"My Mother Bids Me Bind My Hair,"
op. cit.

548. Darcy Maxwell (1742?–1810)

1 It is seldom that we go beyond our teachers.
Quoted in *The Women of
Methodism: Its Three Foundresses* . . .
by Abel Stevens 1866

2 Suffice it to say, I was chosen in the furnace of affliction. The Lord gave me all I desired in this world, then took all from me;* but immediately afterward sweetly drew me to Himself.
Letter to a friend (c. 1776),
Quoted in *Biography of
Distinguished Women*
by Sarah Josepha Hale** 1876

*She was widowed at nineteen; six weeks later her only child died.
**See 703.

549. Anna Seward (1742–1809)

1 O hours! more worth than gold
Untitled (December 1782),
Sonnets 1789

2 This last and long enduring passion for Mrs. Thrale* was, however, composed of cupboard love, Platonic love, and vanity tickled and gratified. Letter, *Letters,*
Vol. II n.d.

*Allusion to Dr. Samuel Johnson's relationship with Hester Lynch Piozzi, aka Mrs. Thrale. See 543.

550. Anna Letitia Barbauld (1743–1825)

1 While Genius was thus wasting his strength in eccentric flights, I saw a person of a very different appearance, named Application.
"The Hill of Science,"
Miscellaneous Pieces in Prose
1773

2 The most characteristic mark of a great mind is to choose some one important object, and pursue it for life. "Against Inconsistency in Our
Expectations,"
op. cit.

3 The awakenings of remorse, virtuous shame and indignation, the glow of moral approbation—if they do not lead to action, grow less and less vivid every time they occur, till at length the mind grows absolutely callous.
"An Inquiry Into Those Kinds of
Distress Which Excite Agreeable
Sensations,"
op. cit.

4 Education, in its largest sense, is a thing of great scope and extent. It includes the whole process by which a human being is formed to be what he is, in habits, principles, and cultivation of every kind. . . . You speak of *beginning* the education of your son. The moment he was able to form an idea his education was already begun. . . . "On Education,"
op. cit.

5 Let us confess a truth, humiliating perhaps to human pride;—a very small part only of the opinions of the coolest philosopher are the result of fair reasoning; the rest are formed by his education, his temperament, by the age in which he lives, by trains of thought directed to a particular track through some accidental association—in short, by *prejudice.*
"On Prejudice,"
op. cit.

6 Forgotten rimes, and college themes,
Worm-eaten plans, and embryo schemes;—
A mass of heterogeneous matter.
A chaos dark, nor land nor water.
"An Inventory of the Furniture
in Dr. Priestley's* Study,"
Poems 1773

*The English chemist Joseph Priestley (1733–1804).

7 Who can resist those dumb beseeching eyes,
Where genuine eloquence persuasive lies?

Those eyes, where language fails, display
  thy heart
Beyond the pomp of phrase and pride of
  art.   "To A Dog,"
                    op. cit.

8 We neither laugh alone, nor weep alone,—
    why then should we pray alone?
          Remarks on Mr. Gilbert
          Wakefield's Enquiry Into the
          Expediency and Propriety of
          Public or Social Worship
          1792

9 But every act in consequence of our faith,
    strengthens faith.   Ibid.

10 The doctrine that all are vile, and equally merit
    a state of punishment, is an idea as conciliatory
    to the profligate, as it is humiliating to the saint;
    and that is one reason why it has always been a
    favourite doctrine.   Ibid.

11 . . . still Afric bleeds,
    Unchecked, the human traffic still proceeds
        "Epistle to William Wilberforce,
                Esq."* (1791),
        The Works of Anna Letitia
        Barbauld, Vol. I
        1826

*English abolitionist; the reference is to slavery (1759–1833).

12 Where seasoned tools of Avarice prevail,
    A Nation's eloquence, combined, must fail
                  Ibid.

13 Yes, injured Woman! rise, assert thy right!
    Woman! too long degraded, scorned, opprest;
    O born to rule impartial Laws despite,
    Resume they native empire o'er the breast!
          "The Right of Woman,"
                op. cit.

14 . . . separate rights are lost in mutual love.
                  Ibid.

15   No line can reach
    To thy unfathomed depths. The reasoning
      sage
    Who can dissect a sunbeam, count the stars,
    And measure distant worlds, is here a child,
    And, humbled, drops his calculating pain.
                "Eternity,"
                op. cit.

16 When trembling limbs refuse their weight,
    And films, slow gathering, dim the sight,
    And clouds obscure the mental light,—
    'Tis nature's precious boon to die.
         "A Thought on Death"
         (November 1814),
                op. cit.

17 Saints have been calm while stretched upon
    the rack,
    And Guatimozin* smiled on burning coals;

But never yet did housewife notable
Greet with a smile a rainy washing-day.
            "Washing-Day,"
            op. cit.

* Aztec emperor, tortured by the conquistadores.

18 . . . [as] a father of three children. I would
    advise you to make a hero, as you have deter-
    mined: another a scholar; and for the third,—
    send him to us, and we will bring him up for a
    Norfolk farmer, which I suspect to be the best
    business of the three.   Letter to Dr. Aiken
               (9 September 1775),
               Vol. II op. cit.

19 To *repair* a ruin carries a better sound with it
    than to *build* a ruin, as we do in England.
            Letter to Dr. Aiken
         (27 February 1786), from
             Thoulouse [sic],
               op. cit.

20 It would be difficult to determine whether the
    age is growing better or worse; for I think our
    plays are growing like sermons, and our sermons
    like plays.   Letter to Miss E. Belshan
            (later Mrs. Kenrick).
         (17 February 1771), from
              London,
              op. cit.

21 Nobody ought to be too old to improve; I should
    be sorry if I was; and I flatter myself I have
    already improved considerably by my travels.
    First, I can swallow gruel soup, egg soup, and
    all manner of soups, without making faces much.
    Secondly, I can pretty well live without
    tea. . . .   Letter to Miss
               Belshan
          (21 October 1785),
            from Geneva,
              op. cit.

22 One hardly knows whether to be frightened or
    diverted on seeing people assembled at a dinner-
    table appearing to enjoy extremely the fare and
    the company, and saying all the while, with the
    most smiling and placid countenance, that the
    French are to land in a fortnight, and that Lon-
    don is to be sacked and plundered for three
    days,—and then they talk of going to watering
    places.   Letter to Miss Dixon
            (later Mrs. Beecroft).
       (28 July 1803), from London,
              op. cit.

23 Here dwell the true magicians. Nature is our
    servant. Man is our pupil. We change, we con-
    quer, we create.   "To Miss C.,"
        A Legacy for Young Ladies
               n.d.

24 Finding out riddles is the same kind of exercise
    to the mind which running and leaping and
    wrestling and sport are to the body.

"On Riddles,"
op. cit.

25 I often murmur, yet I never weep;
I always lie in bed, yet never sleep;
My mouth is large, and larger than my
head,
And much disgorges though it ne'er is fed;
I have no legs or feet, yet swiftly run,
And the more falls I get, move faster on.
Ibid.

26 Between the greater part of those we call the
different classes, there is only the difference of
less and more. . . .   "On Female Studies,
Letter Two,"
op. cit.

27 . . . Taste has one great enemy to contend with
. . . Fashion—an arbitrary and capricious tyrant, who reigns with the most despotic sway
over that department which Taste alone ought
to regulate.   Ibid.

28 . . . a forest was never planted. "On Plants,"
op. cit.

29 How patiently does she support the various burdens laid upon her! We tear her plows and
harrows, we crush her with castles and palaces;
nay we penetrate her very bowels, and bring to
light the veined marble, the pointed crystal, the
ponderous ores and sparkling gems, deep hid in
darkness the more to excite the industry of man.
Yet, torn and harrassed as she might seem to
be, our mother Earth is still fresh and young,
as if she but now came out of the hands of her
Creator.   "Earth,"
op. cit.

30 Friends should consider themselves as the sacred
guardians of each other's virtue; and the noblest
testimony they can give of their affection is the
correction of the faults of those they love.
"On Friendship,"
op. cit.

31 Happy is he to whom, in the maturer season of
life, there remains one tried and constant
friend. . . .   Ibid.

551. Hannah Cowley (1743–1809)

1 DOILEY. No, no; you must mind your P's and
Q's* with him, I can tell you.
Who's the Dupe?,
Act I, Sc. 2   1779

*Originally abbreviation for "pints and quarts," used in
taverns.

2 DOILEY. Well, good fortune never comes in a
hurry. . . .   Ibid.

3 GRADUS. The charms of women were never more
powerful—never inspired such achievements, as

in those immortal periods, when they could
neither read nor write.   Ibid., Sc. 3

4 CHARLOTTE. You know very well, the use of
language is to express one's likes and dislikes—
and a pig will do this as effectually by its
squeak, or a hen with her cackle, as you with
your Latin and Greek.   Ibid.

5 GRADUS. Beauty is a talisman which works true
miracles, and, without a fable, transforms
mankind.   Ibid., Act II, Sc. 1

6 GRANGER. But what is woman?—Only one of
Nature's agreeable blunders.   Ibid.

7 SAVILLE. Five minutes! Zounds! I have been
five minutes too late all my life-time!
The Belle's Strategem,
Act I, Sc. 1   c. 1780s

8 VILLERS. A lady at her toilette is as difficult to
be moved as a quaker.   Ibid., Sc. 3

9 VILLERS. Vanity, like murder, will out. Ibid.

10 SIR GEORGE TOUCHWOOD. Heaven and earth!
with whom can a man trust his wife in the
present state of society? Formerly there were
distinctions of character amongst ye; every class
of females had its particular description! grandmothers were pious, aunts discreet, old maids
censorious! but now, aunts, grandmothers, girls,
and maiden gentlewomen, are all the same creature; a wrinkle more or less is the sole difference
between ye.   Ibid., Act II, Sc. 1

11 COURTALL. But 'tis always so; your reserved
ladies are like ice, 'egad!—no sooner begin to
soften than they melt!   Ibid., Sc. 2

12 MRS. RACKET. Marry first and love will
follow.   Ibid., Act III, Sc. 1

13 LADY FRANCES TOUCHWOOD. Every body about
me seem'd happy—but every body seem'd in a
hurry to be happy somewhere else.
Ibid., Sc. 4

14 FLUTTER. O lord! your wise men are the greatest
fools upon earth; they reason about their enjoyments, and analyse their pleasures, whilst the
essence escapes.   Ibid., Act IV, Sc. 1

15 FLUTTER. "Live to love," was my father's motto:
"Live to laugh," is mine.   Ibid.

16 VILLERS. The charms that helped to catch the
husband are generally laid by, one after another,
till the lady grows a downright wife, and then
runs crying to her mother, because she has
transformed her lover into a downright
husband.   Ibid., Act V, Sc. 1

17 MRS. RACKET. It requires genius to make a good
pun—some men of bright parts can't reach
it.   Ibid., Sc. 5

552. Eibhlín Dhubh Ní Chonaill (1743–1790)

1 Till Art O'Leary returns
  There will be no end to the grief
  That presses down on my heart,
  Closed up tight and firm
  Like a trunk that is locked
  And the key mislaid.   "The Lament for
                                   Arthur O'Leary,"
                                 St. 35, Ellis Dillon, tr.;
                            The Penguin Book of Women Poets,
                              Carol Cosman, Joan Keefe and
                              Kathleen Weaver, tr. and eds.
                                                      1978

553. Abigail Adams (1744–1818)

1 I am more and more convinced that man is a
  dangerous creature. . . .
                                 Letter to John Adams*
                                 (27 November 1775),
                            Letters of Mrs. Adams   1840

*(1735–1826) 2nd president of the United States (1797–1801).

2 We are no ways dispirited here, we possess a
  Spirit that will not be conquered. If our Men
  are all drawn off and we should be attacked,
  you would find a Race of Amazons in
  America.   Letter to John Adams (1776),
                                            op. cit.

3 If perticuliar care and attention is not paid to
  the Laidies we are determined to foment a Re-
  belion, and will not hold ourselves bound by
  any Laws in which we have no voice, or
  Representation.   Letter to John
                            Adams (31 March 1776),
                                            op. cit.

4 Men of Sense in all Ages abhor those customs
  which treat us only as the vassals of your
  Sex.   Ibid.

5 [At] the court of St. James* . . . I seldom meet
  with characters so innofensive as my Hens and
  chickings, or minds so well improved as my
  garden.   Letter to Thomas
                     Jefferson (26 February 1788),
                        Quoted in *The Papers of
                              Thomas Jefferson,**
                        Julian P. Boyd, ed.   *1955*

*Reference to James Madison, 4th president of the United
States (1809–1817).
**3rd president of the United States (1801–1809).

6 . . . had nature formed me of the other Sex, I
  should certainly have been a rover.
                                 Letter to Isaac Smith, Jr.
                                 (20 April 1771),
                              The Adams Papers,
                        L. H. Butterfield, ed.   *1963*

7 The Natural tenderness and Delicacy of our
  Constitution, added to the many Dangers we are
  subject to from your Sex, renders it almost
  impossible for a Single Lady to travel without
  injury to her character.   Ibid.

8 I can not say that I think you very generous to
  the Ladies, for whilst you are proclaiming peace
  and good will to Men, Emancipating all Nations,
  you insist upon retaining an absolute power over
  Wives.   Letter to John Adams
                                 (7 May 1776),
                                            op. cit.

554. Sophie Arnould (1744–1802)

1 We shall be rich as princes. A good fairy has
  given me a talisman to transform every thing
  into gold and diamonds at the sound of my
  voice.   Quoted in *Queens of Song*
                                 by Ellen Creathorne
                                    Clayton   *1865*

2 Oh! that was the good time; I was very unhappy.
  *(Oh! c'était le bon temps; j'étais bien
  malheureuse.)*   Remark to Claude-
                            Carlomande Rulhière,*
                        *Sophie Arnould; d'après sa
                  correspondance et ses mémoires inédits,*
                        Edmond and Jules de Goncourt, eds.
                                                      1884

*French writer and historian (1734–1791).

555. Sarah Bache (1744–1808)

1 The subject now is Stamp Act, and nothing else
  is talked of. The Dutch talk of the "Stamp
  tack," the negroes of the "tamp"—in short,
  every body has something to say.
                     Letter to Benjamin Franklin,* her
                           father (c. November 1764),
                           Quoted in *The Women of the
                                 American Revolution*
                        by Elizabeth F. Ellet   *1848*

*American statesman, author, and scientist (1706–1790).

2 In this country there is no rank but rank
  mutton.   Note to an Englishwoman who
                           ran a school for girls where her
                                 daughters attended,
                                            op. cit.

556. Elizabeth Martin (c. 1745–post-1776)

1 Go, boys; fight for your country! fight till death,
  if you must, but never let your country be
  dishonored. Were I a man I would go with

you. Remark to her seven sons at
the call to arms,
Quoted in *The Women of the
American Revolution*
by Elizabeth F. Ellet *1848*

2 I wish I had fifty. Reply to a British
officer's query regarding her sons
in arms,
op. cit.

557. Hannah More (1745–1833)

1 I shall have nothing to do but go to Bath and
drink like a fish. Letter to David Garrick,*
Quoted in *Garrick
Correspondence,*
Vol. II *1778*

*English actor and theater manager (1717–1779).

2 . . . dost thou know
The cruel tyranny of tenderness?
Percy 1778

3 Honor! O yes, I know him. 'Tis a phantom,
A shadowy figure, wanting bulk and life,
Who, having nothing solid in himself,
Wraps his thin form in Virtue's plundered
robe,
And steals her title. *The Fatal
Falsehood 1779*

4 The keen spirit
Ceases* the prompt occasion,—makes the
thought
Start into instant action, and at once
Plans and performs, resolves and executes!
Daniel 1782

*Seizes.

5 A crown! what is it?
. . . .
It is to sit upon a joyless height,
To ev'ry blast of changing fate expos'd!
Too high for hope! too great for happiness.
Ibid., Pt. VI.

6 No adulation; 'tis the death of virtue;
Who flatters, is of all mankind the lowest
Save he who courts the flattery. *Ibid.*

7 O war!—what, what art thou?
At once the proof and scorge of man's fall'n
state!
After the brightest conquest, what appears
Of all thy glories! for the vanquish'd chains!
For the proud victors, what? alas! to reign
O'er desolated nations! *Ibid., Pt. V 1782*

8 Books, the Mind's food, not exercise!
*"Conversation,"
St. 1, The Bas Bleu*

*[The Blue Stocking]
1784*

9 But sparks electric only strike
On souls electrical alike *Ibid., St. 2*

10 He liked those literary cooks
Who skim the cream of others' books;
And ruin half an author's graces
By plucking *bon-mots* from their places.
Florio 1786

11 And Pleasure was so coy a prude,
She fled the more, the more pursued. . . .
Ibid.

12 He thought the world to him was known,
Whereas he only knew the *town.*
In men this blunder still you find:
All think their little set—mankind. *Ibid.*

13 For you'll ne'er mend your fortunes, nor
help the just cause,
By breaking of windows, or breaking of
laws. Address at Spa Fields (1817),
Quoted in *The Life of Hannah More*
by H. Thompson *1838*

14 Fell luxury! more perilous to youth
Then storms or quicksands, poverty or
chains. *"Belshazzar,"
The Complete Works of Hannah More
1856*

15 That silence is one of the great arts of conversation is allowed by Cicero himself, who says,
there is not only an art, but even an eloquence
in it. *"Thoughts on
Conversation,"
Essays on Various Subjects,*
op. cit.

16 Subduing and subdued, the petty strife,
Which clouds the colour of domestic life;
The sober comfort, all the peace which springs
From the large aggregate of little things;
On these small cares of daugther, wife or
friend,
The almost sacred joys of home depend.
*"Sensibility"
Poems,*
op. cit.

17 If faith produce no works, I see
That faith is not a living tree.
Thus faith and works together grow;
No separate life they e'er can know:
They're soul and body, hand and heart:
What God hath joined, let no man part.
"Dan and Jane,"
op. cit.

18 How short is human life! the very breath
Which frames my words accelerates my
death. *"King Hezekiah,"*
op. cit.

558. Stephanie Félicité Genlis (1746–1830)

1 For which reason, you may observe that the man whose probity consists in merely obeying the laws, cannot be truly virtuous or estimable; for he will find many opportunities of doing contemptible and even dishonest acts, which the laws cannot punish. "Laws," *Tales of the Castle c. 1793*

2 Hence it is that men act ill, and judge well. Feeble and corrupted, they give way to their passions; but when they are cool—that is to say, when they are uninterested—they instantly condemn what they have often been guilty of; they revolt against every thing that is contemptible; they admire every thing generous, and they are moved at every thing affecting. "Virtue," op. cit.

3 Can any one be a connoisseur in music, without knowledge of the science? No; it is absolutely impossible. "Music," op. cit.

4 "A philosopher, desirous of praising a princess, who had been dead these fifty years, could not accomplish his purpose but at the expense of all the princesses, and all the women, who have ever existed or do exist; and that in a single phrase."
"He has been very laconic indeed."
"You shall hear—*Though a woman and a princess*, said he, *she loved learning!*"
"The orator ought to have been answered, that *though a philospher*, and an academician, he did not, on this occasion, show either much politeness or equity."
"The Two Reputations," op. cit.

559. Esther De Berdt Reed (1746–1780)

1 . . . if these great affairs must be brought to a crisis and decided, it had better be in our time than our children's. Letter to Dennis De Berdt, her brother (1775), Quoted in *The Life of Esther De Berdt, Afterwards Esther Reed* by William B. Reed *1853*

560. Frederica de Riedesel (1746–1808)

1 Britons never retrograde. Quoted in *The Women of the American Revolution*, Vol. II, by Elizabeth F. Ellet *1848*

2 Seizing some maize, I begged our hostess to give me some of it to make a little bread. She replied that she needed it for her black people. "They work for us," she added, "and you come to kill us." Ibid.

3 It is astonishing how much the frail human creature can endure. . . .* Ibid.

*Referring to the breakout of a malignant fever in New York in 1780.

561. Susanna Blamire (1747–1794)

1 And ye shall walk in silk attire, And siller* ha'e to spare. "The Siller Crown," *The Poetical Works of Miss Susanna Blamire, the Muse of Cumberland 1842*

*Scottish for "silver."

2 Till soft remembrance threw a veil Across these een o' mine, I closed the door, and sobbed aloud, To think on aul langsyne! "The Nabob," St. 4, op. cit.

3 I come, I come, my Jamie dear; And O! wi' what good will I follow wheresoe'er ye lead! Ye canna lead to ill. "The Waefu' Heart," St. 5, op. cit.

4 Of aw things that is I think thout* is meast queer, It brings that that's by-past and sets it down here. "Auld Robin Forbes," St. 1, op. cit.

*Thought.

562. Anna Gordon Brown (1747–1810)

1 O first he sange a merry song, An then he sang a grave, And then he peckd his feathers gray, To her the letter gave. "The Gay Goshawk," St. '10, *The English and Scottish Popular Ballads*, Francis James Child, ed. *1898*

563. Marie Letitia Bonaparte (1748–1836)

1 Napoleon has never given me a moment's pain, not even at the time which is almost universally woman's hour of suffering.* Quoted in *Biography of Distinguished Women* by Sarah Josepha Hale** *1876*

*Reference to birth of her son, Napoleon Bonaparte (1769–1821).
**See 703.

564. Gertrude Elizabeth Mara (1749–1833)

1 When I give a lesson in singing, I sing with my scholars; by so doing they learn in half the time they can if taught in the usual way—by the master merely playing the tune of the song on the piano. People can not teach what they don't know—my scholars have my singing to imitate—those of other masters seldom any thing but the tinkling of a piano.
Quoted in *Queens of Song*
by Ellen Creathorne Clayton
1865

565. Charlotte Smith (1749–1806)

1 Queen of the silver bowl!   "To the Moon,"
*Elegiac Sonnets and Other
Essays   1782*

2 Sweet poet of the woods. . . .
"The Departure of the
Nightingale,"
op. cit.

3 Another May new buds and flowers shall bring;
Ah! why has happiness—no second Spring?
"The Close of Spring,"
op. cit.

4 Little inmate, full of mirth,
Chirping on my humble hearth "The Cricket,"
St. 1, op. cit.

5 But Reason comes at—Thirty-eight.
"Thirty-Eight,"
St. 4, op. cit.

6 Stripp'd of their gaudy hues by Truth,
We view the glitt'ring toys of youth. . . .
Ibid., St. 7

7 Swift fleet the billowy clouds along the sky,
Earth seems to shudder at the storm aghast;
While only beings as forlorn as I,
Court the chill horrors of the howling blast.
"Montalbert,"
op. cit.

8 . . . the moon, mute arbitress of tides
"Sonnet Written in the Church-
Yard at Middleton, in Sussex,"
op. cit.

9 He was streched upon a sopha—with boots on—
a terrier lay on one side of him, and he occasionally embraced a large hound, which licked his face and hands, while he thus addressed it.—"Oh! thou dear bitchy—thou beautiful bitchy—damme, if I don't love thee better than my mother or my sisters." *Desmond,*
Vol. I, Ch. 5   *1792*

10 " 'Tis an uneasy thing," said he, "a very uneasy thing, for a man of probity and principles to look in these days into a newspaper."
Ibid., Ch. 6

11 Montfleuri . . . said . . . "I reflect with concern on the power of national prejudice and national jealousy, to darken and pervert the understanding."   Ibid., Ch. 9

12 "He [Henry IV of England] had not been taught, that to be born a king is to be born something more than man."   Ibid.

13 When the imagination soars into those regions, where the planets pursue each its destined course, in the immensity of space—every planet, probably, containing creatures adapted by the Almighty, to the residence he has placed them in; and when we reflect, that the smallest of these is of as much consequence in the universe, as this world of our's; how puerile and ridiculous do those pursuits appear in which we are so anxiously busied; and how insignificant the trifles we toil to obtain, or fear to lose.
Ibid., Ch. 12

14 Alas! my friend, there appears to be a strange propensity in human nature to torment itself, and as if the physical inconveniencies with which we are surrounded in this world of ours were not enough, we go forth constantly in search of mental and imaginary evils—This is no where so remarkable as among those who are in what we can affluence and prosperity. . . .
Ibid., Vol. II, Ch. 5

15 Were there, indeed, a sure appeal to the mercies of the rich, the calamities of the poor might be less intolerable; but it is too certain, that high affluence and prosperity have a direct tendency to harden the temper.   Ibid., Ch. 10

16 Having never heard anything but her own praises, she really believed herself a miracle of knowledge and accomplishments. . . .
The Old Manor House   1793

17 The masters of a great school are apt to shew that pupils connected with title and fortune have a more than ordinary share of their regard; yet among boys of the same age there is always established   a   certain   degree   of equality. . . .   *The Young Philosopher,*
Vol. I, Ch. 3   *1798*

18 . . . the wantoness of tyranny, that induces men to exercise power merely because they have it. . . .   Ibid.

19 "If my family are ashamed of me, they have only to leave me out of their genealogical table, as an unworthy branch of the tree, bent towards its native earth, and no longer contributing to their splendid insignificance."   Ibid., Ch. 4

20 "And let me tell you, Mrs. Winslow," said the Doctor, "that you are too apt to fall into these fits of admiration."   Ibid., Ch. 7

21 "These presentiments of evil are often the causes that evil really arrives. . . ."
                Ibid., Vol. II, Ch. 5

22 "Youth, even when deprived of all viable support—makes a long and often a successful stand against calamity."   Ibid., Ch. 6

566. Anne Barnard (1750–1825)

1 The waes o' my heart fa' in showers frae my e'e,
While my gudeman lies sound by me.
                "Auld Robin Gray"   1771

2 My father couldna work, and my mother couldna spin;
I toiled day and night, but their bread I couldna win.   Ibid.

3 They gied him my hand, tho' my heart was at sea.   Ibid.

567. Sophia Burrell (1750?–1802)

1 Blindfold I should to Myra run,
And swear to love her ever;
Yet when the bandage was undone,
Should only think her clever.

With the full usage of my eyes,
I Chloe should decide for;
But when she talks, I *her* despise,
Whom, dumb, I could have died for!"Chloe and Myra,"
Sts. 4, 5,
Poems
1793

2 Cupid and you, 'it is said, are cousins,
(*Au fait** in stealing hearts by dozens,)
                "To Emma,"
                op. cit.

*Proficient.

3 And should you be arraign'd in court
For practising this cruel sport,
In spite of all the plaintiff's fury
Your smile would bribe both judge and jury.   Ibid.

568. Madame du Hausset (fl. 1750–1764)

1 Great people have the bad habit of talking very indiscreetly before their servants.

*The Memoirs of Louis XV, and of Madame de Pompadour**
by Mme. du Hausset
(1802)   *1910 ed.*

*Jeanne-Antoinette Poisson de Pompadour. See 496.

2 See what the Court is; all is corruption there, from the highest to the lowest.
                Remark to Mme. de Pompadour,
                op. cit.

569. Caroline Lucretia Herschel (1750–1848)

1 Many a half or whole holiday he* was allowed to spend with me was dedicated to making experiments in chemistry, where generally all boxes, tops of tea-canisters, pepper-boxes, tea-cups, etc., served for the necessary vessels and the sand-tub furnished the matter to be analyzed. I only had to take care to exclude water, which would have produced havoc on my carpet.
                Memoir and Correspondence of
                Caroline Herschel,
                Mrs. John Herschel, ed.   *1876*

*Her nephew, the astronomer Sir John Frederick Herschel (1792–1871).

2 I am now so enured to receiving honours in my old age, that I take them all upon me without blushing.   Ibid.

570. Mary Jones (fl. 1750)

1 How much of paper's spoil'd! what floods of ink!
And yet how few, how very few, can think!
                I. "Extract from an Epistle to
                Lady Bowyer," St. 1,
                Miscellanies in Prose and Verse
                1750

2 For what is beauty but a sign?
A face hung out, through which is seen
The nature of the goods within.
                II. "To Stella, after the Small-Pox,"
                St. 1, op. cit.

571. Judith Madan (fl. 1750)

1 Doubt not to reap, if thou canst bear to plough.   "Verses. Written in her brother's Coke upon Littleton,"*
                The Female Poets of Great Britain,
                Frederic Rowton, ed.   *1853*

*I.e., a copy of the commentary by the English jurist Sir Edward Coke on the *Tenures* of Sir Thomas Littleton.

572. Elizabeth Peabody (1750–?)

1 Lost to virtue, lost to humanity must that person be, who can view without emotion the complicated distress of this injured land. Evil tidings molest our habitations, and wound our peace. Oh, my brother! oppression is enough to make a wise people mad.
Letter to John Adams, her brother-in-
law,
Quoted in *The Women of the
American Revolution,*
Vol. II, by Elizabeth F. Ellet
1848

573. Caroline Matilda (1751–1775)

1 O God, keep me innocent; make others great! Scratched with a diamond on a window of the castle of Frederiksborg, Denmark *n.d.*

574. Jeanne Isabelle Montolieu (1751–1832)

1 Here lies the child [Voltaire] spoiled by the world which he spoiled. *(Ci git l'enfant gâté due monde qu'il gâta.)* "Epitaph on Voltaire"* *n.d.*

*French author (1694–1778).

575. Judith Sargent Murray (1751–1820)

1 To the absorbing grave I must resign,
All of my first born child that e'er was
mine! "Lines, Occasioned by the Death
of an Infant," St. 4,
*The Massachusetts Magazine
January 1790*

2 Will it be said that the judgment of a male two years old, is more sage that than of a female's of the same age? I believe the reverse is greatly observed to be true. But from that period what partiality! how is the one exalted and the other depressed, by the contrary modes of education which are adopted! the one is taught to aspire, and the other is early confined and limited.
"On the Equality of the Sexes,"
*The Massachusetts Magazine
March and April 1790*

3 I know there are those who assert, that as the animal powers of the one sex are superiour, of course their mental faculties also must be stronger; thus attributing strength of mind to the transient organization of this earth born tenement. But if this reasoning is just, man must be content to yield the palm to many of the brute creation. . . . *Ibid.*

4 I would be Cesar, or I would be nothing.
The Gleaner,
Vol. I *1798*

5 Religion is 'twixt God and my own soul,
Nor saint, nor sage, can boundless thought control. "Lines Prefacing Essay No. XIX. A Sketch of the Gleaner's Religious Sentiment,"
op. cit.

6 I may be accused of enthusiasm, but such is my confidence in the sex, that I expect to see our young women forming a new era in female history. Vol. III, op. cit.

576. Ann Eliza Bleecker (1752–1783)

1 New worlds to find, new systems to explore:
When these appear'd, again I'd urge my flight
Till all creation open'd to my sight.
"On the Immensity of Creation,"
St. 1 (1773), Tomhanick,
*The Posthumous Works of Ann
Eliza Bleecker, in Prose and Verse,*
Margaretta Faugeres, ed.
1793

2 My gods took care of me—not I of them!
"On Reading Dryden's Virgil"
(1778), op. cit.

3 What art thou now, my love!—a few dry bones,
Unconscious of my unavailing moans
"Recollection,"
St. 2 (10 February 1778),
Tomhanick, op. cit.

4 But think not I dislike my situation here; on the contrary, I am charmed with the lovely scene the spring opens around me. Alas! the wilderness is within: I muse so long on the dead until I am unfit for the company of the living.
Letter (8 April 1780), op. cit.

5 . . . Oh leave the city's noxious air.
"To the Same,"
St. 1, op. cit.

6 You've broke th' agreement, Sir, I find;
(Excuse me, I must speak my mind)
It seems in your poetic fit
You mind not jingling, where there's wit
"To Mr. L****,"
op. cit.

577. Fanny Burney (1752–1840)

1 "Do you come to the play without knowing what it is?" "O, yes, Sir, yes, very frequently.

I have no time to read play-bills. One merely comes to meet one's friends, and show that one's alive."

Letter XX
Evelina
1778

2 "What a jabbering they make!" cried Mr. Braughton; "there's no knowing a word they say. Pray what's the reason they can't as well sing [opera] in English?—but I suppose the fine folks would not like it, if they could understand it."

Ibid., Letter XXI

3 Concealment, my dear Maris, is the foe of tranquility. . . .

Ibid., Letter LX

4 Alas, my child!—that innocence, the first, best gift of heaven, should, of all others, be the blindest to its own danger,—the most exposed to treachery,—and the least able to defend itself, in a world where it is little known, less valued, and perpetually deceived!

Ibid., Letter LXVII

5 . . . *Imagination* took the reins, and *Reason,* slow-paced, though sure-footed, was unequal to a race with so eccentric and flighty a companion.

Ibid.

6 . . . but this is not an age in which we may trust to appearances, and imprudence is much sooner regretted than repaired.

Ibid.

7 "If Time thought no more of me, than I do of Time, I believe I should bid defiance, for one while, to old age and wrinkles,—for deuce take me if ever I think about it at all."

Ibid., Letter LXXVII

8 I'd do it as soon as say 'Jack Robinson.'

Ibid., Letter LXXXII

9 "But an old woman . . . is a person who has no sense of decency; if once she takes to living, the devil himself can't get rid of her."

Cecilia,
Bk. I, Ch. 10
1782

10 "How true is it, yet how consistent . . . that while we all desire to live long, we have all a horror of being old!"

Ibid., Bk. II, Ch. 3

11 To a heart formed for friendship and affection the charms of solitude are very short-lived. . . .

Ibid., Ch. 4

12 "Report is mightily given to magnify." Ibid.

13 ". . . men seldom risk their lives where an escape is without hope of recompense."

Ibid., Ch. 6

14 ". . . childhood is never troubled with foresight. . . ."

Ibid., Bk. III, Ch. 2

15 "But if the young are never tired of erring in conduct, neither are the older in erring of judgment. . . ."

Ibid., Bk. IV, Ch. 11

16 ". . . where concession is made without pain, it is often made without meaning. For it is not in human nature to project any amendment without a secret repugnance."

Ibid.

17 The shill I, shall I, of Congreve* becomes shilly shally.

Ibid., Bk. V

*William Congreve, Restoration dramatist (1670–1729).

18 ". . . he looked around him for any pursuit, and seeing distinction was more easily attained in the road to ruin, he galloped along it, thoughtless of being thrown when he came to the bottom, and sufficiently gratified in showing his horsemanship by the way."

Ibid., Ch. 7

19 "True, very true, ma'am," said he, yawning, "one really lives no where; one does but vegetate, and wish it all at an end."

Ibid., Bk. VII, Ch. 5

20 The historian of human life finds less of difficulty and of intricacy to develop, in its accident and adventures, than the investigator of the human heart in its feelings and its changes.

Camilla,
Bk. I, Ch. 1
1796

21 ". . . there is nothing so pleasant as working the indolent; except, indeed, making the restless keep quiet. . . ."

Ibid., Bk. II, Ch. 5

22 "Far from having taken any positive step, I have not yet even formed any resolution."

Ibid., Ch. 13

23 "Happiness is in your power, though beauty is not; and on that to set too high a value would be pardonable only in a weak and frivolous mind; since, whatever is the involuntary admiration with which it meets, every estimable quality and accomplishment is attainable without it. . . ."

Ibid., Bk. IV, Ch. 5

24 "You will live to feel pity for all you now covet and admire. . . ."

Ibid.

25 The artlessness of unadorned truth, however sure in theory of extorting admiration, rarely in practice fails inflicting pain and mortification.

Ibid., Ch. 8

26 As extravagance and good luck, by long custom, go hand-in-hand, he spent as fast as he acquired.

Ibid., Bk. V, Ch. 13

27 Whatever there is new and splendid, is sure of a run for at least a season.

Ibid., Bk. X, Ch. 3

28 Indeed, the freedom with which Dr. [Samuel] Johnson* condemns whatever he disapproves is astonishing.

Diary entry
(23 August 1778),
Diary and Letters of Madame D'Arblay, 1778–1840,

Vol. I, Charlotte Barrett, ed.
1904

*English lexicographer and author (1709–1784).

29 'Tis best to build no castles in the air.
Ibid., Vol. II

30 We are not yet out of the wood.
Ibid., Vol. III

31 All the delusive seduction of martial music. . . . Ibid., (1802) Vol. VIII

578. Jeanne Louise Campan (1752–1822)

1 I have put together all that concerned the domestic life of an unfortunate princess [Marie-Antoinette],* whose reputation is not yet cleared of the stains it received from the attacks of calumny, and who justly merited a different lot in life, a different place in the opinion of mankind after her fall.
Memorandum,
Quoted in
The Memoirs of Marie Antoinette,
Jeanne Louise Campan, ed.
1910

*See 588.

2 His [Louis XVI's] heart, in truth, disposed him towards reforms; but his prejudices and fears, and the clamours of pious and privileged persons, intimidated him, and made him abandon plans which his love for the people had suggested. Ibid., Ch. 6

3 Tremble at the moment when your child has to choose between the rugged road of industry and integrity, leading straight to honour and happiness; and the smooth and flowery path which descends, through indolence and pleasure, to the gulf of vice and misery. It is then that the voice of a parent, or of some faithful friend, must direct the right course.
"To Her Only Son,"
Familiar Letters to her Friends,
n.d.

4 Learn to know the value of money. This is a most essential point. The want of economy leads to the decay of powerful empires, as well as private families. Louis XVI perished on the scaffold for a deficit of fifty millions. There would have been no debt, no assemblies of the people, no revolution, no loss of the sovereign authority, no tragical death, but for this fatal deficit. Ibid.

579. Hannah Mather Crocker (1752–1829)

1 . . . the wise Author of nature has endowed the female mind with equal powers and faculties, and given them the same right of judging and acting for themselves, as he gave to the male sex.
Observations on the
Real Rights of Women   1818

580. Jemima Wilkinson (1752–1819)

1 Live peaceably with all men as much as possible; in an especial manner do not strive against one another for mastery, but all of you keep your ranks in righteousness, and let not one thrust another [aside].
The Universal Friend's Advice, to
Those of the Same Religious
Society   1784

2 It is a Sifting time; Try to be on the Lords side. . . . Letter to John and Orpha Rose
(1789),
Quoted in *Pioneer Prophetess*
by Herbert A. Wisbey, Jr.
1964

3 . . . thou needest not Ask who Shall Ascend up into heaven for to Search the record of Eternity, thou mayest But Descend down into thine own heart and there read what thou art and what thou Shalt Be . . .
"Book of Conscience,"
op. cit.

4 That way the tree inclineth while it groweth that way it pitcheth when it falleth and there it Lieth. . . . So we Lie down to Eternity whether it Be towards heaven or towards hell Being Once fallen there is no removing for as in war an Error is death So in death an Error is damnation therefore Live as you intend to die and die as you intend to Live "As We Live So we Die,"
op. cit.

5 . . . I am weary of them that hate peace.
Letter to James Parker (1788),
op. cit.

581. Catharine Greene (1753–1815?)

1 If you expect to be an inhabitant of this country [Georgia], you must not think to sit down with your netting pins; but on the contrary, employ half your time at the toilet, one quarter to paying and receiving visits; the other quarter to scolding servants, with a hard thump every now and then over the head; or singing, dancing, reading, writing, or saying your prayers. The latter is here quite a phenomenon; but you need not tell how you employ your time.
Letter to Miss Flagg (c. 1783),
Quoted in *The Women of the*
American Revolution,
Vol. II, by Elizabeth F. Ellet
1848

582. Elizabeth Inchbald (1753–1821)

1 LADY MARY. Beauty in London is so cheap, and consequently so common to the men of fashion, (who are prodigiously fond of novelty) that they absolutely begin to fall in love with the ugly women, by way of change.
Appearance is against Them,
Act I, Sc. 1   *1785*

2 HUMPHRY. You can't be at a loss for words, while you are courting!—Women will always give you two for your one.   Ibid., Sc. 2

3 LADY EUSTON. There is as severe a punishment to men of gallantry (as they call themselves) as sword or pistol; laugh at them—that is a ball which cannot miss; and yet kills only their vanity.   *I'll Tell You What,*
Act III, Sc. 1   *1786*

4 LADY EUSTON. "You are the most beautiful woman I ever saw," said Lord *Bandy;* "and your Lordship is positively the most lovely of mankind"—"What eyes," cried he; "what hair," cried I; "what lips," continued he; "what teeth," added I; "what a hand and arm," said he; "and what a *leg* and *foot,*" said I—"Your Ladyship is jesting," was his Lordship's last reply; and he has never since paid me one compliment.   Ibid.

5 MARQUIS. . . . love is a general leveller—it makes the king a slave; and inspires the slave with every joy a prince can taste.
The Midnight Hour,
Act I, Sc. 1   *1787*

6 GENERAL. . . . a man never looks so ridiculous as when he is caught in his own snare.
Ibid., Act III, Sc. 1

7 SIR LUKE TREMOR. . . . he is the slave of every great man, and the tyrant of every poor one.
Such Things Are,
Act I, Sc. 1   *1788*

8 MR. TWINEALL. Why, Madam, for instance, when a gentleman is asked a question which is either troublesome or improper to answer, you don't say you *won't* answer it, even though you speak to an inferior—but you say—"really it appears to me e-e-e-e-e—[mutters and shrugs]—that is—mo-mo-mo-mo-mo—[mutters]—if you see the thing—for my part—te-te-te-te—and that's all I can tell about it at *present.*"   Ibid.

9 DOCTOR. They have refused to grant me a *diploma;* forbid me to practice as a physician, and all because I do not know a parcel of insignificant words; but exercise my profession according to the rules of *reason* and *nature.*—Is it not natural to die? Then, if a dozen or two of my patient *have* died under my hands, is not that natural?   *Animal Magnetism,*
Act I, Sc. 1   *1789*

10 MADAME TICASTIN. What misers are we all of our real pleasures!   *The Massacre,*
Act I, Sc. 1   *1792*

11 SIR ROBERT RAMBLE. We none of us endeavour to *be* happy, Sir, but merely to be *thought* so; and for my part, I had rather be in a state of misery, and envied for my supposed happiness, than in a state of happiness, and pitied for my supposed misery.   *Every One Has his Fault,*
Act II, Sc. 1   *1793*

12 LORD PRIORY. I know several women of fashion, who will visit six places of different amusement on the same night, have company at home besides, and yet, for want of something more, they'll be out of spirits. . . .
*Wives as they Were, and
Maids as they Are,*
Act I, Sc. 1   *1797*

13 COTTAGER. Wife, wife, never speak ill of the dead. Say what you please against the living, but not a word against the dead.

COTTAGER'S WIFE. And yet, husband, I believe the dead care the last what is said about them—   *Lover's Vows,*
Act II, Sc. 1   *1798*

14 VERDUN THE BUTLER. Loss of innocence never sounds well except in verse.
Ibid., Act IV., Sc. 2

15 GIRONE. . . . women's power seldom lasts longer than their complexion.
A Case of Conscience,
Act I, Sc. 1   *1833*

16 GIRONE. My Lord, I *do* know, but I am sworn to secrecy; and 'tis so unmanly to tell! But I will lead you to my wife, who knows also; and being a woman, she would unsex herself as much by keeping the secret, as I should by revealing it.   Ibid., Act II, Sc. 1

17 My present apartment is so small, that I am all over black and blue with thumping my body and limbs against my furniture on every side; but then I have not far to *walk* to reach anything I want, for I can kindle my fire as I lie in bed, and put on my cap as I dine. . . .
From her Journal,
Quoted in
English Women of Letters,
Vol. II, by Julia Kavanagh
1863

583. Phillis Wheatley (1753?–1784)

1 Suppress the deadly serpent in its egg.
Ye blooming plants of human race divine,
An Ethiop tells you 'tis your greatest foe;
Its transient sweetness turns to endless
    pain,
And in immense perdition sinks the soul.

"To the University of Cambridge,
in New-England,"
St. 3 (1767),
*Poems on Various Subjects,
Religious and Moral*   *1773*

2 Some view our sable race with scornful eye,
"Their colour is a diabolic dye."
Remember, *Christians, Negroes* black as
Cain,
May be refin'd, and join th' angelic train.
"On Being Brought From Africa
to America"
(c. 1768), op. cit.

3 I, young in life, by seeming cruel fate
Was snatch'd from Afric's fancy'd happy
seat:
What pangs excruciating must molest,
What sorrows labor in my parent's breast?
Steel'd was that soul and by no misery
mov'd
That from a father seiz'd his babe belov'd:
Such, such my case. And can I then but
pray
Others may never feel tyrannic sway?
"To the Right Honourable William,
Earl of Dartmouth, His
Majesty's Principal Secretary of
State for North America, & C.,"
St. 3, op. cit.

4 The land of freedom's heaven-defended
race!   "To His Excellency General
Washington,"
St. 3, op. cit.

5 . . . civil and religious liberty . . . are so
inseparably united, that there is little or no
enjoyment of one without the other: . . . in
every human breast, God has implanted a principle, which we call love of freedom; it is
impatient of oppression and pants for
deliverance. . . .
Letter to Rev. Samson Occom
(11 February 1774)
Boston Post-Boy
(21 March 1774)

584. Jeanne-Marie Roland (1754–1793)

1 O liberty! what crimes are committed in thy
name!* *(O liberté! que de crimes on commêt
dans ton nom!)*   Last words before being
guillotined (8 November 1793),
Quoted in *Histoire des Girondins,*
Ch. LI, by Alphonse Lamartine
1847

*Words inscribed on front of Statue of Liberty in New
York City; also recorded as: "O Liberty, how you have
been trifled with!" *(O Liberté, comme on t'a jouée!).*

2 I shall soon be there [at the guillotine]; but those
who send me there will follow themselves ere

long. I go there innocent, but they will go as
criminals; and you, who now applaud, will also
applaud them.   Remark en route to execution
(8 November 1793),
Quoted in *Biography of
Distinguished Women*
by Sarah Josepha Hale*   *1876*

*See 703.

3 The more I see of men, the more I admire dogs.
*(Plus je vois les hommes, plus j'admire les
chiens.)*   Attributed*   *n.d.*

*Also attributed to Ouida [See 945.] and to Mme. de
Sévigné [See 387.]

585. Frances Thrynne (?–1754)

1 To thee, all glorious, ever-blessed power,
I consecrate this silent midnight hour.
"A Midnight Hour,"
Miscellanies,
Dr. Watt, ed.   *n.d.*

586. Anne Grant (1755–1838)

1 Gem of the heath! whose modest bloom
Sheds beauty o'er the lonely moor
"On A Sprig of Heath," St. 3,
*The Highlanders and Other Poems
1808*

2 O where, tell me where, is your Highland
laddie gone?
He's gone with streaming banners, where
noble deeds are done,
And my sad heart will tremble till he comes
safely home.
"O Where, Tell Me Where,"*
Scottish Song,
Mary Carlyle Aitken, ed.
1874

*Both this and "The Blue Bells of Scotland" by Dorothea
Jordan (see 619:1) are variants on an older popular song.

587. Anna Maria Lenngren (1755–1817)

1 'Tis plain to see what pride within her
glance reposes,
And mark how nobly curved her nose is!
"The Portraits," St. 2,
*Anthology of Swedish Lyrics from
1750–1915,*
C. W. Stork, ed. and tr.   *1917*

2 The fairer sex possessed a mind
Of sturdy fabric, like her cloak.
Now all is different in our lives—
Other fabrics, other mores!
Taffetas, indecent stories

"Other Fabrics, Other Mores!"
Nadia Christensen and
Mariann Tiblin, trs.;
The Penguin Book of Women Poets,
Carol Cosman, Joan Keefe and
Kathleen Weaver, eds. *1978*

588. Marie-Antoinette (1755–1793)

1 Let them eat cake.* *(Qu'ils mangent de la
brioche.)* Quoted in *Confessions*
by Jean-Jacques Rousseau
1740

*Brioche, or "cake," was equivalent to a round, hard-crusted bread.

2 Courage! I have shown it for years; think you I
shall lose it at the moment when my sufferings
are to end? Remark
(16 October 1793;
on way to guillotine),
Quoted in *Women of Beauty and Heroism*
by Frank B. Goodrich *1858*

3 Adieu, once again, my children, I go to join
your father. Last words, op. cit.

4 I have seen all, I have heard all, I have forgotten
all. Reply to inquisitors
(October 1789),
Quoted in *Biography of
Distinguished Women*
by Sarah Josepha Hale* *1876*

*See 703.

5 I was a queen, and you took away my crown; a
wife, and you killed my husband; a mother, and
you deprived me of my children. My blood
alone remains: take it, but do not make me
suffer long. Remark at the revolutionary
tribunal (14 October 1793),
op. cit.

6 History is busy with us. Ibid.

7 All have contributed to our downfall; the reformers have urged it like mad people, and
others through ambition, for the wildest Jacobin
seeks wealth and office, and the mob is eager
for plunder. There is not one real patriot among
all this infamous horde. the emigrant party have
their intrigues and schemes; foreigners seek to
profit by the dissensions of France; every one
has a share in our misfortunes.
Quoted in *The Memoirs of Marie
Antoinette,*
Ch. 22, *Jeanne Louise Campan*, ed.
1910

*See 578.

589. Renier Giustina Michiel (1755–1832)

1 For me ennui is among the worst evils—I can
bear pain better. Quoted in

*Biography of Distinguished
Women*
by Sarah Josepha Hale* *1876*

*See 703.

2 The world improves people according to the
dispositions they bring into it. Ibid.

3 Time is a better comforter than reflection.
Ibid.

590. Sarah Siddons (1755–1831)

1 I am, as you may observe, acting again: but
how much difficulty to get my money! Sheridan* is certainly the greatest phenomenon that
Nature has produced for centuries. Our theatre
is going on, to the astonishment of everybody.
Very few of the actors are paid, and all are
vowing to withdraw themselves: yet still we go
on. Sheridan is certainly omnipotent.
Letter to a friend
(9 November 1796),
Quoted in *Life of Mrs. Siddons,* Vol. II,
by Thomas Campbell *1834*

*Richard Brinsley Sheridan (1751–1816), playwright es-
pecially noted for *The School for Scandal*, and manager of
the Drury Lane Theatre in London.

2 . . . I know, by sad experience, with what
difficulty a mind, weakened by long and uninterrupted suffering, admits hope, much less
assurance. Letter to Mrs. FitzHugh
(14 July 1801),
from Preston, op. cit.

3 I pant for retirement and leisure, but am doomed
to inexpressible and almost unsupportable
hurry. Letter to Rev. Sedgwick
Whalley (21 June 1784),
from Dublin,
Quoted in *Journals and
Correspondence of Thomas
Sedgwick Whalley,*
Vol. I, Rev. Hill Wickham, ed.
1863

4 This woman* is one of those monsters (I think
them) of perfection, who is an angel before her
time, and is so entirely resigned to the will of
heaven, that (to a very mortal like myself) she
appears to be the most provoking piece of still
life one ever had the misfortune to meet.
Letter to Rev. Whalley
(c. 1787), op. cit.

*The lead character in a new play by Bertie Greatheed.

5 . . . sorry am I to say I have often observed,
that I have performed worst when I most ar-
dently wished to do better than ever.
Letter to Rev. Whalley
(16 July 1781), from Bristol,
Quoted in *The Kembles,*

Vol. I, by Percy
Fitzgerald   *1871*

6 [I] . . . commenced my study of Lady Mac-
beth. As the character is very short, I thought I
should soon accomplish it. Being then only
twenty years of age, I believed, as many others
do believe, that little more was necessary than
to get the words into my head, for the necessity
of discrimination, and the development of character, at that time of my life, had scarcely
entered into my imagination.
Recollection (1785),
op. cit.

7 I have paid severely for eminence.
Letter to the Rev. and Mrs.
Whalley (15 March 1785),
op. cit.

8 Alas! How wretched is the being who depends
on the stability of public favour!
The Reminiscences of Sarah
Kemble Siddons (1824),
William Van Lennep, ed.
1942 reprint

9 The awful consciousness that one is the sole
object of attention to that imense space, lined
as it were with human intellect from top to
bottom, and on all sides round, may perhaps be
imagined but can not be described, and never
never to be forgotten. . . .   Ibid.

10 Alas, why had I enemies, but because to be
prosperous is sufficient cause for enmity.
Ibid.

11 . . . I believe one half of the world is born for
the convenience of the other half. . . .
Letter to Hester Lynch Piozzi*
(27 August 1794),
Quoted in *Sarah Siddons,*
Portrait of an Actress,
Ch. 5, by Roger Manvell
1970

*See 543.

591. Elisabeth Vigée-Lebrun (1755–1842)

1 I was so fortunate as to be on very pleasant
terms with the Queen [Marie Antoinette].* When
she heard that I had something of a voice we
rarely had a sitting without singing some duets
. . . together, for she was exceedingly fond of
music. . . .
Memoirs of Madame Vigée-Lebrun
(1835),
Lionel Strachey, tr.   *1907*

*See 588. Vigée-Lebrun painted several portraits of the
queen, beginning in 1779.

2 The women reigned then; the Revolution dethroned them.   Ibid.

592. Eliza Wilkinson (c. 1755–?)

1 . . . they [soldiers] really merit every thing,
who will fight from principle alone; for from
what I could learn, these poor creatures had
nothing to protect them, and seldom got their
pay; yet with what alacrity will they encounter
danger and hardships of every kind!
Quoted in *The Women of*
the American Revolution,
Vol. II, by Elizabeth F. Ellet
1848

593. Henrietta Luxborough (?–1756)

1 Yon bullfinch, with unvaried tone,
Of cadence harsh, and accent shrill,
Has brighter plumage to atone
For want of harmony and skill.
"The Bullfinch in Town," St. 2,
A Collection of Poems. By Several Hands,
Robert Dodsley, ed.   *1748*

594. Hester Ann Rogers (1756–1794)

1 What I suffered is known only to God.
Quoted in *The Women of*
Methodism: Its Three
Foundress . . .
by Abel Stevens   *1866*

595. Anna Young Smith (1756–1780?)

1 Blest be this humble strain if it imparts
The dawn of peace to but one pensive breast
"An Elegy to the Memory of the
American Volunteers, who Fell
in the Engagement Between the
Massachusetts-Bay Militia, and
the British Troops.
April 19, 1775,"
St. 9 (2 May 1775),
Philadelphia,
Pennsylvania Magazine
June 1775

2 But should we know as much as they,
They fear their empire would decay;
For they know women heretofore
Gained victories, and envied laurel's war.
And now they fear we'll once again
Ambitious be to reign,
And so invade the territories of the brain.
Sylvia's Complaint of her Sex's
Unhappiness   1788

3 But now, so oft filth chokes thy sprightly
fire,
We loathe one instant, and the next admire—

Even while we laugh, we mourn thy wit's
abuse,
And while we praise thy talents, scorn their
use.   "On Reading Swift's* Works"
(1774), Philadelphia,
Universal Asylum & Columbian Magazine
September 1790

*Jonathan Swift, English satirist (1667–1745).

4 Teach my unskilled mind to sing
The feelings of my heart.   "An Ode to
Gratitude,"
Pt. 1 (1770), Philadelphia,
Women Poets in Pre-
Revolutionary America,
Pattie Cowell, ed.   *1981*

5 Oh Sensibility divine!   "Ode to
Sensibility,"
Pt. 1 (1774), Philadelphia,
op. cit.

596. Augusta (1757–1831)

1 How can his [Napoleon's] conscience be quite
in abeyance, with so many thousands of lives
sacrificed to his insane ambition? What would I
not give to read his inner thoughts. If he will
ever awake from his mad dream of power, God
only knows, Who has permitted him to become
the scourge of the nations of the earth.
Diary entry (26 January 1813),
In Napoleonic Days, Extracts
from the private diary of Augusta,
Duchess of Saxe-Coburg-Saalfeld,
Queen Victoria's* maternal grandmother,
1806–1821,
H. R. H., the Princess Beatrice,
ed. and tr.   *1941*

*See 836.

2 When one gets old one is so thankful to be
quiet.   Diary entry (19 December 1817),
op. cit.

597. Georgiana Cavendish (1757–1806)

1 Their Liberty requir'd no rites uncouth,
No blood demanded, and no slaves enchain'd;
Her rule was gentle, and her voice was truth,
By social order form'd, by law restrain'd.
Passage of the Mountain of Saint
Gothard, St. 26
1802

598. Hannah Webster Foster (1758/59–1840)

1 An unusual sensation possesses my breast—a
sensation which I once thought could never

pervade it on any occasion whatever. It is *plea-*
sure, pleasure, my dear Lucy, on leaving my
paternal roof.
The Coquette; or, The History of
Eliza Wharton,
Letter I   *1797*

2 In whatever situation we are placed, our greater
or less degree of happiness must be derived
from ourselves. Happiness is in a great measure the result of our own dispositions and
actions.   Ibid., Letter XXI

3 If the conviction of any misconduct on your part
gives you pain, dissipate it by the reflection that
unerring rectitude is not the lot of mortals; that
few are to be found who have not deviated, in
a greater or less degree, from the maxims of
prudence. Our greatest mistakes may teach lessons which will be useful through life.
Ibid., Letter XLIII

4 How can that be a diversion which racks the
soul with grief, even though that grief be imaginary? The introduction of a funeral solemnity
upon the stage is shocking indeed!
Ibid., Letter LII

599. Elizabeth Hamilton (1758?–1816)

1 "Those who wait till evening for sunrise," said
Mrs. Mason, "will find that they have lost the
day."   Ch. 8, *The Cottagers of*
Glenburnie: A Tale for the
Farmer's Ingle-nook   1808

2 Of a' roads to happiness ever were tried,
There's nane half so sure as ane's ain fireside.
My ain fireside, my ain fireside,
O there's naught to compare wi' ane's ain
fireside.   "My Ain Fireside,"
Scottish Song,
Mary Carlyle Aitken, ed.
1874

3 With expectation beating high,
Myself I now desire to spy;
And straight I in a glass surveyed
An antique lady, much decayed   Untitled,
Quoted in *Biography of*
Distinguished Women
by Sarah Josepha Hale*   *1876*

*See 703.

4 It is only by the love of reading that the evil
resulting from the association with *little* minds
can be counteracted.
"The Benefits of Society,"
Private Letters   n.d.

5 I perfectly agree with you in considering castles
in the air as more useful edifices than they are
generally allowed to be. It is only plodding

matter-of-fact dullness that cannot comprehend
their use.   "Imagination,"
op. cit.

600. Esther Hayden (?–1758)

1 I'm sore distress'd, and greatly 'press'd
With filthy Nature, Sin;
I cannot rise to view the Prize
Of happiness within.   Untitled,
*A Short Account of the Life,
Death and Character of Esther
Hayden, the Wife of Samuel
Hayden of Braintree*
[Mass.]   *1759*

601. Henrietta O'Neill (1758–1793)

1 Hail, lovely blossom! thou canst ease
The wretched victims of Disease;
Canst close those weary eyes in gentle sleep,
Which never open but to weep;
For oh! thy potent charm
Can agonizing Pain disarm;
Expel imperious Memory from her seat,
And bid the throbbing heart forget to beat.
"Ode to the Poppy,"
St. 5,
Quoted in *Elegaic Sonnets
and Other Essays,*
Charlotte Smith, ed.   *1782*

602. Mary Robinson (1758–1800)

1 Yet when love and hope are vanished,
Restless memory never dies.
"Stanzas, written between Dover
& Calais," St. 4,
Poems   *1775*

2 I have wept to see thee weep.   Ibid., St. 13

3 The Snow-drop, Winter's timid child,
Awakes to life, bedew'd with tears.
"The Snow-Drop,"
St. 1, op. cit.

603. Jane West (1758–1852)

1 Great and sudden reverses of fortune are not
frequent; yet little disappointments hourly occur,
which fall with the greatest severity on those,
whose amiable, though dangerous enthusiasm,
induces them to expect too much, and to feel
too severely.   Preface,
*The Advantage of Education; or,
The History of Maria Williams, a*

*tale for Misses and their
Mammas,* Vol. I
1793

2 ". . . your newly acquired taste for reading,
prevents even the hazard of your ever perceiving
time to be an intolerable burden."
Ibid., Ch. 7

3 Oh! gather in life's early prime,
The produce which despises time;
Waste not in pleasure's soothing bowers
Youth's irrecoverable hours   Ibid., Ch. 13,
Untitled poem, St. 4

4 It is in the power of cunning to affect simplicity,
but simplicity itself, when it would assume art,
finds it too thin a disguise.
Ibid., Vol. II, Ch. 1

5 When virtue loses its abhorrence of vice, she
dismisses one of her most vigilant guards. Let
but self-interest surmount principle, and her ruin
is compleat.   Ibid., Ch. 3

6 There are some secrets which scarcely admit of
being disclosed even to ourselves.
A Gossip's Story,
Vol. I, Ch. 8   *1797*

7 As wise people often defeat their aims by too
great caution, cunning also frequently over-
shoots the mark by too much craft.
Ibid., Ch. 11

8 Man, lord of all, beneath the reign of time,
Awaits perfection in a nobler clime.
Ibid., Vol. II, Ch. 24,
"To a Rose Bush"

9 "How disgraceful are these baby quarrels! how
ridiculous these high theatrical passions, which
subject them to the laugh of the neighbourhood!
nay, worse, which point out to artful villany,
means whereby it may *effectually* undermine
domestick happiness."   Ibid., Ch. 31

10 Early in life, before his character was formed,
or his opinions methodized, Mr. Clermont entered into marriage; with vague, floating ideas
of angelick goodness, and consummate bliss. In
proportion as his romantick enthusiasm had raised
the mortal nymph into a goddess, his cooler,
but not more accurate judgment, as the infatu-
ation of love subsided, magnified her errors into
indelible offences.   Ibid., Ch. 35

604. Martha Wilson (1758–post-1848)

1 . . . let it never be forgotten by you that the
reputation established by a boy at school and
college, whether it be of merit or demerit, will
follow him through life.
Letter to C. S. Stewart, her
nephew and adopted son

(16 February 1811),
Quoted in *The Women of the
American Revolution,*
Vol, II, by Elizabeth F. Ellet
1848

2 Press forward, my dear son, in the ways of wisdom—they are ways of pleasantness, and their end is peace.   Letter to C. S. Stewart
(31 May 1814), op. cit.

3 Industry is the handmaid of good fortune. . . .   Ibid.

4 Man can do much for himself as respects his own improvement, unless self-love so blinds him that he cannot see his own imperfections and weaknesses.   Ibid.

5 The exercise of a little self-denial for the time being will be followed by the pleasure of having achieved the greatest of triumphs—a triumph over one's self.   Ibid.

605. Agnes Craig (1759–1841)

1 Talk not of love, it gives me pain,
For love has been my foe;
He bound me with an iron chain,
And plunged me deep in woe.
But friendship's pure and lasting joys,
My heart was formed to prove.
"Talk Not of Love,"
Scottish Song,
Mary Carlyle Aitken, ed.
1874

606. Sarah Wentworth Morton (1759–1846)

1 When life hung quiv'ring on a single hair
"To Constantia," St. 1,
*Massachusetts Magazine
May 1790*

2 To the mere superficial observer, it would seem that man was sent into this breathing world for the purpose of enjoyment—woman for that of trial and of suffering.   "The Sexes,"
My Mind and Its Thoughts   1823

3 More prized than wealth; than worlds more
dear   "Lines to the Breath of Kindness,"
St. 2, op. cit.

4 Expression in its finest utterance lives,
And a new language to creation gives.
"To Mr. [Gilbert] Stuart.* Upon
Seeing Those Portraits Which
were Painted by Him at
Philadelphia, in the Beginning of
the Present Century,"
St. 1, op. cit.

*Famed American portrait painter (1755–1828).

5 Did all the Gods of Afric sleep,
Forgetful of their guardian love,
When the white tyrants of the deep
Betrayed him in the palmy grove?
"The African Chief,"
St. 2, op. cit.

607. Martha Laurens Ramsay (1759–1811)

1 . . . the bucks, the fops, the idlers of college. . . .   *Letters to her Son at college
n.d.*

2 . . . of all the mean objects in creation, a lazy, poor, proud gentleman, especially if he is a dressy fellow, is the meanest. . . .   Ibid.

608. Anna Green Winslow (1759–1780)

1 Those golden arts* the vulgar never knew.
"To her Parents"
(17 March 1772),
*Diary of Anna Green Winslow:
A Boston School Girl of 1771,*
Alice Morse Earle, ed.   *1895*

*Virtues.

609. Mary Wollstonecraft (1759–1797)

1 Perhaps the seeds of false-refinement, immorality, and vanity, have ever been shed by the great. Weak, artificial beings, raised above the common wants and defections of their race, in a premature unnatural manner, undermine the very foundation of virtue, and spread corruption through the whole mass of society!
Introduction to 1st ed.,
*A Vindication of the Rights of
Women   1792*

2 . . . elegance is inferior to virtue. . . .
Ibid.

3 The mind will ever be unstable that has only prejudices to rest on, and the current will run with destructive fury when there are no barriers to break its force.
"The Prevailing Opinion of a
Sexual Character Discussed,"
op. cit.

4 . . . as blind obedience is ever sought for by power, tyrants and sensualists are in the right when they endeavour to keep women in the dark, because the former only want slaves, and the latter a play-thing.   Ibid.

5 But when forebearance confounds right and wrong, it ceases to be a virtue. . . .   Ibid.

6 . . . females . . . have been stripped of the virtues that should clothe humanity . . . their sole ambition is to be fair, to raise emotion instead of inspiring respect; and this ignoble desire, like the servility in absolute monarchies, destroys all strength of character. *Ibid.*

7 From the respect paid to property flow, as from a poisoned fountain, most of the evils and vices which render this world such a dreary scene to the contemplative mind.
"Of the Pernicious Effects which Arise from the Unnatural Distinctions Established in Society," *op. cit.*

8 The preposterous distinctions of rank, which renders civilization a curse by dividing the world between voluptuous tyrants and cunning envious dependents, corrupt, almost equally, every class of people. . . . *Ibid.*

9 When poverty is more disgraceful than even vice, is not morality cut to the quick? *Ibid.*

10 It is a melancholy truth—yet such is the blessed effect of civilization!—the most respectable women are the most repressed. . . . *Ibid.*

11 Would man but generously snap our chains, and be content with rational fellowship instead of slavish obedience, they would find us more observant daughters, more affectionate sisters, more faithful wives, more reasonable mothers—in a word, better citizens. We should then love them with true affection, because we should learn to respect ourselves. . . . *Ibid.*

12 But a child, though a pledge of affection, will not enliven it, if both father and mother be content to transfer the charge to hirelings; for they who do their duty by proxy should not murmur if they miss the reward of duty—parental affection produces filial duty.
"Parental Affection," *op. cit.*

13 I . . . think schools, as they are now regulated, the hot-beds of vice and folly, and the knowledge of human nature supposedly attained there, merely cunning selfishness. "On National Education," *op. cit.*

14 . . . only that education deserves emphatically to be termed cultivation of mind which teaches young people how to begin to think. *Ibid.*

15 The imagination should not be allowed to debauch the understanding before it gains strength, or vanity will become the forerunner of vice: for every way of exhibiting the acquirements of a child is injurious to its moral character. *Ibid.*

16 How I hate this crooked business! This intercourse with the world, which obliges one to see the worst side of human nature! Letter XXX (29 December 1794), *Letters to Imlay* * *n.d.*

*Captain Gilbert Imlay, her lover.

17 Society fatigues me inexpressibly. So much so, that finding fault with everyone, I have only reason enough to discover that the fault is in myself. *Ibid.*, Letter XXXVII (19 February 1795)

18 I never wanted but your heart—That gone, you have nothing more to give. *Ibid.*, Letter LXX, London (November 1795)

19 I begin to love this little creature, and to anticipate his birth as a fresh twist to a knot, which I do not wish to untie. Letter to William Godwin, her husband (March 1797), Quoted in *Godwin and Mary* by Ralph M. Wardle 1966

610. Sally Sayward Wood (1759–1855)

1 Amelia was not a disciple of Mary Woolstonecraft* [sic], she was not a woman of fashion, nor a woman of spirit. She was an oldfashioned wife, and she meant to obey her husband: she meant to do her duty in the strictest sense of the word. *Amelia; or, the Influence of Virtue* 1802

*See 609.

611. Margaret Shippen Arnold (1760–1804)

1 . . . my ambition has sunk with my fortune. Letter to E. Burd (15 August 1801), Quoted in "Life of Margaret Shippen" by Lewis Burd Walker, *Pennsylvania Magazine of History and Biography*, Vol. XXV 1901

2 At one period, when I viewed everything through a false medium, I fancied that nothing but the sacrifice of my life would benefit my children, for that my wretchedness embittered every moment of their lives; and dreadful to say, I was many times on the point of making the sacrifice. Letter to her father (1801), *op. cit.*

612. Charlotte Charke (?–1760)

1 Your two Friends, PRUDENCE and REFLECTION, I am inform'd, have lately ventur'd to

pay you a Visit; for which I heartily congratulate you, as nothing can possibly be more joyous to the Heart than the Return of absent Friends, after a long and painful Peregrination.
Dedication,
A Narrative of the Life of Mrs.
Charlotte Charke　1755

2 'Tis every Parent's Duty to breed their Children with every Advantage their Fortunes will admit of. . . .　　　　　　　　　Text, op. cit.

3 . . . forced again to . . . find fresh means of Subsistence . . . 'till even the last thread of Invention was worn out.　　　　　　　Ibid.

4 Misfortunes are too apt to wear out Friendship. . . .　　　　　　　　　Ibid.

613. Rebecca Franks (c. 1760–1823)

1 I have gloried in my rebel countrymen! Would to God I, too, had been a patriot!
Remark to General Winfield
Scott (c. 1816),
Quoted in *Rebecca Franks: An*
American Jewish Belle of the
Last Century
by Max J. Kohler
1894

614. Anne Douglas Howard (?–1760)

1 Nothing so like as male and female youth;
Nothing so like as man and woman old
A defence of her sex in answer
to [Alexander] Pope's
"Characters of Women,"
The British Female Poets,
George W. Bethune, ed.　*1848*

2 In education all the difference lies; . . .
Ibid.

3 Culture improves all fruits, all sorts we find,
Wit, judgment, sense, fruits of the human mind.　　　　　　　　　　　　　Ibid.

615. Dicey Langston (1760?–?)

1 Shoot me if you dare! I will not tell you.*
Quoted by the Hon. B. F. Perry
in *The Women*
of the American Revolution,
Vol. II, by Elizabeth F. Ellet
1848

*Response to a Loyalist's demand for intelligence concerning the Whigs; Langston was 16 years old at the time.

616. Mary Slocumb (1760–1836)

1 Allow me to observe and prophesy, the only land in these United States which will ever

remain in possession of a British officer, will measure but six feet by two.
Remark to a British colonel,
Quoted in *Women of the*
American Revolution,
Vol. II, by Elizabeth F. Ellet
1848

2 My husband is not a man who would allow a duke, or even a king, to have a quiet [titled] seat upon his ground.　　　　　　　Ibid.

617. Anne Yearsley (1760–1806)

1 Earth by the grizzly tyrant desert made,
The feathered warblers quit the leafless shade;
Quit those dear scenes where life and love began,
And, cheerless seek the savage haunts of man.
"Clifton Hill,"
St. 1 (January 1785),
The British Female Poets,
George W. Bethune, ed.　*1848*

2 All Nature's sweets in joyous circles move
And wake the frozen soul again to love.
Ibid., St. 2

3 The portals of the swelling soul ne'er ope'd
By liberal converse, rude ideas strove
Awhile for vent, but found it not, and died.
Thus rust the minds' best powers.
"A Poem on Mrs. Montague," *
The Female Poets of Great Britain,
Frederic Rowton, ed.　*1853*

*Mary Wortley Montague. See 458.

618. Joanna Baillie (1762–1851)

1 O! who shall lightly say that fame
Is nothing but an empty name?
"The Legend of Christopher
Columbus,"
St. lix, *Fugitive Verses*
1790

2 O lovely Sisters! is it true
That they are all inspired by you,
And write by inward magic charm'd,
And high enthusiasm warm'd?
"Address to the Muses,"
St. xi, op. cit.

3 "Ah! happy is the man whose early lot
Hath made him master of a furnish'd cot;
Who trains the vine that round his window grows,
And after setting sun his garden hoes;
Whose wattled pails his own enclosure shield,
Who toils not daily in another's field."
"A Reverie,"
St. iii, op. cit.

4 "What hollow sound is that?" approaching near,
The roar of many wheels breaks on his ear.
It is the flood of human life in motion!
"London,"
St. iii, op. cit.

5 Sweet bud of promise, fresh and fair,
Just moving in the morning air.
The morn of life but just begun,
The sands of time just set to run!
Sweet babe with cheek of pinky hue,
With eyes of soft ethereal blue,
With raven hair like finest down
Of unfledged bird, and scant'ly shown
Beneath the cap of cumbrous lace,
That circles round thy placid face!
Ah, baby! little dost thou know
How many yearning bosoms glow,
How many lips in blessings move,
How many eyes beam looks of love
At sight of thee!
"To Sophia J. Baillie, an Infant,"
in toto, op. cit.

6 Busy work brings after ease;
Ease brings sport and sport brings rest;
For young and old, of all degrees,
The mingled lot is best.   "Rhymes,"
St. i, op. cit.

7 GEOFFRY. Some men are born to feast and not to fight:
Whose sluggish minds, e'en in fair honours field
Still on their dinner turn—
Let such pot-boiling varlets stay at home,
And wield a flesh-hook rather than a sword.
Basil,
Act I, Sc. 1   1798

8 What custom hath endeared
We part with sadly, tho we prize it not.
Ibid., Sc. 2

9 DUKE. But int'rest, int'rest, man's all-ruling pow'r. . . .   Ibid., Act II, Sc. 3

10 COUNTESS OF ALBINI. For she who only finds her self-esteem
In other's admiration, begs in alms;
Depends on others for her daily food,
And is the very servant of her slaves. . . .
Ibid., Sc. 4

11 COUNT ROSINBERG. The brave man is not he who feels no fear,
For that were stupid and irrational;
But he, whose noble soul its fear subdues,
And barely dares the danger nature shrinks from.   Ibid., Act III, Sc. 1

12 SONG. Child, with many a childish wile,
Timid look, and blushing smile,
Downy wings to steal thy way,

Gilded bow, and quiver gay,
Who in thy simple mien would trace
The tyrant of the human race?   Ibid., Sc. 3

13 Thinks't thou there are no serpents in the world
But those that slide along the grassy sod,
And sting the luckless foot that presses them?
There are who in the path of social life
Do bask their spotted skins in Fortune's sun,
And sting the soul.   De Monfort,
Act I, Sc. 2   1798

14 A willing heart adds feather to the heel.
Ibid., Act III, Sc. 2

15 MR. HARWOOD. . . . the more fools speak the more people will despise them. . . .
The Trial,
Act I, Sc. 2   1798

16 COL. HARDY. It is so seldom that a young fellow has any inclination for the company of an old man. . . .   Ibid., Act IV, Sc. 1

17 COL. HARDY. Nay, heaven defend us from a violent woman; for that is the devil himself!
Ibid.

18 The bliss e'en of a moment still is bliss.
The Beacon,
Act I, Sc. 2   1802

19 ETHWALD. He who will not give
Some portion of his ease, his blood, his wealth,
For other's good is a poor frozen churl.
Ethwald, Part Second,
Act I, Sc. 2   1802

20 SIR CRAFTY SUPPLECOAT. Pride is a fault that great men blush not to own: it is the ennobled offspring of self-love; though, it must be confessed, grave and pompous vanity, like a fat plebeian in a rove of office, does very often assume its name.   The Second Marriage,
Act II, Sc. 4   1802

21 MORGAN. . . . there is nothing but young people now in the world.   Ibid., Act III, Sc. 1

22 MAHOMET. In mortal man
I have no trust; they are all hollow slaves,
Who tremble and detest, and would betray.
Constantine Paleologus,
Act III, Sc. 2   1804

23 RODRIGO. How do men act, when they together stand, on the last perch of this swiftly-sinking wreck?
Do they not bravely give their parting cheer,
And make their last voice loud and boldly sound
Amidst the hollow roarings of the storm?
Ibid., Act V, Sc. 1

24 OTHUS. . . . heaven ofttimes
Success bestows where blessing is denied.
                              Ibid., Sc. 3

25 WORSHIPTON. Curse your snug comfortable ways
of living! my soul abhors the idea of it. I'll pack
up all I have in a knapsack first, and join the
wild Indians in America.   *The Country Inn*,
          Act V, Sc. 2   *1804*

26 The mind doth shape itself to its own wants
And can bear all things.   *Rayner*   *1804*

27 Still on it creeps,
Each little moment at another's heels,
Till hours, days, years, and ages are made up
Of such small parts as these, and men look
     back
Worn and bewilder'd, wondering how it is.
                              Ibid.

28 RAYNER. . . . I have observ'd
That those who bear misfortunes overmeekly
Do but persuade mankind that they and want
     are all too fitly match'd to be
disjoin'd. . . .   Ibid., Act I, Sc. 1

29 EARL OF ARGYLL. That day will come,
When in the grave this hoary head of mine,
And many after heads, in death are laid;
And happier men, our sons, shall live to see
     it.
O may they prize it too with grateful hearts;
And, looking back on these our stormy days
Of other years, pity, admire, and pardon
The fierce, contentious, ill-directed valour
Of gallant fathers, born in darker time!
                   The Family Legend,
          Act V, Sc. 4   *1810*

30 BALTIMORE. O! hang them, but they won't laugh!
I have seen the day, when, if a man made
himself ridiculous, the world would laugh at
him. But now, everything that is mean, disgusting, and absurd, pleases them but so much
the better!   *The Election*,
          Act I, Sc. 2   *1811*

31 Pampered vanity is a better thing perhaps than
starved pride.   Ibid., Act II, Sc. 2

32 CHARLOTTE. I wish I were with some of the
wild people that run in the woods, and know
nothing about accomplishments!
                              Ibid., Act III, Sc. 3

33 ORRA. Can spirit from the tomb, or fiend from
     Hell,
More hateful, more malignant be than man?
                   Orra, Act III, Sc. 2
                              1812

34 ORRA. He was not all a father's heart could
     wish;
But oh, he was my son!—my only son.   Ibid.

35 CRAFTON. Fy, fy! let no man be on his knees
but when he is at his prayers.
                   The Alienated Manor,
          Act V, Sc. 2   *1836*

36 SANCHO. Me care for te laws when te laws care
for me.   Ibid.

37 ARTINA. Misfortune is not dainty in associ-
ates.   *The Bride*,
          Act I, Sc. 2   *1836*

38 SONG. Sweet sleep be with us, one and all!
And if upon its stillness fall
The visions of a busy brain,
We'll have our pleasure o'er again,
To warm the heart, to charm the sight,
Gay dreams to all! good night, good night.
                   The Phantom   *1836*

39 ROBINAIR. This will be triumph! this will be
happiness! yea, that very thing, happiness, which
I have been pursuing all my life, and have never
yet overtaken.   *The Stripling*,
          Act IV, Sc. 1   *1836*

40 Words of affection, howso'er express'd,
The latest spoken still are deem'd the best.
          "Address to Miss Agnes Baillie
               on Her Birthday,"
               ll.125–126,   *n.d.*

41 . . . Some still a thought,
And clip it round the edge, and challenge him
Whose 'twas to swear to it. To serve things
     thus
Is as foul witches to cut up old moons
Into new stars.   *Festus*   *n.d.*

619. Dorothea Jordan (1762–1816)

1 'Oh where, and Oh! where is your Highland
     laddie gone?'
'He's gone to fight the French, for King
     George upon the throne,
And it's Oh! in my heart, how I wish him safe
     at home!'
          "The Blue Bells of Scotland"*   *n.d.*

* Both this and "O Where, Tell Me Where" by Anne Grant
(see 586:2) are variants on an older popular song.

620. Mrs. Lyon (1762–1840)

1. Yet the doctors they do a' agree,
That whiskey's no the drink for me.
Saul! quoth Neil, 'twill spoil my glee,
Should they part me and whiskey, O
          "Neil Gow's Farewell to Whiskey,"
               Scottish Song,
               Mary Carlyle Aitken, ed.
               1874

621. Susanna Haswell Rowson (1762–1824)

1 To raise the fall'n—to pity and forgive,
This is our noblest, best prerogative.
By these, pursuing nature's gentle plan,
We hold—in silken chains—the lordly tyrant
man. *Epilogue,
Slaves in Algiers, or a
Struggle for Freedom 1794*

2 Nay, start not, gentle sirs; indeed, 'tis true,
Poor woman has her rights as well as you;
And if she's wise, she will assert them too.
*"Rights of Women,"
Miscellaneous Poems 1804*

622. Helen Maria Williams (1762–1827)

1 No riches from his scanty store
My lover could impart;
He gave a boon I valued more,
He gave me all his heart. *"Song,"
St. 1,
An Ode to Peace and Other
Poems 1782–1788*

2 The night is dark, the waters deep,
Yet soft the billows roll;
Alas! at every breeze I weep,
The storm is in my soul. *Ibid., St. 5*

3 Come, gentle Hope! with one gay smile
remove
The lasting sadness of an aching heart.
*"Sonnet to Hope,"
Poems, moral, elegant and
pathetic: viz. Essay on Man, by
Pope . . . And Original Sonnets by
Helen Maria Williams 1796*

4 Thy light can visionary thoughts impart,
And lead the Muse to soothe a suffering
heart. *"Sonnet to the Moon,"
op. cit.*

623. Josephine (1763–1814)

1 Trust to me, ladies, and do not envy a splendor
which does not constitute happiness.
*Quoted in Lives of Celebrated Women
by Samuel Griswold Goodrich
1844*

2 . . . patience and goodness will ever in the end
conciliate the goodwill of others.
*Letter to her children (1794),
op. cit.*

624. Anne Willing Bingham (1764–1801)

1 The women of France interfere in the politics
of the Country, and often give a decided Turn
to the Fate of Empires.

*Letter to Thomas Jefferson
(c.1783–1786),
Quoted in The Papers of
Thomas Jefferson,
Vol. XI, Julian P. Boyd, ed.
1955*

625. Catherine Rilliet-Huber (1764–?)

1 All I can say is that she [Germaine de Staël*]
is as lively and brilliant as ever—which proves
the advantage of organizing one's heart in a
system of multiple hiding places.
*Letter to Henri Meister
(13 November 1810),
Quoted in Mistress to an Age: A
Life of Madame de Staël
by J. Christopher Herold
1958*

*See 637.

626. Juliana Krudener (1764–1824)

1 Stay quiet; refuse nothing; flowers grow only
because they tranquilly allow the sun's rays to
reach them. You must do the same.
Remark to Germaine de Staël,
Quoted in Mistress to an Age: A
Life of Madame de Staël
by J. Christopher Herold
1958*

*See 637.

627. Mary Ann Lamb (1764–1847)

1 Who, that e'er could understand
The rare structure of a hand,
With its branching fingers fine,
Work itself of hands divine,
Strong, yet delicately knit,
For ten thousand uses fit *"Cleanliness,"
Poetry for Children 1809*

2 His conscience slept a day or two,
As it is very apt to do
*"The Boy and the Skylark,"
I, St. 5, op. cit.*

3 An infant is a selfish sprite
*"The Broken Doll,"
St. 1, op. cit.*

4 Reproof a parent's province is;
A sister's discipline is this;
By studied kindness to effect
A little brother's young respect. *Ibid., St. 3*

5 This place, methinks, resembleth well
The world itself in which we dwell.

Perils and snares on every ground,
Like these wild beasts, beset us round.
"The Beasts in the Tower," *
II, St. 2, op. cit.

*I.e., the cages in a zoo.

6 A child is fed with milk and praise.
"The First Tooth,"
Brother, op. cit.

7 Shut these odious books up, brother—
They have made you quite another
Thing from what you used to be;
Once you liked to play with me. . . .
"The Sister's Expostulation on
the Brother's Learning Latin,"
op. cit.

8 Know ye not, each thing we prize
Does from small beginnings rise?
"The Brother's Reply,"
I, op. cit.

9 O happy town-bred girl, in fine chaise going
For the first time to see the green grass
growing!
"The First Sight of Green Fields,"
op. cit.

10 Honey and locusts were his* food,
And he was most severely good.
"Salome," **
St. 3 (1808/09), op. cit.

*John the Baptist.
**See 38.

11 A child's a plaything for an hour.
"Parental Recollections," op. cit.

12 Thou straggler into loving arms,
Young climber up of knees,
When I forget thy thousand ways,
Then life and all shall cease.   "A Child,"
St. 3, op. cit.

13 . . . I do not expect or want you to be otherwise
than you are, I love you for the good that is in
you, and look for no change.
Letter to Sarah Stoddart
(21 September 1803),
The Letters of Charles and Mary Lamb,
Vol. II, 1801–1809,
Edwin W. Marrs, Jr., ed.
1976

14 . . . by secrecy I mean you both want the habit
of telling each other at the moment everything
that happens,—where you go—and what you
do—that free communication of letters and opinions, just as they arise, as Charles [her brother]
and I do, and which is after all the only ground-
work of friendship. . . .   Ibid.

15 . . . I never have the power of altering or
amending anything I have once laid aside with
dissatisfaction.   Letter to Dorothy

Wordsworth* (7 May 1805),
op. cit.

*See 661.

16 . . . I have lost all self confidence in my own
actions & one cause of my low spirits is that I
never feel satisfied with any thing I do—a perception of not being in a sane state perpetually
haunts me.   Letter to Sarah
Stoddart (9–14 November 1805),
op. cit.

17 It is but being once thourowly [sic] convinced
one is wrong, to make one resolve to do so no
more. . . .   Letter to Sarah Stoddart
(14 March 1806),
op. cit.

18 Our love for each other* has been the torment
of our lives hitherto. I am most seriously in-
tending to bend the whole force of my mind to
counteract this, and I think I see some prospect
of success.   Ibid.

*Referring to her brother Charles Lamb, English essayist
(1775–1834).

19 I have known many single men I should have
liked in my life (if it had suited them) for a
husband: but very few husbands have I ever
wished was mine which is rather against the
state [of marriage] in general [so] that one is
never disposed to envy their wives their good husbands, So much for marrying—but however get
married if you can.
Letter to Sarah Stoddart
(30 May–2 June 1806), op. cit.

20 If you fancy a very young man, and he likes an
elderly gentlewoman, if he likes a learned &
accomplished lady, and you like a not very
learned youth who may need a little polishing
which probably he will never acquire; it is all
very well & God bless you both together & may
you both be very long in the same mind.
Letter to Sarah
Stoddart (23 October 1806),
op. cit.

21 . . . you must begin the world with ready
money. . . .   Letter to Sarah Stoddart
(21? December 1807),
op. cit.

628. Ann Radcliffe (1764–1823)

1 At first a small line of inconceivable splendour
emerged on the horizon, which, quickly expanding, the sun appeared in all of his glory,
unveiling the whole face of nature, vivifying
every colour of the landscape, and sprinkling
the dewy earth with glittering light. The low
and gentle responses of the birds, awakened by

the morning ray, now broke the silence of the hour, their soft warbling rising by degrees till they swelled the chorus of universal gladness.   *The Romance of the Forest   1791*

2 "We in Italy are not so apt to despair. . . ."   *The Italian   1797*

3 "From my mind the illusion which gave spirit to the colouring of nature is fading fast. . . ."   *Gaston de Blondeville   1826*

4 Then let me stand amidst thy glooms profound
On some wild woody steep, and hear the breeze   "Night,"
St. 8, *Poems 1834*

629. Sun Yün-fêng (1764–1814)

1 Under the waning moon
In the dawn—
A frosty bell.   "Starting At Dawn,"
*The Orchid Boat,
Women Poets of China,*
Kenneth Rexroth and Ling Chung, eds. and trs.   *1972*

2 Along the shore the willows
Wait for their Spring green.
"On the Road Through Chang-te,"
op. cit.

630. Catherine Marie Fanshawe (1765–1834)

1 'Twas whisper'd in heaven, 'twas mutter'd in hell,
And echo caught faintly the sound as it fell;
On the confines of earth 'twas permitted to rest,
And the depths of the ocean its presence confess'd.   "Enigma: The Letter H,"
Memorials   1865

2 At their speed behold advancing
Modern men and women dancing;
Step and dress alike express
Above, below from heel to toe,
Male and female awkwardness.
"The Abrogation of the Birth-Night Ball,"
op. cit.

631. Emma Hamilton (1765–1815)

1 When she [her daughter] comes and looks in my face and calls me "mother," indead [sic] I then truly am a mother. . . .

Letter to Charles Greville (June 1774),
Quoted in *Memoirs of Emma, Lady Hamilton   1815*

632. Ho Xuan Huong (fl. 1765–1799)

1 I am like a jackfruit on the tree.
To taste you must plug me quick, while fresh:
the skin rough, the pulp thick, yes,
but oh, I warn you against touching—
the rich juice will gush and stain your hands.   "The Jackfruit," in toto,
A Thousand Years of Vietnamese Poetry,
Nguyen Ngoc Bich, ed. and tr.   *1975*

2 Pray hard: you too can be a Superior
And squat, proud, on a lotus.
"A Buddhist Priest,"
Nguyen Ngoc Bich and Burton Raffel, trs., op. cit.

633. Nancy Storace (1765–1815)

1 I have as good a right to show the power of my *bomba** as any body else.
Quoted in *Queens of Song*
by Ellen Creathorne
Clayton   *1865*

*Tremolo.

634. Barbara Frietschie (1766–1862)

1 "Shoot, if you must, this old gray head
But spare your country's flag"
Attributed, Quoted by John Greenleaf Whittier* in "Barbara Fritchie,"
Atlantic Monthly   October 1863

* American poet (1807–1892).

635. Carolina Nairne (1766–1845)

1 The Laird o' Cockpen, he's proud an' he's great,
His mind is ta'en up wi' things o' the State. . . .   "The Laird o' Cockpen,"
St. 1, *Lays from Strathearn 1846*

2 A penniless lass wi' a lang pedigree.
Ibid., St. 2

3 Oh, ye may ca' them vulgar farin',
Wives and mithers maist despairin',

Ca' them lives o' men.   "Caller* Herrin',"
                                              op. cit.

*Fresh.

4 Wi' a hundred pipers an' a', an' a',
  Wi' a hundred pipers an' a', an' a',
  We'll up an' gie them a blaw, a blaw,
  Wi' a hundred pipers an' a', an' a'.
                          "The Hundred Pipers,"
                                              op. cit.

5 O, Charlie is my darling,
  My darling, my darling;
  Charlie is my darling,
  The young Chevalier.   "Charlie* Is My
                                       Darling,"
                                  Scottish Song,
                              Mary Carlyle Aitken, ed.
                                             1874

*The reference is to Charles Stuart, aka "Bonnie Prince
Charlie" or The Young Pretender (1720–1788).

636. Nancy Dennis Sproat (1766–1826)

1 How pleasant is Saturday night,
  When I've tried all the week to be good,
  Not spoken a word that is bad,
  And obliged every one that I could.
                          "How Pleasant is Saturday
                                    Night"   n.d.

637. Germaine de Staël (1766–1817)

1 . . . inventiveness is childish, practice sublime.   Réflexions sur la paix intérieure
                      [Reflections on Internal Peace]
                                             1795

2 It is obvious that the most despotic forms of
social organization would be suitable for inert
men who are satisfied with the station fate has
placed them in, and that the most abstract form
of democratic theory would be practicable among
sages guided only by their reason. The only
problem is to what degree it is possible to excite
or to contain the passions without endangering
public happiness.   Preface
                              (1 July 1796),
                De l'influence des passions sur le
                     bonheur des individus et des
                    nations [A Treatise on the
                     Influence of the Passions upon
                     the Happiness of Individuals and
                             of Nations]   1796

3 Love is the whole history of a woman's life, it
is but an episode in a man's.   Ibid.

4 Intellect does not attain its full force unless it
attacks power.   De la littérature
                considérée dans ses rapports avec
                     les institutions sociales [The

Influence of Literature upon
                        Society]   1800

5 [Literature has] ceased to be a mere art; it [has]
become a means to an end, a weapon in the
service of the spirit of man.   Ibid.

6 Every time a new nation, America or Russia for
instance, advances toward civilization, the human race perfects itself; every time an inferior
class emerges from enslavement and degradation, the human race again perfects itself.
                                              Ibid.

7 The decadence of empires is no more in the
natural order of things than is the decadence of
literature and science.   Ibid.

8 Happy the land where the writers are sad, the
merchants satisfied, the rich melancholic, and
the populace content.   Ibid.

9 Scientific progress makes moral progress a necessity; for if man's power is increased, the
checks that restrain him from abusing it must
be strengthened.   Ibid.

10 Why should it not be possible some day to
compile tables that would contain the answer to
all questions of a political nature based on statistical knowledge, on positive facts gathered
for every country?   Ibid.

11 Morality must guide calculation, and calculation
must guide politics.   Ibid.

12 The entire social order . . . is arrayed against
a woman who wants to rise to a man's
reputation.   Ibid.

13 Between God and love, I recognize no mediator
but my conscience.   Delphine   1802

14 "Follow me, let this instant decide our lives!
There are decisions that must be made in the
heat of passion, without giving bitter reflections
the time to revive!"   Ibid.

15 A man must know how to defy opinion; a
woman how to submit to it.   Ibid.

16 Kindness and generosity . . . form the true
morality of human actions.
                              "Reflections of the
                          Moral Aim of Delphine,"
                                  op. cit., 2nd ed.

17 She liked to make others' lives as drab as possible, perhaps so as not to feel too much regret
at the dissolution of her own.
                          Corinne, or Italy   1807

18 Fate persecutes the exalted souls, the poets whose
creative power springs from their capacity for
suffering and love.   Ibid.

19 Love, supreme power of the heart, mysterious
enthusiasm that encloses in itself all poetry, all
heroism, all religion!   Ibid.

20 To understand all makes one very indulgent.
Ibid.

21 Love is above the laws, above the opinion of men; it is the truth, the flame, the pure element, the primary idea of the moral world.
Zulma, and Other Tales   1813

22 Magnificence is the characteristic of everything one sees in Russia.   Dix années d'exil
[Ten Years of Exile]   1821

23 Oh, nothing can equal the emotion that a woman feels when she has the happiness of hearing the name of one beloved repeated by a whole people.   Quoted in Lives of
Celebrated Women
by Samuel Griswold Goodrich
1844

24 The phantom of ennui forever pursues me.
Ibid.

25 Life resembles Gobelin tapestry; you do not see the canvas on the right side; but when you turn it, the threads are visible.   Ibid.

26 If this Old World of ours is to be nothing but a single man [Napoleon], what is the use of staying here?   Letter to Thomas
Jefferson (25 April 1807),
Revue de Littérature
Comparée   1922

27 It is better to be united at a distance.
Letter to Adrien de Mun
(September 1796),
from Coppet,
Revue de Paris   December
1923

28 The greatest happiness is to transform one's feelings into actions. . . .
Letter to de Pange
(c.May 1796),
from Coppet,
Madame de Staël et François de
Pange: lettres et documents
inédits,
Jean de Pange, ed.   1925

29 What I love about noise is that it camouflages life.   Letter to Eric Staël von Holstein,
Revue des Deux Mondes
June/July 1932

30 Money alone determines your entire life, political as well as private.
Letter to Benjamin Constant*
(April 1815),
from Coppet,
Lettres à un ami,
Jean Mistler, ed.   1949

*French writer (1767–1830), Mme. de Staël's lover.

31 I never was able to believe in the existence of next year except as in a metaphysical notion.   Quoted in Mistress to an Age: A Life

of Madame de Staël
by J. Christopher Herold
1958

32 The pursuit of politics is religion, morality, and poetry all in one.   Ibid.

33 Those gentlemen [Lafayette and Sylvain Bailly,* mayor of Paris] are like the rainbow; they always appear after the storm is over.   Ibid.

*French astronomer and politician (1736–1793), guillotined.

34 Genius has no sex!   Ibid.

35 Sir, I understand everything that deserves to be understood; what I don't understand is nothing.   Ibid.

36 There is a kind of physical pleasure in resisting an iniquitous power.   Ibid.

37 If one hour's work is enough to govern France, four minutes is all that is needed for Italy. There is no nation more easily frightened; even its poetic imagination predisposes it to fear, and they look upon power as on an image that fills them with terror.   Ibid. (1804)

38 I shall have to conquer myself once more, despite everything.   Ibid.
(27 September 1810), near Blois

39 You [America] are the vanguard of the human race. You are the world's future.
Spoken to George Ticknow*
(c.Spring 1817), op. cit.

*American author and teacher of languages (1791–1871).

40 What matters in a character is not whether one holds this or that opinion: what matters is how proudly one upholds it.
Letter to Hochet (c.May 1802),
op. cit.

41 In every respect they are two very remarkable men.* If they had been able to be remarkable without trying to be extraordinary, they would have been more remarkable still.
Letter to Johann von
Müller (c.October 1804),
from Coppet, op. cit.

*The German writers and brothers August Wilhelm (1767–1845) and Friedrich (1772–1829) von Schlegel.

42 In matters of the heart, nothing is true except the improbable.   Letter to her cousin
Juliette Récamier
(5 October 1810),
from Fossé, op. cit.

43 I must keep on rowing, not until I reach port but until I reach my grave.
Letter to Albertine Necker de
Saussure [her daughter]
(July 1814),
from Coppet, op. cit.

44 How much past there is in a life, however brief it be. Letter to Récamier (c.February 1816), op. cit.

45 . . . I have always made it a point to adopt the opinions of the man whom I prefer.
Letter to Adolf Ludvig Ribbing (c.1794),
Lettres à Ribbing,
Simone Balaye, ed. *1960*

638. Betty Zane (1766?–1831?)

1 You have not one man to spare.* Quoted in
Chronicles of Border Warfare
by Alexander S. Withers
1831

*Attributed remark as she volunteered to run a dangerous mission.

639. Maria Edgeworth (1767–1849)

1 When one illusion vanishes, another shall appear, and, still leading me forward towards an horizon that retreats as I advance, the happy prospect of futurity shall vanish only with my existence. *Letters of Julia and Caroline* (1787), Letter I *1795*

2 Man is to be held only by the *slightest* chains; with the idea that he can break them at pleasure, he submits to them in sport. . . . Ibid.

3 In strong minds, despair is an acute disease; the prelude to great exertion. In weak minds, it is a chronic distemper, followed by incurable indolence. Ibid., Letter IV

4 "Pleasing for a moment," said Helen, smiling, "is of some consequence; for, if we take care of the moments, the years will take care of themselves, you know." *Mademoiselle Panache 1795*

5 A man who marries a showy entertaining coquette, and expects she will make him a charming companion for life, commits as absurd a blunder as that of the famous nobleman who, delighted with the wit and humour of Punch at a puppet-show, bought Punch, and ordered him to be sent home for his private amusement. Ibid.

6 I've a great fancy to see my own funeral afore I die. *Castle Rackrent,* Ch. 1 *1800*

7 Nothing for nothing. Ibid.

8 "It is quite fitting that charity should *begin* at home," said Wright; "but then it should not end at home; for those that help nobody will find none to help them in time of need."
The Will,
Ch. 2 *1800*

9 How success changes the opinion of men!
Ibid. Ch. 4

10 Business was his aversion; pleasure was his business. *The Contrast,* Ch. 2, *1801*

11 All work and no play makes Jack a dull boy,
All play and no work makes Jack a mere toy.
Harry and Lucy 1801

12 When Paddy heard an English gentleman speaking of the fine echo at the lake of Killarney, which repeats the sound forty times, he very promptly observed, "Faith, that's nothing at all to the echo in my father's garden, in the county of Galway: if you say to it, 'how do you do, Paddy Blake?' it will answer, 'pretty well, I thank you, sir.' " Ch. 1,
Essay on Irish Bulls 1802

13 Bishop Wilkins prophesied that the time would come when gentlemen, when they were to go on a journey, would call for their wings as regularly as they call for their boots.
Ibid., Ch. 2

14 Those who are animated by hope can perform what would seem impossibilities to those who are under the depressing influence of fear.
The Grateful Negro 1802

15 "The law, in our case, seems to make the right; and the very reverse ought to be done—the right should make the law." Ibid.

16 "Those who have lived in a house with spoiled children must have a lively recollection of the degree of torment they can inflict upon all who are within sight or hearing."
The Manufacturers,
Ch. 1 *1803*

17 Children were pretty things at three years old; but began to be great plagues at six, and were quite intolerable at ten. Ibid.

18 The facility with which I learned my lessons encouraged me to put off learning them till the last moment; and this habit of procrastinating, which was begun in presumption, ended in disgrace. *To-Morrow,* Ch. 1 *1803*

19 I was ever searching for some *short cut* to the temple of Fame, instead of following the beaten road. Ibid., Ch. 3

20 I now attempted too much: I expected to repair by bustle the effects of procrastination.
Ibid., Ch. 4

21 . . . when driven to the necessity of explaining, I found that I did not myself understand what I meant. Ibid.

22 What a misfortune it is to be born a woman! . . . Why seek for knowledge, which can prove only that our wretchedness is irremediable? If a ray of light break in upon us, it is but to make darkness more visible; to show us the now limits, the Gothic structure, the impenetrable barriers of our prison.
Leonora,
Letter I 1805

23 A wife who has sense enough to abstain from all reproaches, direct or indirect, by word or look, may reclaim her husband's affections: the bird escapes from his cage, but returns to his nest. Ibid., Letter XXVII

24 It is not so easy to do good as those who have never attempted it may imagine. . . .
Madame De Fleury,
Ch. 2, 1805

25 As a highwayman knows that he must come to the gallows at last, and acts accordingly, so a fashionably extravagant youth knows that, sooner or later, he must come to matrimony.
Ennui (1804),
Ch. 2, 1809

26 "How virtuous we shall be when we have no name for vice!" Ibid., Ch. 10

27 ". . . sometimes the very faults of parents produce a tendency to opposite virtues in their children . . ."
Manoeuvring,
Ch. 1 1809

28 ". . . confidence is the best proof of love. . . ." Ibid., Ch. 16

29 Well! some people talk of morality, and some of religion, but give me a little snug property.
The Absentee,
Ch. 2 1812

30 People usually revenge themselves for having admired too much, by afterward despising and depreciating without mercy—in all great assemblies the perception or ridicule is quickly caught, and quickly too revealed. Ibid., Ch. 3

31 "I believe in the rational, but not in the magical power of education."
Vivian,
Ch. 1 1812

32 "My mother took too much, a great deal too much, care of me; she over-educated, over-instructed, over-dosed me with premature lessons of prudence: she was so afraid that I should ever do a foolish thing, or not say a wise one, that she prompted my every word, and guided my every action. So I grew up, seeing with her eyes, hearing with her ears, and judging with her understanding, till, at length, it was found

out that I had no eyes, or understanding of my own." Ibid.

33 "Fortune's wheel never stands still—the highest point is therefore the most perilous."
Patronage,
Ch. 2 1814

34 "Whenever the honours of professions, civil, military, or ecclesiastical, are bestowed by favour, not earned by merit—whenever the places of trust and dignity in a state are to be gained by intrigue and solicitation—there is an end of generous emulation, and consequently of exertion. Talents and integrity, in losing their reward of glory, lose their vigour, and often their very existence." Ibid., Ch. 8

35 Beauties are always curious about beauties, and wits about wits. Ibid., Ch. 16

36 "Of all men, I think a dissipated clergyman is the most contemptible." Ibid., Ch. 19

37 Alarmed successively by every fashionable medical terror of the day, she dosed her children with every specific which was publicly advertised or privately recommended. No creatures of their age had taken such quantities of Ching's lozenges, Godbold's elixir, or Dixon's anti-bilious pills. The consequence was, that the dangers, which had at first been imaginary, became real: these little victims of domestic medicine never had a day's health: they looked, and were, more dead than alive. Ibid., Ch. 20

38 We must be content to begin at the beginning, if we would learn the history of our own mind; we must condescend to be even as little children, if we would discover or recollect those small causes which early influenced the imagination, and afterward become strong habits, prejudices, and passions.
Harrington,
Ch. 1 1817

39 An orator is the worse person to tell a plain fact. . . . Ibid., Ch. 10

40 ". . . in your vocabulary, that's only a good job where you pocket money and do nothing; now my good jobs never bring me in a farthing, and give me a great deal to do into the bargain."
Ormond,
Ch. 6 1817

41 After a certain age, if one lives in the world, one can't be astonished—that's a lost pleasure. Ibid., Ch. 15

42 A bore is a biped, but not always *unplumed.*
Thoughts On Bores 1826

43 The everlasting quotation-lover dotes on the husks of learning. He is the infant-reciting bore in second childishness. Ibid.

44 His [Sir Walter Scott's] morality is not in purple patches, ostentatiously obtrusive, but woven in through the very texture of the stuff.   *Helen,*
Vol. I, Ch. 12   *1834*

640. Rachel Robards Jackson (1767–1828)

1 Believe me, this country [Florida] has been greatly overrated. One acre of our fine Tennessee land is worth a thousand here.
Letter to friends,
Quoted in *Dames and Daughters of the Young Republic*
by Geraldine Brooks   *1901*

2 To tell you of this city [Washington, D.C.], I would not do justice to the subject. The extravagance is in dressing and running to parties; but I must say they regard the Sabbath and attend preaching, for there are churches of every denomination and able ministers of the gospel.
Letter to friend,
op. cit.

641. Caroline Amelia Elizabeth (1768–1821)

1 I find him* very fat and not half as handsome as his portrait.
Recorded by Lord Malmesbury,
Quoted in *Caroline the Unhappy Queen,*
Ch. 1, by Lord Russell of
Liverpool   *1967*

*Her future husband, King George IV.

2 . . . my dear, Punch's wife is nobody when Punch is present.   Recorded by Lady
Charlotte Bury,
op. cit., Ch. 3

3 The wasp leaves his sting in the wound and so do I.   Recorded by a friend,
op. cit., Ch. 4

642. Charlotte Corday (1768/9–1793)

1 I have done my task, let others do theirs.
Reply during interrogation at
Abbaye Prison,
Paris (13 July 1793),
Quoted in *Biography of
Distinguished Women*
by Sarah Josepha Hale*   *1876*

*See 703.

2 I considered that so many brave men need not come to Paris for the head of one man [Jean

Paul Marat].* He deserved not so much honour: the hand of a woman was enough. . . .
Letter to Barbaroux,
from Abbaye Prison, op. cit.

*Swiss-born French revolutionary (1743–93); assassinated by Corday.

3 . . . we do not execute well that which we have not ourselves conceived.   Remark at her trial
(17 July 1793), op. cit.

643. Dolley Madison (1768–1849)

1 I would rather fight with my hands than my tongue.   *Memoirs and Letters of Dolley
Madison   1886*

2 You may imagine me the very shadow of my husband.*   Letter to Mr. and Mrs.
Barlow (1811), op. cit.

*James Madison (1751–1836), 4th president of the United States (1809–1817).

3 How the crowd jostles!
Quoted in *Dames and Daughters
of the Young Republic*
by Geraldine Brooks   *1901*

4 The profusion of my table is the result of the prosperity of my country, and I shall continue to prefer Virginia liberality to European elegance.   Retort to the wife of
a foreign minister, op. cit.

644. Maria-Louisa Rose Petigny (1768–?)

1 How enviable, thy destiny,
Blessed, nimble butterly!
To live out a stable life,
Then—so change yourself!   "Le Papillon,"
St. 1, Elaine Partnow, tr.;*
Idylles   n.d.

*Author.

645. Madame Necker de Saussure (1768?–1847)

1 . . . there are so many causes of excitement in early life, personal affections and the desire to win the love and esteem of others occupy the mind so fully, that the young rarely press steadily onward to the most elevated mark.
Quoted in *Biography of
Distinguished Women*
by Sarah Josepha Hale*   *1876*

*See 703.

646. Melesina Trench (1768–1827)

1 A fat, fair, and fifty card-playing resident of the Crescent. (18 February 1816), *Letters* c.1820

647. Susannah Farnum Copley (fl. 1769–d. 1836)

1 It was his* own inclination and persevering industry that brought him forward in the art of painting, for he had no instructor. Letter, Quoted in *The Domestic and Artistic Life of John Singleton Copley, R.A.*, Ch.1, by Martha Babcock Amory** 1882

*Her husband, the artist John Singleton Copley (1738–1815).
**Copley's granddaughter.

2 I tell [your father] I don't know what might be the effect if our comfort, as well as our delight, was not so interwoven with the arts, which it is mortifying to know do not find a place among the other refinements of our native country [the United States]. . . . Letter to her daughter, (1 June 1801), op. cit., Ch. 11

3 A happy calm prevails after great apprehension of the reverse. Letter to her daughter (22 March 1821), op. cit., Ch. 16

648. Anne Brunton Merry (1769–1808)

1 The business of the Theatre has been and is very, very bad indeed. Letter to Mrs. Thackerson, Quoted in *The Career of Mrs. Anne Brunton Merry in the American Theatre* by Gresdna Ann Doty 1971

649. Amelia Opie (1769–1853)

1 Thy love, thy fate, dear youth, to share, Must ever be thy happy lot; But thou may'st grant this humble prayer, Forget me not! forget me not! "Go, Youth Beloved," St. 1, (1802), *The Warrior's Return & Other Poems* 1808

2 Yet still enchant and still deceive me, Do all things, fatal fair, but leave me.

"Song," St. 1, op. cit.

3 . . . this *wilderness* of pleasure. . . . Quoted in *English Women of Letters,* Vol. II, by Julia Kavanagh* 1863

*See 864.

4 It usually takes some time for the husband and wife to know each other's humours and habits, and to find what surrender of their own they can make with the least reluctance for their mutual good. "Two Years of Wedded Life," *A Wife's Duty* n.d.

5 Had I been an artful woman, and could I have condescended to make him doubtful of the extent of my love, by a few woman's subterfuges; could I have feigned a desire to return to the world, instead of owning, as I did, that all my enjoyment was comprised in home and him, I do think that I might have been, for a much longer period, the happiest of wives; but then I should have been, in my own eyes, despicable as a woman; and I was always tenacious of my own esteem. Ibid.

650. Anne Newport Royall (1769–1854)

1 Let them be bucktails or cowtails, the nether end of any animal fits them well. *The Black Book; or, A Continuation of Travels in the United States,* Vol. 1 1828

2 . . . the evangelical-tractical-biblical-Sabbath School-prayer meeting—good, honest, pious, sound Presbyterians of Capitol Hill. Remarking on witness at her trial (28 November 1817), *Mrs. Royall's Pennsylvania; or, Travels Continued in the United States,* Vol. II 1829

3 Cards subject you to bad company and bad hours. What is worse? *Letters from Alabama,* Letter I 1830

4 Hitherto I have only learned mankind in theory—but I am now studying him in practice. One learns more in a day, by mixing with mankind, than he can in an age shut up in a closet. Ibid., Letter XIII (22 December 1817)

5 . . . true to their nature, the people, or rabble, rather always think the greatest fool the wisest man. They have proved it in this instance, by

their selecting him [a local politician] to make laws for them. Alas, for my country! all your citizens want is rope.   Letter XLIV
(2 June 1821)   op. cit.

6 The United States Bank [is] not a political machine! It is a despot. It is the rack. It is the inquisition. It is a monster of corruption.
Quoted by Lucille Griffith, ed., in "Anne Royall, Tireless Traveler and Common Nuisance,"
Anne Royall's Letters from Alabama   1969

651. Martha Bratton (fl. 1770s–d. 1816)

1 It was I who did it.* Let the consequence be what it will, I glory in having prevented the mischief contemplated by the cruel enemies of my country.   Quoted in The Women of the American Revolution, Vol. II, by Elizabeth F. Ellet
1848

*Set fire to a cache of ammunition to prevent its falling into the hands of the British.

652. Anna Elliott (fl. 1770s)

1 [It is called] the rebel flower . . . because it always flourishes most when trampled upon.
Remark to a British soldier, Quoted in The Women of the American Revolution, Vol. II, by Elizabeth F. Ellet
1848

2 Let not oppression shake your fortitude, nor the hope of a gentler treatment cause you for a moment to swerve from strict duty.
Remark to her father, Thomas Ferguson, on his removal as a prisoner of war, op. cit.   1848

653. Mrs. Daniel Hall (fl. 1770s–1780s)

1 What is it you wish to look for? [Treason, came the reply.] Then you may be saved the trouble of search, for you may find enough of it at my tongue's end.   Upon handing over the key of her trunk to a British officer, Quoted in The Women of the American Revolution, Vol. II, by Elizabeth F. Ellet
1848

654. Margaret Holford (fl. 1770s)

1 'T is man's pride,
His highest, worthiest, noblest boast,

The privilege he prizes most,
To stand by helpless woman's side.
"Margaret of Anjou,"*
Fanny and Selina, Gresford Vale and Other Poems   1798

*See 211.

655. Mrs. Richard Shubrick (fl. 1770s–1780s)

1 To men of honor, the chamber of a lady should be sacred as a sanctuary!
Remark to British soldiers hunting for an American hiding in her bedroom, Quoted in The Women of the American Revolution, Vol. II, by Elizabeth F. Ellet
1848

656. Mary Wordsworth (1770–1859)

1 O My William! it is not in my power to tell thee how I have been affected by this dearest of all letters—it was so unexpected—so new a thing to see the breathing of thy inmost heart upon   paper   that   I   was   quite overpowered. . . .   Letter to William Wordsworth,* her husband
(1 August 1810), from Grasmere, The Love Letters of William and Mary Wordsworth, Beth Darlington, ed.   1982

*English Poet (1770–1850).

2 Bad as this is, it is some satisfaction to think this act* could only be done by a Lunatic—We were fearful that it was some dreadful Plot which might now bé raging, the first act only being gone through—Alas for this Country [England], Who have we now—I fear a shadow pated Creature** to take his Place. . . .
(13–14 May 1812), op. cit.

*The assassination of British Prime Minister Spencer Perceval (1762–1812) in the House of Commons.
**Robert Banks Jenkinson (1770–1828), second earl of Liverpool; Tory statesman and prime minister (1812–1827).

657. Maria Falconar (1771–?)

1 Once Superstition, in a fatal hour,
O'er Europe rais'd the sceptre of her power;
She reign'd triumphant minister of death,
And Peace and Pleasure faded in her breath;
Deep in monastic solitude entomb'd,

The bud of beauty wither'd ere it bloom'd
> Untitled, *Poems, by Maria and
> Harriet Falconar**   *1788*

*See 665.

658. Margaretta Van Wyck Faugères (1771–1801)

1 *There,* wrapt in musings deep, and steadfast gaze,
In solemn rapture hath she past the night.
> "Winter,"
> *Essays in Prose and Verse
> 1795*

2 "When I am gone—ah! who will care for thee?"   "Elegy to Miss Anna Dundass,"
> op. cit.

659. Elizabeth Holland (1771–1845)

1 Your poetry is bad enough, so pray be sparing of your prose.   Remark to Samuel Rogers,*
> Quoted in *Portraits of Women*
> by Gamaliel Bradford   *1916*

*English poet (1763–1855) known for his wit.

2 I am sorry to hear you are going to publish a poem. Can't you suppress it?
> Remark to Lord Porchester,
> op. cit.

3 There is a sensation in a mother's breast at the loss of an infant that partakes of the feeling of instinct. It is a species of savage despair.
> Letter to her husband,
> Lord Holland, op. cit.

4 . . . as nobody can do more mischief to a woman than a woman, so perhaps might one reverse the maxim and say nobody can do more good.   Ibid.

660. Rachel Levin Varnhagen (1771–1833)

1 My whole day is a feast of doing good!
> *Letters,*   n.d.

661. Dorothy Wordsworth (1771–1855)

1 The half dead sound of the near sheep-bell in the hollow of the sloping coombe, exquisitely soothing.
> *The Alfoxden
> Journal*   *1897*

2 I found a strawberry blossom in a rock. I uprooted it rashly and felt as if I had been committing an outrage, so I planted it again.
> Ibid.

3 One only leaf upon the top of a tree—the sole remaining leaf—danced round and round like a rag blown by the wind.   Ibid. (7 March 1798)

662. Mary Tighe (1772–1810)

1 Oh! how impatience gains upon the soul,
When the long promised hour of joy draws near!
How slow the tardy moments seem to roll!
What specters rise of inconsistent fear!
To the fond doubting heart its hopes appear
Too brightly fair, too sweet to realize;
All seem but day-dreams of delight too dear!
> *Psyche, or the Legend of
> Love   1795–1805*

2 Change is the lot of all.   Ibid.

3 Oh! have you never known the silent charm
That undisturb'd retirement yields the soul
> Ibid.

4 Yes, gentle Time, thy gradual, healing hand
Hath stolen from sorrow's grasp the en-venomed dart;
Submitting to thy skill, my passive heart
> "To Time,"
> "Sonnet,"
> *The British Female Poets,*
> George W. Bethune, ed.   *1848*

5 Who can speak a mother's anguish
> "Hagar* in the Desert,"
> St. 2, op. cit.

*See 2.

6 The careless eye can find no grace,
No beauty in the scaly folds,
Nor see within the dark embrace
What latent loveliness it hold.
Yet in that bulb, those sapless scales,
The lily wraps her silver vest.   "The Lily,"
> Sts. 2, 3,
> *The Female Poets of Great Britain,*
> Frederic Rowton, ed.   *1853*

663. Sophie Cottin (1773–1807)

1 We have resisted a little while, and we think we have done wonders; because we estimate the merit of our resistance, not by its duration, but by the difficulty it has cost us.
> Quoted in *Biography of
> Distinguished Women*
> by Sarah Josepha Hale*   *1876*

*See 703.

2 It is in affliction that the imagination elevates itself to the great thoughts of eternity and supreme justice, and that it takes us out of ourselves, to seek a remedy for our pains.   Ibid.

3 But still, amidst the horror and gloom of an eternal winter, nature displays some of her grandest spectacles. . . .   "The Exiles and
their Home,"
Elizabeth, or the Exile of Siberia,
n.d.

664. Mary Moody Emerson (1774–1863)

1 Rose before light every morn; . . . commented on the Scriptures; . . . touched Shakespeare,—washed, carded, cleaned house, baked.
Diary entry (1805),
Quoted in *Notable American Women,*
Edward T. James, ed.   *1971*

2 Scorn trifles, lift your aims; do what you are afraid to do.   Remark to Ralph Waldo
Emerson,* op. cit.

*American essayist and poet (1803–1882).

665. Harriet Falconar (1774–?)

1 Shall Britain view, unmov'd, sad Afric's shore
Delug'd so oft in streams of purple gore!
Untitled, St. 2,
*Poems, by Maria and Harriet
Falconar**   1788

*See 657.

2 Britain, where science, peace, and plenty smile,
Virtue's bright seat, and freedom's favour'd isle!   Ibid.

666. Cecile Renard (c.1774–1794)

1 I wanted to see how a tyrant looks.
Reply at inquiry on her
attempted assassination of
Robespierre* (1794),
Quoted in *Biography of
Distinguished Women*
by Sarah Josepha Hale**   *1876*

*French revolutionary leader (1758–1794); guillotined.
**See 703.

2 We have five hundred tyrants, [but] I prefer one king.   Ibid.

667. Elizabeth Seton (1774–1821)

1 Afflictions are the steps to heaven.
Quoted in *Notable American Women,*
Edward T. James, ed.   *1971*

668. Louisa Catherine Adams (1775–1852)

1 Go flatter'd image tell the tale
Of years long past away;
Of faded youth, of sorrow wail,
Of times too sure decay. . . .
"To my Sons with my Portrait
by Stuart," *
(18 December 1825), Ch. 3,
Quoted in *Portraits of John
Quincy Adams** and His Wife,*
Ch. 2, by Andrew Oliver   *1970*

*Gilbert Stuart, famed American portrait painter (1755–1828).
**6th president of the United States (1825–1829).

669. Jane Austen (1775–1817)

1 "Beware of the insipid Vanities and idle Dissipations of the Metropolis of England; Beware of the unmeaning Luxuries of Bath and of the stinking fish of South Hampton."
Love and Friendship, Letter Fourth
1790

2 She was nothing more than a mere good-tempered, civil and obliging young woman; as such we could scarcely dislike her—she was only an Object of Contempt—.
Ibid., Letter Thirteenth

3 She is probably by this time as tired of me, as I am of her; but as she is too polite and I am too civil to say so, our letters are still as frequent and affectionate as ever, and our Attachment as firm and sincere as when it first commenced.   *Lesley Castle,*
Letter the Fourth   *1792*

4 An annuity is a very serious business.
Sense and Sensibility,
Pt. I, Ch. 2   *1811*

5 Lady Middleton . . . exerted herself to ask Mr. Palmer if there was any news in the paper.
"No, none at all," he replied, and read on.   Ibid., Ch. 19

6 "It is not time or opportunity that is to determine intimacy; it is disposition alone. Seven years would be insufficient to make some people acquainted with each other, and seven days are more than enough for others."
Ibid., Pt. II, Ch. 12

7 It is a truth universally acknowledged, that a single man in possession of a good fortune, must be in want of a wife.
Pride and Prejudice,
Ch. 1 (first sentence)   *1813*

8 A lady's imagination is very rapid; it jumps from admiration to love, from love to matrimony in a moment.   Ibid., Ch. 6

9 "The power of doing anything with quickness is always much prized by the possessor, and often without any attention to the imperfection of the performance." Ibid., Ch. 10

10 "You have delighted us long enough." Ibid., Ch. 18

11 "It is particularly incumbent on those who never change their opinion, to be secure of judging properly at first." Ibid.

12 "Is not general incivility the very essence of love?" Ibid., Ch. 25

13 . . . where other powers of entertainment are wanting, the true philosopher will derive benefit from such as are given. Ibid., Ch. 42

14 "You ought certainly to forgive them as a Christian, but never admit them in your sight, or allow their names to be mentioned in your hearing." Ibid., Ch. 57

15 I have been a selfish being all my life, in practice, though not in principle. Ibid., Ch. 58

16 ". . . there is not one in a hundred of either sex who is not taken in when they marry. Look where I will, I see that it *is* so; and I feel that it *must* be so, when I consider that it is, of all transactions, the one in which people expect most from others, and are least honest themselves." *Mansfield Park,* Ch. 5 *1814*

17 "What strange creatures brothers are!" Ibid., Ch. 6

18 "Those who see quickly, will resolve quickly, and act quickly. . . ." Ibid.

19 "Selfishness must always be forgiven, you know, because there is no hope of a cure." Ibid., Ch. 7

20 ". . . it will, I believe, be everywhere found, that as the clergy are, or are not what they ought to be, so are the rest of the nation." Ibid., Ch. 9

21 "Oh! do not attack me with your watch. A watch is always too fast or too slow. I cannot be dictated to by a watch." Ibid.

22 An egg boiled very soft is not unwholesome. *Emma,* Ch. 3 *1815*

23 "If I lay it down as a general rule, Harriet, that if a woman *doubts* as to whether she should accept a man or not, she certainly ought to refuse him. If she can hesitate as to 'Yes,' she ought to say 'No,' directly." Ibid., Ch. 7

24 "Vanity working on a weak head produces every sort of mischief." Ibid., Ch. 8

25 It was a delightful visit—perfect, in being much too short. Ibid., Ch. 13

26 . . . but a sanguine temper, for ever expecting more good than occurs, does not always pay for its hopes by any proportion of depression. It soon flies over the present failure, and begins to hope again. Ibid., Ch. 18

27 Nobody who has not been in the interior of a family can say what the difficulties of any individual of that family may be. Ibid.

28 "But, my dear sir," cried Mr. Weston, "if Emma comes away early, it will be breaking up the party." "And no great harm if it does," said Mr. Woodhouse. "The sooner every party breaks up the better." Ibid., Ch. 25

29 Business, you know, may bring money, but friendship hardly ever does. Ibid., Ch. 34

30 "One cannot have too large a party. A large party secures its own amusement." Ibid., Ch. 42

31 "But after all the punishment that misconduct can bring, it is still not less misconduct. Pain is no expiation." Ibid., Ch. 48

32 What did she say? Just what she ought, of course. A lady always does. Ibid., Ch. 49

33 "It is very difficult for the prosperous to be humble." Ibid., Ch. 50

34 "To look *almost* pretty is an acquisition of higher delight to a girl who has been looking plain the first fifteen years of her life than a beauty from her cradle can ever receive." *Northanger Abbey,* Ch. 1 *1818*

35 ". . . I am sure of *this,* that if everybody was to drink their bottle a day, there would be not half the disorders in the world there are now. It would be a famous good thing for us all." Ibid., Ch. 9

36 "But your mind is warped by an innate principle of general integrity, and, therefore, not accessible to the cruel reasonings of family partiality, or a desire for revenge." Ibid., Ch. 27

37 How quick come the reasons for approving what we like! *Persuasion,* Ch. 2 *1818*

38 "In fact, as I have long been convinced, though every profession is necessary and honourable in its turn, it is only the lot of those who are not obliged to follow any, who can live in a regular way, in the country, choosing their own hours, following their own pursuits, and living on their own property, without the torment of trying for more; it is only *their* lot, I say, to hold the blessings of health and a good appearance to the

utmost: I know no other set of men but what lose something of their personableness when they cease to be quite young." Ibid., Ch. 3

39 She had been forced into prudence in her youth, she learned romance as she grew older: the natural sequence of an unnatural beginning.
Ibid., Ch. 4

40 "My idea of good company, Mr. Elliot, is a company of clever, well-informed people, who have a great deal of conversation; that is what I call good company."

"You are mistaken," said he, gently, "that is not good company; that is the best."
Ibid., Ch. 16

41 My sore throats are always worse than anyone's. Ibid., Ch. 18

42 "Man is more robust than woman, but he is not longer lived; which exactly explains my view of the nature of their attachments."
Ibid., Ch. 23

43 ". . . I do not think I ever opened a book in my life which had not something to say upon woman's inconstancy. Songs and proverbs all talk of woman's fickleness. But, perhaps, you will say, these were all written by men."

"Perhaps I shall. Yes, yes, if you please, no reference to examples in books . . . the pen has been in their hands. I will not allow books to prove anything." Ibid.

670. Mary Martha Sherwood (1775–1851)

1 "The book of Nature, my dear Henry, is full of holy lessons, ever new and ever varied; and to learn to discover these lessons should be the work of good education; for there are many persons who are exceedingly wise and clever in worldly matters, and yet with respect to spiritual things are wholly blind and dark, and are as unable to look on divine light as the bats and moles to contemplate the glory of the sun's rays at midday." *The History of Henry Milner,*
Part First, Ch. 16,
from The Works of Mrs.
Sherwood, Vol. I
1856

2 ". . . it is the very nature of sin to prevent man from meditating on spiritual things. . . ." Ibid., Part Second, Ch. 11

3 "We are getting too fine in this country, Lord H———; too fine in our habits. I doubt much whether our intellectual advancement bears a due proportion with the refinements of our habits. If that is the case, as I apprehend, there will be a reaction by-and-by—a reaction in which all that is mere tinsel in the state of society will be reduced to non-entity, and nothing will remain but that which is solid and real."
Ibid., Part Third, Ch. 2

4 "Where the habits are simple, and the mind truly elevated, then is society in the best state. . . ." Ibid.

5 O, how little do children know what parents sometimes endure for their sake!
"The Hedge of Thorns,"
op. cit., Vol. III

6 "And why not?" returned the *fakeer,* "I can read books and men too, and I tell you that the latter is a much more profitable branch of study than the former." *Arzoomund,*
Ch. 5, op. cit.

7 "To speak the plain truth, all religions seem alike to me, one mass of absurdities and lies— . . . I know that there is a God, but I know no more of him; and I believe that all those are liars who pretend to know more than I do."
Ibid.

8 Humility becomes our fallen nature . . .
The Lady of the
Manor; being a Series of
Conversations on the Subject of
Confirmation intended for the use
of the Middle and Higher Ranks
of Young Female,
Vol. I, Ch. 2,
Introductory, op. cit., Vol. IX

9 ". . . whatever station the child may occupy, humility must be enforced, and enforced upon Christian principles. All education, however otherwise excellent, which fails in this point, has, in my opinion, a pernicious tendency; and, humanly speaking, can only produce, at the best, a species of worldly morality, or a mere profession of religion. . . ." Ibid., Ch. 7

10 . . . what is the zest of argument when the antagonist is not allowed to answer?
The Monk of Climiés,
Ch. 5, op. cit., Vol. XIV

11 ". . . my father has lived abroad till he has lost his judgment. . . ." *The History of*
John Marten,
Ch. 1, op. cit., Vol. XVI

12 . . . a dirty exterior is a great enemy to beauty of all descriptions. Ibid., Ch. 13

671. Sydney Owenson Morgan (c.1776–83–1859)

1 There can be no individual happiness but that which harmonizes with the happiness of society—there may be virtue without felicity, but there can be no felicity without virtue. . . .
Ida of Athens *1808*

2 Literary fiction, whether directed to the purpose of transient amusement, or adopted as an indirect medium of instruction, has always in its most genuine form exhibited a mirror of the times in which it is composed; reflecting morals, customs, manners, peculiarity of character, and prevalence of opinion. Thus, perhaps, after all, it forms the best history of nations. . . .
Preface, *O'Donnell: A National Tale*,
Vol. I   *1813.*

3 He stood, indeed, at the head of that class of apathetic men of gallantry, *qui se laissent aimer* [who allow themselves to be loved]; . . . less anxious to be loved than to be adulated—to awaken a sentiment than to expose a triumph;
. . .   Ibid., Vol. III, Ch. 1

4 "That you are an Irishman, *genuine* and thorough bred, there can be no doubt; with your porcupine spirit, rising before it is assailed, and throwing its quill before it receives a wound. . . ."   Ibid., Ch. 3

5 ". . . as is usual among the semi-barbarous, improvement is resisted as innovation; . . . the old muddling system must go on for ever in the same old muddling way."   Ibid.

6 ". . . if foreigners won't understand one another, who do they expect will, I wonder."
Florence Macarthy: An Irish Tale,
Vol. I, Ch. 1   *1819*

7 "Oh! *par exemple,* for fine men," said Lady Dunore, throwing herself into an arm chair, "I think they are really quite extinct with us altogether."   Ibid., Vol. III, Ch. 3

8 "South America," he observed, "is well known to us in the Spanish histories of its early discoverers, when Spain invaded it under the Simoniacal pretext of *religion;* letting loose, at the same time, *bloodhounds and apostles,* while they opened its mineral veins and exterminated its population . . . almost [depriving] these great regions of a place in the history of nations. . . ."   Ibid.

9 "Temporary measures of expediency have nothing to do with general views," replied young Crawley to Mr. Daly's observation. "What is wisdom *to-day* in the conduct of a government may be madness *to-morrow.*"   Ibid.

10 "You are right, madam; the soul is of no sect, no party: it is, as you say, our passions and our prejudices, which give rise to our religious and political distinctions."
The Novice of St. Dominick, Vol. II, Ch. 12   *1823*

11 "All," said he mentally, "sweet child of nature, is pleasing to thee, because all is new: O youth, what a season of delight is thine."
Ibid., Ch. 19

12 "Dreadful to the soul is that moment when the lingering light of hope is finally extinguished, and all its sweet energies of fond expectations are buried in the gloom of despondency."
Ibid., Vol. III, Ch. 24

13 It is under the pressure of great and sudden exigencies that the faculties of a strong and comprehensive mind awaken to a full sense of their own power.   Ibid., Vol. IV, Ch. 35

14 "You see, madam, your wine is like the nepenthe of Helen, for it gives the cares as well as the senses of your guests to oblivion."
Ibid., Ch. 40

15 "For," says O'Brien, who worships his new found sister as a thing enskied, "with woman and music, Abbé, dear, you might proselytize all Ireland, far better than by all the peynals [sic] and all the persecutions that ever were invented:" and wonders that the government never hit upon it.   *The O'Briens and the O'Flahertys,*
Vol. I, Ch. 1   *1827*

672. Adelaide O'Keeffe (1776–1855?)

1 The butterfly, an idle thing,
Nor honey makes, nor yet can sing.
"The Butterfly," *n.d.*

673. Jane Porter (1776–1850)

1 Such, thought she, O Sun, art thou!—The resplendent image of the Giver of All Good. Thy cheering beams, like His All-cheering Spirit, pervades the very soul, and drives thence the despondency of cold and darkness.
Life of Sir William Wallace; or, *The Scottish Chiefs* [a novel]   *1810*

* Scottish hero (c.1270–1305).

2 "The cruel are generally false."   Ibid., Ch. 3

3 "No country is wretched, sweet lady," returned the knight, "till by a dastardly acquiescence it consents to its own slavery."   Ibid., Ch. 9

4 "You would teach confidence to Despair herself. . . ."   Ibid.

5 "For shame, Murray!" was the reply of Wallace; "they are dead, and our enemies no more. They are men like ourselves; and shall we deny them a place in that earth whence we all sprung?"   Ibid., Ch. 13

6 "Earthly crowns are dross to him who looks for a heavenly one."   Ibid., Ch. 33

7 "You are like a bad mirror that, from radical defect, always gives false reflections."
Thaddeus of Warsaw,
Vol. II, Ch. 17   *1835*

8 "The man who dares to be virtuous and great, and appears so, arms the self-love of all common characters against him." Ibid., Ch. 22

9 That sickness which is the consequence of mental pain, usually vanishes with its cause.
Ibid., Ch. 33

674. Hester Lucy Stanhope (1776–1839)

1 If you were to take every feature in my face, and lay them one by one on the table, there is not a single one that would bear examination. The only thing is that, put together and lighted up, they look well enough. It is homogeneous ugliness, and nothing more.
Quoted in *Little Memoirs of the Nineteenth Century*, Pt. I, by George Paston 1902

2 . . . I shall go on making sublime and philosophical discoveries, and employing myself in deep, abstract studies. Letter to Dr.
Meryon (1827), op. cit., Pt. II

3 Nobody is such a fool as to moider [waste] away his time in the slipslop conversation of a pack of women. Remark, op. cit.

4 My roses are my jewels, the sun and moon my clocks, fruit and water my food and drink. I see in your face that you are a thorough epicure; how will you endure to spend a week with me? Remark, op. cit.

675. Ann Chamber (?–1777)

1 But modern quacks have lost the art,
And reach of life the sacred seat;
They know not how its pulses beat,
Yet take their fee and write their bill,
In barb'rous prose resolved to kill.
"To the Duchess of Leeds, who, being ill, desired a copy of my verses to cure her,"
Poems, printed at Strawberry Hill 1764

676. Mary Brunton (1778–1818)

1 . . . —"Let them persecute me, and I will be a martyr." "You may be so now, to-day, every day," returned Mrs. Douglas. "It was not at the stake that these holy men began their self-denial. They had before taken up their cross daily; and whenever, from a regard to duty, you resign anything that is pleasing or valuable to you, you are for the time a little martyr."
"Sketch of the Heroine,"
Self-Control 1811

2 . . . little acquainted with other minds, deeply studious of her own, she concluded that all mankind were like herself engaged in a constant endeavour after excellence. . . . Ibid.

3 The passion which we do not conquer will, in time, reconcile us to any means that can aid its gratification. "The Lover and his Declaration," op. cit.

677. Margaret Hodson (1778–1852)

1 They are solemn and low, and none can hear
The whispers which come to Memory's ear!
"On Memory; Written at Aix-la-Chapelle,"
St. 3, *Poems 1811*

2 "Bright success
May only for a while sustain Man's feeble spirit!" *Margaret of Anjou:* * A Poem in Ten Cantos*, 4th canto 1816

*See 211.

3 "Let me Fate's awful page explore!
Leaf after leaf would I unfold,
E'en to the final word!—till *all* the tale be told!" Ibid., 7th canto

4 And, hark! the signal!—Now begin,
Of those who lose and those who win,
The strife, the shout, the mortal din!
Behold!—they meet!—they clash!—they close!—
They mix!—Sworn friends and deadly foes,
In one dire mass, one struggling host,
All order and distinction lost,
Roll headlong, guideless, blind, like waves together toss'd! Ibid.

5 " 'T is strange
How memory fails with fortune's change!"
Ibid., 10th canto

6 "Monsters! A mother's curse lie strong
And heavy on you! May the tongue,
The ceaseless tongue which well I ween
Live in the murderer's murky breast,
With goading whispers, fell and keen,
Make havoc of your rest!" Ibid.

678. Ann Murry (fl. 1778–1799)

1 Mark but the hist'ry of a modern day,
Composed of nonsense, foppery, and play.
"A Familiar Epistle,"
Poems on Various Subjects 1779

679. Margaret Bayard Smith (1778–1844)

1 Ladies and gentlemen only had been expected at this Levee, not the people en masse. Of all tyrants, they are the most ferocious, cruel and despotic.   Quoted in *First Ladies* by Betty Boyd Caroli
1987

680. Angelica Catalani (1779–1848)

1 For when God has given to a mortal so extraordinary a talent as I possess, people ought to applaud and honour it as a miracle: it is profane to depreciate the gifts of Heaven!
Quoted in *Queens of Song* by Ellen Creathorne Clayton
1865

681. Elizabeth Fry (1780–1845)

1 Does Capital punishment tend to the security of the people?
By no means. It hardens the hearts of men, and makes the loss of life appear light to them; and it renders life insecure, inasmuch as the law holds out that property is of greater value than life.   From her Journal, Quoted in *Biography of Distinguished Women* by Sarah Josepha Hale*   *1876*

*See 703.

2 Punishment is not for revenge, but to lessen crime and reform the criminal.   Ibid.

682. Hannah Farnham Lee (1780–1865)

1 Astronomers tell us of countless worlds;—if we look within our own precincts we shall find an equal multiplication; every class of society talks of *the world*, and every class means something different.   *Elinor Fulton*, Ch. 1   *1837*

2 "I never could bear people that are always striving to rise."   Ibid.

3 No one can have any high degree of virtue, without self-respect; it is the twin-sister of virtue.   Ibid., Ch. 8

4 Liberty has set her foot on our shore, and she is not not to be restricted in her walks.   Ibid.

5 We have arrived at that period when there is no putting a padlock on the human mind; every one is contending for his rights, every one ready to strike for them.   Ibid.

6 "Our good and bad depend much on circumstances."   Ibid., Ch. 9

7 "What is a new bonnet, or a new pelisse [fur piece], to the pleasure of feeling there is something in reserve that you may call your own! Blessings on the Savings Bank! It is truly, to those who resolutely deposit their earnings there, the purse of Fortunatus. . . ."   Ibid., Ch. 11

8 . . . is there no exterminating the shoots of vanity where it has once taken root?   Ibid.

9 Fireside occupation is one of the rights of women that men may envy.   Ibid., Ch. 13

10 A mere compilation of facts presents only the skeleton of History; we do but little for her if we cannot invest her with life, clothe her in the habiliments of her day, and enable her to call forth the sympathies of succeeding generations.   Preface, *The Huguenots in France and America*, Vol. I   *1843*

11 Unless history can be converted to moral uses, it is only "a little book got by heart."   Ibid.

12 He [John Calvin],* who had so loudly declaimed against the tyranny of Rome, was doomed to prove how dangerous an instrument is power in the hands of a human being.   Ibid., Ch. 3

*French religious reformer (1509–1564).

13 It is amusing to observe in every age the ingenuity of dress in changing the human figure.
Ibid., Ch. 13

14 It is those in whom the power of virtue is formed and matured, that are truly great. It matters not how many millions a man may command, the next day may strip him of all; but the *undying principle* of duty is his own, and can only be surrendered by his will.
Ibid., Vol. II, Ch. 29

15 There are principles implanted in the breast that cannot be wholly eradicated. God does not leave himself without witnesses in the heart of every human being.   Ibid., Ch. 31

16 Even under an absolute monarchy men will have an instinctive sense of justice.   Ibid., Ch. 33

17 Trifling circumstances are exciting in still life.   *The Log-Cabin; or, the World Before You*, Part First   *1844*

18 ". . . keep your money if you can, but remember it hath wings . . ."   Ibid.

19 There is nothing old tolerated in this new world [America].   Ibid., Part Second

20 . . . but has not my whole life been made up of trifles?   Ibid.

21 Causes are often disproportioned to effects.
                                                    Ibid.

22 "The school may do much; but alas for the child
where the instructor is not assisted by the influences of home!"   Ibid.

23 Surely we ought to prize those friends on whose
principles and opinions we may constantly rely—
of whom we may say in all emergencies, "I
know what they would think."   Ibid.

24 . . . a good nurse is of more importance than
a physician.   Ibid., Part Third

683. Mary Somerville (1780–1872)

1 And who shall declare the time allotted to the
human race, when the generation of the most
insignificant insect existed for unnumbered ages?
Yet man is also to vanish in the everchanging
course of events. The earth is to be burnt up,
and the elements to melt with fervent heat—to
be again reduced to chaos—possibly to be renovated and adorned for other races of beings.
These stupendous changes may be but cycles in
those great laws of the universe, where all is
variable but the laws themselves and He who
ordained them.   "God and His Works,"
              Physical Geography   1848

2 . . . no circumstance in the natural world is
more inexplicable than the diversity of form and
colour in the human race.
                      "Varieties of the Human Race,"
                                          op. cit.

3 . . . one of the greatest improvements in education is that teachers are now fitted for their
duties by being taught the art of teaching.
                                    "Benevolence,"
                                          op. cit.

4 The moral disposition of the age appears in the
refinement of conversation.
                          "Influence of Christianity,"
                                          op. cit.

684. Frances Milton Trollope (1780–1863)

1 "Is not amusement the very soul of life?"
                      The Life and Adventures of
            Michael Armstrong, the Factory Boy,
                                          Ch. 6
                                          1839

2 "That's nonsense, Michael," said Fanny. "They
can't keep us here for ever. When we die, we
are sure to get away from them."
                                  Ibid., Ch. 17

3 "Times are altered with me now, nurse Trem-
lett," replied Mary; "I have left off living for
myself, and I feel my temper improving already
by it."   Ibid., Ch. 22

685. Lucy Aiken (1781–1864)

1 Their kindness cheer'd his drooping soul;
  And slowly down his wrinkled cheek
  The big round tears were seen to roll,
  And told the thanks he could not speak.
  The children, too, began to sigh,
  And all their merry chat was o'er;
  And yet they felt, they knew not why,
  More glad than they had done before.
                              "The Beggar Man,"
                                     Sts. 9, 10,
              The Female Poets of Great Britain,
                             Frederic Rowton, ed.
                                          1853

2 Shepherd people on the plain
  Pitch their tents and wander free;
  Wealthy cities they disdain,
  Poor,—yet blest with liberty.   "Arabia,"
                                     St. 3, op. cit.

3 That life may not be prolonged beyond the
power of usefulness, is one of the most natural,
and apparently of the most reasonable wishes
man can form for the future. . . .
                                       "Memoirs"
                          (of her father, Dr. Aiken),
                             Quoted in Biography of
                               Distinguished Women
                    by Sarah Josepha Hale*   1876

*See 703.

686. Janet Colquhoun (1781–1846)

1 This day I am thirty years old. Let me now bid
a cheerful adieu to my youth. My young days
are now surely over, and why should I regret
them? Were I never to grow old I might be
always here, and might never bid farewell to sin
and sorrow.   Diary entry (17 April 1811),
                     Quoted in A Memoir of Lady
                               Colquhoun, Ch. 2,
                              by James Hamilton,
                             D. D.   1851

2 The world? it is nothing to me; its pomps, its
pleasures, its vanities—all nothing, nothing.
                        Diary entry (19 July 1816),
                                          op. cit.

3 I feel something within me that lives for God,
that delights in God, that cannot exist without
God, that must be derived from God.

Diary entry (8 September 1844),
op. cit., Ch. 6

687. Anna Jane Vardill (1781–1852)

1 Behold this ruin! 'Twas a skull
One of ethereal spirit full!
This narrow cell was Life's retreat;
This place was Thought's mysterious seat!
What beauteous pictures fill'd that spot,
What dreams of pleasure, long forgot!
Nor Love, nor Joy, nor Hope, nor Fear,
Has left one trace, one record here.
"Lines to a Skull,"
European Magazine
November 1816

688. Susan Edmonstone Ferrier (1782–1854)

1 . . . petty ills; like a troup of locusts, making
up by their number and their stings what they
want in magnitude. *Marriage,*
Ch. 6   *1818*

2 . . . as . . . the surface was covered with
flowers . . . who would have thought of ana-
lysing the soil? Ibid., Ch. 28

3 There are some people who, furious themselves
at opposition, cannot understand the possibility
of others being equally firm and decided in a
gentle manner. Ibid., Ch. 52

4 There are plenty of fools in the world; but if
they had not been sent for some wise purpose,
they wouldn't have been here; and since they
are here they have as good a right to have elbow-
room in the world as the wisest.
Ibid., Ch. 68

5 "Oh, how easy it must be to be good when one
has the power of doing good!"
The Inheritance,
Ch. 4   *1824*

6 Ah! what will not the heart endure e'er it will
voluntarily surrender the hoarded treasure of its
love to the cold dictates of reason or the stern
voice of duty! Ibid., Ch. 33

7 . . . it is not the first stroke of grief, however
heavy it may fall, that can at once crush the
native buoyance of youthful spirit; it is the
continuance of misery which renders its weight
insupportable. . . . Ibid., Ch. 43

8 "The profane and licentious works of Lord B.*
will live only in the minds of the profane and
impure, and will soon be classed amongst

worthless dross, while all that is fine in his
works will be culled by the lovers of virtue, as
the bee gathers honey from even the noxious
plant, and leaves the poison to perish with the
stalk; so shall it be with Burns,** so shall it be
with More."*** Ibid., Ch. 45

*Lord Byron (1788–1824), English poet.
**Robert Burns (1759–1796), Scottish poet.
***Henry More (1614–1687), English poet and philoso-
pher.

9 ". . . the synagogin', the tabernaclin', the
psalmin' that goes on in this hoose, that's enough
to break the spirits o' ony young creature."
Ibid., Ch. 46

10 ". . . passion without passion is an anomaly I
cannot comprehend." Ibid., Ch. 72

11 . . . lovers, it is well known, carry the art of
tautology to its utmost perfection, and even the
most impatient of them can both bear to hear
and repeat the same things time without number,
till the sound becomes the echo to the sense or
the nonsense previously uttered. Ibid.

12 "I am for everything starting into fullblown
perfection at once." Ibid., Ch. 79

13 ". . . there is no doctor like meat and
drink. . . ." Ibid., Ch. 98

14 "Which of all the gifts a liberal Creator has
endowed you with would you exchange for those
empty distinctions which one creature bestows
upon another? Would you exchange your beauty
for rank, your talents for wealth, your greatness
of mind for extended power; for all of them
would you exchange your immortal soul?"
Ibid., Ch. 101

15 . . . the sickness of hope deferred crept like
poison through her veins. Ibid., Ch. 102

16 But who can count the beatings of the lonely
heart? Ibid.

17 "It was the saying, sir, of one of the wisest
judges who ever sat upon the Scottish bench,
that a *poor* clergy made a *pure* clergy—a maxim
which deserves to be engraven in letters of gold
on every manse in Scotland."
"A Bustling Wife,"
Destiny, or the Chief's
Daughter   1831

18 The next day was Sunday—day of rest to the
poor and the toil-worn—of weariness to the rich
and the idle. "Sunday,"
op. cit.

19 "I am no friend to a premature knowledge of
the world; it comes soon enough to most of
us." *Destiny,*
Ch. 15   *(later ed.)*

20 "... I do assure you, it is a very tiresome thing to be trained up to be a person of consequence. . . ."   Ibid., Ch. 47

21 "... the stomach requires to be amused as well as the mind."   Ibid., Ch. 55

22 No generous impulse ever led her beyond the strict line of duty. . . .   Ibid., Ch. 71

23 "... there's no face like the face that loves us."   Ibid., Ch. 78

24 There is no surer mark of a selfish character than that of shrinking from the truth.
Ibid., Ch. 89

25 "... time and eternity are but different periods of the same state. . . ."   Ibid.

689. Ann Taylor (1782–1866)

1 Who ran to help me when I fell,
And would some pretty story tell,
Or kiss the place to make it well?
My mother.   "My Mother," St. 6,
Original Poems for Infant Minds   1804

2 'Tis a *credit* to any good girl to be neat,
But quite a disgrace to be *fine*.   "Neatness,"
op. cit.,
with Jane Taylor* b. 1783

*See 692.

3 Twinkle, twinkle, little star
How I wonder what you are,
Up above the world so high,
Like a diamond in the sky!
"The Star," St. 1,
Rhymes for the Nursery   1806

4 And willful waste, depend upon 't,
Brings, almost always, woeful want!
"The Pin," St. 6,
*Hymns for Infant Minds
1810*

5 Oh, that it were my chief delight
To do the things I ought!
Then let me try with all my might
To mind what I am taught.
"For a Very Little Child,"
op. cit., with Jane Taylor*

*See 692.

690. Theodosia Burr Alston (1783–1813)

1 What a charming thing a bustle is! Oh, dear, delightful confusion! It gives a circulation to the blood, an activity to the mind, and a spring to the spirits.   Letter to her father
(December 1803), Quoted in *Memoirs of Aaron*

Burr, Vol. II,
Matthew L. Davis, ed.
1836–1837

*(1756–1836), 3rd vice president of the United States (1801–1805).

2 You know, I love to convict you of an error, as some philosophers seek for spots in the sun.
Letter to her father
(1 February 1809),
Quoted in *The Private Journal of Aaron Burr,* Vol. I,
Matthew L. Davis, ed.
1838

3 Alas! my dear father, I do live, but how does it happen? Of what am I formed that Live, and why? . . . You talk of consolation. Ah! you know not what you have lost. I think Omnipotence could give me no equivalent for my boy; no, none—none.
Letter to her father on the death of her son (12 August 1812),
op. cit., Vol. II

691. Amelia (1783–1810)

1 Unthinking, idle, wild, and young,
I laugh'd and danc'd and talk'd and sung.
"Youth"   *n.d.*

692. Jane Taylor (1783–1824)

(See also Ann Taylor, 689:2, 5)

1 Though man a thinking being is defined,
Few use the grand prerogative of mind.
How few think justly of the thinking few!
How many never think, who think they do!
"Prejudice, or, Essay on Morals and Manners,"
St. 45, *Original Poems for Infant Minds   1804*

2 How pleasant it is, at the end of the day,
No follies to have to repent;
But reflect on the past, and be able to say,
That my time has been properly spent.
"The Way to be Happy,"
Rhymes for the Nursery   1806

3 I like little Pussy, her coat is so warm;
And if I don't hurt her she'll do me no harm.   "I Like Little Pussy,"
St. 1, op. cit.

693. Mary Austin Holley (1784–1846)

1 How hard it is to be poor.
*Texas: Observations Historical, Geographical and Descriptive
1833*

2 Taste does not spring up in the wilderness, nor in prairies, nor in log cabins!

> Quoted in *Letters of an Early American Traveller: Mary Austin Holley* by Mattie Austin Hatcher
> *1933*

694. Bettina von Arnim (1785–1859)

1 A purple sky my mind, a warm love-dew my words, the soul must come forth like a bride from her chamber, without evil, and avow herself.

> Various letters to Goethe,*
> Quoted in *Correspondence Between Goethe and a Young Girl 1835*

*Johann Wolfgang von Goethe (1749–1832), German poet, dramatist, novelist.

2 Without trust, the mind's lot is a hard one; it grows slowly and needily, like a hot plant betwixt rocks: thus am I—thus was I till to-day. . . .
> Ibid.

3 All which spiritually lays claim on a man, here goes to the senses; therefore is it that through them he feels himself moved to all things.
> Ibid.

4 O yes! the ascending from out of unconscious life into revelation,—that is music!
> Ibid.

5 But this breaking forth of the mind to light, is it not art? This inner man asking for light, to have by the finger of God loosened his tongue; untied his hearing; awakened all senses to receive and to spend: and is love here not the only master, and we its disciples in every work which we form by its inspiration?
> Ibid.

6 They who fancy to understand it [art] will perform no more than what is ruled by understanding; but when senses are submitted to its spirit, he has revelation.
> Ibid.

7 Whoever is come to something in art, did forget his craftiness, his load of experience, became shipwreck, and despair led him to land on the right shore.
> Ibid.

8 To inhale the divine spirit is to engenerate, to produce; to exhale the divine breath is to breed and nourish the mind. . . .
> Ibid.

9 Body is art, art is the sensual nature engenerated into the life of the spirit.
> Ibid.

695. Caroline Lamb (1785–1828)

1 Then, for the first time, Camioli beheld, in one comprehensive view, the universal plan of nature—unnumbered systems performing their various but distinct courses, unclouded by mists, and unbounded by horizon—endless variety in infinite space!
> *Glenarvon,* Vol. I, Ch. 1 *1816*

2 It is the common failing of an ambitious mind to over-rate itself. . . .
> Ibid., Ch. 2

3 . . . . the sins of children rise up in judgment against their parents. .
> Ibid., Ch. 20

4 ". . . she is in love with ruin: it stalks about in every possible shape, and in every shape, she hails it:—woe is it; victim of prosperity, luxury and self indulgence."
> Ibid., Ch. 28

5 Love's blighted flower, can never bloom again.
> Ibid., Vol. II, Ch. 17

6 "I had rather be the cause of her laughter, than of her tears."
> Ibid., Ch. 24

7 But, when the flame [of love] is unsupported by . . . pure feelings, it rages and consumes us, burns up and destroys every noble hope, perverts the mind, and fills with craft and falsehood every avenue to the heart.
> Ibid., Vol. III, Ch. 72

8 Women, like toys, are sought after, and trifled with, and then thrown by with every varying caprice.
> Ibid., Ch. 81

9 ". . . my mind is a world in itself, which I have peopled with my own creatures."
> Ibid., Ch. 94

10 Mad, bad, and dangerous to know.*
> *Journal,* n.d.

*Her description of her lover, Lord Byron, English poet (1788–1824).

696. María Augustín (1786–1857)

1 Death or victory!*
> Speech at siege of Zaragoza (2 June 1808), Quoted in *Women of Beauty and Heroism* by Frank B. Goodrich *1858*

*Cry that led the Spanish resistance to Napoleon's assault.

697. Marceline Desbordes-Valmore (1786–1859)

1 "Has any seen a little child astray among the crowd?
The mother has been seeking it, and weeping long and loud."
> "The Lost Child," 1., St. 1 (refrain), *Elegies and Romances* *1842*

2 It seems that we were born for misery,
And when we are too happy, can but die.
                                    Ibid., St. 10.

3 For still the mother-soul attends the child
                          "Flowers at the Cross,"
                                    St. 3, op. cit.

4 "What?—find my vanished Eden?"
                          "A Woman's Dream,"
                                    St. 1, op. cit.

5 Shall I never play again in my mother's gar-
den-close?   "Tristesse,"
                                    St. 1, op. cit.

6   Ah, when the soul is young,
   It is lightly filled with joy, and the taste is yet
      unknown
   Of the morsel steeped in tears, with honey
      overstrown,
   That leaves a bitter savor on the tongue.
                                    Ibid., St. 10

7 Why are our joys remembered more bitter than
our woes?   Ibid., St. 21

8 "I wonder who will take the oar
   When my poor bark at last is found"
                          "To Alphonse de Lamartine,"*
                                    St. 6, op. cit.

*French poet & statesman (1790–1869)

9 In the vain shows where wit doth win ap-
plause,
   Hushed lies the heart, and hidden:
   To please becomes the first of laws;
   To love is aye forbidden.
                          Untitled poem, St. 2,
                          Quoted in *Memoirs of Madame
                          Desbordes-Valmore,*
                          Ch. 1, by C. A. Sainte-Beuve;
                          Harriet W. Preston, tr.   *1872*

10 "O strange caprice of the unstable crowd!"
                                    Ibid., St. 3

11 "The scattered lights of fame!"   Ibid., St. 4

12 . . . money demoralizes even the giver.
                                    Remark, op. cit.

13 We must make our lives as we sew,—stitch by
stitch.   Ibid.

14   God will gather like bruised flowers
   The souls of babes and women who to him
   Are fled,—the air with outraged souls is dim,
   On earth men wade in blood,—Merciful
      Powers!   "Lyons,"
                          St. 2 (1834), op. cit., Ch. 3

15 Are we* not like the two volumes of one
book?   Letter, op cit., Ch. 4

*Referring to her friend, Pauline Duchambge, composer,
with whom Valmore frequently collaborated on songs.

16 I never see a denizen of that literary world which
forms taste and purifies language. I am my own
sole judge, and I know nothing, so where is my
security?   Letter to M. Antoine de Latour
                          (7 February 1837), op. cit.

17 I am climbing, as best I may, to the goal of an
existence in which I speak very much oftener to
God than to the world.   Ibid.

18 All the miseries of Lyons are added to my
own,—twenty or thirty thousand workmen begging daily for a little bread, a little fire, a
garment, lest they die. Can you realize, monsieur, this universal and insurmountable despair
which appeals to one in God's name, and makes
one ashamed of daring to have food and fire and
two garments, when these poor creatures have
none? I see it all, and it paralyzes me.   Ibid.

19 . . . the more I read, the farther I penetrate into
the shadows which have hidden our great lights
from me, the less I dare to write: I am smitten
with terror,—I am like a glowworm in the
sun.   Letter to her son, Hippolyte
                          (26 October 1840), op. cit.

20 It is certainly true that housekeeping cares bring
with them a thousand endearing compensations.
They are a woman's peculiar joy, and women
are apt to be light-hearted.
                          Letter to Hippolyte and
                          Undine, her son and daughter
                          (1 November 1840), op. cit.

21 . . . if I were not poor, you would not be
so.   Letter to her brother, Felix
                          Desbordes (14 January 1843),
                                    op. cit.

22 In these days the rich will come and tell you
their troubles with such utter candor, such bitter
bewailings, that you are compelled to pity them
more than you do yourself.
                          Letter to Pauline Duchambge
                          (10 February 1843), op. cit.

23 An attack of hope is the same for us as an attack
of fever.   Ibid.

24 Nothing is very clear in my memory, except
that we were very happy, and very
unhappy. . . .   Letter to her brother
                          (14 April 1843), op. cit.

25 But politics poison the mind.
                          Letter to her brother
                          (28 September 1847), op. cit.

26 To gain in strength and elevation of mind, day
by day; to shame, or at least to soften, those
who have despised us, and render them glad to
have been our allies and old friends,—there is
something in all this which may yet sanctify
life.   Ibid.

27 . . . what are grace and wit and wisdom in times like these?   Letter to her brother
(12 January 1848), op. cit.

28 Life certainly is a warfare for all of us.
Letter to M. Richard
(25 February 1850), op. cit.

29 To write what I think, is to betray myself. To write any thing else is to deceive. . . .
Letter to Mme. Derains
(4 October 1852), op. cit.

30 This world of ours grows dizzy.
Letter to her niece, Camille
(26 March 1854), op. cit.

31 . . . another existence swallowed up in the fearful rush of what is called civilization, but is very like chaos.   Ibid.

32 The last result of misfortune is to sow seeds of discord in families which happiness would have united. When it becomes necessary for each member to work hard in order to escape absolute indigence, the wings of the soul are folded, and soaring is postponed to a future day.
Letter to her niece
(6 September 1854), op. cit.

33 . . . the sum and substance of volumes that I feel . . . will remain unwritten, like seeds put away in closets, which dry up and are never sown.   Letter to Mme. Derains
(c.September 1854), op. cit.

34 The rich are no worse than we, but they are utterly unable to understand how one can want for the humblest necessities of life.
Letter to her sister, Cecile
(9 November 1854), op. cit.

35 And what a hard stepmother is life. . . .
Letter to Pauline Duchambge
(27 December 1855), op. cit.

36 You say, my dear and true friend, that poetry is my consolation. On the contrary, it torments me, as with a bitter irony. I am like the Indian who sings at the stake.
Letter to Duchambge (15 January 1856), op. cit.

37 Are we not always young?
Letter to Pauline Duchambge
(5 January 1857), op. cit.

38 Life may become wearisome, but it does not end.   Ibid.

39 Ah, how many stabs are concealed by the smiles and sweet "goodmornings" of the world!
Letter to Duchambge (April 1857), op. cit.

40 There are times when one cannot lift a blade of grass without finding a serpent under it.
Letter to Duchambge
(11 May 1857), op. cit.

41 And our joy, when we meet,
From joy remembered a new bliss will gain.
"Parting at Night," St. 3, *Idyls n.d.*

42 "Flowers o' the home," says he,
"Are daughters."   "Mother and Maiden," St. 15, op. cit.

43 And one hears best, methinks, when one hears blindly   Ibid., St. 17

44 Their fragrance fills my gown this evening, still;
All that remains of a scented
souvenir.   "The Roses of Sa'adi," St. 3, tr. by Elaine Partnow;*
Les poètes maudits, Paul Verlaine, ed.   *1884*

* Author.

698. Caroline Anne Southey (1786–1854)

1 Sleep, little baby! sleep!
Not in thy cradle bed,
Not on thy mother's breast
"To A Dying Infant," St. 1, *Solitary Hours, and Other Poems 1826*

2 She dwelt alone, a cloistered nun,
In solitude and shade.   "The Primrose," St. 5, op. cit.

3 O Grave! we come.   "The Last Journey," St. 1, op. cit.

4 You must love—*not my faults*—but in *spite* of them, me,
For the very caprices that vex ye;
Nay, the more should you chance (as it's likely) to see
'T is my special delight to perplex ye.
"The Threat," St. 6, op. cit.

5 But I have drunk enough of life
(The cup assign'd to me
Dash'd with a little sweet at best,
So scantily, so scantily)   "To Death," St. 4, op. cit.

6 This weak, weak head! this foolish heart! they'll cheat me to the last:
I've been a dreamer all my life, and now that life is past!   "The Dying Mother to her Infant," St. 11., *Autumn Flowers, and Other Poems 1844*

7 How happily, how happily, the flowers die away!
Oh, could we but return to earth as easily as they!   "The Death of the Flowers," St. 1, op. cit.

699. Eliza Lee Follen (1787–1860)

1 The night comes on,
And sleep upon this little world of ours,
Spreads out her sheltering, healing wings; and
man—
The heaven-inspired soul of this fair earth,
The bold interpreter of nature's voice,
Giving a language even to the stars—
Unconscious of the throbbings of his heart,—
Is still   "Winter Scenes in the Country,"
St. 1, *Poems*   *1839*

700. Eliza Leslie (1787–1858)

1 "The truth is," pursued Mr. Culpepper, "I am
travelling for my health, and therefore I am
taking cross-roads, and stopping at out of the
way places. For there is no health to be got by
staying in cities, and putting up at crowded
hotels, and accepting invitations to dinner-par-
ties and tea-parties, or in doing any thing else
that is called fashionable."
                "The Red Box, or, Scenes at the
                General Wayne,"
        *Pencil Sketches; or Outlines of
        Character and Manners   1837*

2 Servility and integrity rarely go together.
                Ibid.

3 "Certainly every body ought to feel on these
occasions; but you know it is impossible to
devote every moment between this and the funeral to tears and sobs. One cannot be crying
all the time—nobody ever does."
                "Constance Allerton; or, the
                Mourning Suits,"
                op. cit.

4 "Excuse me, but innovations on established
customs ought only to be attempted by people
of note—by persons so far up in society that
they may feel at liberty to do any out-of-the-
way thing with impunity."   Ibid.

5 "There is no better cure for folly, and particularly for romantic folly, than a good
burlesque. . . ."   "The Serenades,"
                op. cit.

6 "The pleasure of listening to delightful notes,
with delightful words, uttered with taste and
feeling by an accomplished and intellectual singer,
is one of the most perfect that can fall to the lot
of beings who are unable to hear the music of
the spheres and the songs of Paradise." Ibid.

7 "Why, Pharaoh—my old fellow!" exclaimed
Lindsay, "Is this really yourself?"
                "Can't say, masser," replied Pharaoh. "All
people's much the same—Best not be too personal—But I b'lieve I'm he."
                "The Old Farm House,"
                op. cit.

8 "And the Newman girls mix up their talk with
all sorts of French words that sound very ugly
to me. Instead of 'good night' they say *bone
swear*,* and a 'trifle' they call a *bag-tail*,* and
they are always talking about having a *Gennes-
see Squaw*,* though what they mean by that I
cannot imagine; for I am sure I never saw any
such thing in this part of the country."   Ibid.

* *bon soir; bagatelle; je ne sais quoi.*

9 ". . . you Americans always know more of
every thing than you ought to. I don't wonder
so few of you look plump and ruddy. You all
wear yourselves out with headwork."
                "That Gentleman,"
                op. cit.

10 ". . . there's a considerable difference between
doing without a thing of your own accord, and
being made to do without it."
                "Chase Loring. A Story of the
                Revolution,"
                op. cit.

11 "Aunt Rhoda," observed Tudor, "a cause* that
is sanctioned by the approval of so many wise
and pious men cannot fail to prosper."   Ibid.

* Reference to Boston Tea Party.

12 Our anticipations cannot keep pace with the
realities that are continually overtaking
them. . . .   Quoted in
                *Godey's Lady's Book
                November 1845*

13 Albert Colesbury, of Philadelphia, fell in love
with Catherine Branchely, of New York, at a
quarter past ten o'clock, while dancing opposite
to her on the evening of his arrival at Ballston
Springs. . . .   "Love at First Sight,"
        *Kitty's Relations, and other pencil
                sketches   1847*

14 "Love at first sight is certainly a most amusing
thing," remarked Mrs. Seabright, "at least to
the by-standers."   Ibid.

15 "Some goes by coffee-grounds, which is low
and vulgar; and some goes by the lines on the
parms of your hands, which is nothing but
plexity and puzzledem; and some goes by the
stars and planipos [planets], which is too far off
to be certain. But cards is the only true things,
as all the best judges can scratify [certify]."
                "The Fortune-Teller,"
        *Leonilla Lynmore, and Mr. and
        Mrs. Woodbridge, or A lesson for
                young wives   1847*

701. Mary Russell Mitford (1787–1855)

1 JULIAN. I have been
Sick, brainsick, heartsick, mad I thought—
        I feared—

It was a foretaste of the pains of hell
To be so mad and yet retain the sense
Of that which made me so. *Julian,*
Act II, Sc. 1 *1823*

2 Of all living objects, children, out of doors, seem to me the most interesting to a lover of nature . . . Within doors . . . I am one of the many persons who like children in their places,—that is to say, anyplace where I am not. But out of doors there is no such limitation: from the gypsy urchins under a hedge, to the little lords and ladies in a ducal demesne, they are charming to look at, to watch, and to listen to. Dogs are less amusing, flowers are less beautiful, trees themselves are less picturesque.
"The Carpenter's Daughter,"
Belford Regis; or, Sketches of a
Country Town,
Vol. I *1835*

3 The grave equals all men. . . .
No. III, op. cit., Vol. II

4 COLONNA. The fool's grown wise—
A grievous change. Act II, Sc. 1, *Rienzi,*
1857

5 COLONNA. Joined! by what tie?
RIENZI. By hatred—
By danger—the two hands that tightest grasp
Each other—the two cords that soonest knit
A fast and stubborn tie: your true love knot
Is nothing to it. *Ibid.*

6 I have discovered that our great favourite, Miss [Jane] Austen,* is my countrywoman . . . with whom mamma before her marriage was acquainted. Mamma says that she was then the prettiest, silliest, most affected, husband-hunting butterfly she ever remembers.
Letter to Sir William
Elford (3 April 1815),
Quoted in *Life of Mary Russell Mitford,*
Vol. I, Rev. A. G. L'Estrange, ed.
1870

*See 669.

7 There is a thrilling awfulness, an intense feeling of simple power in that naked colourless beauty which falls on the earth, like the thoughts of death—death pure, and glorious, and smiling—but still death. Sculpture has always had the same effect on my imagination, and painting never. Colour is life. "Walks in the Country:
Frost and Thaw,"
Our Village 1892

702. Emma Hart Willard (1787–1870)

1 Rocked in the cradle of the deep
I lay me down in peace to sleep;
Secure I rest upon the wave,

For Thou, O Lord! hast power to save.
"The Ocean Hymn,"
St. 1, written at sea *14 July*
1831

2 In searching for the fundamental principles of the science of teaching, I find few axioms as indisputable as is the first principles of mathematics. One of these is this, HE IS THE BEST TEACHER WHO MAKES THE BEST USE OF HIS OWN TIME AND THAT OF HIS PUPILS. *For* TIME *is all that is given by God in which to do the work of Improvement.*
"How to Teach,"
Address to the Columbian
Association *n.d.*

3 He is not necessarily the best teacher who performs the most labour; makes his pupils work the hardest, and bustle the most. A hundred cents of copper, though they make more clatter and fill more space, have only a tenth of the value of one eagle of gold. *Ibid.*

4 Reason and religion teach us that we too are primary existences, that it is for us to move in the orbit of our duty around the holy center of perfection, the companions not the satellites of men. Inscribed
beneath her bust in the Hall of
Fame of Great Americans, Bronx,
New York
n.d.

703. Sarah Josepha Hale (1788–1879)

1 O wondrous power! how little understood,
-Entrusted to the mother's mind alone
To fashion genius, form the soul for good,
Inspire a West*, or train a Washington!
The Genius of Oblivion and
Other Poems 1823

*The American painter Benjamin West (1738–1820).

2 And bards and prophets tune their mystic lyres
While listening to the music of the waves!
Ibid.

3 The great error of those who would sever the Union, rather than see a slave within its borders, is that they forget the master is their brother as well as the servant. . . .
Preface *(5th edition, 1852),*
Northwood, A Tale of New
England 1828

4 . . . there is a period when nations as well as individuals quit their minority. . . .
Text, op. cit.

5 You may easily tell a rich Yankee farmer—he is always pleading poverty. *Ibid.*

6 In this age of innovation perhaps no experiment will have an influence more important on the

character and happiness of our society than the granting to females the advantages of a systematic and thorough education. The honour of this triumph, in favour of intellect over long established prejudice, belongs to the men of America.
Editorial,
The Ladies' Magazine
January 1828 *

* First issue of first woman's magazine in the United States.

7 There is no influence so powerful as that of the mother, but next in rank in efficacy is that of schoolmaster.
Ibid.

8 Victoria's reign will be one of the longest in English annals. . . .

She may so stamp her influence on the period in which she flourishes that history shall speak of it as her own. . . .

It will be the Victorian, as a former one now is the Elizabethan age . . .*
Editorial,
The Ladies' Magazine
February 1829

* Predicted two years before Victoria ascended the throne.

9 She was a weak woman—too highly elated in prosperity, too easily depressed by adversity—not considering that *both* are situations of trial. . . .
"Walter Wilson,"
Sketches of American Character 1829

10 Democracies have been, and governments called, *free;* but the spirit of independence and the consciousness of unalienable rights, were never before transfused into the minds of a whole people. . . . The feeling of equality which they proudly cherish does not proceed from an ignorance of their station, but from the knowledge of their rights; and it is this knowledge which will render it so exceedingly difficult for any tyrant ever to triumph over the liberties of our country.
"The Apparition,"
op. cit.

11 So far as the human mind can shake off selfishness and act from a sacred regard to truth, justice and duty, so far will men not only be virtuous, but fearless in virtue.
Ibid.

12 There is something in the decay of nature that awakens thought, even in the most trifling mind.
"A Winter in the Country,"
op. cit.

13 Mary had a little lamb,
Its fleece was white as snow,
And everywhere that Mary went
The lamb was sure to go.

It followed her to school one day,
Which was against the rule.
It made the children laugh and play
To see a lamb at school.

"What makes the lamb love Mary so?"
The eager children cry.
"Oh, Mary loves the lamb, you know,"
The teacher did reply.
"Mary's Little Lamb,"
in toto, *Poems for Our Children 1830*

14 O, beautiful rainbow, all woven of light!
There's not in thy tissue one shadow of night;
Heaven surely is open when thou dost appear,
And bending above thee, the angels draw near,
And sing—"the rainbow! the rainbow!
The smile of God is here."
"Beautiful Rainbow,"
op. cit.

15 We need not power or splendor;
Wide hall or lordly dome;
The good, the true, the tender,
These form the wealth of home.
"Home,"
op. cit.

16 Though Mind Aladdin's lamp might be,
His Geni was the Hand.
"The Hand and Its Work,"
op. cit.

17 I consider every attempt to induce women to think they have a just right to participate in the public duties of government as injurious to their best interests and derogatory to their character. Our empire is purer, more excellent and spiritual. . . .
Editorial,
The Ladies' Magazine and Literary Gazette February 1832

18 There is a deep moral influence in these periodical seasons of rejoicing, in which whole communities participate. They bring out, and together, as it were, the best sympathies in our natures.
Traits of American Life 1835

19 Americans have two ardent passions; the love of liberty and the love of distinction.
Ibid.

20 There is small danger of being starved in our land of plenty; but the danger of being stuffed is imminent.
Ibid.

21 There can be no education without leisure, and without leisure education is worthless.
Godey's Lady's Book (passim) 1837–1877

22 The barbarous custom of wresting from women whatever she possesses, whether by inheritance, donation or her own industry, and conferring it all upon the man she marries, to be used at his discretion and will, perhaps waste it on his wicked indulgences, without allowing her any

control or redress, is such a monstrous perversion of *justice* by *law*, that we might well marvel how it could obtain in a Christian community. "The Rights of Married Women,"
*Godey's Lady's Book
May 1837*

23 . . . man in blessing others finds his highest fame! *Ormond Grosvenor 1838*

24 The temple of our purest thoughts is—
silence! Ibid.

25 . . . rights are liable to be perverted to wrongs when we are incapable of rightly exercising them. Editorial,
*Godey's Lady's Book
January 1850*

26 "You talk to me about educating my children; but what's the use of it. . . . The more they know the wuss it will be for 'em; for they won't keep company with their own color, and white folks won't associate with them, and thar they are shut up by themselves . . . and they won't be any thing but just what I am, a nigger that every body despises."
*Liberia,
Ch. 3 1853*

27 ". . . it's might hard for a man like me, that could be as good as any body, if his skin were a shade or two lighter, to be kept down so all the time, and not get drunk or wicked."
Ibid.

28 ". . . what's de good of strong arms when de heart is a coward's?" Ibid., Ch. 5

29 "Africa . . . is the home . . . of the mysterious Negro races yet lying dormant in the germ, destined, perhaps, to rule this earth when our proud Anglo-Saxon blood is as corrupt as that of the descendents of Homer or Perricles [sic]." Ibid., Ch. 7

30 The belief in witchcraft was and is universal, where the spirit of Christianity has not shed its blessed light. Ibid., Ch. 9

31 If men cannot cope with women in the medical profession let them take an humble occupation in which they can. Editorial,
*Godey's Lady's Book
January 1853*

32 Lambs skip and bound, kittens and puppies seem wild with the joy of life; and little children naturally run, leap, dance and shout in the exhuberance of that capacity for happiness which the young human heart feels as instinctively as the flower buds open to the sun. To repress their natural joyousness, not to direct and train it for good, seems to be the object of most parents. Editorial,
*Godey's Lady's Book
October 1857*

33 Growing old! growing old! Do they say it of me?
Do they hint my fine fancies are faded and fled?
That my garden of life, like the winterswept tree,
Is frozen and dying, or fallen and dead?
"Growing Old"
[written on her 70th birthday],
*Godey's Lady's Book
24 October 1858*

34 . . . the whole process of home-making, housekeeping and cooking, which ever has been woman's special province, should be looked on as an art and a profession. . . . Editorial,
*Godey's Lady's Book
c.1859*

35 The most welcome guest in society will ever be the one to whose mind everything is a suggestion, and whose words suggest something to everybody. "Manners,"
*Godey's Lady's Book
c.1868*

36 The profession of teacher requires . . . as thorough and special training as that of any of the other intellectual professions. The great majority of our teachers are deficient in this training . . . the complaint on this head is indeed universal, and it is coupled with another complaint of the inadequate salaries almost every where paid to teachers, but more especially in rural districts. Editorial,
*Godey's Lady's Book
December 1868*

37 What has made this nation great? Not its heroes but its households. Editorial,
*Godey's Lady's Book
July 1869*

38 Every century has its peculiar tide of thought. *Woman's Record 1877*

704. Marguerite Blessington (1789–1849)

1 "Och! Jim, and is this the way you keep the Bible oath you took over to Father Cahill last Easther Sunday, that you would not dhrink a dhrop in any sheban-house for a year and a day? . . ."
"I did not dhrink a dhrop in the shebanhouse, for I put my head clean out of the window while I was dhrinking, so my oath is safe. . . ." *The Repealers,
Ch. 1 1833*

2 "How is it, Jim dear, that I, who love you betther than ever I loved myself, and you, who say you love me—that we, who have but one heart, can have two minds?" Ibid.

3 "Why liberty, cuishlamachree, manes to do every thing we like ourselves, and hinder everyone else from doing it." Ibid., Ch. 2

4 "Sure there's different roads from this to Dungarvan*—some thinks one road pleasanter, and some think another; wouldn't it be mighty foolish to quarrel for this?—and sure isn't it twice worse to thry to interfere with people for choosing the road they like best to heaven?" Ibid.

* Seaport and seat of Waterford County, Ireland; dating back to 7th Century.

5 "Imagination, which is the eldorado of the poet and of the novel-writer, often proves the most pernicious gift to the individuals who compose the talkers instead of the writers in society." Ibid., Ch. 40

6 Politeness, that cementer of friendship and soother of enmities, is nowhere so much required, and so frequently outraged, as in family circles. . . . Ibid., Ch. 57

7 ". . . he who would remain honest ought to keep away want." Ibid., Ch. 63

8 ". . . chance, the very worst guardian a man can choose for his personal comfort."
  The Two Friends,
  Ch. 1 *1835*

9 "My spaniel Dido is not more submissive," said Scamper; "for though I try Lady Janet by contradicting flatly to-day, what I maintained yesterday, it is all the same to her; she never has any opinion but mine: this is what I call the only solid foundation to build matrimonial happiness upon; and so I have made up my mind to marry." Ibid., Ch. 28

10 This is an autobiographical-loving age. . . .
  *The Confessions of an
  Elderly Gentleman 1836*

11 . . . it is better to die young than to outlive *all* one loved, and *all* that rendered one lovable. Ibid.

12 Love is, I think, like fever; one severe attack leaves the patient subject to relapses through youth; and each succeeding one renders him more weakened, and consequently, more exposed to future assaults. "My Fourth Love,"
  op. cit.

13 Happiness is a rare plant, that seldom takes root on earth: few ever enjoyed it, except for a brief period; the search after it is rarely rewarded by the discovery. But, there is an admirable substitute for it, which all may hope to attain, as its attainment depends wholly on self—and that is, a contented spirit. *The Victims of Society,*
  "Lady Mary Howard to Lady
  Augusta Vernon" *1837*

14 Injurious as are the examples of bad conduct, the impunity which too frequently attends the perpetration is still more fatally pernicious.
  Ibid.,
  "Lord Delaward to Lady
  Delaward"

15 It is a sad thing to look at happiness only through another's eyes. Ibid.,
  "The Countess of Anandale to
  the Countess of Delaward"

16 . . . we [the French] believe that the people who support the ills of life with the most cheerfulness, and forget them with the greatest facility, are the happiest, and, consequently, the wisest. *You* [the English] are above this happiness, and *we* are superior to the *ennui* which sends half your nation wandering into every clime; as if locomotion could relieve a malady that arises in the discontented mind. . . .
  Ibid., "The Marquise Le Villeroi
  to Miss Montressor"

17 You ask me whether English husbands are, in general, bons et aimables? Pas du tout, ma chère; tout au contraire. They are, as far as I can judge from the specimens I have seen, the most selfish beings imaginable. Ibid.,
  "Miss Montressor to La
  Marquise Le Villeroi"

18 It is the motive, and not the results, that constitutes the crime. Ibid.,
  "La Marquise Le Villeroi to
  Miss Montressor"

19 . . . with a good fortune, a brilliant position, and a weak, indulgent husband, what more could she desire? Ibid.

20 How soothing is affection! and how do those who, like me, know little of this sweetener of life, turn, with awakened tenderness, to him who administers the cordial! Ibid.,
  "The Countess of Anandale to
  La Marquise Le Villeroi"

21 A mother's love! O holy, boundless thing! Fountain whose waters never cease to
  spring. "Affection,"
  Gems of Beauty 1837–1838

22 People seem to lose all respect for the past; events succeed each other with such velocity that the most remarkable one of a few years gone by, is no more remembered than if centuries had closed over it.
  *The Confessions of an Elderly
  Lady 1838*

23 . . . modern historians are all would-be philosophers; who, instead of relating facts as they occurred, give us their version, or rather perversions of them, always colored by their political prejudices, or distorted to establish some

theory, and rendered obscure by cumbrous attempts to trace effect from cause.   Ibid.

24 . . . if those only wrote, who were sure of being read, we should have fewer authors; and the shelves of libraries would not groan beneath the weight of dusty tomes more voluminous than luminous.   Ibid.

25 There is no magician like Love. . . .   Ibid.

26 Time, that omnipotent effacer of *eternal* passions. . . .   Ibid.

27 Tears fell from my eyes—yes, weak and foolish as it now appears to me, I wept for my departed youth; and for that beauty of which the faithful mirror too plainly assured me, no remnant existed.   Ibid.

28 Novels and comedies end generally in a marriage, because, after that event, it is supposed that nothing remains to be told.
        "The Honey-Moon,"
        The Works of Lady
        Blessington   1838

29 They perceived that the love, unceasing and ecstatic, of which they had dreamt before their union, was a chimera existing only in imagination; and they awoke, with sobered feelings, to seek content in rational affection, instead of indulging in romantic expectations that never falls to the lot of human beings: each acknowledging, with a sigh, that even in a marriage of love, the brilliant anticipations of imagination are never realised; that disappointment awaits poor mortals even in that brightest portion of existence—The Honey-Moon.   Ibid.

30 Love-matches are made by people who are content, for a month of honey, to condemn themselves to a life of vinegar.
        Commonplace Book   n.d.

31 When the sun shines on you, you see your friends. Friends are the thermometers by which one may judge the temperature of our fortunes.   Ibid.

32 Religion converts despair, which destroys, into resignation, which submits.   Ibid.

705. Charlotte Elliott (1789–1871)

1 Just as I am, without one plea
But that Thy blood was shed for me,
And that Thou bidd'st me come to Thee,
    O Lamb of God, I come! "Just As I Am,"
        Invalid's Hymn Book   1834

2 "Christian! seek not yet repose,"
Hear thy guardian angel say;

Thou art in the midst of foes—
"Watch and pray."   "Christian! Seek
        Not Yet Repose,"
        Morning and Evening
        Hymns   c.1840

706. Hannah Flagg Gould (1789–1865)

1 He went to the windows of those who slept,
And over each pane, like a fairy, crept;
Wherever he breathed, wherever he
    stepped.
    By the light of the morn, were seen
Most beautiful things. . . .   "The Frost,"
        Poems   1832

2 O Thou, who in thy hand dost hold
The winds and waves that wake or sleep,
Thy tender arms of mercy fold
Around the seamen on the deep.
        "Changes on the Deep,"
        op. cit.

707. Ann Hasseltine Judson (1789–1826)

1 Either I have been made, through the mercy of God, a partaker of divine grace, or I have been fatally deceiving myself, and building upon a sandy foundation. Either I have, in sincerity and truth, renounced the vanities of this world, and entered the narrow path which leads to life, or I have been refraining from them for a time only, to turn again and relish them more than ever. God grant that the latter may never be my unhappy case!   Journal entry
        (22 December 1806), Quoted in *Memoir of*
        Mrs. Ann
        H. Judson, Late Missionary to
        Burma by James D. Knowles
        1829

2 I find more real enjoyment in contrition for sin, excited by a view of the adorable moral perfections of God, than in all earthly joys.   Ibid.

708. Catharine Maria Sedgwick (1789–1867)

1 "There is some pure gold mixed with all this glitter; some here that seem to have as pure hearts and just minds as if they had never stood in the dazzling sunshine of fortune."
        "The Opinions of a Yankee
        Spinster," *Redwood*
        1824

2 ". . . contentment is a modest, prudent spirit; and . . . for the most part she avoids the high places of the earth, where the sun burns and the

tempests beat, and leads her favourites along quiet vales to sequestered fountains." Ibid.

3 He who should embody and manifest the virtues taught in Christ's sermon on the Mount, would, though he had never seen a drawingroom, nor even heard of the artificial usages of society, commend himself to all nations, the most refined as well as the most simple. "True Politeness," op. cit.

4 The fountains are with the rich, but they are no better than a stagnant pool till they flow in streams to the labouring people.
"His Advice to his Children,"
The Poor Rich Man and the Rich Poor Man 1836

5 "If parents are civil and kind to one another, if children never hear from them profane or coarse language, they will as naturally grow up well-behaved, as that candle took the form of the mould it was run in.
"His Remarks on Manners,"
op. cit.

709. Eliza Townsend (1789–1854)

1 . . . let that come now,
Which soon or late must come. For light like this
Who would not dare to die?
"The Incomprehensibility of God," St. 1,
The Female Poets of America,
Rufus Griswold, ed. 1849

710. Harriette Wilson (1789–1846)

1 I shall not say why and how I became, at the age of fifteen, the mistress of the Earl of Craven. *Memoirs,*
(first sentence) *n.d.*

711. Ann Eliza Bray (1790–1883)

1 Never fear spoiling children by making them too happy. Happiness is the atmosphere in which all good affections grow . . . unhappiness—the chilling pressure which produces . . . "the mind's green and yellow sickness"—ill temper. Attributed *n.d.*

712. Mary Cole (fl. 1790s)

1 If all the writers upon Cookery had acknowledged from whence they took their receipts, as I do, they would have acted with more candour

by the public. Their vanity to pass for Authors, instead of Compilers, has not added to their reputation. *The Lady's Complete Guide* 1791

713. Louisa Macartney Crawford (1790–1858)

1 Kathleen Mavourneen; what, slumbering still?
Oh, hast thou forgotten how soon we must sever?
O hast thou forgotten this day we must part?
It may be for years, and it may be for ever!
Oh, why art thou silent, thou voice of my heart?
"Kathleen Mavourneen" (Attr.) *n.d.*

714. Eleanor Anne Franklin (c. 1790–1797–1825)

1 "Thine icy heart I well can bear,
But not the love that others share."
Coeur de Lion,* an Epic Poem in Sixteen Cantos 1822

*Richard I (the Lion-Heart), 1157–1199.

2 "The widow'd dove can never rest,
The felon kite has robb'd her nest;
With wing untir'd she seeks her mate,
To share or change his dreadful fate." Ibid.

715. Hannah Godwin (fl. 1790s)

1 Good sense without vanity, a penetrating judgment without a disposition to satire, with about as much religion as my William likes, struck me with a wish that she [Miss Gay] was my Williams' wife. Letter to William Godwin,*
her brother,
Quoted in *William Godwin: His Friends and Contemporaries*
by C. K. Paul 1876

*English political philosopher (1756–1836); married to Mary Wollstonecraft; see 609.

716. Rahel Levin (fl. 1790s–1810s)

1 Poor woman [Germaine de Staël*], she has seen nothing, heard nothing, understood nothing.
Quoted in *Mistress to an Age: A Life of Madame de Staël*
by J. Christopher Herold 1958

*See 637.

717. Rahel Morpurgo (1790–1871)

1 A woman's fancies lightly roam, and weave
Themselves into a fairy web.
Sonnet, *Ugab Rachel
[The Harp of Rachel]*,
I. Castiglione, ed.   *1890*

2 Wherever you go, you will hear all around:
The wisdom of woman to the distaff is
bound.   Untitled, St. 4, op. cit.

3 Better to die—to rest in shadows folded,
Than thus to grope amid the depths in vain!
"And here also I have done
nothing that they should put me
into the dungeon"
(aka "the Dark Valley"),
St. 1 (1867), op. cit.

4 I will tell thee an idea that has come into mind
that "oil from the flinty rock"* is *petroleum,*
and there is nothing new under the sun.
Letter to Isaac Luzzatto (1869),
op. cit.

*From Deuteronomy 32:13.

5 Woe! my knowledge is weak,
My wound is desperate.   Last Poem
(1871), op. cit.

718. Charlotte Elizabeth Tonna (1790–1846)

1 When we name the infliction of a wrong, we
imply the existence of a right. Therefore, if we
undertake to discuss the wrongs of women, we
may be expected to set out by plainly defining
what are the rights of women.
The Wrongs of Women, P. I,
"Milliners and Dress-makers"
Ch. 1   *1833–1834*

2 There is no presumption in taking God at his
word: not to do so, is very
impertinent. . . .   *Personal Recollections,*
Letter I   *1841*

3 There can be no doubt that the hand which first
encloses the waist of a girl in these cruel con-
trivances [stays], supplying her with a fictitious
support, where the hand of God has placed
bones and muscles that ought to be brought into
vigorous action, that hand lays the foundation
of bitter suffering. . . .   Ibid., Letter II

4 How very much do they err who consider the
absence of order and method as implying greater
liberty or removing a sense of restraint!
Ibid., Letter IV

5 . . . the want of punctuality is a want of honest
principle; for however people may think them-

selves authorised to rob God and themselves of
their own time, they can plead no right to lay a
violent hand on the time and duties of their
neighbour.   Ibid.

6 "And how do you feel when you have got
absolution?" "I feel all right; and I go out and
begin again." "And how do you know that God
has really pardoned you?" "He doesn't pardon
me directly; only the priest does. He [the priest]
confesses my sins to the bishop, and the bishop
confesses them to the pope, and the pope sees
the Virgin Mary every Saturday night, and tells
her to speak to God about it."
Ibid., Letter VIII

7 Nothing rights a boy of ten or twelve years like
putting him on his manhood. . . .
Ibid., Letter XIV

8 "He must be sworn. Boy, do you know the
nature of an oath?"
The wretched child answered by repeating
some of the most common and blasphemous
modes of execration, which, to Richard's great
horror, drew forth a peal of laughter, some on
the bench more than smiling.
"Pho!" said the presiding magistrate, angrily, "Do you know, sir, what will become of
those who take a false oath?"
"I have heard some say that it is bad to
swear, sir."   *Helen Fleetwood,*
Ch. 14, from *The Works of Charlotte
Elizabeth*, Vol. I
1844

9 "The weight seemed to be not only on my head,
but all over me; and then the sickening smell
and the whirring noise—I'll tell you what, the
first few days in a factory would make me ill,
and when I got over that, I should become
stupid."   Ibid., Ch. 19

10 Truth is a very aggressive principle; it does not
stand still to be attacked, but marches on, under
the conduct of faith, to assail the enemy, to
make conquests, and to recover what falsehood
has stolen, or violence wrested away.
*Second Causes; or, Up and
be Doing,*
Ch. 7, op. cit.

11 Scorning the rude world's idle toys,
Its faithless vowes and treacherous
joys. . . .   *Posthumous and Other Poems,*
"After a Tempest,"
St. 3, op. cit.

12 A self-sold, suicidal world "The Watchman,"
St. 4, op. cit.

13 Man, the proud sleeper, will not wake.   Ibid.

14 Look upon thy negro brother—
Be one moment *bound with him,*
Slave, in flesh and spirit weary—

Ponder what thy need would be—
Ponder deep the touching query
That thy brother asks of thee!
                    "Anti-Slavery Album,"
                        No. I, op. cit.

15 Haste to set thy people free;
Come; creation groans for thee!
                    "The Millennium,"
    St. 4, *The Female Poets of Great Britain*,
        Frederick Rowton, ed.   *1853*

719. Eliza Ware Farrar (1791–1870)

1 The queen* and princesses were all such com-
mon-looking people that they upset my childish
notions of royalty.
            Recollections of Seventy Years,
                    Ch. 2   *1865*

*Queen Charlotte (1744–1818), consort of George III of
England.

2 . . . Sir William Ellis . . . was at the head of
the great lunatic asylum for paupers at Handwell
near London. . . . No strait-waistcoats, no
strapping patients into beds or chairs, no pun-
ishments of any kind were used,—nothing but
the personal influence of Sir William and Lady
Ellis; and their power over all under their care
was extraordinary. Even persons in the height
of an attack of mania yielded to it. Part of their
system was to keep the patients as fully and as
happily employed as was possible, and the whole
establishment was like a great school of
industry.   Ibid., Ch. 38

720. Anne Marsh (1791–1874)

1 To say nothing of that brief but despotic sway
which every woman possesses over the man in
love with her—a power immense, unaccountable, invaluable; but in general so evanescent as
but to make a brilliant episode in the tale of
life—how almost immeasurable is the influence
exercised by wives, sisters, friends, and, most
of all, by mothers!   "Woman's Influence,"
                        Angela   *1848*

2 He [without education] enters life an ill-trained
steed; and the best that can be hoped for him
is, that the severe lash of disappointment, contradiction, and suffering, will, during the course
of his career, supply the omissions of his youth,
and train him at last, through much enduring,
to that point from which a good education would
have started him.   Ibid.

3 Oh, vice is a hideous thing.
    A hideous, dark mystery—the mystery of
iniquity! Its secret springs are hidden from our
view. . . .   "Sin and its
                            Consequences,"

                    *Mordaunt Hall; or, A September
                        Night   1849*

4 He shall render a heavier account . . . [who]
is great, and gifted, and wise, and powerful,
and fitted to guide a state and rule the interests
of a nation—he shall be the less forgiven, because in the plenitude of his powers he has
chosen to step aside to crush a poor little insect
in its humble path—he shall be the less forgiven,
because the wider the knowledge, and the higher
the intellect, and the larger the observation, so
much the greater is the power of estimating the
claims and appreciating the sufferings of whatever breathes; and that thoughtless cruelty which
we lament and pardon in the untutored child, is
odious, is execrable in the man!   "Seduction,"
                        op. cit.

5 Wherever or howsoever the sacredness of marriage is not reverenced, depend upon it, *there*
the man will ever be found imperfectly
developed.   "Illegitimacy,"
                        op. cit.

721. Sarah Martin (1791–1843)

1 I knew also that it sometimes seemed good in
His sight to try the faith and patience of His
servants, by bestowing upon them very limited
means of support; as in the case of Naomi* and
Ruth;** of the widow of Zarephath and Elijah;
and my mind, in the contemplation of such
trials, seemed exalted by more than human energy; for I had counted the cost; and my mind
was made up.   Article in *Edinburgh
                        Review   1847*

*See 16.
**See 17.

722. Margaret Mercer (1791–1846)

1 *Conversation is to works what the flower is to
the fruit.* A godly conversation shelters and
cherishes the new-born spirit of virtue, as the
flower does the fruit from the cold, chill atmosphere, of a heartless world; and the beauty of
holiness expanding in conversation, gives rational anticipation of nobleminded principles
ripening into the richest fruits of good
works.   *Ethics   n.d.*

2 . . . I confess that the 'unidea-ed chatter of
females' is past my endurance; they are very
capable of better things, but what of that? Is it
not yet more annoying that they will do nothing
better?   Quoted in *Memoirs*
                    by Caspar Morris, M.D.   *n.d.*

3 . . . steady laborious efforts to do good will
doubtless be blessed, although we may in mercy

be denied the luxury of seeing our work under the sun prosper.   Ibid.

723. Lydia Howard Sigourney (1791–1865)

1 "I was a worm till I won my wings"
                "Butterfly on a Child's Grave,"
                        St. 2, *Poems*   1834

2 To evil habit's earliest wile
Lend neither ear, nor glance, nor smile—
Choke the dark fountain ere it flows,
Nor e'en admit the camel's nose.
                        "The Camel's Nose,"
                        St. 4, op. cit.

3 Courage, World-finder!   "Columbus,"*
                                op. cit.

*Christopher C. (1451?–1506) Italian navigator and explorer who opened path to New World.

4 Not on the outer world
    For inward joy depend;
Enjoy the luxury of thought,
    Make thine own self friend
                        "Know Thyself,"
                        op. cit.

5 Flow on forever, in thy glorious robe
Of terror and beauty.   "Niagara," St. 1,
                *Zinzendorff, and Other
                Poems   1836*

6 *Death is the test of life.*—All else is vain.
                        "The Test of Life,"
                        St. 1, op. cit.

7 Bid the long-prisoned mind attain
    A sphere of dazzling day,
Bid her unpinion'd foot
    The cliffs of knowledge climb,
And search for Wisdom's sacred root
    That mocks the blight of time.
                        "Female Education,"
                        St. 3, op. cit.

8   They, perchance,
Did look on woman as a worthless thing,
A cloistered gem, a briefly-fading flower,
Remembering not that she had kingly power
O'er the young soul.   "Establishment of a
                Female College in New-Grenada,
                South America,"
                        St. 1, op. cit.

9 —Oh woman, oft misconstrued!
                        "The Daughter,"
                        St. 8, op. cit.

10 Hope spreads her wing of plumage fair,
    Rebuilds her castle bas'd on air
                        "The Soap Bubble,"
                        op. cit.

11 These were the seeds our mother sowed,—
Let them bear perfect fruit.   "Filial Grief,"
                        St. 4, op. cit.

12 Death's shafts are ever busy.
                        "Death of Mr. Oliver D.
                        Cooke,"
                        St. 1, op. cit.

13 —See, life is but a dream. Awake! Awake!
Break off the trance of vanity. . . .
                        "Dreams,"
                        St. 4, op. cit.

14 Cold world!—the teachings of thy guile
Awhile from these young hearts restrain
                        "Hinder Them Not,"
                        St. 4, op. cit.

15 Like wild flowers among the dells, or clefts of
the rock, they [poems] sprang up wherever the
path of life chanced to lead.
                Preface, *Select Poems*   1841

16   O Man! so prodigal of pride and praise,
Thy works survive thee—dead machines per-
    form
Their revolution, while thy scythe-shorn days
Yield thee a powerless prisoner to the worm—
                        "The Ancient Family
                        Clock,"
                        St. 10, op. cit.

17 —I fear thee. Thou'rt a subtle husbandman,
Sowing thy little seed, of good or ill,
In the moist, unsunn'd surface of the heart.
                        "Thought,"
                        St. 2, op. cit.

18 Memory, with traitor-tread
    Methinks, doth steal away
Treasures that the mind had laid
Up for a wintry day.
                        "Barzillai the Gileadite,"*
                        St. 4, op. cit.

*Aged and wealthy citizen of the city of Gilead, who befriended David when he fled from Absalom (2 Samuel 17: 27–29; 19:32).

19 And yield the torn world to the angel of
    peace.   "The War Spirit,"
                        St. 5, op. cit.

20 This is the parting place; this narrow house
                        "The Tomb,"
                        St. 1, op. cit.

21   Thou who has toiled to earn
The fickle praise of far posterity,
Come, weigh it at the grave's brink, here with
    me,
If thou canst weigh a dream.
                        "The Dying Philosopher,"
                        St. 4, op. cit.

22 But their name is on your waters,
    Ye may not wash it out.   "Indian Names,"
                        St. 1, op. cit.

23 For thou* dost teach us from the dead
    A lesson that all pride should tame;
That genius high and morals base
    Mar the great Giver's plan,
And, like a comet's flaming race,
Make visible the deep disgrace
Of His best gifts to man.
          "The Western Home," St. 52,
          Poems   1854

*Aaron Burr (1756–1836), 3rd vice president of the United States (1801–1805).

24   For fashion, or for thirst of gold.
The venal hand may diamonds link,
In velvet pile the foot may sink
The lips from jewelled chalice drink,
Yet every nerve to joy be dead,
And all the life of feeling fled
In the heart's palsied atrophy.   Ibid., St. 53

25 Man's warfare on the tree is terrible.
          "Fallen Forests,"
          St. 1, op. cit.

26 They say that the cell of the poet should be
Like the breast of the shell that remembers the
    sea   "The Muse,"
          St. 1, op. cit.

27 Nature hath secret lore for those who lean
Upon her breast, with leisure in their soul
          "Listen,"
          St. 2, op. cit.

28 Language is slow. "Unspoken Language,"
          St. 1, op. cit.

29 Then up went the thrush with a trumpet call,
And the martins came forth from their cells on
    the wall,
And the owlets peep'd out from their secret
    bower,
And the swallows conversed on the old
    church-tower,
And the council of blackbirds was long and
    loud,
Chattering and flying from tree to cloud.
          "Birds of Passage," St. 6, op. cit.

30 We dream, but they awake "The Holy Dead,"
          St. 4, op. cit.

31 . . . the few who by example teach,
Making a text-book of their own strong heart
And blameless life.   "The Ivy," St. 4,
          op. cit.

32 For every quarrel cuts a thread
    That healthful Love has spun.
          "The Thriving Family,"
          St. 3, op. cit.

33 The influence which is most truly valuable is
that of mind over mind.
          "Power of a Mother,"
      Letters to Mothers   n.d.

34 Admitting that it is the profession of our sex to teach, we perceive the mother to be first in point of precedence, in degree of power, in the faculty of teaching, and in the department allotted. For in point of precedence she is next to the Creator; in power over her pupil, limitless and without competitor; in faculty of teaching, endowed with the prerogative of a transforming love; while the glorious department allotted is a newly quickened soul and its immortal destiny.   Ibid.

35 This, then, is the patriotism of woman; not to thunder in senates, or to usurp dominion, or to seek the clarion-blast of fame, but faithfully to teach by precept and example that wisdom, integrity, and peace which are the glory of a nation.   "Woman's Patriotism,"
          op. cit.

724. Virginie Ancelot (1792–1875)

1 *"There are no longer any women!* no, my dear, Count, there are no longer any women," mournfully exclaimed the Marchioness de Fontenay-Mareuil. . . ."   *Gabrielle,*
          Ch. 1   *1840*

2 "Saloons* exist no longer; conversation has ceased; good taste has disappeared with it, and mind has lost all its influences."   Ibid.

*Salons.

725. Sarah Moore Grimké (1792–1873)

1 . . . the false translation of some passages [of the New Testament] by the MEN who did that work, and against the perverted interpretation by the MEN who undertook to write commentaries thereon. I am inclined to think, when we [women] are admitted to the honor of studying Greek and Hebrew, we shall produce some various readings of the Bible a little different from those we now have.   Letter, from Haverhill
          (17 July 1837),
      Letters on the Equality of the
      Sexes, and the Condition of
      Woman   1838

2 Ah! how many of my sex feel . . . that what they have leaned upon has proved a broken reed at best, and oft a spear.   Ibid.

3 In most families, it is considered a matter of far more consequence to call a girl off from making a pie, or a pudding, than to interrupt her whilst engaged in her studies.
          Letter, from Brookline
          (1837), op. cit.

4 There is another way in which the general opinion, that women are inferior to men, is mani-

fested. . . . I allude to the disproportionate value set on the time and labor of men and women. Ibid.

5 Woman, instead of being elevated by her union with man, which might be expected from an alliance with a superior being, is in reality lowered. She generally loses her individuality, her independent character, her moral being. She becomes absorbed into him, and henceforth is looked at, and acts through the medium of her husband. Letter, from Brookline (September 1837), op. cit.

6 Brute force, the law of violence, rules to a great extent in the poor man's domicile; and woman is little more than his drudge. Ibid.

7 We cannot push Abolitionism forward . . . *until* we take up the stumbling block [women's rights] out of the road.
Quoted in *Letters of Theodore Dwight Weld,* * Angelina Grimké Weld* * and S. Sarah Grimké, 1822–1844,* Vol. I, Gilbert H. Barnes and Dwight L. Dumond, eds. *1934*

* American abolitionist (1803–1895).
** See 780.

726. Harriet Grote (1792–1878)

1 Politics and theology are the only two really great subjects. Letter to Lord Rosebery* (16 September 1880), Quoted in *Life of Gladstone* by John Morley Morly, Bk. VIII, Ch. 1 *1903*

* Archibald Philip Primrose, 5th earl of Rosebery (1847–1929), English statesman.

727. Anne Isabella Milbanke (1792–1860)

1 Yes! Farewell—farewell forever!
Thou thyself has fixed our doom,
Bade hope's fairest blossoms wither,
Ne'er again for me to bloom.
"Fare Thee Well" (to Lord Byron) *c.January 1816*

728. Caroline Symonds (1792–1803)

1 She planted, she lov'd it, she water'd its head,
And its bloom every rival defied;
But alas! what was beauty or virtue, soon fled,
In Spring they both blossom'd and died.
"The Faded Rose, which grew on the tomb of Zelida," St. 4,

The Female Poets of Great Britain, Frederic Rowton, ed. *1853*

2 Scarce had thy velvet lips imbib'd the dew,
And nature hail'd thee, infant queen of May;
Scarce saw thy opening bloom the sun's broad ray,
And on the air its tender fragrance threw;
When the north wind enamour'd of thee grew,
And from his chilling kiss, thy charms decay. "The Blighted Rosebud," * op. cit.

* Inscribed on the tomb of the writer, who died at the age of 11.

729. Sarah Taylor Austin (1793–1867)

1 It is the peculiar and invaluable privilege of a translator, as such, to have no opinions, and this is precisely what renders the somewhat toilsome business of translating attractive to one who has a profound sense of the difficulty of forming mature and coherent opinions, and of the presumption of putting forth crude and incongruous ones. . . . Translator's Preface, *England in 1835: being a series of Letters written to friends in Germany. . . ,* by Frederick von Raumer *1836*

730. Felicia Dorothea Hemans (1793–1835)

1 We will give the names of our fearless race
To each bright river whose course we trace.
"Song of Emigration," *Works 1839*

2 The stately homes of England!
How beautiful they stand,
Amidst their tall ancestral trees,
O'er all the pleasant land!
"The Homes of England," St. 1, op. cit.

3 The boy stood on the burning deck,
Whence all but he had fled. "Casabianca," St. 1, op. cit.

4 In the busy haunts of men
"Tale of the Secret Tribunal," Pt. I, 1. 203, op. cit.

5 In the music-land of dreams. "The Sleeper," op. cit.

6 Life's best balm—forgetfullness.
"The Caravan in the Desert," op. cit.

7 Home of the Arts! where glory's faded smile
Sheds lingering light o'er many a mouldering
    pile.   "Restoration of the
Works of Art to Italy,"
op. cit.

8 Oh! what a crowded world one moment may
    contain.   "The Last Constantine,"
op. cit.

9   We endow
Those whom we love, in our fond, passionate
    blindness,
With power upon our souls too absolute
To be a mortal's trust.
        "The Siege of Valencia,"
op. cit.

10 They grew in beauty side by side,
They fill'd one home with glee;—
Their graves are severed far and wide
By mount, and stream, and sea.
        "The Graves of a Household,"
op. cit.

11 Oh, lightly, lightly tread!
A holy thing is sleep   "The Sleeper,"
op. cit.

12 Talk not of grief till thou has seen the tears of
    warlike men!   "Bernardo del Carpio,"
1. 26, op. cit.

13 Oh! call my brother back to me!
I cannot play alone;
The summer comes with flower and bee—
Where is my brother gone?
        "The Child's First Grief,"
St. 1, op. cit.

14 Is *all* that we see or seem
But a dream within a dream?
        "A Dream Within a Dream,"
last lines, op. cit.

731. Lucretia Mott (1793–1880)

1 Then, in the marriage union, the independence
of the husband and wife will be equal, their
dependence mutual, and their obligations
reciprocal.   *Discourse on Women*   *1850*

2 Look at the heads of those [Quaker] women;
they can mingle with men; they are not triflers;
they have intelligent subjects of
conversation.   Women's Rights Convention,
Proceedings   *1853*

3 Learning, while at school, that the charge for
the education of girls was the same as that for
boys, and that, when they became teachers,
women received only half as much as men for
their services, the injustice of this distinction
was so apparent, that I resolved to claim for my

sex all that an impartial Creator had bestowed,
which, by custom and a perverted application
of the Scriptures, had been wrested from
woman.   Letter, Quoted in *Biography of
Distinguished Women*
by Sarah Josepha Hale*   *1876*
*See 703.

4 The cause of Peace has had a share of my
efforts, taking the ultra non-resistance ground—
that a Christian cannot consistently uphold, and
actively support, a government based on the
sword, or whose ultimate resort is to the destroying weapon.   *Ibid.*

5 . . . systems by which the rich are made richer,
and the poor poorer, should find no favour
among people professing to "fear God and hate
covetousness."   *Ibid.*

6 Truth for authority, not authority for truth.
        Motto, Quoted in
The Peerless Leader
by Hibben   *n.d.*

732. Almira Lincoln Phelps (1793–1884)

1 What a pledge for virtuous conduct is the character of a mother!   "The Mother's Hopes,"
The Mother's Journal   *1838*

2 So, in the physical world mankind are prone to
seek an explanation of *uncommon* phenomena
only, while the ordinary changes of nature,
which are in themselves equally wonderful, are
disregarded.   "An Infant's First Ideas,"
op. cit.

3 The universe, how vast! exceeding far
The bounds of human thought; millions of
    suns,
With their attendant worlds moving around
Some common centre, gravitation strange!
Beyond the power of finite minds to scan!
        "The Wonders of Nature,"
St. 1, *Poems*   *n.d.*

4 Each opening bud, and care-perfected seed,
Is as a page, where we may read of God.
        Ibid., St. 3

733. Sarah Alden Ripley (1793–1867)

1 What a vista! A whole new language!*
    Quoted in *Notable American Women*,
Edward T. James, ed.   *1971*

*Reaction to Cervantes' *Don Quixote*.

2 The sun looks brighter . . . as the evening of
life draws near.   Letter to her sister-in-law,
op. cit.

734. Catherine Spalding (1793–1858)

1 My heart still clings to the orphans.
Quoted in *Notable American Women*,
Edward T. James, ed. *1971*

735. Caroline Gilman (1794–1888)

1 Changes! Sameness! What a perpetual chime
those words ring on the ear of memory!
Recollections of a Southern
Matron, Ch. 1
1837

2 One clear idea is too precious a treasure to
lose. *Ibid.*, Ch. 3

3 I know how the mind rushes back, in such
moments, to infancy, when those stiffened hands
were wrapped around us in twining love; when
that bosom was the pillow of our first sorrows;
when those ears, now insensible and soundless,
heard our whispered confidence; when those
eyes, now curtained by uplifted lids, watched
our every motion. I know the pang that runs
through the heart, and I can fancy the shrieking
voice within which says, "Thou mightst have
done more for thy mother's happiness, for her
who loved thee so!" *Ibid.*

4 I must ask indulgence of general readers for
mingling so much of the peculiarities of negroes
with my details. Surrounded with them from
infancy, they form a part of the landscape of a
southern woman's life; take them away, and the
picture would lose half its reality. They watch
our cradles; they are the companions of our
sports; it is they who aid our bridal decorations,
and they wrap us in our shroud.
Ibid., Ch. 14

5 . . . it is death—there is its stillness—its
shroud—its fixed and pale repose; the voice tells
not its wants—the eye knows not. We bend over
the stiffened form, and turn away, and come
not again, for it is death; perchance we lift the
bloodless hand, or smooth the straying hair, but
only once, for it is death, and we are
chilled. *Ibid.*, Ch. 23

6 . . . convert schools into places for *teaching*
instead of *recitation*. . . . If the system continue as it is, the name of *teacher* should be
changed to *lesson-hearer*. *Ibid.*, Ch. 28

7 . . . sitting down to *one* plate, that loneliest of
all positions. . . . *Ibid.*, Ch. 35

8 To repress a harsh answer, to confess a fault,
and to stop (right or wrong) in the midst of self-
defence, in gentle submission, sometimes requires a struggle like life and death; but these
three efforts are the golden threads with which
domestic happiness is woven; once begin the

fabric with this woof, and trials shall not break
or sorrow tarnish it. *Ibid.*

9 Space for the sunflower,
Bright with yellow glow
To court the sky. "To the Ursulines,"
Verses of a Life-Time *1849*

736. Anna Brownell Jameson (1794–1860)

1 To think of the situations of these women! . . .
steeped in excitement from childhood, their nerves
for ever in a state of terror between severe
application and maddening flattery; cast on the
world without chart or compass—with energies
misdirected, passions uncontrolled, and all the
inflammable and imaginative part of their being
cultivated to excess as part of their profession—
of their material!
"Women Artists—Singers—
Actresses, &C.,"
Visits and Sketches at Home and
Abroad; With Tales and
Miscellanies *1834*

2 It is this cold impervious pride which is the
perdition of us English, and of England.
"English Pride,"
op. cit.

3 Conversation may be compared to a lyre with
seven chords—philosophy, art, poetry, politics,
love, scandal, and the weather.
"Conversation,"
op. cit.

4 Truth is the golden chain which links the terres-
trial with the celestial, which sets the seal of
heaven on the things of this earth, and stamps
them with immortality.
The Loves of the Poets *c.1835*

5 The true purpose of education is to cherish and
unfold the seed of immortality already sown
within us; to develop, to their fullest extent, the
capacities of every kind with which the God
who made us has endowed us. "Education,"
Winter Studies and Summer
Rambles *1842*

6 He that seeks popularity in art closes the door
on his own genius: as he must needs paint for
other minds, and not for his own.
"Washington Allston," *
Memoirs and Essays Illustrative
of Art, Literature, and Social
Mores *1846*

*American painter (1779–1843).

7 The only competition worthy a wise man is with
himself. *Ibid.*

8 A man may be as much a fool from the want of
sensibility as the want of sense.
Detached Thoughts *n.d.*

9 As the rolling stone gathers no moss, so the
roving heart gathers no affections.
"Sternberg's Novels,"
Studies   n.d.

737. Maria Brooks (1795–1845)

1 My ills are my desert, my good thy gift.
"Hymn," St. 3,
Judith, Esther** and Other
Poems   1820*

*See 31.
**See 34.

2 Day, in melting purple dying.   "Song,"
St. 1, op. cit.

3 Looks are its food, its nectar sighs,
Its couch the lips, its throne the eyes,
The soul its breath: and so possest,
Heaven's raptures reign in mortal breast,
Fratello del mio cor.   "Friendship,"
St. 2, op. cit.

4 Who would not brave a fiend to share an an-
gel's smile?   Canto First,
"Grove of Acadias,"
VIII, St. 1,
*Zóphiël; or the Bride of
Seven   1825*

5 Where passion is not found, no virtue ever
dwelt.   Ibid., X, St. 1

6 "The bird that sweetest sings can least endure
the storm."   Ibid., XIV, St. 1

7 But thou,* too bright and pure for mortal
touch,
Art like those brilliant things we never taste
Or see, unless with Fancy's lip and eye,
When maddened by her mystic spells, we
waste
Life on a thought, and rob reality.
Ibid., XX, Sts. 1, 2

*The passionflower.

8   . . . Reverie,
Sweet mother of the muses, heart and soul are
thine!   Ibid., XXII, St. 1

9 Ye who beheld her hand forgot her face;
Yet in that face was all beside forgot
Ibid., Canto Second,
"Death of Altheëtor,"
LI, St. 1

10 'Tis now the hour of mirth, the hour of love,
The hour of melancholy: Night, as vain
Of her full beauty, seems to pause above,
That all may look upon her ere it wane.
Ibid., Canto Third,
"Palace of Gnomes,"
I, St. 1

11 Soul, I would rein thee in
Ibid., XXXII, St. 1

12 Soul, what a mystery thou art! not one
Admires, or loves, or worships virtue more
Than I; but passion hurls me on, till torn
By keen remorse, I cool, to curse me and
deplore.   Ibid., XXXIII, St. 1

13 How can I longer bear my weary doom?
Alas! what have I gain'd for all I lost?
Ibid., CIX, St. 4

14 . . . cold ambition mimicks love so well,
That half the sons of heaven looked on
deceived   Ibid., Canto Fourth,
"The Storm,"
XLVIII, St. 2

15 How thrills the kiss, when feeling's voice is
mute!   Ibid., Canto Fifth,
"Zameïa," III, St.1

16   "Women may be
Enthrall'd by love, and often will forsake
All other gods for love's idolatry."
Ibid., XXII, St. 3

17   "If evil things can give
Dreams such as mine, let me turn foe to good,
And make a God of *Evil* while I live!"
Ibid., XXIV, St. 1

18 And love and hope are twins. . . .
Ibid., XCVI, St. 1

19 "The frailest hope is better than despair"
Ibid., CII, St. 1

20 But thousand evil things there are that hate
To look on happiness   Ibid., Canto Sixth,
"Bridal of Helon,"
IV, St. 1

738. Frances Manwaring Caulkins (1795–1869)

1 The hand of God is seen in the history of towns
as well as in that of nations. The purest and
noblest love of the olden time is that which
draws from its annals, motives of gratitude and
thanksgiving for the past—counsels and warn-
ings for the future.
Preface, *History of New London,
Connecticut   1852*

2 The tendency of man among savages, without
the watch of his equals and the check of society,
is to degenerate; to decline from the standard of
morals, and gradually to relinquish all Christian
observances.   Ibid., Ch. 6

739. Rebecca Cox Jackson (1795–1871)

1 I always believed that if the Lord had a work

for His children to do, He was able to make it as plain as the light.

From her Autobiography (1833–1836), in *Gift of Powers, The Writings of Rebecca Jackson, Black Visionary, Shaker Eldress,* Jean McMahon Humez, ed. *1981*

2 Jesus, the seed of the woman, is the manhood in which the seed of God dwells. Which seed is called the Godhead dwelling in manhood.

Ibid. (1844–1851)

3 The fear of God is the beginning of Wisdom. . . . Ibid.

740. Frances Wright (1795–1852)

1 The prejudices still to be found in Europe . . . which would confine . . . female conversation to the last new publication, new bonnet, and *pas seul* [nothing else] are entirely unknown here. The women are assuming their place as thinking beings. . . .

Views of Society & Manners in America   1821

2 It is not as of yore. Eve puts not forth her hand to gather the fair fruit of knowledge. The wily serpent now hath better learned his lesson; and, to secure his reign in the garden, beguileth her *not* to eat.

Course of Popular Lectures   1829

3 . . . whenever we establish our own pretensions upon the sacrificed rights of others, we do in fact impeach our own liberties, and lower ourselves in the scale of being! Ibid.

4 Let us enquire—not if a mother be a wife, or a father a husband, but if parents can supply, to the creatures they have brought into being, all things requisite to make existence a blessing.

(1828), Quoted in *Frances Wright, Free Enquirer* by A. J. G. Perkins and Theresa Wolfson   *1939*

741. Sophia Smith (1796–1870)

1 It is my opinion that by the higher and more thoroughly Christian education of women, what are called their "wrongs" will be redressed, their wages will be adjusted, their weight of influence in reforming the evils of society will be greatly increased; as teachers, as writers, as mothers, as members of society, their power for good will be incalculably enlarged.

Last Will and Testament of Miss Sophia Smith,

Late of Hatfield, Massachusetts 1871

742. Annette Elizabeth von Droste-Hülshoff (1797–1848)

1 At night, when heavenly peace is flying
Above the world that sorrow mars,
Ah, think not of my grave with sighing!
For then I greet you from the stars.

"Last Words," St. 3, *The Catholic Anthology,* Thomas Walsh, ed.   *1927*

2 So still the pond in morning's gray,
A quiet conscience is not clearer.

"The Pond" (*"Der Weiher"*), Herman Salinger, tr.; *An Anthology of German Poetry from Hölderlin to Rilke,* Angel Flores, ed.   *1960*

3 O spirit free, entrancing youth,
Here at the very railing, I
Would wrestle, hip to hip, against
Your hold; become alive—or die.

"On the Tower" (*"Am Turme"*), St. 1, James Edward Tobin, tr., op. cit.

4 If heaven listened to my plea,
Made me a man, even though small!
Instead, I sit here—delicate,
Polite, precise, well-mannered child.
Dreams shake my loosened hair—the wind
Lone listener to my spirit wild.   Ibid., St. 4

5 O slumber-waking strange, are you the certain
Curse of delicate nerves or yet their
   blessing?   "Sleepless Night" (*"Durchwachte Nacht"*), St. 4, Herman Salinger, tr., op. cit.

6 . . . dreams release the soul's love urge

Ibid., St. 6

7 . . . all the ghosts within your breast
(Dead love, dead pleasure, and dead time)

"In the Grass" (*"Im Grase"*), St. 2, James Edward Tobin, tr., op. cit.

8 The year is at its close,
A spindle ravels thinning thread;
One strand is left, a single hour.
And time, a glowing, pulsing rose,
Will crumble as a final flower,
Dusty and dead.   "The Last Day of the Year" (*"Am letzten Tage des Jahres"*), St. 1, James Edward Tobin, tr., op. cit.

9   Minutes, like rivers, shake
The city walls, each house, each gate.

Ibid., St. 2

743. Emily Eden (1797–1869)

1 People may go on talking for ever of the jealousies of pretty women; but for real genuine, hard-working envy, there is nothing like an ugly woman with a taste for admiration.
The Semi-Attached Couple,
Pt. I, Ch. 1   *1830*

2 "You will soon see how naturally one acquires a distaste for any ill-judging individual who presumes not to like one's husband."
Ibid., Ch. 3

3 What could be more absurd than to assemble a crowd to witness a man and a woman promising to love each other for the rest of their lives, when we know what human creatures are,—men so thoroughly selfish and unprincipled, women so vain and frivolous?   Ibid., Ch. 7

4 "I said to myself the other day, that one never hears anything new till it is old. . . ."
Ibid., Ch. 17

5 There is nothing so catching as refinement. . . .   Ibid., Ch. 48

6 "I often think, my dear, that it is a great pity you are so imaginative, and still a greater pity that you are so fastidious. You would be happier if you were as dull and as matter-of-fact as I am."   *The Semi-Detached House,* Ch. 1
c.1860s

7 "Now is that so like the Post Office?" she said. "Letters that are of no consequence are always delivered directly, but when Arthur writes to me, they send his letters all over England."
Ibid., Ch. 5

8 At last, there came the joyful whisper, "a fine boy," perhaps the only moment of a fine boy's existence in which his presence is more agreeable than his absence.   Ibid., Ch. 18

744. Kamamalu (1797?–1824)

1 O! heaven; O! earth; O! mountains; O! sea; O! my counsellors and my subjects, farewell! O! thou land for which my father suffered, the object of toil which my father sought. We now leave thy soil; I follow thy command; I will never disregard thy voice; I will walk by the command which thou hast given me.
Farewell address to her
people upon her departure to
England* (27 November 1823),
Quoted in *Biography of
Distinguished Women*
by Sarah Josepha Hale**   *1876*

*She died in England, never returning to her native land.
**See 703.

745. Mary Lyon (1797–1849)

1 There is nothing in the universe that I fear but that I shall not know all my duty, or shall fail to do it.*   Quoted in *Eminent
Missionary Women*
by Mrs. J. T. Gracey   *1898*

*Inscribed on her monument at Mt. Holyoke College, which she founded, in Hadley, Massachusetts.

2 When you choose your fields of labor go where nobody else is willing to go.   Ibid.

3 Oh, how immensely important is this work of preparing the daughters of the land to be good mothers!   Letter to her mother,
from Ipswich (12 May 1834),
Quoted in *Mary Lyon through
Her Letters,* Marion Lansing, ed.
1937

746. Penina Moïse (1797–1880)

1 Lay no flowers on my grave. They are for those who live in the sun, and I have always lived in the shadow.   Last words,
Quoted in *Notable American
Women,* Edward T. James, ed.
1971

747. Madame Pfeiffer (1799–post-1852)

1 A small affair would it have been for me to sail around the world, as many have done; it is my land journeys that render my tour a great undertaking, and invest it with interest.
Quoted in *Biography of
Distinguished Women*
by Sarah Josepha Hale*   *1876*

*See 703.

2 Never betray fear.   Motto, op. cit.

748. Therese Albertine Louise Robinson (1797–post-1852)

1 Not the untamed passion of the human heart, which, bursting out into a flame, spreading ruinously, destroys all barriers; not the unbridled force, which, in wild outbreaks of savage roughness, crushes under foot tender blossoms, lovely flowers,—not these constitute the greatest, the truest evil of the world; it is cold, creeping *egotism,* heartless *selfishness;* which, with its attendants, treachery, deceit, and hypocrisy, easily bears away the palm, because it knows what it is doing, while passion, in blind fury, shatters

its own weapons.   "Selfishness,"
            Life's Discipline; a Tale of the
            Annals of Hungary   1851

2 Losing her faith in the moral worth of the man
she loves, a woman loses all the *happiness* of
love.   "Loving Unworthily,"
                                  op. cit.

3 Love is dead. We are cured,—but are we
happy?   Ibid.

749. Mary Shelley (1797–1851)

1 . . . my dreams were all my own; I accounted
for them to nobody; they were my refuge when
annoyed—my dearest pleasure when free.
                              Introduction
                              (1831 edition),
                *Frankenstein (or, the Modern
                    Prometheus)   1818*

2 I felt that blank incapability of invention which
is the greatest misery of authorship, when dull
Nothing replies to our anxious invocations.
                                      Ibid.

3 To examine the causes of life, we must first
have recourse to death.   Text, Ch. 4,
                                    op. cit.

4 Learn from me, if not by my precepts, at least
by my example, how dangerous is the acquire-
ment of knowledge, and how much happier that
man is who believes his native town to be the
world, than he who aspires to become greater
than his nature will allow.   Ibid.

5 I beheld the wretch—the miserable monster whom
I had created.   Ibid., Ch. 5

6 "Of what a strange nature is knowledge! It
clings to the mind, when it has once seized on
it, like a lichen on the rock."   Ibid., Ch. 13

7 His conversation was marked by its happy
abundance.   Preface,
                        *Collected Edition of
                        Shelley   1839*

8 Mrs. Shelley was choosing a school for her
son,* and asked the advice of this lady, who
gave for advice—to use her own words to me—
"Just the sort of banality, you know, one does
come out with: 'Oh, send him somewhere where
they will teach him to think for himself!' "
. . . Mrs. Shelley answered: "Teach him to
think for himself? Oh, my God, teach him rather
to think like other people!"
                        Quoted in *Essays in
            Criticism, Second Series; Shelley
            by Matthew Arnold   1888*

*Percy Bysshe Shelley (1792–1822), English poet and
husband of Mary.

750. Sojourner Truth (c.1797–1883)

1 Ef women want any rights more'n dey got, why
don't dey jes' *take 'em,* and not be talkin' about
it.   Comment   *c.1863*

2 I . . . can't read a book but I can read de
people.   Address, Tremont Temple,
                        Boston, Massachusetts
                            January 1, 1871

3 It is the mind that makes the body.
                        Interview, Battle Creek,
                        Michigan   *c.1877*

4 Religion without humanity is a poor human
stuff.   Ibid.

5 Wall, childern, whar dar is so much racket dar
must be somethin' out o' kilter.
                        Speech, The Akron, Ohio,
                            Convention (1851),
                        Quoted in *History of Woman
                            Suffrage,* Vol. I,
                        by Elizabeth Cady Stanton,*
                        Susan B. Anthony** and Mathilda
                            J. Gage***   *1881*

*See 811.
**See 840.
***See 876.

6 Dat man ober dar say dat womin needs to be
helped into carriages, and lifted ober ditches,
and to hab de best place everywhar. Nobody
eber helps me into carriages, or ober mud-
puddles, or gibs me any best place! An a'n't I
a woman? Look at me! Look at my arm! I have
ploughed, and planted, and gathered into barns,
and no man could head me! And a'n't I a
woman? I could work as much and eat as much
as a man—when I could get it—and bear de
lash as well! And a'n't I a woman? I have borne
thirteen chilern, and seen 'em mos' all sold off
to slavery, and when I cried out with my mother's grief, none but Jesus heard me! And a'n't
I a woman?   Ibid.

7 Den dat little man in black dar,* he say women
can't have as much rights as men, 'cause Christ
wan't a woman! . . . Whar did your Christ
come from? From God and a woman! Man had
notin' to do wid Him.   Ibid.

*A clergyman in the audience.

8 If de fust woman God ever made was strong
enough to turn the world upside down all alone,
dese women togedder ought to be able to turn
it back, and get it right side up again!   Ibid.

9 I know that it feels a kind o' hissin' and ticklin'
like to see a colored woman get up and tell you
about things, and Woman's Rights. We have all
been thrown down so low that nobody thought
we'd ever get up again; but we have been long

enough trodden now; we will come up again, and now I am here.

> Speech, The Mob Convention, Broadway Tabernacle, New York City (8 September 1853), op. cit.

10 There is a great stir about colored men getting their rights, but not a word about the colored women; and if colored men get their rights, and not colored women theirs, you see the colored men will be masters over the women, and it will be just as bad as it was before. So I am for keeping the thing going while things are stirring; because if we wait till it is still, it will take a great while to get it going again.

> Speech, Annual Meeting of Equal Rights Convention, New York City (9 May 1867), op. cit., Vol. II

11 I know that it is hard for one who has held the reins for so long to give up; it cuts like a knife. It will feel all the better when it closes up again.   Ibid.

12 Truth burns up error.   Comment   c.1882

751. Eliza Vestris (1797–1856)

1 Before you here a 'venturous woman bends—
A warrior woman, who in strife embarks,
The first of all dramatic Joan-of-Arcs!
Cheer on the enterprize thus dared by me,
The first that ever led a company;
What though until this very hour and age,
A Lessee lady never owned a stage,
I'm that *Belle Sauvage*—only rather quieter—
Like Mrs. Nelson, turn'd a stage proprietor.

> Composed for her Olympic Theatre, London, debut (3 January 1831), Quoted in *Enter the Actress* by Rosamond Gilder   *1931*

752. Katharine Augusta Ware (1797–1843)

1 I've looked on thee as thou wert calmly sleeping,
And wished—Oh, couldst thou ever be as blest
As now, when haply all thy cause of weeping
Is for a truant bird, or faded rose!

> "A New-Year Wish, to a child aged five years," St. 1, *The Power of the Passions, and Other Poems*   *1842*

753. Louisa Caroline Tuthill (1798/99–1879)

1 Never ring for a servant unless it is absolutely necessary; consider whether you have a right to

make even your own waiting-maid take forty steps to save yourself one.

> "Behaviour to Servants," *The Young Lady's Home*   n.d.

2 A cumbrous set of rules and maxims hung about one, like the charms which the gree-gree man* sells to the poor African, will not ward off the evils, nor furnish an antidote to the trials of life.   "Home Habits," op. cit.

* Voodoo witch.

754. Catharine Crowe (c.1799/1800–1876)

1 The great proportion of us live for this world alone, and think very little of the next . . . whilst . . . what is generally called the religious world, is so engrossed by its struggles for power or money, or by its sectarian disputes and enmities, and so narrowed and circumscribed by dogmatic orthodoxies, that it has neither inclination nor liberty to turn back or look around, and endeavour to gather up, from past records and present observation, such hints as are now and again dropt in our path, to give us an intimation of what the truth may be.

> *The Night-Side of Nature   1848*

2 A great many things have been pronounced untrue and absurd, and even impossible, by the highest authorities in the age in which they lived, which have afterwards, and, indeed, within a very short period, been found to be both possible and true.   Ibid.

755. Catherine Gore (1799–1861)

1 Waterton, the naturalist . . . asserts that whenever he countered an alligator *tête-à-tête*, in the wilderness, he used to leap on his back, and ride the beast to death. This feat, so much discredited by the stay-at-home critics, was an act of neither bravery nor braggartry—but of necessity. Either the man or the alligator must have had the upper hand. *Il a fallu opter* [He had to choose].

Just so are we situated with regard to the world. Either we must leap upon its back, strike our spur into its panting sides, and, in spite of its scaly defences, compel it to obey our glowing will, or the animal will mangle us with its ferocious jaws, leaving us expiring in the dust.   "How to Manage the World," *Modern Chivalry*   n.d.

2 For the egöist has so far the advantage over every other species of devotee, that his idol is

ever present.   "Society,"
op. cit.

3 Thanks to the march of civilization, privacy has been exploded among us, and individuality effaced. People feel in thousands, and think in tens of thousands. No quiet nook of earth remaining for the modern Cincinnatus* to cultivate his own carrots and opinions, where humours may expand into excrescence, or originality let grow its beard!   *Self*   *n.d.*

*Legendary Roman hero, political leader and farmer (fl. 460 B.C.).

756. Mary Howitt (1799–1888)

1 "Will you walk into my parlor?" said a Spider to a Fly;
" 'Tis the prettiest little parlor that ever you did spy."   "The Spider and the Fly,"
Poems   *c.1822–1831*

2 Old England is our home and Englishmen are we,
Our tongue is known in every clime, our flag on every sea.   "Old England is
Our Home,"
op. cit.

3 Yes! in the poor man's garden grow,
Far more than herbs and flowers,
Kind thoughts, contentment, peace of mind,
And joy for weary hours.
    "The Poor Man's Garden,"
op. cit.

4 Make beauty a familiar guest   Untitled,
Ballads and Other Poems
1847

5 Hunger, and cold, and weariness, these are a frightful three,
But another curse there is beside, that darkens poverty;
It may not have one thing *to love,* how small soe'er it be!
    "The Sale of the Pet Lamb,"
St. 6, op. cit.

6 Sixteen summers had she seen,
A rose-bud just unsealing
    "Tibbie Inglis, or the Scholar's
Wooing," St. 2,
The British Female Poets,
George W. Bethune, ed.   *1848*

7 Snatches of delicious song,
Full of old love-sadness!
    "Beatrice. A Lover's Lay,"
St. 9, op. cit.

8 Ye are neither deep nor wise;
Ye shall ne'er philosophize.   "Village
Children,"
St. 1, op. cit.

9 Oh, hapless heirs of want and woe!
    "Pauper Orphans,"
St. 5, *The Female Poets of Great
Britain,* Frederic Rowton, ed.
1853

10 I love the fields, the woods, the streams,
The wild flowers fresh and sweet,
And Yet I love, no less than these,
The crowded city street   "A City Street,"
St. 1, op. cit.

11   Our lives are all turmoil;
Our souls are in a weary strife and toil,
Grasping and straining—tasking nerve and brain,
—Both day and night for gain!
We have grown worldly: have made gold our god   "English Churches,"
St. 3, op. cit.

12 For visions come not to polluted eyes!   Ibid.

13 Oh! what had death to do with one like thee. . . .?   "The Lost One," St. 3

14 Let us take our proper station;
We, the rising generation,
Let us stamp the age as ours!
    "The Children,"
St. 5,
*Birds and Flowers; or, Lays and
Lyrics of Rural Life*   *1873*

15 How pleasant the life of a bird must be,
Flitting about in a leafy tree;
And away through the air what joy to go,
And to look on the green bright earth below.   "Birds in Summer,"
St. 3, op. cit.

757. Frances Crowe (fl. 1800s)

1 . . . keep on keeping on . . .
    Quoted in "Karen Malpede,"*
*Interviews with Contemporary Women
Playwrights,* Kathleen Betsko**
and Rachel Koenig, eds.   *1987*

*See 2413.
**See 2256.

758. Catharine Esther Beecher (1800–1878)

1 Woman's great mission is to train immature, weak, and ignorant creatures to obey the laws of God; the physical, the intellectual, the social, and the moral—first in the family, then in the school, then in the neighborhood, then in the nation, then in the world. . . .
    "An Address to the Christian Women
of America," *Woman Suffrage and
Women's Professions*   *1871*

2 To open avenues to political place and power for all classes of women would cause [the] humble labors of the family and school to be still more undervalued and shunned.   Ibid.

3 . . . as if *reasoning* were *any kind* of writing or talking which tends to convince people that some doctrine or measure is true and right.
Ibid.

759. Julia Crawford (1800–1885)

1 Kathleen Mavourneen! The grey dawn is breaking
The horn of the hunter is heard on the hill.
"Kathleen Mavourneen," St. 1
(Attr.)   *1835*

2 Oh! Hast thou forgotten how soon we must sever?
Oh! Hast thou forgotten this day we must part?
It may be for years, and it may be forever;
Then why art thou silent, thou voice of my heart?   Ibid.

760. Maria Jane Jewsbury (1800–1833?)

1 But let not thy little heart think, Genie,
Childhood the prophet of life:
It may be life's minstrel, Genie,
And sing sweet songs and clear
"Birth-Day Ballad," St. 4,
Lays for Leisure Hours:
Phantasmagoria   *1824*

2 When the tossed mind surveys its hidden world,
And feels in every faculty a foe,
United but in strife; waves urged and hurled
By passion and by conscience, winds of woe,
Till the whole being is a storm-swept sea—
There's none like thee, O Lord! there's none like thee!   "There Is None Like Unto Thee
(Jeremiah X.6)," St. 3,
op. cit.

3 Unfortunately, I was twenty-one before I became a reader, and I became a writer almost as soon: it is the ruin of all young talent of the day, that reading and writing are simultaneous. We do not educate ourselves for literary enterprise. I would gladly burn almost everything I ever wrote, if so be I might start now with a mind that has seen, read, thought, and suffered somewhat, at least, approaching to a preparation.   Letter to Felicia
Hemans,* *Three Histories*   *1830*

*See 730.

761. Frederika Bremer (1801–1865)

1 Thou mayest own the world, with health
And unslumbering powers;

Industry alone is wealth,
What we do is ours.   "Home"   *1885*

762. Jane Welsh Carlyle (1801–1866)

1 If they had said the sun and the moon was gone out of the heavens, it could not have struck me with the idea of a more awful and dreary blank in the creation than the words: Byron is dead.
Letter to Thomas Carlyle* (1824), *Letters
and Memorials*   *1883*

*English essayist, historian (1795–1881).

2 . . . the only thing that makes one place more attractive to me than another is the quantity of *heart* I find in it. . . .
Letter (1829), op. cit.

3 Some new neighbors, that came a month or two ago, brought with them an accumulation of all the things to be guarded against in a London neighborhood, viz., a pianofort, a lap-dog, and a parrot.   Letter to Thomas Carlyle's
Mother (6 May 1839), op. cit.

4 It is sad and wrong to be so dependent for the life of my life on any human being as I am on you; that I cannot by any force of logic cure myself at this date, when it has become second nature. If I have to lead another life in any of the planets, I shall take precious good care not to hang myself round any man's neck, either as a locket or a millstone.
Ibid., Letter to Thomas Carlyle op. cit. (1850)

5 Never does one feel oneself so utterly helpless as in trying to speak comfort for great bereavement. I will not try it. Time is the only comforter for the loss of a mother.
Ibid. (27 December 1853)

6 When one has been threatened with a great injustice, one accepts a smaller as a favour.
Ibid. (21 November 1855)

7 Men of England, look at your poor girls, many of them fading around you, dropping off in consumption or decline; or, what is worse, degenerating to sour old maids . . . Keep your girls' minds narrow and fettered, they will still be a plague and a care, sometimes a disgrace to you. Cultivate them—give them scope and work—they will be your gayest companions in health, your tenderest nurses in sickness, your most faithful prop in age.
Quoted in *I, Too, Am Here:
Selected Letters of Jane
Welsh Carlyle*, Alan & Mary Simpson,
eds.   *1977*

8 Of all God's creatures, Man alone is poor.
"To a Swallow Building
Under Our Eaves"
n.d.

763. Lydia M. Child (1802–1880)

1 In most nations the path of antiquity is shrouded in darkness, rendered more visible by the wild, fantastic light of fable; but with us, the vista of time is luminous to its remotest point.
Hobomok, Ch. 1   *1824*

2 I sometimes think the gods have united human beings by some mysterious principle, like the according notes of music. Or is it as Plato has supposed, that souls originally one have been divided, and each seeks the half it lost?
Philothea: A Romance, Ch. 1   *1836*

3 No music is so pleasant to my ears as that word—father. Zoroaster tells us that children are a bridge joining this earth to a heavenly paradise, filled with fresh springs and blooming gardens. Blessed indeed is the man who hears many gentle voices call him father!
Ibid., Ch. 19

4 Now twilight lets her curtain down
And pins it with a star.
Obituary for MacDonald Clark
1842

5 Not in vain is Ireland pouring itself all over the earth. . . . The Irish, with their glowing hearts and reverent credulity, are needed in this cold age of intellect and skepticism.
No. 33 (8 December 1842),
Letters from New York, Vol. I
1852

6 None speaks of the bravery, the might, or the intellect of Jesus; but the devil is always imagined as being of acute intellect, political cunning, and the fiercest courage.   *Ibid.*

7 The more women become rational companions, partners in business and in thought, as well as in affection and amusement, the more highly will men appreciate *home*—that blessed work, which opens to the human heart the most perfect glimpse of Heaven, and helps to carry it thither, as on an angel's wings.
Ibid., No. 34 (January 1843)

8 Use is the highest law of our being, and it cannot be disobeyed with impunity.
Ibid., Vol. II, No. 31
(31 December 1844)

9 Ah, my friend, that is the only true church organization, when heads and hearts unite in working for the welfare of the human race!
Letter to Theodore Weld   *1880*

10 Genius hath electric power
Which earth can never tame.
"Marius Amid the Ruins of Carthage"
n.d.

11 Over the river and through the wood,
To grandfather's house we'll go.
"Thanksgiving Day," St. 1
n.d.

764. Dorothea Dix (1802–1887)

1 I have myself seen more than nine thousand idiots, epileptics and insane in the United States . . . bound with galling chains, bowed beneath fetters, lacerated with ropes, scourged with rods.   First Petition to Congress
ca. 1848

2 In a world where there is so much to be done, I felt strongly impressed that there must be something for me to do.
Letters from New York, Vol. II
(1852), Lydia Maria Child,* ed.
31 December 1944

*See 763.

765. Letitia Landon (1802–1838)

1 Few, save the poor, feel for the poor.
"The Poor"
n.d.

2 We might have been—These are but common words,
And yet they make the sum of life's
bewailing.   "Three Extracts from the
Diary of a Week"
n.d.

766. Harriet Martineau (1802–1876)

1 If a test of civilisation be sought, none can be so sure as the condition of that half of society over which the other half has power—from the exercises of the right of the strongest.
"Women," *Society in America*, Vol. III
1837

2 Religion is a temper, not a pursuit.   *Ibid.*

3 . . . the sum and substance of female education in America, as in England, is training women to consider marriage as the sole object in life, and to pretend that they do not think so.
Ibid.

4 Persecution for opinion, punishment for all manifestations of intellectual and moral strength, are still as common as women who have opinions and who manifest strength. . . .   *Ibid.*

5 Marriage . . . is still the imperfect institution it must remain while women continue to be ill-educated, passive, and subservient. . . .
Ibid., "Marriage"

6 I have no sympathy for those who, under any pressure of circumstances, sacrifice their heart's-love for legal prostitution.   *Ibid.*

7 Laws and customs may be creative of vice; and should be therefore perpetually under process of observation and correction: but laws and customs cannot be creative of virtue: they may encourage and help to preserve it; but they cannot originate it.   Ibid.

8 Readers are plentiful: thinkers are rare.
                    Ibid., ''Occupation''

9 What office is there which involves more responsibility, which requires more qualifications, and which ought, therefore, to be more honourable, than that of teaching?   Ibid.

10 The progression or emancipation of any class usually, if not always, takes place through the efforts of individuals of that class. . . .
                    Ibid.

11 . . . I declare that if we are to look for a hell upon earth, it is where polygamy exists: and that, as polygamy runs riot in Egypt, Egypt is the lowest depth of this hell.
        ''The Harem,'' *Eastern Life: Present and Past*   1848

12 I am sure that no traveler seeing things through author spectacles can see them as they are. . . .
        Harriet Martineau's Autobiography,
                    Vol. I   1877

13 I am in truth very thankful for not having married at all.   Ibid.

14 The veneration in which I hold domestic life has always shown me that that life was not for those whose self respect had been early broken down, or had never grown.   Ibid.

15 The older I have grown, the more serious and irremediable have seemed to me the evils and disadvantages of married life as it exists among us at this time.   Ibid.

767. Marjory Fleming (1803–1811)

1 the most Devilish thing is 8 times 8
and 7 times 7 it is what nature itselfe
cant endure. . . .
        Diary of Marjory Fleming, St. 1 (1811)
                    1934

2   love is a very
papithatick thing as well as
troubelsom and tiresome. . . .   Ibid.

768. Sarah B. Judson (1803–1845)

1 Then gird thine armour on, love,
        Nor faint thou by the way—
Till the Boodh* shall fall, and Burmah's sons
Shall own Messiah's sway.

Poem to her husband, departing
on a long voyage, St. 3
(c.1845), Quoted in *Biography of
Distinguished Women* by Sarah
                    Josepha Hale**   1876

*Buddha: Judson was a missionary in Burma.
**See 703.

769. Marie Lovell (1803–1877)

1 INGOMAR. Freedom is hunting, feeding, danger;
        that, that is freedom—that it is which makes
        the veins to swell, the breast to heave
        and glow.
        Aye, that is freedom,—that is pleasure—life!   Act II
        Ingomar, the Barbarian   1896

770. Maria McIntosh (1803–1878)

1 Beneficent Nature, how often does the heart of man, crushed beneath the weight of his sins or his sorrows, rise in reproach against thine unchanged serenity!   *Two Lives,* Ch. 1
                    1846

2 To the inhabitants of the Southern States, not only the New Englander, but everyone who dwelt north of the Potomac was a Yankee—a name which was with him a synonym of meanness, avarice and low cunning—while the native of the Northern States regarded his southern fellow-citizens as an indolent and prodigal race, in comparison with himself but half civilized, and far better acquainted with the sword and the pistol than with any more useful instrument.
        The Lofty and the Lowly, Ch. 1
                    1852

771. Susanna Moodie (1803–1885)

1 I had heard and read much of savages, and have since seen, during my long residence in the bush, somewhat of uncivilized life, but the Indian is one of Nature's gentlemen—he never says or does a rude or vulgar thing. The vicious, uneducated barbarians, who form the surplus of overpopulace European countries, are far behind the wild man in delicacy of feeling or natural courtesy.   *Roughing It in the Bush,*
                    Ch. 1   1852

2 A nose, kind sir! Sure, Mother Nature,
With all her freaks, ne'er formed this feature.
If such were mine, I'd try and trade it,
And swear the gods had never made it.
        Ibid., ''Old Satan and Tom Wilson's Nose,''
                    Ch. 6

3 But hunger's good sauce. Ibid., Ch. 12

4 "I have no wish for a second husband. I had enough of the first. I like to have my own way—to lie down mistress, and get up master."
Ibid.

5 To wean a fellow-creature from the indulgence of a gross sensual propensity, as I said before, we must first convince the mind: the reform must commence there. Merely withdrawing the means of gratification, and treating a rational being like a child, will never achieve a great moral conquest. *Life in the Clearing*, Ch. 2
1853

6 Large parties given to very young children, which are so common in this country [Canada], are very pernicious in the way in which they generally operate upon youthful minds. They foster the passions of vanity and envy, and produce a love of dress and display which is very repulsive in the character of a child.
Ibid., Ch. 19

772. Sarah Childress Polk (1803–1891)

1 It is only the hope that you can live through the campaign that gives me a prospect of enjoyment. Letter to husband, James Polk (1843), Quoted in *First Ladies* by Betty Boyd Caroli
1987

773. Maria W. Stewart (1803–1879)

1 What if I am a woman? Is not the god of ancient times the god of these modern days? Did he not raise up Deborah,* to be a mother, and a judge in Israel? Did not queen Esther** save the lives of the Jews? Essay (1835)
Introduction, *Spiritual Narratives*, Sue E. Houchins
1988

*See 11.
**See 34.

2 O, ye daughters of Africa, awake! awake! arise! no longer sleep nor slumber, but distinguish yourselves. Show forth to the world that ye are endowed with noble and exalted faculties . . . How long shall the fair daughters of Africa be compelled to bury their minds and talents beneath a load of iron pots and kettles?
"Religion and the Pure Principles of Morality"
(1831), op. cit.

774. Flora Tristan (1803–1844)

1 Ne me demandez-pas d'où je viens. (Do not ask from where I come.) Part I, *Méphis* *1838*

2 In the future, when woman is conscious of her power, she will free herself from the need for social approval, and those little tricks which today aid her to deceive men, will become useless; when that time comes, woman will say:—"I choose this man for my lover, because my love will be a powerful force on his intelligence, and our happiness will be reflected on others." Ibid., Part II

3 To love one's fellow-man is rational self-love. Ibid.

775. Sarah Power Whitman (1803–1878)

1 And evening trails her robes of gold
Through the dim halls of the night.
"Summer's Call"
n.d.

2 Star of resplendent front! Thy glorious eye
Shines on me still from out yon clouded
sky. "Arcturus (To Edgar Allan Poe)"*
n.d.

*American poet, author (1809–1849).

776. Delphine de Girardin (1804–1855)

1 Business is other people's money.
Vol. II, *Marguerite* *1852*

777. George Sand (1804–1876)

1 She is Choice at odds with Necessity; she is Love blindly butting its head against all the obstacles set in its path by civilization.
Preface, *Indiana* *1832*

2 "I know that I am a slave, and you are my lord. The law of this country has made you my master. You can bind my body, tie my hands, govern my actions: you are the strongest, and society adds to your power; but with my will, sir, you can do nothing. God alone can restrain it and curb it. Seek then a law, a dungeon, an instrument of torture, by which you can hold it, it is as if you wished to grasp the air, and seize vacancy." Ibid.

3 "Where love is absent there can be no woman." Vol. I, *Lelia* *1833*

4 I had forgotten how to be young, and Nature had forgotten to awaken me. My dreams had moved too much in the world of sublimity, and I could no longer descend to the grosser level of fleshly appetites. A complete divorce had come about, though I did not realize it, between body and spirit. Ibid., Vol. II

5 No one makes a revolution by himself; and there are some revolutions, especially in the

arts, which humanity, accomplishes without quite knowing how, because it is everybody who takes them in hand.

The Haunted Pool, Preface   *1851*

6 Art is not a study of positive reality, it is the seeking for ideal truth. . . .   Ibid., Ch. 1

7 It is sad, no doubt, to exhaust one's strength and one's days in cleaving the bosom of this jealous earth, which compels us to wring from it the treasures of its fertility, when a bit of the blackest and coarsest bread is, at the end of the day's work, the sole recompense and the sole profit attaching to so arduous a toil.

Ibid., Ch. 2

8 He who draws noble delights from the sentiments of poetry is a true poet, though he has never written a line in all his life.   Ibid.

9 "One never knows how much a family may grow; and when a hive is too full, and it is necessary to form a new swarm, each one thinks of carrying away his own honey."

Ibid., Ch. 4

10 For everything, alas! is disappearing. During even my own lifetime there has been more progress in the ideas and customs of my village than had been seen during centuries before the Revolution.   Ibid., Appendix

11 It is extraordinary how music sends one back into memories of the past—and it is the same with smells.   Vol. I, *Story of My Life*
1856

12 The whole secret of the study of nature lies in learning how to use one's eyes. . . .

Nouvelles Lettres d'un Voyageur
1869

13 Classification is Ariadne's clue through the labyrinth of nature.   Ibid.

14 "I hated the pride of men of rank, and thought that I should be sufficiently avenged for their disdain if my genius raised me above them. Dreams and illusions all! My strength has not equalled my mad ambition. I have remained obscure; I have done worse—I have touched success, and allowed it to escape me. I thought myself great, and I was cast down to the dust; I imagined that I was almost sublime, and I was condemned to be ridiculous. Fate took me—me and my audacious dreams—and crushed me as if I had been a reed. I am a most wretched man!"   "The Marquise"   *1869*

15 The beauty that addresses itself to the eyes is only the spell of the moment; the eye of the body is not always that of the soul.

Ch. 1, *Handsome Lawrence*   *1872*

16 There is only one happiness in life, to love and be loved. . . .   Letter to Lina Calamatta

(31 March 1862), *Correspondence,*
Vol. IV   *1883*

17 One is happy as a result of one's own efforts, once one knows the necessary ingredients of happiness—simple tastes, a certain degree of courage, self denial to a point, love of work, and, above all, a clear conscience. Happiness is no vague dream, of that I now feel certain.

Vol. V,
op. cit.

18 Faith is an excitement and an enthusiasm: it is a condition of intellectual magnificence to which we must cling as to a treasure, and not squander on our way through life in the small coin of empty words, or in exact and priggish argument. . . .   Letter to Des Planches
(25 May 1866),
op. cit.

19 One wastes so much time, one is so prodigal of life, at twenty! Our days of winter count for double. That is the compensation of the old.

Letter to Joseph Dessauer
(5 July 1868),
op. cit.

20 I have had my belly full of great men (forgive the expression). I quite like to read about them in the pages of Plutarch, where they don't outrage my humanity. Let us see them carved in marble or cast in bronze, and hear no more about them. In real life they are nasty creatures, persecuters, temperamental, despotic, bitter and suspicious.   Vol. II, *Correspondence,*
1895

21 But if these people of the future are better than we are, they will, perhaps, look back at us with feelings of pity and tenderness for struggling souls who once divined a little of what the future would bring.

Intimate Journal (1834)   *1926*

22 I have the feeling now that one changes from day to day, and that after a few years have passed one has completely altered. Examine myself as I may, I can no longer find the slightest trace of the anxious, agitated individual of those years, so discontented with herself, so out of patience with others.   Ibid.

23 He is unaware that any man who is adored as a god is deceived, mocked and flattered.

Ibid. (13 June 1837)

24 Immodest creature, you do not want a woman who will accept your faults, you want one who pretends that you are faultless—one who will caress the hand that strikes her and kiss the lips that lie to her.   Ibid.

25 For me Communism is the ideal which all progressive societies must set as their goal. It is a religion which will be a living reality centuries

from now.   Quoted in *Women: A Journal of Liberation   Fall, 1970*

26 No religion can be built on force.   Ibid.

27 Education will in time be the same for men and women, but it will be in the female heart par excellence, as it always has been, that love and devotion, patience and pity, will find their true home. On woman falls the duty, in a world of brute passions, of preserving the virtues of charity and the Christian spirit. . . . When women cease to play that role, life will be the loser.
Impressions Littéraires   n.d.

28 The old woman I shall become will be quite different from the woman I am now. Another *I* is beginning, and so far I have not had to complain of her.   *Isadora*, Vol. II   *n.d.*

778. Sarah Flower Adams (1805–1848)

1 And joys and tears alike are sent
To give the soul fit nourishment.
As comes to me or cloud or sun,
Father! thy will, not mine, be done.
    "He Sendeth Sun, He Sendeth Shower"
    n.d.

2 Though like the wanderer,
    the sun gone down,
Darkness be over me,
    my rest a stone;
Yet in my dreams I'd be
Nearer, my God, to Thee,
    Nearer to Thee.
    "Nearer, My God, to Thee," St. 2   *n.d.*

779. Jeanne-Françoise Deroine (1805–1894)

1 Because the revolutionary tempest, in overturning at the same time the throne and the scaffold, in breaking the chain of the black slave, forgot to break the chain of the most oppressed of all— of Woman, the pariah of humanity. . . .
    Letter from Prison of St. Lazare
    (Paris, 15 June 1851), Written with
    Pauline Roland;* Quoted in *History of
    Woman Suffrage*, Vol. I, by Elizabeth
    Cady Stanton,** Susan B. Anthony,*** and
    Mathilda Gage****   *1881*

*See 1006.
**See 811.
***See 840.
****See 876.

2 We have, moreover, the profound conviction that only by the power of association based on solidarity—by the union of the working classes of both sexes to organize labor—can be ac- quired, completely and pacifically, the civil and political equality of women, and the social right for all.   Ibid.

780. Angelina Grimké (1805–1879)

1 I have not placed reading before praying because I regard it more important, but because, in order to pray aright, we must understand what we are praying for. . . .
    "Appeal to the Christian Women of
    the South," *The Anti-Slavery Examiner
    September, 1836*

2 Duty is ours and events are God's.   Ibid.

3 If a law commands me to *sin I will break it;* if it calls me to *suffer,* I will let it take its course *unresistingly.* The doctrine of blind obedience and unqualified submission to any human power, whether civil or ecclesiastical, is the doctrine of despotism, and ought to have no place 'mong Republicans and Christians.   Ibid.

4 Slavery always has, and always will, produce insurrections wherever it exists, because it is a violation of the natural order of things, and no human power can much longer perpetuate it. . . .   Ibid.

5 I am not afraid to trust my sisters—not I.
    Letter No. 11, *Letters to Catherine
    Beecher,** Isaac Knapp, ed.   1836

*See 758.

6 I recognize no rights but *human* rights—I know nothing of men's rights and women's rights; for in Christ Jesus there is neither male nor female. It is my solemn conviction that, until this principle of equality is recognized and embodied in practice, the church can do nothing effectual for the permanent reformation of the world.
    Letter No. 12, op. cit.

7 I am a mystery to myself.
    Letter to Theodore Dwight Weld
    (February, 1838), *Letters of Theodore
    Dwight Weld, Angelina Grimké Weld,
    and Sarah Grimké,** 1822–1844*, Vol.
    II, Gilbert Hobbs Barnes and Dwight
    L. Dumonds, eds.   1934

*See 725.

8 . . . thou art blind to the danger of marrying a woman who feels and acts out the principle of equal rights. . . .   Ibid.

781. Sarah Catherine Martin (fl. 1805)

1 Old Mother Hubbard
Went to the cupboard,

To get her poor dog a bone;
But when she came there
The cupboard was bare,
And so the poor dog had none.
"The Comic Adventures of Old
Mother Hubbard"   1805

782. Elizabeth Barrett Browning (1806–1861)

1 Is it thus,
Ambition, idol of the intellect?
"The Student," 1. 56, The
Seraphim and Other Poems   1838

2 And lips say "God be pitiful,"
Who ne'er said "God be praised."
"The Cry of the Human," St. 1,
Graham's American Magazine   1842

3 I tell you, hopeless grief is passionless. . . .
"Grief," Poems of 1844   1844

4 Life treads on life, and heart on heart;
We press too close in church and mart
To keep a dream or grave apart. . . .
"A Vision of Poets," Conclusion, 1. 820,
op. cit.

5 "Yes," I answered you last night;
"No," this morning, sir, I say:
Colors seen by candle-light
Will not look the same by day.
"The Lady's 'Yes,' " St. 1, op. cit.

6 What I do
And what I dream includes thee, as the wine
Must taste of its own grapes.
Sonnets from the Portuguese, I
1850

7 Because God's gifts put man's best dreams to shame.
XXVI,
op. cit.

8 How do I love thee? Let me count the ways.
I love thee to the depth and breadth and height
My soul can reach. . . .
XLIII,
op. cit.

9 I love thee with a love I seemed to lose
With my lost saints,—I love thee with the breath,
Smiles, tears, of all my life!—and, if God choose,
I shall but love thee better after death.   Ibid.

10 Life, struck sharp on death,
Makes awful lightning.
Aurora Leigh, Bk. I, 1. 210
1857

11 Whoever loves true life, will love true love.
Ibid., 1. 1066

12 Men do not think
Of sons and daughters, when they fall in love. . . .
Ibid., Bk II, 1. 608

13 God answers sharp and sudden some prayers,
And thrusts the thing we have prayed for in our face,
A gauntlet with a gift in 't.—Every wish
Is like a prayer, with God.   Ibid., 1. 952

14 A little sunburnt by the glare of life. . . .
Ibid., Bk. IV, 1. 1140

15 Men get opinions as boys learn to spell,
By reiteration chiefly. . . .
Ibid., Bk. VI, 1. 6

16 Since when was genius found respectable?
Ibid., 1. 275

17 Earth's crammed with heaven,
And every common bush afire with God;
But only he who sees, takes off his shoes—
The rest sit round it and pluck blackberries. . . .   Ibid., Bk. VII, 1. 820

18 Genuine government
Is but the expression of a nation, good
Or less good—even as all society,
Howe'er unequal, monstrous, crazed and cursed,
Is but the expression of men's single lives,
The loud sum of the silent units.
Ibid., Bk. VIII, 1. 867

19 If we tried
To sink the past beneath our feet, be sure
The future would not stand.
Casa Guidi Windows, Pt. 1, 1. 416
1851

20 But "Live the People," who remained and must,
The unrenounced and unrenounceable.
Long live the people! How they lived! and boiled
And bubbled in the cauldron of the street. . . .   Ibid., Pt. II, 1. 115

21 "What monster have we here?
A great Deed at this hour of day?
A great just Deed—and not for pay?
Absurd,—or insincere."
"A Tale of Villafrance," St. 4,
Athenoeum   24 September 1859

22 The thinkers stood aside
To let the nation act.
"Napoleon III in Italy," St. 3,
Poems Before Congress   1860

23 The world goes whispering to its own,
"This anguish pierces to the bone;"
And tender friends go sighing round,
"What love can ever cure this wound?"
My days go on, my days go on.
"De Profundis," St. 5, Last Poems
1862

24 We walked too straight for fortune's end,
We loved too true to keep a friend;

At last we're tired, my heart and I.
"My Heart and I," St. 9,
op. cit.

783. Maria Weston Chapman (1806–1885)

1 As *wives* and *mothers*, as *sisters* and *daughters*, we are deeply responsible for the influence we have on the human race. We are bound to exert it; we are bound to urge man to cease to do evil, and learn to do well. We are bound to urge them to regain, defend and preserve inviolate the rights of all, especially those whom they have most deeply wronged.
Address, Boston Female
Anti-Slavery Society, *Liberator*
13 August 1836

2 Grudge no expense—yield to no opposition—forget fatigue—till, by the strength of prayer and sacrifice, the spirit of love shall have overcome sectional jealousy, political rivalry, prejudice against color, cowardly concession of principle, wicked compromise with sin, devotion to gain, and spiritual despotism. . . .
Ibid.

3 We may draw good out of evil; we must not do evil, that good may come.
Address, "How Can I Help to
Abolish Slavery," New York   *1855*

784. Juliette Drouet (1806–1883)

1 I love you [Victor Hugo] *because* I love you, because it would be impossible for me not to love you. I love you without question, without calculation, without reason good or bad, faithfully, with all my heart and soul, and every faculty.   *Letters to Victor Hugo** (1833)
1915

*French poet, novelist (1802–1885).

2 If I were a clever woman, my gorgeous bird, I could describe to you how you unite in yourself the beauties of form, plumage, and song!
Ibid. (1835)

3 There are no wrinkles in the heart, and you will see my face only in the reflection of your attachment, eh, Victor, my beloved?
Ibid. (19 November 1841)

785. Flora Hastings (1806–1839)

1 Grieve not that I die young. Is it not well
To pass away ere life hath lost its
brightness?   "Swan Song"
n.d.

786. Nomura Motoni (1806–1867)

1 The whistle of the samurai's arrow is changing today to the thunder of cannon.
Untitled Poem   *1855*

2 The song of the warbler, joyful at his release has drawn forth the cry of many other birds.   Untitled Poem   *1863*

787. Julia Pardoe (1806–1862)

1 The heart is a free and fetterless thing—
A wave of the ocean, a bird on the wing.
"The Captive Greek Girl"   *n.d.*

788. Elizabeth Oakes Smith (1806–1893)

1 Faith is the subtle chain
Which binds us to the infinite.
"Faith"   *n.d.*

2 Yes, this is life, and everywhere we meet,
Not victor crowns, but wailings of defeat.
"The Unattained"   *n.d.*

789. Lady Dufferin (1807–1867)

1 The poor make no new friends.
"Lament of the Irish Emigrant"
1894

2 They say there's bread and work for all,
And the sun shines always there:
But I'll not forget old Ireland,
Were it fifty times as fair.   Ibid.

790. Lucretia Maria Davidson (1808–1825)

1 Shakespeare, with all thy faults, (and few have more,)
I love thee still, and still will con thee o'er.
Heaven in compassion to man's erring heart,
Gave thee a virtue, then a vice, apart,
Lest we, in wonder here, should bow before thee,
Break God's commandment, worship, and adore thee.   Untitled (1823),
Loves of Celebrated Women,
Samuel Griswold Goodrich, ed.,
1844

2 O, say, amid this wilderness of life,
What bosom would have throbbed like thine for me?
Who would have smiled responsive? Who, in grief,

Would e'er have felt, and, feeling, grieved
like thee?   "To My Mother"
(November 1824), op. cit.

3 There is a something which I dread;
    It is a dark and fearful thing;
    It steals along with withering tread,
    Or sweeps on wild destruction's wing.

    That thought comes o'er me in the hour
    Of grief, of sickness, or of sadness;
    'Tis not the dread of death; 'tis more,—
    It is the dread of madness.
                  Untitled (1825), op. cit.

791. Frances Dana Gage (1808–1884)

1 The home we first knew on this beautiful
earth,
    The friends of our childhood, the place of our
birth,
    In the heart's inner chamber sung always will
be,
    As the shell ever sings of its home in the sea.
                  "Home"   n.d.

792. Caroline Sheridan Norton (1808–1877)

1 God made all pleasures innocent.
        Pt. 1, The Lady of LaGaraye   *1862*

2 They serve God well, who serve his creatures.
                  Ibid., Conclusion

3 A soldier of the legion lay dying in Algiers—
    There was a lack of woman's nursing,
    There was dearth of woman's tears.
            "Bingen on the Rhine," St. 1
                            n.d.

4 The stranger hath thy bridle-rein, thy master
hath his gold;—
    Fleet limbed and beautiful, farewell; thou'rt
sold, my steed, thou'rt sold.
           "The Arab's Farewell to His
                    Steed"   n.d.

793. Elizabeth Trefusis (fl. 1808)

1 Thus the vain man, with subtle feigning,
    Pursues, o'ertakes poor woman's heart;
    But soon his hapless prize disdaining,
    She dies!—the victim of his art.
             "The Boy and Butterfly,"
             Poems and Tales   *1808*

794. Fanny Kemble (1809–1893)

1 . . . children are made of eyes and ears, and
nothing, however minute, escapes their micro-
scopic observation.   *Journal of a Residence
on a Georgian Plantation in 1838–1839,*
John Scott, ed.   *1961*

2 Just in proportion as I have found the slaves on
this plantation intellectual and advanced beyond
the general brutish level of the majority, I have
observed this pathetic expression of countenance
in them, a mixture of sadness and fear, the
involuntary exhibition of the two feelings, which
I suppose must be the predominant experience
of their whole lives, regret and
apprehension. . . .   Ibid.

3 Better trust all and be deceived,
    And weep that trust, and that deceiving,
    Than doubt one heart that, if believed,
    Had blessed one's life with true believing.
                  "Faith,"   n.d.

4 What shall I do with all the days and hours
    That must be counted ere I see thy face?
    How shall I charm the interval that lowers
    Between this time and that sweet time of
    grace?   "Absence"   n.d.

795. Margaret Fuller (1810–1850)

1 And knowing that there exists, in the world of
men, a tone of feeling towards women as towards
slaves, such as is expressed in the common
phrase, "Tell that to women and
children." . . .
        "The Great Lawsuit. Man Versus Men.
        Woman Versus Women," *The Dial
July 1843*

2 For human beings are not so constituted, that
they can live without expansion; and if they do
not get it one way, must another, or perish.
                            Ibid.

3 Two persons love in one another the future good
which they aid one another to unfold.   Ibid.

4 The well-instructed moon flies not from her orbit
to seize on the glories of her partner.   Ibid.

5 Harmony exists in difference no less than in
likeness, if only the same key-note govern both
parts.   Ibid.

6 The especial genius of women I believe to be
electrical in movement, intuitive in function,
spiritual in tendency.   Ibid.

7 Male and female represent the two sides of the
great radical dualism. But, in fact, they are
perpetually passing into one another. Fluid hardens to solid, solid rushes to fluid. There is no
wholly masculine man, no purely feminine
woman.   Ibid.

8 Nature provides exceptions to every rule.
                            Ibid.

9 If any individual live too much in relations, so that he becomes a stranger to the resources of his own nature, he falls, after a while, into a distraction, or imbecility, from which he can only be cured by a time of isolation, which gives the renovating foundations time to rise up. With a society it is the same.
Woman in the 19th Century 1845

10 It does not follow because many books are written by persons born in America that there exists an American literature. . . . Before such can exist, an original idea must animate this nation and fresh currents of life must call into life fresh thoughts along its shores.
Quoted in the *New York Tribune*
1846

11 Truth is the nursing mother of genius. Ibid.

12 . . . the public must learn how to cherish the nobler and rarer plants, and to plant the aloe, able to wait a hundred years for its bloom, or its garden will contain, presently, nothing but potatoes and pot-herbs. Ibid.

13 POET. Yes, that is always the way. You [critics] understand me, who never have the arrogance to pretend that I understand myself.
"A Dialogue," *Art,*
Literature and the Drama 1858

14 It is not because the touch of genius has roused genius to production, but because the admiration of genius has made talent ambitious, that the harvest is still so abundant.
"The Modern Drama,"
op. cit.

15 . . . there are two modes of criticism. One which . . . crushes to earth without mercy all the humble buds of Phantasy, all the plants that, though green and fruitful, are also a prey to insects or have suffered by drouth. It weeds well the garden, and cannot believe the weed in its native soil may be a pretty, graceful plant. There is another mode which enters into the natural history of every thing that breathes and lives, which believes no impulse to be entirely in vain, which scrutinizes circumstances, motive and object before it condemns, and believes there is a beauty in natural form, if its law and purpose be understood. "Poets of the People,"
op. cit.

16 The lives of the musicians are imperfectly written for this obvious reason. The soul of the great musician can only be expressed in music. . . . We must read them in their works; this, true of artists in every department, is especially so of the high priestesses of sound.
"Lives of the Great Composers," op. cit.

17 We cannot have expression till there is something to be expressed.
"American Literature," op. cit.

18 This was one of the rye-bread days, all dull and damp without.
Diary Entry, *Life of Margaret Fuller-Ossoli,* Ch. 7, Thomas Wentworth Higginson, ed. *1884*

19 Genius will live and thrive without training, but it does not the less reward the watering-pot and pruning-knife. Ibid., Ch. 18

20 I myself am more divine than any I see.
Letter to Emerson (1 March 1838),
The Feminist Papers, Alice Rossi,* ed.
1973
*See 1912.

21 What a difference it makes to come home to a child! Letter to Friends (1849), op. cit.

796. Elizabeth Gaskell (1810–1865)

1 What's the use of watching? A watched pot never boils. Ch. 31, *Mary Barton 1848*

2 A man . . . is *so* in the way in the house!
Ch. 1, *Cranford 1851–1853*

3 I'll not listen to reason. . . . Reason always means what someone else has got to say.
Ibid., Ch. 14

797. Ernestine Rose (1810–1892)

1 Oh, she [Frances Wright]* had her reward!—that reward of which no enemies could deprive her, which no slanders could make less precious—the eternal reward of knowing that she had done her duty; the reward of springing from the consciousness of right, of endeavoring to benefit unborn generations.
Convention Speech, "Petitions Were Circulated" (1860), Quoted in *History of Woman Suffrage,* Vol. I, by Elizabeth Cady Stanton,** Susan B. Anthony*** and Mathilda Gage**** *1881*
*See 740.
**See 811.
***See 840.
****See 876.

798. Fanny Fern (1811–1872)

1 The way to a man's heart is through his stomach. "Willis Parton" *n.d.*

799. Frances Sargent Osgood (1811–1850)

1 Work—for some good, be it ever so slowly;
Cherish some flower, be it ever so lowly;
Labor!—all labor is noble and holy!

Let thy great deeds be thy prayer to thy
god!
"Laborare Est Orare," St. 6   *n.d.*

800. Harriet Beecher Stowe (1811–1896)

1 "Well, I've got just as much conscience as any
man in business can afford to keep—just a little,
you know, to swear by as 't were. . . ."
Ch. 1, *Uncle Tom's Cabin*   *1852*

2 So long as the law considers all these human
beings, with beating hearts and living affections,
only as so many *things* belonging to the master—so long as the failure, or misfortune, or
imprudence, or death of the kindest owner, may
cause them any day to exchange a life of kind
protection and indulgence for one of hopeless
misery and toil—so long it is impossible to make
anything beautiful or desirable in the best-reg-
ulated administration of slavery.   Ibid.

3 "I b'lieve in religion, and one of these days,
when I've got matters tight and snug, I calculate
to 'tend to my soul, and them are
matters: . . .   Ibid., Ch. 8

4 "Treat 'em like dogs, and you'll have dogs'
works and dogs' actions. Treat 'em like men,
and you'll have men's works."   Ibid., Ch. 11

5 If ever Africa shall show an elevated and cultivated race—and come it must, some time, her
turn to figure in the great drama of human
improvement—life will awake there with a gor-
geousness and splendour of which our cold
western tribes faintly have conceived.
Ibid., Ch. 16

6 "Who was your mother?"
"Never had none!" said the child, with an-
other grin.
"Never had any mother? What do you mean?
Where were you born?"
"Never was born?"
"Never was born!" persisted Topsy. . . .
"Do you know who made you?"
"Nobody, as I knows on," said the child
with a short laugh . . . "I 'spect I grow'd.
Don't think nobody never made me."
Ibid., Ch. 20

7 Whipping and abuse are like laudanum: You
have to double the dose as the sensibilities
decline.   Ibid.

8 For how imperiously, how coolly, in disregard
of all one's feelings, does the hard, cold, un-
interesting course of daily reality move on!
Ibid., Ch. 28

9 "Oh, I think," said Clayton, "the African race
evidently are made to excel in that department

which lies between the sensuousness and the
intellectual—what we call the elegant arts. These
require rich and abundant animal nature, such
as they possess; and if ever they become highly
civilised, they will excel in music, dancing and
elocution."   Ch. 29, Ch. 6 *Dred*   *1856*

10 He declared that the gold made in it [slavery]
was distilled from human blood, from mother's
tears, from the agonies and dying groans of
gasping, suffocating men and women, and that
it would sear and blister the soul of him that
touched it; in short, he talked as whole-souled,
impractical fellows are apt to talk about what
respectable people sometimes do. Nobody had
ever instructed him that a slave-ship, with a
procession of expectant sharks in its wake, is a
missionary institution, by which closely-packed
heathen are brought over to enjoy the light of
the Gospel.   Ch. 1, *The Minister's Wooing*
1859

11 So we go, so little knowing what we touch and
what touches us as we talk! We drop out a
common piece of news, "Mr. So-and-so is dead,
Miss Such-a-one is married, such a ship has
sailed," and lo, on our right hand or on our
left, some heart has sunk under the news silently—gone down in the great ocean of Fate,
without even a bubble rising to tell its drowning
pang. And this—God help us!—is what we call
living!   Ibid., Ch. 4

12 And ever and anon came on the still air the soft
eternal pulsations of the distant sea—sound
mournfulest, most mysterious, of all the harp-
ings of Nature. It was the sea—the deep, eternal
sea—the treacherous, soft, dreadful, inexplicable sea. . . .   Ibid., Ch. 5

13 There are some people who receive from Nature
as a gift a sort of graceful facility of sympathy,
by which they incline to take on, for the time
being, the sentiments and opinions of those with
whom they converse, as the chameleon was
fabled to change its hue with every surrounding.
Such are often supposed to be willfully acting a
part, as exerting themselves to flatter and deceive, when in fact they are only framed so
sensitive to the sphere of mental emanation
which surrounds others that it would require an
exertion not in some measure to harmonize with
it. In approaching others in conversation, they
are like a musician who joins a performer on an
instrument—it is impossible for them to strike
a discord; their very nature urges them to bring
into play faculties according in vibration with
those another is exerting.   Ibid., Ch. 16

14 Everyone confesses in the abstract that exertion
which brings out all the powers of body and
mind is the best thing for us all; but practically
most people do all they can to get rid of it, and

as a general rule nobody does much more than circumstances drive them to do.

"The Lady Who Does Her Own Work," *Atlantic Monthly* 1864

15 . . . women are the real architects of society. "Dress, or Who Makes the Fashions," op. cit.

16 Many a humble soul will be amazed to find that the seed it sowed in weakness, in the dust of daily life, has blossomed into immortal flowers under the eye of the Lord.

"The Cathedral," op. cit.

17 "Take us the foxes, the little foxes, that spoil the vines: for our vines have tender grapes." . . . "Little Foxes," by which I mean those unsuspected, unwatched, insignificant *little* causes that nibble away domestic happiness, and make home less than so noble an institution should be. . . . The reason for this in general is that home is a place not only of strong affections, but of entire unreserve; it is life's undress rehearsal, its backroom, its dressing room, from which we go forth to more careful and guarded intercourse, leaving behind us much *debris* of cast-off and everyday clothing.

Ch. 1, *Little Foxes* 1865

18 I am speaking now of the highest duty we owe our friends, the noblest, the most sacred—that of keeping their own nobleness, goodness, pure and incorrupt. . . . If we *let* our friend become cold and selfish and exacting without a remonstrance, we are no true lover, no true friend.

Ibid., Ch. 3

19 Now, if the principle of toleration were once admitted into classical education—if it were admitted that the great object is to read and enjoy a language, and the stress of the teaching were placed on the few things absolutely essential to this result, if the tortoise were allowed time to creep, and the bird permitted to fly, and the fish to swim, towards the enchanted and divine sources of Helicon—all might in their own way arrive there, and rejoice in its flowers, its beauty, and its coolness. Ibid., Ch. 5

20 Every human being has some handle by which he may be lifted, some groove in which he was meant to run; and the great work of life, as far as our relations with each other are concerned, is to lift each one by his own proper handle, and run each one in his own proper groove.

Ibid.

21 "For my part," said my wife, "I think one of the greatest destroyers of domestic peace is Discourtesy. People neglect, with their nearest friends, those refinements and civilities which they practice with strangers." Ibid., Ch. 6

22 Yet there are persons who keep the requirements of life strained up always at concert pitch and

are thus worn out, and made miserable all their days by the grating of a perpetual discord.

Ibid., Ch. 7

23 . . . she's a woman . . . and they are alike. We can't do much for them, but let them come up as they will and make the best of it.

The Pearl of Orr's Island n.d.

801. Sarah Boyle (1812–1869)

1 Here I come creeping, creeping everywhere. . . . "The Voice of Grass" n.d.

802. Sarah Ellis (1812–1872)

1 To act the part of a true friend requires more conscientious feeling than to fill with credit and complacency any other station or capacity in social life. Ch. 4, *Pictures of Private Life* 1834

803. Geraldine Jewsbury (1812–1880)

1 I wish that I had a good husband and a dozen children! Only the difficulty is that "women of genius" require very special husbands—men of noble character, not intellect, but of a character and nature large enough, and strong enough, and wise enough to take them and their genius too, without cutting them down to suit their own crotchets, or reprobating half their qualities because they don't know what to do with them, or what they are intended for.

*Selections from the Letters of Geraldine E. Jewsbury to Jane Welsh Carlyle,** Ireland, ed. 1892

*See 763.

804. Ann Preston (1813–1872)

1 Wherever it is proper to introduce women as patients, there also it is in accordance with the instinct of truest womanhood for women to appear as physicians and students.

Quoted in *The Liberated Woman's Appointment Calendar*, Lynn Sherr and Jurate Kazickas, eds. 1975

805. Ellen Wood (1813–1887)

1 Petty ills try the temper worse than great ones. Ch. 1, *East Lynne* (novel) 1861

2 LEVISON. All strategems are fair in love and war. Act III, Sc. 2, *East Lynne* (play) *1862*

3 "Afflictions are of two kinds—as I class them. The one we bring upon ourselves, through our own misconduct; the other is laid upon us by God for our real advantage. Yes, my boys, we receive many blessings in disguise. Trouble of this sort will only serve to draw out your manly energies, to make you engage vigorously in the business of life, to strengthen your self-dependence and your trust in God."
Vol. I, Ch. 3, *The Channings* *1862*

4 Life has become to the most of us one swift, headlong race—a continuous fight in which there is so much to do that the half of it has to be left undone. . . . It is not so much what we have done amiss, as what we have left undone, that will trouble us, looking back.
Our Children *1876*

5 We are truly indefatigable in providing for the needs of the body, but we starve the soul.
Ch. 1, *About Ourselves* *1883*

806. Anne Botta (1815–1891)

1 The honey-bee that wanders all day long . . .
Seeks not alone the rose's glowing breast,
The lily's dainty cup, the violet's lips,
But from all rank and noxious weed he sips
The single drop of sweetness closely pressed
Within the poison chalice.
"The Lesson of the Bee" *n.d.*

807. Julia Margaret Cameron (1815–1879)

1 I longed to arrest all beauty that came before me, and at length the longing has been satisfied. *Annals of My Glass House* *1874*

808. Eliza Farnham (1815–1864)

1 Our own theological Church, as we know, has scorned and vilified the body till it has seemed almost a reproach and a shame to have one, yet at the same time has credited it with power to drag the soul to perdition.
Pt. I, Ch. 1, *Woman and Her Era* *1864*

2 Again the human face is the organic seat of beauty. . . . It is the register of value in development, a record of Experience, whose legitimate office is to perfect the life, a legible

language to those who will study it, of the majestic mistress, the soul. . . . Ibid.

3 Each of the Arts whose office it is to refine, purify, adorn, embellish and grace life is under the patronage of a Muse, no god being found worthy to preside over them.
Ibid., Pt. II, Ch. 1

809. Elizabeth Phelps (1815–1852)

1 She found out there was no doctor for her like Dr. "Have-To."
"What Sent One Husband to California," *The Tell-Tale* *1853*

2 "You gentlemen," said she, "have such odd ideas of *house-cleaning!* You imagine you can do it up just as you buy and sell—so much labor for so much money. Now, the fact is, the simple labor is the easiest part of it. It is the getting ready for labor—contriving, planning, arranging—that is so wearisome."
"The Old Leather Portfolio," op. cit.

810. Mrs. Henry Rolls (fl. 1815–1825)

1 Whence is that sad, that transient smile
That dawns upon the lip of woe;
That checks the deep-drawn sigh awhile,
And stays the tear that starts to flow?
'T is but a veil cast o'er the heart,
When youth's gay dreams have pass'd away
When joy's faint lingering rays depart,
And the last gleams of hope decay!
"Smiles,"
Sts. 7, 8, *The Female Poets of Great Britain,*
Frederic Rowton, ed.
1853

811. Elizabeth Cady Stanton (1815–1902)

1 It is impossible for one class to appreciate the wrongs of another.
History of Woman Suffrage,
Vol. I, with Susan B. Anthony*
and Mathilda Gage** *1881*
*See 840.
**See 876.

2 But standing alone we learned our power; we repudiated man's counsels forevermore; and solemnly vowed that there should never be another season of silence until we had the same rights everywhere on this green earth, as man. Ibid.

3 But when at last woman stands on an even platform with man, his acknowledged equal everywhere, with the same freedom to express

herself in the religion and government of the country, then, and not until then, . . . will he be able to legislate as wisely and generously for her as for himself.   Ibid.

4 The prolonged slavery of women is the darkest page in human history.   Ibid.

5 . . . woman's discontent increases in exact proportion to her development.   Ibid.

6 Though woman needs the protection of one man against his whole sex, in pioneer life, in threading her way through a lonely forest, on the highway, or in the streets of the metropolis on a dark night, she sometimes needs, too, the protection of all men against this one.   Ibid.

7 Wherever the skilled hands and cultured brain of women have made the battle of life easier for man, he has readily pardoned her sound judgment and proper self-assertion.   Ibid.

8 The queens in history compare favorably with the kings.   Ibid.

9 . . . there is no force in the plea, that "if women vote they must fight." Moreover, war is not the normal state of the human family in its higher development, but merely a feature of barbarism lasting on through the transition of the race, from the savage to the scholar.
                                                   Ibid.

10 Womanhood is the great fact in her life; wifehood and motherhood are but incidental relations.   Ibid.

11 But the love of offspring . . . tender and beautiful as it is, can not as a sentiment rank with conjugal love.   Ibid.

12 Two pure souls fused into one by an impassioned love—friends, counselors—a mutual support and inspiration to each other amid life's struggles, must know the highest human happiness;—this is marriage; and this is the only corner-stone of an enduring home.   Ibid.

13 They who give the world a true philosophy, a grand poem, a beautiful painting or statue, or can tell the story of every wandering star . . . have lived to a holier purpose than they whose children are of the flesh alone, into whose minds they have breathed no clear perceptions of great principles, no moral aspiration, no spiritual life.   Ibid.

14 Modern inventions have banished the spinning-wheel, and the same law of progress makes the woman of to-day a different woman from her grandmother.   Ibid.

15 *Declaration of Sentiments:* . . . We hold these truths to be self-evident: that all men and women are created equal. . . .   Ibid.

16 *Declaration of Sentiments: Resolved,* That all laws which prevent women from occupying such a station in society as her conscience shall dictate, or which place her in a position inferior to that of man, are contrary to the great precept of nature, and therefore of no force or authority.   Ibid.

17 There never was a more hopeful interest concentrated in the legislation of any single State, than when Kansas submitted the two propositions to her people to take the words "white" and "male" from her Constitution.
                          "The Kansas Campaign of 1867,"
                                              op. cit.

18 . . . mothers of the race, the most important actors in the grand drama of human progress. . . .   Ibid.

19 If the Bible teaches the equality of women, why does the church refuse to ordain women to preach the gospel, to fill the offices of deacons and elders, and to administer the Sacraments. . . ?
                       Pt. I, *The Woman's Bible*   1895

20 Why is it more ridiculous to arraign ecclesiastics for their false teaching and acts of injustice to women, than members of Congress and the House of Commons?   Ibid.

21 Come, come, my conservative friend, wipe the dew off your spectacles, and see that the world is moving.   Ibid.

22 For so far-reaching and momentous a reform as her complete independence, an entire revolution in all existing institutions is inevitable.   Ibid.

23 Reformers who are always compromising, have not yet grasped the idea that truth is the only safe ground to stand upon.   Ibid.

24 The Bible and Church have been the greatest stumbling blocks in the way of woman's emancipation.
                     Quoted in *Free Thought Magazine*
                                        September 1896

25 It is a proud moment in a woman's life to reign supreme within four walls, to be the one to whom all questions of domestic pleasure and economy are referred.
                       Eighty Years and More   1898

26 Though motherhood is the most important of all the professions—requiring more knowledge than any other department in human affairs—there was no attention given to preparation for this office.   Ibid., Rev. Ed.   1902

27 So closely interwoven have been our lives, our purposes, and experiences that, separated, we have a feeling of incompleteness—united, such strength of self-assertion that no ordinary obsta-

cles, differences, or dangers ever appear to us insurmountable.   Ibid.

28 I am at a boiling point! If I do not find some day the use of my tongue on this question I shall die of an intellectual repression, a woman's rights convulsion.
Elizabeth Cady Stanton, Vol. II, Theodore Stanton and Harriot Stanton Blatch, eds.   *1922*

29 I never felt more keenly the degradation of my sex. To think that all in me of which my father would have felt a proper pride had I been a man, is deeply mortifying to him because I am a woman.   Ibid.

30 I think if women would indulge more freely in vituperation, they would enjoy ten times the health they do. It seems to me they are suffering from repression.   Ibid.

31 . . . one of the best gifts of the gods came to me in the form of a good, faithful house-keeper.   Ibid.

32 Last evening we spoke of the propriety of women being called by the names which are used to designate their sex, and not by those assigned to males. . . . I have very serious objections, dear Rebecca, to being called Henry. There is a great deal in a name. . . . The custom of calling women Mrs. John This and Mrs. Tom That, and colored men Sambo and Zip Coon, is founded on the principle that white men are lords of all. I cannot acknowledge this principle as just; therefore, I cannot bear the name of another.   Letter to Rebecca R. Eyster
(1 May 1847), op. cit.

33 Man in his lust has regulated long enough this whole question of sexual intercourse. Now let the mother of mankind, whose prerogative it is to set bounds to his indulgence, rouse up and give this whole matter a thorough, fearless examination.   Letter to Susan B. Anthony
(1853), op. cit.

34 Women's degradation is in man's idea of his sexual rights.   (1860), op. cit.

35 I shall not grow conservative with age.   Ibid.

36 I have no sympathy with the old idea that children owe such immense gratitude to their parents that they can never fulfill their obligations to them. I think the obligation is all on the other side. Parents can never do too much for their children to repay them for the injustice of having brought them into the world, unless they have insured them high moral and intellectual gifts, fine physical health, and enough money and education to render life something more than one ceaseless struggle for necessities.
Diary Entry (1880), op. cit.

37 I have been into many of the ancient cathedrals—grand, wonderful, mysterious. But I al-

ways leave them with a feeling of indignation because of the generations of human beings who have struggled in poverty to build these altars to the unknown god.   Ibid. (1882)

38 Our trouble is not our womanhood, but the artificial trammels of custom under false conditions. We are, as a sex, infinitely superior to men, and if we were free and developed, healthy in body and mind, as we should be under natural conditions, our motherhood would be our glory. That function gives women such wisdom and power as no male ever can possess. When women can support themselves, have their entry to all the trades and professions, with a house of their own over their heads and a bank account, they will own their bodies and be dictators in the social realm.   Ibid. (1890)

39 I asked them why . . . one read in the synagogue service every week the "I thank thee, O lord, that I was not born a woman." ". . . It is not meant in an unfriendly spirit, and it is not intended to degrade or humiliate women." "But it does, nevertheless. Suppose the service read, 'I thank thee, O Lord, that I was not born a jackass.' Could that be twisted in any way into a compliment to the jackass?"
Ibid. (1895)

40 Men as a general rule have very little reverence for trees.   Ibid. (1900)

41 In a word, I am always busy, which is perhaps the chief reason why I am always well.   Ibid.

42 I do not know whether the world is quite willing or ready to discuss the question of marriage. . . . I feel, as never before, that this whole question of women's rights turns on the pivot of the marriage relation, and, mark my word, sooner or later it will be the topic for discussion. I would not hurry it on, nor would I avoid it.   Letter to Susan B. Anthony*
(1853), *Feminism*, Miriam Schneir,** ed.
1972

*See 840.
**See 2143.

43 We who like the children of Israel have been wandering in the wilderness of prejudice and ridicule for forty years feel a peculiar tenderness for the young women on whose shoulders we are about to leave our burdens.
Speech, International Council of Women (1888), op. cit.

44 The true woman is as yet a dream of the future.
Speech, International Council of Women (1888), op. cit.

45 . . . put it down in capital letters: SELF-DE-VELOPMENT IS A HIGHER DUTY THAN SELF-SACRIFICE. The thing which most re-

tards and militates against women's self-development is self-sacrifice.

Remark to reporter, Quoted
in *In a Different Voice* by
Carol Gilligan* *1892*

*See 2189.

812. Harriet Tubman (1815?–1913)

1 I had crossed the line. I was *free;* but there was no one to welcome me to the land of freedom. I was a stranger in a strange land; and my home, after all, was down in Maryland; because my father, my mother, my brothers, and sisters, and friends were there. But I was free, and *they* should be free. I would make a home in the North and bring them there, God helping me. Quoted in *Scenes in the Life of Harriet Tubman* by Sarah H. Bradford *1869*

2 I tink dar's many a slaveholder'll git to Heaven. Dey don't know no better. Dey acts up to de light dey hab. You take dat sweet little child—'pears more like an angel dan anyting else—take her down dere, let her nebber know nothing 'bout niggers but they was made to be whipped, an' she'll grow up to use the whip on 'em jus' like de rest. No, Missus, it's because dey don't know no better. Article in the *Boston Commonwealth* (30 June 1863), op. cit.

3 I had reasoned this out in my mind, there was two things I had a right to, liberty and death. If I could not have one, I would have the other, for no man should take me alive.

Quoted in "Lost Women: Harriet Tubman—The Moses of her People" by Marcy Galen, *Ms. August 1973*

813. Charlotte Brontë (1816–1855)

1 Conventionality is not morality. Self-righteousness is not religion. To attack the first is not to assail the last. To pluck the mask from the face of the Pharisee is not to lift an impious hand to the Crown of Thorns. Preface, *Jane Eyre* *1847*

2 Something of vengeance I had tasted for the first time; as aromatic wine it seemed, on swallowing, warm and racy: its after-flavour, metallic and corroding, gave me a sensation as if I had been poisoned. Ibid., Ch. 4

3 It is in vain to say human beings ought to be satisfied with tranquillity: they must have action; and they will make it if they cannot find it. Ibid., Ch. 12

4 "Dread remorse when you are tempted to err, Miss Eyre: remorse is the poison of life." Ibid., Ch. 14

5 "Reason sits firm and holds the reins, and she will not let the feelings burst away and hurry her to wild chasms. The passions may rage furiously, like true heathens, as they are; and the desires may imagine all sorts of vain things, but judgment shall still have the last word in every argument, and the casting vote in every decision." Ibid., Ch. 19

6 Feeling without judgment is a washy draught indeed; but judgment untempered by feeling is too bitter and husky a morsel for human deglutition [sic]. Ibid., Ch. 21

7 "Laws and principles are not for the times when there is no temptation: they arc for such moments as this, when body and soul rise in mutiny against their rigour; stringent are they; inviolate they shall be. If at my individual convenience I might break them, what would be their worth?" Ibid., Ch. 28

8 The soul, fortunately, has an interpreter—often an unconscious, but still a truthful interpreter—in the eye. Ibid.

9 Prejudices, it is well known, are most difficult to eradicate from the heart whose soil has never been loosened or fertilized by education; they grow there, firm as weeds among stones. Ibid., Ch. 38

10 An abundant shower of curates has fallen upon the north of England. Ch. 1, *Shirley* *1849*

11 Give him rope enough and he will hang himself. Ibid., Ch. 3

12 Look twice before you leap. Ibid., Ch. 9

13 . . . nothing moved her [Emily Brontë] more than any insinuation that the faithfulness and clemency, the long-suffering and loving-kindness which are esteemed virtues in the daughters of Eve, become foibles in the sons of Adam. She held that mercy & forgiveness are the divinest attributes of the Great Being who made both man and woman, and that what clothes the Godhead in glory, can disgrace no form of feeble humanity.

Preface to *Wuthering Heights* by
Emily Brontë* *1850*

*See 823.

814. Frances Brown (1816–1864)

1 Oh! those blessed times of old! with their
   chivalry and state;
I love to read their chronicles, which such
   brave deeds relate. . . .

"Oh! The Pleasant Days of Old," St. 7
n.d.

815. Dorothea Primrose Campbell (fl. 1816)

1 The winds of heaven are hushed and mild
As the breath of slumbering child
"Moonlight,"
Poems 1816

2 I dreamed not that a fairer spot
On earth's broad bosom lay;
Nor ever wished my wand'ring feet
Beyond its bounds to stray.
"Address to Zetland
[the Shetlands],"
St. 4, op. cit.

816. Charlotte Saunders Cushman (1816–1876)

1 To me it seems as if when God conceived the
world, that was Poetry; He formed it, and that
was Sculpture; He colored it, and that was
Painting; He peopled it with living beings, and
that was the grand, divine, eternal Drama.
Quoted in Charlotte Cushman
by Emma Stebbins 1879

2 Art is an absolute mistress; she will not be
coquetted with or slighted; she requires the most
entire self-devotion, and she repays with grand
triumphs. *Ibid.*, Ch. 10

817. Ellen Sturgis Hooper (1816–1841)

1 I slept, and dreamed that life was Beauty;
I woke, and found that life was Duty.
"Beauty and Duty" *n.d.*

2 The straightest path perhaps which may be
sought,
Lies through the great highway men call "I
ought." "The Straight Road" *n.d.*

818. Eliza "Mother" Stewart (1816–1908)

1 No power on earth or above the bottomless pit
has such influence to terrorize and make cowards
of men as the liquor power. Satan could not
have fallen on a more potent instrument with
which to thrall the world. Alcohol is king!
Ch. 1, Memories of the Crusade
1888

819. Priscilla Cooper Tyler (1816–1889)

1 I am considered 'charmante' by the Frenchmen,
'lovely' by the Americans and 'really quite nice,
you know' by the English. *Letter, Quoted in*
First Ladies by Betty Boyd
Caroli 1987

820. Jane Montgomery Campbell (1817–1879)

1 We plough the fields and scatter
The good seed on the land,
But it is fed and watered
By God's Almighty hand.
"We Plough the Fields,"
Garland of Songs n.d.

821. Mrs. Cecil Frances Alexander (1818–1895)

1 Jesus calls us, o'er the tumult
Of our life's wild, restless sea.
"Jesus Calls Us" *n.d.*

2 All things bright and beautiful,
All creatures great and small,
All things wise and wonderful,
The Lord God made them all.
"All Things Bright" *n.d.*

822. Amelia Jenks Bloomer (1818–1894)

1 Another cannot make fit to eat without wine or
brandy. A third must have brandy on her apple
dumplings, and a fourth comes out boldly and
says she likes to drink once in a while herself
too well. What flimsy excuses these! brandy and
apple dumplings forsooth! That lady must be a
wretched cook indeed who cannot make apple
dumplings, mince pie, or cake palatable without
the addition of poisonous substances.
Water Bucket 1842

2 The costume of women should be suited to her
wants and necessities. It should conduce at once
to her health, comfort, and usefulness; and,
while it should not fail also to conduce to her
personal adornment, it should make that end of
secondary importance.
Letter to Charlotte A. Joy
3 June 1857

823. Emily Brontë (1818–1848)

1 I'll walk where my own nature would be leading—

It vexes me to choose another guide. . . .
"Often Rebuked"   *1846*

2 Love is like the wild rose-briar;
Friendship like the holly-tree.
The holly is dark when the rose-briar blooms,
But which will bloom most constantly?
"Love and Friendship"   *1846*

3 Vain are the thousand creeds
That move men's hearts: unutterably
vain. . . .   "Last Lines"   *1846*

4 There is not room for Death.   Ibid.

5 "I am now quite cured of seeking pleasure in
society, be it country or town. A sensible man
ought to find sufficient company in
himself."
Ch. 3, *Wuthering Heights*   *1847*

6 "A person who has not done one half his day's
work by ten o'clock, runs a chance of leaving
the other half undone."   Ibid., Ch. 7

7 "My love for Linton is like the foliage in the
woods: time will change it, I'm well aware, as
winter changes the trees. My love for Heathcliff
resembles the eternal rocks beneath: a source of
little visible delight, but necessary. Nelly, I *am*
Heathcliff!"   Ibid., Ch. 9

8 Any relic of the dead is precious, if they were
valued living.   Ibid., Ch. 13

9 I lingered round them [tombstones], under that
benign sky: watched the moths fluttering among
the heath and harebells; listened to the soft wind
breathing through the grass; and wondered how
anyone could ever imagine unquiet slumbers for
the sleepers in that quiet earth.
Ibid., Conclusion

824. Emily Collins (1818?–1879?)

1 It is ever thus; where Theology enchains the
soul, the Tyrant enslaves the body.
"Reminiscences of Emily Collins,"
Quoted in *History of Woman Suffrage,*
Vol. I, by Elizabeth Cady Stanton,*
Susan B. Anthony** and Mathilda Gage***
1881

*See 811.
**See 840.
***See 876.

2 Every argument for the emancipation of the
colored man was equally one for that of women;
and I was surprised that all Abolitionists did not
see the similarity in the condition of the two
classes.   Ibid.

3 Moral Reform and Temperance Societies may
be multiplied *ad infinitum,* but they have about
the same effect upon the evils they seek to cure

as clipping the top of a hedge would have toward
extirpating it.   Letter to Sarah C. Owen
(23 October 1848), op. cit.

825. Eliza Cook (1818–1889)

1 Better build schoolrooms for "the boy,"
Than cells and gibbets for "the man."
"A Song for the Ragged Schools,"
St. 12
n.d.

2 I love it—I love it, and who shall dare
To chide me for loving that old Arm-chair?
"The Old Arm-Chair"
n.d.

3 Oh! much may be done by defying
The ghosts of Despair and Dismay;
And much may be gained by relying
On "Where there's a will there's a way."
"Where There's a Will
There's a Way," St. 4
n.d.

4 On what strange stuff Ambition feeds!
"Thomas Hood"
n.d.

5 Though language forms the preacher,
'Tis "good works" make the man.
"Good Works"
n.d.

6 'Tis well to give honour and glory to Age,
With its lessons of wisdom and truth;
Yet who would not go back to the fanciful
page,
And the fairytale read but in youth?
"Stanzas"   *n.d.*

7 Whom do we dub as Gentleman? The
Knave, the fool, the brute—
If they but own full tithe of gold, and
Wear a courtly suit.
"Nature's Gentleman," St. 1   *n.d.*

826. Mary A. E. Green (1818?–1895)

1 Of all the royal daughters of England who, by
the weight of personal character, or the influence
of advantageous circumstances, had exercised a
permanent bearing on its destiny, few have occupied so prominent a place as Elizabeth, queen
of bohemia, the high-minded but ill-fated daughter
of James I.
Ch. I, *Elizabeth, Queen of Bohemia*
1855

827. Mary Elizabeth Hewitt (1818–?)

1 A sumptuous dwelling the rich man hath.
And dainty is his repast;

But remember that luxury's prodigal hand
Keeps the furnace of toil in blast.
"A Plea for the Rich Man," St. 3,
Poems 1853

2 Then hail! thou noble conquerer!
That, when tyranny oppressed,
Hewed for our fathers from the wild
A land wherein to rest.
"The Axe of the Settler," St. 5, op. cit.

828. Harriet Brent Jacobs (1818–1896)

1 It seems less degrading to give one's self, than
to submit to compulsion. There is something
akin to freedom in having a lover who has no
control over you, except that which he gains by
kindness and attachment.
*Incidents in the Life of a Slave
Girl*, Lydia Maria Child,* ed.
(repr. 1973) 1861

*See 763.

2 You never knew what it is to be a slave; to be
entirely unprotected by law or custom; to have
the laws reduce you to the condition of a chattel,
entirely subject to the will of another. You never
exhausted your ingenuity in avoiding the snares,
and eluding the power of a hated tyrant; you
never shuddered at the sound of his footsteps,
and trembled within hearing of his voice.
Ibid.

829. Mary Todd Lincoln (1818–1882)

1 The change from this gloomy earth, to be forever reunited to my idolized husband & my
darling Willie, would be happiness indeed!
Letter to Mrs. Slataper (29 September
1868), *The Mary Lincoln Letters*,
Justin G. Turner, ed. 1956

2 I am convinced, the longer I live, that life & its
blessings are not so entirely unjustly distributed
[as] when we are suffering greatly, we are inclined to suppose. My home for so many years
was so rich in love and happiness; now I am so
lonely and isolated—whilst others live on in a
careless lukewarm state—not appearing to fill
Longfellow's measure: "Into each life, some
rain must fall." Ibid.

830. Maria Mitchell (1818–1889)

1 We travel to learn; and I have never been in any
country where they did not do something better
than we do it, think some thoughts better than
we think, catch some inspiration from heights
above our own.

Diary Entry (July 1873), *Maria Mitchell,
Life, Letters, and Journals*, Phebe
Mitchell Kendall, ed. 1896

2 . . . to-day I am ready to say, "Give no schol-
arships at all." I find a helping-hand lifts the
girl as crutches do; she learns to like the help
which is not self-help. If a girl has the public
school, and wants enough to learn, she will
learn. It is hard, but she was born to hardness—
she cannot dodge it. Labor is her inheritance. (10 February 1887), op. cit.

3 Health of body is not only an accompaniment
of health of mind, but is the cause; the converse
may be true—that health of mind causes health
of body; but we all know that intellectual cheer
and vivacity act upon the mind. If the gymnastic
exercise helps the mind, the concert or the
theatre improves the health of the body. Ibid.

4 . . . I do think, as a general rule, that teachers
talk too much! A book is a very good institution!
To read a book, to think it over, and to write
out notes is a useful exercise; a book which will
not repay some hard thought is not worth
publishing. (July 1887), op. cit.

5 Every formula which expresses a law of nature
is a hymn of praise to God.
Inscription on Bust in the
Hall of Fame 1905

831. Elizabeth Prentiss (1818–1878)

1 Sleep, baby, sleep!
Thy father's watching the sheep,
Thy mother's shaking the dreamland tree,
And down drops a little dream for thee.
Sleep, baby, sleep. "Cradle Song"
n.d.

832. Lucy Stone (1818–1893)

1 The right to vote will yet be swallowed up in
the real question, viz: has woman a right to
herself? It is very little to me to have the right
to vote, to own property, etc., if I may not keep
my body, and its uses, in my absolute right.
Letter to Antoinette Brown*
1855

*See 869.

2 I know not what you believe of God, but I
believe He gave yearnings and longings to be
filled, and that He did not mean all our time
should be devoted to feeding and clothing the
body. Speech, "Disappointment Is the Lot of
Women" (17–18 October 1855),
Quoted in *History of Woman Suffrage*,

Vol. I, by Elizabeth Cady Stanton,*
Susan B. Anthony,** and Mathilda Gage***
1881

*See 811.
**See 840.
***See 876.

3 In education, in marriage, in religion, in everything, disappointment is the lot of women. It
shall be the business of my life to deepen this
disappointment in every woman's heart until she
bows down to it no longer. Ibid.

4 We want rights. The flour-merchant, the house-
builder, and the postman charge us no less on
account of our sex; but when we endeavor to
earn money to pay all these, then, indeed, we
find the difference. Ibid.

5 Because I know that I shall suffer, shall I, for
this, like Lot's wife, turn back? No, mother, if
in this hour of the world's need I should refuse
to lend my aid, however small it may be, I
should have no right to think myself a Christian,
and I should forever despise Lucy Stone. If,
while I hear the wild shriek of the slave mother
robbed of her little ones, or the muffled groan
of the daughter spoiled of her virtue, I do not
open my mouth for the dumb, am I not
guilty? Letter to Her Mother (c.1847),
Quoted in *Morning Star*, Pt. II, Ch. 6,
by Elinor Rice Hays *1961*

6 "We, the people of the United States." Which
"We, the people"? The women were not
included. Speech, *New York Tribune*
(April 1853), op. cit.

833. George Eliot (1819–1880)

1 Any coward can fight a battle when he's sure
of winning; but give me the man who has pluck
to fight when he's sure of losing. That's my
way, sir; and there are many victories worse
than a defeat. Ch. 6, *Janet's Repentance*
1857

2 Animals are such agreeable friends—they ask
no questions, they pass no criticisms.
"Mr. Gilfi's Love Story," *Scenes of
Clerical Life* *1858*

3 It's but little good you'll do a-watering the last
year's crop. Ch. 18, *Adam Bede*
1859

4 It was a pity he couldna be hatched o'er again,
an' hatched different. Ibid.

5 A maggot must be born i' the rotten cheese to
like it. Ibid., Ch. 29

6 I'm not denyin' the women are foolish: God
Almighty made 'em to match the men.
Ibid., Ch. 43

7 I'm not one o' those as can see the cat 'i the
dairy an' wonder what she's come after.
Ibid., Ch. 52

8 The law's made to take care o' raskills.
Bk. III, Ch. 4, *The Mill on the Floss,*
1860

9 I've never any pity for conceited people, because I think they carry their comfort about
them. Ibid., Bk. V, Ch. 4

10 Nothing is so good as it seems beforehand.
Ch. 18, *Silas Marner* *1861*

11 There is a mercy which is weakness, and even
treason against the common good.
Romola *1863*

12 An ass may bray a good while before he shakes
the stars down. Ibid., Ch. 50

13 There are glances of hatred that stab, and raise
no cry of murder.
Introduction, *Felix Holt, the Radical*
1866

14 'Tis what I love determines how I love.
Bk. I, "The Spanish Gypsy" *1868*

15 Best friend, my well-spring in the wilderness! Ibid., Bk. III

16 Our words have wings, but fly not where we
would. Ibid.

17 Prophecy is the most gratuitous form of
error. Ch. 10, *Middlemarch* *1871–1872*

18 If we had keen vision of all that is ordinary in
human life, it would be like hearing the grass
grow or the squirrel's heart beat, and we should
die of that roar which is the other side of
silence. Ibid., Ch. 22

19 What loneliness is more lonely than distrust?
Ibid., Ch. 44

20 Truth has rough flavors if we bite it
through. Sc. 2, *Armgart* *1871*

21 Gossip is a sort of smoke that comes from the
dirty tobacco-pipes of those who diffuse it; it
proves nothing but the bad taste of the
smoker. *Daniel Deronda*
1876

22 The Jews are among the aristocracy of every
land; if a literature is called rich in the possession of a few classic tragedies, what shall we
say to a national tragedy lasting for fifteen hundred
years, in which the poets and actors were also
the heroes. Ibid.

23 A difference of taste in jokes is a great strain
on the affections. Ibid., Bk. II, Ch. 15

24 ". . . I say that the strongest principle of growth
lies in human choice." Ibid.

25 Blessed is the man who, having nothing to say, abstains from giving wordy evidence of the fact.   Ch. 4, *The Impressions of Theophrastus Such   1879*

26 Few women, I fear, have had such reason as I have to think the long sad years of youth were worth living for the sake of middle age.
 Letter to Mrs. Peter Taylor (31 December 1857), *George Eliot's Life as Related in Her Letters and Journals   1900*

27 The years seem to rush by now, and I think of death as a fast approaching end of a journey— double and treble reason for loving as well as working while it is day.
 Letter to Miss Sara Hennell (22 November 1861), op. cit.

28 I have the conviction that excessive literary production is a social offence.
 Letter to Alexander Main (11 September 1871), op. cit.

29 Oh may I join the choir invisible
 Of those immortal dead who live again
 In minds made better by their presence.
 "Oh May I Join the Choir Invisible," *Poems*

30 'Tis God gives skill,
 But not without men's hands: He could not make
 Antonio Stradivari's violins
 Without Antonio.
 "Stradivarius," l. 140, op. cit.

834. Julia Ward Howe (1819–1910)

1 Mine eyes have seen the glory
 Of the coming of the Lord
 He is trampling out the vintage
 Where the grapes of wrath are stored.
 He hath loosed the fateful lightning
 Of His terrible, swift sword;
 His truth is marching on!
 "Battle Hymn of the Republic" *1862*

2 In the beauty of the lilies
 Christ was born across the sea,
 With a glory in His bosom
 That transfigures you and me:
 As He died to make men holy,
 Let us die to make men free
 His truth is marching on! *Ibid.*

835. Harriet Sewall (1819–1889)

1 Why thus longing, thus forever sighing
 For the far-off, unattain'd, and dim,

While the beautiful all round thee lying
 Offers up its low, perpetual hymn?
 "Why Thus Longing" *n.d.*

836. Queen Victoria (1819–1901)

1 We are not interested in the possibilities of defeat.   Letter to A. J. Balfour *1899*

2 We are not amused.
 Notebooks of a Spinster Lady   1900

3 . . . now let me entreat you seriously not to do this, not to let your feelings (very natural and usual ones) of momentary irritation and discomfort be seen by others; don't (as you so often did and do) let every little feeling be read in your face and seen in your manner, pray don't give way to irritability before your ladies. All this I say with the love and affection I bear you—as I know what you have to contend with and struggle against.
 Letter to Princess Royal (27 September 1858), *Dearest Child*, Roger Fulford, ed. *1964*

4 He [Mr. Gladstone]* speaks to Me as if I was a public meeting.
 Quoted in *Collections and Recollections* by G. W. E. Russell *n.d.*

*British prime minister (1809–1898).

837. Susan Warner (1819–1885)

1 Many a bit we passed in our ignorance, in the days when we could see no metal but what glittered on the surface; and many a good time we went back again, long afterward, and broke our rejected lump with great exultation to find it fat with the riches of the mind.
 Foreword, *The Law and the Testimony 1853*

2 "There is a world there, Winthrop—another sort of world—where people know something; where other things are to be done than running plow furrows; where men may distinguish themselves!—where men may read and write; and do something great; and grow to be something besides what nature made them!—I want to be in that world."
 Ch. 1, *The Hills of the Shatemuc 1856*

3 "Did it ever happen to you to want anything you could not have, Miss Elizabeth?"
 "No—never," said Elizabeth slowly.
 "You have a lesson to learn yet."

"I hope I sha'n't learn it," said Elizabeth.
"It must be learned," said Mrs. Landholm
gently. "Life would not be life without it. It is
not a bad lesson either." *Ibid.*, Ch. 10

4 "And I, Maria—am I not somebody?" her aunt
asked.
"Well, we're all *somebody,* of course, in one
sense. Of course we're not *nobody.*"
"I am not so sure what you think about it,"
said Mrs. Candy. "I think that in your language,
who isn't somebody, is nobody."
Ch. 7, What *She Could* 1870

5 "He who serves God with what costs him nothing, will do very little service, you may depend
on it." *Ibid.*, Ch. 11

838. Amelia C. Welby (1819–1852)

1 As the dew to the blossom, the bud to the bee,
As the scent to the rose, are those memories to
me. "Pulpit Eloquence"
n.d.

2 Ten thousand stars were in the sky,
Ten thousand on the sea.
"Twilight at Sea," St. 4
n.d.

839. Mme. de Launay (fl. 1820s)

1 I forgive the *nonchalance* which you assume
about receiving a pension. . . . It flatters both
the vanity and the purse.
Letter to Desbordes-Valmore*
(1 November 1826), Quoted in *Memoirs of
Marceline Desbordes-Valmore*
by C. A. Sainte-Beuve, Harriet
W. Preston, tr. *1872*

*See 697.

840. Susan B. Anthony (1820–1906)

1 Men their rights and nothing more; women their
rights and nothing less.
Motto, *The Revolution* 1868

2 . . . gentlemen. . . . Do you not see that so
long as society says a woman is incompetent to
be a lawyer, minister or doctor, but has ample
ability to be a teacher, that every man of you
who chooses this profession tacitly acknowl-
edges that he has no more brains than a
woman? Speech, State Convention of
Schoolteachers, *History of
Woman Suffrage,* Vol. I, with
Elizabeth Cady Stanton* and
Mathilda Gage** *1881*

*See 811.
**See 876.

3 Of all the old prejudices that cling to the hem
of the woman's garments and persistently impede
her progress, none holds faster than this. The
idea that she owes service to a man instead of
to herself, and that it is her highest duty to aid
his development rather than her own, will be
the last to die.
"The Status of Women, Past, Present
and Future," *The Arena
May 1897*

4 . . . there never will be complete equality until
women themselves help to make laws and elect
lawmakers. *Ibid.*

5 . . . the day will come when men will recognize
woman as his peer, not only at the fireside, but
in the councils of the nation. Then, and not until
then, will there be the perfect comradeship, the
ideal union between the sexes that shall result
in the highest development of the race. *Ibid.*

6 Those of you who have the talent to do honor
to poor womanhood, have all given yourself
over to baby-making. . . .
Quoted in *Elizabeth Cady Stanton,**
Vol. II, Theodore Stanton and Harriot Stanton Blatch, eds. *1922*

*See 811.

7 Failure is impossible.
Quoted by Carrie Chapman Catt in
Her Speech "Is Woman Suffrage
Progressing?" (1911), *Feminism,*
Miriam Schneir,* ed. *1972*

*See 2143.

841. Urania Locke Bailey (1820–1882)

1 I want to be an angel,
And with the angels stand
A crown upon my forehead,
A harp within my hand.
"I Want to Be an Angel," St. 1
n.d.

842. Anne Brontë (1820–1849)

1 All true histories contain instruction; though, in
some, the treasure may be hard to find, and
when found, so trivial in quantity, that the dry,
shrivelled kernel scarcely compensates for the
trouble of cracking the nut.
Ch. II, *Agnes Grey* 1847

2 I would not send a poor girl into the world,
. . . ignorant of the snares that beset her path;
nor would I watch and guard her, till, deprived
of self-respect and self-reliance, she lost the
power or the will to watch and guard
herself . . .
Ch. III, *The Tenant of Wildfell Hall
1848*

3 "If you would have your son to walk honourable through the world, you must not attempt to clear the stones from his path, but teach him to walk firmly over them—not insist upon leading him by the hand, but let him learn to go alone."
                                                                Ibid.

4 "Oh! I see," said he, with a bitter smile; "it's an act of Christian charity, whereby you hope to gain a higher seat in heaven for yourself, and scoop a deeper pit in hell for me."
                                                    Ibid., Ch. XLVII

5 They say such tears as children weep
    Will soon be dried away;
  That childhood's grief, however strong,
    Is only for a day;
  And parted friends, how dear so e'er,
    Will soon forgotten be:
  It may be so with other hearts;
    It is not so with me.
                        "An Orphan's Lament"
                (1 January 1841), *The Complete
                Poems of Anne Brontë*,
                Clement Shorter, ed.   *1920*

6 Domestic peace! best joy of earth,
    When shall we all thy value learn?
                            "Domestic Peace,"
                St. 7 (11 May 1846), op. cit.

7 Nothing is lost that thou didst give,
    Nothing destroyed that thou hast done.
                            "Severed and Gone,"
                St. 15 (April 1847), op. cit.

8 But he that dares not grasp the thorn
    Should never crave the rose.
                            "The Narrow Way,"
                St. 4 (27 April 1848), op. cit.

843. Alice Cary (1820–1871)

1 Three little bugs in a basket,
  And hardly room for two.   "Three Bugs"
                                        n.d.

2 True worth is in *being*, not *seeming*—
    In doing, each day that goes by,
  Some little good—not in dreaming
    Of great things to do by and by.
                            "Nobility," St. 1
                                        n.d.

3 We cannot bake bargains for blisses,
    Nor catch them like fishes in nets;
  And sometimes the thing our life misses,
    Helps more than the thing which it gets.
                                Ibid., St. 4

4 Work, and your house shall be duly fed:
  Work, and rest shall be won;
  I hold that a man had better be dead
  Than alive when his work is done.   "Work"
                                        n.d.

844. Lucretia Peabody Hale (1820–1900)

1 All the years before, she had lived in a roving, aimless way, and the old love of change came up often to assert its power. Often came back the old longing to live where she would not be bound to anybody—where she might be free, even if she were only free to starve.
                        Ch. 18, *The Struggle for Life
                                            1867*

2 It is so hard to melt away the influences of an early life, to counteract all the lessons of the first ten years, to tear up the weeds that are early planted. There are evil inheritances to be struggled with, childish prejudices and fancies banished.   Ibid., Ch. 33

845. Jean Ingelow (1820–1897)

1 O Land where all the men are stones,
  Or all the stones are men.
                        "A Land That Living Warmth
                                            Disowns"
                                            n.d.

2 You Moon! Have you done something wrong
    in heaven,
  That God has hidden your face?
                        "Seven Times One," St. 4,
                            *Songs of Seven
                                            n.d.*

846. Jenny Lind (1820–1887)

1 I have a brightness in my soul, which strains toward Heaven. I am like a bird!
                    Quoted in *Jenny Lind: The Swedish
                    Nightingale* by Gladys Denny Shultz
                                            1962

2 I have often wished for the blessing of motherhood, for it would have given me a much-needed focal point for my affections. With it, and through the varied experiences that accompany it, I could perhaps have achieved something better than that which I have attained up to now.
                    Letter (11 July 1849), *The Lost
                    Letters of Jenny Lind*, W. Porter Ware
                    and Thaddeus C. Lockard, Jr., eds.
                                            1966

847. Mary Livermore (1820?–1905)

1 For humanity has moved forward to an era when wrong and slavery are being displaced, and reason and justice are being recognized as the rule of life. . . . The age looks steadily to the

redressing of wrong, to the righting of every form of error and injustice; and a tireless and prying philanthropy, which is almost omniscient, is one of the most hopeful characteristics of the time. *Ch. 1, What Shall We Do with Our Daughters?* 1883

2 Above the titles of wife and mother, which, although dear, are transitory and accidental, there is the title human being, which precedes and out-ranks every other. *Ibid., Ch. 7*

848. Princess Mathilde (1820–1904)

1 But I think him lost for ever for any kind of locomotion. Nowadays it is only his mind that travels; his body stays behind on the bank.
Quoted in Revue Bleu
6 August 1863

2 I was born in exile—civically dead. . . .
"Souvenirs des Années d'Exile,"
La Revue des Deux Mondes
15 December 1927

849. Florence Nightingale (1820–1910)

1 No *man*, not even a doctor, ever gives any other definition of what a nurse should be than this— "devoted and obedient." This definition would do just as well for a porter. It might even do for a horse. It would not do for a policeman. *Notes on Nursing* 1859

2 Merely looking at the sick is not observing.
Ibid.

3 It may seem a strange thing to begin a book with:—This Book is not for any one who has time to read it—but the meaning of it is: this reading is good only as a preparation for work. If it is not to inspire life and work, it is bad. Just as the end of food is to enable us to live and work, and not to live and eat, so the end of most reading perhaps, but certainly of mystical reading, is not to read but to work.
Preface; Mysticism 1873

4 For what is Mysticism? Is it not the attempt to draw near to God, not by rites or ceremonies, but by inward disposition? Is it not merely a hard word for "The Kingdom of Heaven is within"? Heaven is neither a place nor a time. *Ibid.*

850. Margaret Preston (1820–1897)

1 Pain is no longer pain when it is past.
"Nature's Lesson" *c.1875*

2 'Tis the motive exalts the action;
'Tis the doing, and not the deed.
"The First Proclamation of Miles Standish"* *c.1875*

*(1584?–1656) English colonial settler in America.

851. Anna Sewell (1820–1878)

1 "I never yet could make out why men are so fond of this sport; they often hurt themselves, often spoil good horses, and tear up the fields, and all for a hare, or a fox, or a stag, that they could get more easily some other way; but we are only horses, and don't know."
Pt. I, Ch. 2, Black Beauty 1877

2 . . . he said that cruelty was the Devil's own trademark, and if we saw anyone who took pleasure in cruelty we might know whom he belonged to, for the Devil was a murderer from the beginning, and a tormentor to the end.
Ibid., Ch. 13

3 I am never afraid of what I know.
Ibid., Pt. II, Ch. 29

4 I said, "I have heard people talk about war as if it was a very fine thing."
"Ah!" said he, "I should think they never saw it. No doubt it is very fine when there is no enemy, when it is just exercise and parade, and sham fight. Yes, it is very fine then; but when thousands of good, brave men and horses are killed or crippled for life, it has a very different look." *Ibid., Pt. III, Ch. 34*

852. Anna Bartlett Warner (1820–1915)

1 Daffy-down-dilly came up in the cold. . . .
"Daffy-Down-Dilly" *n.d.*

2 Jesus loves me, this I know
For the Bible tells me so. "Jesus Loves Me"
n.d.

853. Clara Barton (1821–1912)

1 It is wise statesmanship which suggests that in time of peace we must prepare for war, and it is no less a wise benevolence that makes preparation in the hour of peace for assuaging the ills that are sure to accompany war.
Ch. 1, The Red Cross 1898

2 An institution or reform movement that is not selfish, must originate in the recognition of some evil that is adding to the sum of human suffering, or diminishing the sum of happiness. I

suppose it is a philanthropic movement to try to reverse the process. Ibid.

854. Elizabeth Blackwell (1821–1910)

1 Social intercourse—a very limited thing in a half civilized country, becomes in our centers of civilization a great power. . . .
Medicine as a Profession for Women,
with Emily Blackwell* 1860
* See 874.

2 . . . every advance in social progress removes us more and more from the guidance of instinct, obliging us to depend upon reason for the assurance that our habits are really agreeable to the laws of health, and compelling us to guard against the sacrifice of our physical or moral nature while pursuing the ends of civilization. Ibid.

3 . . . health has its science as well as disease. . . . Ibid.

4 This failure to recognize the equivalent value of internal with external structure has led to such a crude fallacy as a comparison of the penis with such a vestige as the clitoris, whilst failing to recognize that vast amount of erectile tissue, mostly internal, in the female, which is the direct seat of sexual spasm.
The Human Element in Sex 1894

5 . . . the total deprivation of it [sex] produces irritability. Ibid.

6 Do you think I care about medicine? Nay, verily, it's just to kill the devil, whom I hate so heartily—that's the fact, mother.
Letter to Mother, Quoted in
Those Extraordinary Blackwells
by Elinor R. Hays* 1967
* See 574.

855. Mary Baker Eddy (1821–1910)

1 Christian Science explains all cause and effect as mental, not physical.
Science and Health, with Key to the Scriptures (1910 ed.) 1875

2 If materialistic knowledge is power, it is not wisdom. It is but a blind force. Ibid.

3 Jesus of Nazareth was the most scientific man that ever trod the globe. He plunged beneath the material surface of things, and found the spiritual cause. Ibid.

4 You conquer error by denying its verity. Ibid.

5 Sin brought death, and death will disappear with the disappearance of sin. Ibid.

6 Health is not a condition of matter, but of Mind; nor can the material senses bear reliable testimony on the subject of health. Ibid.

7 You command the situation if you understand that mortal existence is a state of self-deception and not the truth of being. Ibid.

8 Truth is immortal; error is mortal. Ibid.

9 Sickness, sin and death, being inharmonious, do not originate in God, nor belong to His government. Ibid.

10 Then comes the question, how do drugs, hygiene, and animal magnetism heal? It may be affirmed that they do not heal, but only relieve suffering temporarily, exchanging one disease for another. Ibid.

11 Disease is an experience of so-called mortal mind. It is fear made manifest on the body. Ibid.

12 I would no more quarrel with a man because of his religion than I would because of his art.
Miscellaneous Writings
(Rev. as *The First Church of Christ, Scientist, and Miscellany* 1913)
1883–1896

13 To live and let live, without clamor for distinction of recognition; to wait on divine Love; to write truth first on the tablet of one's own heart—this is the sanity and perfection of living, and my human ideal.
Message to The Mother Church 1902

14 To live so as to keep human consciousness in constant relation with the Divine, the spiritual and the eternal, is to individualize infinite power; and this is Christian Science.
The First Church of Christ, Scientist and Miscellany 1913

856. Frances P. Cobbe (1822–1904)

1 The time comes to every dog when it ceases to care for people merely for biscuits or bones, or even for caresses, and walks out of doors. When a dog *really* loves, it prefers the person who gives it nothing, and perhaps is too ill ever to take it out for exercise, to all the liberal cooks and active dog-boys in the world.
The Confessions of a Lost Dog 1867

2 I could discern clearly, even at that early age, the essential difference between people who are *kind* to dogs and people who really *love* them. Ibid.

3 . . . I must avow that the halo which has gathered round Jesus Christ obscures Him to my eyes.

Vol. II, Ch. 15, *Life of Frances Power Cobbe*
1894

857. Caroline Dall (1822–1912)

1 I have seen no Hindu who seemed to me prepared intellectually and morally for the freedom
he would find in American society; nor are
Americans prepared for the air of innocence
and exaltation worn by very undeserving
Orientals.
The Life of Doctor Anandabai Joshee *
1888

*See 1120.

2 Why is it that human hearts are so dead to the
heroic?   Pt. I, *Barbara Fritchie* *   1892

*See 634.

3 It was the glorious function of [John Greenleaf]
Whittier* to lift us nearer to the Infinite Spirit,
to keep us intent upon our immortal destiny,
and to fill us with that love of Beauty which is
the love of God.   Ibid., "L'Envoi"

*American author and abolitionist (1807–1892).

858. Julia Carney (1823–1908)

1 Little drops of water, Little grains of sand,
Make the mighty ocean, And the pleasant
land.
So the little minutes, Humble tho' they be,
Make the mighty ages Of Eternity!
"Little Things," St. 1   1845

859. Mary Bokin Chesnut (1823–1886)

1 "You know how women sell themselves and
are sold in marriage, from queens downwards,
eh? You know what the Bible says about slaves,
and marriage. Poor women, poor slaves."
(4 March 1861) *Diary from Dixie*
1949

2 I think this journal will be disadvantageous for
me, for I spend my time now like a spider
spinning my own entrails, instead of reading as
my habit was in all spare moments.
Ibid. (14 March 1861)

3 You see, Mrs. Stowe did not hit the sorest spot.
She makes Legree a bachelor.
Ibid. (27 August 1861)

4 . . . those soul-stirring Negro camp-meeting
hymns. To me this is the saddest of all earthly
music, weird and depressing beyond my power
to describe.   Ibid. (13 October 1861)

5 Conscription has waked the Rip Van Winkles.
To fight and to be made to fight are different
things.   Ibid. (19 March 1862)

860. Margaret Davidson (1823–1838)

1 When left alone, when thou are gone,
Yet still I will not feel alone;
Thy spirit still will hover near,
And guard thy orphan daughter here.
Untitled poem (ca. 1831), *Lives of Cele-
brated Women,* Samuel Griswold Goodrich,
ed.
1844

2 My sister! With that thrilling word
Let thoughts unnumbered wildly spring!
What echoes in my heart are stirred,
While thus I touch the trembling string.
Untitled poem (1836),
op. cit.

3 I cannot weep that thou are fled;
Forever blends my soul with thine   Ibid.

861. Caroline Mason (1823–1890)

1 Do they miss me at home—do they miss me?
'Twould be an assurance most dear,
To know that this moment some loved one
Were saying, "I wish he were here."
"Do They Miss Me at Home," St. 1
1850

2 Ere I am old, O! Let me give
My life to learning how to live.
"When I Am Old," St. 8
n.d.

3 His grave a nation's heart shall be,
His monument a people free!
"President Lincoln's Grave"
n.d.

862. Elizabeth Stoddard (1823–1902)

1 A woman despises a man for loving her, unless
she returns his love.
Ch. 32, *Two Men*   1888

863. Phoebe Cary (1824–1871?)

1   Charley Church, was a preacher who
praught,
Though his enemies called him a screecher
who scraught.   "The Lovers"   n.d.

2 For of all the hard things to bear and grin,
The hardest is being taken in.
"Kate Ketchem"   n.d.

3 I think true love is never blind
  But rather brings an added light,
  An inner vision quick to find
  The beauties hid from common sight.
                    "True Love," St. 1   n.d.

4 Sometimes, I think, the things we see
  Are shadows of the things to be;
  That what we plan we build. . . .
                    "Dreams and Realities," St. 7   n.d.

864. Julia Kavanagh (1824–1877)

1 Most children are aristocratic. . . .
                    Vol. I, *Daisy Burns*   1853

2 Alas! why has the plain truth the power of
  offending so many people. . . . Ibid., Ch. 4

3 It is the culprit who must seek the glance of the
  judge, and not the judge that must look at the
  culprit.   Ch. 1, *Nathalie*   1872

865. Sarah Anna Lewis (1824–1880)

1   The oblivious world of sleep—
    That rayless realm where Fancy never
      beams,
    That nothingness beyond the land of
      dreams.   "Child of the Sea"   n.d.

866. Adeline Dutton Whitney (1824–1906)

1 I bow me to the thwarting gale:
  I know when that is overpast,
  Among the peaceful harvest days
  An Indian Summer comes at last.
                    "Equinoctial," St. 6
                                        n.d.

867. Mrs. Alexander (1825–1902)

1 ". . . it is impossible to rely on the prudence
  or common sense of any man. . . ."
                    Ch. 1, *Ralph Wilton's Weird*   1875

2 "There's nothing more mischievous than mop-
  ing along and getting into the blue devils!—
  nothing more likely to drive a man to suicide or
  matrimony, or some infernal entanglement even
  worse!"   Ibid., Ch. 6

868. Antoinette Brown Blackwell (1825–1921)

1 . . . the sexes in each species of beings . . .
  are always true equivalents—equals but not
  identicals. . . .

The Sexes Throughout Nature
1875

2 Any positive thinker is compelled to see everything in the light of his own convictions.
                                        Ibid.

3 I do not underrate the charge of presumption
  which must attach to any woman who will
  attempt to controvert the great masters of science
  and scientific inference. But there is no
  alternative!   Ibid.

4 If woman's sole responsibility is of the domestic
  type, one class will be crushed by it, and the
  other throw it off as a badge of poverty. The
  poor man's motto, "Women's work is never
  done," leads inevitably to its antithesis—ladies'
  work is never begun.   Ibid.

5 A woman finds the natural lay of the land almost
  unconsciously; and not feeling it incumbent on
  her to be guide and philosopher to any successor, she takes little pains to mark the route by
  which she is making her ascent.   Ibid.

6 The brain is not, and cannot be, the sole or
  complete organ of thought and feeling. Ibid.

7 The law of grab is the primal law of
  infancy.   Ibid.

8 That she is not his peer in all intellectual and
  moral capabilities, cannot at least be very well
  provided until she is allowed an equally untram-
  melled opportunity to test her own strength.
                                        Ibid.

9 If Evolution, as applied to sex, teaches any one
  lesson plainer than another, it is the lesson that
  the monogamic marriage is the basis of all
  progress.   Ibid.

10 It had seemed to both Lucy Stone* and myself
   in our student days that marriage would be a
   hindrance to our public work.
                    Quoted in *Antoinette Brown Blackwell:*
                    Biographical Sketch by Sarah Gibson
                                        1909

*See 832.

11 . . . you asked me one day if it [marriage]
   seemed like giving up much for your sake. Only
   leave me free, as free as you are and everyone
   ought to be, and it is giving up nothing.
                            Letter to future
                            husband, op. cit.

869. Julia Dorr (1825–1913)

1 Grass grows at last above all graves.
                    "Grass-Grown"   n.d.

2 O golden Silence, bid our souls be still,
  And on the foolish fretting of our care
  Lay thy soft touch of healing unaware!
                    "Silence"   n.d.

3 What dost thou bring me, O fair To-day,
   That comest o'er the mountains with swift
   feet?   "To-day"   n.d.

4 The year grows rich as it groweth old,
   And life's latest sands are its sands of gold!
                          "To the 'Bouquet Club' "   n.d.

870. Henrietta Heathorn (1825–1915)

1 Be not afraid, ye waiting hearts that weep,
   For God still giveth His beloved sleep,
   And if an endless sleep He wills—so best.*
                     "Browning's Funeral" **   1889

*Epitaph on T. H. Huxley's tombstone; English scientist
and humanist (1825–1895).
**Robert Browning, English poet (1812–1889).

2 To all the gossip that I hear
   I'll give no faith; to what I see
   But only half, for it is clear
   All that led up is dark to me.
      Learn we the larger life to live,
      To comprehend is to forgive.
                     "Tout Comprendre, C'est Tout
                             Pardonner"   n.d.

871. Adelaide Proctor (1825–1864)

1 Dreams grow holy put in action.
                "Philip and Mildred," The Poems of
                          Adelaide Proctor   1869

2 One dark cloud can hide the sunlight;
   Loose one string, the pearls are scattered;
   Think one thought, a soul may perish;
   Say one word, a heart may break.   Ibid.

3 One by one the sands are flowing,
      One by one the moments fall;
   Some are coming, some are going,
      Do not strive to grasp them all.
                     "One by One," St. 1,
                             op. cit.

4 See how time makes all grief decay.
                     "Life in Death,"
                             op. cit.

5 I know too well the poison and the sting
      Of things too sweet.
                     "Per Pacem ad Lucem,"
                             op. cit.

872. Harriet Robinson (1825–1911)

1 What if she did hunger and thirst after knowledge? She could do nothing with it even if she
   could get it. So she made a *fetish* of some male
   relative, and gave him the mental food for which
   she herself was starving; and devoted all her

energies towards helping him to become what
she felt, under better conditions, she herself
might have been. It was enough in those early
days to be the *mother* or *sister* of somebody.
      "Early Factory Labor in New England,"
            Massachusetts in the Woman Suffrage
                             Movement   1883

2 Skilled labor teaches something not to be found
   in books or in colleges.   Ibid.

873. Laura Towne (1825–1901)

1 I want to agitate, even as I am agitated.
         Journal Entry (1877), Quoted in
                     Woman's True Profession
         by Nancy Hoffman   1981

874. Emily Blackwell (1826–1911)

Co-author of *Medicine as a Profession for Women*
with Elizabeth Blackwell.*

*See 854:1–3.

875. Dinah Mulock Craik (1826–1887)

1 . . . a Brownie is a curious creature. . . .
         The Adventures of a Brownie   1872

2 Altogether, his conscience pricked him a good
   deal; and when people's consciences prick them,
   sometimes they get angry with other people,
   which is very silly, and only makes matters
   worse.   Ibid.

3 Now, I have nothing to say against uncles in
   general. They are usually very excellent people,
   and very convenient to little boys and girls.
         Ch. 2, The Little Lame Prince   1875

4 It seemed as if she had given these treasures
   and left him alone—to use them, or lose them,
   apply them, or misapply them, according to his
   own choice. That is all we can do with children,
   when they grow into big children, old enough
   to distinguish between right and wrong, and too
   old to be forced to do either.   Ibid., Ch. 6

5 Those rooks, dear, from morning till night,
   They seem to do nothing but quarrel and fight,
   And wrangle and jangle, and plunder.
         "The Blackbird and the Rooks," Thirty Years
                                         1881

6 And when I lie in the green kirkyard,
      With mould upon my breast,
   Say not that she did well—or ill,
      Only "she did her best."
                     "Obituary"   1887

7 Duty's a slave that keeps the keys,
  But Love the master goes in and out
  Of his goodly chambers with song and shout,
  Just as he pleases—just as he pleases.
  "Plighted"
  n.d.

8 Faith needs her daily bread.
  Ch. 10, *Fortune's Marriage*
  n.d.

9 Forgotten? No, we never do forget:
  We let the years go by; wash them clean with
    tears,
  Leave them to bleach out in the open day,
  Or lock them careful by, like dead friends'
    clothes,
  Till we shall dare unfold them without pain,—
  But we forget not, never can forget.
  "A Flower of a Day,"
  n.d.

10 God rest ye, little children; let nothing you
    afright,
   For Jesus Christ, your Saviour, was born this
     happy night;
   Along the hills of Galilee the white blocks
     sleeping lay,
   When Christ, the child of Nazareth, was born
     on Christmas day.
   "Christmas Carol," St. 2   *n.d.*

11 Hour after hour that passionless bright face
   Climbs up the desolate blue. "Moon-Struck"

12 Keep what is worth keeping—
   And with the breath of kindness
   Blow the rest away.   "Friendship"   *n.d.*

13 Oh my son's my son till he gets him a wife,
   But my daughter's my daughter all her life.
   "Young and Old"   *n.d.*

14 O the green things growing, the green things
     growing,
   The faint sweet smell of the green things
     growing!
   "Green Things Growing"   . *n.d.*

15 Pierce with thy trill the dark,
   Like a glittering music spark.
   "A Rhyme About Birds"   *n.d.*

16 Tomorrow is, ah, whose?
   "Between Two Worlds"   *n.d.*

876. Mathilda Gage (1826–1898)

1 Co-author of *History of Woman Suffrage,* Vols.
  I and II, with Elizabeth Cady Stanton and Susan
  B. Anthony.*

See 811 and 840.

877. Lucy Larcom (1826–1893)

1 He who plants a tree
  Plants a hope.   "Plant a Tree," St. 1
  n.d.

2 Canst thou prophesy, thou little tree,
  What the glory of thy boughs shall be?   Ibid.

3 I do not own an inch of land,
  But all I see is mine.   "A Strip of Blue"
  n.d.

4 If the world seems cold to you,
  Kindle fires to warm it!   "Three Old Saws"
  n.d.

5 The land is dearer for the sea,
  The ocean for the shore.
  "On the Beach," St. 11
  n.d.

878. Dorothy Nevill (1826–1913)

1 Society to-day and Society as I formerly knew
  it are two entirely different things; indeed, it
  may be questioned whether Society, as the word
  used to be understood, now exists at all. . . .
  Now all is changed, and wealth has usurped the
  place formerly held by wit and learning. The
  question is not now asked, "Is So-and-so clever?"
  but, instead, "Is So-and-so rich?"
  Ch. 8, *The Reminiscences of Lady Dorothy
  Nevill   1907*

2 It is, I think, a good deal owing to the prepon-
  derance of the commercial element in Society
  that conversation has sunk to its present dull
  level of conventional chatter.   Ibid.

879. Jane Francesca Wilde (1826–1896)

1 Weary men, what reap ye?—"Golden corn for
    the stranger."
  What sow ye?—"Human corpses that await
    for the Avenger."
  Fainting forms, all hunger-stricken, what see
    you in the offing?
  "Stately ships to bear our food away amid the
    stranger's scoffing."
  There's a proud array of soldiers—what do
    they round your door?
  "They guard our master's granaries from the
    thin hands of the poor."
  "Ballad on the Irish Famine"   *n.d.*

880. Ethel Lynn Beers (1827–1879)

1 All quiet along the Potomac to-night,
  No sound save the rush of the river,

While soft falls the dew on the face of the
dead,
The picket's off duty forever.
> "The Picket Guard," St. 6 (1861),
> *All Quiet Along the Potomac and*
> *Other Poems* 1879

2 Art thou a pen, whose task shall be
To drown in ink
What writers think?
Oh, wisely write,
That pages white
Be not the worse for ink and thee.
> "The Gold Nugget"
> *n.d.*

881. Rose Terry Cooke (1827–1892)

1 Yet courage, soul! nor hold thy strength in
vain,
In hope o'er come the steeps God set for thee,
For past the Alpine summits of great pain
Lieth thine Italy. "Beyond," St. 4
> *n.d.*

882. Ellen Howarth (1827–1899)

1 Who hath not saved some trifling thing
More prized than jewels rare,
A faded flower, a broken ring,
A tress of golden hair.
> " 'Tis But a Little Faded Flower"
> *n.d.*

883. Johanna Spyri (1827–1901)

1 "You mischievous child!" she cried, in great
excitement. "What are you thinking of? Why
have you taken everything off? What does it
mean?"
"I do not need them," replied the child, and
did not look sorry for what she had done.
> Ch. 1, *Heidi* 1885

2 "Oh, I wish that God had not given me what I
prayed for! It was not so good as I
thought." Ibid., Ch. 11

3 ". . . anger makes us all stupid."
> Ibid., Ch. 23

884. Elizabeth Charles (1828–1896)

1 To know how to say what others only know
how to think is what makes men poets or sages;
and to dare to say what others only dare to think
makes men martyrs or reformers—or both.
> *Chronicle of the Schönberg-*
> *Cotta Family* 1863

885. Mary Jane Holmes (1828–1907)

1 ". . . but needn't tell me that prayers made up
is as good as them as isn't. . . ."
> Ch. 1, *The Cameron Pride* 1867

2 "Keep yourself unspotted from the world,"
Morris had said, and she repeated it to herself
asking "how shall I do that? how can one be
good and fashionable too?" Ibid., Ch. 19

3 "If the body you bring back has my George's
heart within it, I shall love you just the same as
I do now. . . ." Ch. 3, *Rose Mather*
> *1868*

886. Margaret Oliphant (1828–1897)

1 The first thing which I can record concerning
myself is, that I was born. . . . These are
wonderful words. This life, to which neither
time nor eternity can bring diminution—this
everlasting living soul, *began.* My mind loses
itself in these depths. Vol. I, Bk. I,
> Ch. 1, *Memoirs and Resolutions*
> *of Adam Graeme, of Mossgray* 1852

2 "I am perfectly safe—nobody can possibly be
safer than such a woman as I am, in poverty
and middle age," said this strange acquaintance.
"It is an immunity that women don't often prize,
Mr. Vincent, but it is very valuable in its
way." Ch. 9, *Salem Chapel* 1863

3 ". . . the world does not care, though our
hearts are breaking; it keeps its own time."
> Ibid., Ch. 18

4 "There ain't a worm but will turn when he's
trod upon. . . ."
> Vol. II, Ch. 20, *The Perpetual Curate*
> *1864*

5 It *was* a bore to go out into those aimless
assemblies where not to go was a social mistake,
yet to go was weariness of the flesh and
spirit.
Vol. III, Ch. 5, *A Country Gentleman and His*
> *Family* 1886

6 In the history of men and of commonwealth
there is a slow progression, which, however
faint, however deferred, yet gradually goes on,
leaving one generation always a trifle better than
that which preceded it, with some scrap of new
possession, some right assured, some small inheritance gained.
> Introduction, *The Literary History of England*
> *1889*

7 There are many variations in degree of the
greatest human gifts, but they are few in
kind. Pt. IV, Ch. 3, *Royal Edinburgh*
> *1890*

8 The highest ideal [in the fifteenth century] was that of war, war no doubt sometimes for good ends, to redress wrongs, to avenge injury, to make crooked things straight—but yet always war, implying a state of affairs in which the last thing that men thought of was the Golden Rule, and the highest attainment to be looked for was the position of a protector, doer of justice, deliverer of the oppressed.
Ch. 1, *Jeanne d'Arc*   1896

9 It is not necessary to be a good man in order to divine what in certain circumstances a good and pure spirit will do.   Ibid., Ch. 17

887. Martha Johnson Patterson (1828– fl. 1860s)

1 We are plain folks from Tennessee, called here by a national calamity. I hope not too much will be expected of us.   Comment after President Lincoln's assassination, when her father, Andrew Johnson, took office, Quoted in *First Ladies* by Betty Boyd Caroli   1987

888. Elizabeth Doten (1829–?)

1 God of the granite and the rose,
Soul of the sparrow and the bee,
The mighty tide of being flows
Through countless channels, Lord, from
Thee.   "Reconciliation"   *c.1870*

889. Edna Dean Proctor (1829–1923)

1 Now God avenges the life he gladly gave,
Freedom reigns to-day!   "John Brown"*
n.d.

*American militant abolitionist (1800–1859).

2   O there are tears for him,*
O there are cheers for him—
Liberty's champion, Cid of the West.
"Cid of the West"

*Referring to Theodore Roosevelt (1858–1919), 26th president of the United States (1901–1909).

890. Charlotte Barnard (1830–1869)

1 I cannot sing the old songs,
Or dream those dreams again.
"I Cannot Sing the Old Songs"
c.1860

2 Take back the freedom thou cravest,
Leaving the fetters to me.
"Take Back the Heart"   *c.1860*

891. Helen Olcott Bell (1830–1918)

1 To a woman, the consciousness of being well-dressed gives a sense of tranquility which religion fails to bestow.
Letters and Social Aims:
R. W. Emerson *   1876

*American poet and essayist (1803–1882).

892. Emily Dickinson (1830–1886)

1 Success is counted sweetest
By those who ne'er succeed.
No. 67, St. 1 (c.1859), *The Complete Poems of Emily Dickinson,*
Thomas H. Johnson, ed.   *1955*

2 Surgeons must be very careful
When they take the knife!
Underneath their fine incisions
Stirs the Culprit—*Life!*
No. 108 (c.1859), op. cit.

3 Just lost when I was saved!
No. 160, St. 1 (c.1860), op. cit.

4 "Faith" is a fine invention
When Gentlemen can *see*—
But *Microscopes* are prudent
In an Emergency.   No. 185 (c.1860), op. cit.

5 "Hope" is the thing with feathers—
That perches in the soul—
And sings the tune without the words—
And never stops—at all—
No. 254, St. 1 (c.1861), op. cit.

6 There's a certain Slant of light,
Winter Afternoons—
That oppresses, like the Heft
Of Cathedral Tunes—
No. 258, St. 1 (c.1861), op. cit.

7 A single Screw of Flesh
Is all that pins the Soul
No. 262 (c.1861), op. cit.

8 I'm nobody, Who are you?
Are you—Nobody,—too?
No. 288, St. 1 (1861), op. cit.

9 I tasted—careless—then—
I did not know the Wine
Came once a World—Did you?
No. 296, St. 3 (c.1861), op. cit.

10 I reason, Earth is short—
And Anguish—absolute—

And many hurt,
But, what of that?
   No. 301, St. 1 (c.1862), op. cit.

11 The Soul selects her own Society—
Then—shuts the Door—
   No. 303, St. 1 (c.1862), op. cit.

12 I'll tell you how the Sun rose—
A Ribbon at a time—
   No. 318 (c.1860), op. cit.

13 Some keep the Sabbath going to Church—
I keep it, staying at Home—
With a Bobolink for a chorister—
And an Orchard, for a Dome—
   No. 324, St. 1 (c.1860),
   op. cit.

14 After great pain, a formal feeling comes-
   No. 341, St. 1 (c.1862),
   op. cit.

15 Much Madness is divinest Sense—
To a discerning Eye—
Much Sense—the starkest Madness—
   No. 435 (c.1862), op. cit.

16 This is my letter to the World
That never wrote to Me—
   No. 441, St. 1 (c.1862),
   op. cit.

17 I heard a Fly buzz—when I died—
   No. 465, St. 1 (c.1862),
   op. cit.

18 I reckon—when I count at all—
First—Poets—Then the Sun—
Then Summer—Then the Heaven of God—
And then—the List is done—
   No. 569, St. 1 (c.1862),
   op. cit.

19 The Brain—is wider than the Sky—
For—put them side by side—
The one the other will contain
With ease—and You—beside—
   No. 632, St. 1 (c.1862),
   op. cit.

20 I dwell in Possibility—
A fairer House than Prose—
More numerous of Windows—
Superior—for doors—
   No. 657, St. 1 (c.1862), op. cit.

21 The Soul unto itself
Is an imperial friend—
Or the most agonizing Spy—
An Enemy—could send—
   No. 683, St. 1 (c.1862), op. cit.

22 Because I could not stop for Death—
He kindly stopped for me—
   No. 712, St. 1 (c.1863),
   op. cit.

23 My Life had stood—a Loaded Gun—
In Corners . . .   No. 754, St. 1 (c.1863),
   op. cit.

24 If I can stop one Heart from breaking
I shall not live in vain
   No. 919, St. 1 (c.1864),
   op. cit.

25 I never saw a Moor—
I never saw the Sea—
Yet know I how the Heather looks
And what a Billow be.
   No. 1052, St. 1 (c.1865),
   op. cit.

26 The Sweeping up the Heart
And putting Love away
   No. 1078, St. 2 (c.1866),
   op. cit.

27 A great Hope fell
You heard no noise
The Ruin was within
   No. 1123, St. 1 (c.1868),
   op. cit.

28 Tell all the Truth but tell it slant—
Success in Circuit lies
   No. 1129, St. 1 (c.1868), op. cit.

29 A word is dead
When it is said,
Some say.

I say it just
Begins to live
That day.   No. 1212, *in toto* (1872?),
   op. cit.

30 A Deed knocks first at Thought
And then—it knocks at Will—
That is the manufacturing spot
   No. 1216, St. 1 (c.1872),
   op. cit.

31 Not with a Club, the Heart is broken
Nor with a Stone—
A Whip so small you could not see it
I've known
To lash the Magic Creature
Till it fell.   No. 1304, St. 1 (c.1874),
   op. cit.

32 That short—potential stir
That each can make but once—
   No. 1307, St. 1 (c.1874),
   op. cit.

33 A little Madness in the Spring
Is wholesome even for the King,
But God be with the Clown—
   No. 1333, St. 1 (c.1875),
   op. cit.

34 Forbidden Fruit a flavor has
That lawful Orchards mocks—

How luscious lies within the Pod
The Pea that Duty locks—
No. 1377 (c.1876), op. cit.

35 The Pedigree of Honey
Does not concern the Bee—
A Clover, any time, to him,
Is Aristocracy— No. 1627, version II
(c.1884), op. cit.

36 Parting is all we know of heaven,
And all we need of hell.
No. 1732, St. 2 (n.d.),
op. cit.

893. Marie von Ebner Eschenbach (1830–1916)

1 "Good heavens!" said he, "if it be our clothes alone which fit us for society, how highly we should esteem those who make them."
The Two Countesses *1893*

2 He says a learned woman is the greatest of all calamities. Ibid.

3 Fear not those who argue but those who dodge. *Aphorism* *1905*

4 To be content with little is hard, to be content with much, impossible. Ibid.

5 He who believes in freedom of the will has never loved and never hated. Ibid.

6 Whenever two good people argue over principles, they are both right. Ibid.

7 Imaginary evils are incurable. Ibid.

8 We don't believe in rheumatism and true love until after the first attack. Ibid.

9 We are so vain that we even care for the opinion of those we don't care for. Ibid.

10 Privilege is the greatest enemy of right. Ibid.

11 Those whom we support hold us up in life.
Ibid.

12 Only the thinking man lives his life, the thoughtless man's life passes him by. Ibid.

13 You can stay young as long as you can learn, acquire new habits and suffer contradiction.
Ibid.

14 In youth we learn; in age we understand.
Ibid.

15 Oh, say not foreign war! A war is never foreign. Quoted in *War, Peace, and the Future* by Ellen Key* *1916*

*See 1003.

894. Helen Fiske Hunt Jackson (1830–1885)

1 There is nothing so skillful in its own defence as imperious pride. Ch. 13, *Ramona*
1884

2 There cannot be found in the animal kingdom a bat, or any other creature, so blind in its own range of circumstance and connection, as the greater majority of human beings are in the bosoms of their families. Ibid.

3 That indescribable expression peculiar to people who hope they have not been asleep, but know they have. Ibid., Ch. 14

4 My body, eh. Friend Death, how now?
Why all this tedious pomp of writ?
Thou hast reclaimed it sure and slow
For half a century, bit by bit.
"Habeas Corpus," St. 1 *1885*

5 Find me the men on earth who care
Enough for faith or creed today
To seek a barren wilderness
For simple liberty to pray.
"The Pilgrim Forefathers," St. 5 *n.d.*

6 Love has a tide! "Tides" *n.d.*

7 Oh, write of me, not "Died in bitter pains,"
But "Emigrated to another star!"
"Emigravit" *n.d.*

8 O suns and skies and clouds of June,
And flowers of June together,
Ye cannot rival for one hour
October's bright blue weather.
"October's Bright Blue Weather," St. 1 *n.d.*

9 The mighty are brought low by many a thing
Too small to name. Beneath the daisy's disk
Lies hid the pebble for the fatal sling.
"Danger"
n.d.

895. Mother Jones (1830–1930)

1 Sometimes I'm in Washington, then in Pennsylvania, Arizona, Texas, Alabama, Colorado, Minnesota. My address is like my shoes. It travels with me. I abide where there is a fight against wrong. Congressional Hearing, Quoted in *The Rebel Girl*, Pt. II, by Elizabeth Gurley Flynn* *1955*

*See 1410.

2 Sit down and read. Educate yourself for the coming conflicts. Quoted in *Ms.*
November 1981

3 Pray for the dead and fight like hell for the
living.   Motto
                                          n.d.

4 Get it right, I ain't a humanitarian . . . I'm a
hell-raiser!   Comment   *n.d.*

896. Belva Lockwood (1830–1917)

1 I do not believe in sex distinction in literature,
law, politics, or trade—or that modesty and
virtue are more becoming to women than to
men, but wish we had more of it
everywhere.
        Quoted in Pt. II, Ch. 8, *Lady for the Defense*
                            by Mary Virginia
                            Fox   *1975*

2 I know we can't abolish prejudice through laws,
but we can set up guidelines for our actions by
legislation. If women are given equal pay for
Civil Service jobs, maybe other employers will
do the same.   Ibid., Pt. III, Ch. 11

3 If nations could only depend upon fair and
impartial judgments in a world court of law,
they would abandon the senseless, savage practice of war.   Ibid., Ch. 15

4 No one can claim to be called Christian who
gives money for the building of warships and
arsenals.   Address at Westminster Hall,
                      London (c.1886), op. cit.

897. Louise Michel (1830–1905)

1 In rebellion alone, woman is at ease, stamping
out both prejudices and sufferings; all intellectual women will sooner or later rise in
rebellion.   Attributed   *1890*

898. Sarah Agnes Pryor (1830–1912)

1 The public does not tolerate the intrusion of a
man's personal joys and griefs into his official
life.   Comment on Franklin
                    Pierce's* inaugural speech
                    (4 March 1853), Quoted in *First
                    Ladies* by Betty Boyd Caroli
                                      1987

*(1804–1869), 14th president of the United States (1853–
1857).

899. Christina Rossetti (1830–1894)

1 When I am dead, my dearest,
  Sing no sad songs for me;

Plant thou no roses at my head,
  Nor shady cypress tree.
Be the green grass above me
  With showers and dew drops wet:
And if thou wilt, remember,
  And if thou wilt, forget   "Song," St. 1
                                12 December 1848

2 My friends had failed one by one,
  Middle-aged, young, and old,
Till the ghosts were warmer to me
  Than my friends that had grown cold.
                    "A Chilly Night," St. 2
                    11 February 1856

3 Too late for love, too late for joy,
  Too late, too late!
You loitered on the road too long,
  You trifled at the gate. . . .
                    "The Prince's Progress," St. 1
                    11 November 1861

4 "Does the road wind up-hill all the way?"
  "Yes, to the very end."
"Will the day's journey take the whole long
  day?"
"From morn to night, my friend."
                    "Up-Hill," St. 1   *1861*

5 My heart is like a singing bird.
                    "A Birthday," St. 1   *1861*

6 For there is no friend like a sister
  In calm or stormy weather;
To cheer one on the tedious way,
To fetch one if one goes astray,
To lift one if one totters down,
To strengthen whilst one stands.
        "Goblin Market," *Goblin Market*   *1862*

7 One day in the country
  Is worth a month in town.   "Summer,"
                                 op. cit.

8 Better by far that you should forget and smile
  Than that you should remember and be sad.
                    "Remember" (25 July 1849),
                    op. cit.

9 "I ate his life as a banquet,
  I drank his life as new wine,
  I've fattened upon his leanness,
Mine to flourish and his to pine."
                    "Cannot Sweeten," St. 7
                    8 March 1866

10 So gradually it came to pass that, from looking
back together, they took also to looking forward
together.   Ch. 17, *Commonplace, A Tale of
                           Today*   *1870*

11 Glow-worms that gleam but yield no warmth in
gleaming. . . .
                    "Till To-morrow," St. 2   *c.1882*

12 If thou canst dive, bring up pearls. If thou canst
not dive, collect amber.

Prefatory Note, *The Face of the Deep*
1892

13 Hope is like a harebell trembling from its
birth. . . .
"Hope Is Like a Harebell"   *n.d.*

14 Snow had fallen, snow on snow,
Snow on snow,
In the bleak mid-winter,
Long ago.   "Mid-Winter"   *n.d.*

15 Who has seen the wind!
Neither you nor I:
But when the trees bow down their heads,
The wind is passing by.
"Who Has Seen the Wind?," St. 2   *n.d.*

900. Amelia Barr (1831–1919)

1 "There is no corner too quiet, or too far away,
for a woman to make sorrow in it."
Ch. 9, *Jan Vedder's Wife*   *1885*

2 " 'Is she not handsome, virtuous, rich, amiable?' they asked, 'What hath she done to thee?'
The Roman husband pointed to his sandal. 'Is
it not new, is it not handsome and well made?
But none of you can tell where it pinches me.'
That old Roman and I are brothers. Everyone
praises 'my good wife, my rich wife, my handsome wife,' but for all that, the matrimonial
shoe pinches me."   Ibid.

3 "Let me tell thee, time is a very precious gift
of God; so precious that He only gives it to us
moment by moment. He would not have thee
waste it."   Ibid., Ch. 11

4 But the lover's power is the poet's power. He
can make love from all the common strings with
which this world is strung.
Ch. 3, *The Belle of Bolling Green*
1904

5 "When men make themselves into brutes it is
just to treat them like brutes."   Ibid., Ch. 8

6 I entered this incarnation on March-the-twenty-
ninth, A.D. 1831, at the ancient town of Ulver-
ston, Lancashire, England. My soul came with
me. This is not always the case. Every observing
mother of a large family knows that the period
of spiritual possession varies. . . . I brought
my soul with me—an eager soul, impatient for
the loves and joys, the struggles and triumphs
of the dear, unforgotten world.
Ch. 1, *All the Days of My Life*
1913

7 With renunciation life begins.   Ibid., Ch. 9

8 The great difference between voyages rests not
with the ships, but with the people you meet on
them.   Ibid., Ch. 11

9 What we call death was to him only emigration,
and I care not where he now tarries. He is doing
God's will, and more alive than ever he was on
earth.   Ibid., Ch. 23

10 Old age is the verdict of life.   Ibid., Ch. 26

701. Elena Petrovna Blavatsky (1831–1891)

1 We live in an age of prejudice, dissimulation
and paradox, wherein, like dry leaves caught in
a whirlpool, some of us are tossed helpless,
hither and thither, ever struggling between our
honest convictions and fear of that cruelest of
tyrants—PUBLIC OPINION.
"A Paradoxical World," *Lucifer*
February   *1889*

2 We must prepare and study truth under every
aspect, endeavoring to ignore nothing, if we do
not wish to fall into the abyss of the unknown
when the hour shall strike.
Quoted in *La Revue Theosophique*
21 March 1889

3 This idea of passing one's whole life in moral
idleness, and having one's hardest work and
duty done by another—whether God or man—
is most revolting to us, as it is most degrading
to human dignity.
Sec. 5, *The Key to Theosophy*
1893

4 And so the only reality in our conception is the
hour of man's *post mortem* life, when, disembodied—during the period of that pilgrimage
which we call "the cycle of re-births"—he
stands face to face with truth and not the mirages
of his transitory earthly existences.
Ibid., Sec. 9

5 It is the worst of crimes and dire in its results.
. . . Voluntary death would be an abandonment
of our present post and of the duties incumbent
on us, as well as an attempt to shirk karmic
responsibilities, and thus involve the creation of
new Karma.   Ibid., Sec. 12

902. Myra Bradwell (1831–1894/96)

1 [Mary Lincoln*] is no more insane than I
am. .   Comment, Quoted in *First
Ladies* by Betty Boyd Caroli   *1987*

*See 829.

903. Isabel Burton (1831–1896)

1 Without any cant, does not Providence provide
wonderfully for us?

Ch. 15, *Arabia Egypt India*
1879

2 I have no leisure to think of style or of polish, or to select the best language, the best English—no time to shine as an authoress. I must just think aloud, so as not to keep the public waiting.
Foreword, *The Life of Captain Sir Richard F. Burton* 1898

904. Rebecca Harding Davis (1831–1910)

1 The idiosyncrasy of this town is smoke. It rolls solemnly in slow folds from the great chimneys of the iron-foundries, and settles down in black, slimy pools on the muddy streets. Smoke on the wharves, smoke on the dingy boats, on the yellow river—clinging in a coating of greasy soot to the house-front, the two faded poplars, the faces of the passers-by.
"Life in the Iron Mills," *Atlantic Monthly* April 1861

2 Be just—not like man's law, which seizes on one isolated fact, but like God's judging angel, whose clear, sad eye saw all the countless cankering days of this man's life. . . . Ibid.

3 "I tell you, there's something wrong that no talk of 'Liberté' or 'Egalité' will do away. If I had the making of men, these men who do the lowest part of the world's work should be machines—nothing more—hands. It would be kindness. God help them! What are taste, reason, to creatures who must live such lives as that?" Ibid.

4 "Reform is born of need, not pity. No vital movement of the people has worked down, for good or evil; fermented, instead, carried up the heaving, cloggy mass." Ibid.

5 Every child was taught from his cradle that money was Mammon, the chief agent of the flesh and the devil. As he grew up it was his duty as a Christian and a gentleman to appear to despise filthy lucre, whatever his secret opinion of it might be. Ch. 1, *Bits of Gossip* 1904

6 North and South were equally confident that God was on their side, and appealed incessantly to Him. Ibid., Ch. 5

7 We don't look into these unpleasant details of our great struggle [the Civil War]. We all prefer to think that every man who wore the blue or gray was a Philip Sidney at heart. These are sordid facts that I have dragged up. But they are facts. And because we have hidden them our young people have come to look upon war as a kind of beneficent deity, which not only

adds to the national honor but uplifts a nation and develops patriotism and courage. That is all true. But it is only fair, too, to let them know that the garments of the deity are filthy and that some of her influences debase and befoul a people. Ibid.

905. Henrietta Dobree (1831–1894)

1 Safely, safely, gather'd in,
Far from sorrow, far from sin.
"Child's Hymn Book" *n.d.*

906. Amelia Edwards (1831–1892)

1 The Queen has lands and gold, Mother
The Queen has lands and gold,
While you are forced to your empty breast
A skeleton Babe to hold. . . .
"Give Me Three Grains of Corn,
Mother," St. 4 *n.d.*

907. Lucy Webb Hayes (1831–1889)

1 Woman's mind is as strong as man's—equal in all things and his superior in some.
Quoted in *First Ladies* by
Betty Boyd Caroli 1987

908. Nora Perry (1831–1896)

1 But not alone with the silken snare
Did she catch her lovely floating hair,
For, tying her bonnet under her chin,
She tied a young man's heart within.
"The Love-Knot," St. 1 *n.d.*

2 Some day, some day of days, threading the street
With idle, headless pace,
Unlooking for such grace,
I shall behold your face!
"Some Day of Days" *n.d.*

909. Elizabeth Chase Akers (1832–1911)

1 Backward, turn backward, O Time, in your flight,
Make me a child again, just for to-night!
"Rock Me to Sleep, Mother"
1860

2 Blush, happy maiden, when you feel
The lips that press love's glowing seal.
But as the slow years darker roll,

Grown wiser, the experienced soul
Will own as dearer far than they
The lips which kiss the tears away.   "Kisses"
                                                              n.d.

3 Though we be sick and tired and faint and
worn,—
Lo, all things can be borne!
                                      "Endurance," St. 5
                                                              n.d.

910. Louisa May Alcott (1832–1888)

1 A little kingdom I possess,
  Where thoughts and feelings dwell;
And very hard the task I find
  Of governing it well.
                      "My Kingdom," St. 1   *c.1845*

2 "Christmas won't be Christmas without any
presents."   Pt. I, *Little Women*   1868

3 ". . . It seems as if I could do anything when
I'm in a passion. I get so savage I could hurt
anyone and enjoy it. I'm afraid I *shall* do something dreadful some day, and spoil my life, and
make everybody hate me. O Mother, help
me. . . ."   Ibid.

4 "Housekeeping ain't no joke."   Ibid.

5 . . . love is a great beautifier.   Ibid.

6 "My lady" . . . had yet to learn that money
cannot buy refinement of nature, that rank does
not always confer nobility, and that true breeding makes itself felt in spite of external
drawbacks.   Ibid., Pt. II

7 ". . . It's a great comfort to have an artistic
sister."   Ibid.

8 ". . . elegance has a bad effect upon my
constitution. . . ."   Ibid.

9 ". . . Oh dear! How can girls like to have
lovers and refuse them? I think it's
dreadful."   Ibid.

10 ". . . talent isn't genius, and no amount of
energy can make it so. I want to be great, or
nothing. I won't be a commonplace dauber, so
I don't intend to try any more."   Ibid.

11 "It takes two flints to make a fire."   Ibid.

12 . . . when women are the advisers, the lords
of creation don't take the advice till they have
persuaded themselves that it is just what they
intended to do; then they act upon it, and if it
succeeds, they give the weaker vessel half the
credit of it; if it fails, they generously give her
the whole.   Ibid.

13 ". . . I'm not afraid of storms, for I'm learning
how to sail my ship."   Ibid.

14 ". . . What *do* girls do who haven't any mothers to help them through their troubles?"
                                              Ibid.

15 "Help one another, is part of the religion of our
sisterhood, Fan."
                      An Old-Fashioned Girl   1869

16 ". . . women have been called queens for a
long time, but the kingdom given them isn't
worth ruling."   Ibid.

17 "[Molly] remained a merry spinster all her days,
one of the independent, brave and busy creatures
of whom there is such need in the world to help
take care of other people's wives and children,
and to do the many useful jobs that married folk
have no time for."   *Jack and Jill*   1880

18 "[I'm] very glad and grateful that my profession
will make me a useful happy and independent
spinster."   *Jo's Boys*   1886

19 My definition [of a philosopher] is of a man up
in a balloon, with his family and friends holding
the ropes which confine him to the earth and
trying to haul him down.
          *Louisa May Alcott: Her Life, Letters,
          and Journals*, Edna D. Cheney, ed.
                                             1889

20 Father asked us what was God's noblest work.
Anna said *men*, but I said *babies*. Men are often
bad; babies never are.   Early Diary kept at
                              Fruitlands (1843), op. cit.

21 I had a pleasant time with my mind, for it was
happy.   Ibid.

22 I have at last got the little room I have wanted
so long, and am very happy about it. It does
me good to be alone. . . .   Ibid. (1846)

911. Lucretia Rudolph Garfield (1832–1918)

1 My heart almost broke with the cruel thought
that our marriage is based upon the cold, stern
word duty.   Letter to James Garfield
          (1858), Quoted in *First Ladies* by Betty
                              Boyd Caroli   1987

912. Mary Walker (1832–1919)

1 If men were really what they profess to be they
would not compel women to dress so that the
facilities for vice would always be so easy.
              Quoted in *Saturday Review*   1935

913. Mary Woolsey (1832–1864)

1 I lay me down to sleep with little thought or
care

Whether my waking find me here, or there.
"Rest,"
n.d.

914. Gail Hamilton (1833–1896)

1 Whatever an author puts between the two covers
of his book is public property; whatever of
himself he does not put there is his private
property, as much as if he had never written a
word.   Preface, *Country Living and Country
Thinking   1862*

2 What's virtue in man can't be virtue in a
cat.   "Both Sides,"
n.d.

915. Julia Harris May (1833–1912)

1   If we could know
Which of us, darling, would be the first to go,
Who would be first to breast the swelling tide
And step alone upon the other side—
If we could know!   "If We Could Know"
n.d.

916. Emily Miller (1833–1913)

1 Then sing, young hearts that are full of cheer,
With never a thought of sorrow;
The old goes out, but the glad young year
Comes merrily in tomorrow.
"New Year Song," *The Little Corporal*
n.d.

917. Julia Woodruff (1833–1909)

1 Out of the strain of the Doing,
Into the race of the Done.
"Harvest Home," *Sunday at Home
May 1910*

918. Annie Adams Fields (1834–1915)

1 Once men could walk these roads
and hear no sound
Save the sad ocean beating on the shore . . .
"Unchanged," *The Singing Shepherd
1895*

919. Katherine Hankey (1834–1911)

1 Tell me the old, old story
Of unseen things above,

Of Jesus and His glory
Of Jesus and His love.   Hymn   *n.d.*

920. Harriet Kimball (1834–1917)

1 A very rapturing of white;
A wedlock of silence and light:
White, white as the wonder undefiled
Of Eve just wakened in Paradise.
"White Azaleas"   *n.d.*

921. Josephine Pollard (1834–1892)

1 Though he had Eden to live in,
Man cannot be happy alone.
"We Cannot Be Happy Alone," St. 5,
n.d.

922. Ellen Palmer Allerton (1835–1893)

1 Beautiful faces are those that wear
Whole-souled honesty printed there.
"Beautiful Things,"
n.d.

923. Ellen Atherton (1835–1893)

1 Beautiful faces are those that wear
Whole-souled honesty printed there
Untitled   *n.d.*

924. Mary Bradley (1835–1898)

1 Of all the flowers that come and go
The whole twelve months together,
This little purple pansy brings
Thoughts of the sweetest, saddest things.
"Heartsease,"
n.d.

925. Olympia Brown (1835–1900)

1 I comforted her [Mother Cobb] by telling her
that while it was disagreeable and unreasonable
to have our wearing apparel described in the
papers, it was inevitable in this stage of woman's progress, editors and reporters being much
more able to judge of our clothes than they were
of our arguments.
Ch. 10, *Acquaintances, Old and New,
Among Reformers   1912*

2 When I read of the vain discussions of the
present day about the Virgin Birth and other old

dogmas which belong to the past, I feel how great the need is still of a real interest in the religion which builds up character, teaches brotherly love, and opens up to the seeker such a world of usefulness and the beauty of holiness . . .
"Olympia Brown, An Autobiography,"
Gwendolen B. Willis,* ed. (1960),
Ch. 5, *The Annual Journal of the Universalist Historical Society,*
Vol. 4   *1963*

*Daughter of Olympia Brown; see 1007.

3 Our women's colleges are filled with young women, many of whom, with proper encouragement, would make good ministers. We must present the needs of the church and the fitness of the profession for women to these students. The difficulties and discouragements in their way must be overcome by the indefatigable efforts of individual women, so that prejudices will be conquered and church rules, where necessary, amended.   Ibid.

4 I used to say that Susan B. Anthony* was my pole star until I learned to make no one my guide but to follow truth wherever it might lead and to do the duty of the hour at whatever cost.   Ibid., Ch. 6

*See 840.

5 The more we learn of science, the more we see that its wonderful mysteries are all explained by a few simple laws so connected together and so dependent upon each other, that we see the same mind animating them all.   Sermon, Mukwonago, Wisconsin (13 January 1895?), op. cit.

6 In communion with the highest, in *striving* for the best, in losing oneself in others, one is lifted above the common material furniture of life, above its gaudy trappings and encumbering paraphernalia, above its contentions and toils, its antagonisms and weariness into a realm of peace which passeth understanding.   Ibid.

7 Man does not live by bread alone, but by faith, by admiration, by sympathy. 'Tis very shallow to say that cotton or iron or silver or gold are kings of the world. There are rulers that will at any moment make these forgotten. Fear will, love will, character will!   Ibid.

926. Augusta Evans (1835–1909)

1 Money is everything in this world to some people, and more than the next to other poor souls.   Ch. 2, *Beulah*   *1859*

2 Oh! Duty is an icy shadow. It will freeze you. It cannot fill the heart's sanctuary.
            Ibid., Ch. 13

3 Fortuitous circumstances constitute the moulds that shape the majority of human lives, and the hasty impress of an accident is too often regarded as the relentless decree of all ordaining fate. . . .   Ch. 1, *Until Death Us Do Part 1869*

927. Ellen Gates (1835–1920)

1 Sleep sweet within this quiet room,
    O thou! who'er thou art;
And let no mournful yesterday,
    Disturb thy peaceful heart.
            "Sleep Sweet"   *n.d.*

928. Louise Moulton (1835–1908)

1 Bend low, O dusky night,
    And give my spirit rest,
    Hold me deep to your breast,
And put old cares to flight.
            "Tonight"   *n.d.*

2 This life is a fleeting breath. . . .
    "When I Wander Away with Death"   *n.d.*

929. Harriet Spofford (1835–1921)

1 Beauty vanishes like a vapor,
Preach the men of musty morals.
            "Evanescence"   *n.d.*

2 Something to live for came to the place,
    Something to die for maybe,
Something to give even sorrow a grace,
    And yet it was only a baby!
            "Only"   *n.d.*

930. Celia Thaxter (1835–1894)

1 Across the narrow beach we flit,
One little sandpiper and I.
            "The Sandpiper," St. 1
            n.d.

2 Sad soul, take comfort, nor forget
That sunrise never failed us yet!
            "The Sunrise Never Failed Us Yet,"
            St. 4
            n.d.

931. Mary Frances Butts (1836–1902)

2 Build a little fence of trust
    Around today;

Fill the space with loving work,
And therein stay.   "Trust"
                                          n.d.

932. Frances Ridley Havergal (1836–1879)

1 Doubt indulged soon becomes doubt realized.   "The Imagination of the Thoughts of
                  the Heart," *Royal Bounty*
                                          n.d.

2 Love understands love; it needs no talk.
                  "Loving Allegiance," *Royal
                                Commandments*
                                          n.d.

933. Marietta Holley (1836?–1926)

1 We are blind creeters, the fur-seein'est of us;
weak creeters, when we think we are the strong-
mindedest. Now, when we hear of a crime, it
is easy to say that the one who committed that
wrong stepped flat off from goodness into sin,
and should be hung. It is so awful easy and sort
of satisfactory to condemn other folks'es faults
that we don't stop to think that it may be that
evil was fell into through the weakness and
blindness of a mistake.
                  "Kitty Smith and Caleb Cobb," *My
                  Wayward Pardner; or My Trials
                  with Josiah, America, the Widow
                  Bump, and Etcetery*   *1880*

2 But I am a-eppisodin', and a-eppisodin' to a
length and depth almost onprecedented and on-
heard on—and to resoom and go on.
                  *Ch. 4, Samantha at the World's Fair
                                          1893*

3 And I sez, "Children and trees have to be
tackled young, Josiah, to bend their wills the
way you want 'em to go."
        *Ch. 18, Around the World with Josiah Allen's
                                Wife   1899*

934. Jane Ellice Hopkins (1836–1904)

1 Gift, like genius, I often think only means an
infinite capacity for taking pains.
                  *Work Amongst Working Men
                                          1870*

935. Mary Elizabeth Braddon (1837–1915)

1 ". . . it is easy to starve, but it is difficult to
stoop."   *Ch. 23, Lady Audley's Secret
                                          1862*

2 "Let any man make a calculation of his existence, subtracting the house in which he has
been *thoroughly* happy—really and entirely at
his ease, without one *arrièr pensée* to mar his
enjoyment—without the most infinitesimal cloud
to overshadow the brightness of his horizon. Let
him do this, and surely he will laugh in utter
bitterness of soul when he sets down the sum
of his felicity, and discovers the pitiful smallness
of the amount."   Ibid., Ch. 25

3 There can be no reconciliation where there is no
open warfare. There must be a battle, a brave
boisterous battle, with pennants waving and cannon roaring, before there can be peaceful treaties
and enthusiastic shaking of hands.
                                  Ibid., Ch. 32

4 "A priest can achieve great victories with an
army of women at his command."
            Vol. I, Ch. 1, *Hostages to Fortune
                                          1875*

5 ". . . exceptional talent does not always win
its reward unless favoured by exceptional
circumstances."
            Ch. 4, *Dead-Sea Fruit,* Vol. II
                                          1868

6 "Are there not, indeed, brief pauses of mental
intoxication, in which the spirit releases itself
from its dull mortal bondage, and floats starward
on the wings of inspiration?"   Ibid., Ch. 9

7 "I think that most wearisome institution, the
honeymoon, must have been inaugurated by
some sworn foe to matrimony, some vile mis-
ogynist, who took to himself a wife in order to
discover, by experience, the best mode of rendering married life a martyrdom."   Ibid.

8 "A London house without visitors is so
triste."   Ch. 6, *The White House*   *1906*

9 He had compelled her to think of the sons of
toil as she had never thought before, this world
outside the world of Skepton, the lower-grade
labour, the unskilled, uncertain, casual work; a
life in which thrift would seem impossible, since
there was nothing to save, cleanliness and decency impracticable and drunken oblivion the
only possible relief.   Ibid., Ch. 15

10 It may be that Miranda had enjoyed too much
of the roses and the lilies of life, and that a
girlhood of such absolute indulgence was hardly
the best preparation for the battle which has to
come in the lives of women—whatever their
temporal advantages—the battle of the heart, or
of the brain, the fight with fate, or the fight with
man.   Book I, Ch. 2, *Miranda*   *1913*

11 "Love is life, love is the lamp that lights the
universe: without that light this goodly frame
the earth, is a barren promontory and man the
quintessence of dust."   Ibid., Book II, Ch. 9

12 When once estrangement has arisen between those who truly love each other, everything seems to widen the breach.

> Ch. 8, *Run to Earth*
> *1915?*

936. Rosalia de Castro (1837–1885)

1 Give back the flower its fragrant scent
When it is dry;
From the waves that kiss the seashore
And one by one caress it as they die,
Go gather all the murmurs that are spent
And on bronze plates their harmonies
  inscribe.

> "El tiempo pasa" (Life Passes By),
> John A. Crow, tr.   *n.d.*

937. Jeanne Detourbey (1837–1908)

1 Is it necessary to have read Spinoza in order to make out a laundry list?

> Quoted in *Forty Years of Paristan Society* by Arthur Meyer   *1912*

2 Of course, fortune has its part in human affairs, but conduct is really much more important.

> Ibid.

938. Mary E. Bryan (1838/46–1913)

1 Men, after much demur and hesitation, have given women liberty to write; but they cannot yet consent to allow them full freedom. They may flutter out of the cage, but it must be with clipped wings; they may hop about the smooth-shaven lawn, but must, on no account, fly.

> "How Should Women Write?"
> (1860), *Hidden Hands: An Anthology of American Women Writers, 1790–1870,* Lucy M. Freibert & Barbara A. White, eds.   *1985*

2 Women are . . . learning that genius has no sex. . . . How should a woman write? I answer, as men, as all should write to whom the power of expression has been given—honestly and without fear.

> Ibid.

939. Mary Mapes Dodge (1838?–1905)

1 To her mind, the poor peasant-girl Gretel was not a human being, a God-created creature like herself—she was only something that meant poverty, rags and dirt.

> Preface, *Hans Brinker or The Silver Skates*
> *1865*

2 What a dreadful thing it must be to have a dull father. . . .   Ibid., "Boys and Girls"

3 . . . the dame was filled with delightful anxieties caused by the unreasonable demands of ten thousand guilders' worth of new wants that had sprung up like mushrooms in a single night.   Ibid., "A Discovery"

4 "Modern ways are quite alarming,"
Grandma says, "but boys were charming"
(Girls and boys she means, of course) "long
  ago."   "The Minuet," St. 3   *1879*

5 But I believe that God is overhead;
And as life is to the living, so death is to the
  dead.   "The Two Mysteries," St. 5
> *n.d.*

940. Kate Field (1838–1896)

1 They talk about a woman's sphere,
As though it had a limit.
There's not a place in earth or heaven,
There's not a task to mankind given . . .
Without a woman in it.   "Woman's Spirit"
> *n.d.*

941. Lydia Kamekeha Liliuokalani (1838–1917)

1 The Hawaiian people have been from time immemorial lovers of poetry and music, and have been apt in improvising historic poems, songs of love, and chants of worship, so that praises of the living or wails over the dead were with them but the natural expression of their feelings.   Ch. 5, *Hawaii's Story*   *1898*

2 Oh, honest Americans, as Christians hear me for my down-trodden people! Their form of government is as dear to them as yours is precious to you. Quite as warmly as you love your country, so they love theirs. . . . do not covet the little vineyards of Naboth's, so far from your shores, lest the punishment of Ahab fall upon you, if not in your day, in that of your children, for "be not deceived, God is not mocked."   Ibid., Ch. 57

3 Farewell to thee, farewell to thee,
Thou charming one who dwells among the
  bowers,
One fond embrace before I now depart
Until we meet again.   "Aloha Oe"
> *n.d.*

942. Margaret Sangster (1838–1912)

1 And it isn't the thing you do, dear,
It's the thing you leave undone

Which gives you a bit of a heartache
At the setting of the sun.
"The Sin of Omission"   *n.d.*

2 Never yet was a springtime
When the buds forgot to blow.
"Awakening"   *n.d.*

3 Not always the fanciest cake that's there
Is the best to eat!
"French Pastry," St. 3   *n.d.*

943. Victoria Claflin Woodhull (1838–1927)

1 I have an inalienable constitutional and natural right to love whom I may, to love as long or as short a period as I can, to change that love every day if I please!
Article in *Woodhull and Claflin's Weekly*   *20 November 1871*

2 A Vanderbilt may sit in his office and manipulate stocks or declare dividends by which in a few years he amasses fifty million dollars from the industries of the country, and he is one of the remarkable men of the age. But if a poor, half-starved child should take a loaf of bread from his cupboard to appease her hunger, she would be sent to the tombs.
Campaign Speech   *1872*

3 It is a fact terrible to contemplate, yet it is nevertheless true, and ought to be pressed upon the world for its recognition: that fully one-half of all women seldom or never experience any pleasure whatever in the sexual act. Now this is an impeachment of nature, a disgrace to our civilization.   Speech, "The Elixir of Life," American Association of Spiritualists (1873), Chicago, *Feminism, Miriam Schneir,* ed.   *1972*

*See 2134.

944. Mary Clemmer (1839–1884)

1 I lie amid the Goldenrod,
I love to see it lean and nod.   "Goldenrod"
n.d.

2 The Indian Summer, the dead Summer's soul.   "Presence"
n.d.

3 Only a newspaper! Quick read, quick lost,
Who sums the treasure that it carries hence?
Torn, trampled under feet, who counts thy cost,
Star-eyed intelligence?
"The Journalist"   *n.d.*

945. Ouida (1839–1908)

1 . . . with peaches and women, it's only the side next the sun that's tempting.
Strathmore   *1865*

2 To vice, innocence must always seem only a superior kind of chicanery.
"Two Little Wooden Shoes,"
(1874), *Wisdom, Wit and Pathos*   *1884*

3 Petty laws breed great crimes.
"Pipistrello" (1880), op. cit.

4 A cruel story runs on wheels, and every hand oils the wheels as they run.
"Moths," op. cit.

5 Christianity has ever been the enemy of human love.   "The Failure of Christianity"   *n.d.*

6 Christianity has made of death a terror which was unknown to the gay calmness of the Pagan.   Ibid.

946. Frances Willard (1839–1898)

1 Here's a recipe for the abolishment of the Blues which is worth a dozen medical nostrums:
Take one spoonful of Pleasant memories.
Take two spoonfuls of Endeavours for the Happiness of others.
Take two spoonfuls of Forgetfulness of Sorrow.
Mix well with half a pint of Cheerfulness.
Take a portion every hour of the day.
Journal Entry (c.1860), Quoted in Ch. 2,
Frances Willard: Her Life and Works by Ray Strachey
1912

2 The world is wide, and I will not waste my life in friction when it could be turned into momentum.   Ibid., Ch. 6

947. Ann Plato (fl. 1840s)

1 . . . a good education is another name for happiness.   *Essays*   *1841*

948. Elizabeth York Case (1840?–1911)

1 There is no unbelief;
Whoever plants a seed beneath the sod
And waits to see it push away the clod,
He trusts in God.   "There Is No Unbelief"
n.d.

949. Emilia Dilke (1840–1904)

1 [Artistic] work which is not done for its own sake, in which the chief place is claimed by the

historical or the moral, in which attention is seized by the subject rather than the rendering of the subject . . . loses its aesthetic character, and cannot possess those poetic elements which fire the fancy and rouse the emotions.

Quoted in *The Saturday Review*
23 August 1868

2 It was put before me that if I wished to command respect I must make myself *the* authority on some one subject which interested me. I was told, and it was good counsel, not to take hackwork, and to reject even well-paid things that would lead me off the track.

Quoted in "Memoir" by
Sir Charles Dilke, *The Book*
of Spiritual Life   1905

950. Harriet King (1840–1920)

1 Measure thy life by loss instead of gain,
Not by the wine drunk, but by the wine
    poured forth.   "The Disciples"
n.d.

951. Helena Modjeska (1840–1910)

1 Alas! it was not my destiny to die for my country, as was my cherished dream, but instead of becoming the heroine I had to be satisfied with acting heroines, exchanging the armor for tinsel, and the weapon for words.

Pt. I, Ch. 1, *Memories and Impressions*
1910

2 It is never right to be more Catholic than the Pope.   Ibid., Ch. 25

3 . . . the word "great' is not sufficient anymore, if you do not add to it, "Genius!" In Europe the word "genius" is only applied to the greatest of the world, but here [in America] it has become an everyday occurrence.

Ibid., Pt. III, Ch. 51

4 We foreigners, born outside of the magic pale of the Anglo-Saxon race, place Shakespeare upon a much higher pedestal. We claim that, before being English, he was human, and that his creations are not bound either by local or ethnological limits, but belong to humanity in general.   Ibid.

952. Marilla Ricker (1840–1920)

1 The only thing that ever came back from the grave that we know of was a lie.

Vol. XXV, *The Philistine*
c.1901

2 He [Thomas Paine] was as democratic as nature, as impartial as sun and rain.   Ibid.

953. Katharine Walker (1840–1916)

1 The elusiveness of soap, the knottiness of strings, the transitory nature of buttons, the inclination of suspenders to twist and of hooks to forsake their lawful eyes, and cleave only unto the hairs of their hapless owner's head.

"The Total Depravity of Inanimate
Things," *Atlantic Monthly*
September 1864

954. Elizabeth Wordsworth (1840–1932)

1 If all the good people were clever,
And all the clever people were good,
The world would be nicer than ever
We thought that it possibly could.

But somehow, 'tis seldom or never
The two hit it off as they should;
The good are so harsh to the clever,
The clever so rude to the good.

"The Good and the Clever,"
St. Christopher and Other Poems
1890

955. Mary Wood Allen (1841–1908)

1 Women embroiders man's life—Embroider is to beautify—The embroidery of cleanliness—Of a smile—Of gentle words.

Summary, *What a Young Girl Ought to Know*
1897

956. Mathilde Blind (1841–1896)

1 Blossoms of humanity!
                    "The St.-Children's Dance"
n.d.

2 The moon returns, and the spring; birds warble, trees burst into leaf,
But love once gone, goes forever, and all that endures is the grief.

"Love Trilogy," No. 3
n.d.

957. Sarah Knowles Bolton (1841–1916)

1   He alone is great
Who by a life heroic conquers fate.

"The Inevitable"
n.d.

958. Eliza Burt Gamble (1841–1920)

1 . . . with the dawn of scientific investigation it might have been hoped that the prejudices resulting from lower conditions of human society would disappear, and that in their stead would be set forth not only facts, but deductions from facts, better suited to the dawn of an intellectual age . . .

The ability, however, to collect facts, and the power to generalize and draw conclusions from them, avail little, when brought into direct opposition to deeply rooted prejudices.
The Evolution of Woman   1894

959. Mary Lathbury (1841–1913)

1 Children of yesterday,
    Heirs of tomorrow,
What are you weaving?
    Labor and sorrow?   "Song of Hope," St. 1
n.d.

960. Kate Brownlee Sherwood (1841–1914)

1 One heart, one hope, one destiny, one flag
    from sea to sea.
            "Albert Sidney Johnstone,"
            Dreams of the Ages   1893

961. Sarah Sadie Williams (1841–1868)

1 Is it so, O Christ in heaven, that the highest
    suffer most,
That the strongest wander farthest, and more
    hopelessly are lost,
That the mark of rank in nature is capacity for
    pain,
That the anguish of the singer makes the
    sweetness of the strain?
        "Is It So, O Christ in Heaven?"   *n.d.*

962. Marie le Baron (1842–1894)

1 We point with proud, though bleeding hearts,
    to myriads of graves.
They tell the story of a war
    that ended Slavery's night;
And still women struggle for
    our Liberty, our Right.
        "The Yellow Ribbon"   1876

963. Mary Elizabeth Brown (1842–1917)

1 I'll go where you want me to go, dear Lord,
    O'er mountain, or plain, or sea;

I'll say what you want me to say, dear Lord,
    I'll be what you want me to be.
        "I'll Go Where You Want Me to
            Go"   *n.d.*

964. Ina Coolbrith (1842–1928)

1 He walks with God upon the hills!
And sees, each morn, the world arise
New-bathed in light of paradise.
        "The Poet"   *n.d.*

965. May Riley Smith (1842–1927)

1 Strange we never prize the music
Till the sweet-voiced bird has flown. . . .
        "If We Knew," St. 14   *1867*

2 God's plan, like lilies pure and white, unfold.
    We must not tear the close-shut leaves
    apart.
Time will reveal the calyxes of gold.
        "Sometime," *Sometime and Other
            Poems*   *1892*

3 My life's a pool which can only hold
    One star and a glimpse of blue.
        "My Life Is a Bowl," St. 2
            n.d.

966. Sarah Doudney (1843–1926)

1 "There are no such things as mermaids," exclaimed Frank, her schoolboy brother; "and if there are, their company wouldn't suit you, Ada. How do you suppose you would get on under the sea, with no circulating library, no dressmakers and milliners, and knick knacks and fallals?"
        Ch. 19, *Faith Harrowby; or, The Smuggler's
            Cave*   1871

2 We love thee well, but Jesus loves thee
    best.
        "The Christians' Good-Night"   1892

3 But the waiting time, my brothers,
    Is the hardest time of all.
        "The Hardest Time of all,"
            Psalms of Life   *n.d.*

967. Violet Fane (1843–1905)

1 Ah, "All things come to those who wait,"
    (I say these words to make me glad),
But something answers soft and sad,
    "They come, but often come too late."
        "Tout Vient à Qui Sait Attendre"   *n.d.*

2 Let me arise and open the gate,
  To breathe the wild warm air of the heath,
  And to let in Love, and to let out Hate,
  And anger at living and scorn of Fate,
  To let in Life, and to let out Death.
  "Reverie"   *n.d.*

3 Nothing is right and nothing is just;
  We sow in ashes and reap in dust.   Ibid.

968. Anna Hamilton (1843–1875)

1 This learned I from the shadow of a tree,
  That to and fro did sway against a wall,
  Our shadow selves, our influence, may fall
  Where we ourselves can never be.
  "Influence"   *n.d.*

969. Caroline Le Row (1843–?)

1 But I will write of him who fights
  And vanquishes his sins,
  Who struggles on through weary years
  Against himself and wins.
  "True Heroism"   *n.d.*

970. Bertha von Suttner (1843–1914)

1 After the verb "To Love," "To Help" is the
  most beautiful verb in the world!
  "Epigram," *Ground Arms*   *1892*

971. Carmen Sylva (1843–1916)

1 Life was a radiant maiden, the daughter of the
  Sun, endowed with all the charm and grace, all
  the power and happiness, which only such a
  mother could give to her child.
  "The Child of the Sun,"
  Pilgrim Sorrow   *1884*

2 Complaints were heard no longer, for dull dis-
  pair had reduced all men to silence; and when
  the starving people tore one another to pieces,
  no one even told of it.   "Rîul Doamnei,"
  Legends from River and Mountain   *1896*

3 . . . he hesitated to pluck the fruit, for fear it
  should leave a bitter taste behind.
  "A Doubting Lover,"
  op. cit.

4 "Ill could I resign myself to dwell forever shut
  in between four walls. I must be free, free to
  roam where I please, like the birds in the
  woodlands."   "Carma, the Harp-Girl,"
  Real Queen's Fairy Tales   *1901*

5 There was another thing that did not exist in
  these islands; that was money. The swans would
  never have permitted anything so low and degrading to enter their domain. Gold they tolerated, but merely for ornamentation, where it
  could light up some dull surface. But to traffic
  with money, and to bargain, and barter—that
  was unheard of.   "The Swan Lake," op. cit.

6   Great Solitude
  Hath one thousand voices and a flood of light,
  Be not afraid, enter the Sanctuary,
  Thou wilt be taken by the hand and led
  To Life's own fountain, never-ending
  Thought!   "Solitude,"
  Sweet Hours   1904

972. St. Bernadette (1844–1879)

1 I fear only bad Catholics.
  Quoted in *Lourdes* by Edith
  Sanders   *1940*

973. Sarah Bernhardt (1844–1923)

1 Cloister existence is one of unbroken sameness
  for all. . . . The rumor of the outside world
  dies away at the heavy cloister gate.
  Ch. 3, *Memories of My Life   1907*

2 Those who know the joys and miseries of celebrity . . . know. . . . It is a sort of octopus
  with innumerable tentacles. It throws out its
  clammy arms on the right and on the left, in
  front and behind, and gathers into its thousand
  little inhaling organs all the gossip and slander
  and praise afloat to spit out again at the public
  when it is vomiting its black gall.
  Ibid., Ch. 22

974. Madeline Bridges (1844–1920)

1 When Psyche's friend becomes her lover,
  How sweetly these conditions blend!
  But, oh, what anguish to discover
  Her lover has become—her friend!
  "Friend and Lover"   *n.d.*

975. Bertha Buxton (1844–1881)

1 After all, the eleventh commandment (thou shalt
  not be found out) is the only one that is virtually
  impossible to keep in these days.
  Ch. 3, *Jenny of the Princes
  1879*

976. Mary Cassatt (1844–1926)

1 I am independent! I can live alone and I love to work.   Quoted in *Sixteen to Sixty, Memoirs of a Collector* by Louisine W. Havemeyer   *1930*

2 A woman artist must be . . . capable of making the primary sacrifices.
Quoted in "Mary Cassatt" by Forbes Watson, *Arts Weekly*   *1932*

3 Yet in spite of the total disregard of the dictionary of manners, he [Cézanne]* shows a politeness toward us which no other man here would have shown. . . . Cézanne is one of the most liberal artists I have ever seen. He prefaces every remark with *Pour moi* it is so and so, but he grants that everyone may be as honest and as true to nature from their convictions; he doesn't believe that everyone should see alike.
Letter to Mrs. Stillman (1894), Quoted in *Mary Cassatt: A Biography of the Great American Painter* by Nancy Hale**   *1975*

* French impressionist painter (1839–1906).
** See 1687.

4 Why do people so love to wander? I think the civilized parts of the World will suffice for me in the future.   Letter to Louisine Havemeyer (11 February 1911), op. cit.

977. Elizabeth Stuart Phelps (1844–1911)

1 Who originated that most exquisite of inquisitions, the condolence system?
Ch. 2, *The Gates Ajar*   *1869*

2 The meaning of liberty broke upon me like a sunburst. Freedom was in and of itself the highest law. Had I thought that death was to mean release from personal obedience? Lo, death itself was but the elevation of moral claims, from lower to higher.
Ch. 3, *Beyond the Gates*   *1883*

3 The great law of denial belongs to the powerful forces of life, whether the case be one of coolish baked beans, or an unrequited affection.
Ch. 1, *A Singular Life*   *1896*

4 She had accomplished nothing, that she could see, but keep her house in order. . . . Unsatisfied longings for something which she had not attained, often clouded what, otherwise, would have been a bright day to her; and yet the causes of these feelings seemed to lie in a dim and misty region, which her eye could not penetrate.   *The Angel Over the Right Shoulder*   *n.d.*

978. Margaret Sidney (1844–1924)

1 The little old kitchen had quieted down from the bustle and confusion of mid-day; and now, with its afternoon manners on, presented a holiday aspect, that as the principal room in the brown house, it was eminently proper it should have.   "A Home View," *Five Little Peppers and How They Grew*   *1881*

2 "It's better'n a Christmas," they told their mother, "to get ready for it!"
Ibid., "Getting a Christmas for the Little Ones"

3 "You're just the splendidest, *goodest* mamsie in all the world. And I'm a hateful cross old bear, so I am!"
Ibid., "Polly's Dismal Morning"

979. Arabella Smith (1844–1916)

1 Oh, friends! I pray to-night,
Keep not your roses for my dead, cold brow
The way is lonely, let me feel them now.
"If I Should Die To-Night"   *n.d.*

980. Sophie Tolstoy (1844–1919)

1 I am a source of satisfaction to him, a nurse, a piece of furniture, a *woman*—nothing more.
(13 November 1893)
A Diary of Tolstoy's Wife, 1860–1891   *1928*

2 As for me, I both *can* and *want* to do everything, but after a while I begin to realize there is nothing to want, and that I can't do anything beyond eating, drinking, sleeping, nursing the children, and caring for them and my husband. After all, this *is* happiness, yet why do I grow sad and weep, as I did yesterday?
Ibid. (25 February 1865)

3 It makes me laugh to read over this diary. It's so full of contradictions, and one would think I was such an unhappy woman. Yet is there a happier woman than I?   Ibid. (31 July 1868)

4 He would like to destroy his old diaries and to appear before his children and the public only in his patriarchal robes. His vanity is immense!   Ibid. (17 December 1890)

5 It is sad that my emotional dependence on the man I love should have killed so much of my energy and ability; there was certainly once a great deal of energy in me.
Ibid. (31 December 1890)

981. Sarah Winnemucca (1844–1891)

1 I would be the first Indian woman who ever spoke before white people, and they don't know what the Indians have got to stand sometimes. Newspaper interview (1879), Quoted in *Sarah Winnemucca of the Northern Paiutes* by Gae Whitney Canfield   *1983*

2 I assure you that there is an Indian ring; that it is a corrupt ring, and that it has its head and shoulders in the treasury at Washington.
Lecture, op. cit.

3 Everyone knows what a woman must suffer who undertakes to act against bad men. My reputation has been assailed, and it is done so cunningly that I cannot prove it to be unjust.
Lecture, op. cit.

4 If I possessed the wealth of several rich ladies whom you all know, I would place all the Indians of Nevada on ships in our harbor, take them to New York and land them there as immigrants, that they might be received with open arms, blessed with the blessings of universal suffrage, and thus placed beyond the necessity of reservation help and out of the reach of Indian agents.   Lecture (1885), op. cit.

5 Most of teachers have but one object, viz. to draw their salary. I do not think that a teacher should have no salary. But I think they should earn it first and then think of it.
Remark (1885), op. cit.

982. Marie Chona (1845?–1937?)

1 You see, we have power. Men have to dream to get power from the spirits and they think of everything they can—song and speeches and marching around, hoping that the spirits will notice them and give them some power. But we have power . . . Children. Can any warrior make a child, no matter how brave and wonderful he is?   *Papago Woman*, Ruth M. Underhill, ed. (orig. ed., 1936) *1979*

2 It is not good to be old, not beautiful.   Ibid.

983. Tennessee Claflin (1845–1923)

1 At the ballot-box is not where the shoe pinches. . . . It is at home where the husband . . . is the supreme ruler, that the little difficulty arises; he will not surrender this absolute power unless he is compelled.
"Constitutional Equality, a Right of Women"   *1871*

2 A *free* man is a noble being; a *free* woman is a contemptible being. . . . In other terms, the use of this one word, in its two-fold application to men and to women, reveals the unconscious but ever present conviction in the public mind that men tend, of course, heavenward in their natures and development, and that women tend just as naturally hellward.
Article in *Woodhull and Claflin's Weekly*   *1871*

3 The revolt against any oppression usually goes to an opposite extreme for a time; and that is right and necessary.   Ibid.

4 When people had slaves, they expected that their pigs, chickens, corn and everything lying loose about the plantation would be stolen. But the planters began by stealing the liberty of their slaves, by stealing their labor, by stealing, in fact, all they had; and the natural result was that the slaves stole back all they could.
"Which Is to Blame?"   (1872), op. cit.

984. Susan Coolidge (1845–1905)

1 "A commonplace life," we say and we sigh;
But why would we sigh as we say?
The commonplace sun in the commonplace sky
Makes up the commonplace day.
"Commonplace" *n.d.*

2 Men die, but sorrow never dies;
The crowding years divide in vain,
And the wide world is knit with ties
Of common brotherhood in pain.
"The Cradle Tomb in Westminster Abbey"   *n.d.*

985. Emily Hickey (1845–1924)

1 Beloved, it is morn!
A redder berry on the thorn,
A deeper yellow on the corn,
For this good day new-born!
"Beloved, It Is Morn"   *n.d.*

986. Margaret Janvier (1845–1913)

1 You needn't try to comfort me—
I tell you my dolly is dead!
There's no use in saying she isn't, with
A crack like that in her head.
"The Dead Doll," St. 1 *n.d.*

987. Katharine Bradley (1846–1914)

1 Come, mete out my loneliness, O wind,
  For I would know
  How far the living who must stay behind
  Are from the dead who go.
                          "Mete Out My Loneliness," with
                                    Edith Cooper*
                                           n.d.

*See 1099.

2 Sweet and of their nature vacant are the days
    I spend—
  Quiet as a plough laid by at the furrow's
    end.   "Old Age," with Edith Cooper*
                                           n.d.

*See 1099.

988. Anna Dostoevsky (1846–1918)

1 From a timid, shy girl I had become a woman
  of resolute character, who could not longer be
  frightened by the struggle with troubles.
              (c. 1871) Dostoevsky Portrayed by His
                                    Wife   1926

2 It seems to me that he has never loved, that he
  has only imagined that he has loved, that there
  has been no real love on his part. I even think
  that he is incapable of love; he is too much
  occupied with other thoughts and ideas to become strongly attached to anyone earthly.
                                    Ibid. (1887)

989. Anna Green (1846–1935)

1 Hath the spirit of all beauty
  Kissed you in the path of duty?
                          "On the Threshold"
                                           n.d.

990. Princess Kazu-no-miya (1846–1877)

1 Please understand the heart of one who leaves
    as the water in the streams; never to re-
    turn again.   Untitled Poem   1861

2 I wear the magnificent dress of brocade and
    damask in vain, now that you are not here
    to admire it.   Untitled Poem   1866

991. Carry Nation (1846–1911)

1 Who hath sorrow? Who hath woe?
  They who do not answer no;

They whose feet to sin incline,
While they tarry at the wine.
          Ch. 12, Quoted in Cyclone Carry
                    by Carleton Beals   1962

2 A woman is stripped of everything by them
  [saloons]. Her husband is torn from her; she is
  robbed of her sons, her home, her food, and her
  virtue; and then they strip her clothes off and
  hang her up bare in these dens of robbery and
  murder. Truly does the saloon make a woman
  bare of all things!   Ibid. (c. 1893), Ch. 14

3 You have put me in here [jail] a cub, but I will
  come out roaring like a lion, and I will make
  all hell howl!   Ibid. (c. 1901)

992. Leylâ Hanim (?–1847)

1 Leylâ, indulge in pleasure
  With your lovely friend:
  Enjoy yourself in this world,
  Never mind what they say.   Untitled, St. 4,
                        Tâlat S. Halman, tr., The
                        Penquin Book of Women Poets,
                    Carol Cosman, Joan Keefe & Kathleen
                              Weaver, eds.   1978

993. Annie Wood Besant (1847–1933)

1 There is no birthright in the white skin that it
  shall say that wherever it goes, to any nation,
  amongst any people, there the people of the
  country shall give way before it, and those to
  whom the land belongs shall bow down and
  become its servants. . . .
                    Wake Up, India: A Plea for
                        Social Reform   1913

2 . . . when there shall be no differences save by
  merit of character, by merit of ability, by merit
  of service to the country. Those are the true
  tests of the value of any man or woman, white
  or coloured; those who can serve best, those
  who help most, those who sacrifice most, those
  are the people who will be loved in life and
  honoured in death, when all questions of colour
  are swept away and when in a free country free
  citizens shall meet on equal grounds.   Ibid.

994. Mary Catherwood (1847–1901)

1 They [the Chippewa] were a people ruled only
  by persuasive eloquence moving on the surface
  of their passion. . . .
              Pt. I, The White Islander   1893

2 Two may talk together under the same roof for
  many years, yet never really meet; and two
  others at first speech are old friends.

"Marianson," *Mackinac and
Lake Stories   1899*

3 Though in those days of the young century a
man might become anything; for the West was
before him, an empire, and woodcraft was better
than learning.   "The Black Feather,"
op. cit.

4 She might struggle like a fly in a web. He
wrapped her around and around with beautiful
sentences.   "The King of Beaver,"
op. cit.

5 The world of city-maddened people who swarmed
to this lake for their annual immersion in
nature. . . .   "The Cursed Patois,"
op. cit.

995. Alice Meynell (1847–1922)

1   And when you go
There's loneliness in loneliness.   "Song"
n.d.

2 Dear Laws, be wings to me!
The feather merely floats, O be it heard
Through weight of life—the skylark's grav-
ity—
That I am not a feather, but a bird!
"The Laws of Verse"
n.d.

3 I come from nothing: but from where
come the undying thoughts I bear?
"The Modern Poet, or a
Song of Derivations"
n.d.

4 She walks—the lady of my delight—
A shepherdess of sheep
Her flocks are thoughts.
"The Shepherdess," St. 1
n.d.

5 The sense of humour has other things to do
than to make itself conspicuous in the act
of laughter.   "Laughter"
n.d.

996. Julia A. Moore (1847–1920)

1 And now, kind friends, what I have wrote
I hope you will pass over,
And not criticize as some have done
Hitherto herebefore.
"To My Friends and Critics"   *n.d.*

2 Leave off the agony, leave off style,
Unless you've got money by us all the
while.
"Leave Off the Agony in Style"   *n.d.*

997. Annie Rankin Annan (1848–1925)

1 A dandelion in his verse,
Like the first gold in childhood's purse.
"Dandelions"   *n.d.*

998. Alice James (1848–1892)

1 It is so comic to hear oneself called old, even
at ninety I suppose!   Letter to William
James* (14 June 1889),
The Diary of Alice James,
Leon Edel, ed.   *1964*

* American philosopher and psychologist (1842–1910).

2 . . . the immutable law that however great we
may seem to our own consciousness no human
being would exchange his for ours. . . .
Ibid. (7 July 1889)

3 It is an immense loss to have all robust and
sustaining expletives refined away from one! At
. . . moments of trial refinement is a feeble
reed to lean upon.   Ibid. (12 December 1889)

4 I suppose one has a greater sense of intellectual
degradation after an interview with a doctor than
from any human experience.
Ibid. (27 September 1890)

5 The difficulty about all this dying is that you
can't tell a fellow anything about it, so where
does the fun come in?
Ibid. (11 December 1891)

6 . . . physical pain however great ends in itself
and falls away like dry husks from the mind,
whilst moral discords and nervous horrors sear
the soul.   Ibid. (4 March 1892)

999. Catherine Liddell (1848–?)

1 "Isn't this Joseph's son?"—ah, it is He;
Joseph the carpenter—same trade as me.
"Jesus the Carpenter"   *n.d.*

1000. Ellen Terry (1848–1928)

1 Imagination, industry, and intelligence—"the
three I's"—are all indispensable to the actress,
but of these three the greatest is, without any
doubt, imagination.
Ch. 2, *The Story of My Life*   *1908*

2 What is a diary as a rule? A document useful to
the person who keeps it, dull to the contemporary who reads it, invaluable to the student,
centuries afterwards, who treasures it!
Ibid., Ch. 14

3 Wonderful women! Have you ever thought how much we all, and women especially, owe to Shakespeare for his vindication of women in these fearless, high-spirited, resolute and intelligent heroines?
    "The Triumphant Women," Lecture (1911), *Four Lectures on Shakespeare* 1932

1001. Frances Burnett (1849–1924)

1 "Are you a 'publican, Mary?" "Sorra a bit," sez I; "I'm the bist o' dimmycrats!" An' he looks up at me wid a look that ud go to yer heart, an' sez he: "Mary," sez he, "the country will go to ruin." An' nivver a day since thin has he let go by widout argyin' wid me to change me polytics.
    Ch. 1, *Little Lord Fauntleroy* 1888

2 It is astonishing how short a time it takes for very wonderful things to happen.
    Ibid., Ch. 14

1002. Sarah Orne Jewett (1849–1909)

1 This was one of those perfect New England days in late summer where the spirit of autumn takes a first stealthy flight, like a spy, through the ripening country-side, and, with feigned sympathy for those who droop with August heat, puts her cool cloak of bracing air about leaf and flower and human shoulders.
    "The Courting of Sister Wisby," *Atlantic Monthly* 1887

2 "Now I'm a believer, and I try to live a Christian life, but I'd as soon hear a surveyor's book read out, figgers an' all, as try to get any simple truth out o' most sermons." Ibid.

3 Wrecked on the lee shore of age.
    Ch. 7, *The Country of the Pointed Firs and Other Stories* 1896

4 Tact is after all a kind of mind reading.
    Ibid., Ch. 10

5 "Yes'm, old friends is always best, 'less you can catch a new one that's fit to make an old one out of." Ibid., Ch. 12

6 "T'ain't worthwhile to wear a day all out before it comes." Ibid., Ch. 16

7 The road was new to me, as roads always are, going back. Ibid., Ch. 19

1003. Ellen Key (1849–1926)

1 According to my method of thinking, and that of many others, not woman but the mother is the most precious possession of the nation, so precious that society advances its highest wellbeing when it protects the functions of the mother.
    Ch. 2, *The Century of the Child* 1909

2 All philanthropy—no age has seen more of it than our own—is only a savoury fumigation burning at the mouth of a sewer. This incense offering makes the air more endurable to passersby, but it does not hinder the infection in the sewer from spreading. Ibid.

3 At every step the child should be allowed to meet the real experiences of life; the thorns should never be plucked from his roses.
    Ibid., Ch. 3

4 Nothing would more effectively further the development of education than for all flogging pedagogues to learn to educate with the head instead of with the hand. Ibid.

5 Anyone who would attempt the task of felling a virgin forest with a penknife would probably feel the same paralysis of despair that the reformer feels when confronted with existing school systems. Ibid., Ch. 5

6 I wrote in the sand [at age ten], "God is dead." In doing so I thought, If there is a God, He will kill me now with a thunderbolt. But since the sun continued to shine, the question was answered for the time being; but it soon turned up again. Ibid., Ch. 7

7 A destroyed home life, an idiotic school system, premature work in the factory, stupefying life in the streets, these are what the great city gives to the children of the under classes. It is more astonishing that the better instincts of human nature generally are victorious in the lower class than the fact that this result is occasionally reversed. Ibid., Ch. 8

8 Love is moral even without legal marriage, but marriage is immoral without love.
    "The Morality of Woman," *The Morality of Woman and Other Essays* 1911

9 . . . everything which is exchanged between husband and wife in their life together can only be the free gift of love, can never be demanded by one or the other as a right. Man will understand that when one can no longer continue the life of love then this life must cease; that all vows binding forever the life of feeling are a violence of one's personality, since one cannot be held accountable for the transformation of one's feeling. Ibid.

10 Conventionality is the tacit agreement to set appearance before reality, form before content, subordination before principle.
    Ibid., "The Conventional Woman"

11 The educator must above all understand how to wait; to reckon all effects in the light of the future, not of the present. *Ibid.*

12 Woman, however, as the bearer and guardian of the new lives, has everywhere greater respect for life than man, who for centuries, as hunter and warrior, learned that the taking of lives may be not only allowed, but honourable.
Pt. I, Ch. 2, *The Renaissance of Mother-hood,* 1914

13 . . . the child craves of the mother, the work craves of its creator: the vision, the waiting, the hope, the pure will, the faith, and the love; the power to suffer, the desire to sacrifice, the ecstasy of devotion. Thus, man also has his "motherliness," a compound of feelings corresponding to those with which the woman enriches the race, oftener than the work, but which in woman, as in man, constitutes the productive mental process without which neither new works nor new generations turn out well.
Ibid., Pt. II, Ch. 1

14 The socially pernicious, racially wasteful, and soul-withering consequences of the working of mothers outside the home must cease. And this can only come to pass, either through the programme of institutional upbringing, *or* through the intimated renaissance of the home.
Ibid., Pt. III, Ch. 2

15 The belief that we some day shall be able to prevent war is to me one with the belief in the possibility of making humanity *really* human. Preface, *War, Peace, and the Future* 1916

16 But the havoc wrought by war, which one compares with the havoc wrought by nature, is not an unavoidable fate before which man stands helpless. The natural forces which are the causes of war are human passions which it lies in our power to change. *Ibid.*, Ch. 1

17 Formerly, a nation that broke the peace did not trouble to try and prove to the world that it was done solely from higher motives. . . . *Now war has a bad conscience.* Now every nation assures us that it is bleeding for a human cause, the fate of which hangs in the balance of its victory. All now declare themselves to be fighting for right, against might, the very thing that the pacifists urged. No nation will admit that it was solely to insure its own safety and to increase its power that it declared war. No nation dares to admit the guilt of blood before the world. *Ibid.*

18 Everything, everything in war is barbaric. . . . But the worst barbarity of war is that it forces men collectively to commit acts against which individually they would revolt with their whole being. *Ibid.*, Ch. 6

19 . . . feelings of sympathy and admiration are the indispensable mortar that holds the stones of international justice together. *Ibid.*, Ch. 16

1004. Marie La Coste (1849–1936)

1 Into a ward of the whitewashed walls
Where the dead and dying lay—
Wounded by bayonets, shells, and balls—
Somebody's darling was borne one day.
"Somebody's Darling," St. 1 *n.d.*

1005. Emma Lazarus (1849–1887)

1 Give me your tired, your poor,
Your huddled masses yearning to breathe free,
The wretched refuse of your teeming shore,
Send these, the homeless, tempest-tossed to me,
I lift my lamp beside the golden door!
"The New Colossus" *c.1886*

2 Still on Israel's head forlorn,
Every nation heaps its scorn.
"The World's Justice" *n.d.*

1006. Pauline Roland (fl. 1850s)

Co-author with Jeanne-Françoise Deroine.*

*See 779:1–2.

1007. Gwendolyn Willis (185?–18??)

1 When we write the history of our feminists we must begin not with them but with their mothers. Quoted in letter to Elaine Partnow
Nancy S. Prichard,
Unitarian Universalist Women's
Federation 17 *December 1981*

1008. Frances Xavier Cabrini (1850–1917)

1 But don't think that my Institute can be confined to one city or to one diocese. The whole world is not wide enough for me.
Quoted by Bishop Gelmini in Pt. I, Ch. 3,
Too Small a World by Theodore
Maynard, 1945

2 To become perfect, all you have to do is to obey perfectly. When you renounce your personal inclinations you accept a mortification countersigned with the cross of Christ.
Ch. 3, op. cit.

1009. Emma Carleton (1850–1925)

1 Reputation is a bubble which a man bursts when he tries to blow it for himself.
Vol. XI, No. 82, *The Philistine*   *n.d.*

1010. Florence Earle Coates (1850–1927)

1 Age, out of heart, impatient, sighed:——
"I ask what will the *Future* be?"
Youth laughed contentedly, and cried:——
"The future leave to me!"
"Youth and Age"   *n.d.*

2 Fear is the fire that melts Icarian wings.
"The Unconquered Air"   *n.d.*

3 He turned with such a smile to face disaster
That he sublimed defeat.
"The Hero"   *n.d.*

4 I love, and the world is mine!
"The World Is Mine"   *n.d.*

1011. Geneviève (1850–?)

1 The feminine chest was not made for hanging orders on.
Quoted in *Pomp and Circumstance*
by E. de Gramont   *1929*

1012. Margaret Collier Graham (1850–1910)

1 "Harvest's a poor time fer wishin'; it's more prof'table 'long about seedin'-time. . . ."
"Idy," *Stories of the Foot-hills*   *1875*

2 The mind of the most logical thinker goes so easily from one point to another that it is not hard to mistake motion for progress.
Gifts and Givers   *1906*

3 People need joy quite as much as clothing. Some of them need it far more.   Ibid.

4 We are all held in place by the pressure of the crowd around us. We must all lean upon others. Let us see that we lean gracefully and freely and acknowledge their support.   Ibid.

1013. Jane Harrison (1850–1928)

1 Youth and Crabbed Age stand broadly for the two opposite poles of human living, poles equally essential to any real vitality, but always contrasted. . . . The whole art of living is a delicate balance between the two tendencies.

"Crabbed Age and Youth,"
Alpha and Omega   *1915*

2 Your thoughts are—for what they are worth—self-begotten by some process of parthenogenesis. But there comes often to me, almost always, a moment when alone I cannot bring them to birth, when, if companionship is denied, they die unborn.   "Scientiae Sacra Fames,"
op. cit.

3 A child's mind is, indeed, throughout the best clue to understanding of savage magic . . . Like the artist, he goes forth to the work of creation, gloriously alone.
"Darwinism and Religion," op. cit.

4 Whenever at an accusation blind rage burns up within us, the reason is that some arrow has pierced the joints of our harness. Behind our shining armour of righteous indignation lurks a convicted and only half-repentant sinner . . . [and] we may be almost sure some sharp and bitter grain of truth lurks within it, and the wound is best probed.
"Epilogue on the War," op. cit.

5 Here was a big constructive imagination; here was a mere doctor laying bare the origins of Greek drama as no classical scholar had ever done, . . . for generations almost every branch of human knowledge will be enriched and illumined by the imagination of Freud.
"Conclusion," *Reminiscence of a Student's Life*   *1925*

6 I have elsewhere tried to show that Art is not the handmaid of Religion, but that Art in some sense springs out of Religion, and that between them is a connecting link, a bridge, and that bridge is Ritual.   Ibid.

7 Marriage, for a woman at least, hampers the two things that made life to me glorious—friendship and learning.   Ibid.

1014. Laura Howe Richards (1850–1943)

1 "And the storm went on. It roared, it bellowed, and it screeched: it thumped and it kerwhalloped. The great seas would come bunt agin the rocks, as if they were bound to go right through to Jersey City, which they used to say was the end of the world."
Ch. 2, *Captain January*   *1890*

2 "There's times when a man has strength given to him, seemin'ly, over and above human strength. 'Twas like as if the Lord ketched holt and helped me: maybe he did, seein' what 'twas I was doing. Maybe he did!"   Ibid.

3 Be you clown or be you King,
Still your singing is the thing.
"Dedication," *Tirra Lirra*   *1890*

4 Every little wave has its nightcap on.
"Song for Hal," Refrain, op. cit.

5 Once there was an elephant
Who tried to use the telephant—
No! No! I mean an elephone
Who tried to use the telephone.
"Eletelephony," St. 1,
op. cit.

1015. Ellen Swallow (1850?–1911)

1 The power of knowledge is appreciated by manufacturers. They take advantage of every new step in science. The woman must know something of chemistry in self-defense. . . . The housekeeper should know when to be frightened. . . . It is for women to institute reform. Speech (1879), *Ellen Swallow, The Woman Who Founded Ecology* by Robert Clarke 1973

2 For this knowledge of right living, we have sought a new name. . . . As theology is the science of religious life, and biology the science of [physical] life . . . so let *Oekology* be henceforth the science of [our] normal lives . . . the worthiest of all the applied science which *teaches the principles on which to found . . . a healthy . . . and happy life*. Speech (1892), op. cit.

3 Heretofore, civilized man has proclaimed, as his God-like privilege, and as a proof of his superiority to animals, the right to eat what he liked, whether it was suitable or not, and as a result, he has been compelled to employ a band of skilled magicians to exorcise the devils . . . invited to enter his body. But man is . . . only an upright animal, amenable to the same laws of growth and decay as others. . . . The science of human nutrition is to play a larger part in therapeutics than heretofore and it will be of great advantage to the physician [who] . . . at present has less confidence in the cook than in the druggist. Ch. 13, *The New England Kitchen Magazine* (1893), op. cit.

4 The essential principles of health are not understood by the people . . . and, alas! not by all our physicians, who as a rule have been educated to cure disease, not to prevent it. Too many have been taught to fight Nature's Laws, not stand by . . . as her adjutant. Ch. 15, op. cit.

5 Woman was originally the inventor, the manufacturer, the provider. She has allowed one office after another gradually to slip from her hand until she retains, with loose grasp, only the so called housekeeping. . . . she rightly feels that what is left is mere deadening drudg-

ery, and that escape from this condition is essential to her well being as an individual. *The Outlook* (magazine; 1897), op. cit.

6 It is hard to find anyplace in the world where the water does not show the effect of human agencies. Ch. 17, op. cit.

1016. Rose Hartwick Thorpe (1850–1939)

1 And her face so sweet and pleading, yet with sorrow pale and worn,
Touched his heart with sudden pity—lit his eye with misty light;
"Go, your lover lives!" said Cromwell; "Curfew shall not ring tonight!"
"Curfew Shall Not Ring Tonight" 1866

1017. Nellie Cashman (1851–1925)

1 When I saw something that needed doing, I did it. Interview, *Daily British Colonist* 1898

1018. Kate Chopin (1851–1904)

1 In entering upon their new life they decided to be governed by no precedential methods. Marriage was to be a form, that while fixing legally their relation to each other, was in no wise to touch the individuality of either; that was to be preserved intact. Each was to remain a free integral of humanity, responsible to no dominating exactness of so-called marriage laws. And the element that was to make possible such a union was trust in each other's love, honor, courtesy, tempered by the reserving clause of readiness to meet the consequences of reciprocal liberty. "A Point at Issue!" 1889

2 The mother-women seemed to prevail that summer at Grand Isle. It was easy to know them, fluttering about with extended, protecting wings when any harm, real or imaginary, threatened their precious brood. They were women who idolized their children, worshipped their husbands, and esteemed it a holy privilege to efface themselves as individuals and grow wings as ministering angels. Ch. 4, *The Awakening* 1889

3 A certain light was beginning to dawn dimly within her—the light which, showing the way, forbids it. . . . But the beginning of things, of a world especially, is necessarily vague, tangled, chaotic, and exceedingly disturbing. How

few of us ever emerge from such beginning! How many souls perish in its tumult!
                                        Ibid., Ch. 6

4 It sometimes entered Mr. Pontellier's mind to wonder if his wife were not growing a little unbalanced mentally. He could see plainly that she was not herself. That is, he could not see that she was becoming herself and daily casting aside that fictitious self which we assume like a garment with which to appear before the world.   Ibid., Ch. 19

5 Alcée Arobin's manner was so genuine that it often deceived even himself.   Ibid., Ch. 25

6 "There are some people who leave impressions not so lasting as the imprint of an oar upon the water."   Ibid., Ch. 34

7 "The years that are gone seem like dreams—if one might go on sleeping and dreaming—but to wake up and find—oh! well! perhaps it is better to wake up after all, even to suffer, rather than to remain a dupe to illusions all one's life."
                                        Ibid., Ch. 38

8 "I don't hate him," Athenaise answered. . . . "It's jus' being married that I detes' an' despise."   "Athenaise"   1895

1019. Anna Garlin Spencer (1851–1931)

1 And when her biographer says of an Italian woman poet, "during some years her Muse was intermitted," we do not wonder at the fact when he casually mentions her ten children.
    Woman's Share in Social Culture   1912

2 It is not alone the fact that women have generally had to spend most of their strength in caring for others that has handicapped them in individual effort; but also that they have almost universally had to care wholly for themselves.   Ibid.

3 A successful woman preacher was once asked "what special obstacles have you met as a woman in the ministry?" "Not one," she answered, "except the lack of a minister's wife."   Ibid.

1020. Mariana Griswold Van Rensselaer (1851–1934)

1 Let us shun self-analyzation, self-consciousness, morbidness, affectation, attitudinizing. Let us look ahead as little as possible, keeping our eyes on our brushes and on the world of beauty around us.
        "Some Aspects of Contemporary Art,"
        Lippincott's   December 1878

2 . . . we also, and not our artists only, have a duty to perform if we wish the stream of progress to grow wider, deeper, swifter. We must give ourselves more earnestly and intelligently and generously than we have to the happy duty of appreciation.
              The Book of American Figure
                  Painters   1886

1021. Mary Augusta Ward (1851–1920)

1 "Every man is bound to leave a story better than he found it."
            Bk. I, Ch. 3, *Robert Elsmer 1888*

2 In my youth people talked about Ruskin; now they talk about drains.   Ibid., Bk. II, Ch. 12

3 "Put down enthusiasm." . . . The Church of England in a nutshell.   Ibid., Ch. 16

1022. Mary A. Barr (1852–?)

1 I sing the Poppy! The frail snowy weed!
    The flower of Mercy! That within its heart
  Doth keep "a drop serene" of human need,
  A drowsy balm of every bitter smart.
  For happy hours the rose will idly blow
  The Poppy hath a charm of pain and woe.
                                "White Poppies,"
                                        n.d.

1023. Emilia Pardo Bazan (1852–1921)

1 Nature, they call you a mother; they ought to call you a cruel stepmother.
              La madre naturaleza (Mother
                      Nature)   1887

2 I don't know how men are different from hogs. . . . They chase after the same things: food, drink, women. In short, we're all made of the same stuff.   Ibid.

3 Men can hardly form an idea of how difficult it is for a woman to acquire culture and to fill in her education by teaching herself. Boys, from the age they can walk and talk, attend elementary schools, then secondary institutes, the academics, the university. . . . For them, all advantages; for women, all obstacles.
              "Apuntes autobiograficos,"
        Quoted in *Emilia Pardo Bazan* by R. E.
                          Osborne   1964

4 . . . those of us who came into the world a third of a century after Concepcion Arenal found public opinion just as hostile (perhaps more so) to women who were called poetesses or bluestockings, and we read every day furious articles

intended to demonstrate that the object of woman's life is to darn socks.

> "La Lectura" (1907), Quoted in
> *Emila Pardo Bazan* by Walter T.
> Pattison   1971

1024. Martha Jane Burke (1852–1903)

1 During the month of June I acted as a pony express rider carrying the U.S. mail between Deadwood and Custer, a distance of fifty miles. . . . It was considered the most dangerous route in the Hills, but as my reputation as a rider and quick shot was well known, I was molested very little, for the toll gatherers looked on me as being a good fellow, and they knew that I never missed my mark.   *Life and Adventures of Calamity Jane   1896*

2 I Jane Hickok Burke better known as Calamity Jane of my own free will and being of sound mind do this day June 3, 1903 make this confession. I have lied about my past life. . . . People got snoopy so I told them lies to hear their tongues wag. The women are all snakes and none of them I can call friends.

> Document to James O'Neill
> (2 June 1903),
> *Quoted in Calamity Was the
> Name for Jane* by Glenn Clairmonte
> *1959*

1025. Vera Figner (1852–1942)

1 Generally speaking, there was in her* nature both feminine gentleness and masculine severity. Tender, tender as a mother with the working people, she was exacting and severe toward her comrades and fellow-workers, while towards her political enemies, the government, she could be merciless. . . .

> *Memoirs of a Revolutionist   1927*

*Reference Sofia Perovskaya; see 1030.

1026. Mary Wilkins Freeman (1852–1930)

1 . . .it took her a long time to prepare her tea; but when ready it was set forth with as much grace as if she had been a veritable guest to her own self.   *A New England Nun   1891*

2 Louisa's feet had turned into a path . . . so straight and unswerving that it could only meet a check at her grave, and so narrow that there was no room for anyone at her side.   Ibid.

1027. Gertrude Kasebier (1852–1934)

1 . . . from the first days of dawning individuality, I have longed unceasingly to make pictures of people . . . to make likenesses that are biographies, to bring out in each photograph the essential personality that is variously called temperament, soul, humanity.

> Quoted in *The Woman's Eye*
> by Anne Tucker*   1973

*See 2420

1028. Lily Langtry (1853–1929)

1 The sentimentalist ages far more quickly than the person who loves his work and enjoys new challenges.

> Quoted in the *New York Sun   1906*

2 Anyone who limits his vision to his memories of yesterday is already dead.

> Quoted in *Because I Love Him*
> by Noel B. Gerson   *1971*

1029. Mary Lease (1853–1933)

1 What you Kansas farmers ought to do is to raise less corn and raise more hell.

> Political Speech   *1890*

1030. Sofia Perovskaya (1853–1881)

1 . . . my lot is not at all such a dark one. I have lived as my convictions have prompted me; I could not do otherwise; therefore I await what is in store for me with a clear conscience.

> Letter to Her Mother,
> *Woman as Revolutionary,*
> Fred C. Giffin, ed.   *1973*

1031. Emilie Poulsson (1853–1939)

1 Books are keys to wisdom's treasure;
Books are gates to lands of pleasure;
Books are paths that upward lead;
Books are friends. Come, let us read.

> Inscription in Children's Reading
> Room, Hopkington, Massachusetts
> *n.d.*

1032. Jennie Jerome Churchill (1854–1921)

1 Of all nationalities, Americans are the best in adapting themselves. With them, to see is to know—and to know is to conquer.

Quoted in the *New York World*
13 October 1908

2 It is so tempting to try the most difficult thing possible. Quoted in the *Daily Chronicle* (London) *8 July 1909*

3 BASIL. But remember, a man ends by hating the woman who he thinks has found him out.
His Borrowed Plumes *1909*

4 ALMA. I rather suspect her of being in love with him.
MARTIN. Her own husband? Monstrous! What a selfish woman! *Ibid.*

5 All natures are in nature. *Ibid.*

6 Italians love—sun, sin and spaghetti. *Ibid.*

7 . . . we owe something to extravagance, for thrift and adventure seldom go hand in hand. . . . "Extravagance," *October 1915*

8 But I suppose experience of life will in time teach you that tact is a very essential ingredient in all things. Letter to Winston Churchill* (4 October 1895), Quoted in *Jennie,* Vol. II, by Ralph G. Martin *1971*

*(1874–1965) British prime minister (1940–1945 and 1951–1955).

9 One is forever throwing away substance for shadows. Letter to Her Sister, Leonie Leslie (24 July 1914) *op. cit.*

1033. Eva March Tappan (1854–1930)

1 We drove the Indians out of the land,
But a dire revenge those Redmen planned,
For they fastened a name to every nook,
And every boy with a spelling book
Will have to toil till his hair turns gray
Before he can spell them the proper way.
"On the Cape," St. 1, *n.d.*

1034. Edith Thomas (1854–1925)

1 How on the moment all changes!
"Optimi Consiliarii Mortui, XXXIV," Sts. 1–2, *The Inverted Torch* *1890*

2 They troop to their work in the gray of the morning,
Each with a shovel swung over his shoulder . . .
You have cut down their wages without any warning—
Angry? Well, let their wrath smolder!

"Their Argument," St. 2,
The Guest at the Gate
1909

3 The God of Music dwelleth out of doors.
"The God of Music"
n.d.

1035. Mary Dow Brine (1855?–1925?)

1 She's somebody's mother, boys, you know,
For all she's aged, and poor, and slow.
"Somebody's Mother," St. 15,
Harper's Weekly *2 March 1878*

1036. Margaret Wolfe Hungerford (1855?–1897)

1 Beauty is in the eye of the beholder.
Molly Bawn *1878*

1037. Alice Freeman Palmer (1855–1902)

1 Exquisite child of the air.
"The Butterfly," *n.d.*

1038. Olive Schreiner (1855–1920)

1 They are called finishing-schools and the name tells accurately what they are. They finish everything. . . .
"Lyndall," *The Story of an African Farm* *1883*

2 I have seen some souls so compressed that they would have fitted into a small thimble, and found room to move there—wide room. *Ibid.*

3 "It is delightful to be a woman; but every man thanks the Lord devoutly that he isn't one."
Ibid.

4 "Wisdom never kicks at the iron walls it can't bring down." *Ibid.*

5 "Look at this little chin of mine, Waldo, with the dimple in it. It is but a small part of my person; but though I had a knowledge of all things under the sun, and the wisdom to use it, and the deep loving heart of an angel, it would not stead me through life like this little chin. I can win money with it, I can win love; I can win power with it, I can win fame." *Ibid.*

6 "The less a woman has in her head the better she is for climbing." *Ibid.*

7 "We fit our sphere as a Chinese woman's fits her shoe, exactly as though god had made both; and yet He knows nothing of either." *Ibid.*

8 "We were equals once when we lay newborn babes on our nurse's knees. We shall be equals again when they tie up our jaws for the last sleep."   Ibid.

9 "If the bird *does* like its cage, and *does* like its sugar, and will not leave it, why keep the door so very carefully shut?"   Ibid.

10 "The surest sign of fitness is success."   Ibid.

11 *"We* bear the world, and we make it. . . . There was never a great man who had not a great mother—it is hardly an exaggeration."
                                                Ibid.

12 "Men are like the earth and we are the moon; we turn always one side to them, and they think there is no other, because they don't see it—but there is."   Ibid.

13 All day, where the sunlight played on the sea-shore, Life sat.
               "The Lost Joy," *Dreams*   1892

14 "There are only two things that are absolute realities, love and knowledge, and you can't escape them."
                    "The Buddhist Priest's Wife,"
                    Stories, Dreams, and Allegories
                                                1892

15 "I suppose the most absolutely delicious thing in life is to feel a thing needs you, and to give at the moment it needs. Things that don't need you, you must love from a distance."   Ibid.

16 "There is nothing ridiculous in love."   Ibid.

17 There are artists who, loving their work, when they have finished it, put it aside for years, that, after the lapse of time, returning to it and re-viewing it from the standpoint of distance, they may judge of it in a manner which was not possible while the passion of creation and the link of unbroken emotion bound them to it. What the artist does intentionally, life often does for us fortuitiously in other relationships.
               Ch. 1, *Thoughts on South Africa*
                                                1892

18 "Yes, the life of the individual is short, but the life of the nation is long; and it is longer, and stronger, more vigorous and more knit, if it grows slowly and spontaneously than if formed by violence or fraud. The individual cannot afford to wait but the nation can and must wait for true unity, which can only come as the result of internal growth and the union of its atoms, and in no other way whatsoever."
                                        Ibid., Ch. 8

19 I know there will be spring; as surely as the birds know it when they see above the snow two tiny, quivering green leaves. Spring cannot fail us.   "The Woman's Rose"   1893

20 The greatest nations, like the greatest individu-als, have often been the poorest; and with wealth comes often what is more terrible than poverty—corruption.   *An English South African's View
                          of the Situation*   c.1899

21 I suppose there is no man who to-day loves his country who has not perceived that in the life of the nation, as in the life of the individual, the hour of external success may be the hour of irrevocable failure, and that the hour of death, whether to nations or individuals, is often the hour of immortality.   Ibid.

22 We have always borne part of the weight of war, and the major part. . . . Men have made boomerangs, bows, swords, or guns with which to destroy one another; we have made the men who destroyed and were destroyed! . . . *We
pay the first cost on all human life.*
               Ch. 4, *Woman and Labor*   1911

23 I saw a woman sleeping. In her sleep she dreamt life stood before her, and held in each hand a gift—in the one hand love, in the other freedom. And she said to the woman, "Choose." And the woman waited long: and she said, "Free-dom." And life said, "Thou hast well chosen. If thou hadst said "love" I would have given thee that thou didst ask for; and I would have gone from thee, and returned to thee no more. Now, the day will come when I shall return. In that day I shall bear both gifts in one hand." I heard the woman laugh in her sleep.
                            Excerpt   n.d.

1039. Ella Wheeler Wilcox (1855–1919)

1 Laugh and the world laughs with you;
        Weep, and you weep alone;
For the sad old earth must borrow its mirth,
        But has trouble enough of its own.
               "Solitude," St. 1, *New York Sun
                        25 February*   1883

2 'Tis easy enough to be pleasant,
        When life flows along like a song;
But the man worth while is the one who will
        smile
        When everything goes dead wrong.
               "Worth While"   n.d.

3 But with every deed you are sowing a seed,
        Though the harvest you may not see.
               "You Never Can Tell," St. 2
                                        n.d.

4 Give us that grand word "woman" once
        again,
And let's have done with "lady"; one's a term
Full of fine force, strong, beautiful, and firm,
Fit for the noblest use of tongue or pen;

And one's a word for lackeys.   "Woman"
                                        n.d.

5 I love your lips when they're wet with wine
And red with a wicked desire.
                            "I Love You," St. 1
                                        n.d.

6 It ever has been since time began,
     And ever will be, till time lose breath,
That love is a mood—no more—to man,
     And love to a woman is life or death.
                            "Blind," St. 1
                                        n.d.

7 Let there be many windows to your soul,
That all the glory of the world
May beautify it.   "Progress," St. 1
                                        n.d.

8 Sweep up the debris from decaying faiths;
Sweep down the cobwebs of worn-out beliefs,
And throw your soul open to the light
Of Reason and Knowledge.   Ibid., St. 2

9 Love lights more fires than hate extinguishes,
And men grow better as the world grows
     old.   "Optimism"   *n.d.*

10 Keep on with your weary battle against trium-
     phant might;
No question is ever settled until it is settled
     right.
          "Settle the Question Right"   *n.d.*

11 The splendid discontent of God
With chaos, made the world.
And from the discontent of man
     The world's best progress springs.
                            "Discontent"   *n.d.*

12 We flatter those we scarcely know,
     We please the fleeting guest,
And deal full many a thoughtless blow
     To those who love us best.
                    "Life's Scars," St. 3   *n.d.*

13 Whatever is—is best.
                "Whatever Is—Is Best"   *n.d.*

1040. Elisabeth Marbury (1856–1933)

1 I began to realize that the world was divided
into three groups: wasters, mollusks, and
builders.   Ch. 1, *My Crystal Ball*   1923

2 "Ah, daughter," said Mother, "where there is
room in the heart, there is always room on the
hearth."   Ibid.

3 A caress is better than a career.
                "Careers for Women"   *n.d.*

4 No influence so quickly converts a radical into
a reactionary as does his election to power.
                                        Ibid.

1041. Mrs. N. F. Mossell (1856–1946)

1 . . . keeping a clean house will not keep a man
at home.
                *The Work of the Afro-American
                        Women   1894*

2 . . . women must not be blamed because they
are not equal to the self-sacrifice of always
meeting husbands with a smile.   Ibid.

1042. Lizette Reese (1856–1935)

1 A book may be a flower that blows;
A road to a far town;
A roof, a well, a tower;
A book
May be a staff, a crook.   "Books"
                                        n.d.

2 Creeds grow so thick along the way,
Their boughs hide God.   "Doubt"
                                        n.d.

3 The old faiths light their candles all about,
But burly Truth comes by and puts them
     out.   "Truth"   *n.d.*

4 When I consider life and its few years—
A wisp of fog betwixt us and the sun;
A call to battle, and the battle done
Ere the last echo dies within our ears,
I wonder at the idleness of tears.
                            "Tears"   *n.d.*

1043. Kate Douglas Wiggin (1856–1923)

1 Women never hit what they aim at: but if they
just shut their eyes and shoot in the air they
generally find themselves in the bull's eye.
          New Chronicles of Rebecca   1907

1044. Ada Alden (1857–1936)

1 Can this be Italy, or but a dream
     Emerging from the broken waves of
     sleep? . . .
This world of beauty, color, and perfume,
     Hoary with age, yet of unaging bloom.
                    "Above Salerno"   *n.d.*

2 The years shall right the balance tilted wrong,
The years shall set upon his* brows a star.
                            "Ave"   *n.d.*

*Referring to Woodrow Wilson, (1856–1924), 28th pres-
ident of the United States (1913–1921).

1045. Gertrude Atherton (1857–1948)

1 We love the lie that saves their pride, but never
an unflattering truth.
          Bk. III, Ch. 6 *The Conqueror*   1902

2 The perfect friendship of two men is the deepest and highest sentiment of which the finite mind is capable; women miss the best in life.
> Ibid., Ch. 12

1046. Alice Brown (1857–1948)

1 Praise not the critic, lest he think
You crave the shelter of his ink.
> "The Critic"   *n.d.*

2 Yet thou, O banqueter on worms,
Who wilt not let corruption pass!—
Dost search out mildew, mound and stain,
Beneath a magnifying-glass.
> "The Slanderer"   *n.d.*

1047. Mary Lee Demarest (1857–1888)

1 Like a bairn to his mither, a wee birdie to its nest,
I wud fain be ganging nod unto my Saviour's breast;
For he gathers in his bosom witless, worthless lambs like me
An' he carries them himsel' to his ain countree.   "My Ain Countree"
> *n.d.*

1048. Fannie Farmer (1857–1915)

1 Progress in civilization has been accompanied by progress in cookery.
> Ch. 2, *The Boston Cooking-School Cookbook*   *1896*

2 I certainly feel that the time is not far distant when a knowledge of the principles of diet will be an essential part of one's education. Then mankind will eat to live, be able to do better mental and physical work, and disease will be less frequent.
> Ibid., Preface to the First Edition

1049. Minna Irving (1857–1940)

1 He's cheerful in weather so bitterly cold
It freezes your bones to the marrow;
I'll admit he's a beggar, a gangster, a bum,
But I take off my hat to the sparrow.
> "The Sparrow"   *n.d.*

2 The flowery frocks and the ancient trunk,
And Grandmother Granger, too, are dust,
But something precious and sweet and rare
Survives the havoc of moth and rust.
> "The Wedding Gift," St. 6
> *n.d.*

1050. Edna Lyall (1857–1903)

1 Two is company, three is trumpery, as the proverb says.
> Ch. 24, *Wayfaring Men*   *1897*

1051. Agnes Mary Robinson (1857–1944)

1 You hail from dream-land, Dragon-fly?
A stranger hither? So am I.
> "To a Dragonfly"   *n.d.*

1052. Ida Tarbell (1857–1944)

1 The first and most imperative necessity in war is money, for money means everything else— men, guns, ammunition.
> Ch. 1, *The Tariff in Our Times*   *1906*

2 There is no man more dangerous, in a position of power, than he who refuses to accept as a working truth the idea that all a man does should make for rightness and soundness, that even the fixing of a tariff rate must be moral.
> Ibid., Ch. 12

3 Sacredness of human life! The world has never believed it! It has been with life that we settled our quarrels, won wives, gold and land, defended ideas, imposed religions. We have held that a death toll was a necessary part of every human achievement, whether sport, war, or industry. A moment's rage over the horror of it, and we have sunk into indifference.
> Ch. 3, *New Ideals in Business*
> *1914*

4 "Yes, sir; he was what I call a *godly* man. Fact is, I never knew anybody I felt so sure would walk straight into Heaven, everybody welcomin' him, nobody fussin' or fumin' about his bein' let in, as Abraham Lincoln."
> *In Lincoln's Chair*   *1920*

5 "There are more men who see clear now how hard it is for people to rule themselves, more people to determine government by the people shan't perish from the earth, more people willin' to admit that you can't have peace when you've got a thing like slavery goin' on. That something, that's goin' to help when the next struggle comes."
> Ibid.

1053. Martha Thomas (1857–1935)

1 Women are one-half of the world but until a century ago . . . it was a man's world. The laws were man's laws, the government a man's government, the country a man's country. . . .

The man's world must become a man's and a woman's world. Why are we afraid? It is the next step forward on the path to the sunrise, and the sun is rising over a new heaven and a new earth.   Address, North American Woman Suffrage Association, Buffalo, New York   *October 1908*

1054. Clara Zetkin (1857–1933)

1 . . . women must remain in industry despite all narrow-minded caterwauling; in fact the circle of their industrial activity must become broader and more secure daily. . . .
The Question of Women Workers and Women at the Present Time 1889

2 . . . as the liberation of the proletariat is possible only through the abolition of the capitalist productive relation, so too the emancipation of woman is possible only through doing away with private property.
Zur Geschichte der proletarischen Frauenbewegung Deutschlands 1928

3 All roads led to Rome. Every truly Marxist analysis of an important part of the ideological superstructure of society, of an outstanding social phenomenon, had to lead to an analysis of bourgeois society and its foundation, private property. It should lead to the conclusion that "Carthage must be destroyed."
"My Recollections of Lenin"* (1925), Quoted in *The Emancipation of Women*   1966

* Vladimir Lenin (1870–1924) Russian revolutionary leader and statesman.

1055. Anna Julia Cooper (1858/68–1964)

1 Let our girls feel that we expect something more of them than that they merely look pretty and appear well in society. Teach them that there is a race with special needs which they and only they can help; that the world needs and is already asking for their trained, efficient forces.
Preface, *A Voice of the South*   1892

2 If these broken utterances can in any way help to a clearer vision and a truer pulse-beat in studying our Nation's Problem, this Voice by a Black Woman of the South will not have been raised in vain.   Ibid.

1056. Dorothy Gurney (1858–1932)

1 The kiss of sun for pardon,
The song of the birds for mirth—

One is nearer God's Heart in a garden
Than anywhere else on earth.
"The Lord God Planted a Garden"
St. 3
n.d.

1057. Selma Lagerlöf (1858–1940)

1 She began to weep because she would never reach her journey's end. Her whole life long she would travel, travel, travel, and never reach the end of her journey.
Bk. I, Ch. 7, *The Miracles of Anti-Christ 1899*

2 Women can do nothing that has permanence.   Ibid., Bk. II, Ch. 2

3 The fair sun is like a mother whose son is about to set out for a far-off land, and who, in the hour of the leave-taking, cannot take her eyes from the beloved.
"Astrid," Ch. 3, *From a Swedish Homestead 1901*

4 "When I see a stream like this in the wilderness," he thought, "I am reminded of my own life. As persistent as this stream have I been in forcing my way past all that has obstructed my path. Father has been my rock ahead, and Mother tried to hold me back and bury me between moss-tufts, but I stole past both of them and got out in the World. Hey-ho, hi, hi!"
"The Musician," *The Girl from the Marsh Croft 1911*

5 Thinking is never so easy as when one follows a plow up a furrow and down a furrow.
Bk. I, Ch. 1, *Jerusalem*   1915

6 "The ways of Providence cannot be reasoned out by the finite mind," he mused. "I cannot fathom them, yet seeking to know them is the most satisfying thing in all the world."
Ibid., Bk. II

7 Could I ever be happy again now that I knew there was so much evil in the world?
(24 March 1872)
The Diary of Selma Lagerlöf 1936

1058. Edith Nesbit (1858–1924)

1 Little brown brother, oh! little brown brother,
Are you awake in the dark?
"Baby Seed Song"   *n.d.*

2 The chestnut's proud, and the lilac's pretty,
The poplar's gentle and tall,
But the plane tree's kind to the poor dull city—

I love him best of all!
"Child's Song in Spring"   *n.d.*

1059. Emmeline Pankhurst (1858–1928)

1 Those men and women are fortunate who are born at a time when a great struggle for human freedom is in progress.
My Own Story   1914

2 It was rapidly becoming clear to my mind that men regarded women as a servant class in the community, and that women were going to remain in the servant class until they lifted themselves out of it.   Ibid.

3 Women had always fought for men, and for their children. Now they were ready to fight for their own human rights. Our militant movement was established.   Ibid.

4 "I have never felt a prouder woman than I did one night when a police constable said to me, after one of these demonstrations, 'Had this been a man's demonstration, there would have been bloodshed long ago.' Well, my lord, there has not been any bloodshed except on the part of the women themselves—these so-called militant women. Violence has been done to us, and I who stand before you in this dock have lost a dear sister in the course of this agitation."
Ibid.

5 Why is it that men's blood-shedding militancy is applauded and women's symbolic militancy punished with a prison-cell and the forcible feeding horror?   Ibid.

6 There is something that governments care far more for than human life, and that is the security of property, and so it is through property that we shall strike the enemy.
Speech, "I Incite This Meeting to Rebellion" (17 October 1912), op. cit.

7 You have to make more noise than anybody else, you have to make yourself more obtrusive than anybody else, you have to fill all the papers more than anybody else, in fact you have to be there all the time and see that they do not snow you under, if you are really going to get your reform realized.   Speech, "When Civil War Is Waged by Women" (13 November 1913), op. cit.

8 I am what you call a hooligan!
Speech (1909),
Quoted in
The Fighting Pankhursts
by David Mitchell   *1967*

9 I have no sense of guilt. I look upon myself as a prisoner of war. I am under no moral obligation to conform to, or in any way accept, the sentence imposed upon me.
Speech to the Court
(April 1913), op. cit.

10 Over one thousand women have gone to prison in the course of this agitation, have suffered their imprisonment, have come out of prison injured in health, weakened in body, but not in spirit. . . . I ask you . . . if you are prepared to go on doing that kind of thing indefinitely, because that is what is going to happen. There is absolutely no doubt about it. . . . We are women, rightly or wrongly convinced that this is the only way in which we can win power to alter what for us are intolerable conditions, absolutely intolerable conditions. From the moment I leave this court I shall deliberately refuse to eat food—I shall join the women who are already in Holloway [Women's Prison] on the hunger strike. I shall come out of prison, dead or alive, at the earliest possible moment; and once again, as soon as I am physically fit I shall enter into this fight again. Life is very dear to all of us. I am not seeking, as was said by the Home Secretary, to commit suicide. I do not want to commit suicide. I want to see the women of this country enfranchised, and I want to live until that is done.   Speech to the Court
(2 April 1913),
Shoulder to Shoulder,
Midge Mackenzie, ed.   *1975*

11 In time of war the rules of peace must be set aside and we must put ourselves without delay upon a war basis, let the women stand shoulder to shoulder with the men to win the common victory which we all desire.
Speech, London Pavilion
(5 October 1915), op. cit.

12 Better that we should die fighting than be outraged and dishonoured. . . . Better to die than to live in slavery.
Speech, Army and Navy Hall,
Petrograd (August 1917), op. cit.

1060. Agnes Repplier (1858–1950)

1 . . . the children of to-day are favored beyond their knowledge and certainly far beyond their deserts.   "Children, Past and Present,"
Books and Men   1888

2 But self-satisfaction, if as buoyant as gas, has an ugly trick of collapsing when full blown, and facts are stony things that refuse to melt away in the sunshine of a smile.
"Some Aspects of Pessimism," op. cit.

3 It is humiliating fact that, notwithstanding our avaricious greed for novelties, we are forced, when sincere, to confess that *"les anciens ont tout dit,"* and that it is probable the contending schools of thought have always held the same

relative positions they do now: Optimism glittering in the front ranks as a deservedly popular favorite; pessimism speaking with a still, persistent voice to those who, unluckily for themselves, have the leisure and the intelligence to attend. *Ibid.*

4 The pessimist, however—be it recorded to his credit—is seldom an agitating individual. His creed breeds indifference to others, and he does not trouble himself to thrust his views upon the unconvinced. *Ibid.*

5 Memory cheats us no less than hope by hazing over those things that we would fain forget; but who that has plodded on to middle age would take back upon his shoulders ten of the vanished years, with their mingled pleasures and pains? Who would return to the youth he is forever pretending to regret? *Ibid.*

6 Sensuality, too, which used to show itself coarse, smiling, unmasked, and unmistakable, is now serious, analytic, and so burdened with a sense of its responsibility that it passes muster half the time as a new type of asceticism.
"Fiction in the Pulpit,"
Points of View *1891*

7 A villain must be a thing of power, handled with delicacy and grace. He must be wicked enough to excite our aversion, strong enough to arouse our fear, human enough to awaken some transient gleam of sympathy. We must triumph in his downfall, yet not barbarously nor with contempt, and the close of his career must be in harmony with all its previous development. "A Short Defense of Villains,"
Essays in Miniature *1892*

8 It is hard for us who live in an age of careless and cheerful tolerance to understand the precise inconveniences attending religious persecution. Ch. 1,
Philadelphia: The Place and the People *1898*

9 Necessity knows no Sunday. . . .
Ibid., Ch. 18

10 Anyone, however, who has had dealings with dates knows that they are worse than elusive, they are perverse. Events do not happen at the right time, nor in their proper sequence. That sense of harmony with place and season which is so strong in the historian—if he be a readable historian—is lamentably lacking in history, which takes no pains to verify his most convincing statements. Ch. 1, *To Think of Tea!* *1932*

11 The English do not strain their tea in the fervid fashion we [Americans] do. They like to see a few leaves dawdling about the cup. They like to know what they are drinking.
Ibid., Ch. 13

12 People who cannot recognize a palpable absurdity are very much in the way of civilization.
Ch. 9, *In Pursuit of Laughter* *1936*

13 It is not depravity that afflicts the human race so much as a general lack of intelligence.
Ibid.

14 Humour brings insight and tolerance. Irony brings a deeper and less friendly understanding.
Ibid.

15 Science may carry us to Mars, but it will leave the earth peopled as ever by the inept. *Ibid.*

1061. Beatrice Potter Webb (1858–1943)

1 The underlying principle of the industrial revolution—the creed of universal competition—the firm faith that every man free to follow his own self-interest would contribute most effectually to the common weal, with the converse proposition that each man should suffer the full consequence of his own actions—this simple and powerful idea was enabling a rising middle class to break up and destroy those restraints on personal freedom, those monopolies for private gain, with which a Parliament of landowners had shackled the enterprise and weighted the energies of the nation.
Ch. 1, *The Cooperative Movement in Great Britain* *1891*

2 For the committee-man or officer who accepts a bribe or neglects his duty must be fully aware that he is not simply an indifferently honest man, like many of his fellows in private trade, but the deliberate betrayer of the means of salvation to thousands of his fellow-countrymen of this and all future generations. *Ibid., Ch. 7*

3 The inevitability of gradualness.
Presidential Address, British Labour Party Congress *1923*

4 Religion is love; in no case is it logic.
Ch. 2, *My Apprenticeship* *1926*

5 . . . if I had been a man, self-respect, family pressure and the public opinion of my class would have pushed me into a money-making profession; as a mere woman I could carve out a career of disinterested research.
Ibid., Ch. 8

1062. Eva Rose York (1858–1925?)

1 I shall not pass this way again;
Then let me now relieve some pain,
Remove some barrier from the road,
Or brighten some one's heavy load.
"I Shall Not Pass This Way Again,"
St. 2
n.d.

1063. Katherine Lee Bates (1859–1929)

1 O beautiful for spacious skies,
   For amber waves of grain,
For purple mountain majesties
   Above the fruited plain!
America! America!
   God shed His grace on thee
And crown thy good with brotherhood
   From sea to shining sea!
            "America the Beautiful," St. 1
                                      1893

2 Dawn love is silver,
      Wait for the west:
   Old love is gold love—
      Old love is best.
            "For a Golden Wedding"   n.d.

1064. Louise de Koven Bowen (1859–1953)

1 By the time I made my entry into society I was
ignorant in everything and accomplished in
nothing.   Ch. 1, Growing Up with a City
                                      1926

2 It is always a real satisfaction to know that
politics has not yet dominated the Juvenile Court
of Cook County; that we still have these judges
who are incorruptible and devoted to their
work.   Ibid., Ch. 4

1065. Carrie Chapman Catt (1859–1947)

1 There are two kinds of restrictions upon human
liberty—the restraint of law and that of custom.
No written law has ever been more binding than
unwritten custom supported by popular
opinion.   Speech, "For the Sake of Liberty"
         (8–14 February 1900), Quoted in
         History of Woman Suffrage, Vol. IV,
         by Susan B. Anthony* and Ida Husted
                                      1902

*See 840.

2 Once, this movement represented the scattered
and disconnected protests of individual women.
. . . Happily those days are past; and out of
that incoherent and seemingly futile agitation,
which extended over many centuries, there has
emerged a present-day movement possessing a
clear understanding and a definite, positive
purpose.   Speech, "Is Woman Suffrage
          Progressing?" Stockholm   1911

3 When a just cause reaches its flood-tide, as ours
has done in that country, whatever stands in
the way must fall before its overwhelming
power.   Ibid.

1066. Helen Gray Cone (1859–1934)

1 A song of hate is a song of Hell;'
   Some there be who sing it well.
            "Chant of Love for England"
                                      1945

1067. Eleanora Duse (1859–1924)

1 Before passing my lips each word seemed to
have coursed through the ardor of my blood.
There wasn't a fiber in me that did not add its
notes to the harmony. Ah, grace—the state of
grace!   Quoted in Il Fuoco by D'Annunzio
                                      1900

2 I did not use paint, I made myself up
morally.   Quoted by Louis Schneider in
          Le Gaulois   27 July 1922

3 Do you think one can speak about art? It would
be like trying to explain love. There are many
ways of loving and there are as many kinds of
art. There is the love that elevates and leads to
good—there is the love that absorbs all one's
will, all one's strength and intelligence. In my
opinion this is the truest love—but it is certainly
fatal. . . . So is it with art. . .
          Quoted in Eleanora Duse
       by C. Antonia-Traversi   1926

1068. Lady Gregory (1859?–1932)

1 CHRISTIE. It's a grand thing to be able to take
up your money in your hand and to think no
more of it when it slips away from you than
you would of a trout that would slip back into
the stream.   Twenty Five   1903

2 MRS. TARPEY. Business, is it? What business
would the people here have but to be minding
one another's business?
           Spreading the News.   1905

3 MRS. DONOHOE. There is many a thing in the
sea is not decent, but cockles is fit to put before
the Lord!   The Workhouse Ward   1908

4 MRS. BROKDERICK. A splendid shot he was; the
thing he did not see he'd hit it the same as the
thing he'd see.   The Full Moon   1910

5 GIANT. Fru, Fa, Fashog! I smell the smell of a
melodious lying Irishman!
          Act I, Sc. 4, The Golden Apple   1916

6 MOTHER. Them that have too much of it [learn-
ing] are seven times crosser than them that never
saw a book.
          Act I, Aristotle Bellows   1921

7 CELIA. It is better to be tied to any thorny bush
than to be with a cross man.   Ibid.

8 OGRE. I'll take no charity! What I get I'll earn by taking it. I would feel no pleasure it being given to me, any more than a huntsman would take pleasure being made a present of a dead fox, in place of getting a run across country after it.　　Act II, Sc. I, *The Jester,*　　*1923*

9 A theater with a base of reality and an apex of beauty.　　Quoted in "Karen Malpede,"*
Interviews with Contemporary
Women Playwrights,
Kathleen Betsko** & Rachel
Koenig, eds.　　*1987*

*See 2413.
**See 2256.

1069. Florence Kelley (1859–1932)

1 . . . the utter unimportance of children compared with products in the minds of the people. . . .
"My Philadelphia," *The Survey Graphic*
1 October 1926

1070. Nora Archibald Smith (1859–1934)

1 They'd knock on a tree and would timidly say
To the spirit that might be within there that day:
"Fairy fair, Fairy fair, wish thou me well;
'Gainst evil witcheries weave me a spell!'"
"Knocking on Wood," St. 3
n.d.

1071. Mary Gardiner Brainard (f. 1860s)

1 I would rather walk with God in the dark than go alone in the light.
"Not Knowing," St. 1　　*n.d.*

1072. Jane Addams (1860–1935)

1 The new growth in the plant swelling against the sheath, which at the same time imprisons and protects it, must still be the truest type of progress. "Filial Relations," *Democracy and Social Ethics*　　*1907*

2 In our pity for Lear, we fail to analyze his character. . . . His paternal expression was one of domination and indulgence, without the perception of the needs of his children, without any anticipation of their entrance into a wider life, or any belief that they could have a worthy life apart from him.　　Ibid.

3 A city is in many respects a great business corporation, but in other respects it is enlarged housekeeping. . . . May we not say that city housekeeping has failed partly because women, the traditional housekeepers, have not been consulted as to its multiform activities?
"Utilization of Women in City Government," *Newer Ideals of Peace*　　*1907*

4 Old-fashioned ways which no longer apply to changed conditions are a snare in which the feet of women have always become readily entangled.　　Ibid.

5 Private beneficence is totally inadequate to deal with the vast numbers of the city's disinherited.
Twenty Years at Hull House　　*1910*

6 Perhaps I may record here my protest against the efforts, so often made, to shield children and young people from all that has to do with death and sorrow, to give them a good time at all hazards on the assumption that the ills of life will come soon enough. Young people themselves often resent this attitude on the part of their elders; they feel set aside and belittled as if they were denied the common human experiences.　　Ibid.

7 Only in time of fear is government thrown back to its primitive and sole function of self-defense and the many interests of which it is the guardian become subordinated to that.
"Women, War and Suffrage," *Survey*
6 November 1915

1073. Marie Konstantinovna Bashkirtseff (1860–1884)

1 Ah, when one thinks what a miserable creature man is! Every other animal can, at his will, wear on his face the expression he pleases. He is not obliged to smile if he has a mind to weep. When he does not wish to see his fellows he does not see them. While man is the slave of everything and everybody!
(6 May 1873), *The Journal of a Young Artist*　　*1884*

2 Let us love dogs; let us love only dogs! Men and cats are unworthy creatures. . . .
Ibid. (16 July 1874)

3 If I had been born a man, I would have conquered Europe. As I was born a woman, I exhausted my energy in tirades against fate, and in eccentricities.　　Ibid. (25 June 1884)

4 For my own part I think love—impossible—to one who looks at human nature through a microscope, as I do. They who see only what they wish to see in those around them are very fortunate.　　Ibid. (1 August 1884)

1074. Ellen Thorneycroft Fowler (1860–1929)

1 Though outwardly a gloomy shroud,
The inner half of every cloud
  Is bright and shining:
I therefore turn my clouds about
And always wear them inside out
  To show the lining.
            "Wisdom of Folly"   *n.d.*

1075. Charlotte Perkins Gilman (1860–1935)

1 I do not want to be a fly,
I want to be a worm!   "A Conservative,"
            In This Our World   *1893*

2 The labor of women in the house, certainly,
enables men to produce more wealth than they
otherwise could; and in this way women are
economic factors in society. But so are
horses.   Ch. 1, *Women and Economics*
                                    1898

3 The women who do the most work get the least
money, and the women who have the most
money do the least work.   Ibid.

4 To be surrounded by beautiful things has much
influence upon the human creature: to make
beautiful things has more.   Ibid., Ch. 4

5 Specialization and organization are the basis of
human progress.   Ibid.

6 The world is quite right. It does not have to be
consistent.   Ibid., Ch. 6

7 We have built into the constitution of the human
race the habit and desire of taking, as divorced
from its natural precursor and concomitant of
making.   Ibid.

8 When we see great men and women, we give
credit to their mothers. When we see inferior
men and women—and that is a common circumstance—no one presumes to the question of the
motherhood which has produced them.
            Ibid., Ch. 9

9 Maternal instinct, merely as an instinct, is unworthy of our superstitious reverence.   Ibid.

10 A family unity which is only bound together
with a table-cloth is of questionable value
            Ibid., Ch. 11

11 The child learns more of the virtues needed in
modern life—of fairness, of justice, of comradeship, of collective interest and action—in a
common school than can be taught in the most
perfect family circle.   Ibid., Ch. 13

12 Work the object of which is merely to serve
one's self is the lowest. Work the object of
which is merely to serve one's family is the next
lowest. Work the object of which is to serve
more and more people, in widening range . . .
is social service in the fullest sense, and the
highest form of service we can reach.   Ibid.

13 A baby who spent certain hours of every day
among other babies, being cared for because he
was a baby and not because he was "my baby,"
would grow to have a very different opinion of
himself from that which is forced upon each
new soul that comes among us by the ceaseless
adoration of his own immediate family.   Ibid.

14 I am the squaw—the slave—the harem
      beauty—
  I serve and serve, the handmaid of the
  world.
      Introduction, Pt. I, "Two Callings," *The
                              Home   1910*

15 So when the great word "Mother!" rang once
      more,
  I saw at last its meaning and its place;
Not the blind passion of the brooding past,
But Mother—the World's Mother—come at
      last,
To love as she had never loved before—
  To feed and guard and teach the human
  race.   Ibid., Pt. II

16 The original necessity for the ceaseless presence
of the woman to maintain that altar fire—and it
was an altar fire in very truth at one period—
has passed with the means of prompt ignition;
the matchbox has freed the housewife from that
incessant service, but the *feeling* that women
should stay at home is with us yet.
            Ibid., Ch. 3

17 It will be a great thing for the human soul when
it finally stops worshiping backwards.   Ibid.

18 You may observe mother instinct at its height
in a fond hen sitting on china eggs—instinct,
but no brains.   Ibid.

19 Eternity is not something that begins after you
are dead. It is going on all the time. We are in
it now.   Quoted in *The Forerunner Magazine
                              1909–1916*

20 Human life consists in mutual service. No grief,
pain, misfortune, or "broken heart," is excuse
for cutting off one's life while any power of
service remains. But when all usefulness is over,
when one is assured of an unavoidable and
imminent death, it is the simplest of human
rights to choose a quick and easy death in place
of a slow and horrible one.
            Suicide Note   *17 August 1935*

21 One may have a brain specialized in its grasp of ethics, as well as of mechanics, mathematics or music.
The Living of Charlotte Perkins Gilman 1935

22 Death? Why this fuss about death. Use your imagination, try to visualize a world *without* death! . . . Death is the essential condition of life, not an evil. Ibid.

23 The first duty of a human being is to assume the right functional relationship to society—more briefly, to find your real job, and do it. Ibid.

24 . . . love grows by service. Ibid.

25 We are told to hitch our wagons to a star, but why pick on Betelgeuse?* Ibid.

*Largest star in the galaxy.

26 . . . New York . . . that unnatural city where every one is an exile, none more so than the American. Ibid.

27 There is no female mind. The brain is not an organ of sex. As well speak of a female liver. Quoted in *The Liberated Woman's Appointment Calendar*, Lynn Sherr and Jurate Kazickas, eds. 1975

28 A concept is stronger than a fact.
"Human Work" n.d.

29 I ran against a Prejudice.
That quite cut off the view.
"An Obstacle," St. 1 n.d.

30 The people people have for friends
Your common sense appall,
But the people people marry
Are the queerest folks of all.
"Queer People" n.d.

1076. Florence Kling Harding (1860–1924)

1 If the career is the husband's, the wife can merge her own with it, if it is to be the wife's as it undoubtedly will be in an increasing proportion of cases, then the husband may, with no sacrifice of self respect or of recognition by the community, permit himself to be the less prominent and distinguished member of the combination.
Remark (1922), Quoted in *First Ladies* by Betty Boyd Caroli 1987

2 They can't hurt you now.
Posthumous remark to her husband, Warren Harding,* op. cit.

*29th president of the United States (1921–1923).

1077. Amy Leslie (1860–1939)

1 No animal is so inexhaustible as an excited infant. *Amy Leslie at the Fair 1893*

2 When these marvels of art and architecture begin to crumble the hearts of nations will stand still. Now the city blooms apace like a great white rose perfuming the clouds and smiling out upon the waters, but it is to fade! It is to die and that is one of its most exquisite enchantments.
Ibid.

1078. Juliette Low (1860–1927)

1 To put yourself in another's place requires real imagination, but by so doing each Girl Scout will be able to live among others happily.
Letter to Girl Scouts of America (31 October 1923),* *Juliette Low and the Girl Scouts*, Anne Hyde Choate and Helen Ferris, eds. 1928

2 I hope that during the coming year we shall all remember the rules of this Girl Scouting game of ours. They are: To play fair.To play in your place. To play for your side and not for yourself. And as for the score, the best thing in a game is the fun and not the result. . . .
Ibid. (31 October 1924)*

*Ms. Low's birthday.

1079. Harriet Monroe (1860–1936)

1 Great ages of art come only when a widespread creative impulse meets an equally widespread impulse of sympathy. . . . The people must grant a hearing to the best poets they have else they will never have better.
Quoted in "Harriet Monroe," *Famous American Women* by Hope Stoddard 1970

2 . . . poetry, "The Cinderella of the Arts."
Ibid.

1080. Grandma Moses (1860–1961)

1 I don't advise any one to take it [painting] up as a business proposition, unless they really have talent, and are crippled so as to deprive them of physical labor, Then with help they might make a living, But with taxes and income tax there is little money in that kind of art for the ordinary artis [sic] But I will say that I have did remarkable for one of my years, and experience, As for publicity, that Im [sic] too old to care for

now. . . . "How Do I Paint?" *The New York Times* *11 May 1947*

2 What a strange thing is memory, and hope; one looks backward, the other forward. The one is of today, the other is the Tomorrow. Memory is history recorded in our brain, memory is a painter, it paints pictures of the past and of the day.
Ch. 1, *Grandma Moses, My Life's History,* Aotto Kallir, ed. *1947*

3 If I didn't start painting, I would have raised chickens. Ibid., Ch. 3

1081. Annie Oakley (1860–1926)

1 I can shoot as well as you [her husband].
Quoted in Ch. 4, *Annie Oakley: Woman at Arms* by Courtney Ryley Cooper *1927*

2 The contents of his [Sitting Bull's]* pockets were often emptied into the hands of small, ragged little boys, nor could he understand how so much wealth should go brushing by, unmindful of the poor. Ibid., Ch. 7

*Dakota Indian leader (1834?–1890).

1082. Henrietta Zolde (1860–1915)

1 In the life of the spirit there is no ending that is not a beginning. Comment *n.d.*

1083. Minna Antrim (1861–?)

1 A homely face and no figure have aided many women heavenward.
Naked Truth and Veiled Allusions 1902

2 Man forgives woman anything save the wit to outwit him. Ibid.

3 Experience has no text books nor proxies. She demands that her pupils answer her roll-call personally. Ibid.

4 To know one's self is wisdom, but to know one's neighbor is genius. Ibid.

5 Smiles are the soul's kisses. . . . Ibid.

6 To control a man a woman must first control herself. Ibid.

7 Golden fetters hurt as cruelly as iron ones. Ibid.

1084. Mary Byron (1861–?)

1 On gossamer nights when the moon is low,
And stars in the mist are hiding,

Over the hill where the foxgloves grow
You may see the fairies riding.
"The Fairy Thrall" *n.d.*

1085. Mary Coleridge (1861–1907)

1 The fruits of the tree of knowledge are various; he must be strong indeed who can digest all of them. *Gathered Leaves from the Prose of Mary E.Coleridge 1910*

2 Solitude affects some people like wine; they must not take too much of it, for it flies to the head. Ibid.

3 And in her lurid eyes there shone
The dying flame of life's desire,
Made mad because its hope was gone,
And kindled at the leaping fire
Of jealousy, and fierce revenge,
And strength that could not change nor tire. "The Other Side of the Mirror," St. 4 *n.d.*

4 Mother of God! No lady thou:
Common woman of common earth!
"Our Lady" *n.d.*

5 We were young, we were merry, we were very, very wise,
And the door stood open at our feast,
When there passed us a woman with the West in her eyes,
And a man with his back to the East.
"Unwelcome" *n.d.*

1086. Clemence Dane (1861–1965)

1 DR. ALLIOT. That young, young generation found out, out of their own unhappiness, the war taught them, what peace couldn't teach us—that when conditions are evil it is not your duty to submit—that when conditions are evil, your duty, in spite of protests, in spite of sentiment, your duty, though you trample on the bodies of your nearest and dearest to do it, though you bleed your own heart white, your duty is to see that those conditions are changed. If your laws forbid you, you must change your laws. If your church forbids you, you must change your church. And if your god forbids you, why then, you must change your God.
Act II, *A Bill of Divorcement* *1921*

2 ZEDEKIAH. How else should I treat an idol but tread on it?
Act I, Sc. 1, *Naboth's Vineyard* *1925*

3 JEZEBEL. How often must I stoop to hold you up? Ibid., Sc. 2

4 JEZEBEL. What is it to sit on a throne? Weariness! But to shift the dolls that sit there, that's a game, Jehu, for a man or a woman! Let me teach you my game! Ibid., Act II, Sc. 1

1087. Dorothy Dix (1861–1951)

1 Now one of the great reasons why so many husbands and wives make shipwreck of their lives together is because a man is always seeking for happiness, while a woman is on a perpetual still hunt for trouble.
Ch. 1, *Dorothy Dix, Her Book,*
1926

2 So many persons think divorce a panacea for every ill, who find out, when they try it, that the remedy is worse than the disease.
Ibid., Ch. 13

3 Confession is always weakness. The grave soul keeps its own secrets, and takes its own punishment in silence. Ibid., Ch. 20

4 In reality, the mother who rears her children up to be monsters of selfishness has no right to expect appreciation and gratitude from them because she has done them as ill a turn as one human being can do another. She has warped their characters. Ibid., Ch. 44

5 For in all the world there are no people so piteous and forlorn as those who are forced to eat the bitter bread of dependency in their old age, and find how steep are the stairs of another man's house. Ibid., Ch. 69

1088. Louise Imogen Guiney (1861–1920)

1 Quotations (such as have point and lack triteness) from the great old authors are an act of filial reverence on the part of the quote, and a blessing to a public grown superficial and external.
Quoted in *Scribner's Magazine*
January   1911

2 A short life in the saddle, Lord!
Not long life by the fire.
"The Knight Errant," St. 2   *n.d.*

3 High above hate I dwell,
O storms! Farewell.
"The Sanctuary"   *n.d.*

4 The fool who redeemed us once of our folly,
And the smiter that healed us, our right John Brown!*
"John Brown: A Paradox"   *n.d.*
* American abolitionist (1800–1859)

1089. Gracy Hebard (1861–1936)

1 These indians [Shoshones] believe also that God pulled out the upper teeth of the elk because the elk were meant to be eaten by the indians, and not the indians by the elk.
Washakie   1930

2 The buffaloes were the original engineers, as they followed the lay of the land and the run of the water. These buffalo paths became indian trails, which always pointed out the easiest way across the mountain barriers. The white man followed in these footpaths. The iron trail finished the road.
Ch. 9, *The Pathbreakers from River to*
Ocean   1932

1090. Katharine Tynan Hinkson (1861–1931)

1 O you poor folk in cities,
A thousand, thousand pities!
"June Song"   *n.d.*

2 To me the wonderful charge was given,
I, even a little ass, did go
Bearing the very weight of heaven;
So I crept cat-foot, sure and slow.
"The Ass Speaks"   *n.d.*

1091. Alice Hubbard (1861–1915)

1 [Thomas] Paine* was a Quaker by birth and a friend by nature. The world was his home, mankind were his friends, to do good was his religion.   Introduction, *An American Bible*
1911

* English-born American revolutionary leader (1737–1809).

1092. Jessie Brown Pounds (1861–?)

1 Somewhere, Somewhere, Beautiful Isle of Somewhere,
Land of the true, where we live anew,
Beautiful Isle of Somewhere.
"Beautiful Isle of Somewhere"
1901

1093. Corinne Roosevelt Robinson (1861–1933)

1 Though Love be deeper, Friendship is more wide. . . .
"Friendship," *The Call of Brotherhood and*
Other Poems
1912

2 Is life worth living?
Aye, with the best of us,
Heights of us, depths of us,—
Life is the test of us!
"Life, A Question," *One Woman to Another*   1914

3 Nothing is as difficult as to achieve results in this world if one is filled full of great tolerance and the milk of human kindness. The person who achieves must generally be a one-ideaed individual, concentrated entirely on that one idea, and ruthless in his aspect toward other men and other ideas.
Ch. 1, *My Brother Theodore Roosevelt**   1921

*(1858–1919), 26th president of the United States.

1094. Edith Carow Roosevelt (1861–1948)

1 Women who marry pass their best and happiest years in giving life and fostering it.
American Backlogs, quoted in *First Ladies* by Betty Boyd Caroli   1987

1095. Ernestine Schumann-Heink (1861–1936)

1 One can never either hear or see himself, and there is a need—if one would make real progress in art—for constant criticism.
Quoted in *Schumann-Heink, the Last of the Titans* by Mary Lawton   1935

2 This shall be my parting word—know what you want to do—then do it. Make straight for your goal and go undefeated in spirit to the end.
Ibid.

1096. Helen Herron Taft (1861–1943)

1 I have thought that a woman should be independent and not regard matrimony as the only thing to be desired in life.
Diary entry (at 22), Quoted in *First Ladies* by Betty Boyd Caroli   1987

2 I do not dislike teaching when the boys behave themselves.
Ibid.

1097. Helen Bannerman (1862–1946)

1 But the Tiger said, "What would your shoes be to me? I've got four feet, and you've got only two; you haven't got enough shoes for me."

But Little Black Sambo said, "You could wear them on your ears."
"So I could," said the Tiger: "that's a very good idea. Give them to me, and I won't eat you this time."
The Story of Little Black Sambo   1899

2 And there he saw all the Tigers fighting, and disputing which of them was the grandest. And at last they got so angry that they jumped up and took off all the fine clothes, and began to tear each other with their claws, and bite each other with their great big white teeth.   Ibid.

1098. Carrie Jacobs Bond (1862–1946)

1 When God made up this world of ours,
He made it long and wide,
And meant that it should shelter all,
And none should be denied.
"Friends," St. 1, *Little Stories in Verse*   1905

2 And we find at the end of a perfect day,
The soul of a friend we've made.
"A Perfect Day," St. 2   1926

1099. Edith Cooper (1862–1913)

Co-author with Katharine Bradley. See 987:1–2.

1100. Ella Higginson (1862–1940)

1 Forgive you?—Oh, of course, dear,
A dozen times a week!
"Wearing Out Love," St. 1   *n.d.*

2 One leaf is for hope, and one is for faith,
And one is for love, you know,
And God put another in for luck.
"Four-Leaf Clover," St. 2   *n.d.*

1101. Ada Leverson (1862–1933)

1 Absurdly improbable things happen in real life as well as in weak literature.
The Twelfth Hour   1907

1102. Ts'ai-t'ien Chang (1862–1945)

1 ". . . I wanted to study and not to marry. My brother and Mao Tse-tung also hated marriage and declared they would never marry. . . ."

Quoted in *Women in Modern China*
by Helen Foster Snow*   *1967*

*See 1675.

1103. Ida B. Wells (1862–1931)

1 Let the Afro-American depend on no party, but on himself for his salvation. Let him continue to education, character, and above all, put money in his purse.   "Iola's Southern Field,"
The New York Age
11 November 1892

2 The first excuse given to the civilized world for the murder of unoffending Negroes was the necessity of the white man to repress and stamp out "race riots." . . . It was always a remarkable feature in these insurrections and riots that only Negroes were killed during the rioting, and that all the white men escaped unharmed.
A Red Record   *1895*

3 True chivalry respects all womanhood. . . . Virtue knows no color lines, and the chivalry which depends upon complexion of skin and texture of hair can command no honest respect.   *Ibid.*

4 I felt that one had better die fighting against injustice than to die like a dog or a rat in a trap. I had already determined to sell my life as dearly as possible if attacked. I felt if I could take one lyncher with me, this would even up the score a little bit.
Crusade for Justice: The Autobiography of Ida B. Wells, Alfreda M. Duster, ed.   *1970*

1104. Edith Wharton (1862–1937)

1 A New York divorce is in itself a diploma of virtue. . . .   Ch. 1, "The Other Two,"
The Descent of Man   *1904*

2 "It feels uncommonly queer to have enough cash to pay one's bills. I'd have sold my soul for it a few years ago!"   Ibid., Ch. 3

3 "I don't know as I think a man is entitled to rights he hasn't known how to hold on to. . . ."   Ibid., Ch. 4

4 Her pliancy was beginning to sicken him. Had she really no will of her own . . . ? She was "as easy as an old shoe"—a shoe that too many feet had worn.   Ibid.

5 If he paid for each day's comfort with the small change of his illusions, he grew daily to value the comfort more and set less store upon the coin.   Ibid.

6 She keeps on being queenly in her own room with the door shut.   *The House of Mirth*
1905

7 When she spoke it was only to complain, and to complain of things not in his power to remedy; and to check a tendency to impatient retort he had first formed the habit of not answering her, and finally of thinking of other things while she talked.   Ch. 4, *Ethan Frome*   *1911*

8 My little old dog:
A heart-beat at my feet.
"A Lyrical Epigram"   *n.d.*

9 There are two ways of spreading light: to be
The candle or the mirror that receives it.
"Vesalius in Zante"   *n.d.*

1105. Annie Jump Cannon (1863–1941)

1 . . . a life spent in the routine of science need not destroy the attractive human element of a woman's nature.   Quoted in *Science*
30 June 1911

1106. Elaine Goodale (1863–1953)

1 We feel our savage kind,—
And thus alone with conscious meaning wear
The Indian's moccasin.
"Moccasion Flower," *In Berkshire with the Wild Flowers*   *1879*

1107. Mary Church Terrell (1863–1954)

1 Lynching is the aftermath of slavery.
"Lynching from a Negro's Point of View," *North American Review*
June 1904

2 As a colored woman I might enter Washington any night, a stranger in a strange land, and walk miles without finding a place to lay my head. . . . The colored man alone is thrust out of the hotels of the national capital like a leper.
"What It Means to Be Colored in the Capital of the United States" (1907),
A Colored Woman in a White World
1940

3 It is impossible for any white person in the United States, no matter how sympathetic and broad, to realize what life would mean to him if his incentive to effort were suddenly snatched away. To the lack of incentive to effort, which is the awful shadow under which we live, may be traced the wreck and ruin of scores of colored youth.   Ibid.

4 Please stop using the word "Negro." . . . We are the only human beings in the world with fifty-seven variety of complexions who are classed together as a single racial unit. Therefore, we

are really truly colored people, and that is the only name in the English language which accurately describes us.   Letter to the Editor, *The Washington Post* 14 May 1949, op. cit.

1108. Margot Asquith (1864–1945)

1 Riches are overestimated in the Old Testament: the good and successful man received too many animals, wives, apes, she-goats and peacocks.   *The Autobiography of Margot Asquith,* Vols. I and II *1920–1922*

2 One can only influence the strong characters in life, not the weak; and it is the height of vanity to suppose that you can make an honest man of anyone.   Ibid., Ch. 6

3 The first element of greatness is fundamental humbleness (this should not be confused with servility); the second is freedom from self; the third is intrepid courage, which, taken in its widest interpretation, generally goes with truth; and the fourth—the power to love—although I have put it last, is the rarest.   Ibid., Ch. 7

4 Journalism over here [in America] is not only an obsession but a drawback that cannot be overrated. Politicians are frightened of the press, and in the same way as bull-fighting has a brutalising effect upon Spain (of which she is unconscious), headlines of murder, rape, and rubbish, excite and demoralise the American public.   Ch. 10, *My Impressions of America 1922*

5 The ingrained idea that, because there is no king and they despise titles, the Americans are a free people is pathetically untrue. . . . There is a perpetual interference with personnal liberty over there that would not be tolerated in England for a week.   Ibid., Ch. 17

6 . . . her one idea was to exercise a moderating influence; and without knowing it she would in a subtle and disparaging manner check the enthusiasm, dim the glow, and cramp the extravagance of everyone round her.   Ch. 1, *Octavia   1928*

7 She was not an individual when she was with him, she was an audience—   Ibid., Ch. 12

1109. Mary Berenson (1864–1945)

1 Love in whatever form it comes is a god, and even if it destroys all one's so-called "moral nature," it remolds the world nearer to the heart's desire. Why should we put faithfulness above it?   Diary entry (1895), *Mary Berenson: A Self-Portrait from Her Letters and Diaries,* Barbara Strachey and Jayne Samuels, eds.   *1984*

1110. Elinor Glyn (1864–1943)

1 Marriage is the aim and end of all sensible girls, because it is the meaning of life.   "Letters to Caroline," *Harper's Bazaar September   1913*

1111. Margaret P. Sherwood (1864–1955)

1 Whisper some kindly word, to bless
A wistful soul who understands
That life is but one long caress
Of gentle words and gentle hands.
    "In Memoriam—Leo: A Yellow Cat," *n.d.*

1112. Wenonah Stevens Abbott (1865–1950)

1 To-day the journey is ended,
    I have worked out the mandates of fate;
Naked, alone, undefended,
    I knock at the Uttermost Gate.
    "A Soul's Soliloquy"   *n.d.*

1113. Evangeline Booth (1865–1950)

1 Drink has drained more blood,
Hung more crepe,
Sold more houses,
Plunged more people into bankruptcy,
Armed more villains,
Slain more children,
Snapped more wedding rings,
Defiled more innocence,
Blinded more eyes,
Twisted more limbs,
Dethroned more reason,
Wrecked more manhood,
Dishonored more womanhood,
Broken more hearts,
Blasted more lives,
Driven more to suicide, and
Dug more graves than any other poisoned
Scourge that ever swept its death-
Dealing waves across the world.
    "Good Housekeeping"   *n.d.*

1114. Mrs. Patrick Campbell (1865–1940)

1 I believe I was impatient with unintelligent people from the moment I was born: a tragedy—for I am myself three-parts a fool.
Ch. 2, *My Life and Some Letters*
1922

2 To be made to hold his [George Bernard Shaw's*] tongue is the greatest insult you can offer him—though he might be ready with a poker to make you hold yours. Ibid., Ch. 16

*Irish-born English author (1856–1950).

3 Wedlock—the deep, deep peace of the double bed after the hurly-burly of the chaise-longue. (1914), Quoted in *Jennie*, Vol. II, by Ralph G. Martin *1971*

1115. Edith Louisa Cavell (1865–1915)

1 I realize that patriotism is not enough. I must have no hatred or bitterness towards anyone.
Last Words, Quoted in
The Times (London)
23 October 1915

1116. Elsie De Wolfe (1865–1950)

1 It is the personality of the mistress that the home expresses. Men are forever guests in our homes, no matter how much happiness they may find there. Ch. 1, *The House in Good Taste*
1920

2 It does not matter whether one paints a picture, writes a poem, or carves a statue, simplicity is the mark of a master-hand. Don't run away with the idea that it is easy to cook simply. It requires a long apprenticeship.
"Why I Wrote This Book," *Recipes for Successful Dining* *1934*

1117. Minnie Fiske (1865–1932)

1 You must make your own blunders, must cheerfully accept your own mistakes as part of the scheme of things. You must not allow yourself to be advised, cautioned, influenced, persuaded this way and that. Letter to Alexander Woollcott* (1908), Quoted in *Mrs. Fiske* by Alexander Woollcott *1917*

*American journalist and author (1887–1943).

2 Among the most disheartening and dangerous of . . . advisors, you will often find those closest to you, your dearest friends, members

of your own family, perhaps, loving, anxious, and knowing nothing whatever. . . . Ibid.

3 The essence of acting is the conveyance of truth through the medium of the actor's mind and person. The science of acting deals with the perfecting of that medium. The great actors are the luminous ones. They are the great conductors of the stage. Ibid., Ch. 5

1118. Yvette Guilbert (1865–1944)

1 Try to make a woman who does badly on the stage understand that she might do better in trade, or in any other occupation. She will never believe you. It seems impossible to her to make linen garments or millinery, but very simple to enact the dandy on the stage.
La Vedette *1902*

2 One cannot remain the same. Art is a mirror which should show many reflections, and the artist should not always show the same face, or the face becomes a mask. Ibid.

1119. Laurence Hope (1865–1904)

1 For this is wisdom: to love, to live,
To take what Fate, or the Gods, may give.
"The Teak Forest,"
India's Love Lyrics *1922*

2 Less than the dust beneath thy chariot wheel,
Less than the weed that grows beside thy door,
Less than the rust that never stained thy
sword,
Less than the need thou hast in life of me,
Even less am I.
"Less Than the Dust," St. 1,
op. cit.

3 Pale hands I loved beside the Shalimar,
Where are you now? Who lies beneath your
spell? "Kashmiri Song," St. 1,
op. cit.

4 Yet I, this little while ere I go hence,
Love very lightly now, in self-defence.
"Verse by Taj Mahomed"
n.d.

5 Your work was waste? Maybe your share
Lay in the hour you laughed and kissed;
Who knows but that your son shall wear
The laurels that his father missed?
"The Masters"
n.d.

1120. Anandabai Joshee (1865–1887)

1 Holes are bored through the lower part of the left nostril for the nose-ring, and all around the

edge of the ear for jewels. This may appear barbarous to the foreign eye; to us it is a beauty! Everything changes with the clime.

> Letter to Mrs. Carpenter (1880),
> Quoted in *The Life of Anandabai
> Joshee* by Caroline H. Dall *1888*

2 Had there been no difficulties and no thorns in the way, then man would have been in his primitive state and no progress made in civilization and mental culture. Letter to Her Aunt (27 August 1881), op. cit.

3 . . . I regard irreligious people as pioneers. If there had been no priesthood the world would have advanced ten thousand times better than it has now. Ibid.

1121. Nellie Melba (1865?–1931)

1 The first rule in opera is the first rule in life: see to everything yourself.
> *Melodies and Memories* *1925*

2 One of the drawbacks of Fame is that one can never escape from it. Ibid.

1122. Baroness Orczy (1865–1947)

1 A surging, seething, murmuring crowd of beings that are human only in name, for to the eye and ear they seem naught but savage creatures, animated by vile passions and by the lust of vengeance and of hate.
> Ch. 1, *The Scarlet Pimpernel* *1905*

2 Marguerite St. Just was from principle and by conviction a republican—equality of birth was her motto—inequality of fortune was in her eyes a mere untoward accident, but only inequality she admitted was that of talent. "Money and titles may be hereditary," she would say, "but brains are not. . . ." Ibid., Ch. 6

3 "I sometimes wish you had not so many lofty virtues. . . . I assure you little sins are far less dangerous and uncomfortable." Ibid., Ch. 7

4 "We seek him here, we see him there,
Those Frenchies seek him everywhere.
Is he in heaven?—Is he in hell?
That damned elusive Pimpernel?"
> Ibid., Ch. 12

5 "But a wife! . . . What matters what she thinks and feels? if she be cold or loving, gentle or shrewish, sensitive to a kind word or callous to cruelty? A wife! . . . Well! so long as no other man hath ever kissed her lips—for that would hurt masculine vanity and wound the pride of possession!"
> Bk. I, Ch. 3, *Leatherface* *1918*

1123. Emily James Putnam (1865–1944)

1 But the typical lady everywhere tends to the feudal habit of mind. In contemporary society she is an archaism, and can hardly understand herself unless she knows her own history.
> Introduction, *The Lady* *1910*

2 Until changing economic conditions made the thing actually happen, struggling early society would hardly have guessed that woman's road to gentility would lie through doing nothing at all. Ibid.

1124. Kathe Schirmacher (1865–1930)

1 In the greater part of the world woman is a slave and a beast of burden. . . . In most cases she is overworked, exploited, and (even when living in luxury) the oppressed sex. . . . These conditions are opposed by the woman's right movement. . . . Most men do not understand this ideal; they oppose it with unconscious egotism. *The Modern Rights Movement* *1905*

1125. Louisa Thomas (1865–?)

1 Charm is the measure of attraction's power
To chain the fleeting fancy of the hour.
> "What Is Charm?" St. 1 *n.d.*

1126. Mary A. Arnim (1866–?)

1 A marriage, she found, with someone of a different breed is fruitful of small rubs. . . . Ch. 1, *Mr. Skeffington* *1940*

2 Life was certainly a queer business—so brief, yet such a lot of it; so substantial, yet in a few years, which behaved like minutes, all scattered and anyhow. Ibid.

3 . . . without it [love], without, anyhow, the capacity for it, people didn't seem to be much good. Dry as bones, cold as stones, they seemed to become, when love was done; inhuman, indifferent, self-absorbed, numb. Ibid., Ch. 5

4 Strange that the vanity which accompanies beauty—excusable, perhaps, when there is such great beauty, or at any rate understandable—should persist after the beauty was gone.
> Ibid., Ch. 6

1127. Martha Dickinson Bianchi (1866–1943)

1 Deeper than chords that search the soul and die,

Mocking to ashes color's hot array,—
Closer than touch,—within our hearts they
   lie—
The words we do not say.
                    "The Words We Do Not Say"
                                        n.d.

1128. Voltairine de Cleyre (1866–1912)

1 [Anarchism] . . . not only the denial of authority, not only a new economy, but a revision
of the principles of morality. It means . . . self-
responsibility, not leader-worship.
                    "The Burial of My Past Self"
                    (c. 1887), *The Selected Works of*
                    Voltairine de Cleyre   1914

2 Consider the soul reflected on the advertising
page. . . . Commercial man has set his image
therein; let him regard himself when he gets
time.   Ibid.

3 [Language] . . . this great instrument which
men have jointly built . . . every word the
mystic embodiment of a thousand years of vanished passion, hope, desire, thought.   Ibid.

4 Do I repent? Yes, I do; but wait till I tell you
of what I repent and why. I repent that I ever
believed a man could be anything but a living
lie!   "Betrayed,"
                                        op. cit.

1129. Annie Johnson Flint (1866–1932)

1 Have you come to the Red Sea place in your
   life
   Where, in spite of all you can do,
There is no way out, there is no way back,
   There is no other way but through?
      "At the Place of the Sea," St. 1   *n.d.*

1130. Eleanor Prescott Hammond (1866–1933)

1 Prone on my back I greet arriving day,
   A day no different than the one just o'er;
When I will be, to practically say,
   Considerably like I have been before.
Why then get up? Why wash, why eat, why
   pray?
   —Oh, leave me lay!
"Oh, Leave Me Lay,"
                            Atlantic Monthly
                            August 1922

1131. Beatrix Potter (1866–1943)

1 Once upon a time there were four little Rabbits,
and their names were—Flopsy, Mopsy, Cotton-
tail, and Peter.   *The Tale of Peter Rabbit*
                                        1904

2 The water was all slippy-sloppy in the larder
and the back passage. But Mr. Jeremy liked
getting his feet wet; nobody ever scolded him,
and he never caught a cold.
                    The Tale of Mr. Jeremy Fisher
                                        1906

1132. Annie Sullivan (1866–1936)

1 I have thought about it a great deal, and the
more I think the more certain I am that obedience is the gateway through which knowledge,
yes, and love, too, enter the mind of the
child.   Letter (11 March 1887),
                    Quoted in *The Story of My Life*
                    by Helen Keller*   1903

*See 1287.

2 My heart is singing for joy this morning. A
miracle has happened! The light of understanding has shone upon my little pupil's mind, and
behold, all things are changed!
                            Ibid. (20 March 1887)

3 I am beginning to suspect all elaborate and
special systems of education. They seem to me
to be built upon the supposition that every child
is a kind of idiot who must be taught to
think.   Ibid. (8 May 1887)

4 . . . people seldom see the halting and painful
steps by which the most insignificant success is
achieved.   Ibid. (30 October 1887)

5 Language grows out of life, out of its needs and
experiences. . . . *Language* and *knowledge* are
indissolubly connected; they are interdependent.
Good work in language presupposes and depends on a real knowledge of things.
                    Speech, American Association
                    to Promote the Teaching of Speech to
                    the Deaf (July 1894), op. cit.

6 I never taught language for the PURPOSE of
teaching it; but invariably used language as a
medium for the communication of *thought;* thus
the learning of language was *coincident* with the
acquisition of knowledge.   Ibid.

1133. Pearl Craigie (1867–1906)

1 Women may be whole oceans deeper than we
are, but they are also a whole paradise better.
She may have got us out of Eden, but as a
compensation she makes the earth very
pleasant.   Act III, *The Ambassador*
                                        1898

2 A false success made by the good humor of
outside influences is always peaceful; a real

success made by the qualities of the thing itself is always a declaration of war.
The Dream and the Business *1906*

1134. Marie Curie (1867–1934)

1 All my life through, the new sights of Nature made me rejoice like a child.
*Pierre Curie** *1923*

* French chemist (1859–1906).

2 . . . I was taught that the way of progress is neither swift nor easy. . . . *Ibid.*

3 You cannot hope to build a better world without improving the individuals. To that end each of us must work for his own improvement, and at the same time share a general responsibility for all humanity, our particular duty being to aid those to whom we think we can be most useful. *Ibid.*

4 One never notices what has been done; one can only see what remains to be done. . . .
Letter to Her Brother
(18 March 1894),
op. cit.

5 After all, science is essentially international, and it is only through lack of the historical sense that national qualities have been attributed to it. "Intellectual Co-operation,"
Memorandum (magazine)
16 June 1926

1135. Edith Hamilton (1867–1963)

1 . . . the seed never explains the flower.
Ch. 1, The Greek Way *1930*

2 Mind and spirit together make up that which separates us from the rest of the animal world, that which enables a man to know the truth and that which enables him to die for the truth.
Ibid.

3 The English method [of poetry] is to fill the mind with beauty; the Greek method was to set the mind to work. *Ibid., Ch. 4*

4 None but a poet can write a tragedy. For tragedy is nothing less than pain transmuted into exaltation by the alchemy of poetry, and if poetry is true knowledge and the great poet's guides safe to follow, this transmutation has arresting implications. *Ibid., Ch. 11*

5 A people's literature is the great textbook for real knowledge of them. The writings of the day show the quality of the people as no historical reconstruction can.
Preface, The Roman Way *1932*

6 Theories that go counter to the facts of human nature are foredoomed. *Ibid., Ch. 1*

7 "Bless me," he [Socrates]* said, looking around the market where all an Athenian wanted lay piled in glowing profusion, "what a lot of things there are a man can do without."
Ch. 1, Witness to the Truth *1948*

* Greek philosopher (470?–399 B.C.)

8 Ages of faith and of unbelief are always said to mark the course of history. *Ibid., Ch. 9*

9 But it is not hard work which is dreary; it is superficial work. That is always boring in the long run, and it has always seemed strange to me that in our endless discussions about education so little stress is ever laid on the pleasure of becoming an educated person, the enormous interest it adds to life. To be able to be caught up into the world of thought—that is to be educated. Quoted in the *Bryn Mawr School*
Bulletin *1959*

1136. Käthe Kollwitz (1867–1945)

1 No longer diverted by other emotions, I work the way a cow grazes.
(April 1910), Diaries and Letters
Hans Kollwitz, ed. *1955*

2 For the last third of life there remains only work. It alone is always stimulating, rejuvenating, exciting and satisfying. *Ibid. (1 January 1912)*

3 Men without joy seem like corpses.
Ibid. (19 September 1918)

4 I am afraid of dying—but being dead, oh yes, that to me is often an appealing prospect.
Ibid. (December 1941)

5 Although my leaning toward the male sex was dominant, I also felt frequently drawn toward my own sex—an inclination which I could not correctly interpret until much later on. As a matter of fact I believe that bisexuality is almost a necessary factor in artistic production; at any rate, the tinge of masculinity within me helped me in my work. *Ibid. (1942)*

1137. Emmeline Pethick-Lawrence (1867–?)

1 Under the flagstones of the pavements in London lie the dormant seeds of life—ready to spring into blossom if the opportunity should ever occur. And under our cruel and repressive financial and economic system lie dormant human energy and joy that are ready to burst into flower. So far as a drop may be compared to the ocean,

we witnessed in many individual cases that releasing of the spirit that is possible when the conditions of life afford some modicum of dignity and of leisure.
Ch. 7, *My Part in a Changing World*
1938

2 A change of heart is the essence of all other change and it is brought about by a re-education of the mind. Ibid., Ch. 23

1138. Laura Ingalls Wilder (1867–1957)

1 It was so hard to be good all the time, every day, for a whole year.
Ch. 4, *Little House in the Big Woods*
1932

2 "Did little girls have to be as good as that?" Laura asked, and Ma said: "It was harder for little girls. Because they had to behave like little ladies all the time, not only on Sundays. Little girls could never slide downhill, like boys. Little girls had to sit in the house and stitch on samplers." Ibid., Ch. 5

1139. Mary Hunter Austin (1868–1934)

1 When a woman ceases to alter the fashion of her hair, you guess that she has passed the crisis of her experience.
The Land of Little Rain *1903*

2 Life set itself to new processions of seed-time and harvest, the skin newly turned to seasonal variations, the very blood humming to new altitudes. The rhythm of walking, always a recognizable background for our thoughts, altered from the militaristic stride to the jog of the wide unrutted earth.
The American Rhythm *1923*

1140. Alexandra David-Néel (1868–1969)

1 I wish to live philosophy on the spot and undergo physical and spiritual training, not just read about them. Quoted in "*Walker in the Sky*"
by Jane Dedman, *Quest*
May/June 1978

2 Whatever those unacquainted with it may think, solitude and utter loneliness are far from being devoid of charm. Words cannot convey the almost voluptuous sweetness of the feelings experienced . . . Mind and senses develop their sensibility in this contemplative life made up of continual observations and reflections. Does one become a visionary or, rather, is it not that one has been blind until then? Ibid.

3 To the one who knows how to look and feel, every moment of this free wandering life is an enchantment. Ibid.

1141. Guida Diehl (1868–?)

1 Never did Hitler* promise to the masses in his rousing speeches any material advantage whatever. On the contrary he pleaded with them to turn aside from every form of advantage-seeking and serve the great thought: Honor, Freedom, Fatherland!
The German Woman and National Socialism *1933*

*Adolf Hitler, Austrian-born Nazi dictator (1889–1945).

1142. Maude Glasgow (1868–1955)

1 When new-born humanity was learning to stand upright, it depended much on its mother and stood close to her protecting side. Then women were goddesses, they conducted divine worship, woman's voice was heard in council, she was loved and revered and genealogies were reckoned through her. . . .
As the race grew older, rationality flourished at the expense of moral sense.
The Subjection of Women and the Traditions of Men *1940*

1143. Florence Prag Kahn (1868–1948)

1 Preparedness never caused a war and unpreparedness never prevented one.
Quoted in *American Political Women*
by Esther Stineman *1980*

1144. Agnes Lee (1868–1939)

1 Bed is the boon for me!
It's well to bake and sweep,
But hear the word of old Lizette:
It's better than all to sleep.
"Old Lizette on Sleep," St. 1 *n.d.*

2 But I'll not venture in the drift
Out of this bright security,
Till enough footsteps come and go
To make a path for me.
"Convention" *n.d.*

1145. Caroline "La Belle" Otero (1868–1965)

1 . . . Paco took care of me; protected me; taught me to dance and sing, and was my lover. It was

the first time in over two years that I knew where I was going to sleep every night, and the first time in my life that I knew there would be something for me to eat when I woke up. Then Paco fell in love with me; wanted me to marry him, and spoiled everything.

> Quoted in the *Pittsburgh Leader*
> *11 April 1904*

1146. Eleanor H. Porter (1868–1920)

1 "Oh, yes, the game was to just find something about everything to be glad about—not matter what 'twas," rejoined Pollyanna earnestly. "And we began right then—on the crutches."

"Well, goodness me! I can't see anythin' ter be glad about—gettin' a pair of crutches when you wanted a doll!" . . .

"Goosey! Why, just be glad because you *don't—need—'em!* . . ." Ch. 5, *Pollyanna*
1912

2 "Oh, but Aunt Polly, Aunt Polly, you haven't left me any time at all just to—to live."

"To live, child! What do you mean? As if you weren't living all the time!"

"Oh, of course I'd be *breathing* all the time I was doing those things, Aunt Polly, but I wouldn't be living. You breathe all the time you're sleep, but you aren't living. I mean *living*—doing the things you want to do. . . . That's what I call living, Aunt Polly. Just breathing isn't living!"   Ibid., Ch. 7

3 "What men and women need is encouragement. . . . Instead of always harping on a man's faults, tell him of his virtues. Try to pull him out of his rut of bad habits. Hold up to him his better self, his *real* self that can dare and do and win out . . . People radiate what is in their minds and in their hearts."   Ibid., Ch. 5

1147. Margaret Fairless Barber (1869–1901)

1 . . . Earth, my Mother, whom I love.
> Dedication, *The Roadmender*, Vol. I
> *1900*

2 The people who make no roads are ruled out from intellectual participation in the world's brotherhood.   Ibid., Ch. 5

3 Revelation is always measured by capacity.
        Ibid., Vol. III, Ch. 3

4 To look backward for a while is to refresh the eye, to restore it, and to render it the more fit for its prime function of looking forward.
        Ibid.

1148. Elsa Barker (1869–1954)

1 They never fail who light
Their lamp of faith at the unwavering flame
Burnt for the altar service of the Race
Since the beginning.
        "The Frozen Grail"   *1910*

1149. Nancy Ford Cones (1869–1962)

1 Lonely? Dull? At Road's End [her home]? Not as long as I can see the catkins from my door and our maple trees in early spring, or tramp through the misty April wood in search of wildflowers to photograph and color, or watch the birds nesting about our house. Not as long as I can have our friends gather around our fireplace or about our stone table for a picnic under the maples in the summer.

> Quoted in "Rediscovering the Lady
> from Loveland" by Owen Findsen
> in *The Cincinnati Enquirer*
> *9 November 1980*

1150. Olive Dargan (1869–1968)

1 Be a God, your spirit cried;
Tread with feet that burn the dew;
Dress with clouds your locks of pride;
Be a child, God said to you.
        "To William Blake"*   *n.d.*

*English artist and poet (1757–1827).

2 The mountains lie in curves so tender
I want to lay my arm about them
As God does.   "Twilight"   *n.d.*

1151. Anna Bunston De Bary (1869–?)

1 Close to the sod there can be seen
A thought of God in white and green.
        "The Snowdrop"
        n.d.

1152. Emma Goldman (1869–1940)

1 Merely external emancipation has made of the modern woman an artificial being. . . . Now, woman is confronted with the necessity of emancipating herself from emancipation, if she really desires to be free.

> "The Tragedy of Women's Emancipation," *Anarchism and
> Other Essays   1911*

2 Corruption of politics has nothing to do with the morals, or the laxity of morals, of various political personalities. Its cause is altogether a material one.   Ibid.

3 Politics is the reflex of the business and industrial world. . . . Ibid.

4 These internal tyrants [conscience] . . . these busybodies, moral detectives, jailers of the human spirit, what will they say? Ibid.

5 If love does not know how to give and take without restrictions, it is not love, but a transaction that never fails to lay stress on a plus and a minus. Ibid.

6 . . . true emancipation begins neither at the polls nor in courts. It begins in woman's soul. Ibid.

7 . . . the most vital right is the right to love and be loved. Ibid.

8 The important and only God of practical American life: Can the man make a living? Can he support a wife? That is the only thing that justifies marriage.
"Marriage and Love," op. cit.

9 Love, the strongest and deepest element in all life, the harbinger of hope, of joy, of ecstasy; love, the defier of all laws, of all conventions; love, the freest, the most powerful moulder of human destiny; how can such an all-compelling force be synonymous with that poor little State and Church-begotten weed, marriage? Ibid.

10 Man has bought brains, but all the millions in the world have failed to buy love. Man has subdued bodies, but all the power on earth has been unable to subdue love. Man has conquered whole nations but all his armies could not conquer love. Man has chained and fettered the spirit, but he has been utterly helpless before love. High on a throne, with all the splendor and pomp his gold can command, man is yet poor and desolate, if loves passes him by. And if it stays, the poorest hovel is radiant with warmth, with life and color. Thus love has the magic power to make of a beggar a king. Yes, love is free; it can dwell in no other atmosphere. In freedom it gives itself unreservedly, abundantly, completely. Ibid.

11 Capitalism . . . has . . . grown into a huge insatiable monster.
"The Social Aspects of Birth Control,"
Mother Earth   April 1916

12 . . . the soldier's business is to take life. For that he is paid by the State, eulogized by political charlatans and upheld by public hysteria. But woman's function is to give life, yet neither the State nor politicians nor public opinion have ever made the slightest provision in return for the life woman has given. Ibid.

13 No, it is not because woman is lacking in responsibility, but because she has too much of the latter that she demands to know how to prevent conception. Ibid.

14 After all, that is what laws are for, to be made and unmade. Ibid.

15 But even judges sometimes progress. Ibid.

16 . . . all wars are wars among thieves who are too cowardly to fight and who therefore induce the young manhood of the whole world to do the fighting for them.
"Address to the Jury,"
Mother Earth   July 1917

17 . . . no great idea in its beginning can ever be within the law. How can it be within the law? The law is stationary. The law is fixed. The law is a chariot wheel which binds us all regardless of conditions or place or time. Ibid.

18 . . . democracy must first be safe for America before it can be safe for the world. Ibid.

19 Anarchy stands for the liberation of the human mind from the dominion of religion; the liberation of the human body from the dominion of property; liberation from the shackles and restraints of government.   Anarchism
1917

20 . . . the experience of Russia, more than any theories, has demonstrated that all government, whatever its forms or pretenses, is a dead weight that paralyzes the free spirit and activities of the masses.
My Disillusionment in Russia   1923

21 The ultimate end of all revolutionary social change is to establish the sanctity of human life, the dignity of man, the right of every human being to liberty and well-being.
My Further Disillusionment in Russia
1924

22 Are we really courageous, we who do not know fear, if we remain firm in the face of danger?   Vol. II, Ch. 39, Living My Life
1939

23 Revolution is but thought carried into action.
Quoted in The Feminist Papers,
Alice Rossi,* ed.   1973

*See 1912.

24 There's never been a good government.
Quoted by Katherine Anne Porter* in
the Los Angeles Times
7 July 1974

*See 1417.

1153. Corra May Harris (1869–1935)

1 The deadly monotony of Christian country life . . .   Ch. 3, A Circuit Rider's Wife
1910

2 This is the wonderful thing about the pure in heart—they do see God. *Ibid., Ch. 6*

3 No one has yet had the courage to memorialize his wealth on his tombstone. A dollar mark would not look well there. *Ibid., Ch. 11*

1154. Else Lasker-Schuler (1869–1945)

1 We shall rest from love like two rare beasts
In the high reeds behind this world.
"A Love Song" (c.1902),
The Other Voices,
Carol Cosman, ed. *1975*

1155. Charlotte Mew (1869–1928)

1   . . . Oh! my God! the down,
The soft young down of her, the brown,
The brown of her. . . .
"The Farmer's Bride," St. 5,
Collected Poems 1916

1156. Jessie Rittenhouse (1869–1948)

1 I worked for a menial's hire,
    Only to learn, dismayed,
That any wage I had asked of life,
    Life would have paid.
"My Wage" *n.d.*

2 My debt to you, Beloved,
    Is one I cannot pay
In any coin of any realm
    On any reckoning day.
"Debt" *n.d.*

1157. Carolyn Wells (1869–1942)

1 Total is a book. We find it
    Just a little past its prime;
And departing leaves behind it
    Footprints on the sands of time.
"Four," St. 3, *At the Sign of the
Sphinx 1896*

2 A Tutor who tooted the flute
Tried to teach two young tutors to toot;
    Said the two to the Tutor,
    "Is it harder to toot, or
To tutor two tutors to toot?"
"Limericks," No. 6, *The Book of
Humorous Verse 1920*

3 A canner can can
    Anything that he can,
But a canner can't can a can, can he?
"The Canner"
n.d.

4 The books we think we ought to read are
    poky, dull, and dry;
The books that we would like to read we are
    ashamed to buy;
The books that people talk about we never can
    recall;
And the books that people give us, oh, they're
    the worst of all. "On Books" *n.d.*

1158. Elizabeth Botume (fl. 1870s)

1 It was not an unusual thing to meet a woman coming from the fields, where she had been hoeing cotton, with a small bucket or cup on her head, and a hoe over her shoulder, contentedly smoking a pipe and briskly knitting as she strode along. I have seen, added to all these, a baby strapped to her back.
*First Days Amongst the
Contrabands 1893*

1159. Mrs. Edmund Craster (d. 1874)

1 The Centipede was happy quite,
Until the Toad in fun
Said, "Pray which leg goes after which?"
And worked her mind to such a pitch,
She lay distracted in a ditch
Considering how to run.
"Pinafore Poems," *Cassell's Weekly
1871*

1160. Clara Dolliver (fl. 1870s)

1 No merry frolics after tea,
No baby in the house.
"No Baby in the House,"
*No Baby in the House and Other
Stories for Children 1868*

1161. Mary Pyper (fl. 1870s)

1 I sat me down; 'twas autumn eve,
    And I with sadness wept;
I laid me down at night, and then
    'Twas winter, and I slept.
"Epitaph: A Life"
n.d.

1162. Sarah Ann Sewell (fl. 1870s)

1 It is a man's place to rule, and a woman's to yield. He must be held up as the head of the house, and it is her duty to bend so unmurmur-

ingly to his wishes, that the rest of the household will follow her example, and treat him with the due respect his sex demands.
Woman and the Times We Live In
1869

1163. Jessie Tarbox Beals (1870–1942)

1 I have learned that to get a job done and have fun in it is about all you can get out of life.
Quoted in *Jessie Tarbox Beals:
First Woman News Photographer*
by Alexander Alland   *1978*

2 I had too many keys that opened too many doors in too many places.   Ibid.

3 Mere feminine, delicate, Dresden china type of women get nowhere in business or professional life. They marry millionaires, if they are lucky. But if a woman is to make headway with men, she must be truly masculine.   Ibid.

4 I miss New York and its fairy-like towers
With Liberty's torch high in the air
I'd give all of California's damn flowers
For the sight of Washington Square.
Poem in Diary (1936), op. cit.

1164. Sharlot Mabridth Hall (1870–1943)

1 I stayed not, I could not linger; patient, resistless, alone,
I hewed the trail of my destiny deep in the hindering stone.
"Song of the Colorado," *Cactus Pine*
1910

1165. Florence Hurst Harriman (1870–1967)

1 Next to entertaining or impressive talk, a thoroughgoing silence manages to intrigue most people.   Ch. 4, *From Pinafores to Politics*
1924

1166. Grace Hibbard (1870?–1911)

1 "An Honest Lawyer"—book just out—
What can the author have to say?
Reprint perhaps of ancient tome—
A work of fiction anyway.
"Books Received"
n.d.

1167. Mary Johnston (1870–1936)

1 "I am weary of swords and courts and kings.
Let us go into the garden and watch the minister's bees."
Ch. 9, *To Have and to Hold*   *1899*

1168. Marie Lloyd (1870–1922)

1 A little of what you fancy does you good.
Song   *n.d.*

2 I'm one of the ruins that Cromwell knocked about a bit.   Ibid.

1169. Rosa Luxemburg (1870–1919)

1 . . . profits are springing, like weeds, from the fields of the dead.   *The Crisis in the German
Social Democracy*   *1919*

2 Shamed, dishonored, wading in blood and dripping with filth, thus capitalist society stands.
Ibid.

3 Self-criticism, cruel, unsparing criticism that goes to the very root of the evil, is life and breath for the proletarian movement.   Ibid.

4 Reduced to its objective historic significance, the present world war as a whole is a competitive struggle of a fully developed capitalism for world supremacy, for the exploitation of the last remnant of noncapitalistic world zones.   Ibid.

5 The high stage of world-industrial development in capitalistic production finds expression in the extraordinary technical development and destructiveness of the instruments of war. . . .   Ibid.

6 Without general elections, without freedom of the press, freedom of speech, freedom of assembly, without the free battle of opinions, life in every public institution withers away, becomes a caricature of itself, and bureaucracy rises as the only deciding factor.
Quoted in *Die Russische Revolution*
by Paul Froelich   *1940*

1170. Lucia Clark Markham (1870–?)

1 To-night from deeps of loneliness I wake in wistful wonder
To a sudden sense of brightness, an immanence of blue.
"Bluebells"   *n.d.*

1171. Maria Montessori (1870–1952)

1 . . . in nature nothing creates itself and nothing destroys itself.
The Secret of Childhood   *1939*

2 . . . humanity is still far from that stage of maturity needed for the realization of its aspirations, for the construction, that is, of a harmo-

nious and peaceful society and the elimination of wars. Men are not yet ready to shape their own destinies, to control and direct world events, of which—instead—they become the victims.
The Absorbent Mind 1967

3 And if education is always to be conceived along the same antiquated lines of a mere transmission of knowledge, there is little to be hoped from it in the bettering of man's future. For what is the use of transmitting knowledge if the individual's total development lags behind? Ibid.

4 If help and salvation are to come, they can only come from the children, for the children are the makers of men. Ibid.

5 We teachers can only help the work going on, as servants wait upon a master. Ibid.

6 The child endures all things. Ibid.

1172. Alice Caldwell Rice (1870–1942)

1 To him work appeared a wholly artificial and abnormal action, self-imposed and unnecessary. The stage of life presented so many opportunities for him to exercise his histrionic ability, that the idea of settling down to a routine of labor seemed a waste of talent.
Ch. 6, *A Romance of Billy-Goat Hill,* 1912

2 The arbitrary division of one's life into weeks and days and hours seemed, on the whole, useless. There was but one day for the men, and that was pay day, and one for the women, and that was rent day. As for the children, every day was theirs, just as it should be in every corner of the world. Ibid., Ch. 15

1173. Helena Rubinstein (1870–1965)

1 I have always felt that a woman has the right to treat the subject of her age with ambiguity until, perhaps, she passes into the realm of over ninety. Then it is better she be candid with herself and with the world.
Pt. I, Ch. 1, *My Life for Beauty* 1966

2 There are no ugly women, only lazy ones.
Ibid., Pt. II, Ch. 1

1174. Maud Younger (1870–1936)

1 "See here. How am I ever going to get experience if everyone tells me that I must have it before I begin?" "New York, May 6, 1907,"
McClure's Magazine 1907

2 "Then why don't all girls belong to unions?" I asked, feeling very much an outsider; but she of the gents' neckwear replied: "Well, there's some that thinks it ain't fashionable; there's some that thinks it ain't no use; and there's some that never thinks at all."
"New York, June 8," op. cit.

3 A trade unionist—of course I am. First, last, and all the time. How else to strike at the roots of the evils undermining the moral and physical health of women? How else grapple with the complex problems of employment, overemployment, and underemployment alike, resulting in discouraged, undernourished bodies, too tired to resist the onslaughts of disease and crime?
Speech, Quoted in *Ms.*
January 1973

1175. Emily Carr (1871–1945)

1 You come into the world alone and you go out of the world alone yet it seems to me you are more alone while living than even going and coming. (16 July 1933)
Hundreds and Thousands 1966

2 Oh, the glory of growth, silent, mighty, persistent, inevitable! To awaken, to open up like a flower to the light of a fuller consciousness!
Ibid. (17 October 1933)

3 Twenty can't be expected to tolerate sixty in all things, and sixty gets bored stiff with twenty's eternal love affairs. Ibid. (12 August 1934)

4 It is wonderful to feel the grandness of Canada in the raw, not because she is Canada but because she is something sublime that you were born into, some great rugged power that you are a part of. Ibid. (16 April 1937)

5 I am not half as patient with old women now that I am one. Ibid. (6 March 1940)

1176. Maxine Elliott (1871–1940)

1 Beauty, what is that? There are phalanxes of beauty in every comic show. Beauty neither buys food nor keeps up a home.
News Item 1908

1177. Margaret Witter Fuller (1871–1954)

1 I am immortal! I know it! I feel it!
Hope floods my heart with delight!
Running on air, mad with life, dizzy, reeling,

Upward I mount—faith is sight, life is feeling,
Hope is the day-star of might!
"Dryad Song"   *n.d.*

1178. Pamela Glenconner (1871–1928)

1 Giving presents is a talent; to know what a person wants, to know when and how to get it, to give it lovingly and well. Unless a character possesses this talent there is no moment more annihilating to ease than that in which a present is received and given.
Ch. 5, *Edward Wyndhan Tennant:
A Memoir*   *1919*

2 Bitter are the tears of a child:
Sweeten them.
Deep are the thoughts of a child:
Quiet them.
Sharp is the grief of a child:
Take it from him.
Soft is the heart of a child:
Do not harden it.   "A Child"   *n.d.*

1179. Georgiana Goddard King (1871–1939)

1 English spelling is an affair of memory, not of reason.   *The Bryn Mawr Spelling Book
1909*

2 Like other things that came out of the East, it [architecture] is always a little intoxicating.
"Castles in Spain,"
*The Journal of the American
Institute of Architects,*
Vol. 9   *1921*

1180. Agnes C. Laut (1871–1936)

1 They had reached the fine point where it is better for the weak to die trying to overthrow strength, than to live under the iron heel of brute oppression.   Ch. 4, *Vikings of the Pacific
1905*

2 The ultimate umpire of all things in life is—Fact.   Ch. 20, *The Conquest of the
Great Northwest   1908*

3 Yet when you come to trace when and where national consciousness awakened, it is like following a river back from the ocean to its mountain springs. . . . You can guess the eternal striving, the forward rush and the throwback that have carved a way through the solid rock; but until you have followed the river to its source and tried to stem its current you can not know.   Ch. 1, *The Canadian Commonwealth
1915*

1181. Florence Sabin (1871–1953)

1 The prohibition law, written for weaklings and derelicts, has divided the nation, like Gaul, into three parts—wets, drys and hypocrites.
Speech   *9 February 1931*

1182. Ella S. Stewart (1871–?)

1 The real goddesses of Liberty in this country do not spend a large amount of time standing on pedestals in public places; they use their torches to startle the bats in political cellars.
Quoted in *New Directions for Women
November/December 1980*

1183. Maude Adams (1872–1953)

1 If I smashed the traditions it was because I knew no traditions.
Quoted in *Maude Adams: A Biography*
by Ada Patterson   *1907*

2 Genius is the talent for seeing things straight. It is seeing things in a straight line without any bend or break or aberration of sight, seeing them as they are, without any warping of vision. Flawless mental sight! That is genius.   *Ibid.*

1184. Mary Reynolds Aldis (1872–1949)

1 They flush joyously like a cheek under a lover's kiss;
They bleed cruelly like a dagger-wound in the breast;
They flame up madly of their little hour,
Knowing they must die.   "Barberries"
n.d.

1185. Eva Gore-Booth (1872–1926)

1 The little waves of Breffney go stumbling through my soul.
"The Little Waves of Breffney,"
*Poems
n.d.*

1186. Mildred Howells (1872–1966)

1 And so it criticized each flower,
This supercilious seed;
Until it woke one summer hour,
And found itself a weed.
"The Different Seed," St. 5   *n.d.*

1187. Aleksandra Kollontai (1872–1952)

1 The "upper" elements may divert the masses from the straight road of history which leads

toward communism only when the masses are mute, obedient, and when they passively and credulously follow their leaders.

> *The Workers' Opposition in Russia*
> *c.1921*

2 Bureaucracy, as it is, is a direct negation of mass self-activity. . . .   Ibid.

3 Fear of criticism and freedom of thought by combining together with bureaucracy quite often produce ridiculous forms.   Ibid.

1188. Julia Morgan (1872–1957)

1 The building should speak for itself.

> Quoted in "Some Examples of the Work of Julie Morgan" by Walter T. Steilberg, *Architect and Engineer November 1918*

2 Never turn down a job because you think it's too small, you don't know where it can lead.   Ibid.

1189. Grace Seton-Thompson (1872–1959)

1 I know what it means to be a miner and a cowboy, and have risked my life when need be, *but,* best of all, I have felt the charm of the glorious freedom, the quick rushing blood, the bounding motion, of the wild life, the joy of the living and of the doing, of the mountain and the plain; I have learned to know and feel some, at least, of the secrets of the Wild Ones.

> Ch. 18, *A Woman Tenderfoot*
> *1900*

2 Courage! Speed the day of world perfection.
Straining from the Wheel of Things,
Let us break the bonds of lost direction!
Godward! Borne on Freedom's wings!

> "The Wheel of Life," St. 6,
> *The Singing Traveler*   *1947*

3 My Mother is everywhere . . .
In the perfume of a rose,
The eyes of a tiger,
The pages of a book,
The food that we partake,
The whistling wind of the desert,
The blazing gems of sunset,
The crystal light of full moon,
The opal veils of sunrise.

> "Hindu Chant," St. 4, op. cit.

4 Butterflies and birds fly over me unconcerned . . .
The forest accepts me.

> "Forest," St. 4, op. cit.

5 Many times I have looked into the eyes of wild animals
And we have parted friends.
What did they see, and recognize,
Shining through the windows of a human soul?

> "Windows of the Soul," St. 9, op. cit.

1190. Leonora Speyer (1872–1956)

1 I'll sing, "Here lies, here lies, here lies—"
Ah, rust in peace below!
Passers will wonder at my words,
But your dark dust will know.

> "I'll Be Your Epitaph,"
> *Fiddler's Farewell*   *1926*

2 Poor patch-work of the heart,
This healing love with love;
Binding the wound to wound,
The smart to smart!

> "Therapy," St. 3, op. cit.

3 Houses are like the hearts of men,
I think;
They must have life within,
(This is their meat and drink),
They must have fires and friends and kin,
Love for the day and night,
Children in strong young laps:
Then they live—then!

> "Abrigada," St. 10, op. cit.

4 You gave me wings to fly;
Then took away the sky.

> Introduction, Pt. V, op. cit.

5 . . . no amount of study will contrive a talent, that being God's affair; but having the gift, "through Grace," as John Masefield says, it must be developed, the art must be learned.

> "On the Teaching of Poetry,"
> *The Saturday Review of Literature*
> *1946*

6 There is not much stitching and unstitching in some of the hasty and cocksure writing of today.   Ibid.

7 . . . to be exact has naught to do with pedantry or dogma. . . .   Ibid.

1191. Willa Cather (1873–1947)

1 No one can build his security upon the nobleness of another person.

> Ch. 8, *Alexander's Bridge*   *1912*

2 There are only two or three human stories, and they go on repeating themselves as fiercely as if they had never happened before.

> Pt. II, Ch. 4, *O Pioneers!*   *1913*

3 The history of every country begins in the heart of a man or woman. Ibid.

4 I like trees because they seem more resigned to the way they have to live than other things do. Ibid., Ch. 8

5 Artistic growth is, more than it is anything else, a refining of the sense of truthfulness. The stupid believe that to be truthful is easy; only the artist, the great artist, knows how difficult it is.
Pt. VI, Ch. 11,
The Song of the Lark   1915

6 That is happiness; to be dissolved into something completely great.
Bk. I, Ch. 2, Epitaph, *My Antonia*   1918

7 This was a lie, but Paul was quite accustomed to lying; found it, indeed, indispensable for overcoming friction.
"Paul's Case," *Youth and the Bright Medusa*   1920

8 Art, it seems to me, should simplify. That, indeed, is very nearly the whole of the higher artistic process; finding what conventions of form and what details one can do without and yet preserve the spirit of the whole. . . .
On the Art of Fiction   1920

9 The dead might as well try to speak to the living as the old to the young.
Bk. II, Ch. 6,
One of Ours
1922

10 Yes, inside of people who walked and worked in the broad sun, there were captives dwelling in darkness,—never seen from birth to death. Ibid., Bk. III, Ch. 2

11 Theoretically he knew that life is possible, maybe even pleasant, without joy, without passionate griefs. But it had never occurred to him that he might have to live like that.
The Professor's House   1925

12 That irregular and intimate quality of things made entirely by the human hand.
Bk. I, Ch. 3,
Death Comes for the Archbishop
1927

13 The universal human yearning for something permanent, enduring, without shadow of change. Ibid., Bk. III, Ch. 3

14 CECILE. Do you think it wrong for a girl to know Latin?

PIERRE. Not if she can cook a hare or a partridge as well as Mademoiselle Auclaire! She may read all the Latin she pleases.
Shadows on the Rock   1931

15 Only solitary men know the full joys of friendship. Others have their family; but to a solitary and an exile his friends are everything.
Ibid., Bk. III, Ch. 5

16 There are all those early memories; one cannot get another set; one has only those.
Ibid., Bk. IV, Ch. 2

17 One made a climate within a climate; One made the days—the complexion, the special flavor, the special happiness of each day as it passed; one made life. Ibid., Ch. 3

18 Sometimes a neighbor whom we have disliked a lifetime for his arrogance and conceit lets fall a single commonplace remark that shows us another side, another man, really; a man uncertain, and puzzled, and in the dark like ourselves. Ibid., Epilogue

19 "Nothing really matters but living—accomplishments are the ornaments of life, they come second." *Lucy Gayheart*   1935

20 The revolt against individuals naturally calls artists severely to account, because the artist is of all men the most individual; those who were not have long been forgotten.
On Writing   1949

21 Religion and art spring from the same root and are close kin. Economics and art are strangers. Ibid.

22 Oh, this is the joy of the rose:
That it blows,
And goes. "In Rose-Time"   n.d.

1192. Colette (1873–1954)

1 All those beautiful sentiments I've uttered have made me feel genuinely upset.
"The Journey"   1905

2 I look like a discouraged beetle battered by the rains of a spring night. I look like a molting bird. I look like a governess in distress. I look—Good Lord, I look like an actress on tour, and that speaks for itself.
"On Tour," *Music Hall Sidelights*
1913

3 How can one help shivering with delight when one's hot fingers close around the stem of a live flower, cool from the shade and stiff with newborn vigor! Ibid.

4 Nothing ages a woman like living in the country. Ibid.

5 A bed, a nice fresh bed, with smoothly drawn sheets and a hot-water bottle at the end of it, soft to the feet like a live animal's tummy.
"Arrival and Rehearsal," op. cit.

6 Privation prevents all thought, substitutes for any other mental image that of a hot, sweet-smelling dish, and reduces hope to the shape of a rounded loaf set in rays of glory.
"A Bad Morning," op. cit.

7 I hate guests who complain of the cooking and leave bits and pieces all over the place and cream-cheese sticking to the mirrors.

Cheri 1920

8 Years of close familiarity rendered silence congenial. . . . *Ibid.*

9 . . . they had become mistrustful, self-indulgent, and cut off from the world, as women are who have lived only for love. *Ibid.*

10 . . . her smile was like a rainbow after a sudden storm. *Ibid.*

11 Give me a dozen such heart-breaks, if that would help me to lose a couple of pounds. *Ibid.*

12 You aren't frightened when a door slams, though it may make you jump. It's a snake creeping under it that's frightening. *Ibid.*

13 . . . the sudden desire to look beautiful made her straighten her back. "Beautiful? For whom? Why, for myself, of course." *Ibid.*

14 Let's go out and buy playing-cards, good wine, bridge-scorers, knitting needles—all the paraphernalia to fill a gaping void, all that's required to disguise that monster, an old woman.

Ibid.

15 "What a nuisance! Why should one have to eat? And what shall we eat this evening?"

"Jealousy,"
My Mother's House 1922

16 Blushing beneath the strands of her graying hair, her chin trembling with resentment, this little elderly lady is charming when she defends herself without so much as a smile against the accusations of a jealous sexagenarian. Nor does he smile either as he goes on to accuse her now of "gallivanting." But I can still smile at their quarrels because I am only fifteen and have not yet divined the ferocity of love beneath his old man's eyebrows, or the blushes of adolescence upon her fading cheeks. *Ibid.*

17 "What are you thinking about, Bel-Gazou?"
"Nothing, Mother."
An excellent answer. The same that I invariably gave when I was her age.
"The Priest on the Wall," op. cit.

18 It is not a bad thing that children should occasionally, and politely, put parents in their place. *Ibid.*

19 It's pretty hard to retain the characteristics of one's sex after a certain age.
"My Mother and Illness," op. cit.

20 You'll understand later that one keeps on forgetting old age up to the very brink of the grave. *Ibid.*

21 . . . she has lost her torturer, her tormentor, the daily poison, the lack of which may well kill her. *Ibid.*

22 . . . the telephone shone as brightly as a weapon kept polished by daily use. . . .

The Last of Cheri 1926

23 If one wished to be perfectly sincere, one would have to admit there are two kinds of love— well-fed and ill-fed. The rest is pure fiction.

Ibid.

24 Whenever I feel myself inferior to everything about me, threatened by my own mediocrity, frightened by the discovery that a muscle is losing its strength, a desire its power, or a pin the keen edge of its bite, I can still hold up my head and say to myself: . . . "Let me not forget that I am the daughter of a woman who bent her head, trembling, between the blades of a cactus, her wrinkled face full of ecstasy over the promise of a flower, a woman who herself never ceased to flower, untiringly, during three quarters of a century."

Break of Day 1928

25 A second place [setting]. . . . If I say that it is to be taken away for good, no pernicious blast will blow suddenly from the horizon to make my hair stand on end and alter the direction of my life as once it did. If that plate is removed from my table, I shall still eat with appetite.

Ibid.

26 My true friends have always given me that supreme proof of devotion, a spontaneous aversion for the man I loved. *Ibid.*

27 I have suffered, oh yes, certainly I learned how to suffer. But is suffering so very serious? I have come to doubt it. It may be quite childish, a sort of undignified pastime—I'm referring to the kind of suffering a man inflicts on a woman or a woman on a man. It's extremely painful. I agree that it's hardly bearable. But I very much fear that this sort of pain deserves no consideration at all. *Ibid.*

28 . . . that wild, unknown being, the child, who is both bottomless pit and impregnable fortress. . . . "Look!" 1929

29 I have not forgotten how I used to take a child every year to the sea, as to a maternal element better fitted than I to teach, ripen, and perfect the mind and body that I had merely rough-hewn. *Ibid.*

30 I am seized with the itch to possess the secrets of a being who has vanished forever. . . .
"The Savages," *Sido* 1929

31 He was such an inoffensive little boy, she could find no fault with him, except his tendency to disappear. *Ibid.*

32 When ordinary parents produce exceptional children they are often so dazzled by them that they push them into careers that they consider superior, even if it takes some lusty kicks on their behinds to achieve this result. Ibid.

33 She [the cat] hasn't had her full ration of kisses-on-the-lips today. She had the quarter-to-twelve one in the Bois, she had the two o'clock one after coffee, she had the half-past-six one in the garden, but she's missed tonight's.
The Cat 1933

34 He loved his dreams and cultivated them. Ibid.

35 "She never misses an opportunity to shrink away from anything that can be tasted or touched or smelled." "Armande" *1944*

36 He wondered why sexual shyness, which excites the desire of dissolute women, arouses the contempt of decent ones. Ibid.

37 "If only her brain worked as well as her jaws!" *Gigi 1944*

38 "Call your mother, Gigi! Liane d'Exelmans has committed suicide."
The child replied with a long drawn-out "Oooh!" and asked, "Is she dead?"
"Of course not. She knows how to do things." Ibid.

39 "The telephone is of real use only to important businessmen or to women who have something to hide." Ibid.

40 "Instead of marrying 'at once,' it sometimes happens that we marry 'at last.'" Ibid.

41 "All that's in the past. All that's over and done with."
"Of course, Tonton, until it begins again." Ibid.

42 . . . he was always ready to part with twenty francs or even a "banknote," so much so that he died poor, in the arms of his unsuspected honesty.
"The Photographer's Missus" *1944*

43 "Don't be too nice to me. When anyone's too nice to me, I don't know what I'm doing—I boil over like a soup." Ibid.

44 The unexpected sound of sobbing is demoralizing. Ibid.

45 In the matter of furnishing, I find a certain absence of ugliness far worse than ugliness. Ibid.

46 Like so many saviors, heavenly or earthly, the angel tended to overdo her part. Ibid.

47 It is easy to relate what is of no importance. Ibid.

48 "Such a happy woman, why exactly, that's what I would have been if, here and there, in my trivial little life, I'd had something great. What do I call great? I've no idea, madame, because I've never had it!" Ibid.

49 "But once I had set out, I was already far on my way." Ibid.

50 "Madame, people very seldom die because they lost someone. I believe they die more often because they haven't had someone." Ibid.

51 A mouth is not always a mouth, but a bit is always a bit, and it matters little what it bridles. "The Sick Child" *1944*

52 Exhausted under the burden of universal kindness, he shut his eyes. . . . Ibid.

53 A time comes when one is forced to concentrate on living. A time comes when one has to renounce dying in full flight. Ibid.

1193. Mary Elizabeth Crouse (1873–?)

1 How often do the clinging hands, though weak,
Clasp round strong hearts that otherwise would break. "Strength of Weakness"
n.d.

1194. Marie Dressler (1873–1934)

1 Fate cast me to play the role of an ugly duckling with no promise of swanning. Therefore, I sat down when a mere child—fully realizing just how *utterly* "mere" I was—and figured out my life early. Most people do it, but they do it too late. At any rate, from the beginning I have played my life as a comedy rather than the tragedy many would have made of it.
Ch. 1, *The Life Story of an Ugly Duckling 1924*

2 I was born serious and I have earned my bread making other people laugh.
Ch. 1, *My Own Story 1934*

3 In order to represent life on the stage, we must rub elbows with life, live ourselves.
Ibid., Ch. 3

4 Love is not getting, but giving. It is sacrifice. And sacrifice is glorious! I have no patience with women who measure and weigh their love like a country doctor dispensing capsules. If a man is worth loving at all, he is worth loving generously, even recklessly. Ibid., Ch. 7

1195. Nellie McClung (1873–1951)

1 When they felt tired, they called it laziness and felt disgraced and thus they had spent their days,

working, working from the grey dawn, until the darkness came again, and all for what? When in after years these girls, broken in health and in spirits, slipped away to premature graves, or, worse still, settled into chronic invalidism, of what avail was the memory of the cows they milked, the mats they hooked, the number of pounds of butter they made.
Sowing Seeds in Danny 1908

1196. Virginia Taylor McCormick (1873–1957)

1 Not any leaf from any book
Can give what Pan, in going took.
"Regret from Pan" *n.d.*

2 Now she is dead she greets Christ with a nod,—
(He was a carpenter)—*but she knows God.*
"The Snob" *n.d.*

1197. Elizabeth Reeve Morrow (1873–1955)

1 My friend and I have built a wall
Between us thick and wide:
The stones of it are laid in scorn
And plastered high with pride.
"Wall," St. 1,
n.d.

1198. Daisy, Princess of Pless (1873–?)

1 Either of my parents would have done anything in the world for me—except tell me the truth.   Ch. 1, *Daisy, Princess of Pless*
1923

2 How seldom people find their happiness on a darkened stage; they must turn up all the limelights to find it.   Entry (16 August 1903),
From My Private Diary 1926

3 No theatre is prosperous, or a play complete, unless there is a bedroom scene in the second act. . . .   Ibid. (28 April 1904)

4 The Irish sit by a peat fire; the English by a coal one. That is the unbridgeable difference between the two peoples: We prefer the glamorous, the quick, the pungent; they the lasting and substantial.
Ch. 1, *What I Left Unsaid* 1936

1199. Emily Post (1873–1960)

1 To the old saying that man built the house but woman made of it a "home" might be added

the modern supplement that woman accepted cooking as a chore but man has made of it a recreation.   Ch. 34, *Etiquette* 1922

2 The honor of a gentleman demands the inviolability of his word, and the incorruptibility of his principles. He is the descendant of the knight, the crusader; he is the defender of the defenseless and the champion of justice—or he is not a gentleman.   Ibid., Ch. 48

3 To tell a lie in cowardice, to tell a lie for gain, or to avoid deserved punishment—are all the blackest of black lies. On the other hand, to teach him to try his best to avoid the truth— even to press it when necessary toward the outer edge of the rainbow—for a reason of kindness, or of mercy, is far closer to the heart of truth than to repeat something accurately and mercilessly that will cruelly hurt the feelings of someone.
Ch. 11, *Children Are People* 1940

1200. Dorothy Miller Richardson (1873–1957)

1 "There; how d'ye like that, eh? A liberal education in twelve volumes, with an index."
Vol. II, Ch. 24, *Pilgrimage* 1938

2 If there was a trick, there must be a trickster.   Ibid.

3 It will all go on as long as women are stupid enough to go on bringing men into the world. . . .   Ibid.

4 No future life could heal the degradation of having been a woman. Religion in the world had nothing but insults for women.   Ibid.

5 *Coercion.* The unpardonable crime.
Ibid., Vol. IV, Ch. 9

6 "Women carry all the domesticity they need about with them. That is why they can get along alone so much better than men."   Ibid.

1201. Margaret Baillie Saunders (1873–1949?)

1 I've often known people more shocked because you are not bankrupt than because you are.
A Shepherd of Kensington 1907

1202. Janet Scudder (1873–1940)

1 I don't believe artists should be subjected to experiences that harden the sensibilities; without sensibility no fine work can ever be done.
Ch. 2, *Modeling My Life* 1925

2 Someone has said that even criticism is better than silence. I don't agree to this. Criticism can be very harmful unless it comes from a master; and in spite of the fact that we have hundreds of critics these days, it is one of the most difficult of professions. *Ibid.*

1203. Edith Franklin Wyatt (1873–1958)

1 Every true poem is a lone fount, of whose refreshment the traveler himself must drink, if he is to quench his thirst for poetry.
"Modern Poetry," *Art and the Worth-While*, Baker Brownell, ed. *1929*

1204. Ch'iu Chin (1874–1907)

1 We'll follow Joan of Arc—*
With our own hands our land we shall regain! "Ch'iu Chin—A Woman Revolutionary," Quoted in *Women of China* by Fan Wen-Lan—*1956*

*See 206.

1205. Olive Custance (1874–1944)

1 Spirit of Twilight, through your folded wings
I catch a glimpse of your averted face,
And rapturous on a sudden, my soul sings
"Is not this common earth a holy place?"
"Twilight" *n.d.*

1206. Zona Gale (1874–1938)

1 They were all dimly aware that something was escaping them, some inheritance of joy which they had meant to share. How was it they were not sharing it? Ch. 1, *Birth* *1918*

2 DWIGHT. Energy—it's the driving power of the nation. Act I, Sc. 1, *Miss Lulu Bett* *1920*

2 NINIAN. Education: I ain't never had it and I ain't never missed it. *Ibid.*, Sc. 2

4 He faced the blind wall of human loneliness. He was as one who, expecting to be born, is still-born, and becomes aware not of the cradle, but of eternity. "The Biography of Blade," *Century Magazine* *1924*

5 The unexpressed, then, is always of greater value than the expressed.
"Modern Prose," *Art and the Worth-While*, Baker Brownell, ed. *1929*

1207. Theodosia Garrison (1874–1944)

1 I never crossed your threshold with a grief
But that I went without it.
"The Closed Door," St. 1 *n.d.*

2 The hardest habit of all to break
Is the terrible habit of happiness.
"The Lake" *n.d.*

3 When the red wrath perisheth, when the dulled swords fail,
These three who have walked with death—these shall prevail.
Hell bade all its millions rise; Paradise sends three:
Pity, and self-sacrifice, and charity.
"This Shall Prevail" *n.d.*

1208. Ellen Glasgow (1874–1945)

1 And the spring passed into Nicholas also. The wonderful renewal of surrounding life thrilled through the repression of his nature. With the flowing of the sap the blood flowed more freely in his veins. New possibilities were revealed to him; new emotions urged him into fresh endeavours. All his powerful, unspent youth spurred on to manhood.
Bk. II, Ch. 3, *The Voice of the People* *1900*

2 It was not the matter of the work, but the mind that went into it, that counted—and the man who was not content to do small things well would leave great things undone.
Ibid., Ch. 4

3 "A farmer's got to be born, same as a fool. You can't make a corn pone out of flour dough by the twistin' of it." *Ibid.*

4 "What a man marries for's hard to tell," she returned; "an' what a woman marries for's past findin' out." *Ibid.*, Bk. III, Ch. 1

5 "I ain't never seen no head so level that it could bear the lettin' in of politics. It makes a fool of a man and a worse fool of a fool. The government's like a mule, it's slow and it's sure; it's slow to turn, and it's sure to turn the way you don't want it." *Ibid.*, Ch. 2

6 "I d'clare if it don't beat all—one minute we're thar an' the next we're here. It's a movin' world we live in, ain't that so, Mum?"
Bk. I, Ch. 1, *The Deliverance* *1904*

7 "But the war wasn't the worst thing," he concluded grimly. "The worst thing is this sense of having lost our way in the universe. The worst thing is that the war has made peace seem

so futile. It is just as if the bottom had dropped out of idealism. . . .''
> Pt. I, Ch. 1, *They Stooped to Folly*
> *1929*

8 "Oh, but it feels so nice to be hard! If I had known how nice it felt, I should have been hard all my life."   Ibid., Ch. 12

9 Women like to sit down with trouble as if it were knitting.   *The Sheltered Life*   *1932*

10 "Grandpa says we've got everything to make us happy but happiness."
> Pt. I, Ch. 1, *In This Our Life*
> *1941*

11 "I don't like human nature, but I do like human beings."   Ibid., Pt. II, Ch. 1

12 "We didn't talk so much about happiness in my day. When it came, we were grateful for it, and, I suppose, a little went farther than it does nowadays. We may have been all wrong in our ideas, but we were brought up to think other things more important than happiness."
> Ibid., Ch. 10

1209. Beatrice Hinkle (1874–1953)

1 Fundamentally the male artist approximates more to the psychology of woman, who, biologically speaking, is a purely creative being and whose personality has been as mysterious and unfathomable to the man as the artist has been to the average person.
> "The Psychology of the Artist,"
> *Recreating the Individual*   *1923*

2 . . . woman is a being dominated by the creative urge and . . . no understanding of her as an individual can be gained unless the significance and effects of that great fact can be grasped.   Ibid.

3 When one looks back over human existence, however, it is very evident that all culture has developed through an *initial resistance against adaptation to the reality in which man finds himself.*   Ibid.

4 The creator does not create only for the pleasure of creating but . . . he also desires to subdue other minds.   Ibid.

5 The attitude and reactions of artists toward their art children reveal an attitude similar to that which mothers in general possess toward their children. There is the same sensitivity to any criticism, the same possessive pride, the same devotion and love, with the accompanying anxiety and distress concerning them.   Ibid.

1210. Lou Henry Hoover (1874–1944)

1 My chief hobbies are my husband and my children.   Comment, Quoted in
> *First Ladies* by Betty Boyd
> Caroli *1987*

2 Boys, remember you are just as great factors in the home making of the family as are the girls.   Radio speech to 4-H Club (June 1929), op. cit.

1211. Bettina von Hutten (1874–1957)

1 A good many women are good tempered simply because it saves the wrinkles coming too soon.   *The Halo*   *1907*

1212. Yamamuro Kieko (1874–1915)

1 . . . I realize that were I a man, I would be at the battlefront fighting amidst bullets and explosives, instead of sitting serenely at my desk.
> Untitled Essay   *1895*

1213. Amy Lowell (1874–1925)

1 All books are either dreams or swords,
You can cut, or you can drug, with words.
> "Sword Blades and Poppy Seeds," St. 3
> *Sword Blades and Poppy Seeds*
> *1914*

2 My God, but you keep me starved! You write "No Entrance Here," over all the doors. . . . Hating bonds as you do, why should I be denied the rights of love if I leave you free?
> "The Basket," III, op. cit.

3 My words are little jars
For you to take and put upon a shelf.
> "Gift," op. cit.

4 You are beautiful and faded,
Like an old opera tune
Played upon a harpsichord.
> "A Lady," St. 1,
> op. cit.

5 I too am a rare
Pattern. As I wander down
The garden paths.
> "Patterns," *Men, Women and*
> *Ghosts*   *1916*

6   A pattern called a war.
Christ! What are patterns for?   Ibid., St. 7

7 Youth condemns; maturity condones.
> *Tendencies in Modern American*
> *Poetry*   *1917*

8 Let the key-guns be mounted, make a brave
show of waging war, and pry off the lid of
Pandora's box once more.
"Guns as Keys: And the
Great Gate Swings," Pt. I,
Can Grande's Castle 1918

9 A wise man,
Watching the stars pass across the sky,
Remarked:
In the upper air the fireflies move more slowly.
"Meditation," *Picture of the
Floating World* 1919

10 There are few things so futile, and few so
amusing,
As a peaceful and purposeless sort of perusing
Of old random jottings set down in a blank-
book
You've unearthed from a drawer as you looked
for your bank-book. . . .
"A Critical Fable," St. 1,
A Critical Fable 1922

11 And what are we?
We, the people without a race,
Without a language;
Of all races, and of none;
Of all tongues, and one imposed;
Of all traditions and all pasts,
With no tradition and no past.
A patchwork and an altar-piece. . . .
"The Congressional
Liberty," St. 1,
What's O'Clock 1925

12 Love is a game—yes?
I think it is a drowning. . . .
"Twenty-four Hokku on a
Modern Theme," XIX, op. cit.

13 Sappho* would speak, I think, quite openly,
And Mrs. Browning** guard a careful silence,
But Emily*** would set doors ajar and slam
them
And love you for your speed of observation.
"The Sisters," St. 2, op. cit.

*See 50.
**See 782.
***Emily Dickinson; see 892.

14 Finally, most of us [imagist poets] believe that
concentration is the very essence of poetry.
"Imagist Poetry"
n.d.

15 For books are more than books, they are the
life
The very heart and core of ages past,
The reason why men lived and worked and
died,
The essence and quintessence of their lives.
Untitled Poem, *The Boston
Athenoeum
n.d.*

1214. Dorothy Reed Mendenhall (1874–1964)

1 My early life had been fed with dreams and a
deep feeling that if I waited, did my part and
was patient, love would come to me and with it
such a family life as fiction depicted and romance built up. It seems to me that I have
always been waiting for something better—
sometimes to see the best I had snatched from
me. Quoted in "Dorothy Mendenhall:
'Childbirth Is Not a Disease' "
by Gena Corea, *Ms.* April 1974

1215. Alice Duer Miller (1874–1942)

1 And now too late, we see these things are one:
The art is sacrifice and self-control,
And who loves beauty must be stern of soul.
"An American to France,"
Welcome Home 1928

2 When a woman like that whom I've seen so
much
All of a sudden drops out of touch,
Is always busy and never can
Spare you a moment, it means a Man.
"Forsaking All Others,"
Forsaking All Others 1931

3 The white cliffs of Dover, I saw rising steeply
Out of the sea that once made her [England]
secure. "The White Cliffs," St. 1,
The White Cliffs 1940

1216. Lucy Montgomery (1874–1942)

1 "Isn't it splendid to think of all the things there
are to find out about? It just makes me feel glad
to be alive—it's such an interesting world. It
wouldn't be half so interesting if we knew all
about everything, would it? There'd be no scope
for imagination then, would there?"
Ch. 2, *Anne of Green Gables*
1908

2 "There's such a lot of different Annes in me. I
sometimes think that is why I'm such a troublesome person. If I was just one Anne it would
be ever so much more comfortable, but then it
wouldn't be half so interesting."
Ibid., Ch. 20

3 "As for Horace Baxter, he was in financial
difficulties a year ago last summer, and he
prayed to the Lord for help; and when his wife
died and he got her life insurance he said he
believed it was the answer to his prayer. Wasn't
that like a man?"
Ch. 15, *Anne's House of Dreams*
1917

1217. Roselle Mercier Montgomery (1874–1933)

1 I would always be with the thick of life,
Threading its mazes, sharing its strife;
Yet—somehow, singing!
"Somehow, Singing,"
Ulysses Returns 1925

2 Never a ship sails out of the bay
But carries my heart as a stowaway.
"The Stowaway,"
op. cit.

3 The facts are not quite obdurate.
They have a grim, sardonic way
Of granting men who supplicate
The things they wanted—yesterday!
"The Fates," *Many Devices* 1929

1218. Angela Morgan (1874?–1957)

1 I will hew great windows for my soul.
"Room"
n.d.

2 The signals of the century
Proclaims the things that are to be—
The rise of woman to her place,
The coming of a nobler race.
"Today," St. 3
n.d.

3 Praised be the gods that made my spirit mad;
Kept me aflame and raw to beauty's touch.
"June Rapture"
n.d.

4 Work!
Thank God for the swing of it,
For the clamoring, hammering ring of it,
Passion of labor daily hurled
On the mighty anvils of the world.
"Work: A Song of Triumph" *n.d.*

1219. Rose O'Neill (1874–1944)

1 Remember, men of guns and rhymes,
And kings who kill so fast,
That men you kill too many times
May be too dead at last.
"When the Dead Men Die,"
The Master's Mistress 1922

2 "My face is a caricature of her, and her soul is
a caricature of mine. In fact, she has no soul.
She is my substance. She robbed me of substance in the womb. That's why I named her
Narcissa. . . . She grew her beauty on me like
a flower on a dunghill. She is my material. I
am her soul. We are that perilous pair."
Ch. 1, *Garda* 1929

3 They lose least who have least to lose.
Ibid., Ch. 11

1220. Josephine Preston Peabody (1874–1922)

1 That you should follow our poor humanhood,
Only because you would!
"To a Dog" *n.d.*

2 . . . The elements rehearse
Man's urgent utterance, and his words traverse
The spacious heav'ns like homing birds.
"Wireless" *n.d.*

1221. Gertrude Stein (1874–1946)

1 "You are so afraid of losing your moral sense
that you are not willing to take it through anything more dangerous than a mud—
puddle."
"Adele," *Q. E. D.*, Bk. I 1903

2 "I could undertake to be an efficient pupil if it
were possible to find an efficient teacher."
Ibid.

3 I am writing for myself and strangers. This is
the only way that I can do it.
The Making of Americans
1906–1908

4 "Rose is a rose is a rose is a rose."
"Sacred Emily" 1913

5 You are all a lost generation.
Letter to Ernest Hemingway 1926

6 Pigeons on the grass alas.
Four Saints in Three Acts 1927

7 Before the flowers of friendship faded friendship
faded. *Before the Flowers of Friendship*
Faded Friendship Faded 1931

8 Remarks are not literature.
The Autobiography of
Alice B. Toklas 1933

9 She always says she dislikes the abnormal, it is
so obvious. She says the normal is so much
more simply complicated and interesting.
Ibid.

10 In the United States there is more space where
nobody is than where anybody is. That is what
makes America what it is.
The Geographical History of
America 1936

11 Everybody knows if you are too careful you are
so occupied in being careful that you are sure
to stumble over something.
Ch. 1, *Everybody's Autobiography*
1937

12 . . . native always means people who belong
somewhere else, because they had once belonged somewhere. That shows that the white
race does not really think they belong anywhere
because they think of everybody else as
native. Ibid.

13 . . . one never discusses anything with anybody who can understand, one discusses things with people who cannot understand. . . .   Ibid.

14 . . . if anything is a surprise then there is not much difference between older or younger because the only thing that does make anybody older is that they cannot be surprised.
                                        Ibid., Ch. 2

15 . . . money . . . is really the difference between men and animals, most of the things men feel animals feel and vice versa, but animals do not know about money, money is purely a human conception and that is very important to know very very important.   Ibid.

16 . . . considering how dangerous everything is nothing is really very frightening.   Ibid.

17 . . . what is the use of thinking if after all there is to be organization.   Ibid.

18 It takes a lot of time to be a genius, you have to sit around so much doing nothing, really doing nothing.   Ibid.

19 I am also fond of saying that a war of fighting is like a dance because it is all going forward and back, and that is what everybody likes; they like that forward and back movement, that is the reason that revolutions and Utopias are discouraging they are up and down and not forward and back.   Ibid., Ch. 3

20 Too few is as many as too many.   Ibid.

21 America is not old enough yet to get young again.   Ibid.

22 Counting is the religion of this generation it is its hope and its salvation.   Ibid.

23 I understand you undertake to overthrow my undertaking.   Ibid.

24 . . . I do want to get rich but I never want to do what there is to do to get rich.   Ibid.

25 . . . what is the use of being a little boy if you are going to grow up to be a man.
                                        Ibid., Ch. 4

26 Everybody gets so much information all day long that they lose their common sense.
                                Untitled Essay (1946),
                            Reflection on the Atomic Bomb,
                                        Vol. I   1973

1222. Etsu Inagaki Sugimoto (1874?– 1950)

1 A careless or perturbed state of mind always betrays itself in the intricate shadings of ideographs, for each one requires absolute steadiness and accuracy of touch. Thus, in careful guidance

of the hand were we children taught to hold the mind in leash.
                            Ch. 2, A Daughter of the Samurai
                                        1925

2 "Look in the mirror every day," she said, "for if scars of selfishness or pride are in the heart, they will grow into the lines of the face. Watch closely."   Ibid., Ch. 6

1223. Mary McLeod Bethune (1875– 1955)

1 If our people are to fight their way up out of bondage we must arm them with the sword and the shield and the buckler of pride. . . .
                            "Clarifying Our Vision with the Facts,"
                                Journal of Negro History
                                    January   1938

2 Mr. Lincoln* had told our race we were free, but mentally we were still enslaved.
                            "Faith That Moved a Dump Heap,"
                                Who, The Magazine About People
                                    June   1941

* Abraham Lincoln (1809–65). 16th president of the United States (1861–65); assassinated.

3 I never stop to plan. I take things step by step.
                                        Ibid.

4 For I am my mother's daughter, and the drums of Africa still beat in my heart. They will not let me rest while there is a single Negro boy or girl without a chance to prove his worth.
                                        Ibid.

5 The true worth of a race must be measured by the character of its womanhood. . . .
                                Address, "A Century of
                                Progress of Negro Women,"
                                Chicago Women's Federation
                                    (3 June 1933)
                                Black Women
                        in White America, Gerda Lerner,* ed.
                                        1973

* See 1882.

1224. Anna Hempstead Branch (1875– 1937)

1 God wove a web of loveliness,
    Of clouds and stars and birds,
But made not anything at all
    So beautiful as words.
                            "Songs for My Mother:
                            Her Words," St. 5   n.d.

2 If there is no God for thee
Then there is no God for me.
                            'To a Dog"   n.d.

3   Order is a lovely thing;
On disarray it lays its wing,

Teaching simplicity to sing.
          "The Monk in the Kitchen"   *n.d.*

1225. Abbie Farwell Brown (1875–1927)

1 No matter what my birth may be,
     No matter where my lot is cast,
  I am the heir in equity
     Of all the precious past.
          "The Heritage," St. 1   *n.d.*

1226. Louise Driscoll (1875–1957)

1 Power and gold and fame denied,
  Love laughs glad in the paths aside.
          "The Highway"   *n.d.*

2 There you will find what
     Every man needs,
  Wild religion
  Without any creeds.
          "Spring Market," St. 5   *n.d.*

1227. Alice Dunbar-Nelson (1875–1935)

1 In its dark bosom many secrets lie buried. It is
  like some beautiful serpent, languorous, sinister.
  It ripples in the sunshine, sparkles in the moonlight, glooms in the dusk and broods in the dark.
  But it thinks unceasingly, and below its brightest
  sparkle you feel its unknown soul.
          Sketch about a Louisiana bayou,
          The Schomburg Library of
          Nineteenth-Century Black
          Women Writers, Henry Louis Gates,
          Jr., ed.   *1988*

1228. Anne Crawford Flexner (1875?– 1955)

1 *Mrs. Frost:* If there were no women in the
  world, what would become of you men?
  Frost: We would be scarce, Emily, but we might
  be happier.   Act I, *The Marriage Game*
                              1913

2 *Keats:* One must have health! You may banish
  money—banish sofas—banish wine! but right
  Jack Health, true Jack Health, honest Jack
  Health—banish health, and you banish all the
  world!   Act II, Sc. 3, *Aged Twenty-six*
                              1937

1229. Minnie Haskins (1875–1957)

1 And I said to the man who stood at the gate of
  the year:

"Give me a light that I may tread safely into
  the Unknown."
And he replied: "Go out into the darkness and
  put your hand
Into the hand of God. That shall be to you
  better than light
And safer than a known way."
          "The Desert"   *1908*

1230. Helen Huntington (1875?–1950)

1 With the bitter past I will deck to-morrow.
          "The Wayfarer"   *n.d.*

1231. Marie Lenéru (1875–1940)

1 To be deaf is perhaps not to hear, but certainly
  it is this: to hold your tongue. Whatever spontaneous feelings may move you, to resist the
  impulse to communicate them, to remember that
  your world, your moment, are not other people's: to hold your tongue . . . a *haute école*
  of self-control, of nonspontaneousness, of solitude and indifference.   *Journal*
                              1945

2 One *sees* intelligence far more than one hears
  it. People do not always say transcendental things,
  but if they are *capable* of saying them, it is
  always visible.   Ibid.

3 I will never abdicate. I shall always want everything. To accept my life I must prefer it.
          Ibid. (1898)

4 If I were honest, I would admit that money is
  one half of happiness; it makes it so much more
  attractive!   Ibid.

1232. Belle Livingstone (1875–1957)

1 That winter two things happened which made
  me see that the world, the flesh, and the devil
  were going to be more powerful influences in
  my life after all than the chapel bell. First, I
  tasted champagne; second, the theatre.
          Belle Out of Order   *1959*

2 Like Moses, I wasn't born. I was found.
          Ibid., Pt. I, Ch. 1

3 Odd how the erotic appeal has swung away
  from legs; today a smart girl takes her legs for
  granted and gets herself a good sweater.
          Ibid., Ch. 2

4 Much has been written about the beauty, the
  stillness, the terror of the desert but little about
  its flies.   Ibid., Ch. 5

1233. Vilda Sauvage Owens (1875–1950)

1 If ever I have time for things that matter,
If ever I have the smallest chance,
I'm going to live in
Little Broom Gardens,
Moat-by-the-Castle,
Nettlecombe, Hants.
"If Ever I Have Time for Things
That Matter," St. 1,
n.d.

1234. Anne Goodwin Winslow (1875–?)

1 And how can curses make him yours
When kisses could not make him so?
"The Beaten Path,"
n.d.

1235. Josephine Dodge Bacon (1876–1961)

1 Life in all its phases possessed for him unsounded depths of entertainment, and in the intervals of uncontrolled laughter at the acts and words of his astonished elders he gave way to frequent subtle smiles resulting from subjectively humorous experiences unguessed by the world at large.
Ch. 2, *The Memoirs of a Baby*
1904

2 You mark my words, Toots, if you ever hear a darn-fool thing to-day, you can make up your mind some woman said it that writes books. . . . It ought to be a crime for any woman to have children that writes books.
Ch. 2, *The Biography of a Boy*
1910

3 I do not see how there can be any real respect, Or any real privacy such as women love, When you marry a man.
A man makes trouble.
Ch. 20, *Truth o'Women*   *1923*

1236. Mary Ritter Beard (1876–1958)

1 In their quest for rights they [women] have naturally placed emphasis on their wrongs, rather than their achievements and possessions, and have retold history as a story of their long Martyrdom.   Ch. 1, *Understanding Women*
1931

2 In other words, those who sit at the feast will continue to enjoy themselves even though the veil that separates them from the world of toiling reality below has been lifted by mass revolts and critics.   Ibid., Ch. 6

3 The dogma of woman's complete historical subjection to men must be rated as one of the most fantastic myths ever created by the human mind.   *Woman as a Force in History*
1946

4 . . . history has been conceived—and with high justification in the records—as the human struggle for civilization against barbarism in different ages and places, from the beginning of human societies.   Ibid., Ch. 12

5 Beneath the surface of civilian interests and capitalistic enterprises smoldered embers of the world's war spirit—humanity's traditional flare—now to be enflamed by new instruments for fighting and the associated aspiration for world trade and world power.
Ch. 9, *The Force of Women in Japanese History*   *1963*

1237. Anne Bronaugh (1876–1961)

1 Life is a patchwork—here and there,
Scraps of pleasure and despair
Join together, hit or miss.   "Patchwork" *n.d.*

1238. Sarah Norcliffe Cleghorn (1876–1959)

1 Since more than half my hopes came true
And more than half my fears
Are but the pleasant laughing-stock
Of these my middle years . . .
Shall I not bless the middle years?
Not I for youth repine
While warmly round me cluster lives
More dear to me than mine.
"Contented at Forty"   *1916*

2 Come, Captain Age,
With your great sea-chest full of treasure!
Under the yellow and wrinkled tarpaulin
Disclose the carved ivory
And the sandalwood inlaid with pearl:
Riches of wisdom and years.
"Come, Captain Age,"
Three Score   *1936*

1239. Mata Hari (1876–1917)

1 The dance is a poem of which each movement is a word.   *Scrapbook*   *1905*

2 I am a woman who enjoys herself very much; sometimes I lose, sometimes I win.

Quoted in *Mata Hari, The*
True Story by
Russell Howe   1986

1240. Norah M. Holland (1876–1925)

1 Life has given me of its best—
Laughter and weeping, labour and rest,
Little of gold, but lots of fun;
Shall I then sigh that all is done?   "Life"
n.d.

1241. Sally Kinsolving (1876–?)

1 Ships, young ships,
I do not wonder men see you as women—
You in the white length of your loveliness
Reclining on the sea!
"Ships," *Many Waters*   1942

1242. Mary Sinton Leitch (1876–1954)

1 And deaf, he sings of nightingales
Or, blind, he sings of stars.   "The Poet"
n.d.

2 He who loves the ocean
And the ways of ships
May taste beside a mountain pool
Brine on his lips.
"He Who Loves the Ocean"   *n.d.*

1243. Grace Fallow Norton (1876–1926)

1 I have loved many, the more and the few—
I have loved many that I might love you.
"Song of the Sum of All"
n.d.

2 Take me upon thy breast,
O River of Rest.
Draw me down to thy side,
Slow-moving tide.   "O Sleep"   *n.d.*

1244. Mary Roberts Rinehart (1876–1958)

1 Conscription may form a great and admirable
machine, but it differs from the trained army of
volunteers as a body differs from a soul. But it
costs a country heavy in griefs, does a volunteer
army; for the flower of the country goes.
Introduction, *Kings, Queens, and Pawns*
1915

2 It is easier to die than to send a son to death.
Ibid., Ch. 37

3 "You're a perfect child, a stubborn child! Your
mind's in pigtails, like your hair."
"The Family Friend,"
Affinities and Other
Stories   1920

4 The great God endows His children variously.
To some He gives intellect—and they move the
earth. To some He allots heart—and the beating
pulse of humanity is theirs. But to some He
gives only a soul, without intelligence—and
these, who never grow up, but remain always
His children, are God's fools, kindly, elemental,
simple, as if from His palette the Artist of all
had taken one colour instead of many.
"God's Fool," *Love Stories*
1920

5 Men deceive themselves; they look back on the
children who were once themselves, and attempt
to reconstruct them. But they can no longer
think like the child, and against the unpleasant
and the horrid the mind has set up the defensive
machinery of forgetfulness.
Ch. 1, *My Story*   1931

1245. Helen Rowland (1876–1950)

1 Woman: the peg on which the wit hangs his
jest, the preacher his text, the cynic his grouch,
and the sinner his justification.
Reflections of a Bachelor Girl
1903

2 When you see what some girls marry, you realize how they must hate to work for a living.
Ibid.

3 Love, the quest; marriage, the conquest; divorce, the inquest.   Ibid.

4 Marriage: a souvenir of love.   Ibid.

5 The follies which a man regrets most in his life
are those which he didn't commit when he had
the opportunity.   Ibid.

6 It takes a woman twenty years to make a man
of her son, and another woman twenty minutes
to make a fool of him.   Ibid.

7 One man's folly is another man's wife.   Ibid.

8 Never trust a husband too far, nor a bachelor
too near.   *The Rubaiyat of a Bachelor*
1915

9 The woman who appeals to a man's vanity may
stimulate him; the woman who appeals to his
heart may attract him; but it's the woman who
appeals to his imagination who *gets* him.
"Personally Speaking,"
The Book of Diversion,
F. P. Adams, D. Taylor,
J. Bechdolt, eds.   1925

10 At twenty, a man feels awfully aged and blasé; at thirty, almost senile; at forty, "not so old"; and at fifty, positively skittish. Ibid.

11 Alas, why will a man spend months trying to hand over his liberty to a woman—and the rest of his life trying to get it back again? Ibid.

12 Marriage is the only thing that affords a woman the pleasure of company and the perfect sensation of solitude at the same time. Ibid.

1246. Helen L. Sumner (1876–1933)

1 . . . the history of women's work in this country shows that legislation has been the only force which has improved the working conditions of any large number of women wage-earners.
Senate Report, *History of Women in Industry in the United States*, Vol. IX
1911

1247. Katharine Anthony (1877–1965)

1 For mothers who must earn, there is indeed no leisure time problem. The long hours of earning are increased by the hours of domestic labor, until no slightest margin for relaxation or change of thought remains.
Ch. 6, *Mothers Who Must Earn*
1914

2 Beyond all superficial differences and incidental forms, the vision of the emancipated woman wears the same features, whether she be hailed as *frau, fru,* or *woman.*
Ch. 1, *Feminism in Germany and Scandinavia* *1915*

3 The cult of "arms and the man" must reckon with a newer cult, that of "schools and the woman." Schools, which exalt brains above brawn, and women, who exalt life-giving above life-taking, are the natural allies of the present era. Ibid., Ch. 2

4 The struggle for self-consciousness is the essence of the feminist movement. Slowly but inevitably, the soul of a sex is emerging from the dim chamber of instinct and feeling into the strong sunshine of reason and will.
Ibid., Ch. 9

5 There can be no doubt as to who began the literary war between the sexes. Also there is no comparison between the severity and harshness of the tone of criticism in the opposing camps. If we search the polemic writings of the most militant feminists, we can nowhere find expressions which compare in venom and ruthlessness with the woman-eating sentiments of certain medieval "saints" and modern "philosophers." Ibid.

6 Principles are a dangerous form of social dynamite. . . . Introduction,
The Endowment of Motherhood
1920

7 Foremost among the barriers to equality is the system which ignores the mother's service to Society in making a home and rearing children. The mother is still the unchartered servant of the future, who receives from her husband, at *his* discretion, a share in *his* wages. Ibid.

1248. Grace Noll Crowell (1877–1965?)

1 God wrote His loveliest poem on the day
He made the first tall silver poplar tree.
"Silver Poplars," St. 1 *n.d.*

2 The woman who can move about a house,
Whether it be a mansion or a camp,
And deftly lay a fire, and spread a cloth,
And light a lamp,
And by the magic of a quick touch give
The look of home wherever she may be—
Such a woman always will seem great
And beautiful to me.
"The Home Makers," St. 1
n.d.

1249. Isabelle Eberhardt (1877–1904)

1 For those who know the value and the exquisite taste of solitary freedom (for one is only free when alone), the act of leaving is the bravest and most beautiful of all.
Journal Entry, Quoted in *The Destiny of Isabelle Eberhardt* by Cecily Mackworth *1975*

2 I love to dive into the bath of street life, the waves of the crowds flowing over me, to impregnate myself with the fluids of the people.
Ibid.

1250. Rose Fyleman (1877–1957)

1 There are fairies at the bottom of our garden.
"The Fairies," St. 1
n.d.

1251. Mary Garden (1877?–1967)

1 If I ever had complete charge of an opera house, the chances are I wouldn't get anybody to sing

for me. I would be very emphatic about some things. I would never have a curtain call. I would never allow an encore. I would never permit a claque. There would be only art in my theatre. Ch. 11, *Mary Garden's Story,* with Louis Biancolli *1951*

2 I used my voice to color my roles. Salomé was blood red. Melissande was ice, melting ice. . . . Ibid, Ch. 21

1252. Virginia Gildersleeve (1877–1965)

1 Medicine is a profession which naturally appeals deeply to women, as they are instinctively concerned with conserving life.
"The Advancement of Women," *Many a Good Crusade* *1954*

2 Now our witchhunters are trying to drive students and teachers into conformity with a rigid concept of Americanism defined by ignorant and irresponsible politicians. If we do not check this movement, we shall become a totalitarian state like the Fascist and Communist models and our colleges and universities will produce frightened rabbits instead of scholars with free minds.
"The Inescapable Desert," op. cit.

1253. Mathilda von Kemnitz (1877–?)

1 Since the fundamental principle of eroticism imperiously governs every human life, since the manner of the first erotic happiness determines in a far-reaching manner the laws of the individual's eroticism throughout his entire life, the majority of men have become entirely incapable of concentrating their erotic will consistently on one human being; therefore, they have become incapable of monogamy.
The Triumph of the Immortal Will *1932*

2 The man experiences the highest unfolding of his creative powers not through asceticism but through sexual happiness. Ibid.

1254. Marian Le Sueur (1877–1954)

1 The American destiny is what our fathers dreamed, a land of the free, and the home of the brave; but only the brave can be free. Science has made the dream of today's reality for all the earth if we have the courage and vision to build it. American Democracy must furnish the engineers of world plenty—the builders of world peace and freedom.

Quoted in *Crusaders* by Meridel Le Sueur* *1955*

*See 1558.

1255. Anne Shannon Monroe (1877–1942)

1 I have never been much cheered by the "stenciled smile," the false front, the pretending that there was no trouble when trouble stalked, that there was no death when Death laid his cold hand upon one dearer to us than life: but I have been tremendously cheered by the *brave* front; the imagination that could travel past the trouble and see that there were still joys in the world. . . . Ch. 1, *Singing in the Rain* *1926*

2 "Don't get hung up on a snag in the stream, my dear. Snags alone are not so dangerous— it's the debris that clings to them that makes the trouble. Pull yourself loose and go on."
Ibid., Ch. 13

1256. Maude Royden (1877–1956)

1 The belief that the personality of men and women are of equal dignity in the sight of God is necessary to a right moral standard.
The Church and Woman *c.1920*

1257. Rosika Schwimmer (1877–1948)

1 I am no uncompromising pacifist. . . . I have no sense of nationalism, only a cosmic consciousness of belonging to the human family.
Court Testimony, Citizenship Hearings *1928*

2 Women's rights, men's rights—human rights— all are threatened by the ever-present spectre of war so destructive now of human material and moral values as to render victory indistinguishable from defeat.
Speech, Centennial Celebration of Seneca Falls Convention of Women's Rights *July 1948*

3 Women's function of homemaker, we once dreamed, would extend into politics and economics our highest creative and conserving instincts. Let us go back to the task of building that safe, decent and wholesome home for the entire human family to which we once pledged ourselves. Ibid.

1258. Alice B. Toklas (1877–1967)

1 What is sauce for the goose may be sauce for the gander, but is not necessarily sauce for the

chicken, the duck, the turkey or the guinea hen. *The Alice B. Toklas Cook Book*
1954

2 Haven't you learned yet that it isn't age but lack of experience that makes us fall off ladders or have radiators fall on us.
Letter to Princess Dilkusha de Rohan (5 March 1955), *Staying On Alone*, Ed Burns, ed.
1973

3 . . . the past is not gone—nor is Gertrude.*
Letter to Samuel Steward (7 August 1958), op. cit.

*Gertrude Stein; see 1221.

4 Dawn comes slowly but dusk is rapid.
Letter to Virginia Knapik (9 August 1960), op. cit.

1259. Elizabeth Arden (1878–1966)

1 Nothing that costs only a dollar is worth having. Quoted in "In Cosmetics the Old Mystique Is No Longer Enough" by Eleanore Carruth, *Fortune October 1973*

1260. Florence Ayscough (1878–1942)

1 Ideals determine government, and government determines social life, and social life, with all that the term connotes, is the essence of every literature. Introduction, *Fir-Flower Tablets*
1921

1261. Amelia Burr (1878–1940?)

1 Because I have loved life, I shall have no sorrow to die. "A Song of Living," St. 3, *Life and Living* 1916

2 Swift and sure go the lonely feet,
And the single eye sees cold and true,
And the road that has room and to spare for one
May be sorely narrow for two.
"To Lovers" *n.d.*

1262. Grace H. Conkling (1878–1958)

1 I have an understanding with the hills.
"After Sunset" *n.d.*

2 Mountains are good to look upon
But do not look too long.

They are made of granite. They will break your heart. "Mountains"
n.d.

3 The forest looks the way
Nightingales sound. "Frost on a Window,"
n.d.

1263. Adelaide Crapsey (1878–1914)

1 If I'd as much money as I could tell,
I never would cry my songs to sell.
"Vendor's Song"
n.d.

2 These be
Three silent things:
The falling snow . . . the hour
Before the dawn . . . the mouth of one
Just dead. "Cinquain: Triad"
n.d.

1264. Isadora Duncan (1878–1927)

1 You were once wild here. Don't let them tame you! Curtain Speech, Symphony Hall, Boston 1922

2 All Puritan vulgarity centers in Boston. The Back Bay conservatives are impoverished by custom and taboo. They are the lifeless and sterile of this country. Interview, Boston
1922

3 . . . [I] would rather live in Russia on black bread and vodka than in the United States at the best hotels. America knows nothing of food, love or art. Interview Aboard Ship 1922

4 . . . the artist is the only lover, he alone has the pure vision of beauty, and love is the vision of the soul when it is permitted to gaze upon immortal beauty. . . . *My Life*
1927

5 I have discovered the dance. I have discovered the art which has been lost for two thousand years. Ibid.

6 . . . I believe, as a wage-earning woman, that if I make the great sacrifice of strength and health and even risk my life, to have a child, I should certainly not do so if, on some future occasion, the man can say that the child belongs to him by law and he will take it from me and I shall see it only three times a year! Ibid.

7 Any intelligent woman who reads the marriage contract, and then goes into it, deserves all the consequences. Ibid.

8 No composer has yet caught this rhythm of America—it is too mighty for the ears of most. Ibid.

9 And this dance will have nothing in it of the inane coquetry of the ballet, or the sensual convulsion of the Negro. It will be clean.
                                          Ibid.

1265. Edith Ronald Mirrielees (1878–1962)

1 In the thinking out of most stories, the thing the story is about, as apart from merely what happens in it, is of the utmost importance. For a story is not the sum of its happenings.
                    "The Substance of the Story,"
                              Story Writing   *1947*

2 Incident piled on incident no more makes life than brick piled on brick makes a house.
                                          Ibid.

1266. Ethel Watts Mumford (1878–1940)

1 There was a young person of Tottenhem,
  Whose manners, good Lord! she'd forgotten
  'em.   "Good Manners,"
                          The Limerick Up to
                          Date Book   *1903*

2 Said a Rooster, "I'd have you all know
  I am nearly the whole of the show;
    Why, the Sun every morn
    Gets up with the dawn
  For the purpose of hearing me crow!"
                  "Know Your Own Worth," op. cit.

1267. Bertha Runkle (1878–1958)

1 We own the right of roaming, and the world is wide.
            "Songs of the Sons of Essau"   *n.d.*

1268. Nancy Astor (1879–1964)

1 I can conceive of nothing worse than a man-governed world—except a woman-governed world.
              "America," Ch. 1, *My Two Countries*
                                            1923

2 It is no use blaming the men—we made them what they are—and now it is up to us to try and make ourselves—the makers of men—a little more responsible.   Ibid.

3 In passing, also, I would like to say that the first time Adam had a chance he laid the blame on woman. . . .   Ibid.

4 The most practical thing in the world is common sense and common humanity.   Ibid., Ch. 7

1269. Ethel Barrymore (1879–1959)

1 That's all there is, there isn't any more.
              Curtain Speech After Performance of
                              Sunday   *1904*

2 For an actress to be a success she must have the face of Venus, the brains of Minerva, the grace of Terpsichore, the memory of Macaulay, the figure of Juno, and the hide of a rhinoceros.
              Quoted in *The Theatre in the Fifties*
                    by George Jean Nathan   *1953*

3 You grow up the day you have your first real laugh at yourself.   Comment   *n.d.*

1270. Margarete Bieber (1879–1978)

1 Hope for the best, and expect the worst.
                  Quoted in "Margarete Bieber:
                    An Archaeologist in Two Worlds"
                    by Larissa Bonfante, *Women*
              as Interpreters of the Visual Arts,
              Claire Richter Sherman, ed. *1981*

2 Sweets are good for the nerves.   Ibid.

1271. Catherine Carswell (1879–1946)

1 . . . it wasn't a woman who betrayed Jesus with a kiss.   *The Savage Pilgrimage*
                                            1932

1272. Grace Goodhue Coolidge (1879–1957)

1 This was I and yet not I—this was the wife of the President of the United States and she took precedence over me; my personal likes and dislikes must be subordinated to the consideration of those things which were required of her.
              Quoted in *First Ladies* by Betty
                              Boyd Caroli
                                            1987

1273. Mabel Dodge (1879–1962)

1 . . . I knew instinctively that the strongest, surest way to the soul is through the flesh.
                              Lorenzo in Taos
                                            1932

2 A mania of love held me enthralled. . . . Nothing counted for me but Reed* . . . to lie close

to him and to empty myself over and over, flesh against flesh. And I was proud I had saved so much to spill lavishly, without reckoning, passion unending.   *Movers and Shakers*   *1936*

*John "Jack" Reed (1887–1920), American poet, adventurer, revolutionary writer.

3 Something in us wants men to be strong, mature, and superior to us so that we may admire them, thus consoled in a measure for our enslavement to them. But something else in us wants them to be inferior, and less powerful than ourselves, so that obtaining the ascendancy over them we gain possession, not only of them, but of our own souls, once more.   Quoted in "The Passions of Mabel Dodge" by Rusty Brown, *Ms.*   *March 1984*

4 Nature is so strong here [Taos, New Mexico] that one has to be on one's guard not to be absorbed by it.   Ibid.

1274. Dorothy Canfield Fisher (1879–1958)

1 "I am thinking that I am being present at a spectacle which cynics say is impossible, the spectacle of a woman delighting—and with most obvious sincerity—in the beauty of another."   Bk. III, Ch. 23, *The Bent Twig* *1915*

2 A mother is not a person to lean on but a person to making leaning unnecessary.
Her Son's Wife   *1926*

3 This was a nightmare memory, one of those that never come to you at all in daylight, but when you get about so far asleep, start to unroll themselves in the dark.
Pt. I, Ch. 2, *The Deepening Stream* *1930*

4 "Father sticks to it that anything that promises to pay too much can't help being risky."
Ibid., Pt. II, Ch. 1

5 The skull of life suddenly showed through its smile.   *Bonfire*   *1933*

1275. Katherine Gerould (1879–1944)

1 There are only three things worth while—fighting, drinking, and making love.
"The Tortoise," *Vain Oblations* *1914*

2 . . . I have always, privately and humbly, thought it a pity that so good a word [as culture] should go out of the best vocabularies; for when

you lose an abstract term, you are very apt to lose the thing it stands for.
"The Extirpation of Culture," *Modes and Morals*   *1920*

3 Politics, which, the planet over, are the fly in the amber, the worm in the bud, the rift in the loot, had, with great suddenness, deprived Wharton Cameron of a job.
Ch. 1, *Conquistador*   *1923*

1276. Wanda Landowska (1879–1959)

1 Obviously the good lady [melody] has a tough constitution. The more attempts made against her, the more she blooms with health and rotundity. It is interesting to note that all those accused of being her murderers are becoming, in turn, her benefactors and her saviors.
"Why Does Modern Music Lack Melody?" (9 February 1913), *Landowska on Music,* Denise Resout, ed.   *1964*

2 The most beautiful thing in the world is, precisely the conjunction of learning and inspiration. Oh, the passion for research and the joy of discovery!   Letter to a Former Pupil (1950) op. cit.

1277. Frieda Lawrence (1879–1956)

1 Everything he* met had the newness of a creation, just that moment come into being.
Not I, But the Wind . . .   *1934*

*D. H. Lawrence, English author, 1885–1930.

2 He loved me absolutely, that's why he hates me absolutely. . . .   Letter to Edward Garnett (c. 1914), *Frieda Lawrence: The Memoirs and Correspondence,* E. W. Tedlock, ed. *1961*

1278. Lilian Leveridge (1879–1953)

1 Over the hills of home, laddie, over the hills of home. "A Cry from the Canadian Hills," St. 9, *Over the Hills of Home* *1918*

1279. Sarojini Naidu (1879–1949)

1 *To-day* it is spring!
"Ecstasy," *The Golden Threshold* *1890*

2 The voice of the wind is the voice of our
  fate. "Wandering Singers," St. 3, op. cit.

3 O Bird of Time on your fruitful bough
  What are the songs you sing?
                          "The Bird of Time," St. 1
                          The Bird of Time 1912

4 Shall hope prevail where clamorous hate is
  rife,
  Shall sweet love prosper or high dreams find
  place
  Amid the tumult of reverberant strife.
                          "At Twilight," St. 2, op. cit.

5 What do you know in your blithe, brief season
  Of dreams deferred and a heart grown old?
                          "A Song in Spring," St. 2, op. cit.

6 The Indian woman of to-day is once more awake
  and profoundly alive to her splendid destiny as
  the guardian and interpreter of the Triune Vision
  of national life—the Vision of Love, the Vision
  of Faith, the Vision of Patriotism.
                          Foreword, *The Broken Wing*
                          1916

1280. Alma Mahler Werfel (1879–1964)

1 He soured my enjoyment of life and made it an
  abomination. That is, he tried to. Money—
  rubbish! Clothes—rubbish! Beauty—rubbish!
  Traveling—rubbish! Only the spirit was to count.
  I know today that he was afraid of my youth
  and beauty. He wanted to make them safe for
  himself by simply taking from me any atom of
  life in which he himself played no part. I was a
  young thing he had desired and whose education
  he now took in hand.
                          "Marriage and Life Together,"
                          *Gustav Mahler**
                          1946

*Austrian composer, 1860–1911.

1281. Beth Slater Whitson (1879–1930)

1 Meet me in Dreamland, sweet dreamy Dream-
  land,
  There let my dreams come true.
                          "Meet Me To-Night in Dreamland"
                          1909

1282. Alice Williams Brotherton
   (fl. 1880s–1930)

1 Books we must have though we lack bread.
                          "Ballade of Poor Bookworms" *n.d.*

2 Heap high the board with plenteous cheer, and
  gather to the feast,

And toast the sturdy Pilgrim band whose courage never ceased.
                          "The First Thanksgiving Day" *n.d.*

1283. Mrs. E. T. Corbett (fl. 1880s)

1 Ef you want to be sick of your life,
  Jest come and change places with me a spell—
  for I'm an inventor's wife.
                          The Inventor's Wife 1883

1284. Ellen M. Hutchinson (fl. 1880s–
   1933)

1 They are all in the lily-bed, cuddled close to-
  gether—
  Purple, yellow-cap, and baby-blue;
  How they ever got there you must ask the
  April weather,
  The morning and the evening winds, the
  sunshine and the dew.
                          "Vagrant Pansies" *n.d.*

1285. Meta Orred (fl. 1880s)

1 In the gloaming, O, my darling!
  When the lights are dim and low,
  And the quiet shadows falling
  Softly come and softly go.
                          "In the Gloaming" 1890

1286. Miles Franklin (1880–1956)

1 Bravely you jog along with the rope of class
  distinction drawing closer, closer, tighter, tighter
  around you. . . . I see it and know it, but I
  cannot help you. . . . I am only an unnecessarily, little, bush commoner, I am only a—
  woman.   *My Brilliant Career* 1901

1287. Helen Keller (1880–1968)

1 . . . we could never learn to be brave and
  patient, if there were only joy in the world.
                          Quoted in the *Atlantic Monthly*
                          May 1890

2 Literature is my Utopia. Here I am not disenfranchised. No barrier of the senses shuts me
  out from the sweet, gracious discourse of my
  book friends. They talk to me without embarrassment or awkwardness.
                          The Story of My Life 1903

3 Everything has its wonders, even darkness and
  silence, and I learn, whatever state I may be in,
  therein to be content.   Ibid., Ch. 22

4 . . . a people's peace—a peace without victory, a peace without conquests or indemnities.
Ibid.

5 . . . militarism . . . is one of the chief bulwarks of capitalism, and the day that militarism is undermined, capitalism will fail. *Ibid.*

6 One can never consent to creep when one feels an impulse to soar. Speech, Mt. Airy, op. cit.

7 Study the hand, and you shall find in it the true picture of man, the story of human growth, the measure of the world's greatness and weakness. "The Hand of the World"
American Magazine
December 1912

8 . . . as the eagle was killed by the arrow winged with his own feather, so the hand of the world is wounded by its own skill. *Ibid.*

9 The only moral virtue of war is that it compels the capitalist system to look itself in the face and admit it is a fraud. It compels the present society to admit that it has no morals it will not sacrifice for gain.
"Menace of the Militarist Program,"
New York Call 20 December 1915

10 I look upon the whole world as my fatherland, and every war has to me a horror of a family-feud. I look upon true patriotism as the brotherhood of man and the service of all to all.
Ibid.

11 Security is mostly a superstition. It does not exist in nature, nor do the children of men as a whole experience it. Avoiding danger is no safer in the long run than outright exposure. Life is either a daring adventure, or nothing.
The Open Door 1957

1288. Sophie Kerr (1880–1965)

1 The longing to produce great inspirations didn't produce anything but more longing.
Ch. 1, *The Man Who Knew the Date*
1951

2 If peace, he thought (as he had often thought before), only had the music and pageantry of war, there'd be no more wars. Ibid., Ch. 8

1289. Edith Lewis (1880?–1955?)

1 . . . it is not in any form of biographical writing, but in art alone, that the deepest truth about human beings is to be found.
Willa Cather* Living 1953

*See 1191.

1290. Kathleen Norris (1880–1966)

1 "If you have children, you never have anything else!" Ch. 2, *Mother* 1911

2 We cooked, cleaned, laboured, worried, planned, we wept and laughed, we groaned and we sang—but we never despaired. All this was but a passing phase; "we will certainly laugh at this someday," we all said buoyantly, laughing even then. Ch. 1, *Noon* 1924

3 And so came middle-age, for I have discovered that middle-age is not a question of years. It is that moment in life when one realizes that one has exchanged, by a series of subtle shifts and substitutes, the vague and vaporous dreams of youth for the definite and tangible realization. Ibid., Ch. 3

4 When they were going to be flagrantly, brutally selfish, how men did love to talk of being fair! Ch. 2, *Bread into Roses* 1936

5 "There seems to be so much more winter than we need this year." Ibid., Ch. 14

1291. Christabel Pankhurst (1880–1958)

1 We are not ashamed of what we have done, because, when you have a great cause to fight for, the moment of greatest humiliation is the moment when the spirit is proudest. The women we do pity, the women we think unwomanly, the women for whom we have almost contempt, if our hearts could let us have that feeling, are the women who can stand aside, who take no part in this battle—and perhaps even more, the women who know what the right path is and will not tread it, who are selling the liberty of other women in order to win the smiles and favour of the dominant sex.
Speech, Albert Hall, London
19 March 1908

2 What we suffragettes aspire to be when we are enfranchised is ambassadors of freedom to women in other parts of the world, who are not so free as we are. Speech, "America and the War,"
Carnegie Hall, New York
25 October 1915

3 Some people are tempted to say that all war is wrong, and that both sides to every war must be in the wrong. I challenge that statement and deny it utterly, absolutely, and with all the power I have at my disposal. All wars are not wrong. Was your war against a British Government wrong? As an Englishwoman, I say that when you fought us for the principle of freedom, for the right of self-government, you did right. I am glad you fought us and I am glad you beat us. *Ibid.*

4 Never lose your temper with the Press or the public is a major rule of political life.
Unshackled 1959

5 The spirit of the movement was wonderful. It was joyous and grave at the same time. Self seemed to be laid down as the women joined us. Loyalty, the greatest of the virtues, was the keynote of the movement—first to the cause, then to those who were leading, and member to member. Courage came next, not simply physical courage, though so much of that was present, but still more the moral courage to endure ridicule and misunderstandings and harsh criticism and ostracism. There was a touch of the "impersonal" in the movement that made for its strength and dignity. Humour characterized it, too, in that our militant women were like the British soldier who knows how to joke and smile amid his fighting and trials.   Ibid.

1292. Jeannette Rankin (1880–1973)

1 As a woman I can't go to war, and I refuse to send anyone else.   Prologue (c. 1941),
Quoted in Jeannette Rankin: First Lady in Congress by Hannah Josephson 1974

2 You take people as far as they will go, not as far as you would like them to go.   Ibid.

3 Establish democracy at home, based on human rights as superior to property rights. . . .
Ibid., Ch. 6

4 You can no more win a war than you can win an earthquake.   Ibid., Ch. 8

5 Men and women are like right and left hands: it doesn't make sense not to use both.
Quoted in American Political Women by Esther Stineman 1980

1293. Ruth St. Denis (1880–1968)

1 I used to say that if a person wanted to keep alive, in distinction to merely existing, he should change his occupation every ten years.
Ch. 3, *Ruth St. Denis: An Unfinished Life* 1939

2 We were a Poet* and a Dancer; and we became lovers. And let it be said of us that Beauty was our god whom we worshipped in rites of such pure loveliness that he became my Emperor and I became Moon to his Imperial Sun. Poems, like shy white birds, rose from our union: records of the strange drama of our love.
Ibid., Ch. 15

*Referring to her husband, Ted Shawn.

1294. Marie Carmichael Stopes (1880–1958)

1 An impersonal and scientific knowledge of the structure of our bodies is the surest safeguard against prurient curiosity and lascivious gloating.   Ch. 5, *Married Love* 1918

2 . . . each coming together of man and wife, even if they have been mated for many years, should be a fresh adventure; each winning should necessitate a fresh wooing.   Ibid., Ch. 10

3 So deeply are we woven I can lend
You outwardly to other hands who clutch
Small corners of your heart, greedy that such
Resplendence should its rays to darkness send.
"You," St. 2, *Joy and Verity* 1952

1295. Nancy Byrd Turner (1880–1954?)

1 Burn, wood, burn—
    Wood that once was a tree, and knew
Blossom and sheaf, and the Spring's return,
    Nest, and singing, and rain, and dew—
Burn, wood, burn!   "Flame Song"   n.d.

2 Death is only an old door
Set in a garden wall.
"Death Is a Door"   n.d.

1296. Margaret Widdemer (1880–1978)

1 To grown people a girl of fifteen and a half is a child still; to herself she is very old and very real; more real, perhaps, than ever before or after. . . .   "The Changeling,"
The Boardwalk 1920

2 But the young are improvident—not having yet learned how hard to come by money is and of how little account are other things.
"The Congregation," op. cit.

3 No one had told them that Age was a place
Where you sat with a curious mask on your
    face.   "Old Ladies," St. 6, *Hill Garden* 1936

4 "It only was gifts that I let them take.
I never gave dreams away."
"Spendthrift Nancy," St. 3, op. cit.

1297. Mary Antin (1881–1949)

1 "So at last I was going to America! Really, really going, at last! The boundaries burst. The arch of heaven soared. A million suns shone out of every star. The winds rushed into outer space, roaring in my ears, 'America! America!' "
The Promised Land 1912

1298. Mary Breckinridge (1881–1965)

1 To meet the needs of the frontierman's child, you must begin before he is born and carry him through the hazards of childbirth. His care not only means the care of the mother before, during and after his birth, but the care of his whole family as well. . . . Health teaching must also be on a family basis—in the homes.

Quoted in "Birth Control Gains in the Mountains of Kentucky" by Kenneth Reich, *Los Angeles Times* 9 May 1975

1299. Grace Stone Coates (1881–?)

1 Now, no doubt, my friend and I
Will proceed to lie and lie
To ourselves, till we begin
To act the truth and call it sin. "As It Is" *n.d.*

1300. Alice Corbin (1881–1949)

1 Then welcome Age and fear not sorrow;
Today's no better than tomorrow.
"Two Voices" *n.d.*

1301. Esther Lape (1881–1981)

1 We have no illusions about the flexibility of the Nobel Committee. Its statements reflect a rigidity *extraordinaire*.

Letter to A. David Gurewitsch (30 December 1964), Quoted in *Eleanor:* The Years Alone* by Joseph P. Lash 1972

*Eleanor Roosevelt; see 1341.

1302. Rose Macaulay (1881–1958)

1 Decades have a delusive edge to them. They are not, of course, really periods at all, except as any other ten years would be. But we, looking at them, are caught by the different name each bears, and give them different attributes, and tie labels on them, as if they were flowers, in a border.

Pt. II, Ch. 1, *Told by an Idiot* 1923

2 Sleeping in a bed—it is, apparently, of immense importance. Against those who sleep, from choice or necessity, elsewhere society feels righteously hostile. It is not done. It is disorderly, anarchical. "Beds and 'Omes," *A Casual Commentary* 1925

3 Does conduct rank with food, wine, and weather as a department of life in which goodness is almost universally admired?
"A Platonic Affection," op. cit.

4 . . . he desired to exaggerate. And here we have what may be called a primary human need, which should be placed by psychologists with the desire for nourishment, for safety, for sense-gratifications, and for appreciation, as one of the elemental lusts of man.
Catchwords and Claptrap 1926

5 . . . the desire not to work; indeed, I share it to the full. As to one's country, why should one feel any more interest in its welfare than in that of any other countries? And as to the family, I have never understood how that fits in with the other ideals—or, indeed, why it should be an ideal at all. A group of closely related persons living under one roof; it is a convenience, often a necessity, sometimes a pleasure, sometimes the reverse; but who first exalted it as admirable, an almost religious ideal?
Ch. 20, *The World My Wilderness* 1950

1303. Eleanor "Cissy" Patterson (1881–1948)

1 Perhaps a woman editor is resented because an editor is supposed to possess wisdom, and something in the masculine mind objects to the suggestion that a woman can know anything except what she has already been told by a man.
Quoted in *Cissy* by Ralph G. Martin 1979

1304. Anna Pavlova (1881–1931)

1 . . . although one may fail to find happiness in theatrical life, one never wishes to give it up after having once tasted its fruits. To enter the School of the Imperial Ballet is to enter a convent whence frivolity is banned, and where merciless discipline reigns.
"Pages of My Life," *Pavlova: A Biography,* A. H. Franks, ed. 1956

2 To tend, unfailingly, unflinchingly, towards a goal, is the secret of success. But success? What exactly is success? For me it is to be found not in applause, but in the satisfaction of feeling that one is realising one's ideal. When a small child . . . I thought that success spelled happiness. I was wrong. Happiness is like a butterfly which appears and delights us for one brief moment, but soon flits away. Ibid.

1305. Margaret Sackville (1881–1963)

1 When all is said and done, monotony may after all be the best condition for creation.
Introduction,
The Works of Susan Ferrier, *
Vol. 1   *1929*

*See 688.

2 Great imaginations are apt to work from hints and suggestions and a single moment of emotion is sometimes sufficient to create a master-piece.   Ibid.

3 . . . extreme modernity is apt very quickly to become old-fashioned.   Ibid.

4 Noble natures can adapt themselves to any change without loss of dignity; but those who are naturally insignificant make themselves ridiculous by taking refuge in their own sense of self-importance.   Ibid.

1306. Mary Heaton Vorse (1881–1966)

1 "Some folks is born in the world feeling it and knowing it in their hearts that creation don't stop where the sight of the eyes stop, and the thinner the veil is the better, and something in them sickens when the veil gets too thick."
"The Other Room" *McCall's*   *1919*

1307. Mary Webb (1881/83?–1927)

1 It made me gladsome to be getting some education, it being like a big window opening.
Bk. I, Ch. 5, *Precious Bane*   *1924*

2 Saddle your dreams afore you ride 'em.
Ibid., Ch. 6

3 If you stop to be kind, you must swerve often from your path.   Ibid., Bk. II, Ch. 3

1308. Marie Bonaparte (1882–1962)

1 On the one hand, then, in the reproduction functions proper—menstruation, defloration, pregnancy and parturition—woman is biologically doomed to suffer. Nature seems to have no hesitation in administering to her strong doses of pain, and she can do nothing but submit passively to the regimen prescribed. On the other hand, as regards sexual attraction, which is necessary for the act of impregnation, and as regards the erotic pleasure experienced during the act itself, the woman may be on equal footing with the man.

"Passivity, Masochism, and Femininity" (1934), *International Journal of Psycho-Analysis,*
Vol. 16   *1935*

1309. Charlotte Brown (1882–1961)

1 A few of us must be sacrificed perhaps in order to get a step further.
Letter to F. P. Hobgood, Jr.
(19 October 1921), *Black Women in White America,* Gerda Lerner,* ed.
1972

*See 1882.

2 Now that things are turning and many are opening their eyes to what I've tried to do and desiring to have a share in the same, the question in my heart and mind, and God only knows how it hurts, is just what are they going to ask me to submit to as a negro woman to get their interest for there are some men who occupy high places who feel that no negro woman whether she be cook, criminal or principal of a school should ever be addressed as *Mrs.*
Letter Fragment, op. cit.

1310. Susan Glaspell (1882–1948)

1 HENRIETTA. It is through suppression that hells are formed in us.
Sc. 1, *Suppressed Desires*   *1914*

2 MABEL. Why, if it wasn't for psychoanalysis you'd never find out how wonderful your own mind is!   Ibid., Sc. 2

3 We all go through the same things—it's all just a different kind of the same thing!"
"A Jury of Her Peers," *Every Week*
1917

4 Those who were neither mourning nor rejoicing were being kept awake by mourners or rejoicers. All the while, diluted whiskey that could be bought on the quiet was in use for the deadening or the heightening of emotion.
"Government Goat," *The Pictorial Review*   *1919*

5 GRANDMOTHER. Seems nothing draws men together like killing other men.
Act I, *Inheritors*   *1921*

1311. Emma Jung (1882–1955)

1 Neither arrogance nor presumption drives us to the audacity of wanting to be like God—that is, like man; we are not like Eve of old, lured by

the beauty of the fruit of the tree of knowledge, nor does the snake encourage us to enjoy it. No, ere has come to us something like a command; we are confronted with the necessity of biting into this apple, whether we think it good to eat or not, confronted with the fact that the paradise of naturalness and unconsciousness, in which many of us would only too gladly tarry, is gone forever. "On the Nature of Animus" (1931),
Animus and Anima 1957

2 And now we come to the magic of words. A word, also, just like an idea, a thought, has the effect of reality upon undifferentiated minds. Our Biblical myth of creation, for instance, where the world grows out of the spoken word of the Creator, is an expression of this. Ibid.

3 Learning to cherish and emphasize feminine values is the primary condition of our holding our own against the masculine principle. . . . Ibid.

1312. Winifred Letts (1882–?)

1 God rest you, happy gentlemen,
  Who laid your good lives down,
Who took the khaki and the gun
  Instead of cap and gown.
    "The Spires of Oxford," St. 4,
      *The Spires of Oxford and
      Other Poems* 1917

2 I do be thinking God must laugh
The time he makes a boy,
All element the creatures are,
And divilment and joy. "Boys" *n.d.*

1313. Anne O'Hare McCormick (1882?–1954)

1 Whoever goes to Russia discovers Russia,
    Ch. 1, *The Hammer and the Scythe*
      1927

2 There is no place where you can see more human nature in a few hours than in a session of the Parliament of Italy.
    "A Papal Consistory and a Political Debut" (24 July 1921), *Vatican Journal, 1921–1954*, Marion Turner Sheehan, ed. 1957

3 One little angry, brooding man [Hitler] has put the whole world on wartime. A man who could never keep step with anybody has forced millions of free and intelligent human beings to keep the time he sets.
    "Reflections in Time of War" (4 April 1942), op. cit.

1314. Sylvia Pankhurst (1882–1960)

1 English is the most modern of the great languages, the most widely spoken, and the most international. . . . Its swiftness and transparent accuracy of expression, and especially the fact that it has shed most of the old grammatical forms which time has rendered useless and scarcely intelligible, have made English a model, pointing the way which must be followed in building the Interlanguage. . . .
    Ch. 5, *Delphos* 1926

2 I could not give my name to aid the slaughter in this war, fought on both sides for grossly material ends, which did not justify the sacrifice of a single mother's son.
    Ch. 25, *The Home Front* 1932

3 Racked with pain, prostrate with headache, at times I might be, yet within me was a rage at this merciless War, this squalor of poverty! Oh! that all the wealth and effort the nation was squandering might be to rebuild these slums, to restore these faded women, these starved and stunted children. Ibid., Ch. 58

4 I have gone to war too. . . . I am going to fight capitalism even if it kills me. It is wrong that people like you should be comfortable and well fed while all around you people are starving. Courtroom Speech (January 1921), Quoted in *The Fighting Pankhursts**   by David Mitchell 1967

*See Adela, 1339, Christabel, 1291, and Emmeline, 1059, Pankhurst.

5 Love and freedom are vital to the creation and upbringing of a child. I do not advise anyone to rush into either legal or free marriage without love, sympathy, understanding, friendship and frankness. These are essentials, and having these, no legal forms are necessary.
    Article in *News of the World* (April 1928), op. cit.

6 Socialism is the greatest thing in life for me. You will never crush it out of me or kill it. I am only one of thousands or millions. Socialists make it possible to practise what you say in church, that we should love our neighbours as ourselves. If you work against socialism, you are standing with reaction against life, standing with the dead past against the coming civilization. Pt. II, Ch. 4, op. cit.

7 The emancipation of today displays itself mainly in cigarettes and shorts. There is even a reaction from the ideal of an intellectual and emancipated womanhood, for which the pioneers toiled and sufffered, to be seen in painted lips and nails, and the return of trailing skirts and other absur-

dities of dress which betoken the slave-woman's intelligent companionship.

Pt. V, Ch. 3, op. cit.

1315. Frances Perkins (1882–1965)

1 In America, public opinion is the leader.
Sec. I, *People at Work*   1934

2 But with the slow menace of a glacier, depression came on. No one had any measure of its progress; no one had any plan for stopping it. Everyone tried to get out of its way.
Ibid., Sec. IV

3 The quality of his [F. D. Roosevelt]* being one with the people, of having no artificial or natural barriers between him and them, made it possible for him to be a leader without ever being or thinking of being a dictator.
Ch. 7, *The Roosevelt I Knew*   1946

*32nd president of the United States (1933–45).

1316. Gisela Richter (1882–1972)

1 . . . a series of failures may culminate in the best possible result.
My Memoirs: Recollection of an Archaeologist's Life   1972

1317. Mabel Ulrich (1882?–?)

1 It can't be so easy being the husband of a "modern" woman. She is everything his mother wasn't—and nothing she was.
"A Doctor's Diary, 1904–1932,"
Scribner's Magazine   June 1933

2 But, oh, what a woman I should be if an able young man would consecrate his life to me as secretaries and technicians do to their men employers.
Ibid.

3 Verily what bishops are to the English, bankers are to Americans.
Ibid.

1318. Virginia Verona (1882–   )

1 I blame the unions, first, last and all the time. The nation has gotten to the place where unskilled labor is getting paid more than skilled. The unions have gone too far. They rule this country, and they have no compassion, no mercy for people, not even other union members.
Quoted in "Fighting for Her—and Our—Rights" by Ursula Vils,
Los Angeles Times
5 January 1975

2 People are too easygoing. The American people will not stand up for their rights. They'll be violent, of course, but they will not stand up for their rights.
Ibid.

1319. Virginia Woolf (1882–1941)

1 But when the self speaks to the self, who is speaking?—the entombed soul, the spirit driven in, in, in to the central catacomb; the self that took the veil and left the world—a coward perhaps, yet somehow beautiful, as it flits with its lantern restlessly up and down the dark corridors.
"An Unwritten Novel," *Monday or Tuesday*   1921

2 Life's bare as a bone.
Ibid.

3 The older one grows the more one likes indecency.   "The String Quartet," op. cit.

4 In people's eyes, in the swing, tramp, and trudge; in the bellow and uproar; the carriages, motor cars, omnibuses, vans, sandwich men shuffling and swinging; brass bands; barrel organs; in the triumph and the jingle and the strange high singing of some aeroplane overhead was what she loved; life; London; this moment in June.   *Mrs. Dalloway*   1925

5 The word-coining genius, as if thought plunged into a sea of words and came up dripping.
"An Elizabethan Play,"
The Common Reader   1925

6 Those comfortably padded lunatic asylums which are known, euphemistically, as the stately homes of England.   "Lady Dorothy Nevill,"
op. cit.

7 If truth is not to be found on the shelves of the British Museum, where, I asked myself, picking up a notebook and a pencil, is truth?
Ch. 2, *A Room of One's Own*   1929

8 Why are women . . . so much more interesting to men than men are to women?   Ibid.

9 When an arguer argues dispassionately he thinks only of the argument.   Ibid.

10 Women have served all these centuries as looking-glasses possessing the magic and delicious power of reflecting the figure of man at twice its natural size.   Ibid.

11 Indeed, I thought, slipping the silver into my purse, it is remarkable, remembering the bitterness of those days, what a change of temper a fixed income will bring about.   Ibid.

12 Great bodies of people are never responsible for what they do.   Ibid.

13 . . . for fiction, imaginative work that is, is not dropped like a pebble upon the ground, as sci-

ence may be; fiction is like a spider's web, attached ever so lightly perhaps, but still attached to life at all four corners. . . . But when the web is pulled askew, hooked up at the edge, torn in the middle, one remembers that these webs are not spun in midair by incorporeal creatures, but are the work of human beings and are attached to grossly material things, like health and money and the houses we live in.

Ibid., Ch. 3

14 When, however, one reads of a witch being ducked, of a woman possessed by devils, of a wise woman selling herbs, or even a very remarkable man who had a mother, then I think we are on the track of a lost novelist, a suppressed poet . . . indeed, I would venture to guess that Anon, who wrote so many poems without signing them, was often a woman.

Ibid.

15 The history of men's opposition to women's emancipation is more interesting perhaps than the story of that emancipation itself.   *Ibid.*

16 . . . the mind of an artist, in order to achieve the prodigious effort of freeing whole and entire the work that is in him, must be incandescent. . . . There must be no obstacle in it, no foreign matter unconsumed.   *Ibid.*

17 It is fatal to be a man or woman pure and simple; one must be woman-manly or man-womanly.   *Ibid., Ch. 6*

18 His clothes seemed to melt into each other with the perfection of their cut and the quiet harmony of their color. Without a single point of emphasis everything was distinguished. . . . he was the personification of freshness and cleanliness and order.   "Beau Brummell," *The Second Common Reader   1932*

19 I have sometimes dreamt, at least, that when the Day of Judgment dawns and the great conquerors and lawyers and statesmen come to receive their rewards—their crowns, their laurels, their names carved indelibly upon imperishable marble—the Almighty will turn to Peter and will say, not without a certain envy when he sees us coming with our books under our arms, "Look, these need no reward. We have nothing to give them here. They have loved reading."
"How Should One Read a Book?," op. cit.

20 But what have I done with my life? thought Mrs. Ramsay, taking her place at the head of the table, and looking at all the plates making white circles on it.   *To the Lighthouse 1937*

21 If people are highly successful in their professions they lose their senses. Sight goes. They have no time to look at pictures. Sound goes. They have no time to listen to music. Speech goes. They have no time for conversation. They lose their sense of proportion—the relations between one thing and another. Humanity goes. . . .   *Three Guineas   1938*

22 "I will not cease from mental fight," Blake* wrote. Mental fight means thinking against the current, not with it. The current flows fast and furious. It issues a spate of words from the loudspeakers and the politicians. Every day they tell us that we are a free people fighting to defend freedom. That is the current that has whirled the young airman up into the sky and keeps him circulating there among the clouds. Down here, with a roof to cover us and a gas mask handy, it is our business to puncture gas bags and discover the seeds of truth.

Article in the *New Republic 21 October 1940*

*William Blake (1757–1827), English poet and engraver.

23 If you do not tell the truth about yourself you cannot tell it about other people.
The Moment and Other Essays 1952

24 It is worth mentioning, for future reference, that the creative power which bubbles so pleasantly in beginning a new book quiets down after a time, and one goes on more steadily. Doubts creep in. Then one becomes resigned. Determination not to give in, and the sense of an impending shape keep one at it more than anything.   (11 May 1919) *A Writer's Diary* Leonard Woolf, ed.   *1954*

25 I mark Henry James' sentence: observe perpetually. Observe the oncome of age. Observe greed. Observe my own despondency. By that means it becomes serviceable.
Ibid. (8 March 1941)

26 My own brain is to me the most unaccountable of machinery—always buzzing, humming, soaring, roaring, diving, and then buried in mud.   *Letters of Virginia Woolf, Vol. V: (1932–1935)*, Nigel Nicolson, ed.   *1979*

1320. Dorothy Brett (1883–1977)

1 She [Mabel Dodge*] had an insatiable appetite for tasting life in all its aspects. She tasted and spat it out.
"My Long and Beautiful Journey," *South Dakota Review Summer 1967*

*See 1273.

1321. Nannie Helen Burroughs (1883–1961)

1 In fact, America will destroy herself and revert to barbarism if she continues to cultivate the things of the flesh and neglect the higher virtues.   "With All They Getting,"
The Southern Workman
July 1927

2 When the Negro learns what manner of man he is spiritually, he will wake up all over. He will stop playing white even on the stage. He will rise in the majesty of his own soul. He will glorify the beauty of his own brown skin. He will stop thinking white and go to thinking straight and living right. He will realize that wrong-reaching, wrong-bleaching and wrong-mixing have "most nigh ruin't him" and he will redeem his body and rescue his soul from the bondage of that death. . . .   Ibid.

3 Don't wait for deliverers. . . . I like that quotation, "Moses, my servant, is dead. Therefore, arise and go over Jordan." There are no deliverers. They're all dead. We must arise and go over Jordan. We can take the promised land.   Article in *Louisiana Weekly*
23 December 1933

4 The framers of the Declaration of Independence prophesied that uprisings would occur "in the course of human events," if people are denied those inalienable rights to which the "laws of nature and of nature's God entitle them." Reread their prophecy. . . . If that's Red, then the writers of the Declaration of Independence were very Red. They told Americans not to stand injustice after "patient sufferance."
'Declaration of 1776 Is Cause of Harlem Riot," *The Afro-American*
13 April 1935

5 We specialize in the wholly impossible.
Motto, National Training School for Girls, Washington, D.C. (c.1909),
Black Women in White America,
Gerda Lerner,* ed.   *1972*

*See 1882.

1322. Coco Chanel (1883–1971)

1 A fashion for the young? That is a pleonasm: there is no fashion for the old.
Quoted in *Coco Chanel, Her Life, Her Secrets* by Marcel Haedrich   *1971*

2 My friends, there are no friends.   Ibid.

3 Since everything is in our heads, we had better not lose them.   Ibid.

4 "Where should one use perfume?" a young woman asked. "Wherever one wants to be kissed," I said.   Ibid.

5 Fashion is architecture: it is a matter of proportions.   Ibid.

1323. Imogen Cunningham (1883–1976)

1 People who are living aren't famous—they're just infamous.   Quoted in *Never Give Up,*
a Film by Ann Hershey   *1975*

2 One thing about being born without beauty—you don't look for it.   Ibid.

1324. Clementine Hunter (1883?–   )

1 My papa taught me how to pick cotton when I was 8 years old. I didn't mind it. I'd rather pick cotton than to paint.
Quoted in "Clementine Hunter" by Mimi Read, *Dixie Magazine*
14 April 1985

2 Work don't kill nobody. It make you tired though.   Ibid.

1325. Elsa Maxwell (1883–1963)

1 I married the world—the world is my husband. That is why I'm so young. No sex. Sex is the most tiring thing in the world.
"I Married the World," *This Fabulous Century: 1930–1940*   *1940*

2 First I want a woman guest to be beautiful. Second, I want her to be beautifully dressed. Third, I demand animation and vivacity. Fourth, not too many brains. Brains are always awkward at a gay and festive party.
Interview, *New York Mirror*   *1938*

3 Most rich people are the poorest people I know.   Ch. 1, *R.S.V.P.*   *1954*

1326. Frances Newman (1883?–1928)

1 . . . she did not understand how her father could have reached such age and such eminence without learning that all mothers are as infallible as any pope and more righteous than any saint.   *The Hard-Boiled Virgin*   *1926*

1327. Mabel Louise Robinson (1883?–1962)

1 "Can't you have sense?"
Thankful, [the girl] hurried him on. "Not if I can have anything else."
Pt. I, *Bright Island*   *1937*

2 What if the truth does make them sad, what if it haunts them? Better be saddened than dead. "Writing for the Younger Generation,"
The Writer's Book,
Helen Hull, ed. *1950*

1328. Margaret Sanger (1883–1966)

1 Women of the working class, especially wage workers, should not have more than two children at most. The average working man can support no more and the average working woman can take care of no more in decent fashion.
Family Limitations 1917

2 The problem of birth control has arisen directly from the effort of the feminine spirit to free itself from bondage.
Women and the New Race 1920

3 Women are too much inclined to follow in the footsteps of men, to try to think as men think, to try to solve the general problems of life as men solve them. . . . The woman is not needed to do man's work. She is not needed to think man's thoughts. . . . Her mission is not to enhance the masculine spirit, but to express the feminine; hers is not to preserve a man-made world, but to create a human world by the infusion of the feminine element into all of its activities. Ibid.

4 Diplomats make it their business to conceal the facts. . . . Ibid.

5 Upon women the burden and the horrors of war are heaviest. . . . When she sees what lies behind the glory and the horror, the boasting and the burden, and gets the vision, the human perspective, she will end war. She will kill war by the simple process of starving it to death. For she will refuse longer to produce the human food upon which the monster feeds. Ibid.

6 When motherhood becomes the fruit of a deep yearning, not the result of ignorance or accident, its children will become the foundation of a new race. Ibid.

7 Like begets like. We gather perfect fruit from perfect trees. . . . Abused soil brings forth stunted growths. Ibid.

8 Awaken the womanhood of America to free the motherhood of the world!
"Awakening and Revolt,"
My Fight for Birth Control 1931

9 . . . there was not a darkened tenement, hovel, or flat but was brightened by the knowledge that motherhood could be voluntary; that children need not be born into the world unless they are wanted and have a place provided for them.

"A Public Nuisance,"
op. cit.

1329. Marguerite Wilkinson (1883–1928)

1 God bless pawnbrokers!
They are quiet men.
"Pawnbrokers" *n.d.*

2 My father got me strong and straight and slim
And I give thanks to him.
My mother bore me glad and sound and sweet,
I kiss her feet! "The End" *n.d.*

1330. Laura Benét (1884–1979)

1 Lost in the spiral of his conscience, he
Detachedly takes rest. "The Snail,"
n.d.

2 No voice awoke. Dwelling sedate, apart
Only the thrush, the thrush that never spoke,
Sang from her bursting heart. "The Thrush,"
n.d.

1331. Helene Deutsch (1884–1982)

1 They have an extraordinary need of support when engaged in any *activity directed outward,* but are absolutely independent in such feeling and thinking as related to their inner life, that is to say, in their *activity directed inward.* Their capacity for identification is not an expression of inner poverty but of inner wealth.
Vol. I, *The Psychology of Women*
1944–1945

2 After all, the ultimate goal of all research is not objectivity, but truth. Ibid.

3 It is no exaggeration to say that among all living creatures, only man, because of his prehensile appendages, is capable of rape in the full meaning of this term—that is, sexual possession of the female against her will. Ibid., Ch. 6

4 The vagina—a completely passive, receptive organ—awaits an active agent to become a functioning excitable organ. Ibid.

1332. Caroline Giltinan (1884–?)

1 Betrayer of the Master,
He sways against the sky,
A black and broken body,
Iscariot—or I? "Identity" *n.d.*

2 Let me keep my eyes on yours;
I dare not look away
Fearing again to see your feet
Cloven and of clay. "Disillusioned" *n.d.*

1333. Texas Guinan (1884–1933)

1 Fifty million Frenchmen can be wrong.
Quoted in the
New York World-Telegram
21 March 1931

2 I've been married once on the level, and twice in America. Nightclub Act *n.d.*

3 Success has killed more men than bullets.
Ibid.

1334. Rose Henniker Heaton (1884–?)

1 She left no little things behind
Except loving thoughts and kind.
"The Perfect Guest" *n.d.*

1335. Edith Summers Kelley (1884–1956)

1 . . . the barnyard was an expression of something that was real, vital, and fluid, that . . . was of natural and spontaneous growth, that . . . turned with its surroundings, that . . . was a part of the life that offered itself to her. *Weeds* *1923*

1336. Fanny Heaslip Lea (1884–1955)

1 It's odd to think we might have been
Sun, moon and stars unto each other—
Only, I turned down one little street
As you went up another. "Fate," St. 5
n.d.

1337. Alice Roosevelt Longworth (1884–1980)

1 He [Coolidge*] looks as if he had been weaned on a pickle. *Crowded Hours* *1934*

*Calvin Coolidge (1872–1933), 30th president of the United States (1923–29).

2 I have a simple philosophy. Fill what's empty. Empty what's full. And scratch where it itches. Quoted in *The Best* by Peter Russell and Leonard Ross *1974*

1338. Mountain Wolf Woman (1881–1960)

1 I cried as loud as I could and cried as much as I wanted to. That is the way I cried. Then when I got enough crying, I stopped crying. When I stopped crying my anxiety seemed to be re-lieved. Then, after I cried it out, this pain in my heart, I felt better.
Mountain Wolf Woman, Sister of Thunder,
Nancy Oestreich Lurie, ed.
1961

2 I do not know why, but whatever the white people say, that is the way it has to be. I guess it must be that way. Ibid.

1339. Adela Pankhurst (1884?–?)

1 We have no religious doctrine to preach, only a morality that is big enough to include all religions and that should give offence to none.
Quoted in *The Fighting Pankhursts**
by David Mitchell *1967*

*Also see Christabel, 1291, Emmeline, 1059, and Sylvia, 1314, Pankhurst.

2 Profits and prostitution—upon these empires are built and kingdoms stand. . . .
"Communism and Social Purity," *Deadnought,* London (February 1921), op. cit

3 Their [politicians'] most outstanding characteristic, I should say, would be their inability to manage anything properly. What industry have they ever promoted but the gambling industry? What have they ever produced but strife and deficits? What resolve have they shown but a determination to grab for themselves, their friends and supporters whatever is available to grab?
Speech (c. 1929), op. cit.

4 Capital and labour in alliance will require neither government control nor political interference, and the vast network of government which is impoverishing us today will become useless and will shrivel up and die away. Ibid.

1340. Ruth Mason Rice (1884–1927)

1 An oval, placid woman who assuaged men's lives;
Her comely hands wrought forth a century
Of oval, placid women who engaged, as wives,
In broideries and tea.
"Queen Victoria," *Afterward* *1927*

2 Where are you going, multitude of feet?
"New York," op. cit.

1341. Eleanor Roosevelt (1884–1962)

1 No one can make you feel inferior without your consent. *This Is My Story* *1937*

2 A democratic form of government, a democratic way of life, presupposes free public education

over a long period; it presupposes also an education for personal responsibility that too often is neglected.
"Let Us Have Faith in Democracy,"
Land Policy Review, Department of
Agriculture *January 1942*

3 We must be willing to learn the lesson that cooperation may imply compromise, but if it brings a world advance it is a gain for each individual nation.
"My Day" Newspaper Column
21 January 1946

4 None of us has lived up to the teachings of Christ. *14 February 1946,* op. cit.

5 It is not fair to ask of others what you are not willing to do yourself. *15 June 1946,* op. cit.

6 . . . a trait no other nation seems to possess in quite the same degree that we do—namely, a feeling of almost childish injury and resentment unless the world as a whole recognizes how innocent we are of anything but the most generous and harmless intentions.
"My Day" Newspaper Column
11 November 1946

7 It is very difficult to have a free, fair and honest press anywhere in the world. In the first place, as a rule, papers are largely supported by advertising, and that immediately gives the advertisers a certain hold over the medium which they use. *If You Ask Me 1946*

8 Franklin* had a good way of simplifying things. He made people feel that he had a real understanding of things they felt they had about the same understanding. Interview in *PM*
6 April 1947

*Franklin Delano Roosevelt (1882–1945), 32nd president of the United States (1933–45), her husband.

9 Justice cannot be for one side alone, but must be for both. . . . .
"My Day" Newspaper Column
15 October 1947

10 . . . certain rights can never be granted to the government, but must be kept in the hands of the people. Quoted in *The New York Times*
3 May 1948

11 A society in which everyone works is not necessarily a free society and may indeed be a slave society; on the other hand, a society in which there is widespread economic insecurity can turn freedom into a barren and vapid right for millions of people. Speech, "The Struggle for Human Rights," Paris
27 September 1948

12 For it isn't enough to talk about peace. One must believe in it. And it isn't enough to believe in it. One must work at it.
Broadcast, Voice of America
11 November 1951

13 Too often the great decisions are originated and given form in bodies made up wholly of men, or so completely dominated by them that whatever of special value women have to offer is shunted aside without expression.
Speech, United Nations
December 1952

14 As for accomplishments, I just did what I had to do as things came along.
Quoted in *The New York Times*
8 October 1954

15 A mature person is one who does not think only in absolutes, who is able to be objective even when deeply stirred emotionally, who has learned that there is both good and bad in all people and in all things, and who walks humbly and deals charitably with the circumstances of life, knowing that in this world no one is all-knowing and therefore all of us need both love and charity. *It Seems to Me 1954*

16 Could we have the vision of doing away in this great country with poverty? . . . what can make us not only the nation that has some of the richest people in the world, but the nation where there are no people that have to live at a substandard level. That would be one of the very best arguments against Communism that we could possibly have.
Speech, Democratic National
Convention *13 August 1956*

17 I have always felt that anyone who wanted an election so much that they would use those* methods did not have the character that I really admired in public life.
"Meet the Press," NBC-TV
16 September 1956

*Referring to Richard Nixon's smear campaign against Helen Gahagan Douglas; see 1545.

18 Where, after all, do universal human rights begin? In small places, close to home—so close and so small that they cannot be seen on any maps of the world. Yet they *are* the world of the individual persons; the neighborhood he lives in; the school or college he attends; the factory, farm or office where he works. Such are the places where every man, woman and child seeks equal justice, equal opportunity, equal dignity without discrimination. Unless these rights have meaning there, they have little meaning anywhere. Without concerned citizen action to uphold them close to home, we shall look in vain for progress in the larger world.
Speech, "The Great Question,"
United Nations *1958*

19 You can't move so fast that you try to change the mores faster than people can accept it. That

doesn't mean you do nothing, but it means that you do the things that need to be done according to priority. *On My Own*
1958

20 We cannot exist as a little island of well-being in a world where two-thirds of the people go to bed hungry every night.
Speech, Democratic Fund-Raising Dinner *8 December 1959*

21 We have to face the fact that either all of us are going to die together or we are going to learn to live together and if we are to live together we have to talk.
Quoted by A. David Gurewitsch in *The New York Times* *15 October 1960*

22 Everybody wants something.
Interview with Maureen Corr *1960*

23 You gain strength, courage, and confidence by every experience in which you really stop to look fear in the face.
"You Learn by Living" *1960*

24 You must do the thing you think you cannot do. Ibid.

25 . . . I could not, at any age, be content to take my place in a corner by the fireside and simply look on. Life was meant to be lived. Curiosity must be kept alive. The fatal thing is the rejection. One must never, for whatever reason, turn his back on life.
Quoted by Emma Bugbee in the *New York Herald Tribune* *11 October 1961*

26 They [Israelis] are still dreamers, but they make their dreams come true. . . .
Quoted by Ruth G. Michaels in *Hadassah* *December 1962*

27 This I know. This I believe with all my heart. If we want a free and peaceful world, if we want to make the deserts bloom and man grow to greater dignity as a human being—*we can do it!* *Tomorrow Is Now* *1963*

28 I cannot believe that war is the best solution. No one won the last war, and no one will win the next war. Letter to Harry S. Truman* (22 March 1948), Quoted in *Eleanor: The Years Alone* by Joseph P. Lash *1972*

*33rd president of the United States (1945–53).

29 We need our heroes*. . . .
Letter to Joseph Lash (21 January 1952), op. cit.

*Referring to General Dwight D. Eisenhower (1890–1969), 34th president of the United States (1954–61).

30 The Jews in their own country are doing marvels and should, once the refugee problem is settled, help all the Arab countries.
Letter to Maude Gray (5 March 1952), op. cit.

31 Television has completely revolutionized what should go on at a convention.
Letter to Frank E. McKinney (13 July 1952), op. cit.

32 It isn't within my hands to resign or not to resign. Each of us does that automatically. . . . Letter to Bernard Baruch* (18 November 1952), op. cit.

*American stockbroker and economic and political adviser (1870–1965).

33 It is always hard to tell people that it is the causes of war which bring about such things as Hiroshima, and that we must try to eliminate these causes because if there is another Pearl Harbor there will be undoubtedly another Hiroshima. Letter to John Golden (12 June 1953), op. cit.

34 I believe that it is essential to our leadership in the world and to the development of true democracy in our country to have no discrimination in our country whatsoever. This is most important in the schools of our country.
Letter to Richard Bolling (20 January 1956), op. cit.

35 I doubt if Eisenhower can stand a second term and I doubt if the country can stand Nixon as President. Letter to Lord Elibank (20 January 1956), op. cit.

36 It seems to me . . . we have reached a place where it is not a question of "can we live in the same world and cooperate" but "we must live in the same world and learn to cooperate." Letter to Queen Juliana* of the Netherlands (14 February 1958), op. cit.

*See 1703.

37 I cannot, of course, ever feel safe . . . because with Mr. Nixon* I always have the feeling that he will pull some trick at the last minute.
Letter to John F. Kennedy** (27 August 1960), op. cit.

*Richard M. Nixon (1913–), 37th president of the United States (1969–74); resigned.
**(1917–1963), 35th president of the United States (1961–63); assassinated.

38 You seem to think that everyone can save money if they have the character to do it. As a matter

of fact, there are innumerable people who have a wide choice between saving and giving their children the best possible opportunities. The decision is usually in favor of the children.
Letter to Franklin Roosevelt III
(15 January 1962), op. cit.

1342. Florida Scott-Maxwell (1884–)

1 Age puzzles me. I thought it was a quiet time. My seventies were interesting and fairly serene, but my eighties are passionate. I grow more intense as I age.   *The Measure of My Days*
1972

2 No matter how old a mother is she watches her middle-aged children for signs of improvement.   Ibid.

3 I wonder why love is so often equated with joy when it is everything else as well. Devastation, balm, obsession, granting and receiving excessive value, and losing it again. It is recognition, often of what you are not but might be. It sears and it heals. It is beyond pity and above law. It can seem like truth.   Ibid.

4 Is life a pregnancy? That would make death a birth.   Ibid.

5 We who are old know that age is more than a disability. It is an intense and varied experience, almost beyond our capacity at times, but something to be carried high. If it is a long defeat it is also a victory . . .   Ibid.

6 When a new disability arrives I look about me to see if death has come, and I call quietly, "Death, is that you? Are you there?" So far the disability has answered, "Don't be silly, it's me."   Ibid.

7 You need only claim the events of your life to make yourself yours. When you truly possess all you have been and done, which may take some time, you are fierce with reality.
Quoted in *The Finishing School*
by Gail Godwin*   *1984*

*See 2217.

1343. Sara Teasdale (1884–1933)

1 My soul is a broken field
Ploughed by pain.
"The Broken Field"   *n.d.*

2 No one worth possessing
Can be quite possessed.
"Advice to a Girl"   *n.d.*

3 Spend all you have for loveliness.   "Barter"
n.d.

4 Then, like an old-time orator
Impressively he rose;
"I make the most of all that comes
And the least of all that goes."
"The Philosopher," St. 4
n.d.

5 When I can look Life in the eyes,
Grown calm and very coldly wise,
Life will have given me the Truth,
And taken in exchange—my youth.
"Wisdom"
n.d.

1344. Sophie Tucker (1884–1966)

1 From birth to age eighteen, a girl needs good parents. From eighteen to thirty-five, she needs good looks. From thirty-five to fifty-five, she needs a good personality. From fifty-five on, she needs good cash.   Attributed   *1953*

2 Keep breathing.   Anniversary Speech
13 January 1964

1345. Sophie Tunnell (1884–?)

1 Fear is a slinking cat I find
Beneath the lilacs of my mind.   "Fear"
n.d.

1346. Anna Wickham (1884–1947)

1 I desire Virtue, though I love her not—
I have no faith in her when she is got:
I fear that she will bind and make me slave
And send me songless to the sullen grave.
"Self-Analysis," St. 3,
The Contemplative Quarry   *1915*

2 I smother in the house in the valley below,
Let me out to the night, let me go!
"Divorce," *The World Split Open*,
Louise Bernikow,* ed.   *1974*

*See 2289.

3 Alas! For all the pretty women who marry dull men,
Go into the suburbs and never come out again.   "Meditation at Kew"   *n.d.*

4 Desire and longing are the whips of God.
"Sehnsucht"   *n.d.*

1347. Helen M. Cam (1885–1968)

1 We must not read either law or history backwards.   Introduction to *Selected Essays of F. W. Maitland*, H. D. Hazeltine, G. Gapsley, P. H. Winfield, eds.
1936

2 If civilisation is the art of living together with people not entirely like oneself, the first step in civilisation is not so much the invention of material tools as the regularisation of social habits. As soon as you begin to say "We always do things this way" the foundations are laid. "Custom is before all law." As soon as you begin to say "We have always done things this way—perhaps *that* might be a better way," conscious law-making is beginning. As soon as you begin to say "*We* do things this way—*they* do things that way—what is to be done about it?" men are beginning to feel towards justice, that resides between the endless jar of right and wrong.   Lecture, "Law as It Looks to a Historian," Gurton College *18 February 1956*

3 Historical fiction is not only a respectable literary form: it is a standing reminder of the fact that history is about human beings.
Historical Novel   1961

4 . . . every historian knows that belief itself is a historical fact, and that legend and myth cannot be left out of account in tracing the sequence of cause and effect.
Lecture, "Magna Carta—Event or Document?," Old Hall of Lincoln's Inn   *7 July 1967*

1348. Gladys Cromwell (1885–1919)

1 Sorrow can wait,
For there is magic in the calm estate
Of grief; lo, where the dust complies
Wisdom lies.   "Folded Power"   *n.d.*

1349. Isak Dinesen (1885–1962)

1 "What is man, when you come to think upon him, but a minutely set, ingenious machine for turning, with infinite artfulness, the red wine of Shiraz* into urine?"   *Seven Gothic Tales 1934*

*City in Iran famous for its wine.

2 Woman. I understand the word itself, in that sense, has gone out of the language. Where we talk of woman . . . you talk of women, and all the difference lies therein. . . .
"The Old Chevalier," op. cit.

3 I do not know if you remember the tale of the girl who saves the ship under mutiny by sitting on the power barrel with her lighted torch . . . and all the time knowing that it is empty? This has seemed to me a charming image of the women of my time. There they were, keeping the world in order . . . by sitting on the mystery

of life, and knowing themselves that there was no mystery.   Ibid.

4 I have seen a herd of elephants traveling through dense native forest . . . pacing along as if they had an appointment at the end of the world.
Pt. I, Ch. 1, *Out of Africa   1938*

5 The giraffe, in their queer, inimitable, vegetating gracefulness, as if it were not a herd of animals but a family of rare, long-stemmed, speckled gigantic flowers slowly advancing.
Ibid.

6 I have before seen other countries, in the same manner, give themselves to you when you are about to leave them.   Ibid., Pt. V, Ch. 1

7 "But the trouble is not as you think now, that we have put up obstacles too high for you to jump, and how could we possibly do that, you great leaper? It is that we have put up no obstacles at all. The great strength is in you, Lulu, and the obstacles are within you as well, and the thing is, that the fullness of time has not yet come."   Ibid.

1350. Malvina Hoffman (1885–1966)

1 My true center of work was not commissions.
It was an enormous capacity for falling in love with everything around me. . . .
Quoted in "Malvina Hoffman," *Famous American Women* by Hope Stoddard   *1970*

2 . . . at heart we are really working for the angels. . . . What counts is the lasting integrity of the artist and the enduring quality of his work.   Ibid.

1351. Karen Horney (1885–1952)

1 Psychoanalysis is the creation of a male genius, and almost all those who have developed his ideas have been men. It is only right and reasonable that they should evolve more easily a masculine psychology and understand more of the development of men than of women.
"The Flight from Womanhood," *Feminine Psychology   1926*

2 Is not the tremendous strength in men of the impulse to creative work in every field precisely due to their feeling of playing a relatively small part in the creation of living beings, which constantly impels them to an overcompensation in achievement?   Ibid.

3 But miracles occur in psychoanalysis as seldom as anywhere else.   *Self-Analysis   1942*

4 Fortunately [psycho]analysis is not the only way to resolve inner conflicts. Life itself still remains a very effective therapist.
Our Inner Conflicts   *1945*

1352. Frances Parkinson Keyes (1885–1970)

1 "I can't see that the Nazis are any different from the Communists, except that they're cleaner and better looking and better drilled. They're both stirring up trouble, they're both bent on destruction and despotism, they're both ready to go to any lengths to gain their ends!"
Pt. V, Ch. 15,
The Great Tradition
1939

2 Folks with their wits about them knew that advertisements were just a pack of lies—you had only to look at the claims of patent medicines!
Pt. 1, Ch. 3, *Blue Camellia*   *1957*

3 ". . . young folks, them, don' never think 'bout nothin' only spend, spend, spend money, instead of save, save, save money, like us used to do, us. It's education, or either it's clothes, or either it's something else, as long as somebody got to spend, spend, spend. Boys is plenny bad, I got to admit, yes, but girls is even worser."
Ibid., Pt. V, Ch. 22

1353. Marie Laurencin (1885–1956)

1 Why should I paint dead fish, onions and beer glasses? Girls are so much prettier.
Quoted in *Time*   *18 June 1956*

1354. Ettie Lee (1885–1974)

1 Every child has a right to a good home.
Quoted in the *Los Angeles Times*
27 April 1974

1355. Alice Paul (1885–1977)

1 It is better, as far as getting the vote is concerned I believe, to have a small, united group than an immense debating society.
Letter to Eunice R. Oberly
(6 March 1914), Quoted in
*Alice Paul and the National
Woman's Party, 1912–1920*
by Loretta Ellen Zimmerman
1964

2 Equality of rights under the law shall not be denied or abridged by the United States or by any State on account of sex.
Equal Rights Amendment*   *1923*

*The wording of the proposed amendment was likely contributed to by several members of the National Women's Party, of which Paul was founder and president.

1356. Elizabeth Madox Roberts (1885–1941)

1 The wind found out my coat was thin.
It tried to tear my clothes away.
And the cold came in.
"Cold Fear," St. 3, *Under the
Tree*   *1922*

1357. Constance Rourke (1885–1941)

1 Ardent and tired and overwrought, in that sensitive state where the imagination grows fluid, where inner and outer motives coalesce. . . .
The Trumpets of Jubilee   *1927*

2 An emotional man may possess no humour, but a humorous man usually has deep pockets of emotion, sometimes tucked away or forgotten.   Ch. 1, *American Humor*   *1931*

3 It is a mistake to look for the social critic—even Manqué—in Mark Twain. In a sense the whole American comic tradition had been that of social criticism: but this had been instinctive and incomplete, and so it proved to be in Mark Twain. . . . He was primarily a *raconteur*. . . . He was never the conscious artist, always the improvisor.   Ibid., Ch. 7

1358. Marjorie Allen Seiffert (1885–1968)

1 And when I search your soul until
I see too deeply and divine
That you can never love me—Still
I hold you fast for you are mine!
"Possession," St. 3, *A Woman of
Thirty*   *1919*

2 And love is worth what it cost you, nothing more.
"The Horse-Leech's Daughter," *The King
with Three Faces and Other
Poems*   *1929*

3 Lust is the oldest lion of them all.
"An Italian Chest"
n.d.

1359. Clare Sheridan (1885–?)

1 At the end of her days, she became superbly squaw-like, and would sit impassively for hours, staring into the fire, her head shrouded in a

shawl. A figure of great moral fortitude and self-oblation was gradually fading out.
To the Four Winds   1955

1360. Bess Truman (1885–1982)

1 A woman's place in public is to sit beside her husband, be silent, and be sure her hat is on straight.   Quoted in *Bess W. Truman* by Margaret Truman*   1986

*See 1942.

2 I'm not used to this awful public life.
          Comment to Frances Perkins,* Quoted in *First Ladies* by Betty Boyd Caroli   1987

*See 1315.

1361. Elinor Wylie (1885–1928)

1 I was, being human, born alone;
I am, being woman, hard beset;
I live by squeezing from a stone
The little nourishment I get.

In masks outrageous and austere
The years go by in single file;
But none has merited my fear,
And none has quite escaped my smile.
          "Let No Charitable Hope,"
          Sts. 2–3 (1923),
          Collected Poems   1932

2   Honeyed words like bees,
Gilded and sticky, with a little sting.
          "Pretty Words," op. cit.

3 I love smooth words, like gold-enameled fish
Which circle slowly with a silken
     swish. . . .   Ibid.

4 The worst and best are both inclined
To snap like vixens at the truth;
But, O, beware the middle mind
That purrs and never shows a tooth!
          "Nonsense Rhyme," St. 2, op. cit.

1362. Zoë Akins (1886–1958)

1 LADY HELEN. To accuse is so easy that it is infamous to do so where proof is impossible!   Act I, *Déclassé   1919*

2 LADY HELEN. My life is like water that has gone over the dam and turned no mill wheels. Here I am, not happy, but not unhappy, as my days run on to the sea, idly—but not too swiftly—for I love living.   Ibid.

3 MRS. DAHLGREN. Shutting one's eyes is an art, my dear. I suppose there's no use trying to make you see that—but that's the only way one *can* stay married.

          Act, II, *Daddy's Gone A-Hunting*
          1921

4 CANAVA. The success-haters. . . . That's what I call them—the people who have never got what they want and turned sour on everybody who has. The world's full of them. . . . As soon as you've made good they begin to watch for you to fail. . . .   Act I, *Greatness*
          1922

5 RAYMOND. No one can ever help loving anyone.   Ibid., Act III

6 SENTONI. My cousin Cleofante does not believe in inspiration. She shuns the false energy of all stimulants, even those of criticism and sympathy, when she sets herself to a task. What she does, she does alone—unencouraged, unadvised, unmoved.
          The Portrait of Tiero   1924

7 CLEOFANTE. Work alone qualifies us for life, Sentoni.   Ibid.

8 Indifferent to all the fun of chance
I watched black spiders of inertia spin
The far-flung web which I was strangling in.
          "Indifference," St. 1, *The Hills Grow
          Smaller   1937*

9 In all my locked-up songs
No one but you belongs.
          "To H. R.," St. 1, op. cit.

1363. Margaret Ayer Barnes (1886–1967)

1 There they were. Opinions. Jane bumped into them, tangible obstacles in her path, things to be recognized, and accepted or evaded, as the exigencies of the situation demanded.
          Pt. I, Ch. 1, *Years of Grace   1930*

2 Childless women, Olivia reflected, slipped gracefully into middle age. There was no one particular awkward moment when they climbed up on the shelf.   Ch. 1, *Westward Passage*
          1931

3 "There's nothing half so real in life as the things you've done," she whispered. "Inexorably, unalterably *done*."   Ibid., Ch. 4

4 "Character comes before scholarship.
. . ."   Pt. I, Ch. 1
          Within This Present
          1933

1364. Frances Darwin Cornford (1886–?)

1 O fat white woman whom nobody loves,
Why do you walk through the fields in
     gloves?

"To a Fat Lady Seen from the Train,"
n.d.

2 Magnificently unprepared
For the long littleness of life.
"Rupert Brooke"
n.d.

1365. Hilda Doolittle (1886–1961)

1 Egypt had maimed us,
offered dream for life,
an opiate for a kiss,
and death for both. "Egypt,"
n.d.

1366. Florence Kiper Frank (1886?–?)

1 The canny among the publishers know that an
enormous popular appetite for the insulting of
the famous must be gratified, and the modern
biographer emerges from the editorial conference a sadist and a wiser man.
Morrow's Almanac 1929

2 Pooh-Men!
We are done with them now,
Who had need of them then,—
I and you! "Baby"
n.d.

1367. Hazel Hall (1886–1924)

1 *I am the dance of youth, and life is fair!*
Footfall, footfall;
I am a dream, divinely unaware!
Footfall, footfall;
I am the burden of an old despair!
Footfall. "Footsteps" *n.d.*

1368. Radclyffe Hall (1886–1943)

1 Acknowledge us, o God, before the whole world.
Give us also the right to our existence.
The Well of Loneliness 1928

2 "You're neither unnatural, nor abominable, nor
mad; you're as much a part of what people call
nature as anyone else; only you're unexplained
as yet—you've not got your niche in creation." Ibid.

3 They had sought among the ruins of a dead
civilization for the beauty they missed subconsciously in their own.
Ch. 1, *A Saturday Life* 1930

4 But when told that to appear naked in a drawingroom might be considered somewhat odd, since

it was no longer the custom, she had argued
that our bodies were very unimportant, only
there so that people might perceive us. "We
couldn't see each other without them, you know,"
she had said, smiling up at her mother. Ibid.

1369. Elizabeth Kenny (1886–1952)

1 . . . panic plays no part in the training of a
nurse. *And They Shall Walk*, with
Martha Ostenso* 1943

*See 1563.

2 O sleep, O gentle sleep, I thought gratefully,
Nature's gentle nurse! Ibid., Ch. 2

3 I was wholly unprepared for the extraordinary
attitude of the medical world in its readiness to
condemn anything that smacked of reform or
that ran contrary to approved methods of
practice. Ibid., Ch. 6

4 Some minds remain open long enough for the
truth not only to enter but to pass on through
by way of a ready exit without pausing anywhere
along the route. Ibid.

5 My mother used to say, "He who angers you,
conquers you!" But my mother was a saint.
Ibid., Ch. 7

6 His response was remarkable for its irrelevance,
if for nothing else. Ibid.

1370. Frances Marion (1886–1973)

1 This is not dead land, it is only thirsty land.
Pt. II, Ch. 22, *Westward the Dream*
1948

2 "A coin, Mr. Fox, can only fall heads or tails,
and I'll gamble on heads, they last longer."
Off with Their Heads 1972

3 Promises that you make to yourself are often
like the Japanese plum tree—they bear no
fruit. "1914 Through 1924,"
Ibid.

4 We have a little catch phrase in our family which
somehow fits almost everyone in the movie
colony: "Spare no expense to make everything
as economical as possible." Ibid.

5 One thing you learned when you wrote for the
movies: all nationalities were sensitive except
Americans. The Arabs were always to be pic-
tured as sweet, friendly people. so were the
Greeks, the Dutch, Turks, Laps, Eskimoes, and
so on down the line. Everyone was honest and
virtuous, except Americans. You could make
them the most sinister villains and never hear a

word of protest from Washington, Chicago, Kalamazoo, or all points south. But should you describe a villain belonging to any country but America, you found yourself spread-eagled between the Board of Censors and the diplomatic service of some foreign power.
"1925 Through 1928," op. cit.

1371. Mary Wigman (1886–1973)

1 Art is communication spoken by man for humanity in a language raised above the everyday happening. "The New German Dance," *Modern Dance,* Virginia Stewart, ed. *1935*

2 During the process of artistic creation, man descends into the primoridal elements of life. He reverts to himself to become lost in something greater than himself, in the immediate, indivisible essence of life. Ibid.

1372. Anzia Yezierska (1886–1970)

1 "If you have no luck in this world, then it's better not to live." "The Fat of the Land," *The Century* *1919*

2 "The world is a wheel always turning," philosophized Mrs. Pelz. "Those who were high go down low, and those who've been low go up higher." Ibid.

1373. Ruth Benedict (1887–1948)

1 No man ever looks at the world with pristine eyes. He sees it edited by a definite set of customs and institutions and ways of thinking. Ch. 1, *Patterns of Culture* *1934*

2 If we justify war, it is because all peoples always justify the traits of which they find themselves possessed, not because war will bear an objective examination of its merits. Ibid.

3 Racism is the new Calvinism which asserts that one group has the stigmata of superiority and the other has those of inferiority. . . . For racism is an *ism* to which everyone in the world today is exposed; for or against, we must take sides. And the history of the future will differ according to the decision which we make. Ch. 1, *Race: Science and Politics* *1940*

4 Racism in its nationalistic phase, therefore, has been a politician's plaything. . . . It is a dangerous plaything, a sword which can be turned in any direction to condemn the enemy of the moment. Ibid., Ch. 7

5 Everybody repeats the proverbial maxim: "In this world everything changes except good deeds and bad deeds; these follow you as the shadow follows the body." Pt. II, Ch. 5, *Thai Culture and Behavior,* *1943*

6 The Japanese are, to the highest degree, both aggressive and unaggressive, both militaristic and aesthetic, both insolent and polite, rigid and adaptable, submissive and resentful of being pushed around, loyal and treacherous, brave and timid, conservative and hospitable to new ways. Ch. 1, *The Chrysanthemum and the Sword* *1946*

7 I have always used the world of make-believe with a certain desperation. Quoted in *An Anthropologist at Work* by Margaret Mead* *1951*

*See 1576.

8 I long to speak out the intense inspiration that comes to me from the lives of strong women. Ibid. (January 1917)

9 . . . work even when I'm satisfied with it is never my child I love nor my servant I've brought to heel. It's always busy work I do with my left hand, and part of me watches grudging the wastes of a lifetime. Ibid. (9 June 1934)

1374. Elizabeth Drew (1887–1965)

1 But though personality is a skin that no writer can slip, whatever he may write about: though it is a shadow which walks inexorably by his side, so also is the age he lives in. "The Novel and the Age," *The Modern Novel* *1926*

2 The world is not run by thought, nor by imagination, but by opinion. . . . "Sex Simplexes and Complexes," op. cit.

3 The test of literature is, I suppose, whether we ourselves live more intensely for the reading of it. . . . "Is There a 'Feminine' Fiction?", op. cit.

4 How poetry comes to the poet is a mystery. Quoted in "On the Teaching of Poetry" by Leonora Speyer,* *The Saturday Review of Literature* *1946*

*See 1190.

5 We read poetry because the poets, like ourselves, have been haunted by the inescapable tyranny of time and death; have suffered the pain of loss, and the more wearing, continuous pain of frustration and failure; and have had moods of unlooked-for release and peace.

Pt. II, Ch. 7, *Poetry: A Modern Guide to Its Understanding and Enjoyment* *1959*

6 Propaganda has a bad name, but its root meaning is simply to disseminate through a medium, and all writing therefore is propaganda for *something*. It's a seeding of the self in the consciousness of others. Ibid., Ch. 10

1375. Edna Ferber (1887–1968)

1 Roast Beef, Medium, is not only a food. It is a philosophy. Seated at Life's Dining Table, with the menu of Morals before you, your eye wanders a bit over the entrées, the hors d'oeuvres, and the things *à la* though you know that Roast Beef, Medium, is safe and sane, and sure.
Foreword, *Roast Beef, Medium* *1911*

2 From supper to bedtime is twice as long as from breakfast to supper. Ibid., Ch. 1

3 "There are only two kinds of people in the world that really count. One kind's wheat and the other kind's emeralds."
Ch. 1, *So Big* *1924*

4 "Woman's work! Housework's the hardest work in the world. That's why men won't do it."
Ibid., Ch. 8

5 "But 'most any place is Baghdad if you don't know 'what will happen in it." Ibid., Ch. 10

6 "Any piece of furniture, I don't care how beautiful it is, has got to be lived with, kicked about, and rubbed down, and mistreated by servants, and repolished, and knocked around and dusted and sat on or slept in or eaten off of before it develops its real character," Salina said. "A good deal like human beings." Ibid., Ch. 15

7 . . . the Negroes whose black faces dotted the boards of the Southern wharves as thickly as grace notes sprinkle a bar of lively music.
Ch. 2 *Show Boat* *1926*

8 Wasn't marriage, like life, unstimulating and unprofitable and somewhat empty when too well ordered and protected and guarded. Wasn't it finer, more splendid, more nourishing, when it was, like life itself, a mixture of the sordid and the magnificent; of mud and stars; of earth and flowers; of love and hate and laughter and tears and ugliness and beauty and hurt?
Ibid., Ch. 19

9 It had no definite expression. It was not in their bearing; it could not be said to look out from the dead, black, Indian eye, nor was it anywhere about the immobile, parchment face. Yet somewhere black implacable resentment smoldered in the heart of this dying race.
Ch. 3, *Cimarron* *1929*

10 "If American politics are too dirty for women to take part in, there's something wrong with American politics." Ibid., Ch. 23

11 "I am not belittling the brave pioneer men, but the sunbonnet as well as the sombrero has helped to settle this glorious land of ours." Ibid.

12 "You lose in the end unless you know how the wheel is fixed or can fix it yourself."
Ch. 14, *Saratoga Trunk* *1941*

13 It was part of the Texas ritual. We're rich as son-of-a-bitch stew but look how homely we are, just as plain-folksy as Grandpappy back in 1836. We know about champagne and caviar but we talk hog and hominy.
Ch. 2, *Giant* *1952*

1376. Florence Luscomb (1887–   )

1 . . . there is no end to what you can accomplish if you don't care who gets the credit.
Quoted in *Moving the Mountain* by Ellen Cantarow *1980*

2 The tragedy in the lives of most of us is that we go through life walking down a high-walled land with people of our own kind, the same economic situation, the same national background and education and religious outlook. And beyond those walls, all humanity lies, unknown and unseen, and untouched by our restricted and impoverished lives. Oral History Project, University of Rhode Island (1972/1973), op. cit.

3 And when women are working side by side with them on all the great public issues, and carrying on the life of humanity, I think that men are going to get comradeship that only the really advanced men have now. And when we have amended the Declaration of Independence so that it reads, "All men and women are created equal," this new force of men and women will be able to go forward and create a society of peace and of social justice and of beauty we haven't ever known in this world. Ibid.

4 I have come face-to-face with the question, "Is America still a democracy? Is it ruled by the people, by their votes?" and I have been forced to answer, "No." Behind the screen of the ballot, the real holders of power who decide national policies and laws, and control public opinion by their ownership of all the mass media of information are the great industrial and monetary monopolies who own our national economic life. They, together with the armed forces—the military industrial complex—are the real rulers of our country today. Ibid.

5 Capitalism, by definition, sets money as the sole model of power which keeps us running. Every man for himself. From my lifetime experiences, I have reached the firm conviction that the only possible basis for a successful, just, and peaceful world society is a cooperative economy of production for human needs, not for individual profits. That is the basic principle of communism.　　　　　　　　　　　　　　Ibid.

6 It is subversive to set up inquisitions like this, state or national, into the thoughts and consciences of Americans. . . . It is subversive for commissions like this to spread such hysteria and intimidation throughout the land that Americans are afraid to sign petitions, afraid to read progressive magazines, afraid to make out checks for liberal causes, afraid to join organizations, afraid to speak their minds on public issues. Americans dare not be free citizens! This is the destruction of democracy.
　　　　　　　　Statement to Commission to
　　　　Investigate Communism in Massachusetts
　　　　　　　　(7 January 1955), op. cit.

1377. Agnes Meyer (1887–1970?)

1 When you travel through the wheat fields of Kansas for a day and a night and see endless herds grazing on the pastureland, when you have spent weeks visiting factory after factory in city after city producing at top speed, when you have seen the tireless effort, the intelligent application of management and labor and their ever-increasing co-operation, you realize that there are enough resources, actual and potential, enough brains and good will in this country to turn the whole world into a paradise.
　　　　　　　　"Juvenile Delinquency and Child
　　　　　　　Labor," *Washington Post*
　　　　　　　　　14 March 1943

2 What the Nation must realize is that the home, when both parents work, is non-existent. Once we have honestly faced the fact, we must act accordingly.　　　　"Living Conditions of the
　　　　　　　Woolworker," *10 April 1943*
　　　　　　　　　　op. cit.

3 An orderly existence creates primarily an unconscious relation to the silent progression of the days, seasons, and the music of the spheres.
　　　　　　　　Out of These Roots　　1953

4 In the pursuit of an educational program to suit the bright and the not-so-bright we have watered down a rigid training for the elite until we now have an educational diet in many of our public high schools that nourishes neither the classes nor the masses.　　　　　　　Ibid., Ch. 2

5 Let us hope that in the process of integration in our society, which fortunately is now well underway, the Negro will not allow the American steam roller of conformity to destroy his creative gifts.　　　　　　　　　　　Ibid., Ch. 8

6 The children are always the chief victim of social chaos.　　　　　　　　Ibid., Ch. 13

7 There is a need for heroism in American life today.　　Ch. 1, *Education for a New Morality*
　　　　　　　　　　　　　　　1957

1378. Marianne Moore (1887–1972)

1 I, too, dislike it: there are things that are important beyond all this fiddle.
　　　　"Poetry," *Collected Poems*　　1935

2 I wonder what Adam and Eve
　think of it by this time.　"Marriage," op. cit.

3 My father used to say,
　"Superior people never make long visits,
　Have to be shown Longfellow's* grave
　or the glass flowers at Harvard."
　　　　　　　　"Silence," op. cit.

*Henry Wadsworth Longfellow, American poet (1807–82).

4　What is our innocence,
　what is our guilt? All are
　naked, none is safe.
　　　　　　"What Are Years?," St. 1,
　　　　　　　Collected Poems　　1941

5　Among animals, one has a sense of humor.
　Humor saves a few steps, it saves years.
　　　　　　　"The Pangolin," St. 1,
　　　　　　　　　op. cit.

6　As contagion
　of sickness make sickness,
　contagion of trust can make trust.
　　　　　　"In Distrust of Merits," St. 2,
　　　　　　　Collected Poems　　1944

7 [The] whirlwind fife-and-drum of the storm
　bends the salt
　marsh grass, disturbs stars in the sky and
　the star on the steeple; it is a privilege to
　see so much confusion.
　　　　　　　"The Steeple-Jack,"
　　　　　　　Collected Poems　　1951

8　O to be a dragon
　a symbol of the power of Heaven—of
　silkworm
　size or immense; at times invisible.
　Felicitous phenomenon!
　　　　　　　"O to Be a Dragon"　　1959

9 To wear the arctic fox
　you have to kill it.
　　　　　　"The Arctic Fox (Or Goat)"　1959

1379. Georgia O'Keeffe (1887–1986)

1 Those hills! They go on and on—it was like looking at two miles of gray elephants.

Quoted in *Time*
12 October 1970

2 . . . nobody sees a flower—really—it is so small—we haven't time—and to see takes time like to have a friend takes time. If I could paint the flower exactly as I see it no one would see what I see because I would paint it small like the flower is small. So I said to myself—I'll paint what I see—what the flower is to me but I'll paint it big and they will be surprised into taking time to look at it—I will make even busy New Yorkers take time to see what I see of flowers. . . . Well, I made you take time to look at what I saw and when you took time to really notice my flower you hung all your own associations with flowers on my flower and you write about my flower as if I think and see what you think and see of the flower—and I don't.
(c.1939) Quoted in *Georgia O'Keeffe* by Lloyd Goodrich and Doris Bry   1970

3 The desert is the last place you can see all around you. The light out here makes everything close, and it is never, never the same. Sometimes the light hits the mountains from behind and front at the same time, and it gives them the look of Japanese prints, you know, distances in layers.   Quoted in "A Visit with Georgia O'Keeffe" by Beth Coffelt, *San Francisco Examiner & Chronicle* 11 April 1971

4 Where I was born, and where and how I lived is unimportant. It is what I have done and where I have been that should be of interest.
Georgia O'Keeffe   1985

5 My first memory is of the brightness of light, light all around.   Ibid.

1380. Rebecca Shelley (1887–?)

1 Humanity above all nations!
"Bicentennial Prayer for Peace"   1976

1381. Edith Sitwell (1887–1964)

1 Daisy and Lily
Lazy and silly. . . .
"Facade" (1922), *Facade and Other Poems 1920–1935*   1950

2 But a word stung him like a mosquito. . . .
"I do like to be beside the Seaside" (1922), op. cit.

3 Alas, that he who caught and sang the sun in flight, yet was the sun's brother, and never grieved it on its way, should have left us with no good-by, good night.

"Dylan Thomas," *Atlantic Monthly* February 1954

4 After the first death, there is no other. . . .
Ibid.

5 I'm not the man to baulk at a low smell,
I'm not the man to insist on asphodel.
This sounds like a He-fellow, don't you think?
It sounds like that. I belch, I bawl, I drink.   "One-Way Song," *Collected Poems* 1954

6 Jane, Jane
Tall as a crane,
The morning light creaks down again.
"Aubade," op. cit.

7 A lady asked me why, on most occasions, I wore black. "Are you in mourning?"
"Yes."
"For whom are you in mourning?"
"For the world."
Ch. 1, *Taken Care Of*   1965

8 At last the day drifted into a long lacquered afternoon.   Ibid., Ch. 13

9 MR. MUGGLEBY LION. I hate to disturb you, but I have just finished a *Little Sonnet*, that I *must* read to you.

HIERATIC WOMAN (coldly). It can't be a *Little* Sonnet, Mr. Muggleby Lion. Sonnets are all of the same size.   Ibid.

10 Rhythm is one of the principal translators between dream and reality. Rhythm might be described, as to the world of sound, what light is to the world of sight. It shares and gives new meaning. Rhythm was described by Schopenhauer as melody deprived of its pitch.
Ibid., Ch. 14

11 . . . the heartless stupidity of those who have never known a great and terrifying poverty.
Ibid., Ch. 22

12 When we think of cruelty, we must try to remember the stupidity, the envy, the frustration from which it has arisen.   Ibid.

13 Remember only this of our hopeless love
That never till time is done
Will the fire of the heart and the fire of the mind be one.   "Heart and Mind"   n.d.

1382. Vicki Baum (1888–1960)

1 Fame always brings loneliness. Success is as ice cold and lonely as the north pole.
Grand Hotel   1931

2 Marriage always demands the greatest understanding of the art of insincerity possible be-

tween two human beings.   *And Life Goes On*
                                                    1932

3 To be a Jew is a destiny.   Ibid.

1383. Marjorie Bowen (1888–1952)

1   "But will it last?"
       "What a ridiculous question," returned the
colonel blandly. "Will you, or I, or anything
last? Flesh is grass, my dear Count."
                           Ch. 1, *General Crack*   *1928*

2   "If you live in the world you must live on the
world's terms."   Ibid., Ch. 10

3   "If you can't command your own soul, how
can I give you enlightenment how to do
so?"   Ibid.

4   "What is the most dangerous possession in
the world, Mr. Falkland?"
       "No use at riddles," replied the young man
cautiously.
       Dobree picked up the speaking-tube.
       "Someone   else's   secret,"   he
remarked. . . .
                   Ch. 2, *The Shadow on Mockways*
                                                    1932

5   . . . she was cured of love as she was cured of
drunkenness. Indulgence had soon brought her
to a point of nausea; she had never given anyone
tenderness or affection, and the recollection of
dead passions that had ended in disgust or rage
was like the recollection of the stench of
decay.   *Moss Rose*   *1935*

6   As civilisation advanced, people began to discover that more was to be gained by flattery
than by force—and that flattery had a larger
purchasing power than coin of the realm.
                              "The Art of Flattery,"
                              World's Wonder   *1937*

7   "Leave well alone, my dear Miss Lawne."
       "But perhaps we are leaving evil alone,"
replied the lady, smiling.
       "In that case, also, have nothing to do with
it."   Ch. 1, *Mignonette*   *1948*

1384. Edith Evans (1888–1976)

1   When a woman behaves like a man, why doesn't
she behave like a nice man?
                   Quoted in "Sayings of the Week,"
                   Observer   *30 September 1956*

1385. M. Esther Harding (1888–1971)

1   The chief characteristic of the goddess in her
crescent phase is that she is a virgin. Her instinct

is not used to capture or possess the man whom
she attracts. . . . Her divine power does not
depend on her relation to a husband-god, and
thus her actions are not dependent on the need
to conciliate such a one or to accord with his
qualities and attitudes. For she bears her divinity
in her own right.
       In the same way the woman who is virgin,
one-in-herself, does what she does—not because
of any desire to please, not to be liked, or to be
approved, even by herself; not because of any
desire to gain power over another, to catch his
interest or love, but because what she does is
true.   *Woman's Mysteries*   *1935*

1386. Aline Murray Kilmer (1888–1941)

1   I'm sorry you are wiser,
       I'm sorry you are taller;
    I liked you better foolish,
       And I liked you better smaller.
                   "For the Birth of a Middle-Aged
                                           Child," St. 1

2   I cannot see myself as I once was;
       I would not see myself as I am now.
                           "To Aphrodite: With a Mirror"
                                                    n.d.

3   I sing of little loves that glow
       Like tapers shining in the rain,
    Of little loves that break themselves
       Like moths against the window-pane.
                           "Prelude"   *n.d.*

1387. Olga Knopf (1888–   )

1   The art of being a woman can never consist of
being a bad imitation of a man.
                   The Art of Being a Woman   *1932*

2   The outer limitations to woman's progress are
caused by the fact we are living in a man's
culture.   *Woman on Their Own*   *1935*

1388. Clare Kummer (1888–1948)

1   STEIN. It's the public. You can't count on it.
Give 'em something good and they'll go to see
something bad. Give 'em something bad and
they don't like that either.
                   Act I, Sc. 1, *Rollo's Wild Oat*
                                                    1922

2   AUNT MIN. He should have started worrying
before he had things to worry about.
                   Act I, *Her Master's Voice*   *1933*

3   Oh, there was a woman-hater hated women all
he could,

And he built himself a bungle in a dingle in
the wood;
Here he lived and said of ladies things I do not
think he should,
"If they're good they're not good-looking; if
good-looking, they're not good.
"In the Dingle-Dongle Bell"   *n.d.*

1389. Lotte Lehmann (1888–1976)

1 But to me the actual sound of the words is all-
important; I feel always that the words complete
the music and must never be swallowed up in
it. The music is the shining path over which the
poet travels to bring his song to the world.
"The Singing Actor," *Players at
Work*, Morton Eustis, ed.   *1937*

2 Do not become paralyzed and enchained by the
set patterns which have been woven of old. No,
build from your own youthful feeling, your own
groping thought and your own flowering perception—and help to further that beauty which
has grown from the roots of tradition. . . .
Introduction, *More Than Singing
1945*

3 For what mission can be greater than that of
giving to the world hours of exaltation in which
it may forget the misery of the present, the cares
of everyday life and lose itself in the eternally
pure world of harmony. . . .   Ibid.

1390. Anita Loos (1888–1981)

1 "I really think that American gentlemen are the
best after all, because . . . kissing your hand
may make you feel very, very good, but a
diamond and sapphire bracelet lasts
forever."   Ch. 4, *Gentlemen Prefer Blondes
1925*

2 So this gentlemen said, "A girl with brains
ought to do something else with them besides
think."   Ibid.

3 . . . I always say that a girl never really looks
as well as she does on board a steamship, or
even a yacht.   Ibid.

4 JUDGE. Always go to a solitary drinker for the
truth!   Act I, *Happy Birthday*   *1947*

5 ADDIE. Why, Benjamin Franklin says a man
without a woman is like a half a pair of
scissors.   Ibid., Act II

6 So after a Star has received five or six million
of those Fan letters, you begin to realize you
must be wonderful without having to read all
those monitinous [sic] letters.
Ch. 1, *A Mouse Is Born*   *1951*

7 So I am beginning to wonder if maybe girls
wouldn't be happier if we stopped demanding
so much respeckt for ourselves and developped
[sic] a little more respeckt for husbands.
Ibid., Ch. 19

8 . . . memory is more .lelible than ink.
Ch. 1, *Kiss Hollywood Goodby
1974*

9 That our popular art forms become so obsessed
with sex has turned the U.S.A. into a nation of
hobbledehoys; as if grown people don't have
more vital concerns, such as taxes, inflation,
dirty politics, earning a living, getting an education, or keeping out of jail. It's true that the
French have a certain obsession with sex, but
it's a particularly adult obsession. France is the
thriftiest of all nations; to a Frenchman sex
provides the most economical way to have fun.
The French are a logical race.   Ibid., Ch. 21

1391. Katherine Mansfield (1888–1923)

1 How idiotic civilization is! Why be given a body
if you have to keep it shut up in a case like a
rare, rare fiddle?
"Bliss," *Bliss and Other Stories
1920*

2 ". . . Why! Why! Why is the middle-class
so stodgy—so utterly without a sense of
humour!"   Ibid.

3 Hundreds, yes, literally hundreds, had come out
in a single night; the green bushes bowed down
as though they had been visited by archangels.   "The Garden Party"   *1922*

4 How on earth could he have slaved, denied
himself, kept going all those years without the
promise for ever before him of the boy's stepping into his shoes carrying on where he left
off?   "The Fly," *The Dove's Nest*   *1923*

5 It is as though God opened his hand and let you
dance on it a little, and then shut it . . . so
tight that you could not even cry.
(February 1914) *The Journal of Katherine
Mansfield*   *1927*

6 There is no limit to human suffering. When one
thinks "Now I have touched the bottom of the
sea—now I can go no deeper," one goes deeper.
. . . Suffering is boundless, is eternity. One
pang is eternal torment. Physical suffering is—
child's play.   Ibid. (19 December 1920)

7 Risk! Risk anything! Care no more for the opinions of others, for those voices. Do the hardest
thing on earth for you. Act for yourself. Face
the truth.   Ibid. (14 October 1922)

8 *Important.* When we can begin to take our
failures nonseriously, it means we are ceasing

to be afraid of them. It is of immense importance to learn to laugh at ourselves.
Ibid. (October 1922)

9 Whenever I prepare for a journey I prepare as though for death. Should I never return, all is in order. This is what life has taught me.
Ibid. (1922)

10 I feel like a fly who has been dropped into the milk-jug and fished out again, but is still too milky and drowned to start cleaning up yet.
Katherine Mansfield's Letters to John Middleton Murry, 1913–1922
1951

1392. Carlotta Monterey O'Neill (1888–1970)

1 To understand his [Eugene O'Neill's*] work you must understand the man, for the work and the man are one.
Quoted in *O'Neill* by Arthur and Barbara Gelb   *1960*

*American playwright (1888–1953).

2 I had to work like a dog. I was Gene's secretary, I was his nurse. His health was always bad. I did everything. He wrote the plays, but I did everything else. I loved it. It was a privilege to live with him, because he was mentally stimulating. My God, how many women have husbands who are very stimulating?   Ibid, Ch. 4

1393. Agnes Sligh Turnbull (1888–   )

1 "Now ain't that funny! I thought it was you, an' you thought it was me; an' begob, it's *nayther* of us!"
Bk. I, Ch. 6, *The Rolling Years*
1936

2 "There is still vitality under the winter snow, even though to the casual eye it seems to be dead."   Ibid., Bk. II, Ch. 4

3 "Wasn't it [religion] invented by man for a kind of solace? It's as though he said, 'I'll make me a nice comfortable garment to shut out the heat and the cold'; and then it ends by becoming a straitjacket."   Ibid., Ch. 6

4 "I don't know that I care so much about going far," he said at last; "but I should like to go *deep* where I go."   Ibid., Epilogue

5 "You can put city polish *on* a man, but by golly, it seems you can't ever rub it off him."   Ch. 2, *The Golden Journey*   *1955*

6 "The idea of perfection always gives one a chance to talk without knowing facts."
Ibid., Ch. 4

7 "Do you know that the tendrils of graft and corruption have become mighty interlacing roots so that even men who would like to be honest are tripped and trapped by them?"
Ibid., Ch. 11

8 "Dogs' lives are too short. Their only fault, really."   Ch. 2, *The Flowering*   *1972*

9 Girls! Girls! Girls!
With platted hair an' mebbe curls
Singin' in a *chorus!*
Lord have mercy o'er us.   Ibid., Ch. 4

1394. Mary Day Winn (1888–1965)

1 Sex is the tabasco sauce which an adolescent national palate sprinkles on every course in the menu.   *Adam's Rib*   *1931*

1395. Anna Akhmatova (1889–1966)

1 There is a sacred, secret line in loving which attraction and even passion cannot cross,—
Untitled, St. 4 (1915), *White Flock,* Jane Kenyon, tr.
1917

2 I remember how the gods turned people into things, not killing their consciousness.
And now, to keep these glorious sorrows alive,
you have turned into my memory of you.
Untitled, st. 3 (1916),
op. cit.

3 How quiet it is after the volley!
Death sends patrols into every courtyard.
Untitled (1917), *Plantain,*
Jane Kenyon, tr.   *1921*

4   O great language we love:
It is you, Russian tongue, we must save, and we swear
We will give you unstained to the sons of our sons.   "Courage"   *1942*

5 It is not with the lyre of someone in love that I go seducing people.
The rattle of the leper
is what sings in my hands.
Untitled, in toto, *Twenty Poems of Anna Akhmatova,* Jane Kenyon, tr.   *1985*

6 And the sun goes down in waves of ether in such a way that I can't tell
if the day is ending, or the world,
or if the secret of secrets is within me again.
"On the Road," st. 3 (1964),
op. cit.

1396. Enid Bagnold (1889–1981)

1 "She keeps 'er brains in 'er 'eart. An' that's where they ought ter be. An' a man or woman who does that's one in a million an' as got my backing." *National Velvet* 1935

2 "Things come suitable to the time. Childbirth. An' bein' in love. An' death. You can't know 'em till you come to them. No use guessing an' dreading." *Ibid.*

3 "There's men . . . as can see things in people. There's men . . . as can choose a horse, an' that horse'll win. It's not the look of the horse, no, nor of the child, nor of the woman. it's the thing *we* can see. . . . *Ibid.*

4 "Love don't seem dainty on a fat woman." *Ibid.*

5 MAITLAND. Madame loves the unusual! It's a middle-class failing—she says—to run away from the unusual.
Act I, *The Chalk Garden* 1953

6 MRS. ST. MAUGHAM. You can't fit false teeth to a woman of character. As one gets older and older, the appearance becomes such a bore. *Ibid.*

7 MRS. ST. MAUGHAM. Privilege and power make selfish people—but gay ones. *Ibid.*

8 MAITLAND. Praise is the only thing that brings to life again a man that's been destroyed. *Ibid.*

9 OLIVIA. The thoughts of a *daughter* are a kind of memorial. *Ibid.*, Act III

10 ALICE. Oh—a girl's looks are *agony!*
Act I, Sc. 1, *The Chinese Prime Minister* 1964

11 SIR GREGORY. Marriage. The beginning and the end are wonderful. But the middle part is hell. *Ibid.*, Act II

12 BENT. So few people achieve the final end. *Most* are caught napping. *Ibid.*, Act III

13 SHE. We were so different that when two rooms separated us for half an hour—we met again as strangers. *Ibid.*

14 SHE. And if I die in ten years—or ten minutes— you can't measure Time! In ten minutes everything can be felt! In four minutes you can be born! Or live. In two minutes God may be understood! And what one woman grasps—all men may get nearer to. *Ibid.*

1397. Mildred Cram (1889–?)

1 Publicity tripped upon the heels of publicity.
"Billy," *Harper's Bazaar* 1924

2 He was capitalized, consolidated, incorporated, copyrighted, limited, protected, insured, and all rights reserved, including the Scandinavian. *Ibid.*

1398. Fannie Hurst (1889–1968)

1 It's hard for a young girl to have patience for old age sitting and chewing all day over the past. "Get Ready the Wreaths," *Cosmopolitan* 1917

2 "I always say he wore himself out with conscientiousness." "She Walks in Beauty," *Cosmopolitan* 1921

3 To housekeep, one had to plan ahead and carry items of motley nature around in the mind and at the same time preside, as mother had, at table, just as if everything, from the liver and bacon, to the succotash, to the French toast and strawberry jam, had not been matters of forethought and speculation.
Ch. 2, *Imitation of Life* 1932

4 Papa lived so separately within himself that I retreated to Mama, who wore herself on the outside. Everything about her hung in view like peasant adobe houses with green peppers and little shrines, drying diapers and cooking utensils on the façade. Bk. I, *Anatomy of Me* 1958

1399. Elsie Janis (1889–1956)

1 When I think of the hundreds of things I might be,
I get down on my knees and thank God that I'm me.
"Compensation," *Poems Now and Then* c. 1927

2 Why do we do it?
Oh, Hell! What's the use?
Why battle with the universe?
Why not declare a truce? "Why?," op. cit.

1400. Dorothy McCall (1889–?)

1 One cannot have wisdom without living life.
Quoted in the *Los Angeles Times* 14 March 1974

2 Technology dominates us all, diminishing our freedom. *Ibid.*

1401. Gabriela Mistral (1889–1957)

1 Let me be more maternal than a mother; able to love and defend with all of a mother's fervor

the child that is not flesh of my flesh. Grant that I may be successful in molding one of my pupils into a perfect poem, and let me leave within her deepest-felt melody that she may sing for you when my lips shall sing no more.
"La Oracion de la Maestra" (The Teacher's Prayer), *Desolacion* *1922*

2 Let me make my brick schoolhouse into a spiritual temple. Let the radiance of my enthusiams envelop the poor courtyard and the bare classroom. Let my heart be a stronger column and my goodwill purer gold than the columns and gold of rich schools. Ibid.

3 A son, a son, a son! I wanted a son of yours and mine, in those distant days of burning bliss when my bones would tremble at your least murmur and my brow would glow with a radiant mist. "Poem of the Son," St. 1, op. cit.

4 he kissed me and now I am someone else
"He Kissed Me," St. 1, op. cit.

5 My grief and my smile begin in your face, my son. "Eternal Grief," St. 2, op. cit.

6 The crimson rose
plucked yesterday,
the fire and cinnamon
of the carnation,

the bread I baked
with anise seed and honey,
and the goldfish
flaming in its bowl.

All these are yours, baby born of woman,
if you'll only go to sleep.
"If You'll Only Go To Sleep," Sts. 1–3, *Tenura* (Tenderness) *1924*

7 Of the enemies of the soul—
the world, the devil, the flesh—
the *world* is the most serious and most dangerous. "Todas Ibamos a Ser Reinas" (We Were All to Be Queens), *Tala* (Felling) *1938*

8 I have all that I lost
and I go carrying my childhood
like a favorite flower
that perfumes my hand. Ibid.

9 And I wished I were born with them.
Could it not be so another time?
To leap from a clump of banana plants
one morning of wonders—
a dog, a coyote, a deer;
to gaze with wide pupils, to run, to stop, to run, to fall,
to whimper and whine and jump with joy,
riddled with sun and with barking,
a hallowed child of God, his secret, divine servant.
"Ocho Perritos" (Eight Puppies), op. cit.

10 I will leave behind me the dark ravine, and climb up gentler slopes toward that spiritual mesa where at last a wide light will fall upon my days. From there I will sing words of hope, without looking into my heart. As one who was full of compassion wished: I will sing to console men. Quoted in Introduction to *Tala* in *Selected Poems of Gabriela Mistral*, Doris Dana, tr. and ed. *1971*

1402. Julia Seton (1889–?)

1 Dancing is a universal instinct—zoölogic, a biologic impulse, found in animals as well as in man. "Why Dance?," *The Rhythm of the Redman* *1930*

2 In its natural, primitive form, dancing is vigorous muscular action to vent emotion. Originally, it was the natural expression of the basic impulses of a simple form of life. Triumph, defeat, war, love, hate, desire, propitiation of the gods— all were danced by the hero or the tribe to the rhythm of beaten drums.
"Dance in the Animal World," op. cit.

3 But life has taught me that it knows better plans than we can imagine, so that I try to submerge my own desires, apt to be too insistent, into a calm willingness to accept what comes, and to make the most of it, then wait again. I have discovered that there is a Pattern, larger and more beautiful than our short vision can weave. . . . Epilogue, *By a Thousand Fires* *1967*

1403. Madeline Talmage Astor (fl. 1890–1945)

1 [Being helped over the rail of the Titanic*] "I rang for ice, but *this* is ridiculous!"
Attr. *15 April 1912*

*British luxury passenger liner that sank during its maiden voyage after it struck an iceberg near Newfoundland; 1,513 lives were lost.

1404. Mary E. Buell (fl. 1890s)

1 Something made of nothing, tasting very sweet,
A most delicious compound, with ingredients complete;
But if, as on occasion, the heart and mind are sour,
It has no great significance, and loses half its power. "The Kiss" *n.d.*

1405. Harriet L. Childe-Pemberton (fl. 1890s)

1 As I allays say to my brother,
  If it isn't one thing it's the tother.
        "Geese: A Dialogue," *Dead Letters
        and Other Narrative and Dramatic
                Pieces   1896*

2 O beautiful earth! alive, aglow,
  With your million things that grow,
  I would lay my head on your ample
  knee. . . .
        "Songs of Earth," I, St. 1, *Nenuphar
                                1911*

3 For passion has come to the verge and leaps
  Headlong to the blind abyss,
  Yet gathers thereby the strength of deeps,
  And eddies a moment and swirls and sweeps
  Till peril is one with bliss!
        "Songs of Water," IV, St. 4, op. cit.

1406. Anita Owen (fl. 1890s)

1 And in these eyes the love-light lies
  And lies—and lies and lies!
        "Dreamy Eyes"   *c.1894*

2 . . . Daisies won't tell.
        "Sweet Bunch of Daisies"   *1894*

1407. Hattie Starr (fl. 1890s)

1 Nobody loves me, well do I know,
  Don't all the cold world tell me so?
        "Nobody Loves Me"   *1893*

2 Somebody loves me; How do I know?
  Somebody's eyes have told me so!
        "Somebody Loves Me"   *1893*

1408. Daisy Ashford (1890?–1972)

1 I am parshial [sic] to ladies if they are nice. I
  suppose it is my nature. I am not quite a gentleman but you would hardly notice it.
        Ch. 1, *The Young Visitors*,*   *1919*

*Written when the author was nine years old.

2 My life will be sour grapes and ashes without
  you.   Ibid., Ch. 8

1409. Hallie Flanagan (1890–1969)

1 We were a violent lot,* a thorn in the body
  bureaucratic. Possibly that is one function of art

in society. In the midst of learning the necessary
lingo of procedures, allotments, authorizations,
we found time for exchange of ideas, ideas for
salvaging the quickly receding past of our country, capturing it in plays, pictures, books; ideas
for penetrating and illuminating our own age,
finding quicksilver ways in which to express the
mercurial present.
        "Danger: Men Not Working," *Arena,
        The Story of the Federal
                Theatre,   1940*

*The Federal Theatre of the New Deal's W.P.A.

2 We live in a changing world: man is whispering
  through space, soaring to the stars in ships,
  flinging miles of steel and glass into the air.
  Shall the theatre continue to huddle in the confines of a painted box set? The movies, in their
  kaleidoscopic speed and juxtaposition of external objects and internal emotions are seeking to
  find visible and audible expression for the tempo
  and the psychology of our time. The stage too
  must experiment—with ideas, with psychological relationship of men and women, with speech
  and rhythm forms, with dance and movement,
  with color and light—or it must and should
  become a museum product.   Ibid.
        (Comment at Meeting,
        8/9 October 1935)

3 It was ended because Congress, in spite of
  protests from many of its own members, treated
  the Federal Theatre not as a human issue or a
  cultural issue, but as a political issue.   Ibid,
        "Blasting: Work Suspended"

4 The greatest achievement of these public thea-
  tres was in their creation of an audience of many
  millions, a waiting audience. . . . Neither should
  the theatre in our country be regarded as a
  luxury. It is a necessity because in order to
  make democracy work the people must increasingly participate; they can't participate unless
  they understand; and the theatre is one of the
  great mediums of understand.   Ibid.

1410. Elizabeth Gurley Flynn (1890–1964)

1 Time was, when the ACLU was young, they
  were Anarchists, Socialists, Christian pacifists,
  trade unionists, I.W.W., Quaker, Irish, Republican and Communist! Today, they are no longer
  heretics, non-conformists, radicals,—they are
  respectable.
        "I Am Expelled from Civil Liberties!,"
        Sunday Worker   *17 March 1940*

2 History has a long-range perspective. It ultimately passes stern judgment on tyrants and
  vindicates those who fought, suffered, were im-

prisoned, and died for human freedom, against political oppression and economic slavery. Pioneers who were reviled, persecuted, ridiculed, and abused when they fought for free public schools, woman's suffrage against chattel slavery, for labor unions, are honored and revered today.   *Labor's Own: William Z. Foster**
1949

*American labor leader and Communist Party leader (1881–1961).

3 So confident was he [Nicola Sacco*] of his innocence that sunny afternoon that he had no fear. He was sure when he told his story in court he would go free. He did not know that he was approaching the valley of the shadow of death. He feared no evil because the truth was with him. But greed, corruption, prejudice, fear and hatred of radical foreign-born workingmen were weaving a net around him.
Pt. VII, *The Rebel Girl*   *1955*

*Italian-born American anarchist (1891–1927); executed.

4 I was a convict, a prisoner without rights, writing a censored letter. But my head was unbowed. Come what may, *I was a political prisoner* and proud of it, at one with some of the noblest of humanity who had suffered for conscience's sake. I felt no shame, no humiliation, no consciousness of guilt. To me my number 11710 was a badge of honor.
Ch. 3, *The Alderson Story**   *1963*

*The Federal Reformatory for Women at Alderson, West Virginia.

5 One of my correspondents asked me: "What do you think are the main differences between a women's prison and a men's prison?" I replied: "You would never see diapers hung on a line at a men's prison or hear babies crying in the hospital on a quiet Sunday afternoon." The physiological differences—menstruation, menopause, and pregnancy—create intense emotional problems among many women in prison.
Ibid., Ch. 13

6 A popular saying in Alderson went as follows: "They work us like a horse, feed us like a bird, treat us like a child, dress us like a man—and then expect us to act like a lady."
Ibid., Ch. 25

1411. Frances Noyes Hart (1890–1943)

1 "I cried at first . . . and then, it was such a beautiful day, that I forgot to be unhappy."
"Green Garden," *Scribner's Magazine*
1921

1412. Hedda Hopper (1890–1966)

1 His footprints* were never asked for, yet no one has ever filled his shoes.
From Under My Hat   *1952*

*Referring to D. W. Griffith, American filmmaker (1875–1948), and Grauman's Theatre in Hollywood.

2 In Hollywood gratitude is Public Enemy Number One.   Ibid.

1413. Rose Fitzgerald Kennedy (1890–   )

1 The secret of the Kennedy successes in politics was not money but meticulous planning and organization, tremendous effort and the enthusiasm and devotion of family and friends.
Times to Remember   *1974*

2 Sedentary people are apt to have sluggish minds. A sluggish mind is apt to be reflected in flabbiness of body and in a dullness of expression that invites no interest and gets none.   Ibid.

3 Birds sing after a storm; why shouldn't people feel as free to delight in whatever remains to them?   Ibid.

1414. Beatrice Llewellyn-Thomas (1890–?)

1 O We have a desperate need of laughter! Give us laughter, Puck!*
"To Puck"   *n.d.*

*Character from Shakespeare's *A Midsummer's Night Dream.*

1415. Maria, Grand Duchess of Russia (1890–1958)

1 . . . death, the mysterious disillusion and disappearance, of a human being.
Ch. 1, *Education of a Princess*
1930

2 Russia still writhed and stumbled. The wave of revolts and uprisings, the constant agitations, the incessant inflammatory orations of men possessed of little political competence. . .
Ibid., Ch. 8

1416. Aimee Semple McPherson (1890–1944)

1 O Hope! dazzling, radiant Hope!—What a change thou bringest to the hopeless; brightening

the darkened paths, and cheering the lonely way.   Pt. I, Ch. 1, *This Is That*   *1923*

2 We are all making a crown for Jesus out of these daily lives of ours, either a crown of golden, divine love, studded with gems of sacrifice and adoration, or a thorny crown, filled with the cruel briars of unbelief, or selfishness, and sin, and placing it upon His brow.
Pt. II, "What Shall I Do with Jesus," op. cit.

1417. Katherine Anne Porter (1890–1980)

1   "*What* could you buy with a hundred dollars?" she asked fretfully.
"Nothing, nothing at all," said their father, "a hundred dollars is just something you put in the bank."   Pt. II, *Old Mortality*   *1936*

2 "It don't *look* right," was his final reason for not doing anything he did not wish to do.
Noon Wine   *1937*

3 "I don't see no reason to hold it against a man because he went loony once or twice in his lifetime and so I don't expect to take no steps about it. Not a step. I've got nothin' against the man, he's always treated me fair. They's things and people," he went on, "'nough to drive any man loony. The wonder to me is, more men don't wind up in straitjackets, the way things are going these days and times."   Ibid.

4 Nothing is mine, I have only nothing but it is enough, it is beautiful and it is all mine. Do I even walk about in my own skin or is it something I have borrowed to spare my modesty?
Pale Horse, Pale Rider   *1939*

5 After working for three years on a morning newspaper she had an illusion of maturity and experience; but it was fatigue merely. . . .
Ibid.

6 "The mind and the heart sometimes get another chance, but if anything happens to the poor old human frame, why, it's just out of luck, that's all."   Ibid.

7 No more war, no more plague, only the dazed silence that follows the ceasing of the heavy guns; noiseless houses with the shades drawn, empty streets, the dead cold light of tomorrow. Now there would be time for everything.
Ibid.

8 Miracles are instantaneous, they cannot be summoned, but come of themselves, usually at unlikely moments and to those who least expect them.   Pt. III, *Ship of Fools*   *1962*

9 "The real sin against life is to abuse and destroy beauty, even one's own—even more, one's own, for that had been put in our care and we are responsible for its well-being. . . ."   Ibid.

10 Such ignorance. All the boys were in military schools and all the girls were in the convent, and that's all you need to say about it.
Quoted in "Lioness of Literature Looks Back" by Henry Allen, *Los Angeles Times*   *7 July 1974*

11 I do not understand the world, but I watch its progress.   Ibid.

1418. Rachel (1890–1931)

1 Like a bird in the butcher's palm you flutter in my hand, insolent pride.
"Revolt," *Poems from the Hebrew*, Robert Mezey, ed.   *1973*

2 This is a bond nothing can ever loosen.
What I have lost: what I possess forever.
"My Dead," op. cit.

1419. Ellen West (1890?–1923?)

1 I am twenty-one years old and am supposed to be silent and grin like a puppet.
Diary Entry (c.1911), Quoted in *Women and Madness* by Phyllis Chesler*   *1972*

*See 2293.

1420. Margaret Culkin Banning (1891–1982)

1 I get a little angry about this highhanded scrapping of the looks of things. What else have we to go by? How else can the average person form an opinion of a girl's sense of values or even of her chastity except by the looks of her conduct?   *Letters to Susan*   *1936*

2 It isn't easy to be the person who sometimes has to try to preserve your happiness at the expense of your fun.   Ibid.

1421. Fanny Brice (1891–1951)

1 Your audience gives you everything you need. They tell you. There is no director who can direct you like an audience.

Quoted in Ch. 6, *The Fabulous Fanny*
by Norman Katkov   *1952*

2 When love is out of your life, you're through in a way. Because while it is there it's like a motor that's going, you have such vitality to do things, big things, because love is goosing you all the time.   Ibid., Ch. 19

3 Let the world know you as you are, not as you think you should be, because sooner or later, if you are posing, you will forget the pose, and then where are you?   Ibid., Ch. 24

1422. Agatha Christie (1891–1975)

1 Curious things, habits. People themselves never knew they had them.
        Witness for the Prosecution   *1924*

2 It is completely unimportant. That is why it is so interesting.   *The Murder of Roger Ackroyd*   *1926*

3 TREVES. If one sticks too rigidly to one's principles one would hardly see anybody.
        Act I, *Toward's Zero*   *1957*

4 Is there ever any particular spot where one can put one's finger and say, "It all began that day, at such a time and such a place, with such an incident?"   Bk. I, Ch. 1, *Endless Night* *1967*

5 . . . money isn't so hot, after all. What with incipient heart attacks, lots of bottles of little pills you have to take all the time, and losing your temper over the food or the service in hotels. Most of the rich people I've known have been fairly miserable.   Ibid., Ch. 3

6 I didn't want to work. It was as simple as that. I distrusted work, disliked it. I thought it was a very bad thing that the human race had unfortunately invented for itself.   Ibid.

7 "Look here," I said, "people like to collect disasters."   Ibid., Ch. 5

8 To put it quite crudely . . . the poor don't really know how the rich live, and the rich don't know how the poor live, and to find out is really enchanting to both of them.
        Ibid., Bk. II, Ch. 9

1423. Laura Gilpin (1891–1979)

1 A river seems a magic thing. A magic, moving, living part of the very earth itself—for it is from the soil, both from its depth and from its surface, that a river has its beginning.
        Introduction, *The Rio Grande*   *1949*

2 . . . much earnest philosophical thought is born of the life which springs from close association with nature.   "The Source,"
        op. cit.

1424. Vivian Yeiser Laramore (1891–?)

1 Talk to me tenderly, tell me lies;
I am a woman and time flies.
        "Talk to Me Tenderly"   *n.d.*

1425. Irene Rutherford McLeod (1891–1964?)

1 I'm a lean dog, a keen dog, a wild dog, and alone.   "Lone Dog," *Songs to Save a Soul* *1919*

1426. Anne Nichols (1891–1966)

1 MRS. COHEN. How early it iss of late!
        Act I, *Abie's Irish Rose*   *1922*

2 FATHER WHALEN. Shure, we're all trying to get to the same place when we pass on. We're just going by different routes. We can't all go on the same train.

RABBI. And just because you are not riding on my train, why should I say your train won't get there?   Ibid., Act II

1427. Victoria Ocampo (1891–1979)

1 He [T. E. Lawrence] was of the same stuff as the saints, and like them he had to find perfection in himself, and not like a great artist in the work he had conceived and executed.
        "Childhood," *338171TE (Lawrence of Arabia)**   *1947*

*T. E. Lawrence, British soldier and writer (1888–1935).

2 Moral, like physical, cleanliness is not acquired once and for all: it can only be kept and renewed by a habit of constant watchfulness and discipline.   Ibid., "Scruples and Ambitions"

3 This eagerness to seek hidden but necessary connections, connections that revealed a close relationship between the world where I was born in the flesh and the other worlds where I was reborn, has been the enterprise of my whole life.   Speech, American Academy of Arts and Letters, New York   *1973*

1428. Ruth Law Oliver (1891–1970)

1 I had a great desire to take off and go somewhere in flight, never having done it.

Quoted in Ch. 4, *The American Heritage History of Flight* 1962

1429. Marie Rambert (1891–1982)

1 We want to create an atmosphere in which creation is possible.
Quoted in "Ballet Rambert: The Company That Changed Its Mind" by John Percival, *Dancemagazine February 1973*

1430. Nelly Sachs (1891–1970)

1 O you chimneys,
O you fingers
And Israel's body as smoke though the air!
"O the Chimneys," St. 4,
O the Chimneys 1967

2 When sleep leaves the body like smoke
and man, sated with secrets,
drives the overworked nag of quarrel
out of its stall,
then the fire-breathing union begins
anew. . . . "When Sleep Enters the Body Like Smoke," St. 3, op. cit.

3 You, the inexperienced, who learn nothing in the nights.
Many angels are given you
But you do not see them.
"Chorus of Clouds," *The Seeker and Other Poems* 1970

4 Are graves breath-space for longing?
"Are Graves Breath-Space for Longing?," op. cit.

1431. Brenda Ueland (1892–1985)

1 Everybody is talented, original and has something important to say.
Ch. 1, *If You Want To Write* 1938

2 You know how all children have this creative power. You have all seen things like this: the little girls in our family used to give play after play. . . . these small ten-year-olds were working with feverish energy and endurance. . . . If they had worked that hard for school it probably would have killed them. They were working for nothing but fun, for that glorious inner excitement. It was the creative power working in them. It was hard, hard work but there was no pleasure or excitement like it and it was something never forgotten. Ibid.

3 For when you come to think of it, the only way to love a person is not, as the stereotyped Christian notion is, to coddle them and bring them soup when they are sick, but by listening to them and seeing and believing in the god, in the poet, in them. For by doing this, you keep the god and the poet alive and make it flourish.
Ibid.

4 . . . orthodox criticism . . . is a murderer of talent. And because the most modest and sensitive people are the most talented, having the most imagination and sympathy, these are the very first ones to get killed off. It is the brutal egotists that survive. Ibid.

5 Self-trust is so important. When you launch on a story, make your neck loose, feel free, good-natured. And be lazy. Feel that you are going to throw it away. Try writing utterly unplanned stories and see what comes out.
Ibid., Ch. 16

1432. Mary Ambrose (1892–?)

1 The true vocation [of a nun is] settled on the day the girl looks around her and sees a young woman her own age in pretty clothes wheeling a baby carriage by the convent. Then her heart takes an awful flop and she knows what it is God really is asking of her.
Quoted in *Life* 15 March 1963

1433. Djuna Barnes (1892–1982)

1 She knew what was troubling him, thwarted instincts, common beautiful instincts that he was being robbed of.
"A Night Among the Horses," *The Little Review* 1918

2 She wanted to be the reason for everything and so was the cause of nothing.
Nightwood 1936

3 She defied the very meaning of personality in her passion to be a person. Ibid.

4 No man needs curing of his individual sickness; his universal malady is what he should look to. Ibid.

1434. Stella Benson (1892–1933)

1 Call no man foe, but never love a stranger.
Build up no plan, nor any star pursue.
Go forth in crowds, in loneliness is danger.
Thus nothing fate can send,
And nothing fate can do
Shall pierce your peace, my friend.
"To the Unborn," St. 3,
This Is the End 1917

2 Family jokes, though rightly cursed by strangers, are the bond that keeps most families alive.
Ch. 9, *Pipers and a Dancer*   *1924*

1435. Pearl S. Buck (1892–1973)

1 It is better to be first with an ugly woman than the hundredth with a beauty.
Ch. 1, *The Good Earth*   *1931*

2 "Hunger makes a thief of any man."
Ibid., Ch. 15

3 "Men do not take good iron to make nails nor good men to make soldiers."
Ch. 8, *The Young Revolutionist*
1932

4 "But that land—it is one thing that will still be there when I come back—land is always there. . . ."
Ch. 1, *A House Divided*
1935

5 I feel no need for any other faith than my faith in human beings.   *I Believe*   *1939*

6 There were many ways of breaking a heart. Stories were full of hearts broken by love, but what really broke a heart was taking away its dream—whatever that dream might be.
Pt. II, *The Patriot*   *1939*

7   "We shall fight until all anti-Japanese feeling is stamped out and the Chinese are ready to co-operate with us."
I-wan stared at him, not believing what he heard.
"You mean," he repeated, "you will kill us and bomb our cities—and—and—rape our women—until we learn to love you?"   Ibid.

8 When hope is taken away from the people moral degeneration follows swiftly after.
Letter to the Editor,
The New York Times
14 November 1941

9 For our democracy has been marred by imperialism, and it has been enlightened only by individual and sporadic efforts at freedom.
Speech, "Freedom for All," New York
14 March 1942

10   I remember as a child hearing my impatient missionary father . . . [as] he explained to an elderly Chinese gentleman, "Does it mean nothing to you that if you reject Christ you will burn in hell?"
The Chinese gentleman smiled as he replied, "If, as you say, my ancestors are all in hell at this moment, it would be unfilial of me not to be willing to suffer with them."
Speech, "The Chinese Mind and India," Boston   *28 April 1942*

11 Every era of renaissance has come out of new freedoms for peoples. The coming renaissance will be greater than any in human history, for this time all the peoples of the earth will share in it.
Introduction, *What America Means to Me*
1942

12 Every great mistake has a halfway moment, a split second when it can be recalled and perhaps remedied.   Ibid., Ch. 10

13 But when you remember the suffering, which you have not deserved, do not think of vengeance, as the small man does. Remember, rather, as the great remember, that which they have unjustly suffered, and determine only that such suffering shall not be possible again for any human being anywhere.
"A Letter to Colored Americans,"
American Unity and Asia   *1942*

14 "Believing in gods always causes confusion."   Ch. 1, *The Bondsmaid*   *1949*

15 Endurance can be a harsh and bitter root in one's life, bearing poisonous and gloomy fruit, destroying other lives. Endurance is only the beginning. There must be acceptance and the knowledge that sorrow fully accepted brings its own gifts. For there is an alchemy in sorrow. It can be transmuted into wisdom. . . .
Ch. 1, *The Child Who Never Grew*
1950

16 Americans are all too soft. I am not soft. It is better to be hard, so that you can know what to do.   Ibid.

17 Euthanasia is a long, smooth-sounding word, and it conceals its danger as long, smooth words do, but the danger is there, nevertheless.
Ibid., Ch. 2

18 Children who never grow are human beings, and suffer as human beings, inarticulately but deeply nevertheless. The human creature is always more than an animal.   Ibid., Ch. 3

19 What is a neglected child? He is a child not planned for, not wanted. Neglect begins, therefore, before he is born.
Ch. 3, *Children for Adoption*
1964

20 The community must assume responsibility for each child within its confines. Not one must be neglected whatever his condition. The community must see that every child gets the advantages and opportunities which are due him as a citizen and as a human being.   Ibid., Ch. 4

21 If our American way of life fails the child, it fails us all.   Ibid., Ch. 9

22 Nothing and no one can destroy the Chinese people. They are relentless survivors. They are

the oldest civilized people on earth. Their civilization passes through phases but its basic characteristics remain the same. They yield, they bend to the wind, but they never break.

> Ch. 1, *China, Past and Present*
> *1972*

23 Ah well, perhaps one has to be very old before one learns how to be amused rather than shocked.

> Ibid., Ch. 6

24 "A hand is not only an implement, it's a sense organ. It's the eye of a blind man, it's the tone of those who cannot speak."

> Pt. II, *The Goddess Abides*   *1972*

25 Go out and be born among gypsies or thieves or among happy workaday people who live with the sun and do not think about their souls.

> "Advice to Unborn Novelists"   *n.d.*

1436. Ivy Compton-Burnett (1892–1969)

1 "But a gentlewoman is not able to spin gold out of straw; it required a full princess to do that."

> Ch. 1, *A House and Its Head*
> *1935*

2 "We do not discuss the members of our family to their faces. . . ."

> Ibid., Ch. 11

3 "Parents have too little respect for their children, just as the children have too much for the parents. . . ."

> Ch. 5, *Two Worlds and Their Ways*
> *1949*

4 "We can build upon foundations anywhere, if they are well and truly laid."

> Ibid., Ch. 7

5 "If I were not a child with my parents, they would be more unloving towards me," said Gwendolen.

> Ibid.

6 "My youth is escaping without giving me anything it owes me."

> Ch. 1, *A Heritage and Its History*
> *1959*

7 "Civilised life exacts its toll."

> Ibid., Ch. 9

8 "A thing is not nothing, when it is all there is."

> Ibid., Ch. 10

9 "She should be thinking of higher things."
"Nothing could be higher than food," said Leah.

> Ch. 1, *The Mighty and Their Fall*
> *1961*

10 "They must release each other in time for their lives to grow."

> Ibid., Ch. 3

11 When an age is ended you see it as it is.

> Quoted in *The Life of Ivy Compton-Burnett* by Elizabeth Sprigge
> *1973*

1437. Diana Cooper (1892–1986)

1 Naturally good until now, I had never lied, for nothing tempted me to lie except fear of wounding and I had nothing to fear. But now with the advent of the young men—benign serpents—came the apple . . . Childhood was over.

> Ch. 5, *The Rainbow Comes and Goes*
> *1958*

2 In astrology there is room for precaution and obstruction; the disaster is not inevitable. One can dodge the stars in their courses.

> *Trumpets from the Steep*   *1960*

3 I'll write no more memories. They would get too sad, tender as they are. Age wins and one must learn to grow old. As I learnt with the loss of a nurse to put childish things behind me, as I learnt when the joys of dependence were over to embrace with fear the isolation of independence, so now I must learn to walk this long unlovely wintry way, looking for spectacles, shunning the cruel looking-glass, laughing at my clumsiness before others mistakenly condole, not expecting gallantry yet disappointed to receive none, apprehending every ache of shaft of pain, alive to blinding flashes of mortality, unarmed, totally vulnerable.

> Ibid., Ch. 8

1438. Janet Flanner (1892–1978)

1 Paris is now the capital of limbo.

> "Paris Germany," *The New Yorker*
> *7 December 1940*

2 The German passion for bureaucracy—for written and signal forms, for files, statistics, and lists, and for printed permissions to do this or that, to go here or there, to move about, to work, to exist—is like a steel pin pinning each French individual to a sheet of paper, the way an entymologist pins each specimen insect past struggling to his laboratory board.

> Ibid.

3 By jove, no wonder women don't love war nor understand it, nor can operate in it as a rule; it takes a man to suffer what other men have invented . . . Women have invented nothing in all that, except the men who were born as male babies and grew up to be men big enough to be killed fighting.

> Letter to Natalia Danesi Murray (1944), *Darlinghissima: Letters to a Friend*   *1985*

1439. Edna St. Vincent Millay (1892–1950)

1 For my omniscience paid I toll
In infinite remorse of soul.

"Renascence," St. 2, *Renascence and
Other Poems*   *1917*

2 God, I can push the grass apart
And lay my finger on Thy heart.   Ibid., St. 7

3 The soul can split the sky in two,
And let the face of God shine through.
Ibid., St. 8

4 Life goes on forever like the gnawing of a
mouse.   "Ashes of Life," St. 3, op. cit.

5 O world, I cannot hold thee close enough!
"God's World," St. 1, op. cit.

6 COLUMBINE. I cannot *live*
Without a macaroon! *Aria Da Capo*   *1920*

7 PIERROT. I am become a socialist. I love
Humanity; but I hate people.   Ibid.

8 PIERROT. Your mind is made of crumbs. . . .
Ibid.

9 I had a little Sorrow,
Born of a little Sin.
"The Penitent," St. 1, *A Few Figs
from Thistles*   *1920*

10 My candle burns at both its ends;
It will not last the night;
But oh, my foes, and oh, my friends—
It gives a lovely light.   "First Fig,"
op. cit.

11 All my life,
Following Care along the dusty road,
Have I looked back at loveliness and
sighed. . . .   "Journey," St. 1,
Second April   *1921*

12 I make bean-stalks, I'm
A builder, like yourself.
"The Bean-Stalk," St. 4, op. cit.

13 Life is a quest and love a quarrel. . . .
"Weeds," St. 1, op. cit.

14 My heart is what it was before,
A house where people come and
go. . . .   "Alms," St. 1, op. cit.

15 Life must go on;
I forget just why.   "Lament," op. cit.

16 Always I climbed the wave at morning,
Shook the sand from my shoes at night,
That now am caught beneath great buildings,
Stricken with noise, confused with light.
"Exiled," St. 4
op. cit.

17 Your body was a temple to Delight. . . .
"As to some lovely temple,
tenantless,"
op. cit.

18 I only know that summer sang in me
A little while, that in me sings no more.

"What lips my lips have kissed,
and where, and why,"
*The Harp-Weaver
and Other Poems*   *1923*

19 Pity me that the heart is slow to learn
What the swift mind beholds at very turn.
"Pity me not because the
light of day,"
op. cit.

20 If ever I said, in grief or pride,
I tired of honest things, I lied. . . .
"The Goose-Girl,"
op. cit.

21 I know I am but summer to your heart,
And not the full four seasons of the
year. . . .   "I know I am but summer
to your heart,"
op. cit.

22 Music my rampart, and my only one.
"On Hearing a Symphony of
Beethoven," St. 1, *The Buck
in the Snow*   *1928*

23 The anguish of the world is on my tongue.
My bowl is filled to the brim with it; there is
more than I can eat.
Happy are the toothless old and the toothless
young,
That cannot rend this meat.
"The Anguish," St. 2,
op. cit.

24 Not for you was the pen bitten,
And the mind wrung, and the song written.
"To Those Without Pity,"
op. cit.

25 Life has no friend. . . .
"Fatal Interview," VIII
Fatal Interview   *1931*

26 Youth, have no pity; leave no farthing here
For age to invest in compromise and fear.
Ibid., XXIX

27 Desolate dreams pursue me out of sleep;
Weeping I wake; waking, I weep, I weep.
Ibid., XXXIII

28 My kisses now are sand against your mouth,
Teeth in your palm and pennies on your
eyes.   Ibid., XXXIX

29 To be grown up is to sit at the table with
people who have died, who neither listen
nor speak. . . .
"Childhood Is the Kingdom
Where Nobody Dies," III, St. 6
Wine from These Grapes   *1934*

30 I shall die, but that is all that I shall do for
Death: I am not on his pay-roll.
"Conscientious Objector," St. 3, op. cit.

31 East has demoralized us, nearly so; we know
Nothing of the rigours of winter. . . .
"Underground System," St. 2,
Huntsman, What Quarry? 1939

32 Heart, do not stain my skin
With bruises; go about
Your simple function. Mind,
Sleep now; do not intrude;
And do not spy; be kind.

Sweet blindness, now begin.
"Theme and Variations,"
II, Sts. 5–6, op. cit.

33 . . . my heart is set
On living—I have heroes to beget
Before I die. . . .
"Thou famished grave, I will
not fill thee yet," op. cit.

34 No, no, not love, not love. Call it by name,
Now that it's over, now that it is gone and
cannot hear us.
It was an honest thing. Not noble. Yet no
shame.
"What Savage Blossom," Sts. 3–4, op. cit.

35 Parrots, tortoises and redwoods
Live a longer life than men do,
Men a longer life than dogs do,
Dogs a longer life than love does.
"Pretty Love I Must Outlive You," op. cit.

36 See how these masses mill and swarm
And troop and muster and assail:
God! we could keep this planet warm
By friction, if the sun should fail.
"Three Sonnets in
Tetrameter," I, op. cit.

37 Love does not help to understand
The logic of the bursting shell.   Ibid., III

38 You think we build a world; I think we leave
Only these tools, wherewith to strain and
grieve.   "Count them unclean, these
tears that turn no mill," op. cit.

39 It's not true that life is one damn thing after
another—its one damn thing over and
over.   *Letters of Edna St. Vincent Millay,*
Allen R. Macdougall, ed.   1952

1440 Vita Sackville-West (1892–1962)

1 So prodigal was I of youth,
Forgetting I was young;
I worshipped dead men for their strength,
Forgetting I was strong.
"MCMXIII," St. 1, *Poems of
West and East*   1917

2 Travel is the most private of pleasure. There is
no greater bore than the travel to bore. We do
not in the least want to hear what he has seen
in Hong-Kong.
Ch. 1, *Passenger to Teheran*   1926

3 . . . besides, the fingers which had once grown
accustomed to a pen soon itch to hold one again:
it is necessary to write, if the days are not to
slip emptily by. How else, indeed, to clap the
net over the butterfly of the moment? for the
moment passes, it is forgotten; the mood is gone;
life itself is gone. That is where the writer scores
over his fellows: he catches the changes of his
mind on the hop. Growth is exciting; growth is
dynamic and alarming. Growth of the soul,
growth of the mind. . .
Ch. 1, *Twelve Days*   1928

4 Perhaps it would be better to go the whole hog
and cut oneself off entirely from the outside
world. A merely negative form of protest, I
fear, against conditions one does not like; for
resentment is vain unless one has an alternative
to offer. Flight is no alternative; it is only a
personal solution. But as a personal experiment
it certainly offers material for reflection to the
curious.   Ibid., Ch. 15

5 For a young man to start his career with a love
affair with an older woman was quite *de rigueur.*
. . . Of course, it must not go on too long.
Ch. 3, *The Edwardians*   1930

6 Click, clack, click, clack, went their conversation, like so many knitting-needles, purl, plain,
purl plain, achieving a complex pattern of references, cross-references, Christian names, nicknames, and fleeting allusions. . . .
Ibid., Ch. 6

7 Men do kill women. Most women enjoy being
killed; so I'm told.
All Passion Spent   1931

8 Now to my little death the pestering clock
Beckons—but who would sleep when he might
wake?   "Solitude"   1938

9 Nothing shows up the difference between the
things said or read, so much as the daily experience of it.   *Country Notes*   1940

10 It is very necessary to have makers of beauty
left in a world seemingly bent on making the
most evil ugliness.   Ibid.

11 I have come to the conclusion, after many years
of sometimes sad experience, that you cannot
come to any conclusion at all.
"May," *In Your Garden Again*
1953

12 "It is lucky for some people," I say to Laura,
"that they can live behind their own faces."
No Signposts in the Sea   1961

13 When, and how, and at what stage of our development did spirituality and our strange no-

tions of religion arise? the need for worship which is nothing more than our frightened refuge into propitiation of a Creator we do not understand? A detective story, the supreme Whodone-it, written in undecipherable hieroglyphics, no Rosetta stone supplied, by the consummate mystifier to tease us poor fumbling unravellers of his plot.   Ibid.

1441. Alfonsina Storni (1892–1938)

1 Miles overhead there is a light in space:
   He sees a star; aroused, inspired, he reaches
      up to hold it,
   And then another hand cuts off the hand he
      raises.
                         "Man," John A. Crow, tr., *El dulce
                             dano* (The sweet injury)   *1918*

2 I gutted your belly as I would a doll's
   Examining its artifice of cogs
   And buried deep within its golden pulleys
   I found a trap bearing this label: sex.
                         "To Eros," *Mask and Trefoil*
                                                c.1930

3 . . . Ah, one favor:
   If he telephones again,
   Tell him it's no use, that I've gone out. . . .
                         "I Shall Sleep,"* *La Nacion*
                         (Buenos Aires newspaper)   *1938*

*Sent to *La Nacion* the day before she drowned herself.

4 You want me to be white
   (God forgive you)
   You want me to be chaste
   (God forgive you)
   You want me to be immaculate!
                         "You Want Me White"   *n.d.*

1442. Ruth Suckow (1892–1960)

1 To have someone tell his boys to do this and that! To take away his help on the farm just when he needed it most! To have somebody just step in and tell him where they had to go! Was that what happened in this country? Why had his people left the old country, then if things were going to be just the same?
                         Pt. II, Ch. 4, *Country People*   *1924*

2 To most of the people it [World War I] had seemed far away, something that could never come close. Some resented it, others seized upon it now to help break break up the long monotony of everyday living—more terribly thrilling than a fire in the business district, a drowning in the river, or the discovery that the cashier of the Farmers' Bank had been embezzling. Something had come, it seemed, to shake

up that placid, solid, comfortable life of home, changing things around, shifting values that had seemed to be fixed.
                         Pt. IV, Ch. 3, *The Odyssey of a Nice Girl*
                                                1925

3 Exercises, songs and recitations—pieces by children whose mothers would be offended if they were left off the program: good or bad, the audience clapped.
                         "Eminence," *Children and Other
                             People*   *1931*

1443. Marina Tsvetaeva (1892–1941)

1 So they wait for—
   a letter.

   A ragged scrap
   circled by sticky tape. Inside—

   a scribble,
   and happiness.
   And that's all.
                         "A Letter," Sts. 2–3, adapted
                             by Denise Levertov,* *Pages
                 from Tarusa,* Andrew Field, ed.   *1963*

*See 1927.

2 Word-creation . . . is only a journeying in the track of the hearing ear of nation and nature. A journey by ear.   "Art in the Light of
                         Conscience," *Russian
                         Poets on Poetry*   *1976*

3 I feel possessive only toward my children and my notebooks.
                         Marina Tsvetaeva, *A Captive Spirit:
                             Selected Prose,* Janet Marin
                             King, ed. & tr.,
                         intro. by Susan Sontag*   *1983*

*See 2136.

4 Art does not pay its victims. It does not even know them. The worker is paid by the master, not by the lathe. The lathe can only leave you without an arm. How many of them I have seen, poets without an arm. With an arm lost for any other work.   Ibid.

5 I have been trying on death for a year. It's all ugly and terrifying. Poison is vile, drowning—repulsive. . . . I do not want to die, I [just] want not to be.*
                         Diary entry (September 1940),
                                                op. cit.

*She hanged herself on 31 August 1941.

6 The word, which for me is already the thing, is all I want.   Letter to Rilke,* *Letters: 1926,*
                                                198?

*Rainer Maria Rilke, Swiss poet (1875–1926).

1444. Mae West (1892–1980)

1 "You're a fine woman, Lou, One of the finest women that ever walked the streets."
She Done Him Wrong   1932

2 TIRA. She's the kind of girl who climbed the ladder of success, wrong by wrong.
I'm No Angel   1933

3 FRISCO DOLL. Between two evils, I always pick the one I never tried before.
Klondike Annie   1936

4 FLOWER BELLE LEE. I generally avoid temptation unless I can't resist it.
My Little Chickadee   1940

5 It is better to be looked over than overlooked.
The Wit and Wisdom of Mae West,
Joseph Weintraub, ed.   1967

6 It's not the men in my life that counts—it's the life in my men.   Ibid.

7 Too much of a good thing can be wonderful.   Ibid.

8 I used to be Snow White . . . but I drifted.   Ibid.

9 The best way to hold a man is in your arms.   Ibid.

10 When women go wrong, men go right after them.   Ibid.

11 I've always had a weakness for foreign affairs.   Quoted in *Time*   1959

12 Is that a gun in your pocket, or are you just glad to see me?   *Sextette*   1978

13 I've made it my business to make business my business.   Quoted in "My Side" by M. George Haddad, *Working Woman* February 1979

14 Men have structured society to make a woman feel guilty if she looks after herself. Well, I beat men at their own game. I don't look down on men but I certainly don't look up to them either. I never found a man I could love—or trust—the way I loved myself.   Ibid.

1445. Rebecca West (1892–1983)

1 Literature must be an analysis of experience and a synthesis of the findings into a unity.
Ending in Earnest   1931

2 Yes, if an age would deal fairly well with its children and let them do what they can!
"Manibus Date Lilia Plenis," op. cit.

3 Infantilism is not a happy state. The childhood of the individual and the race is full of fears, and panic-stricken attempts to avert what is feared by placating the gods with painful sacrifices.   "Journey's End," op. cit.

4 Most works of art, like most wines, ought to be consumed in the district of their fabrication.
" 'Journey's End' Again," op. cit.

5 "We're on a permanent plateau of prosperity. There's never been anything like it before. It's America."   *The Abiding Vision*   1935

6 There is no such thing as conversation. It is an illusion. There are intersecting monologues, that is all.   Ch. 1, *There Is No Conversation* 1935

7 It is queer how it is always one's virtues and not one's vices that precipitate one into disaster.   Ibid.

8 "Why must you always try to be omnipotent, and shove things about? Tragic things happen sometimes that we just have to submit to."
Ch. 2, *The Salt of the Earth*   1935

9 But the Slav knows . . . that life . . . is an essence unpredictable, that she often produces events for which there is no apt prescription, and that she can be as slippery as an eel when wise men attempt to control her; and they know that it is life, not power or authority, that gives us joy, and this often when she is least predictable.
"Dalmatia," *Black Lamb and Grey Falcon*   1941

10 But there are other things than dissipation that thicken the features. Tears, for example.
"Serbia," op. cit.

11 Now different races and nationalities cherish different ideals of society that stink in each other's nostrils with an offensiveness beyond the power of any but the most monstrous private deed.   Epilogue, op. cit.

12 . . . any authentic work of art must start an argument between the artist and his audience.
Pt. I, Ch. 1, *The Court and the Castle* 1957

1446. Margaret Anderson (1893–1973)

1 My unreality is chiefly this: I have never felt much like a human being. It's a splendid feeling.   *My Thirty Years' War*   1930

2 I didn't know what to do about life—so I did a nervous breakdown that lasted many months.   Ibid.

3 In real love you want the other person's good.
In romantic love you want the other person.
The Fiery Fountains   *1969*

1447. Faith Baldwin (1893–1978)

1 Sometimes entering the ward he felt himself a
god, with the gifts of life, of hope, of allevia-
tion, of promise in his hands.
Pt. V, Ch. 28, *Medical Center*   *1938*

2 . . . it is hard to convince editors . . . that
people of—or past—forty are not senile, and
might even have problems, emotions and—*mir-
abile dictu*—romances, licit and illicit.
"Writing for the Women's Magazines,"
The Writer's Book, Helen Hull, ed.
1950

3 Oh well, one must adopt a New England attitude, saying not yea, nor nay, but perhaps,
maybe, and sometimes.   Ibid.

4 Men's private self-worlds are rather like our
geographical world's seasons, storm, and sun,
deserts, oases, mountains and abysses, the end-
less-seeming plateaus, darkness and light, and
always the sowing and the reaping.
"April," *Harvest of Hope*   *1962*

5 Character builds slowly, but it can be torn down
with incredible swiftness.   "July,"
op. cit.

6 I think that life has spared these mortals
much—
And cheated them of more—who have not
kept
A breathless vigil by the little bed
Of some beloved child.   "Vigil"   *n.d.*

1448. Bessie Breuer (1893–1975)

1 Hollywood . . . scripts . . . a medium where
both syntax and the language itself were subjected to horrid mutilation by young men who
thought of themselves as writers and who proved
it by the enormous salaries they received from
those higher up who were even less knowledge-
able of the mother tongue.
Ch. 15, *The Actress*   *1955*

2 Did I stay with him the very next night because
I, way deep down, thought I would learn the
secret of acting by sleeping with him; was that
it—the way women are always snatching at
poets and composers and writers to bedizen
themselves with a rag, a knuckle, a toe, the
sacred toe of art?   Ibid., Ch. 32

3 Lust, this muscular dilation and contraction, this
in itself, was that it—the *ding an sich,* memory
of a college course?   Ibid., Ch. 36

1449. Vera Brittain (1893–1970)

1 I thought that spring must last forevermore,
For I was young and loved, and it was
May.   "May Morning," St. 4 (May 1916),
Poems of the War and After   *1934*

2 I found in you a holy place apart,
Sublime endurance, God in man revealed,
Where mending broken bodies slowly healed
My broken heart.   "Epitaph on My Days in
Hospital" (1919), op. cit.

3 Meek wifehood is no part of my profession;
I am your friend, but never your possession.
"Married Love" (1926),
op. cit.

4 For the courage of greatness is adventurous
and knows not withdrawing,
But grasps the nettle, danger, with resolute
hands,
And ever again.
Gathers security from the sting of pain.
"Evening in Yorkshire," St. 4
(December 1932), op. cit.

5 The idea that it is necessary to go to a university
in order to become a successful writer, or even
a man or woman of letters (which is by no
means the same thing), is one of those phanta-
sies that surround authorship.
Ch. 2, *On Being an Author*   *1948*

6 His secret realisation of his physical cowardice
led him to underrate his exceptional moral
courage. . . .   Pt. I, Ch. 1, *Born*   *1949*

7 It is probably true to say that the largest scope
for change still lies in men's attitude to women,
and in women's attitude to themselves.
Ch. 15, *Lady into Woman*   *1953*

8 Politics are usually the executive expression of
human immaturity.   Ch. 1, *The Rebel Passion*
1964

9 The pacifists' task today is to find a method of
helping and healing which provides a revolutionary constructive substitute for war.
Ibid., Ch. 12

1450. Elizabeth Coatsworth (1893–1986)

1 Only of one thing I am sure:
when I dream
I am always ageless
Personal Geography   *1976*

2 To a life that seizes
Upon content,
Locality seems
But accident.
"To Daughters, Growing Up,"
St. 1   *n.d.*

1451. Elizabeth Cotten (1893–1987)

1 Freight train, freight train, goin' so
   fast. . . .   "Freight Train."
                              n.d.

2 This life I been livin' is very hard.
  Work all the week, honey
  and I give it all to you.
  Honey, baby, what more can I do?
            "Babe, It Ain't No Lie"
                             n.d.

1452. Lillian Day (1893–?)

1 A lady is one who never shows her underwear
unintentionally.   *Kiss and Tell*   1931

1453. Marie Gilchrist (1893–?)

1 But the life of poetry lies in fresh relationships
between words, in the spontaneous fusion of
hitherto unrelated words.
           Ch. 1, *Writing Poetry*
                            1932

2 All American Indian poems are songs, and an
Indian was once asked which came first, the
words or the music. "They come together," he
replied.   *Ibid., Ch. 3*

3 Nouns and verbs are almost pure metal; adjec-
tives are cheaper ore.
     Quoted in "On the Teaching of Poetry" by
                  Leonora Speyer,* *The*
           Saturday Review of Literature
                            1946

*See 1190.

1454. Helen Hathaway (1893–1932)

1 More tears have been shed over men's lack of
manners than their lack of morals.
                 Manners for Men
                              n.d.

1455. Margery Eldredge Howell (1893–?)

1 There's dignity in suffering—
Nobility in pain—
But failure is a salted wound
That burns and burns again.   "Wormwood,"
                               n.d.

1456. Suzanne LaFollette (1893–1983)

1 There is nothing more innately human than the
tendency to transmute what has become customary into what has been divinely ordained.
        "The Beginnings of Emancipation,"
            Concerning Women   *1926*

2 The revolutionists did not succeed in establishing human freedom; they poured the new wine
of belief in equal rights for all men into the old
bottle of privilege for some; and it soured.
                            Ibid.

3 . . . where divorce is allowed all . . . society
demands a specific grievance of one party against
the other. . . . The fact that marriage may be
a failure spiritually is seldom taken into
account.   *Ibid.*

4 If responsibility for the upbringing of children
is to continue to be vested in the family, then
the rights of children will be secured only when
parents are able to make a living for their families with so little difficulty that they may give
their best thought and energy to the child's
development. . . .   *Ibid.*

5 For man, marriage is regarded as a station; for
women, as a vocation.
          "Women and Marriage," op. cit.

6 . . . nothing could be more grotesquely unjust
than a code of morals, reinforced by laws, which
relieves men from responsibility for irregular
sexual acts, and for the same acts drives women
to abortion, infanticide, prostitution and self-
destruction.   *Ibid.*

7 . . . when one hears the argument that marriage
should be indissoluble for the sake of children,
one cannot help wondering whether the protag-
onist is really such a firm friend of
childhood. . . .   *Ibid.*

8 No system of government can hope to survive
the cynical disregard of both law and principle
which government in American regularly
exhibits.   "What Is to Be Done," op. cit.

9 No one . . . who has not known that inesti-
mable privilege can possibly realize what good
fortune it is to grow up in a home where there
are grandparents.
          Letter to Alice Rossi* (July 1971),
       The Feminist Papers, Alice Rossi, ed;
                            1973

*See 1912.

1457. Margaret Leech (1893–1974)

1 England was the friend whose policy stood like
a bulwark against Continental animosity to the
ambitions of the American republic.
        Ch. 11, *In the Days of McKinley**
                            1959

*(1843–1901), 25th president of the United States (1897–
1901); assassinated.

2 Charity stood ready to atone for the heartlessness of the War Department. Ibid., Ch. 13

3 Yet, for a space, Americans turned from the challenge and the strangeness of the future. Entranced and regretful, they remembered McKinley's firm, unquestioning faith; his kindly, frock-coated dignity; his accessibility and dedication to the people: the federal simplicity that would not be seen in Washington.
Ibid., Ch. 26

1458. Hesper Le Gallienne (1893–?)

1 The loose foot of the wanderer
    Is curst as well as blest!
It urges ever, ever on
    And never gives him rest.
        "The Wanderer"   n.d.

1459. Dorothy Parker (1893–1967)

1 (All your life you wait around for some damn man!)   "Chant for Dark Hours,"
        Enough Rope   1927

2 By the time you swear you're his,
    Shivering and sighing,
And he vows his passion is
    Infinite, undying—
Lady, make a note of this:
    One of you is lying.
        "Unfortunate Coincidence," op. cit.

3 Four be the things I am wiser to know:
Idleness, sorrow, a friend, and a foe.

Four be the things I'd be better without:
Love, curiosity, freckles, and doubt.
        "Inventory," Sts. 1–2,
            op, cit.

4 Men seldom make passes.
A girls who wear glasses.   "News Item,"
            op. cit.

5 Oh, life is a glorious cycle of song,
A medley of extemporanea;
And love is a thing that can never go wrong;
And I am Marie of Roumania.   "Comment,"
            op. cit.

6 Razors pain you
Rivers are damp;
Acids stain you;
And drugs cause cramp.
Guns aren't lawful;
Nooses give;
Gas smells awful;
You might as well live.   "Resumé,"
            op. cit.

7 Scratch a lover, and a foe.
        "Ballade of a great Weariness,"
            St. 1, op. cit.

8 Where's the man could ease a heart
Like a satin gown?
        "The Satin Dress," St. 1,
            op. cit.

9 Authors and actors and artists and such
Never know nothing, and never know much.
        "Bohemia," Sunset Gun   1928

10 Byron and Shelley and Keats
Were a trio of lyrical treats.
        "A Pig's-Eye View of
            Literature,"
            op. cit.

11 Her mind lives tidily, apart
    From cold and noise and pain,
And bolts the door against her heart,
    Out wailing in the rain.   "Interior," St. 3,
            op. cit.

12 They sicken of the calm, who knew the
    storm.   "Fair Weather," St. 1,
            op. cit.

13 This living, this living, this living
    Was never a project of mine.   "Coda,"
            op. cit.

14 There was nothing separate about her days.
Like drops upon a window-pane, they ran
together and trickled away.
        "Big Blonde," Pt. I, Laments for the
            Living   1929

15 She was always pleased to have him come and never sorry to see him go.   Ibid., Pt. II

16 She had spent the golden time in grudging its going.   "The Lovely Leave," op. cit.

17 Scratch a king and find a fool!
        "Salome's Dancing-Lesson," St. 3,
            Death and Taxes   1931

18 There was nothing more fun than a man!
        "The Little Old Lady
            in Lavendar Silk," St. 3,
            op. cit.

19 Brevity is the soul of lingerie.
        Quoted in While Rome Burns
        by Alexander Woollcott   1934

20 She [Katharine Hepburn*] runs the gamut of emotions from A to B.
        Quoted in Publisher's Weekly
            19 June 1967

* See 1702.

21 I heard someone say, and so I said it too, that ridicule is the most effective weapon. Well, now I know. I know that there are things that never have been funny, and never will be. And I know

(308)

that ridicule may be a shield, but it is not a weapon.   Quoted in *You Might As Well Live* by John Keats   *1970*

22 Excuse my dust.   "Epitaph"   *n.d.*

1460. Mary Pickford (1893–1979)

1 I was forced to live far beyond my years when just a child, now I have reversed the order and I intend to remain young indefinitely.
Quoted in "How Mary Pickford Stays Young" by Athene Farnsworth, *Everybody's Magazine*   *May 1926*

2 I left the screen because I didn't want what happened to Chaplin* to happen to me. When he discarded the little tramp, the little tramp turned around and killed him.
Quoted in "America's Sweetheart Lives" by Aljean Harmetz, *The New York Times 28 March 1971*

*Charlie Chaplin (1889–1977). American motion picture actor and producer.

1461. Dorothy L. Sayers (1893–1957)

1 "A man goes and fights for his country, gets his inside gassed out, and loses his job, and all they give him is the privilege of marching past the Cenotaph once a year and paying four shillings in the pound income-tax."
Ch. 1, *The Unpleasantness at the Bellona Club*   *1928*

2 "Very dangerous things, theories."
Ibid., Ch. 4

3 "People who make some other person their job are dangerous."   *Gaudy Night*   *1936*

4 "There is perhaps one human being in a thousand who is passionately interested in his job for the job's sake. The difference is that if that one person in a thousand is a man, we say, simply, that he is passionately keen on his job; if she is a woman, we say she is a freak."
Ibid.

5 ". . . of all devils let loose in the world there [is] no devil like devoted love. . . ."   Ibid.

6 ". . . love's a nervous, awkward, overmastering brute; if you can't rein him it's best to have no truck with him."   Ibid.

7 "The only sin passion can commit is to be joyless."   *Busman's Honeymoon*   *1947*

8 "Lawyers enjoy a little mystery, you know. Why, if everybody came forward and told the truth, the whole truth, and nothing but the truth straight out, we should all retire to the workhouse."   Ch. 3, *Clouds of Witness 1956*

9 "She always says, my lord, that facts are like cows. If you look them in the face hard enough they generally run away.   Ibid., Ch. 4

10 "Well-bred English people never have imagination. . . ."   Ibid., Ch. 11

11 "Time and trouble will tame an advanced young woman, but an advanced old woman is uncontrollable by any earthy force."   Ibid., Ch. 16

1462. Evelyn Scott (1893–1963)

1 If I could only *feel* the child! I imagine the moment of its quickening as a sudden awakening of my own being which has never before had life. I want to *live* with the child, and I am as heavy as a stone.   *Escapade*   *1913*

2 I realized a long time ago that a belief which does not spring from a conviction in the emotions is no belief at all.   Ibid.

3 It is impossible to control creation.   Ibid.

1463. Madame Sun Yat-sen (1893–1981)

1 Liberty and equality, those two inalienable rights of the individual . . . but there is still Fraternity to be acquired. . . . And it may be for China, the oldest of nations, to point the way to this Fraternity.   Quoted in *The Wesleyan April 1912*

2 In the last analysis, all revolutions must be social revolutions, based upon fundamental changes in society; otherwise it is not revolution, but merely a change of government. . . .
Article in the *People's Tribune 14 July 1927*

3 Let us exert every ounce of man's energy and everything produced by him to ensure that everywhere the common people of the world get their due from life. This is to say that our task does not end until every hovel has been rebuilt into a decent house, until the products of the earth are within easy reach of all, until the profits from the factories are returned in equal amount to the effort exerted, until the family can have complete medical care from the cradle to the grave.   Address (21 September 1949), "The Chinese Women's Fight for Freedom," *Asia July–August 1956*

1464. Clara Thompson (1893–1958)

1 Although this is a special group within the culture [the upper classes], it is an important group because, on the whole, it is a thinking group, nonconformist, and seeking to bring about changes in the cultural situation.
"The Role of Women in This Culture," *Psychiatry*, Vol IV   *1941*

2 Industry has been taken out of the home.
Ibid.

3 The fact that one is married by no means proves that one is a mature person.
"Changing Concepts of Homosexuality in Psychoanalysis," *A Study of Interpersonal Relations, New Contributions to Psychiatry*, Patrick Mullahy, ed.   *1949*

1465. Sylvia Townsend Warner (1893–1978)

1 Blest fertile Dullness! mothering surmise, rumor, report, as stagnant water, flies, whose happy votaries, stung by every hatch, divinely itch, and more divinely scratch!
Opus Seven   1931

2 You are only young once. At the time it seems endless, and is gone in a flash; and then for a very long time you are old.
"Swans on an Autumn River," *Swans on an Autumn River   1966*

3 . . . Audrey carried in *The Daily Telegraph*. Mother turned with avidity to the Deaths. When other helpers fail and comforts flee, when the senses decay and the mind moves in a narrower and narrower circle, when the grasshopper is a burden and the postman brings no letters, and even the Royal Family is no longer quite what it was, an obituary column stands fast.
"Their Quiet Lives," op. cit.

1466. Katherine Bowditch (1894–1933)

1 And what am I but love of you made flesh,
Quickened by every longing love may bring,
A pilgrim fire, homeless and wandering.
"Reincarnation"   *n.d.*

1467. Rachel Lyman Field (1894–1942)

1 You won't know why, and you can't say now
Such a change upon you came,
But—once you have slept on an island
You'll never be quite the same!

"If Once You Have Slept on an Island," *Taxis and Toadstools 1926*

2 Doorbells are like a magic game,
Or the grab-bag at a fair—
You never know when you hear one ring
Who may be waiting there.   "Doorbells,"
n.d.

1468. Esther Forbes (1894–1967)

1 Women have almost a genius for anticlimaxes.   *O Genteel Lady!   1926*

2 Most American heroes of the Revolutionary period are by now two men, the actual man and the romantic image. Some are even three men—the actual man, the image, and the debunked remains.   *Paul Revere   1942*

1469. Martha Graham (1894–1991)

1 Nothing is more revealing than movement.
"The American Dance," *Modern Dance*, Virginia Stewart, ed.   *1935*

2 America does not concern itself now with Impressionism. We own no involved philosophy. The psyche of the land is to be found in its movement. It is to be felt as a dramatic force of energy and vitality. We move; we do not stand still. We have not yet arrived at the stocktaking stage.   *Ibid.*

3 We look at the dance to impart the sensation of living in an affirmation of life, to energize the spectator into keener awareness of the vigor, the mystery, the humor, the variety, and the wonder of life. This is the function of the American dance.   *Ibid.*

1470. Agnes Kendrick Gray (1894–?)

1 Sure, 'tis God's ways is very quare,
An' far beyont my ken,
How o' the selfsame clay he makes
Poets an' useful men.
"The Shepherd to the Poet," St. 4
n.d.

1471. Osa Johnson (1894–1953)

1 "A woman that's too soft and sweet is like tapioca pudding—fine for them as likes it."
Ch. 10, *I Married Adventure   1940*

2 "Animals and primitive people are alike in one thing," he said. "They know when you are

friendly, they can sense it. . . . They can even smell fear."
Ch. 18, *Bride in the Solomons*   1944

1472. Sister Pascalina (1894–?)

1 The Pope* should stop all overt political activity by the clergy.
Ch. 5, *La Popessa*, Paul I. Murphy with R. Rene Arlington   1983

*Pius XII (1876–1958); Pope (1939–1958).

2 Pius spurned ecumenism and feared the increasing democratization of ecclesiastical decision-making. The vernacular Mass, the growing role of the laity in Church policies, and the rising debate over the Holy See's sexual ethics [are] signs of decadence and profanation of Catholic heritage.
Ibid., Epilogue

1473. Jean Rhys (1894–1979)

1 . . . Miss Bruce, passing by a shop, with the perpetual hunger to be beautiful and that thirst to be loved which is the real curse of Eve. . . . Then must have begun the search for *the* dress, the perfect Dress, beautiful, beautifying, possible to be worn. And lastly, the search for illusion—a craving, almost a vice, the stolen waters and the bread eaten in secret of Miss Bruce's life.
"Illusion," *The Left Bank*   1927

2 She respected Americans: they were not like the English, who, under a surface of annoying moroseness of manner, were notoriously timid and easy to turn round your finger.
"Mannequin," op. cit.

3 Next week, or next month, or next year I'll kill myself. But I might as well last out my month's rent, which has been paid up, and my credit for breakfast in the morning.
Pt. II, *Good Morning, Midnight* 1939

4 "I often want to cry. That is the only advantage women have over men—at least they can cry."
Ibid.

1474. Dora Russell (1894–?)

1 Marriage, laws, the police, armies and navies are the mark of human incompetence.
The Right to Be Happy 1927

1475. Adela Rogers St. Johns (1894–1988)

1 The modern woman is the curse of the universe. A disaster, that's what. She thinks that before her arrival on the scene no woman ever did anything worthwhile before, no woman was ever liberated until her time, no woman really ever amounted to anything. . . .
Quoted in "Some Are Born Great" by Mert Guswiler, *Los Angeles Herald-Examiner*   13 October 1974

2 About twenty-five years ago . . . I made three resolutions of what I would never do again. They were: to put on a girdle, to wear high heels, and to go out to dinner.
Ibid.

3 Mrs. [Margaret] Sanger* said the best birth control is to make your husband sleep on the roof.
Some Are Born Great   1974

*See 1328; Sanger *reported* this advice—she did not give it.

4 I wish women would stand together and shackle the men who want to move us backwards.
Quoted in *Time*   22 August 1988

1476. Agnes Smedley (1894?–1950)

1 The gossips specialized most of all in the gruesome . . .
Bk. I, "The Pattern," *Battle Hymn of China*   1943

2 I have always detested the belief that sex is the chief bond between man and woman. Friendship is far more human.
Ibid.

3 There's something dreadfully decisive about a beheading.
Bk. IX, "Farewell!," op. cit.

4 . . . commercialism seemed to have eaten into the very heart of American life and culture.
Bk. X, "Hong Kong," op. cit.

5 There was waste and softness on every hand.
Ibid.

1477. Genevieve Taggard (1894–1948)

1 Try tropic for your balm,
Try storm,
And after storm, calm.
Try snow of heaven, heavy, soft and slow,
Brilliant and warm.
Nothing will help, and nothing do much harm.
"Of the Properties of Nature for Healing an Illness," St. 1   n.d.

1478. Dorothy Thompson (1894–1961)

1 But I do not think that Communism as a belief, apart from overt and illegal actions, can be

successfully combatted by police methods, persecution, war or a mere anti spirit. The only force that can overcome an idea and a faith is another and better idea and faith, positively and fearlessly upheld.

> Quoted in the *Ladies' Home Journal*
> *October 1954*

2 Of all forms of government and society, those of free men and women are in many respects the most brittle. They give the fullest freedom for activities of private persons and groups who often identity their own interests, essentially selfish, with the general welfare.

> *On the Record   May 1958*

3 They have not wanted *Peace* at all; they have wanted to be spared war—as though the absence of war was the same as peace.   Ibid.

1479. Babette Deutsch (1895–1974)

1 But the poet's job is, after all, to translate God's poem (or is it the Fiend's?) into words.

> "Poetry at the Mid-Century,"
> *The Writer's Book,*
> Helen Hull, ed.   *1950*

2 . . . the poet . . . like the lover . . . is a person unable to reconcile what he knows with what he feels. His peculiarity is that he is under a certain compulsion to do so.   Ibid.

3 Their memories: a heap of tumbling stones, Once builded stronger than a city wall.

> "Old Women"
> *n.d.*

4 You, also laughing one, Tosser of balls in the sun, Will pillow your bright head By the incurious dead.   "A Girl"
> *n.d.*

1480. Anna Freud (1895–1982)

1 The war acquires comparatively little significance for children so long as it only threatens their lives, disturbs their material comfort or cuts their food rations. It becomes enormously significant the moment it breaks up family life and uproots the first emotional attachments of the child within the family group.

> *War and Children, w/*
> Dorothy Burlingham
> *1943*

2 . . . it is normal for an adolescent to behave for a considerable length of time in an inconsistent and unpredictable manner; to fight his impulses and to accept them; to ward them off successfully and to be overrun by them; to love

his parents and to hate them; to revolt against them and to be dependent on them; to be deeply ashamed to acknowledge his mother before others and, unexpectedly, to desire heart-to-heart talks with her; to thrive on imitation of and identification with others while searching unceasingly for his own identity; to be more idealistic, artistic, generous and unselfish than he will ever be again, but also the opposite: self-centered, egoistic, calculating. Such fluctuations between extreme opposites would be deemed highly abnormal at any other time of life. At this time they may signify no more than that an adult structure of personality takes a long time to emerge . . .   "Adolescence," *The*
> *Psychoanalytic Study of the*
> *Child,* Vol. 13   *1958*

1481. Juana de Ibarbourou (1895–1989)

1 I give you my naked soul Like a statue unveiled.

> "The Hour," *Diamond Tongues*
> *1919*

2 For if I am so rich, if I have so much, If they see me surrounded by every luxury, It is because of my noble lineage That builds castles on my pillow.

> "Small Woman," op. cit.

1482. Dolores Ibarruri (1895–1989)

1 It is better to die on your feet than to live on your knees!   Radio Speech
> *18 July 1936*

2 Wherever they pass they [the fascists] sow death and desolation.

> *Speeches and Articles* (1936–1938)
> *1938*

3 We dip our colours in honour of you, dear women comrades, who march into battle together with the men.   Ibid.

4 *!No pasaran!*   Quoted in Ch. 4, *The*
> *Passionate War, the Narrative*
> *History of the Spanish Civil War,*
> (1936–39) by Peter Wyden   *1983*

5 It is better to be the widow of a hero than the wife of a miserable coward.

> Speech, Valencia (1936), op. cit.

6 I am a simple woman; granddaughter, daughter and sister of miners. A woman who has fought much and hard to bring socialism to Spain.

> Quoted in
> "Entrevista" by Antonio del
> Corral, *Carta de España,*
> Hélène Lopez, tr.
> *15 December 1985*

1483. Bessie Rowland James (1895–1974)

1 No matter how lofty you are in your department, the responsibility for what your lowliest assistant is doing is yours. *Adlai's Almanac n.d.*

1484. Dorothea Lange (1895–1965)

1 These [country women] are women of the American soil. They are a hardy stock. They are the roots of our country. . . . They are not our well-advertised women of beauty and fashion. . . . These women represent a different mode of life. They are of *themselves* a very great American style. They live with courage and purpose, a part of our tradition.
Quoted in *The Woman's Eye* by Anne Tucker* 1973

*See 2240.

2 The camera is an instrument that teaches people how to see without a camera.
Quoted in "The Photographer Who Showed Americans How to See Themselves" by Robert Kirsch, *Los Angeles Times* 13 August 1978

3 . . . being disabled gave me an immense advantage. People are kinder to you. It puts you on a different level than if you go into a situation whole and secure. Ibid.

4 The megalopolis is not just an American phenomenon, it's international and we are creating this environment, teeming with unfamiliar ways of living, almost without scrutiny. Ibid.

1485. Susanne K. Langer (1895–1985)

1 Feeling, in the broad sense of whatever is felt in any way, as sensory stimulus or inward tension, pain, emotion or intent, is the mark of mentality
Vol. 1, Pt. I, Ch. 1, *Mind, An Essay on Human Feeling* 1967

2 Art is the objectification of feeling. . . .
Ibid., Pt. II, Ch. 4

3 "Consciousness" is not an entity at all, let alone a special cybernetic mechanism. It is a condition built up out of mental acts of a particular life episode. . . . Ibid., Ch. 11

1486. Monica Baldwin (1896–?)

1 . . . all the magic of the countryside which is ordained from the healing of the soul.
I Leap Over the Wall 1950

1487. Mamie Doud Eisenhower (1896–1979)

1 I stayed busy all the time and loved being in the White House, but I was never expected to do all the things you have to do.
Comment to Rosalyn Carter* (1977), Quoted in *First Ladies* by Betty Boyd Caroli 1987

*See 1992.

1488. Ruth Gordon (1896–1985)

1 MAX. Say, is it too early for a drink?

POLLY. What's early about it? It's tomorrow in Europe and yesterday in China.
Act III, *Over Twenty-One* 1943

2 POLLY. Do you realize you've come damn close to breaking a man's spirit?

GOW. Well, it was his spirit or my bank account. Ibid.

3 CLYDE. I'm sure the way to be happy is to live well beyond your means!
Act I, *The Leading Lady* 1948

4 CLYDE. The best impromptu speeches are the ones written well in advance. Ibid.

5 GAY. So easy to fall into a rut, isn't it? Why should ruts be so comfortable and so unpopular? Ibid., Act II

6 BENJY. The kiss. There are all sorts of kisses, lad, from the sticky confection to the kiss of death. Of them all, the kiss of an actress is the most unnerving. How can we tell if she means it or if she's just practicing? Ibid.

7 MRS. GILSON. Up and the world is your oyster! This time you can't miss! Whack comes down the old shillaly and you're down again bitin' the dust! Can't face it! Screeching into your pillow nights! Put back your smile in the morning, trampin' to managers' offices! Home again in the evenin' ready to give up the ghost. Somebody comes by, to tell you: "Go see Frohman nine-thirty sharp!" Luck's turned, you're on the trolley again! Curl up your ostrich feathers! Sponge off the train of your skirt! Because it's all aboard tomorrow. . . . Ibid., Act III

1489. Vivien Kellems (1896–1975)

1 Of course I'm a publicity hound. Aren't all crusaders? How can you accomplish anything

unless people know what you're trying to do? Quoted in "Unforgettable Vivien Kellems" by Gloria Swanson,* *Reader's Digest* October 1975

*See 1535.

2 Men always try to keep women out of business so they won't find out how much fun it really is. Ibid.

1490. Martha Martin (1896–1959)

1 I killed a sea otter today. I actually did kill a sea otter. I killed him with the ax, dragged him home, and skinned him.
O Rugged Land of Gold 1952

2 I told her the deer are our helpers and our friends, our subjects and our comfort, and they will give us food and clothing according to our needs. I told her of the birds. . . . Told her of the fishes. . . . Told her of the mink and the otter, and the great brown bear with his funny, furry cub. Told her of the forest and of the things it will give us . . . of the majestic mountain uprising behind us with a vein of goldbearing ore coming straight from its heart. Told her that all these things were ours to have and to rule over and care for. Ibid.

3 The Indians have come, good, good Indians. Shy, fat, smelly, friendly, kindhearted Indians. Ibid.

1491. Tina Modotti (1896–1942)

1 . . . I never realized before that a letter—a mere sheet of paper—could be such a spiritual thing—could emanate so much feeling—you gave a soul to it!
Letter to Edward Weston* (25 April 1921), Quoted in Ch. 1, *Tina Modotti, A Fragile Life* by Mildred Constantine 1975

*English/American photographer (1850–1936) with whom she collaborated and who was her companion.

2 The love of revolutionaries is not separate from their other activities; it is related to their political ideals. Courtroom interrogation* (16 January 1929), op. cit.

*After the shooting death of Julio Antonio Mella, Cuban revolutionary, in Mexico, who was her companion.

3 I consider myself a photographer, nothing more . . . Photography, precisely because it can only be produced in the present and because it is based on what exists objectively before the camera, takes its place as the most satisfactory medium of registering life in all its aspects, and from this comes its documental value. If to this is added sensibility and understanding and, above all, a clear orientation as to the place it should have in the field of historical development, I believe that the result is something worthy of a place in social production, to which we should all contribute.
Comment at exhibition, Mexico City (December 1929), op. cit.

1492. Beata Rank (1896–1967)

1 Because she is so barren of spontaneous manifestations of maternal feelings, she studies vigilantly all the new methods of upbringing and reads treatises about physical and mental hygiene. "Adaptation of the Psychoanalytical Technique . . . ," *American Journal of Orthopsychiatry* January 1949

1493. Marjorie Kinnan Rawlings (1896–1953)

1 You can't change a man, no-ways. By the time his mammy turns him loose and he takes up with some innocent woman and marries her, he's what he is. "Benny and the Bird-dogs," *When the Whippoorwill* 1931

2 When she settled down for a life-time's quarreling at him, it was for the same reason syrup sours—the heat had just been put to her too long. Ibid.

3 Sorrow was like the wind. It came in gusts, shaking the woman. She braced herself.
Ch. 9, *South Moon Under* 1933

4 The game seemed for him to be two different animals. On the chase, it was the quarry. He wanted only to see it fall. . . . When it lay dead and bleeding, he was sickened and sorry. . . . Then when it was cut into portions . . . his mouth watered at its goodness. He wondered by what alchemy it was changed, so that what sickened him one hour, maddened him with hunger the next. It seemed as though there were either two different animals or two different boys. Ch. 8, *The Yearling* 1938

5 "A woman has got to love a bad man once or twice in her life, to be thankful for a good one." Ibid., Ch. 12

6 "Ever' man wants life to be a fine thing, and a easy. 'Tis fine, boy, powerful fine, but 'tain't easy. Life knocks a man down and he gits up and it knocks him down again. I've been uneasy all my life." Ibid., Ch. 33

7 They were all too tightly bound together, men and women, creatures wild and tame, flowers,

fruits and leaves, to ask that anyone be spared. As long as the whole continued, the earth could go about its business.

Ch. 20, *The Sojourner*   1953

1494. Ida P. Rolf (1896–1979)

1 Word's going around Esalen that Ida Rolf thinks the body is all there is. Well, I want it known that I think there's more than the body, but the body is all you can get your hands on.

Quoted in *The Protean Body*
By Don Johnson   1977

2 Form and function are a unity, two sides of one coin. In order to enhance function, appropriate form must exist or be created.

Preface, *Rolfing: The Integration of Human Structures*   1977

3 Twentieth-century medicine, which has worked so many miracles, has been chemically not structurally oriented. Hence, the lay mind thinks of chemistry as the only outstanding healing medium—a drug for this, a shot for that. But any mirror photograph would reveal that a great many problems are matters of structure, of physics . . .   Ibid.

1495. Elsa Schiaparelli (1896–1973)

1 So fashion is born by small facts, trends, or even politics, never by trying to make little pleats and furbelows, by trinkets, by clothes easy to copy, or by the shortening or lengthening of a skirt.

Ch. 9, *Shocking Life*
1954

2 A good cook is like a sorceress who dispenses happiness.   Ibid., Ch. 21

3 Eating is not merely a material pleasure. Eating well gives a spectacular joy to life and contributes immensely to goodwill and happy companionship. It is of great importance to the morale.   Ibid.

1496. Betty Smith (1896–1972)

1 There's a tree that grows in Brooklyn. Some people call it the Tree of Heaven. No matter where its seed falls, it makes a tree which struggles to reach the sky. It grows in boarded-up plots and out of neglected rubbish heaps. It grows up out of cellar gratings. It is the only tree that grows out of cement. It grows lushly . . . survives without sun, water, and seemingly without earth. It would be considered

beautiful except that there are too many of it.   *A Tree Grows in Brooklyn*   1943

2 Miss Gardner had nothing in all the world excepting a sureness about how right she was.

Ibid. Ch. 42

3 "The difference between rich and poor," said Francie, "is that the poor do everything with their own hands and the rich hire hands to do things."   Ibid., Ch. 45

4 "Is it not so that a son what is bad to his mother," he said "is bad to his wife?"

Ch. 1, *Maggie—Now*   1958

5 She felt, vaguely, that she had given away her childhood that night. She had given it to him or he had taken it from her, and made it into something wonderful. In a way, her life was his now.   Ibid., Ch. 23

1497. Dodie Smith (1896–?)

1 I have found that sitting in a place where you have never sat before can be inspiring.

I Capture the Castle   1948

2 Noble deeds and hot baths are the best cures for depression.   Ibid., Ch. 3

3 . . . miserable people cannot afford to dislike each other. Cruel blows of fate call for extreme kindness in the family circle.   Ibid., Ch. 6

4 ". . . she happens to belong to a type [of American woman] I frequently met—it goes to lectures. And entertains afterwards. . . . Amazing, their energy," he went on. "They're perfectly capable of having three or four children, running a house, keeping abreast of art, literature and music—superficially of course, but good lord, that's something—and holding down a job into the bargain. Some of them get through two or three husbands as well, just to avoid stagnation."   Ibid., Ch. 7

5 What a difference there is between wearing even the skimpiest bathing-suit and wearing nothing! After a few minutes I seemed to live in every inch of my body as fully as I usually do in my head and my hands and my heart. I had the fascinating feeling that I could think as easily with my limbs as with my brain. . . .

Ibid., Ch. 12

1498. Charlotte Whitton (1896–1975?)

1 Whatever women do they must do twice as well as men to be thought half as good. Luckily, this is not difficult.   Quoted in *Canada Month*
June 1963

1499. Dixie Willson (1896–?)

1 He may look just the same to you,
  And he may be just as fine,
  But the next-door dog is the next-door dog,
  And mine—is—mine!
  　　　　　"Next-Door Dog"   *n.d.*

1500. Wallis Simpson Windsor (1896–1986)

1 One can never be too thin or too rich.
  　　　　　Comment   *n.d.*

1501. Elizabeth Asquith Bibesco (1897–1945)

1 Being in a hurry is one of the tributes he pays
  to life.   "Balloons"   *1922*

2 It is sometimes the man who opens the door
  who is the last to enter the room.
  　　　　Ch. 13, *The Fir and the Palm*
  　　　　　　　　　　1924

3 It is never any good dwelling on good-byes.
  It is not the being together that it prolongs, it
  is the parting.   *Ibid.*, Ch. 15

1502. Louise Bogan (1897–1970)

1 The art of one period cannot be approached
  through the attitudes (emotional or intellectual)
  of another. "Reading Contemporary Poetry,"
  　　College English   *February 1953*

2 True revolutions in art restore more than they
  destroy.   *Ibid.*

3 It is a dangerous lot, that of the charming,
  romantic public poet, especially it if falls to a
  woman. . . . it is almost impossible for the
  poetess, once laurelled, to take off the crown
  for good or to reject values and taste of those
  who tender it.*   "Unofficial Feminine
  Laurate" (1939) *Selected Criticism*
  　　　　　　　　　　1955

*Referring to Edna St. Vincent Millay; see 1439.

4 But childhood prolonged, cannot remain a fairy-
  land. It becomes a hell.*
  　　　　　"Childhood's False Eden"
  　　　　　　　　(1940), op. cit.

*Referring to Katherine Mansfield; see 1391.

5 The intellectual is a middle-class product; if he
  is not born into the class he must soon insert
  himself into it, in order to exist. He is the fine
  nervous flower of the bourgeoisie.

"Some Notes on Popular and
Unpopular Art" (1943), op. cit.

6 Once form has been smashed, it has been smashed
  for good, and once a forbidden subject has been
  released it has been released for good.
  　　　"Experimentalists of A New
  　　　　　Generation," (1957),
  　　　　A Poet's Alphabet   *1970*

7 How fortunate the rich and/or married, who have
  servants and *wives* to expedite matters.
  　　　*What the Woman Lived: Selected
  　　　Letters 1920–1970*, Ruth Limmer, ed.
  　　　　　　　　　　1974

8 I don't like quintessential certitude.
  　　　　　Letter to Rolfe Humphries,
  　　　　　　　　　　op. cit.

9 A second blooming and the bough can scarcely
  bear it.   *Ibid.*

10 I cannot believe that the inscrutable universe
  turns on an axis of suffering; surely the strange
  beauty of the world must somewhere rest on
  pure joy!   Letter to John
  　　　　　　　　Hall Wheelock,
  　　　　　　　　　op. cit.

11 Women have no wilderness in them,
  They are provident instead,
  Content in the tight hot cell of their hearts
  To eat dusty bread.   "Women"
  　　　　　　　　　　n.d.

1503. Catherine Drinker Bowen (1897–1973)

1 I know what these people want; I have seen
  them pick up my violin and turn it over in their
  hands. They may not know it themselves, but
  they want music, not by the ticketful, the purse-
  ful, but music as it should be had, music at
  home, a part of daily life, a thing as necessary,
  as satisfying, as the midday meal. They want to
  play. And they are kept back by the absurd, the
  mistaken, the wicked notion that in order to play
  an instrument one must be possessed by that
  bogey called Talent. . . .
  　　　Ch. 2, *Friends and Fiddlers*   *1934*

2 "We don't want her to take music too seriously." Real concern came into her voice. "We
  don't want her to become intense over something, and warped and queer. Such women are
  unhappy in later life. They don't" she rang the
  bell for more tea, "they don't make good
  wives."   *Ibid.*, Ch. 4

3 Many a man who has known himself at ten
  forgets himself utterly between ten and
  thirty. . . .   *Ibid.*, Ch. 9

4 The professors laugh at themselves, they laugh
  at life; they long ago abjured the bitch-goddess

Success, and the best of them will fight for his scholastic ideals with a courage and persistence that would shame a soldier. The professor is not afraid of words like *truth;* in fact he is not afraid of words at all.
Ch. 5, *Adventures of a Biographer*
1946

5 For your born writer, nothing is so healing as the realization that he has come upon the right word. Ibid., Ch. 11

6 Great artists treasure their time with a bitter and snarling miserlines.
Speech, "The Nature of the Artist," Scripps College
27 April 1961

1504. Catherine Cate Coblentz (1897– 1951)

1 Life is an archer, fashioning an arrow
With anxious care, for in it life must trust;
A single flash across the earthly spaces
Straight to the throat of death—one conquering thrust! "Life" *n.d.*

1505. Dorothy Day (1897–1980)

1 . . . who were the mad and who the sane? . . . People sold themselves for jobs, for the pay check, and if they only received a high enough price, they were honored. If their cheating, their theft, their lies, were of colossal proportions, if it were successful, they met with praise, not blame. Pt. I, *The Long Loneliness* *1952*

2 In our disobedience we were trying to obey God rather than men, trying to follow a higher obedience. We did not wish to act in a spirit of defiance and rebellion.
Ch. 16, *Loaves and Fishes* *1963*

3 The greatest challenge of the day is: how to bring about a revolution of the heart, a revolution which has to start with each one of us? When we begin to take the lowest place, to wash the feet of others, to love our brothers with that burning love, that passion, which led to the Cross, then we can truly say, "Now I have begun." Ibid., Ch. 19

4 The best thing to do with the best things in life is to give them up.
Quoted in "Saints Among Us,"
Time *29 December 1975*

1506. Hermione Gingold (1897–1987)

1 My father dealt in stocks and shares and my mother also had a lot of time on her hands.
Pt. I, *The World is Square* *1945*

2 To call him a dog hardly seems to do him justice, though inasmuch as he had four legs, a tail, and barked, I admit he was, to all outward appearances. But to those of us who knew him well, he was a perfect gentleman.
Ibid., Pt. II

1507. Iréne Joliot-Curie (1897–1956)

1 That one must do some work seriously and must be independent and not merely amuse oneself in life—this our mother [Marie Curie]* has told us always, but never that science was the only career worth following.
Quoted in Ch. 10, *A Long Way from Missouri,*
by Mary Margaret McBride**
1959

*See 1134.
**See 1533.

1508. Caroline Lejeune (1897–1973)

1 Nothing is said that can be regretted. Nothing is said that can even be remembered.
"Dietrich as an Angel,"
The Observer (London) *1936*

2 Sometimes it seems to me as if the only quality admired in modern writing, or play-making, or film-making, is truth-and-ugliness. This, for some reason, is described as realism; as if nothing could be real that is not sordid, disagreeable or violent. Ch. 21, *Thank You for Having Me*
1964

3 When you finish with a job it is wiser to make the break completely. Cut off the old life, clean and sharp. If your mind is tired, that is the only way. If your mind is lively you will soon find other interests. Ibid., Ch. 22

1509. Margaret Mahler (1897–1985)

1 . . . the emotional growth of the mother in her parenthood, her emotional willingness to let go of the toddler—to give him, as the mother bird does, a gentle push, an encouragement toward independence—is enormously helpful. It may even be a *sine qua non* of normal (healthy) individuation. *The Psychological Birth of the Human Infant*
1975

1510. Ruth Pitter (1897–?)

1 I go about, but cannot find
The blood-relations of the mind.
"'The Lost Tribe," St. 1
n.d.

2 Though our world burn, the small dim words
 Stand here in steadfast grace,
And sing, like the indifferent birds
 About a ruined place.
"On an Old Poem," St. 2
n.d.

1511. Lillian Smith (1897–1966)

1 Faith and doubt both are needed—not as antag-
onists but working side by side—to take us
around the unknown curve.
The Journey   1954

2 To believe in something not yet proved and to
underwrite it with our lives: it is the only way
we can leave the future open. Man, surrounded
by facts, permitting himself no surprise, no
intuitive flash, no great hypothesis, no risk, is
in a locked cell. Ignorance cannot seal the mind
and imagination more securely.   Ibid.

3 . . . I am caught again in those revolving doors
of childhood.
Foreword, *Killers of the Dream*
(Rev. Ed.)   1961

4 The human heart dares not stay away too long
from that which hurt it most. There is a return
journey to anguish that few of us are released
from making.   Ibid., Pt. I, Ch. 1

5 Man, born of woman, has found it a hard thing
to forgive her for giving him birth. The patriarchal protest against the ancient matriarch has
borne strange fruit through the years. . . .
Ibid., Pt. II, Ch. 4

6 Education is a private matter between the person
and the world of knowledge and experience, and
has little to do with school or college. . . .
"Bridges to Other People, *Redbook*
September 1969

1512. Margaret Chase Smith (1897–   )

1 I believe that in our constant search for security
we can never gain any peace of mind until we
secure our own soul.   Essay in *This I Believe*,
Raymond Swing, ed.   1952

2 My creed is that public service must be more
than doing a job efficiently and honestly. It must
be a complete dedication to the people and to
the nation with full recognition that every human
being is entitled to courtesy and consideration,
that constructive criticism is not only to be
expected but sought, that smears are not only to
be expected but fought, that honor is to be
earned but not bought.   "My Creed," *Quick*
11 November 1953

3 Strength, the American way, is not manifested
by threats of criminal prosecution or police state
methods. Leadership is not manifested by coercion, even against the resented. Greatness is not
manifested by unlimited pragmatism, which
places such a high premium on the end justifying
any means and *any* methods.
Address, National Republican
Women's Conference Banquet
16 April 1962

4 The key to security is public information.
"It's Time to Speak Up for National
Defense," *Readers Digest*
March 1972

1513. Berenice Abbott (1898–1991)

1 Photography can never grow up if it imitates
some other medium. It has to walk alone; it has
to be itself.   "It Has to Walk Alone,"
Infinity (magazine)   1951

2 I took to photography like a duck to water. I
never wanted to do anything else. Excitement
about the subject is the voltage which pushes
me over the mountain of drudgery necessary to
produce the final photograph.
Preface, *The Berenice Abbott
Portfolio*   1976

3 Photography helps people to see.
Quoted in "Berenice Abbott: An
American Master," *ASMP Bulletin
October 1989*

4 I am so fascinated with this century it will help
keep me alive. I'll be there until the last minute,
fighting.   Ibid.

1514. Judith Anderson (1898–1992)

1 There is nothing enduring in the life of a woman
except what she builds in a man's heart.
News Item   *8 March 1931*

1515. Madame Chiang Kai-shek (1898–?)

1 Of all the inventions that have helped to unify
China perhaps the airplane is the most outstanding. Its ability to annihilate distance has been in
direct proportion to its achievements in assisting
to annihilate suspicion and misunderstanding
among provincial officials far removed from one
another or from the officials at the seat of
government.
"Wings Over China," *Shanghai
Evening Post*   *12 March 1937*

2 This changing world is rolling towards the abyss of self-destruction with a breath-taking rapidity. Speech, International Women's Conference, Sydney, Australia (February 1938), *War Messages and Other Selections* 1938

3 Machinery should be used to make necessities which hands cannot make, but there it should stop. Letter to a Friend (14 May 1938), op. cit.

4 I am convinced that we must train not only the head, but the heart and hand as well. Sec. II, *This Is Our China* 1940

5 Cliques seem to hold sway in many places. They are like dry rot in the administration. They stifle enterprise and initiative. They operate to oust honesty and efficiency by preventing a patriotic "outsider," or a stranger to the clique, from gaining a position, no matter how capable he may be. And they eject, or try to, anyone of any independence of character or mind who may happen to be near them but not of them. Every clique is a refuge for incompetence. It fosters corruption and disloyalty, it begets cowardice, and consequently is a burden upon and a drawback to the progress of the country. Its instincts and actions are those of the pack. Pt. I, Ch. 8, *China Shall Rise Again* 1941

6 America is not only the cauldron of democracy, but the incubator of democratic principles. Speech, U.S. House of Representatives *18 February 1943*

7 China's struggle now is the initial phase of a gigantic conflict between good and evil, between liberty and communism. Radio Address, New York *9 January 1950*

1516. Ariel Durant* (1898–1981)

1 You** love me because you know I love you to distraction. Quoted in "The Philosopher and the Schoolgirl" by Jim Bishop, *Reader's Digest October 1969*

*Since the lion's share of Ms. Durant's monumental work was in collaboration with her husband, historian **Will Durant, (1885?–1981), little can be found that is purely her own work.

1517. Amelia Earhart (1898–1937)

1 Courage is the price that Life exacts for granting peace. *Courage* 1927

2 There are two kinds of stones, as everyone knows, one of which rolls. Ch. 1, *20 Hours: 40 Minutes—Our Flight in the Friendship* 1928

3 In soloing—as in other activities—it is far easier to start something than it is to finish it. Ibid., Ch. 2

1518. Gracie Fields (1898–1979)

1 You can get good fish and chips at the Savoy; and you can put up with fancy people once you understand that you don't have to be like them. Ch. 4, *Sing as We Go* 1960

2 Now sometimes it can be a very dangerous thing to go in search of a dream for the reality does not always match it. . . . Ibid.

1519. Cecily R. Hallack (1898–1938)

1 Make me a saint by getting meals, and washing up the plates! "The Divine Office of the Kitchen," St. 1 *c.1928*

1520. Lotta Lenya (1898–1981)

1 [I have] a heavenly vase full of autumn leaves today. They look so beautiful. How much closer to God can one get? And a beautiful blue heron flew over the brook. Nature can make me cry faster than anything. Letter to Mary Daniel (April 1957), Quoted in *Lenya, a Life,* by Donald Spoto 1989

2 I don't like holidays, not here [the U.S.A.]— it's a giant supermarket, and I'm thinking with nostalgia of my childhood with a tiny Christmas tree . . . Ibid., Christmas card to Hilde Halpern (1980)

1521. Beatrice Lillie (1898–1989)

1 I'll simply say here that I was born Beatrice Gladys Lillie at an extremely tender age because my mother needed a fourth at meals. Ch. 1, *Every Other Inch a Lady* 1927

2 I took up knitting from time to time as a relaxation, but I always put it down again before going out to buy a rocking chair. Ibid., Ch. 15

3 The vows one makes privately are more binding than any ceremony or even a Shubert contract. Ibid.

1522. Golda Meir (1898–1978)

1 Can we today measure devotion to husband and children by our indifference to everything else? Is it not often true that the woman who has given up all the external world for her husband and her children has done it not out of a sense of duty, out of devotion and love, but out of incapacity, because the soul is not able to take into itself the many-sidedness of life, with its sufferings but also with its joys?
The Plough Woman   *c.1930*

2 I want to say to you, friends, that the Jewish community in Palestine is going to fight to the very end. If we have arms to fight with, we will fight with those, and if not, we will fight with stones in our hands.
"In the Midst of Battle: 1948," Speech, Council of Jewish Chicago
21 January 1948

3 We desire nothing more than peace, but we cannot equate peace merely with an apathetic readiness to be destroyed. If hostile forces gather for our proposed destruction, they must not demand that we provide them with ideal conditions for the realization of their plans. . . . The concept of annihilating Israel is a legacy of Hitler's war against the Jewish people, and it is no mere coincidence that the soldiers of Nasser had an Arabic translation of *Mein Kampf* in their knapsacks.
"The Israeli Action in Sinai: 1956," statement, General Assembly of the United Nations   *5 December 1956*

4 We have not the slightest doubt that eventually there will be peace and cooperation between us. This is a historic necessity for both peoples. We are prepared; we are anxious to bring it about now.
"A Solemn Appeal to the Arabs," Statement, General Assembly of United Nations
7 October 1957

5 . . . The deserts of the Middle East are in need of water, not bombers.   Ibid.

6 There is only one way: he who is Zionist, he who cannot rest in the *Galuth** must come here, but he must be ready for anything.
Quoted in *Golda Mier: Woman with a Cause* by Marie Syrkin   *1984*

*Forced exile.

7 We only want that which is given naturally to all peoples of the world, to be masters of our own fate, only of *our* fate, not of others, and in cooperation and friendship with others.
Address, Anglo-American Committee of Inquiry (25 March 1946),
op. cit.

8 Those that perished in Hitler's gas chambers were the last Jews to die without standing up to defend themselves.
"In the Hour of Deliverance: 1967" Speech, United Jewish Appeal rally at Madison Square Garden, New York
11 June 1967

9 But the individual was not a tool for something. He was the maker of tools. He was the one who must build. Even for the best purpose it is criminal to turn an individual into simply a means for some ultimate end. A society in which the dignity of the individual is destroyed cannot hope to be a decent society.
"The Zionist Purpose," Speech at Dropise College   *26 November 1967*

10 When peace comes we will perhaps in time be able to forgive the Arabs for killing our sons, but it will be harder for us to forgive them for having forced us to kill their sons.
Press conference, London   *1969*

11 A leader who doesn't hesitate before he sends his nation into battle is not fit to be a leader.
(1967), Quoted in *As Good as Golda* Israel and Mary Shenker, eds.   *1970*

12 We intend to remain alive. Our neighbors want to see us dead. This is not a question that leaves much room for compromise.
Quoted in "The Indestructible Golda Meir" by David Reed, *Reader's Digest*   *July 1971*

13 Women's Liberation is just a lot of foolishness. It's the men who are discriminated against. They can't bear children. And no one's likely to do anything about that.   Quoted in *Newsweek* *23 October 1972*

14 I believe there are a couple of gross injustices in the world: against African blacks and against Jews. Moreover, I think there two instances of injustice can only be remedied by Socialist principles.   Quoted by Oriana Fallaci* in *Le'Europeo*   *1973*

*See 2060.

15 At work, you think of the children you've left at home. At home, you think of the work you've left unfinished. Such a struggle is unleashed within yourself: your heart is rent.   Ibid.

16 Those who do not know how to weep with their whole heart don't know how to laugh either.
Ibid.

17 I must govern the clock, not be governed by it.   Ibid.

18 . . . old age is like a plane flying through a storm. Once you're aboard, there's nothing you can do. You can't stop the plane, you can't stop

the storm, you can't stop time. So one might as well accept it calmly, wisely.   Ibid.

19 . . . there's no difference between one's killing and making decisions that will send others to kill. It's exactly the same thing, or even worse.   Ibid.

20 I have had enough.
                          Statement upon Resignation
                          as Prime Minister of Israel
                                        11 April 1974

21 I think women often get not so much an unfair deal as an illogical one. Once in the Cabinet we had to deal with the fact that there had been an outbreak of assaults on women at night. One minister (a member of an extreme religious party) suggested a curfew. Women should stay at home after dark. I said: "But it's the men who are attacking the women. If there's to be a curfew, let the men stay at home, not the women."   Speech   *n.d.*

1523. Isabel Briggs Myers (1898–1980)

1 We cannot safely assume that other people's minds work on the same principles as our own. All too often, others with whom we come in contact do not reason as we reason, or do not value the things we value, or are not interested in what interests us.
                    Pt, I, Ch. 1, *Gifts Differing,*
                    with Peter B. Myers   *1980*

2 Whatever the circumstances of your life, whatever your personal ties, work, and responsibilities, the understanding of type can make your perceptions clearer, your judgments sounder, and your life closer to your heart's desire.
                    Ibid., Part IV, Ch. 19

1524. Lily Pincus (1898–1981)

1 Why not acknowledge and satisfy without shame the baby needs stirred up by bereavement?
                    Death and the Family
                                        1974

2 Regression in grief must be seen and supported as a means toward adaptation and health.
                                            Ibid.

1525. Helen Sekaquaptewa (1898–?)

1 We were as stubborn about going back to the old ways as they were about changing their way.   *Me and Mine*   *1969*

2 I was stuck here, so I might as well learn everything.

Interview,
    3 June 1981, Quoted in
*American Indian Women, Telling Their
Lives,* Gretchen M. Bataille &
            Kathleen Mullen Sands, eds.   *1984*

1526. Anna Moore Shaw (1898–1975)

1 We were not allowed to speak the Pima tongue at school. Some students would report on those who spoke in Indian and as a punishment our mouths would be taped. We did not mind, for the matron, teachers, and other employees were good to us, despite our naughty ways.
                    A Pima Past   *1974*

2 The educations they had strived so hard to give us had prepared us to bring in money from the white man's work; it would be wrong to waste all those years of schooling on a life of primitive farming.   Ibid.

1527. Bessie Smith (1898–1937)

1 No time to marry, no time to settle down;
I'm a young woman, and I ain't done runnin' aroun'.
                    "Young Woman's Blues"   *1927*

2 While you're living in your mansion, you
    don't know what hard times mean.
Poor working man's wife is starving; your
    wife is living like a queen.
                    "Poor Man's Blues"   *1930*

3 It's a long old road, but I know I'm gonna
find the end.   "Long Old Road"   *1931*

1528. Elizabeth Bowen (1899–1973)

1 "The best type of man is no companion."
                    The Hotel   *1928*

2 "There being nothing was what you were frightened of all the time, eh? Yes."
                    The Little Girls   *1963*

3 "Did you exchange embraces of any kind?"
"No. She was always in a hurry."
                    Eva Trout   *1968*

1529. Indra Devi (1899–?)

1 Like an ugly bird of prey, tension hovers over the heads of millions of people, ready to swoop down on all its victims at any time and in any place. More and more men, women, and even children are caught up in its cold grip and held

for years, sometimes for the whole of their lives. Tension, in fact, is probably one of the greatest menaces the civilized world must face these days.　　Ch. 1, *Renewing Your Life Through Yoga*　　*1963*

2 Tranquilizers . . . dull the keen edge of the angers, fears, or anxiety with which we might otherwise react to the problems of living. Once the response has been dulled, the irritating surface noise of living muted or eliminated, the spark and brilliance are also gone.　　Ibid.

3 Like water which can clearly mirror the sky and the trees only so long as its surface is undisturbed, the mind can only reflect the true image of the Self when it is tranquil and wholly relaxed.　　Ibid.

4 Our body is a magnificently devised, living, breathing mechanism, yet we do almost nothing to insure its optimal development and use. . . . The human organism needs an ample supply of good building material to repair the effects of daily wear and tear.　　Ibid., Ch. 2

5 Yoga is not a religion, nor is it a magic formula or some form of calisthenics. In the country of its origin it is called a science—the science of living a healthy, meaningful, and purposeful life—a method of realizing the true self when the body, mind, and spirit blend into one harmonious whole. . . . Yoga is a philosophy, a way of life, and organized religion forms no part of it.　　Ibid., Ch. 10

1530. Hildegarde Flanner (1899–?)

1 I saw a hawk devour a screaming bird,
Devour the little ounce sugared with song.
　　"Hawk Is a Woman,"
　　If There is Time　　*1942*

2 May she, the very she, may that hawk hear
The ugly female laughter of a hawk.　　Ibid.

1531. Marguerite Harris (1899–1978)

1 In tidy terminal homes,
agape at the stalking Rorschach
shapes that menace our cosmos,
pawns, now, we itch and surmise.
　　"The Chosen," St. 1, *The East Side Scene*, Allen de Loach, ed.　　*1968*

1532. Eva Le Gallienne (1899–1991)

1 . . . no mechanical device can ever, it seems to me, quite take the place of that mysterious communication between players and public, that sense of an experience directly shared, which gives to the living theatre its unique appeal.
　　Ch. 1, *The Mystic in the Theatre: Eleanora Duse**　　*1965*

*See 1067.

2 Innovators are inevitably controversial.　　Ibid.

3 People who are born even-tempered, placid and untroubled—secure from violent passions or temptations to evil—those who have never needed to struggle all night with the Angel to emerge lame but victorious at dawn, never become great saints.　　Ibid., Ch.2

1533. Mary Margaret McBride (1899–1976)

1 This country began with people moving, and we've been moving ever since. . . . As long as we keep at that I guess we'll be all right.
　　Ch. 2, *America for Me*　　*1941*

2 "Terrible things happen to young girls in New York City. . . ."
　　Ch. 1, *A Long Way from Missouri*
　　1959

1534. Helen Hill Miller (1899–?)

1 France prides itself on being very old, on being not only the first-born among modern nations but the heir of the ancient world, the transmitter to the West of Mediterranean civilization.
　　Pamphlet, "The Spirit of Modern France"　　*1934*

2 Logical clarity is the genius of the French language.　　Ibid.

1535. Gloria Swanson (1899–1983)

1 When I die, my epitaph should read: *She Paid the Bills*. That's the story of my private life.
　　Quoted in "Gloria Swanson Comes Back" By S. Frank, *Saturday Evening Post*　　*22 July 1950*

1536. Diana Vreeland (1899/1904?–1989)

1 Elegance is innate . . . it has nothing to do with being well dressed.　　Quoted in *Time*
　　4 September 1989

1537. Lena Guilbert Ford (fl. early 1900s–1916?)

1 Keep the home fires burning,
While your hearts are yearning,

Though your lands are far away
They dream of home.
There's silver lining
Through the dark cloud shining:
Turn the dark cloud inside out,
Till the boys come home.
"Keep the Homes Fires Burning"
1915

1538. Eva Lathbury (fl. early 1900s)

1 The fall, like the serpent, was mythical: the apple was sound and Eve hysterical.
My Meyer's Pupil 1907

2 I can't help it . . . that's what we all say when we don't want to exert ourselves. Ibid.

1539. Moira O'Neill (fl. early 1900s)

1 Youth's for an hour,
Beauty's a flower,
But love is the jewel that wins the world.
"Beauty's a Flower," *Songs of the Glens of Antrim* 1901

2 The memory's fairly spoilt on me
Wild mindin' to forget. "Forgettin'," St. 5,
op. cit.

1540. Lady Troubridge (fl. early 1900s– 1946)

1 A bad woman always has something she regards as a curse—a real bit of goodness hidden away somewhere. *The Millionaire* 1907

2 If I had had a pistol I would have shot him— either that or fallen at his feet. There is no middle way when one loves. Ibid.

1541. Grace Adams (1900–?)

1 Whenever serious intellectuals, psychologists, sociologists, practicing physicians, Nobel prize novelists take time off from their normal pursuits to scrutinize and appraise the Modern American Woman, they turn in unanimously dreary reports. "American Women Are Coming Along," *Harper's* 1939

1542. Polly Adler (1900–1962)

1 Too many cooks spoil the brothel.
A House Is Not a Home 1953

2 The degree to which a pimp, if he's clever, can confuse and delude a prostitute is very nearly unlimited. Ibid., Ch. 4

3 What it comes down to is this: the grocer, the butcher, the baker, the merchant, the landlord, the druggist, the liquor dealer, the policeman, the doctor, the city father and the politician— these are the people who make money out of prostitution, these are the real reapers of the wages of sin. Ibid., Ch. 9

4 The women who take husbands not out of love but out of greed, to get their bills paid, to get a fine house and clothes and jewels; the women who marry to get out of a tiresome job, or to get away from disagreeable relatives, or to avoid being called an old maid—these are whores in everything but name. The only difference between them and my girls is that my girls gave a man his money's worth. Ibid., Ch. 10

1543. Dorothy Arzner (1900–1980)

1 I was led by the grace of God to the movies. I would like the industry to be more aware of what they're doing to influence people. . . . Quoted in *Popcorn Venus* by Marjorie Rosen* 1973

*See 2356.

1544. Taylor Caldwell (1900–1985)

1 "Honest men live on charity in their age; the almhouses are full of men who never stole a copper penny. Honest men are the fools and the saints, and you and I are neither."
Bk. I, Ch. 12, *Dynasty of Death* 1938

2 Men who retain irony are not to be trusted, thought Ernest. They can't always resist an impulse to tickle themselves.
Ibid., Bk. II, Ch. 78

3 "He that hath no rule over his own spirit is like a city that is broken down and without walls." Pt. I, Ch. 5, *This Side of Innocence* 1946

4 "Learning," he would say, "should be a joy and full of excitement. It is life's greatest adventure; it is an illustrated excursion into the mind's noble and learned men, not a conducted tour through a jail. So its surroundings should be as gracious as possible, to complement it."
Pt. I, Ch. 9, *The Sound of Thunder* 1957

5 But what was a body? Dust, dung, urine, itches. It was the light within which was important,

and it was not significant if that light endured after death, or if the soul was blinded eternally in the endless night of the suspired flesh.

> Pt. I, Ch. 1, *Great Lion of God*
> *1970*

6 The old [Roman] gods understood that life was reasonable and favors were exchanged for favors, and that is how it should be.

> Ibid., Pt. III, Ch. 53.

7 At the end—and as usual—God had betrayed the innocent and had left them comfortless.

> Pt. I, Ch. 1, *Captains and the Kings*
> *1972*

8 It was business, and none of them had allegiances or attachments or involvements with any nation, not even their own. . . . Joseph immediately called them "the gray and deadly men," and did not know why he detested them, or why he found them the most dangerous of all among the human species.   Ibid., Ch. 21

9 "Once power is concentrated in Washington—admittedly not an immediate prospect—America will take her place as an empire and calculate and instigate wars, for the advantage of all concerned. We all know, from long experience, that progress depends on war."   Ibid.

10 "Mankind is the most selfish species this world has ever spewed up from hell, and it demands, constantly, that neighbors and politicians be 'unselfish,' and allow themselves to be plundered—for its benefit."   Ibid., Pt. II, Ch. 13

1545. Helen Gahagan Douglas (1900–1980)

1 If I go to Congress, it won't be to spar with anybody, man or woman. I'm not a wit. I'm not a fencer. I don't enjoy that kind of thing. It's all nonsense and an insult to the intelligence of the American people.   News Item   *1944*

2 Such pip-squeaks as Nixon and McCarthy are trying to get us so frightened of Communism that we'll be afraid to turn out the lights at night.   Speech   *1950*

3 The Eleanor Roosevelt* I shall always remember was a woman of tenderness and deep sympathy, a woman with the most exquisite manners of anyone I have known—one who did what she was called upon to do with complete devotion and rare charm.

> *The Eleanor Roosevelt We Remember*
> *1963*

*See 1341.

4 I know the force women can exert in directing the course of events.   Ibid.

1546. Queen Elizabeth (1900–   )

1 The children will not leave unless I do. I shall not leave unless their father does, and the King will not leave the country in any circumstances whatever.   Attributed   *1940*

2 I'm glad we've been bombed [Buckingham Palace]. It makes me feel I can look the East End in the face.   Attributed   *1940*

1547. Joanna Field (1900–   )

1 I used to trouble about what life was for—now being alive seems sufficient reason.

> (8 June) *A Life of One's Own*
> *1934*

2 I came to the conclusion then that "continual mindfulness" . . . must mean, not a sergeant-major-like drilling of thoughts, but a continual readiness to accept whatever came.

> Ibid., (10 October)

3 I began to suggest that thought, which I had always before looked on as a cart-horse to be driven, whipped and plodding between shafts, might be really a Pegasus, so suddenly did it alight beside me from places I had no knowledge of.   Ibid.

4 . . . the growth of understanding follows an ascending spiral rather than a straight line.

> Ibid. (Undated)

1548. Zelda Fitzgerald (1900–1948)

1 Most people hew the battlements of life from compromise, erecting their impregnable keeps from judicious submissions, fabricating their philosophical drawbridges from emotional retractions and scalding marauders in the boiling oil of sour grapes.

> Ch. 1, *Save Me the Waltz*   *1932*

2 Wasn't any art the expression of the inexpressible? And isn't the inexpressible always the same, though variable—like the *Time* in physics?   Ibid., Ch. 3

3 "Oh, the secret life of man and woman—dreaming how much better we would be than we are if we were somebody else or even ourselves, and feeling that our estate has been unexploited to its fullest. I have reached the point where I can only express the inarticulate, taste food without taste, smell whiffs of the past, read statistical books, and sleep in uncomfortable positions."   Ibid., Ch. 4

4 "By the time a person has achieved years adequate for choosing a direction, the die is cast

and the moment has long since passed which determined the future.'' Ibid.

5 ''. . . We grew up founding our dreams on the infinite promise of American advertising. I *still* believe that one can learn to play the piano by mail and that mud will give you a perfect complexion.'' Ibid.

6 Don't you think I was made for you? I feel like you had me ordered—and I was delivered to you—to be worn—I want you to wear me, like a watch-charm or a button hole boquet [sic]— to the world.
Letter to F. Scott Fitzgerald* (1919),
Quoted in *Zelda* by Nancy Mitford**
1970

*American author, 1896–1940.
**See 1626.

7 . . . I have often told you that I am that little fish who swims about under a shark and, I believe, lives indelicately on its offal. Anyway, that is the way I am. Life moves over me in a vast black shadow and swallow whatever it drops with relish . . .
Letters to F. Scott Fitzgerald (1932)
op. cit.

8 I take a sun bath and listen to the hours, formulating, and disintegrating under the pines, and smell the resiny hardi-hood of the high noon hours. The world is lost in a blue haze of distances and the immediate sleeps in a thin and finite sun. Journal (1938), op. cit.

1549. Lisa Gardiner (1900–1956)

1 And remember, expect nothing and life will be velvet. Quoted in *Don't Fall Off the Mountain* by Shirley MacLaine*
1970

*See 2159.

1550. Elizabeth Goudge (1900–1984)

1 Her birthdays were always important to her; for being a born lover of life, she would always keep the day of her entrance into it as a very great festival indeed. . . .
Pt, II, Ch. 1, Bk. I, *Green Dolphin Street*
1944

2 His hatred of his wife horrified him. It was the first hatred of his life, it was growing in bitterness and intensity day by day, and he had no idea what to do about it.
Ibid., Bk. II, Pt. III, Ch.1

3 She had a deep sense of justice and sometimes this made her feel as uncomfortable in her spirit

if she deserved a whipping and did not get it as she felt in her body if she did get it, and of the two she preferred to suffer in body.
Bk. I, Ch. 1, *The Child from the Sea*
1970

4 ''. . . The travail of creation of course exaggerates the importance of our work while we engage in it; we know better when the opus is finished and the lion is perceived to be only a broken-backed mouse. . . .''
Ibid., Pt. III, Ch. 2

1551. Helen Hayes (1900–)

1 An actress's life is so transitory—suddenly you're a building.* News Item
November 1955

*Referring to a New York theater named for her.

2 We rely upon the poets, the philosophers, and the playwrights to articulate what most of us can only feel, in joy or sorrow. They illuminate the thoughts for which we only grope; they give us the strength and balm we cannot find in ourselves. Whenever I feel my courage wavering I rush to them. They give me the wisdom of acceptance, the will and resilience to push on. Introduction, *A Gift of Joy*, with
Lewis Funke *1965*

3 Actors cannot choose the manner in which they are born. Consequently, it is the one gesture in their lives completely devoid of self-consciousness. Ch. 1, *On Reflection*, with
Sandford Dody *1968*

1552. Laura Z. Hobson (1900–1986)

1 Did it never occur to one of them to write about a fine guy who was Jewish? Did each one feel some savage necessity to pick a Jew who was a swine in the wholesale business, a Jew who was a swine in the movies, a Jew who was a swine in bed? Ch. 3, *Gentlemen's Agreement*
1946

2 Where did ideas come from, anyway? This one leaped at him when he'd been exhausted, AWOL from his search. Ibid., Ch. 4

3 We are born in innocence. . . . Corruption comes later. The first fear is a corruption, the first reaching for a something that defies us. The first nuance of difference, the first need to feel better than the different one, more loved, stronger, richer, more blessed—these are corruptions.
Ibid., Ch. 6

4 What was it, this being ''a good father''? To love one's sons and daughters was not enough;

to carry in one's bone and blood a pride in them, a longing for their growth and development—this was not enough. One had to be a ready companion to games and jokes and outings, to earn from the world this accolade. The devil with it.
Pt. I, Ch. 2, *The First Papers.*
1964

5 Why didn't children ever see that they could damage and harm their parents as much as parents could damage and harm children?
Consenting Adult
1975

1553. Kathryn Hulme (1900–1981)

1 I saw more of them [concentration-camp brands] on that first day. I saw so many that I was sure my memory was branded forever and that never again would I be able to think of mankind with that certain friendly ease which characterizes Americans like a birthright.
Ch. 2, *The Wild Place*   *1953*

2 Interior silence, she repeated silently. That would be her Waterloo. How without brain surgery could you quell the rabble of memories? Even as she asked herself the question, she heard her psychology professor saying quite clearly across a space of years, "No one, not even a saint, can say an *Ave* straight through without some association creeping in; this is a known thing."
Ch. 1, *The Nun's Story*
1956

3 "You must never lose the awareness that in yourself you are nothing, you are only an instrument. An instrument is nothing until it is lifted."
Ibid., Ch. 8

4 Then there had been the inspection of their child from head to toe as he watched Annie undress the baby before bedtime. The tiny perfect fingernails and toenails astonished him the most. They were like the small pink shells you scuffed up in the sands of tropical beaches, he whispered, counting them.
Ch. 9, *Annie's Captain*
1961

1554. Loran Hurnscot (1900?–1970)

1 It came over me, blindingly, for the first time in my life, that suicide was a wrong act, was indeed "mortal sin." In that moment, God stopped me. I did not want my life, but I knew I was suddenly forbidden by something outside myself to let it go.
(9 July 1939), *A Prison, a Paradise,*
Vol. II   *1959*

2 It had always been pride that had held me off from Him. Now it was broken the obstacle was gone. One is never simple enough, while things go well.
Ibid.

1555. Guion Griffis Johnson (1900–   )

1 Government existed for the best people—the intelligent, educated and wealthy. In a society where all are equally free and share alike in political privileges, there are some more fit for the exercise of good government than others.
"Southern Paternalism Toward Negroes After Emancipation,"
The Journal of Southern History
November 1957

2 The argument against mixing in the schools stresses again the concept of superior and inferior races and the obligation of the superior to give the inferior equal but separate facilities so that the Negro may have the opportunity to rise within his own social system.
Ibid.

1556. Wilhelmina Kemp Johnstone (1900–   )

1 But how glad I am, how very glad and grateful for that window looking out upon the sea!
"My Window," *Bahamian Jottings*
1973

2 The dawn artist was already out, tipping the clouds with glory, and transforming the sky into a glow of wonder.   "Our Trip to Green Cay,"
op. cit.

1557. Estee Lauder (1900?–   )

1 I would give the woman a sample of whatever she did not buy as a gift. It might be a few teaspoonsful of powder in a wax envelope. I just knew, even though I had not yet named the technique, that a gift with a purchase was very appealing.   *Estee: A Success Story*   *1985*

1558. Meridel Le Sueur (1900–?)

1 In the mid-centre of America a man can go blank for a long, long time. There is no community to give him life; so he can go lost as if he were in a jungle. No one will pay any attention. He can simply be as lost as if he had gone into the heart of an empty continent.
"Corn Village" (1930),
Salute to Spring   *1940*

2 "I put my hand where you lie so silently. I hope you will come glistening with life power, with

it shining upon you as upon the feathers of birds. I hope you will be a warrior and fierce for change, so all can live."

"Annunciation," op. cit.

3 Every generation must go further than the last or what's the use in it?

"The Dead in Steel," op. cit.

4 Hard times ain't quit and we ain't quit.

"Salute to Spring," op. cit.

5 . . . the history of an oppressed people is hidden in the lies and the agreed-upon myth of its conquerors.   Ch. 3, *Crusaders* 1955

6 Memory in America suffers amnesia.

Ibid., Ch. 6

7 Money is only money, beans tonight and steak tomorrow. So long as you can look yourself in the eye.   Ibid., Ch. 7

1559. Paula Ludwig (1900–1974)

1 Because I betrayed myself there in the dim
no leaf moved
no drop fell
But in the stillness could be heard
my hands growing toward you.

"To the Dark God," St. 3,
Candice L. McRee, tr.   *n.d.*

1560. Margaret Mitchell (1900–1949)

1 "I'm tired of everlastingly being unnatural and never doing anything I want to do. I'm tired of acting like I don't eat more than a bird, and walking when I want to run and saying I feel faint after a waltz, when I could dance for two days and never get tired. I'm tired of saying, 'How, wonderful you are!' to fool men who haven't got one-half the sense I've got and I'm tired of pretending I don't know anything, so men can tell me things and feel important while they're doing it. . . ."

Pt. I, Ch. 5, *Gone with the Wind* 1936

2 "Until you've lost your reputation, you never realize what a burden it was or what freedom really is."   Ibid., Pt. II, Ch. 9

3 "What most people don't seem to realize is that there is just as much money to be made out of the wreckage of a civilization as from the upbuilding of one."   Ibid.

4 "Death and taxes and childbirth! There's never any convenient time for any of them!"

Ibid., Pt. IV, Ch. 38

5 "You kin polish a mule's feets an' shine his hide an' put brass all over his harness an' hitch him ter a fine cah'ige. But he a mule jes' de same. He doan fool nobody."   Ibid., Ch. 48

6 "My pet, the world can forgive practically anything except people who mind their own business."   Ibid.

7 "I won't think of it now. I can't stand it if I do. I'll think of it tomorrow at Tara. Tomorrow's another day."   Ibid., Pt. V, Ch. 57

8 "What is broken is broken—and I'd rather remember it as it was at its best than mend it and see the broken places as long as I lived."

Ibid., Ch. 63

1561. Barbara Morgan (1900–   )

1 The Navajo and Pueblo Indian tribes who danced the rituals . . . as partners in the cosmic process, attuned me to the universally primal—rather than to either the "primitive" or the "civilized."   Quoted in *The Woman's Eye* by Anne Tucker*   1973

*See 2420.

2 . . . as the life style of the Space Age grows more inter-disciplinary, it will be harder for the "one-track" mind to survive. . . . I see simultaneous intake, multiple-awareness, and synthesized comprehension as inevitable, long before the year 2000 A.D.   Ibid.

1562. Louise Nevelson (1900–1988)

1 The freer that women become, the freer will men be. Because when you enslave someone—you *are* enslaved.   Quoted in *AFTRA* Summer   1974

1563. Martha Ostenso (1900–1963)

1 Far overhead sounded a voluminous prolonged cry, like a great trumpet call. Wild geese flying still farther north, to a region beyond human warmth . . . beyond even human isolation.

Ch. 1, *Wild Geese*   1925

2 Wherever the wind was bound, Elsa thought, there the whole world seemed to be going.

Ch. 4, *The Mad Carews*   1927

3 She was especially happy in the violence, the stride of the great, obstreperous city [Chicago], the fierce roar of the wind that was its voice, the white-green tumult of the waves breaking on the shore of Lake Michigan, its soul.

Ibid., Ch. 21

4 "You have stirred the soil with our plow, my
   friend. It will never be the same again."
                Ch. 4, *O River, Remember*   *1943*

5 Pity the Unicorn,
  Pity the Hippogriff,
  Souls that were never born
  Out of the land of If!   "The Unicorn and the
                               Hippogriff," St. 1
                                              n.d.

1564. Vijaya Lakshmi Pandit (1900–1990)

1 It [political imprisonment] is a slow daily sacrifice which can be so much more deadly than
  some big heroic gesture made in a moment of
  emotional upheaval. . . .
                (3 May 1943), *Prison Days*
                                        1946

2 When my public activities are reported it is very
  annoying to read how I looked, if I smiled, if a
  particular reporter liked my hair style.
                Quoted in *The Scotsman* (Glasgow)
                                  29 August 1955

3 You know, what happens to anybody who has
  been in these two places [Moscow and Washington, D. C.] and looked at them objectively,
  is the horrifying thought—if I may use that word
  in quotes—that they are so similar. . . . Take
  that passion for science—they're both absolutely
  dedicated to the machine, they are both extro-
  verts, they both function in much the same
  way. . . .   Ibid.

4 Difficulties, opposition, criticism—these things
  are meant to be overcome, and there is a special
  joy in facing them and in coming out on top. It
  is only when there is nothing but praise that life
  loses its charm and I begin to wonder what I
  should do about it.
                Quoted in *The Envoy Extraordinary*
                by Vera Brittain *   *1965*

* See 1449.

5 Freedom is not for the timid.
                          Ibid. (c. 1964)

1565. Malvina Reynolds (1900–1978)

1 Where are you going, my little one, little one,
  Where are you going, my baby, my own?
  Turn around and you're two,
  Turn around and you're four,
  Turn around and you're a young girl going out
  of my door.   "Turn Around"   *1958*

2 Everybody thinks my head's full of nothing,
  Wants to put his special stuff in,
  Fill the space with candy wrappers,

Keep out sex and revolution,
But there's no hole in my head,
Too bad.   "No Hole in My Head"   *1965*

3 While that baby is a child it will suffer from
   neglect,
  Be picked up and pecked, run over and
   wrecked,
  And its head will be crowned with the thorn,
  But while it's inside her it must remain intact,
  And it cannot be murdered till it's born.
                "Rosie Jane"   *1973*

4 There's inflation and pollution.
  Everything's been bought on credit
  In this rotten institution.
  And they waste the gentle people
  'Cause the system has no soul.
  They've got the world in their pocket,
  But their pocket's got a hole.
                "World in their Pocket,"
                Verse 1   *1975*

5 Celebrate my death for the good times I've
   had,
  For the work that I've done
   and the friends that I've made
  Celebrate my death, of whom it could be said,
  "She was a working class woman, and a
   red."   Last song, untitled   *1978*

1566. Nathalie Sarraute (1900–   )

1 Those who live in a world of human beings can
  only retrace their steps.
                "From Dostoievski to Kafka"
                            (October 1947)
                The Age of Suspicion   *1956*

2 Neither reproaches nor encouragements are able
  to revive a faith that is waning.
                "The Age of Suspicion"
                (February 1950),
                op. cit.

3 . . . what is hidden beneath the interior monologue: an immense profusion of sensations, images, sentiments, memories, impulses, little lar-
  val actions that no inner language can convey,
  that jostle one another on the threshold of consciousness, gather together in compact groups
  and loom up all of a sudden, then immediately
  fall apart, combine otherwise and reappear in
  new forms; while unwinding inside us, like the
  ribbon that comes clattering from a telescriptor
  slot, in an uninterrupted flow of words.
                "Conversation and Sub-conversation"
                (Jan.–Feb. 1956), op, cit.

4 "We're swallowed up only when we are willing
  for it to happen."
                The Planetarium, Maria Jolas, tr.
                                        1959

5 "But there are no more holy of holies, no more sacred places, no more magic, no more mirages for the thirsty, no more unsatisfied desires . . ."   Ibid.

6 "There are people we should not allow to come near us, not for anything. Parasites who devour our very substance . . . Microbes that settle on us . . ."
The Golden Fruits, Maria Jolas, tr.   1963

1567. Opal Whiteley (1900?–   )

1 The mamma where I love
says I am a new sance.
I think it is something grown-ups
don't like to have around.
The Story of Opal *   1920

* Written between the ages of five and twelve.

2 Potatoes are very interesting folks
I think they must see a lot
of what is going on in the earth
They have so many eyes.   Ibid.

3 And this I have learned
grown-ups do not know the language
of shadows.   Ibid.

1568. Frances Winwar (1900–   )

1 In her [Eleonora Duse]* intellectual acquisitiveness she selected people as a bee chooses its flowers, for what they had to offer. Her lack of formal education made her the eternal disciple.   Ch. 14, *Wingless Victory*
1956

* See 1067.

1569. Yocheved Bat-Miriam (1901–   )

1 Singing like a hope, shining like a tear,
Silent the echo of what will befall.
"Parting," St. 1, *Poems from the Hebrew*, Robert Mezey, ed.   1973

2 Not to be, to be gone—I pray for this
At the gates of infinity, like a fey child.
"Distance Spills Itself," St. 5, op. cit.

1570. Miriam Beard (1901–   )

1   "Haven't you some small article I could send her, very attractive—typically American?"

The sales expert looked depressed. . . .
"American, you say? . . . Why, my dee-ur, *we* don't carry those *Colonial* goods. All *our* things are *imported*."
Ch. 1, *Realism in Romantic Japan*
1930

1571. Margaret Craven (1901–1980)

1 The tide-book open by the compass because you came with the tide, you went with the tide, you waited for the tide, and sometimes you prayed for the tide.   Part 1, Ch. 1, *I Heard the Owl Call My Name*   1973

2 "Where there is no written language, anything which must be remembered must be said."
Ibid., Ch. 2

3 Here in the village my people are at home as the fish in the sea, as the eagle in the sky. When the young leave, the world takes them, and damages them. They no longer listen when the elders speak. They go, and soon the village will go also."   Ibid., Pt. II, Ch. 8

4 "The church belongs in the gutter. It is where it does some of its best work."
Ibid., Pt. III, Ch. 12

5 Here every bird and fish knew its course. Every tree had its own place upon this earth. Only man had lost his way.   Ibid., Ch. 16

6 Past, the village flowed the river, like time, like life itself, waiting for the swimmer [salmon] to come again on his way to the climax of his adventurous life, and to the end for which he had been made.   *Wa Laum* (That is all)
Ibid., Pt. IV, Ch. 23

1572. Doris Fleeson (1901–1970)

1 It is occasionally possible to charge Hell with a bucket of water but against stupidity the gods themselves struggle in vain.
Newspaper Column
17 February 1964

1573. Marie-Luise Fleisser (1901–1974)

1 WOLLANK. These women are dreadful, the way they swarm around you and each one dies performing a different service.
TÜTU I don't see why I shouldn't take what I can get. I have turned it into a system. Everything that is able to stimulate me is brought to me without my having to live a finger. I am spared all the painstaking work which wears out the nerves unnecessarily.

WOLLANK. Doesn't it make you afraid?
TÜTU. Afraid of what?
WOLLANK. Man, you'll shrivel up this way.
TÜTU. Quite the contrary, I'm developing faster.
The high points in my life become concentrated
so that I experience it more intensively. My
energies are freed for what is essential. . . . I
can devote myself completely to pursuing my
instincts, bright ideas, my appetite for
action.   *Tiefseefisch* (Deep-Sea
        Fish), Jan van Heurck, tr.   *1972*

2 I have seized on you the way a male animal
corners his mate. I defend my prey. I will think
about you so rigorously that it will keep you at
my side, spellbound.   Ibid.

3 Mine is a nature that sees ahead. I can renounce
things.   Ibid.

4 I am always forced to see the abyss. I could
scratch the eyes out of my head.   Ibid.

1574. Elinor Hays (1901?–   )

1 It was not childbearing that wore away women's
lives. There were slower erosions.
            Pt. I, Ch. 1, *Morning Star*   *1961*

2 Those most dedicated to the future are not always the best prophets.   Ibid., Pt. IV, Ch. 29

1575. Gertrude Lawrence (1901–1952)

1 In London I had been by terms poor and rich,
hopeful and despondent, successful and down-
and-out, utterly miserable and ecstatically diz-
zily happy. I belonged to London as each of us
can belong to only one place on this earth. And,
in the same way, London belonged to me.
            Ch. 1, *A Star Danced*   *1945*

2 "So this is America!" I exclaimed. "Look at
that bath, will you? Feel that delicious warmth.
Central heating, my girl. No wonder they call
this the most luxurious country on earth."
                        Ibid., Ch. 11

1576. Margaret Mead (1901–1978)

1 The negative cautions of science are never
popular.   Ch. 1, *Coming of Age in Samoa*
                                    1928

2 A society which is clamouring for choice, which
is filled with many articulate groups, each urging
its own brand of salvation, its own variety of
economic philosophy, will give each new generation no peace until all have chosen or gone

under, unable to bear the conditions of choice.
The stress is in our civilization. . . .
                        Ibid., Ch. 14.

3 The removal of all legal and economic barriers
against women's participating in the world on
an equal footing with men may be in itself a
standardizing move towards the wholesale
stamping-out of the diversity of attitudes that is
such a dearly bought product of civilization.
            Sex and Temperament in Three
                Primitive Societies   *1935*

4 If we are to achieve a richer culture, rich in
constrasting values, we must recognize the whole
gamut of human potentialities, and so weave a
less arbitrary social fabric, one in which each
diverse human gift will find a fitting place.
                                    Ibid.

5 We know of no culture that has said, articu-
lately, that there is no difference between men
and women except in the way they contribute
to the creation of the next generation. . . .
                Male and Female   *1948*

6 Living in the modern world, clothed and muffled, forced to convey our sense of our bodies
in terms of remote symbols like walking sticks
and umbrellas and handbags, it is easy to lose
sight of the immediacy of the human body
plan.   Ibid.

7 Man's role is uncertain, undefined, and perhaps
unnecessary. By a great effort man has hit upon
a method of compensating himself for his basic
inferiority.   Ibid.

8 Women, it is true, make human beings, but only
men can make men.   Ibid.

9 Women want mediocre man, and men are working to be as mediocre as possible.
                    Quoted in *Quote Magazine*
                                15 May 1958

10 . . . most people prefer to carry out the kinds
of experiments that allow the scientist to feel
that he is in full control of the situation rather
than surrendering himself to the situation, as
one must in studying human beings as they
actually live.   *Blackberry Winter*   *1972*

11 . . . I had no reason to doubt that brains were
suitable for a woman. And as I had my father's
kind of mind—which was also his mother's—I
learned that the mind is not sex-typed.   Ibid.

12 We are living beyond our means. As a people
we have developed a life-style that is draining
the earth of its priceless and irreplaceable resources without regard for the future of our
children and people all around the world.
        "The Energy Crises—Why Our World
            Will Never Again Be the Same"
                Redbook   *April 1974*

13 The contempt for law and the contempt for the human consequences of lawbreaking go from the bottom to the top of American society.
> Quoted in "Impeachment?" by Claire Safran, op. cit.

14 A city is a place where there is no need to wait for next week to get the answer to a question, to taste the food of any country, to find new voices to listen to and familiar ones to listen to again.
> Ch. 2, *World Enough*   1975

15 In this country, some people start being miserable about growing old while they are still young.
> Quoted in "Growing Old in America" by Grace Hechinger, *Family Circle*   26 July 1977

16 There are far too many children in America who are badly afraid of older people because they never see any. Old people are not a regular part of their everyday lives.
> Ibid.

17 If I were to be taken hostage, I would not plead for release nor would I want my government to be blackmailed. I think certain government officials, industrialists and celebrated persons should make it clear they are prepared to be sacrificed if taken hostage. If that were done, what gain would there be for terrorists in taking hostages?
> Quoted in "Comment" *Parade*   20 May 1979

1577. Grace Moore (1901–1947)

1 There, in repressed defiance, lies the natural instinct to tell the world where to get off: an instinct, alas, that too often takes itself out in the tardy retort framed *sotto voce,* or the year-in, year-out threat mumbled to oneself, "Just wait till I write that book!"
> Ch. 1, *You're Only Human Once* 1944

2 I think that to get under the surface and really appreciate the beauty of any country, one has to go there poor.
> Ibid., Ch. 4

1578. Ruth Rowland Nichols (1901–1961)

1 Many newspaper articles . . . discussed the supposed rivalry between Amelia Earhart* and me. I have no hesitation in stating that they were exaggerated or slanted or untrue. . . . We were united by common bond of interest. We spoke each other's language—and that was the language of pioneer women of the air.
> *Wings for Life*   1957

*See 1517.

2 It was a great source of concern, to put it mildly, when I finally had reached my altitude peak and discovered that I was down to my last five gallons of gasoline.
> Quoted in Ch. 7, *The American Heritage History of Flight*   1960

1579. Laura Riding (1901–1991)

1 We must distinguish better
Between ourselves and strangers.
> "The Why of the Wind," *Collected Poems*   1938

2 I met God.
"What," he said, "you already?"
"What," I said, "you still?"
> "Then Follows," op. cit.

3 You have pretended to be seeing.
I have pretended that you saw.
> "Benedictory," op. cit.

4 Conversation succeeds conversation,
Until there's nothing left to talk about
Except truth, the perennial monologue,
And no talker to dispute it but itself.
> "The Talking World," op. cit.

5 Until the missing story of ourselves is told, nothing besides told can suffice us: we shall go on quietly craving it.
> "The Telling," *The Telling*   1967

6 Art, whose honesty must work through artifice, cannot avoid cheating truth.
> Preface, *Selected Poems: In Five Sets* 1975

1580. Cornelia Otis Skinner (1901–1979)

1 There are compensations for growing older. One is the realization that to be sporting isn't at all necessary. It is a great relief to reach this stage of wisdom.
> "Bonnie Boating Weather," *Dithers and Jitters* 1937

2 It's not that I don't want to be a beauty, that I don't yearn to be dripping with glamor. It's just that I can't see how any woman can find time to do to herself all the things that must apparently be done to make herself beautiful and, having once done them, how anyone without the strength of mind of a foreign missionary can keep up such a regime.
> "The Skin-Game," op. cit.

3 Courtesy is fine and heaven knows we need more and more of it in a rude and frenetic world, but mechanized courtesy is as pallid as Pablum . . . in fact, it isn't even courtesy. One can put

up with "Service with a Smile" if the smile is genuine and not mere compulsory toothbaring. And while I am hardly advocating "Service with a Snarl," I find myself occasionally wishing for "Service with a Deadpan," or just plain Service, executed with efficiency and minus all the Charm School garnish.
"Production-Line Courtesy," *The Ape in Me*   *1959*

4 Woman's virtue is man's greatest invention.
Quoted in *Paris '90*
n.d.

1581. Edith Mendel Stern (1901–1975)

1 The role of the housewife is, therefore, analogous to that of the president of a corporation who would not only determine policies and make over-all plans but also spend the major part of his time and energy in such activities as sweeping the plant and oiling the machines. . . . For a woman to get a rewarding sense of total creation by way of the multiple monotonous chores that are her daily lot would be as irrational as for an assembly line worker to rejoice that he had created an automobile because he tightened a bolt.
"Women Are Household Slaves,"
American Mercury   *January 1949*

1582. Jan Struther (1901–1953)

1 It took me forty years on earth
To reach this sure conclusion:
There is no Heaven but clarity,
No Hell except confusion.
"All Clear," *The Glass Blower and Other Poems*   *1940*

2 She saw every personal religion as a pair of intersecting circles. . . . Probably perfection is reached when the area of the two outer crescents, added together, is exactly equal to that of the leaf-shaped piece in the middle. On paper there must be some neat mathematical formula for arriving at this; in life, none.
Mrs. Miniver   *1940*

1583. Edith Summerskill (1901–1980)

1 I learned that economics was not an exact science and that the most erudite men would analyze the economic ills of the world and derive a totally different conclusion. . . . [Yet] governments still pin their faith to some new economic nostrum which is produced periodically by some bright young man. Only time proves that his alleged magic touch is illusory.
Ch. 5, A Woman's World   *1967*

2 Prize-fighting is still accepted as a display worthy of a civilized people despite the fact that all those connected with it are fully aware it caters to the latent sadistic instincts.   Ibid., Ch. 12

3 The practice of abortion is as old as pregnancy itself. . . . Today, literate people of the space age, in well-populated countries, are not prepared to accept taboos without question; and in the matter of abortion the human rights of the mother with her family must take precedence over the survival of a few weeks' old foetus without sense or sensibility   Ibid., Ch. 19

1584. Marian Anderson (1902–   )

1 Where there is money, there is fighting.
Quoted in *Marian Anderson, a Portrait* by Kosti Vehanen
1941

2 As long as you keep a person down, some part of you has to be down there to hold him down, so it means you cannot soar as you otherwise might.   Interview on CBS-TV
30 December 1957

1585. Barbara Cartland (1902?–   )

1 What did we in our teens realize of war? Only that we were unsatisfied after our meals, bored, in the selfishness of youth, with mourning and weeping, sick of being told plaintively that the world would "never be the same again."
Ch. 1, *The Isthmus Years*   *1942*

2 I always say what I think and feel—it's got me into a lot of trouble but only with women. I've never had a cross word with a man for speaking frankly but women don't like it—I can't think why, unless it's natural love of subterfuge and intrigue.   Ibid., Ch. 8

1586. Stella Gibbons (1902–   )

1 Graceless, Pointless, Feckless and Aimless waited their turn to be milked.
Ch. 3, *Conference at Cold Comfort Farm*
1932

2 Something nasty in the woodshed.
Ibid., Ch. 8

1587. Madeline Gray (1902–   )

1 Sex, as I said, can be summed up in three P's: procreation, pleasure, and pride. From the long-

range point of view, which we must always consider, procreation is by far the most important, since without procreation there could be no continuation of the race. . . . So female orgasm is simply a nervous climax to sex relations . . . and as such it is a comparative luxury from nature's point of view. It may be thought of as a sort of pleasure-prize like a prize that comes with a box of cereal. It is all to the good if the prize is there, but the cereal is valuable and nourishing if it is not.
The Normal Woman   *1967*

1588. Irene Handle (1901/2–1987)

1 "The Dauphin has a truly terrifying sense of gratitude. You'll be annihilated by it, my poor Vince. Nothing can stand up against this terrible, slow gratitude of the Dauphin."
The Sioux   *1965*

1589. Elsa Lanchester (1902–1986)

1 If I can't be a good artist without too much pain, then I'm damned if I'll be an artist at all.   *Charles Laughton and I*   *1938*

2 Comedians on the stage are invariably suicidal when they get home.   *Ibid.*

3 Every artist should be allowed a few failures.   *Ibid.*

1590. Barbara McClintock (1902–)

1 They* thought I was crazy, absolutely mad.
Quoted in "Honoring a Modern Mendel" by Claudia Wallis, *Time*   *24 October 1983*

*The National Academy of Sciences, 1944, in response to her theory that genes could "jump" around on a chromosome; she later won the Nobel Prize for Medicine (1983).

2 When you know you're right, you don't care what others think. You know sooner or later it will come out in the wash.   *Ibid.*

3 I know [my corn plants] intimately, and I find it a great pleasure to know them.
Quoted in *A Feeling for the Organism: The Life and Work of Barbara McClintock* by Evelyn Fox Keller   *1983*

1591. Alva Reimer Myrdal (1902–1986)

1 An established tendency to drive values underground, to make the analysis appear scientific

by omitting certain basic assumptions from the discussion, has too often emasculated the social sciences as agencies for rationality in social and political life. To be truly rational, it is necessary to accept the obvious principles that a social program, like a practical judgment, is a conclusion based upon premises of values as well as upon facts.   Pt. I, Ch. 1, *Nation and Family*
1941

2 In the new era the scope of social policy will be widened to include general social solicitude for all human beings, not only for the indigent.   *Ibid.*, Pt. II, Ch. 10

3 The family of old could rightly be called the mutually supported family. All family members, without calculation as to exact shares, took part in both production and consumption. The nature and the degree of dependency were relatively similar for all. Only in the transition stage, when the male heads of households had surrendered to industrialism but that process had not yet markedly changed the functions of women, did the special dilemma of wives [as wage earner] appear.   *Ibid.*, Ch. 22

4 The plight of the hitherto less privileged nations is beginning to weigh heavily on our conscience. Today, when all the modern means of communication keep us supplied with an incessant, vivid flow of information, we can no longer ignore that plight, as our forefathers did. Such is the dilemma of our time . . .
"A Scientific Approach to International Welfare," *America's Role in International Welfare*   *1955*

5 The overpopulation scourge is the very symptom of an unbalanced development. It is as if it were Nature's own revenge when humans interfere in an unskillful way. The connection is a simple one: some of the most easily instituted measures of welfare lead to decreased mortality. This overthrows the balance which at a very low existence level is upheld by high mortality and high fertility checking each other.   *Ibid.*

6 It's not worthy of human beings to give up.
Quoted in "Sissela Bok," * *A World of Ideas* by Bill Moyers   *1989*

*See 2145.

1592. Iris Origo (1902–)

1 It is only comparatively seldom that the so-called "turning points" in a country's history—so convenient to the historian—are actually observable by those present at the time.
War in Val d'Orcia (2 February 1943)
1947

2 It is odd how used one can become to uncertainty for the future, to a complete planlessness, even in one's most private mind. What we shall do and be, and whether we shall, in a few month's time, have any home or possessions, or indeed our lives, is so clearly dependent on events outside our own control as to be almost restful.   Ibid. (9 February 1944)

3 A life-sentence can be pronounced in many ways; and there are as many ways of meeting it. What is common to all who have received it—the consumptive, the paralyzed, the deaf, the blind—is the absence of a fixed point on the mind's horizon.
                    Introduction, *A Measure of Love*
                    1957

4 All of my past life that has not faded into mist has passed through the filter, not of my mind, but of my affections.   *Images and Shadows*
                    1970

1593. Leni Riefenstahl (1902–)

1 I state precisely: it is *film-verité*. It reflects the truth that was then, in 1934, history. It is therefore a documentary. Not a propaganda film. Oh! I know very well what propaganda is. That consists of recreating certain events in order to illustrate a thesis or, in the face of certain events, to let one thing go in order to accentuate another.   Quoted by Michel Delahaye in
                    Cahiers du Cinema, No. 5   *1966*

2 My life became a tissue of rumors and accusations through which I had to beat a path. . . .   Ibid.

1594. Christina Stead (1902–)

1 The City is a machine miraculously organised for extracting gold from the seas, airs, clouds, from barren lands, holds of ships, mines, plantations, cottage hearth-stones, trees and rocks; and he, wretchedly waiting in the exterior halls, like the porters, or the newsboys, could not even get his finger on one tiny, tiny lever.
                    "The Sensitive Goldfish,"
                    The Salzburg Tales   *1934*

2 . . . the waste, the insane freaks of these money men, the cynicism and egotism of their life . . . I'll show that they are not brilliant, not romantic, not delightful, not intelligent.
                    The House of All Nations
                    1938

3 "I know your breed; all your fine officials debauch the young girls who are afraid to lose their jobs; that's as old as Washington."

Ch. 4, *The Man Who Loved Children*
1940

4 "'There are so many ways to kill yourself, they're just old-fashioned with their permanganate: do you think I'd take permanganate? I wouldn't want to burn my insides out and live to tell the tale as well; idiots! It's simple. I'd drown myself. . . . Why be in misery at the last?"   Ibid., Ch. 5

5 She was able to feel active creation going on around her in the rocks and hills, where the mystery of lust took place; and in herself, where all was yet only the night of the senses and wild dreams, the work of passion was going on.
                    For Love Alone   *1944*

6 "We are primitive men; we taboo what we desire and need. How did the denying of love come to be associated with the idea of morality?"   Ibid.

7 "When Europe's ruined after the war and the kids are starving and the old people dropping dead like flies, everybody sick, and without any hats or shoes, you'll see, we'll make a fortune."   *A Little Tea, A Little Chat*
                    1948

8 "Ye want to tell the plain truth all your life, woman, and speak straight and see straight; otherwise ye get to seein' double."
                    Dark Places of the Heart
                    1966

9 "Loneliness is a terrible blindness."   Ibid.

1595. Jessamyn West (1902–1984)

1 "After a good heart," she said, "the least a woman can do is pick a face she fancies. Men's so much alike and many so sorry, that's the very least. If a man's face pleasures thee, that doesn't change. That is something to bank on."   "Lead Her Like a Pigeon,"
                    The Friendly Persuasion   *1945*

2 She intended to forgive. Not to do so would be un-Christian; but she did not intend to do so soon, nor forget how much she had to forgive.   Ibid., "The Buried Leaf"

3 "Men ain't got any heart for courting a girl they can't pass—let alone catch up with."
                    Ibid., "A Likely Exchange"

4 "It's better to learn to say good-by early than late. . . ."   "Learn to Say Good-by,"
                    Love, Death, and the Ladies'
                    Drill Team   *1955*

5 Being consistent meant not departing from convictions already formulated; being a leader meant making other persons accept these convictions.

It was a narrow track, and a one-way, but a person might travel a considerable distance on it. A number of dictators have.
        Ch. 7, The See the Dream   *1956*

6 We want the facts to fit the preconceptions. When they don't, it is easier to ignore the facts than to change the preconceptions.
        Introduction, *The Quaker Reader*
        1962

7 Friends [Quakers] refused to take legal oaths, since by doing so they acquiesced in the assumption that, unless under oath, one was not obliged to tell the truth.   *Ibid.*

8 A religious awakening which does not awaken the sleeper to love has roused him in vain.
        Ibid.

9 Fiction reveals truths that reality obscures.
        Quoted in *Reader's Digest*
        April 1973

10 "He should have put his wife to work. That's the way doctors and lawyers pay for their education nowadays."   *Ch. 1, Hide and Seek*
        1973

11 Visitors to Los Angeles, then and now, were put out because the residents of Los Angeles had the inhospitable idea of building a city comfortable to live in, rather than a monument to astonish the eye of jaded travelers.
        Ibid., Ch. 22

1596. Marya Zaturenska (1902–)

1 The cold dream melts, the frost
Dissolves—the dream has sown
A harvest never lost.
        "Song," St. 5   *1960*

2 Once they were flowers, and flame, and living bread;
Now they are old and brown and all but dead.   "Spinners at Willowsleigh"
        n.d.

1597. Brooke Astor (1903–)

1 I am beginning to think 1929 is going to be a great year for us. There is nothing that makes me feel more alive than making money
     The Last Blossom on the Plum Tree
        1986

1598. Ella Baker (1903–)

1 I don't think it ever occurred to our immediate family to indoctrinate children against sharing.

Because they had had the privilege of growing up where they'd raised a lot of food. They were never hungry. They could share their food with people. And so, you share your *lives* with people.   Quoted in *Moving the Mountain*
        by Ellen Cantarow   *1980*

2 The best country in the world, you hear them say. I guess it may be. I haven't lived anywhere else. But it's not good enough as far as I'm concerned.   *Ibid.*

1599. Bettina Ballard (1903–1961)

1 None of the people I wrote about were as exciting in reality as I imagined them to be.
        Ch. 3, In My Fashion   *1960*

2 The feeling about time and what to do with it has changed. What has become of those long hours when we brushed our hair, fooled with our nails, tried for the most effective place of a beauty spot? Fashion is one of the great sacrifices of the jet age—there just isn't time to play at it.   *Ibid., Ch. 21*

1600. Tallulah Bankhead (1903–1968)

1 I have three phobias which, could I mute them, would make my life as slick as a sonnet, but as dull as ditch water: I hate to go to bed, I hate to get up, and I hate to be alone.
        Ch. 1, Tallulah   *1952*

2 Here's a rule I recommend. Never practice two vices at once.   *Ibid., Ch. 4*

3 I've been called many things, but never an intellectual.   *Ibid., Ch. 15*

4 I am as pure as the driven slush.
        Comment   *n.d.*

1601. Jessie Shirley Bernard (1903–)

1 Women may think like men, act like men, live the rules of the male world, and think they live in the male world until something happens that shows how wide the chasm really is.
        The Female World   *1981*

2 Many women find female solidarity hard to reconcile with almost any other of the many competing pulls on them; ethnic, racial, religious—and male. Perhaps especially male. Men seem better able to "gang up" against women than vice versa.   *Ibid.*

3 There are two marriages, then, in every marital union, his and hers.
        The Future of Marriage   *1982*

1602. Dorothy Dow (1903–)

1 Shall I tremble at a gray hair. . . .
"Unbeliever," *Time and Love*   1942

2 Things that are lovely
Can tear my heart in two—
Moonlight on still pools,
You.   "Things," op. cit.

1603. Barbara Hepworth (1903–1975)

1 . . . I rarely draw what I see. I draw what I
feel in my body.
Quoted in A. M. Hammersmith in the
World of Art Series   1968

1604. Clare Boothe Luce (1903–1987)

1 MAGGIE. Marriage is a business of taking care
of a man and rearing his children. . . . It ain't
meant to be no perpetual honeymoon.
Act II, *The Women*
1936

2 MARY Reno's full of women who all have their
pride.   Ibid.

3 LITTLE MARY. You know, that's the only good
thing about divorce; you get to sleep with your
mother.   Ibid., Act III

4 EDITH. Always remember, Peggy, its matrimonial suicide to be jealous when you have a really
good reason.   Ibid.

5 Much of what Mr. [Vice-President Harry] Wallace calls his global thinking is, no matter how
you slice it, still Globaloney.
Speech, U.S. House of Representatives
9 February 1943

6 I am for lifting everyone off the social bottom.
In fact, I am for doing away with the social
bottom altogether.   Quoted in *Time*
14 February 1964

7 BLACK WOMAN'S VOICE. There's no human being
a man can buy anymore—except a woman.
Slam the Door Softly   1970

8 NORA. But if God had wanted us to think with
our wombs, why did He give us a brain?
Ibid.

9 NORA. When a man can't explain a woman's
actions, the first thing he thinks about is the
condition of her uterus.   Ibid.

10 NORA. Know what Freud wrote in his diary when
he was 77? "What do women want? My God,
what do they want?" Fifty years this giant brain
spends analyzing women. And he still can't find
out what they want. So this makes him the

world's greatest expert on female psychology?   Ibid.

11 The American Republic is now almost 200 years
old, and in the eyes of the law women are still
not equal with men. The special legislation which
will remedy that situation is the Equal Rights
Amendment. Its language is short and simple:
*Equality of rights under the law shall not be
abridged in the United States or by any state on
account of sex.* *
Quoted in the *Bulletin of the Baldwin
School*, Pennsylvania
September 1974

*See Alice Paul, 1355.

12 A man's home may seem to be his castle on the
outside; inside, it is more often his nursery.
Ibid.

13 In politics women . . . type the letters, lick the
stamps, distribute the pamphlets and get out the
vote. Men get elected.
Quoted in *Saturday Review/World*
15 September 1974

14 Male supremacy has kept woman down. It has
not knocked her out.   Ibid.

1605. Virginia Moore (1903–)

1 Fortunately there is excess in greatness: it can
lose more than mediocrity possesses, and still
be great.   "Sappho," * *Distinguished
Women Writers*   1934

*See 50.

2 A poet is a state of mind.   "Saint
Teresa," * op. cit.

*See 256.

3 Suspicion is the badge of base-born minds,
And calculation never understands.
"Tragic Conclusions,"
n.d.

1606. Empress Nagako (1903–)

1 We have always been trained in the past to a
life of service and I am afraid that as these new
changes come about there may be a loss of real
values.   Meeting with Eleanor Roosevelt *
(1953), Quoted in *Eleanor: The Years
Alone* by Joseph P. Lash   1972

*See 1341.

1607. Anaïs Nin (1903–1977)

1 The imagination is far better at inventing tortures
than life because the imagination is a demon
within us and it knows where to strike, where

it hurts. It knows the vulnerable spot, and life does not, our friends and loves do not, because seldom do they have the imagination equal to the task.   *Winter of Artifice   1945*

2 He had a mania for washing and disinfecting himself. . . . For him the only danger came from the microbes which attacked the body. He had not studied the microbe of conscience which eats into the soul.   Ibid.

3 He wants to interfere with his instruments, while I struggle with nature, with myself, with my child and with the meaning I put into it all, with my desire to give and to hold, to keep and to lose, to live and to die.
          "Birth," *Under a Glass Bell   1948*

4 There is blood in my eyes. A tunnel. I push into this tunnel, I bite my lips and push. There is a fire and flesh ripping and no air. Out of the tunnel! All my blood is spilling out. Push! Push! Push! It is coming! It is coming! I feel the slipperiness, the sudden deliverance, the weight is gone.   Ibid.

5 She hated him because she could not remain detached. . . .   Ibid.

6 I stopped loving my father a long time ago. What remained was the slavery to a pattern.
          Ibid.

7 She* lacks confidence, she craves admiration insatiably. She lives on the reflections of herself in the eyes of others. She does not dare to be herself.   (30 December 1931)
          The Diary of Anaïs Nin, Vol I
          1966

* Referring to author Henry Miller's wife, June.

8 Woman does not forget she needs the fecundator, she does not forget that everything that is born of her is planted in her.   (August 1937)
          The Diary of Anaïs Nin, Vol II
          1967

9 The art of woman must be born in the wombcells of the mind. She must be the link between synthetic products of man's mind and the elements.   Ibid.

10 For the womb has dreams. It is not as simple as the good earth.   Ibid.

11 The crowd is a malleable thing, it can be dominated, dazzled, it's a public, it is faceless. This is the opposite of relationship.   Ibid.
          (October 1937)

12 Inner chaos, like those secret volcanoes which suddenly lift the neat furrows of a peacefully plowed field, awaited behind all disorders of face, hair and costume, for a fissure through which to explode.
          A Spy in the House of Love   1968

13 What I consider my weaknesses are feminine traits: incapacity to destroy, ineffectualness in battle.   (January 1943)
          The Diary of Anaïs Nin, Vol. III
          1969

14 . . . we cannot cure the evils of politics with politics. . . . Fifty years ago if we had gone the way of Freud (to study and tackle hostility within ourselves) instead of Marx, we might be closer to peace than we are.
          Letter to Geismar, "San Francisco,"
          The Diary of
          Anaïs Nin, Vol. V   *1974*

15 If we are unable to make passion a relationship of duration, surviving the destruction and erosions of daily life, it still does not divest passion of its power to transform, transfigure, transmute a human being from a rather limited, petty, fearful creature to a magnificent figure reaching at moments the status of a myth.   Ibid.

16 Anxiety is love's greatest killer, because it is like the strange hold of the drowning.   Ibid.

17 I will not be just a tourist in the world of images, just watching images passing by which I cannot live in, make love to, possess as permanent sources of joy and ecstasy.   "Sierra Madre,"
          op. cit.

18 The drugs, instead of bringing fertile images which in turn can be shared with the world . . . have instead become a solitary vice, a passive dreaming which alienates the dreamer from the whole world, isolates him, ultimately destroys him.   Ibid.

1608. Nelly Ptaschkina (1903–1920)

1 Youth does not know how to concentrate, and, on the other hand, does not want to confide in others. Hence the diary. The old work out everything in themselves.   (23 January 1918)
          The Diary of Nelly Ptaschkina
          1923

2 It seems to me that man at birth does not represent a lump of clay, which can be shaped at will: for instance, either he is born intelligent or he is born stupid. Goodness can, on the other hand, be acquired.   Ibid., (26 January 1918)

3 Give women scope and opportunity, and they will be no worse than men.
          Ibid. (1 October 1918)

1609. Leonor Kretzer Sullivan (1903–1988)

1 Millions of American women would like to see the nation which can dress men in the garments

necessary to withstand the hostile environment of the moon help women to get through a day without a bag, sag, wrinkle or tear in an expensive and frequently essential article of wearing apparel here on earth.
The Congressional Record
1970

2 A woman with a woman's viewpoint is of more value than when she forgets she's a woman and begins to act like a man. Ibid.

1610. Teng Ying-ch'ao (1903–)

1 . . . in order to fight the Japanese we must study Japanese!
Quoted in *Women in Modern China* by Helen Foster Snow* *1967*

*See 1675.

1611. Thyra Samter Winslow (1903–1961)

1 Platonic love is love from the neck up.
Quoted by James Simpson in *Interview* *19 August 1952*

1612. Marguerite Yourcenar (1903–1987)

1 One reaches all great events of life a virgin.
Fires *1935*

2 One doesn't know what to do with delirium while experimenting with the mingling and mixing of bodies. Ibid.

3 And you are going? You are going? . . . No, you are not going: I am keeping you . . . you leave your soul, like a coat, in my hands. Ibid.

4 We say: made with joy. We should say: wise with grief. Ibid.

5 To possess is the same thing as to know: the Bible is always right. Ibid.

6 Thieves are only after our rings, lovers our bodies, preachers our souls, murderers our lives. Ibid.

7 "Life is atrocious, we know. But precisely because I expect little of the human condition, man's periods of felicity, his partial progress, his efforts to begin over again and continue, all seem to me like so many prodigies which nearly compensate for the monstrous mass of ills and defeats, of indifference and error. Catastrophe and ruin will come; disorder will triumph, but order will too, from time to time."
Memoirs of Hadrian *1954*

8 This morning it occurred to me for the first time that my body, my faithful companion and friend, truly better known too me than my own soul, may be after all only a sly beast who will end by devouring his master.
"Animula Vagula Blandula," op. cit.

9 I have done much rebuilding. To reconstruct is to collaborate with time gone by, penetrating or modifying its spirit, and carrying it toward a longer future. Thus beneath the stones we find the secret of the springs. "Tellus Stabilita," op. cit.

1613. Margery Allingham (1904–1966)

1 We—he and thee and the parson and all the other lads of the village—constitute the public, and the politicians are our servants. They apply for the job (often rather obsequiously, we notice with instant suspicion), we give it to them, we pay them in honours or cash, and we judge them solely by results.
Ch. 1, *The Oaken Heart* *1941*

2 It is always difficult to escape from youth; its hopefulness, its optimistic belief in the privileges of desire, its despair, and its sense of outrage and injustice at disappointment, all these spring on a man inflicting indelicate agony when he is no longer prepared. Ibid., Ch. 21

3 Normally he was the happiest of men. He asked so little of life that its frugal bounty amazed and delighted him. . . . He believed in miracles and frequently observed them, and nothing astonished him. His imagination was as wild as a small boy's and his faith ultimate. In ordinary life he was, quite frankly, hardly safe out.
Ch. 2, *The Tiger in the Smoke* *1952*

4 Chemists employed by the police can do remarkablĕ things with blood. They can find it in shreds of cloth, in the interstices of floor boards, on the iron of a heel, and can measure it and swear to it and weave it into a rope to hang a man. Ibid., Ch. 9

1614. Elaine Frances Burton (1904–)

1 A woman in authority is often unpopular, only because she is efficient.
What of the Women? *1941*

2 If you get a good woman, you get the finest thing on earth. Ibid.

1615. Mary Calderone (1904–)

1 Sex had to be brought out of the Victorian closet—freed from the guilt and fear, bigotry

and misconceptions which shrouded it, if America was to recover from its deep-rooted sexual trouble. SIECUS* Fund-raising Letter
*1979**

*Sex Information and Education Council of the United States.

2 Interference with self-pleasure is a very bad thing for children.
"Sixty Minutes," CBS-TV
25 October 1981

3 I don't want to control anybody's mind or anybody's heart—I just want to help free people from the concept of sex as evil instead of a gift from God. Ibid.

1616. Ève Curie (1904–   )

1 We discovered that peace at any price is no peace at all. . . . We discovered that life at any price has no value whatever; that life is nothing without the privileges, the prides, the rights, the joys which make it worth living, and also worth giving. And we also discovered that there is something more hideous, more atrocious than war or than death; and that is to live in fear.
Address, American Booksellers Association, New York
9 April 1940

2 Public opinion waged the war. Statesmen, diplomats, government officials waged the war. To beat the Axis, it was not enough to win battle in the field, to kill millions of men. We also had to kill ideas that knew no frontiers and spread like disease
Pt. V, Ch. 26, *Journey Among Warriors*
1943

1617. Lilly Daché (1904–   )

1 When I was six I made my mother a little hat—out of her new blouse.
Newspaper Interview *3 December 1954*

2 Glamour is what makes a man ask for your telephone number. But it also is what makes a woman ask for the name of your dressmaker. Quoted in *Woman's Home Companion* *July 1955*

1618. Adelle Davis (1904–1974)

1 Nutrition is a young subject; it has been kicked around like a puppy that cannot take care of itself. Food faddists and crackpots have kicked it pretty cruelly. . . . They seem to believe that

unless food tastes like Socratic hemlock, it cannot build health. Frankly, I often wonder what such persons plan to do with good health in case they acquire it.
Ch. 1, *Let's Eat Right to Keep Fit*
1954

2 When the blood sugar is extremely low, the resulting irritability, nervous tension, and mental depression are such that a person can easily go berserk. . . . And a few guns, gas jets, or razor blades, and you have the stuff murders and suicides are made of. The American diet has become dangerous in many more ways than one. Ibid., Ch.2

3 Thousands upon thousands of persons have studied disease. Almost no one has studied health. Ibid., Ch. 29

4 If this county is to survive, the best-fed-nation myth had better be recognized for what it is: propaganda designed to produce wealth but not health. Ibid., Ch. 30

1619. Marlene Dietrich (1901–1992)

1 The average man is more interested in a woman who is interested in him than he is in a woman—any woman—with beautiful legs.
News Item *13 December 1954*

2 Latins are tenderly enthusiastic. In Brazil they throw flowers at you. In Argentina they throw themselves. Quoted in *Newsweek*
24 August 1959

1620. Margaret Fishback (1904–1985)

1 At six weeks Baby grinned a grin
That spread from mouth to eyes to chin,
And Doc, the smartie, had the brass
To tell me it was only gas!
"Infant Prodigy," *Look Who's A Mother* *1945*

2 The same old charitable lie
Repeated as the years scoot by
Perpetually makes a hit—
"You really haven't changed a bit!"
"The Lie of the Land" *n.d.*

1621. Hayashi Fumiko (1904–1951)

1 Kin refused to forget her femininity.
Death itself was preferable to the
blowsiness of the average old woman.
There was a poem—composed, they said, by
some famous woman of the past—

Never could human form
Aspire, I know,
To beauty ripe as that now bends
This rose. Yet, somewhere here,
I see myself.   "Late Chrysanthemum," John
Bester, tr.   *1948*

2 Love in itself, she felt should be like the creation
of a succession of works of art.   Ibid.

1622. Sheilah Graham (1904–1988)

1 . . . you have to really drink a lot to enjoy
parties.   Quoted in"Sheilah Graham:
Still Upwardly, Verbally
Mobile" by Kathleen Hendrix,
Los Angeles Times
13 October 1974

2 You just never know when you're going into
eternity.   Ibid.

3 I won't be remembered for my writing. I'll be
remembered as Scott's* mistress.
Comment, Quoted in
Milestones, *Time*
28 November 1988

*F. Scott Fitzgerald. American writer (1896–1940).

1623. Helen Lawrenson (1904–1982)

1 Most of today's film actress are typical of a
mass-production age: living dolls who look as
if they came off an assembly line and whose
uniformity of appearance is frequently a triumph
of modern science, thanks to which they can be
equipped with identical noses, breast, teeth, and
hair.   "Where Did It Go?," *Latins*
Are Still Lousy Lovers   *1968*

1624. Marya Mannes (1904–   )

1 Promiscuous. . . . That was a word I had never
applied to myself. Possibly no one ever does,
for it is a sordid word, reducing many valuable
moments to nothing more than dog-like
copulation.
"The Second Month," *Message from a*
Stranger   *1948*

2 The real demon is success—the anxieties engen-
dered by this quest are relentless, degrading,
corroding. What is worse, there is no end to
this escalation of desire. . . .
"The Roots of Anxiety in Modern
Women," *Journal of Neuropyschiatry*
May 1964

3 Affuent as it was for the majority, the society
we had produced was not admirable. It might

be better than others, but it was nowhere near
what it should have been. It was, in fact, going
rotten. The private gain had for so long triumphed
over the public need that the cities had become
unlivable, the country desecrated, the arteries
choked, and pollution—of air, of water, yes, of
spirit too—a daily, oppressive, fact. And who
else but our generation (if not ourselves) had
made it so?   *Them*   *1968*

4 Timing and arrogance are decisive factors in the
successful use of talent. The first is a matter of
instinct, the second part carapace and part self-
hypnosis; the shell that protects, the ego that
assumes, without question, that the talent possessed is not only unique but important, the
particular vision demanding to be shared.
Preface, *Out of My Time*
1971

5 The barbarian weapon is fission: the splitting
asunder. It has been perfected for death. Our
only weapon is fusion: an imperfect process still,
though designed for life.   Ibid., Ch. 9

1625. Dorothy Eugenia Miner (1904–1973)

1 The book with pages was the stimulus to everything that we think of when we discuss book
design.   *The History of Bookbinding,*
525-1950 A.D.   *1957*

2 . . . labels—a favorite device by which insig-
nificant things can *reflect* significance.
Letter to Eleanor P. Spencer
(3 November 1970), Quoted in
"The Varied Career of a Medievalist"
by Claire Richter Sherman, *Women*
As Interpreters of the Visual Arts,
Claire Richter Sherman, ed.   *1981*

1626. Nancy Mitford (1904–1973)

1 "I simply don't see the point of getting up at
six all the time you are young and working
eighteen hours a day in order to be a millionaire,
and then when you are a millionaire still getting
up at six and working eighteen hours a day.
. . . What does it all mean?"
Ch. 1, *Pigeon Pie*   *1940*

2 An aristocracy in a republic is like a chicken
whose head has been cut off: it may run about
in a lively way, but in fact it is dead.
Noblesse Oblige   *1956*

3 Americans relate all effort, all work, and all of
life itself to the dollar. Their talk is of nothing
but dollars. The English seldom sit happily chat-
ting for hours on end about pounds. In England,

public business is its own reward, nobody would go into Parliament in order to become rich, neither do riches bring public appointment.
Ibid.

1627. Virgilia Peterson (1904–1966)

1 In Reno, there is always a bull market, never a bear market for the stocks and bonds of happiness.
A Matter of Life and Death 1961

2 A lady, that is an enlightened, cultivated, liberal lady—the only kind to be in a time of increasing classlessness—could espouse any cause: wayward girls, social diseases, unmarried mothers, and/or birth control with impunity. But never by so much as the shadow of a look should she acknowledge her own experience with the Facts of Life.
Ibid.

1628. Anne Roe (1904–   )

1 Nothing in science has any value to society if it is not communicated. . . .
Ch. 1, *The Making of a Scientist* 1952

2 Freedom breeds freedom. Nothing else does.
Ibid., Ch. 16

1629. Sally Stanford (1904–1982)

1 Well, there's a Book that says we're all sinners and I at least chose a sin that's made quite a few people happier than they were before they met me, a sin that's left me with very little time to consider other extremely popular moral misdemeanors, like usury, intolerance, bearing false tales, extortion, racial bigotry, and the casting of that first stone. And, I might add, a hell of a lot worse. Ch. 4, *The Lady of the House* 1966

2 No man can be held throughout the day by what happens throughout the night.   Ibid., Ch. 13

3 Romance without finance is a nuisance. Few men value free merchandise. Let the chippies fall where they may.
Ibid.

1630. Charlotte Wolff (1904–   )

1 I have no doubt that lesbianism makes a woman virile and open to *any* sexual stimulation, and that she is more often than not a more adequate and lively partner in bed than a "normal" woman.   *Love Between Women* 1971

1631. Jane Ace (1905–1974)

1 Home wasn't built in a day.
Comment, "Easy Aces" Radio show (c. 1928–1945), Quoted in *The Fine Art of Hypochondria* by Goodman Ace* 1966

* American humorist and radio personality; her husband.

2 Familiarity breeds attempt.   Ibid.

3 He's a ragged individualist.   Ibid.

4 Time wounds all heels.   Ibid.

1632. Shulamit Aloni (1905–   )

1 According to civil law, women are equal to men. But I have to go to a religious court as far as personal affairs are concerned. Only men are allowed to be judges there—men who pray every morning to thank God He did not make them women. You need prejudice before you open your mouth. And because they believe women belong in the home, you are doubly discriminated against if you work.
Quoted in "Women in Israel" (November 1973), *Crazy Salad* by Nora Ephron* 1975

* See 2317.

1633. Ilka Chase (1905–1978)

1 She knew that no human being is immune to sorrow and she wanted me to be tough, the way a green branch is tough, and to be independent, so that if anything happened to her I would be able to take hold of my own life and make a go of it.   Ch. 6, *I Love Miss Tilli Bean* 1946

2 The very fact that we make such a to-do over golden weddings indicates our amazement at human endurance. The celebration is more in the nature of a reward stamina. . . .
Ch. 15, *Free Admission* 1948

1634. Viña Delmar (1905–   )

1 "We have strict orders on how to teach. There are certain methods that must be employed. Your way is easier to learn, but it hasn't been approved by the school board for use in the classroom."   *The Becker Scandal* 1968

2 . . . her plumpness was so neat and firm that she was rather like one of the better apples that are purchased for fruit-bowl display.   Ibid.

1635. Dorothy Fields (1905–1974)

1 To think the highest-brow,
Which I must say is he,
Should pick the lowest-brow,
Which there's no doubt is me . . .
  "If My Friends Could See Me Now,"
   Act I, Scene 6, *Sweet Charity*
    1966

2 No matter where I run,
I meet myself there. "Where Am I Going?"
   Act II, Scene 6, op. cit.

1636. Frances Frost (1905–1959)

1 I am the keeper of wall and sill,
I kneel on the hearth to a tempered fire:
(Flesh that was wild can learn to be still,
But what of a heart that was born to briar?)
  "Capture," St. 4, *Hemlock Wall*
    1929

2 But the trees that lost their apples
In the early windy year—
Hard-checked little apples,
Round and green and clear,—
They have nothing more to lose
And nothing more to fear.
  "Loss," St. 2, op. cit.

1637. Enchi Fumiko (1905–?)

1 Chigako had no interest in pornographic pictures
and books; even in the first days of their marriage, when Keisaku had shown her his private
store of pictures she had, far from enjoying
them, ended by shutting the book unread, thus
affording her husband simultaneously both disappointment and a sense of relief at his wife's
lack of the lecherous instinct.
  "Enchantress," John
  Bestor, tr. *n.d.*

2 . . . their daughter was gone. Kiriko had been
invaluable—a solid, flesh-and-blood barrier between them. Now she had vanished, and the
gap she had left must, whatever happened, be
filled with something else.   Ibid.

3 Spectacles, false teeth eventually, false locks
made of other people's hair—all kinds of things
foreign to her own flesh which she donned like
armor in her hungry craving to appear young,
to be beautiful. What kind of creature was
she?   Ibid.

1638. Greta Garbo (1905–1990)

1 There are many things in your heart you can
never tell to another person. They are you, your
private joys and sorrows, and you can never tell

them. You cheapen yourself, the inside of yourself, when you tell them.
  Quoted in *The Story of Great Garbo*
  by Bruce Biery *1928*

2 I never said, "I want to be alone." I only said,
"I want to be *left* alone." There is all the
difference. Quoted in *Garbo* by John
  Bainbridge *1955*

1639. Ethel Jacobson (1905?–)

1 Behind every man who achieves success
Stand a mother, a wife and the IRS.
  Quoted in *Reader's Digest*
  April 1973

1640. Adelaide Johnson (1905–1960)

1 The neurotic needs of the parent . . . are va-
cariously gratified by the behavior of the
child.   "The Genesis of Antisocial Acting
  Out in Children and Adults,"
  Psychoanalytic Quarterly, Vol. 21
    1952

2 Firmness bespeaks a parent who has learned
. . . how all of his major goals may be reached
in some creative course of action. . . . Ibid.

1641. Maggie Kuhn (1905–)

1 Our [old people's] citizenship is not served when
we take ourselves out of the mainstream of
society and consign ourselves to a life of play.
. . . Arbitrary retirement at a fixed age ought
to be negotiated and decided according to the
wishes of the people involved. Mandatory retirement ought to be illegal.
  Quoted in "Profile of a Gray Panther"
  by Carol Offen, *Retirement Living*
    December 1972

2 One reason our society has become such a mess
is that we're isolated from each other. The old
are isolated by government policy. So we have
all sorts of stereotypes floating around about
blacks, old people, and women.
  Quoted in "How to Forget Age Bias,"
  Ms. *June 1975*

3 Power should not be concentrated in the hands
of so few, and powerlessness in the hands of so
many.   Ibid.

4 I think of age as a great universalizing force.
It's the only thing we all have in common. It
doesn't begin when you collect your social security benefits. Aging begins with the moment
of birth, and it ends only when life itself has
ended. Life is a continuum; only, we—in our

stupidity and blindness—have chopped it up into little pieces and kept all those little pieces separate.   Quoted in "Liberating Aging" by Ken Dychtwald, *New Age   February 1979*

5 There are lots of people and programs that have purported to serve us but instead treat us like wrinkled babies, powerless and dependent. Our goal should be responsible adulthood. We're the elders of the tribe, and the elders are charged with the tribe's survival and well being!   Ibid.

6 Our technological society scrap-piles old people as it does automobiles. . . .   Ibid.

7 Learning and sex until rigor mortis.
                                        Motto   *n.d.*

1642. Eirka Mann (1905–1969)

1 I want the child to become a human being, a good and decent man who knows the difference between lies and truth, aware of liberty and dignity and true reason, not the opportunistic reason 'dictated by policy' which turns black white if it's useful at the moment. I want the boy to become a decent human being—a man and not a Nazi!"
                Prologue, *School for Barbarians*
                                        1938

2 Music, theatre, the beauty of men and things, a fine day, a child, an attractive animal—from all these he [Thomas Mann] drew much pleasure, provided he was getting on with his work. Without work—that is, without active hope—he would not have known how to live.
                The Last Year of Thomas Mann, a Revealing Memoir by His Daughter
                                        1958

*German American author, 1875–1955.

1643. Phyllis McGinley (1905–1978)

1 Oh, shun, lad, the life of an author.
    It's nothing but worry and waste.
Avoid that utensil,
The laboring pencil,
    And pick up the scissors and paste.
                "A Ballad of Anthologies,"
                A Ballad of Anthologies   1941

2 Compromise? Of course we compromise. But compromise, if not the spice of life, is its solidity. It is what makes nations great and marriages happy and Spruce Manor the pleasant place it is.   "Suburbia, of Thee I Sing,"
                The Province of the Heart   1959

3 It's this no-nonsense side of women that is pleasant to deal with. They are the real sports-

men. They don't have to be constantly building up frail egos by large public performances like over-tipping the hat-check girl, speaking fluent French to the Hungarian waiter, and sending back the wine to be recooled.
                "Some of My Best Friends . . . ,"
                                        op. cit.

4 Sin . . . has been made not only ugly but passé. People are no longer sinful, they are only immature or under privileged or frightened or, more particularly, sick.   "In Defense of Sin,"
                                        op. cit.

5 Yet who could deny that privacy is a jewel? It has always been the mark of privilege, the distinguishing feature of a truly urbane culture.   "A Lost Privilege,"
                                        op. cit.

6 . . . "I am he
Who champions total liberty—
Intolerance being, ma'am, a state
No tolerant man can tolerate.
                "The Angry Man," St. 2,
                Times Three: 1932–1960   1960

7 Pressed for rules and verities
All I recollect are these:
Feed a cold to starve a fever.
Argue with no true believer.
Think too-long is never-act.
Scratch a myth and find a fact.
                "A Garland of Precepts," St. 2, op. cit.

8 The thing to remember about fathers is,
    they're men.   "Girls-Eye View of
                        Relatives," St. 3, op. cit

9 We might as well give up the fiction
    That we can argue any view.
For what in me is pure Conviction
    Is simple Prejudice in you.
                "Note to My Neighbor,"
                                        op. cit.

10 For the wonderful thing about saints is that they were *human*. They lost their tempers, got hungry, scolded God, were egotistical or testy or impatient in their turns, made mistakes and regretted them. Still they went on doggedly blundering toward heaven.
                "Running to Paradise,"
                Saint-Watching   1969

11 We live in the century of the Appeal. . . . One applauds the industry of professional philanthropy. But it has its dangers. After a while the private heart begins to harden. We fling letters into the wastebasket, are abrupt to telephone solicitations. Charity withers in the incessant gale.   "Aspects of Sanctity," op. cit.

2 Benevolent, stormy, patient, or out of sorts.
God knows which God is the God God
    recognizes
                "The Day After Sunday"   *n.d.*

1644. Eileen O'Casey (1905?–)

1 I was liberated but not too liberated. I was Catholic, you see, and my conscience always bothered me. Quoted in "Eileen O'Casey Remembers" by Lee Grant, *Los Angeles Times* *13 November 1974*

1645 Gretta Brooker Palmer (1905–1953)

1 Happiness is a by-product of an effort to make someone else happy. *Permanent Marriage n.d.*

1646. Ivy Baker Priest (1905–1975)

1 We women ought to put first things first. Why should we mind if men have their faces on the money, as long as we get our hands on it? Ch. 1, *Green Grows Ivy* 1958

2 My father had always said that there are four things a child needs—plenty of love, nourishing food, regular sleep, and lots of soap and water— and after those, what he needs most is some intelligent neglect. Ibid., Ch. 11

1647. Ayn Rand (1905–1982)

1 "Civilization is the progress toward a society of privacy. The savage's whole existence is public, ruled by the laws of his tribe. Civilization is the process of setting man free from men." *The Fountainhead* 1943

2 "Creation comes before distribution—or there will be nothing to distribute." Ibid.

3 "Has any act of selfishness ever equalled the carnage perpetrated by disciples of altruism?" Ibid.

4 Great men can't be ruled. Ibid.

5 If you learn how to rule one single man's soul, you can get the rest of mankind. Ibid.

6 Kill reverence and you've killed the hero in man. Ibid.

7 "Throughout the centuries there were men who took first steps down new roads armed with nothing but their own vision. Their goals differed, but they all had this in common: that the step was first, the road new, the vision unborrowed, and the response they received—hatred. The great creators—the thinkers, the artists, the scientists,the inventors—stood alone against the men of their time." Ibid.

8 "We are one in all and all in one. There are no men but only the great WE. One, indivisible and forever." Ch. 1, *Anthem* 1946

9 My happiness is not the means to any end. It is the end. It is its own goal. It is its own purpose. Neither am I the means to any end others may wish to accomplish. I am not a tool for their use. I am not a servant of their needs. I am not a bandage for their wounds. I am not a sacrifice on their altars. Ibid., Ch. 9

10 The word which can never die on this earth, for it is the heart of it and the meaning and the glory. The sacred word: EGO. Ibid., Ch. 12

11 "Disunity, that's the trouble. It's my absolute opinion that in our complex industrial society, no business enterprise can succeed without sharing the burden of the problems of other enterprises." Part I, Ch. 3, *Atlas Shrugged* 1957

12 "The entire history of science is a progression of exploded fallacies, not of achievements." Ibid., Pt. II, Ch. 1

13 "To demand 'sense' is the hallmark of nonsense. Nature does not make sense. Nothing makes sense." Ibid.

14 "People don't look for *kinds* of work anymore, ma'am," he answered impassively. "They just look for work." Ibid., Ch. 10

15 The modern mystics of muscle who offer you the fraudulent alternative of "human rights" versus "property rights," as if one could exist without the other, are making a last, grotesque attempt to revive the doctrine of soul versus body. Only a ghost can exist without material property; only a slave can work with no right to the product of his effort. Ibid., Pt. III, Ch. 7

16 Man's unique reward, however, is that while animals survive by adjusting themselves to their background, man survives by adjusting his background to himself. *For the New Intellectual* 1961

17 Professional intellectuals are the voice of a culture and are, therefore, its leaders, its integrators and its bodyguards. Ibid.

18 The hippies were taught by their parents, their neighbors, their tabloids and their college professors that faith, instinct and emotion are superior to reason—and they obeyed. They were taught that material concerns are evil, that the State or the Lord will provide, that the Lilies of the Field do not toil—and they obeyed. They were taught that love, indiscriminate love, for one's fellow-men is the highest virtue—and they obeyed. They were taught that the merging of one's self with a herd, a tribe or a community

is the noblest way for men to live—and they obeyed. There isn't a single basic principle of the Establishment which they do not share—there isn't a belief which they have not accepted.
"Apollo and Dionysus," *The New Left*   1968

1648. Mary Renault (1905–   )

1 Miss Searle had always considered boredom an intellectual defeat.   Ch. 1, *North Face* 1948

2 Exchanging ideas with women was always an illusion; they tagged everything on to some emotion, they were all incapable of the thing in itself.   Ibid., Ch. 5

3 Which of youth's pleasures can compare with the making ready for one's first big war?
Bk. II, Ch. 3, *The King Must Die* 1958

4 "Go with your fate, but not beyond. Beyond leads to dark places."
"Marathon," *The Bull from the Sea* 1962

5 I thought of my life, the good and evil days; of the gods, and fate; how much of a man's life and of his soul they make for him, how much he makes for himself. . . . Fate and will, will and fate, like earth and sky bringing forth the grain together; and which the bread tastes of, no man knows.   "Skyros," op. cit.

1649. Anna F. Trevisan (1905–   )

1 ELZA. Some things are very important and some are very unimportant. To know the difference is what we are given life to find out. . . .
Easter Eve 1946

2 ELZA. The mother! She is what keeps the family intact. . . . It is proved. A fact. Time and time again. The father, no matter how good . . . a father cannot keep the family intact.   Ibid.

3 MRS. GRISWOLD. The world is exhausted
In the Valley of the Shadow 1946

1650. Margaret Webster (1905–1972)

1 When an actor says a line, he makes his point and his thought moves on to the next; but a singer has to repeat the same words over a dozen times, the emotional shading varying with the

music, the thought progressing only in terms of sound.   *Don't Put Your Daughter On the Stage* 1972

1651. Hannah Arendt (1906–1975)

1 In an ever-changing, incomprehensible world the masses had reached the point where they would . . . think that everything was possible and that nothing was true.
Origins of Totalitarianism 1951

2 Thought . . . is still possible, and no doubt actual, wherever men live under the conditions of political freedom. Unfortunately . . . no other human capacity is so vulnerable, and it is in fact far easier to act under conditions of tyranny than it is to think.
The Human Condition 1958

3 With the loss of tradition we have lost the thread which safely guided us through the vast realms of the past, but this thread was also the chain fettering each successive generation to a predetermined aspect of the past. It could be that only now will the past open up to us with unexpected freshness and tell us things that no one as yet had ears to hear.   *Nomos I: Authority*, Carl J. Frederich, ed.   1958

4 Have we now come to the point where it is the children who are being asked to change or improve the world?   "Reflections on Little Rock" 1959

5 Our tradition of political thought had its definite beginning in the teachings of Plato and Aristotle. I believe it came to a no less definite end in the theories of Karl Marx.
Ch. 1, *Between Past and Future* 1961

6 Immortality is what nature possesses without effort and without anybody's assistance, and immortality is what the mortals must therefore try to achieve if they want to live up to the world into which they were born, to live up to the things which surround them and to whose company they are admitted for a short while.   Ibid., Ch. 2

7 . . . under conditions of terror most people will comply but *some people will not*. . . . Humanly speaking, no more is required, and no more can reasonably be asked, for this planet to remain a place fit for human habitation.
Ch. 14, *Eichmann in Jerusalem* 1963

8 The trouble with Eichmann was precisely that so many were like him, and that the many were neither perverted nor sadistic, that they were, and still are, terribly and terrifyingly normal. . . . this new type of criminal, who is in actual fact *hostis generis humani*, commits his crimes

under circumstances that make it well-nigh impossible for him to know or to feel that he is doing wrong. op. cit., Epilogue

9 Wars and revolutions . . . have outlived all their ideological justifications. . . . No cause is left but the most ancient of all, the one, in fact, that from the beginning of our history has determined the very existence of politics, the cause of freedom versus tyranny.
Introduction, *On Revolution*   1963

10 . . . What makes it so plausible to assume that hypocrisy is the vice of vices is that integrity can indeed exist under the cover of all other vices except this one. Only crime and the criminal, it is true, confront us with the perplexity of radical evil; but only the hypocrite is really rotten to the core. Ibid., Ch. 2

11 When we were told that by freedom we understood free enterprise, we did very little to dispel this monstrous falsehood. . . . it is a minor blessing compared with the truly political freedoms, such as freedom of speech and thought, of assembly and association, even under the best conditions. Economic growth may one day turn out to be a curse rather than a good, and under no conditions can it either lead into freedom or constitute a proof for its existence.
Ibid., Ch. 6

12 . . . be loyal to life, don't create fiction but accept what life is giving you, show yourself worthy of whatever it may be by recollecting and pondering over it, thus repeating it in imagination: "this is the way to remain alive."
Men in Dark Times   1968

13 For the trouble with lying and deceiving is that their efficiency depends entirely upon a clear notion of their truth that the liar and deceiver wishes to hide. In this sense, truth, even if it does not prevail in public, possesses an ineradicable primacy over all falsehoods.
"Lying in Politics," *Crises of the Republic*   1972

14 The defiance of established authority, religious and secular, social and political, as a worldwide phenomenon may well one day be accounted the outstanding event of the last decade. "Civil Disobedience," op. cit.

15 When we were young enough to have children, we had no money. And when we had money, we were too old.
Quoted in *Hannah Arendt: For Love of the World* by Elisabeth Young-Bruehl   1981

1652. Dorothy Gillam Baker (1906–   )

1 We are living today at the climax of history, when the main line of human history has con-

verged to a balance of terror between the two superpowers. The United States and the Soviet Union find themselves in an accelerating arms race beyond their power to control, and appear trapped by the binding power of tradition, habit, and the very nature of power. In the past no dominant political, economic, religious or military power has voluntarily relinquished its position. *Transformation or Catastrophe?*   1978

2 I am convinced that the promise of harmonious resolution as a united people of the world, capable of living on a higher level of consciousness . . . is not a utopian vision, but the new revolutionary form that lies within our grasp. Ibid.

1653. Josephine Baker (1906–1975)

1 I like Frenchmen very much, because even when they insult you they do it so nicely.
Remark   *n.d.*

1654. Margaret Bourke-White (1906–1971)

1 Usually I object when someone makes overmuch of men's work versus women's work, for I think it is the excellence of the results which counts. *Portrait of Myself*   1963

2 . . . war correspondents . . . see a great deal of the world. Our obligation is to pass it on to others. Quoted in *The Woman's Eye* by Anne Tucker*   1973

*See 2240.

1655. Jacqueline Cochran (1906/10?–1981)

1 I can cure your men of walking off the [flight] program. Let's put on the girls.
Quoted in Ch. 8, *The American Heritage History of Flight*   1962

1656. Catherine Cookson (1906–   )

1 "Catholic, be damned! They tell 'em to have bairns, but do they bloody well keep them?'" Ch. 1, *The Fifteen Streets*   1952

2 "It's no good saying one thing and thinking another." Ibid., Ch. 8

1657. Anna Roosevelt Halsted (1906–1975)

1 There are so many indignities to being sick and helpless. . . .

Letter to David Gray (1 November 1962), Quoted in *Eleanor: The Years Alone** by Joseph P. Lash *1972*

*Eleanor Roosevelt; see 1341.

1658. Lillian Hellman (1906–1984)

1 MRS. MORTAR. But the cinema is a shallow art. It has no—no—no fourth dimension.
Act I, *The Children's Hour* *1934*

2 HANNAH. Lucy, there were people made to think and people made to listen. I ain't sure either you or Lundee were made to do either.
Act I, *Days to Come* *1936*

3 EASTER. When you got nothin' to do, we can't do it for you. Ibid., Act II, Sc. 1

4 WILKIE. You're a noble lady, and I am frightened of noble ladies. They usually land the men they know in cemeteries. Ibid., Sc. 3

5 ANDREW. Polite and blind, we lived.
Ibid., Act III

6 Cynicism is an unpleasant way of saying the truth. Act I, *The Little Foxes* *1939*

7 God forgives those who invent what they need. Ibid.

8 Fashions in sin change. *Watch on the Rhine* *1941*

9 KOYLA. You are what you are. It is my opinion the trouble in the world comes from people who do not know what they are, and pretend to be something they're not.
The North Star *1943*

10 MARCUS. Carry in your own valise, son. It is not seemly for a man to load his goods on other men, black or white.
Act I, *Another Part of the Forest* *1946*

11 BIRDIE. You lose your manners when you're poor. Ibid., Act II

12 LAVINIA. But maybe half a lie is worse than a real lie. Ibid., Act III

13 LAVINIA. I'm not going to have any Bibles in my school. That surprise you all' It's the only book in the world but it's just for grown people, after you know it don't mean what it says.
Ibid.

14 I am not willing, now or in the future, to bring bad trouble to people who, in my past association with them, were completely innocent of any talk or any action that was disloyal or subversive. . . . I cannot and will not cut my conscience to fit this year's fashions, even though I long ago came to the conclusion that I was not a political person and could have no comfortable place in any political group.
Letter to the House Committee on Un-American Activities, *The Nation* *31 May 1952*

15 CARRIE. Not like the country. My. I never heard anybody say a thing like that before. It takes courage to just up and say you don't like the country. Everybody likes the country.
Act I, *Toys in the Attic* *1959*

16 ALBERTINE. You do too much. Go and do nothing for a while. Nothing. Ibid., Act II

17 CARRIE. I read in a French book that there was nothing so abandoned as a respectable young girl. Ibid.

18 CARRIE. There are lives that are shut and should stay shut. . . . Ibid., Act III

19 ANNA. Well, people change and forget to tell each other. Too bad—causes so many mistakes. Ibid.

20 I didn't know what she was saying when she moved her lips in a Baptist church or a Catholic cathedral or, less often, in a synagogue, but it was obvious that God could be found anywhere. . . .
An Unfinished Woman *1969*

21 Mamma seemed to do only what my father wanted, and yet we lived the way my mother wanted us to live. Ibid.

22. . . . the first sexual stirrings of little girls, so masked, so complex, so foolish as compared with the sex of little boys. Ibid.

1659. Grace Murray Hopper (1906–1992)

1 We're just getting started. We're just beginning to meet what will be the future—we've got the model T.
60 Minutes, ABC-TV *24 August 1986*

2 It's just as well to be told you're too old at 40. Then you're over it.*
Quoted in *Time* by Sara C. Medina *25 August 1986*

*Ref. to regular Navy's rejection of her in 1946.

1660. Hsieh Ping-ying (1906–)

1 Ah! Mother really loved me, but why did she beat me so hard? Is not a child a person too? Can she never have her own way? Must she obey every word a grown-up says? These questions went round and round in my head.
Girl Rebel, Adet & Anor Lin, trs. *1940*

2 The spring came, warm and intoxicating, and planted the seeds of love in the hearts of many young boys and girls. But it also sprayed the dew of blood on the young bodies of boy and girl soldiers. The call to "fight on" had waked young people from their dreams. They came out of the pink palace of romance, going to the social front which was covered with corpses and reeked with the smell of blood. They gave up their idea of love, and substituted for it the love of the masses suffering under suppression, the love of the poor, the love of their comrades.

Ibid.

1661. Mirra Komarovsky (1906–   )

1 What are we educating women for? To raise this question is to face the whole problem of womens' role in society. We are uncertain about the end of women's education precisely because the status of women in our society is fraught with contradictions and confusion.

Women in the Modern World   1953

2 Today the survival of some . . . stereotypes is a psychological strait jacket for both sexes.

Ibid.

3 Were our knowledge of human relationships a hundredfold more reliable than it is now, it would still be foolish to seek ready-made solutions for problems of living in the index of a book.   *Ibid., Ch. 6*

4 The most elusive knowledge of all is self-knowledge and it is usually acquired laboriously through experience outside the classroom   *Ibid.*

5 The greatest danger of traditional education is that learning may remain purely verbal.

Ibid., Ch. 7

1662. Dilys Laing (1906–1960)

1 Proud inclination of the flesh,
most upright tendency, salute
in honor of the secret wish.
    "Villanelle," St. 1, *Collected Poems*
    1967

2 . . . memory is a storm I can't repel.
    "Venus Petrified," St. 3,
    op. cit.

3 The women took a train
away away from herself.
    "The Double Goer," St. 1,
    op. cit.

4 I was a child who clutched the amulet
of childhood in a terror of time. I saw

archangels, worshipped trees, expected God
    "The Little Girls," St. 2, op. cit.

5 Women receive
the insults of men
with tolerance,
having been bitten
in the nipple
by their toothless gums.   "Veterans," op. cit.

6   To be a woman and a writer
is double mischief, for
the world will slight her
who slights "the servile house," and who
    would rather
make odes than beds.
    "Sonnet to a Sister in Error,"
    St. 2, op. cit.

1663. Anne Morrow Lindbergh (1906–   )

1 Travelers are always discoverers, especially those who travel by air. There are no signposts in the sky to show a man has passed that way before. There are no channels marked. The flier breaks each second into new uncharted seas.
    Ch. 1, *North to the Orient   1935*

2 . . . the fundamental magic of flying, a miracle that has nothing to do with any of its practical purposes—purposes of speed, accessibility, and convenience—and will not change as they change.   *Ibid., Ch. 23*

3 Lost time was like a run in a stocking. It always got worse.   Ch. 3, *The Steep Ascent*
    1944

4 Perhaps middle-age is, or should be, a period of shedding shells; the shell of ambition, the shell of material accumulations and possessions, the shell of the ego.   *Gift from the Sea*
    1955

5 One cannot collect all the beautiful shells on the beach.   *Ibid.*

6 It isn't for the moment you are struck that you need courage, but for the long uphill climb back to sanity and faith and security.
    Hours of Gold, Hours of Lead
    1973

7 Love is a force. . . . It is not a result; it is a cause. It is not a product; it produces. It is a power, like money, or steam or electricity. It is valueless unless you can give something else by means of it.   *Locked Rooms and Open Doors*
    1974

8 People talk about love as though it were something you could give, like an armful of flowers.   *Ibid.*

1664. Maria Goeppert Mayer (1906–1972)

1 Of course my father always said I should have been a boy. He said, Don't grow up to be a woman, and what he meant by that was, a housewife . . . without any interests.
Quoted in "Maria Goeppert-Mayer,"
A Life of One's Own
By Joan Dash   *1973*

2 Mathematics began to seem too much like puzzle solving. Physics is puzzle solving, too, but of puzzles created by nature, not by the mind of man.   Ibid.

1665. Rita Boumy Pappas (1906–   )

1 I did not let them nail my soul as they do butterflies.   "Roxane M."   *1975*

1666. Ting Ling (1906–   )

1 In the Chinese family system, there is superficial quiet and calmness and quarreling is frowned upon, but in reality all is in conflict.
Quoted in *Women in Modern China*
by Helen Foster Snow*   *1967*

*See 1675.

2 I wanted to escape from love but didn't know how.   Ibid.

3 The Red Army soldiers are a totally new type that cannot be found anywhere else in China. They have never known anything but revolution. Because they originally lived in the Sovietized areas, they have no ideology of private property and no domestic ideas. No unhappiness ever comes to mind. They think only of how to overcome the difficulties of their work and never of their troubles.   Ibid.

1667. Dorothy Baker (1907–1968)

1 In the first place maybe he shouldn't have got himself mixed up with Negroes. It gave him a funny slant on things and he never got over it. It gave him a feeling for undisciplined expression, a hot, direct approach, a full-throated ease that never did him any final good in his later dealings with those of his race, those whom civilization has whipped into shape, those who can contain themselves and play what's written.
Ch. 1, Bk. I, *Young Man with a Horn*
1938

2 "She wastes herself, she drifts, all she wants to do with her life is lose it somewhere."
Cassandra at the Wedding   *1962*

3 "Same thing everywhere I'd looked. Large amounts of safety, very few risks. Let nothing endanger the proper marriage, the fashionable career, the nonirritating thesis that says nothing new and nothing true."   Ibid.

1668. Rachel Carson (1907–1964)

1 Beginnings are apt to be shadowy and so it is the beginnings of that great mother of life, the sea.   Pt. I, Ch. 1, *The Sea Around Us*
1951

2 For the sea lies all about us. . . . In its mysterious past it encompasses all the dim origins of life and receives in the end, after, it maybe, many transmutations, the dead husks of that same life. For all at last return to the sea—to Oceanus, the ocean river, like the everflowing stream of time, the beginning and the end.
Ibid., Pt. III, Ch. 14

3 Always the edge of the sea remains an elusive and indefinable boundary. The shore has a dual nature, changing with the swing of the tides, belonging now to the land, now to the sea.
"The Marginal World,"
The Edge of the Sea   *1955*

4 The discipline of the writer is to learn to be still and listen to what his subject has to tell him.   Speech, American Association of University Women   *22 June 1956*

5 In every outthrust headland, in every curving beach, in ever grain of sand there is a story of the earth.   "Our Every-Changing Shore,"
Holiday   *July 1958*

6 As cruel a weapon as the cave man's club, the chemical barrage has been hurled against the fabric of life.   *The Silent Spring*   *1962*

7 For the first time in the history of the world, every human being is now subjected to contact with dangerous chemicals, from the moment of conception until death.   Ibid., Ch. 3

8 If we are going to live so intimately with these chemicals—eating and drinking them, taking them into the very marrow of our bones—we had better know something about their nature and their power.   Ibid.

9 Under the philosophy that now seems to guide our destinies, nothing must get in the way of the man with the spray gun.   Ibid., Ch. 7

10 Over increasingly large areas of the United States, spring now comes unheralded by the return of the birds, and the early mornings are strangely

silent where once they were filled with the beauty of bird song. *Ibid., Ch. 8*

11 The "control of nature" is a phrase conceived in arrogance, born of the Neanderthal age of biology and convenience of man.
Ibid., Ch. 17

1669. Daphne Du Maurier (1907–)

1 . . . like most sleepers I knew that I dreamed. *Ch. 1, Rebecca   1938*

2 We can never go back again, that much is certain. The past is still too close to us. The things we have tried to forget and put behind us would stir again, and that sense of fear, of furtive unrest . . . might in some manner unforeseen become a living companion, as it had been before. *Ibid., Ch. 2*

3 She could not separate success from peace of mind. The two must go together; her observation pointed to this truth. Failure meant poverty, poverty meant squalor, squalor led, in the final stages, to the smells and stagnation of Bowling Inn Alley.
Pt. 1, Ch. 10, Mary Anne   1954

4 The pair were playing a game that defied intervention, they were matched like reel and rod and there was no unwinding. They juggled in jargon, dabbled in *double-entendres,* wallowed in each other's witticisms, and all at the expense of the Defendant. *Ibid., Pt. IV, Ch. 2*

5 . . . the little festive atmosphere of strangeness, of excitement, that only a holiday bedroom brings. This is ours for the moment, but no more. While we are in it we bring it life. When we have gone it no longer exists, it fades into anonymity. *Don't Look Now   1970*

6 "The trouble is," said Laura, "walking in Venice becomes compulsive once you start. Just over the next bridge, you say, and then the next one beckons." *Ibid.*

1670. Eugenia Ginzburg (1907?–1967)

1 Maternal feelings are a splendid rational for misbehavior.
Pt. I, Ch. 1, Eugenia Ginzburg: Within the Whirlwind (1979), Ian Boland, tr.   1981

2 When you have lived for years on end without any sense of the future or any real feeling for the reality of the morrow, the whole idea of putting something aside, of saving, goes clean out of your head. There had been periods when

we had been earning quite a lot of money. We could have saved up for a rainy day. But when every day is rainy, you somehow don't think about it. And how we were ourselves astonished at where all the money had gone; all at once we were without means. *Ibid., Pt. II, Ch. 14*

3 One way or another the book had entered upon a new phase in its existence . . . The total alienation of the product from its author had been accomplished. The book had become a grown-up daughter off on her continental tour, without so much as a look over her shoulder or a thought to spare for her old mother left to fend for herself at home. *Ibid., Epilogue*

1671. Edith Head (1907–1981)

1 The subjective actress thinks of clothes only as they apply to her; the objective actress thinks of them only as they affect others, as a tool for the job. *The Dress Doctor,* with Jane Kesner Ardmore   *1959*

1672. Zora Neale Hurston (1907–1960)

1 Ships at a distance have every man's wish on board. For some they come in with the tide. For others they sail forever on the horizon, never out of sight, never landing, until the Watcher turns his eyes away in resignation, his dreams mocked to death by Time. That is the life of men. Now, women forget all those things they don't want to remember, and remember everything they don't want to forget. The dream is the truth. Then they act and do things accordingly. *Ch. 1, Their Eyes Were Watching God   1937*

2 "You love like a coward. Don't take no steps at all. Just stand around and hope for things to happen outright. Unthankful and unknowing like a hog under an acorn tree. Eating and grunting with your ears hanging over your eyes, and never even looking up to see where the acorns are coming from." *Seraph on the Suwanee 1948*

3 "Don't you realize that the sea is the home of water? All water is off on a journey unlessen it's in the sea, and it's homesick, and bound to make its way home someday." *Ibid., Ch. 27*

1673. Violette Leduc (1907–1972)

1 "She is killing me and there's nothing I can accuse her of.' *La Bâtarde 1965*

2 The pearl wanted what I wanted. I was discovering the little male organ we all of us have. A eunuch taking heart again.
Therese and Isabelle 1968

3 To give oneself, one must annihilate oneself. Ibid.

4 To write is to inform against others.
Mad in Pursuit 1971

5 "I desire, am only able to desire, myself."
Ibid.

1674. Lee Miller (1907–1977)

1 I'm not Cinderella. I can't force my foot into the glass slipper. Quoted in *The Lives of Lee Miller* by Antony Penrose* 1985

*Her son.

2 In all the great sieges, the defenders eat rats, and if I have to eat rats, they are going to be well spiced!* Ibid.

*Remark to store manager on purchasing a basketful of spices at start of Blitz in London, 1940.

1675. Helen Foster Snow (1907–)

1 The war between the artist and writer and government or orthodoxy is one of the tragedies of humankind. One chief enemy is stupidity and failure to understand anything about the creative mind. For a bureaucratic politician to presume to tell any artist or writer how to get his mind functioning is the ultimate in asininity. The artist is no more able to control his mind than is any outsider. Freedom to think requires not only freedom of expression but also freedom from the threat of orthodoxy and being outcast and ostracized. "Women and Kuomintang,"
Women in Modern China 1967

2 . . . one can judge a civilization by the way it treats its women. "Bound Feet and Straw Sandals," op. cit.

1676. Barbara Stanwyck (1907–1990)

1 Sponsors obviously care more about a ninety-second commercial and *want* to pay you more than any guest star gets for a ninety-minute *acting* performance. Quoted in *McCall's* March 1965

2 There is a point in portraying surface vulgarity where tragedy and comedy are very close.
Quoted in *Starring Miss Barbara Stanwyck* by Ella Smith 1974

1677. Anna Anastasi (1908–)

1 . . . it is apparent that we cannot speak of inferiority and superiority, but only of specific differences in aptitudes and personality between the sexes. These differences are largely the result of cultural and other experiential factors. . . .
Differential Psychology 1937

1678. Harriette Arnow (1908–)

1 "If a religion is unpatriotic, it ain't right."
Ch. 4, *The Dollmaker* 1954

2 "I've been readen th Bible an a hunten God fer a long while—off an on—but it ain't so easy as picken up a nickel off th floor."
Ibid., Ch. 15

3 Christ had had no money, just his life. Life and money: could a body separate the two? What had Judas done for his money? Whispered a little, kept still as she did now. Ibid., Ch. 37

4 "Supposen the rebels lose. They'll try again. Supposen they win? How can they ever stick together in one nation? They'll be jarren and fighten around over slavery, trade and a lot of other things. Right now the East don't want the West, and the North is a different world from the South. And they've got Spain on their doorstep. But supposen they do clean out Spain, kill every Indian, plow up every acre a ground from the Atlantic to the Pacific? They'll still have their wars." *The Kentucky Trace* 1974

1679. Sylvia Ashton-Warner (1908–)

1 Love interferes with fidelities.
Teacher 1963

2 When love turns away, now, I don't follow it. I sit and suffer, unprotesting, until I feel the tread of another step. Ibid.

3 I've got to relearn what I was supposed to have learned. (February 1941) *Myself* 1967

4 I flung my tongue round like a cat-o'-nine-tails so that my pleasant peaceful infant room became little less than a German concentration camp as I took out on the children what life should have got. Ibid. (August 1941)

5 I am my own Universe, I my own Professor. Ibid.

6 Love has the quality of informing almost everything—even one's work.
Ibid. (12 November 1942)

7 In mind I lay a hand on his arm but only in mind. That would be revealing a feeling, an offense against London.   *Three   1970*

8 As the blackness of the night recedes so does the nadir of yesterday. The child I am forgets so quickly.   Ibid.

9 "God, the illogic! The impossibility of communication in this house. The sheer operation alone of getting something through to somebody."   Ibid.

1680. Simone de Beauvoir (1908–1986)

1 To attain his truth, man must not attempt to dispel the ambiguity of his being but, on the contrary, accept the task of realizing it. He rejoins himself only to the extent that he agrees to remain at a distance from himself.
      Ch. 1, *The Ethics of Ambiguity 1948*

2 . . . the time that one gains can not be accumulated in a storehouse; it is contradictory to want to save up existence, which, the fact is, exists only by being spent, and there is a good case for showing that airplanes, machines, the telephone, and the radio do not make men of today happier than those of former times.
      Ibid., Ch. 3

3 A man would never get the notion of writing a book on the peculiar situation of the human male.   *The Second Sex   1953*

4 For him she is sex—absolute sex, no less. She is defined and differentiated with reference to man and not he with reference to her; she is the incidental, the inessential as opposed to the essential. He is the Subject, he is the Absolute— she is the Other.   Ibid.

5 . . . the only public good is that which assures the private good of the citizens. . . .   Ibid.

6 There is no justification for present existence other than its expansion into an indefinitely open future.   Ibid.

7 Refusal to make herself the object is not always what turns women to homosexuality; most lesbians, on the contrary, seek to cultivate the treasures of their femininity. . . .   Ibid.

8 Between women love is contemplative. . . . There is no struggle, no victory, no defeat; in exact reciprocity each is at once subject and object, sovereign and slave; duality becomes mutuality.   Ibid.

9 Society, being codified by man, decrees that woman is inferior; she can do away with this inferiority only by destroying the male's superiority.   Ibid.

10 All oppression creates a state of war.   Ibid.

11 . . . justice can never be done in the midst of injustice.   Ibid.

12 . . . the effort to inhibit all sex curiosity and pleasure in the child is quite uesless; one succeeds only in creating repressions, obsessions, neuroses.   Ibid.

13 . . . when we abolish the slavery of half of humanity, together with the whole system of hypocrisy that it implies, then the "division" of humanity will reveal its genuine significance and the human couple will find its true form.   Ibid.

14 "Ah! if only there were two of me," she thought, one who spoke and the other who listened, one who lived and the other who watched, how I would love myself! I'd envy no one."
      Prologue, Ch. 1, *All Men Are Mortal 1955*

15 This stale taste of my life will never change. Always the same past, the same feelings, the same rational thoughts, the same boredom. For thousands of years! Never will I escape from myself!   Ibid., Bk. III

16 She was trying to get rid of a religious hangover.
      Pt. IV, *Memoirs of a Dutiful Daughter 1959*

17 "There won't be a war. The gap between the capitalist and socialist countries will soon be done away with. Because now we're in the great twentieth-century revolution: producing is more important than possessing."
      Ch. 1, *Les Belles Images   1966*

18 Whatever the country, capitalist or socialist, man was everywhere crushed by technology, made a stranger to his own work, imprisoned, forced into stupidity. The evil all arose from the fact that he had increased his needs rather than limited them; . . . As long as fresh needs continued to be created, so new frustrations would come into being. When had the decline begun? The day knowledge was preferred to wisdom and mere usefulness to beauty. . . . Only a moral revolution—not a social or a political revolution—only a moral revolution would lead man back to his lost truth.   Ibid., Ch. 3

19 It's frightening to think that you mark your children merely by being yourself. . . . It seems unfair. You can't assume the responsibility for everything you do—or don't do.   Ibid.

20 I had grown very fond of this dying woman [her mother]. As we talked in the half-darkness I assuaged an old unhappiness; I was renewing the dialogue that had been broken off during my adolescence and that our differences and our

liknenesses had never allowed us to take up again. And the early tenderness that I had thought dead for ever came to life again . . .
A Very Easy Death   1966

21 I find it absurd to assume that all coitus is rape. By saying that, one agrees to the masculine myth that a man's sex is a sword, a weapon.   Quoted in "The Radicalization of Simone de Beauvoir" by Alice Schwarzer, *The First Ms. Reader*, Francine Klagsbrun, ed.   1972

22 Both today and throughout history, the class struggle governs the manner in which old age takes hold of a man: there is a great gulf between the aged slave and the aged patrician, . . . and these two classes are brought into being by the conflict between the exploiters and the exploited. Any statement that claims to deal with old age as a whole must be challenged, for it tends to hide this chasm.
The Coming of Age   1972

23 . . . it is old age, rather than death, that is to be contrasted with life. Old age is life's parody, whereas death transforms life into a destiny: in a way it preserves it by giving it the absolute dimension—"As into himself eternity changes him at last." Death does away with time.
Ibid., Conclusion

24 One is not born a genius, one becomes a genius.   Quoted in *The Woman's Eye* by Anne Tucker*   1973

*See 2420.

25 I tore myself away from the safe comfort of certainties through my love for truth; and truth rewarded me.   *All Said and Done*   1974

26 Patience [is one of those] "feminine" qualities which have their origin in our oppression but should be preserved after our liberation.
Interview by Alice Schwarzer in
Marie-Claire   October 1976

1681. Constance Carrier (1908–)

1 They recognize their own elect discriminate, appraise, condemn, and, with no hint of disrespect, almost unconsciously they come to change *One should be* to *I am.*
"Seminary," St. 5, *The Middle Voice*   1955

1682. Bette Davis (1908–1989)

1 I have always been driven by some distant music—a battle hymn no doubt—for I have been at war from the beginning. I've never looked back before. I've never had the time and it has always seemed so dangerous. To look back is to relax one's vigil.
Ch. 1, *The Lonely Life*   1962

2 The male ego with few exceptions is elephantine to start with.   Ibid., Ch. 9

3 If you have never been hated by your child, you have never been a parent.   Ibid., Ch. 19

4 This become a credo of mine . . . attempt the impossible in order to improve your work.
Ch. 10, *Mother Goddamn*   1974

5 Writers don't know how to write scripts today. They don't know what to write about. . . . There are no scripts. That's why they do all these damn docu-dramas, because our lives are more interesting than anything they can make up.   Quoted in "The Story of a Winner" by Dotson Rader, *Parade Magazine*
6 March 1983

6 Don't you hate people who drink white wine? I mean, my dear, every alcoholic in town is getting falling-down drunk on white wine. They think they aren't drunks because they only drink wine. Never, never trust anyone who asks for white wine. It means they're phonies.   Ibid.

7 I'm very religious, though I've never been a big churchgoer. Being a working woman, I decided God would allow me Sundays off.   Ibid.

8 I am a woman meant for a man, but I never found a man who could compete.
Newspaper Interview
n.d.

1683. Agnes DeMille (1908–)

1 I learned three important things in college—to use a library, to memorize quickly and visually, to drop asleep at any time given a horizontal surface and fifteen minutes. What I could not learn was to think creatively on schedule.
Dance to the Piper   1952

2 No trumpets sound when the important decisions of our life are made. Destiny is made known silently.   Ibid.

3 A good education is usually harmful to a dancer. A good calf is better than a good head.
News Item   1 February 1954

4 The truest expression of a people is in its dances and its music. Bodies never lie.
"Do I Hear a Waltz?," *The New York Times Magazine*   11 May 1975

1684. Hildegarde Dolson (1908–1981)

1 Perhaps the surest way to tell when a female goes over the boundary from childhood into

meaningful adolescence is to watch how long it takes her to get to bed at night.

> "How Beautiful with Mud," *We Shook the Family Tree* 1946

2 I too would be beautiful. I would also be Flower-Fresh, Fastidious ad Dainty—a triple-threat virtue obviously prized above pears by the entire male sex, as depicted in the *Ladies' Home Journal*   Ibid.

1685. M.F.K. Fisher (1908–1992)

1 A true karmic force is supposed to build up its strength through centuries of both evil and good, in order to prevent its transmigration into another and lesser form, and this may well explain why Marseilles has always risen anew from the ashes of history.

> Ch. I, *A Considerable Town*   1964

2 "In France we have lived with the law for so long that we know how and when to make use of it. We are not afraid of it. In your country you are still so inexperienced, that you are in awe of it. The law is your stern parent, like God, and you fear its punishment. Here we respect it, but only if we respect ourselves more. We use it when we need it."   Ibid., Ch. 5

3 There are many people like me who believe firmly if somewhat incoherently that pockets on this planet are filled with what humans have left behind them, both good and evil, and that any such spiritual accumulation can stay there forever, past definition of such a stern word. . . . there are kindlier and even restorative places, which like the bad or merely disturbing ones influence people whether or not they are aware of their vulnerability before such old forces.

> Ibid., Ch. 8

4 . . . our dispassionate acceptance of attribution [by age needs to] be matched by a full use of everything that has ever happened in all the long wonderful-ghastly years to free a person's mind from his body . . . to use the experience, both great and evil, so that physical annoyances are surmountable in an alert and even mirthful appreciation of life itself.   *Sister Age*   1983

5 "There is a communion of more than our bodies when bread is broken and wine is drunk. And that is my answer when people ask me: Why do you write about hunger, and not wars or love?"   Quoted in

> "With Bold Pen and Fork" by Mimi Sheraton, *Time* 26 January 1987

1686. Joan Fleming (1908–1980)

1 "It's the money," Molly said clumsily, "if you've once had no money, and I mean no money at all, it means something always ever afterwards."

> Ch. 7, *The Chill and the Kill*   1964

2 "Folk love being told things about themselves they already know."   Ibid.

1687. Nancy Hale (1908–   )

1 She could never get used to the idea that most people don't use their eyes except to keep from running into things.

> "Eyes or No Eyes, or The Art of Seeing," *The Life in the Studio* 1957

2 After my mother's death I began to see her as she had really been. . . . It was less like losing someone than discovering someone.

> "A Good Light," op. cit.

3 . . . this mysterious thing, artistic talent; the key to so much freedom, the escape from so much suffering.   Pt. I, Ch. 4, *Mary Cassatt:* A Biography of the Great American Painter* 1975

*See 976.

4 An artist's originality is balanced by a corresponding conservatism, a superstitiousness, about it; which might be boiled down to "What worked before will work again."   Ibid., Pt. II, Ch. 6

5 I had wanted to say then to the young man, "Painting one picture—even a mediocre picture—is more important than collecting a hundred." I'd wanted to say, "You couldn't have any collections at all unless you first had pictures."   Ibid., Epilogue

1688. Josephine Jacobsen (1908–   )

1 Kneel at the window.
Wait under the thorntree
for the sun. Go away
carrying your difference, you
  cannot leave it.
Say, Not God
himself would dare to lay it
  on you without
relief.
Tell your secret bones: Wait.

> "Short Views of Africa."   n.d.

2 Galaxies are simpler. There is an awful grace in such mystery.   "Presence I"   n.d.

3 Life is absolutely brimming with terror.
> Quoted in interview by
> Betty Parry in *Belles Lettres*
> *May/June 1986*

4 For me, it's like Jacob wrestling with the angel. In every encounter with a poem there is a possibility of an abysmal failure. It's like the difficulty of trying to climb a mountain: the chances that you are going to fall are very steep, and the sense of triumph if you get there is very strong.
> Ibid.

5 The essence of poetry is the unique view—the unguessed relationship, suddenly manifest. Poetry's eye is always aslant, oblique.
> Lecture, "One Poet's
> Poetry," op. cit.

1689. Amy Johnson (1908?–1941)

1 Had I been a man I might have explored the Poles or climbed Mount Everest, but as it was my spirit found outlet in the air. . . .
> Essay in *Myself When Young,*
> Margot Asquith,* ed.   *1938*

*See 1108.

1690. Betty MacDonald (1908–1958)

1 Men are quite humorless about their own businesses.
> "I Learn to Hate Even Baby Chickens," *The
> Egg and I*   1945

2 Gammy used to say, "Too much scrubbing takes the life right out of things" . . .   Ibid.

3 Nobody knows how old Mrs. Piggle-Wiggle is. She says doesn't know herself. She says, "What difference does it make how old I am when I shall never grow any bigger?"
> Ch. 1, *Mrs. Piggle-Wiggle*
> *1947*

1691. Jean Sutherland MacLeod (1908–   )

1 Oh! why does the wind blow upon me so wild?
Is it because I'm nobody's child?
> "Nobody's Child"   *1954*

1692. Madeline Mason-Manheim (1908–   )

1   Know you Silence, my friend?
It is the dumbness of the tongue when the heart would be heard;

It is the muteness of the lips when the spirit speaks loudest.
It is the uttering of the unutterable.
> "Silence," St. 1, *Hill Fragments*
> *1925*

2 Your destiny, O River,
It is even as the destiny of man.
O, ye are brethren,
Souls unharboured,
Seeking to regain the Sea.   "The River,"
> op. cit.

3 Sleep, companion of Silence, walks in her garden;
Walks 'midst her deathless poppies and gathers them to her breast.   "Sleep,"
> op. cit.

4 They call you barren
Who, unseeing, gaze upon you.
Yet! Time's most secret thoughts,
The jewels of the ages
Are buried in your breast
As in your loneliness you lie
Beneath the everlasting heights.
> "The Desert," St. 1,
> op. cit.

1693. Ethel Merman (1908–1984)

1 Broadway has been very good to me—but then, I've been very good to Broadway.
> Quoted in "She Had Rhythm and Was
> the Top" by William A. Henry III,
> *Time*   *27 February 1984*

2 I take a breath when I have to.   Ibid.

1694. Alice Neel (1908–1984)

1 But we are all creatures in a way, aren't we?
And both men and women are wretched.
> Quoted in "Alice Neel: Portraits of
> Four Decades" by Cindy Nemser, *Ms.*
> *October 1973*

2 You can't leave humanity out. If you didn't have humanity, you wouldn't have anything.
> Ibid.

1695. Peace Pilgrim (1908–1981)

1 I wish that every child could have growing space because I think children are a little like plants. If they grow too close together they become thin and sickly and never obtain maximum growth. We need room to grow.
> Ch. 1, *Peace
> Pilgrim: Her Life and Work in
> Her Own Words*   *1982*

2 I don't eat junk foods and I don't think junk thoughts.　　　　　　　　　　Ibid., Ch. 2

3 This is the way of peace—overcome evil with good, and falsehood with truth, and hatred with love.　　　　　　　　Ibid., Motto, Ch. 3

4 Truth is the pearl without price. . . . Those who have the truth would not be packaging it and selling it, so anyone who is selling it, really does not possess it.　　　　　　　　Ibid.

5 Life is like a mirror. Smile at it and it smiles back at you.　　　　　　　　　　Ibid.

6 If you feed a man a meal, you only feed him for a day—but if you teach a man to grow food, you feed him for a lifetime.　　　　Ibid.

7 Prayer is a concentration of positive thought.　　　　　　　　　　　　Ibid.

8 I would say to the military: yes, we need to be defended; yes, we need you. The Air Force can clean up the air, the Marines can take care of the despoiled forests, the Navy can clean the oceans, the Coast Guard can take care of the rivers, and the Army can be used to build adequate drainage projects to prevent disastrous floods, and other such benefits for mankind.　　　　　　　　　　　　Ibid., Ch. 8

9 We seem always ready to pay the price for war. Almost gladly we give our time and our treasure—our limbs and even our lives—for war. But we expect to get peace for nothing.　Ibid.

10 The price of peace is to abandon fear and replace it with faith—faith that if we obey God's laws we will receive God's blessing. The price of peace is to abandon hate and allow love to reign supreme in our hearts—love for all our fellow human beings over the world. The price of peace is to abandon arrogance and replace it with repentance and humility, remembering that the way of peace is the way of love. The price of peace is to abandon greed and replace it with giving, so that none will be spiritually injured by having more than they need while others in the world still have less than they need.　Ibid.

11 You have much more power when you are working for the right thing than when you are working against the wrong thing.　　　　　　　　　　　　Ibid., Ch. 11

1696. Ann Ronell (1908–)

1 Who's afraid of the big bad wolf?
　　　　"Who's Afraid of the Big Bad Wolf?"
　　　　from Walt Disney's *Three Little Pigs*
　　　　　　　　　　　　　　1933

1697. Amy Vanderbilt (1908–1974)

1 Ceremony is really a protection, too, in times of emotional involvement, particularly at death. If we have a social formula to guide us and do not have to extemporize, we feel better able to handle life.
　　　　Introduction, Pt. I, *New Complete Book of
　　　　　　　　　　　　Etiquette
　　　　　　　　　　　　1963*

2 Good manners have much to do with the emotions. To make them ring true, one must feel them, not merely exhibit them.
　　　　　　　　Ibid., Pt II, Introduction

3 One face to the world, another at home makes for misery.　　Ibid., Pt. VI, Introduction

1698. Yang Ping (1908–)

1 That I should think, even now, of wanting to continue to exist only as the vessel of a chemical experimentation heartlessly, inexorably formulating itself within me! And against my will . . . And yet I love this little life! With all the pain of it, I long for the wonderful thing to happen, for a tiny human creature to spring from between my limbs bravely out into the world. I need it, just as a true poet *needs* to create a great undying work.
　　　　　　"Fragment from a Lost Diary,"
　　　　　*Fragment from a Lost Diary and
　　　　　Other Stories,* Naomi Katz and
　　　　　　Nancy Milton, eds.　*1973*

2 Women and revolution! What tragic, unsung epics of courage lie silent in the world's history!　　　　　　　　　　Ibid.

1700. Anne Fremantle (1909–)

1 Among the most truly responsible for all people are artists and revolutionaries, for they most of all prepared to pay with their lives.
　　　　　　Introduction to *Woman as
　　　　　Revolutionary,* Fred. C. Giffin, ed.
　　　　　　　　　　　　　　1973

2 The revolutionary attempts a secular denial of mortality, the artist a spiritual one.　　Ibid.

1701. Eleanor Hamilton (1909–)

1 Good lovers have known for centuries that the hand is probably the primary sex organ.
　　　　　Quoted in "Hue & Cry," *San
　　　　　　　　　　　Francisco Chronicle
　　　　　　　　　　　29 October 1978*

1702. Katharine Hepburn (1909–)

1 Trying to be fascinating is an asinine position
to be in. Dick Cavett Show, ABC-TV
2 April 1975

2 Without discipline, there's no life at all.
Ibid. *4 April 1975*

3 You never feel that you have fame. It's always
in back of you. Ibid.

4 As for me, prizes mean nothing. My prize is
my work. Quoted in *Kate* by Charles
Higham *1975*

5 Our Constitution was not intended to be used
by . . . any group to foist its personal religious
beliefs on the rest of us.
Planned Parenthood Federation
Fund-raising Letter
November 1981

1703. Queen Juliana (1909–)

1 You people of the United States of America
have the wonderfully farseeing conception of
being Democracy's material and spiritual arsenal, to save the world's highest values from
annihilation. Radio Address, NBC
13 April 1941

2 I want to emphasize that for a queen the task of
being a mother is just as important as it is for
every other Netherlands woman.
Inauguration Address, Amsterdam
6 September 1948

1704. Gabrielle Roy (1909–)

1 When there was enough money for their needs,
the ties between them had been strong, but once
the money was lacking, what a strain was put
on their love!
Ch. 32, *The Tin Flute* *1947*

2 Oh! The matchless release of the man asleep!
Who has not realized through experience that
sleep tells the truth about us? In sleep a human
being is finally brought back to himself, having
sloughed off everything else. Bound hand and
foot fettered with fatigue, he at last drifts toward
the cavern of the unknown. Some men have
returned therefrom with poems fully written, or
with equations solved.
Ch. 12, *The Cashier* *1955*

1705. Simone Weil (1909–1943)

1 Just as a person who is always asserting that he
is too good-natured is the very one from whom

to expect, on some occasion, the coldest and
most unconcerned cruelty, so when any group
sees itself as the bearer of civilization this very
belief will betray it into behaving barbarously
at the first opportunity.
"Hitler and Roman Foreign Policy,"
Nouveaux Cahiers *1 January 1940*

2 There is something else which has the power to
awaken us to the truth. It is the works of writers
of genius. . . . They give us, in the guise of
fiction, something equivalent to the actual density of the real, that density which life offers us
every day but which we are unable to grasp
because we are amusing ourselves with lies.
"Morality and Literature,"
Cahiers du Sud *January 1944*

3 Obvious and inexorable oppression that cannot
be overcome does not give rise to revolt but to
submission. *La Condition Ouvrière* *1951*

4 Money destroys human roots wherever it is able
to penetrate, by tuning desire for gain into the
sole motive. It easily manages to outweigh all
other motives, because the effort it demands of
the mind is so very much less. Nothing is *so*
clear *and so* simple as a row of figures.
"L'Enracinement," Pt. II (1949),
The Deed for Roots *1952*

5 Propaganda is not directed towards creating an
inspiration: it closes, seals up all the openings
through which an inspiration might pass; it fills
the whole spirit with fanaticism. Ibid., Pt. III

6 Evil becomes an operative motive far more easily than good; but once pure good has become
an operative motive in the mind, it forms there
the fount of a uniform and inexhaustible impul-
sion, which is never so in the case of evil.
Ibid.

7 The idea of a snare set for man by God is also
the meaning of the myth of the labyrinth . . .
that path where man, from the moment he enters
upon it, loses his way and finds himself equally
powerless, at the end of a certain time, to return
upon his steps or to direct himself anywhere.
He errs without knowing where, and finally
arrives at the place where God waits to devour
him. *Intimations of Christianity,*
Elisabeth Chase Geissbuhler, ed. *1957*

8 War, which perpetuates itself under the form of
preparation for war, has once and for all given
the State an important role in production.
"Revolution Proletarienne"
(25 August 1933),
Oppression and Liberty *1958*

9 . . . man alone can enslave man.
"Reflections Concerning the
Causes of Liberty and Social Oppression"
(1934), op. cit.

10 He [Marx*] labelled this dream "dialectical materialism." This was sufficient to shroud it in mystery. These two words are of an almost impenetrable emptiness. A very amusing game—though rather a cruel one—is to ask a Marxist what they mean.
"Is There a Marxist Doctrine?" (1943), op. cit.

*Karl Marx, German political philosopher and economist (1818–83).

11 The payment of debts is necessary for social order. The non-payment is quite equally necessary for social order. For centuries humanity has oscillated, serenely unaware, between these two contradictory necessities.
"On Bankruptcy" (1937), *Selected Essays* (1934–1953)   *1962*

12 . . . when a man's life is destroyed or damaged by some wound or privation of soul or body, which is due to other men's actions or negligence, it is not only his sensibility that suffers but also his aspiration toward the good. Therefore there has been sacrilege towards that which is sacred in him.   "Draft for a Statement of Human Obligation" (1943), op. cit.

13 At the bottom of the heart of every human being from earliest infancy until the tomb, there is something that goes on indomitably expecting, in the teeth of all experience of crimes committed, suffered, and witnessed, that good and not evil will be done to him. It is this above all that is sacred in every human being.
"Human Personality" (1943), op. cit.

14 The future is made of the same stuff as the present.   "Some Thoughts on the Love of God" (October 1940–May 1942), *On Science, Necessity, and the Love of God,* Richard Rees, ed.   *1968*

15 . . . if we are suffering illness, poverty, or misfortune, we think we shall be satisfied on the day it ceases. But there too, we know it is false; so soon as one has got used to not suffering one wants something else.   Ibid.

16 Evil being the root of mystery, pain is the root of knowledge.   "The New York Notebook" (1942), *First and Last Notebooks,* Richard Rees, ed.   *1970*

17 To get power over is to defile. To possess is to defile.   Ibid.

18 Charity. To love human beings in so far as they are nothing. That is to love them as God does.   Ibid.

19 Truth is not discovered by proofs but by exploration. It is always experimental. But necessity also is an object of exploration.   Ibid.

20 Joy fixes us to eternity and pain fixes us to time. But desire and fear hold us in bondage to time, and detachment breaks the bond.   Ibid.

21 The proper method of philosophy consists in clearly conceiving the insoluble problems in all their insolubility and then in simply contemplating them, fixedly and tirelessly, year after year, without any hope, patiently waiting.
"London Notebook" (1943), op. cit.

1706. Eudora Welty (1909–   )

1 This time, when his heart leapt, something—his soul—seemed to leap too, like a little colt invited out of a pen.
"Death of a Travelling Salesman," *A Curtain of Green and Other Stories*   *1936*

2 How intensified, magnified, really vain all attempt at expression becomes in the afflicted!
"The Key," op. cit.

3 Radio, sewing machine, book ends, ironing board and that great big piano lamp—peace, that's what I like. Butterbean vines planted all along the front where the strings are.
"Why I Live at the P.O.," op. cit.

4 "No, babe, it ain't the truth. . . . Truth is something worse, I ain't said what, yet. It's something hasn't come to me, but I ain't saying' it won't."   "Powerhouse," op. cit.

5 His memory could work like the slinging of a noose to catch a wild pony.
"First Love," *The Wide Net and Other Stories*   *1943*

6 In a shadowy place something white flew up. It was a heron, and it went away over the dark treetops. William Wallace followed it with his eyes and Brucie clapped his hands, but Virgil gave a sigh, as if he knew that when you go looking for what is lost, everything is a sign.   "The Wide Net," op. cit.

7 "I rather a man be anything, than a woman be mean."   "Livvie," op. cit.

8 Haven't you noticed it prevail, in the world in general? Beware of a man with manners.
Ch. 1, *The Golden Apples*   *1949*

9 Attrition was their wisdom.   Ibid., Ch. 7

10 He loved being happy! He loved happiness like I love tea.   *The Ponder Heart*   *1954*

11 "Never think you've seen the last of anything. . . ."

Pt. I, Ch. 1, *The Optimist's
Daughter   1969*

12 All they could see was sky, water, birds, light
and confluence. It was the whole morning world.
And they themselves were a part of the confluence. Their own joint act of faith had brought
them here at the very moment and matched its
occurrence, and proceeded as it proceeded. Direction itself was made beautiful, momentous.
They were riding as one with it, right up
front.   Ibid., Pt. IV

13 What I do in the writing of any character is to
try to enter into the mind, heart and skin of a
human being who is not myself. Whether this
happens to be a man or a woman, old or young,
with skin black or white, the primary challenge
lies in making the jump itself. It is the act of a
writer's imagination that I set most high.
          Preface, *The Collected Stories of Eudora
                              Welty   1980*

14 She has spent her life trying to escape from the
parlorlike jaws of self-consciousness.
              "Old Mr. Marblehall," op. cit.

15 They were not really old—they were only 50;
still, their lives were filled with tiredness, with
a great lack of necessity to speak, with poverty
which may have bound them like a disaster too
great for any discussion but left them still separate and undesirous of sympathy. Perhaps, years
ago, the long habit of silence may have been
started in anger or passion. Who could tell
now?   "The Whistle," op. cit.

1707. Gale Wilhelm (1909–   )

1 "I'm going to turn on the light and we'll be
two people in a room looking at each other and
wondering why on earth they were afraid of the
dark."   *We Too Are Drifting
                                          1935*

1708. Bertha Adams Backus (fl. 1910s)

1 Build for yourself a strong-box,
   Fashion each part with care;
When it's strong as your hand can make it,
   Put all your troubles there.
                      "Then Laugh," St. 1   *1911*

1709. Janet Begbie (fl. 1910s)

1 Carry on, carry on, for the men and boys are
      gone,
But the furrow shan't lie fallow while the
   women carry on.   "Carry On" *n.d.*

1710. Esther Lilian Duff (fl. 1910s)

1 Some of the roofs are plum-color
Some of the roofs are gray,
Some of the roofs are silverstone,
And some are made of clay;
But under every gabled close
There's a secret hid away.
              "Not Three, But One,"
              Bohemian Glass   1916

1711. Hsiang Chin-yu (fl. 1910s–1927)

1 . . . the emancipation of women can only come
with a change in the social structure which frees
men and women alike.
          Quoted in *Women in Modern China*
              by Helen Foster Snow*   *1967*

*See 1675.

1712. Annie Kenney (fl. 1910s)

1 . . . Paradise would be there once the vote*
was won! I honestly believed every word I said.
I had yet to learn that Nature's works are very
slow but very sure. Experience is indeed the
best though the sternest teacher.
              Memoirs of a Militant   1924

*Woman's suffrage was granted in 1918 in Great Britain,
subject to limitations; full enfranchisement came in 1928.

2 Prison. It was not prison for me. Hunger-strikes.
They had no fears for me. Cat and Mouse Act.
I could have laughed. A prison cell was quiet—
no telephone, no paper, no speeches, no sea
sickness, no sleepless nights. I could lie on my
plank bed all day and all night and return once
more to my day dreams.   Ibid.

1713. Dora Alonso (1910–   )

1 The shadow, the color of the man, and the kind
of living, all arc thc same; black in one hundred
tones, either so light as to be cinnamon flesh or
as dark as black coffee, it carries the sign of
subjection.
              "Time Gone By," *Fragment from a
              Lost Diary and Other Stories,* Naomi
              Katz and Nancy Milton, eds.   *1973*

2 Life goes on, buried in pain for those who wait;
swollen with haughtiness and arrogance for those
who fear.   Ibid.

3 Her body broke down like the collapse of forked
poles which could no longer bear the weight of
an entire life dedicated to obedience, without a
single pillar of rebellion to hold up the
structure.   Ibid.

1714. Myrtie Lillian Barker (1910–)

1 The idea of strictly minding our own business is moldy rubbish. Who could be so selfish?
I Am Only One 1963

1715. Mary Ingraham Bunting (1910–)

1 When her last child is off to school, we don't want the talented woman wasting her time in work far below her capacity. We want her to come out running.
Quoted in *Life* 13 January 1961

1716. Hilda Conkling (1910–)

1 The hills are going somewhere;
They have been on the way a long time.
They are like camels in a line
But they move more slowly.
"Hills," *n.d.*

2 The world turns softly
Not to spill its lakes and rivers.
"Water" *n.d.*

1717. Elizabeth Gould Davis (1910–1974)

1 The deeper the archeologists dig, the further back go the origins of man and society—and the less sure we are that civilization has followed the steady upward course so thoroughly believed in by the Victorians. It is more likely that the greatest civilizations of the past have yet to be discovered. Prologue, *The First Sex* 1971

2 Maleness remains a recessive genetic trait like color-blindness and hemophilia, with which it is linked. The suspicion that maleness is abnormal and that the Y chromosome is an accidental mutation boding no good for the race is strongly supported by the recent discovery by geneticists that congenital killers and criminals are possessed of not one but *two* Y chromosomes, bearing a double dose, as it were, of genetically undesirable maleness. Ibid., Pt. I, Ch. 1

3 When man substituted God for the Great Goddess he at the same time substituted authoritarian for humanistic values. Ibid., Ch. 7

4 It is men, not women, who have promoted the cult of brutal masculinity; and because men admire muscle and physical force, they assume that women do too. Ibid., Pt. IV, Ch. 21

5 If the human race is unhappy today, as all modern philosophers agree that it is, it is only because it is uncomfortable in the mirror image society man has made—the topsy-turvy world in which nature's supporting pillar is forced to serve as the cornice of the architrave, while the cornice struggles to support the building.
Ibid., Ch. 22

1718. Millicent Fenwick (1910–)

1 The curious fascination in this job* is the illusion that either you are being useful or you could be—and that's so tempting.
"Sixty Minutes," CBS-TV 1 February 1981

*U.S. Representative.

2 When you're old, everything you do is sort of a miracle. Ibid.

3 Party organization matters. When the door of a smoke-filled room is closed, there's hardly ever a woman inside. Ibid.

4 We cannot continue to deny American women the full rights and responsibilities of citizenships.
Quoted by the National Women's Political Caucus *n.d.*

1719. Edith Starrett Green (1910–)

1 I have never believed that race, sex, religion, or national origin are valid criteria for either "favorable" or "unfavorable" treatment. This is one reason why I have been opposed to programs which give an advantage in job consideration and promotion to members of those groups who have suffered historic discrimination. Speech, Brigham Young University 1977

2 I've always argued that it is just as desirable, just as possible, to have philosopher plumbers as philosopher kings.
Quoted in *American Political Women* by Esther Stineman 1980

1720. Margaret Halsey (1910–)

1 . . . she blushed like a well-trained sunrise.
With Malice Toward Some 1938

2 These people . . . talk simply because they think sound is more manageable than silence. Ibid.

3 Humility is not my forte, and whenever I dwell for any length of time on my own shortcomings, they gradually begin to seem mild, harmless, rather engaging little things, not at all like the staring defects in other people's characters.
Ibid.

4 All of Stratford, in fact, suggests powdered history—add hot water and stir and you have a delicious, nourishing Shakespeare.   Ibid.

5 . . . in England, having had money . . . is just as acceptable as having it, since the upper-class mannerisms persist, even after the bankroll has disappeared. But never having had money is unforgivable, and can only be atoned for by never trying to get any.   Ibid..

6 The whole flavor and quality of the American representative government turns to ashes on the tongue, if one regards the government as simply an inferior and rather second-rate sort of corporation.   *The Folks at Home*
1952

7 What I know about money, I learned the hard way—by having had it.   Ibid.

1721. Jacquetta Hawkes (1910–   )

1 The young are now kinder than they were and are more tender towards old age, more aware perhaps with the growth of self-consciousness that it will come also to them.
A Land   1952

2 We live in a world made seemingly secure by the four walls of our houses, the artificiality of our cities, and by the four walls of habit. Volcanoes speak of insecurity, of our participation in process. They are openings not any longer into a properly appointed hell, but into an equally alarming abysm of thought.   Ibid.

1722. Frida Kahlo (1910–1954)

1 I never painted dreams. I painted by own reality.   Quoted in *Frida: A Biography of Frida Kahlo* by Hayden Herrera   *1983*

2 I rather sit on the floor in the market of Toluca and sell tortillas, than to have anything to do with these ''artistic'' bitches of Paris. They sit for hours on the ''cafes'' warming their precious behinds, and talk without stopping about ''culture'' ''art'' ''revolution'' and so forth thinking themselves the gods of the world. . . . Gee whiz! It was worthwhile to come here only to see why Europe is rottening.   Letter to Nikolas Muray (1939), op. cit.

1723. Mary Keyserling (1910–   )

1 There shouldn't be a single little child in America left alone to fend for himself.
Ch. 2, *Windows on Day Care   1972*

2 Our ultimate goal as a nation should be to make available comprehensive, developmental child-care services to all families that wish to use them.   Ibid., Ch. 9

1725. Elizabeth Layton (1910–   )

1 I never did dislike the world. I just disliked myself.   Quoted in ''A Hidden Talent'' by Michael Ryan, *Parade Magazine   28 May 1989*

2 There's a wonderful story. There was a little sparrow, lying out on the ground with his feet up in the air. Somebody asked him what he was doing, and he said, 'The sky is going to fall.' And this person said, 'What do you think you can do about it?' And the little sparrow said, 'One must do what one can.'   Ibid.

1726. Alicia Markova (1910–   )

1 . . . glorious bouquets and storms of applause. . . . These are the trimmings which every artist naturally enjoys. But to *move* an audience in such a role, to hear in the applause that unmistakable note which breaks through good theatre manners and comes from the heart, is to feel that you have won through to life itself. Such pleasure does not vanish with the fall of the curtain, but becomes part of one's own life.   Ch. 18, *Giselle and I   1960*

1727. Mother Teresa (1910–   )

1 Loneliness and the feeling of being unwanted is the most terrible poverty.
Quoted in ''Saints Among Us,'' *Time 29 December 1975*

2 Our intellect and other gifts have been given to be used for God's greater glory, but sometimes they become the very god for us. That is the saddest part: we are losing our balance when this happens. We must free ourselves to be filled by God. Even God cannot fill what is full.
Ibid.

3 To keep a lamp burning we have to keep putting oil in it.   Ibid.

4 Jesus loved every one, but he loved children most of all. Today we know that unborn children are the targets of destruction. We must thank our parents for wanting us, for loving us and for taking such good care of us.
Speech, Awakening Conference, Colorado   *15 June 1986*

5 I don't claim anything of the work. It is his work. I am like a little pencil in his hand. That

is all. He does the thinking. He does the writing. The pencil has nothing to do with it. The pencil has only to be allowed to be used.   Ibid.

6 We have very little, so we have nothing to be preoccupied with. The more you have, the more you are occupied, the less you give. But the less you have, the more free you are. Poverty for us is a freedom.   Ibid.

7 The hunger for love is much more difficult to remove than the hunger for bread.   Ibid.

1728. Adeline Wanatee (1910–?)

1 Men have visions, women have children.
      Oral Interview (Feb 28, 1980), *American Indian Women, Telling Their Lives*, Ch. 2, Gretchen M. Bataille & Kathleen Mullen Sands *1984*

1729. Annie Dodge Wauneka (1910–   )

1 I ask them [Navajo youth], "what is your biggest problem?" They tell me alcohol, drugs.
  I ask them, "What is the most beautiful machine?" They tell me they don't know how to answer.
  I tell them it's their heads, and they must not let alcohol and drugs ruin that machine.
      Quoted in " 'Our Mother' " Shepherds A Nation of Navajos" by Rusty Brown, *The Albuquerque Tribune* *1 May 1984*

1730. Margaret R. Wilcox (prob. 1910–   )

1 Children ask the world from us.
      Women's Action of Nuclear Disarmament (WAND), Boston *n.d.*

1731. Virginia Mae Axline (1911–   )

1 "So much to say. And so much not to say! Some things are better left unsaid. But so many unsaid things can become a burden."
      Ch. 8, *Dibs: In Search of Self,* *1965*

2 Asking questions in therapy would be so helpful if anyone ever answered them accurately. But no one ever does.   Ibid., Ch. 12

1732. Lucille Ball (1911–1989)

1 Luck? I don't know anything about luck. I've never banked on it, and I'm afraid of people who do. Luck to me is something else: Hard work—and realizing what is opportunity and what isn't.
      Quoted in Ch. 1, *The Real Story of Lucille Ball*, by Eleanor Harris *1954*

2 I think knowing what you can *not* do is more important than knowing what you can do. In fact, that's good taste.   Ibid., Ch. 7

1733. Elizabeth Bishop (1911–1979)

1 It is like what we imagine knowledge to be:
dark, salt, clear, moving, utterly free,
drawn from the cold hard mouth
of the world, derived from the rocky breast
forever, flowing and drawn, and since
our knowledge is historical, flowing, and
  flow.   "At the Fishhouses," *A Cold Spring*
      1955

2 Icebergs behoove the soul
(Both being self-made from elements least visible)
to see themselves: fleshed, fair, erected
  indivisible.
      "The Imaginary Iceberg," *North and South* *1955*

3 We stand as still as stones to watch
  the leaves and ripples
while light and nervous water hold their
  interview.   "Quai d'Orleans,"
      op. cit.

4 Brazilians are very quick, both emotionally and physically. Like the heroes of Homer, men can show their emotions without disgrace.
      Ch. 1, *Brazil* *1962*

5 The masses of poor people in the big cities, and the poor and not-so-poor of the "backlands," love their children and kill them with kindness by the thousands. The wrong foods, spoiled foods, warm medicines, sleeping syrups—all exact a terrible toll. . . .   Ibid.

1734. Hortense Calisher (1911–   )

1 A happy childhood can't be cured. Mine'll hang around my neck like a rainbow, that's all, instead of a noose.   Pt. I, *Queenie* *1971*

2 Every sixteen-year-old is a pornographer, Miss Piranesi. We had to know what was open to us.   Ibid.

3 . . . the circulation of money is different from the circulation of the blood. Some eras obscure that; now it was nakedly appearing. I began to understand why the banker had jumped. A circulatory failure.   Pt. I, *Herself* *1972*

4 Every art is a church without communicants, presided over by a parish of the respectable. An

artist is born kneeling; he fights to stand. A critic, by nature of the judgment seat, is born sitting. *Ibid.*, Pt. IV

5 When anything gets freed, a zest goes round the world. *Ibid.*

1735. Raya Dunayevskaya (1911?–)

1 Ever since the myth of Eve giving Adam the apple was created, women have been presented as devils or as angels, but definitely not as human beings. "We Speak in Many Voices," *Notes on Women's Liberation 1970*

2 It is not labor or "socialism" which acted as catalyst for . . . the anti-war movement and, indeed, gave birth to a whole new generation of revolutionaries, but the black revolution which was both catalyst and reason, *and continues to be that ceaseless movement today.* *Ibid.*

3 The first act of liberation is to demand back our own heads. *Ibid.*

1736. Leah Goldberg (1911–1970)

1 There is a law of life in her hands milking,
For quiet seamen hold a rope like her.
"Of Bloom," Pt. II, St. 2,
Poems from the Hebrew,
Robert Mezey, ed. *1973*

2 Land of low clouds, I belong to you.
I carry in my heart your every drop of rain.
"Song of the Strange Woman,"
Pt. III, St. 1, op. cit.

1737. Hsiao Hung (1911–1941)

1 "I've never abused her all the time she's been in my home. Where else will you find another family that has not abused its child-bride by giving her beatings and tongue lashings all day long? Now I may have beaten her a little, but just to get her started off on the right foot, and I only did that for a little over a month. Maybe I beat her pretty severely sometimes, but how was I expected to make a well-mannered girl out of her without being severe once in a while? Believe me, I didn't enjoy beating her so hard, what with all her screaming and carrying on. But I was doing it for her own good, because if I didn't beat her hard, she'd never be good for anything." "The Child Bride," *Tales of Hulan River,* Howard Goldblatt, tr. *1940*

2 "Each of the 360 trades in this world of ours has its share of miseries." *Ibid.*

1738. Mahalia Jackson (1911–1972)

1 It's easy to be independent when you've got money. But to be independent when you haven't got a thing—that's the Lord's test.
Ch.1, *Movin' On Up,* with Evan McLoud Wylie *1966*

2 Blues are the songs of despair, but gospel songs are the songs of hope. *Ibid.*, Ch. 6

3 The grass is still green. The lawns are as neat as ever. The same birds are still in the trees. I guess it didn't occur to them to leave just because we moved in.
Quoted in "Unforgettable Mahalia Jackson" by Mildred Falls, *Reader's Digest March 1973*

1739. Ruth McKenney (1911–1972)

1 If modern civilization had any meaning it was displayed in the fight against Fascism.
Letter to George Seldes, *The Great Quotations,* George Seldes, ed. *1960*

1740. Josephine Miles (1911–)

1 All our footsteps, set to make
Metric advance,
Lapse into arcs in deference
To circumstance.
"On Inhabiting an Orange," St. 2,
Poems (1930–1960) 1960

2 This weight of knowledge dark on the brain is never
To be burnt out like fever,
"Physiologus," St. 2, op. cit.

3 Where is the world? not about.
The world is in the heart
And the heart is closed in the sea lanes out of port. "Merchant Marine," St. 1, op. cit.

4 Accustomed as we are to change, or unaccustomed, we think of a change of heart, of clothes, of life, with some uncertainty. We put off the old, put on the new, yet say that the more it changes the more it remains the same. Every age is an age of transition.
Introduction, *Poetry and Change 1974*

1741. Anna Russell (1911–)

1 The reason that there are so few women comics is that so few women can bear being laughed at. Quoted in the *Sunday Times* (London) *25 August 1957*

1742. Rosalind Russell (1911–1976)

1 . . . taste. You cannot buy such a rare and wonderful thing. You can't send away for it in a catalogue. And I'm afraid it's becoming obsolete.
> Quoted in "Rosalind Russell: Screen's Career Career Girl," *Los Angeles Times*   *31 March 1974*

2 Sex for sex's sake on the screen seems childish to me, but it's violence that really bothers me. I think it's degrading. It breeds something cancerous in our young people. We have a great responsibility to the future in what we're communicating.   Ibid.

1743. Viola Spolin (1911?–)

1 In a culture where approval/disapproval has become the predominant regulator of effort and position, and often the substitute for love, our personal freedoms are dissipated.
> Ch. 1, *Improvisation for the Theater* *1963*

2 It stands to reason that if we direct all our efforts towards reaching a goal, we stand in grave danger of losing everything on which we have based our daily activities. For when a goal is superimposed on an activity instead of evolving out of it, we often feel cheated when we reach it.   Ibid.

3 The audience is the most revered member of the theater. Without an audience there is no theater. . . . They are our guests, our evaluators, and the last spoke in the wheel which can then begin to roll. They make the performance meaningful.   Ibid.

4 It is the avant-garde teachers who . . . have come to realize that body release, not body control, is what is needed for natural grace to emerge, as opposed to artificial movement.
> Ibid., Ch. 5

5 First teach a person to develop to the point of his limitations and then—pfft!—break the limitation.   Quoted in "Spolin Game Plan for Improvisational Theater" by Barry Hyams, *Los Angeles Times* *26 May 1974*

1744. Madeleine Bingham (1912–)

1 In every country the organization of society is like a section of a rock face, with new layers and old layers built one upon the other. The decay of old ways of behaving and old laws does not take place within a few years; it is a gradual process of erosion.
> Ch. 2, *Scotland Under Mary Stuart** *1971*

*See 285.

2 Once the fervour has gone out of it, a revolution can turn out to be dull work for the ordinary people.   Ibid., Ch. 7

1745. Julia Child (1912–)

1 Sometimes . . . it takes me an entire day to write a recipe, to communicate it correctly. It's really like writing a little short story. . . .
> Quoted in "The Making of a Masterpiece" by Patricia Simon, *McCall's*   *October 1970*

2 Learn how to cook! That's the way to save money. You don't save it buying hamburger helpers, and prepared foods; you save it buying fresh foods in season or in large supply, when they are cheapest and usually best, and you prepare them from scratch at home. Why pay for someone else's work, when if you know how to do it, you can save all that money for yourself?   Introduction, *Julia Child's Kitchen* *1975*

3 Too many cooks may spoil the broth, but it only takes one to burn it.   *The Bad Cook's Guide* *n.d.*

1745.1 Amalia Fleming (1912–1986)

1 So much sorrow should certainly not come to a man who has given so much of value to humanity.   Letter to Ben May (5 November 1949), Quoted in *The Life of Sir Alexander Fleming** by André Maurois *1959*

*English bacteriologist (1881–1955).

2 I am working on a problem which fascinates me but I keep failing to do what I try. Still there is an end even to failures.
> Ibid. (December 1954)

3 I respect every ideology, including communism, provided they are not trying to impose their will through force. I am against any totalitarian regime.   Quoted in *Newsweek* *11 October 1971*

4 The innocent people who have nothing to say are tortured the most because when a prisoner admits something, the torture stops.
> Quoted in "Greece: Survival of the Shrewdest" by Susan Margolis, *Ms.* *October 1973*

1746. Lucille Fletcher (1912–   )

1 Such amazing things happened to the female sex on an ocean cruise. The sea air acted like an aphrodisiac. Or maybe it was the motion. Or the carnival atmosphere. Whatever it was, and he had never seen it otherwise, the ladies, married or single, young or old, simply went to pieces aboard the *S.S. Columbia*. They toppled like tenpins—into bed.
Ch. 2, *The Girl in Cabin B54, 1968*

2 "The brain, of course, is still an unknown country in many respects—like outer space. And as a psychologist, I myself can believe that certain people, extraordinarily sensitive people, may possess special mental equipment which can tune in, as it were, certain waves, vibrations, even imagery, which other people cannot sense at all."
Ibid., Ch. 8

1747. Virginia Graham (1912–   )

1 Good shot, bad luck and hell are the five basic words to be used in a game of tennis, though these, of course, can be slightly amplified.
Ch. 8, *Say Please 1949*

2 In society it is etiquette for ladies to have the best chairs and get handed things. In the home the reverse is the case. That is why ladies are more sociable than gentlemen.
Ibid., Ch. 14

3 Be blind. Be stupid. Be British. Be careful.
Ibid., Ch. 25

1748. Martha Wright Griffiths (1912–   )

1 This amendment [the Equal Rights Amendment*], if passed, would be like a beacon which should awaken nine sleeping Rip Van Winkles to the fact that the twentieth century is passing into history. It is a different world and they [the Supreme Court] should speak for justice, not prejudice. . . . I seek justice, not in some distant tomorrow, not in some study commission, but now while I live.
Quoted in *American Political Women* by Esther Stineman   *1980*

*See Alice Paul, 1355.

2 My grandmother wanted to live long enough to vote for a woman president. I'll be satisfied if I live to see a woman go before the Supreme Court and hear the justices acknowledge, "Gentlemen, she's human. She deserves the protection of our laws."
Ibid.

1749. Lady Bird Johnson (1912–   )

1 It all began so beautifully. After a drizzle in the morning, the sun came out bright and clear. We were driving into Dallas. In the lead car were President and Mrs. Kennedy. . . .
A White House Diary (22 November 1963)*   *1970*

*The day John F. Kennedy, 35th president of the United States, was assassinated.

2 This was one of those terrific, pummeling White House days that can stretch and grind and use you—even I, who only live on the periphery. So what must it be like for Lyndon!*
Ibid. (14 March 1968)

*Lyndon Baines Johnson (1908–1973), 36th president of the United States (1963–69).

3 I've had a long love affair with the environment. It is my sustenance, my pleasure, my joy. Flowers in a city are like lipstick on a woman—it just makes you look better to have a little color.   Quoted in *Time*   *5 September 1989*

1750. Dena Justin (1912–   )

1 Mythologically speaking, the ancients scooped our modern-day biologists by unknown thousands of years in their recognition of the female principle as the primal creative force. And they too buried the truth, restructuring the myths to accommodate male ideology.
"From Mother Goddess to Dishwasher," *Natural History*   *February 1973*

2 Although the witch, incarnate or in surrogate mother disguise, remains a universal bogey, pejorative aspects of the wizard, her masculine counterpart, have vanished over the patriarchal centuries. The term *wizard* has acquired reverential status—wizard of finance, wizard of diplomacy, wizard of science.   Ibid.

1751. Mary Lavin (1912–   )

1 "Take my own father! You know what he said in his last moments? On his deathbed, he defied me to name a man who had enjoyed a better life. In spite of the dreadful pain, his face *radiated* happiness!" said Mother, nodding her head comfortably. "Happiness drives out pain, as fire burns out fire."
"Happiness," *The New Yorker 14 December 1968*

2 Our father, while he lived, had cast a magic over everything, for us as well as for her. He held his love up over us like an umbrella and kept off the troubles that afterward came down on us, pouring cats and dogs!   Ibid.

3 "Life is a vale of tears," they said. "You are privileged to find it out so young!" Ugh! After I staggered onto my feet and began to take hold of life once more, they fell back defeated. And the first day I gave a laugh—pouf, they were blown out like candles. They weren't living in a real world at all; they belonged to a ghostly world where life was easy: all one had to do was sit and weep. It takes effort to push back the stone from the mouth of the tomb.   Ibid.

1752. Mary McCarthy (1912–1989)

1 I felt caught in a dilemma that was new to me then but which since has become horribly familiar: the trap of adult life, in which you are held, wriggling, powerless to act because you can see both sides. On that occasion, as generally in the future, I compromised.
Memories of a Catholic Girlhood   1946

2 The American, if he has a spark of national feeling, will be humiliated by the very prospect of a foreigner's visit to Congress—these, for the most part, illiterate hacks whose fancy vests are spotted with gravy, and whose speeches, hypocritical, unctuous, and slovenly, are spotted also with the gravy of political patronage, these persons are a reflection on the democratic process rather than of it; they expose it in its underwear.   "America the Beautiful,"
Commentary   September 1947

3 "You mustn't force sex to do the work of love or love to do the work of sex."
Ch. 2, *The Group 1954*

4 She had tried to bind him with possessions, but he slipped away like Houdini.   Ibid., Ch. 13

5 Sometimes she felt that he was postponing being a success till he could wear out her patience; as soon as she gave up and left him, his name would mock her in lights.   Ibid.

6 Labor is work that leaves no trace behind it when it is finished, or if it does, as in the case of the tilled field, this product of human activity requires still more labor, incessant, tireless labor, to maintain its identity as a "work" of man.   "The *Vita Activa*," *The New Yorker   18 October 1958*

7 There are no new truths, but only truths that have not been recognized by those who have perceived them without noticing.   Ibid.

8 . . . bureaucracy, the rule of no one, has become the modern form of despotism.   Ibid.

9 . . . Americans do not dissemble what they are up to. They do not seem to feel the need, except through verbiage; *e.g.,* napalm has become "Inciderjell," which makes it sound like Jello-O.

And defoliants are referred to as weedkillers—something you use in your driveway. The resort to euphemism denotes, no doubt, a guilty conscience or—the same thing nowadays—a twinge in the public relations nerve.
"The Home Program," *Vietnam 1967*

10 In politics, it seems, retreat is honorable if dictated by military considerations and shameful if even *suggested* for ethical reasons. . . .
"Solutions," op. cit.

1753. Pat Nixon (1912–   )

1 I have sacrificed everything in my life that I consider precious in order to advance the political career of my husband.
Quoted in *Women at Work*
by Betty Medsger   1975

1754. Ann Petry (1912–   )

1 It took me quite a while to realize that there were fashions in literary criticism and that they shifted and changed much like the fashions in women's hats.
"The Novel as Social Criticism," *The Writer's Book,* Helen Hull, ed.
1950

2 It seems to me that all truly great art is propaganda. . . .   Ibid.

3 I told myself that if I were a maker of perfumes I would make one and call it "Spring," and it would smell like this cool, sweet, early-morning air and I would let only beautiful young brown girls use it, and if I could sing I would sing like the song sparrow and I would let only beautiful young brown boys hear me.   "The New Mirror," *Miss Muriel and Other Stories   1971*

1755. May Sarton (1912–   )

1 Learning is such a very painful business. It requires humility from people at an age where the natural habitat is arrogance.
The Small Room   1961

2 Excellence cost a great deal.   Ibid.

3 "There was such a thing as women's work and it consisted chiefly, Hilary sometimes thought, in being able to stand constant interruption and keep your temper. . . ."
Mrs. Stevens Hears the Mermaids Singing   1965

4 Women's work is always toward wholeness.   Ibid.

5 Women have moved and shaken me, but I have been nourished by men.   Ibid.

6 True feeling justifies, whatever it may cost.
                                                    Ibid.

1756. Kate Simon (1912–   )

1 One assumes that foreign ladies, English and Americans particularly, because they are tremulous, neurotic bags of bone reduced by sexual malnutrition, find all Italians irresistible.
                        Italy: The Places In Between
                        n.d.

2 Girls' prayers counted for nothing; like animals, they had no souls and no voices to God's ear.   *Bronx Primitive;*
                        Portraits in A Childhood
                        1982

3 Here I stand,hobbled in a sack of doom, determined to tear out of it, knowing that I will.
                        A Wider World:
                        Portraits in Adolescence
                        1986

4 I had no time for step-by-step projects; the urgent need was for swift voyages, with short stops at many ports of call.   Ibid.

1757. Barbara Tuchman (1912–1989)

1 Honor wears different coats to different eyes. . . .
                        Ch. 7, The Guns of August   *1962*

2 . . . out of the excited fancy produced by the fears and exhaustion and panic and violence of a great battle a legend grew. . . .
                        Ibid., Ch. 11

3 For one August in its history Paris was French— and silent.   Ibid., Ch. 20

4 When at last it was over, the war had many diverse results and one dominant one transcending all others; disillusion.   Ibid., Afterword

5 The core of the military profession is discipline and the essence of discipline is obedience. Since this does not come naturally to men of independent and rational mind, they must train themselves in the habit of obedience on which lives and the fortunes of battle may someday depend. Reasonable orders are easy enough to obey; it is capricious, bureaucratic or plain idiotic demands that form the habit of discipline.
                        Pt. I, Ch. I, Stilwell* and the
                        American Experience
                        in China: 1911–1945
                        1970

*Joseph W. Stilwell, American army general (1883–1946).

6 Friendship of a kind that cannot easily be reversed tomorrow must have its roots in common interests and shared beliefs, and even between nations, in some personal feeling.
                        "Friendship with Foreign Devils,"
                        Harper's   *December 1972*

7 In a country where misery and want were the foundation of the social structure, famine was periodic, death from starvation common, disease pervasive, thievery normal, and graft and corruption taken for granted, the elimination of these conditions in Communist China is so striking that negative aspects of the new rule fade in relative importance.
                        Ch. 1, Notes from China   *1972*

8 The farmer is the eternal China.   Ibid., Ch. 3

9 Our sins in the twentieth century—greed, violence, inhumanity—have been profound, with the result that the pride and self-confidence of the nineteenth century have turned to dismay and self-disgust.
                        "On Our Birthday—America As Idea,"
                        Newsweek   *12 July 1976*

10 In the United States we have a society pervaded from top to bottom by contempt for the law.
                                                    Ibid.

11 Our government . . . learns no lessons, employs no wisdom and corrupts all who succumb to Potomac fever.   Ibid.

12 Every French town has an Avenue Victor Hugo. We never have Mark Twain Street.
                        Quoted in "Nothing Wicked About
                        Being Elite . . ." by Nan Robertson,
                        The New York Times
                        28 February 1979

13 Halfway "between truth and endless error," the mold of the species is permanent.
                        The First Salute   *1988*

14 Nineteen-fourteen was the birthday of us all, the moment when the clock struck, and the war that followed is the chasm between our world and a world that died forever.
                        Interview (1962), Quoted in "Noted historian
                        Tuchmandies,"Knight-Ridder Newspapers
                        7 February 1989

15 I ask myself, have nations ever declined from a loss of moral sense rather than from physical reasons or the pressure of barbarians? I think that they have.
                        Quoted in"Barbara Tuchman," *A World of*
                        Ideas by Bill Moyers   *1989*

16 You can't govern without having the training in it. Even Plato said that a long time ago. You need to be trained in government, to exercise it, to practice it. But the American public is now satisfying itself with entertainers.   Ibid.

17 We're a public that is brought up on deception, through advertising. . . . we're accustomed to being deceived. We allow ourselves to be deceived. Advertising is really responsible for a lot in the deterioration of American public perceptions. Ibid.

18 We have gained a lot in social freedom and individual rights, which is the thing that I personally believe in more intensely than anything else—the right of the individual to guide his own life, to think for himself, to live where he wants. We have created a society in which the individual is self-managing and insofar as he can economically manage, he can determine his own fate. Ibid.

1758. Charleszetta Waddles (1912–)

1 You can't give people pride, but you can provide the kind of understanding that makes people look to their inner strengths and find their own sense of pride.
> Quoted in "Mother Waddles: Black Angel of the Poor" by Lee Edson, *Reader's Digest* October 1972

2 God knows no distance. Ibid.

1759. Eleanor Clark (1913–)

1 "He was the kind of man, if a mule kicked somebody down the street, he'd work till he gut it on his conscience."
> Pt. III, Ch. 2, *Baldur's Gate* 1955

2 "We Occidentals have a congenital, it may even be a fatal, need for good manners, or you might say ceremony, in our approach to meaning, I suppose to make up for our crudeness in living." Ibid., Ch. 3

1760. Nathalia Crane (1913–)

1 But my heart is all aflutter like the washing on the line.
> "The Flathouse Roof," St. 1, *n.d.*

2 Crumpling a pyramid, humbling a rose,
The dust has its reasons wherever it goes.
> "The Dust"
> *n.d.*

3 There is a glory
In a great mistake. "Imperfection"
> *n.d.*

4 You cannot choose your battlefield,
The gods do that for you,
But you can plant a standard
Where a standard never flew. "The Colors"
> *n.d.*

1761. Ruth Beebe Hill (1913–)

1 I live in a world of reason and choice as opposed to faith and force.
> Quoted in " 'Hanta Yo': The Book of the Indian" by Kathleen Hendrix, *Los Angeles Times* 4 February 1979

2 Bear with me. I'll get back on the track. Actually I'm not off the track. I'm off the train, but not off the track. Ibid.

3 I own my life. And only mine. And so I shall appreciate my person. And so I shall make proper use of my self. *Hanta Yo* 1979

4 I am Ahbleza. I own the earth. Ibid.

1762. Elizabeth Janeway (1913–)

1 . . . it is through the ghost [writer] that the great gift of knowledge which the inarticulate have for the world can be made available.
> Ch. 29, *The Writer's Book*
> Helen Hull, ed. 1950

2 Poets are the leaven in the lump of civilization. Ibid., Ch. 30

3 After the city, where we had always lived, those country years were startling. . . . The surprise of animals . . . in and out, cats and dogs and a milk goat and chickens and guinea hens, all taken for granted, as if man was intended to live on terms of friendly intercourse with the rest of creation instead of huddling in isolation on the fourteenth floor of an apartment house in a city where animals occurred behind bars in the zoo.
> "Steven Benedict," *Accident* 1964

4 The Goddamn human race deserves itself, and as far as I'm concerned it can have it.
> "Charles Benedict," op. cit.

5 American women are not the only people in the world who manage to lose track of themselves, but we do seem to mislay the past in a singularly absent-minded fashion.
> "Reflections on the History of Women," *Women: Their Changing Roles* 1973

6 Like their personal lives, women's history is fragmented, interrupted; a shadow history of human beings whose existence has been shaped by the efforts and the demands of others. Ibid.

7 We have to see, I think, that questioning the value of old rules is different from simply breaking them.
> *Between Myth and Morning* 1974

8 When dealing with adultery becomes a matter of private choice instead of public rules, middle-class morality, that bastion of social stability, has ceased to function. *Ibid.*

9 With the old rules for masculine superiority fading in the public sphere, how can men face the feminine superiority they have posited in the private world? *Ibid.*

10 Love between women is seen as a paradigm of love between equals, and that is perhaps its greatest attraction. *Ibid.*

11 Loyalty, friendship, family ties, the duty owed to an ideal—in our time, these obligations seem to have lost their force as motivators and connectors. "Incest: A Rational Look at the Oldest Taboo," *Ms. November 1981*

12 I am not sure how many "sins" I would recognize in the world. Some would surely be defused by changed circumstances. But I can imagine none that is more irredeemably sinful than the betrayal, the exploitation, of the young by those who should care for them. *Ibid.*

1763. Margo Jones (1913–1955)

1 Neither the building, nor the organization, nor the finest plays and actors in the whole world will help you create a fine theatre if you have no consistent approach of your own, a true philosophy of the theatre.
Theatre in the Round 1951

2 Everything in life is theatre.
Quoted in *The New York Times 26 July 1955*

3 The theatre has given me a chance not only to live my own life but a million others. In every play there is a chance for one great moment, experience or understanding. *Ibid.*

4 With imagination and a tremendous willingness for hard work, it is possible to create a great theatre, a vigorous and vital theatre, in the second half of the twentieth century.
"Theatre '50: A Dream Come True," *Ten Talents in the American Theatre,* David H. Stevens, ed. *1957*

1764. Dorothy Kilgallen (1913–1965)

1 The chief product of Baghdad is dates . . . and sheiks. *Girl Around the World 1936*

2 The world is grand, awfully big and astonishingly beautiful, frequently thrilling. But I love New York. *Ibid.*

1765. Vivien Leigh (1913–1967)

1 In Britain, an attractive woman is somehow suspect. If there is talent as well it is overshadowed. Beauty and brains just can't be entertained; someone has been too extravagant.
Quoted by Robert Ottaway in *Light of a Star* by Gwen Robyns *1968*

1766. Mary Morris (1913–)

1 "It's like dependency on foreign oil. . . . We should be able to live alone, even if we don't want to." "Summer Share," *The Bus of Dreams 1985*

2 . . . how easy it is for a heart to turn to stone. "The Hall of Meteorites," op. cit.

1767. Tillie Olsen (1913–)

1 And when is there time to remember, to sift, to weigh, to estimate, to total?
"I Stand Here Ironing" (1954), *Tell Me a Riddle 1960*

2 My wisdom came too late. *Ibid.*

3 It is a long baptism into the seas of humankind, my daughter. Better immersion than to live untouched. . . . "O Yes" (1956), op. cit.

4 For forty-seven years they had been married. How deep back the stubborn, gnarled roots of the quarrel reached, no one could say—but only now, when tending to the needs of others no longer shackled them together, the roots swelled up visible, split the earth between them, and the tearing shook even the children, long since grown. Ch. 1, "Tell Me a Riddle" (1960), op. cit.

5 He could not, could not turn away from this desire: to have the troubling of responsibility, the fretting with money, over and done with; to be free, to be *care*free where success was not measured by accumulation. . . . *Ibid.*

6 The television is shadows. Mrs. Enlightened! Mrs. Cultured! A world comes into your house— and it is shadows. People you would never meet in a million lifetimes. Wonders. *Ibid.*

7 "Vinegar he poured on me all his life; I am well marinated; how can I be honey now?" *Ibid.*

8 Heritage. How have we come from the savages, now no longer to be savages—this to teach. To look back and learn what humanizes man—this to teach. To smash all ghettos that divide us—

not to go back, not to go back—this to
teach.   Ibid., Ch. 2

9 The mute inglorious Miltons: those whose waking hours are all struggle for existence; the
barely educated; the illiterate; women—their silence the silence of centuries as to how life was,
is, for most of humanity.
                  Silences: When Writers Don't Write
                                              1965

10 More than in any other human relationship,
overwhelmingly more, motherhood means being
instantly interruptible, responsive, responsible.
. . .   Ibid.

11 Time granted does not necessarily coincide with
time that can be most fully used.   Ibid.

1768. Rosa Parks (1913–   )

1 My only concern was go get home after a hard
day's work.*   Quoted in *Time*
                                   15 December 1975

*Referring to her refusal to give up her seat on a bus in
Montgomery, Alabama, in 1955 to a white who was standing. From her act of defiance grew the Montgomery bus
boycott and the leadership of Martin Luther King, Jr.

1769. Sylvia Porter (1913–   )

1 The average family exists only on paper and its
average budget is a fiction, invented by statisticians for the convenience of statisticians.
            Ch. 1, *Sylvia Porter's Money Book*
                                              1975

2 Money never remains just coins and pieces of
paper. It is constantly changing into the comforts
of daily life. Money can be translated into the
beauty of living, a support in misfortune, an
education, or future security. It also can be
translated into a source of bitterness.   Ibid.

3 For millions, the retirement dream is in reality
an economic nightmare. For millions, growing
old today means growing poor, being sick, living in substandard housing, and having to scrimp
merely to subsist. And this is the prospect not
only for the one out of every ten Americans
now over sixty-five . . . but also for the sixty-
five million who will reach retirement age within
the next thirty-three years.   Ibid., Ch. 19

1770. Nancy Reeves (1913–   )

1 Today the hemisphere of the public has been
assigned to the male and the hemisphere of the
private to the female. Each sex has become a
symbol for its territory. The conflict between
them can then be seen as a reflection of the

longing of each to be part of the other's sphere,
to link the public with the private in our schizoid
world, to embrace the whole of life.
              Womankind Beyond the Stereotypes
                                              1971

1771. Muriel Rukeyser (1913–1980)

1 Women in drudgery knew
They must be one of four:
Whores, artists, saints, and wives.
                  "Wreath of Women," *Beast in*
                                   View   1944

2 However confused the scene of our life ap-
    pears,
however torn we may be who now do face that
    scene,
it can be faced, and we can go on to be
whole.   *The Life of Poetry   1949*

3 Those women who stitch their lives to their
    machines
and daughters at the symmetry of looms.
              "Ann Burlak," St. 4, *Waterlily*
                      Fire (1935–1962)   *1962*

4 . . . the seeking marvelous look
Of those who lose and use and know their
    lives.   "Nine Poems for the
                          Unborn Child," II,
                                        op. cit.

5 The strength, the grossness, spirit and gall of
    choice.   Ibid., VI, St. 1

6 I have forgotten what it was
that I have been trying to remember.
                          "Woman as Market,"
                  The Speed of Darkness   1968

7 my lifetime
listens to yours.
                  "Käthe Kollwitz," * I, St. 1,
                                        op. cit.

*See 1136.

8 What would happen if one woman told the
    truth about her life?
The world would split open   Ibid., III, St. 4

9 The universe is made of stories,
not of atoms.
              "The Speed of Darkness," IX, St. 2,
                                        op. cit.

10 Whatever we stand against
We will stand feeding and seeding.
              "Wherever," St. 3, *Breaking Open*
                                              1973

1772. Honor Tracy (1913–   )

1 He was a member of the eccentric race of
fiscophobes, Englishmen who would do any-

thing and live anywhere, no matter how bored and miserable they might be, rather than stay at home and pay English taxes.
Ch. 1, *The Butterflies of the Province* 1970

2 "Early upbringing," David moaned. "One struggles against it in vain." Ibid., Ch. 5

1773. Julia de Burgos (1914/16?–1953)

1 You curl your hair and paint your face.
Not I:
I am curled by the wind, painted by the sun.
"To Julia de Burgos," *The Nation* 1972

1774. Agnes "Sis" Cunningham (1914–   )

1 We . . . were young radicals who felt that by singing ideas straightforwardly we could get more said in five minutes than in hours, or days, of talking. "Songs of Hard Years," with Madeline B. Rose, *Ms.* March 1974

2 Oh, it's good to be living and working
when we know the land's our own
To know that we have got a right to
all the crops we've grown.
"When We Know the Land's Our Own" *n.d.*

1775. Marguerite Duras (1914–   )

1 "Do you think it is ever possible to be successful in love, if one doesn't make an effort to help things along?" *The Vice-Consul*, Eileen Ellenbogen, tr. 1966

2 One must talk. That's how it is. One must.
Ibid.

3 Thousands on the causeways, carrying their loads, laying them down, returning empty-handed. People surrounding the bare, watery spaces of the rice-field, fields of upright stalks. People everywhere, ten thousand, a hundred thousand, crowded like grains of millet, walking along the causeways, an endless procession, continually on the move, each one with his tools of naked flesh hanging down on either side. Ibid.

4 I'm still there watching . . . as far away from the mystery now as I was then. I've never written, though I thought I wrote, never loved, though I thought I loved, never done anything but wait outside the closed door.
The Lover 1984

5 From time to time, I wrote for the outside world, when the outside world overwhelmed me, when things outside in the street, drove me crazy.
Introduction, *Outside* 1986

1776. Gypsy Rose Lee (1914–1970)

1 Mother, in a feminine way, was ruthless. She was, in her own words, a jungle mother, and she knew too well that in a jungle it doesn't pay to be nice. "God will protect us," she often said to June and me. "But to make sure," she would add, "carry a heavy club."
Ch. 1, *Gypsy* 1957

2 [He] often said I was the greatest no-talent star in the business. Ibid.

1777. Catherine Marshall (1914–   )

1 Often God has to shut a door in our face, so that He can subsequently open the door through which He wants us to go.
Ch. 2, *A Man Called Peter* 1951

2 . . . truth could never be wholly contained in words. All of us know it: At the same moment the mouth is speaking one thing, the heart is saying another. . . . Prologue, *Christy* 1967

3 So once I shut down my privilege of disliking anyone I chose and holding myself aloof if I could manage it, greater understanding, growing compassion came to me. . . . Ibid., Ch. 12

4 . . . in rejecting secrecy I had also rejected the road to cynicism. Ibid., Ch. 33

1778. Abigail McCarthy (1914?–   )

1 For those of us whose lives have been defined by others—by wifehood and motherhood—there is no individual achievement to measure, only the experience of life itself.
Private Faces/Public Places 1972

1779. Dixy Lee Ray (1914–   )

1 My answer to why did I choose the Democratic Party is that I spent three years in Washington under a Republican administration.
Quoted in *The Wall Street Journal* 15 March 1976

2 Everybody's in favor of resolving the energy crisis and everybody is in favor of preserving the environment. But the people in the Northwest, where the big coal deposits are, don't

want their terrain upset; and the people in the Northeast, who need heating fuel the most, don't want an oil port and refineries on their coast, and some of the Nader people don't want any nuclear plants at all generating electric power because of some theoretical dangers. I understand these conflicts, but this isn't a perfect world. Somebody—and I mean every one of us—has to make some sacrifices.
> Interview (1974), Quoted in
> *American Political Women*
> by Esther Stineman   *1980*

3 The reality is that zero defects in products plus zero pollution plus zero risk on the job is equivalent to maximum growth of government plus zero economic growth plus runaway inflation.   Speech, Scientists and Engineers for Secure Energy (1980), op. cit.

1780. Hazel Brannon Smith (1914–1981)

1 I ain't no lady. I'm a newspaperwoman.
> Quoted in "The 11-Year Siege of Mississippi's Lady Editor" by T. George Harris, *Look*
> *16 November 1965*

2 I can't think of but one thing that's worse than being called a nigger-lover. And that's a nigger-hater!   Ibid.

1781. Barbara Ward (1914–1981)

1 All archaic societies feel themselves bound to a "melancholy wheel" of endless recurrence. . . . No vision of reality as progressing forward to new possibilities, no sense of the future as better and fuller than the present, tempered the underlying fatalism of ancient civilization. It is only in the Jewish and Christian faith that a Messianic hope first breaks upon mankind.
> Ch. 1, *The Rich Nations and the Poor Nations   1962*

2 It is very much easier for a rich man to invest and grow richer than for the poor man to begin investing at all. And this is also true of nations.   Ibid.

3 We . . . live in an epoch in which the solid ground of our preconceived ideas shakes daily under our uncertain feet.
> "Only One Earth," *Who Speaks for Earth?*, Maurice F. Strong, ed.
> *1973*

4 We can all cheat on morals. . . . But today the morals of respect and care and modesty come to us in a form that we cannot evade. We cannot cheat on DNA. We cannot get round photosyn-

thesis. We cannot say I am not going to give a damn about phytoplankton. All these tiny mechanisms provide the preconditions of our planetary life. To say we do not care is to say in the most literal sense that "we choose death."   Ibid.

1782. Molly Yard (1914–)

1 I thought it would be different in this country [than it is in China], but I learned quickly that females weren't valued in this society, either. It is indeed a worldwide problem.
> Quoted in "NOW Head Assails President's Policies" by Alex Tizon, *Seattle Times   February 1989*

1783. Babe Didrikson Zaharias (1914–1956)

1 Boy, don't you men wish you could hit a ball like that!   Quoted in " 'Babe' Didrikson Zaharias," *Famous American Women* by Hope Stoddard   *1970*

2 All my life I've been competing—and competing to win. I came to realize that in its way, this cancer was the toughest competition I'd faced yet. I made up my mind that I was going to lick it all the way. I not only wasn't going to let it kill me, I wasn't even going to let it put me on the shelf.   Ibid.

1784. Hortensia Bussi de Allende (1915–)

1 We want a Chile where the rights of man will be fully respected. Our message is not fear but hope, not hate but joy. It is not the past, but the future, that we will build together.
> Speech,
> Santiago, Chile   *24 September 1988*

1785. Phyllis Shand Allfrey (1915–)

1 She went out on the portico and looked down on the land, sighing as if her heart had broken and the wind was whistling through it. "Beauty grows like a weed here," she said, "and so does disease."   *The Orchid House   1953*

1786. Ingrid Bergman (1915–1982)

1 . . . I saw my wrinkles in their wrinkles. You know, one looks at herself in the mirror every morning, and she doesn't see the difference, she doesn't realize that she is aging. But then she

finds a friend who was young with her, and the friend isn't young anymore, and all of a sudden, like a slap on her eyes, she remembers that she, too, isn't young anymore.

Quoted in"Ingrid Bergman," *The Egotists* by Oriana Fallaci*   *1963*

* See 2060.

2 I've never sought success in order to get fame and money; it's the talent and the passion that count in success.   Ibid.

1787. Caroline Bird (1915–   )

1 The contraceptive pill may reduce the importance of sex not only as a basis for the division of labor, but as a guideline in developing talents and interests.   Foreword, *Born Female 1968*

2 A career woman who has survived the hurdle of marriage and maternity encounters a new obstacle: the hostility of men.   Ibid., Ch. 3

3 Secretaries may be specially prized, and the top secretaries exceptionally well paid, because they give men who can afford to pay well the subservient, watchful and admiring attention that Victorian wives used to give their husbands.
Ibid., Ch. 4

4 Equity speaks softly and wins in the end. But it is expedience, with its loud voice, that sets the time of victory.   Ibid., Ch. 10

5 To keep their mammoth plants financially solvent, many [educational] institutions have begun to use hard-sell, Madison Avenue techniques to attract students. They sell college like soap. . . .
The Case Against College   1975

1788. Fawn M. Brodie (1915–1981)

1 There is, of course, a gold mine or a buried treasure on every mortgaged homestead. Whether the farmer ever digs for it or not, it is there, haunting his daydreams when the burden of debt is most unbearable.
Ch. 2, *No Man Knows My History 1945*

2 The paradise of the prophet [Joseph Smith]* had much of the earth in it.   Ibid., Ch. 13

* American prophet and founder of Mormons (1805–1844).

3 Mormon theology was never burdened with otherworldliness. There was a fine robustness about it that smelled of the frontier and that rejected an asceticism that was never endemic to America.   Ibid.

4 A man's memory is bound to be a distortion of his past in accordance with his present interests,

and the most faithful autobiography is likely to mirror less what a man was than what he has become.   Ibid., Ch. 19

5 Housework is a breeze. Cooking is a pleasant diversion. Putting up a retaining wall is a lark. But teaching is like climbing a mountain.
Quoted in "Home Q&A" by Marshall Berges in *Los Angeles Times Home Magazine 20 February 1977*

1789. Marie-Louise von Franz (1915–   )

1 Unfortunately the conscious representation we make of the Godhead undergoes the same fate as all other contents of our consciousness: it suffers from the tendency to wear out, and becomes mere words which lose their emotional and feeling substructure.
Ch. 4, *Individuation in Fairytales   1977*

2 The inner experience consolidates, and instead of being a kind of emotional spiritual experience, it becomes a realization in the most literal sense of the word. We use the word "realization" rather too lightly; but if we "realize" something in its basic meaning, it becomes a real thing forever.   Ibid., Ch. 5

3 The only way the Self can manifest is through conflict. To meet one's insoluble and eternal conflict is to meet God, which would be the end of the ego with all its blather.
Alchemy: An Introduction to the Symbolism and the Psychology   1980

4 You think God has published general rules which He keeps Himself, and we think He is a living spirit appearing in man's psyche who can always create something new. . . . To a theologian God is bound to His own books and is incapable of further publications. That is where we lock horns.   Ibid.

5 Every content of the unconscious with which one is not properly related tends to obsess one for it gets at us from behind. If you can talk to it you get into relationship with it. You can either be possessed by a content constellated in the unconscious, or you can have a relationship to it. The more one represses it, the more one is affected by it.
Redemption Motifs in Fairytales, n.d.

1790. Janet Harris (1915–   )

1 I'm the ultimate in the throwaway society, the disposable woman.
The Prime of Ms. America   1975

2 . . . one searches the magazines in vain for women past their first youth. The middleaged face apparently sells neither perfume nor floor wax. The role of the mature woman in the media is almost entirely negative.   Ibid.

3 We were born in an era in which it was a disgrace for women to be sexually responsible. We matured in an era in which it was an obligation.   Ibid.

4 Quite a few women told me, one way or another, that they thought it was sex, not youth, that's wasted on the young. . . .   Ibid.

1791. Billie Holiday (1915–1959)

1 Southern trees bear a strange fruit,
  Blood on the leaves and blood at the root,
  Black bodies swinging in the Southern breeze,
  Strange fruit hanging from the poplar trees.
                          "Strange Fruit"   1939

2 Mama may have
  Papa may have
  But God bless the child that's got his own
  That's got his own.
                          "God Bless the Child"   1941

3 And when you're poor, you grow up fast.
        Ch. 1, *Lady Sings the Blues,* with William
                                  Dufty   1956

4 You can be up to your boobies in white satin, with gardenias in your hair and no sugar cane for miles, but you can still be working on a plantation.   Ibid., Ch. 11

5 Sometimes it's worse to win a fight than to lose.   Ibid., Ch. 13

1792. Lena Jeger (1915–   )

1 . . . no legislation can compel anybody to give the unmarried mother what she usually most needs—friendship, understanding and companionship in what is almost inevitably a lonely and deeply traumatic experience.
        Foreword, *Illegitimate Children and Their
                                  Parents   1951*

2 The child is different, not because he is illegitimate, but because he is fatherless and he is going to miss a father in the same way that any child who loses his father early, through death or separation, misses him.   Ibid.

3 . . . we feel that there is often too little concern with the unmarried father. In our social records he is an elusive figure, often anonymous, alternately reviled, beloved or blackmailed. . . . Often he needs as much help as the mother to regain a mental and emotional equilibrium and

so to make subsequently a good husband to somebody, if not to the mother of his first child.   Ibid.

1793. Isobel Lennart (1915–1971)

1 FANNY. Look—suppose all you ever had for breakfast was onion rolls. All of a sudden one morning, in walks a bagel. You'd say, "Ugh! What's that?" Until you tried it. *That's* my trouble. I'm a bagel on a plate full of onion rolls!   Act I, Sc. 3, *Funny Girl   1964*

1794. Margaret Millar (1915–   )

1 As soon as she opened her eyes Priscilla could feel in her bones that it was Saturday. The air smelled different, and it seemed to quiver with anticipation.
                  "A Problem in Economics," *It's
                      All in the Family   1948*

2 "And when I was eleven and wanted ten cents I went out and got me a ten-cent task to do."
  "I can't think of any ten-cent task except just plain being good."
  "In this world you don't get paid for being good."   Ibid.

1795. Nien Cheng (1915–   )

1 The [Chinese] leaders who ordered this killing of innocent people* will never ever recover the good reputation they'd worked so hard for and gained in the eyes of the world and the Chinese people.   Quoted in "China Hears a Voice of
                        Experience" by Judi Hunt,
                          *Seattle Post-Intelligencer
                                  10 June 1989*

*Referring to the gunning down by the military of Chinese students and workers demonstrating for democracy in Tiananmen Square, Beijing, 15 April 1989.

2 I think the democratic movement will be repressed for now, only to erupt again somewhere down the line.
  And more blood will be shed, just like it was when Americans fought and died to bring independence, democracy and freedom to the United States. It's not something you can sit back and wait for someone to give to you voluntarily.   Ibid.

1796. Eleanor Perry (1915–1981)

1 "We've all known each other so long there's not even anyone to flirt with."
                  The Swimmer (screenplay)   1967

2 Rape has become a kind of favor done to the female—a fairly commonplace male fantasy.
> Quoted in "Rebirth" by Kay Loveland and Estelle Changas, *The Hollywood Screenwriters,* Richard Corliss, ed.
> *1972*

3 . . . so long as a woman is dependent on a man for her self-image or her self-esteem she will remain without any sense of her own worth—can never be a fully realized human being.
> Ibid.

1797. Janet Mary Riley (1915–   )

1 We [women law students] bore the burden of representing womankind, whether we liked it or not.
   If you goofed, if you failed, if you cried in public or received bad grades, they'd say, "What do you expect: She's only a woman."
   So we didn't cry in public. We didn't get bad grades. The result was that the woman students did remarkably well. For years, the women were the tops in their class.
   There was a lot of self-inflicted pressure not to cry. But I did my share of crying in the women's lounge.
> Quoted in "Women Win Their Case as Legal Eagles" by Jean Blake, *The Times-Picayune*
> *2 November 1986*

2 The role of mother is probably the most important career a woman can have. Ibid.

1798. Ethel Rosenberg (1915–1953)

1 Together we hunted down the answers to all the seemingly insoluble riddles which a complex and callous society presented. . . . And yet for the sake of these answers, for the sake of American democracy, justice and brotherhood, for the sake of peace and bread and roses, and children's laughter, we shall continue to sit here [in prison] in dignity and in pride—in the deep abiding knowledge of our innocence before God and man, until the truth becomes a clarion call to all decent humanity.
> Letter to Julie Rosenberg, Sing Sing (27 May 1951), *Death House Letters of Ethel and Julius Rosenberg*
> *1953*

2 Work and build, my sons, and build
a monument to love and joy,
to human worth, to faith we kept
for you, my sons, for you.
> "If We Die" (24 January 1953), op. cit.

1799. Natalie Shainess (1915–   )

1 At a recent meeting devoted to the theme of dissent, a Negro analyst pointed to the analyst's blind spot, in studying only the dissenters, but not the people or ideas dissented against. How valid a perception!
> "A Psychiatrist's View: Images of Woman—Past and Present, Overt and Obscured," *American Journal of Psychotherapy* *January 1969*

2 As we have become a thing-oriented, impulse-ridden, narcissistically self-preoccupied people, we are increasingly dedicated to the acquisition of things, and cultivate little else. Ibid.

1800. Jean Stafford (1915–1979)

1 There were two subjects of conversation; one was the food they were eating and the other was the food they had eaten at other times . . .
> "Maggie Meriwether's Rich Experience," *The Innocents Abroad,* from *The Collected Stories of Jean Stafford* *1969*

2 Abby's preconception of gambling derived from scenes in movies, and as she moved from table to table, endeavoring to understand the games, she realized that either her memory was at fault or Hollywood had carelessly added an apocryphal glitter and subtracted an essential gloom. "The Children's Game," op. cit.

3 . . . , "From time to time, I need a rest from the exercitation of my intellect."
> "The Echo and the Nemesis," op. cit.

4 . . . (they revered education and, even when married, even when pregnant, took graduate courses in political science and Eastern philosophy), . . . "Polite Conversation," *The Bostonians,* op. cit.

1801. Margaret Walker (1915–   )

1 For my people thronging 47th Street in Chicago and Lenox
Avenue in New York and Rampart Street in
   New
Orleans, lost disinherited dispossessed and
   happy
people filling the cabarets and taverns and
   other
people's pocket. . . .
> "For My People," St. 6, *For My People* *1942*

2 Old women working by an age-old plan to make their bread in ways as best they can.
> "Whores," St. 1, op. cit.

3 Hurry up, Lucille, Hurry up
We're Going to Miss Our Chance to go to
Jail.   "Street Demonstration," St. 2,
         Prophets for a New Day   1970

4   . . . the filthy
privies marked "For Colored Only"
and the drinking-soda-fountains
tasting dismal and disgusting
with a dry and dusty flavor
of the deep humiliation. . . .
                          "Now," op. cit.

1802. Helen Yglesias (1915–   )

1 They never ask the patient. The patient is anesthetized on the operating table, cut open. They
call in the husband. "We think it best to remove
this precancerous breast. Since this is your hunk
of meat, do we have your permission,
husband?"   Ch. 1, *How She Died*
                                     1972

2 "Life is too short to understand God altogether,
especially nowadays."   Ibid.

3 Listening was a three times a day ritual with
her, the news made even more nightmarish in
the repetition: the war, the official statements,
the enemy's denial, the traffic deaths, conspiracy charges, abortion reform fights, kidnap-
pings, terrorism, peace talks, negotiations of all
kinds, hijackings, charges and countercharges
of anti-Semitism, Panther trials, civilian massacre trials, murder trials, riots, demonstrations,
flaring wars between nations in corners of the
world that didn't seem to really exist, the nonsense item they always found to end each broadcast with—and then the weather, reported as if
every dip of the wind was a judgment day
warning.   Ibid., Ch. 16

1803. Dorothy Salisbury Davis
   (1916–   )

1 There are seasons in Washington when it is even
more difficult than usual to find out what is
going on in the government. Possibly it is because nothing is going on, although a great many
people seem to be working at it.
            Ch. 1, *Old Sinners Never Die*   1959

2 We are all at the mercy of God as well as of
one another. And for that we can be grateful,
He has so much more of it than we have.
         Ch. 7, *Black Sheep Among White Lamb*
                                        1963

3 She dressed more severely than was her fashion,
needing herringbone for backbone. . . .
         "The Purple Is Everything," *Ellery
         Queen's Mystery Magazine*   1964

4 The law is above the law, you know.
            Ch. 8, *The Little Brothers*   1973

5 You know what truth is, gentlemen? Truth
is self-justification. That is everybody's
truth. . . .   Ibid.

1804. Betty Furness (1916–   )

1 You fellows have got to get this [phosphate-
pollution problem] straightened out, because the
laundry's piling up.
            Quoted in *Bella!,* * Mel Ziegler, ed.
                                        1972

*Bella Abzug; see 1873.

1805. Natalia Ginzburg (1916–1991)

1 I haven't managed to become learned about
anything, even the things I've loved most in
life: in me they remain scattered images, which
admittedly feed my life of memories and feelings, but fail to fill my empty cultural
wasteland.
            "He and I" (1963), *Italian Writing
            Today,* Raleigh Trevelyan, ed.
                                        1967

2 . . . it hurts me not to love music, because I
feel my spirit is hurt by not loving it. But there's
nothing to be done about it; I shall never understand music, and never love it. If I occasionally hear music I like, I can't remember it; so
how could I love a thing I can't remember?
                                        Ibid.

3 My tidiness, and my untidiness, are full of regret
and remorse and complex feelings.   Ibid.

1806. Françoise Giroud (1916–   )

1 Are there still virgins? One is tempted to answer
no. There are only girls who have not yet crossed
the line, because they want to preserve their
market value. . . . Call them virgins if you
wish, these travelers in transit.
            Quoted in *Coronet
            November 1960*

2 Nothing is more difficult than competing with a
myth.   *I Give You My Word*   1974

3 . . . the present evolution of women . . . is to
my mind the most profound revolution that highly
developed societies will have to contend
with. . . .   Ibid.

4 As though femininity is something you can lose
the way you lose your pocketbook: hmm, where
in the world did I put my femininity?   Ibid.

5 . . . I don't for one moment believe that over the centuries some universal plot has been hatched by men to keep women in a state of servitude. Ibid.

6 When mores are no longer founded on the law of civilization but on habit, then comes the revolt. Ibid.

1807. Elizabeth Hardwick (1916–)

1 Letters are above all useful as a means of expressing the ideal self; and no other method of communication is quite so good for this purpose. . . . In letters we can reform without practice, beg without humiliation, snip and shape embarrassing experiences to the measure of our own desires. . . .
"Anderson, Millay and Crane*
in Their Letters" (1953),
A View of My Own 1962

*Margaret Anderson, see 1446; Edna St. Vincent Millay, see 1439; Nathalia Crane, see 1760.

2 Mothers born on relief have their babies on relief. Nothingness, truly, seems to be the condition of these New York people. . . . They are nomads going from one rooming house to another, looking for a toilet that functions.
"The Insulted and Injured:
Books About Poverty" (1961), op. cit.

3 Hedda [Gabler],* rather than Nora [of A Doll's House],** was the real prophecy.
Seduction and Betrayal: Women in
Literature 1974

*Play by August Strindberg, Swedish (1849–1912).
**Play by Henrik Ibsen, Norwegian (1828–1906).

4 Women, wronged in one way or another, are given the overwhelming beauty of endurance, the capacity for high or low suffering, for violent feeling absorbed, finally tranquilized, for the radiance of humility, for silence, secrecy, impressive acceptance. Heroines are, then, heroic. Ibid.

5 The raging productivity of the Victorians, shattered nerves and punctured stomachs, but it was a thing noble, glorious, awesome in itself. Ibid.

6 They [the F. Scott Fitzgeralds]* had created themselves together, and they always saw themselves, their youth, their love, their lost youth and lost love, their failures and memories, as a sort of living fiction. Ibid.

*American author, 1896–1940, and his wife Zelda; see 1548.

7 The "book"—a plaguing growth that does not itself grow, but attaches, hangs on, a tumorous companion made up of the deranged cells of learning, experience, thinking.
Sleepless Nights 1979

1808. Jane Jacobs (1916–)

1 But look what we have built . . . low-income projects that become worse centers of delinquency, vandalism and general social hopelessness than the slums they were supposed to replace. . . . Cultural centers that are unable to support a good bookstore. Civic centers that are avoided by everyone but bums. . . . Promenades that go from no place to nowhere and have no promenaders. Expressways that eviscerate great cities. This is not the rebuilding of cities. This is the sacking of cities.
Introduction, The Death and Life of Great
American Cities 1961

2 There is a quality even meaner than outright ugliness or disorder, and this meaner quality is the dishonest mask of pretended order, achieved by ignoring or suppressing the real order that is struggling to exist and to be served. Ibid.

3 To keep the city safe is a fundamental task of a city's streets and its sidewalks.
Ibid., Pt. I, Ch. 2

4 The only possible way to keep open the economic opportunities for new activities [in a city] is for a "third force" to protect their weak and still incipient interests. Only governments can play this economic role. And sometimes, for pitifully brief intervals, they do. But because development subverts the status quo, the status quo soon subverts governments.
Ch. 8, The Economy of Cities
1969

5 The bureaucratized, simplified cities, so dear to present-day city planners and urban designers, and familiar also to readers of science fiction and utopian proposals, run counter to the processes of city growth and economic development. Conformity and monotony, even when they are embellished with a froth of novelty, are not attributes of developing and economically vigorous cities. They are attributes of stagnant settlements. Ibid.

1809. Natasha Josefowitz (1916–)

1 Even though awareness must precede action, they are very different processes, and what we are experiencing today is the time lag between the two. For modern women, this time lag between heightened awareness and the need for action presents a new problem. Many are ex-

periencing a real gap between how they are supposed to feel and act and how they actually feel and act. All these discrepancies reinforce the inability of many women to identify the cause of their powerlessness.

Ch. 1, *Paths to Power*   1980

2 Speaking is the most visible of the four uncommon skills. You may not be well read, you may not know how to count, you may write poorly, but as soon as you open your mouth people get an impression of you based both on the content of your message and on the way you deliver it.   Ibid., Ch. 4

1810. Florynce R. Kennedy (1916–   )

1 . . . there can be no really pervasive system of oppression, such as that in the United States, without the consent of the oppressed.
"Institutionalized Oppression vs. the Female," *Sisterhood Is Powerful*, Robin Morgan,* ed.   1970

*See 2327.

2 Women are dirt searchers; their greatest worth is eradicating rings on collars and tables. Never mind real-estate boards' corruption and racism, here's your soapsuds. Everything she is doing is peripheral, expendable, crucial, and nonnegotiable. Cleanliness is next to godliness.
Ibid.

3 Being a mother is a noble status, right? Right. So why does it change when you put "unwed" or "welfare" in front of it?
Quoted in "The Verbal Karate of Florynce R. Kennedy, Esq." by Gloria Steinem,* *Ms.*   *March 1973*

*See 2164.

4 The biggest sin is sitting on your ass.   Ibid.

5 Don't agonize. Organize.   Ibid.

6 If men could get pregnant, abortion would be a sacrament.   Ibid.

7 There are very few jobs that actually require a penis or vagina. All other jobs should be open to everybody.
Quoted in "Freelancer with No Time to Write" by John Brady, *Writer's Digest   February 1974*

1811. Bella Lewitzky (1916–   )

1 Making social comment is an artificial place for an artist to start from. If an artist is touched by some social condition, what the artist creates will reflect that, but you can't force it.

Quoted in "Modern Dance Group Plants Western Roots" by Didi Moore, *San Francisco Chronicle 4 March 1979*

2 When you dance, it's only for now. When you choreograph, it's with you day and night. But when you get through, the creation leaves you like a child.   Ibid.

1812. Patricia McLaughlin (1916–   )

1 Discoveries have reverberations. A new idea about oneself or some aspect of one's relations to others unsettles all one's other ideas, even the superficially related ones. No matter how slightly, it shifts one's entire orientation. And somewhere along the line of consequences, it changes one's behavior.
Quoted in *American Scholar Autumn 1972*

1813. Cicely Saunders (1916–   )

1 Deception is not as creative as truth. We do best in life if we look at it with clear eyes, and I think that applies to coming up to death as well.
Quoted in "Dying With Dignity" by David Brand, *Time 5 September 1988*

1814. Anya Seton (1916–   )

1 People in England seemed to think nothing of false teeth, even when they got them from the National Health.
Pt. I, Ch. 1, *Green Darkness*   1972

2 "As I grew up I got cynical. I'd see Mother enthusiastic and involved with charlatans. Numerologists and astrologers who charged five hundred dollars for a 'reading' which was so vague you could twist the meaning any way you wanted. And faith healers who couldn't seem to heal themselves, and a Yogi in California who preached purity, sublimity and continence, and then tried to seduce me one day while Mother was out."   Ibid., Ch. 2

3 "Truth is naturally universal," said Akananda, "and shines into many different windows, though some of them are clouded."
Ibid., Pt. III, Ch. 19

1815. Frances Silverberg (1916–   )

1 It was better not to speak, nor let your face or eyes show what you were feeling, because if

people didn't know how you felt about them, or things, or maybe thought you had no feelings at all, they couldn't hurt you as much, only a little.   "Rebecca by Any Other Name,"
American Scene: New Voices,
Don Wolfe, ed.   *1963*

1816. Annie Skau (1916?–   )

1 The old Christian who has lived and walked with the Lord for many years is living in a treasure chamber.
Quoted in"Saints Among Us," *Time*
29 December 1975

1817. Helen Suzman (1916/18–   )

1 Liberalism has a future in South Africa, but fundamental changes will take a lot longer than most people think.
Quoted in World Notes, *Time*
29 May 1989

1818. Patricia Swerda (1916–   )

1 Go to nature. Once you learn how plants grow, you will know how to arrange them.
Quoted in "Ikebana, A Zen way with flowers" by Karen Mathieson,
Pacific (magazine)
28 May 1989

2 The only difference between a rut and a grave are the dimensions.   Ibid.

1819. Hiltgunt Zassenhaus (1916–   )

1 If they bomb my home in Hamburg, all I have left is what I can carry with me. . . . [But] there was something no suitcase could hold. It was intangible and the prisoners hungered for it. Only our minds and hearts could give truth and hope.   *Walls: Resisting the Third Reich—*
One Woman's Story   1974

1820. Maeve Brennan (1917–   )

1 She had found that the more the child demanded of her, the more she had to give. Strength came up in waves that had their source in a sea of calm and unconquerable devotion. The child's holy trust made her open her eyes, and she took stock of herself and found that everything was all right, and that she could meet what challenges arose and meet them well, and that she

had nothing to apologize for—on the contrary, she had every reason to rejoice.
"The Eldest Child," *The New Yorker*
23 June 1968

2 She . . . enjoyed the illusion that life had nothing to teach her.   Ibid.

3 He wished they could go back to the beginning and start all over again, but the place where they had stood together, where they had been happy, was all trampled over and so spoiled that it seemed impossible ever to make it smooth again.   Ibid.

1821. Gwendolyn Brooks (1917–   )

1 Abortions will not let you forget.
You remember the children you got that you
did not get. . . .   "The Mother," St. 1,
A Street in Bronzeville   1945

2 I hold my honey and I store my bread
In little jars and cabinets of my will.
I label clearly, and each latch and lid
I bid, Be firm till I return from hell.
I am very hungry. I am incomplete.
And none can tell when I may dine again.
"My dreams, my works,
must wait till after hell,"
op. cit.

3 People like definite decisions,
Tidy answers, all the little ravellings
Snipped off, the lint removed, they
Hop happily among their roughs
Calling what they can't clutch insanity
Or saintliness.
"Memorial to Ed Blanc," St. 3,
Annie Allen   1949

4 What she wanted was to donate to the world a good Maude Martha. That was the offering, the bit of art, that could not come from any other. She would polish and hone that.
Ch. 6, *Maude Martha   1953*

5 She had a tremendous impatience with other people's ideas—unless those happened to be exactly like hers; even then, often as not, she gave hurried, almost angry, affirmative, and flew onto emphatic illumination of her own.
Ibid., Ch. 23

6 We real cool. We
Left school. We

Lurk late. We
Strike straight. We

Sing sin. We
Thin gin. We

Jazz June. We
Die soon.

"We Real Cool," *The Bean
Eaters   1960*

7 I wonder if the elephant
Is lonely in his stall
When all the boys and girls are gone
And there's no shout at all,
And there's no one to stamp before,
No one to note his might.
Does he hunch up, as I do,
Against the dark of night?   "Pete at the Zoo,"
op. cit.

8 He opened us—
who was a key,

who was a man.
"Malcolm X," Sts. 4–5, *In the
Mecca   1968*

9 Does man love Art? Man visits Art, but
squirms
Art hurts. Art urges voyages—
and it is easier to stay at home,
the nice beer ready.
"The Chicago Picasso," St. 1,
op. cit.

1822. Barbara Deming (1917–   )

1 It is particularly hard on us as pacifists, of
course, to face our own anger. It is particularly
painful for us—hard on our pride, too—to have
to discover in ourselves murderers.
"On Anger," *We Cannot Live
Without Our Lives   1974*

2 If men put from them in fear all that is "wom-
anish" in them, then long, of course, for that
missing part in their natures, so seek to possess
it by possessing us; and because they have feared
it in their own souls seek, too, to dominate it in
us—seek even to slay it—well, we're where we
are now, aren't we?   "Two Perspectives on
Women's Struggles,"
op. cit.

1823. Phyllis Diller (1917–   )

1 Cleaning your house while your kids are still
growing
Is like shoveling the walk before it stops
snowing.
*Phyllis Diller's Housekeeping Hints
1966*

2 Never go to bed mad. Stay up and fight.
Ibid.

3 You know you're getting old, when your back
starts going out more than you do.   Quoted in
Earl Wilson's "Broadway" column
8 September 1978

1824. Indira Gandhi (1917–1984)

1 Peace we want because there is another war to
fight against poverty, disease and ignorance. We
have promises to keep to our people of work,
food, clothing, and shelter, health and
education.
Radio Broadcast (26 January 1966),
Quoted in *Indira Gandhi*
by Mithrapuram K. Alexander
1968

2 The young people of India must recognize that
they will get from their country tomorrow what
they give her today.   Ibid.

3 You cannot shake hands with a clenched
fist.   Press Conference, New Delhi
(19 October 1971), Quoted in
Indira Speaks by Dhiren Mullick
1972

4 Martyrdom does not end something; it is only
the beginning.   Address to Parliament,
New Delhi (12 August 1971), op. cit.

5 One cannot but be perturbed when fire breaks
out in a neighbour's house.
Address in Kremlin,
Moscow (28 September 1971), op. cit.

6 To natural calamities of drought, flood and cy-
clone has been added the man-made tragedy of
vast proportions. I am haunted by tormented
faces in our overcrowded refugee camps reflecting grim events, which have compelled exodus
of these millions from East Bengal.
Meeting with Richard Nixon,*
Washington, D.C. (4 November 1971), op.
cit.

*1913–   ; 37th president of the United States, 1969–
1974; resigned.

7 You must learn to be still in the midst of activity
and to be vibrantly alive in repose.
Quoted in "The Embattled Woman"
by James Shepherd, *People
30 June 1975*

8 As for Western women, it seems to me that they
have often had to struggle to obtain their own
rights. That did not leave them much time to
prove their abilities. The time will come.
Quoted in "Conversation with
Indira Gandhi" by José-Luis de
Vilallonga, *Oui   1975*

9 I think that the highly industrialized Western
world has neglected to the utmost degree to
leave room for man. The infernal production-
consumption cycle has completely dehumanized
life. The individual has become a tool. He
hardly has any contact with nature anymore.
That is, with himself. He has lost his soul and
is not even trying to find it again.   Ibid.

10 Never forget that when we are silent, we are one. And when we speak, we are two.   Ibid.

11 I have no admiration for military feats. Defeats are always pitiful. Victories are always last resources.   Ibid.

1825. Katharine Graham (1917–   )

1 If one is rich and one's a woman, one can be quite misunderstood.
Quoted in "The Power That Didn't Corrupt" by Jane Howard,* *Ms.* *October 1974*

*See 2171.

2 So few grown women like their lives.   Ibid.

3 To love what you do and feel that it matters— how could anything be more fun?   Ibid.

1826. Fannie Lou Hamer (1917–1977)

1 Let's face it. What's hurtin' the Black folks that's without, is hurtin' the white folks that's without. If the white folk fight for theyself, and the Black folk for theyself, we gonna crumble apart. These are things that we gonna have to fight together. We got to fight in America for ALL the people . . . and I'm perfectly willing to make this country what it have to be.
Slogan, Women for Racial & Economic Equality   *n.d.*

1827. Lena Horne (1917–   )

1 It's ill-becoming for an old broad to sing about how bad she wants it. But occasionally we do.   Quoted in *Time*   *17 October 1988*

2 Always be smarter than the people who hire you.   Remark   *n.d.*

1828. Sybil Leek (1917–1982)

1 You can't be sure who the Devil is these days. He might be a TV or movie producer in disguise.   Ch. 1, *Diary of a Witch*   *1968*

2 Perhaps telepathy will remain a mystery for many more years but it has always been within the power of a few people in every generation to transmit and receive thoughts. People in love often claim this power. Maybe we are being forced to realize that love is in itself a magical power and that awareness may be instrumental in preventing our own destruction.
Ibid., Ch. 6

3 Reincarnation is nothing more than the law of evolution applied to the consciousness of the individual. . . . The spirit is our only link with the Godhead, the divine force of life, and it is the indestructible part of ourselves.
Ibid., Ch. 12

1829. Carson McCullers (1917–1967)

1 "There are those who know and those who don't know. And for every ten thousand who don't know there's only one who knows. That's the miracle of all time—that these millions know so much but don't know this."
Pt. I, Ch. 2, *The Heart Is a Lonely Hunter* *1940*

2 The inside room was a very private place. She could be in the middle of a house full of people and still feel like she was locked up by herself.   Ibid., Pt. II, Ch. 5

3 "Today we are not put up on the platforms and sold at the courthouse square. But we are forced to sell our strength, our time, our souls during almost every hour that we live. We have been freed from one kind of slavery only to be delivered into another."   Ibid., Ch. 6

4 An army post in peacetime is a dull place. Things happen, but then they happen over and over again. . . . But perhaps the dullness of a post is caused most of all by insularity and by a surfeit of leisure and safety, for once a man enters the army he is expected only to follow the heels ahead of him.
Ch. 1, *Reflections in a Golden Eye* *1941*

5 Three words were in the captain's heart. He shaped them soundlessly with his trembling lips, as he had not breath to spare for a whisper: "I am lost." And having given up life, the Captain suddenly began to live.   Ibid., Ch. 3

6 This August she was twelve and five-sixths years old. She was five feet and three-quarter inches tall, and she wore a Number 7 shoe. . . . If she reached her height on her eighteenth birthday, she had five and one-sixth growing years ahead of her. Therefore, according to mathematics and unless she could somehow stop herself, she would grow to be over nine feet tall. And what would be a lady who was over nine feet high? She would be a Freak.
Pt. I, *The Member of the Wedding* *1946*

7 "We all of us somehow caught. We born this way or that way and we don't know why. But we caught anyhow. . . . And maybe we wants to widen and bust free. But no matter what we

do we still caught. Me is me and you is you and he is he. We each one of us somehow caught all by ourself.''   Ibid., Pt. II, Ch. 2

8 Sweet, casual intimacy, the soft-fleshed loveliness indisputably possessed.
            ''The Sojourner,'' *The Ballad of the Sad Cafe*   *1951*

9 Ferris glimpsed the disorder of his life: the succession of cities, of transitory loves; and time, the sinister glissando of the years, time always.   Ibid.

1830. Jessica Mitford (1917–   )

1 Things on the whole are much faster in America; people don't *stand for election*, they *run for office*.   Ch. 11, *Sons and Rebels 1960*

2 O death where is thy sting? O grave where is thy victory? Where, indeed? Many a badly stung survivor, faced with the aftermath of some relative's funeral, has ruefully conceded that the victory has been won hands down by a funeral establishment—in disastrously unequal battle.   *The American Way of Death 1963*

3 When is conduct a crime, and when is a crime not a crime? When Somebody Up There—a monarch, a dictator, a Pope, a legislator—so decrees.
          Ch. 5, *Kind and Unusual Punishment 1971*

4 One of the nicest American scientists I know was heard to say, ''Criminals in our penitentiary are fine experimental material—much cheaper than chimpanzees.'' I hope the chimpanzees don't come to hear of this.   Ibid., Ch. 9

5 Radical and revolutionary ideologies are seeping into the prisons. Whereas formerly convicts tended to regard themselves as unfortunates whose accident of birth at the bottom of the heap was largely responsible for their plight, today many are questioning the validity of the heap.
          Ibid., Ch. 13

1831. Raisa Davydovna Orlova (1917–1964)

1 Beliefs and convictions reach out from the past, and they cannot be altered by fervent desire alone. They possess their own logic and illogic, their own organic existence, their own rhythm of development.   Introduction, *Memoirs*, Samuel Cioran, tr. *1983*

2 The fate of a song that has become part of folklore is inscrutable.   Ibid., Ch. 10

3 The working morning. Now I love the morning more than the evening, the spring more than the fall. The promise more than the fulfillment.
          Ibid., Ch. 24

1832. Violeta Parra (1917–1967)

1 I do not play the guitar for applause. I sing the difference that there is between what is true and is false; otherwise I do not sing.
          Remark   *n.d.*

1833. Estelle R. Ramey (1917–   )

1 . . . what is human and the same about the males and females classified as *Homo sapiens* is much greater than the differences.
          ''Men's Monthly Cycles (They Have Them Too, You Know),'' *The First Ms. Reader*, Francine Klagsbrun, ed. *1972*

2 In man, the shedding of blood is always associated with injury, disease, or death. Only the female half of humanity was seen to have the magical ability to bleed profusely and still rise phoenix-like each month from the gore.   Ibid.

3 Women's chains have been forged by men, not by anatomy.   Ibid.

4 I don't mind . . . the fun and games of being treated like a fragile flower. But as a physiologist working with the unromantic scientific facts of life, I find it hard to delude myself about feminine frailty.
          Quoted in *The Prime of Ms. America* by Janet Harris*   *1975*

*See 1790.

5 It is said, for instance, that men are innately more aggressive than women. But conditioning, not sex hormones, makes them that way. Anyone seeing women at a bargain-basement sale—where aggression is viewed as approp-riate, even endearing—sees aggression that would make Attila the Hun turn pale.
          Quoted in ''Are Men and Women Different?'' by Judith Viorst,* *Redbook November 1978*

*See 2092.

1834. Christiane Rochefort (1917–   )

1 CELINE. It's not only that you are killing grass and trees. . . . You are killing LIFE.
          Les Stances à Sophie   *1970*

2 JULIA. Never argue with them. You're always forgetting you're a woman. They never listen to what you're saying, they just want to listen to the music of your voice.   Ibid.

3 You can go to the hospital. If you don't go to the hospital, you can go to marriage. And if you don't go to marriage you can go to the women's movement.

> Quoted in "Les Stances à Sophie"
> by Annette Levy, *Women and Film*
> (Vol. I, Nos. 3 and 4)   *1973*

1835. Han Suyin (1917–   )

1 What we loved best about England was the grass—the short, clean, incredibly green grass with its underlying tough, springy turf, three hundred years growing.

> Ch. 2, *Destination Chungking*   *1942*

2 The city hums with noise and work and hope. This is Chungking, not dead Pompeii—five hundred thousand Chinese with a will to withstand, to endure and build again. Next year, next spring, the planes will lay it waste again. Next autumn we shall be building. . . .

> Ibid., Ch. 12

3 "Your laws are ineffective," Wen declared. "Why? Because no system of control will work as long as most of those administering the law against an evil have more than a finger dipped into it themselves."   Ibid., Ch. 13

4 "I'd sell my love for food any day. The rice bowl is to me the most valid reason in the world for doing anything. A piece of one's soul to the multitudes in return for rice and wine does not seem to me a sacrilege."

> Preface, *A Many-Splendored Thing*
> *1950*

5 Afterwards, as happens when a man is safely dead, they sang his praise.   Ibid., Pt. IV

6 "I'm nicely dead," she told Leo, and it was his turn to find nothing to say.

> Pt. I, Ch. 1, *The Mountain Is Young*
> *1958*

7 . . . all humans are frightened of their own solitude. Yet only in solitude can man learn to know himself, learn to handle his own eternity of aloneness. And love from one being to another can only be that two solitudes come nearer, recognize and protect and comfort each other.   Ibid., Pt. V, Ch. 1

8 For exploitation and oppression is not a matter of *race*. It is the system, the apparatus of worldwide brigandage called imperialism, which made the Powers behave the way they did. I have no illusions on this score, nor do I believe that any Asian nation or African nation, in the same state of dominance, and with the same system of colonial profit-amassing and plunder, would have behaved otherwise.

> Pt. I, Ch. 9, *The Crippled Tree*
> *1965*

9 These ways to make people buy were strange and new to us, and many bought for the sheer pleasure at first of holding in the hand and talking of something new. And once this was done, it was like opium, we could no longer do without this new bauble, and thus, though we hated the foreigners and though we knew they were ruining us, we bought their goods. Thus I learned the art of the foreigners, the art of creating in the human heart restlessness, disquiet, hunger for new things, and these new desires became their best helpers.

> Ibid., Ch. 15

10 "Goldfish are flowers," said Papa, "flowers that move."   Ibid., Pt. II, Ch. 26

1836. Pearl Bailey (1918–1986)

1 There's a period of life when we swallow a knowledge of ourselves and it becomes either good or sour inside.

> Ch. 13, *The Raw Pearl*   *1968*

2 The fact is that it takes more than ingredients and technique to cook a good meal. A good cook puts something of *himself* into the preparation—he cooks with enjoyment, anticipation, spontaneity, and he is willing to experiment.

> Preface, *Pearl's Kitchen*   *1973*

3 My kitchen is a mystical place, a kind of temple for me. It is a place where the surfaces seem to have significance, where the sounds and odors carry meaning that transfers from the past and bridges to the future.   Ibid., "Sanctuary"

4 Hungry people cannot be good at learning or producing anything, except perhaps violence.   Ibid., Epilogue

1837. Peg Bracken (1918–   )

1 . . . unnecessary dieting is because everything from television to fashion ads have made it seem wicked to cast a shadow. This wild, emaciated look appeals to some women, though not to many men, who are seldom seen pinning up a *Vogue* illustration in a machine shop.

> *The I Hate to Cook Book*   *1960*

1838. Gertrude Louise Cheney (1918–   )

1 All people are made alike.
They are made of bone, flesh and dinners.

Only the dinners are different.
                              "People"   *1927*

1839. Tove Ditlevsen (1918–1976)

1. When you have
   once had
   a great joy
   it lasts always
   quivers gently
   on the edge of all the
   insecure adult days
   subdues inherited dread
   makes sleep deeper.
                    "Self-Portrait," St. 1, tr. *Ann
                    Freeman, In the Midst of
                    Winter: Selections from the
                    Literature of Mourning,*
                Mary Jane Moffat,* ed.   1982

*See 2245.

1840. Jeane L. Dixon (1918–   )

1 The rare and beautiful experiences of divine
  revelation are moments of special gifts. Each of
  us, however, lives each day with special gifts
  which are a part of our very being, and life is a
  process of discovering and developing these
  God-given gifts within each of us.
              Ch. 4, *My Life and Prophecies,* with Rene
                    Noorbergen   *1969*

1841. Betty Ford (1918–   )

1 In our society, we get to know one another over
  drinks, we associate feasts and celebrations with
  liquor. We think we have to drink, that it's a
  social necessity . . . It's romantic as long as
  you can handle it—for years I could and did—
  but it's misery when you become addicted.
                    The Times of My Life,
              with Chris Chase   *1979?*

2 My makeup wasn't smeared, I wasn't dishev-
  eled, I behaved politely, and I never finished
  off a bottle, so how could I be alcoholic? And
  I wasn't on heroin or cocaine, the medicines I
  took—the sleeping pills, the pain pills, the re-
  laxer pills, the pills to counteract the side effects
  of other pills—had been prescribed by doctors,
  so how could I be a drug addict?
                    Ch. 2, *Glad Awakening,* with
                    Chris Chase   *1987*

3 . . . a woman . . . told us she was forever
  getting herself into trouble. "But I just keep
  coming back," she said. "I just keep showing
  up for my life."

Showing up for life. Being blessed with the
rebirth that recovery brings.
  One day at a time.   Ibid., Ch. 17

1842. Selma Fraiberg (1918–1981)

1 But the neurotic conscience behaves like a gestapo
  headquarters within the personality, mercilessly
  tracking down dangerous or potentially dangerous ideas and every remote relative of these
  ideas, accusing, threatening, tormenting in an
  interminable inquisition to establish guilt for
  trivial offenses or crimes committed in dreams.
  Such guilt feelings have the effect of putting the
  whole personality under arrest . . .
                    The Magic Years   *1959*

1843. Fay Kanin (1918–   )

1 While other crafts have to sit around chewing
  their fingernails waiting for a movie to be put
  together, writers have one great strength. They
  can sit down and generate their own employment
  and determine their own fate to a great extent
  by the degree of their disciplines, their guts,
  and their talents.
              Quoted in "Fay Kanin," *The Screen-
                    writer Looks at the Screenwriter*
                    by William Froug   *1972*

2 Only an insatiable ego or an intolerable sense
  of inferiority could lead a director to ignore the
  basic creativity of the man or woman who thought
  it up, sweated it out, and delivered those precious pages into his hands.   Ibid.

1844. Corita Kent (1918–   )

1 There are so many hungry people that God
  cannot appear to them except in the form of
  bread.   "Enriched Bread" (silkscreen)
                                        1965

2 One of the things Jesus did was to step aside
  from the organized religion of his time because
  it had become corrupt and bogged down with
  rules. Rules became more important than feeding the hungry.
              Quoted in "A Time of Transition for
                    Corita Kent" by Lucie Kay Scheuer,
                    Los Angeles Times   *11 July 1974*

3 Women's liberation is the liberation of the feminine in the man and the masculine in the
  woman.   Ibid.

4 The real circus with acrobats, jugglers and bare-
  back riders = also an empty field transformed,
  and in the tent artists and freaks, children and

pilgrims and animals are gathered in communion = us   Poster, New York Urban Coalition, Inc.   *n.d.*

1845. Ann Landers (1918–)

1 Women complain about sex more often than men. Their gripes fall into two major categories: (1) Not enough. (2) Too much.
Ch. 2, *Ann Landers Says Truth Is Stranger . . .   1968*

2 What the vast majority of American children needs is to stop being pampered, stop being indulged, stop being chauffeured, stop being catered to. In the final analysis it is not what you do for your children but what you have taught them to do for themselves that will make them successful human beings.   Ibid., Ch. 3

3 All married couples should learn the art of battle as they should learn the art of making love. Good battle is objective and honest—never vicious or cruel. Good battle is healthy and constructive, and brings to a marriage the principle of equal partnership.   Ibid., Ch. 11

4 The mail grew me up in a hurry.
Quoted in "Living By the Letter" by Elizabeth Taylor, *Time   21 August 1989*

5 I don't want anybody calling me Ms.   Ibid.

1846. Ida Lupino (1918–)

1 And believe me, *Bring it in on time* is such a major factor in television that I'd sometimes get absolutely sick to my stomach days beforehand. . . . So any ladies who want to take over men's jobs—if that's what they really want— had better have strong stomachs.
Quoted in *Popcorn Venus* by Marjorie Rosen*   1973

*See 2356.

1847. Anna Magnani (1918–1973)

1 Great passions, my dear, don't exist: they're liars' fantasies. What do exist are little loves that may last for a short or a longer while.
Quoted in "Anna Magnani," *The Egotists* by Oriana Fallaci*   1963

2 . . . I might use foul language, but I do hate bad breeding.   Ibid.

3 Children are like puppies: you have to keep them near you and look after them if you want to have their affection.   Ibid.

1848. Mary McGrory (1918–)

1 But he [Richard M. Nixon]* was like a kamikaze pilot who keeps apologizing for the attack.   Syndicated Newspaper Column
8 November 1962

*(1913–), 37th president of the United States (1969–1974); resigned.

2 Somehow it sounded as though his [Richard M. Nixon's] zeal in providing a generation of peace rather than his efforts to cover up a generation of corruption had gotten him into trouble.
Syndicated Newspaper Column
9 August 1974

3 He [John F. Kennedy]* came on, composed as a prince of the blood, chestnut thatch carefully brushed, facts straight, voice steady. "Look at him," breathed the proud Irishman next to me in the audience. "He's a thoroughbred."
Ibid.

*(1917–1963), 35th president of the United States (1961–1963); assassinated.

1849. Martha Mitchell (1918–1976)

1 I'm not certain that we should have Democrats in the Cabinet.
Interview, "Today Show," NBC-TV
11 February 1971

2 I've never said I was against integration. It should have started right after the Civil War. But why single out the South? The South has been imposed on long enough. It's the orphan of the nation.
Quoted in *Martha: The Mouth That Roared* by Charles Ashman and Sheldon Engelmayer   *1973*

1850. Penelope Mortimer (1918–)

1 In all the years of her marriage, a long war in which attack, if not happening, was always imminent, she had learned an expert cunning. The way to avoid being hurt, to dodge unhappiness, was to run away.
Ch. 1, *Daddy's Gone A-Hunting 1958*

2 It was intensely boring, but they all made a great fuss over me and I began to think that perhaps it was better to be bored and admired than interested and miserable.
Ch. 10, *The Pumpkin Eater 1962*

3 "What do your patients do while you're away? Commit suicide, murder their wives, or do they

just sit and cry and take pills and think about what they told you last time? . . . If I'm sane enough to be left alone with my *thoughts* for two weeks then I'm too sane to need these futile, boring conversations—because my God, they bore me—at six guineas a time."

Ibid., Ch. 11

4 "I have arguments with myself."
"About what?"
"Between the part of me that believes in things, and the part that doesn't."
"And which wins?"
"Sometimes one. Sometimes the other."
"Then stop arguing." Ibid., Ch. 23

1851. June Singer (1918–   )

1 And so Multi-media Man, the contemporary successor to Renaissance Man . . .

Ch. 1, *Boundaries of the Soul, The Practice of Jung's Psychology*   1972

2 As a man's image of the world changes, so a man changes himself. Ibid.

3 In learning to sail you do not change the current of the water nor do you have any effect on the wind, but you learn to hoist your sail and turn it this way and that to utilize the greater forces which surround you. By understanding them, you become one with them, and in doing so are able to find your own direction—so long as it is in harmony with, and does not try to oppose, the greater forces in being. Ibid.

4 The modern man needs to rescue himself from his cultural provincialism. Ibid., Ch. 4

5 Despite the continuing expansion or even explosion of information, there will forever be limits beyond which the devices of science cannot lead a man. Ibid., Ch. 13

6 To begin with, I was first attracted by psychology in general around the age of twelve when I discovered that the psychology books in the public library were kept under lock and key in a glass case and you could only see the titles. That rather intrigued me. Interview
(27 October 1982), *Contemporary Authors,* Vol. ?   1983

1852. Muriel Spark (1918–   )

1 "Being over seventy is like being engaged in a war. All our friends are going or gone and we survive amongst the dead and the dying as on a battlefield." Ch. 4, *Memento Mori* 1959

2 There was altogether too much candour in married life; it was an indelicate modern idea, and frequently led to upsets in a household, if not divorce. Ibid., Ch. 12

3 "Give me a girl at an impressionable age, and she is mine for life."
Ch. 1, *The Prime of Miss Jean Brodie* 1961

4 "One's prime is elusive. You little girls, when you grow up, must be on the alert to recognize your prime at whatever time of your life it may occur. You must then live it to the full."
Ibid.

5 "Art and religion first; then philosophy; lastly science. That is the order of the great subjects of life, that's their order of importance."
Ibid., Ch. 2

6 Kathleen, speaking from that Catholic point of view which takes some getting used to, said, "She was at Confession only the day before she died—wasn't she lucky?"
"The Portobello Road," *Collected Stories: I*   1968

7 She did not know then that the price of allowing false opinions was the gradual loss of one's capacity for forming true ones.
"Bang-Bang You're Dead," op. cit.

8 Oh, the trifles, the people, that get on your nerves when you have a neurosis!
"Come Along, Marjorie," op. cit.

9 New York, home of the vivisectors of the mind, and of the mentally vivisected still to be reassembled, of those who live intact, habitually wondering about their states of sanity, and home of those whose minds have been dead, bearing the scars of resurrection. . . .
Ch. 1, *The Hothouse by the East River* 1973

10 So far as I knew to date, forever was slip-stitch, split-stitch, cross-stitch, back-stitch; and also buttonhole and running stitches . . . all along the dipping and rising hemline, as if for always and always.
"The Dragon," *The Stories of Muriel Spark*   1985

1853. Abigail Van Buren (1918–   )

1 People who fight fire with fire usually end up with ashes.
"Dear Abby" Newspaper Column 7 March 1974

2 Some people are more turned on by money than they are by love. . . . In one respect they're alike. They're both wonderful as long as they last. 26 April 1974, op. cit.

3 Religion, like water, may be free, but when they pipe it to you, you've got to help pay for the piping. And the piper!
28 April 1974, op. cit.

4 Psychotherapy, unlike castor oil, which will work no matter how you get it down, is useless when forced on an uncooperative patient.
11 July 1974, op. cit.

1854. Joy Adamson (1919–1980)

1 How could she [Elsa, the lion] know that it needed all the strength of my love for her to leave her now and give her back to nature—to let her learn to live alone until she might find her pride—her real pride?
"The Second Release,"
Born Free 1960

1855. Isidora Aguirre (1919–)

1 CAROLINA. Besides, when I say "nothing," what I mean is: everything.
Express for Santiago 1960

2 CAROLINA. It's awful to be the wife of a lawyer. *Ibid.*

1856. Jessie Lopez De La Cruz (1919–)

1 I'd hear them scolding their kids and fighting their husbands and I'd say, "Gosh! Why don't you go after the people that have you living like this? Why don't you go after the growers that have you tired from working out in the fields at low wages and keep us poor all the time? Let's go after them! *They're* the cause of our misery!" Quoted in *Moving the Mountain* by Ellen Cantarow 1980

2 They tell us there's no money for food stamps for poor people. But if there is money enough to fight a war in Vietnam, and if there is money enough for Governor Reagan's* wife** to buy a $3,000 dress for the Inauguration Ball, there should be money enough to feed these people. The nutrition experts say surplus food is full of vitamins. . . . But you know, we don't call them vitamins, we call them weevils! *Ibid.*

*Ronald Reagan (1911–), governor of California (1967–75), 40th president of the United States (1980–88), actor;
**Nancy Reagan; see 1893.

3 America was built with small farms. They keep saying that the farmer is the country's backbone. I never heard anything about agribusiness being the backbone of the country, or corporations being the backbone. *Ibid.*

1857. Zsa Zsa Gabor (1919–)

1 Husbands are like fires. They go out when unattended. Quoted in *Newsweek*
28 March 1960

2 I'm a vunderful housekeeper. Effry time I get a divorce I keep the house. Remark *n.d.*

1858. Ella Grasso (1919–1981)

1 I'm opposed to abortion because I happen to believe that life deserves the protection of society. Quoted in "Ella Grasso of Connecticut" by Joseph B. Treaster, *Ms.*
October 1974

2 I would not be President because I do not aspire to be President. But I'm sure that a woman will be President. When? I don't know. It depends. I don't think the woods are full of candidates today. Quoted in *Newsweek*
4 November 1974

1859. Uta Hagen (1919–)

1 More than in the other performing arts the lack of respect for acting seems to spring from the fact that every layman considers himself a valid critic. Introduction, Pt. I, *Respect for Acting*
1973

2 Talent is an amalgam of high sensitivity; easy vulnerability; high sensory equipment (seeing, hearing, touching, smelling, tasting—*intensely*); a vivid imagination as well as a grip on reality; the desire to communicate one's own experience and sensations, to make one's self heard and seen. *Ibid., Ch. I*

3 To maintain one's ideals in ignorance is easy. . . . *Ibid.*

1860. Pauline Kael (1919–)

1 Movies have been doing so much of the same thing—in slightly different ways—for so long that few of the possibilities of this great hybrid art have yet been explored.
Pt. I, "Movies as Opera,"
Going Steady 1968

2 Art is still what teachers and ladies and foundations believe in, it's civilized and refined, cultivated and serious, cultural, beautiful, Eu-

ropean, Oriental: it's what America isn't, and it's especially what American movies are not.   *Ibid.*, Pt. II, Ch. 4

3 The lowest action trash is preferable to wholesome family entertainment. When you clean them up, when you make movies respectable, you kill them. The wellspring of their *art*, their greatness, is in not being respectable.
                                   Ibid., Ch. 6

4 The words "Kiss Kiss Bang Bang," which I saw on an Italian movie poster, are perhaps the briefest statement imaginable of the basic appeal of movies.   Title Note, *Kiss Kiss Bang Bang*
                                                     1968

5 . . . banality and luxuriant wastefulness . . . are so often called the superior "craftsmanship" of Hollywood.   *Ibid.*, Pt. I

6 We may be reaching the end of the era in which individual movies meant something to people. In the new era, movies may just mean a barrage of images.   *Ibid.*, Pt. V

7 Los Angeles, a mock paradise, is so perversely beautiful and so fundamentally unsatisfying that maybe just about everybody there secretly longs to see it come rattling down.
                   "The Current Cinema," *The New Yorker*
                                        2 December 1974

1861. Elizabeth Duncan Koontz
(1919–   )

1 . . . like steel that has been passed through fire, the century will be stronger for having been tested.   Quoted in "Impeachment?"
                            by Claire Safran, *Redbook*
                                           April 1974

1862. Doris Lessing (1919–   )

1 . . . he went onto remark gently that some women seemed to imagine birth control was a sort of magic; if they bought what was necessary and left it lying in a corner of a drawer, nothing more was needed. To this attitude of mind, he said, was due a number of births every year which would astound the public.
                         Pt. I, Ch. 1, *A Proper Marriage*
                                                1952

2 Love had brought her here, to lie beside this young man; love was the key to every good; love lay like a mirage through the golden gates of sex.   *Ibid.*

3 "In university they don't tell you that the greater part of the law is learning to tolerate fools."
                    Pt. III, Ch. 2, *Martha Quest*   *1952*

4 . . . she envied her lost capacity for making the most of time—that was how she put it, as if time were a kind of glass measure which one could fill or not.   *Ibid.*, Pt. IV, Ch. 1

5 What of October, that ambiguous month, the month of tension, the unendurable month?
                                              Ibid.

6 "Sometimes I look at a young man in the States who has a certain resemblance, and I ask myself: Perhaps he is my son? Yes, yes, my friend, this is a question that every man must ask himself, sometimes, is it not?"
                   Ch. 3, *The Habit of Loving*   *1957*

7 Effort, after days of laziness, seemed impossible.   *Ibid.*, Ch. 15

8 . . . he hated her for his ineptitude.
                               "One Off the Short List,"
                         A Man and Two Women   *1958*

9 . . . the rifle, justified by utility. . . .   *Ibid.*

10 "Small things amuse small minds. . . ."
                               "A Woman on a Roof,"
                                           op. cit.

11 "Don't you think there's something awful in two grown people stuck together all the time like Siamese twins?"
                              "A Man and Two Women,"
                                           op. cit.

12 It's not a terrible thing—I mean it may be terrible, but it's not damaging, it's not poisoning to do without something one really wants. . . . What's terrible is to pretend that the second-rate is first-rate. To pretend that you don't need love when you do; or you like your work when you know quite well you're capable of better.
                         The Golden Nootbook   *1962*

13 After a certain age—and for some of us that can be very young—there are no new people, beasts, dreams, faces, events: it has all happened before . . . and everything is an echo and a repetition; and there is no grief even that it is not a recurrence of something long out of memory.
                            Ch. 2, *Particularly Cats*
                                              1967

14 If a fish is the movement of water embodied, given shape, then cat is a diagram and pattern of subtle air.   *Ibid.*

15 Oh cat; I'd say, or pray: be-*oooo*tiful cat! Delicious cat! Exquisite cat! Satiny cat! Cat like a soft owl, cat with paws like moths, jewelled cat, miraculous cat! Cat, cat, cat, cat.   *Ibid.*

16 ". . . that is what learning is. You suddenly understand something you've understood all your life, but in a new way."
                            The Four-Gated City   *1969*

17 This was a happy and satisfactory marriage because both she and Michael had understood,

and very early on, that the core of discontent, or of hunger, if you like, which is unfailingly part of every modern marriage . . . was fed and heightened by what people were educated to expect of marriage, which was a very great deal because the texture of ordinary life . . . was thin and unsatisfactory. Marriage had had a load heaped on it which it could not sustain.
The Summer Before the Dark 1973

18 [I wanted] a simultaneous knowledge of vastness and of smallness.
The Memoirs of a Survivor 1975

19 It's almost impossible for anyone in the West not to see the West as the God-given gift to the world.
Quoted in "Doris Lessing on Feminism, Communism and 'Space Fiction' " by Lesley Hazleton, *The New York Times Magazine* 25 July 1982

20 There are certain types of people who are political out of a kind of religious reason. I think it's fairly common among socialists: they are, in fact, God-seekers, looking for the kingdom of God on earth. A lot of religious reformers have been like that, too. It's the same psychological set, trying to abolish the present in favor of some better future—always taking it for granted that there is a better future. If you don't believe in heaven, then you believe in socialism.
Ibid.

21 The human community is evolving. . . . We can survive anything you care to mention. We are supremely equipped to survive, to adapt and even in the long run to start thinking. Ibid.

1863. Iris Murdoch (1919–)

1 "What are you famous *for*?"
"For nothing. I am just famous."
The Flight from the Enchanter 1955

2 "We can only learn to love by loving. . . ." *The Bell* 1958

3 "You cannot have both civilization and truth. . . ." *A Severed Head* 1961

4 "To be a complete victim may be another source of power." *The Unicorn* 1963

5 Love can't always do work. Sometimes it just has to look into the darkness.
The Nice and the Good 1968

6 He led a double life. Did that make him a liar? He did not feel a liar. He was a man of two truths.
The Sacred and Profane Love Machine 1974

1864. Françoise Parturier (1919–)

1 In general all curvaciousness strikes men as incompatible with the life of the mind.
Open Letter to Men 1968

2 And the more deodorants there are in the drugstores, the worse [woman] smells in literature. Ibid.

3 That the most intelligent, discerning and learned men, men of talent and feeling, should finally put all their pride in their crotch, as awed as they are uneasy at the few inches sticking out in front of them, proves how normal it is for the world to be crazy. . . . Ibid.

4 . . . we've never been in a democracy; we've always been in a phallocracy! Ibid.

1865. Eva Perón (1919–1952)

1 Our President [General Juan Perón] has declared that the only privileged person in our country are the children. Speech, "My Labour in the Field of Social Aid," American Congress of Industrial Medicine 5 December 1949

2 Almsgiving tends to perpetuate poverty; aid does away with it once and for all. Almsgiving leaves a man just where he was before. Aid restores him to society as an individual worthy of all respect and not as a man with a grievance. Almsgiving is the generosity of the rich; social aid levels up social inequalities. Charity separates the rich from the poor; aid raises the needy and sets him on the same level with the rich. Ibid.

1866. May Swenson (1919–1989)

1 We play in the den of the Gods and snort at death "To Confirm A Thing," St. 2, *New and Selected Things Taking Place* 1978

2 The summer that I was ten—
Can it be there was only one summer that I was ten? It must
have been a long one then—
"The Centaur," Sts. 1 & 2, *To Mix with Time* 1963

3 I was the horse and the rider . . .
Ibid., St. 13

1867. Mary Carolyn Davies (fl. 1920s–1930s)

1 A trap's a very useful thing:
Nature in our path sets Spring. "Traps" *n.d.*

2 If I had known what trouble you were bearing;
What griefs were in the silence of your face;
I would have been more gentle, and more car-
ing,
And tried to give you gladness for a space.
                    "If I Had Known"   n.d.

3 The talking oak
to the ancient spoke.
But any tree
Will talk to me.
                    "Be Different to Trees"   n.d.

4 Women are doormats and have been,
   The years these mats applaud—
They keep the men from going in
   With muddy feet to God.
                    "Door-Mats"   n.d.

1868. Mary J. Elmendorf (fl. 1920s)

1 Beauty's the thing that counts
In women; red lips
And black eyes are better than brains.
                    "Beauty's the Thing"   n.d.

1869. Elizabeth Shane (fl. 1920s)

1 But every road is tough to me
That has no friend to cheer it.   "Sheskinbeg"
                                         n.d.

1870. Margaret Turnbull (fl. 1920s–d. 1942)

1 No man is responsible for his father. That is
entirely his mother's affair.   *Alabaster Lamps*
                                         1925

2 When a man confronts catastrophe on the road,
he looks in his purse—but a woman looks in
her mirror.   *The Left Lady*
                              1926

1871. Violeta Chamorro (192?–   )

1 Isn't it strange that during Somoza* we were
called a yellow, communist paper. Now we are
called a Reagan paper.
            Quoted in "Once-lively paper is
               dead under Sandinistas" by
            Rick Raber, *The Times-Picayune*
                              22 February 1987

*Anastasio Somoza (1896–1956), soldier/politician who
was dictator of Nicaragua, (1936–1956); succeeded by son,
Luis Anastasio Somoza (1922–1967), president (1957–
1963).

2 We [the newspaper staff] will die here.   Ibid.

1872. Betty Rollin (192?–   )

1 . . . biological *possibility* and desire are not the
same as biological *need*. Women have childbearing equipment. For them to choose not to
use the equipment is no more blocking what is
instinctive than it is for a man who, muscles or
no, chooses not to be a weightlifter.
            "Motherhood: Who Needs It," *Look*
                              16 May 1971

2 How can birth-control programs really be effective as long as the concept of glorious motherhood remains unchanged? (Even poor old Planned
Parenthood has to euphemize—why not Planned
Unparenthood?)   Ibid.

3 Motherhood affords an instant identity. First,
through wifehood, you are somebody's wife;
then you are somebody's mother. Both give not
only identity and activity, but status and stardom
of a kind.   Ibid.

1873. Bella Abzug (1920–   )

1 I am not elevating women to sainthood, nor am
I suggesting that all women share the same
views, or that all women are good and all men
bad. Women have screamed for war. Women,
like men, have stoned black children going to
integrated schools. Women have been and are
prejudiced, narrowminded, reactionary, even
violent. *Some* women. They, of course, have a
right to vote and a right to run for office. I will
defend that right, but I will not support them or
vote for them.
            Speech, National Women's Political
               Caucus, Washington, D.C.
                              10 July 1971

2 I've been described as a tough and noisy woman,
a prize fighter, a man-hater, you name it. They
call me Battling Bella, Mother Courage, and a
Jewish mother with more complaints than Port-
noy. There are those who say I'm impatient,
impetuous, uppity, rude, profane, brash, and
overbearing. Whether I'm any of those things,
or all of them, you can decide for yourself. But
whatever I am—and this ought to be made very
clear at the outset—I am a very serious
woman.
Introduction, *Bella!*, Mel Ziegler, ed.   *1972*

3 One thing that crystallized for me like nothing
else this year is that Congress is a very *unrep-
resentative* institution. . . . These men in Congress . . . represent their *own* point of view—
by reason of their sex, background, and
class.   Epilogue, op. cit.

4 You can't have a Congress that responds to the needs of the workingman when there are practically no people here who represent him. And you're not going to have a society that understands its humanity if you don't have more women in government.
Quoted in "Impeachment?" by Claire Safran, *Redbook*   *April 1974*

1874. Rosemary Brown (1920–   )

1 I'm not committed to welfare measures. I don't think they get at the root of the problem. I'm committed to the eradication of all poverty, to its being wiped out. I'm not hung up on guaranteed incomes and that kind of thing, because I don't think that's the solution. We've got to change the system and make it impossible to be poor.   Quoted in "The Radical Tradition of Rosemary Brown" by Sharon Batt, *Branching Out*   *July/August 1975*

2 We cannot swing our vote. We have to swing our party.   Ibid.

1875. Liz Carpenter (1920–   )

1 I thought that we would wake up this morning and have the same rights as our husbands, grandsons and garbagemen—but we are still begging to be let into our country's Constitution.*   Speech, Thursday Caucus, New York City *22 March 1979*

*After the defeat of the Equal Rights Amendment; see 1355:2.

2 And what was a shy, retiring homebody like me doing, bounding around between fifteen unratified states? I do it because I can't not do it. I do it because of indignation that women were left out in the first place and have always fought other people's battles in lieu of their own. I do it because I figure life has been good to me and I have the chance to say thanks. The Lord won't like me very well if I don't. And I won't like myself very well, either.
Speech, National Women's Political Caucus Conference, Albuquerque, New Mexico   *July 1981*

1876. Alice Childress (1920–   )

1 OLDTIMER. Child, when hard luck fall it just keep fallin'. *Wine in the Wilderness*   1969

2 TOMMY. I'm independent as a hog on ice and a hog on ice is dead, cold, well-preserved and don't need a mother'grabbin' thing.   Ibid.

3 TOMMY. I'm just sick-a hair, hair, hair. Do it this way, don't do it, leave it natural, straighten it, process, no process. I get sick-a hair and talkin' 'bout it and foolin' with it. That's why I wear the wig.   Ibid.

4 Today our youngsters can freely discuss sex. Soon they will even be able to openly discuss one of the results of sex-life.
"Alice Childress," *Interviews with Contemporary Women Playwrights*, Kathleen Betsko* & Rachel Koenig   *1987*

*See 2256.

5 . . . "the good old days." The only good days are ahead.   Ibid.

6 I think women need kindness more than love. When one human being is kind to another, it's a very deep matter.   Ibid.

1877. Rosalind Franklin (1920–1958)

1 This was my first continental holiday by car . . . and I confirmed my impression that cars are undesirable. . . . Travelling around in a little tin box isolates one from the people and the atmosphere of the place in a way that I have never experienced before. I found myself eyeing with envy all rucksacks and tents.
Quoted in *Rosalind Franklin and DNA* by Anne Sayre   *1975*

1878. Barbara Guest (1920–   )

1 I wonder if this new reality is going to destroy me.   "The Hero Leaves His Ship," St. 1, *The Location of Things*   1962

2 I am talking to you
With what is left of me written off,
On the cuff, ancestral and vague,
As a monkey walks through the many fires
Of the jungle while the village breathes in its sleep.   "Sunday Evening," St. 3, op. cit.

3 Then you took my hand. You told me that love was a sudden disturbance of the nerve ends that startled the fibers and made them new again.   "Sadness," St. 3, op. cit.

1879. Mary Anne Guitar (c. 1920–   )

1 We have to stop being so teacher-centered, and become student-centered. It's not what you think they need, but what they think they need. That's the functional approach.

"College Marriage Courses—Fun or
Fraud?," *Mademoiselle*
February 1961

1880. Helen Hudson (1920–   )

1 A white casket with silver handles, she thought.
Not a soft bed with a pink quilt but four sides
and a lid that closes. To be shipped like a shoe
in a box from this world to the next.
"Sunday Morning," *American Scene:
New Voices,* Don Wolfe, ed.   *1963*

2 As he worked, putting the mask of sleep over
the faces of death, he felt a vague excitement,
as though he were, indeed, reviving her, as
though the eyes he had closed so carefully might
open again and see him, without reproach: a
kindly man who knew his trade and did it
well.   Ibid.

1881. Shirley Jackson (1920–1965)

1 I believe that all women, but especially housewives, tend to think in lists. . . . The idea of
a series of items, following one another docilely,
forms the only possible reasonable approach to
life if you have to live it with a home and a
husband and children, none of whom would
dream of following one another docilely.
Pt. II, *Life Among the Savages*
1953

2 "Cocoa," she said. "Cocoa. Damn miserable
puny stuff, fit for kittens and unwashed boys.
Did *Shakespeare* drink cocoa?"
Pt. I, *The Bird's Nest*   *1954*

3 . . .I saw that Beth now, looking about her and
drawing herself together, was endeavoring to
form herself, as it were; let my reader who is
puzzled by my awkward explanations close his
eyes for no more than two minutes, and see if
he does not find himself suddenly not a compact
human being at all, but only a consciousness on
a sea of sound and touch; it is only with the
eyes open that a corporeal form returns, and
assembles itself firmly around the hard core of
sight.   Ibid., Pt. IV

4 Her manner of dress, of speech, of doing her
hair, of spending her time, had not changed
since it first became apparent to a far younger
Morgen that in all her life to come no one was,
in all probability, going to care in the slightest
how she looked, or what she did, and the minor
wrench of leaving humanity behind was more
than compensated for by her complacent freedom from a thousand small irritations.
Ibid., Pt. V

5 It has long been my belief that in times of great
stress, such as a four-day vacation, the thin
veneer of family unity wears off almost at once,
and we are revealed in our true personalities. . . .
Pt. IV, *Raising Demons.*   *1956*

6 She looked out the window . . . savoring the
extreme pleasure of being on a moving train
with nothing to do for six hours but read and
nap and go into the dining-car, going farther
and farther every minute from the children, from
the kitchen floor, with even the hills being
incredibly left behind, changing into fields and
trees too far away from home to be daily.
"Pillar of Salt," *The Magic of Shirley
Jackson,* Stanley Edgar Hyman, ed.
1966

1882. Gerda Lerner (1920–   )

1 Black people cannot and will not become integrated into American society on any terms but
those of self-determination and autonomy.
Preface, *Black Women in White America*
1972

2 . . . black women . . . are trained from childhood to become workers, and expect to be
financially self-supporting for most of their lives.
They know they will have to work, whether
they are married or single; work to them, unlike
to white women, is not a liberating goal, but
rather an imposed lifelong necessity.   Ibid.

3 . . . American social movements: they rise fast,
they wane fast, and they seem to disappear.
History tells us that this is not really true.
Quoted in "On the Future of Our
Past" by Catharine R. Stimpson,
Ms.   *September 1981*

4 . . . women's history is the primary tool for
women's emancipation.   Ibid.

5 Today, we can be defeated in regard to laws, to
appropriations, to representation, but if we are
truly transforming consciousness, we cannot be
defeated.   Ibid.

6 Everything that explains the world has in fact
explained a world that does not exist, a world
in which men are at the center of the human
enterprise and women are at the margin "helping" them. Such a world does not exist—never
has.   Ibid.

1883. Elaine Morgan (1920–   )

1 The trouble with specialists is that they tend to
think in grooves.
Ch. 1, *The Descent of Woman*
1972

2 We had taken the first step along the tortuous road that led to the sex war, sado-masochism, and ultimately to the whole contemporary snarl-up, to prostitution, prudery, Casanova, John Knox, Marie Stopes, white slavery, women's liberation, *Playboy* magazine, *crimes passionels,* censorship, strip clubs, alimony, pornography, and a dozen different brands of mania. This was the Fall. It had nothing to do with apples.   Ibid., Ch. 4

3 Housewives and mothers seldom find it practicable to come out on strike. They have no union, anyway.   Ibid., Ch. 11

1884. Gabriela Roepke (1920–)

1 AMANDA. I just can't seem to go on—without a good morning in a big baritone voice.
A White Butterfly   1960

2 SMITH. . . . the reflection in my shaving mirror tells me things nobody else ever would.   Ibid.

3 OLD LADY. The best thing others can do for us is to tell us lies.   Ibid.

1885. Hazel Scott (1920–1981)

1 There's only one free person in this society, and he is white and male.
Quoted in "Great (Hazel) Scott!" by Margo Jefferson, *Ms.* November 1974

2 Who ever walked behind anyone to freedom? If we can't go hand in hand, I don't want to go.   Ibid.

1886. Dinah Shore (1920–)

1 I earn and pay my own way as a great many women do today. Why should unmarried women be discriminated against—unmarried men are not.   Quoted in "Dinah," *Los Angeles Times* 16 April 1974

2 I have never thought of participating in sports just for the sake of doing it for exercise or as a means to lose weight. And I've never taken up a sport just because it was a social fad. I really enjoy playing. It is a vital part of my life.
Ibid.

1887. Harriet Van Horne (1920–)

1 Cooking is like love. It should be entered into with abandon or not at all.   Quoted in *Vogue* October 1956

1888. Carol Emshwiller (1921–)

1 As a mother I have served longer than I expected.
"Autobiography," *Joy in Our Cause* 1974

2 Mother wants me to write something nice she can show to her friends.   Ibid.

1889. Betty Friedan (1921–)

1 Over and over women heard in voices of tradition and Freudian sophistication that they could desire no greater destiny than to glory in their own femininity [and] to pity the neurotic, unfeminine, unhappy women who wanted to be poets or physicians or presidents.
Ch. 1, *The Feminine Mystique*   1963

2 American women no longer know who they are.   Ibid., Ch. 3

3 The most powerful influence on modern women, in terms of both functionalism and the feminine protest, was Margaret Mead.* . . . She was, and still is, the symbol of the woman thinker in America.   Ibid., Ch. 6

*See 1579.

4 Female biology, women's "biological career-line," may be changeless . . . but the nature of the human relationship to biology *has* changed.   Ibid.

5 For, of course, the natural childbirth-breastfeeding movement Margaret Mead* helped to inspire was not at all a return to primitive earth-mother maternity. It appealed to the independent, educated, spirited . . . woman . . . because it enabled her to experience childbirth not as a mindless female animal, an object manipulated by the obstetrician, but as a whole person, able to control her own body with her aware mind.   Ibid.

*See 1579.

6 Instead of fulfilling the promise of infinite orgastic bliss, sex in the America of the feminine mystique is becoming a strangely joyless national compulsion, if not a contemptuous mockery.   Ibid., Ch. 11

7 It is easier to live through someone else than to become complete yourself.   Ibid., Ch. 14

8 The problem that has no name—which is simply the fact that American women are kept from growing to their full human capacities—is taking a far greater toll on the physical and mental health of our country than any known disease.   Ibid.

9 If divorce has increased one thousand percent, don't blame the woman's movement. Blame our obsolete sex roles on which our marriages were based.   Speech   20 January 1974

10 Sexual war against men is an irrelevant, self-defeating acting out of rage.
                    The Second Stage   1981

11 The most important effect of transcending those old sex roles may be an evolution of morality and religious thought. . . .   Ibid.

12 This uneasy sense of battles won, only to be fought over again, of battles that should have been won, according to all the rules, and yet are not, of battles that suddenly one does not really want to win, and the weariness of battle altogether—how many women feel it?   Ibid.

13 Today the problem that has no name,* is how to juggle work, love, home and children.
                    Ibid.

*See quotation 2.

1890. Juanita Kreps (1921–   )

1 I'd like to get to the point where I can be just as mediocre as a man.
                    Quoted in American Political Women
                    by Esther Stineman   1980

1891. Eeva-Liisa Manner (1921–   )

1 MAIJA. Artfulness is a kind of capital.
                    Act I, Sc. 1, Snow in May   1966

2 LASSI. Love makes intelligent beings depressed and flat. Only women, ostriches and monkeys are made happy by love. Oh yes, and parrots.   Ibid., Act II, Sc. 1

3 LASSI. The female is designed on the same principle as the starfish. Those creatures that the woman doesn't swallow she melts outside her body until the soft parts dissolve and only the shell remains.   Ibid.

4 PAAVO. Illusions! Illusions. Illusion of innocent love. Illusion of the heart's goodness, illusion of the sacredness of the pure life. But your virtuousness is only love of comfort, bourgeois self-satisfaction. Give up what you hold so dear: your illusions, and you can return to reality and become your real self.   Ibid., Sc. 2

5 HELENA. If hope shows the depth of sorrow, then hopelessness must cure sorrow.   Ibid.

6 PAAVO. Great men are born in stable straw and they are put in a basket of reeds for the river to carry away. They are allowed to form their own

souls—God looks after their bodies. They're not fed with warm milk, they must drink from the streams of the world, they do dirty work; the polisher of the mirror has dirty hands.
                    Ibid., Sc. 3

7 LASSI. Women! There isn't anything so bad that they don't soon start to enjoy it. Even if they lived in a barrel of shit they'd start making a home out of it, with everything nice and cozy.   Ibid., Act III, Sc. 1

1892. Del Martin (1921–   )

1 To understand the lesbian as a sexual being, one must understand woman as a sexual being.
                    Lesbian/Woman, with Phyllis Lyon*
                    1972

*See 1937.

2 It is only when she can denounce the idiocy of religious scriptures and legal strictures that bind her and can affirm her Lesbian nature as but a a single facet of her whole personality that she can become fully human.   Ibid.

3 There is nothing mysterious or magical about lesbian lovemaking . . . The mystery and the magic come from the person with whom you are making love.   Ibid.

4 The higher on the evolutionary scale you are, the less instinctive are your sexual relations. So our life experiences "teach" us our sexuality, which may turn out to be hetero, homo, or bi.   Ibid.

1893. Nancy Reagan (1921–   )

1 The Sixties, of course, was the worst time in the world to try and bring up a child. They were exposed to all these crazy things going on.
                    Quoted in "Reflections of a
                    Woman in Love" by Dotson Rader,
                    Parade   8 November 1981

2 Where would we be without the movies?
                    Filmex Tribute to Elizabeth Taylor,*
                    Quoted in "The Great Life"
                    by George Cristy, The Hollywood
                    Reporter   November 1981

*See 2120.

1894. Donna Reed (1921–1986)

1 If nuclear power plants are safe, let the commercial insurance industry insure them. Until these most expert judges of risk are willing to

gamble with their money, I'm not willing to gamble with the health and safety of my family. Quoted in the *Los Angeles Times* *12 March 1974*

1895 Hannah Senesh (1921–1944)

1 One needs something to believe in, something for which one can have whole-hearted enthusiasm. One needs to feel that one's life has meaning, that one is needed in this world.
Diary entry (1938), *Hannah Senesh: Her Life and Diary* *1966*

2 I dream and plan as if there was nothing happening in the world, as if there was no war, no destruction, as if thousands upon thousands were not being killed daily. . . .
Ibid. (2 November 1940)

3 There are events without which one's life becomes unimportant, a worthless toy; and there are times when one is commanded to do something, even at the price of one's life.
Ibid. (25 December 1943)

1896. Mona Van Duyn (1921–)

1 I pray that the great world's flowering
stay as it is. "The Gardener to His God," St. 1, *A Time of Bees*   *n.d.*

2 There is no disorder but the heart's.
Ibid., St. 2

1897. Alison Wyrley Birch (1922–)

1 There are sounds to seasons. There are sounds to places, and there are sounds to every time in one's life. Quoted in *The Christian Science Monitor* *23 January 1974*

1898. Ruth Brinker (1922–)

1 You have to go out and beg.*
Quoted in "Open Heart, Open Hand," *Time* *9 January 1989*

*Referring to fundraising for her Project Open Hand, which feeds victims of AIDS.

1899. Helen Gurley Brown (1922–)

1 You may marry or you may not. In today's world that is no longer the big question for women. Those who glom on to men so that they can collapse with relief, spend the rest of their days shining up their status symbol and figure they never have to reach, stretch, learn, grow, face dragons or make a living again are the ones to be pitied. They, in my opinion, are the unfulfilled ones.
Sex and the Single Girl   *1963*

1900. Eugenie Clark (1922–)

1 Not many appreciate the ultimate power and potential usefulness of basic knowledge accumulated by obscure, unseen investigators who, in a lifetime of intensive study, may never see any practical use for their findings but who go on seeking answers to the unknown without thought of financial or practical gain.
Ch. 1, *The Lady and the Sharks* *1969*

2 In the beginning, I wanted to enter what was essentially a man's field. I wanted to prove I could do it. Then I found that when I did as well as the men in the field I got more credit for my work because I am a woman, which seems unfair. Quoted in "Shark Tamer" by Madeleine Lundberg, *Ms.   August 1979*

3 It seems as though women keep growing. Eventually they can have little or nothing in common with the men they chose long ago.   Ibid.

1901. Judith Crist (1922–)

1 The critics who love are the severe ones . . . we know our relationship must be based on honesty.
Introduction, *The Private Eye, the Cowboy and the Very Naked Girl* *1968*

2 In this lovely land of corrugated cartons and plastic bags, we want our entertainment packaged as neatly as the rest of our consumer goods: an attractive label on the outside, a complete and accurate detailing of contents there or on the inside, no loose ends, no odd parts, nothing left out. "*Hud:* Unpackaged Reality" (2 June 1963), op. cit.

3 In this era of affluence and of permissiveness, we have, in all but cultural areas, bred a nation of overprivileged youngsters, saturated with vitamins, television and plastic toys. But they are nurtured from infancy on a Dick-and-Jane literary and artistic level; and the cultural drought, as far as entertainment is concerned, sets in when they are between six and eight.

"Forgotten Audience: American Children" (2 May 1965), op. cit.

4 . . . the outcry against the current spate of sadism and violence in films is . . . more than justified by the indecencies that we are being subjected to on the big screen (and more and more on the little one at home), by the puddles of blood and piles of guts pouring forth from the quivering flesh that is being lashed and smashed, by the bouncing of breast and grinding of groin, by the brutalizing of men and desecration of women being fed to us by the hour for no possible social, moral or intellectual purpose beyond our erotic edification and sensual delight and, above all, the almighty box-office return. "Against the Groin" (December 1967), op. cit.

1902. Mavis Gallant (1922–)

1 Flor looked at his closed fist. "Why do people keep things?" she said.
"I don't know," said George. "I guess it proves you were somewhere."
Ch. 1, *Green Water, Green Sky* 1959

2 Success can only be measured in terms of distance traveled. . . . Ibid.

3 No people are ever as divided as those of the same blood. . . . *Its Image on the Mirror* 1964

4 Until the time of my own marriage I had sworn I would settle for nothing less than a certain kind of love. However, I had become convinced, after listening to my mother and to others as well, that a union of that sort was too fantastic to exist; nor was it desirable. The reason for its undesirability was never plain. It was one of the definite statements of rejection young persons must learn to make; "Perfect love cannot last" is as good a beginning as any. Ibid.

5 The Knights had been married nearly sixteen years. They considered themselves solidly united. Like many people no longer in love, they cemented their relationship with opinions, pet prejudices, secret meanings, a private vocabulary that enabled them to exchange amused glances over a dinner table and made them feel a shade superior to the world outside the house. "Bernadette," *My Heart Is Broken* 1964

6 She had the loaded handbag of someone who camps out and seldom goes home, or who imagines life must be full of emergencies. Ch. 5, *A Fairly Good Time* 1970

7 Nobody in movies ever runs out of cigarettes or has to look for parking space. Ibid., Ch. 12

8 The worst punishment I can imagine must be solitary confinement with nothing for entertainment except news of the world. Ibid.

9 She had gone into captivity believing in virtue and learned she could steal. Went in loving the poor, came out afraid of them; went in generous, came out grudging; went in with God, came out alone. "The Pegnitz Junction," *The Pegnitz Junction* 1973

10 Now that he was rich he was not thought ignorant any more, but simply eccentric. Ibid.

1903. Judy Garland (1922–1969)

1 . . . they [MGM] had us working days and nights on end. They'd give us pep-up pills to keep us on our feet long after we were exhausted. Then they'd take us to the studio hospital and knock us cold with sleeping pills— Mickey [Rooney] sprawled out on one bed and me on another. Then after four hours they'd wake us up and give us the pep-up pills again so we could work another seventy-two hours in a row. Half of the time we were hanging from the ceiling, but it became a way of life for us. Quoted in Ch. 11, *Judy Garland* by Anne Edwards* 1975

*See 1995.

2 Before every free conscience in America is subpoenaed, please speak up! Ibid., Ch. 19 (c.1947)

3 How strange when an illusion dies
It's as though you've lost a child. . . . "An Illusion," op. cit.

4 For 'twas not into my ear you whispered but into my heart.
'Twas not my lips you kissed, but my soul. "My Love Is Lost," op. cit.

1904. Blanche H. Gelfant (1922–)

1 Friendships, like geraniums, bloom in kitchens. Love runs up and down a flight of stairs and enters one flat and another in the housing projects. *Women Writing in America: Voices in Collage* 1985

2 [I have a] preference for criticism that is open-ended, capable of surprise, and subversive of

traditional standards and forms . . . Juxtaposition of disparate pieces allows for new ways of seeing, for re-vision [sic], the activity central to feminist criticism. *Ibid.*

1905. Grace Hartigan (1922–)

1 . . . the face the world puts on to sell itself to the world.
> Quoted by Cindy Nemser in *Art Talk* (magazine) *1975*

2 I'd like to think that there are some things that . . . can't be analyzed to the point where they're finished off, either. *Ibid.*

3 There's a time when what you're creating and the environment you're creating it in come together. *Ibid.*

1906. Gladys Heldman (1922–)

1 Players are always in the foreground, and they should be . . . anything else would be like Sol Hurok thinking that *he* was the star when it is really the ballet.
> Quoted in "Queen of the Long-Way Babies" by Dan Rose, *Signature August 1974*

1907. Gertrude Himmelfarb (1922–)

1 The old feminism spoke the language of liberation. . . . The new feminism speaks the language of power.
> Quoted in "Are women leaders wielding power differently than men?" by Georgie Anne Geyer,* *Seattle Times 14 May 1989*

*See 2170.

1908. Eda J. LeShan (1922–)

1 . . . most of us carry into marriage not only our childlike illusions, but we bring to it as well the demand that is *has* to be wonderful, because it's *supposed* to be. Of course the biggest illusion of all is that we are going to do the job of parenthood so well: it will all be fun and always deeply satisfying.
> Ch. 2, *How to Survive Parenthood 1965*

2 Psychotherapy can be one of the greatest and most rewarding adventures, it can bring with it the deepest feelings of personal worth, of purpose and richness in living. It doesn't mean that one's life situation will change dramatically or suddenly. . . . It does mean that one can develop new capacities and strengths with which to meet the natural vicissitudes of living; that one may gain a sense of inner peace through greater self-acceptance, through a more realistic perspective on one's relationships and experiences.
> *Ibid.*, Ch. 11

3 . . . in all our efforts to provide "advantages" we have actually produced the busiest, most competitive, highly pressured and over-organized generation of youngsters in our history— and possibly the unhappiest. We seem hell-bent on eliminating much of childhood.
> Ch. 1, *The Conspiracy Against Childhood 1967*

4 Babies are necessary to grown-ups. A new baby is like the beginning of all things—wonder, hope, a dream of possibilities. In a world that is cutting down its trees to build highways, losing its earth to concrete . . . babies are almost the only remaining link with nature, with the natural world of living things from which we spring.
> *Ibid.*, Ch. 2

5 We are not asking our children to do their own best but to be *the* best. Education is in danger of becoming a religion based on fear; its doctrine is to compete. The majority of our children are being led to believe that they are doomed to failure in a world which has room only for those at the top.
> *Ibid.*, Ch. 5

1909. Carmen McRae (1922–)

1 Blues is to jazz what yeast is to bread—without it, it's flat. Speech, "Blues Is A Woman,"
> Newport Jazz Festival Concert, Avery Fisher Hall, New York City *2 July 1980*

1910. Grace Paley (1922–)

1 He had had a habit throughout the twenty-seven years of making a narrow remark which, like a plumber's snake, could work its way through the ear down the throat, halfway to my heart. He would then disappear, leaving me choking with equipment.
> *Enormous Changes at the Last Minute 1960*

2 . . . a very large family. Four brothers and three sisters, they wouldn't touch birth control with a basement beam. Orthodox. Constructive fucking. Builders, baby. *Ibid.*

3 I don't believe civilization can do a lot more than educate a person's senses. If it's truth and

honor you want to refine, I think the Jews have some insight. Make no images, imitate no God. After all, in His field, the graphic arts, He is pre-eminent. Then let that One who made the tan deserts and the blue Van Allen belt and the green mountains of New England be in charge of Beauty, which He obviously understands, and let man, who was full of forgiveness at Jerusalem, and full of survival at Troy, let man be in charge of Good.   Ibid.

4 Rosiness is not a worse windowpane than gloomy gray when viewing the world.   Ibid.

5 I was a fantastic student until ten, and then my mind began to wander.
Quoted in Grace Paley: "Art Is on the Side of the Underdog" by Harriet Shapiro, *Ms.*   *March 1974*

6 There isn't a story written that isn't about blood and money. People and their relationship to each other is the blood, the family. And how they live, the money of it.   Ibid.

7 Nobody lives without a personal life.
"Grace Paley: Fragments for a Portrait in Collage," *Women Writing in America: Voices in Collage* by Blanche H. Gelfant*   *1984*

*See 1904.

8 I believe in a kind of fidelity to your own early ideas; it's a kind of antagonism in me to prevailing fads.   Ibid.

9 But the fun of talking, Ruthy. What about that? It's as good as fucking lots of times. Isn't it?
Oh boy, Ruth said, if it's that good, then it's got to be that bad.
"The Expensive Moment," *Later the Same Day   1985*

1911. Vera Randal (1922–   )

1 Time, dough in a bowl, rose, doubling, trebling in bulk, and I was in the middle of the swelling, yeasty mass—lost.
"Alice Blaine," *The Inner Room 1964*

2 ". . . If this is July, what, precisely, happened to June, and a sizable slice of May?"   Ibid.

3 "John is dead."
"Yes."
"I am also dead," I said numbly.
"You're not dead. You're very far from dead."
"I feel dead."
"That's different."
"Is it?" I said. "Is it really?"
"It is. Really."   Ibid.

4 "I believe in people, which I suppose is a way of believing in God."   Ibid.

1912. Alice Rossi (1922–   )

1 A really radical break from the confinement of sex roles might lie in women's search for mates from very different social and intellectual circles, men who are not vain, self-centered and ambitious but tenderly devoted to home and children and the living of life.
Pt. I, "The Making of a Cosmopolitan Humanist," *The Feminist Papers   1973*

2 As economic affluence increased with the growth of the new industrialism and expansion of trade, women's worth declined as producers and increased as consumers.
Ibid., Pt. II, Introduction

3 It is curious that it may be the help of a housekeeper and a friend that facilitates a woman's life's work, while the closest analogy . . . one would find from the pen of a man is typically a tribute to his wife.
Ibid., "A Feminist Friendship"

4 Equal pay for equal work continues to be seen as applying to equal pay for men and women in the same occupation, while the larger point of continuing relevance in our day is that some occupations have depressed wages because women are the chief employees. The former is a pattern of sex discrimination, the latter of institutionalized sexism.   Ibid.

5 The single most impressive fact about the attempt by American women to obtain the right to vote is how long it took.
Ibid., "Along the Suffrage Trail"

6 Without the means to prevent, and to control the timing of conception, economic and political rights have limited meaning for women. If women cannot plan their pregnancies, they can plan little else in their lives. . . .
Ibid., "The Right to One's Body"

7 The drum-beating martial mood of wartime is often followed by a pot-stirring and baby-rocking domestic ethos in its aftermath.
Ibid., Pt. IV, Introduction

8 Abridgement of any published book or essay is an assault, a cutting or pruning by one mind of the work of another.
Ibid., "Guineas and Locks"

1913. Renee Winegarten (1922–   )

1 The book of the faults and complexities of the present cannot be closed like that containing the difficulties and errors of the past. . . .
"The Idea of Decadence," *Commentary September 1974*

2 The mighty are fallen and we shall not look upon their like again. Ibid.

3 We still tend to share the idea that civilization must be either growing and pressing ever onward and upward, or else disintegrating into nothingness, instead of going on, variously developing and changing in a multitude of different areas, in ways not always perceptible to the human eye. Ibid.

4 . . . the quest for origin and end, zenith and nadir, growth and decline, rise and fall, florescence and decadence. Where would writers be without these essential props for their narrative? Ibid.

1914. Shelley Winters (1922–)

1 It was so cold I almost got married.
Quoted in *The New York Times*
29 April 1956

1915. Diane Arbus (1923–1971)

1 I really believe there are things nobody would see if I didn't photograph them.
Diane Arbus 1972

2 Most people go through life dreading they'll have a traumatic experience. Freaks are born with their trauma. They've already passed it. They're aristocrats. Ibid.

3 My favorite thing is to go where I've never been. Ibid.

1916. Ylena Georgievna Bonner (1923–)

1 Since I never at any time anywhere under any circumstances deliberately spread slanderous fabrications defaming the Soviet state or social system, or the state or social system of other countries, or private persons, I will not participate in the investigation and will not answer the question. *Alone Together* 1986

2 Living under the surveillance of the KGB* is very strange and unpleasant. Wherever you go, you feel the KGB watching, sometimes making films, sometimes harassing. Ibid.

Komitet Gosudarstvennoy Bezopasnosti (Committee of State Security), Soviet intelligence agency.

1917. Ursula Reilly Curtiss (1923–)

1 It was the old principle of getting back on the horse that had thrown you (although why, Kate had always wondered? Why not just take up some other sport?) but sometimes, like a number of laudable things, it was wearing.
Ch. 1, *The Wasp* 1963

2 After a second's astonishment, Kate let the lie stand. Like most lies it was much easier than the truth, and to contradict it might turn out to be a very wearying affair. Ibid., Ch. 3.

3 This was not love; it was exactly what Georgia had said: ownership. If you owned a race horse, you got the winner's stakes. If you owned a play, you got the royalties. If you owned a son. . . . Ibid., Ch. 17

1918. Antoinette DeWit (1923–)

1 Grab the Hope when it flies by, we* say.
Letter to Elaine Partnow
16 June 1989

*Enabled Artists Guild, Portland, Oregon.

2 I really cannot, and never will, presume to "educate" the public . . . that being disabled never means "disabled en toto," but to recognize that "disabled" also means "enabled," and that I would like to see the public become more aware of.
Quoted in "She's got Art and Soul" by Kathy Brock, *Lake Oswego (Oregon) Review*
April 1989

1919. Dorothy Dinnerstein (1923–)

1 . . . a sense of deep strain between women and men has been permeating our species' life as far back into time as the study of myth and ritual permits us to trace human feeling.
The Mermaid and the Minotaur
1977

2 So long as the first parent is a woman, then, woman will inevitably be pressed into the dual role of indispensable quasi-human supporter and deadly quasi-human enemy of the human self. She will be seen as naturally fit to nurture other people's individuality; as the born audience in whose awareness other people's subjective existence can be mirrored; as the being so peculiarly needed to confirm other people's worth, power, significance that if she fails to render them this service she is a monster, anomalous and useless. And at the same time she will also be seen as the one who will not let other people be, the one who beckons her loved ones back from selfhood, who wants to engulf, dissolve, drown, suffocate them as autonomous persons. Ibid.

3 . . . renunciation of what has been inexorably outlived is by definition affirmative.   Ibid.

1920. Mari Evans (1923–)

1 It don't do
to wake up
quick . . .
                "The Alarm Clock," *I Am a Black
                Woman*   1970

1921. Nadine Gordimer (1923–)

1 I'm forty-nine but I could be twenty-five except
for my face and my legs.
                "Good Climate, Friendly
                Inhabitants," *Not for
                Publication and Other Stories*
                1965

2 These [teenage] girls had dropped childhood,
with its bond of physical dependency on parents,
behind them. They had forgotten what they had
been, and they did not know that they would
become what their parents were. For the brief
hiatus they occupied themselves with preparations for a state of being very different—a world
that would never exist.
                "Vital Statistics," op. cit.

3 The two women gazed out of the slumped and
sagging bodies that had accumulated around
them.   Ibid.

4 Oh we bathed and perfumed and depilated white
ladies, in whose wombs the sanctity of the white
race is entombed! What concoction of musk and
boiled petals can disguise the dirt done in the
name of that sanctity?
                The Late Bourgeois World   1966

5 "There's nothing moral about beauty."   Ibid.

6 It is in opposition (the disputed territory of the
argument, the battle for self-definition that goes
on beneath the words) . . . that intimacy takes
place.   *The Conservationist*   1975

7 She filled her house with blacks, and white
parsons who went around preaching Jesus was
a revolutionary, and then when the police walked
in she was surprised.   Ibid.

1922. Marcella Hazan (1923–)

1 You don't cook? What do you do? Starve?
                Quoted in "Battling
                Spaghetti O Taste Buds" by
                Cathy Booth, *Time
                29 May 1989*

2 Cooking is an art, but you eat it too.   Ibid.

1923. Jane Screven Heyward (fl. 1923–1939)

1 More brightly must my spirit shine
Since grace of Beauty is not mine.
                "The Spirit's Grace"
                n.d.

2 The dear old ladies whose cheeks are pink
In spite of the years of winter's chill,
Are like the Autumn leaves, I think,
A little crumpled, but lovely still.
                "Autumn Leaves"
                n.d.

1924. Carolina Maria de Jesus (1923?–)

1 Actually we are slaves to the cost of living.
                Diary Entry (15 July 1955), *Child of the Dark:
                The Diary of
                Carolina Maria de Jesus
                1962*

2 I classify Sao Paulo this way: The Governor's
Palace is the living room. The mayor's office is
the dining room and the city is the garden. And
the *favela** is the back yard where they throw
the garbage.   Ibid. (15 May 1958)

* Barrio or ghetto.

3 "You had faith, and now you don't have it any
more?
  "No, my son, democracy is losing its follow-
ers. In our country everything is weakening.
The money is weak. Democracy is weak and
the politicians are very weak. Everything that is
weak dies one day."   Ibid. (20 May 1958)

4 She neglects children and collects men.
                Ibid. (1 June 1958)

5 A child is the root of the heart.   Ibid.

1925. Shirley Kaufman (1923–)

1 Through every night we hate,
preparing the next day's
war. . . .   "Mothers, Daughters,"
                The Floor Keeps Turning   1970

1926. Jean Kerr (1923–)

1 MARY. It was hard to communicate with you.
You were always communicating with yourself.
The line was busy.   Act II, *Mary, Mary 1960*

2 SYDNEY. You don't seem to realize that a poor person who is unhappy is in a better position than a rich person who is unhappy. Because the poor person has hope. He thinks money would help. *Act I, Poor Richard 1963*

3 SYDNEY. Even though a number of people have tried, no one has yet found a way to drink for a living. *Ibid.*

4 RICHARD. See, I believe in words. I think when they're put together they should mean something. They have an exact meaning, a precise meaning. There is more precision in one good sonnet than there is in an Atlas missile. *Ibid., Act III*

5 JEFF. Man is the only animal that learns by being hypocritical. He pretends to be polite and then, eventually, he *becomes* polite. *Act I, Finishing Touches 1973*

6 FELICIA. Hope is the feeling you have that the feeling you have isn't permanent. *Ibid., Act III*

1927. Denise Levertov (1923–   )

1 To reach those shining pebbles,
that soil where uncommon men
have labored in their virtue
and left a store
of seeds for planting!
    "A Common Ground," I, Sts. 3 & 4, *The Jacob's Ladder   1961*

2 Man gets his daily bread
in sweat, but no one said
in daily death. Don't eat
those nice green dollars your wife
gives you for breakfast.
    "The Part," Sts. 7 & 8, op. cit.

3   Images
split the truth
in fractions.
    "A Sequence," III, St. 2, op. cit.

4 two by two in the ark of
the ache of it.
    "The Ache of Marriage," *O Taste and See   1963*

5 "Life after life after life goes by
without poetry,
without seemliness,
without love."
    The Mutes," *The Sorrow Dance   1966*

6   The day's blow
rang out, metallic—or it was I, a bell awakened,
and what I heard was my whole self
saying and singing what it knew: *I can.*

"Variation on a Theme by Rilke," * Pt. I, *Breathing the Water   1989*

*Rainer Maria Rilke, Swiss poet (1875–1926).

7 I hear the books in all the rooms
breathing calmly . . .
    "August Daybreak," St. 1, op. cit.

8 Much happens when we're not there.
    "Window-Blind," op. cit., Pt. II

9 Every day, every day I hear
enough to fill
a year of nights with wondering.
    "Every Day," Pt. III, St. 6, op. cit.

10   The bees
care for the allium, if you don't—
hear them now, doing their research,
humming the arias
of a honey opera . . . "In Praise of Allium,"
    Pt. VI, op. cit.

1928. Inge Trachtenberg (1923?–   )

1 Decent was more than moral, decent was also being a good sport, a good friend, having a sense of humor, being tough. *Ch. 14, So Slow the Dawning   1973*

2 I did a lot of writing that winter. . . . Putting things down lent them a sense of permanence, it seemed to stem the feeling of rushing time which was suddenly so compelling that I fancied hearing its sound. *Ibid., Ch. 16*

1929. Lauren Bacall (1924–   )

1 The purity of Jewish upbringing—the restrictions that one carries through life being a "nice Jewish girl"—what a burden. *Lauren Bacall By Myself 1978*

2 A man's illness is his private territory and, no matter how much he loves you and how close you are, you stay an outsider. You are healthy. *Ibid.*

1930. Sarah Caldwell (1924–   )

1 If you approach an opera as though it were something that always went a certain way, that's what you get. I approach an opera as though I didn't know it.
    Quoted in "Sarah Caldwell: The Flamboyant of the Opera" by Jane Scovell Appleton, *Ms.   May 1975*

2 We must continuously discipline ourselves to remember how it felt the first moment.   Ibid.

3 It [Tanglewood, summer home of the Boston Symphony Orchestra] was a place where gods strode the earth.
> Quoted in "Music's Wonder Woman,"
> *Time*   *10 November 1975*

1931. Shirley Chisholm (1924–   )

1 I was well on the way to forming my present attitude toward politics as it is practiced in the Untied States; it is a beautiful fraud that has been imposed on the people for years, whose practitioners exchange gilded promises for the most valuable thing their victims own. their votes. And who benefits most? The lawyers.
> Pt. I, Ch. 4, *Unbought and Unbossed*   *1970*

2 I am a candidate for the Presidency of the United States. I make that statement proudly, in the full knowledge that, as a black person and as a female person, I do not have a chance of actually gaining that office in this election year.
> Speech   *4 June 1972*

3 We Americans have a chance to become someday a nation in which all racial stocks and classes can exist in their own self hoods, but meet on a basis of respect and equality and live together, socially, economically, and politically. We can become a dynamic equilibrium, a harmony of many different elements, in which the whole will be greater than all its parts and greater than any society the world has seen before. It can still happen.
> Ch. 14, *The Good Fight*   *1973*

4 I am particularly struck by the number of aged men who represent America. It seems we are not taking into consideration what is happening in this country today. We are not giving bright young people—who are often so much in touch with the time—a sufficient chance to break into politics and be heard.   Quoted in *Shirley Chisholm,* Susan Brownmiller* *197?*

*See 2166.

1932. Janet Frame (1924–   )

1 Every morning I woke in dread, waiting for the day nurse to go on her rounds and announce from the list of names in her hand whether or not I was for shock treatment, the new and fashionable means of quieting people and of making them realize that orders are to be obeyed and floors are to be polished without anyone

protesting and faces are made to be fixed into smiles and weeping is a crime.
> Ch. 1, *Faces in the Water*   *1961*

2 Electricity, the peril the wind sings to in the wires on a gray day.   Ibid., Ch. 2

3 . . . . very often the law of extremity demands an attention to irrelevance. . . .   Ibid., Ch. 3

1933. Patricia Roberts Harris (1924–   )

1 I am one of them [society's disadvantaged citizens]. I am a black woman, the daughter of a dining car waiter. You do not seem to understand who I am.
> Congressional Confirmation Hearings
> (addressing Senator William Proxmire)*
> *25–26 July 1979*

*American politician, (1915–   ).

1934. Ruth Hubbard (1924–   )

1 Every theory is a self-fulfilling prophecy that orders experience into the framework it provides.   "Have Only Men Evolved?,"
> *Women Look at Biology Looking at Women,* Ruth Hubbard, Mary Sue Henifin and Barbara Fried, eds.
> *1979*

2 The mythology of science asserts that with many different scientists all asking their own questions and evaluating the answers independently, whatever personal bias creeps into their individual answers is cancelled out when the large picture is put together. This might conceivably be so if scientists were women and men from all sorts of different cultural and social backgrounds who came to science with very different ideologies and interests. But since, in fact, they have been predominantly university-trained white males from privileged social backgrounds, the bias has been narrow and the product often reveals more about the investigator than about the subject being researched.   Ibid.

1935. Alice Koller (1924–   )

1 I stare into the mirror. I don't have a life: I'm just using up a number of days somehow. There is no *reason* for me to be here.
> *An Unknown Woman*   *1981*

2 If I could learn how to see with my own eyes, I'd be able to make a comparable leap, leaving behind everybody else's rules. . . . I don't

know what I want, or want to do. I don't know how to use my own evidence . . . I don't know what to look for inside me. I don't know how to identify that I'm feeling something, let alone give it a name. I think I've been anesthetized, deadened.   Ibid.

1936. Cloris Leachman (1924–)

1 Why can't we build orphanages next to homes for the elderly? If someone's sitting in a rocker, it won't be long before a kid will be in his lap.   Quoted in "I Love My Career and I Love My Children . . . ." by Jane Wilkie, *Good Housekeeping* October 1973

1937. Phyllis Lyon (1924–)

Co-author with Del Martin. See 1892.

1938. Bess Myerson (1924–)

1 . . . the accomplice to the crime of corruption is frequently our own indifference.
Quoted in "Impeachment?" by Claire Safran, *Redbook* April 1974

1939. Harriet Rochlin (1924–)

1 "Laughter can be more satisfying than honor; more precious than money; more heart cleansing than prayer."   Ch. 1, *So Far Away* 1981

2 "Family life is a training ground," intoned Miss O'Hara, "for life in the world. Learn to get along at home, and you can get along everywhere."   Ibid., Ch. 8

3 "A Jew is supposed to chase God, not gold."   Ibid., Ch. 18

1940. Alma Routsong (1924–)

1 Time enough later to teach her that it's better to be a real woman than an imitation man, and that when someone chooses a woman to go away with it's because a woman is what's preferred.   *A Place for Us*   1969

2 [I] wonder if what makes men walk lordlike and speak so masterfully is having the love of women.   Ibid.

1941. Phyllis Schlafly (1924–)

1 The advance planning and sense stimuli employed to capture a $10 million cigarette or soap market are nothing compared to the brainwashing and propaganda blitzes used to ensure control of the largest cash market in the world: the Executive Branch of the Untied States Government.   Ch. 1, *A Choice Not an Echo* 1964

2 The moral sickness of the Federal Government becomes more apparent every day. Public officials are caught in a giant web of payoffs, bribes, perversion, and conflicts of interest, so that few dare speak out against the establishment.   Ch. 1, *Safe—Not Sorry*   1967

3 The left wing forces—both obvious and hidden—which have been running our country for the last seven years understand and appreciate the importance of *political action*. Their long tentacles reach out in many fields: to "orchestrate" propaganda through the communications media, to indoctrinate youth in our schools and universities, to create a Socialist intellectual climate through tax-exempt foundations, and to bend business into line with Government contracts.   Ibid., Ch. 12

4 The claim that American women are downtrodden and unfairly treated is the fraud of the century.   Quoted by Lisa Cronin Wohl in *Ms.* March 1974

1942. Margaret Truman (1924–)

1 I know from experience that the barbs of the critics are more painful for a President's family to endure than they are for the President.
Women of Courage   1977?

1943. Sally Weinraub (1924–)

1 Architects believe less and less in doors these days, so that houses were becoming like beehives, arches leading into chambers and more arches. It was lucky that Americans were still puritan in their habits. You could be alone in the bathroom.
"Knifed with a Black Shadow," *American Scene: New Voices,* Don Wolfe, ed.   1963

1944. Shana Alexander (1925–)

1 The sad truth is that excellence makes people nervous.   "Neglected Kids—the Bright Ones" (June 1966), *The Feminine Eye*   1970

2 Mankind still has monsters, of course. The trouble is that they are no longer mythological. Rather, they are the terrifying things man creates with his technology and then cannot control—things like Peenemünde; things like smog, that foul thousand-mile blob visible from any jet; things like the cataclysmic, coiling, deadly dragon that is Vietnam. "More Monsters, Please!" (December 1967), op. cit.

3 . . . when two people marry they become in the eyes of the law one person, and that one person is the husband!
Introduction, *State-by-State Guide to Women's Legal Rights* 1975

4 The law changes and flows like water, and . . . the stream of women's rights law has become a sudden rushing torrent. Ibid.

1945. Dede Allen (1925–)

1 Editing [film] is really a creative art. Any editor needs to know certain techniques, but the real decisions are made in her or his head.
Quoted in "The Power Behind the Screen" by Geraldine Febrikant, *Ms.* *February 1974*

1946. Svetlana Alliluyeva (1925–)

1 Moscow, breathing fire like a human volcano with its smoldering lava of passion, ambition and politics, its hurly-burly of meetings and entertainment. . . . Moscow seethes and bubbles and gasps for air. It's always thirsting for something new, the newest events, the latest sensation. Everyone wants to be the first to know. It's the rhythm of life today.
Introduction (16 July 1963), *Twenty Letters to a Friend* 1967

2 He [her father, Stalin]* is gone, but his shadow still stands over all of us. It still dictates to us and we, very often, obey. Ibid., Ch. 2

*Joseph Stalin Soviet Communist revolutionary and political leader (1879–1953).

3 . . . as a result of half a century of Soviet rule people have been weaned from a belief in human kindness. "The Journey's End," *Only One Year* 1969

1947. Helen Barolini (1925–)

1 When you don't read, you don't write.
The Dream Book: An Anthology of

Writings by Italian American Women 1985

1948. Marilyn Bender (1925–)

1 Female clothing has been disappearing literally and philosophically.
Ch. 1, *The Beautiful People* 1967

2 To whip up desire for something that people don't really need, at least not in endless quantity, glamorous idols are essential. If desire begets need, then envy begets desire. The stimulation of envy or a longing to imitate is the function of the idol. The fashion industry, through its press agents and an eagerly cooperative, self-serving press, had to manufacture new goddesses. Ibid., Ch. 3

3 Just as the court flunky tasted the king's food to screen it for poison, so today the corporate sovereign has his literary fare digested and presented in capsule form or laced into his speeches by his ghost writer.
"The Business of Reading About Business," *Saturday Review of the Society* *April 1973*

1949. Barbara Bush (1925–)

1 I got away with murder [as Second Lady]. I'm now slightly more careful about what I say. Slightly. Quoted in "The Silver Fox" by Michael Duffy, *Time* *23 January 1989*

2 Why would he tell me any secrets when he says I begin every sentence with "Don't tell George* I told you this, but . . .'' Ibid.

*Her husband, George Bush (1924–); 41st president of the United States (1989–).

1950. Kathryn Clarenbach (1925?–)

1 The overemphasis on protecting girls from strain or injury and underemphasis on developing skills and experiencing teamwork fits neatly into the pattern of the second sex. . . . Girls are the spectators and the cheerleaders. . . . Perfect preparation for the adult role of woman—to stand decoratively on the sidelines of history and cheer on the men who make the decisions. . . .
Sex Role Stereotyping in the Schools 1973

2 Women who have had the regular experience of performing before others, of learning to win and

lose, of cooperating in team efforts, will be far less fearful of running for office, better able to take public positions on issues in the face of public opposition.

> Quoted in "Old School System Curbed Sportswomen," *Los Angeles Times* 24 April 1974

1951. Pam Gems (1925–)

1 All the stories have been told long ago. Your job is retelling. Relighting.
> "Pam Gems," *Interviews with Contemporary Women Playwrights,* Kathleen Betsko* & Rachel Koenig 1987

*See 2256.

2 The nature of the dramatic mode is the withholding of information, in the creation of a puzzle for the audience to solve. Clues. Ibid.

3 What you have to control, in the writing, is silence. You have to orchestrate that important member of the cast, the audience. Orchestrate, and conduct. One joke too many and they become flatulent, blowzy. One thought too many and they begin to move, restless, oppressed. The audience *must* be working, as hard as the actors. The audience must be alive, must create the play. Ibid.

1952. Eleanor Hoover (c. 1925–)

Co-author with Marie Edwards. See 1966.

1953. Huang Zongying (1925–)

1 The woman growing wild herbs* aroused my interest for some unknown reason. Perhaps for her frankness, her composure, or perhaps because she looked as ordinary as any country midwife, who interrupts her pig-feeding and washes her hands before picking up her sterilized instruments.
> "The Flight of the Wild-Geese," Yu Fanqin & Wang Mingjie, trs., *Seven Contemporary Chinese Women Writers,* Gladys Yang,** ed. 1982

*Qin Guanshu Chinese botanist (1929–). See 2033.
**See 2076.

2 God! In the world of plants, no two leaves have the same pattern of veins. But in the world of human beings, people have to be classified and tagged all over the country. But how can these

tags express the complications of Chinese society? After all, class origin is not terribly important. Ibid.

1954. Carolyn Kizer (1925–)

1 We don't lack people here on the Northern coast,
But they are people one meets, not people one cares for.
> "Amusing Our Daughters," St. 1, *Knock Upon Silence* 1963

2 We waken and count our daughters.
Otherwise, nothing happens. Ibid., St. 3

1955. Maxine Kumin (1925–)

1 I plucked the memory splinter from your spine
as we played at being normal, who
had eased each other in the cold zoo
of childhood. "The Man of Many L's," *Our Ground Time Here Will Be Brief* 1982

2 They've
been here
for thousands of years.
You're
the visitor "You Are in Bear Country," *The Long Approach* 1985

3 Cherish
your wilderness. Ibid.

4 Everything pays for growing tame
> "Sunday in March," op. cit.

5 caring is small
susceptible fits in a pocket
nor is it one thing to save animals
and people another
but seamless "Caring: A Dream," op. cit.

6 Already we have had snow lucid,
snow surprising, snow bees
and lambswool snow.
> "Getting Through," op. cit.

7 Let me put my faith in the bean.
> "Shelling Jacob's Cattle Beans," op. cit.

8 I'm going home the old way with a light hand
on the reins
making the long approach.
> "The Long Approach," op. cit.

1956. Melina Mercouri (1925–)

1 When you are born and they tell you "what a pity that you are so clever, so intelligent, so

beautiful but you are not a man," you are ashamed of your condition as a woman. I wanted to act like a man because the man was the master.   Quoted in "Greece: Survival of the Shrewdest" by Susan Margolis, *Ms.*   *October 1973*

1957. Tharon Musser (1925–   )

1 It's the lighting of moving sculpture. . . . Dance is heaven to light . . .
"The Facts of Light" by Arnold Aronson, *American Theatre* *January 1986*

2 All design in theatre is a supportive art. It's there to help, to underline, to emphasize.
Ibid.

1958. Flannery O'Connor (1925–1964)

1 "I'm going to preach there was no Fall because there was nothing to fall from and no Redemption because there was no Fall and no Judgment because there wasn't the first two. Nothing matters but that Jesus was a liar."
Ch. 6, *Wise Blood*   *1949*

2 She felt justified in getting anything at all back that she could, money or anything else, as if she had once owned the earth and been dispossessed of it. She couldn't look at anything steadily without wanting it, and what provoked her most was the thought that there might be something valuable hidden near her, something she couldn't see.
Ibid., Ch. 14.

3 "I call myself The Misfit," he said, "because I can't make what all I done wrong fit what all I gone through in punishment."
"A Good Man Is Hard to Find," *A Good Man Is Hard to Find*   *1955*

4 "Lady, a man is divided into two parts, body and spirit. . . . A body and a spirit," he repeated. "The body, lady, is like a house it don't go anywhere; but the spirit, lady, is like a automobile: always on the move, always. . . ."   "The Life You Save May Be Your Own," op. cit.

5 Then the revelation came, silent, implacable, direct as a bullet. He did not look into the eyes of any fiery beast or see a burning bush.
Pt. I, Ch. 3, *The Violent Bear It Away* *1955*

6 She was a good Christian woman with a large respect for religion, though she did not, of course, believe any of it was true.
"Greenleaf," *Everything That Rises Must Converge*   *1965*

7 He would have hastened his end but suicide would not have been a victory. Death was coming to him legitimately, as a justification, as a gift from life. That was his greatest triumph.
"The Enduring Chill," op. cit.

8 He had stuffed his own emptiness with good work like a glutton.
"The Lame Shall Enter First," op. cit.

9 I believe that there are many rough beasts now slouching toward Bethlehem to be born and that I have reported the progress of a few of them.
Flannery O'Connor: Collected Works, Sally Fitzgerald, ed.   *1988*

1959. Ru Zhijuan (1925–   )

1 The desolate grassland stretched out as if to the end of the world. On a piece of uncultivated land as vast as this, one could have made straight for anywhere . . .   "The Path Through the Grassland," tr. Yu Fanqin, *Seven Contemporary Chinese Women Writers,* Gladys Yang,* ed.   *1982*

*See 2076.

2 "The hardest thing for a person to bear is not a dressing-down or beating, but loneliness, ostracism."
Ibid.

3 Love needed a full stomach, but the two were quite different things.
Ibid.

1960. Naomi Streshinsky (1925–   )

1 The danger of a gift is an intriguing concept. Primitive man may have believed that the gift contained the spirit of the donor and therein lay its potential harm. The belief in the donor's spirit dissolved from modern man but the danger is still very much present.
Ch. 2, *Welfare Rights Organizations* *1970*

1961. Margaret Thatcher (1925–   )

1 *Détente* sounds a fine word. And, to the extent that there has really been a relaxation in international tension, it is a fine thing. But the fact remains that throughout this decade of *détente,* the armed forces of the Soviet Union have increased, are increasing, and show no signs of diminishing.
Speech, Chelsea Conservative Association (July 1975), Quoted in *Margaret*

Thatcher, A Tory and her Party
by Patrick Cosgrave   *1978*

2 I have reason to believe that the tide is beginning to turn against collectivism, socialism, statism, dirigism, whatever you call it. And this turn is rooted in a revulsion against the sour fruit of socialist experience.   Speech, Zurich
Economic Society (March 1977), op. cit.

3 You will only achieve higher growth, only release enterprise, only spur people to greater effort, only obtain their full-hearted commitment to reform, when people have the dignity and enjoyment of personal and political liberty, when they have the freedom of expression, freedom of association and the right to form free and independent trade unions.
Remark to Gen. Wojciech Jaruzelski,*
State Banquet, Warsaw, Poland
3 November 1988

*(1923–   ), Polish premier (1981–   ).

4 The best compliment they [men] can give a woman is that she thinks like a man. I say she does not; she thinks like a woman.
Quoted in Interview, *Los Angeles Times*
9 May 1989

5 The great battle now is to prevent the smaller minority ruining the lives of the majority by violence, by dirtiness, by graffiti, by everyday surliness . . . Graciousness has been replaced by surliness in much of everyday life.
Quoted in Interview, *The Washington Post*
25 May 1989

6 Battles in life are never won. I mean, you don't have your household budget permanently balanced; you have to balance it every year. Life's a continuous business, and so is success, and requires continuous effort.
Quoted in Interview, London, *The New York Times*   *28 September 1989*

7 If you want anything said, ask a man. If you want anything done, ask a woman.
Quoted in "Free to Fly Inside the Cage"
by Michael Kramer, *Time*
2 October 1989

1962. Ingeborg Bachmann (1926–1973)

1 For the facts that make up the world need the non-factual as a vantage point from which to be perceived.   *Der Fall*
Franza (The Franza Case), Jan
van Heurck, tr.   *n.d.*

2 He has taken my possessions from me. My laughter, my tenderness, my ability to feel joy, my compassion, my ability to help, my animality, my radiance; he has stamped out every

sprout of all these things, until they stopped sprouting. But why does someone do that, I don't understand.   *Ibid.*

3 The whites are coming. The whites are landing. And if they are repulsed again, they will return again once more. No revolution and no resolution and no foreign currency statute will help; they will come in spirit if they can no longer come in any other way. And they will be resurrected in a brown and a black brain; it will still always be the whites, even then. They will continue to own the world in this roundabout way.   *Ibid.*

4 your heart has business elsewhere,
your mouth is annexing new languages.
"Explain to Me, Love," St. 1,
Jan van Heurck, tr.   *n.d.*

5 Explain nothing to me. I see the
salamander
go through every fire.
No shudder pursues him, and nothing gives
him pain.   *Ibid., St. 6*

1963. Toni Carabillo (1926–   )

1 But powerlessness is still each woman's most critical problem, whether or not she is a social activist. It is at the root of most of her psychological disorders.
Address, "Power Is the Name of the Game," California NOW* State Conference, San Diego
28 October 1973

*Natl. Organization for Women.

2 We know that poverty in this country is primarily the problem of *all* women—that most women are only a husband away from welfare.
Address, "Sharing the Power, the Glory—and the Pain," NOW Western Regional Conference, Long Beach, California   *24 November 1974*

3 Rock music consistently degrades women and makes it clear her place in this man's world is limited to the kitchen and bedroom. Rock music has been rightly characterized, in our view, as a "frenzied celebration of masculine supremacy."   Address, "Womanpower and the Media," National Association of Broadcasters   *1974*

4 Not only the CIA, but the FBI, as well as many state and community police departments, have devoted vast resources to monitoring the activities of concerned citizens working in concert to make social changes within our system. The "flatfoot mentality" insists that any individual or organization that wants to change *anything* in our present system is somehow subversive of

"the American way," and should be under continuous surveillance—a task that appears to absorb most of our resources for fighting genuine crime.
"The 'Flatfoot Mentality,' " *Hollywood NOW News* *August 1975*

1964. Elizabeth Douvan (1926–)

1 The dream of college apparently serves as a substitute for more direct preoccupation with marriage: girls who do not plan to go to college are more explicit in their desire to marry, and have a more developed sense of their own sex role. "Motivational Factors in College Entrance," *The American College*, with Carol Kaye*

*See 2067.

1965. Rosalyn Drexler (1926–)

1 "I'm just a dog. Look, no opposable thumb." *The Cosmopolitan Girl* *1975*

2 He visited the Museum of Modern Art, and was standing near the pool looking at his dark reflection when a curator of the museum noticed him. "My, my, what a fine work of art that is!" the curator said to himself. "I must have it installed immediately." *Ibid.*

3 Acknowledging the body is acknowledging what is real. . . . It's such a strain, a struggle, to appear to be without physical blemish . . . to remain young as the relentless years add up. It's time consuming and emotionally depleting.
"Rosalyn Drexler," *Interviews with Contemporary Women Playwrights*, Kathleen Betsko* & Rachel Koenig *1987*

*See 2256.

4 As Hemingway* once said, or was thought to have said, [to write well] one must have a built-in shit detector. But to have that, one must have smelled shit at least a few times. *Ibid.*

*American writer (1899–1961).

5 Pornography is not a safety valve, it is a writ of permission. . . . *Ibid.*

1966. Marie Edwards (1926?–)

1 Books, magazines, counselors, therapists sell one message to unmarrieds: "Shape up, go where other singles are, entertain more, raise your sex quotient, get involved, get closer, be

more open, more honest, more intimate, above all, find Mr. Right or Miss Wonderful and *get married.*" *The Challenge of Being Single*, with Eleanor Hoover* *1975*

*See 1952.

1967. Elizabeth II of England (1926–)

1 My whole life, whether it be long or short, shall be devoted to your [the public's] service and the service of our great imperial family to which we all belong. But I shall not have strength to carry out this resolution alone unless you join in it with me. Radio Broadcast *21 April 1947*

1968. Sissy Farenthold (1926–)

1 I am working for the time when unqualified blacks, browns and women join the unqualified men in running our government.
Quoted in the *Los Angeles Times* *18 September 1974*

2 There is no question that under the Equal Rights Amendment there will be debates at times, indecision at times, litigation at times. Has anyone proposed that we rescind the First Amendment on free speech because there is too much litigation over it? Has anyone suggested the same for the Fourteenth Amendment (I don't suppose there has ever been a constitutional amendment with so much litigation)?
Speech for International Women's Year, "Legal Rights," Vermont College *26 February 1977*

3 You change laws by changing lawmakers.
Quoted in "Interview with Sissy Farenthold" by Dave Anast, *The Bakersfield Californian* *22 April 1978*

1969. Wilma Scott Heide (1926–)

1 The only jobs for which no man is qualified are human incubator and wet nurse. Likewise, the only job for which no woman is or can be qualified is sperm donor.
Quoted in *NOW* Official Biography* *1971*

*National Organization for Women.

2 . . . we whose hands have rocked the cradle, are now using our heads to rock the boat. . . . *Ibid.*

3 . . . we will no longer be led only by that half of the population whose socialization, through

toys, games, values and expectations, sanctions violence as the final assertion of manhood, synonymous with nationhood. Ibid.

4 Now that we've organized [NOW] . . . all over the United States and initiated an international movement and actions, it must be apparent that feminism is no passing fad but indeed a profound, universal behavior revolution.

Quoted in "About Women,"
Los Angeles Times
12 May 1974

1970. Carolyn Heilbrun (1926–   )

1 Ideas move fast when their time comes.
Toward a Recognition of Androgyny
1973

2 What is important now is that we free ourselves from the prison of gender and, before it is too late, deliver the world from the almost exclusive control of the masculine impulse.
Ibid., Introduction

3 Great periods of civilization, however much they may have owed their beginning to the aggressive dominance of the male principle, have always been marked by some sort of rise in the status of women. This in its turn is a manifestation of something more profound: the recognition of the importance of the "feminine" principle, not as other, but as necessary to wholeness. Ibid., Pt. I

4 Today's shocks are tomorrow's conventions.
Ibid., Pt. II

5 The genuine solitaries of life fear intimacy more than loneliness. The married are those who have taken the terrible risk of intimacy and, having taken it, know life without intimacy to be impossible. "Marriage Is the Message," *Ms.*
August 1974

6 Only a marriage with partners strong enough to risk divorce is strong enough to avoid it. . . . Ibid.

1971. Aileen Clarke Hernandez (1926–   )

1 My comments to the thousands of persons at the peace march [the 1971 Another Mother for Peace march in Los Angeles] were directed not just against the Vietnam War, but against *all* war, against the masculine mystique which glorifies violence as a solution to problems, and against the vast diverting of American energies and resources from socially needed programs into social destructive wars.

Letter to Eve Norman, Quoted in
the NOW* Newsletter
29 April 1971

*National Organization for Women.

2 There are no such things as women's issues! All issues are women's issues. The difference that we bring to existing issues of our society, the issues of war and peace; the issues of poverty; the issues of child care; the issues of political power—the difference that we bring is that we are going to bring the full, loud, clear determined voice of women into deciding how those issues are going to be addressed.
Address, National Conference of
NOW, Los Angeles
3–6 September 1971

1972. Sue Kaufman (1926–   )

1 I was afraid that if I opened my mouth, like Gerald McBoing-Boing, terrible inhuman sounds would come out—brakes screeching, metal clashing, tires skidding, trains roaring past in the night. "Saturday, October 7,"
Diary of a Mad Housewife
1967

2 Every since she had gotten out of hospital, her eye kept seeking out and fastening on the cruel, the ugly, the sordid—trying to turn every nasty little incident or detail into some sort of concrete proof of just how rotten the world had become. *Falling Bodies* 1974

3 "In violent and chaotic times such as these, our only chance for survival lies in creating our own little islands of sanity and order, in making little havens of our homes." Ibid.

1973. Gertrude Lemp Kerbis (1926–   )

1 It was hell for women architects then. They didn't want us in school or in the profession. . . . One thing I've never understood about this prejudice is that it's so strange in view of the fact that the drive to build has always been in women. Quoted in *Women at Work*
by Betty Medsger 1975

1974. Elisabeth Kübler-Ross (1926   )

1 The more we are making advancements in science, the more we seem to fear and deny the reality of death. Ch. 1, *On Death and Dying*
1969

2 . . . we have to ask ourselves whether medicine is to remain a humanitarian and respected

profession or a new but depersonalized science in the service of prolonging life rather than diminishing human suffering. . . .
Ibid., Ch. 2

3 Acceptance should not be mistaken for a happy stage. It is almost void of feelings. It is as if the pain had gone, the struggle is over. . . .   Ibid., Ch. 7

4 Dying is hard under any circumstances, but dying in the familiar surroundings of one's home, with those you love and who love you, can take away much of the fear.
Ch. 3, *Death: The Final Stage
of Growth   1975*

5 Those who have been immersed in the tragedy of massive death during wartime, and who have faced it squarely, never allowing their senses and feelings to become numbed and indifferent, have emerged from their experiences with growth and humanness greater than that achieved through almost any other means.   Ibid., Ch. 5

6 It is not the end of the physical body that should worry us. Rather, our concern must be to *live* while we're alive—to release our inner selves from the spiritual death that comes with living behind a façade designed to conform to external definitions of who and what we are.
Ibid., "Omega"

7 The world is in desperate need of human beings whose own level of growth is sufficient to enable them to learn to live and work with others cooperatively and lovingly, to care for others— not for what those others can do for you or for what they think of you, but rather in terms of what you can do for them.   Ibid.

8 Death is the final stage of growth in this life. There is no total death. Only the body dies. The self or spirit, or whatever you may wish to label it, is eternal.   Ibid.

9 Learn to get in touch with silence within yourself and know that everything in this life has a purpose. There are no mistakes, no coincidences; all events are blessings given to us to learn from. There is no need to go to India or anywhere else to find peace. You will find that deep place of silence right in your room, your garden or even your bathtub.
(Speech, 1976), Quoted in
"Elisabeth Kübler-Ross" by Lennie
Kronisch, *Yoga Journal
November/December 1976*

1975. Margaret Laurence (1926–   )

1 The bird had no name. She did not believe in bestowing names upon non-humans, for a name

to her meant a christening, possible only for Christians.
"The Sound of Singing," *Winter's Tales,*
A. D. Maclean, ed.   *1963*

2 Privacy is a privilege not granted to the aged or the young.   Ch. 1, *The Stone Angel   1964*

3 Even if heaven were real, and measured as Revelation says, so many cubits this way and that, how gimcrack a place it would be, crammed with its pavements of gold, its gates of pearl and topaz, like a gigantic chunk of costume jewelry.   Ibid., Ch. 4

4 "Death's unmentionable?"
"Not exactly unmentionable, but let's face it, most of us could get along without it."
"I don't see how."
Ch. 7, *A Jest of God* (later known as
Rachel, Rachel)   *1966*

5 How strange to have to keep on retreating to the only existing privacy, the only place one is permitted to be unquestionably alone, the lavatory.   Ibid., Ch. 9

6 "You are out of danger," he said. I laughed, I guess, and said, "How can I be—I don't feel dead yet."   Ibid., Ch. 11

7 God's mercy on reluctant jesters. God's grace on fools. God's pity on God.   Ibid., Ch. 12

1976. Harper Lee (1926–   )

1 A day was twenty-four hours long but seemed longer. There was no hurry, for there was no-where to go, nothing to buy and no money to buy it with, nothing to see outside the bound-aries of Maycomb County. But it was a time of vague optimism for some of the people: May-comb County had recently been told that it had nothing to fear but fear itself.
Pt. I, Ch. 1, *To Kill a Mockingbird
1960*

2 "People in their right minds never take pride in talents," said Miss Maudie.   Ibid., Ch. 10

3 "The one thing that doesn't abide by majority rule is a person's conscience."   Ibid., Ch. 11

4 Never, never, never, on cross-examination ask a witness a question you don't already know the answer to, was a tenet I absorbed with my baby-food. Do it, and you'll often get an answer you don't want, an answer that might wreck your case.   Ibid., Ch. 17

5 "As you grow older, you'll see white men cheat black men every day of your life, but let me tell you something and don't you forget it— whenever a white man does that to a black man, no matter who he is, how rich he is, or how

fine a family he comes from, that white man is trash." Ibid., Ch. 23

1977. Carolyn Leigh (1926–1983)

1 When you arouse the need in me
My heart says yes, indeed, to me
Proceed with what you're leading me to
"Witchcraft" *n.d.*

2 Out of the tree of life
I done picked me a plum
"The Best Is Yet to Come"
n.d.

3 It's hard, you will find
To be narrow of mind
If you're young at heart
"Young at Heart" *n.d.*

1978. Pat Loud (1926–)

1 College for women was a refinement whose main purpose was to better prepare you for your ultimate destiny . . . to make you a more desirable product.
Pat Loud: A Woman's Story, with Nora Johnson 1974

2 Life was diapers and little jars of pureed apricots and bottles and playpens and rectal thermometers, and all those small dirty faces and all those questions. Ibid.

1979. Alison Lurie (1926–)

1 "You see, actually, Roger, the very second a plant is cut from its roots, or pulled out of the ground, it starts to die and lose its nutritive values. That's why I've started growing my own, as much as I've got room for, and so's Elsie." Ch. 16, *Imaginary Friends* 1967

2 But intellectual and personal force—even genius—are not guarantees of sanity. Ibid., Ch. 17

3 Then last year, when Jeffrey turned fourteen and Matilda twelve, they had begun to change; to grow rude, coarse, selfish, insolent, nasty, brutish, and tall. It was as if she were keeping a boarding house in a bad dream, and the children she had loved were turning into awful lodgers— lodgers who paid no rent, whose leases could not be terminated.
Ch. 1, *The War Between the Tates* 1974

4 Since she is an authority on children's literature, people assume that Vinnie must love children, and that her own lack of them must be a tragedy. For the sake of public relations, she seldom denies these assumptions outright. But the truth is otherwise. In her private opinion most contemporary children—especially American ones— are competitive, noisy, and shallow, at once jaded and ignorant as a result of overexposure to television, baby-sitters, advertising, and video games. Vinnie wants to be a child, not to have one; she isn't interested in the parental role, but in an extension or recovery of what for her is the best part of life. Ch. 5, *Foreign Affairs* 1984

5 As an American friend of hers once put it at a high point of their brief relationship . . . : "Sometimes I think we're the same person." "Oh, I know," Vinnie had replied, equally deluded. . . .
Even more often, outsiders conflate the couple, and credit them with each other's characteristics. If a radical takes up with a conservative, both will be perceived as more moderate politically, regardless of whether their views have in fact altered. The man or woman who becomes involved with a much younger person seems younger, the latter more mature.
Ibid., Ch. 9

1980. Joyce McDougall (1926–)

1 Psychic reality will always be structured around the poles of absence and difference; and . . . human beings will always have to come to terms with that which is forbidden and that which is impossible. Quoted in *Necessary Losses* by Judith Viorst* 1986

*See 2092.

1981. Marilyn Monroe (1926–1962)

1 I've been on a calendar, but never on time.
Quoted in *Look* 16 January 1962

2 I have too many fantasies to be a housewife.
. . . I guess I *am* a fantasy.
Quoted in "Marilyn: The Woman Who Died Too Soon" by Gloria Steinem,* *The First Ms. Reader,* Francine Klagsbrun, ed. 1972

*See 2164.

3 I don't want to make money. I just want to be wonderful. Ibid.

4 I am always running into peoples' unconscious. Quoted in *Marilyn* by Norman Mailer 1973

1982. Jan Morris (1926–)

1 To me gender is not physical at all, but is altogether insubstantial. It is soul, perhaps, it is talent, it is taste, it is environment, it is how one feels, it is light and shade, it is inner music. . . .   Ch. 3, *Conundrum*   *1974*

2 I had reached the conclusion myself that sex was not a division but a continuum, that almost nobody was altogether of one sex or another, and that the infinite subtlety of the shading from one extreme to the other was one of the most beautiful of nature's phenomena. Sex was like a biological pointer, but the gauge upon which it flickered was that very different device, gender.   Ibid., Ch. 5

3 Nothing is more flexibly resilient than Chineseness.   *Hong Kong*   *1988*

1983. Patricia Neal (1926–)

1 It [Hollywood] always sounds glamorous when you're young.   Quoted in *Time*   *20 March 1964*

2 It's very important not to pamper or indulge them [brain-injured or handicapped children] or to treat them differently from the other children in the family. But this is very difficult . . .
    Quoted in "Triumph Over Tragedy"
    by Patricia Baum,
    Parents' Magazine   *November 1975*

3 Tennessee hillbillies don't conk out that easily.   Ibid.

1984. Charlotte Painter (1926–)

1 We are looking for some way to live in a world gone mad. We have left America the beautiful. But not because we know a better place.
    Confession from the Malaga
    Madhouse   *1971*

2 If a thing is absolutely true, how can it not also be a lie? An absolute must contain its opposite.   Ibid.

3 I don't know where in this shrunken world to take you, son, to let you grow to manhood.
    Ibid.

4 . . . as awareness increases, the need for personal secrecy almost proportionately decreases.
    Afterword, *Revelations: Diaries of Women,*
    with Mary Jane Moffat*   *1974*

*See 2245.

1985. Cynthia Propper Seton (1926–)

1 To Angela her grandmother was old but had not grown older and was never younger. This is a usual way with grandmothers.
    Ch. 1, *The Sea Change of Angela Lewes*
    1971

2 "It sometimes looks to me," said Angela, "that a middle-class marriage is a careful mismatching of two innocents—and the game is called Making the Best of It, while in actual fact each one does a terrible thing to the spirit of the other. . . . And you wonder why they endure each other, why they stand for it? And the explanation is that they really answer each other's needs, unconscious needs, and are in fact often admirably suited to each other, and that, unbelievable as it might seem from the outside, they do really *love* each other"   Ibid., Ch. 12

3 To pursue yourself is an interesting and absorbing thing to do. Once you have caught the scent of a hidden being, your own hidden being, you won't readily be deflected from the tracking down of it.   Ibid., Ch. 25

4 She had trouble defining herself independently of her husband, tried to talk to him about it, but he said nonsense, he had no trouble defining her at all.   *The Half-Sisters*   *1974*

1986. Dorothy E. Smith (1926–)

1 In the social sciences the pursuit of objectivity makes it possible for people to be paid to pursue a knowledge to which they are otherwise indifferent.   "Women's perspective as a radical critique of sociology," *Sociological Inquiry 44* *1974*

2 The exclusion of women from the making of our culture is not the product of a biological deficiency or a biological configuration of some kind. As we learn more of our women's history we discover that a powerful intellectual and artistic current moves like an underground stream through the history of the last few centuries. it appears sometimes merely as a missing potentiality . . . We learn of the subordination of genius to the discipline of service in the home and in relation to children, and of the fragmentary realization of extraordinary powers of mind and dedication . . .
    Ch. 1, *The Everyday Woman as*
    Problematic   *1987*

1987. Joan Sutherland (1926–)

1 If I weren't reasonably placid, I don't think I could cope with this sort of life. To be a diva, you've got to be absolutely like a horse.

Quoted in "Joan Sutherland," *Divas:
Impressions of Six Opera Superstars*
by Winthrop Sargeant   *1959*

1988. Johnnie Tillmon (1926–   )

1 I'm a woman. I'm a black woman. I'm a poor
woman. I'm a fat woman. I'm a middle-aged
woman. And I'm on welfare. In this country, if
you're any one of those things, you count less
as a person. If you're *all* those things, you just
don't count, except as a statistic.
"Welfare Is a Woman's Issue,"
The First Ms. Reader,
Francine Klagsbrun, ed.   *1972*

2 Women aren't supposed to work. They're supposed to be married.   Ibid.

3 Wages are the measure of dignity that society
puts on a job.   Ibid.

1989. Erma Bombeck (1927–   )

1 You hear a lot of dialogue on the death of the
American family. Families aren't dying. They're
merging into big conglomerates.
"Empty Fridge, Empty Nest,"
San Francisco Examiner
1 October 1978

2 I worry about scientists discovering that lettuce
has been fattening all along. . . .
*If Life is a Bowl of Cherries—
What am I Doing in the Pits?*
1978

3 The Rose Bowl is the only bowl I've ever seen
that I didn't have to clean.   Remark   *n.d.*

1990. Joyce Brothers (1927/28–   )

1 Marriage is not just spiritual communion and
passionate embraces; marriage is also three-meals-
a-day and remembering to carry out the
trash.   "When Your Husband's Affection
Cools," *Good Housekeeping*
May 1972

2 Anger repressed can poison a relationship as
surely as the cruelest words.   Ibid.

1991. Lynn Caine (1927–1987)

1 Our society is set up so that most women lose
their identities when their husbands die.
Widow   *1974*

2 After my husband died, I felt like one of those
spiraled shells washed upon the beach . . .

Poke a straw through the twisting tunnel, around
and around, and there is nothing there. No flesh.
No life. Whatever lived there is dried up and
gone.   Ibid.

3 "Widow" is a harsh and hurtful word. It comes
from the Sanskrit and it means "empty." I have
been empty too long.   Ibid.

1992. Rosalynn Smith Carter (1927–   )

1 Jimmy* and I were always partners.
Remark, Quoted in *First Ladies*
by Betty Boyd Caroli   *1987*

*James Carter (1924–   ), 39th president of the United
States (1977–81); her husband.

2 If we have not achieved our early dreams, we
must either find new ones or see what we can
salvage from the old. If we have accomplished
what we set out to do in our youth, then we
need not weep like Alexander* the Great that
we have no more worlds to conquer. There is
clearly much left to be done, and whatever else
we are going to do, we had better get on with
it.   *Something to Gain*   *1987*

*King of Macedonia (336–323 B.C.).

3 I had already learned from more than a decade
of political life that I was going to be criticized
no matter what I did, so I might as well be
criticized for something I wanted to do. (If I
had spent all day 'pouring tea,' I would have
been criticized for that too.)
Response to her attending
Cabinet meetings,
op. cit.

1993. Nora Dauenhauer (1927–   )

1 Trying to write
about you is like dragging
a fishing line through bushes.
I go a short distance
and my line hooks
on underbrush.   "Jessy," *in toto, That's
What She Said,* Rayna Green,* ed.
1984

*See 2284.

1994. Midge Decter (1927–   )

1 The hatred of the youth culture for adult society
is not a disinterested judgment but a terror-
ridden refusal to be hooked into the, if you will,
ecological chain of breathing, growing, and dying.
It is the demand, in other words, to remain

children. Ch. 1, *The New Chastity and Other Arguments Against Women's Liberation*   *1972*

2 Women's Liberation calls it enslavement but the real truth about the sexual revolution is that it has made of sex an almost chaotically limitless and therefore unmanageable realm in the life of women.   Ibid., Ch. 2

3 It might sound a paradoxical thing to say—for surely never has a generation of children occupied more sheer hours of parental time—but the truth is that we neglected you. We allowed you a charade of trivial freedoms in order to avoid making those impositions on you that are in the end both the training ground and proving ground for true independence. We pronounced you strong when you were still weak in order to avoid the struggles with you that would have fed your true strength. We proclaimed you sound when you were foolish in order to avoid taking part in the long, slow, slogging effort that is the only route to genuine maturity of mind and feeling. Thus, it was no small anomaly of your growing up that while you were the most indulged generation, you were also in many ways the most abandoned to your own meager devices by those into whose safe-keeping you had been given.
        Ch. 1, *Liberal Parents/Radical Children*   *1975*

4 All they wished for her was that she should turn herself into a little replica of them.
        Ibid., Ch. 3

1995. Anne Edwards (1927–   )

1 What a difficult swallowing of ego and pride she [Judy Garland]* must have suffered with each pill—what a frightening loss of self.
        Judy Garland   *1975*

*See 1903.

1996. Althea Gibson (1927–   )

1 I don't want to be put on a pedestal. I just want to be reasonably successful and live a normal life with all the conveniences to make it so. I think I've already got the main thing I've always wanted, which is to be somebody, to have identity. I'm Althea Gibson, the tennis champion. I hope it makes me happy.
        Ch. 9, *I Always Wanted to Be Somebody*   *1958*

1997. Ruth Prawer Jhabvala (1927–   )

1 "... what she wants is a live guru—someone to inspire her . . . snatch her up and out of

herself—simultaneously destroy and create her."   *Travelers*   *1973*

2 "It is only," he says, "when you have given up all enjoyment that it is no longer enjoyment, it is only then that you can have these things back again."   Ibid.

3 "India . . . is not a place that one can pick up and put down again as if nothing had happened. In a way it's not so much a country as an experience, and whether it turns out to be a good or a bad one depends, I suppose, on oneself."   Ibid.

4 I had come to India to be in India. I wanted to be changed. Henry didn't—he wanted a change, that's all, but not be changed.
        "An Experience of India," *Out of India*   *1986*

1998. Beverly Jones (1927–   )

1 Now, as always, the most automated appliance in a household is the mother.
        "The Dynamics of Marriage and Motherhood," *The Florida Paper on Women's Liberation*   *1970*

2 If enforced wakefulness is the handmaiden and necessary precursor to serious brainwashing, a mother—after her first child—is ready for her final demise.   Ibid.

3 Romance, like the rabbit at the dog track, is the illusive, fake, and never-attained reward which for the benefit and amusement of our masters keeps us running and thinking in safe circles.   Ibid.

1999. Coretta Scott King (1927–   )

1 There is a spirit and a need and a man at the beginning of every great human advance. Each of these must be right for that particular moment of history, or nothing happens.
        Ch. 6, *My Life with Martin Luther King, Jr.*   *1969*

2 My husband* often told the children that if a man had nothing that was worth dying for, then he was not fit to live.
        Ibid., Press Conference (April, 1968)

*Martin Luther King, Jr., American civil rights leader (1929–68); assassinated.

2000. Jean Baker Miller (1927–   )

1 Women are quite validly seeking something more complete than autonomy as it is defined by men,

a fuller not lesser ability to encompass relationships to others, simultaneously with the fullest development of oneself.

Toward a New Psychology of Women
1976

2 Most so-called women's work is not recognized as real activity. One reason for this attitude may be that such work is usually associated with helping others' development, rather than with self-enhancement or self-employment. This is seen as *not doing anything*.　　　Ibid., Ch. 5

3 The very essence of all life is growth, which means change. . . . Some societies, particularly ours, attempt to divert the need for change by entertainment, and a rapid succession of fads. All of these "circuses" may convey the illusion of change, but in fact they accomplish the opposite. They do not meet the need for growth and enlargement of the mind. Instead, they often confuse us so much that we overlook the terrible frustration of this true need. They thwart rather than fulfill it.　　　Ibid.

4 Practically everyone now bemoans Western man's sense of alienation, lack of community, and inability to find ways of organizing society for human ends. We have reached the end of the road that built on the set of traits held out for male identity—advance at any cost, pay any price, drive out all competitors, and kill them if necessary.　　　Ibid., Pt. III, Ch. 8

5 Authenticity and subordination are totally incompatible.　　　Ibid., Ch. 9

2001. Patsy Takemoto Mink (1927–　　)

1 We self-righteously expect all others to admire us for our democracy and our traditions. We are so smug about our superiority, we fail to see our own glaring faults, such as prejudice and poverty amidst affluence.

Speech, National Association for
Student Affairs Conference,
Atlanta　　*May 1972*

2 National security is not only building war machines to kill. National security is as much a policy of the living who prefer life over death, wellness over sickness, work over idleness, education over illiteracy, and food over hunger.　　　"Gazette News," *Ms.*
October 1981

2002. Leontyne Price (1927–　　)

1 I think that recording is in a way much more personal than stage performance. In a theater the audience sees and hears you. So the costumes and the general *mise en scène* help you do the job, because they can see. In recording, you have to see and hear for them with the voice—which makes it much more personal.

Quoted in "Leontyne Price," *Divas:*
Impressions of Six Opera Superstars
by Winthrop Sargeant　　*1959*

2 All token blacks have the same experience. I have been pointed at as a solution to things that have not *begun* to be solved, because pointing at us token blacks eases the conscience of millions, and I think this is dreadfully wrong.
　　　Ibid.

2003. Lillian Ross (1927–　　)

1 Good will was stamped on the faces of all, but there was no indication as to whom or what it was directed toward. As they entered, the guests exchanged quick glances, as though they were assuring each other and themselves that they were there.　　　Ch. 1, *Picture*
1952

2004. Una Stannard (1927–　　)

1 Woman's mask of beauty is the face of the child, a revelation of the tragic sexual immaturity of both sexes in our culture.

"The Mask of Beauty," *Woman in*
Sexist Society, Vivian Gornick* and
Barbara Moran, eds.　　*1971*

*See 2241.

2 Woman officially lost her head in Judeo-Christian cultures in Genesis 3, interestingly enough, for trying to acquire knowledge, for which sin God decided a woman's head was good for nothing since it only got man into trouble.

Mrs. Man　　*1977*

3 . . . wives are a dying breed.　　　Ibid.

4 Freud, living at a time when women were proving their heads were no different from men's, substituted the penis for the head as the organ of male superiority, an organ women could never prove they had.　　　Ibid.

2005. Jane Wagner (1927–　　)

1 LILY.* One thing I have no worry about is
　　whether
God exists.
But it has occurred to me that God has Alzheimer's and has
forgotten

we exist.　　　　Part I, *The Search for Signs of Intelligent Life in the Universe*　1986

*Lily Tomlin; see 2206.

2 KATE. I am sick of being the victim of trends I reflect
but don't even understand.　　　Ibid.

3 TRUDY. See, it's not so much what we know,
but how we know, and what
it is about us that needs to know.
The intriguing part: Of all the things
we've learned, we still
haven't learned
where did this desire to want to know
come from?　　　Ibid., Part II

2006. Maya Angelou (1928–)

1 She said that I must always be intolerant of ignorance but understanding of illiteracy. That some people, unable to go to school, were more educated and even more intelligent than college professors. She encouraged me to listen carefully to what country people called mother wit. That in those homely sayings was couched the collective wisdom of generations.
　　　Ch. 15, *I Know Why the Caged Bird Sings*
　　　1969

2 Children's talent to endure stems from their ignorance of alternatives.　　　Ibid., Ch. 17

3 The fact that the adult American Negro female emerges a formidable character is often met with amazement, distaste and even belligerence. It is seldom accepted as an inevitable outcome of the struggle won by survivors, and deserves respect if not enthusiastic acceptance.　　Ibid., Ch. 34

4 My life has been one great big joke,
A dance that's walked
A song that's spoke,
I laugh so hard I almost choke
When I think about myself
　　　"When I Think About Myself,"
　　　Just Give Me a Cool Drink of Water 'fore I Diiie　1971

5 A textured guilt was my familiar, my bed mate to whom I had turned my back. My daily companion whose hand I would not hold. The Christian teaching dinned into my ears. . . .
　　　Preface, *Gather Together in My Name*
　　　1974

6 "I probably couldn't learn to cook creole food, anyway. It's too complicated."
"Sheeit. Ain't nothing but onions, green peppers and garlic. Put that in everything and you got creole food."　　　Ibid., Ch. 3

7 "You a cherry, ain't you?"
"Yes." Lying would get me nothing.
"Well, that's a thirty-second business. When you turn the first trick, you'll be a 'ho. A stone 'ho. I mean for life. . . . I'm a damn good one. I'm a mud kicker. In the streets I make more money by accident than most bitches make on purpose."　　　Ibid., Ch. 27

8 Separate from my boundaries, I had not known before that he had and would have a life beyond being my son, my pretty baby, my cute doll, my charge. In the plowed farmyard near Bakersfield, I began to understand the uniqueness of the person. He was three and I was nineteen, and never again would I think of him as a beautiful appendage of myself.　Ibid., Ch. 29

2007. Shirley Temple Black (1928–)

1 Won't the new "Suggested for Mature Audience" protect our youngsters from such films? I don't believe so. I know many forty-five-year-old men with the mentalities of six-year-olds, and my feeling is that they should not see such pictures, either.
　　　Quoted in *McCall's*　January 1967

2 Our whole way of life today is dedicated to the *removal of risk*. Cradle to grave we are supported, insulated, and isolated from the risks of life—and if we fall, our government stands ready with Bandaids of every size.
　　　Speech, Kiwanis International Convention, Texas (June 1967),
　　　Quoted in *The Sinking of the Lollipop* by Rodney G. Minott　1968

3 No country has washed more dirty laundry in public than we have.
　　　Quoted in *American Political Women* by Esther Stineman
　　　1980

4 I was very sophisticated when I was 17. When I was 14, I was the oldest I ever was.
　　　Quoted in "What Do You Do After You've Been Shirley Temple?" by Dotson Rader,
　　　Parade　7 December 1986

5 One has to handle these negative experiences alone.* You can't get help from your friends or family. You're finally alone with it, and you have to come to grips with misfortune and go on.　　　Ibid.

*Reference to her mastectomy.

2008. Antonia Brenner (1928–)

1 The Lord was a prisoner, just as you are a prisoner. You have something in common.

Comment to prisoner, Quoted
in "She Brings Hope to
Prisoners" by Arnie Weissman,
Parade Magazine 19 January 1986

2 I lived what most people call the good life. I
was happy, but deep inside I always felt that,
with the short amount of time we are given to
live and love in this world, we spend too much
time loving things instead of people. Ibid.

3 I love America, but charity knows no border. Ibid.

2009. Barbara B. Brown (1928–)

1 The critical and quite new element that biofeed-
back brings to medical and psychologic therapeutics is the capacity to manipulate one's own
body (and mind) by one's own mind. The implications of this newly discovered capacity are
enormous. The uses are obvious, but the misuses
are not obvious at all. *New Mind, New Body,*
Bio-Feedback: New Directions
for the Mind 1974

2 Inner misery does not officially qualify for the
curing magic of the healing arts. Yet we are not
well at all. Prologue, *Between Health and*
Illness 1984

3 Stress is a phenomenon generated almost exclusively by society's mad pace of the twentieth
century. Diminished well being is the social
Pac-Man that devours coping and psychic energy and inner strength. Before it wins the game
of our lives, it needs some serious, sober attention. Ibid.

2010. Mary Daly (1928–)

1 It is the creative potential itself in human beings
that is the image of God.
Ch. 1, *Beyond God the Father 1973*

2 . . . "God's plan" is often a front for men's
plans and a cover for inadequacy, ignorance and
evil. Ibid.

3 Why indeed must "God" be a noun? Why not
a verb—the most active and dynamic of all.
Ibid., Ch. 2

4 The image of Mary as Virgin, moreover, has an
(unintended) aspect of pointing to independence
for women. This aspect of the symbol is of
course generally unnoticed by theologians.
Ibid., Ch. 3

5 I had explained that a woman's asking for equality in the church would be comparable to a black
person's demanding equality in the Ku Klux

Klan. "New Autobiographical Preface"
(1968), *The Church and the*
Second Sex 1975

6 The liberation of language is rooted in the liberation of ourselves. Ibid.

7 Phallic lust is seen as a fusion of obsession and
aggression. As obsession it specializes in genital
fixation and fetishism, causing broken consciousness, broken heartedness, broken connections among women and between women and
the elements. As aggression it rapes, dismem-
bers, and kills women and all living things
within its reach. Phallic lust begets phallocratic
society, that is sadosociety, which is, in fact,
pseudo-society.
Introduction, *Pure Lust 1984*

8 Elemental female Lust is intense longing/craving
for the cosmic concrescence that is creation. It
is charged, tense, in tension with the tenses of
fabricated "father time." Incensed, it burns
through the shallow impressions of insipid senses,
sensing the Sources, Astral Forces, Angels and
Graces that call from the Deep. This Lusting is
divining: foreseeing, foretelling, forecasting.
Unlike the dim divines and divinities, the dead-
heads of deadlands whose ill-illuminations blind
us, Lusty women portend with luster, our radiance from within that radiates from and toward
Original Powers of creation. Ibid.

9 The tidiness inflicted upon women, together
with orders to impose this torture upon each
other, combine to produce a climate of tidy
torture. Ibid., Ch. 8

2011. Takako Doi (1928–)

1 The people are aware of how politics affects
their daily life. It's the politicians who are behind the times. Quoted in "A
Mountain Moves" by Jill Smolowe,
Time 7 August 1989

2012. Muriel Fox (1928–)

1 Women and men have to fight together to change
society—and both will benefit. We [her husband
and herself] are strongly pro-marriage. I think
it is a grave mistake for young girls to think
that it has to be a career versus marriage, equality versus love. Partnership, not dependence, is
the real romance in marriage.
Quoted in "Wait Late to Marry"
by Barbara Jordan Moore,
New Woman October 1971

2 Total commitment to family and total commitment to career is possible, but fatiguing.
Ibid.

2013. Griselda Gambaro (1928–   )

1 Through balkanization, regimes are able to employ horror and fear. The fact that everybody is isolated helps the purposes of any dictatorship. Every dictatorship is based on that principle. One starts being afraid of one's shadow.
> "Griselda Gambaro,"
> Alberto Minero, tr., *Interviews with Contemporary Women Playwrights,* Kathleen Betsko* & Rachel Koenig
> 1987

*See 2256.

2 . . . what feminism means is to change our optic, our vision, which means we must also change our ethics.   Ibid.

3 Theater is very much connected with the society, with the social situation. . . . A theater piece, of itself, demands a confrontation with an audience. It demands that you connect with other people; it demands a collective and social effort with the company and later with the audience.   Ibid.

2014. Rita Liljestrom (1928–   )

1 What good does it do to treat women and men alike if the whole system is permeated by a male culture? If all of society's prioritized values rest on a collective male consciousness, then what is equality but assimilation in the dominant culture?   Quoted in *Sisterhood is Global,* Robin Morgan,* ed.   1984

See 2327.

2015. Thea Musgrave (1928–   )

1 Music is a human art, not a sexual one. Sex is no more important than eye color.
> Quoted in "A Matter of Art, Not Sex,"
> *Time*   10 November 1975

2016. Anna Maria Ortese (1928?   )

1 It was the easiest and at the same time the most sinister thing possible that was happening to me: when one thing recalls another, and so on, till your present vanishes, and everything before you is purely past, the echo of a life that was more real than this one.
> "The Lights of Genoa," *Italian Writing Today,* Raleigh Trevelyna, ed.   1967

2 I was searching for a piece of luggage that seemed to have been mislaid, as my own life had for some time seem slightly mislaid. . . .   Ibid.

3 . . . in order to feel anything you need strength. . . .   Ibid.

2017. Beah Richards (1928?   )

1 Having grown up in a racist culture where two and two are not five, I have found life to be incredibly theatrical and theatre to be profoundly lifeless.   Preface, *A Black Woman Speaks and Other Poems*   1974

2 Heaven and earth!
How is it that bodies join
but never meet?
> "It's Time for Love," St. 2, op. cit.

3 Lord,
there is no death,
no numb, no glacial sorrow
like the love of loveless love,
a tender grunting, sweating horror of
obscenity.   "Love Is Cause It Has to Be,"
> St. 6, op. cit.

2018. Anne Sexton (1928–1974)

1 love your self's self where it lives.
> "The Double Image,"
> *To Bedlam and Partway Back*   1960

2 You, Dr. Martin,* walk from breakfast to madness.   "You, Dr. Martin," St. 1, op. cit.

*Martin Luther King, Jr. American civil rights leader, (1929–68); assassinated.

3 Today life opened inside me like an egg. . . .   "Live," *Live or Die*   1966

4 The trouble with being a woman,
Skeezis,
is being a little girl
in the first place.
> "Hurry Up Please It's Time,"
> *The Death Notebooks*   1974

5 Even without wars, life is dangerous.   Ibid.

6 It doesn't matter who my father was; it matters who I remember he was.
> (1 January 1972, 12:30 A.M.),
> *The Poet's Story,*
> Howard Moss, ed.   1974

7 God owns heaven
but He craves the earth.
> "The Earth," St. 2, *The Awful Rowing Toward God*   1975

8 The tongue, the Chinese say,
    is like a sharp knife:
    it kills
    without drawing blood.
                    "The Dead Heart," St. 3,
                                    op. cit.

9 Each night I am nailed into place and forget
    who I am.   "Sleeping Beauty"   *n.d.*

2019. Agnes Varda (1928–   )

1 You ask me, is it difficult to be a woman
    director? I'd say that it's difficult to be a direc-
    tor, period! It's difficult to be free; it's difficult
    not to be drowned in the system. It's difficult
    for women, and it's difficult for men, the same
    way.   Quoted in "An Interview with
        Agnes Varda" by Barbara Confino,
            Saturday Review   *12 August 1972*

2 The image of woman is crucial, and in the . . .
    movies that image is always switching between
    the nun and the whore, the mama and the bitch.
    We have put up with that for years, and it has
    to be changed. It is the image that is important,
    not so much who is making the film.   Ibid.

2020. Marion Woodman (1928–   )

1 Leap—leap—remembering my journal that looks
    like a Beethoven manuscript—blots, blue ink,
    red, yellow and green, pages torn by an angry
    pen, smudged with tears, leaping with joy from
    exclamation marks to dashes that speak more
    than the words between, my journal that dances
    with the heartbeat of a process in motion. How
    does one fashion a pipe that can contain that
    honesty, and be at the same time professionally
    credible?   Introduction, *The Pregnant Virgin,*
                    A Process of Psychological
                        Transformation   1985

2 Without an understanding of myth or religion,
    without an understanding of the relationship
    between destruction and creation, death and re-
    birth, the individual suffers the mysteries of life
    as meaningless mayhem—alone.
                            Ibid., Ch. 1.

3 Many people can listen to their cat more intel-
    ligently than they can listen to their own de-
    spised body. Because they attend to their pet in
    a cherishing way, it returns their love. Their
    body, however, may have to let out an earth-
    shattering scream in order to be heard at all.
                                    Ibid.

4 Rage and bitterness do not foster femininity.
    They harden the heart and make the body
    sick.   Ibid., Ch. 5.

5 Healing depends on listening with the inner
    ear—stopping the incessant blather, and *listen-
    ing.* Fear keeps us chattering—fear that wells
    up from the past, fear of blurting out what we
    really fear, fear of future repercussions. It is our
    very fear of the future that distorts the *now* that
    could lead to a different future if we dared to
    be whole in the present.   Ibid., Ch. 6

6 Detachment liberates the heart from the past and
    from the future. It gives us the freedom to be
    who we are, loving others for who they are. It
    is the leap into *now,* the stream of Being in
    which everything is possible. It is the domain
    of the pregnant virgin.   Ibid.

7 As human creatures, not gods, we must go for
    the grey, the steady solid line that makes its
    serpentine way only slightly to left and right
    down the middle course between the opposites.
        And that's the differentiated ego, whether
    male or female, cutting a course between wind
    and water.
        Ch. 1, *Addiction to Perfection, The Still
                Unravished Bride*   1982

8 It takes great courage to break with one's past
    history and stand alone.   Ibid., Ch. 2

9 The aim in analysis is to bring the magnificent
    energy of the wild horse under the control of
    the rider, without using a whip that will kill its
    spirit.   Ibid., Ch. 5

10 The experience of the feminine is the psycho-
    logical key to both the sickness of our time and
    its healing.   Ibid., Ch. 7

11 Moreover, perfectionist standards do not allow
    for failure. They do not even allow for life, and
    certainly not for death.   Ibid.

2021. Zong Pu (1928–   )

1 "But I can't play the cello all day long. I must
    read some books too. Since I can't find any
    good ones, I'm reading these, even though they're
    bad. It's like food. When there's nothing deli-
    cious, I eat anything. So there!"
            Ch. 3, "Melody in Dreams,"
                    Song Shouquan, tr.,
        *Seven Contemporary Chinese Women
            Writers,* Gladys Yang,* ed.   1982

*See 2076.

2 Yuejun was outraged thinking how many fami-
    lies had been ruined by the gang*; how many
    young people had been deprived of their lives.
    They wouldn't even leave the premier** alone.
    Our great hero had left nothing of himself after
    his death. Even his ashes had been scattered

over the mountains and rivers. Now they intended to blacken his reputation.   Ibid., Ch. 4

*The Gang of Four.
**Mao-Tse Tung (or Mao Zedong), Chinese Communist leader (1893–1976).

2022. Anne Frank (1929–1945)

1 I soothe my conscience now with the thought that it is better for hard words to be on paper than that Mummy should carry them in her heart.   Entry (2 January 1944),
The Diary of a Young Girl
1952

2 I think what is happening to me is so wonderful, and not only what can be seen on my body, but all that is taking place inside. I never discuss myself or any of these things with anybody; that is why I have to talk to myself about them.   Ibid.

3 We all live with the objective of being happy; our lives are all different and yet the same.
Ibid. (6 July 1944)

4 Parents can only give good advice or put them on the right paths, but the final forming of a person's character lies in their own hands. . . .   Ibid. (15 July 1944)

2023. Marilyn French (1929–   )

1 There are thousands of snails, and mussels too, among the heaped boulders, clustering together like inhabitants of an ancient city . . . they don't have to create their order, they don't have to create their lives, those things are just programmed into them. All they have to do is live.   Pt. 1, Ch. 4, *The Women's Room*
1977

2 "I hate discussions of feminism that end up with who does the dishes," she said. So do I. But at the end, there are always the damned dishes.   Ibid., Ch. 21

3 "Well, love is insanity. The ancient Greeks knew that. It is the taking over of a rational and lucid mind by delusion and self-destruction. You lose yourself, you have no power over yourself, you can't even think straight."
Ibid., Pt. 4, Ch. 10

4 "And this goddamned school is antifemale, they look down on women, especially women my age. It's a goddamned monastery that's been invaded by people in skirts and the men who run it only hope that the people in skirts are pseudomen, so they won't disturb things, won't

insist that feeling is as important as thinking and body as important as mind. . . ."
Ibid., Ch. 12

5 "When they kept you out it was because you were black; when they let you in, it is because you are black. That's progress?"
Ibid., Ch. 19

6 In a patriarchal world, power is not just the highest but the only value.
Beyond Power; On Men, Women,
and Morals   1985

7 And I thought: so that is what a peasant is. Or anyway, what *peasant* meant to my grandmother. Subhuman. The man may have been intelligent enough—he certainly knew crops and weather, and animal husbandry—things I didn't know. But intelligence didn't appear in his gaping face; I could not imagine him speaking. He was a creature immured in blue sky, the wind, wheat fields, shaky wood-fenced yards full of dung. Circumscribed within nature, and benighted, benighted. I was shocked by him. I was shocked that the word *subhuman* crossed his mind. So this is what they meant, the old ones, when they talked of peasants.
Pt. I, Ch. 2, Section 3,
Her Mother's Daughter   1987

8 . . . when the juices are running strong, it seems sinful not to let them run their course. It seems a waste of youth and vigor, and damming up of what should run free.
Ibid., Ch. 3, Section 2

9 The truth is it is not the sins of the fathers that descend unto the third generation, but the sorrows of the mothers.
Ibid., Pt. II, Ch. 6, Section 4

2024. Linda Goodman (1929?–   )

1 It seems to be quite a leap from the . . . lost continent of Atlantis to the jet-propelled twentieth century. But how far is it really? Perhaps only a dream or two.
Afterword, *Linda Goodman's Sun Signs*
1968

2025. Lee Grant (1929–   )

1 One's art adjusts to economic necessity if your metabolism does.
"Selling Out to Hollywood, or Home,"
The New York Times
12 August 1973

2 As more of us [actresses] are moving into producing and directing, the level of creativity among women has become very high, and there-

fore our relationships have changed—have themselves become more creative.
"Art Catches Up to Life," *Ms.*
November 1975

3 . . . art always seems to be catching up to life.   Ibid.

2026. Shirley Ann Grau (1929–   )

1 I know that I shall hurt as much as I have been hurt. I shall destroy as much as I have lost. It's a way to live, you know. It's a way to keep your heart ticking under the sheltering arches of your ribs. And that's enough for now.
"Abigail," *The Keepers of the House*
1964

2 Why does it take so much trouble to keep your stomach full and quiet?   "Margaret,"
op. cit.

3 And isn't it funny, she thought, that it takes two generations to kill off a man? . . . First him, and then his memory. . . .   Ibid.

4 Me? What am I? Nothing. The legs on which dinner comes to the table, the arms by which cocktails enter the living room, the hands that drive cars. I am the eyes that see nothing, the ears that don't hear. I'm invisible too. They look and don't see me. When they move, I have to guess their direction and get myself out of the way. If they were to walk into me—all six feet of black skin and white bone—they'd never again be able to pretend that I wasn't there. And I'd be looking for another job.
"Stanley," *The Condor Passes*
1971

5 He had to humor his body occasionally so that the rest of the time it obeyed his will.
"The Old Man," op. cit.

6 Her Father was waiting. When she saw him, she felt the usual shift in her feelings. A lift, a jump, a tug. Pleasure, but not totally. Love, but not completely. Dependence. Fear, familiarity, identification. That's part of me there, walking along. Tree from which I sprang. His spasm produced me. Shake of his body and here I am. . . .   "Margaret," op. cit.

7 "You forget places you've been and you forget women you've had, but you don't forget fighting."
"Homecoming," *The Wind Shifting West*   *1973*

8 Quite detached from her body, her mind stole out, prowling like a cat in the shadows, searching. And it found that there was nothing on any side of her, that she hung like a point, like a star in the empty sky.   "Sea Change,"
op. cit.

9 Women use children as excuses not to do anything.
Quoted in "Profile . . . Shirley Ann Grau" by Louis Gallo, *New Orleans*
February 1974

10 One of my current pet theories is that the writer is a kind of evangelist, more subtle than Billy Graham, of course, but of the same stuff.
Ibid.

11 The realization that something is good material for a story is no big bang. No need to dignify it with an explosion. Instant bangs never happen. No writer I know talks about it in those terms. Nonwriters tend to think of it that way, but writing is day to day grubby hard work. It's isolated and time consuming.   Ibid.

2027. Jill Johnston (1929–   )

1 It's necessary in order to attract attention, to dazzle at all costs, to be disapproved of by serious people and quoted by the foolish.
Lesbian Nation: The Feminist Solution   1973

2 Bisexuality is not so much a copout as a fearful compromise.   Ibid.

3 . . . we as womenfolk can't as i see it be all that smug and satisfied about where we're at anyhow until the ascending female principle is better established at large.
Gullible's Travels   1974

4 . . . i want these women in office who're in touch with their feelings and who know perfectly well when they're bullshitting and who don't have to displace their concealed feelings by dropping bombs on people who live thousands of miles away. . . .   Ibid.

2028. Ursula K. LeGuin (1929–   )

1 When action grows unprofitable, gather information; when information grows unprofitable, sleep.   Ch. 3, *The Left Hand of Darkness*
1969

2 . . . primitiveness and civilization are degrees of the same thing. If civilization has an opposite, it is war. Of those two things, you have either one, or the other. Not both.   Ibid., Ch. 8

3 To oppose something is to maintain it.
Ibid., Ch. 11

4 What is more arrogant than honesty?
Ibid., Ch. 15

5 It is good to have an end to journey towards; but it is the journey that matters, in the end.
Ibid.

6 He had grown up in a country run by politicians who sent the pilots to man the bombers to kill the babies to make the world safe for children to grow up in.
Ch. 6, *The Lathe of Heaven*   *1971*

7 A person who believes, as she did, that things fit: that there is a whole of which one is a part, and that in being a part one is whole: such a person has no desire whatever, at any time, to play God. Only those who have denied their being yearn to play at it.   *Ibid., Ch. 7*

8 Love doesn't just sit there, like a stone, it has to be made, like bread; re-made all the time, made new.   *Ibid., Ch. 10.*

9 "Night. Country's the only place where they have night left."   "A Week in the Country,"
The Little Magazine
Spring 1976

10 "What would we do with freedom if we had it, Kosta? What has the West done with it? Eaten it. Put it in its belly. A great wondrous belly, that's the West."   *Ibid.*

11 It seems a pity to have a built-in rite of passage* and to dodge it, evade it, and pretend nothing has changed. That is to dodge and evade one's womanhood, to pretend one's like a man. Men, once initiated, never get the second chance. They never change again. That's their loss, not ours. Why borrow poverty?
"The Space Crone,"
The Co-Evolution Quarterly
Summer 1976

*Menopause.

12 The men thought everything, did every-thing, ran everything, made everything, made the laws, broke the laws, punished the lawbreakers; and there was no room left for the women, no City for the women. Nowhere, nowhere, but in their own rooms, alone.   Ch. 1,
The Eye of the Heron   *1978*

13 "His soul is about the size of a toenail."
Ibid., Ch. 7

14 We like to think we live in daylight, but half the world is always dark; and fantasy, like poetry, speaks the language of the night.
"Fantasy, Like Poetry,
Speaks the Language of the Night,"
World Magazine   *21 November 1979*

15 Theory is not enough. There must be stones.
Introduction, *The Language of the Night,*
Essays on Fantasy and Science Fiction,
Susan Wood, ed. & intro.   *1979*

16 Art, like sex, cannot be carried on indefinitely solo; after all they have the same mutual enemy, sterility.
Pt. I, "A Citizen of Mondath," op. cit.

17 For the story—from *Rumpelstilskin* to *War and Peace*—is one of the basic tools invented by the mind of man, for the purpose of gaining understanding. There have been great societies that did not use the wheel, but there have been no societies that did not tell stories.
Pt. II, "On Fantasy and Science Fiction,"
op. cit.

18 Now, I doubt that the imagination can be suppressed. If you truly eradicated it in a child, he would grow up to be an eggplant. Like all our evil propen-sities, the imagination will out. But if it is rejected and despised, it will grow into wild and weedy shapes; it will be deformed.
"Why Are Americans
Afraid of Dragons?," op. cit.

19 Fake realism is the escapist literature of our time. And probably the ultimate escapist reading is that masterpiece of total unreality, the daily stock market report.   Ibid.

20 Sure it's simple, writing for kids. Just as simple as bringing them up.   "Dreams Must Explain
Themselves," op. cit.

21 Fantasy is nearer to poetry, to mysticism, and to insanity than naturalistic fiction is. It is a real wilderness, and those who go there should not feel too safe.
"From Elfland to Poughkeepsie," op. cit.

22 In art, "good enough" is not good enough.
Ibid.

23 Almost anything carried to its logical extreme becomes depressing, if not carcinogenic.
Pt. III,
Introduction to *The Left Hand of Darkness,*
op. cit.

24 Pop art, so called, was the pure essence of art as commodity: soup cans. Genuine newness, genuine originality, is suspect. Unless it's something familiar rewarmed, or something experimental in form but clearly trivial or cynical in content, it is unsafe. And it must be safe. It mustn't hurt the consumer. It mustn't change the consumer. . . . The publishers, the gallery owners, the entrepreneurs, the producers, the marketers, . . . are happier if art is not taken seriously. Soup cans are much easier. They want products to sell, quick turnover, built-in obsolescence. They do not want large, durable, real, frightening things.
Pt. V, "The Stalin in the Soul," op. cit.

25 The worst walls are never the ones you find in your way. The worst walls are the ones you put there—you build your-self. Those are the high ones, the thick ones, the ones with no doors in.
"The Stone Ax and the Muskoxen," op. cit.

26 Hating gets going, it goes round, it gets older and tighter and older and tighter, until it holds a person inside it like a fist holds a stick.
Four Histories, "Old Women Hating," *Always Coming Home* 1985

27 O brave new world, that has no people in it!
Ibid., "Time in the Valley"

28 Almost everything is double like that for adolescents; their lies are true and their truths are lies, and their hearts are broken by the world. They gyre and fall; they see through everything, and are blind. Stone Telling, Part II, op. cit.

2029. Imelda Marcos (1929–)

1 I was no Marie Antoinette.* I was not born to nobility, but I had a human right to nobility.
Quoted on *Sixty Minutes* with Diane Sawyer** *21 September 1986*

*See 588.
**See 2417.

2 If you know how much you've got, you probably haven't got much. Ibid.

2030. Jeanne Moreau (1929–)

1 Success is like a liberation or the first phase of a love story. . . .
Quoted in "Jeanne Moreau," *The Egotists* by Oriana Fallaci* 1963

*See 2060.

2 I don't think success is harmful, as so many people say. Rather, I believe it indispensable to talent, if for nothing else than to increase the talent. Ibid.

3 When people are alive, they have many deaths: not only cowards die a million deaths. What is incredible about existence is its toughness in extremity.
Quoted in "Profiles: A Sense of Dream" by Penelope Gilliatt,* *The New Yorker* 13 March 1978

*See 2102.

4 Mystery is a taste that we have lost, but it will come back. Maybe the longing to see the naked body is a longing to know everything about someone. But you find then that the body itself is a cover. That's the reason the way one is dressed has meaning. Ibid.

2031. Nel Noddings (1929–)

1 Many of the practices embedded in the masculine curriculum masquerade as essential to the maintenance of standards, . . . [but in fact] they accomplish quite a different purpose: the systematic dehumanization of both female and male children through the loss of the feminine. *Caring* 1984

2 It is time for the voice of the mother to be heard in education. Ibid.

2032. Jacqueline Kennedy Onassis (1929–)

1 Can anyone understand how it is to have lived in the White House, and then, suddenly, to be living alone as the President's widow?
Quoted by Billy Baldwin in *McCall's* December 1974

2033. Quin Guanshu (1929–)

1 Wasting time is an unbearable punishment.
Quoted by Huang Zongying* in "The Flight of the Wild-Geese," tr. Yu Fanqin & Wang Mingjie, *Seven Contemporary Chinese Women Writers*, Gladys Yang,** ed. 1982

*See 1953.
**See 2076.

2034. Adrienne Rich (1929–)

1 A thinking woman sleeps with monsters.
"Snapshots of a Daughter-in-Law," Pt. III, St. 1 (1958–1960), *Snapshots of a Daughter-in-Law* 1963

2 Only to have a grief equal to all these tears!
"Peeling Onions," St. 1 (1961), op. cit.

3 I'd call it love if love didn't take so many years but lust too is a jewel a sweet flower. . . .
"Two Songs," Pt. I (1964), *Necessities of Life* 1966

4 Posterity trembles like a leaf and we go on making heirs and heirlooms.
"The Demon Lover," *Leaflets* 1969

5 Humans lived here once; it became sacred only when they went away.
"Shooting Script Part I," Pt. IV, St. 9 (November 1969– February 1970), *The Will to Change* 1971

6 The victory carried like a corpse
from town to town
begins to crawl in the casket.
                    "Letters: March 1969: 1"
                        (1969), op. cit.

7 the moment of change is the only
poem. . . .   "Images for Godard,"
                    Pt. V, St. 7 (1970)
                        op. cit.

8 The woman I needed to call my mother was
silenced before I was born.
                "Reforming the Crystal," *Poems:*
                    Selected and New
                    (1950–1974)   *1974*

9 The friend I can trust is the one who will let
me have my death.
The rest are actors who want me to stay and
further the plot.   Untitled (1960s),
                        op. cit.

10 Every journey into the past is complicated by
delusions, false memories, false namings of real
events.   Foreword, *Of Woman Born*
                        1976

11 My children cause me the most exquisite suffering of which I have any experience. It is the
suffering of ambivalence: the murderous alter-
nation between bitter resentment and raw-edged
nerves, and blissful gratification and tenderness.
Sometimes I seem to myself, in my feelings
toward these tiny guiltless beings, a monster of
selfishness and intolerance.   Ibid., Ch. I

12 The ocean, whose tides respond, like women's
menses, to the pull of the moon, the ocean
which corresponds to the amniotic fluid in which
human life begins, the ocean on whose surface
vessels (personified as female) can ride but in
whose depth sailors meet their death and monsters conceal themselves . . . it is unstable and
threatening as the earth is not; it spawns new
life daily, yet swallows up lives; it is changeable
like the moon, unregulated, yet indestructible
and eternal.   Ibid., Ch. IV

13 For months for years each one of us
had felt her own yes growing in her
slowly forming as she stood at windows
    waited
For trains mended her rucksack combed her
hair   "Phantasia for
    Elvira Shatayev," * *The Dream
    of a Common Language, Poems
        (1974–1977)   1978*

*Leader of a women's climbing team, all of whom died in
a storm on Lenin Peak, August 1974.

14 She* died a famous woman denying
    her sounds
    denying
    her wounds came from the same

source as her power
                Pt. I, "Power" (1974), op. cit.

*Marie Curie; See 1134.

15 No one lives in this room
without confronting the whiteness of the wall
behind the poems, planks of books,
photographs of dead heroines.
Without contemplating last and late
the true nature of poetry. The drive
to connect. The dream of a common
    language.   "Origins and History of
                Consciousness" (1972–1974), op. cit.

16 Marriage is lonelier than solitude.
                    Pt. III, "Paula Becker to
            Clare Westhoff" (1975–1976), op. cit.

17 how sister gazed at sister
reaching through mirrored pupils
back to the mother
            Pt. IV, St. 6, "Sibling Mysteries"
                        (1963), op. cit.

18 But gentleness is active
gentleness swabs the crusted stump
invents more merciful instruments
to touch the wound beyond the wound
                    "Natural Resources,"
            Pt. VIII, Sts. 3 & 4 (1979), op. cit.

19 But to be a female human being trying to fulfill
traditional female functions in a traditional way
is in direct conflict with the subversive function
of the imagination.   *On Lies, Secrets and
                        Silence   1979*

20 I am a feminist because I feel endangered,
psychically and physically, by this society and
because I believe that the women's movement
is saying that we have come to an edge of history
when men—insofar as they are embodiments of
the patriarchal idea—have become dangerous to
children and other living things, themselves
included.   Ibid.

21 It seems to me that the form of many communications in academia, both written and verbal,
is such as to not only obscure the influence of
the personal or subjective but also to give the
impres-sion of divine origin—a mystification
composed of syballine statements—from beings
supposedly emptied of the "dross" of the
self.   Ibid.

2035. Beverly Sills (1929–   )

1 In a way, retarded children are satisfying.
Everything is a triumph. Even getting Bucky to
manage to get a spoon to his mouth was a
triumph. God compensates.
            Quoted in "Beverly Sills," *Divas:
        Impressions of Six Opera Superstars*
            by Winthrop Sargeant   *1959*

2 I would willingly give up my whole career if I could have just one normal child. . . . Ibid.

3 A happy woman is one who has no cares at all; a cheerful woman is one who has cares but doesn't let them get her down.
Interview, "60 Minutes," CBS-TV
1975

2036. Patricia Meyer Spacks (1929–   )

1 Theories by women about women have only recently begun to appear in print. Theories by men about women are abundant.
Ch. 1, *The Female Imagination* 1975

2 Dependency invites encroachment.
Ibid., Ch. 2

3 Like the adolescent, the artist is a dreamer and a revolutionary; like the adolescent, he often finds his accomplishment inadequate to his imaginings. But his dream, setting him apart, helps him to escape the burden of the real.
Ibid., Ch. 5

4 The cliché that women, more consistently than men, turn inward for sustenance seems to mean, in practice, that women have richly defined the ways in which imagination creates possibility; possibility that society denies.
Ibid., "Afterword"

5 One discourses from a height, gossips around the kitchen table.
"In Praise of Gossip," *Hudson Review,* 35 1982

6 Gossip, like poetry and fiction, penetrates to the truth of things. Ibid.

2037. Mabel Elsworth Todd (fl. 1929–37)

1 In the expiratory phase lies renewal of vigor through some hidden form of muscular release. . . . *The Balancing of Forces in the Human Body* 1929

2 Emotion constantly finds expression in bodily position. . . . Ibid.

2038. Alisa Wells (1929–   )

1 Now the real beginnings of the "freedom" which we have discussed for many years—and a heady freedom it is, coming after so many years of reaching outward for it—to finally discover all I had to do was reach inward, and it was there waiting all the time for me!

Quoted in *The Woman's Eye*
by Anne Tucker* 1973

*See 2420.

2039. Christa Wolf (1929–   )

1 Ten years of war. That was long enough to forget completely the question of how the wars started. In the middle of a war you think of nothing but how it will end. And put off living. When large numbers of people do that, it creates a vacuum within us which the war flows in to fill. *Cassandra,* Jan van Heurck, tr. 1983

2 I could not have dreamed what my limbs replied to the questions of his lips, or what unknown inclinations his scent would confer on me. And what a voice my throat had at its command. Ibid.

3 " 'Try to understand, Mother,'' he said. "We want to spare you. The things we have to talk about in our council, now in wartime, are no longer the concern of women.' "
"Quite right," said Anchises. "Now they are the concern of children." Ibid.

4 . . . We foreigners . . . incapable of deciphering even the signs outside the shops, must rely on pictures, smells.
But isn't the word the very thing that has taken over control of our inner life? The fact that I lack words here: doesn't this mean that I am losing myself? How quickly does lack of speech turn into lack of identity? Ibid.

5 The atomic threat, if it has brought us to the brink of annihilation, must then have brought us to the brink of silence too, to the brink of endurance, to the brink of reserve about our fear and anxiety, and our true opinions.
"3: A Work Diary, about the Stuff Life and Dreams Are Made Of," op. cit.

6 About reality. The insane fact that in all the "civilized" industrialized nations, literature, if it is realistic, speaks a completely different language from any and all public disclosures. As if every country existed twice over. As if every resident existed twice over: once as himself and as the potential perceiver of an artistic presentation; second, as an object of statistics, publicity, agitation, advertisement, political propaganda. Ibid.

7 To what extent is there really such a thing as "women's writing" To the extent that women, for historical and biological reasons, experience a different reality than men. Experience a different reality than than men and express it. To the extent that women belong not to the ruler

but to the ruled, and have done so for centuries. To the extent that they are the objects of objects, second-degree objects, frequently the objects of men who are themselves objects, and so, in terms of their social position, unqualified members of the subculture. To the extent that they stop wearing themselves out trying to integrate themselves into the prevailing delusional systems. To the extent that, writing and living, they aim at autonomy. In this case they encounter the men who aim at autonomy. Autonomous people, nations, and systems can promote each other's welfare; they do not have to fight each other like those whose inner insecurity and immaturity continually demand the demarcation of limits and postures of intimidation.   Ibid.

8 Magic, though, was once exclusively the art of women (who, when driven to lovelessness, revert, not without reason, to magic spells). It was the art of the female tribal elders in the early agricultural societies; then, for a long time, of the priestesses, from whom the first priests could entice away the ritual only by pushing their way into the magical clothing of women. It would seem comical to me to point out these things in a tone of indignation, for humanity could not stay at the level of magic and sorcery. But what I ask myself is: Was it necessary that man should come to stand "alone" before Nature—opposite Nature, not in it?*   "4: A Letter about Unequivocal and Ambiguous Meaning, Definiteness and Indefiniteness; about Ancient Conditions and New View-Scopes; about Objectivity," op. cit.

*Ref. to Goethe's *Faust*, Act 5, Pt. II: "If, Nature, I stood before you a man alone."

9 Awe is composed of reverence and dread. I often think that people today have nothing left but the dread.   Ibid.

2040. Maria Castellani (fl. 1930s)

1 Fascism recognizes women as a part of the life force of the country, laying down a division of duties between the two sexes, without putting obstacles in the way of those women who by their intellectual gifts reach the highest positions.   *Italian Women, Past and Present*
                                                      1937

2041. Elisabeth Craigin (fl. 1930s)

1 A so-called Lesbian alliance can be of the most rarefied purity, and those who do not believe it are merely judging in ignorance of the facts.
                                        Either Is Love   *1937*

2042. Lydia Gottschewski (fl. 1930s)

1 It is a curious fact that pacifism . . . is a mark of an age weak in faith, whereas the people of religious times have honored war as God's rod of chastisement . . . Only the age of enlightenment has wished to decide the great questions of world history at the table of diplomats.
                                        Women in the New State
                                                      1934

2043. Frances Newton (fl. 1930s)

1 There, in that manufactured park with its ghoulish artificiality, with its interminable monuments to bad taste, wealth and social position, we were planning to place the body of a beautiful and dignified old man who had lived generously and loved beauty.   *Light, Like the Sun*   *1937*

2 I can stand what I know. It's what I don't know that frightens me.   Ibid.

2044. Alice M. Shepard (fl. 1930s)

1 They shall not pass, tho' battleline
May bend, and foe with foe combine,
     Tho' death rain on them from the sky
     Till every fighting man shall die,
France shall not yield to German Rhine.
                                        "They Shall Not Pass"
                                                      n.d.

2045. Bertye Young Williams (fl. 1930s– 1951)

1 He who follows Beauty
Breaks his foolish heart.
                                        "Song Against Beauty"   *n.d.*

2046. Isabel Allende (193?–   )

1 It was a long week of penitence and fasting, during which there were no card games and no music that might lead to lust or abandon; and within the limits of possibility, the strictest sadness and chastity were observed, even though it was precisely at this time that the forked tail of the devil pricked most insistently at Catholic flesh.   Ch. 1, *The House of the Spirits*,
                                        Magda Bogin, tr.   *1982*

2 A bone in Nivea's corset snapped and the point jabbed her in the ribs. She felt she was choking in her blue velvet dress, with its high lace collars, its narrow sleeves, and a waist so tight that when she removed her belt her stomach

jumped and twisted for half an hour while her organs fell back in place.   Ibid.

3 "The Congress and the armed forces are above corruption. It would be better if we used the money to buy the mass media. That would give us a way to manipulate public opinion, which is the only thing that really counts."
                                   Ibid., Ch. 12

4 They were unable to bribe the members of Congress, and on the date stipulated by law the left calmly came to power. And on that date the right began to stockpile hatred.   Ibid.

2047. Sandra Burton (1934?–   )

1 [Marcos*] was the kind of lawyer you would hire to get you off if you were really in trouble— particularly if you were guilty.
                          Impossible Dream:
                the Marcoses, the Aquinos,
        and the Unfinished Revolution   1989

*Ferdinand Marcos (1917–1989), Philippine president (1966–1986).

2048. Shirley Trusty Corey (193?–   )

1 The arts must be considered an essential element of education, not an optional or lesser element in the consideration of time, materials or appropriate teaching staff. They are the content and process by which we bring unity to isolated knowledge and feelings. They are tools for living life reflectively, joyfully, and with the ability to shape the future.
                     Letter to Elaine Partnow*
                             19 December 1989

*Author.

2 The arts personalize knowledge and visions, demanding an ever growing development of the mind and spirit. We do our children and our country ill service by not supporting them adequately in our schools.   Ibid.

2049. Maureen Fiedler (193?–   )

1 Why organize? First, because it ends isolation. Many women feel treated as second-class citizens—in church, in society. In organizing we lose the sense of being alone. Second, in organizing the whole is greater than the sum of its parts, and our energy is increased when we come together. And third, we are building base communities which struggle for change and give us a place to talk.
                   Speech, National Assembly of
                             Religious Women
                Annual Conference   *1985*

2050. Raisa Gorbachev (193?–   )

1 Soviet people are putting into practice plans of revolutionary restructuring. We want our public life . . . to be worthy of a human being.
                             Quoted in *Time*
                             20 March 1989

2051. Norma Meacock (193?–   )

1 . . . in all my life I have never found reasoning satisfactory as a means of progress.
                       Thinking Girl   1968

2 If the texture of our daily life gets any thinner, it'll disappear up its own arsehole.   Ibid.

2052. Alice Miller (193?–   )

1 Society chooses to disregard the mistreatment of children, judging it to be altogether normal because it is so commonplace.
          "Childhood and Creativity," *Pictures of a
            Childhood,* Hildegarde Hannum, tr.
                                         1986

2 Technical mastery and skill may be helpful to many, but they are not necessarily so. They can even become a prison for those who are afraid to express themselves, for such artists may cling to their technical proficiency and hide behind it. I have seen drawings that are true to nature down to the last detail, with scarcely a single flaw, yet they seem lifeless because the person who drew them is not sensed there at all.
                                         Ibid.

3 We are often imprisoned in the cage of our own abilities and routines, which provides us with a sense of security. We are afraid to break free; yet we must gasp for air and keep seeking our way, probably over and over again, if we do not want to be smothered in the womb of what is familiar and well known to us, but rather to be born along with our new work.   Ibid.

2053. Muriel Resnik (193?–   )

1 JOHN. . . . that's nothing but a tax dodge! . . . This is what the Internal Revenue Service expects. It's all part of the game. They play their part, we have to play ours. It's our duty as American citizens!
              Act I, Sc. 1, *Any Wednesday
                                    1963*

2 JOHN. But she doesn't *know* I'm hurting her, so I'm not. Is that a happy woman? Is she? You see? We're not hurting her, we're not taking anything away from her. In point of fact, having you in my life makes me happy, a happy hus-

band for Dorothy! Far from hurting her, pet, we're *helping* her. . . . If I didn't have you, Dorothy would be *miserable!*
Ibid., Act II, Sc. 1

3 JOHN. I happen to feel that suburbia is as much of a blight as billboards on country roads.
Ibid., Sc. 2

2054. Marjorie Tuite (193?–1986)

1 I think to work on one issue is a luxury in a global analogy. Because there is a basic problem: militarism out of a patriarchal structure, a world view of militarism that nurtures cultural violence.
Speech, National Assembly of
Religious Women Annual
Conference 1985

2055. Nguyen Thi Binh (1930–)

1 I was tortured [in the 1950s] by the Vietnamese, with the French directing, just as now it is with the Americans directing.
Quoted in "Madame Binh" by Beca
Wilson, *New York Review of Books*
25 June 1975

2 We tell our children that the bombs cannot kill everyone, that they must not be afraid. . . . We know our sacrifice is necessary. If the bombs do not fall on you, they fall on friends. We accept fate. We are calm. It is useless to be a pessimist. Some day we will win a beautiful life, if not for ourselves, then for our children.
Ibid.

2056. Julie Anne Bovasso (1930–1991)

1 BEBE. I want to know you. And I want you to know me and understand me. What good is love without understanding? How can we love each other if we don't know each other and understand each other? How can we understand each other if we don't know each other? And how can we know each other if we don't love each other?
Schubert's Last Serenade
1972

2057. Marion Zimmer Bradley (1930–)

1 And as men believe, so their world goes. And so the worlds which once were one are drifting apart.
Bk. I, Ch. 1,
The Mists of Avalon 1982

2 . . . one of the old priestesses had once said that the House of Maidens was for little girls whose whole duty in life was to spill things, break things, and forget things, the rules of their daily life among them, until they had spilled, broken, and forgotten everything they could, and thus made room in their lives for a little wisdom.
Ibid., Ch. 12

3 Some knowledge and some song and some beauty must be kept for those days before the world again plunges into darkness.
Ibid., Bk. IV, Ch. 7

4 "The truth is not so good a story."
Prologue, *The Firebrand* 1987

5 Men had no divine power; they neither bred nor bore; yet somehow they felt they had some natural right in the fruit of their women's bodies, as if coupling with a woman gave them some power of ownership, as if children did not naturally belong to the woman whose body had sheltered and nourished them.
Ibid.

2058. Evan Burrows (1930–)

1 If we're not growing,* we must feel guilty, because we are not fulfilling Christ's demand.
Quoted in "A New General Takes
Charge" by Richard N.
Ostling, *Time* 11 August 1986

*Ref. Salvation Army.

2059. Blythe M. Clinchy (1930–)

See Mary Belenky, 2124, Quotations 1–4.

2060. Oriana Fallaci (1930–)

1 Listening to someone talk isn't at all like listening to their words played over on a machine. What you hear when you have a face before you is never what you hear when you have before you a winding tape.
Foreword, *The Egotists* 1963

2 If I were to give human semblance to the America of today, this hated and often misunderstood country, I would choose Norman Mailer to be the model. . . . One tries to catch America—Mailer's stare—and one doesn't know which eye to choose, which eye to respond to. As a result one cannot reach a moral decision about him. But the practical dilemma remains: Should one be his friend or his enemy? Most people consider him an enemy; to be his friend is anything but easy.
"Norman Mailer,"* op. cit.

*American author (1923–).

3 Glory is a heavy burden, a murdering poison, and to bear it is an art. And to have that art is rare. "Federico Fellini," * op. cit.

*Italian film director (1920–   ).

4 I'm going to show you the real New York—witty, smart, and international—like any metropolis. Tell me this—where in Europe can you find old Hungary, old Russia, old France, old Italy? In Europe you're trying to copy America, you're almost American. But here you'll find Europeans who immigrated a hundred years ago—and we haven't spoiled them. Oh, Gio! You must see why I love New York. Because the whole world's in New York. . . .
Ch. 8, *Penelope at War*   1966

5 "America's a hard school, I know, but hard schools make excellent graduates."
Ibid., Ch. 16

6 But here's what I learned in this war, in this country, in this city: to love the miracle of having been born.
Ch. 3, *Nothing, and So Be It*   1972

7 Have you ever thought that war is a madhouse and that everyone in the war is a patient? Tell me, how can a normal man get up in the morning knowing that in an hour or a minute he may no longer be there? How can he walk through heaps of decomposing corpses and then sit down at the table and calmly eat a roll? How can he defy nightmare-like risks and then be ashamed of panicking for a moment? Ibid., Ch. 6

8 It was a big magnolia, with big branches and big leaves and big flowers which opened like clean handkerchiefs. . . .
Letter to a Child Never Born   1975

9 Equality, Child, like freedom, exists only where you are now. Only as an egg in the womb are we all equal. Ibid.

10 But what is this life by which you, who exist still incomplete, count for more than I, who exist complete already? What is this respect for you that removes respect for me? What is this right of yours to exist that takes no account of my right to exist? Ibid.

11 To have realized your dream makes you feel lost Ibid.

2061. Maria Irene Fornes (1930–   )

1 . . . the playwright is the "woman" of the theater. . . . The playwright is the woman and the director is the husband.
"Maria Irene Fornes," *Interviews with Contemporary Women*

Playwrights, Kathleen Betsko * & Rachel Koenig   *1987*

* See 2256.

2 I feel that the older I get, the more shameless I feel. And in a sense, more pure. Ibid.

3 Writing is an intellectual process, so it is good to *root* the process into your stomach, your heart, your bowels. Ibid.

4 When I'm not doing something that comes deeply from me, I get bored. When I get bored I get distracted, and when I get distracted, I become depressed. It's a natural resistance, and it insures your integrity. You die when you are faking it, and you are alive when you are truthful.
Ibid.

2062. Francine Du Plessix Gray (1930–   )

1 Woman—as tender of the hearth, custodian of most ethnic rituals and religious customs, safeguarder of tribal memory—stand in contrast to man the explorer, innovator, technocrat, who in his nomadic obsession for power and control tends to neglect many time-honored traditions. "Women's Rites," *Vogue September 1980*

2 If I were to describe the decline in quality of life enjoyed by women in the West, I'd say that it decreased in proportion to the decrease of meaningful rituals in their lives. Ibid.

3 This is indeed the nadir of women's history, the idle and lonely housewife, surrounded by kitchen appliances, who increasingly resorts, as medical figures show, to Valium and alcohol and the equally drugging effects of daytime television to relieve her sense of powerlessness and isolation. Ibid.

4 The act of nutrition is not a purely physiological event. It remains, in its more civilized form, a way of communion. The family meal is a formality that cultivates in us from earliest age a curb of natural greed, a capacity for sharing, generosity, thoughtfulness, a talent for civilized conversation. It is a custom that can enrich our knowledge of our historic roots by carefully prepared food from our own ethnic tradition, that can enlarge our love of literature by readings of poetry easily adaptable to the beginning or the end of a meal Ibid.

2063. Lorraine Hansberry (1930–1965)

1 WALTER. Baby, don't *nothing* happen for you in this world 'less you pay *somebody* off!
Act I, Sc. 1, *A Raisin in the Sun 1958*

2 asagai. Ah, I like the look of packing crates! A household in preparation for a journey! . . . Something full of the flow of life. . . . Movement, progress. . . .   Ibid., Act III

3 beneatha. While I was sleeping in my bed in there, things were happening in this world that directly concerned me—and nobody asked me, consulted me—they just went out and did things—and changed my life.   Ibid.

4 beneatha. Don't you see there isn't any real progress, Asagai, there is only one large circle that we march in, around and around, each of us with our own little picture—in front of us—our own little mirage that we think is the future.   Ibid.

2064. Barbara C. Harris (1930–   )

1 A fresh wind is blowing across this church* of ours.   Sermon, Church of the
Advocate, Philadelphia,
Quoted in "First Anglican Woman
Bishop . . ." by Bruce Rule, The
Associated Press
26 September 1988

*Anglican Communion.

2065. Maureen Howard (1930–   )

1 When I go home my mother and I play a cannibal game; we eat each other over the years, tender morsel by morsel, until there is nothing left but dry bone and wig.
Bridgeport Bus   1966

2 . . . my mother is soothed at last by her television, watching lives much more professional than ours.   Ibid.

3 She was a survivor, frail, helpless, but a survivor: the past was one prop, the bottle another.   "Three Cheers for Mr. Spears,"
Before My Time   1974

4 "The process of losing my faith was so gradual," said Mr. Spears, "I didn't seem to notice it. I've thought since that it was a counterpart of attaining my physical growth, which I never noticed either. One day it was complete—my height and my loss of faith—and it was easy, painless. I wish that I had suffered."   Ibid.

2066. Dolores Huerta (1930–   )

1 . . . if you haven't forgiven yourself something, how can you forgive others?

Quoted in "Stopping Traffic: One
Woman's Cause" by Barbara L. Baer,
The Progressive   September 1975

2 Don't be a marshmallow. Walk the street with us into history. Get off the sidewalk. Stop being vegetables. Work for justice. *Viva* the boycott!   Ibid.

3 But we want to change people's lives. Farmworkers kill themselves working, living nowhere, traveling all the time, putting up with the pesticides because the growers want it that way. It's a feudal system which higher wages won't change. *We* know the work can be organized so people settle down in one place with their families, and control their lives through political power and their own union—which they run themselves.   Quoted in "Dolores
Huerta: La Pasionaria* of the
Farmworkers" by Judith Coburn,
Ms.   November 1976

*Dolores Ibarruri [see 1482] was known as La Pasionaria during the Spanish Civil War.

4 I consider myself a feminist, and the Women's Movement has done a lot toward helping me not feel guilty about my [two] divorces. But among poor people, there's not any question about women being strong—even stronger than men—they work in the fields right along with the men. When your survival is at stake, you don't have these questions about yourself like middle-class women do.   Ibid.

5 Women are getting afraid to have kids. I still believe you are supposed to conceive children. Don't you want to leave something of yourself, belong to something, do that for your man?
Ibid.

6 That's why Cesar* always reminds us of that *dicho: Hay mas tiempo que vida* (the saying: there is more time than life).   Ibid.

*Cesar Chavez, American labor leader, union organizer (1927–   ).

2067. Carol Kaye (1930?–   )

Co-author with Elizabeth Douvan. See 1964: 1–2.

2068. Abbey Lincoln (1930–   )

1 The fact that white people readily and proudly call themselves "white," glorify all that is white, and whitewash all that is glorified, becomes unnatural and bigoted in its intent only when these same whites deny persons of African her-

itage who are Black the natural and inalienable right to readily—proudly—call themselves "black," glorify all that is black, and blackwash all that is glorified.

"Who Will Revere the Black Woman?,"
Negro Digest   *September 1966*

2069. Gay Gaer Luce (1930–   )

1 Swept along in the concepts of their business-oriented culture, many people berate themselves if they are not as consistent and productive as machines.   Preface, *Body Time*
1971

2 . . . people are beginning to resist the rhythm of the machine and suspect that the path of inner harmony and health demands an inward attention.   "Trust Your Body Rhythms,"
Psychology Today   *April 1975*

2070. Ann McGovern (1930–   )

1 Dumb. Dumb. Tiny drum beats. Dumb. Dumb. Her sister's favorite word. She called her dumb more than she called her Jane.
"Wonder Is Not Precisely Knowing,"
American Scene: New Voices,
Don Wolfe, ed.   *1963*

2 She shared much with her sister—the absence of a father, the presence of a shadowy unhappy mother. They had one bike and one sled between them and had learned long ago that these possessions were not worth the fights.   Ibid.

3 In those days, people did not think it was important for girls to read. Some people thought too much reading gave girls brain fever.
The Secret Soldier   *1975*

2071. Sandra Day O'Connor (1930–   )

1 There is no question that the [Supreme] Court has now made clear that it will no longer view as benign archaic and stereotypic notions concerning the roles and abilities of males and females. Despite the encouraging and wonderful gains and the changes for women which have occurred in my lifetime, there is still room to advance and to promote correction of the remaining deficiencies and imbalances.
Conference speech,
Atlanta, Quoted in *New York Times*
12 February 1989

2 The more education a woman has, the wider the gap between men's and women's earnings for the same work.   *Phoenix Magazine*   *1971*

2072. Dory Previn (1930–   )

1 men wander
women weep
women worry
while men are asleep
"Men Wander"   *1971*

2 I said
your words
till my throat
closed up
and I had
no voice
and I had
no choice
but to do your song
I was you baby
I was you too long   "I Was You"   *1971*

3 Would you care to stay till sunrise
it's completely your decision
it's just the night cuts through me like a knife
would you care to stay awhile and save my
life?   "The Lady with the Braid"   *1971*

2073. Dorothy Semenow (1930–   )

1 I share with the client how I arrive at my responses. In so doing, I demonstrate that analytic methods are knowable and imply that the client too can master them. This demystifies my utterances and punctures the myth often held over from childhood by the client (and by many of the rest of us too) that *big people,* originally *her parents* and now *the analyst,* can read her mind and heart with their powerful x-ray vision and thus know her sins *and* her destiny.
Address, "Principles of Feminist
Psychoanalysis," Cedars-Sinai
Hospital, Los Angeles   *May 1975*

2074. June L. Tapp (1930–   )

1 Now about the totalitarian liberal. . . . What I found . . . were groups who in principle or on paper were committed to religious values that looked liberal, but who held these views with a ferocity that would not, could not, allow for a truly democratic interpretation of the rights of others. Their liberality was more apparent than real.   Quoted in "The Notion of Conspiracy Is Not Tasty to Americans" by
Gordon Bermant, *Psychology Today*
May 1975

2 The liberal view, it seems to me, encourages a diversity of views and open confrontation among them. . . . The due process of law as we use it, I believe, rests squarely on the liberal idea of conflict and resolution.   Ibid.

2075. Hilma Wolitzer (1930–)

1 I was drawn into the back seat of his father's green Pontiac and the pattern of those seat covers stays in my head forever.
"Waiting for Daddy," *Esquire*
July 1971

2 It seemed strange that I could do all those things with him, discover all those sensations and odors and that new voice that came from the dark pit of my throat *(Don't—oh, yes, oh God)* and that my mother and grandmother didn't know.
Ibid.

2076. Gladys Yang (c.1930–fl. 1950s– 1980s)

1 In China, literature is not viewed as a form of entertainment or simply as a source of aesthetic enjoyment, but as an effective means of education, of inspiring readers with high ideals and the belief that these can be attained.
Preface, *Seven Contemporary Chinese Women Writers*   *1982*

2077. Sally Gearhart (1931–)

1 I look forward with great anticipation to the death of the church. The sooner it dies, the sooner we can be about the business of living the gospel.   "The Lesbian and God-the-Father or All the Church Needs Is a Good Lay—on Its Side"   *1972*

2078. Ossie Guffy (1931–)

1 I'm a woman, I'm black, I'm a little under forty, and I'm more of black America than Ralph Bunche* or Rap Brown** or Harry Belafonte,*** because I'm one of the millions who ain't bright, militant, or talented.
Ossie: The Autobiography of a Black Woman   *1971*

*Am. founder and key diplomat of the United Nations and recipient of the 1950 Nobel Peace Prize (1904–1971).
** An American Civil rights activist (194?–).
***West Indian/American actor, singer, director (1927–).

2 I got more children than I can rightly take care of, but I ain't got more than I can love.   Ibid.

2079. Shirley Hazzard (1931–)

1 One would always want to think of oneself as being on the side of love, ready to recognize it and wish it well—but, when confronted with it in others, one so often resented it, questioned its true nature, secretly dismissed the particular instance as folly or promiscuity. Was it merely jealousy, or a reluctance to admit so noble and enviable a sentiment in anyone but oneself?
Ch. 9, *The Evening of the Holiday*   *1965*

2 "Sometimes, surely, truth is closer to imagination—or to intelligence, to love—than to fact? To be accurate is not to be right."
Ibid., Ch. 11

3 "Do you ever notice," asked Luisa, "how easy it is to forgive a person any number of faults for one endearing characteristic, for a certain style, or some commitment to life—while someone with many good qualities is insupportable for a single defect if it happens to be a boring one?"   Ibid., Ch. 13

4 Algie was collecting contradictions in terms: to a nucleus of "military intelligence" and "competent authorities" he had added such discoveries as the soul of efficiency, easy virtue, enlightened self-interest, Bankers Trust, and Christian Scientist.
"Nothing in Excess," *People in Glass Houses*   *1967*

5 Nothing, Izmet thought, makes a more fanatical official than a Latin. Organization is alien to their natures, but once they get the taste for it they take to it like drink.
"Official Life," op. cit.

6 When I was a child . . . I would think it must be marvellous to issue those proclamations of experience—"It was at least ten years ago" or "I hadn't seen him for twenty years." But chronological prestige is tenacious: once attained, it can't be shed; it increased moment by moment, day by day, pressing its honours on you until you are lavishly, overly endowed with them. Until you literally sink under them.
Ch. 1, *The Bay of Noon*   *1970*

7 Like many men who are compulsively cruel to their womenfolk, he also shed tears at the cinema, and showed a disproportionate concern for insects.   Ibid., Ch. 7

8 "People resort to violence," she said. . . . "not to relieve their feelings, but their thoughts. The demand for comprehension becomes too great, one would rather strike somebody than have to go on wondering about them."
Ibid., Ch. 8

2080. Margaret O'Shaughnessy Heckler (1931–)

1 When you undermine faith in a system, your child may not necessarily see the difference

between the politician who is no longer respected and the policeman, the teacher, the parent.   Quoted in "Impeachment?" by Claire Safran, *Redbook* *April 1974*

2 Once you start to separate public service form the enormous influence of the fat cats of society, you rob the vested interests of their most powerful weapons.   Ibid.

2081. Kristin Hunter (1931–   )

1 "A landlord is supposed to be brutal, stingy, insulting, and arrogant. Like the police, like the magistrates, like all the authority-figures of white society. That's what we're used to. That's what we understand. We're accustomed to our enemies, we know how to deal with them. A landlord who tries to be a friend only confuses us."   *The Landlord* *1966*

2 "Love can't last around poverty. Neither can a woman's looks."   Ibid.

3 "But generally speaking I've always been too confused about who I was to decide who I was better than."   Ibid.

4 Life was both simpler and more complicated than he had imagined. One did not, after all, change one's skin or one's society. One was given both, along with one's identity, at birth. And all things ossified as one grew older. But within the rigid framework were loopholes of possibility, spaces in which small miracles might occur.   Ibid.

2082. Adrienne Kennedy (1931–   )

1 SARAH. As for myself I long to become even a more pallid Negro than I am now; pallid like Negroes on the covers of American Negro magazines; soulless, educated and irrelevant. I want to possess no moral value, particularly value as to my being. I want not to be. I ask nothing except anonymity.   *Funnyhouse of a Negro   1964*

2 SARAH. I find there are no places only my *funnyhouse*.   Ibid.

3 SARAH. I wanted to live in Genesis in the midst of golden savannas, nim and white frankopenny trees and white stallions roaming under a blue sky. I wanted to walk with a white dove. I wanted to be a Christian.   Ibid.

4 To me, menstrual periods, no matter how long you've been having them, are traumatic—simply the fact that you bleed once a month. I

wanted to write about the fear* . . . the fear that you will get blood on your clothes.
"Adrienne Kennedy, *Interviews with Contemporary Women Playwrights,* Kathleen Betsko** & Rachel Koenig *1987*

*In her play *Lesson in a Dead Language.*
**See 2356.

2083. Ella Leffland (1931–   )

1 How could [the diplomats] keep from flinging themselves across the table and smashing each other's faces? Why had [innocent families] been killed if these leaders didn't even let go with a clenched fist? In such restraint, in such cordiality, there was something more horrifying than death itself.   *Rumors of Peace   1979*

2 Each century was the same; history was the same record played over and over. War was war, and peace was preparation for war; it was as if man were crazy, had always been, would always be, and the people on the street were man in his daily and abiding craziness.   Ibid.

2084. Toni Morrison (1931–   )

1 "Which you want? A whipping and no turnips or turnips and no whipping?" *The Bluest Eye   1961*

2 The difference between white and black females seemed to me an eminently satisfactory one. White females were *ladies,* said the sign maker, worthy of respect. And the quality that made ladyhood worthy? Softness, helplessness and modesty—which I interpreted as a willingness to let others do their labor and their thinking. Colored females, on the other hand, were *women*—unworthy of respect, independent and immodest.   "What the Black Woman Thinks About Women's Lib," *The New York Times Magazine 22 August 1971*

3 And like any artist with no art form, she became dangerous.   *Sula* *1974*

4 "I don't know everything, I just do everything."   Ibid.

5 "I know what every colored woman in this country is doing."
"What's that?"
"Dying."   Ibid.

6 He meant that if you take a life, then you own it. You responsible for it. You can't get rid of

nobody by killing them. They still there, and they yours now. *Song of Solomon* 1977

7 "How come it [peacock] can't fly no better than a chicken?" Milkman asked.
"Too much tail. All that jewelry weighs it down. Like vanity. Can't nobody fly with all that shit. Wanna fly, you got to give up the shit that weighs you down." Ibid., Ch. 8

8 Bryn Mawr had done what a four-year dose of liberal education was designed to do: unfit her for eighty per cent of the useful work of the world. Ibid., Ch. 9

9 "Grab this land! Take it, hold it, my brothers, make it, my brothers, shake it, squeeze it, turn it, twist it, beat it, kick it, kiss it, whip it, stomp it, dig it, plow it, seed it, reap it, rent it, buy it, sell it, own it, build it, multiply it, and pass it on—can you hear me? Pass it on!" Ibid., Ch. 10

10 . . . "I wished I'd a knowed more people. I would of loved 'em all. If I'd a knowed more, I would a loved more. Ibid., Ch. 15

11 But I think women dwell quite a bit on the duress under which they work, on how hard it is just to do it at all. We are traditionally rather proud of ourselves for having slipped creative work in there between the domestic chores and obligations. I'm not sure we deserve such big A-pluses for all that.
Quoted in "Toni Morrison's Black Magic" by Jean Strouse, *Newsweek* 30 March 1981

12 Fog came to that place in wisps sometimes, like the hair of maiden aunts. . . .
Tar Baby 1981

13 What they took for inattentiveness was a miracle of concentration. Ibid.

14 "How come everybody run off from Sweet Home can't stop talking about it? Look like if it was so sweet you would have stayed."
"Girl, who you talking to?"
Paul D laughed. "True, true. She's right, Sethe. It wasn't sweet and it sure wasn't home." He shook his head.
"But it's where we were," said Sethe. "All together. Comes back whether we want it to or not." Pt. I, *Beloved* 1987

15 Once upon a time she had known more and wanted to. Ibid.

16 She couldn't read clock time very well, but she knew when the hands were closed in prayer at the top of the face she was through for the day. Ibid., Pt. II

17 "Tell me this one thing. How much is a nigger supposed to take? Tell me. How much?"

"All he can," said Stamp Paid. "All he can."
"Why? Why? Why? Why? Why?" Ibid.

18 Two parents can't raise a child any more than one. You need a whole community—everybody—to raise a child. And the little nuclear family is a paradigm that just doesn't work. It doesn't work for white people or for black people. Why we are hanging onto it, I don't know. It isolates people into little units—people need a larger unit.
Quoted in "The Pain of Being Black" by Bonnie Angelo, *Time* 22 May 1989

2085. Alice Munro (1931–)

1 Lovers. Not a soft word, as people thought, but cruel and tearing.
"Something I've Been Meaning to Tell You," *Something I've Been Meaning to Tell You* 1974

2 Now that she was sure of getting away, a layer of loyalty and protectiveness was hardening around every memory she ever had.
The Beggar Maid 1981

3 They were intimate. They had found out so much about each other that everything had got cancelled out by something else. That was why the sex between them could seem so shamefaced, merely and drearily lustful, like sex between siblings.
The Progress of Love 1986

4 Moments of kindness and reconciliation are worth having, even if the parting has to come sooner or later. Ibid.

2086. Nisa (1931–)

1 There isn't a child whose birth is painless. It hurts like a terrible sickness.
Quoted in *The Life and Words of a !Kung Woman* by Marjorie Shostak 1981

2 When your child dies, you think . . . "This God . . . his ways are foul! Why did he give me a little one and then take her away?"
It is the same if it is your mother. You cry for her as you do for your child. You pull off your beads and ornaments so your neck and body are bare. You mourn for her, you miss her, and your heart is miserable. Ibid.

2087. Cynthia Ozick (1931–)

1 He had once demonstrated that, since God had made the world, and since there was no God,

the world in all logic could not exist.
                        Pt. I, Ch. 1, *Trust*   *1966*

2 "He knows nothing about literature—most great writers don't: all they know is life."
                        Ibid., Pt. III, Ch. 1

3 Moral: In saying what is obvious, never choose cunning. Yelling works better.
                        "We Are the Crazy Lady and Other Feisty Feminist Fables," *The First Ms. Reader,* Francine Klagsbrun, ed.
                        1972

4 I'm not afraid of facts, I welcome facts *but a congeries of facts is not equivalent to an idea.* This is the essential fallacy of the so-called "scientific" mind. People who mistake facts for ideas are incomplete thinkers; they are gossips.   Ibid.

5 Wondrous hole! Magical hole! Dazzlingly influential hole! Noble and effulgent hole! From this hole everything follows logically: first the baby, then the placenta, then, for years and years and years until death, a way of life. It is all logic, and she who lives by the hole will live also by its logic. It is, appropriately, logic with a hole in it.   "The Hole/Birth Catalog,"
                        op. cit.

6 Judaism has no dying god, no embalming of dead bodies, above all no slightest version of death-instinct—"Choose life."   Ibid.

2088. Amanda Row (1931–   )

1 Jocelyn's childhood stood on the bookcase: *Pollyanna, The Bobbsey Twins, Now We Are Six, Black Beauty,* and *The Little Minister* beside *Heidi.*   *Where No Sea Runs*   *1963*

2089. Jane Rule (1931–   )

1 ". . . I think everything has value, absolute value, a child, a house, a day's work, the sky. But nothing will save us. We were never meant to be saved."
    "What were we meant for then?"
    "To love the whole damned world . . ."
                        Desert of the Heart   *1964*

2 Ann did not want to accept the view of the world she sometimes revealed to herself.
                        Ibid.

3 I believe only in art and failure.
                        This is Not for You   *1970*

4 Cleaving is an activity which should be left to snails for cleaning ponds and aquariums.
                        Introduction, *Lesbian Images*   *1975*

5 Morality, like language, is an invented structure for conserving and communicating order. And morality is learned, like language, by mimicking and remembering.
                        "Myth and Morality, Sources of Law and Prejudice," op. cit.

6 What is is my domain. What ought to be is the business of politicians and preachers.
                        "Lesbian and Writer,"
                        A Hot-Eyed Moderate   *1985*

2090. Maxine Singer (1931–   )

1 . . . science is one of the grand human activities. It uses the same kind of talent and creativity as painting pictures and making sculptures. It's not really very different, except that you do it from a base of technical knowledge.
    Science is not an inhuman or superhuman activity. It's something that humans invented, and it speaks to one of our great needs—to understand the world around us.
                        Quoted in *A World of Ideas* by Bill Moyers   *1989*

2 A society that turns its back on science has to face decay and deterioration.   Ibid.

3 The reasons we know that we will discover things that we can't describe now is that this has been the history of science. We do things to learn something we can define, and we wind up knowing things we never imagined even asking about.   Ibid.

4 If the knowledge that is gained is misused, it is not because of science or the scientists, it is because of the same old human problems that have caused evil for eons. . . . And whether evil uses technology that's new or technology that's old, what motivates it are human problems that have nothing to do with the developments in technology.   Ibid.

2091. Merlin Stone (1931–   )

1 It is difficult to grasp the immensity and significance of the extreme reverence paid to the Goddess over a period of (at least) seven thousand years and over miles of land cutting across national boundaries and vast expanses of sea. Yet it is vital to do just that to fully comprehend the longevity as well as the widespread power and influence this religion once held.
                        When God Was A Woman   *1976*

2 We may find ourselves wondering to what degree the suppression of women's rites has actually been the suppression of women's rights.   Ibid.

3 They had so hoped that when the beings of Earth began to think about a very long past, it would help them to conceive of a very long future ahead.
> "The Plasting Project," *Hear the Silence,*
> Irene Zahava, ed. *1986.*

2092. Judith Viorst (1931–)

1 The suburbs are good for the children,
But no place for grown-ups to be.
> "The Suburbs Are Good for
> the Children," *It's Hard*
> *to Be Hip Over Thirty and Other*
> *Tragedies of Married Life* *1968*

2 But it's hard to be hip over thirty
When everyone else is nineteen . . .
> "It's Hard to Be Hip Over
> Thirty," op. cit.

3 Love is much nicer to be in than an automobile accident, a tight girdle, a higher tax bracket or a holding pattern over Philadelphia.
> "What IS This Thing Called Love?,"
> *Redbook* *February 1975*

4 Brevity may be the soul of wit, but not when someone's saying, "I love you." Ibid.

5 And I'm working all day and I'm working all night
To be good-looking, healthy, and wise.
And adored.
And contented.
And brave.
And well-read.
And a marvelous hostess,
Fantastic in bed,
And bilingual,
Athletic,
Artistic . . .
Won't someone please stop me?
> "Self-Improvement Program," St. 4, *How*
> *Did I Get to Be Forty*
> *and Other Atrocities* *1973*

6 Guilt: Although it is sometimes better to sin and feel guilty than never to sin at all, it is pretty ratty to sin and not feel guilty.
> *Love and Guilt and*
> *the Meaning of Life* *1979*

7 When we think of loss we think of the loss, through death, of people we love. But loss is a far more encompassing theme in our life. For we lose not only through death, but also by leaving and being left, by changing and letting go and moving on. And our losses include not only our separations and departures from those we love, but our conscious and unconscious losses of romantic dreams, impossible expectations, illusions of freedom and power, illusions of safety—and the loss of our own younger self,

the self that thought it always would be unwrinkled and invulnerable and immortal.
> Introduction, *Necessary Losses*
> *1986*

8 We begin life with loss. We are cast from the womb without an apartment, a charge plate, a job or a car. We are sucking, sobbing, clinging, helpless babies. Our mother interposes herself between us and the world, protecting us from overwhelming anxiety. We shall have no greater need than this need for our mother.
> Ibid., Ch. 1

9 Growing up means letting go of the dearest megalomaniacal dreams of our childhood. Growing up means knowing they can't be fulfilled. Growing up means gaining the wisdom and skills to get what we want within the limitations imposed by reality—a reality which consists of diminished powers, restricted freedoms and, with the people we love, imperfect connections.
> Ibid., Ch. 11

2093. Barbara Walters (1931–)

1 . . . I happen to disagree with the well-entrenched theory that the art of conversation is merely the art of being a good listener. Such advice invites people to be cynical with one another and full of fake; when a conversation becomes a monologue, poked along with tiny cattle-prod questions, it isn't a conversation any more.
> *How to Talk with Practically Anybody*
> *About Practically Anything* *1970*

2 Parents of young children should realize that few people, and maybe no one, will find their children as enchanting as they do.
> Ibid., Ch. 4

3 Success can make you go one of two ways. It can make you a prima donna, or it can smooth the edges, take away the insecurities, let the nice things come out.
> Quoted in "Barbara Walters—Star of
> the Morning," *Newsweek*
> *6 May 1974*

2094. Liliane Atlan (1932–)

1 We have all become little sharks.
> *The Carriage of Flames and*
> *Voices* *1971*

2 My goal is to arrive at a nonegoistic type of writing: objective writing which would reawaken a love of life. I would like to be able to write for an *empty heart,* that is, emptied of myself—but filled with others.
> *Theater*
> *Winter 1981*

3 At first, men wrote on the walls of their caves, then on papyrus, then paper; why, in an age such as ours, should we not write with waves of sound and light?
> "Liliane Atlan," Antoine Bootz & Catherine Ruello, trs., *Interviews with Contemporary Women Playwrights,* Kathleen Betsko* & Rachel Koenig *1987*

*See 2256.

4 Video is a great instrument—the cassette and television are small and intimate. I am convinced that the new mode of communication is not the theater play, the novel, or cinema, but videotexts. Ibid.

5 When we return to pure language we are given great visions. Ibid.

2095. Bai Fengxi (1932?–)

1 Women are not the moon. Emit your own light. *Return of an Old Friend on a Stormy Night 1983*

2 If a woman is strong, there will be no peace in the house. Ibid.

3 My love of the stage is like my love for my mother: a love that grows with age . . .
> "Bai Fengxi" by Corinne Jacker,* *Interviews with Contemporary Women Playwrights,* Kathleen Betsko** & Rachel Koenig *1987*

*See 2131.
**See 2256.

4 I don't think a writer can give the answer, or make a judgment as to which solution is right or wrong. All a writer can do is raise the question. Ibid.

2096. Beverly Butcher Byron (1932–)

1 Legislation is not going to change discrimination. That is like trying to legislate morality. The quality of representation is neither hindered nor helped by gender; the quality is with the individual. *Speech, 96th Congress January 1979*

2097. Olga Connolly (1932–)

1 Society feels that sport must be justified, and we have gotten away from the Greek concept of mind and body. That is a failure of the physical education process.
> Quoted in "Women in Sports: The Movement Is Real," *Los Angeles Times 23 April 1974*

2 Women must be accepted as human beings, and it can't be done until women are physically strong enough to stand on their own feet. Ibid.

2098. Patricia Cumming (1932–)

1 We thought we could banish
the faceless

dark, the sticky
cobwebs in the hall:
we thought the
hollowness would go away.
> "Further Notes for the Alumni Bulletin," Sts. 3 & 4, *Quartet,* Vol. VI, no's. 15–16 *Winter/Spring 1974*

2099. Eva Figes (1932–)

1 The "cured" [psychiatric] patient is actually brainwashed, a walking automaton, as good a dead. *Patriarchal Attitudes 1970*

2 Sadly, man recognises that the ideal, submissive woman he has created for himself is somehow not quite what he wanted. Ibid.

3 When modern woman discovered the orgasm it was (combined with modern birth control) perhaps the biggest single nail in the coffin of male dominance.
> Quoted in *The Descent of Woman* by Elaine Morgan* *1972*

*See 1883.

4 The law of individualism and private enterprise is that God helps those who help themselves; what is more, He is actually on their side, since it is a sin not to make use of the talents God gave you. So poverty definitely implies not only laziness but a fall from grace: God disapproves of paupers. Ibid.

5 Providing for one's family as a good husband and father is a water-tight excuse for making money hand over fist. Greed may be a sin, exploitation of other people might, on the face of it, look rather nasty, but who can blame a man for "doing the best" for his children?
> "A View of My Own," *Nova January 1973*

2100. Dian Fossey (1932–1985)

1 The more you learn about the dignity of the gorilla, the more you want to avoid people.
> Quoted in "Case of the Gorilla Lady Murder" by William E. Smith, *Time 1 September 1986*

2101. Antonia Fraser (1932–   )

1 . . . as with all forms of liberation, of which the liberation of women is only one example, it is easy to suppose in a time of freedom that the darker days of repression can never come again.   "Epilogue: How Strong?," *The Weaker Vessel*   1984

2 It is however an almost universal fact of history that women have done well in wartime when they have been able or compelled to act as substitutes for men, showing themselves resourceful, courageous and strong in every sense of the words; in short displaying without much difficulty all those qualities generally described as masculine. It is another fact that the post-war period has generally seen a masculine retreat from this view of the female sex when the vacuum no longer needs to be filled.   Ibid.

2102. Penelope Gilliatt (1932–   )

1 ALEX. I can't see why having an affair with someone on and off is any worse than being married for a course or two at mealtimes.
    "Monday," *Sunday Bloody Sunday*   1971

2 ALEX. I've had this business that anything is better than nothing. There are times when nothing has to be better than anything.
    Ibid., "Saturday"

3 The odd thing is, whatever you've been stingy about is something you never use anyway. It's like life itself . . . spend it—spend it because you have it.
    Quoted in "Rebirth?" by James Childs, *The Hollywood Screenwriters*, Richard Corliss, ed.   1972

4 It would be difficult for a woman to be, I should think, the production head of a studio or a manager without being called a bull-dyke.
    Ibid.

2103. Hannah Green (1932–   )

1 A child's independence is too big a risk for the shaky balance of some parents.
    Ch. 5, *I Never Promised You a Rose Garden* 1964

2 She had opened her mind to the words the way an eye used to darkness, veiled with its lashes, opens cautiously to the light, and, finding it even a little blinding, closes itself too late. The light had come, and come invincibly, even after the eye had renounced it. It was too late to unsee.   Ibid., Ch. 8

3 "Look here," Furii said. "I never promised you a rose garden. I never promised you perfect justice. . . ."   Ibid., Ch. 13

4 The girl . . . was a gentle, generous veteran of mechanical psychiatry in a dozen other hospitals. Her memory had been ragged, but her sickness was still intact.   Ibid., Ch. 27

5 "The senses are not discreet!"   Ibid., Ch. 28

2104. Barbara Howar (1932/35–   )

1 . . . the cocktail party remains a vital Washington institution, the official intelligence system.   Ch. 5, *Laughing All the Way*   1973

2 Eventually most television stations around the country achieved their minority quota by hiring "twofers," which is a trade expression meaning a "black, female, on-air personality," two television unthinkables, at one salary—a salary, I might add, that generally falls short of the "equal pay for equal work" cliché.   Ibid., Ch. 15

3 Those complicated people that make Washington the mysterious jungle it is, those famous men and women who to the rest of the world are glamorous and powerful, even ruthless, public figures, have in them a specialness that is inconsistent with the city's official image—a combination of worldly involvement and personal commitment that makes Washington genuine despite its reach for power.
    Ibid., Ch. 21

2105. Jacquelyne Jackson (1932–   )

1 Those black males who try to hold women down are expression in sexist terms the same kinds of expressions in racist terms which they would deny. . . .
    Speech, First National Conference on Black Women   March 1974

2106. Jenny Joseph (1932–   )

1 When I am an old woman I shall wear purple
With a red hat which doesn't go, and doesn't suit me,
And I shall spend my pension on brandy and summer globes
And satin sandals, and say we've no money for butter.
I shall sit down on the pavement when I'm tired
And gobble up samples in shops and press alarm bells

And run my stick along the public railings
And make up for the sobriety of my youth.
"Warning," St. 1, *The Oxford
Book of Twentieth Century
English Verse,* Philip Larkin,
ed. *1973*

2107. Nancy Kassebaum (1932–)

1 The professional politician, with his eye on the next election, quite naturally seeks to temporize or completely avoid potentially controversial issues. . . . The result is often the subjugation of the nation's common welfare.
Quoted in *American
Political Women,* Esther
Stineman *1980*

2108. Judith Krantz (1932–)

1 "It's that or get fat again," she told herself, as she walked up Rodeo or down Camden, feeling a sexual buzz as she searched the windows for new merchandise. The thrill was in the trying on, in the buying. The moment after she had acquired something new it became meaningless to her. . . . Ch. 6, *Scruples 1978*

2 Billy thought privately that the rich are different only because people treat them as if they were. Sometimes she wondered why people bothered. It was not as if knowing someone rich rubbed off on them, put more money in their own bank accounts. Yet, there it was, that slight self-consciousness, the faint over-consideration, that eagerness to charm, the instinctive putting-the-best-foot-forward that she heard all day.
Ibid., Ch 8

2109. Loretta Lynn (1932–)

1 A woman's two cents worth is worth two cents in the music business.
Quoted in "Sexism Seen But Not
Heard" by Tracy Hotchner,
Los Angeles Times 26 May 1974

2110. Miriam Makeba (1932–)

1 I look at an ant and I see myself: a native South African, endowed by nature with a strength much greater than my size so I might cope with the weight of a racism that crushes my spirit. I look at a bird and I see myself: a native South African, soaring above the injustices of apartheid on wings of pride, the pride of a beautiful people. I look at a stream and I see myself: a native South African, flowing irresistibly over hard obstacles until they become smooth and, one day, disappear—flowing from an origin that has been forgotten toward an end that will never be. Prologue, *Makeba, My
Story,* with James Hall *1987*

2 Ours was a marriage, a love affair—the land would nurture us, and we would honor the land.
But the land was too rich and too good. The powerful and greedy invaders saw this at once. . . . We Africans were not consulted or even paid attention to. We were pushed aside, robbed of our land. When we protested we were massacred. A handful of whites took power, and with their boots they pressed the faces of an entire people to the dirt. Ibid.

3 *"Age ain't nothin' but a number."* But age is other things, too. It is wisdom, if one has lived one's life properly. It is experience and knowledge. And it is getting to know all the ways the world turns, so that if you cannot turn the world the way you want, you can at least get out of the way so you won't get run over.
Ibid., Ch. 16

4 Africa has her mysteries, and even a wise man cannot understand them. But a wise man respects them. Ibid., Ch. 20

5 People in the United States still have a 'Tarzan' movie view of Africa. That's because in the movies all you see are jungles and animals or occasionally the pictures from South Africa of people being beaten by police. You don't realize that we live 'normal' lives there, just as Americans and Europeans do. We watch television and listen to the radio and go to dances and fall in love. Quoted in "Miriam Makeba
is set to take the U.S. by Storm
Once Again" by J. Poet, New York Times
Syndicate *18 August 1988*

2111. Joan Manley (1932–)

1 The best direction is the least possible direction. Quoted in "Hooked on Books"
by Jurate Kazickas, *Working Woman
February 1979*

2 Selling is the final step of the creative process—since I didn't have the ability to be in on the beginning of a book, the writing of it, then I wanted to be in on the end.
Quoted in "Wistful View From the
Corporate Heights" by Lynn Darling,
*The Washington Post
8 April 1979*

3 I would have made a terrible mother. For one thing, I hate to repeat myself. Ibid.

4 Sometimes you wonder how you got on this mountain. But sometimes you wonder, "How will I get off?" *Ibid.*

2112. Nobuko Mori (1932–)

1 Let the voice from the kitchen be heard in government. Quoted in "A Mountain Moves" by Jill Smolowe, *Time* 7 August 1989

2113. Edna O'Brien (1932–)

1 When something has been perfect . . . . there is a tendency to try hard to repeat it.
The Love Object 1963

2 There is something about holding on to things that I find therapeutic. *Ibid.*

3 I suppose you wonder why I torment myself like this, but I need it, I cannot let go of him now, because if I did, all our happiness and my subsequent pain . . . will have been nothing, and nothing is a dreadful thing to hold on to. *Ibid.*

4 Later she came in the house and sat in front of the telephone, staring at it, waiting for it to come to life, hoping, beseeching, lifting it from time to time to make sure it was not out of order, then, relieved at its regular purr, she would drop it suddenly in case he should be dialing at that very moment, which he wasn't.
Ch. 3, *August Is a Wicked Month* 1965

5 "After the rich, the most obnoxious people in the world are those who serve the rich."
Ibid., Ch. 8

6 Kindness. The most unkindest thing of all.
Ibid., Ch. 11

7 There are times when the thing we are seeing changes before our very eyes, and if it is a landscape we praise nature, and if it is spectre, we shudder or cross ourselves, but if it is a loved one that defects, we excuse ourselves and say we have to be somewhere, and are already late for our next appointment.
"A Scandalous Woman," *A Scandalous Woman* 1974

8 But it is not good to repudiate the dead because they do not leave you alone, they are like dogs that bark intermittently at night.
"Love-Child," op. cit.

9 I would grow to forget him, the him that I believed had broken my heart, but in my saner moments I recognized as being probably the last to partake with me at that fount of sensuality,

and vertigo and earthly love.
The High Road 1988

10 In the evenings when I had a drink or two I would allow myself to think of her, as I might a painting or a beautiful garden. I would dwell on her body the way I never allowed myself to dwell on my own, exploring it with invisible hands, invisible eyes, touching her tentatively and without shame. *Ibid.*

11 It hurt, with a raw hurt, to recall our gadfly days, and yet I did, our days, nights, beaded jackets, shawls, sometimes had our hands read . . . those days when every new love affair brought us, as we thought, to the brink of a sustained happiness. I thought of the day I too had gone a bit mad, slipped from behind this girl with all these hopes to the woman who would count in morsels from that moment onward the pleasures and excitements of her life. *Ibid.*

2114. Linda Pastan (1932–)

1 Grief is a circular staircase
"The Five Stages of Grief," *The Five Stages of Grief* 1978

2 You have grown wings of pain
and flap around the bed like a wounded gull
calling for water, calling for tea, for grapes
whose skins you cannot penetrate.
Remember when you taught me
how to swim? Let go, you said,
the lake will hold you up.
I long to say, Father let go
and death will hold you up . . .
"Go. Gentle," *PM/AM* 1982

2115. Sylvia Brinton Perera (1932–)

1 . . . so much of the power and passion of the feminine has been dormant in the underworld— in exile for five thousand years.
Introduction, *Descent to the Goddess, A Way of Initiation for Women* 1981

2 For what has been valued in the West in women has too often been defined only in relation to the masculine: the good, nurturant mother and wife; the sweet, docile, agreeable daughter; the gently supportive or bright, achieving partner. As many feminist writers have stated through the ages, this collective model (and the behavior it leads to) is inadequate for life; we mutilate, depotentiate, silence, and enrage ourselves trying to compress our souls into it, just as surely as our grandmothers deformed their fully breathing bodies with corsets for the sake of an ideal.
Ibid., Ch. 1

3 Our planet is passing through a phase—the return of the goddess . . .   *Ibid.*

2116. Sylvia Plath (1932–1963)

1 . . . I guess I feel about a hot bath the way those religious people feel about holy water. . . . The longer I lay there in the clear hot water the purer I felt, and when I stepped out at last and wrapped myself in one of the big, soft, white, hotel bath-towels I felt pure and sweet as a new baby.   Ch. 2, *The Bell Jar*
                                                       1963

2   "Do you know what a poem is, Esther?"
"No, what?" I would say.
"A piece of dust."
Then just as he was smiling and starting to look proud, I would say, "So are the cadavers you cut up. So are the people you think you're curing. They're dust as dust as dust. I reckon a good poem lasts a whole lot longer than a hundred of those people put together."
                                     Ibid., Ch. 5

3 I never wanted to get married. The last thing I wanted was infinite security, and to be the place an arrow shoots off from. I wanted change and excitement and to shoot off in all directions myself, like the colored arrows from a Fourth of July rocket.   *Ibid.*, Ch. 7

4 I took a deep breath and listened to the old brag of my heart. I am, I am, I am.   *Ibid.*, Ch. 20

5 A living doll, everywhere you look.
It can sew, it can cook,
It can talk, talk, talk.

It works, there is nothing wrong with it.
You have a hole, it's a poultice
You have an eye, it's an image.
My boy, it's your last resort.
Will you marry it, marry it, marry it.
                      "The Applicant," *Ariel*   *1966*

6 Out of the ash
I rise with my red hair
and I eat men like air.
                         "Lady Lazarus," op. cit.

7 Viciousness in the kitchen!
                              "Lesbos," op. cit.

8 How long can I be a wall around my green
    property?
How long can my hands
Be a bandage to his hurt, and my words
Bright birds in the sky, consoling? consoling?
It is a terrible thing
To be so open: it is as if my heart
Put on a face and walked into the
    world. . . .
                "A Poem for Three Voices"   *1968*

9 Spiderlike, I spin mirrors,
Loyal to my own image,
Uttering nothing but blood.
                       "Childless Woman," *Ibid.*

10 Widow. The word consumes itself. . . .
     "Widow," *Crossing the Water*   *1971*

11 Is there no way out of the mind?
                   "Apprehensions"   *n.d.*

2117. Harriet Rosenstein (1932?–   )

1 . . . violent outrage and equally violent despair seem inevitable responses to our era. All the horrors committed in the name of national honor or the sanctity of the family or individual integrity have caught up with us.
            "Reconsidering Sylvia Plath," * *The
                    First Ms. Reader*, Francine
                    Klagsbrun, ed.   *1972*

* See 2116.

2 Destiny is something men select; women achieve it only by default or stupendous suffering.
               Quoted in *Ms.*   *July 1974*

2118. Alix Kates Shulman (1932–   )

1 Why was everything nice he did for me a bribe or a favor, while my kindnesses to him were my duty?   Ch. 1, *Memoirs of an Ex-Prom
                              Queen*   *1972*

2 If, as the girls always said, it's never too early to think about whom to marry, then it could certainly not be too early to think about who to be. Being somebody had to come first, because, of course, somebody could get a much better husband than nobody.   *Ibid.*, Ch. 2

2119. Muriel Siebert (1932–   )

1 I know a twenty-eight-year-old woman, a recent graduate of Harvard Business School. She asked me the other day if I wasn't afraid of what people will say if I associate with the women's movement. What she doesn't understand is that it's because of the movement and people like me that it's now not as difficult for her to make it.   Quoted in *Women at Work*
                   by Betty Medsger   *1975*

2120. Elizabeth Taylor (1932–   )

1 When people say: she's got everything, I've only one answer: I haven't had tomorrow.
                       Elizabeth Taylor   *1965*

2 I want to be known as an actress. I'm not royalty.   Interview in *The New York Times*

(1964), Quoted in *Elizabeth*
by Dick Sheppard   *1974*

2121. Megan Terry (1932–   )

1 CHESTER. My God, the human baby! A few weeks after birth, any other animal can fend for itself. But *you!* A basket case till you're twenty-one.   *The Magic Realist   1968*

2 CHESTER. Fourteen mewling brats and not a business brain in a bucketful.   Ibid.

3 Broadway is just a showcase for television now. Broadway is no longer the place I was taught about when I went to college, i.e., the place where The Theater was kept alive, the Theater of Ideas. A place where one could be in touch with human feelings, where you could see yourself, where society could see itself. Broadway is now a place for the tourists to go and be beguiled by stagecraft.
     "Megan Terry," *Interviews with Contemporary Women Playwrights,*
     Kathleen Betsko* & Rachel
     Koenig   *1987*

*See 2256.

4 I think you have to *submit* to art. One must submit the ego to the work, or the work never gets done. That's the positive side of submission. The only utopias that ever lasted very long were those where people submitted to an idea greater than the individual.   Ibid.

5 I think that people are too rarified in New York. They've been too long away from animals and plants and trees.   Ibid.

6 Isn't it strange that this American culture has valued everything but the people who create something out of thin air? What is left when a civilization dies? Only its art and a few tool fragments.   Ibid.

2122. Robin Worthington (1932–   )

1 Mental health, like dandruff, crops up when you least expect it.
     Thinking About Marriage   1971

2 The battle to keep up appearances unnecessarily, the mask—whatever name you give creeping perfectionism—robs us of our energies.   Ibid.

2123. Corazon Aquino (1933–   )

1 The politicians think that I have not included enough of them; the nonpoliticians think that I have gone back to the old ways; and the mass public groups think I have forgotten them.

Interview with Sandra Burton,*
Quoted in *Time   10 March 1986.*

*See 2047.

2 No one can say Cory did not give it her all.
     Ibid.

3 It wasn't until we [she and her incarcerated husband]* got over the self-pity that we were able to accept suffering as part of our life with Christ. A man or woman reaches this plane only when he or she ceases to be the "hero" playing to the gallery and becomes the humble Christian praying to God to fix the direction of his or her actions.   Speech (1984), Quoted in
     "The Passage of Corazon Aquino"
     by Gail Sheehy,**
     Parade Magazine   8 June 1986

*Benigno ("Ninoy") Aquino Jr., Philippine senator & hero (1933–1983).
**See 2228.

4 Marcos* underestimated me—and look where it got him!   Interview with Diane
     Sawyer,** *60 Minutes,* ABC-TV
     14 September 1986

*Ferdinand Marcos (1917–1989), Philippine president (1966–1986).
**See 2417.

5 I think Ninoy's joy is the knowledge that he pulled a fast one on me. Once more he has gone on his merry way and left me to pick up the mess.   Speech, St.
     Ignatius Roman Catholic Church,
     Newton, Massachusetts
     21 September 1986

2124. Mary Field Belenky (1933–   )

1 Language—even literacy—alone does not lead automatically to reflective, abstract thought. In order for reflection to occur, the oral and written forms of language must pass back and forth between persons who both speak and listen or read and write—sharing, expanding, and reflecting on each other's experiences. Such interchanges lead to ways of knowing that enable individuals to enter into the social and intellectual life of their community. Without them, individuals remain isolated from others; and without tools for representing their experiences, people also remain isolated from the self.
     Pt. I, Ch. 1,
     The Ways of Knowing, with
     Blythe McVicker Clinchy,*
     Nancy Rule Goldberger,**
     and Jill Mattuck Tarule,***
     1986

*See 2059.
**See 2151.
***See 2380.

2 That they can strengthen themselves through the empowerment of others is essential wisdom often gathered by women. Ibid., Ch. 2

3 Connected knowers do not measure other people's words by some impersonal standard. Their purpose is not to judge but to understand.
Ibid., Ch. 6

2125. Maureen Duffy (1933–   )

1 We all have to rise in the end, not just one or two who were smart enough, had will enough for their own salvation, but all the halt, the maimed and the blind of us which is most of us. *The Microcosm* 1966

2 All reduction of people to objects, all imposition of labels and patterns to which they must conform, all segregation can lead only to destruction. *Rites* 1969

3 The pain of love is the pain of being alive. It's a perpetual wound. *Wounds* 1969

4 Love is the only effective counter to death.
Ibid.

5 I think basically I just think I want everyone and don't really want anybody.
Love Child 1971

2126. Cynthia Fuchs Epstein (1933–   )

1 During World War II, for instance, when the young men were off at war, dating did not consume the time of the college co-ed and she redirected her energies to study. . . . Work became an alternative even for those who did marry. Once engaged in an occupation, many had so firm a foothold they were loath to give it up. *Woman's Place* 1970

2127. Pozzi Escot (1933–   )

1 In our [Peruvian] schools we teach Bach, Beethoven and Brahms but nothing that has been composed in the past 70 years.
Quoted in "A Matter of Art, Not Sex,"
Time 10 November 1975

2128. Dianne Feinstein (1933–   )

1 This city [San Francisco] typifies the American dream of a sense of tolerance and openness, with different people living closely together, carefully, with respect for the law, not impinging their will on others but living with a growing mutual respect. Quoted in "Dianne Feinstein: Learning the Lessons of the

Phoenix" by Mildred Hamilton,
San Francisco Examiner
4 March 1979

2129. Barbara C. Gelpi (1933–   )

1 . . . the masculine and feminine principles are not simply arbitrary manila folders for filing certain qualities; they are transcendent functions, spiritual realities which must be taken into account in the psychological makeup of every human being.
"The Androgyne," *Women and Analysis,* Jean Strouse, ed. 1974

2 If women could help society to throw off the heavy yoke of the Fathers they might eventually move humanity forward. . . . Ibid.

3 With myths, dreams, visions, poems, stories, conversations we must imagine a race in which both mind and soul are of equal importance and may be equally fulfilled for both sexes. Ibid.

2130. Ruth Bader Ginsberg (1933–   )

1 In commercial law, the person duped was too often a woman. In a section on land tenure, one 1968 textbook explains that "land, like women, was meant to be possessed."
Quoted in "Portia Faces Life—The Trials of Law School" by Susan Edmiston, *Ms.* April 1974

2 The emphasis must be not on the right to abortion but on the right to privacy and reproductive control. Ibid.

2131. Corinne Jacker (1933–)

1 It's true that women tend to think of domestic, encapsulated incidents as crucial. We look at the microcosm rather than the macrocosm. . . . Perhaps women find their metaphors in domestic experience because we are still new to the world of action.
"Corinne Jacker," *Interviews with Contemporary Women Playwrights*, Kathleen Betsko* & Rachel Koenig 1987
*See 2256.

2132. Yoko Ono (1933–   )

1 I wonder why men can get serious at all. They have this delicate long thing hanging outside their bodies, which goes up and down by its own will. . . . If I were a man I would always be laughing at myself.
"On Film No. 4," (1967),
Grapefruit 1970

2 Don't be too clever or we'll scratch your goodies out . . . or we'll blow your sillies off.
                              "Catman" *n.d.*

3 Keep your intentions in a clear bottle and leave it on the shelf when you rap.
                              "Peter the Dealer" *n.d.*

4 What a bastard the world is.
                              "What a Bastard the World Is" *n.d.*

2133. Suzy Parker (1933–)

1 I thank God for high cheekbones every time I look in the mirror in the morning.
          Quoted in *This Fabulous Century* (1950–1960)   *1970*

2134. Miriam Schneir (1933–)

1 The decline of feminism after the First World War is attributable at least in part to the eventual concentration of the women's movements on the single narrow issue of suffrage—which was won.
          Introduction, *Feminism: The Essential Historical Writings*   *1972*

2 . . . centuries of slavery do not provide a fertile soil for intellectual development or expression.   Ibid.

2135. Mary Jane Sherfey (1933–)

1 The nature of female sexuality as here presented makes it clear that . . . woman's inordinate orgasmic capacity did not evolve for monogamous, sedentary cultures.
          "A Theory on Female Sexuality,"
          Journal of the American Psychoanalytical Association   *1966*

2 The strength of the drive determines the force required to suppress it.   Ibid.

2136. Susan Sontag (1933–)

1 Ambition if it feeds at all, does so on the ambition of others.
          Ch. 1, *The Benefactor*   *1963*

2 I was not looking for my dreams to interpret my life, but rather for my life to interpret my dreams.   Ibid., Ch. 4

3 Unfortunately, moral beauty in art—like physical beauty in a person—is extremely perishable. It is nowhere so durable as artistic or intellectual beauty. Moral beauty has a tendency to decay

very rapidly into sententiousness or untimeliness.   "Camus' Notebooks" (1963), *Against Interpretation*   *1966*

4 *Transparence* is the highest, most liberating value in art—and in criticism—today. Transparence means experiencing the luminousness of the thing in itself, of things being what they are.   "Against Interpretation" (1964), op. cit.

5 Interpretation is the revenge of the intellect upon art.   Ibid.

6 The relation between boredom and Camp taste cannot be overestimated. Camp taste is by its nature possible only in affluent societies, in societies or circles capable of experiencing the psychopathology of affluence.
          "Notes on 'Camp' "
          (1964), op. cit.

7 Camp is a vision of the world in terms of style. . . . It incarnates a victory of 'style' over 'content,' 'aesthetics' over 'morality,' or irony over tragedy.   Ibid   *1966*

8 Persons who merely have-a-life customarily move in a dense fluid. That's how they're able to conduct their lives at all. Their living depends on not seeing.   *Death Kit*   *1967*

9 Foreigners extol the American "energy," attributing to it both our unparalleled economic prosperity and the splendid vivacity of our arts and entertainments. But surely this is energy bad at its source and for which we pay too high a price, a hypernatural and humanly disproportionate dynamism that flays everyone's nerves raw.   "What's Happening in America" (1966), *Styles of Radical Will*   *1969*

10 Experiences aren't pornographic; only images and representations—structures of the imagination—are.   "The Pornographic Imagination" (1967), op. cit.

11 Bending the mind and shaking loose the body makes someone a less willing functionary of the bureaucratic machine. Rock, grass, better orgasms, freaky clothes, grooving on nature—really grooving on anything—unfits, maladapts a person for the American way of life.
          Quoted in *Recreation*
          by Marc Estrin   *1971*

12 Most men experience getting older with regret, apprehension. But most women experience it even more painfully: with shame. Aging is a man's destiny, something that must happen because he is a human being. For a woman, aging is not only her destiny . . . it is also her vulnerability.
          "The Double Standard of Aging,"
          Saturday Review   *October 1972*

13 . . . cancer patients are lied to, not just because the disease is (or is thought to be) a death sentence, but because it is felt to be obscene— in the original meaning of that word: ill-omened, abominable, repugnant to the senses.
Ch. 1, *Illness as Metaphor*   1977

14 "At the beginning of the world, everything was America." How far from the beginning are we? When did we first start to feel the wound?
I, Etcetera   1978

15 Sisyphus, I. I cling to my rock, you don't have to chain me. Stand back! I roll it up—up, up. And . . . down we go. I knew that would happen. See, I'm on my feet again. See, I'm starting to roll it up again. Don't try to talk me out of it. Nothing, nothing could tear me away from this rock.
"Debriefing," *I*, Ibid.   1978

16 Communism is fascism with a human face.
Speech, Forum for Poland's Solidarity, New York City   1982

2137. Rosalie Sorrels (1933–)

1 Let her discover all the things that she can do.
Sooner or later she's gonna discover
She can do without you.
"She Can Do Without You"   1974

2 What can I say, but that it's not easy?
I cannot lift the stones out of your way,
And I can't cry your bitter tears for you.
I would if I could, what can I say?
"Apple of My Eye"   1974

3 I like to sing for my friends; I don't want to sing in fucking stadiums. I like to be able to see who I'm singing to, look them right in the eye and talk to them. . . . I can't get into that thing where you keep swelling up bigger and bigger, publicity, super-hype, higher prices, more equipment. . . . If you come around with a seven-piece band, three roadies, a manager, and groupies . . . you lose your mobility and miss all the *good* times.
Quoted in "Rosalie Sorrels" by Amie Hill, *Rolling Stone* 28 January 1975

4 It's not that I don't love the darlings
I'd do anything for my kids, but
If I had to go through all that one more time
I'd jump off the Golden Gate Bridge tra la la.   "Mother's Day Song"   1980

2138. Minnie Thomas (1933?–)

1 Crack has taken away these women's pride.
By the time they find their way here,*

they'll beg, steal and trade their bodies to the dope man for more.
Quoted in "A Hand and a Home for Pregnant Addicts" by Dennis Wyss, *Time* 27 February 1989

*Mandela House, a halfway house for pregnant crack addicts in Oakland, California.

2 I tell the women constantly that I'm part of them. I tell them, 'I was you.'   Ibid.

2139. Dorothy Uhnak (1933–)

1 The only people left when the blacks and Puerto Ricans came spilling in were the old people who still paid nearly the same rents as they had for more than twenty-five years. Who had been fixed in income, fixed in a particular neighborhood, in a particular building, in a particular apartment. They stayed as though serving a life sentence; their next and only move would be in a box.
Part I, Ch. 7, *The Investigation*   1977

2 I like to deliver more than I promise instead of the other way around. Which is just one of my many trade secrets.   Ibid., Ch. 13

3 He maintained that the case was lost or won by the time the final juror had been sworn in; his summation was set in his mind before the first witness was called. It was all in the orchestration, he claimed: in knowing how and where to pitch each and every particular argument; who to intimidate; who to trust, who to flatter and court; who to challenge; when to underplay and exactly when to let out all the stops.
Ibid., Ch.14

4 There weren't many unusual events to clutter up her memory, so she hung on to the ones she had.   Ibid., Part II, Ch. 10

2140. Helen Vendler (1933–)

1 It is a crushing burden . . . to reinterpret in a personal, and personally acceptable, way every conventional liturgical and religious act; to make devotion always singular, never simply communal . . . to particularize, not to merge; to individuate, not to accede.
Introduction, *The Poetry of George Herbert*   1975

2141. Nina Voronel (1933–)

1 In Russia today, anything new is dangerous.
Quoted in "Russia: No Exit for These Four Women" by Ruth Gruber, *Ms.* April 1974

2 The echoes of pogroms sob in my verses
Making contact with history.
"I Am A Jew," op. cit.

2142. Fay Weldon (1933–   )

1 We shelter children for a time; we live side by
side with men; and that is all. We owe them
nothing, and are owed nothing. I think we owe
our friends more, especially our female
friends.   *Praxis*   *1978*

2 You end up as you deserve. In old age, you
must put up with the face, the friends, the health
and the children you have earned.   Ibid.

3 Women who live by the good will of men have
no control over their lives, and that's the truth
of it.   *The Heart of the Country*   *1989*

4 The heart of the country is rotten.   Ibid.

5 I am an ordinary person, but carried to
extremes.   *Leader of the Band*   *1989*

6 I make myself deaf to the pleas of the unborn.
As many as my father brought into existence, I
will keep out of it.   Ibid.

2143. Freda Adler (1934–   )

1 The phenomenon of female criminality is but
one wave in this rising tide of female assertive-
ness—a wave which has not yet crested and
may even be seeking its level uncomfortably
close to the high-water mark set by male
violence.
          Prologue, *Sisters in Crime*   *1975*

2 Of all the tyrannies which have usurped power
over humanity, few have been able to enslave
the mind and body as imperiously as drug
addiction.   Ibid., Ch. 5

3 Stripped of ethical rationalizations and philosophical pretensions, a crime is anything that a
group in power chooses to prohibit.
          Ibid., Ch. 7

4 It is little wonder that rape is one of the least
reported crimes. Perhaps it is the only crime in
which the victim becomes the accused and, in
reality, it is she who must prove her good
reputation, her mental-soundness, and her im-
peccable propriety.   Ibid., Ch. 9

2144. Brigitte Bardot (1934–   )

1 I leave before being left. I decide.
          Quoted in *Newsweek*
          5 March 1973

2145. Sissela Bok (1934–   )

1 If you combine lying and secrecy, and if you
also bring in violence so that secrecy covers up
for schemes of lying and violence, then I think
a republic can die. I don't think it's possible for
citizens to have very much of an effect if they
literally don't know what's going on.
          Quoted in *A World of*
          Ideas by Bill Moyers   *1989*

2 The predicament we're in now and that we have
been in for some time is the threat of extinction
from nuclear weapons, and the threat of extinction from environmental sources. It has simply
never been the case before in human history that
all of life—not just human life but really all of
life—could be wiped out. That has made an
enormous change for us. At the same time, this
is also an extraordinary opportunity.   Ibid.

3 Our century has been unbelievably violent and
brutal and filled with tyranny, but it has also
brought forth countervailing powers. We've had
popular movements seeking change nonviolently
and, in fact, succeeding more and more
often. . . . We have better history. We know
much more about how wars start and how they
can get out of hand.   Ibid.

2146. Diana Chang (1934–   )

1 The old are girlish now
Going to their grooms
They marry mysteries
          "On Seeing My Great-Aunt in a
          Funeral Parlor," St. 5,
          The American Scholar, Vol. 28,
          No. 1 *Winter 1958/59*

2147. Sherry Suib Cohen (1934–   )

1 What have been the costs of blind, cutthroat,
unaffiliating competition? Lagging productivity,
as the import figures reveal, a huge turnover of
the best people, distrust and suspicion within
the ranks, political infighting and sabotage,
workers who expect to be ignored and who
expect to fail (and who do exactly these two
things). These are the costs the American corporation is paying.
          Ch. 3, *Tender Power*   *1989*

2 Power is not a sorority for working women
alone. A certain inner confidence is to be gained
when, knowing one is following one's strongest
instincts, one chooses, in defiance of current
dogma, to stay home. For some, heeding that
call is power. Moreover, those who decide they
can afford to stay home, at least for a few years,

are not alone in the wisdom of their decision. Ibid., Ch. 10

2148. Arlene Croce (1934?–)

1 At least some of the men who write sex books admit that they really don't understand female sexuality. Freud was one. Masters is another— that was why he got Johnson.
Quoted in *Commentary n.d.*

2149. Diane Di Prima (1934–)

1 We buy the arms and the armed men, we have placed them
on all the thrones of South America
we are burning the jungles, the beasts will rise up against us "Goodbye Nkrumah," St. 4,
Intrepid #VI 1966

2 Had you lived longer than your twenty-six years
You, too, wd have come up against it like a wall—
That the Beauty you saw was bought
At too great a price
Even in those days. . . .
"Ode to Keats," St. 1, *The East Side Scene,* Allen De Loach, ed. 1968

2150. Sheila Fugard (1934?–)

1 In a way it is much simpler to take upon oneself a discipline without the consolation of a visionary guide.
I believe now that there is no need to find him, the Buddhist, that all I must do is progress in the knowledge of the void, the perennial nothingness of the moment.
Pt. III, Last Lines,
The Castaways 1972

2 I talk of the lives of others. I am fertilized, but not fulfilled, and my life insists on its own voice. Part I, *A Revolutionary Woman* 1985

3 Racism is enshrined here.* Ibid.

*Ref. the Union of South Africa.

4 The Karoo* is all space. The trees fail to fill the emptiness, and the fences are useless too. The Karoo swallows up everything; Brahmins and Untouchables, the flocks of sheep and goats, as well as the houses and possessions. There is much to contend with here. Ibid.

*The harsh landscape of South Africa.

5 The butcher is mistaken. Justice is not weighed on a scale like a pound of steak. I'm aware of

the cost of justice, and it's not measured in pounds. It's got to do with men's hearts.
Ibid., Part III

2151. Nancy Rule Goldberger (1934–)

See Mary Field Belenky, 2124: 1–4.

2152. Jean Harris (1934?–)

1 The problems of administering a prison or living in one as an inmate appear to me to be quite similar . . . mental illness, physical illness, ignorance, drugs and alcohol, racism, overcrowding, inadequate vocational training, incompetent staff and homosexuality.
Were I to be asked to choose, I would put mental illness at the top of the list. There are days on my floor when the shrieks and screams and banging on the metal doors and throwing of furniture against a wall make my blood run cold, leave me touching a blanket or a book or something that represents sanity and a degree of permanence in a world gone mad.
"They Always Call Us Ladies": Stories from Prison 1988

2 My own observations is that many of the women here [in Bedford Hills Correctional Facility, New York] fall loosely into two groups. The first made up of those so damaged in childhood they have never learned to trust and love or even feel small pangs of compassion for others; the second made up of those in whom the need to love and be loved is the overriding drive in their lives. Ibid.

2153. Nancy M. Henley (1934–)

1 The humiliation of being a subordinate is often felt most sharply and painfully when one is ignored or interrupted while speaking, towered over or forced to move by another's bodily presence or cowed unknowingly into dropping the eyes, the head, the shoulders. Conversely, the power to manipulate others' lives, to take graft, price gouge, or plan the bombing of far-off peasants is conferred in part by others' snapping to attention in one's presence, their smiling, fearing to touch or approach, their following one around for information and favors. These are the trivia that make up the batter for that great stratified waffle that we call our society. Ch. 1, *Body Politics: Power, Sex, and Non-Verbal Communication* 1977

2 Feminine atmosphere projects the image of immobility; these accoutrements are ones that one can only look beautiful in, not move, feel strong, or be active in. . . . It is no accident that coffins puff out with satin pads, lace, and frills . . . ., and the funeral parlor is filled with flowers. These signs of femininity, common also to the beauty parlor, are symbolic of the powerlessness of the dead, as they are of the powerlessness of women.   Ibid., Ch. 4

3 "Polite" company, that is, the social elite and those who would imitate them, are so removed from their bodies undoubtedly a sign of spirituality and near-divinity that they are expected not to feel the need to itch, belch, or fart.
                                                     Ibid., Ch. 6

4 The history of power in fact shows us that victims of unfathomable oppression have arisen to claim their rights, that power is persistently being broken down and overturned. Every new insight into its workings may provide a new road to its overthrow.   Ibid., Ch. 11

2154. Marilyn Horne (1934–   )

1 Ninety percent of what's wrong with singers today is that they don't breathe right.
                    Quoted in "Marilyn Horne," *Divas: Impressions of Six Opera Superstars* by Winthrop Sargeant   1959

2 The thing to do [for insomnia] is to get an opera score and read *that*. That will bore you to death.   Ibid.

2155. Louise Kapp Howe (1934–   )

1 Despite the focus in the media on the affluent and the poor, the average man is neither. Despite the concentration in TV commercials on the blond, blue-eyed WASP, the real American prototype is of Italian or Irish or Polish or Greek or Lithuanian or German or Hungarian or Russian or any of the still amazing number of national origins represented in this country—a "white ethnic," sociologists somberly call him.
                    Introduction, *The White Majority*   1970

2 We all know what the American family is supposed to look like. We can't help it. The picture has been imprinted on our brains since we were tiny, . . . Now, the striking point about our model family is not simply the compete-compete, consume-consume style of life it urges us to follow. . . . The striking point, in the face of all the propaganda, is how few Americans actually live this way.

                    Introduction, *The Future of the Family*   1972

3 . . . the assumption of a male-breadwinner society . . . ends up determining the lives of everyone within a family, whether a male breadwinner is present or not, whether one is living by the rules in suburbia or trying to break them on a commune.   Ibid.

4 While politicians carry on about the sanctity of the American family, we learn . . . that in the scale of national priorities our children and families really come last. After freeways. After pork subsidies. After the billions spent on munitions in the name of national defense. It is now time . . . to reverse the usual procedure. It is time to *change the economy* to meet the needs of American families.   Ibid.

2156. Diane Johnson (1934–   )

1 Waiting to be murdered has given me you might say something to live for.
                    The Shadow Knows   1974

2 We are surrounded by the enraged.   Ibid.

3 A lesser life does not seem lesser to the person who leads one. His life is very real to him; he is not a minor figure in it. He looks out of his eyes at our poet, our chronicled statesman. . . . And he is our real brother.
                    Lesser Lives   n.d.

2157. Audre Lorde (1934–   )

1 Since Naturally black is Naturally Beautiful
I must be proud
And, naturally,
Black and
Beautiful

Who always was a trifle
Yellow
And plain though proud
Before.   "Naturally," St. 1, *Cables to Rage*
                                                     1970

2 There are so many roots to the
     tree of anger
that sometimes the branches
     shatter
before they bear.
          "From a Land Where Other People
          Live," *From a Land Where
          Other People Live*   1975

3 . . . Which me will survive all these liberations.   Ibid.

4 Black feminism is not white feminism in blackface.

"Sexism: An American Disease in Blackface,"
Sister Outsider   n.d.

5 What woman here is so enamoured of her own oppression that she cannot see her heelprint upon another woman's face?
"Uses of Anger," op. cit.

2158. Sophia Loren (1934–   )

1 Getting ahead in a difficult profession requires avid faith in yourself. You must be able to sustain yourself against staggering blows and unfair reversals. There is no code of conduct to help beginners. That is why some people with mediocre talent, but with great inner drive, go much further than people with vastly superior talent. I'm convinced that this inner drive is something you are born with, and no one can teach you how to acquire it.
Quoted in *Sophia: Living and Loving* by A. E. Hotchner
1979

2159. Shirley MacLaine (1934–   )

1 The pain of leaving those you grow to love is only the prelude to understanding yourself and others.   *Don't Fall Off the Mountain*
1970

2 For if the talent or individuality is there, it should be expressed. If it doesn't find its way out into the air, it can turn inward and gnaw like the fox at the Spartan boy's belly.
Ibid., Ch. 4

3 Africa seemed the harmonious voice of creation. Everything alive was inextricably intertwined until death. And even death was part of the life harmony.   Ibid., Ch. 13

4 Freedom, with her front windows open and unlocked, with breezes and challenges blowing in. I wished that she [MacLaine's daughter, Sasha] would know herself through freedom. I wished that underneath she would understand that there is no such thing as being safe—that there are no safe havens for anyone who wants to know the TRUTH, *whatever* it is, about himself or others.   Ibid., Ch. 19

5 Hollywood always had a streak of the totalitarian in just about everything it did.
Ch. 2, *You Can Get There from Here*   *1975*

6 China was proud now—of herself and of her potential. She had pulled herself to dignity and unity and that spirit literally pervaded the communes, the backbone of China. The Chinese countryside was where the revolution was won

and the countryside was the secret of China's future.   Ibid., Ch. 20

7 In some ways, America had grown up to be a masterpiece of self-concern.   Ibid., Epilogue

8 I was not a soldier or a philosopher or a politician; I could cure no disease, solve no economic problems or lead any revolution. But, I could dance I could sing. I could make people laugh. I could make people cry.   Ibid.

9 Within the family environment was every human conflict that could ultimately lead to a willingness, or a nonwillingness, to wage war. Most attitudes of, and toward, violence and hostility are spawned in the family. Just as attitudes of love and compassion are.
Ch. 2, *Dancing in the Light*   *1985*

10 Experimentation in front of the big black giant* is enough to reduce an accomplished and seasoned performer to the rank of blithering idiot. . . . The audience never responds to artifice. They can detect sham immediately and just as swiftly respond positively to something you do that comes out of your gut. They want you to be real. That's what they're there for.
Ibid., Ch. 6

*Reference to song "The Big Black Giant" from Rogers and Hammerstein's musical, *Me and Juliet.*

11 Nothing should be permanent except struggle with the dark side within ourselves.
Ibid., Ch. 11

12 If I could know me, I could know the universe.   Ibid., Epilogue

2160. Winnie Mandela (1934–   )

1 I am a living symbol of whatever is happening in the country. I am a living symbol of the white man's fear.   "My Little Siberia," *Part of My Soul*   *1984*

2 The Afrikaner in the Free State—for him a black is something that site on their tractor or plods behind their plough. What is more important to that farmer is his tractor and not that laborer. . . .   Ibid.

3 We never had him* physically to share that love he exudes so much of. I knew when I married him that I married the struggle, the liberation of my people.   "Life with Him Was Always a Life without Him," op. cit.

*Nelson Mandela, South African hero and civil rights leader (1918–   ); incarcerated 1962–1990.

2161. Kate Millett (1934–   )

1 The care of children, even from the period when their cognitive powers first emerge, is infinitely

better left to the best-trained practitioners of both sexes who have chosen it as a vocation, rather than to harried and all too frequently unhappy persons with little time or taste for the work of educating minds however young or beloved. . . . The family, as that term is presently understood, must go.
Sexual Politics   1969

2 Perhaps nothing is so depressing an index of the inhumanity of the male supremacist mentality as the fact that the more genial human traits are assigned to the underclass: affection, response to sympathy, kindness, cheerfulness.   Ibid.

3 . . . I see the function of true Erotica (writing which is pro-, not antisexual) as one not only permissible but worthy of encouragement and social approval, as its laudable and legitimate function is to increase sexual appetite just as culinary prose encourages other appetites.
Ibid.

4 Aren't women prudes if they don't and prostitutes if they do?   Speech, Women's Writer's Conference, Los Angeles
22 March 1975

5 Whores are the political prisoners of the feminist movement. . . . They are considered criminals for no other reason than the fact that they are women . . . men aren't jailed for solicitation. . . . Women are jailed. And they're jailed because they have cunts.
Quoted in *Radical Lifestyles* by Claudia Dreifus*   1971

* See 2388.

6 All the agony of that severance fresh as a dismembered limb.   *Sita   1976*

7 In sex one wants or one does not want. And the grief, the sorrow of life is that one cannot make or coerce or persuade the wanting, cannot command it, cannot request it by mail order or finagle it through bureaucratic channels.   Ibid.

2162. Carol Lee Sanchez (1934–)

1 For fifty years, children in this country have been raised to kill Indians mentally, subconsciously through the visual media, until it is an automatic reflex. That shocks you? Then I have made my point . . . the cheap western is still rolling out of Hollywood, the old shoot-'em-up westerns playing on afternoon kid shows, late night T.V. Would you allow your children to play Nazis and Jews? Blacks and KKKs?
"Sex, Class and Race Intersections Visions of Women of Color," *A Gathering of Spirit,* Beth Brant,* ed.   1984

* See 2134.

2 We have been displaced, relocated, removed, terminated, educated, acculturated and in our hearts and minds we will always "go back to the blanket" as long as we are still connected to our families, our Tribes and our land.
Ibid.

3 yo soy india
  pero no soy
  yo soy anglo
  pero no soy
  yo soy arabe
  pero no soy
  yo soy chicana
  pero no soy   "Tribal Chant," St. 5, *That's What She Said,* Rayna Green,* ed.   1984

* See 2284.

4 how come you kees me by
  the reever, & on the strit
  jou don told me hallo?
      "The Way I Was. . . .," St. 2, op. cit.

5 love longs to touch the ordinary places—
  momentary what-nots scattered through the
      years
  from dresser drawer
  to china closet
  and way up high on the linen
  closet shelf.   Untitled, St. 2, op. cit.

2163. Patricia Simon (1934–)

1 An old French farm built on levels up and down a hillside near Grasse—overlooking, in the middle distance, the quiet cluster of the town and, in the further distance, hills, and beyond them other hills, and other hills, in a gentle, fertile, dreamlike landscape that continued forever—the Alpes-Maritimes.
"The Making of a Masterpiece," *McCall's   October 1970*

2 Flowers and sunlight, air and silence—*"luxe, calme et volupté."*   Ibid.

2164. Gloria Steinem (1934–)

1 The first problem for all of us, men and women, is not to learn, but to unlearn.
"A New Egalitarian Life Style," *The New York Times 26 August 1971*

2 It's clear that most American children suffer too much mother and too little father.   Ibid.

3 . . . no man can call himself liberal, or radical, or even a conservative advocate of fair play, if

his work depends in any way on the unpaid or underpaid labor of women at home, or in the office. Ibid.

4 God knows (*she* knows) that women try.
"Sisterhood," *The First Ms. Reader,* Francine Klagsbrun, ed. *1972*

5 I have met brave women who are exploring the outer edge of human possibility, with no history to guide them, and with a courage to make themselves vulnerable that I find moving beyond words. Ibid.

6 The definition of woman's work is shitwork.
Quoted in "Freelancer with No Time to Write" by John Brady, *Writer's Digest February 1974*

7 A government's responsibility to its young citizens does not magically begin at the age of six. It makes more sense to extend the free universal school system downward—with the necessary reforms and community control that child care should have from the start.
"Victory with Honor," *Ms. April 1974*

8 Erotica is about sexuality, but pornography is about power and sex-as-weapon—in the same way we have come to understand that rape is about violence, and not really about sex at all. "Erotica and Pornography, A Clear and Present Difference," *Ms. November 1978*

9 We must understand the difference between what we mean by family and what the Right Wing means by family. . . . Women are the means of production, owned by the husband. Children are the labor, owned by the husband. And that's what they mean by family. Consequently, they oppose any direct guarantee of right between wife and the law or children and the law, because that is antithetical to their definition of family. Speech, National Women's Political Caucus Conference, Albuquerque, New Mexico *July 1981*

10 . . . the family is the basic cell of government: it is where we are trained to believe that we are human beings or that we are chattel, it is where we are trained to see the sex and race divisions and become callous to injustice even if it is done to ourselves, to accept as biological a full system of authoritarian government. Ibid.

11 Some of us are becoming the men we wanted to marry. Speech, Yale University *23 September 1981*

12 If the men in the room would only think how they would feel graduating with a "spinster of arts" degree they would see how important this [language reform] is. Ibid.

13 . . . the authority of any governing institution must stop at its citizen's skin.
"Night Thoughts of a Media-Watcher," *Ms. November 1981*

14 Finding language that will allow people to act together while cherishing each other's individuality is probably the most feminist and therefore truly revolutionary function of writers.
Introduction, *Outrageous Acts and Every Day Rebellions 1983*

15 Living in India made me understand that a white minority of the world has spent centuries conning us into thinking a white skin makes people superior, even though the only thing it really does is make them more subject to ultraviolet rays and wrinkles.
"If Men Could Menstruate" (1978), op. cit.

16 Logic has nothing to do with oppression.
Ibid.

17 If men start taking care of children, the job will become more valuable.
Quoted in "Onward, Women!" by Claudia Wallis, *Time 4 December 1989*

18 A woman without a man is like a fish without a bicycle. Attr. *n.d.*

2165. Shirley Hill Witt (1934–)

1 I want to weep for La Vieja
Two booths away,
But I can't: she is me.
"Punto Final," St. 6, *That's What She Said*, Rayna Green, ed. *1984*

2 The campesinos tend to smooth out the wrinkled places of legend for the better telling and also for their own better understanding. In this way, they discharge those questions left unanswered in their time as so much uselessness: the tale weaves better the more simply told, anyway. "La Mujer de Valor," op. cit.

2166. Susan Brownmiller (1935–)

1 Man's discovery that his genitalia could serve as a weapon to generate fear must rank as one of the most important discoveries of prehistoric times, along with the use of fire and the first crude stone axe. From prehistoric times to the present, I believe, rape has played a critical function. It is nothing more or less than a conscious process of intimidation by which all men keep all women in a state of fear.
Against Our Will: Men, Women, and Rape 1975

2 It has been argued that, when killing is viewed as not only permissible but heroic behavior sanctioned by one's government or cause, the fine distinction between taking a human life and other forms of impermissible violence gets lost, and rape becomes an unfortunate but inevitable by-product of the necessary game called war. Ibid.

3 My purpose in this book has been to give rape its history. Now we must deny it a future. Ibid.

2167. Gretchen Cryer (1935–)

1 Music is my one salvation
Singin' is my celebration
And playin' with a rock 'n roll band
Is a natural high
"Natural High," *I'm Getting My Act Together And Taking It On The Road* 1977

2 MOTHER. I prayed and prayed that my father would die before mother so that she could have a little time to herself, a little time to be happy. But he didn't, he held on, the old coot. Finally she died first and he died the next day. He just couldn't let her have anything. op. cit.

3 HEATHER. You see, men would rather have a shitty thing than a good thing. It's less binding. As long as a relationship is shitty, they have a sense of freedom because they can say to themselves, "This is shitty and I really should get out of it." But if a relationship is good, that's very frightening, because then they don't have an excuse to get out. So the trick becomes to stay in a relationship and keep it shitty so the door is always open. Ibid.

4 Until men learn that nurturing is all part of the human condition, and that they have an equal responsibility to share in it, they are going to be stuck with their wars. "Gretchen Cryer," *Interviews with Contemporary Women Playwrights*, Kathleen Betsko* & Rachel Koenig 1987

See 2256

5 It's lucky happenstance that women's liberation came along just when it did so that women can participate in the world arena and rescue the planet. Just in the nick of time. Ibid.

2168. Joan Didion (1935–)

1 New York is full of people on this kind of leave of absence, of people with a feeling for the tangential adventure, the risk adventure, the interlude that's not likely to end in any doublering ceremony.
"New York: The Great Reprieve," *Mademoiselle* February 1961

2 "I think nobody owns land until their dead are in it. . . ." Ch. 8, *Run River* 1963

3 She *knew* clocks weren't supposed to stop, don't be silly. She knew they needed a clock. But she could not work with it going every second. When it was going every second that way she could not seem to take her eyes off it, and because it made no noise she found herself making the noise for it in her mind. Ibid., Ch. 18

4 . . . the day that I did not make Phi Beta Kappa nonetheless marked the end of something, and innocence may well be the word for it. I lost the conviction that lights would always turn green for me . . . lost a certain touching faith in the totem power of good manners, clean hair, and proven competence on the Stanford-Binet scale. To such doubtful amulets had my self-respect been pinned, and I faced myself that day with the nonplussed apprehension of someone who has come across a vampire and has no crucifix at hand.
"On Self-Respect" (1961) *Slouching Towards Bethlehem* 1968

5 As an adjective, the very word "Hollywood" has long been pejorative and suggestive of something referred to as "the System." . . . the System not only strangles talent but poisons the soul, a fact supported by rich webs of lore. "I Can't Get That Monster Out of My Mind" (1964), op. cit.

6 . . . California is a place in which a boom mentality and sense of Chekhovian loss meet in uneasy suspension; in which the mind is troubled by some buried but ineradicable suspicion that things had better work here, because here, beneath that immense bleached sky, is where we run out of continent.
"Notes From a Native Daughter" (1965), op. cit.

7 "I am what I am. To look for 'reasons' is beside the point. *Play It As It Lays* 1970

8 "Hear that scraping, Maria?" the doctor said. "That should be the sound of music to you. . . ." Ibid., Ch. 25

9 . . . she had deliberately not counted the months but she must have been counting them unawares, must have been keeping a relentless count somewhere, because this was the day, the day the baby would have been born. Ibid., Ch. 54

10 To hear someone's voice she looked in the telephone book and dialed a few prayers . . .   Ibid., Ch. 64

11 Some nights he said that he was tired, and some nights she said that she wanted to read, and other nights no one said anything.
                                   Ibid., Ch. 69

12 I know Las Vegas to be a theater dedicated to the immediate gratification of every impulse, but I also know it to be a theater designed to numb those very impulses it promised to gratify. Nobody in this theater rushes the stage.
                     "Getting the Vegas Willies,"
                        Esquire   *May 1977*

13 We all have the same dreams.
            Part II, Ch. 1, *The Book of Common
                        Prayer*   *1977*

14 . . . the freeway experience . . . is the only secular communion Los Angeles has. . . . Actual participation requires a total surrender, a concentration so intense as to seem a kind of narcosis, a rapture-of-the-freeway. The mind goes clean. The rhythm takes over. A distortion of time occurs. . . .   "Bureaucrats"
        (1976), *The White Album*   *1979*

15 We were that generation called "silent," but we were silent neither, as some thought, because we shared the period's official optimism nor, as others thought, because we feared its official repression. We were silent because the exhilaration of social action seemed to many of us just one more way of escaping the personal, of masking for a while that dread of the meaningless which was man's fate.   "On the Morning After the Sixties" (1970), op. cit.

2169. Ann Faraday (1935–   )

1 I believe we have entered a new age of self-reliance and personal responsibility in which former reticence about the inner life is being abandoned and the demand for external conformity is being relaxed. The need in this new age is for more deliberate inquiry into the hidden forces of the personality which shape our waking behavior and for communication of our insights for public discussion.
            Introduction, *Dream Power
                                    1972*

2 In forming a bridge between body and mind, dreams may be used as a springboard from which man can leap to new realms of experience lying outside his normal state of consciousness and enlarge his vision not only of himself, but also of the universe in which he lives.
                              Ibid., Pt. 1, Ch. 1

3 Thus, learning to understand our dreams is a matter of learning to understand our heart's language.   *The Dream Game*   *1974*

2170. Georgia Anne Geyer (1935–   )

1 . . . not only does the world scarcely know who the Latin American man is, the world has barely *cared*.   Introduction, *The New
                                    Latins   1970*

2 . . . the more revolutions occur, the less things change.   Ibid.

3 Orderly northern man looked south and he saw a cluster of basically untroubled countries with simple, passionate people; a fiesta of the senses; people unencumbered by the moral chains of the Puritan North; men living out their lives in sensual celebration.   Ibid.

4 Because it was when "reporters" became "journalists" and when "objectivity" gave way to "searching for truth," that an aura of distrust and fear arose around the New Journalist.
            "Whatever Happened to Lois
                Lane?," *Los Angeles Times
                            4 February 1979*

5 Would women leaders wield power differently? Would they be more humane? Would they perhaps even usher in some gleaming, renascent era? And would men accept them?
    Now that we have this veritable club of women leaders across the globe—ruling, scheming, changing the rules and the world—we can begin to answer those questions. But the answers are no simpler than the questions themselves.
            "Are Women Leaders Wielding
            Power Differently Than Men?"
            Seattle Times   14 May 1989

2171. Jane Howard (1935–   )

1 An encounter group is a gathering, for a few hours or a few days, of twelve or eighteen personable, responsible, certifiably normal and temporarily smelly people. Their destination is intimacy, trust and awareness of why they behave as they do in groups; their vehicle is candor.   "Whatever Possessed Me,"
                        Please Touch   1970

2 Parents, however old they and we may grow to be, serve among other things to shield us from a sense of our doom. As long as they are around, we can avoid the fact of our mortality; we can still be innocent children.
                     A Different Woman   1973

3 New links must be forged as old ones rust.
                                   Ibid., Ch. 1

4 Wholesomeness is exotic to me. I pretended to like the era of strobe lights and deafening acid rock in discotheques but a lot of that sixties frenzy really just made me nervous. More and more I am drawn toward stillness.

Ibid., Ch. 34

2172. Beverly Hungry Wolf (1935–)

1 In the years since I began following the ways of my grandmothers I have come to value the teachings, stories, and daily examples of living which they shared with me. I pity the younger girls of the future who will miss out on meeting some of these fine old women.

The Ways of My Grandmothers 1980

2173. Sarah Kirsch (1935–)

1 This autumn the atomic mushrooms became such a common sight in the newspapers that aesthetic categories began to form

"Year's End," St. 1, tr. Jan van Heurck *n.d.*

2174. Anne Richardson Roiphe (1935–)

1 . . . despite my concern for civil liberties, for equality, for justice in Mississippi—I am blond, and blond is still beautiful, and if I have one life to lead it will be as a white, and I am a mass of internal contradictions, all of which cause me to finally attempt some rite which will bring salvation, save me from a system I despise but still carry within me like any other of my vital organs.

"Out of Week One," *Up the Sandbox!* 1970

2 "What the world needs," he said, "is not a Joan of Arc,* the kind of woman who allows herself to be burned on the cross. That's just a bourgeois invention meant to frighten little girls into staying home. What we require is a real female military social leader."

"But that"—I smiled at him—"is just impossible. Women are tied to husband and children. Women are constructed to be penetrated; a sword or a gun in their hands is a joke or a mistake. They are open holes in which things are poured. Occasionally, it's true, a woman can become a volcano, but that's about it."

Ibid., "Out of Week Two"

*See 206

3 She tried to be respectable because respectabilty kept away the chaos that sometimes over-

whelmed her, causing her to call out in her sleep, screaming wild sounds, a warning to the future, a mourning for the past.

Long Division 1972

2175. Judith Rossner (1935–)

1 It is easier to betray than to remain loyal. It takes far less courage to kill yourself than it takes to make yourself wake up one more time. It's harder to stay where you are than to get out. (For everyone but you, that is.)

Pt. II, *Nine Months in the Life of an Old Maid* 1969

2 Love is the direct opposite of hate. By *definition* it's something you can't feel for more than a few minutes at a time, so what's all this bullshit about loving somebody for the rest of your life? Ibid.

3 So often I heard people paying blind obeisance to change—as though it had some virtue of its own. Change or we will die. Change or we will stagnate. Evergreens don't stagnate. Ibid.

4 "Self-government is a form of self-control, self-limitation. It goes against our whole grain. We're [Americans] supposed to go after what we want, not question whether we really need it."

Any Minute I Can Split 1972

5 He always said she was smart, but their conversations were a mined field in which at any moment she might make the wrong verbal move and find her ignorance exploding in her face. *Looking for Mr. Goodbar* 1975

6 A lie was something that hadn't happened but might just as well have. Ibid.

2176. Sara Ruddick (1935–)

1 I seemed to learn new ways of attending to the natural world and to people, especially children. This kind of attending was intimately concerned with caring; because I cared I reread slowly, then I found myself watching more carefully, listening with patience, absorbed by gestures, moods, and thoughts. The more I attended, the more deeply I cared. The domination of feeling by thought, which I had worked so hard to achieve, was breaking down. Instead of developing arguments that could bring my feelings to heel, I allowed feeling to inform my most abstract thinking. "New Combinations: Learning from Virginia Woolf,"* *Between Women*, with C. Asher & L. DeSalvor 1984

*See 1319.

2177. Françoise Sagan (1935–   )

1 It is healthier to see the good points of others
than to analyze our own bad ones.
Pt. I, Ch. 5, A Certain Smile   1956

2 We had the same gait, the same habits and lived
in the same rhythm; our bodies suited each
other, and all was well. I had no right to regret
his failure to make the tremendous effort required of love, the effort to know and shatter
the solitude of another.   *Ibid., Pt. II, Ch. 2*

2178. Shen Rong (1935–   )

1 Never having imagined love could be so intox-
icating, she almost regretted not finding it
earlier.   "At Middle Age,"
*Ch. 3 (1980), Yu Fanqin
& Wang Mingjie, trs. Seven
Contemporary Chinese Women Writers,
Gladys Yang,* ed.*   1982

*See 2076.

2 "Who are you?" Liu was really half tipsy.
"You live in cramped quarters and slave away
regardless of criticism, not seeking fame or
money. A hard-working doctor like you is an
ox serving the children, as Lu Xun said, eating
grass and providing milk.   *Ibid., Ch. 9*

3 "I don't want a medal or a citation. I just wish
your hospital understood how hard it is to be a
doctor's husband. As soon as the order comes
to go out on medical tours or relief work, she's
up and off, leaving the family. She comes back
so exhausted from the operating theatre, she
can't raise a finger to cook a meal. That being
the case, if I don't go into the kitchen, who
will? I should really be grateful to the 'cultural
revolution' for giving me all that time to learn
to cook."   *Ibid.*

4 "There's no pleasing you!" laughed Jiang.
"When you're not used, you complain that your
talents are wasted, you live at the wrong time.
When you're fully used, you gripe that you're
overworked and underpaid!"   *Ibid.*

5 She had performed such operations umpteen
times, but every time she picked up her instruments, she felt like a raw recruit on the
battlefield.   *Ibid., Ch. 13*

6 So this was dying, no fear, no pain, just life
withering away, the senses blurring, slowly
sinking, like a leaf drifting on a river.
Ibid., Ch. 17

2179. Joan Micklin Silver (1935–   )

1 Standing erect, like overgrown bookends on
either side of Mr. MacAfee's desk, were two
Air Force officers.

Ch. 1, *Limbo*, with Linda Gottlieb*
1972

*See 2318.

2 The mother of an eighteen-year-old boy who
had had to secure his mother's consent for en-
listing in the Army, she now cried at the slightest
provocation. "How could I tell him not to go?"
she once asked Fay Clausen, the tears brimming
in her eyes. "He always loved guns—from the
time he was just a little boy he would play with
toy guns, BB guns—you know, pretended he
was in the marines and things. I once got him
that big illustrated history of the Second World
War—it cost seventeen dollars—from American
Heritage, and he read it over and over
again."   *Ibid., Ch. 8*

2180. Audrey Thomas (1935–   )

1 How could I tell her that she was wrong about
things when essentially she was right? Life was
cruel, people hurt and betrayed one another,
grew old and died alone.
*Songs My Mother Taught Me
1973*

2 . . . cats everywhere asleep on the shelves like
motorized bookends.   *Ibid.*

2181. Marina vonNeumann Whitman
(1935–   )

1 I never took a lifetime view at 20 and decided
where I wanted to be at 50. Since I was trail-
blazing, there weren't many rules about what
you were and were not supposed to do. Young
women today feel such a burden to prove
themselves.   Quoted in "The Corporate Guru
of Global Economics" by Beth
McGoldrick, *Working Woman
November 1988*

2 I've learned only that you never say never.
Ibid.

2182. Monique Wittig (1935/36–   )

1 There was a time when you were not a slave,
remember that. . . . You say there are no words
to describe this time. You say it does not exist.
But remember. Make an effort to remember.
Or, failing that, invent.
*Les Guerillières**   1969

*Female guerrilla warriors.

2 The women say that they perceive their bodies
in their entirety. They say that they do not favor

any of its parts on the grounds that it was formerly a forbidden object. They say that they do not want to become prisoners of their own ideology.   Ibid.

3 The language you speak poisons your glottis tongue palate lips. They say, the language you speak is made up of words that are killing you. They say, the language you speak is made up of signs that rightly speaking designate what men have appropriated.   Ibid.

2183. Jean M. Auel (1936?–   )

1 "You cannot see the spirit of your totem because he is part of you, inside you. Yet, he will tell you. Only you must learn to understand. If you have a decision to make, he will help you. He will give you a sign if you make the right choice. . . . It may be a stone you have never seen before or a root with a special shape that has meaning for you. You must learn to understand with your heart and mind, not your eyes and ears, then you will know."
Ch. 9, *The Clan of the*
Cave Bear   1980

2 Six men, pitifully weak by comparison, using skill and intelligence and cooperation and daring, had killed the gigantic creature no other predator could. No matter how fast or how strong or how cunning, no four-legged hunter could match their feat.   Ibid., Ch. 14

3 Zoug's pride was the pride of a true teacher for a pupil who exceeded; a student who paid attention, learned well, and then did the master one better.   Ibid., Ch. 15

2184. Rose Bird (1936–   )

1 The role of the press and the protections which we afford it are today more important than ever before, because we dwell in a society where belief in our governments and in the strength of our institutions is declining.   Quoted in
"Hue & Cry," *San Francisco*
Chronicle   13 May 1979

2 Courts are an aristocratic institution in a democracy. That's the dilemma for an institution that has the function of reviewing the will of the people. We're bound to be "anti-majoritarian." Quoted in "Calm at the center of the storm" by Anthony Lewis, The New York Times News Service
23 October 1986

3 In an age of television, of personalities and black-and-white issues, we [judges] are a col-

legial body that speaks through the written word and in complexities.   Ibid.

2185. Jean Shinoda Bolen (1936–   )

1 There is a potential heroine in every woman.
Ch. 14, *Goddesses in Every Woman, A New*
Psychology Of Women   1984

2 . . . the necessity for choosing a "path with heart." I feel that one must deliberate and then act, must scan every life choice with rational thinking but then base the decision on whether one's heart will be in it. No other person can tell you if your heart is involved, and logic cannot provide an answer.   Ibid.

2186. Sandy Boucher (1936–   )

1 My father's voice says, Watch out for little men. They are more aggressive, meaner, nastier, trickier, more combative. A big man is secure in his strength, so he doesn't push it. A little man is always proving something. The same goes for little dogs versus big dogs.
"Mountain Radio," *Assaults and*
Rituals   1975

2 Thus we were equally, though differently, sophisticated, and our game was the same: not to *care*—to arrive at each other without being there.   Ibid.

2187. Carol Burnett (1936?–   )

1 When someone who is known for being comedic does something straight, it's always "a big breakthrough" or "a radical departure." Why is it no one ever says that if a straight actor does comedy? Are they presuming comedy is easier?   Quoted in "Death by 'Friendly Fire' and a Mother's Search" by Ellen Farley, *San Francisco Chronicle   5 October 1978*

2 I don't consider [the Equal Rights Amendment] a political issue. It is a moral issue as far as I am concerned. Where are women mentioned in the Constitution except in the Nineteenth Amendment, giving us the right to vote? When they said all *men* were created equal, they really meant it—otherwise, why did we have to fight for the Nineteenth Amendment?
Quoted in "Hue & Cry,"
San Francisco Chronicle
29 April 1979

2188. Sandra Gilbert (1936–)

1 Examining the psychosocial implications of a "haunted" ancestral mansion, such a tale* explores the tension between parlor and attic, the psychic split between the lady who submits to male dicta and the lunatic who rebels. But in examining these matters the paradigmatic female story inevitably considers also the equally uncomfortable spatial options of expulsion into the cold outside or suffocation in the hot indoors, and in addition it often embodies an obsessive anxiety both about starvation to the point of disappearance and about monstrous inhabitation.
The Madwoman in the Attic: The Woman Writer and The Nineteenth-Century Literary Imagination, w/Susan Gubar,** p. 86   *1979*

Jane Eyre by Charlotte Brontë (see 813).
**See 2392.

2189. Carol Gilligan (1936-)

1 Implicitly adopting the male life as the norm, they have tried to fashion women out of a masculine cloth. It all goes back, of course, to Adam and Eve—a story which shows, among other things, that if you make a woman out of man, you are bound to get into trouble. In the life cycle, as in the Garden of Eden, the woman has been the deviant.
Ch. 1, *In a Different Voice* *1982*

2 The blind willingness to sacrifice people to truth, however, has always been the danger of an ethics abstracted from life. This willingness links Gandhi to the biblical Abraham, who prepared to sacrifice the life of his son in order to demonstrate the integrity and supremacy of his faith. Both men, in the limitations of their fatherhood, stand in implicit contrast to the woman* who comes before Solomon and verifies her motherhood by relinquishing truth in order to save the life of her child. . . . the ethics of . . . adulthood . . . has become principled at the expense of care. . .   Ibid., Ch. 3

*Prostitute of Jerusalem, mother of the living child; see 26.

3 Thus changes in women's rights change women's moral judgments, seasoning mercy with justice by enabling women to consider it moral to care not only for others but for themselves.   Ibid., Ch. 5

4 . . . while men represent powerful activity as assertion and aggression, women in contrast portray acts of nurturance as acts of strength.   Ibid., Ch. 6

5 While an ethic of justice proceeds from the premise of equality—that everyone should be treated the same—an ethic of care rests on the premise of nonviolence—that no one should be hurt.   Ibid.

2190. Natalya Gorbanevskaya (1936–)

1 Opening the window, I open myself.
Untitled Poem, *Poems, the Trial, Prison* 1972

2 I am awaiting the birth of my child quite calmly, and neither my pregnancy nor the birth will prevent me from doing what I wish—which includes participating in every protest against any act of tyranny.
Red Square at Noon 1972

2191. Judith Guest (1936–)

1 The small seed of despair cracks open and sends experimental tendrils upward to the fragile skin of calm holding him together.
Ch. 1, *Ordinary People* 1976

2 Riding the train gives him too much time to think, he has decided. Too much thinking can ruin you.   Ibid., Ch. 4

3 He had left off being a perfectionist then, when he discovered that not promptly kept appointments, not a house circumspectly clean, not membership in Onwentsia, or the Lake Forest Golf and Country Club, or the Lawyers' Club, not power, or knowledge, or goodness—not *anything*—cleared you through the terrifying office of chance; that it is chance and not perfection that rules the world.   Ibid., Ch. 11

4 How would you describe your marriage, in terms of knowing each other? In terms of being friends? Of understanding that hopelessly intricate network of clash and resolution that has been woven over the last twenty years? Two separate, distinct personalities, not separate at all, but inextricably bound, soul and body and mind, to each other, how did we get so far apart so fast?   Ibid., Ch. 19

5 "Geez, if I could get through to you, kiddo, that depression is not sobbing and crying and *giving vent*, it is plain and simple *reduction of feeling*. Reduction, see? Of all feeling. People who keep stiff upper lips find that it's damn hard to smile.   Ibid., Ch. 27

2192. Sandra Hochman (1936–)

1 What I wanted
Was to be myself again.
"The Inheritance," *Love Letters
from Asia* 1967

2193. Xaviera Hollander (1936?–)

1 *Mundus vult decipi decipiatur ergo.* The world
wants to be cheated, so cheat.
Ch. 1, *The Happy Hooker*, with Robin Moore
and Yvonne Dunleavy 1972

2 There is only one other profession that outranks
bankers as dedicated clients, and that is the
stockbroker. . . . When the stocks go up, the
cocks go up! *Ibid., Ch. 11*

3 . . . if my business could be made legal . . .
I and women like me could make a big contri-
bution to what Mayor Lindsay* calls "Fun
City," and the city and state could derive the
money in taxes and licensing fees that I pay off
to crooked cops and political figures.
Ibid., Ch. 14

* John Lindsay, mayor of New York City (1966–1974).

2194. Sonia Johnson (1936?–)

1 I liked the *name* of the amendment. I couldn't
help feeling uneasy that the church was opposing
something with a name as beautiful as the *Equal
Rights* Amendment.
*From Housewife to Heretic
1981*

2 In our patriarchal world, we are all taught—
whether we like to think we are or not—that
God, being male, values maleness much more
than he values femaleness . . . that in order to
propitiate God, women must propitiate men.
After all, God won't like us if we don't please
those nearest his heart, if we don't treat his
cronies well. *Ibid.*

3 I am a warrior in the time of women warriors;
the longing for justice is the sword I carry, the
love of womankind my shield. *Ibid.*

4 Women cannot serve two masters at once who
are urgently beaming antithetical orders. . . .
Either we believe in patriarchy—the rule of men
over women—or we believe in equality.
Ibid.

2195. Barbara Jordan (1936–)

1 . . . if I have anything special that makes me
"influential" I simply don't know hot to define

it. If I knew the ingredients I would bottle them,
package them and sell them, because I want
everyone to be able to work together in a spirit
of cooperation and compromise and accommo-
dation without, you know, any caving in or
anyone being woefully violated personally or in
terms of his principles.
Quoted in "Barbara Jordan" by
Charles L. Sanders, *Ebony
February 1975*

2 If you're going to play the game properly you'd
better know every rule. *Ibid.*

3 The code of morality is to do unto others as you
would have them do unto you. If you make that
the central theme of your morality code, it will
serve you well as a moral individual.
Quoted in "Where Is
Barbara Jordon Today?" by Malcolm Boyd
Parade 16 February 1986

4 I live a day at a time. Each day I look for a
kernel of excitement. In the morning, I say:
"What is my exciting thing for today?" Then,
I do the day. Don't ask me about tomorrow.
Ibid.

2196. June Jordan (1936–)

1 There was no loneliness in the living room. So
it was a good part, and maybe the best part, of
the house. *New Life, New Room
1975*

2 "But what's more important. Building a bridge
or taking care of a baby?" *Ibid.*

3 . . . the intimate face of the universal struggle.
You begin with your family and the kids on the
block, and next you open your eyes to what you
call your people and that leads you into land
reform, into Black English, into Angola, leads
you back to your own bed where you lie by
yourself, wondering if you deserve to be
peaceful. *Civil Wars 1981*

2197. Evelyn Fox Keller (1936–)

1 The need to dominate nature is, in this view, a
project of the need to dominate other human
beings. *Reflections on Gender and
Science 1985*

2 In my vision of science, it is not the taming of
nature that is sought, but the taming of
hegemony. *Ibid.*

2198. Dacia Maraini (1936–)

1 He talked and talked because he didn't know
what to say. Ch. 1, *The Holiday 1962*

2 "Our strength is like the sea," Pompei announced, lifting his chin up proudly. "Nothing can divert it."   *Ibid.*, Ch. 8

3 the nausea of being the thing I was leapt from my throat like sobbing. . . .
"His Foot on the Sand,"
Crudelta all Aria' Aperia   1966

2199. Barbara Ann Mikulski (1936–   )

1 America is not a melting pot. It is a sizzling cauldron.   Speech, First National Conference of the National Center for Urban and Ethnic Affairs, Quoted in *American Political Women* by Esther Stineman   *1980*

2 As we move from an economy of affluence to an economy of scarcity, we must be careful that the people who make $5,000 a year are not pitted against those who make $25,000 a year by those who make $900,000. The two-martinis-for-lunch bunch would love for us to fight each other over the resources they have made scarce.   Campaign Speech (1974), op. cit.

2200. Jane O'Reilly (1936–   )

1 . . . the click! of recognition, that parenthesis of truth around a little thing that completes the puzzle of reality in women's minds—the moment that brings a gleam to our eyes and means the revolution has begun.
"The Housewife's Moment of Truth,"
The First Ms. Reader, Francine Klagsbrun, ed.   *1972*

2 . . . housewives, the natural people to turn to when there is something unpleasant, inconvenient or inconclusive to be done.   Ibid.

3 Men will always opt for things that get finished and stay that way—putting up screens, but not planning menus.   Ibid.

2201. Rochelle Owens (1936–   )

1 CY. I don't want no sow with two feet but with four! Them repeats true things with their grunts not like you human-daughter.
Sc. 1, *Futz*   *1958*

2 CY. I wasn't near people. They came to me and looked under my trousers all the way up to their dirty hearts. They minded my *own* life.
Ibid., Sc. 2

3 MRS. LOOP. A son and his mother are godly.
Ibid.

4 MARX. Labor! Sucking Capital! Capital! The exploiting class! The milking class—the ruling class!   *The Karl Marx* Play   1971*

*German political philosopher and economist (1818–83).

5 MARX. Little rolls with butter is good! Viennese torte is good! And a revolution is good!   Ibid.

6 MARX. Machinery sweeps away every moral and material restriction, in its blind unrestrainable passion, its werewolf hunger.   Ibid.

7 CHUCKY. My own failings are enmeshed in the times. . . .   *Chucky's Hunch   1981*

8 It's as if I was a chemist, an alchemist, mixing and playing around with fluids, living tissue, vapors, always testing the viability of the matter—language.
"Rochelle Owens," *Interviews with Contemporary Women Playwrights*, Kathleen Betsko* & Rachel Koenig   *1987*

*See 2256.

9 A writer must have sympathy with the devil; that is literature, and that is what is exciting about art.   Ibid.

2202. Marge Piercy (1936–   )

1 Reflecting the values of the larger capitalistic society, there is no prestige whatsoever attached to actually working. Workers are invisible.
"The Grand Coolie Damn,"
Sisterhood Is Powerful,
Robin Morgan,* ed.   *1970*

*See 2327.

2 The ruling class isn't dissatisfied: they are healthy, well-fed, live in beauty, enjoy their own importance: fun-loving cannibals.   Ibid.

3 "You're not pretty, Miriam-mine, so you better be smart. But not too smart."
Small Changes   1973

4 "All women hustle. Women watch faces, voices, gestures, moods. The person who has to survive through cunning."   Ibid.

5 She must learn again to speak
starting with I
starting with Wc
starting as the infant does
with her own true hunger
and pleasure
and rage.   "Unlearning to Not Speak" *To Be of Use   1973*

2203. Jill Robinson (1936–   )

1 The fame fraud is so complete that all the Hollywood kids think everyone else has money.

It is the suburban delusion. But then, suburbia was invented by Hollywood.
Pt. I, *Bed/Time/Story*   *1974*

2 I could hear the lovely, tiny swallowing gulps— you cover all ages in the sex-play cycle, from nursing infant to death in one terrifying swoop of the sexual plot.   Ibid.

3 "Everyone's parent is only a fantasy finally, neither as magical as, forgive me, you are, nor as prosaic. It is the image one has created in the head that one is fighting. Not the real parent at all."   Ibid. Pt. II

4 "It's a big risk—to stop drinking, going straight. Who knows? What you've got in mind could be very boring."   Ibid.

2204. Rosemary Radford Ruether
(1936–   )

1 Feminist theology cannot be done from the existing base of the Christian Bible.
Womanguides: Reading Toward A Feminist Theology   *1985*

2 It is through generating stories of our own crisis and hope and telling them to one another that we light the path.   Ibid.

2205. Becky Simpson (1936–   )

1 What I wanted was justice for poor people. Then I realized that can also mean putting a good pair of shoes on somebody's feet, a meal on their table, clothes on their back—that's justice to me. I know it's ground level, but that's where I want to be.   Quoted in "You Just Have to Try" by Michael Ryan, *Parade Magazine* *28 May 1989*

2206. Lily Tomlin (1936–   )

1 If you have a psychotic fixation and you go to the doctor and you want these two fingers amputated, he will not cut them off. But he *will* remove your genitals. I have more trouble getting a prescription for Valium than I do having my uterus lowered and made into a penis.
Quoted by David Felton in *Rolling Stone*   *24 October 1974*

2 If you can't be direct, why be?
Ibid., "Mary Jean"*

3 Once poor, always wantin'. Rich is just a way of wantin' bigger.   Ibid., "Wanda V."*

4 Lady . . . Lady, I do not make up things. That is lies. Lies is not true. But the truth could be

made up if you know how. And that's the truth.   Ibid., "Edith Ann"*

*Characters created by Lily Tomlin.

2207. Sidney Abbot (1937–   )

1 Lesbianism is far more than a sexual preference: it is a political stance.
Sappho Was a Right-on Woman*, with Barbara J. Love**   *1972*

*See 50.
**See 2221.

2 . . . a woman who wants a woman usually wants a woman.   Ibid.

3 Multiple relationships made it possible to comprehend people, not acquire them or own them.   Ibid.

2208. Bella Akhmadulina (1937–   )

1 But your eyes have changed
since those terrible old days
a hundred years ago,
when you died, alone in the house here,
poor, without work or friends."
"A Dream," Sts. 6 & 7, Adapted by Jean Valentine, *Poets on Street Corners*, Olga Carlisle   *1968*

2209. Margaret Lowe Benston
(1937–   )

1 In sheer quantity, household labor, including child care, constitutes a huge amount of socially necessary production. Nevertheless, in a society based on commodity production, it is not usually considered as "real work" since it is outside of trade and the marketplace. . . . In a society in which money determines value, women are a group who work outside the money economy.   "The Political Economy of Women's Lib," *Monthly Review* *September 1969*

2 Once women are freed from private production in the home, it will probably be very difficult to maintain for any long period of time a rigid definition of jobs by sex.   Ibid.

2210. Sallie Bingham (1937–   )

1 . . . he wondered again, how much of her desire was passion and how much grasping: girls

used sex to get a hold on you, he knew—it was so easy for them to pretend to be excited.
"Winter Term," *Mademoiselle*
July 1958

2211. Toni Cade (1937?–   )

1 Personally, Freud's "anatomy is destiny" has always horrified me. *Kirche, Kusse, Kuche, Kinde* made me sick. Career woman versus wife-mother has always struck me as a false dichotomy. The-pill'll-make-you-gals-run-wild a lot of male chauvinist anxiety. Dump-the-pill a truncated statement. I think most women have pondered, those who have the heart to ponder at all, the oppressive nature of pregnancy, the tyranny of the child burden, the stupidity of male-female divisions, the obscene nature of employment discrimination. And day-care and nurseries being what they are, paid maternity leaves being rare, the whole memory of wham bam thank you ma'am and the big Getaway a horrible nightmare, poverty so ugly, the family unit being the last word in socializing institutions to prepare us all for the ultimate rip-off and perpetuate the status quo, and abortion fatalities being what they are—of course the pill.   "The Pill," *Onyx*   *August 1969*

2 We are involved in a struggle for liberation: liberation from the exploitive and dehumanizing system of racism, from the manipulative control of a corporate society; liberation from the constrictive norms of "mainstream" culture, from the synthetic myths that encourage us to fashion ourselves rashly from without (reaction) rather than from within (creation).
Preface, *The Black Woman*   *1970*

3 The genocidal bloodbath of centuries and centuries of witch hunts sheds some light on the hysterical attitude white men have regarding their women.   Lecture, "The Scattered Sopranoes," Livingston College Black Women's Seminar (December 1969), op. cit.

4 Revolution begins with the self, in the self.
Ibid.

2212. Helene Cixous (1937–   )

1 Write your self. Your body must be heard.
"The Laugh of the Medusa," *Signs*   *1976*

2 You only have to look at the Medusa straight on to see her,
And she's not deadly. She's beautiful and she's laughing.   *Ibid.*

2213. Marian Wright Edelman (1937–   )

1 Just because a child's parents are poor or uneducated is no reason to deprive the child of basic human rights to health care, education, proper nutrition. Clearly we ignore the needs of black children, poor children, and handicapped children in the country.
Quoted in "Society's Pushed-Out Children" by Margie Casady,
Psychology Today   *June 1975*

2 I've been struck by the upside-down priorities of the juvenile-justice system. We are willing to spend the least amount of money to keep a kid at home, more to put him in a foster home, and the most to institutionalize him.   *Ibid.*

2214. Jane Fonda (1937–   )

1 I don't care about the Oscar. I make movies to support the causes I believe in, not for any honors. I couldn't care less whether I win an Oscar or not.
Quoted in Prologue, *Jane: An Intimate Biography of Jane Fonda* by
Thomas Kiernan   *1973*

2 Before I went into analysis, I told everyone lies—but when you spend all that money, you tell the truth. . . . Analysis has also taught me that you should know who to love and who to hate and who to just plain like, and it's important to know the difference.
Ibid., Pt. II, Ch. 13   "c.1962"

3 But the whole point of liberation is that you get out. Restructure your life. Act by yourself.
Quoted in "At Home with Tom and Jane" by Danae Brook,
Los Angeles Weekly
28 November–4 December 1980

4 When a child enters the world through you, it alters everything on a psychic, psychological and purely practical level. You're just not free anymore to do what you want to do. And it's not the same again. Ever.   *Ibid.*

5 I am not a do-gooder. I am a revolutionary. A revolutionary woman.
Comment (1971), op. cit.

2215. Kathleen Fraser (1937–   )

1 He is all of him urge.
Untitled Poem, *What I Want*   *1974*

2 I think you have many shelves but never put love there.
Untitled Poem, op. cit.

3 "Personal things is all I care about."
Untitled Poem, op. cit.

2216. Nancy Friday (1937–   )

1 Anger broke the pane of glass between us.
Ch. 1, *My Mother, My Self*
1977

2 Spontaneous and honest love admits errors, hesitations, and human failings; it can be tested and repaired. Idealized love ties us because we already intuit that it is unreal and are afraid to face this truth.
Ibid.

3 The older I get, the more of my mother I see in myself.
Ibid.

4 We are the loving sex; people count on us for comfort, nurturing warmth. We hold the world together with the constant availability of our love when men would tear it apart with their needs for power.
Ibid.

5 It was the promise of men, that around each corner there was yet another man, more wonderful than the last, that sustained me. You see, I had men confused with life. . . . You can't get what I wanted from a man, not in this life.
Ibid., Ch. 8

2217. Gail Godwin (1937–   )

1 "The only reason people forget is because they want to. If we were all clear, with no aberrations, we could remember everything, before we were born, even."
Ch. 1, *The Perfectionists*   1970

2 . . . life is a disease. . . .
The Odd Woman   1974

3 "Good teaching is one-fourth preparation and three-fourths theatre. . . ."
Ibid.

4 I turn into an anachronism every time I come home, she thought angrily. I start measuring myself by standards thirty, fifty, a hundred years old.
Ibid.

5 I believe that dreams transport us through the undersides of our days, and that if we wish to become acquainted with the dark side of what we are, the signposts are there, waiting for us to translate them. Dreams say what they mean, but they don't say it in daytime language.
Ch. 1, *The Finishing
School*   1984

6 Actors between plays are like ghosts looking for bodies to inhabit.
Ibid., Ch. 7

7 Did I have to drive one hundred miles, and another hundred back, to discover that memory does not reside in places? Places have their own continuing lives. Memory lives in the brain of the rememberer.
Ibid.

8 Death is not the enemy; age is not the enemy. These things are inevitable, they happen to everybody. But what we ought to fear is the kind of death that happens in life. It can happen at any time. You're going along, and then, at some point, you congeal. You know, like jelly. You're not fluid anymore. You solidify at a certain point and from then on your life is doomed to be a repetition of what you have done before. That's the enemy.
Ibid.

9 "The best antidote I have found is to yearn for something. As long as you yearn, you can't congeal: there is a forward motion to yearning.
Ibid.

2218. Lois Gould (1937–   )

1 Danny Mack got past the nurses at two-fifteen by impersonating a doctor. All he did was clip four ballpoint pens on his vest pocket and march in looking preoccupied.
Such Good Friends   1970

2 "Hogamous, Higamous, men are polygamous, Higamous, Hogamous, women monogamous."
Ibid.

3 Life is the only sentence which doesn't end with a period.
Ibid.

4 *Things* have squatter's rights; why else do we call them *belongings*?
Ibid.

5 What it is, I guess, is that I don't really miss *him;* I miss something that must have been *us.* Because we *were* something, in spite of each other, weren't we?
Ibid.

6 She hated the powdered oil smell they put on the baby. Rubbing away all his natural sourness and anointing him with foreign substances that were all ironically labeled *Baby.* So that he would never recognize his own body in the dark, the way she could recognize hers now. Small victory, discovering your acrid identity after eighteen years. Buried alive under thousands of layers of powdered oil.
Necessary Objects   1972

7 Make up. Meaning invent. Make up something more acceptable, because that face you have on right there will not do.
Final Analysis   1974

8 The only reason I hated him was that I had needed him so much. That's when I found out about need. It goes much better with hate than with love.
Ibid.

2219. Brooke Hayward (1937–)

1 I thought for a whole minute while my heart stopped and my eyes blinked and my face flushed with fury. It was a trick question, two-sided, flipping back and forth, now-you-see-it-now-you-don't, the trick of a supreme magician who could—with cunning legerdemain under a silk handkerchief—transform a few seconds of tranquility into an eternity of chaos. The truth: no, I did not, under any circumstance whatsoever, wish to share the doll's house with Bridget. . . . Or the truth: yes, of course I wanted to share the doll's house with Bridget, because not only would that please Mother and demonstrate how generous and grown up I really was but because I knew that I loved Bridget very deeply and identified with her yearning as she tentatively touched the miniature grandfather's clock in the miniature hallway. (Get your nasty little fingers out of there, I wanted to scream, until I give you permission.) *Haywire* 1978

2220. Bessie Head (1937–)

1 And if the white man thought that Asians were a low, filthy nation, Asians could still smile with relief—at least, they were not Africans. And if the white man thought that Africans were a low, filthy nation, Africans in southern Africa could still smile—at least, they were not bushmen. They all have their monsters.
Pt. I, *Maru* 1971

2 Love is mutually feeding each other, not one living on another like a ghoul.
A Question of Power 1973

2221. Barbara J. Love (1937–)

Co-author with Sidney Abbot. See 2207: 1–4.

2222. Marabel Morgan (1937–)

1 Be prepared mentally and physically for intercourse every night this week.
The Total Woman 1973

2223. Liane Norman (1937–)

1 If conscience is regarded as imperative, then compliance with its dictates commends a society not to forgive, but to celebrate, its conscientious citizens. "Selective Conscientious Objection,"
The Center Magazine
May/June 1972

2 While the State may respectfully require obedience on many matters, it cannot violate the moral nature of a man, convert him into a serviceable criminal, and expect his loyalty and devotion.
Ibid.

3 Whenever government's interests become by definition more substantial than the humanity of its citizens, the drift toward government by divine right gathers momentum.
Ibid.

2224. Eleanor Holmes Norton (1937–)

1 Racial oppression of black people in America has done what neither class oppression nor sexual oppression, with all their perniciousness, has ever done: destroyed an entire people and their culture. "For Sadie and Maude,"
Sisterhood Is Powerful,
Robin Morgan,* ed. 1970

*See 2327.

2 There is no reason to repeat bad history.
Ibid.

3 There are not many males, black or white, who wish to get involved with a woman who's committed to her own development.
Quoted in "The Black Family and Feminism" by C. Ware, *The First Ms. Reader,* Francine Klagsbrun, ed. 1972

4 But feminist change is both irresistible and irreversible. American women are part of an international movement that affects virtually every country in the world.
Speech, National Women's Political Caucus Conference, Albuquerque, New Mexico *July 1981*

2225. Jill Ruckelshaus (1937?–)

1 Women's rights in essence is really a movement for freedom, a movement for equality, for the dignity of all women, for those who work outside the home and those who dedicate themselves with more altruism than any profession I know to being wives and mothers, cooks and chauffeurs, decorators and child psychologists and loving human beings.
Quoted in "Jill Ruckelshaus: Lady of Liberty" by Frederic A. Birmingham, *Saturday Evening Post* *3 March 1973*

2 I have no hostility towards men. Some of my best friends are men. I married a man, and my father was a man.
Ibid.

3 It occurred to me when I was thirteen and wearing white gloves and Mary Janes and going to dancing school, that no one should have to dance backward all their lives.
Speech   *1973*

4 The Equal Rights Amendment* is designed to establish in our Constitution the clear moral value judgment that all Americans, women and men, stand equal under the law.
Quoted in "Forum," *Ladies' Home Journal   August 1975*

*See Alice Paul, 1355.

2226. Margo St. James (1937–   )

1 A conservative estimate would be that 90 percent of politicians patronize public women. Imagine the wealth of information available for bringing "undercover" pressure to bear regarding passage of certain legislation concerning minors, women, minorities, religious and political freedoms.
Quoted in *The Realist*, No. 94   *October 1972*

2 I did not find the business [prostitution] all that disgusting. You pick your customers, you meet interesting people and youth is not a prerequisite.
Quoted in "St. James Still Hustling In Grand Old Party Style" by Allison Engel, *San Jose Mercury 23 October 1978*

3 Punishing the prostitute promotes the rape of all women. When prostitution is a crime, the message conveyed is that women who are sexual are "bad," and therefore legitimate victims of sexual assault. Sex becomes a weapon to be used by men.
Quoted in "Margo" by Mildred Hamilton, *San Francisco Examiner 29 April 1979*

2227. Dinae B. Schulder (1937–   )

1 Law is a reflection and a source of prejudice. It both enforces and suggests forms of bias.
"Does the Law Oppress Women?," *Sisterhood Is Powerful*, Robin Morgan,* ed.   *1970*

*See 2327.

2 Legislation and case law still exist in some parts of the United States permitting the "passion shooting" by a husband of a wife; the reverse, of course, is known as homicide.   Ibid.

2228. Gail Sheehy (1936–   )

1 Into this anonymous pit they climb—a fumbling, frightened, pathetic man and a cold, contemp-

tuous, violated woman—prepared to exchange for twenty dollars no more than ten minutes of animal sex, untouched by a stroke of their common humanity.   Ch. 3, *Hustling   1971*

2 It is a silly question to ask a prostitute why she does it. . . . These are the highest-paid "professional" women in America.   Ibid., Ch. 4

3 The best way to attract money, she had discovered, was to give the appearance of having it.   Ibid., Ch. 9

4 It is fitting that speed should be our chemical superstar. With the only certainty in our daily existence being change, and a rate of change growing always faster in a kind of technological leapfrog game, speed helps people to think they are keeping up.   *Speed Is of the Essence 1971*

5 Safe but stifled, these are the most familiar men.   Pt. V, Ch. 15, *Passages 1976*

6 It is a paradox that as we reach our prime, we also see there is a place where it finishes.
Ibid., Pt. VI, Ch. 17

2229. Evelyn Elizabeth Smith (1937?–   )

1 Enemies whispered that he had bewitched the voting machines, but that wasn't true; he'd won fair and square through mass hypnosis.
The Martian and the Magician 1952

2 That's always the way when you discover something new; everybody thinks you're crazy.
Ibid.

2230. Jennifer Tipton (1937–   )

1 I often do feel that theatre might truly save the world. It is that expression on a stage in front of an audience—not the global communication that film and television can give—that tells us how we see ourselves, how we can better ourselves. It doesn't mean that all plays should be beautiful—we can better ourselves by picturing the worst, too. I'm deeply committed to theatre in all its forms.
"The Facts of Light" by Arnold Aronson, *American Theatre January 1986*

2 You have to see the dancer to know what is going on, whereas in theatre that's not necessarily true; information can come from language.   Ibid.

2231. Diane Wakoski (1937–)

1 thinking how cage life drove an animal into
   mazes of himself,
   his cage mates chosen for him his life circumscribed and focused
   on eating, his play watched by it-doesn't-mat-
   ter-whom, just
   watched, always watched.
>   "The Birds of Paradise Being Very
>   Plain Birds," St. 5, *The East Side
>   Scene*, Allen De Loach, ed.   *1968*

2 My face
   that my friends tell me is so full of character;
   my face
   I have hated for so many years;
   my face
   I have made an angry contract to live with
   though no one could love it
>   "I Have Had to Learn to Live with
>   My Face," St. 2, *The Motorcycle
>   Betrayal Poems*   *1971*

3 When I touch the man
   I love,
   I want to thank my mother for giving me
   piano lessons
   all those years,
   keeping the memory of Beethoven,
   a deaf tortured man,
   in mind;
     of the beauty that can come
   from even an ugly
   past.
>   "Thanking My Mother For Piano Lessons,"
>   St. 12, op. cit.

2232. Zhang Jie (1937–)

1 I am thirty, the same age as our People's Republic. For a republic thirty is still young. But
   a girl of thirty is virtually on the shelf.
>   "Love Must Not Be
>   Forgotten" (1979), Gladys Yang,
>   tr., *Seven Contemporary Chinese
>   Women Writers*, Gladys
>   Yang,* ed.   *1982*

*See 2076.

2 Though not bound together by earthly laws or
   morality, though they never once clasped hands,
   each possessed the other completely. Nothing
   could part them. Centuries to come, if one white
   cloud trails another, two grasses grow side by
   side, one wave splashes another, a breeze follows another . . . believe me, that will be
   them.   Ibid.

3 I long to shout: "Mind your own business! Let
   us wait patiently for our counterparts. Even
   waiting in vain is better than willy-nilly marriage. To live single is not such a fearful disaster. I believe it may be a sign of a step forward
in culture, education and the quality of
life."   Ibid.

4 No human emotion can transcend the social
   conditions around it.
>   Quoted in "The Art of a
>   Chinese Writer" by Bruce
>   Shenitz, *Newsweek*   *26 May 1986*

5 In China since the founding of the People's
   Republic, women have won equal rights in the
   political and economical spheres. But in social
   consciousness there is still a skepticism of wom-
   en's abilities and there is still a degree of disrespect for women's dignity. But I don't think
   this problem can be solved by feminism alone.
   It depends on the progress of mankind as a
   whole, and that includes both material and spiritual progress.   Ibid.

6 . . . there's no absolute freedom anywhere in
   the world. Freedom is always relative.   Ibid.

2233. Renata Adler (1938–)

1 I . . . doubt that film can ever argue effectively
   against its own material: that a genuine antiwar
   film, say, can be made on the basis of even the
   ugliest battle scenes. . . . the medium is somehow unsuited to moral lessons, cautionary tales
   or polemics of any kind. If you want to make a
   pacifist film, you must make an exemplary film
   about peaceful men.
>   "The Movies Make heroes of Them
>   All"   (7 January 1968),
>   *A Year in the Dark*   *1969*

2 The writer has a grudge against society, which
   he documents with accounts of unsatisfying sex,
   unrealized ambition, unmitigated loneliness, and
   a sense of local and global distress. The square,
   overpopulation, the bourgeois, the bomb and
   the cocktail party are variously identified as
   sources of the grudge. There follows a little
   obscenity here, a dash of philosophy there, considerable whining overall, and a modern satirical
   novel is born.
>   "Salt into Old Scars" (22 June 1963),
>   *Toward a Radical Middle*   *1971*

3 If anything has characterized the [peace] movement, from its beginning and in all its parts, it
   has been a spirit of decentralization, local autonomy, personal choice, and freedom from
   dogma.   "Early Radicalism: The Price
>   Of Peace Is Confusion"
>   (11 December 1965), op. cit.

4 At six one morning, Will went out in jeans and
   frayed sweater to buy a quart of milk. A tourist
   bus went by. The megaphone was directed at

him. "There's one," it said. That was in the 1960s. Ever since, he's wondered. There's one what? *Speedboat* 1976

2234. Ti-Grace Atkinson (1938?–)

1 The continuance of the inheritance idea—the idea of living on through things, property, children—subverts any possibility of the communal society succeeding. For people to live communally instead of competitively, the bonds of inheritance must be completely broken.
Quoted in "The Second Feminist Wave" by Martha Weinman Lear, *New York Times Magazine* 10 March 1968

2235. Rona Barrett (1938–)

1 It's ironic, but until you can free those final monsters within the jungle of yourself, your life, your soul is up for grabs.
Prologue, *Miss Rona: An Autobiography,* 1974

2 . . . the *healthy,* the *strong* individual, is the one who asks for help when he needs it. Whether he's got an abscess on his knee or in his soul. Ibid., Ch. 15

2236. Judy Blume (1938–)

1 "Are you there God? It's me, Margaret.
I just told my mother I want a bra.
Please help me grow God. You know where.
I want to be like everyone else."
Are You There, God? It's Me, Margaret 1970

2237. Helen Caldicott (1938–)

1 We are the curators of life on earth. We hold it in the palm of our hand. Remark *n.d.*

2238. Caryl Churchill (1938–)

1 Most theaters are still controlled by men and people do tend to be able to see promise in people who are like themselves.
"Caryl Churchill," *Interviews with Contemporary Women Playwrights,* Kathleen Betsko* & Rachel Koenig 1987

*See 2256.

2 [Margaret] Thatcher* had just become prime minister; there was talk about whether it was an advance to have a woman prime minister if it was someone with policies like hers: She may be a woman but she isn't a sister, she may be a sister but she isn't a comrade. Ibid.

*See 1961.

3 JOAN. Women, children and lunatics can't be Pope. Act I, Scene 1, *Top Girls* 1982

4 NELL. Because that's what an employer is going to have doubts about with a lady as I needn't tell you, whether she's got the guts to push through to a closing situation. They think we're too nice. They think we listen to the buyer's doubts. They think we consider his needs and his feelings. Ibid., Act II, Scene 1

2239. Colette Dowling (1938–)

1 I tell you, the great divide is still with us, the awful split, the Us and Them. Like a rubber band tautened to the snapping point, the polarization of the sexes continues, because we lack the courage to face our likenesses and admit to our real need.
"A Woman Sounds Off on Those Sexy Magazines," *Redbook* April 1974

2 Here it was—the Cinderella Complex. It used to hit girls of sixteen or seventeen, preventing them, often, from going to college, hastening them into early marriages. Now it tends to hit women after college—after they've been out in the world a while. When the first thrill of freedom subsides and anxiety rises to take its place, they begin to be tugged by that old yearning for safety: the wish to be saved.
The Cinderella Complex 1982

3 Without being conscious of it she looks for a situation in which she can give up her facade of self-sufficiency and ease back into that warm, cradled state reminiscent of childhood that's so seductive to women—a home. Ibid., Ch. 3

4 Like the youngest child obsessing on the negative treatment received from the family, women use the unfairness with which they've historically been treated to wall themselves off from further negative treatment. Isolated by their feelings of victimization, they remain trapped. Ibid., Ch. 4

5 Once a man is on hand, a woman tends to stop believing in her own beliefs. Ibid., Ch. 6

2240. Mary Ann Glendon (1938–)

1 Laws are ways that society makes sense of things.   Quoted in *A World of Ideas* by Bill Moyers   *1989*

2 Certainly, the American woman is very well off as an individual and a possessor of rights. But many European women are better off as mothers and members of interdependent family units. This difference of opinion on what better off means makes it very difficult to say what is a feminist in the United States at the present time.   Ibid.

3 Apparently we just don't feel that all American children of all colors and social classes are our children, the way I think a Swede quite easily feels that a child up in Lapland is very precious to a worker in Stockholm.   Ibid.

4 Pro-choice has some silent support among men who don't want to take responsibility for fatherhood, among persons involved in a profit-making abortion industry, and, maybe saddest of all, among taxpayers who see abortion as a way of keeping down the size of an underclass. So there's a lot of unspoken support for the status-quo. On other hand, pro-life has this dark side of punitiveness toward women that I find absolutely incomprehensible, but it seems to be there, as well as a certain unwillingness to recognize that if you're going to be pro-life, it shouldn't be with a view that life begins at conception and ends at birth. You have to be pro-life all the way, and that means supporting maternity, childbirth, and child raising, which has become very difficult in our society, where both parents are usually in the labor force.   Ibid.

5 There is always the danger that if you speak a language that recognizes only individual rights, you will become a people that can think only about individuals.   Ibid.

2241. Vivian Gornick (1938–)

1 Behind the "passive" exterior of many women there lies a growing anger over lost energies and confused lives, an anger so sharp in its fury but so diffuse in its focus that one can only describe it as the price society must pay for creating a patriarchal system in the first place, and for now refusing to let it go. And make no mistake, it is not letting go.   "Why Women Fear Success," *The First Ms. Reader,* Francine Klagsbrun, ed.   *1972*

2 The subjection of women, in my view, lies most deeply in the ingrained conviction—shared by both men and women—that for women marriage is the pivotal experience. It is this conviction, primarily, that reduces and ultimately destroys in women that flow of psychic energy that is fed in men from birth by the anxious knowledge given them that one is alone in this world; that one is never taken care of; that life is a naked battle between fear and desire, and that fear is kept in abeyance only through the recurrent urge of desire. . .   "Toward a Definition of the Female Sensibility," *The Village Voice*   *31 May 1973*

3 She takes daily walks on the land that was once the bottom of the sea, marking and classifying, sifting through her thoughts the meaning of the jagged edges of discontent that have begun to make inroads anew inside her.   "Stillness at the Center," *Ms. October 1973*

4 If the word for London is decency and the word for New York is violence, then, beyond doubt, the word for Cairo is tenderness. Tenderness is what pervades the air here.   Pt. I, *In Search of Ali-Mahmoud*   *1973*

5 I lived once in the American desert. The solitude opens up. It becomes an enormous surrounding comfort. But the solitude in the city is a confusing and painful thing.   Ibid., Pt. II

2242. Tina Howe (1938?–)

1 Young mothers inhabit rather wild territory.   "Tina Howe," *Interviews with Contemporary Women Playwrights,* Kathleen Betsko* & Rachel Koenig   *1987*

*See 2256.

2 The reason to pick up the pen or the paint brush is to fight back.   Ibid.

3 I've always thought women were much more dangerous than men.   Ibid.

2243. Jane Kramer (1938?–)

1 Dawia maintained that the Europeans were . . . favored by Allah because Allah liked automobiles and was hoping that the Europeans would bring their cars to Heaven with them. Omar, however, said no, that Allah loved the Europeans because the Europeans always got to their appointments on time.   Pt. I, *Honor to the Bride*   *1973*

2 "It is a burden to have daughters," Dawia said, sighing. "My husband looks at Jmaa now and

he says, 'What can I expect from her? More of the same problems I have suffered with the first two.' "

"He has a point," Musa remarked. "Having daughters is not profitable."   Ibid., Pt. II

2244. Bette Bao Lord (1938–)

1 "If your heart did not break now and then, Spring Moon, how would you know it is there? Hearts break, then mend and break and mend again in a cycle without beginning, without end. As surely as dawn sows the evening, twilight sows the morn."   Prologue, *Spring Moon*
1981

2 "I fear, Lustrous Jade, that in broadening your mind, you have narrowed your heart."
Ibid., Jade Phoenix, Ch. 27

3 "If mortals wait until the gods remake the world to their liking to be happy, they are already in hell."   Ibid., Sowing Dawn, Ch. 38

4 "There is a season for sun, another for shadow. A season to sing, another to be silent. And, in all seasons, parting and reunion.

"In yielding we are like the water, by nature placid, conforming to the hollow of the smallest hand; in time, shaping even the mountains to its will.

"Thus we keep duty and honor. We cherish clan and civilization.

"We are Chinese."   Ibid.

2245. Mary Jane Moffat (1938?–)

1 Why do women keep diaries? . . . The form has been an important outlet for women partly because it is an analogue to their lives: emotional, fragmentary, interrupted, modest, not to be taken seriously, private, restricted, daily, trivial, formless, concerned with self, as endless as their tasks.
Foreword, *Revelations: Diaries of Women,*
with Charlotte Painter*   *1974*

*See 1984.

2246. Joyce Carole Oates (1938–)

1 This is a work of history in fictional form—that is, in personal perspective, which is the only kind of history that exits.
Author's Note, *Them*   *1969*

2 She ransacked her mind but there was nothing in it.   Pt. I, Ch. 15, op. cit.

3 ". . . women don't understand these things. They only understand money when they can see it. They're very crude essentially. They don't understand where money comes from or what it means or how a man can be worth money though he hasn't any at the moment. But a man understands all that."   Ibid., Pt. II, Ch. 2

4 She would have a baby with her husband, to make up for the absence of love, to locate love, to fix herself in a certain place, but she would not really love him.   Ibid., Pt. III, Ch. 1

5 Old women snore violently. They are like bodies into which bizarre animals have crept at night; the animals are vicious, bawdy, noisy. How they snore! There is no shame to their snoring. Old women turn into old men.
"What Is the Connection Between Men and Women?," *Mademoiselle*
February 1970

6 In love there are two things: bodies and words.   Ibid.

7 Her mind churns so that she can't hear, she can't think.   Ibid.

8 "Loneliness is dangerous. it's bad for you to be alone, to be lonely, because if aloneness does not lead to God, it leads to the devil. It leads to the self."
"Shame" (1968), *The Wheel of Love and Other Stories*
1970

9 Night comes to the desert all at once, as if someone turned off a light.
"Interior Monologue" (1969), op. cit.

10 When a marriage ends, who is left to understand it?   "Unmailed, Unwritten Letters" (1969), op. cit.

11 Before falling in love, I was defined. Now I am undefined, weeds are growing between my ribs.   "I Was in Love" (1970), op. cit.

12 "I don't think that California is a healthy place. . . . Things disintegrate there."
Pt. I, Ch. 8, *Do with Me What You Will*
1970

13 The worst cynicism: a belief in luck.
Ibid., Pt. II, Ch. 15

14 . . . he believed in the justice of his using any legal methods he could improvise to force the other side into compromise or into dismissals of charges, or to lead a jury into the verdict he wanted. Why not? He was a defense lawyer, not a judge or a juror or a policeman or a legislator or a theoretician or an anarchist or a murderer.   Ibid.

15 . . . like all virtuous people he imagines he must speak the truth. . . .   Ibid.

16 Nothing is accidental in the universe—this is one of my Laws of Physics—except the entire universe itself, which is Pure Accident, pure divinity. "The Summing Up: Meredith Dawe," op. cit.

17 What relationship had a dagger to the human hand, that it must be invented, imagined out of the shape of the hand?—where did the sharpness come from, was it from the soul and its unstoppable imaginings?—because the hand in itself was so defenseless, so vulnerable in its flesh. "Elena," op. cit.

18 Our house is made of glass . . . and our lives are made of glass; and there is nothing we can do to protect ourselves.
American Appetites 1988

2247. Diane Ravitch (1938–   )

1 The ladder was there, "from the gutter to the university," and for those stalwart enough to ascend it, the schools were a boon and a path out of poverty. The Great School Wars 1974

2248. Nancy Simpson (1938–   )

1 In hearing distance of a wave's yes, earth is a woman with plans.
"Skin Underwater," Night Student 1985

2249. Liv Ullman (1938–   )

1 . . . we have to work to be good people, . . . goodness always involves the choice to be good. Quoted in Necessary Losses by Judith Viorst* 1986

*See 2092.

2250. Luisa Valenzuela (1938–   )

1 In Victor's life, monotomy and boredom had nothing to do with one another. He repeated his repertoire so often that even from miles away, Clara could follow his conversation with anyone who happened to be sitting next to him.
"The Body," Ch. 1, Clara (1967), Thirteen Short Stories and a Novel by Luisa Valenzuela, Hortense Carpentier and J. Jorge Castello, trs. 1976

2 How good can freedom be if you're alone and broke, with just a few coins in the bottom of your purse, hidden in the lining, the forgotten coins nobody cares about. Ibid., Ch. 4

3 I am superior. I don't need any drugs, although at times I share those of others out of pure sociability, so as not to seem different. And to keep my business going: I produce drugs—no longer through my pores but in an industrial way, so others can attain, even if only in fleeting flashes, a little of the light that illuminates me.
For my personal use, I am the drug, the drug is I.
"The One," The Lizard's Tail (El Brujo Hormiga Roja Señor Del Tacurú), Gregory Rabassa, tr. 1983

4 The initial path can be repeated forever. Ibid.

2251. Natalie Wood (1938–1981)

1 The only time a woman really succeeds in changing a man is when he is a baby.
Remark n.d.

2252. Paula Gunn Allen (1939–   )

1 The best of the world slumps before
    me—minds
that eighteen years ago first turned
    earthward,
blinking.
oh yeah.
Wasted.
Turned off.
Tuned in to video narcosis,
stereophonic flight, transfixed.
naked angels burning their hopes, mine,
    on dust and
beer.
"Star Child Suit," II, St. 4, That's What She Said, Rayna Green,* ed., 1984

*See 2284.

2 beautiful woman. beautiful
corn woman. woman like corn:
ripe and full. sweet. self
generating. tasseled.
blowing in the wind. meeting.
"The Beautiful Woman Who Sings," op. cit.

3 We are the women of daylight; of clocks
    and steel
foundries, of drugstores and street-
    lights,
of superhighways that slice our days in
    two.

Our dreams are pale memories of themselves,
and nagging doubt is the false measure of
our days.   "Kopis'taya," St. 3, op. cit.

4 There was a man who had come into her
life, into her,
feeding her, feeding on her.
                    "The Bearer of the Sun Arises,"
                                        op. cit.

5 The serene presence of the state, the faceless
shadow of authority, of power, of those who
controlled because they had seen fit to entomb
themselves and their sacred honor in the vast
caverns of city hall.   Untitled Story, op. cit.

6 "I pay for my loving and I refuse to pay when
they refuse to love. Shit."   Ibid.

2253. Margaret Atwood (1939–   )

1 He has realized he was an intruder; the cabin,
the fences, the fires and paths were violations;
now his own fence excludes him, as logic excludes love.   *Surfacing*   *1983*

2 We are for breeding purposes: we aren't con-
cubines, geisha girls, courtesans. On the contrary: everything possible has been done to remove us from that category. There is supposed
to be nothing entertaining about us.
                    The Handmaid's Tale   *1986*

3 Who knows, your very flesh may be polluted,
dirty as an oily beach, sure death to shore birds
and unborn babies. Maybe a vulture would die
of eating you. . . . Women took medicines,
pills, men sprayed trees, cows ate grass, all that
souped-up piss flowed into the rivers. Not to
mention the exploding atomic power plants.
                                        Ibid.

4 Nobody dies from lack of sex. It's lack of love
we die from. There's nobody here I can
love. . . . I too am a missing person.   Ibid.

2254. Maria Isabel Barreno (1939–   )

1 . . . all friendship between women has a uterine
air about it, the air of a slow, bloody, cruel,
incomplete exchange, of an original situation
being repeated all over again.
                    New Portuguese Letters, with Maria
                        Fatima Velho da Costa* and Maria
                            Teresa Horta**   1972

*See 2309.
**See 2269.

2 The time of discipline began. Each of us the
pupil of whichever one of us could best teach
what each of us needed to learn.   Ibid.

3. . . . we are still the property of men, the spoils
today of warriors who pretend to be our comrades in the struggle, but who merely seek to
mount us. . . .   Ibid.

4 One lives and endures one's life with others,
within matrices, but it is only alone, truly alone
that one bursts apart, springs forth.   Ibid.

5 Let no one tell me that silence gives consent,
because whoever is silent dissents.   Ibid.

2255. Mary Catherine Bateson (1939–   )

1 The family is changing, not disappearing. We
have to broaden our understanding of it, look
for the new metaphors.
                    Quoted in *The World of Ideas* by
                            Bill Moyers   *1989*

2 There are few things as toxic as a bad metaphor.
You can't think without metaphors.   Ibid.

3 Fear is not a good teacher. The lessons of fear
are quickly forgotten.   Ibid.

4 Either we have to make the leap to a vision that
includes all human beings, or we are locked up
in tiny, local self-interest and prejudices—and
at that point, why not just get rich and enjoy
yourself? It's as if the time had come to recognize that we are one.   Ibid.

5 This is the century of the refugee.   Ibid.

2256. Kathleen Betsko (1939–   )

1 Most war tales have been about male bravery.
National history seen through men's militaristic
eyes. I want to record the history of England's
mothers at war . . . children at war.
                    "Kathleen Betsko," *Interviews*
                        with Contemporary Women
                        Playwrights, Kathleen Betsko &
                            Rachel Koenig   1987

2 I think the theater should be a place to "get
down and dirty" . . . passionate, visceral. Even
unfair if necessary. Fairness is the opposite of
passion.   Ibid.

3 We* were delirious with learning, discovering
art, growing in self-esteem, and still doing the
laundry.   Ibid.

*(Disadvantaged Women for a Higher Education [DWHE]
at the University of New Hampshire.)

4 In my own opinion, women think and write
differently than men because they have different
experiences, different myths, different needs and
desires and dreams and memories. As feminist

scholars have pointed out, we exist as a separate culture within the dominant culture. A culture distinct from men's, no matter how intimately we may live with or love them. *Ibid.*

5 When women are free to be completely honest, the theater will be rocked to its foundations; far from destroying it, I think there'll be a glorious rebirth. *Ibid.*

2257. Rosellen Brown (1939–   )

1 "Do you think there could be something like victims without crimes?"
"A Letter to Ismael in the Grave,"
Street Games   1974

2 "I wish you were alive, I wish, I wish, so I could hate you and get on with it." *Ibid.*

3 I know how he dreams me. I know because I dream his dreams. "How to Win,"
op. cit.

4 . . . I remember sort of half dreaming as if I had dozed for a few unlikely minutes down by the bay and some sea animal had crawled up, slimy, from below the pilings, had bit me painfully between the legs, and had retreated to its secret life, invisible under the water, covered with blood like something wounded. For an initiation, I assume it was about average.
"Street Games,"
op. cit.

2258. Gro Harlem Brundtland (1939–   )

1 We need a wider definition of national security . . . The destruction of the planet's environment is making the world a less stable place, politically, economically and militarily . . . Our environmental management practices have focussed largely upon after-the-fact repair of damage . . . The ability to anticipate and prevent environmental damage will require that the ecological dimensions of policy be considered at the same time as the economic, trade, energy, agricultural and other dimensions.
From TV broadcast, "Only One Earth," Quoted in *Ms.*
January 1989

2 There is resentment [against the "minimum gender" rule*]. There are only so many jobs. It is a question of power.
Quoted in "Are Women Leaders Wielding Power Differently Than Men?" by Georgia Anne Geyer,**
Seattle Times   14 May 1989

*The Social Democrat rule in Norway by which 40 percent of Cabinet and Parliament posts are assured for women.
**See 2170.

3 There is a very close connection between being a doctor and being a politician. The doctor first tries to prevent illness, then tries to treat it if it comes. It's exactly the same as what you try to do as a politician, but with regard to society. Quoted in
"Norway's Radical Daughter" by Nancy Gibbs, *Time   25 September 1989*

4 I do not know of any environmental group in any country that does not view its government as an adversary. *Ibid.*

2259. Judy Chicago (1939–   )

1 We have made a space to house our spirit, to give form to our dreams. . . .
"Let Sisterhood Be Powerful,"
Womanspace   February/March 1973

2 I did not understand that wanting doesn't always lead to action
Ch. 4, *Through the Flower: My Struggle as a Woman Artist   1975*

3 The acceptance of women as authority figures or as role models is an important step in female education. . . . It is this process of identification, respect, and then self-respect that promotes growth. *Ibid., Ch. 5*

2260. Judy Collins (1939–   )

1 In the future we will have pop song cycles like classical Lieder, but we will create our own words, music and orchestrations, because we are a generation of whole people.
Quoted in *Rock and Other Four Letter Words* by ?,
1968

2 I look in the mirror through the eyes of the child that was me. "Secret Gardens of the Heart"
1972

2261. Yaël Dayan (1939–   )

1 Within me I would be the mistress; outside, if necessary, a slave. I would knit my world together, make contact with the outside world, write the right kind of letters, and be as I thought appropriate to different people.
New Face in the Mirror   1959

2 My father,* I remembered, had no fears at all. In that he differed greatly from me. But he could not be called a courageous man because he had no fears to overcome. *Ibid.*

*Moshe Dayan, 1915–1981, Israeli political and military leader.

3 He picked up some earth and poured it into the boy's palm. "Grasp it, feel it, taste it. There is your God. If you want to pray, boy, pray to the sky to bring rain to our land and not virtue to your souls."
Ch. 4, *Envy the Frightened*   *1960*

4 How long it takes us to gather the component parts of our memory—the problems, self-appraisals, the self-analysis, our little daily dilemmas, petty quests for comfort. And how quickly they all can disappear.
Israel Journal (June 1967)   *1967*

2262. Shelagh Delaney (1939–   )

1 HELEN. The only consolation I can find in your immediate presence is your ultimate absence.   Act I, Sc. 1, *A Taste of Honey*
1959

2 JO. In this country [England] there are only two seasons, winter and winter.   Ibid., Sc. 2

3 GEOF. You need somebody to love you while you're looking for someone to love.
Ibid., Act II, Sc. 2

4 I am here and I am safe and I am sick of it.
"Sweetly Sings the Donkey," *Sweetly Sings the Donkey*   *1963*

5 He didn't play with his food anymore till it got cold; instead, down it went like fuel into a furnace keeping the ovens hot, and the energy at boiling point, as Tom hurtled through his life catching up with himself at last.
"Tom Riley," op. cit.

6 We teach you the pleasure of physical exercise—the team-spirit of games, too, for when you leave school finally you will find that life is a game, sometimes serious, sometimes fun, but a game that must be played with true team-spirit—there is no room for the outsider in life.   "The Teacher," op. cit.

7 "There aren't enough secrets to go round anymore. Some spies are having to invent secrets in order to earn a living."
"My Uncle, the Spy," op. cit.

2263. Margaret Drabble (1939–   )

1 If I need to understand what I am doing, if I cannot act without my own approbation—and I must act, I have changed, I am no longer capable of inaction—then I will invent a morality that condones me. Though by doing so, I risk condemning all that I have been.
The Waterfall   *1969*

2 It appalled him, the complacency with which such friends would describe the advantages of living in a mixed area. As though they licensed seedy old ladies and black men to walk their streets, teaching their children of poverty and despair, as their pet hamsters and guinea pigs taught them of sex and death.
Pt. I, *The Needle's Eye*   *1972*

3 How easy it was to underestimate what had been endured.   Ibid., Pt. II

4 We seek a utopia in the past, a possible if not ideal society. We seek golden worlds from which we are banished, they recede infinitely, for there never was a golden world, there was never anything but toil and subsistence, cruelty and dullness.   *The Realms of Gold*   *1975*

5 . . . the human mind can bear plenty of reality but not too much unintermittent gloom.   Ibid.

6 As a geologist, he took a long view of time: even longer than Frances Wingate, archaeologist, and very much longer than Karel Schmidt, historian.   Ibid.

7 But his heart was another matter. It beat in his chest, soft and treacherous. It was invisible. Nobody had ever seen it. He had been unaware of it most of the time, until it had reminded him of its existence. And now he thought of it often, he nursed it carefully, as though it were a baby or a bird, a delicate creature that must not be shocked or offended.   Part I, *The Ice Age*
1977

8 People like blowing things up these days, thought Len. They prefer blowing up to building.
Ibid.

9 When nothing is sure, everything is possible.   *The Middle Ground*   *1980*

10 We gamble on the present, what else can we do?   Ibid.

2264. Roxanne Dunbar (1939–   )

1 Man, in conquering nature, conquered the female, who had worked with nature, not against it, to produce food and to reproduce the human race.   "Feminine Liberation as the Basis for Social Revolution," *Sisterhood Is Powerful*, Robin Morgan,* ed.   *1970*

*See 2327.

2 We live under an international caste system, at the top of which is the Western white male ruling class, and at the very bottom of which is the female of the nonwhite colonized world.
Ibid.

3 In reality, the family has fallen apart. Nearly half of all marriages end in divorce, and the

family unit is a decadent, energy-absorbing, destructive, wasteful institution for everyone except the ruling class for which the institution was created. *Ibid.*

2265. Terry Garthwaite (1939–)

1 from bessie to bebe to billie to boz
there's a lot more power than the wizard of
oz   "Rock and Roller" *1975*

2266. Joan Goulianos (1939–)

1 . . . these . . . women [of history] . . . wrote in a world which was controlled by men, a world in which women's revelations, if they were anything but conventional, might not be welcomed, might not be recognized, and they wrote nevertheless.
Introduction (February 1972),
By a Woman Writt
1973

2 But, overall, it was men who were the critics, the publishers, the professors, the sources of support. It was men who had the power to praise women's works, to bring them to public attention, or to ridicule them, to doom them . . . to obscurity. *Ibid.*

2267. Germaine Greer (1939–)

1 What is the arms race and the cold war but the continuation of male competitiveness and aggression into the inhuman sphere of computer-run institutions? If women are to cease producing cannon fodder for the final holocaust they must rescue men from the perversities of their own polarization.   "The Psychological Sell,"
The Female Eunuch   1971

2 As soon as we find ourselves working at being indispensable, rigging up a pattern of vulnerability in our loved ones, we ought to know that our love has taken the socially sanctioned form of egotism. *Ibid.,* "Egotism"

3 Love, love, love—all the wretched cant of it, masking egotism, lust, masochism, fantasy under a mythology of sentimental postures.
Ibid., "Obsession"

4 Shared, but secret behavior will cement any group into a conspiracy. . . . *Ibid.,* "Family"

5 There is no such thing as security. There never has been. . . . Security is when everything is settled, when nothing can happen to you; security is the denial of life. *Ibid.,* "Security"

6 Loneliness is never more cruel than when it is felt in close propinquity with someone who has ceased to communicate. *Ibid.*

2268. Matina Horner (1939–)

1 Unusual excellence in women was clearly associated for them with the loss of femininity, social rejection, personal or societal destruction or some combination of the above.
Women and Success: The Anatomy
of Achievement   1964

2269. Maria Teresa Horta (1939–)

Co-author with Maria Isabel Barreno and Maria Fatima Velho da Costa. See 2254; 2309.

2270. Barbara Kolb (1939–)

1 . . . composing a piece of music is very feminine. It is sensitive, emotional, contemplative. By comparison, doing housework is positively masculine.
Quoted in "A Matter of Art, Not Sex,"
Time   10 November 1975

2271. Kathrin Perutz (1939–)

1 The true man or woman must be deeply sexual; the only true intercourse between humans is sexual; levels of pleasure have almost become notches in the yardstick of goodness; and sexual variation is as necessary to marriage now as once social graces were. . . . Love must be made—or sex must be had—a prescribed number of times a week; otherwise one falls from grace and competition.
Marriage Is Hell   1972

2272. Letty Cottin Pogrebin (1939–)

1 . . . lifestyles and sex roles are passed from parents to children as inexorably as blue eyes or small feet.
"Down with Sexist Upbringing,"
The First Ms. Reader, Francine
Klagsbrun, ed.   *1972*

2 In school books, the Dick and Jane syndrome reinforced our emerging attitudes. The arithmetic books posed appropriate conundrums: "Ann has three pies . . . Dan has three rockets. . . ." We read the nuances between the lines: Ann

keeps her eye on the oven; Dan sets his sights on the moon. Ibid.

3 . . . children's liberation is the next item on our civil rights shopping list. Ibid.

2273. Willie Mae Reid (1939–   )

1 [There is an] insidious, contradictory belief that Black women have always had it better than Black men, and still do. For example, there is the story that Black women have always enjoyed "sexual liberation," . . . The truth is that Black women, from the time of slavery to this very day, have been victimized the most by the warped sexual ideas of this racist society. As slaves, we were raped, abused, and beaten at the whim of the slave owners . . . We were bred like cattle . . . Black women were assumed to be the sexual property of the owner, his friends, visitors, and relatives.
> "Changing Attitudes Among Black
> Women," *International*
> *Socialist Review   March 1975*

2 What must be recognized is that the status of black women places us at the intersection of all the forms of subjugation in this society—racial oppression, sexual oppression, economic exploitation. We are a natural part of many different struggles—as Black people, as union members, as unemployed, as parents, as women. Ibid.

3 The oppression of women, like the oppression of blacks, is one of the pillars of the capitalist system of exploitation. The fight to weaken any one of these pillars contributes to weakening the entire structure that victimizes all of us. Ibid.

2274. Joan Rivers (1939–   )

1 The psychic scars caused by believing that you are ugly have a permanent mark on your personality.   Quoted in "An Ugly Duckling
> Complex" by Lydia Lane,
> *Los Angeles Times*
> *10 May 1974*

2 There is not one female comic who was beautiful as a little girl. Ibid.

3 Can we talk?   Catchphrase   *n.d.*

4 Your anger can be 49 percent and your comedy 51 percent, and you are okay. If the anger is 51 percent, the comedy is gone.
> *Enter Talking   1986*

2275. Susan Sherman (1939–   )

1 Analysis. Cross-reference analysis. The age of analysis.
Psychological, philosophical, poetic analysis. Not the
event, but the picturing of the event.
> "The Fourth Wall," St. 2, *El Corno*
> *Emplumado   1966*

2276. Grace Slick (1939–   )

1 Remember what the dormouse said:
"Feed your head.
Feed your head.
Feed your head."   "White Rabbit"   *1965*

2277. Eleanor Smeal (1939–   )

1 Just think—guns have a constitutional amendment protecting them and women don't.
> Fundraising letter, Fund
> for the Feminist Majority   *1989*

2 Any system that produces 95% men members and 5% women members—like Congress—is sex discriminatory. We must show how the election rules lock women out, and we must change these rules!   Ibid.

2278. Loretta Swit (1939–   )

1 So much of life is luck. One day you make a right turn and get hit by a car. Turn left and you meet the love of your life. I think I made the correct turn.
> Quoted in "M*A*S*H Supporting
> Players About Ready for Civilian
> Careers" by Bob Wisehart in
> *The Times/Picayune*
> *17 September 1981*

2279. Naomi Weisstein (1939–   )

1 . . . there isn't the tiniest shred of evidence that . . . fantasies of servitude and childish dependence have anything to do with woman's true potential. . . ."
> Address, " 'Kinder, Kuche, Kirche' as
> Scientific Law: Psychology Constructs
> the Female," American Studies
> Association, California
> *26 October 1968*

2 . . . in order to understand why people do what they do, and certainly in order to change what

people do, psychologists must turn away from the theory of the causal nature of the inner dynamic and look at the social context within which individuals live. *Ibid.*

3 The problem with insight, sensitivity and intuition is that they tend to confirm our biases. At one time people were convinced of their ability to identify witches. All it required was sensitivity to the workings of the devil. Clinical experience is not the same thing as empirical evidence. "Woman as Nigger," *Psychology Today October 1969*

4 . . . a typical minority-group stereotype—woman as nigger—if she knows her place (home), she is really a quite lovable, loving creature, happy and childlike. *Ibid.*

5 Evidence and reason: my heroes and my guides.
"Adventures of a Woman in Science," *Women Look at Biology Looking at Women,* Ruth Hubbard,* Mary Sue Henifin and Barbara Fried, eds. *1979*

*See 1934.

2280. Moira Bachman (fl. 1940s)

1 In my apron, I carry nails, pliers, a heavy hammer, and pride. Organization for Equal Education of the Sexes, *n.d.*

2281. Kate Braverman (194?–   )

1 Except for a small group of organically damaged individuals, doing nothing at all indefinitely is quite rare. For one thing, fate and external circumstances usually don't leave us completely alone. There are always some new demands from that place out there. Sometimes the demands can be quite minimal, like getting yourself together enough to pick up your unemployment check.
"Dropping What," *Dropping In, Putting It All Back Together 1973*

2 We've been raised by books which told our parents when we were supposed to move, sit, walk, read, stop hitting the kid next door and start making out instead. We grew up with them watching to see if we were on the right page at the right age. *Ibid.,* "Splitting"

3 Los Angeles is a new cosmopolitan refugee city for the world. It's a city of confluences.
Quoted in "From the Tropic of L.A." by Cristina Garcia, *Time 20 November 1989*

4 California is looked at the way Italy used to be viewed in England. It's sexual and dangerous. Something could happen. A person could change. *Ibid.*

5 I find women as writers and as characters are operating within narrow confines. They inherit a kind of ghetto of the soul. *Ibid.*

6 I have to protect myself from the toxicity of this culture. *Ibid.*

7 To be one woman, truly, wholly, is to be all women. Tend one garden and you will birth worlds. *Palm Latitudes 1989?*

2282. Anne Commire (194?–   )

1 Funny, if I have any pride in my writing, it's not in what I wrote. It's because I dare to write, dare to face my demons and that enormously frightening machine daily. After fifteen years, I still face that machine with fear. Dreading there'll be nothing there. Dreading that today I'll find out I don't have an original thought left in my brain, that I squandered it on postcards to friends. "Anne Commire," *Interviews with Contemporary Women Playwrights,* Kathleen Betsko* & Rachel Koenig *1987*

*See 2256.

2 Theater risks every night. It has the possibility of soaring in the air or landing on its ass. People come for the spectacle, for the danger. Some with holly in their hearts; some like spectators at the Colosseum, rooting for the lion. *Ibid.*

3 Books have been written *ad infinitum* on male-female misunderstandings. Most of Hollywood's success is based on it. And yet we've never dealt with that on a level of male critic/female writer. We pretend that it's not even going on. *Ibid.*

2283. Betty Edwards (fl. 1940s)

1 Training in perception has the same function as teaching people to read and write—that is, it reins those skills so they are honed up and useable at a conscious level, and useful for things other than just looking around, just as language skills are trained up through reading and writing, in ways that one doesn't achieve just talking.
Quoted in "Betty Edwards: Teaching The Tricks of Perception" by John Crutcher, *Common Ground of Puget Sound Fall 1989*

2 My work essentially is involved with teaching people how to better control their own brains. This is what I'm interested in. And drawing is as incidental to being an artist in that sense, as learning to read and write is to being a poet. Drawing is simply a path towards really becoming a better Captain Kirk*—of the space voyage.   Ibid.

*Fictitious character from the longlived *Star Trek* television series.

3 Somehow or other in this century, we have psychologically blocked the training of right hemisphere, especially for drawing, which is one of its main functions.   Ibid.

4 Computers can do all the left hemisphere processing better and faster than the human brain. So what's left for the human brain is global thinking, creative thinking, intuitive-problem solving, seeing the whole picture. All of that can not be done by the computer. And yet the school system goes on, churning out reading, writing and arithmetic, spelling, grammer.
                                      Ibid.

2284. Rayna Green (194?–   )

1 But "identity" is never simply a matter of genetic make-up or natural birthright. Perhaps once, long ago, it was both. But not now. For people out on the edge, out on the road, identity is a matter of will, a matter of choice, a face to be shaped in a ceremonial act.
                        Introduction, *That's What She Said*, Rayna Green, ed.   *1984*

2 women's hands are never empty
  women's mouths are never empty
  women's arms are never empty
                   "Spider Woman," op. cit.

3 Indian silence
  leaves no room to hide
  except in dreams
  visions of light and spirit
  to wipe terror away
            "Old Indian Trick," St. 6, op. cit.

4 He's run everybody's patience out, and if he'd been on fire, not a soul would have pissed on him to save him.
                "High Cotton" (story), op. cit.

5 There's nothing like funerals for good eating.   Ibid.

2285. Joreen (194?–   )

1 Bitches are aggressive, assertive, domineering, overbearing, strong-minded, spiteful, hostile, direct, blunt, candid, obnoxious, thick-skinned, hard-headed, vicious, dogmatic, competent, competitive, pushy, loud-mouthed, independent, stubborn, demanding, manipulative, egoistic, driven, achieving, overwhelming, threatening, scary, ambitious, tough, brassy, masculine, boisterous and turbulent. . . . A Bitch takes shit from no one. You may not like her, but you cannot ignore her.
                        The Bitch Manifesto
                                  196?

2 The mythology that women are inferior and need to be protected by men went out with the mythology about the superiority of the Aryan race.   "The 51 Percent Minority
                Group," *The Voice of the
Women's Liberation Movement*   *196?*

2286. Harriet Goldhor Lerner
   (1944–   )

1 Perhaps we should first take time to contemplate why tending to relationships, like changing diapers, is predominately women's work. . . . *in relationships between dominant and subordinate groups, the subordinate group members always possess a far greater understanding of dominant group members and their culture than vice versa.*   Ch. 1, *The Dance of Intimacy*
                                  1989

2 In our rapidly changing society we can count only two things that will never change. What will never change is the will to change and the fear of change.   Ibid., Ch. 2

3 Men chart the stars, create language and culture as we know it, record history as they see it, build and destroy the world around us, and continue to run every major institution that generates power, policy, and wealth. Men define the very "reality" that—until the current feminist movement—I, for one, accepted as a given. and although women throughout history have exercised a certain power as mothers, we have not created the conditions in which we mother, nor have we constructed the predominant myths and theories about "good mothering."
                             Ibid., Epilogue

4 Women often choose a spouse who will express just those traits and qualities they most need to deny within themselves, or those qualities they wish they could express themselves but can't. A woman may then rage against her spouse as he expresses the very qualities she chose him for.   Quoted in "What Qualities Do Women Most Value in Husbands?," *Viewpoints*,
                Vol. 16, No. 5   *n.d.*

2287. Beverly Lowry (194?–)

1 Gardening and scholarship were not so different; both took long hours and singlemindedness, resiliency in the face of major setbacks, a gift for tedium and a flair for the marriage of the unusual. Both strained the eyes and lower back and depended to some degree on fate, prejudice, perspective and the intuitive flash.
Breaking Gentle 1988

2 "Soup's on," she said in so low a voice not even the broccoli could have heard her. Ibid.

2288. Nobuko Albery (1940?–)

1 "Many may argue it's the lowest of the low amongst living creatures, to be performers. But don't forget, Buddha put us there, and we actors live in service to the gods. . . . We, the humblest leeches of temples and shrines, though called untouchables, beggars and dung-worms, by singing, dancing, giving happiness to thousands of miserable souls should be the first amongst holy herons and peace blossoms to be allowed into Heaven of Blissful Peace."
Ch. 1, *The House of Kanze* 1986

2 "I'd rather forgo sleep today than sleeplessly lament my lost fortune tomorrow."
Ibid., Ch. 9

3 "When you forget the beginner's awe, you start decaying." Ibid., Ch. 10

4 "Of course it is true that our art exists only when we are seen; we are slaves to our audiences. But at the same time, we must always be a step ahead of them. We must tantalize, not bore them To shock, Motomasa, is a Flower of our art, like a sting of a certain bee that is said to revive the dead."
Ibid., Ch. 21

2289. Louise Bernikow (1940–)

1 Pep is what happened in American history before *vigah*, but it only applied to females. Pep was cheerfulness. It mysteriously resided in the Ipana smile. "Confessions of an Ex-Cheerleader," *Ms.*
October 1973

2 Everytime I say "sure" when I mean "no," every time I smile brightly when I'm exploding with rage, every time I imagine my man's achievement is my own, I know the cheerleader never really died. I feel her shaking her ass inside me and I hear her breathless, girlish voice mutter "T-E-A-M, Yea, Team." Ibid.

3 The question arises as to whether it is possible *not* to live in the world of men and still to live in the world. The answer arises nearly as quickly that this can only happen if men are not thought of as "the world."
Introduction, *The World Split Open*
1974

4 A witch was a woman with enormous power, a woman who might change the natural world. She was "uncivilized" and in opposition to the world of the King, the court, polite society. She had to be controlled. Ch. 1, *Among Women*
1980

5 Acknowledging the tension, distance, and conflict, where is a map of the nurturance, the connection, the ways in which the torch is passed from mother to daughter or from daughter to mother? In Colette.*
Collette is the Poet of Passion Between Mother and Daughter. Colette Paints the Portrait of Mother as the Tree of Life. Ibid., Ch. 2
*See 1192.

6 I say you hurt me. You say I scorned you. We say we care. It begins. The conversation begins. Ibid., Ch. 6

2290. Maria Campbell (1940–)

1 Cheechum [grandmother] would often say scornfully of this God that he took more money from us than the Hudson's Bay store.
Halfbreed 1973

2 She taught me to see beauty in all things around me; that inside each thing a spirit lived, that it was vital too, regardless of whether it was only a leaf or a blade of grass, and by recognizing its life and beauty I was accepting God. . . . that when my body became old my spirit would leave and I'd come back and live again. She said God lives in you and looks like you, and not to worry about him floating around in a beard and white cloak; that the Devil lives in you and all things, and that he looks like you and not like a cow. . . . Her explanation made much more sense than anything Christianity had ever taught me. Ibid.

3 Dreams are so important in one's life, yet when followed blindly they can lead to the disintegration of one's soul. Ibid.

4 My Cheechum used to tell me that when the government gives you something, they take all that you have in return—your pride, your dignity, all the things that make you a living soul. When they are sure they have everything they give you a blanket to cover your shame. She said that the churches with their talk about God,

the Devil, heaven and hell, and schools that taught children to be ashamed, were all part of that government. . . . She used to say that all our people wore blankets, each in his own way.   Ibid.

5 I no longer need my blanket to survive.   Ibid.

2291. Isabel do Carmo (1940–)

1 The movement must be accompanied by force. . . . There must be an armed insurrection.
Quoted in *Time*   30 October 1975

2 There can be no halfway solutions, no half measures. That won't work. We must have either pure socialism or we will go back to fascism.   Ibid.

3 In our party, being a woman is no problem. After all, it is a revolutionary party.   Ibid.

2292. Kim Chernin (1940–)

1 The obsession [of slenderness] . . . might well be considered one of the most serious forms of suffering affecting women in America today.   *The Obsession*   1981

2 They could not see they were too thin because slenderness had become a statement of power. There could never be too much of it, since more implied that the will had grown even stronger in its relentless struggle to dominate matter.
Ibid.

3 And so we leave home, we leave the apron and . . . put on . . . tailored executive suits. . . . And now we take ourselves in hand, tailoring ourselves to the specifications of this world we are so eager to enter. We strip our bodies of flesh, our hearts of the overflow of feeling, our language of exuberant and dramatic imprecisions. We cut back the flight of our fancy, make our thoughts rigorous and subject it (this marvelous rushing intuitive leaping capacity of ours) to measures of demonstration and proof, trying not to talk with our hands, trying hard to subdue our voices, getting our bursts of laughter under control.   *The Hungry Self*   1985

2293. Phyllis Chesler (1940–)

1 At this moment in history only women can (if they will) support the entry or re-entry of women into the human race.
Women and Madness   1972

2 There is a double standard of mental health— one for men, another for women—existing among most clinicians. . . . For a woman to be healthy, she must "adjust" to and accept the behavioral norms of her sex—passivity, acquiescence, self-sacrifice, and lack of ambition—even though these kinds of "loser" behaviors are generally regarded as socially undesirable (i.e., nonmasculine).   Ibid.

3 While [women] live longer than ever before, and longer than men, there is less and less use for them in the only place they have been given— within the family. Many newly useless women are emerging more publicly and visibly into insanity and institutions.   Ibid.

2294. Lydia Dunn (1940–)

1 China will let Hong Kong survive not because it is just or right but because of our economic value.   Quoted in "Whither Hong Kong?" by
Margaret Scott, *The New York Times Magazine*   October 1989

2 We [Hong Kongers] have been told to stay out of politics and if we did we could make money. We did.   Ibid.

2295. Frances Fitzgerald (1940–)

1 By intervening in the Vietnamese struggle the United States was attempting to fit its global strategies into a world of hillocks and hamlets, to reduce its majestic concerns for the containment of Communism and the security of the Free World to a dimension where governments rose and fell as a result of arguments between two colonels' wives.
Pt. I, Ch. 1, *Fire in the Lake*   1972

2 Americans see history as a straight line and themselves standing at the cutting edge of it as representatives for all mankind. They believe in the future as if it were a religion; they believe that there is nothing they cannot accomplish, that solutions wait somewhere for all problems, like brides.   Ibid.

3 In a sense, the design of the Confucian world resembled that of a Japanese garden where every rock, opaque and indifferent to itself, takes on significance from its relation to the surrounding objects.   Ibid.

4 For most Americans, Southeast Asia came to look like the most complicated place in the world. And naturally enough, for the American official effort to fit the new evidence into the old official assumptions was something like the effort of the seventeenth-century astronomers to fit their observations of the planets into the Ptolemaic theory of the universe.
Ibid., Ch. 2

5 . . . the Americans were once again embarked upon a heroic and (for themselves) almost painless conquest of an inferior race. . . . [They] were white men in Asia, and they could not conceive that they might fail in their enterprise, could not conceive that they could be morally wrong.   *Ibid.*, Pt. II, Ch. 13

2296. Maria Mazziotto Gillan
(1940–   )

1 Remember me, ladies,
the silent?
I have found my voice
and my rage will blow
your house down.   "Public School 18:
Paterson, New Jersey,"
*The Dream Book: An Anthology of
Writings by Italian American
Women,* Helen Barolini,* ed.   *1985*

*See 1947.

2297. Judy Grahn (1940–   )

1 a woman is talking to death. . . .
"A Woman Is Talking to Death"
1974

2 . . . I looked into the mirror
and nobody was there to testify.   *Ibid.*

3 the woman who has the tattoo of a bird
the woman who puts things together
the woman who squats on her haunches
the woman whose children are all
different colors

singing   i am the will of the
woman   the woman
            my will is unbending

when She-Who-moves-the-earth will turn over
when She Who moves, the earth will turn
over.   "She Who," St. 10–12, *The Work
of a Common Woman*   *1980*

2298. Joan Haggerty (1940–   )

1 It was the novelty of the attraction that captivated her as much as the woman herself.
Daughters of the Moon   *1971*

2 Afterwards, you know, afterwards, I often feel like being fucked by a man too. . . . You *tune* me, d'you see, and then I want a man to counter me, but we together, we just keep traveling to strung out space. We can't comfort each other.   *Ibid.*

2299. Molly Haskell (1940–   )

1 . . . the propaganda arm of the American Dream machine, Hollywood. . . .
From Reverence to Rape   *1973*

2 The mammary fixation is the most infantile—and most American—of the sex fetishes.
. . .   *Ibid.*

3 Our sexual emancipators and evangelists sometimes miss half of the truth: that if puritanism is the source of our greatest hypocrisies and most crippling illusions it is, as the primal anxiety whose therapy is civilization itself, the source of much, perhaps most, of our achievement.   *Ibid.*

4 There have been very few heroines in literature who defined their lives morally rather than romantically and likewise but a handful in film.
. . .   *Ibid.*

5 The idea that acting is quintessentially "feminine" carries with it a barely perceptible sneer, a suggestion that it is not the noblest or most dignified of professions. Acting is role-playing, role-playing is lying, and lying is a woman's game.   *Ibid.*

6 . . . her [Marilyn Monroe's] suicide, as suicides do, casts a retrospective light on her life. Her "ending" gives her a beginning and middle, turns her into a work of art with a message and a meaning.   *Ibid.*

2300. Arlie Hochschild (1940–   )

1 It has become a sad commonplace to associate being old with being alone. We call isolation a punishment for the prisoner, but perhaps a majority of American old people are in some degree isolated or soon will be.
"Communal Living in Old Age," *The
Future of the Family,* Louise Kapp
Howe,* ed.   *1972*

*See 2155.

2 . . . the decline of the extended family creates the need for a new social shelter, another pool of friendships, another bond with society apart from family.   *Ibid.*

2301. Maxine Hong Kingston
(1940–   )

1 "Where's our jazz? Where's our blues? Where's our ain't-taking-no-shit-from-nobody street-strutting language? I want so bad to be the first bad-jazz China Man bluesman of America."
*Tripmaster Monkey: His Fake
Book*   *1989*

2 "You're going through the delusion of clarity
. . ." Ibid.

2302. Juliet Mitchell (1940–)

1 Socialism should properly mean not the abolition of the family, but the diversification of the
socially acknowledged relationships . . . which
matched the free invention and variety of men
and women.
"Women—The Longest Revolution,"
New Left Review
November/December 1966

2 Anatomy may, at its point of hypothetical nor-
mality, give us two opposite but equal sexes
(with the atrophied sex organs of the other
present in each), but Freudian psychoanalytic
theory does not.
"On Freud and the Distinction
Between the Sexes," *Women and
Analysis,* Jean Strouse, ed. *1974*

2303. Anne Moody (1940–)

1 I sat on the grass and listened to the speakers
[28 August 1963 March on Washington], to
discover we had "dreamers" instead of leaders
leading us. Just about every one of them stood
up there dreaming. Martin Luther King* went
on and on talking about his dream. I sat there
thinking that in Canton [Mississippi] we never
had time to sleep, much less dream.
Coming of Age in Mississippi
1968

*American civil rights leader (1929–1968); assassinated.

2 . . . the [Civil Rights] Movement was not in
control of its destiny. We were like an angry
dog on a leash who had turned on its master. It
could bark and howl and snap, and sometimes
even bite, but the master was always in
control. Quoted in *Contemporary Authors,*
Vol. 65–68 *1977*

2304. Gail Parent (1940–)

1 Do you want to live in a world where a man
lies about calories?
"The Facts," *Sheila Levine Is Dead
and Living in New York* *1972*

2 Don't we realize we're a business, we single
girls are? There are magazines for us, special
departments in stores for us. Every building that
goes up in Manhattan has more than fifty percent
efficiency apartments . . . for the one million
girls who have very little use for them.
Ibid., "On Jobs and Apartments"

3 Actually, I have only two things to worry about
now: afterlife and reincarnation.
Ibid., "The End"

2305. Jane Quick-To-See-Smith
(1940–)

1 The glaciers pushed
and the People moved.
"The Ronan Robe Series," Pt. I,
That's What She Said, Rayna
Green,* ed. *1984*

*See 2284.

2306. Patricia Schroeder (1940–)

1 However useless a defense concept, however
premature its implementation, however extravagant its cost, an argument to proceed is deemed
conclusive on one of two grounds. Either the
Russians are doing it and therefore we must do
it in order to avoid falling behind, or the Russians are not doing it and therefore we must in
order to stay ahead.
Quoted in *American Political
Women* by Esther Stineman
1980

2 Everyone is always talking about our defense
effort in terms of defending women and children, but no one ever asks the women and
children what they think. Ibid.

3 I have a brain and a uterus and I use them
both. (1973),
op. cit.

4 The government has an obligation to protect the
family so that it can care for itself during a
crisis. But the Reagan administration has turned
its back on parents who have lost their jobs
because they have missed too many days at
work caring for a child dying of cancer.
The administration has shown no concern for
young mothers who have returned to work after
having a baby only to find that they don't have
a job. It makes no allowances for parents who
need time off to adopt a child.
That's certainly no way to be pro-family.
"Parental Leave
Promises Big Return for Nation's
Families," *Seattle Post-Intelligencer*
October 1988

5 There is an ancient Indian saying: "We do not
inherit the earth from ancestors; we borrow it
from our children." If we use this ethic as a
moral compass, then our rendezvous with reality can also become a rendezvous with
opportunity. Quoted in *Ms.*
February 1989

2307. Stephanie Matthews-Simonton (1940–)

1 The most powerful tool we have for changing our environment is our ability to change ourselves.
Quoted in "The Good News About Cancer," by Peggy Elman Roggenbuck, *New Age* May 1978

2 Too often we associate healing only with medical treatment . . . [but] healing is more than just physiological . . . the patient can take part in his own recovery. The family can offer a vital supportive environment in this effort.
Introduction, *The Healing Family* 1984

3 Hope is essential; human beings can't live long without it. . . . When hope is taken away, people become so depressed that no matter what the outcome, their lives are miserable.
Ibid., Ch. 3

2308. Valerie Solanis (1940–)

1 Life in this society being, at best, an utter bore and no aspect of society being at all relevant to women, there remains to civic-minded, responsible, thrill-seeking females only to overthrow the government, eliminate the money system, institute complete automation and destroy the male sex.
SCUM Manifesto* 1967–1968

*SCUM is an acronym for Society for Cutting Up Men.

2 Dropping out gives control to those few who don't drop out; dropping out is exactly what the establishment leaders want; it plays into the hands of the enemy; it strengthens the system instead of undermining it, since it is based entirely on non-participation, passivity, apathy and non-involvement. . . .
Ibid.

2309. Maria Fatima Velho da Costa (1940?–)

Co-author with Maria Isabel Barreno, see 2254, and Maria Teresa Horta; see 2269.

2310. Michelene Wandor (1940–)

1 However it is true so far that on the whole women playwrights have tended to choose to write about their own sex—and actually, there is nothing at all unusual about that. Most male playwrights choose to write about their own sex—it is just that they rarely see that that is what they are doing.
Introduction, *Plays by Women* 1984

2 If someone accuses me of ghettoizing women playwrights, I have two answers: one is unprintable, the other is that no one ever accuses the editor of an all-male anthology of plays of ghettoizing playwrights.
"Michelene Wandor," *Interviews with Contemporary Women Playwrights*, Kathleen Betsko* & Rachel Koenig 1987

*See 2256.

2311. Margot Adler (1941–)

1 Although we know that on some level we are always connected, our most common experience is one of estrangement.
Drawing Down the Moon 1986

2 Just as ecological theory explains how we are interrelated with all other forms of life, rituals allow us to re-create that unity in an explosive, non-abstract, gut-level way. Rituals have the power to reset the terms of our universe until we find ourselves suddenly and truly "at home."
Ibid.

2312. Gloria Allred (1941–)

1 Lots of men, you see, simply aren't ready for assertive women. They expect us to tiptoe in, trembling and pleading for our rights and when those rights are denied, they expect us not to cause a furor but to tiptoe away quietly. But they underestimate how much we care.
Quoted in "Home Question and Answer" by Marshal Berges, *Los Angeles Times Home Magazine* 7 January 1979

2 There are enough high hurdles to climb, as one travels through life, without having to scale artificial barriers created by laws or silly regulations . . .
Ibid.

2313. Joan Baez (1941–)

1 Powerful Jesus gold and silver with young, hundred-year-old eyes.
You look around and you know you must have failed somewhere.
"Farewell Angelina" 1965

2 . . . hypothetical questions get hypothetical answers.
Daybreak 1966

3 War was going on long before anybody dreamed up Communism. It's just the latest justification for self-righteousness. Ibid.

4 If it's natural to kill why do men have to go into training to learn how? Ibid.

5 That's all nonviolence is—organized love.
Ibid.

6 By the middle of the twentieth century men had reached a peak of insanity. They grouped together in primitive nation-states, each nation-state condoning organized murder as the way to deal with international differences. . . .
Ibid.

7 Instead of getting hard ourselves and trying to compete, women should try and give their best qualities to men—bring them softness, teach them how to cry.
Quoted in "Sexism Seen But Not Heard" by Tracy Hotchner,
Los Angeles Times
26 May 1974

8 And if you're offering me diamonds and rust I've already paid.
"Diamonds and Rust" *1975*

9 We're the children of the eighties;
Haven't we grown?
We're softer than a lotus
and tougher than stone*
And the age of our innocence
Is somewhere in the garden.
"(For the) Children of the Eighties," *Live Europe 83* (album)
1983

*Adapted from phrase by Gandhi, Indian nationalist and spiritual leader (1869–1948); assassinated.

10 We are the warriors of the sun
Fighting postwar battles
That somehow never were won.
"Warriors of the Sun," op. cit.

2314. Beth Brant (1941–)

1 Because in the unraveling, the threads become more apparent, each one with its distinct color and texture. And as I unravel, I also weave. I am the storyteller and the story.
Introduction, *A Gathering of Spirit*,
Beth Brant, ed. *1984*

2 We have a spirit of rage. We are angry women. Angry at white men and their perversions. Their excessive greed and abuse of the earth, sky, and water. Their techno-christian approach to anything that lives, including our children, our people. We are angry at Indian men for their refusals of us. For their limited vision of what constitutes a strong Nation. We are angry at a

so-called "women's movement" that always seems to forget we exist. Except in romantic fantasies of earth mother, or equally romantic and dangerous fantasies about Indian-woman-as victim. Ibid.

3 I truly believe that white man hates and craves what is inside those of us who are colored. They envy our connections to the spirit, to the earth, to a community, to a people. Because they envy that; they hate us, and will do anything to get rid of us. So all the things . . . slavery, genocide of Indians on this continent, as well as in Latin America; the Holocaust, missionaries in China, the Vietnam War . . . all of these a calculated program of extermination. And I add to that, the millions of women burned at the stake centuries ago, because we were women, because we were lesbians.
Letter to Raven* (28 December 1982), op. cit.

*Doris Ann Foster, aka Raven; See 2059.

2315. Blanche Weisen Cook (1941–)

1 Revolution is a process and not an event. The power of women to come together, to support each other in community, in creative self-criticism and love, gives us the power to intensify the economic and political struggle. Wherever groups of women come together to define their own visions, economic and personal, and make connections with other groups of women working in our own interests, politically accountable to our own needs and wants, we are affirming a network of change. We are building the future. *Women and Support Networks* *1979*

2316. Bridget Rose Dugdale (1941–)

1 For how long you sentence me is of no relevance; I regard it with the contempt it deserves. I am guilty and proudly so if guilty has come to describe one who takes up arms to defend the people of Ireland against the English tyrant.
Quoted in "Englishwoman Trips on Revolutionary Road" by Tom Lambert,
Los Angeles Times
26 June 1974

2317. Nora Ephron (1941–)

1 We have lived through the era when happiness was a warm puppy, and the era when happiness was a dry martini, and now we have come to

the era when happiness is "knowing what your uterus looks like."
"Vaginal Politics" (December 1972),
Crazy Salad   1975

2 She [Rose Mary Woods]* has often said that she was very much impressed by him [Nixon] before she even knew him, because he kept such neat expense accounts.
"Rose Mary Woods—The Lady or the Tiger?" (March 1974), op. cit.

* President Richard Nixon's secretary, held responsible for 20 missing minutes of vital recorded tape related to the Watergate scandal.

2318. Linda Gottlieb (1941?–   )

Co-author with Joan Silver. See 2179.

2319. Toni Grant (1941–   )

1 There is a profound sense of alienation and loneliness here [in Southern California], and few traditional guidelines for behavior. I don't have any grand solutions, just my own idiosyncratic ones.   "Dial Dr. Toni for Therapy,"
Time   26 May 1980

2 . . . sometimes you have to give up an intense heat for a continuing warmth.
Quoted in "Sexy Guru for Kvetches" by Elaine Warren, *Los Angeles Herald Examiner* 20 July 1980

2320. Barbara Grizzuti Harrison (1941–   )

1 Profoundly ignorant, we were obliged to invent.   "Talking Dirty," *Ms.* October 1973

2 True revolutionaries are like God—they create the world in their own image. Our awesome responsibility to ourselves, to our children, and to the future is to create ourselves in the image of goodness, because the future depends on the nobility of our imaginings.
Ch. 9, *Unlearning the Lie: Sexism in School*   1973

3 Women's propensity to share confidences is universal. We confirm our reality by sharing.
"Secrets Women Tell Each Other," *McCall's*   August 1975

4 I refuse to believe that trading recipes is silly. Tuna-fish casserole is at least as real as corporate stock.   Ibid.

5 There is no way to take the danger out of human relationships.   Ibid.

2321. Marie Herbert (1941–   )

1 Unlike children in other countries, the Eskimos played no games of war. They played with imaginary rifles and harpoons, but these were never directed against people but against the formidable beasts that haunted the vast wastes of their land.
Ch. 5, *The Snow People*   1973

2322. Elizabeth Holtzman (1941–   )

1 If the mood of the country is for fiscal responsibility, then let's get at that area of government which is the biggest waster of funds—the Defense Department.   Quoted in *American Political Women*, Esther Stineman   1980

2323. Shirbey Johnson (1941–   )

1 . . . women are carrying a new attitude. They've cast aside the old stereotypes. They don't believe you have to be ugly or have big muscles to play sports.
Quoted in "Women in Sports: The Movement Is Real," *Los Angeles Times*   23 April 1974

2324. Carole King (1941–   )

1 When my soul was in the lost-and-found
You came along to claim it.
"A Natural Woman"   1967

2 You've got to get up every morning with a
  smile on your face
And show the world all the love in your heart
Then people gonna treat you better
You're gonna find, yes you will
That you're beautiful as you feel.
"Beautiful"   1971

3 Doesn't anybody stay in one place any
  more?   "So Far Away"   1971

4 Winter, spring, summer or fall
All you have to do is call
And I'll be there,
You've got a friend.
"You've Got a Friend"   1971

2325. Julia Kristeva (1941–   )

1 But Judaism was founded through and beyond this tradition, when, around 2000 BC, Egyptian

refugees, nomads, brigands and insurgent peasants banded together, it seems, without any coherent ethnic origin, without land or State, seeking at first merely to survive as a wandering community. Jewish monotheism is undoubtedly rooted in this will to create a community in the face of all the unfavorable concrete circumstances: an abstract, nominal symbolic community beyond individuals and their beliefs, but beyond their political organization as well.

> "On This Side," *Des Chinoises*
> *1974*

2 FLASH—instant of time or of dream without time; inordinately swollen atoms of a bond, a vision, a shiver, a yet formless, unnameable embryo. Epiphanies. Photos of what is not yet visible and that language necessarily skims over from afar, allusively. Words that are always too distant, too abstract for this underground swarming of seconds, folding in unimaginable spaces. Writing them down is an ordeal of discourse, like love. What is loving, for a woman, the same thing as writing. Laugh. Impossible. Flash on the unnameable, weavings of abstractions to be torn. Let a body venture at last out of its shelter, take a chance with meaning under a veil of words. WORD FLESH. From one to the other, eternally, broken up visions, metaphors of the invisible.

> "Héréthique de l'amour," *Tel*
> *Quel, 74*
> *Winter 1977*

3 Our philosophies of language, embodiments of the idea, are nothing more than the thoughts of archivists, archaeologists, and necrophiliacs. Fascinated by the remains of a process which is partly discursive, they substitute this fetish for what actually produced it. Egypt, Babylon, Mycenae: we see their pyramids, their carved tablets, and fragmented codes in the discourse of our contemporaries, and think that by codifying them we can possess them.

> "Prolegomenon," *Revolution in*
> *Poetic Language (La revolution du*
> *langage poetique* [1974]),
> Margaret Waller, tr.   *1984*

4 I think that in the imaginary, maternal continuity is what guarantees identity. One may imagine other social systems where it would be different . . . The imaginary of the work of art, that is really the most extraordinary and the most unsettling imitation of the mother-child dependence. [It is] its substitution and its displacement towards a limit which is fascinating because inhuman. The work of art is independence conquered through inhumanity. The work of art cuts off natural filiation, it is patricide and matricide, it is superbly solitary. But look backstage, as does the analyst, and you will find a

dependence, a secret mother on whom this sublimation is constructed.

> "Entretien avec Julia Kristeva,
> réalisé par Francoise Collin," *Les*
> *Cahiers due GRIF, 32*   *1985*

2326. Donna de Matteo (1941–   )

1 A new play is like a child.

> "Donna de Matteo," *Interviews with*
> *Contemporary Women Playwrights,*
> Kathleen Betsko* & Rachel
> Koenig   *1987*

See 2256.

2 Watching Miss [Uta] Hagen* during rehearsals is comparable to watching a superb musician playing a fine instrument. She is a master at her craft, very detailed, and patient in her approach to a character; but at the same time, she never loses sight of her instincts and emotions, and when you see her blend all of these elements together, it all looks so natural and effortless . . . It transcends life. It's art at its best.

> Ibid.

See 1859.

3 The wonderful thing about music is that it immediately evokes certain eras of one's life, brings you back to where you've been, even if you don't want to go there.   Ibid.

4 Women, generally, are apt to put things together rather than tear them apart.   Ibid.

2327. Robin Morgan (1941–   )

1 . . . although every organized patriarchal religion works overtime to contribute its own brand of mysogyny to the myth of woman-hate, woman-fear, and woman-evil, the Roman Catholic Church also carries the immense power of very directly affecting women's lives everywhere by its stand against birth control and abortion, and by its use of skillful and wealthy lobbies to prevent legislative change. It is an obscenity—an all-male hierarchy, celibate or not, that presumes to rule on the lives and bodies of millions of women.   Introduction, *Sisterhood Is Powerful*
> *1970*

2 There's something contagious about demanding freedom.   Ibid.

3 Don't accept rides from strange men,
and remember that all men are strange as
hell.

> "Letter to a Sister Underground," op. cit.

4 And I will speak less and less to you
And more and more in crazy gibberish you
  cannot understand:
witches' incantations, poetry, old women's
  mutterings. . . .
                    "Monster," *Monster*   *1972*

5 All the secretaries hunch at their IBM's, snick-
  ering at keys.
What they know could bring down the
  government.
              "On the Watergate Women," St. 7
                                        1974

6 Only she who attempts the absurd can achieve
the impossible.
              Sisterhood Is Global   *1984*

2328. Pamela Painter (1941–   )

1 For his father it had all been said, as if words
had been stripped away like coal from the hol-
lows and hills that had once been farms. And
he too had nothing to say as he kept his father's
silence.   "Winter Evenings: Spring
                  Night," *Getting to Know the
                  Weather*   *1985*

2329. Sally Quinn (1941–   )

1 Washington is . . . a company town. Most of
the interesting people in Washington either work
for the government or write about it.
              We're Going to Make You a Star
                                        1975

2330. Judith Rascoe (1941–   )

1 "There are more important rights than the so-
called right to know. That is not the right that
is being violated nowadays. People have the
right to know *something*. They have the right to
know that something is being done. That is more
important than the right to know. They have the
right to know how long they will have to wait
until something is done. That is more important
than the right to know. I know you would rather
know that I am doing something than know
what I am doing."
              "Evening's Down Under,"
              Yours and Mine   *1973*

2 . . . the grandmother opens the envelope with
the letter-opener that Helen's first husband gave
her and finds a colored photograph of Helen's
second husband and his new wife, Myrna, surrounded by Myrna's children from her first mar-

riage: "Season's Greetings from the
Hannibals!"   "Yours and Mine," op. cit.

2331. Helen Reddy (1941–   )

1 If I have to, I can do anything
I am strong, I am invincible, I am Woman.
                    "I Am Woman"   *1972*

2 Glamour to me is being spotlessly clean and
courteous at all times.
              Quoted in the *Los Angeles Times*
                                    23 April 1974

2332. Buffy Sainte-Marie (1941–   )

1 He's five feet two and he's six feet four.
He fights with missiles and with spears.
He's all of thirty-one and he's only seventeen.
He's been a soldier for a thousand years.

He's a Cath'lic, a Hindu, an atheist, a Jain,
A Buddhist and a Baptist and a Jew.
And he knows he shouldn't kill
and he knows he always will
Kill you for me my friend and me for you.
              "The Universal Soldier"   *1963*

2 We'll make a space in the lives that we
  planned
And here I'll stay until it's time for you to
  go.   "Until It's Time for You to Go"
                                        1965

3 And yet where in your history books is the tale
of the genocide basic to this country's birth?
of the preachers who lied?
how the Bill of Rights failed.
              "My Country 'Tis of Thy People
                  You're Dying"   *1966*

4 You have to sniff out joy, keep your nose to
the joy-trail.   Quoted by Susan Braudy in *Ms.*
                                    March 1975

5 . . . red, I mean, *white* tape. . . .   Ibid.

6 Here the melting pot stands open—if you're
willing to get bleached first.   Ibid.

2333. Susan Fromberg Schaeffer
(1941–   )

1 The sky is reduced,
A narrow blue ribbon banding the lake.
Someone is wrapping things up.
              "Post Mortem," St. 1, *The Witch and
                  the Weather Report*   *1972*

2 What can be wrong
That some days I hug this house

Around me like a shawl, and feel
Each window like a tatter in its skin,
Or worse, bright eyes I must not look
    through?   "Housewife," St. 1, op. cit.

3 In her drugged state, she felt only a euphoria,
as if all the pain of her life had become a vast
salty water, buoying up, where she floated on
the great blue waves of a vast, melodramatic
sea.   Ch. 1, *Falling*   1973

2334. Vicki Sears (1941–   )

1 Now
    at 57 years
    she sits crying for a
    barren womb stolen by Nagasaki.
    tears bumping down her rippled skin
    bound in pain thirty years past its time
    unable to answer why.
                "Nagasaki Elder," St. 4, *Backbone*
                    Vol. 1, No. 1   *Fall 1984*

2 They went to the city   only once
    understanding
    they had all they needed.

    the city never fooled them.
                "Mem & Pep," *Ikon,* second series, #4
                        Winter/Summer 1985

3 Almost every recent day my mind tongue tasted
the bitter heat of scotch. I salivated. It seemed
real again. That getting drunk would make
everything better. All the world issues and ordinary life problems would fade to oblivion.
Nothing would hurt. I would have control of
my environment again. Fool's talk on a fool's
walk. Splurges of dirges, I mused.
                "Sticktalk" (1984), *Hear the
                Silence,* Irene Zahava, ed.   *1986*

4 My father had repeatedly proven, when I was a
child, that all things have their own spirits and
lessons to share. I am just as the sticks and
rocks. I may not always know my purpose, but
it will be clear to me when I need to know. I
will behave just as I am supposed to at that
moment.   Ibid.

5 "You can't possess anything but yourself. Let
me loose."   Ibid.

2335. Anne Tyler (1941–   )

1 . . . she thought of the hall lamp she used to
leave on so they wouldn't be scared in the dark.
Then later she'd left just the bathroom light on,
further down the hall of whatever house they'd
been living in; and later still just the downstairs

light if one of them was out for the evening.
Their growing up amounted, therefore, to a
gradual dimming of the light at her bedroom
door, as if they took some radiance with them
as they moved away from her.
                        Ch. 1, *Dinner at the
                        Homesick Restaurant
                        1982*

2 "You almost died," a nurse told her. But that
was nonsense. Of course she wouldn't have
died; she had children. When you have children,
you're obliged to live.   Ibid.

3 He was back to his boyhood, it seemed, fearing
that his mother could read his mind as unhesi-
tatingly as she read the inner temperature of a
roasting hen by giving its thigh a single, contemptuous pinch.   Ibid., Ch. 10

4 The effort of typing made the corners of his
mouth turn down, so that no one could have
guessed how much he was enjoying himself. I
am happy to say that it's possible now to buy
Kentucky Fried Chicken in Stockholm.
                The Accidental Tourist   1985

5 "It's just time to marry, that's all . . . I'm so
tired of dating! I'm so tired of keeping up a
good front! I want to sit on the couch with a
regular, normal husband and watch TV for a
thousand years."   *Breathing Lessons
                                1988*

6 "It used to be 'Love Me Forever' and now it's
'Help Me Make It Through the Night.' "
                                        Ibid.

2336. Yuliya Voznesenskaya
        (1941?–   )

1 In the West they had invented disposable nap-
pies and plastic pants long ago. Our people were
supposed to be involved in industrial espionage,
so why couldn't they steal some useful secret
instead of always going for electronics?
                *The Women's Decameron (Damskii
                Dekameron),* W. B. Linton, tr.
                                1985

2 "I think, Larissa," she said, "that all your
strength comes precisely from your insecurity.
It happens to a lot of women these days. It's
not so much that we're striving to be strong
ourselves, but the weakness of the men forces
us to be. It's frightening how unmanly they
have become. A husband in the home is just
another child, only greedier."
                Ibid., The First Day, Story Two

3 "When a saint does something holy there's
nothing surprising about it."
                Ibid., The Eighth Day, Story Five

2337. Judy Wenning (1941?–)

1 Women are freer to express their competitiveness now. Women's competitiveness in the past has been limited to competing for men, but those days are over. It's no longer a totally negative thing. Quoted in "Women in Sports: The Movement Is Real," *Los Angeles Times* 23 April 1974

2338. Anne Wortham (1941–)

1 A civilized society is one whose members expect that each will address at all times, as far as possible, the rational in man; that even when I may want to bash you over the head, I will be checked by my awareness of you as a rational entity, and I will not resort to force as an expression of my disagreement with you or even my feeling that you have been unjust to me; that in my disagreements with you, I will rely on the power of persuasion. Quoted in *A World of Ideas* by Bill Moyers *1989*

2 Rationality has the capacity for betraying itself. Rational men have the capacity to be irrational and to institutionalize irrationality. We've seen that in Nazi Germany. Ibid.

3 Respect means that you leave me alone, that you don't build up in your own mind scenarios for my salvation and that you respect me enough to trust me, even when I'm an idiot, even when I'm wrong. Ibid.

4 Government is not a savior—the American federal government has not acted as a liberator. Civil rights for minorities was no great favor, for Christ's sake! This is what they should have done two hundred years ago. Ibid.

2339. Ama Ata Aidoo (1942–)

1 People are worms, and even the God who created them is immensely bored with their antics. *No Sweetness Here* *1970*

2 . . . tears . . . one of the most potent weapons in woman's bitchy and inexhaustible arsenal. Ibid.

3 Eternal death has worked like a warrior rat, with a diabolical sense of duty, to gnaw at my bottom. "The Message," *Fragment from a Lost Diary and Other Stories,* Naomi Katz and Nancy Milton, eds. *1973*

4 It's a sad moment, really, when parents first become a bit frightened of their children. Ibid.

2340. Alta (1942–)

1 [Of] course, if you think only terrible people go to prison, that solves that problem. Untitled Poem *1972*

2 if you come in me
a child is likely to
come back out.
my name is alta.
i am a woman. Untitled Poem *1969–1973*

2341. Eve Babitz (1942?–)

1 Culturally, Los Angeles has always been a humid jungle alive with seething L.A. projects that I guess people from other places can't see. It takes a certain kind of innocence to like L.A., anyway. "Daughters of the Wasteland," *Eve's Hollywood* *1974*

2 When they reach the age of *fifteen* and their beauty arrives, it's very exciting—like coming into an inheritance. . . . "The Sheik," op. cit.

3 Packaging is all heaven is. "Rosewood Casket," op. cit.

4 But by the time I'd grown up, I naturally supposed that I'd grown up. "The Academy," op. cit.

2342. Charlotte Bingham (1942–)

1 I was thinking in bed the other night I must have been out with nearly three hundred men, and I still haven't found a Superman. I don't know what a Superman is, but I know there must be one somewhere. Ch. 1, *Coronet Among the Weeds* *1963*

2 I think it must have been quite fun when women were rather mysterious and men didn't know all about them. Look at the end product of women being free. I mean, go on, look at it. It's a poor old career girl sitting in her digs wondering whether she ought to ring up her boyfriend or not. Ibid.

3 An isolated outbreak of virginity like Lucinda's is a rash on the face of society. It arouses only pity from the married, and embarrassment from the single. Ch. 1, *Lucinda* *1966*

4 "And the only way to avoid playing the game is never to belong to a club, class, set, or trade union. As soon as you do, you're accepting someone else's rules, and as soon as you do that, you start looking down on the other chap with different rules."   Ibid., Ch. 3

2343. Mary Bricker-Jenkins (1942–   )

1 Having been so long in ascendancy, patriarchal ideology has also determined the interpretation and recording of history. Therefore, we women must reclaim history, exposing the myths that distort our experiences and limit our vision of our capabilities.   "A Feminist World View,"
Not For Women Only, w/Nancy R. Hooyman,* eds.   *1986*

*See 2409.

2 The notion that the personal is political is a primary analytic tool in feminist practice—a precision instrument with which we examine the myths and structures of oppression that contain us. It also is another of the fundamental organizing principles of our practice: we change our world by changing our selves as we change our world. It is by this process that fundamental structural changes may occur.   Ibid.

3 We have a long and enduring history of struggle to implement such values as egalitarianism, consensus democracy, nonexploitation, cooperation, collectivism, diversity, and nonjudgmental spirituality even though these values are not ascendant in the American tradition. In the fabric of our society, these values can be reclaimed and rewoven into a transformed social order. That is the feminist agenda.   Ibid.

2344. Barbara Garson (1942–   )

1 JOHN. The Pox Americana, a sweet haze
Shelt'ring all the world in its deep shade.
                    MacBird, Act I, Sc. 2
                              1966

2 JOHN. Consensus is the thing.   Ibid., Sc. 3

3 4th VOICE. Let's get the facts. Let's go and
watch TV.   Ibid., Sc. 7

4 EGG OF HEAD. Security makes cowards of us
all.   Ibid., Act II, Sc. 1

5 EGG OF HEAD. I know you think I'm acting
   like a toad
But still I choose the middle of the road.
                              Ibid.

2345. Carol Glassman (1942?–   )

1 For its recipients, the welfare system carried with it most of the hazards of "housewife and mother," and a few of the rewards. Domination by a husband was replaced with control over every aspect of a woman's life by the welfare agency. Strangers could knock at any hour to pass judgment on her performance as mother, housekeeper, and cook—as well as her fidelity to the welfare board. The welfare board, like a jealous husband, doesn't want to see any men around who might threaten its place as provider and authority.
             "Women and the Welfare System,"
                    Sisterhood Is Powerful,
             Robin Morgan,* ed.   *1970*

*See 2327.

2 Throughout the welfare department one finds the combined view that poverty is due to individual *fault* and that *something is wrong with women who don't have men.*   Ibid.

3 It is the woman who is ultimately held responsible for pregnancy. While not being allowed to have control over her body, she is nevertheless held responsible for its products.   Ibid.

2346. J. B. Goodenough (1942–   )

1 Wisteria ties the roof
of the porch down; morning-
Glory anchors the mailbox;
Green peas keep the garden
Fence from taking off.
             "Among Vines," St. 1, *Dower
                              Land   1984*

2 No, they said,
You cannot be a tree.
You are a human child.   "Changes," op cit.

2347. Marilyn Hacker (1942–   )

1 The child of wonder, deep in his
gut, knows how long forever is,
and, like a haunted anarchist,
hears a repeated order hissed
not to exist.
             "Chanson de L'Enfant Prodigue,"
                    Presentation Piece   1974

2 I am in exile in my own land.
                    "Exiles," St. 1, op cit.

3 Between us on our wide bed we cuddle an
   incubus
whom we have filled with voyages. We wake
more apart than before, with open hands.
             "The Navigators, I," St. 1, op. cit.

4   "Have you done
flaunting your cunt and your pen in her face
when she's not looking? high above your bed,

like a lamppost with eyes, stern as a pay
  toilet,
she stands, waiting to be told off
and tolled out.''
          ''For Elektra,'' St. 2, op. cit.

5 I wish I had a lover instead of letters
from strangers. The arrival of the mail
is the only time that someone hands
me movement. Nothing real is going to happen
yet, except this dessicated ritual.
          ''Waiting,'' St. 5, op cit.

2348. Judith Lewis Herman (1942–)

1 This idea of the child's right to her own body
is a radical one. In the traditional patriarchal
family, there is no such concept. The child is
the legal property of the father. Only in the last
century have reforms in law and custom recognized the *mother's* custodial rights to her child.
The concept that the child, too, might have some
individual rights or interests not represented by
either parent is even more recent.
         Father-Daughter Incest
         1981

2 As long as fathers rule but do not nurture, as
long as mothers nurture but do not rule, the
conditions favoring the development of father-
daughter incest will prevail.   Ibid.

2349. Erica Jong (1942–)

1 Everyone has talent. What is rare is the courage
to follow the talent to the dark place where it
leads.   ''The Artist as Housewife: The
      Housewife as Artist,'' *The First
      Ms. Reader,* Francine
      Klagsbrun, ed.   *1972*

2 If sex and creativity are often seen by dictators
as subversive activities, it's because they lead
to the knowledge that you own your own body
(and with it your own voice), and that's the
most revolutionary insight of all.   Ibid.

3 Perhaps all artists were, in a sense, housewives:
tenders of the earth household.   Ibid.

4 I can live without it all—
love with its blood pump,
sex with its messy hungers,
men with their peacock strutting,
their silly sexual baggage,
their wet tongues in my ear
and their words like little sugar suckers
with sour centers.
      ''Becoming a Nun,'' *About Women,*
      Stephen Berg and S. J. Marks, eds.
      1973

5 Q: Why does a Jew always answer a question
with a question?
   A: And why should a Jew *not* answer a
question with a question?
        Ch. 1, *Fear of Flying*   *1973*

6 Phallocentric, someone once said of Freud. He
thought the sun revolved around the penis. And
the daughter, too.   Ibid., Ch. 2

7 Throughout all of history, books were written
with sperm, not menstrual blood.   Ibid.

8 Gossip is the opiate of the oppressed.
         Ibid., Ch. 6

9 There is nothing fiercer than a failed artist. The
energy remains, but, having no outlet, it im-
plodes in a great black fart of rage which smokes
up all the inner windows of the soul.
         Ibid., Ch. 9

10 Coupling doesn't always have to do with sex.
. . . Two people holding each other up like
flying buttresses. Two people depending on each
other and babying each other and defending each
other against the world outside. Sometimes it
was worth all the disadvantages of marriage just
to have that: one friend in an indifferent
world.   Ibid., Ch. 10

11 The cure for starvation in India *and* the cure for
overpopulation—both in one big swallow!
         Ibid., Ch. 17

12 Surviving meant being born over and over.
         Ibid., Ch. 19

13 Each month
the blood sheets down
like good red rain.

I am the gardener.
Nothing grows without me.
      ''Gardener,'' *Half-Lives*   *1973*

14 He had been in analysis for seven years and he
regarded life as a long disease, alleviated by
little fifty-minute bloodlettings of words from
the couch.   *How to Save your Own Life*
      1977

15 Advice is what we ask for when we already
know the answer but wish we didn't. . . .
         Ibid.

16 All the cosmetics names seemed obscenely obvious to me in their promises of sexual bliss.
They were all firming or uplifting or invigorat-
ing. They made you *tingle.* Or *glow.* Or feel
young. They were all prepared with hormones
or placentas or royal jelly. All the juice and joy
missing in the lives of these women were to be
supplied by the contents of jars and bottles.
         Ibid.

17 *''How do I save my own life?'' the poet asked.
''By being a fool,'' God said.*   Ibid.

18 "The trick is not how much pain you feel—but how much joy you feel. Any idiot can feel pain. Life is full of excuses to feel pain, excuses not to live, excuses, excuses, excuses." Ibid.

19 Books go out into the world, travel mysteriously from hand to hand, and somehow find their way to the people who need them at the *times* when they need them. . . . Cosmic forces guide such passings-along. Ibid.

20 "Do you want me to tell you something really subversive? Love *is* everything it's cracked up to be. That's why people are so cynical about it." Ibid.

21 The only difference between men and women is that women are able to create new little human beings in their bodies while simultaneously writing books, driving tractors, working in offices, planting crops—in general, doing everything men do.
Quoted in "Are Men and Women Different" by Judith Viorst,* *Redbook November 1978*

*See 2092.

2350. Temma E. Kaplan (1942–   )

1 By placing human need above other social and political requirements and human life above property, profit, and even individual rights, female consciousness creates the vision of a society that has not yet appeared. "Female Consciousness and Collective Action: the case of Barcelona, 1910–1918," *Signs, 7 Spring 1982*

2351. Sarah J. McCarthy (1942–   )

1 On close scrutiny, the beast within us looks suspiciously like a sheep.
"Why Johnny Can't Disobey," *The Humanist September/October 1979*

2 Despite our rich literature of freedom, a pervasive value instilled in our society is obedience to authority. Unquestioning obedience is perceived to be in the best interests of the schools, churches, families, and political institutions. Nationalism, patriotism, and religious ardor are its psychological vehicles. Ibid.

3 Religions, which are often nothing more than cults that grew, set the stage for the credulity and gullibility required for membership in cults. Ibid.

4 The concept of religious tolerance has been stretched to its outer limits, implying freedom from criticism and the nonpayment of taxes. Neither patriotism nor religion should be justification for the suspension of reason. Ibid.

5 Contrary to previous theories that the instinct for self-preservation was the most basic and powerful of human drives, the Guyana* suicides demonstrate that the socialization process is even more powerful.
"Pornography, Rape, and the Cult of Macho," *The Humanist September/October 1980*

*Mass suicide (18 November 1978) at the behest of James Jones, American religious cult leader.

6 There is a long macho tradition in this culture that pronounces certain kinds of violence as perfectly appropriate, even expected. . . .
Ibid.

2352. Kate Michelman (1942–   )

1 [Roe vs. Wade]* is solely responsible for saving women's lives, saving women's health, and saving women from shame and degradation. It is an important milestone in the quest for equality and liberty.
Quoted in interview in *USA Today 22 January 1989*

*The U.S. Supreme Court case legalizing abortions, 1973.

3 Nobody likes abortion. It's a difficult choice. Women don't have abortions they want. They have abortions they need.
Quoted in "Whose Life Is It?" by Richard Lacayo, *Time 1 May 1989*

2353. Hedda Nussbaum (1942–   )

1 I worshipped him.*
Comment, Manhattan courtroom, Quoted in 'Hedda's Hellish Tale" by David Ellis, *Time 12 December 1988*

*Response to lawyer's inquiry as to why she never left Joel Steinberg, abuser and murderer.

2354. Flora Purim (1942–   )

1 Clear days, feel so good and free
So light as a feather can be. . . .
"Light as a Feather" 1973

2355. Phyllis Rose (1942–   )

1 There comes a time in your life when you dead end on the search for your identity as something

unique. At that point, you start looking around for what connects you to other people, not what distinguishes you alone.
Writing of Women, Essays in a Renaissance 1985

2 . . . whether you choose to destroy or to redeem what you perceive as Other, the problem begins with perceiving it as Other.
Ibid., "Helen Bannerman"*

* Author of *Little Black Sambo;* 1899, see 1097.

3 In starkly political terms, biography is a tool by which the dominant society reinforces its values. It has ignored women; it ignores the poor and working class; it ignores the unprivileged; it ignores noncelebrities. Such a formulation is useful only up to a point, because in fact biography ignores almost everyone.
Ibid., "Fact and Fiction in Biography"

2356. Marjorie Rosen (1942–)

1 Does art reflect life? In movies, yes. Because more than any other art form, films have been a mirror held up to society's porous face.
Preface, *Popcorn Venus* 1973

2 Which is strongest—the reality out of which the illusion is created, the celluloid illusion itself, or the need for illusion? Do we hold the mirror up and dive in? And if we do, what are the consequences? And what are the responsibilities of the illusion makers? Ibid., Pt. I, Ch. 2

3 Women were the sacrificial lambs of the Depression, but amid the collective pain of the nation's empty bellies, they scarcely felt the knife.
Ibid., Pt. III, Ch. 8

4 Studios, purporting to ease the anguish of Depression reality, transformed movies into the politics of fantasy, the great black-and-white opiate of the masses. Ibid., Ch. 9

5 On December 7, 1941, the Japanese bombed hell out of Pearl Harbor. Johnny got his gun. America mobilized. And social roles shifted with a speed that would have sent Wonder Woman into paroxysms of power pride.
Ibid., Pt. IV, Ch. 12

6 Women's films [in the fifties] became "how-to's" on catching and keeping a man. Veneer. Appearance. Sex Appeal. Hollywood descended into mammary madness. Ibid., Pt. V, Ch. 17

2357. Susan C. Ross (1942–)

1 The brutal fact is that convicted women . . . have not yet won the right to equal treatment in the criminal and juvenile justice system.
Ch. 5, *The Rights of Women* 1973

2 . . . alimony is one way of compensating women for those financial disabilities aggravated, or caused, by marriage: unequal educational opportunities; unequal employment opportunities; and an unequal division of family responsibilities, with no compensation for the spouse who works in the home. . . . Thus, women should not be cowed into believing that to ask for alimony is to be unliberated, or that their husbands provide alimony out of the largesse of their noble hearts. Ibid., Ch. 7

3 Law then is not a preordained set of doctrines, applied rigidly and unswervingly in every situation. Rather, law is molded from the arguments and decisions of thousands of persons. It is very much a human process, a game of trying to convince others . . . that your view of what the law requires is correct. Ibid., Ch. 10

2358. Sally E. Shaywitz (1942–)

1 . . . just as breast milk cannot be duplicated, neither can a mother.
"Catch 22 for Mothers," *The New York Times Magazine* 4 March 1973

2 To be somebody, a woman does not have to be more like a man, but has to be more of a woman. Ibid.

2359. Barbra Streisand (1942–)

1 Success to me is having ten honeydew melons and eating only the top half of each one.
Quoted in *Life* 20 September 1963

2360. Barrie Thorne (1942–)

1 In working for political change, feminists seek to create organizations based on power understood as energy and initiative, while challenging institutions that embody power understood as domination. Although fraught with contradictions, the feminist process uses methods of organization as a strategy for redefining political power itself. "Review of Building Feminist Theory: Essays from Quest," *Signs,* 7 1982

2361. Susan Witkovsky (1942–)

1 All children are musicians; all children are artists. Quoted in "A New Era in Day Care"

by Mildred Hamilton, *San Francisco Chronicle* , *19 December 1971*

2 I am opposed to the custodial idea of day care. That is a mistake. Enrichment is what we are after. Ibid.

3 The merits of good child care for all who need it or want it are many. The health and well-being of our society depends on it. Those unconvinced are people who have no need of high quality public programs, and who choose not to see the children and parents who suffer from lack of them.
"The Impediments to Public Day Care Programs in San Francisco" *1974*

2362. Charlotte Bonny Cohen
(1943–)

1 For the Chinese Communists, ideology is always ahead of practice.
"Chung-kuo Fu Nu (Women of China)," *Sisterhood Is Powerful*, Robin Morgan,* ed. *1970*

*See 2327.

2 China is not our model. . . . But Mao and the Chinese Communists do show us that society is changed by changing people's daily lives. Working side by side with men partially liberates women. Freedom—however you want it—comes from new ways of living together.
Ibid.

2363. Cecilia Danieli (1943–)

1 It's the company that's important, not me as an individual.   Quoted in "Italy's First Lady of Steel" by Gordon M. Henry, *Time*   *19 May 1986*

2364. China Galland (1943?–)

1 Going into the wilderness involves the wilderness within us all. This may be the deepest value of such an experience, the recognition of our kinship with the natural world.
Women in the Wilderness, p. 5   *1980*

2365. Nikki Giovanni (1943–)

1 you see, my whole life is tied up to unhappiness . . .
it's having a job
they won't let you work
or no work at all
castrating me

(yes it happens to women too)
"Woman Poem," *Black Feeling*   *1968*

2 Why, LBJ has made it
quite clear to me
He doesn't give a
Good goddamn what I think
(else why would he continue to *masterbate* in public?)
"A Historical Footnote to Consider Only When All Else Fails," St. 2, *Black Feeling/Black Talk/Black Judgement*   *1970*

3 But we can't be Black
And not be crazy
"A Short Essay of Affirmation Explaining Why," St. 7, op. cit.

4 Mistakes are a fact of life
It is the response to error that counts
"Of Liberation," St. 16, op. cit.

5 And you will understand all too soon
That you, my children of battle, are your heroes
You must invent your own games and teach us old ones
how to play   "Poem for Black Boys," St. 8, op. cit.

6 His headstone said
FREE AT LAST, FREE AT LAST
But death is a slave's freedom
"The Funeral of Martin Luther King, Jr.,"* op. cit.

*American civil rights leader (1929–1968); assassinated.

7 In the name of peace
They waged the wars
ain't they got no shame
"The Great Pax Whitie," St. 3, op cit.

8 and nothing is worse
than a
dream deferred   "From a Logical Point of View," St. 1, op. cit.

9 You could say we've lost our innocence. That's a little worse than losing the nickel to put in Sunday school, though not quite as bad as losing the dime for ice cream afterward.
Introduction, *Spin a Soft Black Song*   *1971*

2366. Susan Griffin (1943–)

1 In no state can a man be accused of raping his wife. How can any man steal what already belongs to him?   Quoted in *Ramparts September 1971*

2 I've been inside institutions,
my family,

kindergarten,
grammar school, high
school, college and then
marriage, waiting
to be
grown up, graduated, & divorced,
but before I
turned around,
here I am
back in as the
jailor, a
mother and a
teacher.
    "Letters to the Outside," *Dear Sky 1973*

3 sleep leads to dreaming
waking to imagination and to
imagine what we
could be, o,
what we could be.
    "To Gather Ourselves," op cit.

4 . . . rape is a form of mass terrorism, for the
victims of rape are chosen indiscriminately, but
the propagandists for male supremacy broadcast
that it is women who cause rape by being un-
chaste or in the wrong place at the wrong time—
in essence, by behaving as though they were
free. . . . The fear of rape keeps women off
the streets at night. Keeps women at home.
    Keeps women passive and modest for fear
that they be thought provocative
    "Rape: The All-American Crime,"
    Women: A Feminist Perspective,
    Jo Freeman, ed.   *1975*

5 The legal answer
to the problem of feeding children
is ten free lunches every month,
being equal, in the child's real life,
to eating lunch every other day.
Monday but not Tuesday.
I like to think of the President
eating lunch Monday, but not
Tuesday.
And when I think of the President
and the law, and the problem of
feeding children, I like to
think of Harriet Tubman*
and her revolver.   "I Like to Think of
    Harriet Tubman," St. 2,
    Like the Iris of an Eye   *1976*

* See 812.

2367. Barbro Hedstrom (1943–   )

1 Art should awaken the senses and compassion
in people. We *shall* interfere, we *shall* protest,
the rebellion must be kept alive! We must not
disintegrate to silent agreement to deeds that are

damaging and destructive for the earth and
humanity.   Interview by Annika E.
    Ortmark, *Kvinna Nu,* No. 2   *1989*

2 I am one who carves away rather than builds
up.   Ibid.

3 If Picasso could then I can.
    Interview by Nicole de Bouczan,
    Karlstads Tidningen
    6–12 July 1989

4 I had a "real" job for seven months. My soul
fell asleep.   Ibid.

2368. Susan Isaacs (1943–   )

1 He wore white shirts so starched they could
carry on a life of their own.
    Shining Through   *1988*

2369. Janis Joplin (1943–1970)

1 They ain't never gonna love you any better,
  babe
And they're nee-eever gonna love you ri-ight
So you better dig it right now, right now.
    "Kozmic Blues"   *1969*

2 You got to get it while you can. . . .
    "Get It While You Can"
    n.d.

3 Oh Lord won't you buy me a night on the
town?   "Oh Lord Won't You Buy Me a
    Mercedes-Benz"
    n.d.

2370. Rosabeth Moss Kanter (1943–   )

1 The [commune] movement is part of a reawak-
ening of belief in the possibilities for utopia that
existed in the nineteenth century and exist again
today, a belief that by creating the right social
institution, human satisfaction and growth can
be achieved.
    "Getting It All Together: Communes
    Past, Present, Future," *The Future of*
    the Family, Louise Kapp Howe,* ed.
    1972

* See 2155.

2371. Sally Kempton (1943?–   )

1 I became a feminist as an alternative to becoming a masochist.   "Cutting Loose," *Esquire*
    July 1970

2 All children are potential victims, dependent
upon the world's good will.   Ibid.

3 Men define intelligence, men define usefulness, men tell us what is beautiful, men even tell us what is womanly. Ibid.

4 And yet wherever there exists the display of power there is politics, and in women's relations with men there is a continual transfer of power, there is, continually, politics. Ibid.

5 Women are natural guerrillas. Scheming, we nestle into the enemy's bed, avoiding open warfare, watching the options, playing the odds. Ibid.

6 It is hard to fight an enemy who has outposts in your head. Ibid.

2372. Billie Jean King (1943–)

1 I've always wanted to equalize things for us. . . . Women can be great athletes. And I think we'll find in the next decade that women athletes will finally get the attention they deserve.
Interview   *September 1973*

2 I think self-awareness is probably the most important thing towards being a champion.
Quoted by Marlene Jensen in
The Sportswoman
November/December 1973

3 No one changes the world who isn't obsessed.
Quoted in "For Billie Jean, Is There Life After Tennis" by Jane Gross, *San Francisco Chronicle*
8 August 1978

2373. Jane Lazarre (1943–)

1 . . . there is only one image in this culture of the "good mother." At her worst, this mother image is a tyrannical goddess of stupefying love and murderous masochism which none of us can or should hope to emulate. But even at her best, she is . . . quietly receptive and intelligent in only a moderate, concrete way; she is of even temperament, almost always in control of her emotions. She loves her children completely and unambivalently. Most of us are not like her.
Preface, *The Mother Knot*
1976

2374. Susan Lydon (1943?–)

1 The Victorians had needed to repress sexuality for the success of Western industrialized society; in particular, the total repression of woman's sexuality was crucial to ensure her subjugation. So the Victorian, . . . supported by Freud, passed on to us the heritage of the double standard. "The Politics of Orgasm,"
Ramparts   December 1968

2 Our society treats sex as a sport, with its record-breakers, its judges, its rules and its spectators. Ibid.

2375. Joni Mitchell (1943–)

1 I've looked at life from both sides now
From up and down, and still somehow
It's life's illusions I recall
I really don't know life at all
"Both Sides, Now"   *1969*

2 Oh, won't you stay
We'll put on the day
And we'll talk in present tenses
"Chelsea Morning"   *1969*

3 if you're feeling contempt
well then you tell it
if you're tired of the silent night
Jesus, well then you yell it
"Judgement of the Moon and Stars"
1972

4 Golden in time
Cities under sand
Power, ideals and beauty
Fading in everyone's hands.
"The Hissing of Summer Lawns"
1975

5 We are stardust, we are golden.
"Woodstock"   *1975*

2376. Elaine Pagels (1943–)

1 When you look at the history of Christianity, you see that what the Bible says has been interpreted so many ways that one has to acknowledge that one chooses an interpretation.
Quoted in *A World of Ideas* by Bill Moyers
1989

2 There's practically no religion that I know of that sees other people in a way that affirms the others' choices. But in our century we're forced to think about a pluralistic world. Ibid.

3 I began to reflect on how our culture has taught us that suffering and death and disease are not natural, are not part of nature, but were brought in because of human guilt and sin. That belief can lead people to blame themselves in ways that are not constructive. Ibid.

4 Guilt involves a sense of importance in the drama. To say that one is not guilty is also to acknowledge that one is in fact quite powerless.

. . . Dealing with that sense of helplessness is very much part of our condition. Religion is often a way of disguising it, a way of avoiding it, a way of pretending that we're not helpless.   Ibid.

2377. Gail Thain Parker (1943–   )

1 . . . Quaker meetings [were] the first enclaves in American society in which women were encouraged to speak out in public . . . [with] the faith . . . that each individual, regardless of sex, had to act according to his inner lights. . . .
                    Introduction, Pt. I, *The Oven Birds*
                                                    1972

2 Literature was a great factor in the socialization of women, and without novels (and poems) which portrayed women on an heroic scale, whole generations of nascent feminists might be stunted in their development.   Ibid.

3 Sentimentalism restructured the Calvinist model of salvation, making the capacity to feel, and above all to weep, in itself evidence of redemption.   Ibid.

2378. Susan Shnall (1943–   )

1 The professed purpose of the United States military is to maintain the peace, but its methods toward this goal are destructive and have resulted in the promotion of suffering and death of foreign peoples, as well as of its own.
                          "Women in the Military,"
                              Sisterhood Is Powerful,
                       Robin Morgan,* ed.   *1970*

*See 2327.

2 Because I wore a peace symbol, I had to have an extra interview to determine my suitability as a member of the military.   Ibid.

2379. Jill Tarule (1943–   )

See Mary Belenky, 2143: 1–4.

2380. Viva (1943–   )

1 If Mother had let us go to bed whenever we wanted, not forced us to go to church, allowed us to masturbate, go to bars at night, see any movie we wanted, eat whenever we felt like it, sleep with her and Daddy, then I'm sure we'd now be exactly the way she had hoped us to be.   *The Baby*   *1975*

2381. Faye Wattleton (1943–   )

1 If we can't preserve the privacy of our right to procreate, I can't imagine what rights we will be able to protect.
                  Quoted in "Nothing Less Than
                  Perfect" by Richard Stengel, *Time*
                                  11 December 1989

2 Social change rarely comes about through the efforts of the disenfranchised. The middle class creates social revolutions. When a group of people are disproportionately concerned with daily survival, it's not likely that they have the resources to go to Washington and march.
                                                    Ibid.

3 The stakes are higher for us as African-American women. It will be African-American women who will die first. We suffer disproportionately from poverty. We suffer disproportionately from despair.   Address, Chicago, op. cit.

2382. Judith Barrington (1944–   )

1 They want women to be like gardens
  cultivated possessed
  perfected by man.
                  "A Remarkably Vigorous Rose,"
                        Trying to be an Honest
                              Woman   *1985*

2 Awful truths can mutter under the
      breastbone
  hide their heads, grow fat on opulent
      time.   "Sonnet for a Stiff Upper
                              Lip," op. cit.

2383. Ingrid Bengis (1944?–   )

1 No amount of evidence is ever sufficient to compensate for the deviousness with which human beings manage to conceal themselves. . . .
                  "Monroe* According to Mailer,"** *Ms.*
                                      October 1973

*See 1981.
**American writer, (1923–   ).

2 The form that our bodies take, particularly with women, dictates more often than we wish it would the form that a portion of our lives will take.   Ibid.

3 The real questions are the ones that obtrude upon your consciousness whether you like it or not, the ones that make your mind start vibrating like a jackhammer, the ones that you "come to terms with" only to discover that they are still there. The real questions refuse to be placated. They barge into your life at the times when it

seems most important for them to stay away. They are the questions asked most frequently and answered most inadequately, the ones that reveal their true natures slowly, reluctantly, most often against your will.

"Man-Hating," *Combat in the Erogenous Zone 1973*

4 For me words still possess their primitive, mystical, incantatory healing powers. I am inclined to use them as part of an attempt to make my own reality more real for others, as part of an effort to transcend emotional damage. For me words are a form of action, capable of influencing change. Their articulation represents a complete, lived experience.   Ibid.

5 When all of the remedies and all of the rhetorical armor have been dropped, the absence of love in our lives is what makes them seem raw and unfinished.   "Love," op. cit.

2384. Rita Mae Brown (1944–)

1 One doesn't get liberated by hiding. One doesn't possess integrity by passing for "white."
Untitled Essay   *March 1970*

2 To love without role, without power plays, is revolution.   Ibid.

3 I move in the shadow of the great guillotine
That rhythmically does its work
On heads remaining unbowed.
"The Self Affirms Herself" (1966),
The Hand That Cradles the Rock 1971

4 An army of lovers shall not fail.
"Sappho's* Reply" (1970), op. cit.

*See 50.

5 I am a comic writer, which means I get to slay the dragons, and shoot the bull.
Speech, San Jose, California
18 November 1978

2385. Charlotte Bunch (1944–)

1 Feminism is an entire world view or gestalt, not just a laundry list of "women's issues."
"Understanding Feminist Theory,"
New Directions for Women September/October 1981

2386. Mary Coombs (1944–)

1 The law has been written with men in mind. Feminist jurisprudence puts women at the center

and asks, "To what extent is this doctrine or this area of law designed in a way that implicitly assumes people are men?"
Quoted in "Now for a Woman's
Point of View" by
Anastasia Touflexis, *Time
17 April 1989*

2387. Angela Davis (1944–)

1 Expending indispensable labor for the enrichment of her [the black woman's] oppressor, she could attain a practical awareness of the oppressor's utter dependence on her—for the master needs the slave far more than the slave needs the master.
"Reflections on the Black Woman's
Role in the Community of Slaves,"
*The Black Scholar
December 1971*

2 The master subjected her to the most elemental form of terrorism distinctly suited to the female: rape.   Ibid.

3 We, the black women of today, must accept the full weight of a legacy wrought in blood by our mothers in chains. As heirs to a tradition of perseverance and heroic resistance, we must hasten to take our place wherever our people are forging toward freedom.   Ibid.

4 . . . the brother . . . had painted a night sky on the ceiling of his cell, because it had been years since he had seen the moon and stars.
An Autobiography   1974

5 Jails and prisons are designed to break human beings, to convert the population into specimens in a zoo—obedient to our keepers, but dangerous to each other.   Ibid.

6 Racism, in the first place, is a weapon used by the wealthy to increase the profits they bring in by paying Black workers less for their work.
Ibid.

2388. Claudia Dreifus (1944–)

1 We spent a winter learning the feminist basics from the textbook of each other's lives. . . .
Introduction, *Woman's Fate   1973*

2 . . . girls enforce the cultural code that men invent.
"The Adolescent Experience," op. cit.

2389. Delia Ephron (1944?–)

1 If you are a girl, worry that your breasts are too round. Worry that your breasts are too pointed.

Worry that your nipples are the wrong color. Worry that your breasts point in different directions.

If you are a boy, worry that you will get breasts.

. . . If you are a boy, worry that you'll never be able to grow a mustache.

If you are a girl, worry that you have a mustache.   *Teenage Romance   1981*

2390. Anne Fausto-Sterling (1944–   )

1   . . . in modern usage, a cuckhold is the husband of an unfaithful wife—a far nastier and more humiliating state, apparently, than being the wife of a philanderer, for which in fact no word exists.   *Myths of Gender   1985*

2   . . . to take even very extensive animal research, define it according to uniquely human behavior, and then use it to analyze human behavior is both logically flawed and politically dangerous . . .   Ibid.

2391. Marcia Gillespie (1944–   )

1   We have been looking at it [feminism] warily. Black women need economic equality but it doesn't apply for me to call a black man a male chauvinist pig. Our anger is not at our men. I don't think they have been the enemy.
    Quoted in "About Women," *Los Angeles Times   12 May 1974*

2392. Susan Gubar (1944–   )

See Sandra Gilbert, 2188.

2393. Frances Moore Lappé (1944–   )

1   . . . much agricultural land which might be growing food is being used instead to "grow" money (in the form of coffee, tea, etc.).
    Foreword, *Diet for a Small Planet   1971*

2   The act of putting into your mouth what the earth has grown is perhaps your most direct interaction with the earth.   Ibid., Part I

3   After eleven years of research, I have come to see that *food production and food distribution are in the midst of a revolution,* a revolution that puts people's needs for food *last.* And, the revolution is led by the largest corporations on earth and elite-based governments. It isn't fought in the name of liberty or equality or fraternity, but in the name of profit.
    Food First/Institute for Food and Development Policy Fund-raising Letter   *1980*

4   . . . the outrage of hunger amidst plenty will never be solved by "experts" somewhere. It will only be solved when people like you and me decide to act.   Ibid.

2394. Sara Lawrence Lightfoot (1944–   )

1   Part of teaching is helping students learn how to tolerate ambiguity, consider possibilities, and ask questions that are unanswerable.
    Quoted in *A World of Ideas* by Bill Moyers   1989

2   Good schools have a sense of mission that kids and adults can all articulate. They have an identity. They have a character, a quality that's their own, that feels quite sturdy. They have a set of values . . . Good schools are also disciplined places. I don't mean by that just behavioral discipline, but a place where people set goals and standards and hold each other accountable.   Ibid.

3   Somehow the American public has to get back to the great richness and mystery of learning, the playfulness and seriousness of learning, and how that can be nurtured in schools by teachers in classrooms.   Ibid.

4   Schooling is what happens inside the walls of the school, some of which is educational. Education happens everywhere, and it happens from the moment a child is born—and some people say before—until a person dies.   Ibid.

2395. Tatyana Mamonova (1944?–   )

1   I, Tatyana Mamonova, the chief editor of *Woman and Russia,* the first free feminist publication in the Soviet Union, call the women of the whole world to solidarity with our struggle for our rights. I have been stripped of my Soviet citizenship and exiled from the Soviet Union, and now, as a citizen of the world . . . I hope that all people of good will will support . . . women's moral resistance to the forces of evil and violence.   Quoted in *New Directions for Women*
    November/December 1980

2396. Ann Oakley (1944–   )

1   Being a "good" mother does not call for the same qualities as being a "good" housewife,

and the pressure to be both at the same time may be an insupportable burden. Children may suffer, because the goals of housework may become the goals of child-care, and a dedication to keeping children clean and tidy may override an interest in their separate development as individuals.　　Ch. 5, *Woman's Work: The Housewife, Past and Present*　　*1974*

2 In our defence of biology and its mystique we are blind to the dangers of power. Women as the guardians of children possess great power. They are the molders of their children's personalities and the arbiters of their development.
Ibid., Ch. 8

3 The family's gift to women is a direct apprenticeship in the housewife role. For this reason, the abolition of the housewife role requires the abolition of the family, and the substitution of more open and variable relationships: not man-provider, woman-housewife and dependent children, but people living together in a chosen and freely perpetuated intimacy, in a space that allows each to breathe and find her or his own separate destiny.　　*Ibid., Ch. 9*

2397. Julia Phillips (1944?–)

1 Here's how I define the role of producer: the producer is there long before the shooting starts, and way after the shooting stops.
Quoted in *American Film Magazine December 1975*

2398. Arlene Raven (1944–)

1 In my view, the content of feminist art, and its deepest meaning, is consciousness: a woman's full awareness of herself as an entity, including her sensations, her emotions, and her thoughts—mind in its broadest sense.
"Woman's Art: The Development of a Theoretical Perspective," *Womanspace February/March 1973*

2 The artist who shows us his/her world without this essential sense of optimism is without hope and without power: We can empathize with that art, but it cannot inspire in us the high level of human aspiration that we need to enrich ourselves, to grow, and to change.　　*Ibid.*

3 Animals which are traditionally referred to as female include the cow, sow, bitch and cat—all derogatory words in our language when they are applied to human beings. English does not use gender extensively, but its linguistic sexism is intact because sexism is intact.　　*Ibid.*

2399. Lee Smith (1944–)

1 I hate all this active-listening shit. Ever since they learned it last year in that class, you can't have a decent conversation with them. If you ever could. But now I mean you come home from school really pissed, and they say something like, "Gee, son, you're very angry!" and then if you say "Well yes, I am pretty goddamn angry," they say "Yes! Yes, you are! I can tell you're angry!" and that's it.
Family Linen　　*1985*

2400. Robyn Smith (1944–)

1 Don't ever call me a jockette.
Quoted in "Sportswomanlike Conduct," *Newsweek 3 June 1974*

2401. Alma Villanueva (1944?–)

1 Who is this woman with
words dangling from
the ends of her
hair? leaping
out from her
eyes? dripping
from her
breasts? seeping
from her
hands? Her

left foot, a
question mark.
Her right
foot, an
exclamation.
Her body, a
dictionary dying
to define life,
growth, a
yearning.　　Untitled, *Bloodroot*　　*c. 1977*

2402. Alice Walker (1944–)

1 The sight of a Black nun strikes their sentimentality; and as I am unalterably rooted in native ground they consider me a work of primitive art, housed in a magical color; the incarnation of civilized, anti-heathenism, and the fruit of a triumphing idea.
"The Diary of an African Nun," *Freedomways*　　*Summer 1968*

2 Be nobody's darling;
Be an outcast

"Be Nobody's Darling," *Revolutionary Petunias and Other Poems* 1973

3 They stumbled blindly through their lives: creatures so abused and mutilated in body, so dimmed and confused by pain, that they considered themselves unworthy even of hope . . . exquisite butterflies trapped in an evil honey, toiling away their lives in an era, a century, that did not acknowledge them, except as "the *mule* of the world."
"In Search of Our Mother's Gardens," *Ms.* May 1974

4 In search of my mother's garden I found my own. Ibid.

5 We are together, my child and I, Mother and child, yes, but *sisters* really, against whatever denies us all that we are.
"*One* Child of One's Own," *Ms.* August 1979

6 We will be ourselves and free, or die in the attempt. Harriet Tubman* was not our great-grandmother for nothing. *You Can't Keep a Good Woman Down* 1981

*See 812.

7 . . . the inner voice; the human compulsion when deeply distressed to seek healing counsel within ourselves, and the capacity within ourselves both to create this counsel and to receive it. "A Letter of the Times," op. cit.

8 But I don't know how to fight. All I know how to do is stay alive.
Letter 11, *The Color Purple* 1982

9 But evil all over her today. She smile, like a razor opening. Ibid., Letter 27

10 I think Africans are very much like white people back home, in that they think they are the center of the universe and that everything that is done is done for them. Ibid., Letter 65

11 Anyhow, I say, the God I been praying and writing to is a man. And act just like all the other mens I know. Trifling, forgitful and lowdown. Ibid., Letter 73

12 She say, Celie, tell the truth, have you ever found God in church? I never did. I just found a bunch of folks hoping for him to show. Any God I ever felt in church I brought in with me. And I think all the other folks did too. They come to church to share God, not find God. Ibid.

13 Yeah, It. God ain't a he or a she, but a It. But what do it look like? I ast. Don't look like nothing, she say. It ain't a picture show. It ain't something you can look at apart from anything else, including yourself. I believe God is everything, say Shug. Everything that is or ever was or ever will be. And when you can feel that, and be happy to feel that, you've found it. Ibid.

14 It [marijuana] just like whiskey, I say. You got to stay ahead of it. You know a little drink now and then never hurt nobody, but when you can't git started without asking the bottle, you in trouble.
You smoke it much, Miss Celie? Harpo ast.
Do I look like a fool? I ast. I smoke when I want to talk to God. I smoke when I want to make love. Lately I feel like me and God make love just fine anyhow. Whether I smoke reefer or not. Ibid., Letter 78

15 And I try to teach my heart not to want nothing it can't have. Ibid., Letter 87

16 The diamonds on Liz's* bosom
are not as bright
as his eyes
the morning they took him
to work in the mines . . .
"The Diamonds on Liz's Bosom," *Horses Make A Landscape Look More Beautiful* 1985

*Ref. Elizabeth Taylor; see 2120.

17 In consorting with man, as he had become, woman was bound to lose her dignity, her integrity. *The Temple of My Familiar* 1989

18 . . . the reasons millions of Africans are exterminating themselves in wars is that the superpowers have enormous stores of outdated weapons to be got rid of. Ibid.

19 She was soon meditating and masturbating and finding herself dissolved into the cosmic All. Delicious. Ibid.

2403. Aung San Suu Kyi (1945–)

1 The country [Burma] accepts me because they trust me and they associate me with my father.* Quoted in "The Armed Forces Seize Power" by William Stewart, *Time* 26 September 1988

*Aung San, Burmese nationalist hero (1915–1947).

2 Let the world know that under this administration the Burmese people are like prisoners in their own homes. Letter to various political parties, Quoted in *Time* 31 July 1989

2404. Victoria Billings (1945–)

1 Whether he admits it or not, a man has been brought up to look at money as a sign of his virility, a symbol of his power, a bigger phallic symbol than a Porsche. "Getting It Together," *The Womansbook* 1974

2 The best thing that could happen to motherhood already has. Fewer women are going into it.
Ibid., "Meeting Your Personal Needs"

3 Constant togetherness is fine—but only for Siamese twins. Ibid., "A Love to Believe In"

2405. Annie Dillard (1945–)

1 We wake, if we ever wake at all, to mystery, rumors of death, beauty, violence.
Ch. 1, *Pilgrim at Tinker Creek* 1974

2 Every live thing is a survivor on a kind of extended emergency bivouac. Ibid.

3 I am an explorer, then, and I am also a stalker, or the instrument of the hunt itself. Ibid.

4 The world's spiritual geniuses seem to discover universally that the mind's muddy river, this ceaseless flow of trivia and trash, cannot be dammed, and that trying to dam it is a waste of effort that might lead to madness.
Ibid., Ch. 2

5 The secret of seeing is to sail on solar wind. Hone and spread your spirit till you yourself are a sail, whetted, translucent, broadside to the merest puff. Ibid.

6 It is ironic that the one thing that all religions recognize as separating us from our creator—our very self-consciousness—is also the one thing that divides us from our fellow creatures. It was a bitter birthday present from evolution. . . . Ibid., Ch. 6

7 No; we have been as usual asking the wrong question. It does not matter a hoot what the mockingbird on the chimney is singing. . . . The real and proper question is: Why is it beautiful? Ibid., Ch. 7

8 Somewhere, and I can't find where, I read about an Eskimo hunter who asked the local missionary priest, "If I did not know about God and sin, would I go to hell?" "No," said the priest, "not if you did not know." "Then why," asked the Eskimo earnestly, "did you tell me?"
Ibid.

9 I don't know what it is about fecundity that so appalls. I suppose it is the teeming evidence that birth and growth, which we value, are

ubiquitous and blind, that life itself is so astonishingly cheap, that nature is as careless as it is bountiful, and that with extravagance goes a crushing waste that will one day include our own cheap lives. . . . Ibid., Ch. 10

10 Every day is a god, each day is a god, and holiness holds forth in time.
Part 1, *Holy the Firm* 1977

11 The day is real; the sky clicks securely in place over the mountains, locks round the islands, snaps slap on the bay. Ibid.

12 The universe is illusion merely, not one speck of it real, and we are not only its victims, falling always into or smashed by a planet slung by its sun—but also its captives, bound by the mineral-made ropes of our senses. Ibid., Part II

2406. Buchi Emecheta (1945–)

1 That was life, she said to herself. Be as cunning as a serpent and as harmless as a dove.
Ch. 2, *Second-Class Citizen* 1974

2 But how was she to tell this beautiful creature that in her society she could only be sure of the love of her husband and the loyalty of her parents-in-law by having and keeping alive as many children as possible, and that though a girl may be counted as one child, to her people a boy was like four children put together? And if the family could give the boy a good university education, his mother would be given the status of a man in the tribe. How was she to explain all that? Ibid., Ch. 6

3 The whole world seemed so unequal, so unfair. Some people were created with all the good things ready-made for them, others were just created like mistakes. God's mistakes.
Ibid., Ch. 9

4 I am a woman and a woman of Africa. I am a daughter of Nigeria and if she is in shame, I shall stay and mourn with her in shame.
Destination Biafra 1982

5 . . . shame kills faster than disease.
The Rape of Shavi 1985

2407. Shulamith Firestone (1945–)

1 Perhaps it is true that a presentation of only the female side of things . . . is limited. But . . . is it any more limited than the prevailing male view of things, which—when not taken as absolute truth—is at least seen as "serious," relevant and important.
The Dialectic of Sex 1970

2 I submit that women's history has been hushed up for the same reason that black history has been hushed up . . . and that is that a feminist movement poses a direct threat to the establishment. From the beginning it exposed the hypocrisy of the male power structure.   Ibid., Ch. 2

3 The bar is the male kingdom. For centuries it was the bastion of male privilege, the gathering place for men away from their women, a place where men could go to freely indulge in The Bull Session . . . a serious political function: the release of the guilty anxiety of the oppressor class.   "The Bar as Microcosm,"
Voices from Women's Liberation,
Leslie B. Tanner, ed.   *1970*

2408. Nancy R. Hooyman (1945–   )

See Mary Bricker-Jenkins, 2343:1-3.

2409. Ruth Iskin (1945–   )

1 In the dealer-critic system, galleries exist primarily for sale purposes and it is the critic's role to promote the art product by establishing its value and providing a justification for its importance.
"A Space of Our Own, Its Meaning and Implications," *Womanspace February/March 1973*

2410. Kathy Kahn (1945–   )

1 There is still a natural tendency for the people of one class to look down on people who they think are lower class—as if they are less than human.   Quoted in "Kathy Kahn: Voice of Poor White Women" by Meridee Merzer, *Viva   April 1974*

2 In places like the textile mills, where superhuman production rates are set, the people have to take speed (amphetamines) in order to keep up production. . . . Virtually every factory in this country is run on speed, grass, or some other kind of upper.   Ibid.

3 I do not believe in being paid for organizing . . . because a revolution is a revolution. And nobody—*nobody*—gets paid for making a revolution.   Ibid.

2411. Jamaica Kincaid (1945?–   )

1 And what are my fears? What large cows! When I see them coming, shall I run and hide face down in the gutter? Are they really cows? Can I stand in a field of tall grass and see nothing for miles and miles? On the other hand, the sky, which is big and blue as always, has its limits.   "Wingless," *At the Bottom of the River   1985*

2 Wash the white clothes on Monday and put them on the stone heap; wash the color clothes on Tuesday and put them on the clothesline to dry; . . . soak your little cloths right after you take them off; . . . always eat your food in such a way that it won't turn someone else's stomach; on Sundays try to walk like a lady, and not like the slut you are so bent on becoming; . . . this is how you smile to someone you don't like too much; this is how you smile to someone you don't like at all; this is how you smile to someone you like completely; . . . this is how to make a good medicine for a cold; this is how to make a good medicine to throw away a child before it even becomes a child; . . . this is how to bully a man; this is how a man bullies you; this is how to love a man, and if this doesn't work there are other ways, and if they don't work don't feel too bad about giving up . . .   "Girl," op. cit.

2412. Karen Malpede (1945–   )

1 . . . in order for me to reveal the divine in "man" I had to come to feminism. There was no other way, I had to come to an understanding of the divine in women. Now I can truly be one within a long tradition of people who believe that theater is a way to reveal the spirit, the deep essence, the unrealized desires, the true holiness of humankind.
"Karen Malpede," *Interviews with Contemporary Women Playwrights,* Kathleen Betsko* & Rachel Koenig   *1987*

*See 2256.

2 Pacifism is an active, assertive way of being which, when used effectively disarms. It has to do with holding to a sense of self and of community and with refusing to be part of the victor/victim scenario.   Ibid.

3 The great artist speaks a truth so personal it becomes universal. There's no way you can do that with one eye on the market place.   Ibid.

4 I think artists, like most other people, don't want to face the fact that we are very close to our extinction as a species and we intend to take with us all the life on earth.   Ibid.

5 Pregnancy can be a tremendously creative time in the life of a woman; the body itself is tied up

in the act of creation so it's easy for the mind and heart to be similarly engaged. *Ibid.*

6 The true artist is bisexual; I'm not necessarily talking about whom you choose to sleep with but about how deeply you can enter into both your own psyche and that of someone unlike you. *Ibid.*

2413. Wilma Pearl Mankiller (1945–)

1 Cherokees have stated that they are ready for female leadership. . . . We all knew this was coming. . . . The issues are our programs, the breaking of the circle of poverty, not me.
Inaugural Speech
5 December 1985

2414. Bette Midler (1945–)

1 For Tillie had been (in the Days of her Youth)
Adored as a Terpsichorine.
She danced with Abandon and not too much else,
Yet never approached the Obscene.
The Saga of Baby Divine, St. 16
1983

2 "A good laugh is good for the spirits it's true,
But a good cry is good for the soul."
Ibid., St. 114

3 "Make sure that your Life is a Rare Entertainment!
It doesn't take anything drastic.
You needn't be gorgeous or wealthy or smart
Just Very Enthusiastic!" *Ibid.*, St. 153

4 There's a kind of emotional exploration you plumb with a friend that you don't really do with your family.
Quoted in "I Can't Play the Victim" by Tom Seligson,
Parade Magazine *5 February 1989*

5 Marriage involves big compromises all the time. International-level compromises. You're the U.S.A., he's the USSR, and you're talking nuclear warheads. *Ibid.*

2415. Honor Moore (1945–)

1 I have thought the cancer was in my control. If I decide she will recover, it will go away. . . . *Mourning Pictures* (verse play)
1974

2 A ring or two.
Her turquoise beads
The green-striped chair
What will she leave me
Except alone. . . .
"What Will She Leave Me?," op. cit.

2416. Paula Nelson (1945–)

1 Women's battle for financial equality has barely been joined, much less won. Society still traditionally assigns to woman the role of money-handler rather than money-maker, and our assigned specialty is far more likely to be home economics than financial economics.
Ch. 1, *The Joy of Money* *1975*

2 A credit card is a money tool, *not* a supplement to money. The failure to make this distinction has "supplemented" many a poor soul right into bankruptcy. *Ibid.*, Ch. 4

3 . . . launching your own business is like writing your own personal declaration of independence from the corporate beehive, where you sell bits of your life in forty-hour (or longer) chunks in return for a paycheck. . . . Going into business for yourself, becoming an entrepreneur, is the modern-day equivalent of pioneering on the old frontier. *Ibid.*, Ch. 6

2417. Diane Sawyer (1945–)

1 When someone's life is shattered, there is only humanity.* *Quoted in "Star Power" by Richard Zoglin, Time*
7 August 1989

*Referring to Richard Nixon (1913–), 37th president of the United States (1969–1974), forced to resign after the Watergate scandel.

2 We're a Madison Avenue country. I'm not sure that we make a distinction between newspeople and celebrities. And I think there is a distinction. The distinction lies in what you do every day— what you do to get stories and how far you will go and how much you will dig for them. All of the rest of the attention that comes to you because you're on the air seems to me an irrelevance. *Ibid.*

2418. Karin Sheldon (1945–)

1 Environment, in all its forms and relations, sustains us. We depend upon it. I truly believe that the fundamental principles of ecology gov-

ern our lives, wherever we live, and that we must wake up to this fact or be lost.

Quoted in "Found Women: Defusing the Atomic Establishment" by Anna Mayo, *Ms.* *October 1973*

2419. Carly Simon (1945–)

1 You're so vain, I'll bet you think this song is about you. . . .
"You're So Vain" *1972*

2 The thing that drugs do is they break down the barrier that's tense between people. People want to feel as *comfortable* as they possibly can and if you take drugs it makes you feel more at ease with your friends. But in fact, there is a certain thing to be gained from being *tense* with your friends. *The Dick Cavett Show,* PBS-TV *1977*

2420. Anne Tucker (1945–)

1 All art requires courage.
Introduction, *The Woman's Eye* *1973*

2 Exploration, whether of jungles or minds, is considered unfeminine. Ibid.

3 For centuries men have defined themselves in terms of other men, but women have been defined by and in terms of men. . . . The ubiquitous nature of masculine images of Woman has contributed significantly to the struggles of woman artists because that which is publicly acceptable art does not conform with their own needs and experiences, and their own art does not conform with popular standards. Ibid.

2421. Joan Barfoot (1946–)

1 I remember now that in the old life, I watched clocks. They told me everything: when to do each thing, walking, cooking, laundering, watching television, reading the newspaper, even having a cigarette. And sleeping. Time was how I counted off my life.

Now I see that it was time I was accomplishing. I was not timing my tasks, but making the tasks into time; and all that is gone.
Ch. 3, *Gaining Ground (aka Abra)* *1978*

2 "I've often thought that if we just put all our energy into raising the next generation, and they do the same and so on and so on, it makes us no better than ants, really, or bees. Save something for yourself." Ibid., Ch. 5.

3 "I can't know anything about you if you're doing something that's a lie, and I can't be myself if I have to keep worrying about whether or not you're happy." Ibid., Ch. 14

2422. Candice Bergen (1946–)

1 Hollywood is like Picasso's bathroom.
Quoted by Sheila Graham* in the *New York Post* *14 February 1967*

*See 1622.

2 THE MAN. You've been renovated, my sweet, like an urban renewal project!
The Freezer *1968*

3 THE MAN. Can't they realize that mankind was founded on two basic principles? *Religion and Death?* The one motivates the other. *Both* motivate the man! Ibid.

2423. Jacqueline Bisset (1946–)

1 Character contributes to beauty. It fortifies a woman as her youth fades. A mode of conduct, a standard of courage, discipline, fortitude and integrity can do a great deal to make a woman beautiful. Quoted by Lydia Lane in the *Los Angeles Times* *16 May 1974*

2424. Sharon Doubiago (1946–)

1 Men create war to compete with women, who create life. "The Football Players and the Poet: Mother and Child Reunion," *Clinton Street Quarterly* *Fall 1986*

2 "Ever since you were born, I've tried to understand why, since women birth and raise the boys, they grow up to be soldiers. Why isn't the world a more sensuous, loving place? A more feminine place? and you know what Danny? There's almost nothing on this subject. Women and war, mothers and soldiers—the most fundamental, crucial issue." Ibid.

3 "The football player in America is like the artist in America! The same loner, the same heroic figure so outside the mainstream, but performing for it. Both are like the shaman, the one who heals oneself, who comes back transformed from the mutilating experience to show the world how.

"Still I have these funny moments. Is this
what I birthed and raised my child for? Football?
What would my son be, with his perfect giant
body, in a perfect society? And there remains
the other great mystery. What is the function of
this game for the spectators? Why do Americans
love football?''   Ibid.

4 What happens to your American soul when,
despite all your efforts, laying your body and
soul on the line, you keep losing?   Ibid.

2425. Andrea Dworkin (1946–   )

1 Institutionalized in sports, the military, acculturated sexuality, the history and mythology of
heroism, it [violence] is taught to boys until
they become its *advocates*.
                    *Photography: Men Possessing
                           Women   1981*

2 She is the pinup, the centerfold, the poster, the
postcard, the dirty picture, naked, half-dressed,
laid out, legs spread, breast or ass protruding.
She is the thing she is supposed to be: the thing
that makes him erect.   Ibid.

3 The sexually liberated woman is the woman of
pornography. . . . Freedom is the mass-mar-
keting of woman as whore. Free sexuality for
the woman is in being massively consumed,
denied an individual nature, denied any sexual
sensibility other than that which serves the
male.   Ibid.

4 In [the work of the Marquis de] Sade, the
authentic equation is revealed: the power of the
pornographer is the power of the rapist batterer
is the power of the man.   Ibid.

2426. Elizabeth Fee (1946–   )

1 The voice of the scientific authority is like the
male voice-over in commercials, a disembodied
knowledge that cannot be questioned, whose
author is inaccessible.
            "Women's Nature and Scientific
            Objectivity," *Woman's Nature:
            Rationalizations of Inequality*, M.
            Loew & R. Hubbard, eds.   *1983*

2427. Kimi Gray (1946–   )

1 Poor people are allowed the same dreams as
everyone else.
            Quoted in "Turning Public Housing
            Over to Resident Owners" by
            Jerome Cramer, *Time*
            12 December 1988

2 People don't throw trash on the ground when
they know it soon will be their turn to pick it
up.   Ibid.

2428. Sylvia Ann Hewlett (1946?–   )

1 How did the most independent and best-edu-
cated women in the world come to have the
least good conditions of life?
                    *A Lesser Life, The Myth of
                    Women's Liberation in
                    America   198?*

2429. Carter Heyward (1946–   )

1 I'm a priest, not a priestess. . . . "Priestess"
implies mumbo jumbo and all sorts of pagan
goings-on. Those who oppose us would love to
call us priestesses. They can call us all the names
in the world—it's better than being
invisible.   Quoted in "Who's Afraid of
            Women Priests?" by Malcolm Boyd,
            Ms.   December 1974

2 It's obvious throughout secular and church history that significant legislation follows only after
dramatic action.   Ibid.

2430. Susan Jacoby (1946–   )

1 Political détente notwithstanding, the Soviet
Union is still a nation with a deeply ingrained
suspicion of foreign influence.
                    Inside Soviet Schools   1974

2 I have always regarded the development of the
individual as the only legitimate goal of
education. . . .   Ibid.

3 Soviet schools are extraordinarily good at
squeezing the fight out of the individuals they
process.   Ibid.

2431. Marcia Kaptur (1946–   )

1 The American people have the right to know
who holds the mortgage on America.
            Congressional Speech   *October 1988*

2432. Candy Lightner (1946–   )

1 Death by drunken driving is a socially acceptable form of homicide.
            Quoted in "Legislature Eyes Harsher
            Laws . . ." by Chuck Buxton,
            *San Jose Mercury
            20 April 1981*

2 Victims of drunk drivers have no place to turn. Judges drink and drive, juries drink and drive, D.A.'s drink and drive. They're going to have sympathy for the drunk driver. They don't have sympathy for the rapist, the murderer, the mugger.   Quoted in "Mother's Crusade to Get Drunk Drivers Off the Streets" by Beverly Beyette, *Los Angeles Times* *11 June 1981*

2433. Jessica Tuchman Mathews (1946–)

1 The automobile reaches to the heart of the American self-image in the way the horse once did in the West. It's going to be hard to change.   Quoted in *A World of Ideas* by Bill Moyers   *1989*

2 Countries are starting to see that they can't have economic growth without protecting their resource base The economic growth disappears as the fisheries disappear, as the forest disappears, as soil erosion progresses. They can't have real growth without environmental management. *Ibid.*

3 We're going to need a new sense of shared destiny, that we're in this together. We, the family of nations, are going to have to develop somehow some shared sense, almost like a joint business venture, that we work together, or we're all going to suffer.   *Ibid.*

4 It is hard to think abstractly about a crisis. *Ibid.*

2434. Mary McCaslin (1946?–)

1 Bury me out on the lone prairie
Near the mountains I could never see

The speakers, they all gasp to clear their lungs
for their luncheon speeches
This year's new campaign is save the canyons
and the beaches   "The Dealers"   *1975*

2435. Laura Nyro (1946–)

1 And when I die
and when I'm gone
there'll be one child born
and a world to carry on. . . .
"And When I Die"   *1966*

2 I was born from love
and my poor mother worked the mines
I was raised on the good book Jesus

till I read between the lines. . . .
"Stoney End"   *1966*

3 Nothing cures like time and love. . . .
"Time and Love"   *1970*

4 money money money
do you feel like a pawn
in your own world?
you found the system
and you lost the pearl. . . .
"Money"   *1975*

5 They say a woman's place
is to wait and serve
under the veil
submissive and dear
but I think my place is in a ship from space
to carry me
the hell out of here
"The Right to Vote"   *n.d.*

6 . . . you will find
your own way
hard and true
And I'll find mine
cause I'm growing with you
"To a Child. . . ."   *n.d.*

2436. Dolly Parton (1946–)

1 I've been like a captured eagle.
You know an eagle's born to fly,

Now that I have won my freedom, like an
eagle,
I am eager for the sky.   "Light of a Clear Blue
Morning"   *1976*

2 Butterflies are colorful and bright and gentle and have no way to harm you. They go about their business and bring others pleasure while doing it, because just seeing one flying around makes people happy. I'd like to think of myself as bringing people happiness while I do my business, which is my music. I'm content with what I am, and butterflies seem to be content to be just what they are, too. They're gentle, but determined.   Quoted in "Introduction: Hello, Dolly," *Dolly* by Alanna Nash   *1978*

3 Sure we had runnin' water. When we'd run and get it!   *Ibid., Ch. 1*

2437. Minnie Bruce Pratt (1946–)

1 She has three sisters, Lethean, Evie, and Ora Gilder.
When they aggravate her she wants to pinch their habits off like potato bugs off the leaf.

But she meets them each weekend for cards
and jokes
while months go by without her speaking to
her brother.   "My Mother Loves Women,"
The Sound of One Fork   *1981*

2 You had not acted like a man
and I never loved you better
"Love Poem to an
Ex-Husband," St. 4, op. cit.

2438. Gilda Radner (1946–1989)

1 [Audiences] all applaud, but none of them will
come home with you and look at your back
someplace to see if you have a pimple.
Quoted in "The Many Faces of
Gilda" by Roy Blount, Jr.,
Rolling Stone
2 November 1978

2 I'd much rather be a woman than a man. Women
can cry, they can wear cute clothes, and they're
first to be rescued off sinking ships.
Quoted in "My Fair City"
By Merla Zellerbach,
San Francisco Chronicle
6 June 1979

3 I think of my illness [ovarian cancer] as a
school, and finally I've graduated.
Quoted in *Life*   *1988*

2439. Shulamit Reinharz (1946–   )

1 I will never know the experience of others, but
I can know my own, and I can approximate
theirs by entering their world. This approxima-
tion marks the tragic, perpetually inadequate
aspect of social research.
On Becoming a Social Scientist
1984

2440. Linda Ronstadt (1946–   )

1 The thing you have to be prepared for is that
other people don't always dream your
dream.
Quoted in
"Ronstadt Backed into Her
Notoriety" by Lawrence DeVine,
Knight-Ridder Newspapers
3 October 1986

2 The great temper tantrum of the 60's . . .
Ibid.

3 We were raised with the idea that we had limitless chances and we got very shocked to learn
that wasn't the case.   Ibid.

2441. Judee Sill (1946?–   )

1 The great storm raged and the power kept
growin',
Dragons rose from the land below
And even now I wonder where I'm goin'
Ever since a long time ago,
I've tried to let my feelin's show.
"The Phoenix"   *1969*

2442. Barbara Smith (1946–   )

1 Then there was the magazine called LIFE which
promised more about the Deaths.
"Poem for My Sister (One) Birmingham
Sunday (1963)," *Southern Voices*
August/September 1974

2443. Sue Townsend (1946–   )

1 I was racked with sexuality but it wore off when
I helped my father put manure on our rose
bed.   *The Diary of Adrian Mole,*
Ten & Three-Quarters.
1984

2 Babies hardly take any space at all. They are
only about 21 inches long.   Ibid.

2444. Anna Lee Walters (1946–   )

1 The ever swollen hills in Oklahoma have given
birth many times. . . . It is a land that drinks
a lot of water and never seems to swallow
much.
"Autobiography" (1977), Quoted in *American*
Indian Women, Telling
Their Lives, Gretchen M.
Bataille & Kathleen Mullen Sands, eds.
1981

2 The old folks are all gone. They were tired,
prepared and they went on. Life goes on. Nothing diminishes it. We have been taught also that
life is a fragile thing. Grandma always said that
it almost feels too good to be alive.   Ibid.

2445. Marina Warner (1946–   )

1 For while Mary provides a focus for the steeliest
asceticism, she is also the ultimate of fertility
symbols. The mountain blossoms spontaneously; so does the mother maid.
Alone of All Her Sex   *1978*

2 The Virgin Mary has inspired some of the loftiest
architecture, some of the most moving poetry,

some of the most beautiful paintings in the world; she has filled men and women with deep joy and fervent trust; she has been an image of the ideal that has entranced and stirred men and women to the noblest emotions of love and pity and awe. But the reality her myth describes is over; the moral code she affirms has been exhausted. . . .

As an acknowledged creation of Christian mythology, the Virgin's legend will endure in its splendor any lyricism, but it will be emptied of moral significance, and thus lose its present real powers to heal and to harm.　　　　Ibid.

2446. Laurie Anderson (1947–)

1 Paradise
is exactly like
Where you are right now
Only much much
Better　　　　"Language is a Virus,"
　　　　　　　　Laurie Anderson　　n.d.

2 Well I dreamed there was an island
That rose up from the sea.
And everybody on the island
Was somebody from TV.
And there was a beautiful view
But nobody could see.
'Cause everybody on the island
Was saying: Look at me! Look at me!
　　　　　　"Look at me! Look at me!,"
　　　　　　　　　　　　op. cit.

2447. Karen Brodine (1947–)

1 "will you hold please? I'll see if he's in."
(are you in?)
"I'm sorry, sir, he's out."

the receptionist is by definition underpaid to lie.　　"The Receptionist Is By Definition,"
St. 3, *Workweek: Poems by Karen Brodine*　　1977

2448. Sara Davidson (1947–)

1 Overexposure to women's liberation leads, I found, to headaches, depression and a fierce case of the shakes.　　　　Quoted in
　　　　　　　　Interview, *Life*　　1969

2 In that time [the Sixties], that decade which belonged to the young, we had thought life was free and would never run out. There were good people and bad people and we could tell them apart by a look or by words spoken in code. We were certain we belonged to a generation that

was special. We did not need or care about history because we had sprung from nowhere.　　*Loose Change: Three Women
of the Sixties*　　1977

3 "I've always been so rational, so damn well-adjusted. My problem is that I don't have any problems."　　　　Ibid., Ch. 9

4 He had attacked hypocrisy everywhere but at home. He couldn't deal with pain. He was always telling stories, playing with the energy and ranting about capitalist society. But he couldn't face himself, Susie, their life or his problems.　　　　Ibid., Ch. 20

5 "I can't even deal with that picture," Susie said. "People love it, they think it's an image of courage. But pictures lie."　　Ibid., Ch. 27

2449. Bernadette Devlin (1947–)

1 To gain that which is worth having, it may be necessary to lose everything else.
　　　　Preface, *The Price of My Soul*
　　　　　　　　　　　　1969

2450. Mary Gallagher (1947–)

1 Publication is the only thing that makes me stop rewriting.　　"Mary Gallagher," *Interviews
with Contemporary Women Playwrights*,
Kathleen Betsko* & Rachel
Koenig　　1987

*See 2256.

2 Healthy people aren't that interesting.　　Ibid.

3 Good theater incorporates the personal, the social, the political, seamlessly.　　Ibid.

4 The theater brigades are a major tool for unifying the Nicaraguan people. Music, dance, poetry are taught in every community because the Sandinistas believe that Nicaraguans can't explore their national identity till they are making art.　　　　Ibid.

2451. Linda Hogan (1947–)

1 On the bus two elderly women sat in front of her. They were both speaking and neither one listened to the other. They carried on two different conversations the way people did in the city, without silences, without listening. Trying to get it all said before it was too late, before they were interrupted by thoughts.
　　"New Shoes" (story), *A Gathering of Spirit*,
Beth Brant,* ed.　　1984

*See 2314.

2　This land is the house
　　we have always lived in.
　　The women,
　　their bones are holding up the earth.
　　　　　　　　"calling myself home," st. 4,
　　　　　　　　That's What She Said, Rayna
　　　　　　　　　　　　Green,* ed.　*1984*

*See 2284.

3　We're full of bread and gas, getting fat on the
　　　outside
　　while inside we grow thin.
　　　　　　　　　　　　"Oil," St. 5, op. cit.

4　From my mother, the antique mirror
　　where I watch my face take on her lines.
　　　　　　　　　　　　"Heritage," St. 1, op. cit.

2452. Keri Hulme (1947–　　)

1　They were nothing more than people, by them-
　　selves. Even paired, any pairing, they would
　　have been nothing more than people by them-
　　selves. But all together, they have become the
　　heart and muscles and mind of something per-
　　ilous and new, something strange and growing
　　and great.
　　　　Together, all together, they are the instru-
　　ments of change.　Prologue, *The Bone People*
　　　　　　　　　　　　　　　　　　1983

2　"I have everything I need, but I have lost the
　　main part."　　　　　Ibid., Part I, Ch. 2

3　She thought of the tools she had gathered to-
　　gether, and painstakingly learned to use. Future
　　probes, Tarot and I Ching and the wide wispfin-
　　gers from the stars . . . all these to scry and
　　ferret and vex the smokethick future. A broad
　　general knowledge, encompassing bits of his-
　　tory, psychology, ethology, religious theory and
　　practices of many kinds. Her charts of self-
　　knowledge. Her library. The inner thirst for
　　information about everything that had lived or
　　lives on Earth that she'd kept alive long after
　　childhood had ended.
　　　　None of them helped make sense of
　　living.　　　　　　　　　　　　Ibid.

4　A man can find satisfaction with enough."
　　　　　　　　　　　　Ibid., Part IV, Ch. 10

2453. Melanie (1947–　　)

1　don't hold the sprout against the seed
　　don't hold this need against me. . . .
　　　　　　　　"Gather on a Hill of Wildflowers"
　　　　　　　　　　　　　　　　　　1975

2454. Elizabeth Morgan (1947–　　)

1　For the average middle-class American, living
　　in the D.C. jail* is a horror. It's dirty, it's
　　noisy, it's crowded, and you have no privacy.
　　But I chose this because the middle-class Amer-
　　ican existence is worthless to me if my daughter
　　is being raped. The destruction of my child is
　　not worth any possessions. Just having her safe
　　makes me happy.
　　　　　　　　Quoted in "A Hard Case of
　　　　　　Contempt" by Jon Elson, *Time*
　　　　　　　　　　　18 September 1989

*Incarcerated in Washington, D.C. for refusing to disclose
the whereabouts of her allegedly sexually abused five-year-
old daughter.

2455. Marsha Norman (1947–　　)

1　It's all time, see, and learning how to tell.
　　　　　　　　　　　　Circus Valentine
　　　　　　　　　　　　　　n.d.

2　Most people get their information about the
　　theater from the critics, not from the theater
　　itself. . . . Too often, reviews answer one
　　question, "Should you buy it or not?" When
　　critics approach a piece of theater with a "buy
　　it or not" attitude, our plays are reduced to
　　products . . .
　　　　　　　　"Marsha Norman," *Interviews*
　　　　　　　　with Contemporary Women
　　　　　　Playwrights, Kathleen Betsko* &
　　　　　　　　Rachel Koenig　*1987*

*See 2256.

3　There are things that music can do that language
　　could never do, that painting can never do, or
　　sculpture. Music is capable of going directly to
　　the source of the mystery. It doesn't have to
　　explain it. It can simply celebrate it.　Ibid.

4　My attitude toward the computer has changed.
　　In the first year I owned it, I was a true believer.
　　I wrote articles and gave interviews saying it
　　was our only hope as writers. Now I've gone
　　back to the yellow pad. . . . I found I was
　　having conversations with the screen, rather than
　　with the audience, or with myself. The screen
　　appreciates a very particular kind of talk. You
　　might say I was talking head-to-head rather than
　　heart-to-heart.　　　　　　　　　Ibid.

5　As women, our historical role has been to clean
　　up the mess. Whether it's the mess left by war
　　or death or children or sickness. I think the
　　violence you see in plays by women is a direct
　　reflection of that historical role. We are not
　　afraid to look under the bed, or to wash the
　　sheets; we know that life is messy. We know

that somebody has to clean it up, and that only if it is cleaned up can we hope to start over, and get better. **Ibid.**

6 Success is always something that you have to recover from. **Ibid.**

2456. Martha Nussbaum (1947–)

1 To be a good human being is to have a kind of openness to the world, an ability to trust uncertain things beyond your own control, that can lead you to be shattered in very extreme circumstances for which you were not to blame.
Quoted in A World of Ideas by
Bill Moyers 1989

2 But the life that no longer trusts another human being and no longer forms ties to the political community is not a human life any longer.
Ibid.

3 The stories that we sometimes tell ourselves, that the free will is free no matter what conditions people are living in, and that these people in misery are really okay because they have free will—those are evasive and pernicious stories, because they prevent us from looking with the best kind of compassion at the lives of other people. **Ibid.**

4 The role of politics is to provide conditions of support for all the richly diverse elements in the full human life. **Ibid.**

5 Often, when people are measuring the quality of life, what they're doing is measuring the opulence of the society. **Ibid.**

6 Advertising simplifies us, when I think what we want to do is to become more aware of complexity, nuance, and the complicated messiness of human situations. Advertising gives us a simple, two-second message in language that has to be grasped right away whereas the great works of literature draw us into a complex, highly textured language that is much more adequate for a grasp of ethical reality. **Ibid.**

2457. Susan Partnow (1947–)

1 It is within the families themselves where peace can begin. If families can learn to respect their members, and deal with conflict resolution, that would be the first step to keeping peace on a global level. *"Families For Peace," Puget*
Consumers Coop Newsletter
Spring 1986

2 War toys and [children's television] cartoons dehumanize the enemy, really glamorizing war.

The opponent has a legitimate point-of-view, too, and these cartoons don't resolve issues of conflict. There are no treaties, and no solutions in cartoons. There is no consideration given to the opponent. *Quoted in "Locals Seek*
Alternatives to War Toys" by Denise
Fisk-Park, The North Seattle Press
30 December 1987/12 January 1988

3 Children learn about the world through their play. When we choose toys and games that encourage creativity, problem solving and learning, and we resolve to keep violence and racial stereotypes out of our homes, we are taking important steps towards a world without hatemongers. *Letter to the editor, The*
Seattle Times 3 December 1988

2458. Sally Priesand (1947–)

1 Clergy are father figures to many women, and sometimes they are threatened by another woman accomplishing what they see as strictly male goals. But I can see them replacing that feeling with a sense of pride that women can have that role. *Quoted in Women at Work*
by Betty Medsger 1975

2459. Lynn Thomas (1947–)

1 There are for starters, grandeur and silence, pure water and clean air. There is also the gift of distance . . . the chance to stand away from relationships and daily ritual . . . and the gift of energy. Wilderness infuses us with its own special brand of energy. I remember lying by the Snake River in Idaho once and becoming aware I could not sleep . . . nature's forces had me in hand. I was engulfed by a dance of ions and atoms. My body was responding to the pervasive pull of the moon.
The Backpacking Woman 1980

2460. Ann-ping Chin (1948–)

1 One cannot say that all China's cultural symbols and cultural assumptions were reduced to ruins. They seem to be endowed with a life of their own. *Children of China 1989*

2461. Deirdre English (1948–)

1 The fact remains that, no matter how disturbing violent fantasies are, as long as they stay within

the world of pornography they are still only fantasies. The man masturbating in a theater showing a snuff film is still only watching a movie, not actually raping and murdering.

> Quoted in *Mother Jones*
> *April 1980*

2 There is something wrong with attacking people not because of their actions but because of their fantasies—or their particular commercial style of having them. Ibid.

2462. Connie Field (1948–   )

1 Many people think that the women who responded to the call to "do the job he left behind," were surburban housewives who trotted back to their homes after the war. The newsreels would have you believe that too. But for a majority, the women were working before, and had to work after.

> Quoted in " 'Rosies' Were There When U.S. Needed Them" by Anita Alverio, *New Directions for Women July/August 1981*

2 . . . making a [documentary] film is not writing a textbook. Someone can have a terrifically wonderful story, but if they can't say it in a way that makes you want to listen, then it's not useful. Ibid.

2463. Shakti Gawain (1948–   )

1 Creative visualization is magic in the truest and highest meaning of the word. It involves understanding and aligning yourself with the natural principles that govern the workings of our universe, and learning to use these principles in the most conscious and creative way.

> *Creative Visualization   1978*

2464. Christa McAuliffe (1948–1986)

1 What are we doing here? We're reaching for the stars.

> Remark upon entering astronaut program,*
> Quoted in *Time,*
> *10 February 1986*

*Killed in explosion of spacecraft Challenger, 28 January 1986.

2 I touch the future. I teach.

> Speech (August 1985), op. cit.

2465. Wendy Rose (1948–   )

1 I am hungry enough
to eat myself and you

"The Indian Women Are Listening: To the Nuke Devils," St. 2, *A Gathering of Spirit,* Beth Brant,* ed.   *1984*

*See 2314.

2 the hope or the lie
all the gods gave us that
pain is a vitamin
to make us grow.
> "Well You Caught Me Unprepared,"
> St. 4, op. cit.

3 . . . . chained
to the glamor of speed   Ibid., St. 6

4 I am still convinced no matter what
that I am stronger than any storm.
Every song straining against the shackles
I creep the ocean floor and don't believe
anything about me can drown.   Ibid., St. 8

5 Nothing is old
about us yet;
we are still waiting.
> "Walking on the Prayerstick," St. 1,
> *That's What She Said,* Rayna
> Green,* ed.   *1984*

*See 2284.

6 It's our blood that give you
those southwestern skies.
> "Long Division: A Tribal
> History," op. cit.

2466. Nora Astorga (1949–1989)

1 I want it to be known that I participated in the operation of bringing to justice the bloody henchman.*   Quoted in
> "Nora and the Dog," *Time*
> *2 April 1984*

*Ref. assassination of General Reynaldo Perez Vega, 1978.

2467. Victoria Bond (1949–   )

1 The conductor traditionally has been anything but a mother figure. The conductor is much more like a general than a mother or teacher. It's a kind of enforced leadership, the kind of leadership more likely to be expected of men than women. A woman conductor, because of those traditions, must rely completely on being able to transmit authority purely on the grounds of her musical ability.

> Quoted in *Women at Work*
> by Betty Medsger   *1975*

2468. Mary Hyde (fl. 1949–1982)

1 The art of managing men has to be learned from birth. . . . It depends to some extent on one's distribution of curves, a developed instinct, and a large degree of sheer feline cunning.
How to Manage Men 1955

2469. Gayl Jones (1949–)

1 "My great-grandmama told my grandmama the part she lived through that my grandmama didn't live through and my grandmama told my mama what they both lived through and my mama told me what they all lived through and we were suppose to pass it down like that from generation to generation so we'd never forget."
Corregidora 1975

2 It was as if the words were helping her, as if the words repeated again and again could be a substitute for memory, were somehow more than the memory.
Ibid.

2470. Alicia Bay Laurel (1949–)

1 When we depend less on industrially produced consumer goods, we can live in quiet places. Our bodies become vigorous; we discover the serenity of living with the rhythms of the earth. We cease oppressing one another.
Living on the Earth 1971

2 Let's all go out into the sunshine, take off our clothes, dance and sing and make love and get enlightened.
Quoted in *Contemporary Authors* 1974

2471. Holly Near (1949?–)

1 Get off me baby, get off and leave me alone
I'm lonely when you're gone but I'm lonelier when you're home. . . .
"Get Off Me Baby" 1973

2 Well if you think traveling three is a drag
Pack up loner
I've got my own bag full of dreams for this little child of wonder
and you can only stay if you start to understand. . . .
"Started Out Fine" 1973

3 Can we be like drops of water falling on the stone
Splashing, breaking, dispersing in air
Weaker than the stone by far

But be aware that as time goes by
The rock will wear away
And the water comes again
"The Rock Will Wear Away,"
St. 3, w/Meg Christian* 1976

*See 2496.

4 You were being Isadora,* I was being you
Did I know that I'd grow to say:
You've got me flying, I'm flying . . .
You inspired a sister song . . .
"You've Got Me Flying"
1976

*Isadora Duncan. See 1264.

5 Why do we kill people who are killing people
to show that killing people is wrong?
"Foolish Notion" 1980

2472. Judith Resnik (1949–1986)

1 I think something is only dangerous if you are not prepared for it or if you don't have control over it or if you can't think through how to get yourself out of a problem.
Quoted in *Time* 10 February 1986

2473. Georgia Sassen (1949–)

1 . . . [I'd gained] a heightened perception of the "other side" of competitive success, that is, the great emotional costs at which success achieved through competition is often gained—an understanding which, though confused, indicates some underlying sense that something is rotten in the state in which success is defined as having better grades than everyone else.
"Success Anxiety in Women: A
Constructivist Interpretation of Its
Sources and Its Significance,"
Harvard Educational Review, No. 50
1980

2474. Ntozake Shange (1949–)

1 ooooooooooooooh the sounds
sneakin in under age to slug's
to stare ata real 'artiste'
& every word outta imamu's mouth waz gospel
& if Jesus couldnt play a horn like shepp
waznt no need for colored folks to bear no cross at all
"now i love somebody more than,"
*for colored girls
who have considered suicide/when
the rainbow is enuf* 1977

2 TOUSSAINT L'OUVERTURE*
became my secret lover at the age of 8
i entertained him in my bedroom
widda flashlight under my covers

way inta the night/we discussed strategies
how to remove white girls from my hopscotch
  games
& etc.   "toussaint," op. cit.

*Leader of Haitian independence and emancipator of black
slaves (c.1743–1803).

3 i found god in myself
   & I loved her/i loved her fiercely
                              "a laying on
                           of hands," op. cit.

4 I am gonna write poems til i die and when i
   have gotten outta this body i am gonna hang
   round in the wind and knock over everybody
   who got their feet on the ground.
                      "advice," *Nappy Edges*
                                        1979

5 Where there is a woman there is magic. If there
   is a moon falling from her mouth, she is a
   woman who knows her magic, who can share
   or not share her powers. A woman with a moon
   falling from her mouth, roses between her legs
   and tiaras of Spanish moss, this woman is a
   consort of the spirits.
        Sassafras, Cypress and Indigo   *1982*

5 I know we got to fight the white people and be
   better than them, Gina. It's just I'm so tired of
   them and I feel so much better when I'm with
   the colored.   *Betsey Brown*   *1985*

2475. Theadora Van Runkle
   (1949?–   )

1 Death is very sophisticated. It's like a Noel
   Coward comedy. You light a cigarette and wait
   for it in the library.
           Quoted in "People You Should Know"
           by Mary Reinholz, *Viva*   *April 1974*

2476. Joan Borysenko (195?–   )

1 The work of healing is in peeling away the
   barriers of fear and past conditioning that keep
   us unaware of our true nature of wholeness and
   love.   Introduction, *Minding the Body,*
                     Mending the Mind   *1987*

2 It's only through our relations with others that
   we develop the outlook of hardiness and come
   to believe in our own capabilities and inner
   goodness.   Ibid., Ch. 1

2477. Michelle Cliff (195?–   )

1 When did we (the light-skinned middle-class
   Jamaicans) take over for them [the whites] as
   oppressors? I need to see when and how this
   happened. When what should have been reality
   was overtaken by what was surely unreality.
   When the house nigger became master.
            "If I Could Write This In fire,
               I Would Write This In
       Fire," *The Land of Look Behind,*
                                        1985

2478. Tsitsi Dangarembga (195?–   )

1 They played the new rumba that, as popular
   music will, pointed unsystematic fingers at the
   conditions of the times: 'I'll beat you up if you
   keep asking for your money,' 'Father, I am
   jobless, give me money for roora,' 'My love,
   why have taken a second wife?' There was
   swaying of hips, stamping of feet to the pulse
   of these social facts.
         Ch. 1, *Nervous Conditions*   *1988*

2 Words like 'always' and 'never' were meaningful to my father, who thought in absolutes and
   whose mind consequently made great leaps in
   antagonistic directions when it leapt at all.
                            Ibid., Ch. 2

3 "Money is a difficult thing to keep, especially
   when it is scarce."   Ibid.

4 The victimization, I saw, was universal. It didn't
   depend on poverty, on lack of education or on
   tradition. It didn't depend on any of the things
   I had thought it depended on. Men took it
   everywhere with them. Even heroes like Baba-
   mukuru did it. And that was the problem. . . .
   Femaleness as opposed and inferior to
   maleness.   Ibid., Ch. 6

2479. Doris Davenport (195?–   )

1 it is not your business,
   how i came and i can't stand
   nosey people but
   this is your business.

   i am not going back.
   so here i am.
   but what
   i am, really,
   ain't your business.
            "To The 'Majority' from A
                 'Minority'," Sts. 2 & 3
       Eat Thunder and Drink Rain   *1982*

2480. Laura Farabough (195?–)

1 A strong woman artist who is not afraid of herself, her sexuality, passion, symbols, language, who is fearless, willing to take any and all risks, often produces work that is staggeringly beautiful and at the same time frightening, dangerous, something to be reckoned with.
"Laura Farabough, *"Interviews with Contemporary Women Playwrights*, Kathleen Betsko* &Rachel Koenig   *1987*

*See 2256.

2481. Arden Fingerhut (195?–)

1 It's a cellular, biological reaction. We understand images because of who we are physically.   "The Facts of Light" by Arnold Aronson, *American Theatre   January 1986*

2482. Catherine Risingflame Moirai (195?–)

1 Every morning touch the earth.
Every night praise the worms.
Listen.   "How To Make A Garden in the City," St. 2, *Fominary*, Vol. 12, No. 1   *1982*

2483. Merle Woo (195?–)

1 Abrasive teacher, incisive comedian,
Painted Lady, dark domestic—
Sweep minds' attics; burnish our senses;
keep house, make love, wreak vengeance.
"Yellow Woman Speaks," St. 5, *Breaking Silence: An Anthology of Contemporary Asian American Poets*, Joseph Bruchac, ed.   *1982*

2484. Gloria Naylor (1950–)

1 Like his father, he saw where the future of Wayne County—the future of America—was heading. It was going to be white: white money backing wars for white power because the very earth was white—look at it—white gold, white silver, white coal running white railroads and steamships, white oil fueling white automotives. Under the earth—across the earth—and one day, over the earth. Yes, the very sky would be white. He didn't know exactly how, but it was the only place left to go. And when they got there, they weren't taking anyone black with them—and why should they?
"Linden Hills," *Linden Hills 1985*

2 "If my brothers saw me writing poems, they'd call me a queer and then it'd be all over school and I'd have to fight my way home every day. You know, most guys think you're a sissy if you like this stuff."   Ibid., "December 19th"

3 Geometry forgotten, they sat in Lester's room for hours, reciting to each other the lines that helped to harness the chaos and confusions in their fourteen-year-old worlds. Bloody noses had made them friends, but giving sound to the bruised places in their hearts made them brothers.   Ibid.

4 Willie had left school after the ninth grade. He said there was really nothing more they could teach him. He knew how to read and write and reason. And from here on in, it was all propaganda. He was not free to read the books that were important to him, not to some rusty-minded teacher. And if you wanted to write about life, you had to go where life was, among the people.   Ibid.

5 Xavier Donnell was falling in love with a black woman. It was one of the most terrifying experiences of his life.   Ibid., "December 21st"

6 Maxwell had discovered long ago that he doubled the odds of finishing first if he didn't carry the weight of that milligram of pigment in his skin. There was no feasible reason why it should have slowed him down since in mass it weighed so little, and even that was consistently distributed over his six-foot frame. But the handicap had been set centuries before it was his turn at the gate. And since he knew no tract of ground but the planet earth and no competition but the human race, he had to use the rules as written and find a way to turn a consequence into an inconsequence in his struggle to reach the finish line as a man.   Ibid.

7 "She's got this real funny idea about a diet: you don't get fat if no one sees you eating."
Ibid., "December 22nd"

8 "You there, Sister?"   *Mama Day   1988*

2485. Gigliola Pierobon (1950?–)

1 It is horrible to listen to men in black togas (in court) having discussions about your morals, your cystitis, your feelings, your womb, the way you straddled your legs.
"Gazette News: Abortion in Italy," *Ms.   October 1973*

2486. Arianna Stassinopoulos
(1950–)

1 It would be futile to attempt to fit women into a masculine pattern of attitudes, skills and abilities and disastrous to force them to suppress their specifically female characteristics and abilities by keeping up the pretense that there are no differences between the sexes.
"The Natural Woman,"
The Female Woman 1973

2 Our current obsession with creativity is the result of our continued striving for immortality in an era when most people no longer believe in an after-life. "The Working Woman," op. cit.

3 Liberation is an evershifting horizon, a total ideology that can never fulfill its promises. . . . It has the therapeutic quality of providing emotionally charged rituals of solidarity in hatred—it is the amphetamine of its believers.
"The Liberated Woman? . . .
and Her Liberators," op. cit.

2487. Wendy Wasserstein (1950–)

1 RITA. The only problem with menstruation for men is that some sensitive schmuck could write about it for the *Village Voice,* and become the new expert on women's inner life.
*Uncommon
Women and Others* 1978?

2 LEILAH. Sometimes it's difficult having sympathy with everyone's point of view. Ibid.

3 PAUL STUART. Now you girls have careers and *you* want a wife. *Isn't It Romantic* n.d.

4 LILLIAN. You tell me who has to leave the office when the kid bumps his head or slips on a milk carton. Ibid.

5 The real reason for comedy is to hide the pain. Ibid.
"Wendy Wasserstein,"
*Interviews with Contemporary
Women Playwrights,*
Kathleen Betsko* & Rachel Koenig
1987

*See 2256.

2488. Zhang Kangkang (1950–)

1 People can trace the causes and effects of the human comedies and tragedies of their times by studying history. On the other hand history is history, a pile of classical files, a science with no material benefits. Who would be interested in studying it?

"The Wasted Years," Shen Zhen,
tr., *Seven Contemporary Chinese
Women Writers,* Gladys Yang,*
ed. *1982*

*See 2076.

2 "But I think history is like a mirror reflecting the truth. We understand many things better after studying it." Ibid.

2489. Christine Bell (1951–)

1 If heat had a smell, it would smell like this: layers upon layers of rotting vegetation steaming on the jungle floor. . . . If heat had a sound, it would be this manic staccato of unseen birds and the on-again, off-again static of insects.
Saint 1985

2 And Rosa . . . she is far from idle and far from sulking. She is sweating with responsibility. She is everywhere at once and nowhere at all. She supervises, directs, organizes, aids, like a saint in religious heat. Even when she just sits and sweats, the wheels of responsibility are turning in her head. Sometimes I hear a cluck of her tongue when the wheel hits a rut. If sweat had a sound, it would be Rosa's tongue clucking. Ibid.

2490. Joy Harjo (1951–)

1 i am a dangerous woman
but the weapon is not visible
security will never find it
they can't hear the clicking
of the gun
        inside my head
"I Am a Dangerous Woman,"
St. 4, *That's What She Said,*
Rayna Green, ed.* 1984

*See 2284.

2 He's half Creek, half plains.
I'm part Creek and white.
"Which part do you want tonight?"
I ask him.
"It's the Same at Four A.M.,"
St. 1, op. cit.

3 Remember the earth whose skin you are.
Red earth yellow earth white earth brown earth
black earth we are earth.
Remember the plants, trees, animal life who
all have their
tribes, their families, their histories, too. Talk
to them,
listen to them. They are alive poems.
"Remember," op. cit.

4   But she needs
the feel of danger,
          for life.   (It Helps Her Remember.)
               "Noni Daylight Remembers the
               Future," Sts. 3 & 4, op. cit.

5 The woman hanging from the 13th floor window
on the east side of Chicago is not alone.
. . . .
She is all the women of the apartment
building who stand watching her, watching
themselves
               "The Woman Hanging from the 13th
               Floor Window," St. 3, op. cit.

2491. Barbara Holland (1951–   )

1 Speech that is but percussion under melody is
bones to music. I do not understand a word you
say, and yet you tell me in your rhythms, your
harmonies, and richness of their structure.
                    "Translation," St. 1
                    The East Side Scene,
               Allen De Loach, ed.   *1968*

2492. Janis Ian (1951–   )

1   How do you do
     would you like
     to be friends?
No I just want a bed for the night
someone to tell me they care.
You can fake it, that's all right
In the morning I won't be here.
                    "The Come On"   *1974*

2493. Miriam Simos (1951–   )

1 Ritual is the original womb of art; its waters
continue to nourish creativity.
                    Truth or Dare   *1987*

2494. Phoebe Snow (1951–   )

1 I'd like to be a willow, a lover, a mountain
Or a soft refrain
But I'd hate to be a grownup
And have to try to bear
My life in pain.
          "Harpo's Blues," *Phoebe Snow*   *1973*

2 Sometimes this face looks so funny
That I hide it behind a book
Sometimes this face has so much class
That I have to sneak a second look.
                    "Either or Both," op. cit.

3 It must be Sunday
Everybody's telling the truth. . . .
               "It Must Be Sunday," op. cit.

2495. Denise M. Boudrot (1952–   )

1 I don't ride to beat the boys, just to win.
               Quoted in *Women at Work*
               by Betty Medsger   *1975*

2496. Meg Christian* (1952?–   )

1 Mama, oh, my Mama, well, do you under-
stand
Why I've not bound myself to a man?
Is something buried in your old widow's mind
That blesses my choice of our own kind?
Oh, Mama, Mama.
          "Song to My Mama," Verse 3, *I Know
                    You Know* (album)   *1974*

2 She was a big tough woman, the first to come
along
That showed me being female meant you still
could be strong;
And though graduation meant that we had to
part,
She'll always be a player on the ballfield of
my heart.
          "Ode to a Gym Teacher," Chorus, op. cit.

* Also see 2471:3.

2497. Mildred Clingerman (fl. 1952)

1 Nobody really looks at a bartender. . . . Even
the bar philosophers (the dreariest customers of
all) prefer to study their own faces in the back-
bar mirror. And however they accept their reflected images, whether shudderingly or with
secret love, it is to this aloof image that they
impart their whisky-wisdom, not to the
bartender.   *Stair Trick*   *1952*

2 She faced him as if he were Judgment and she
standing up pleading for mankind.   Ibid.

2498. Ferron (1952–   )

1 But by our light be we spirit,
And by our hearts be we women,
And by our eyes be we open,
And by our hands be we wide.
                    "Testimony"   *1980*

2499. Beth Henley (1952–   )

1 CHICK. They say each cigarette is just a little
stick of cancer. A little death stick.

MEG. That's what I like about it, Chick—taking a drag off of death. Mmm! Gives me a sense of controlling my own destiny. What power! What exhilaration! Want a drag?

Act I, Crimes of the Heart   1979

2 BABE. He started hating me, 'cause I couldn't laugh at his jokes. I just started finding it impossible to laugh at his jokes the way I used to. And then the sound of his voice got to where it tired me out awful bad to hear it. I'd fall asleep just listening to him at the dinner table.   Ibid.

3 . . . I find it fascinating to think about what the world is going to be like when people won't talk anymore. There are probably brilliant people, geniuses, alive today who don't even know how to say, "Hello, how do you do?" because their minds are absorbed with electronic images.   "Beth Henley," *Interviews with Contemporary Women Playwrights,* Kathleen Betsko* & Rachel Koenig   1987

*See 2256.

4 And all writing is creating or spinning dreams for other people so they won't have to bother doing it themselves.   Ibid.

2500. Michele Wallace (1952–   )

1 On April 4 King* was shot and the rioting began again, worse than ever. Praying, waiting, singing, and everything white were out. Rioting was viewed as urban guerrilla warfare, the first step toward the complete overthrow of the honky, racist government. On the cultural level everything had to be rehauled. Black poems, plays, paintings, novels, hairstyles, and apparel were springing up like weeds in Central Park. Brothers, with softly beating drums in the background, were talking about beautiful black Queens of the Nile and beautiful full lips and black skin and big asses.   Pt. I, Ch. 1, *Black Macho and The Myth of the Superwoman   1978*

*Martin Luther King, Jr., American civil rights leader and minister (1929–1968); Nobel Peace Prize, 1964.

2 I am saying, among other things, that for perhaps the last fifty years there has been a growing distrust, even hatred, between black men and black women. It has been nursed along not only by racism on the part of whites but also by an almost deliberate ignorance on the part of blacks about the sexual politics of their experience in this country.   Ibid.

3 The driving force behind the [Black Power] movement had really very little to do with bread and butter needs. The motive was revenge. It was not equality that was primarily being pur-

sued but a kind of superiority—black manhood, black macho. . . . And when the black man went as far as the adoration of his own genitals could carry him, his revolution stopped. A big Afro, a rifle, and a penis in good working order were not enough to lick the white man's world after all.   Ibid., Ch. 2

4 From the intricate web of mythology which surrounds the black woman, a fundamental image emerges. It is of a woman of inordinate strength, with an ability for tolerating an unusual amount of misery and heavy, distasteful work. This woman does not have the same fears, weaknesses, and insecurities as other women, but believes herself to be and is, in fact, stronger emotionally than most men. Less of a woman in that she is less "feminine" and helpless, she is really more of a woman in that she is the embodiment of Mother Earth, the quintessential mother with infinite sexual, life-giving, and nurturing reserves. In other words, she is a superwoman.   Ibid., Pt. II, Ch. 1

2501. Benazir Bhutto (1953–   )

1 Every dictator uses religion as a prop to keep himself in power.

Interview, 60 Minutes, CBS-TV 8 August 1986

2 A ship in port is safe, but that is not what ships are built for.   Ibid.

3 When a government is run at gunpoint, the youth of the country get the impression that real power comes from holding a gun, not from laws. With the restoration of free debate, students' minds will automatically switch from guns to books.   Inaugural Speech, Quoted by Barbara Crossette in *The New York Times   3 December 1988*

4 What is not recorded is not remembered.

Daughter of Destiny   1989

5 You can't be fueled by bitterness. It can eat you up, but it cannot drive you.   Ibid.

2502. Susan Seidelman (1953–   )

1 Failure is a luxury not yet afforded to women.   Quoted in "Calling Their Own Shots" by Richard Corliss, *Time   24 March 1986*

2503. Marilyn Waring (1953–   )

1 What I find so offensive about it [the Moral Majority] in terms of Christian dogma is that it plays on fear, not love.

Quoted in "Gazette News: Marilyn Waring—New Zealand's Feisty M.P." by Robin Morgan,*
Ms.   December 1981

*See 2327.

2 I don't use all the operative academic words, but it seems you can have power *to,* or you can have power *for,* or you can have power *over,* or you're power*less.*   Ibid.

3 Since the patriarchy has designated to us power as consumers, then let's do actions that break down national boundaries.   Ibid.

2504. Louise Erdrich (1954–   )

1 She can't keep much trash in a Mustang, and that's what she likes. Travel light.
  Don't keep
what does not have immediate uses. The road thinks ahead.
              "The Lady in the Pink Mustang,"
                st. 3, *That's What She Said*
              Rayna Green,* ed.   *1984*

*See 2284.

2 The drum breaks. There will be no parlance.
Only arrows whining, a death-cloud of nerves swarming down on the settlers
who die beautifully, tumbling like dust weeds
into the history that brought us all here
together: this wide screen beneath the sign of
  the bear.   "Dear John Wayne," St. 3,
                            op. cit.

3 Our tribe unraveled like a coarse rope, frayed at either end as the old and new among us were taken.   *Tracks   1988*

4 Land is the only thing that lasts life to life. Money burns like tinder, flows off like water. And as for government promises, the wind is steadier.   Ibid.

5 Even when you plan to have a family, you never know who the person is going to be that you decide to become a parent to. We're accidentally born to our own parents.
                    Quoted in *A World of
              Ideas* by Bill Moyers   *1989*

6 Columbus only discovered that he was in some new place. He didn't discover America.   Ibid.

7 The ordained push West was supposed to clear the land of the native inhabitants. They were supposed to vanish before progress. That never happened. There are over three hundred tribes surviving and somehow managing to keep together language, culture, and religion. These are not visible people.   Ibid.

2505. Rickie Lee Jones (1954–   )

1 Ask me if you want to know
  The way to Coolsville
                  "Coolsville," *RLJ   1979*

2 And if she don't know your name
She knows what you got
From your matzo balls
To the chicken-in-the-pot
              "Danny's All-Star Joint"
                (1978), op. cit.

3 There are wounds that stir up the force of gravity:
a cold that will wipe the hope from your eyes.   "Gravity" (1983) *The
                        Magazine   1984*

4 Draw the Weird Beast
  everywhere you go.
Death speaks the foreign
  language we don't know.
Make sure they hear him
  breathing.   "Rorschachs B. The Weird
                    Beast" (1984)
                        op. cit.

2506. Wang Anyi (1954–   )

1 How a comfortable life can improve one's tolerance of others! "Life in a Small Courtyard,"
              Ch. 1, Hu Zhihui, tr.,
          *Seven Contemporary Chinese
            Women Writers,* Gladys
              Yang,* ed.   *1982*

*See 2076.

2 How I long for some hot soup! Aping held my hands tenderly. Though I had worn two pairs of gloves, my hands were still cold. He put them into the pockets of his overcoat. I drew them out at once. I didn't want such tenderness. What I needed badly was a stable family life, not embraces and kisses!   Ibid., Ch. 3

3 "Our life was so beautiful and we were so deeply in love. So we're not poor at all."
  "We're only short of money," Ziao Ji added drily. We all laughed.   Ibid., Ch. 4

2507. Sherley Anne Williams (1954–   )

1 "Oh, we have paid for our children's place in the world again, and again . . ."
                  Dessa Rose   1986

2508. Chris Evert Lloyd (1955–   )

1 Once you've been No. 1, you can never be satisfied with less.

Quoted in "Fire Over Ice"
by Tom Callahan, *Time*
15 July 1985

2 My whole career, people have been talking about how tough I am. Now that I'm losing some, I can see how tough I was—the killer instinct, the single-mindedness, playing like a machine. Boy, that's what made me a champion. Quoted in "I Can See How Tough I Was" by William A. Henry III, *Time* *11 September 1989*

2509. Raven (1955–)

1 I'm dying slowly. I need to feel the earth under my feet. This place resembles a tomb. I'm sealed way from the things that make living, living. I need fresh air and space to move. I often asks the guards to bring me a cup of fresh air . . . Letter to Beth Brant* (6 January 1983) *A Gathering of Spirit*, Beth Brant, ed. *1984*

*See 2314.

2 Many christians write [to me], but I do not believe the way they do. They are really weird sometimes. I usually ignore them. They only want to save my soul. I need to save my life. Letter to Beth Brant (26 January 1983), op. cit.

2510. Margaret Casey (1956–1985)

1 It hurts not being a contender.
Quoted in *Time* *10 June 1985*

2510.1 Anita Hill (1956–)

1 I had to tell the truth.
Quoted in "A Moment of Truth," *Newsweek*
21 October 1991

2 I would have preferred not to endure what I endured . . .*
Speech, Hunter College, New York City (25 April 1992),
Quoted in *New York Times*
by Deborah Sontag
26 April 1992

*Referring to the Clarence Thomas sexual harassment hearings held by the U. S. Senate Judiciary Committee, October 1991.

3 . . . we need to turn the question around to look at the harasser, not the target. We need to be sure that we can go out and look anyone who is a victim of harassment in the eye and say, "You do not have to remain silent anymore." Ibid.

2511. Naomi Littlebear (1956?–)

1 You can't kill the spirit
It's like a mountain
old and strong; it lives on and on.
"Like A Mountain" *1976*

2512. Aurelia Potor (fl. 1956)

1 Middle-aged rabbits don't have a paunch, do have their own teeth and haven't lost their romantic appeal.
Quoted in *The New York Times*
22 September 1956

2513. Martha Kegel (1958–)

1 The proponents of this law [scientific creationism] are trying to sneak religion into the public schools. They are trying to disguise the religious nature of the doctrine of creationism. They have dressed this law with verbal fig leaves, nicesounding phrases like "equal time" and "nondiscrimination." But the fact remains that creationism is a Bible story and teaching it as science in public schools violates the rights of religious minorities.
Quoted in *Hammond Daily Star*
3 December 1981

2514. Florence Griffith Joyner (1959–)

1 I don't think a person has to use drugs [to excel in athletics]. There is no substitute for hard work. Quoted in "For Speed and Style, Flo with the Go" by Ellie McGrath, *Time*
19 September 1988

2515. Marjorie Karmel (fl. 1959)

1 It is a great pity that a man should stand back, helpless and inadequate, *de trop,* while his wife alone knows the profound experience of the birth of the child they have created together.
Ch. 3, *Thank You, Dr. Lamaze*
1959

2 Who ever said that doctors are truthful or even intelligent? You're getting a lot if they know their profession. Don't ask any more from them. They're only human after all—which is to say, you can't expect much. Ibid., Ch. 7

3 "One-way first-name calling always means inequality—witness servants, children and dogs." Ibid.

2516. Maya Lin (1959–)

1 You really can't function as a celebrity. Entertainers are celebrities. I'm an architect. I'm an artist, I make things.
Quoted in "First She Looks Inward"
by Jonathan Coleman, *Time*
6 November 1989

2 Architecture is like a mythical fantastic. It *has* to be experienced. It can't be described. We can draw it up and we can make models of it, but it can only be experienced as a complete whole. Ibid.

3 If you don't remember history accurately, how can you learn? Ibid.

2517. Suzanne Vega (1959–)

1 Today I am
a small blue thing
Like a marble
or an eye   "Small Blue Thing," *Suzanne*
Vega   1985

2 Solitude stands by the window
She turns her head as I walk in the room
I can see by her eyes she's been waiting
Standing in the slant of the late afternoon
"Solitude Standing"   *1987*

3 I believe right now if I could
I would swallow you whole
I would leave only bones and teeth
We could see what was underneath
And we could be free then.
"The Undertow"   *n.d.*

2518. Frances M. Beal (fl. 1960s)

1 The advertising media in this country continuously informs the American male of his need for indispensable signs of his virility . . .
"Double Jeopardy: To Be Black and
Female" (1969), *Sisterhood Is*
Powerful, Robin Morgan,* ed.
1970

*See 2327.

2 Let me state here and now that the black woman in America can justly be described as a "slave of a slave." Ibid.

3 Men may be cruelly exploited and subjected to all sorts of dehumanizing tactics on the part of the ruling class, but they have someone who is below them—at least they're not women. Ibid.

4 To die for the revolution is a one-shot deal; to live for the revolution means taking on the more

difficult commitment of changing our day-to-day life patterns. Ibid.

2519. Christine Billson (fl. 1960s)

1 I am admired because I do things well. I cook, sew, knit, talk, work and make love very well. So I am a valuable item. Without me he would suffer. With him I am alone. I am as solitary as eternity and sometimes as stupid as clotted cream. Ha ha ha! Don't think! Act as if all the bills are paid. *You Can Touch Me*
1961

2520. Enriqueta Longauex y Vasquez (fl. 1960s)

1 A woman who has no way of expressing herself and of realizing herself as a full human has nothing else to turn to but the owning of material things.   "The Mexican-American Woman,"
Sisterhood Is Powerful,
Robin Morgan,* ed.   *1970*

*See 2327.

2 The Anglo woman is always there with her superiority complex. Ibid.

3 When a family is involved in a human rights movement, as is the Mexican-American family, there is little room for a woman's liberation movement alone. Ibid.

2521. Susanna Millar (fl. 1960s)

1 If animals play, this is because play is useful in the struggle for survival; because play practices and so perfects the skills needed in adult life.   Ch. 1, *The Psychology of Play*
1968

2 For the healthy, a monotonous environment eventually produces discomfort, irritation and attempts to vary it. Ibid., Ch. 4

3 The social life of a child starts when he is born. Ibid., Ch. 7

2522. Octavia Waldo (fl. 1960s)

1 The rain fell like a cascade of pine needles over Rome. Rain—thirty days of it. It marked the interlude between winter and spring, and spring was late in coming. There was nothing to do about it but wait. There is nothing to do about most things that are late in Rome, whether it be

an appointment, or a bus, or a promise. Or even hope.
> "Roman Spring," Ch. 1 *American Scene: New Voices*, Don Wolfe, ed. *1963*

2 ". . . Adam Maxwell, age twenty-four, husband to Ruth. A boy who wants to go to the top. As if the world has a top!" *Ibid.*

3 The lazy pattern of living had reinstated itself, had returned an assuagement made of compromises and complacency. It had made things safe again between them. *Ibid.*, Ch. 2

2523. Edie Brickell (1966?–)

1 Philosophy is the talk on a cereal box
> "What I Am" *n.d.*

2 There's nothing I hate more than nothing
Nothing keeps me up at night
I toss and turn over nothing
Nothing could cause a great big fight
> "Nothing" *n.d.*

2524. Tanita Tikaram (196?–)

1 Look my eyes are just holograms
> "twist in my sobriety"
> *n.d.*

2 Chances, changes are all that you have
> "i love you"
> *n.d.*

2525. Brigit Dressel (1961–1987)

1 These are all harmless drugs.* All athletes take them. It's really nothing special.
> Comment to mother,
> Quoted in "An Athlete Dying
> Young," *Time* *10 October 1988*

*Referring to use of steroids.

2526. Jackie Joyner-Kersee (1962–)

1 Ask any athlete: we all hurt at all times. I'm asking my body to go through seven different tasks. To ask it not to ache would be too much. Quoted in "Regal Masters of Olympic
> Versatility" by Tom Callahan,
> *Time* *19 September 1988*

2 Jumping has always been the thing to me. It's like leaping for joy. . . . *Ibid.*

3 I don't think being an athlete is unfeminine. I think of it as a kind of grace. *Ibid.*

2527. Beatrice Conrad (fl. 1963)

1 Their lives had intertwined into a comfortable dependency, like the gnarled wisteria on their front porch, still twisted around the frail support which long ago it had outgrown.
> "The Night of the Falling Star,"
> *American Scene: New Voices,*
> Don Wolfe, ed. *1963*

2 We are poor helpless creatures on an undistinguished plant in an obscure corner of a small and fading universe. *Ibid.*

2528. Tracy Chapman (1964–)

1 I love you
is all that you can't say
> "Baby Can I Hold You" (1982), *Tracy Chapman* *1988*

2 It won't do no good to call
The police
Always come late
If they come at all
> "Behind the Wall" (1983), op. cit.

3 And those whose sole misfortune
Was having mountains o' nothing at birth
> "Mountains O' Things" (1987),
> op. cit.

2529. Virginie des Rieux (fl. 1967)

1 "Gentlemen, in life, there is one thing that fascinates everybody, and that's rear ends. Talk about backsides and only backsides, and you will have friends everywhere always."
> Ch. 1, *La Satyre* *1967*

2 Marriage is a lottery in which men stake their liberty and women their happiness. Epigram
> *n.d.*

2530. Geneviève Antoine-Dariaux (fl. 1968–1973)

1 [Habit]
is the chloroform of love.
is the cement that unites married couples.
is getting stuck in the mud of daily routine.
is the fog that masks the most beautiful scenery.
is the end of everything.
> "The Men in Your Life" *1968*

2 A stranger loses half his charm the day he is no longer a stranger. *Ibid.*

3 She began to think about her friends' happy tranquillity, of their affection, of their two non-

problem children: the boy wasn't on drugs; the girl wasn't a nymphomaniac; they weren't even quarrelsome. The kind of children nobody had any more. *Ch. 1 The Fall Collection* *1973*

2531. Alice Embree (fl. 1970s)

1 Shortly after the turn of the century, America marshalled her resources, contracted painfully, and gave birth to the New Technology. The father was a Corporation, and the New Technology grew up in the Corporate image.
"Media Images I: Madison Avenue Brainwashing—The Facts," *Sisterhood Is Powerful,* Robin Morgan,* ed. *1970*

*See 2327.

2 Humans must breathe, but corperations must make money. *Ibid.*

3 The message of the media is the commercial. *Ibid.*

4 America's technology has turned in upon itself; its corporate form makes it the servant of profits, not the servant of human needs. *Ibid.*

2532. Annette Motley (fl. 1970s–1980s)

1 "Ah, Second Daughter, your imagination takes you journeying as far as any traveller."
"Is that a curse, or a blessing, do you think?"
"A blessing, surely as long as imagination outstrips desire." *Pt. 1, Ch. 3, Green Dragon, White Tiger* *1986*

2 How the Chinese man loved to build such walls. It was part of his temperament. He built them around his cities and his houses; around his women; and most of all around his inmost thoughts. *Ibid., Ch. 4*

2533. Judy Syfers (fl. 1970s)

1 My God, who *wouldn't* want a wife?
"I Want a Wife," *The First Ms. Reader,* Francine Klagsbrun, ed. *1972*

2534. Loma Chandler (fl. 1973)

1 Sometimes asylums are just what they should be—a resting place for people who get lost in life. "They're Expecting Us," *Reader's Digest* *October 1973*

2 A smile appeared upon her face as if she'd taken it directly from her handbag and pinned it there. *Ibid.*

2535. Helen Dudar (fl. 1973)

1 Contrary to the folklore of abortion as lifelong trauma, it is not necessarily a profoundly scarring one either.
"Abortion for the Asking," *Saturday Review of the Society* *April 1973*

2 In this era of radicalized and politicized clergy, it is no longer even surprising when a woman shows up at [an abortion] clinic with the blessing of her priest. *Ibid.*

2536. Merle Shain (fl. 1973)

1 We tend to think of the rational as a higher order, but it is the emotional that marks our lives. One often learns more from ten days of agony than from ten years of contentment. . . .
Pt. 1, Ch. 1, Some Men are More Perfect Than Others *1973*

2 Most women would rather have someone whisper their name at optimum moments than rocket with contractions to the moon. . . . *Ibid., Ch. 3*

3 So mistresses tend to get a steady diet of whipped cream, but no meat and potatoes, and wives often get the reverse, when both would like a bit of each. *Ibid., Pt. II, Ch. 4*

2537. Sonya Rudikoff (fl. 1974)

1 Although there are countless alumni of the school of hard knocks, there has not yet been a move to accredit that institution.
"Women and Success," *Commentary* *October 1974*

2 The embattled gates to equal rights have indeed opened up for modern women, but I sometimes think to myself: "That is not what I meant by freedom—it is only 'social progress.' " *Ibid.*

3 There are surely lives which display very few of the signs of success until very late, or after life is over. There are lives of great significance which go unrecognized by peers for a very long time, there are those who achieve nothing for themselves but leave a legacy for others who come after, there are lives sacrificed for causes. *Ibid.*

4 Should we, perhaps, see the development of the commune movement in another light, as a less

expensive form of summer camp for a growing population—post-adolescent, post-industrial, post-Christian and unemployed?

Article in *Commentary* 1974

2538. Carol Polowy (fl. 1975)

1 Educational institutions mirror the stereotypes of the larger society. The fact that education has become known as a "woman's field" stems at least in part from the identification of childcare and child-rearing as woman's work. Men frequently view teaching as a stepping stone to educational administration while women look to careers as classroom teachers.

Address, 'Sex Discrimination: The Legal Obligations of Educational Institutions," *Vital Speeches 1 February 1975*

2 When textbooks are examined in terms of their presentation and reinforcement of a social order, women and minority groups are dissatisfied with the lack of reality in the presentation. Ibid.

2539. Margaret Sloan (fl. 1975)

1 We feel that there can't be liberation for less than half a race. We want *all* black people in this country to be free.

Manifesto, National Black Feminist Organization 1975

2 It has been hard for black women to emerge from the myriad of distorted images that have portrayed us as grinning Beulahs, castrating Sapphires, and pancake-box Jemimahs. Ibid.

2540. Brita Westergaard (fl. 1980s)

1 We are not just changing Norway.* When people realize that this is possible in the Cabinet of one country, they must realize it is possible everywhere. Quoted in "An Experiment in Woman Power" by Michael S. Serrill, *Time* 6 October 1986

*Reference to stunning increase in the number of women selected to serve on the Norwegian Cabinet by Gro Brundtland; See 2258.

BIOGRAPHICAL INDEX

Notes to Biographical Index

Every contributor is listed alphabetically and her contributor number given (these numbers will be found in page headings throughout the Quotations sections). Women well known by a name other than the one used at the heading of their entries in the Quotations section are cross-indexed here. All co-authors are listed except "as told to" authors.

Brief biographical information is given for each woman: her full name (those parts of her name not used at the heading of her quotations are in brackets), and any hereditary or honorary title she is known to hold; her nationality, and—if different—her country of residence (e.g., Am./It. indicates a woman was born in the United States but has lived most of her life in Italy); her profession(s); other names by which she is or may have been known; her family relationship to other well-known persons, along with biographical data on them (names of relatives followed by an asterisk indicate contributors in this book); any "firsts" or outstanding achievements for which she is responsible; any major awards or honors she is known to have received.

Abbreviations (other than nationality which, I believe, are quite clear) are as follows: h.— name by marriage; m.—mother of; w.—wife of; d.—daughter of; s.—sister of; pseud.—fictitious name used specifically in her work; aka (also known as)—nicknames, aliases, and any other names by which she may be known; asa (also seen as)—alternate spellings.

The term educator encompasses teachers, professors—whether full, associate or assistant— and other instructors; college administrators are specifically designated. The term composer is used in reference to classical music; composers of popular music are designated as songwriters. A word about the alphabetization of names: many women nobles, women of the Middle Ages, and many Asian women are alphabetized by family names (or what appears to the contemporary Western eye as a "first" name).

A

Abbott, Berenice (1898–1991) 1513
  Am. photographer, writer; technical pioneer of photographic equipment
Abbott, Sidney (1937–) 2207
  Am. writer.
Abbott, Wenonah Stevens (1865–1950) 1112
  Am. journalist, poet
Abel of Beth-maacah, Woman of (fl. c.1040–970 B.C.) 24
  Isr. peacemaker
Abergavenny, [Lady] Frances (fl. 1580s) 319
  Eng. poet; asa Bergavenny, aka Elizabeth Fane, Frances Manners; m. Lady Marie Fane
Abigail (fl. c.990 B.C.) 20
  Judean; w. Naval (1) and David (2), m. Chileah

Abzug, Bella (1920–) 1873
  Am. lawyer, politician; née Savitsky
Ace, Jane (1905–1974) 1631
  Am. comedian, radio personality; née Sherwood; w. Goodman A- (1899–1982, television and radio comedy writer)
Adams, Abigail (1744–1818) 553
  Am. first lady, letter writer, feminist; née Smith; w. John A- (2nd U.S. pres.), m. John Quincy A- (6th U.S. pres.), m-in-law Louisa Catherine A-,* s. Elizabeth Peabody*
Adams, Grace (1900–?) 1541
  Am. psychologist; née Kinckle
Adams, Louisa Catherine (1775–1852) 668
  Eng./Am. first lady; née Johnson; w. John Quincy A- (6th U.S. pres.), d.-in-law Abigail A-,* grandm. Henry A-

B

Babitz, Eve (1942?–)   2341
  Am. writer
Bacall, Lauren (1924–)   1929
  Am. actor, author; née Betty Joan Perske;
  widow of Humphrey Bogart (actor), ex-w.
  Jason Robards (actor); Antoinette Perry
  (Tony) Award, 1970; Natl. Book Award,
  1980
Bache, Sarah (1744–1808)   555
  Am. letter writer; d. Benjamin Franklin,
  great aunt of Gertrude Atherton*
Bachman, Moira (fl. 1940s)   2280
  Am. labor activist?
Bachmann, Ingeborg (1926–1973)   1962
  Ger. writer, novelist
Backus, Bertha Adams (fl. 1910s)   1708
  Poet
Bacon, Anne Cooke (c.1528–1610?)   272
  Eng. author, translator; d. Anthony Cooke,
  s. Elizabeth Hoby Russell,* Catherine Kil-
  ligrew,* and Lady Mildred Burleigh, m.
  Francis B- and Anthony B-
Bacon, Josephine Dodge [Daskam] (1876–
  1961)   1235
  Am. writer, poet, humorist
Baez, Joan (1941–)   2313
  Am. singer, songwriter, civil rights activist;
  founder of Institute for the Study of Non-
  violence, California
Bagnold, Enid (1889–1981)   1396
  Eng. playwright, writer; h. Lady Jones
Bai, Mira (1498–1547)   240
  Ind. Hindu saint, poet, princess
Bai, Mukta (fl. 13th cen.)   173
  Ind. poet, beggar
Bai Fengxi (1932?–)   2095
  Chin. playwright, actor
Bailey, Pearl [Mae] (1918–1986)   1836
  Am. singer; h. Bellson
Bailey, Urania Locke [Stoughton] (1820–1882)   841
  Am. evangelist, writer; pseud. Julia Gill,
  Una Locke
Baillie, Grisell (see Home, Grisell)
Baillie, Joanna (1762–1851)   618
  Scot./Eng. poet, dramatist
Baillie, Margaret (see Saunders, Margaret
  Baillie)
Baker, Dorothy [Dodds] (1907–1968)   1667
  Am. writer
Baker, Dorothy Gillam (1906–)   1652
  Am. educator, peace activist; née Gillam
Baker, Ella (1903–)   1598
  Am. civil rights activist; founding member
  of Young Negroes Cooperative League,
  1932, Student Nonviolent Coordinating
  Committee (SNCC), 1960, and Mississippi
  Freedom Democratic Party, 1964
Baker, Josephine (1906–1975)   1653
  Am./Fr. exotic dancer

Baldwin, Faith (1893–1978)   1447
  Am. writer; h. Cuthrell
Baldwin, Monica (1896–)   1486
  Eng. writer, ex-nun
Ball, Lucille (1911–1989)   1732
  Am. actor, comedian, television producer;
  Emmy Award, 1952, 1955, 1967, 1968
Ballard, Bettina (1903–1961)   1599
  Am. editor
Bankhead, Tallulah (1903–1968)   1600
  Am. actor
Bannerman, Helen (1862–1946)   1097
  Am. writer
Banning, Margaret Culkin (1891–1982)   1420
  Am. writer
Barbauld, Anna Letitia (1743–1825)   550
  Eng. poet, essayist, editor, bluestocking;
  née Aiken, aunt of Lucy Aiken*
Barber, Margaret Fairless (1869–1901)   1147
  Eng. writer; pseud. Michael Fairless
Barber, Mary (1690?–1757)   459
  Ir./Eng. poet; aka Sapphira
Bard, Ann Elizabeth Campbell (see Mac-
  Donald, Betty)
Bardot, Brigitte (1934–)   2144
  Fr. actor
Barfoot, Joan (1946–)   2421
  Can. novelist, journalist
Barker, Elsa (1869–1954)   1148
  Am. poet, writer
Barker, Jane (fl. 1688–1715)   457
  Eng. poet, novelist
Barker, Myrtie Lillian (1910–)   1714
  Am. journalist, writer
Barnard, A. M. (see Alcott, Louisa May)
Barnard, Anne, Lady (1750–1825)   566
  Scot. poet, letter writer; née Lindsay
Barnard, Charlotte [Arlington] (1830–1869)   890
  Eng. ballad writer; pseud. Claribel
Barnes, Djuna (1892–1982)   1433
  Am. writer, journalist, playwright, artist,
  illustrator; pseud. Lydia Steptoe
Barnes, Julians (see Berners, [Dame] Juliana)
Barnes, Margaret Ayer (1886–1967)   1363
  Am. writer; Pulitzer Prize, 1931
Barolini, Helen (1925–)   1947
  Am. writer, translator; née Mollica
Baron, Marie le (see le Baron, Marie)
Barr, Amelia [Edith Huddleston] (1831–1919)   900
  Eng./Am. writer
Barr, Mary A. (1852–?)   1022
  Scot. writer
Barreno, Maria Isabel (1939–)   2254
  Port. writer, poet
Barrett, Rona (1938–)   2235
  Am. columnist, television personality
Barrington, Judith [M.] (1944–)   2382
  Eng./Am. poet
Barrymore, Ethel (1879–1959)   1269
  Am. actor; Academy Award, 1944

Barton, Clara (1821–1912) 853
Am. nurse, writer; aka "The Angel of the Battlefield"; founder of the American Red Cross; Hall of Fame, 1976

Bashkirtseff, Marie Konstantinovna (1860–1884) 1073
Russ. artist, diarist

Bates, Katherine Lee (1859–1929) 1063
Am. poet, educator

Bateson, Mary Catherine (1939–) 2255
Am. anthropologist, scholar, author, educator; d. Margaret Mead* and Gregory B- (1904–1980, anthropologist)

Bathsheba (fl. c.1000–970 B.C.) 25
Judean queen; w. Ukiah (1) and David, king of Israel (2), m. Solomon

Bat-Miriam, Yocheved (1901–) 1569
Isr. poet

Baudonivia (fl. 6th cen.) 92
Frankish nun, biographer; founder of the Abbey of the Holy Cross

Baum, Vicki (1888–1960) 1382
Austr./Am. writer, playwright, scenarist

Bayly, Ada Ellen (see Lyall, Edna)

Baynard, Anne (1672–1697) 442
Eng. scholar

Bazan, Emilia Pardo, Condesa de (1852–1921) 1023
Sp. novelist, educator, stateswoman, feminist

B. B. [Mrs. Bogan of Bogan] (see Nairne, Carolina)

Beal, Frances M. (fl. 1960s) 2518
Am. civil rights activist

Beals, Jessie Tarbox (1870–1942) 1163
Am. photographer; first woman press photographer in U.S.

Beard, Mary Ritter (1876–1958) 1236
Am. historian; w. Charles Austin B-

Beard, Miriam (1901–) 1570
Am. writer, humorist, feminist

Beatritz de Dia (c.1140–post–1189?) 161
Provençal trobairitz; asa Beatrice, aka countess of Die; d.? Marguerite de Bourgogne and Comte Guigues IV (dauphin of the Viennois and count of Albon), w. Guillem de Poitiers (count of Valentinois?), m. Aymar (count of Dia), lover of Raimbaut of Orange

Beauveau, Marie [Françoise Catherine] de (1711–1786) 482
Fr. poet; aka marquise de Boufflers

Beauvoir, Simone [Lucie Ernestine Marie Bertrand] de (1908–1986) 1680
Fr. writer, philosopher, feminist; lover of Jean Paul Sartre (1905–1980, philosopher, playwright); Prix Goncourt, 1954

Bedford, Countess of (see Harington, Lucy)

Beecher, Catharine Esther (1800–1878) 758
Am. educator, writer

Beers, Ethel Lynn (1827–1879) 880
Am. poet; née Eliot; pseud. Ethelinda Eliott

Begbie, Janet (fl. 1910s) 1709
Eng. poet

Behn, Aphra (1640–1689) 406
Eng. novelist, dramatist, poet, translator, spy; née Johnson or Amis, asa Afra, Aphara, Ayfara, aka Astrea

Belenky, Mary Field (1933–) 2124
Am. educator, researcher, author

Bell, Acton (see Bronte, Emily)

Bell, Christine (1951–) 2489
Am. writer

Bell, Currer (see Bronte, Charlotte)

Bell, Helen Olcott (1830–1918) 891
Am. writer; d. Rufus Choates

Bender, Marilyn (1925–) 1948
Am. journalist; h. Altschul

Benedict, Ruth [Fulton] (1887–1948) 1373
Am. anthropologist, biographer, poet; pseud. Anne Singleton

Benét, Laura (1884–1979) 1330
Am. poet, writer, biographer

Benet, Mother (fl. 1558) 298
Eng. commoner

Bengis, Ingrid (1944?–) 2383
Am. writer

Benson, Stella (1892–1933) 1434
Eng. writer, poet

Benston, Margaret Lowe (1937–) 2209
Am. physical chemist, educator

Berenson, Mary [Logan Whitall Costelloe] (1864–1945) 1109
Am. art historian, writer; w. Bernard B-

Bergen, Candice (1946–) 2422
Am. actor, playwright, writer, photographer; d. Edgar Bergen (ventriloquist), w. Louis Malle (Fr. film director)

Bergman, Ingrid (1915–1982) 1786
Swed. actor; w. Robert Rosselini (Ital. film director); Academy Awards, 1944, 1956, 1974; Antoinette Perry Award, 1947; Emmy Award, 1960

Bernadette, Saint (1844–1879) 972
Fr. Roman Catholic saint; née Marie-Bernarde Soubirous

Bernard, Jessie Shirley (1903–) 1601
Am. sociologist, author; w. L. L. B- (1881–?, collaborator)

Berners, Juliana, Dame (1388?–?) 201
Eng. poet; asa Bernes, aka Julians Barnes; first known English woman poet and author

Bernhardt, Sarah (1844–1923) 973
Fr. actor, writer; aka "The Divine Sarah"

Bernikow, Louise (1940–) 2289
Am. journalist, poet

Berry, Dorothy (fl. 1630s) 391
Eng. poet; pseud. only

Bertegund (fl. 530s) 96
Merovingian nun?

Berthold, Ernst (see Robinson, Therese A. L.)

Bertinora, Countess de (see Aldrude)

Bertken, Sister (c.1427–c.1514) 210
Dutch poet, mystic, nun; aka Bertha Jacobs

Beruriah (fl. 1210–1280) 180
Isr. Biblical scholar, author; w. Rebbe Meir

Besant, Annie Wood (1847–1933) 993
Eng. religious leader, political activist; pseud.
Ajax; active exponent of Theosophy; founder of Central Hindu College, 1898, and
Indian Home Rule League, 1916; president,
India National Congress, 1917

Bethune, Mary McLeod (1875–1955) 1223
Am. educator, writer, lecturer, organizer;
founder of Bethune-Cookman College, 1904;
co-founder of National Association of Colored Women's Clubs; Spingarn Medal,
1935

Betsko, Kathleen (1939–) 2256
Eng. playwright, editor, theater historian

Bhutto, Benazir (1953–) 2501
Pakistani prime minister, political activist;
d. Zulfikar Ali Bhutto (Pakistani Prime
Minister, 1971–1977; assassinated, 1979)

Bianchi, Martha [Gilbert] Dickinson (1866–1943) 1127
Am. poet, writer, editor; niece and literary
heir of Emily Dickinson*

Bibesco, Elizabeth Asquith, Princess (1897–1945) 1501
Eng./Rum. writer, poet

Bieber, Margarete (1879–1978) 1270
W. Prussian/Ger./Am. archaeologist, educator

Billings, Victoria (1945–) 2404
Am. journalist, writer

Billson, Christine (fl. 1960s) 2519
Eng. writer

Bingen, Hildegard von (1098–1179) 145
Ger. poet, painter, composer, mystic, abbess; aka Sibyl of the Rhine

Bingham, Anne Willing (1764–1801) 624
Am. social figure; w. William B- (U.S.
Senator and Representative)

Bingham, Charlotte (1942–) 2342
Eng. writer; d. Madeleine* and John B-,
aka Lord and Lady Clanmorris

Bingham, Madeleine (1912–1988) 1744
Eng. writer, playwright; h. Baroness Clanmorris, pseud. Julia Mannering; m. Charlotte B-*

Bingham, Sallie (1937–) 2210
Am. writer; h. Ellsworth

Binh, Nguyen Thi (1930–) 2055
Viet. politician; foreign minister of the South
Vietnamese National Liberation Front

Birch, Alison Wyrley [Greenbie] (1922–) 1897
Am. writer, journalist

Bird, Caroline (1915–) 1787
Am. writer, lecturer

Bird, Rose [Elizabeth] (1936–) 2184
Am. judge, lawyer; Chief Justice, California Supreme Court

Bishop, Elizabeth (1911–1979) 1733
Am./Braz. poet, writer; Pulitzer Prize, 1956;
Natl. Book Award, 1970

Bisset, Jacqueline (1946–) 2423
Eng. actor

Black, Shirley Temple (1928–) 2007
Am. diplomat, actor; first woman appointed
Chief of Protocol in U.S. State Dept.; Special Academy Award, 1934

Blackwell, Antoinette Brown (1825–1921) 868
Am. feminist, writer, minister; s.-in-law
Elizabeth* and Emily* B-

Blackwell, Elizabeth (1821–1910) 854
Am./Eng. physician, feminist, writer; s.
Emily B-,* s.-in-law Antoinette Brown
B-* and Lucy Stone*; first woman physician
in U.S.; co-founder of New York Infirmary
for Women (first woman's health center),
1857

Blackwell, Emily (1826–1911) 874
Am. physician, educator, writer, feminist;
s. Elizabeth B-,* s.-in-law Antoinette Brown
B-* and Lucy Stone*; co-founder of New
York Infirmary for Women (first woman's
health center), 1857

Blackwell, Helen (see Dufferin, Lady Helen)

Blamire, Susanna (1747–1794) 561
Eng./Scot. poet

Bland, Mrs. Hubert (see Nesbit, Edith)

Blavatsky, Elena Petrovna (1831–1891) 901
Russ. religious leader, writer; née Hahn;
founder of Theosophical Society in U.S.
and India

Bleecker, Ann Eliza (1752–1783) 576
Am. author; née Schuyler, asa Bleeker; m.
Margaretta Van Wyck Faugere*

Blessington, Marguerite, Lady (1789 1849) 704
Ir. novelist, poet, salonist; d. Edmund Power;
w. Capt. Maurice St. Leger Farmer (1) and
Charles John Gardner, first earl of Blessington (2)

Blind, Mathilde (1841–1896) 956
Ger./Eng. poet, biographer; née Cohen

Blixen, Karen, Baroness (see Dinesen, Isak)

Bloomer, Amelia Jenks (1818–1894) 822
Am. temperance leader, reformer, writer;
founder of Lily (first newspaper published
by and for women in U.S.), 1848; first
woman Deputy Postmaster; introduced
"bloomers"

Blume, Judy (1938–) 2236
Am. fiction writer; née Sussman

Boadicea (fl. c.40–65) 74
Eng. queen; w. Prasutagas (king of Iceni:
i.e., Norfolk, Suffolk, Cambridge and Huntingdonshire)

Bogan, Louise (1897–1970) 1502

Clark, Eugenie (1922–)   1900
Am. marine biologist, author; gold medal,
Society of Women Geographers

Clarkstone, Bessie (?–1625)   384
Eng. householder

Cleghorn, Sarah Norcliffe (1876–1959)   1238
Am. poet, socialist, pacifist

Clemence (see Michel, Louise)

Clementine (see Howarth, Ellen)

Clemmer, Mary (1839–1884)   944
Am. poet, writer; h. Hudson

Cleopatra VII (69 B.C.–A.D. 30)   68
Macedonian/Egypt. queen; d. Ptolemy XII,
s. and w. Ptolemy XIII (1), lover of Julius
Caesar, w. Mark Antony (2), m. Cleopatra
Selene (queen of Mauretania)

Cleora (see Thrynne, Frances)

Cleyre, Voltairine de (1886–1912)   1128
Am. anarchist, feminist, writer, poet, educator

Cliff, Michelle (195?–)   2477
Jamaican writer

Clifford, Anne, Lady (1590–1676)   335
Eng. diarist, poet; aka Diana Primrose (?);
grandd. Francis Russell, 2nd earl of Pembroke, d. Margaret Russell and George C-,
3rd earl of Cumberland, w. Richard Sackville, earl of Dorset (1) and Philip Herbert,
earl of Bedford (2), niece of Ann, countess
of Warwick

Clinchy, Blythe M. (1930–)   2059
Am. professor of psychology, author

Clingerman, Mildred (fl. 1952)   2497
Am. writer

Clinton, Elizabeth (1574–1630?)   317
Eng. noble, author; aka countess of Lincoln;
w. Thomas C-, 3rd earl of Lincoln

Clitherow, Margaret (1556?–1586)   294
Eng. Catholic martyr; née Middleton, asa
Clitheroe; d. Thomas Middleton, w. John
C-

Clive, Catherine (1711–1785)   483
Eng. playwright, actor; née Rafter, aka Kitty
C-

Coates, Florence Earle (1850–1927)   1010
Am. poet

Coates, Grace Stone (1881–?)   1299
Am. writer

Coatsworth, Elizabeth [Jane] (1893–1986)   1450
Am. poet, novelist; Newbery Award, 1931

Cobbe, Frances P. (1822–1904)   856
Eng. writer

Coblentz, Catherine Cate (1897–1951)   1504
Am. writer

Cochran, Jacqueline (1906/10?–1980)   1655
Am. aviator; h. Odium; head of U.S. Woman's Airforce Service Pilots (WASP); broke
several world speed records

Cockburn, Alicia (1713–1794)   486
Scot. songwriter, poet, playwright, society
leader; née Rutherford, aka Alison

Cockburn, Catherine (1679–1749)   448
Eng. poet, playwright, essayist; née Trotter

Cohen, Charlotte Bonny (1943–)   2362
Am. political activist

Cohen, Sherry Suib (1934–)   2147
Am. journalist, teacher, lecturer, author

Coignard, Gabrielle de (?–d. 1594)   341
Fr. poet

Cole, Mary (fl. 1790s)   712
Am. author

Coleridge, Mary [Elizabeth] (1861–1907)   1085
Eng. poet, writer, biographer, educator

Colette (1873–1954)   1192
Fr. writer; née Sidonie Gabrielle C-; first
president of Goncourt Academy

Coligny, Henriette de (1613?–1673)   368
Fr. poet; h. Hamilton (1), Suze (2), aka
countess de La Suze

Collins, Anne (fl. 1653)   420
Eng. poet

Collins, Emily (1818?–1879?)   824
Am. suffragist

Collins, Judy [Marjorie] (1939–)   2260
Am. folksinger, songwriter, Grammy Award,
1968

Colonna, Vittoria de (1490/2?–1547/49?)   235
Ital. poet; aka marchesa de Pescara; d. Fa-
brizio C-, w. Ferrante Francesco d'Avalos,
friend of Michelangelo

Colquhoun, Janet (1781–1846)   686
Scot. writer, diarist, philanthropist; née Sin-
clair, aka Lady of Rossdhu; founded School
of Industry near Rossdhu, Scotland

Commire, Anne (194?–)   2282
Am. playwright

Compiuta Donzella, La (fl. 13th cen.)   174
Ital. poet; aka Accomplished Maid of Tuscany, The Divine Sibyl, The Perfect Maid

Compton, Elizabeth, Lady (fl. 1595)   342
Eng. maid of honor to Elizabeth I*; d. John
Spencer (mayor of London, 1584/85), w.
William, 2nd Lord C- (later earl of North-
ampton)

Compton-Burnett, Ivy, Dame (1892–1969)   1436
Eng. writer, satirist

Concépcion, Francisca Josepha de la, Sister
(see Castillo y Guevara, Francisca J. del)

Cone, Helen Gray (1859–1934)   1066
Am. poet, educator

Cones, Nancy Ford (1869–1962)   1149
Am. photographer

Conkling, Grace [Walcott] H. (1878–1958)   1262
Am. writer, poet, lecturer; née Hazard; m.
Hilda C-*

Conkling, Hilda (1910–)   1716
Am. poet; d. Grace C-*

Connolly, Olga (1932–)   2097

Czech./Am. athlete; née Fikotova; Olympic champion, discus throwing

Conrad, Beatrice (fl. 1963) 2527
Am. educator, writer

Constantia (*see* 1. Morton, Sarah Wentworth; 2. Murray, Judith Sargent)

Cook, Blanche Weisen (1941–) 2315
Am. professor of history, journalist, author, poet

Cook, Eliza (1818–1889) 825
Eng. poet

Cooke, Rose Terry (1827–1892) 881
Am. poet

Cookson, Catherine [McMullen] (1906–) 1656
Eng. writer; aka Catherine Marchant

Coolbrith, Ina [Donna] (1842–1928) 964
Am. poet

Coolidge, Grace Goodhue (1879–1957) 1272
Am. hostess; w. Calvin C- (U.S. President, 1923–29)

Coolidge, Susan (1845–1905) 984
Am. writer; née Sarah Chauncey Woolsey

Coombs, Mary (1944–) 2386
Am. professor of law

Cooper, Anna Julia [Haywood] (1858/68–1964) 1055
Am. writer, educator, scholar

Cooper, Diana, Lady (1892–1986) 1437
Eng. writer, society leader, actor; nurse; née Manners, aka viscountess of Norwich; w. Alfred Duff C- (d. 1952, diplomat, politician)

Cooper, Edith [Emma] (1862–1913) 1099
Eng. writer

Cooper, Elizabeth (fl. 1730s) 517
Eng. playwright, anthologist

Copley, Mary Singleton (*see* Pelham, Mary Singleton Copley)

Copley, Susannah Farnum (fl. 1769–d. 1836) 647
Am./Eng. householder, letter writer; née Clarke; w. John Singleton C- (1738–1815, painter), m. John Singleton C-, Jr., Baron Lyndhurst (statesman)

Corbett, E. T., Mrs. (fl. 1880s) 1283
Poet

Corbin, Alice (1881–1949) 1300
Am. poet, editor; h. Henderson

Corday, Charlotte (1768/69–1793) 642
Fr. noble, intellectual; née Maria-Anne Charlotte Corday d'Armont; assassin of Jean Paul Marat

Corey, Martha (?–1692) 461
Eng.?/Am. alleged witch

Corey, Shirley Trusty (193?–) 2048
Am. educator, arts-in-education specialist

Corinna (c.520–c.420 B.C.) 52
Grk. lyric poet; asa Crinna, Korinna, Korina, aka The Lyric Muse, The Fly, The Boeotian Sow; d. Acheloodoros and Hipokrateia (contemporaries of Pindar, lyric poet)

Corinna (*see* Thomas, Elizabeth)

Cornelia (fl. 160–140 B.C.) 64
Rom. letter writer, scholar; aka Mother of the Gracchi; w. Tiberius Sempronius Gracchus II (statesman), m. Tiberius Sempronius Gracchus III, Gaius IV and Sempronia (w. Scipio Africanus the Younger)

Cornelia (*see* Hale, Sarah Josepha)

Cornford, Frances Darwin (1886–1960) 1364
Eng. poet

Cornuel, A. M. Bigot de (c.1605/14–1694) 361
Fr. wit, letter writer

Cortissoz, Ellen Mackay (*see* Hutchinson, Ellen Mackay)

Costa, Maria Fatima Velho da (1940?–) 2309
Port. writer

Cotten, Elizabeth (1892–1987) 1451
Am. songwriter, guitarist; aka "Sis" Cotten

Cottin, Sophie (1773–1807) 663
Fr. author; née Ristaud

Countess Temple (*see* Chamber, Anna)

Cowley, Hannah (1743–1809) 551
Eng. playwright, poet; née Parkhouse, aka Anna Matilda

Craig, Agnes (1759–1841) 605
Scot. poet; h. McLehose; aka Clarinda (heroine of Robert Burns' songs)

Craigie, Pearl [Mary Teresa] (1867–1906) 1133
Am./Eng. writer, playwright; pseud. John Oliver Hobbes

Craigin, Elisabeth (fl. 1930s) 2041
Am. writer

Craik, Dinah [Maria] Mulock (1826–1887) 875
Eng. writer, poet

Cram, Mildred (1889–?) 1397
Am. writer

Crane, Nathalia [Clara Ruth] (1913–) 1760
Am. poet; h. Black

Crapsey, Adelaide (1878–1914) 1263
Am. poet, educator

Craster, Edmund, Mrs. (fl. 1870s–d. 1874) 1159
Eng. poet

Craven, Margaret (1901–1980) 1571
Am. fiction writer, journalist

Crawford, Julia (1800–1885) 759
Ir. poet

Crawford, Louisa Macartney (1790–1858) 713
Eng. poet, songwriter

Crist, Judith (1922–) 1901
Am. film critic; née Klein

Croce, Arlene (1934?–) 2148
Am. dance critic, writer, editor

Crocker, Hannah Mather (1752–1829) ·579
Am. author; great-grandd. Increase Mather, grandd. Cotton Mather, niece of Thomas Hutchinson (royal governor of Massachusetts)

Cromwell, Gladys (1885–1919) 1348
Am. poet

Am. humanitarian, reformer; Natl. Women's Hall of Fame, 1980

Dix, Dorothy (1861–1951)   1087
Am. journalist, columnist; née Elizabeth Meriwether; h. Gilmer

Dixon, Jeane L. (1918–)   1840
Am. psychic, writer

Dobree, Henrietta [Octavia de Lisle] (1831–1894)   905
Hymnist

Dodge, Mabel (1879–1962)   1273
Am. writer, patron of arts; née Ganson; h. Luhan

Dodge, Mary Abigail (see Hamilton, Gail)

Dodge, Mary [Elizabeth] Mapes (1838?–1905)   939
Am. writer, editor

Doi, Takako (1928–)   2011
Jap. politician, lawyer; first Japanese woman to lead a major political party

Dolliver, Clara (fl. 1870s)   1160
Am. poet

Dolson, Hildegarde (1908–1981)   1684
Am. fiction writer; aka Hildegarde Lockridge

Domna H. (fl. c.12th cen.)   149
Fr. trobairitz

Doolittle, Hilda (1886–1961)   1365
Am. poet; pseud. H.D.; h. Aldington

Dorr, Julia [Caroline] (1825–1913)   869
Am. writer, poet; née Ripley

Dorset, F. H. (see Llewellyn-Thomas, Beatrice)

Dostoevsky, Anna (1846–1918)   988
Russ. diariest; w. Feodor D- (1821–81, novelist)

Doten, Elizabeth (1829–?)   888
Am. poet; asa Lizzie D-

Doubiago, Sharon (1946–)   2424
Am. poet, fiction writer, essayist

Doudney, Sarah (1843–1926)   966
Eng. writer, poet

Douglas, Alford, Lady (see Custance, Olive)

Douglas, Anne (see Howard, Anne)

Douglas, Eleanor (see Audeley, Eleanor)

Douglas, Helen Gahagan (1900–1980)   1545
Am. writer, lecturer, politician, actor; w. Melvyn D- (actor); U.S. delegate to United Nations, 1946, U.S. Representative, 1944–1950, D-Calif.

Douvan, Elizabeth [Ann Malcolm] (1926–)   1964
Am. psychologist

Dow, Dorothy [Minerva] (1903–)   1602
Am. poet

Dowling, Colette (1938–)   2239
Am. writer

Dowriche, Anne (fl. 1589)   334
Eng. poet; s. Pearse Edgecombe of Devon

Drabble, Margaret (1939–)   2263
Eng. writer

Draper, Mary (c.1718–1810)   492
Am. patriot

Dreifus, Claudia (1944–)   2388
Am. writer, labor organizer, editor, lecturer

Dressel, Brigit (1961–1987)   2525
Ger. athlete

Dressler, Marie (1873–1934)   1194
Can. actor; née Koerber; Academy Award, 1931

Drew, Elizabeth (1887–1965)   1374
Eng./Am. writer, literary citic

Drexler, Rosalyn (1926–)   1965
Am. novelist, playwright, sculptor; Obie Award, 1964, 1979, 1980, 1985; Emmy Award, 1974

Driscoll, Louise (1875–1957)   1226
Am. poet, writer

Droste-Hülshoff, Annette Elisabeth von (1797–1848)   742
Ger. poet, novelist

Drouett, Juliette (1806–1883)   784
Fr. society leader; lover of Victor Hugo

Duchess, The (see Hungerford, Margaret Wolfe)

Dukes, Marie, Dame (see Rambert, Marie)

Duclaux, Anges Mary Frances (see Robinson, Agnes Mary)

Dudar, Helen (fl. 1973)   2535
Am. writer

Dudevant, Baronne (see Sand, George)

Duff, Esther Lilian (fl. 1910s)   1710
Eng. poet

Dufferin, [Helen], Lady (1807–1867)   789
Ir. songwriter; née Blackwood; h. Helen Selina Sheridan, Countess of Dufferin and Gifford; pseud. Impulsia Gushington

Duffy, Maureen (1933–)   2125
Eng. writer, playwright

Dugdale, Bridget Rose (1941–)   2316
Ir. revolutionary

Du Maurier, Daphne (1907–1989)   1669
Eng. writer, playwright

Dunayevskaya, Raya (1910–1987)   1735
Am. author, philosopher

Dunbar, Roxanne (1939–)   2264
Am. political activist, writer

Dunbar-Nelson, Alice Ruth (1875–1935)   1227
Am. author, editor, social worker; née Moore

Duncan, Isadora (1878–1927)   1264
Am. dancer, dance teacher, writer; innovator of modern dance

Dunlap, Jane (see Davis, Adelle)

Dunn, Lydia [Selina], Dame (1940–)   2294
Hong Kong Chin. business executive, stateswoman; aka "The Iron Lady of the East"; Commander of the Order of the British Empire, 1983

Dupin, Amandine Aurore Lucile (see Sand, George)

Durant, Ariel (1898–1981)   1516
Russ./Am. historian, author; née Ada Kaufman; w. Will D- (1885–1981, historian); Pulitzer Prize, 1968; Presidential Medal of Freedom, 1977

Duras, Marguerite (1914–)   1775
Indoch./Fr. novelist, screenwriter; née Donnadieu; Prix Goncourt, 1984

Durham, Helen (see Hathaway, Helen)

Duse, Eleonora [Guilia Amalia] (1859–1924) 1067
Ital. actor; lover of Gabriele D'Annunzio

Dworkin, Andrea (1946–)   2425
Am. author, journalist; née Spiegel

Dyer, Mary (fl. 1633–d. 1660)   398
Eng./Am. Quaker martyr; née Barrett, asa Dyre

E

Earhart, Amelia (1898–1937)   1517
Am. aviator, social worker; writer; w. George Putnam; first woman to make solo transAtlantic and Pacific flights; first woman to receive the Distinguished Flying Cross; Women's Sports Hall of Fame, 1980

Eberhardt, Isabelle (1877–1904)   1249
Adventurer

Ebner-Eschenbach, Marie von, Baroness (1830–1916)   893
Austr. novelist; née Dubsky

Eddy, Mary Baker (1821–1910)   855
Am. theologian, writer, pastor; founder of Christian Science, 1866, and The Christian Science Monitor, 1908

Edelman, Marian Wright (1937–)   2213
Am. civil rights activist, lawyer; founder of Children's Defense Fund

Eden, Emily (1797–1869)   743
Eng./Ind. novelist; aka Lady Auckland; d. William E-, 1st baron of Auckland, s. George E-, earl of Auckland

Edgeworth, Maria (1767–1849)   639
Ir. novelist, essayist

Edwards, Amelia (1831–1892)   906
Eng. writer, Egyptologist

Edwards, Anne (1927–)   1995
Am. writer, scenarist

Edwards, Betty (fl. 1940s)   2283
Am. artist, author, researcher

Edwards, Marie (1926?–)   1966
Am. psychologist; née Babare

Egburg (fl. 8th cen.)   105
Eng. nun

Egeria (fl. 381–384)   88
Sp. abbess

Egeria (see Hemans, Felicia Dorothea)

Eifuku, Empress (1271–1342)   187
Jap. poet, noble

Eisenhower, Mamie [Geneva Doud] (1896–1979)   1487

Am. first lady, society leader; w. Dwight D. E- (U.S. President, 1953–61)

Eleanor of Aquitaine (c.1122–1204)   156
Fr./Eng. queen; w. Louis VII of France (1) and Henry II of England (2), m. Richard I (the Lion Heart) and John of England

Elia, Bridget (see Lamb, Mary Ann)

Eliot, George (1819–1880)   833
Eng. writer; née Marian Evans; h. Cross

Eliott, Ethelinda (see Beers, Ethel Lynn)

Elisabeth, Saint (fl. c.20 B.C.–A.D. 1)   40
Judean; w. Zechariah, m. John the Baptist, cousin of the Virgin Mary*

Elisabeth of Brandenburg (1485–1545)   233
Ger. noble; s. Christian II of Denmark, w. Joachim I (Elector of Brandenburg), m. Elisabeth of Braunschweig*

Elisabeth of Braunschweig, Duchess (1510–1558)   250
Ger. noble; d. Elisabeth of Brandenburg,* w. Erich, duke of Braunschweig-Calenberg, m. Anna Maria of B-*

Elizabeth (see Arnim, Mary A.)

Elizabeth, Queen Mother (1900–)   1546
Eng. queen; née Elizabeth Angela Marguerite Bowes-Lyon; w. King George VI; mother of Elizabeth II*

Elizabeth I of England (1533–1603)   277
Eng. queen; d. Henry VIII and Ann Boleyn,* half-s. Mary I of England* and Edward VI of England, grandd. Elizabeth of York,* first cousin of Mary, Queen of Scots*

Elizabeth II of England (1926–)   1967
Eng. queen, 1952– ; d. Queen Mother Elizabeth* and King George VI; w. Philip Mountbatten, Duke of Edinburgh

Elizabeth of Rumania (see Sylva, Carmen)

Elizabeth of Thuringia, Saint (1206/07–1231)   179
Ger. queen, Franciscan tertiary; d. Andrew II of Hungary, w. Ludwig (landgrave of Thuringia)

Elizabeth of York (1465/66–1503)   220
Eng. queen, poet; d. Edward IV and Elizabeth Woodville-Grey,* m. Henry VIII, grandm. Elizabeth I*

Elliot, Jean (1727–1805)   509
Scot. poet, songwriter; asa Jane E.

Elliott, Anna (fl. 1770s)   652
Am. householder

Elliott, Charlotte (1789–1871)   705
Eng. hymnist

Elliott, Maxine (1871–1940)   1176
Am. actor, theater owner-manager

Ellis, Sarah [Stickney] (1812–1872)   802
Eng. missionary, writer; w. William E-; cofounder of Rawdon House School for Girls

Elmendorf, Mary J[ohnson] (fl. 1920s)   1868
Am. poet

Fletcher, Julia A. (*see* Carney, Julia A.)

Fletcher, Lucille (1912–)   1746
Am. scenarist, writer

Fletcher, Mary (1739–1815)   537
Eng. philanthropist, née Bosanquet, asa Basquet

Flexner, Anne Crawford (1875?–1955)   1228
Am. playwright

Flint, Annie Johnson (1866–1932)   1129
Am. poet

Flynn, Elizabeth Gurley (1890–1964)   1410
Am. Communist leader, civil rights activist, writer; aka "The Rebel Girl"

Follen, Eliza Lee (1787–1858)   699
Ger./Am. poet, author; née Cabott

Fonda, Jane [Seymour] (1937–)   2214
Am. actor, fitness expert, political activist; d. Henry F- (1905–82, actor), s. Peter F- (actor), ex-w. Roger Vadim (1, Fr. film director), Tom Hayden (2, activist, politician); w. Ted Turner (3, media mogul); Academy Award, 1971, 1978

Forbes, Esther (1894–1967)   1468
Am. writer; Pulitzer Prize, 1943; Newbery Award, 1944

Forcalquier, Garsenda de (*see* Garsenda de Forcalquier)

Ford, Betty (1918–)   1841
Am. First Lady, civic leader; née Elizabeth Bloomer; w. Gerald R. F- (U.S. President, 1974–1977)

Ford, Lena Guilbert (fl. early 1900s–1916?)   1537
Am. poet

Fornes, Maria Irene (1930–)   2061
Cuban/Am. playwright, stage director; Obie Award, 1965, 1977, 1979, 1982

Fossey, Dian (1932–1985)   2100
Am. anthropologist

Foster, Hannah Webster (1758/59–1840)   598
Am. novelist

Fowler, Ellen Thorneycroft (1860–1929)   1074
Eng. writer; h. Felkin

Fox, Muriel (1928–)   2012
Am. business executive, feminist; h. Aronson

Fradonnet, Catherine (1547–1587)   288
Fr. poet, playwright; aka, with her mother, Les Dames Des Roches; d. Madeleine F-*

Fradonnet, Madeleine (c.1520–1587)   262
Fr. poet; née Neveu, aka, with her daughter, Les Dames Des Roches; w. André F- (1), François Eboissard (2), m. Catherine F-*

Fraiberg, Selma (1918–1981)   1842
Am. child psychoanalyst, clinician, researcher, author; née Horwitz

Frame, Janet (1924–)   1932
New Zeal. writer, poet

Franco, Veronica (1546–1591)   287
Ital. poet, courtesan; founder of hospice for "fallen women"; friend of Tintoretto

Frank, Anne (1929–1945)   2022
Ger. diarist; executed by Nazis

Frank, Florence Kiper (1886?–?)   1366
Am. poet, playwright

Franklin, Eleanor Anne (c.1790/97–1825)   714
Eng. poet; née Porden

Franklin, Miles (1880–1956)   1286
Austral. novelist; aka Brent of Bin Bin

Franklin, Rosalind (1920–1958)   1877
Eng. physicist; co-discoverer of DNA

Franks, Rebecca (c.1760–1823)   613
Am./Eng. social figure; aka Lady Johnson

Franz, Marie-Louise von (1915–)   1789
Swiss Jungian analyst, scholar, author; founder C.G. Jung Institute, Zurich

Fraser, Antonia, Lady (1932–)   2101
Eng. historian, biographer, novelist, social activist, television personality; nee Antonia Pakenham; d. Lord Longford (former Labour Cabinet minister), w. Hugh Fraser (1; politician), Harold Pinter (2; playwright)

Fraser, Kathleen (1937–)   2215
Am. poet

Freeman, Mary [Eleanor] Wilkins (1852–1930)   1026
Am. writer, poet

Freer, Otto, Mrs. (*see* Less, Agnes)

Fremantle, Anne [Jackson] (1909/10–)   1700
Am. educator, writer, poet

French, Marilyn (1929–)   2023
Am. novelist, writer; critic; née Edwards

Freud, Anna (1895–1982)   1480
Austr./Eng. psychoanalyst, author; d. Sigmund F- (1856–1939); founder Hampstead Child Therapy Clinic, London; Commander of British Empire, 1967; pioneer in the field of child psychoanalysis

Friday, Nancy (1937–)   2216
Am. writer; née Colbert

Friedan, Betty [Naomi] (1921–)   1889
Am. feminist, writer; née Goldstein; founder of National Organization for Women (NOW), 1966

Frietschie, Barbara (1766–1862)   634
Am. patriot; née Hauer, asa Frietchie; subject of Whittier's poem "Barbara Fritchie"

Frost, Frances (1905–1959)   1637
Am. poet

Fry, Elizabeth (1780–1845)   681
Eng. social and prison reformer

Fugard, Sheila [Meiring] (1934?–)   2150
Eng./So.Afr. writer; w. Athol F- (1932– playwright)

Fukuzoyo Chiyo (c.1701/03–1775)   472
Jap. poet, painter; aka Chiyoni, Chiyojo, Kaga no Chiyo

Fulke-Greville, Frances (*see* Greville, Frances Fulke)

Fuller, [Sarah] Margaret (1810–1850)   795
Am. journalist, social critic, educator,

translator, editor, feminist; h. Marchesa Ossoli

Fuller, Margaret Witter (1871–1954)　1177
Am. poet, writer

Fumiko, Enchi (1905–?)　1635
Jap. novelist, playwright; Women's Writer's Prize, 1952, 1966

Fumiko, Hayashi (1904–1951)　1621
Jap. writer; Women's Prize for Literature, 1948

Furness, Betty (1916–)　1804
Am. columnist, government official, actor

Fyleman, Rose (1877–1957)　1250
Eng. poet

G

Gabor, Zsa Zsa [Sari] (1919–)　1857
Hung./Am. actor, business executive; ex.w. Conrad Hilton (1), George Sanders (2), etc.; Miss Hungary, 1936

Gabrielli, Caterina (1730–1796)　518
Ital. singer

Gage, Frances Dana (1808–1884)　791
Am. social reformer, lecturer, poet

Gage, Mathilda J. (1826–1898)　876
Am. suffragist, writer

Gale, Zona (1874–1938)　1206
Am. writer; h. Breese; Pulitzer Prize, 1921

Gallagher, Mary (1947–)　2450
Am. actor, stage director, playwright, novelist

Galland, China (1943?–)　2364
Am. naturalist?, writer

Gallant, Mavis (1922–)　1902
Eng./Can. writer

Gambara, Veronica (1485–1550)　234
Ital. poet, governor; w. Gilberto X, lord of Correggio, friend and correspondent of Pietro Bembo

Gambaro, Griselda (1928–)　2013
Argen. writer, playwright

Gamble, Eliza Burt (1841–1920)　958
Am. author

Gandhi, Indira [Priyadarshini] (1917–1984)　1824
Ind. politician; née Nehru; d. Jawaharlal Nehru (1889–1964, first prime minister of India); first woman prime minister of India, 1966–1977 and 1980–1984; assassinated.

Garbo, Greta (1905–1990)　1638
Swed./Am. actor

Garden, Mary (1877?–1967)　1251
Scot./Am. opera singer

Gardiner, Lisa (1900–1956)　1549
Am. dancer, choreographer, educator; founder of Washington School of Ballet

Garfield, Lucretia Rudolph (1832–1918)　911
Am. First Lady, society leader; w. James G- (1831–81); U.S. President, 1881; assassinated); s. Lucy Hayes*

Garland, Judy (1922–1969)　1903
Am. singer, actor; née Frances Gumm; ex-w. Sidney Luft (1), Vincente Minnelli (2); m. Liza Minnelli, Lorna Luft; Academy Award, 1939; Grammy Award, 1961

Garrick, Eva Maria (1725–1822)　506
Ital./Eng. dancer, actor; née Viegel, aka Violette; w. David Garrick

Garrison, Theodosia (1874–1944)　1207
Am. poet, writer; h. Mrs. Frederick Faulks

Garsenda de Forcalquier (c.1170–?)　166
Provençal trobairitz; w. Alphonse II, lord of Provence

Garson, Barbara (1942–)　2344
Am. playwright; Obie Award, 1977

Garthwaite, Terry (1939–)　2265
Am. singer, lyricist

Gaskell, Elizabeth [Cleghorn] (1810–1865)　796
Eng. novelist; née Stevenson

Gates, Ellen [Huntington] (1835–1920)　927
Am. poet, writer

Gawain, Shakti (1948–)　2463
Am. dance teacher, therapist, workshop leader, writer

Gearhart, Sally [Miller] (1931–)　2077
Am. writer

Gelfant, Blanche H[ousman] (1922–)　1904
Am. teacher, literary scholar

Gelpi, Barbara C[harlesworth] (1933–)　2129
Am. educator

Gems, Pam[ela Iris] (1925–)　1951
Eng. playwright

Genêt (see Flanner, Janet)

Geneviève (1850–?)　1011
Fr. society leader; h. Straus; d. Jacques François Halévy, w. Georges Bizet (1838–75, composer)

Genlis, Stephanie Félicité, Countess (1746–1830)　558
Fr. harpist, author, tutor; née Du Crest de St. Aubin

Gentileschi, Artemisia (1593–1652/53)　340
Ital. painter; d. Orazio Gentileschi (1563–1639, painter)

Geoffrin, Marie Thérèse Rodet (1669–1757)　441
Fr. wit, salonist

Gerould, Katherine (1879–1944)　1275
Am. writer; née Fullerton

Gertrude the Great (fl. 1256–1302)　184
Ger. Benedictine mystic, author; aka Saint Gertrude of Hefta

Geyer, Georgia Anne (1935–)　2170
Am. columnist, author, educator

Gibbons, Stella [Dorothea] (1902–)　1586
Eng. writer, poet; h. Webb

Gibson, Althea (1927–)　1996
Am. tennis and golf pro; Olympic champion; Women's Sports Hall of Fame, 1980; first black woman to win both the U.S. Open, 1950, and Wimbledon, 1957.

Gilbert, Mrs. (*see* Taylor, Ann)

Gilbert, Sandra [Mortola] (1936–)   2188
Am. educator, poet, writer

Gilchrist, Marie [Emilie] (1893–?)   1453
Am. writer, researcher

Gildersleeve, Virginia [Crocheron] (1877–1965)   1252
Am. educator, administrator; dean of Barnard College, 1911–47; U.S. delegate to United Nations, 1945

Gill, Julia (*see* Bailey, Urania Locke Stoughton)

Gill, Sarah Prince (1728–1771)   511
Am. poet, diarist; s. Deborah Prince (poet)

Gillan, Maria Mazziotti (1940–)   2296
Am. poet, educator

Gillespie, Marcia [Ann] (1944–)   2391
Am. editor

Gilliatt, Penelope [Ann Douglass] (1932–)   2102
Eng. writer, film critic, scenarist

Gilligan, Carol (1936–)   2189
Am. psychologist, author

Gilman, Caroline (1794–1888)   735
Am. author, educator, poet; née Howard, pseud. Mrs. Clarissa Packard; w. Samuel G- (poet), m. Caroline Howard (author)

Gilman, Charlotte Perkins (1860–1935)   1075
Am. writer, poet, lecturer, social critic, publicist

Gilmer, Elizabeth Merriwether (*see* Dix, Dorothy)

Gilpin, Laura (1891–1979)   1423
Am. photographer

Giltinan, Caroline (1884–?)   1332
Am. poet; h. Harlow

Gingold, Hermione [Ferdinanda] (1897–1987)   1506
Eng. actor, comedian; Grammy Award, 1976

Ginsberg, Ruth Bader (1933–)   2130
Am. educator, lawyer

Ginzburg, Eugenia [Semyonovna] (1907?–1967)   1670
Soviet social critic, author

Ginzburg, Natalia [Levi] (1916–1991)   1805
Ital. writer; aka Alessandra Tornimparte; Premio Strega Prize, 1963

Giovanni, Nikki (1943–)   2365
Am. poet

Girardin, Delphine de (1804–1855)   776
Fr. writer; née Gay; pseud. Vicomte Charles de Launay

Giroud, Françoise (1916–)   1806
Swiss/Fr. politician, journalist, editor; Minister of Women; co-founder of *Elle* and *L'Express* magazines

Glasgow, Ellen [Anderson Gholson] (1874–1945)   1208
Am. writer; Pultizer Prize, 1942

Glasgow, Maude (1868–1955)   1142
Am. physician, writer

Glaspell, Susan (1882–1948)   1310
Am. writer, playwright, actor; widow of George Cram Cook, w. Norman H. Matson; co-founder of Provincetown Players; Pulitzer Prize, 1931

Glassman, Carol (1942?–)   2345
Am. civil rights activist, judge

Glenconner, Pamela [Wyndham], Lady (1871–1928)   1178
Eng. writer; née Gray

Glendon, Mary Ann (1938–)   2240
Am. lawyer, educator, author

Gloriana (*see* Morgan, Sydney Owenson)

Glyn, Elinor (1864–1943)   1110
Eng. writer; née Sutherland

Goddard, Mary Katherine (1736/38–1816)   531
Am. printer, newspaper publisher, postmaster; d. Sarah Updike G-,* s. William G- (publisher, postmaster); first printed copy of Declaration of Independence with signatures came from her press; probably the first woman postmaster in American colonies

Goddard, Sarah Updike (c.1700–1770)   471
Am. printer; m. Mary Katherine G-* and William G- (printers)

Godolphin, Margaret [Blagge] (1652–1678)   419
Eng. maid of honor, letter writer

Godwin, Gail (1937–)   2217
Am. writer, journalist, educator, lecturer

Godwin, Hannah (fl. 1790s)   715
Eng. letter writer; s. William G- (1756–1836, political philosopher)

Goeppert Mayer, Maria (*see* Mayer, Maria Goeppert)

Goldberg, Leah (1911–1970)   1736
Isr. poet

Goldberger, Nancy Rule (1934–)   2151
Am. professor of psychology, author

Goldman, Emma (1869–1940)   1152
Russ./Am. anarchist, political agitator and organizer, lecturer, editor; founder of *Mother Earth*, 1906

Gonzaga, Elisabetta (1471–1526)   224
Ital. art and literary patron; aka duchess of Urbino; s. Francisco G-, marquis of Mantua, s.-in-law Isabella d'Este,* w. Guidobaldo da Montefeltre, duke of Urbino; cultivated a genteel court that inspired Castiglione's book *The Courtier*

Gonzaga, Giulia (1513–1566)   253
Ital. art patron; s.-in-law Pico della Mirandola (philosopher), w. Vespasiano Colonna

Gonzaga, Lucrezia [di Bozzolo e Sabbioneta] (1522–pre-1552)   266
Ital. letter writer; cousin Ippolita G-, w. Gianpaolo Manfrone

Goodale, Elaine (1863–1953)   1106
Am. poet; h. Eastman; s. Dora Read G- (poet)

Goodenough, J[udith]. B. (1942–)   2346
Am. poet; née Beach

Goodman, Linda (1929?–)   2024
Am. astrologer, writer

Gorbachev, Raisa Maximovna (193?–)   2050
Soviet First Lady; w. Mikhail Sergeyevich G- (1931– , General Secretary of Soviet Union, 1985–)

Gorbanevskaya, Natalya (1936–)   2190
Sov. poet, political activist

Gordimer, Nadine (1923–)   1921
So. Afr. writer, lecturer; Nobel Prize for Literature, 1991

Gordon, Ruth (1896–1985)   1488
Am. actor, playwright, screenwriter; née Jones; w. Garson Kanin (screenwriter, producer); Academy Award, 1968; Emmy Award, 1979

Gore, Catherine [Grace Frances] (1799–1861)   755
Eng./Fr. poet, novelist, playwright, composer; née Moody

Gore-Booth, Eva (1872–1926)   1185
Ir. poet

Gorenko, Anna Andreevna (see Akhmatova, Anna)

Gormley (fl. 10th cen.)   127
Ir. queen, poet; asa Gormphley

Gornick, Vivian (1938–)   2241
Am. writer

Gossamer, Lady (see Michitsuna, Mother of)

Gottlieb, Linda (1941?–)   2318
Am. writer, film producer

Gottschewski, Lydia (fl. 1930s)   2042
Ger. political activist

Goudge, Elizabeth [de Beauchamp] (1900–1984)   1550
Eng./Am. writer

Gould, Hannah Flagg (1789–1865)   706
Am. poet

Gould, Lois (1937?–)   2218
Am. writer, editor

Goulianos, Joan (1939–)   2266
Am. writer, educator, literary critic; née Rodman Gourielli-Tchkonia, Princess (see Rubinstein, Helena)

Gournay, Demoiselle de (see Jars, Marie de)

Gracia, Princeps (see Aspasia)

Graham, Isabelle (1742–1814)   546
Scot./Am. poet, letter writer, educator, philanthropist; née Marshall; founded N.Y. Widow's Society, N.Y. Orphan's Asylum, N.Y. Society for the Promotion of Industry

Graham, Janet (1723/24–1805)   503
Scot. poet

Graham, Katharine (1917–)   1825
Am. newspaper publisher, editor; née Meyer

Graham, Margaret Collier (1850–1910)   1012
Am. writer

Graham, Martha (1894–1991)   1469
Am. dancer, choreographer, educator; direct descendant of Miles Standish; founder of Martha G- Dance Company; Presidential Medal of Freedom, 1976; pioneer of modern dance

Graham, Sheilah (1904–1988)   1622
Eng./Am. columnist, writer

Graham, Virginia (1912–)   1747
Am. writer, playwright, television/radio commentator

Grahn, Judy (1940–)   2297
Am. poet, feminist

Grant, Anne (1755–1838)   586
Scot./Am. poet, author; née MacVicar, aka Anne Grant of Loggan (or Laggan)

Grant, Lee (1929–)   2025
Am. actor, director; née Lyova Haskell Rosenthal; Obie Award, 1964; Emmy Award, 1966, 1971; Academy Award, 1975

Grant, Toni [Gale] (1941–)   2319
Am. psychologist, radio commentator

Granville-Barker, Helen (see Huntington, Helen)

Grasso, Ella (1919–1981)   1858
Am. politician; née Tambussi; U.S. House of Representatives, 1971–1974, governor, 1975–1980, D-Connecticut

Grau, Shirley Ann (1929–)   2026
Am. writer; h. Feibelman; Pulitzer Prize, 1965

Gray, Agnes Kendrick (1894–)   1470
Ir. poet

Gray, Francine Du Plessix (1930–)   2062
Pol./Am. author

Gray, Kimi (1946–)   2427
Am. social activist

Gray, Madeline (1902–)   1587
Am. writer

Green, Anna [Katherine] (1846–1935)   989
Am. writer

Green, Edith Starrett (1910–)   1719
Am. politician; U.S. Representative, D-Oregon, 1955–75

Green, Hannah (1932–)   2103
Am. writer; née Joanne Greenberg

Green, Mary A. E. (1818?–1895)   826
Eng. writer, historian, editor; née Everett

Green, Rayna (194?–)   2284
Am. writer, poet, historian, editor

Greenberg, Joanne (see Green, Hannah)

Greene, Catharine (1753–1815?)   581
Am. householder; née Littlefield; h. Miller (2); w. Genl. Nathanael G-; patron of Eli Whitney (inventor)

Greer, Germaine (1939–)   2267
Austral. writer, feminist, educator

Gregoria, Francisca (1653–1736)   421
Sp. nun, poet

Gregory, Augusta, Lady (1859?–1932)   1068
Ir. writer, playwright, director; née Persse; co-founder of Irish National Theatre Society, 1902; director of Abbey Theatre

H

Hagen, Uta (1919–)   1859
  Ger./Am. actor, teacher; w. Herbert Berghof;
  co-founder, Herbert Berghof Studios, New
  York; Antoinette Perry Award, 1951, 1963;
  London Critics Award, 1963, 1964
Haggerty, Joan (1940–)   2298
  Can. writer
Hale, Lucretia Peabody (1820–1900)   844
  Am. writer; s. Edward Everett H-
Hale, Nancy (1908–1988)   1687
  Am. writer, editor
Hale, Sarah Josepha (1788–1879)   703
  Am. editor, writer, poet; née Buell, aka
  Cornelia; first woman magazine editor in
  U.S., established Thanksgiving as national
  holiday, established Mount Vernon as na-
  tional shrine
Hall, Daniel, Mrs. (fl. 1770s–80s)   653
  Am. householder
Hall, Hazel (1886–1924)   1367
  Am. poet
Hall, Radclyffe (1886–1943)   1368
  Eng. writer, poet
Hall, Sharlot Mabridth (1870–1943)   1164
  Am. poet, writer, editor
Hallack, Cecily R. (1898–1938)   1519
  Eng. writer, poet
Halsey, Margaret F. (1910–)   1720
  Am. writer; h. Stern
Halsted, Anna Roosevelt (1906–1975)   1657
  Am. editor, civil and women's rights activ-
  ist; d. Eleanor* and Franklin D. Roosevelt,
  grandniece Theodore Roosevelt (U.S. Pres-
  ident, 1901–09) and Corinne R. Robinson,*
  niece, Edith Carow Roosevelt*
Hamer, Fannie Lou (1917–1977)   1826
  Am. civil rights activist, farmer; founder of
  the Mississippi Freedom Democratic Party
Hamilton, Anna E. (1843–1875)   968
  Ir. poet
Hamilton, Edith (1867–1963)   1135
  Am. classical scholar, writer, translator
Hamilton, Eleanor (1909–)   1701
  Am. sex therapist, marriage counselor, au-
  thor; née Poorman
Hamilton, Elizabeth (1758?–1816)   599
  Ir./Scot. poet, author, governess
Hamilton, Emma, Lady (1765–1815)   631
  Eng. beauty, adventurer; née Emily Lyon,
  aka Emily Hart; w. Sir William H-, mistress
  of Horatio Nelson, m. Horatia Nelson
Hamilton, Gail (1833–1896)   914
  Am. writer, humorist; née Mary Abigail
  Dodge
Hammond, Eleanor Prescott (1866–1933)   1130
  Am. writer, scholar
Handle, Irene (1901/02–1987)   1588
  Eng. actor, author
Hanim, Leylâ (?–1847)   992
  Poet

Hankey, Katherine (1834–1911)   919
  Eng.? hymnist
Hansberry, Lorraine (1930–1965)   2063
  Am. playwright
Han Suyin (1917–)   1835
  Chin. writer, physician, researcher
Han Ts'ui-p'in (fl. 850s)   124
  Chin. poet, courtier
Hannah (fl. c.1040 B.C.)   18
  Hebr.; w. Elkanah, son of Jeroham, m.
  Samuel
Hapsburg, Maria (see Maria of Hungary and
Bohemia)
Harding, Florence Kling (1860–1924)   1076
  Am. First Lady, society leader; w. Warren
  H- (U.S. President, 1921–23)
Harding, Mary (fl. c.1591)   336
  Eng. waiting woman to Lady Rose Man-
  ners, countess of Rutland
Harding, M. Esther (1888–1971)   1385
  Am. author, psychologist?, psychoanalytic
  writer
Hardwick, Elizabeth (1916–)   1807
  Am. writer, educator, drama and literary
  critic
Hari, Mata (1876–1917)   1239
  Dutch spy, dancer; née Margaretha Geer-
  truida Zelle; aka "The Red Danger"; h.
  MacLeod
Harima, Young Woman of (fl. c.715–719)   115
  Jap. poet
Harington, Lucy (1581–1627)   322
  Eng. poet, patron of poets; aka countess of
  Bedford, Lady Russell, Selena; d. Sir John
  H- (translator), w. Edward Russell, earl of
  Bedford
Harjo, Joy (1951–)   2490
  Am. filmmaker, screenwriter, artist, poet
Harley, Brilliana, Lady (1600–1643)   350
  Eng. letter writer; d. Sir Edward Conway,
  baron of Ragley, third w. Sir Robert H-
  (Member of Parliament)
Harlow, Leo P., Mrs. (see Gilinan, Caroline)
Harriman, Florence [Jaffray] Hurst (1870–1967)   1165
  Am. public servant; U.S. Minister to Nor-
  way, 1937–1940
Harris, Barbara C. (1930–)   2064
  Am. priest; first woman bishop in Anglican
  Communion
Harris, Corra May (1869–1935)   1153
  Am. writer; née White
Harris, Janet [Dorothea] (1915–)   1790
  Am. writer, educator, civil rights activist;
  official of NOW and CORE
Harris, Jean (1934?–)   2152
  Am. school administrator, teacher, author;
  née Struven
Harris, Marguerite (1899–1978)   1531
  Am. poet; founder of Woodstock Poetry
  Festival

Home, Anne (1742–1821) 547
Scot. poet, bluestocking; aka Anne Hunter; w. John Hunter, m. John Hunter of Glasgow (physiologist, anatomist)

Home, Grisell, Lady (1665–1746) 431
Scot. poet, author, spy; asa Hume, aka Grizel Baillie

Homespun, Prudentia (*See* West, Jane)

Hŏ Nansŏrhŏn (1563–1589) 308
Korean poet; s. Hŏ Kyun (novelist)

Honnamma (fl. 1665–1699) 432
Ind. (Kannada) poet

Honora or Honora-Martesia (*see* Murray, Judith Sargent)

Hooper, Ellen Sturgis (1816–1841) 817
Am. poet

Hoover, Eleanor (c.1925–) 1952
Am. writer

Hoover, Lou Henry (1874–1944) 1210
Am. First Lady, society leader, translator; w. Herbert H- (U.S. President, 1929–33)

Hooyman, Nancy R. (1945–) 2408
Am. feminist social worker, educator, college administrator

Hope, Laurence (1865–1904) 1119
Eng. poet; aka Adela Florence Nicolson

Hoper, Mrs. (fl. 1740s) 539
Eng. actor, playwright

Hopkins, Jane Ellice (1836–1904) 934
Eng. social reformer, writer

Hopper, Grace Murray (1906–1992) 1659
Am. Rear Admiral of Navy, mathematician, educator; née Brewster; helped program Mark I, first large scale automatic calculator; coined computer term "bugs"; Data Processing Management Association's first "Man of the Year" award, 1969

Hopper, Hedda (1890–1966) 1412
Am. columnist, writer

Horikawa, Lady (fl. 1135–1165) 159
Jap. poet, attendant of Empress Dowager Taiken

Horne, Lena (1917–) 1827
Am. singer, actor, civil rights activist; w. Lennie Hayton (music director); Antoinette Perry Award, 1981

Horne, Marilyn (1934–) 2154
Am. opera singer

Horner, Matina (1939–) 2268
Am. psychologist, educator, college administrator, writer; née Souretis

Horney, Karen (1885–1952) 1351
Ger./Am. psychiatrist, writer, educator; née Danielson

Horta, Maria Teresa (1939–) 2269
Port. writer, poet

Hortensia (85 B.C.–?) 67
Rom. orator, reformer; d. Quintus Hortensius (orator)

Ho Shuang-ch'ing (1712–?) 484
Chin. poet

Houdetot, Sophie de la Briche, Countess (1730–1813) 519
Fr. poet, wit, musician

Howar, Barbara (1932/35–) 2104
Am. society leader, writer

Howard, Anne Dacre (1557–1630) 296
Eng. poet; aka duchess of Arundel; w. Philip H-, earl of Arundel

Howard, Anne Douglas (?–1760) 614
Eng. poet; aka Viscountess Irwin

Howard, Isabella (c.1722–c.1793/95) 500
Eng.? poet, née Byron, aka countess of Carlisle

Howard, Jane [Temple] (1935–) 2171
Am. writer

Howard, Maureen [Keans] (1930–) 2065
Am. writer

Howarth, Ellen [Clementine Doran] (1827–1899) 882
Am. poet; pseud. Clementine

Howe, Julia Ward (1819–1910) 834
Am. writer, lecturer, social reformer, civil and women's rights activist, suffragist, poet

Howe, Louise Kapp (1934–) 2155
Am. writer, editor

Howe, Tina (1938?–) 2242
Am. playwright, educator; Obie Award, 1983

Howell, Margery Eldredge (1893–?) 1455
Am. poet

Howells, Mildred (1872–1966) 1186
Am. painter, poet; d. William Dean H-

Howitt, Mary (1799–1888) 756
Eng./Ital. poet, essayist, translator; née Botham; m. William H-, frequent collaborator; honored by Literary Academy of Stockholm for translation of works of Frederika Bremer*

Howland, Robert Shaw, Mrs. (*see* Woolsey, Mary)

Ho Xuan Huong (fl. 1765–1799) 632
Vietnamese poet

Hroswitha of Gandersheim (c.935–1000) 131
Ger. nun, poet, playwright; née Helena von Rossen, asa Hrosvitha, Rosvitha, Hrotsvit; earliest woman poet of the middle ages whose works are preserved, first playwright and first female poet of Germany

Hsiang Chin-yu (fl. 1910s–1927) 1711
Chin. militant

Hsiao Hung (1911–1941) 1737
Chin. novelist; née Chang Nai-ying

Hsi-chün (fl. c.105 B.C.) 65
Chin. poet; w. K'un Mo, king of Wu-sun

Hsieh Ping-Ying (1906–) 1660
Chin. novelist, political activist

Hsüeh T'ao (768–831) 118
Chin. poet, singer

Huang O (1498–1569) 241
Chin. poet; w. Yang Shen (poet)

Johnson, Amy (1908?–1941) 1689
Eng. aviator

Johnson, [Claudia Alta] Lady Bird (1912–) 1749
Am. First Lady, environmental activist, cattle rancher; née Taylor; w. Lyndon B. J-
(U.S. President, 1963–1969); Presidential
Medal of Freedom, 1977

Johnson, Diane (1934–) 2156
Am. writer, educator

Johnson, Guion Griffis (1900–) 1555
Am. writer, educator

Johnson, Osa [Helen] (1894–1953) 1471
Am. explorer, writer; née Leighty; w. Martin J-

Johnson, Shirbey (1941–) 2323
Am. athletics director

Johnson, Sonia (1936?–) 2194
Am. author, feminist

Johnston, Henrietta (c.1665–1728/29) 433
Ir.?/Am. painter; née Deering; possibly the
first woman artist in America

Johnston, Jill (1929–) 2027
Eng./Am. writer, feminist; pseud. F. J.
Crowe

Johnston, Mary (1870–1936) 1167
Am. writer

Johnstone, Wilhelmina Kemp (1900–) 1556
Bahamian poet, writer

Joliot-Curie, Iréne (1897–1956) 1507
Fr. chemist; d. Marie* and Pierre C-, s.
Éve C-*, w. Frederic Joliet (physicist); Nobel Prize for Chemistry, 1935

Jones, Beverly (1927–) 1998
Am. writer, feminist

Jones, Gayl (1949–) 2469
Am. writer

Jones, Lady (see Bagnold, Enid)

Jones, Margo (1913–1955) 1763
Am. theater producer, director; founder of
Theater '47–'50, Dallas, Texas

Jones, Mary (fl. 1750) 750
Eng. poet

Jones, Mother [Mary Harris] (1830–1930) 895
Ir./Am. labor organizer, humanitarian; née
Harris

Jones, Rickie Lee (1954–) 2505
Am. singer, songwriter; Grammy Award,
1979

Jong, Erica (1942–) 2349
Am. poet, writer; née Mann

Joplin, Janis (1943–1970) 2369
Am. singer, songwriter

Jordan, Barbara (1936–) 2195
Am. politician; U.S. House of Representatives, 1973–78, D-Texas; first black and
first woman to give keynote address at Democratic National Convention, 1976

Jordan, Dorothea (1762–1816) 619
Scot. poet

Jordan, June [Meyer] (1936–) 2196

Am. poet, writer, filmmaker, educator, environmentalist

Joreen (194?–) 2285
Am. feminist

Josefowitz, Natasha (1916–) 1809
Fr./Am. syndicated columnist, consultant,
lecturer, author; née Chapro

Joseph, Jenny (1932–) 2106
Eng. poet, fiction writer

Josephine (1763–1814) 623
Fr. empress; née Marie Josephe Rose Tascher
de la Pagerie; w. Alexandre, vicomte de
Beauharnais (1) and first w. Napoleon I (2),
m. Eugene and Hortense (by de Beauharnais)

Joshee, Anandabai (1865–1887) 1120
Ind. physician; née Yumna; first Hindu
woman and first Indian woman to receive
medical degree

Joyner, Florence Griffith (see Griffith Joyner,
Florence)

Joyner-Kersee, Jackie [Jacqueline] (1962–) 2526
Am. track & field athlete; s. Al Joyner
(Olympic medalist), s.-in-law, Florence
Griffith Joyner*; two-time Olympic medalist

Judith (c.600–495 B.C.) 31
Isr. hero; d. Merari (son of Ox), w. Manasseh; killed Holofernes (commander of
Assyrian forces) and brought peace to Israel

Judson, Ann Hasseltine (1789–1826) 707
Am. missionary; aka Nancy J.; one of the
first women to leave the U.S. for foreign
missionary work

Judson, Sarah [Hall] B[oardman] (1803–1845) 768
Eng. poet

Juliana Louise Emma Marie Wilhelmina, Queen
(1909–) 1703
Queen of the Netherlands, 1948–1980; d.
Queen Wilhelmina, m. Beatrix Wilhelmina
Armgard (1938– ; Queen of the Netherlands, 1980–)

Juliana of Norwich (c.1342–1417?) 191
Eng. author; aka Dame Julian; first Englishwoman of letters; retired in seclusion to
Church of St. Julian

Jung, Emma (1882–1955) 1311
Swiss scholar, lecturer; née Rauschenbach;
w. Carl J- (psychoanalyst)

Justin, Dena (1912–) 1750
Am. writer, educator, lecturer

K

Kael, Pauline (1919–) 1860
Am. film critic, writer; Natl. Book Award,
1974

Kaga no Chiyo (see Fukuzoyo Chiyo)

Kahlo, Frida (1910–1954) 1722
Mex. painter; w. Diego Rivera (1886–1957,
muralist)

Kahn, Florence Prag (1868–1948) 1143
Am. politician, lawyer; U.S. House of Representatives, 1925–1937, R-California
Kahn, Kathy (1945–) 2410
Am. social worker, songwriter, musician, writer
Kai-shek, Madame Chiang (*see* Chiang Kai-shek, Madame)
Kamamalu (1797?–1824) 744
Hawaiian queen; d. King Kamehameha, s. and w. King Liholiho
Kanin, Fay (1918–) 1843
Am. scenarist, union activist; née Mitchell; president of Writers Guild of America; Emmy Award, 1974 (2), 1979
Kanter, Rosabeth Moss (1943–) 2370
Am. educator, sociologist, writer
Kaplan, Temma E. (1942–) 2350
Am. historian, educator, feminist; née Thane?
Kaptur, Marcia Carolyn (1946–) 2431
Am. congresswoman; U.S. Representative, 1983–
Karmel, Marjorie (fl. 1959) 2515
Am. writer
Kasa no Iratsume (fl. 8th cen.) 106
Jap. noble, poet; w. Otomo no Yakamochi (poet)
Kasebier, Gertrude (1852–1934) 1027
Am. photographer
Kasmuneh (fl. c.12th–13th cen.) 151
Sp. (Moorish/Andalusian) poet; d. Ishmael, poet
Kassebaum, Nancy (1932–) 2107
Am. politician; U.S. Senator, 1979– ; d. Alfred Mossman Landon (1887–1987, governor of Kansas)
Kassia (fl. c.840) 121
Byzantine poet
Kaufman, Shirley (1923–) 1925
Am. poet
Kaufman, Sue (1926–) 1972
Am. writer, editor; h. Barondess
Kavanagh, Julia (1824–1877) 864
Ir. writer
Kawai Chigetsu-Ni (1632–1736) 396
Jap. poet
Kaye, Carol (1930?–) 2067
Am. educator
Kazu-no-miya, Princess (1846–1877) 990
Jap. princess, political activist, poet
Keating, Sarah Sayward (*see* Wood, Sally Sayward)
Kegel, Martha (1958–) 2513
Am. administrator, journalist, civil rights activist
Kellems, Vivien (1896–1975) 1489
Am. industrialist, feminist, lecturer
Keller, Evelyn Fox (1936–) 2197
Am. mathematician, writer, educator
Keller, Helen [Adams] (1880–1968) 1287

Am. writer, lecturer; deaf and blind from infancy; student of Annie Sullivan*; Presidential Medal of Freedom, 1964
Kelley, Edith Summers (1884–1956) 1335
Can/Am. novelist
Kelley, Florence (1859–1932) 1069
Am. writer, civic reformer
Kemble, Fanny [Frances Anne] (1809–1893) 794
Eng. actor, writer, poet; h. Butler
Kemnitz, Mathilda von (1877–?) 1253
Ger. writer; aka Mathilde Spiess Ludendorff
Kempe, Margery (1373–1438?) 200
Eng. author, mystic; née Burnham; w. John K-; author of first known English autobiography
Kempton, Sally (1943?–) 2371
Am. writer, feminist; d. Murray K- (1918– , writer, journalist)
Kennedy, Adrienne (1931–) 2082
Am. playwright; Obie Award, 1964
Kennedy, Florynce (1916–) 1810
Am. lawyer, civil rights activist, feminist
Kennedy, Jacqueline Bouvier (*see* Onassis, Jacqueline K.)
Kennedy, Rose Fitzgerald (1890–) 1413
Am. public figure; w. Joseph P. K-, Sr., m. John F. (U.S. President, 1961–63; assassinated), Robert F. (1925–68; lawyer and politician; assassinated), and Edward (1932– , lawyer and politician)
Kenney, Annie (fl. 1910s) 1712
Eng. suffragist
Kenny, Elizabeth (1886–1952) 1369
Austral. nurse; aka Sister K-; developed method of treatment for poliomyelitis
Kent, Corita (1918–) 1844
Am. graphic artist, former nun
Keppel, Caroline, Lady (1735–?) 529
Scot. poet
Kerbis, Gertrude Lemp (1926–) 1973
Am. architect; designed Seven Continents Bldg. at O'Hare Internatl. Airport, Chicago
Kerr, Jean (1923–) 1926
Am. playwright; née Collins; w. Walter K-
Kerr, Sophie (1880–1965) 1288
Am. writer; h. Underwood
Key, Ellen [Karolina Sofia] (1849–1926) 1003
Swed. writer, feminist
Keyes, Frances Parkinson (1885–1970) 1352
Am. writer, editor
Keyserling, Mary [Dublin] (1910–) 1723
Am. economist, government official; director of Women's Bureau, 1964–69
Khatun, Padeshah (fl. 14th cen.) 189
Iranian poet
Kieko, Yamamuro (1874–1915) 1212
Jap. evangelist, philanthropist
Kii, Lady (fl. 8th cen.) 107
Jap. poet
Kilgallen, Dorothy (1913–1965) 1764

Am. columnist, radio and television personality; w. Dick Kollmar (actor)

Killigrew, Anne (1660–1685) 424
Eng. poet, painter, lady-in-waiting; d. Dr. Henry K-, cousin of Charles and Thomas K- (playwrights)

Killigrew, Catherine (1530?–1583) 275
Eng. poet; d. Anthony Cooke, s. Anne Cooke Bacon,* Lady Mildred Burleigh and Elizabeth Hoby Russell*

Kilmer, Aline Murray (1888–1941) 1386
Am. poet; w. Joyce K- (poet)

Kimball, Harriet [McEwan] (1834–1917) 920
Am. poet

Kincaid, Jamaica (1945?–) 2411
Antiguan/Am. writer

King, Billie Jean (1943–) 2372
Am. tennis pro; founder and developer, World Tennis Team, 1976, and Women's Professional Softball League, 1975; co-founder, Virginia Slims Women's Pro Tennis Tour; won 19 titles at Wimbledon; Women's Sports Hall of Fame, 1980; pioneer in raising recognition and pay for professional women athletes

King, Carole (1941–) 2324
Am. songwriter, singer; Grammy Award, 1971

King, Coretta Scott (1927–) 1999
Am. lecturer, author, concert singer, diplomat, civil rights activist; widow of Martin Luther K., Jr. (1926–1968; civil rights leader; assassinated); founder and president, Martin Luther King, Jr., Center for Non-Violent Social Change, 1971

King, Georgianna Goddard (1871–1939) 1179
Am. art and literary critic, educator, poet, scholar, author; asa G. G. K-; founded art dept. at Bryn Mawr College, 1912

King, Harriet [Eleanor] (1840–1920) 950
Eng. poet

Kingston, Maxine [Ting Ting] Hong (1940–) 2301
Am. nonfiction writer, educator

Ki no Tsurayuki, Daughter of (fl. 947–967) 132
Jap. poet

Kinsky, Countess (see Suttner, Bertha von)

Kinsolving, Sally [Bruce] (1876–1962) 1241
Am. poet

Kirsch, Sarah (1935–) 2173
Ger. writer, poet

Kizer, Carolyn (1925–) 1954
Am. poet, editor, educator; née Ashley

Klopstock, Margaret (1728–1758) 512
Ger. author; née Meta Moller; w. Frederick Gottlieb K- (1724–1803, poet)

Knesebeck, Eleonora von dem (fl. 1684–1713) 452
Ger./Eng. lady-in-waiting to Sophia Dorothea of Celle*

Knight, Sarah Kemble (1666–1727) 435
Am. diarist, poet, businesswoman

Knollys, Lettice (1540–1634) 282
Eng. maid of honor to Elizabeth I of England*; aka countess of Leicester; w. Walter Devereaux, 1st Earl of Essex (1), Robert Dudley, earl of Leicester (2), and Christopher Bount (3); m. Robert Devereaux, 2nd earl of Essex (favorite of Elizabeth I) and Penelope Devereaux Rich*

Knopf, Olga (1888–?) 1387
Austr./Am. psychiatrist, writer

Knowles, Mary (1733–1807) 524
Eng. letter writer; friend of Samuel Johnson and James Boswell

Koghtnatsi, Khosrovidoukht (?–737) 116
Armenian poet; d. Khosrov (prince of the Koghten region)

Kōka [Mon-in no Bettō], Stewardess of the Empress (fl. 12th cen.) 154
Jap. poet; d. Fujiwara no Toshitaka

Kolb, Barbara (1939–) 2270
Am. composer

Koller, Alice (1924–) 1935
Am. philosopher

Kollontai, Aleksandra [Mikhailovna] (1872–1952) 1187
Russ. writer, diplomat, propagandist, government official; first commissar of Public Welfare for Bolshevik government, 1917–1918; Order of Lenin

Kollwitz, Käthe (1867–1945) 1136
E. Prussian painter, sculptor, graphic artist; née Schmidt; first woman elected full member of Prussian Academy of Arts, 1919

Komarovsky, Mirra (1906–) 1661
Russ./Am. college professor, sociologist, author, editor; w. Marcus A. Heyman

Koontz, [Elizabeth Duncan] Libby (1919–) 1861
Am. government official; director of Women's Bureau, 1969–73 (first black woman to hold position)

Kouchak, Nahabed (fl. 15th cen.) 203
Armenian poet

Kramer, Jane (1938?–) 2243
Am. writer

Krantz, Judith (1932–) 2108
Am. novelist, editor; née Tarcher

Kreps, Juanita M. (1921–) 1890
Am. government official, educator, administrator; née Morris; vice president of Duke University, 1973–77; U.S. Secretary of Commerce, 1977–79 (first woman to hold position)

Kristeva, Julia (1941–) 2325
Fr. psychoanalyst, author

Krudener, Juliana, Baroness (1764–1824) 626
Russ. novelist, mystic; aka Barbara Juliana von Vietinghoff

Kshetrayya (fl 17th cen.) 347
Ind. (Telugu) poet

Kuan Tao-shêng (1262–1319) 186
Chin. poet, painter, calligrapher
Kubatum (fl. c.2032 B.C.) 44
Sumerian poet
Kübler-Ross, Elisabeth (1926–) 1974
Swiss/Am. thanatologist, psychiatrist, author
Kuhn, [Margaret E.] Maggie (1905–) 1641
Am. civil rights activist, author; founder of Gray Panthers, 1970
Kumin, Maxine (1925–) 1955
Am. poet, author; née Winokur; Pulitzer Prize for Poetry, 1973
Kummer, Clare [Rodman Beecher] (1888–1948) 1388
Am. playwright, songwriter

L

Labé, Louise (1524/25–1566) 269
Fr. poet, linguist, feminist, soldier; asa Labbé; aka La belle Amazone, La belle Cordière (The Beautiful Ropemaker), Captain Lays (title and pseud. while in the army); w. Ennemond Perrin
La Coste, Marie [Ravene] de (1849–1936) 1004
Am. writer, poet
Lactilla (see Yearsley, Anne)
La Fayette, Marie Madeleine de, Countess (1634–1692/93) 400
Fr. novelist, salonist; née Pioche de La Vergne; w. François Motier, comte de La Fayette
LaFollette, Suzanne (1893–1983) 1456
Am. feminist, writer, editor; d. William L. L- (U.S. Congressman)
Lagerlöf, Selma [Ottiliana Lovisa] (1858–1940) 1057
Swed. writer; first woman elected to and director of Swedish Academy; Nobel Prize for Literaure, 1909 (first woman to receive award)
Laing, Dilys (1906–1960) 1662
Can. poet, editor
Lal Ded (see Ded, Lal)
Lalleswari (fl. 1365–1399) 197
Ind. (Kashmiri) poet, saint; aka Lalla
Lamb, Caroline, Lady (1785–1828) 695
Eng. novelist; d. Frederick Ponsonby, 3rd earl of Bessborough, w. Sir William L-, 2nd viscount Melbourne, mistress of Lord Byron (1788–1824, poet), niece of Georgiana Cavendish*
Lamb, Mary Ann (1764–1847) 627
Eng. poet, author, letter writer, dressmaker; aka Sempronia, Bridget Elia; s. Charles L- (1775–1834, essayist)
Lambrun, Margaret (fl. 1587) 332
Scot. courtier; aka Anthony Sparke
Lanchester, Elsa (1902–1986) 1589
Eng./Am. actor; née Elizabeth Sullivan; widow of Charles Laughton (d. 1962, actor)

Landers, Ann (1918–) 1845
Am. columnist; née Esther "Eppie" Friedman; h. Lederer; s. Abigail Van Buren*
Landon, Letitia [Elizabeth] (1802–1838) 765
Eng. poet; h. Maclean; asa L. E. L-
Landowska, Wanda (1877/79–1959) 1276
Pol./Fr./Am. harpsichordist, composer, music scholar; w. Henry Lew (d. 1919, writer); Recording Academy Hall of Fame; founder, l'Ecole de Musique Ancienne
Lange, Dorothea (1895–1965) 1484
Am. photographer
Langer, Susanne K[nauth] (1895–1985) 1485
Am. educator, philosopher, writer
Langston, Dicey (1760?–?) 615
Am. Revolutionary war hero
Langtry, Lily (1853–1929) 1028
Eng. actor; née Emily Charlotte Le Breton; aka "The Jersey Lily"
Lanier, Emilia (1569/70–c.1640/45) 312
Eng. poet; asa Aemelia Lanyer; d. Baptista Bassano (musician) and Margaret Johnson, w. Alphonso L- (musician), m. Henry L- (musician); probably the "Dark Lady" addressed in Shakespeare's sonnets #127–152
La Pasionaria (see Ibarruri, Dolores)
Lape, Esther [Everett] (1881–1981) 1301
Am. educator, editor, author, social activist, suffragist, researcher; director, American Foundation for Studies in Government, 1924–55
Lappé, Frances Moore (1944–) 2393
Am. author, activist, ecologist; w. Marc L-; founder of Food First/Institute for Food and Development Policy, 1975
Laramore, Vivian Yeiser (1891–?) 1424
Am. poet
Larcom, Lucy (1826–1893) 877
Am. editor, poet, mill worker
Lasker-Schuler, Else (1869–1945) 1154
Ger./Swiss poet
La Suze, countess de (see Coligny, Henriette de)
Lathbury, Eva (fl. early 1900s) 1538
Eng. writer
Lathbury, Mary [Artemisia] (1841–1913) 959
Am. poet, hymnist; aka "The Chautauqua Laureate"
Lauder, Estée (1900?–) 1557
Am. business executive, philanthropist; née Josephine Estée Mentzer; founder and chair, Estée Lauder, Inc., 1946
Launay, Mme de (fl. 1820s) 839
Fr. actor; aka Mlle Hopkins; friend of Marceline Desbordes-Valmore*
Launay, Charles de, Vicomte (see Girardin, Delphine de)
Laurel, Alicia Bay (1949–) 2470
Am. naturalist, writer, illustrator

MacLeod, Mairi (1569–1674?)　　313
　Scot. poet, nurse; d. Red Alastair (poet)

Macuilxochitl (1435–1499?)　　212
　Aztec poet; d. Tlacaelel (counselor to Itzcoatl)

Madan, Judith (fl. 1750)　　571
　Eng. poet; née Cowper; s. William Cowper (?–1723, lord high chancellor of England, 1707–19 and 1714–18)

Madison, Dolley (1768–1849)　　643
　Am. First Lady, society leader; née Dorothea Payne; w. John Todd (1) and James M- (2; 4th U.S. President, 1809–17)

Magdeburg, Mechtild von (see Mechtild von Magdeburg)

Magdelene, Mary (see Mary Magdelene)

Magnani, Anna (1918–1973)　　1847
　Egypt./Ital. actor; Academy Award, 1955

Mahādēviyakka (fl. 12th cen.)　　152
　Ind. (Kannada) poet, Hindu saint; asa Mahadevi; w. King Kausika

Mahlah (see Zelophehad)

Mahler, Alma (see Werfel, Alma Mahler)

Mahler, Margaret (1897–1985)　　1509
　Hung./Am. psychoanalyst, psychiatrist, nonfiction writer, lecturer; née Schoenberger

Mahodahi (fl. c.700–1050)　　109
　Ind. (Sanskrit) poet

Mahsati (fl. 12th cen.)　　153
　Iran. poet

Maintenon, Françoise de (1635–1719)　　401
　Fr. letter writer; née d'Aubigné, asa marquise or Mme de M-; w. Paul Scarron (1), mistress and w. Louis XIV of France (2); founded school for daughters of impoverished noblemen at St.-Cyr, 1686

Makeba, Miriam (1932–)　　2110
　So. Afr./Am./Ghanaian singer, political activist; aka Mama Africa; ex-w. Stokely Carmichael (Am. civil rights activist)

Makhfi (1639–1703)　　405
　Ind. (Farsi) princess, poet, patron of poets and scholars; aka Zibu'n-Nisa (asa Zeb-un-Nissa)

Makin, Bathsua (1612?–1674?)　　367
　Eng. scholar, author; d. John Pell, s. John Pell II (mathematician); tutor to the children of Charles II of England

Malpede, Karen (1945–)　　2412
　Am. playwright, theater historian, educator, peace activist

Mamonova, Tatyana (1944?–)　　2395
　Soviet/Austr. painter, poet, translator, critic, feminist

Mancini, Maria Anna (1649–1714)　　415
　Ital./Fr. salonist; d. Michele Lorenzo M- and Girolama Mazzarino, s. Laure, Olympe, Marie and Hortense M-, w. Godefroy Maurice de la Tour, duc de Bouillon, niece of Cardinal Mazarin; patron of La Fontaine, Corneille, and Molière

Mandela, Winnie (1934–)　　2160
　So. Afr. civil rights activist; w. (separated) Nelson M- (activist and hero)

Mankiller, Wilma Pearl (1945–)　　2413
　Am. Chief of Cherokee Nation of Oklahoma, 1985–

Manley, Joan [Adele] (1932–)　　2111
　Am. publisher; née Daniels; chair of the board, Time-Life Books, 1976–

Manley, Mary de la Rivière (1663–1724)　　428
　Eng. author, playwright, editor; first Englishwoman to be a political journalist, to author a bestseller, and to be arrested for her writings

Mann, Erika (1905–1969)　　1642
　Ger. writer, journalist, lecturer; d. Thomas M-, w. W. H. Auden (1907–73, Eng./Am. author)

Manner, Eeva-Liisa (1921–)　　1891
　Fin. poet, writer, playwright

Mannering, Julia (see Bingham, Madeleine)

Manners, Diane (see Cooper, Lady Diana)

Manners, Frances, Lady (see Abergavenny, Lady Frances)

Mannes, Marya (1904–)　　1624
　Am. writer, journalist

Mansfield, Katherine (1888–1923)　　1391
　Eng. writer, literary critic; née Kathleen Beauchamp Murry

Mantua, marquise de (see Este, Isabella d')

Mara, Gertrude Elizabeth (1749–1833)　　564
　Ger. singer; née Schmaling

Maraini, Dacia (1935–)　　2198
　Ital. poet, playwright, feminist, political activist

Marbury, Elisabeth (1856–1933)　　1040
　Am. playwright, literary agent, theater manager, translator

Marcelle, countess de (fl. c.1540s)　　283
　Fr. nun

Marchant, Catherine (see Cookson, Catherine)

Marchocka, Anna Maria (1603–1652)　　358
　Pol. Carmelite nun; aka Sister Teresa

Marcos, Imelda (1929/31–)　　2029
　Philippine public figure; née Romualdez; w. Ferdinand M- (1917–89, president of Philippines, 1966–86); Miss Manila, 1953; governor of Metropolitan Manila, 1975–?, Cabinet Member, 1978–86

Margaret of Alençon and Margaret of Angouleme (see Marguerite of Navarre)

Margaret of Anjou (1430–1482)　　211
　Eng. queen, military hero; w. Henry VI of England, m. Edward, prince of Wales

Margaret of Austria (1480–1530)　　231
　Austr. regent of the Netherlands; d. Maxi-

milian of Austria, w. Charles VIII of France (1), Don Juan of Castile and Aragon (2) and Philibert, duke of Savoy (3)

Margaret of Nassau (fl. 1367)   198
Ger. noble?; friend of Matilda of Cleves

Margot (*see* Marguerite of Valois)

Marguerite of Navarre (1492–1549)   237
Fr. poet, author, scholar, religious reformer, patron of literature; aka Margaret of Angouleme, of Alençon, The Tenth Muse, The Pearl, Parlamente (her pseud. in the *Heptameron*); s. Francis I of France, w. duke of Alençon (1) and Henry d'Albret (2; titular king of Navarre), m. Jeanne d'Albret,* grandm. Henry IV of France

Marguerite of Valois (1553–1615)   293
Fr. queen, diarist; aka Margot; d. Catherine de' Medici,* s. Francis II of France, Charles IX of France and Henry III of France, first w. Henry of Navarre (later Henry IV of France)

Maria, Laura (*see* Robinson, Mary)

Maria de Jesus, Sister (*see* Agreda, Maria de)

Maria of Hungary and Bohemia (1505–1558)   246
Austr. queen, poet; aka Maria Hapsburg; s. Charles V (Holy Roman Emperor, aka Charles I of Spain), Ferdinand of Austria, Elizabeth (aka Isabel) of Denmark, and Eleanore of Portugal; w. Louis II of Bohemia and Hungary

Maria Theresa (1717–1780)   490
Austr. queen, empress, reformer, philanthropist, letter writer; aka archduchess of Austria, queen of Hungary and Bohemia, empress of the Holy Roman Empire; d. Charles VI of Austria, w. Francis of Lorraine (grand-duke of Tuscany later Francis I, Holy Roman Emperor), m. Joseph II (Holy Roman Emperor, co-regent of Austria) and Marie-Antoinette*

Marie-Antoinette (1755–1793)   588
Austr./Fr. queen; née Josephe Jeanne Marie-A-; d. Francis I (Holy Roman Emperor) and Empress Marie Theresa,* w. Louis XVI of France, m. Louis, dauphin of France

Marie de France (1160?–1215?)   163
Fr./Eng. noble, author, translator; first European female author of fiction

Maria, Grand Duchess of Russia (1890–1958)   1415
Russ. duchess

Marinda (*see* Monk, Mary)

Marinella, Lucrezia (fl. 1600)   351
Ital. author

Marion, Frances (1886–1973)   1370
Am. scenarist, journalist; Academy Award, 1932

Marissa (*see* Lee, Mary Chudleigh)

Markham, Lucia Clark (1870–?)   1170
Am. poet

Markova, Alicia, Dame (1910–)   1726
Eng. ballet dancer

Marsh, Anne (1791–1874)   720
Eng. author; née Caldwell, pseud. "An Old Man"

Marshall, [Sarah] Catherine (1914–1983)   1777
Am. writer, editor; née Wood

Martin, Del (1921–)   1892
Am. civil rights activist, feminist, writer; co-founder of Daughters of Bilitis

Martin, Elizabeth (c.1745—post-1776)   556
Am. patriot; née Marshall

Martin, Martha (1896–1959)   1490
Am. diarist, adventurer; aka Helen Boylan

Martin, Sarah (1791–1843)   721
Eng. prison reformer, dressmaker

Martin, Sarah Catherine (fl. 1805)   781
Eng. poet

Martineau, Harriet (1802–1876)   766
Eng. writer, social critic, feminist

Marula (fl. c.1156)   162
Ind. (Sanskrit) poet

Mary, Countess of Warwick (1624–1678)   382
Ir. society leader; née Mary Boyle, aka Mary Rich

Mary, Queen of Scots (1542–1587)   285
Scot./Fr. queen, poet; aka Mary Stuart; d. James V of Scotland and Mary of Guise, w. Francis II of France (1), Henry Stuart (2; Lord Darnley), and James Hepburn (3; 4th earl of Bothwell), m. James VI of Scotland (later James I of England), first cousin of Elizabeth I of England*

Mary, Virgin (fl. c.7 B.C.–A.D. 25)   39
Nazarene; d. Anna and Joachim, w. Joseph, m. Jesus Christ, cousin of St. Elisabeth*

Maryam bint Abi Ya'qub al-Ansari (fl. 1000–1035)   140
Arabic/Sp. poet

Mary Magdalene (fl. c.A.D. 25)   42
Biblical; first person to learn of the resurrection

Mary I of England (1516–1558)   257
Eng. queen; aka Bloody Mary, Mary Tudor; d. Henry VIII and Catherine of Aragon,* half-s. Elizabeth I* and Edward VI, w. Philip II of Spain

Mary II of England (1662–1694)   426
Eng. queen; d. James II of England and Anne Hyde, s. Anne of England,* w. William II of Orange (later William III of England)

Mary of France (1496–1533)   238
Eng. queen; aka The White Queen, Mary Tudor, duchess of Suffolk; d. Henry VII of England, s. Henry VIII of England, w. Louis XII of France (1) and Charles Brandon, duke of Suffolk (2), grandm. Lady Jane Grey*

Mary of the Gaels (*see* Brigid of Kildare)

Mason, Caroline [Atherton Briggs] (1823–1890)   861
Am. poet

Mason-Manheim, Madeline (1908–)   1692
Am. poet, writer, literary critic

Masters, Mary (fl. 1733–1755)   525
Eng. poet, letter writer

Mathews, Jessica Tuchman (1946–)   2433
Am. environmental scientist, research center executive; d. Barbara Tuchman*

Mathilde, Princess (1820–1904)   848
Fr. princess, writer; niece of Napoleon I

Matilda, Anna (*see* Cowley, Hannah)

Matilda of Magdeburg (*see* Mechtild von Magdeburg)

Matraini, Chiara Cantarini (1514–post–1597)   255
Ital. poet; asa Clara M- ; w. Vicenzo Contarini

Matthews-Simonton, Stephanie (1940?–)   2307
Am. psychotherapist; w. John S- ; pioneer in cancer psychotherapy

Maximilla (c.465–1465)   91
Religious leader

Maxtone Graham, Joyce Anstruther (*see* Struther, Jan)

Maxwell, Darcy, Lady (1742?–1810)   548
Scot.?/Eng.? religious leader, philanthropist, courtier; née Brisbane; friend of John Wesley

Maxwell, Elsa (1883–1963)   1325
Am. society leader, writer

Maxwell, Mary Elizabeth (*see* Braddon, Mary Elizabeth)

May, Julia Harris (1833–1912)   915
Am. poet

Mayer, Maria Goeppert (1906–1972)   1664
Ger./Am. physicist; w. J. A. Jensen; discovered shell structure of atomic nuclei; Nobel Prize, 1963

McAuliffe, [Sharon] Christa [Corrigan] (1948–1986)   2464
Am. teacher, astronaut

McBride, Mary Margaret (1899–1976)   1533
Am. columnist, writer, radio personality

McCall, Dorothy (1889–?)   1400
Am. political activist

McCarthy, Abigail [Eleanor] (1914?–)   1778
Am. author; née Quigley; ex-w. Eugene M- (politician)

McCarthy, Mary [Therese] (1912–1989)   1752
Am. writer, editor, drama and social critic; s. Kevin M- (actor); ex-w. Edmund Wilson (3; critic), James West (4; diplomat)

McCarthy, Sarah J. (1942–)   2351
Am. writer, educator, activist; aka Sally M-

McCaslin, Mary (1946?–)   2434
Am. singer, songwriter

McClintock, Barbara (1902–)   1590
Am. botanist, geneticist, educator; Natl. Medal of Science, 1970, Nobel Prize, 1983

McClung, Nellie (1873–1951)   1195
Can. feminist, writer

McCormick, Anne O'Hare (1882?–1954)   1313
Am. journalist, writer; Pulitzer Prize, 1937

McCormick, Virginia Taylor (1873–1957)   1196
Am. poet

McCorquodale, Barbara (*see* Cartland, Barbara)

McCullers, Carson (1917–1967)   1829
Am. writer, playwright; née Smith

McDougall, Joyce (1926–)   1980
New Zeal./Fr. psychoanalyst, author; née Carrington

McGinley, Phyllis (1905–1978)   1643
Am. poet, humorist; Pulitzer Prize, 1961

McGovern, Ann (1930–)   2070
Am. editor, writer

McGrory, Mary (1918–)   1848
Am. columnist; Pulitzer Prize, 1975

McIntosh, Maria (1803–1878)   770
Am. writer

McKenney, Ruth (1911–1972)   1739
Am. writer

McLaughlin, Patricia (1916–)   1812
Ir./Am. civic leader, editor

McLeod, Irene Rutherford (1891–1964?)   1425
Eng. poet; h. De Selincourt

McPherson, Aimee Semple (1890–1944)   1416
Can./Am. evangelist; aka Sister Aimee; founder of Internatl. Church of the Foursquare Gospel

McRae, Carmen (1922–)   1909
Am. jazz singer

Meacock, Norma (193?–)   2051
Eng. writer

Mead, Margaret (1901–1978)   1576
Am. anthropologist, writer, editor, museum curator; w. Gregory Bateson (1904–80, anthropologist), m. Mary Catherine Bateson*; Presidential Medal of Freedom, 1979

Mechain, Gwerfyl (c.1460–1500)   217
Welsh poet

Mechtild von Magdeburg (c.1212–1283)   181
Ger. mystic, author, church reformer; aka Matilda of Magdeburg; member of Beguines

Medici, Catherine de' (1519–1589)   258
Ital./Fr. queen; d. Lorenzo de Medici, duke of Urbino; grandd. Lucrezia de' Medici,* w. Henry II of France, m. Marguerite of Valois,* Francis II of France, Charles IX of France and Henry III of France

Medici, Lucrezia de' (1425–1482)   208
Ital. poet, patron of the arts; née Tournabuoni; w. Piero de' Medici, m. Lorenzo de' Medici (the Magnificent), grandm. Catherine de' Medici,* great grandm. Marguerite of Valois*

Mehri (c.1404–1447)   204

Iran. poet; aka Mihru'n-Nisa of Herat

Meir, Golda (1898–1978)　　　　　　1522
　Russ./Am./Isr. politician; née Mabovitch;
　h. Meyerson; first prime minister of Israel,
　1969–1974

Melanie (1947–　)　　　　　　　　2453
　Am. singer, songwriter; née Melanie Safka

Melba, Nellie, Dame (1865?–1911)　　1121
　Austral. opera singer; née Helen Porter
　Mitchell

Melvill, Elizabeth (fl. 1603)　　　　　359
　Scot. poet; aka Lady Culross, Lady Colvill
　of Culross; d. Sir James M., w. Colvill of
　Culross

Mendel, Lady (see De Wolfe, Elsie)

Mendenhall, Dorothy Reed (1874–1964)　1214
　Am. physician, civil rights activist, govern-
　ment official; director of U.S. Children's
　Bureau; innovator in obstetrics

Mercer, Margaret (1791–1846)　　　　722
　Am. educator, philanthropist, abolitionist

Mercis (see Pharoah's Daughter)

Mercouri, Melina (1925–　)　　　　　1956
　Grk. actor, government official, political
　activist; w. Jules Dassin (Am. film director)

Mère, Madame (see Bonaparte, Marie L.)

Merian, Maria Sibylla (1647–1717)　　412
　Ger. painter, entomologist, botanist; h. Graff

Merman, Ethel (1908–1984)　　　　　1693
　Am. singer, actor; née Ethel Agnes Zim-
　mermann; Antoinette Perry Award, 1951;
　Grammy Award, 1959

Merry, Anne Brunton (1769–1808)　　648
　Eng./Am. actor, theater manager; aka Mrs.
　Wignell, Mrs. Warren; w. Robert M- (1;
　poet, playwright, politician), Thomas Wig-
　nell (2; theater producer, manager), and
　William Warren (3; theater producer, man-
　ager)

Mew, Charlotte [Mary] (1869–1928)　　1155
　Eng. poet, writer

Meyer, Agnes [Elizabeth Ernst] (1887–1970?) 1377
　Am. writer, journalist, translator, social
　worker

Meynell, Alice (1847–1922)　　　　　995
　Eng. poet, literary critic; née Thompson

Michal (fl. c.1010–970 B.C.)　　　　21
　Benjamite queen; d. Saul, king of Israel, s.
　Merab (first betrothed to David), first w.
　David, king of Israel

Michel, Louise (1830–1905)　　　　　897
　Fr. revolutionary; pseud. Clemence

Michelman, Kate (1942–　)　　　　　2352
　Am. women's rights activist, civic organi-
　zation administrator; executive director of
　the National Abortion Rights Action League
　(NARAL), 1985–

Michiel, Renier Giustina (1755–1832)　589
　Ital. botanist, noble

Michiner, Harry, Mrs. (see Irving, Minna)

Michitsuna, Mother of (fl. 954–974)　　133
　Jap. diarist; aka Lady Gossamer; mistress
　of Fujiwara no Kane-iye (statesman), w.
　Regent Kaneie, m. Udaishō Michitsuna no
　haba

Midler, Bette (1945–　)　　　　　　2414
　Am. singer, actor, writer; aka The Divine
　Miss M; Grammy Award, 1973, 1980 (2),
　Antoinette Perry Award, 1973, Emmy
　Award, 1978

Mihru'n-Nisa of Herat (see Mehri)

Mikulski, Barbara Ann (1936–　)　　2199
　Am. politician; U.S. House of Representa-
　tives, 1977– , D-Maryland

Milan, duchess of (see Este, Beatrice d')

Milbanke, Anne Isabella (1792–1860)　727
　Eng. poet; aka Lady Byron, Annabella; w.
　George Gordon (aka Lord Byron, 1788–
　1824, poet); m. Augusta Ada Byron

Milcah (see Zelophehad)

Mildmay, Lady (see Sherrington, Grace)

Miles, Josephine (1911–1985)　　　　1740
　Am. poet, educator, literary critic

Millar, Margaret Ellis (1915–　)　　1794
　Can./Am. fiction writer; née Sturm; w.
　Kenneth M- (pseud. Ross Macdonald, writer)

Millar, Susanna (fl. 1960s)　　　　　2521
　Eng. psychologist, writer

Millay, Edna St. Vincent (1892–1950)　1439
　Am. poet, playwright, writer; h. Boisse-
　vain; pseud. Nancy Boyd; Pulitzer Prize,
　1923

Miller, Alice (193?–　)　　　　　　2052
　Ger. painter, arts-in-education specialist

Miller, Alice Duer (1874–1942)　　　1215
　Am. writer, poet; h. Wise

Miller, Emily (1833–1913)　　　　　916
　Am. journalist, writer, poet, editor, social
　reformer; aka Emily Clark Huntington

Miller, Helen [Day] Hill (1899–?)　　1534
　Am. journalist, writer

Miller, Isabel (see Routsong, Alma)

Miller, Jean Baker (1927–　)　　　　2000
　Am. psychoanalyst, psychiatrist, editor,
　teacher, author

Miller, Lee (1907–1977)　　　　　　1674
　Am. photographer, model; w. Sir Roland
　Algernon Penrose (1900–84, Eng. art critic,
　collector, painter)

Miller, Margaret (1915–　)　　　　　1794
　Am. writer

Millet, Kate (1934–　)　　　　　　2161
　Am. sculptor, writer, feminist

Milner, Marion (see Field, Joanna)

Miner, Dorothy Eugenia (1904–1973)　1625
　Am. librarian, scholar

Mink, Patsy Takemoto (1927–　)　　2001
　Am. politician, lawyer; Hawaiian territorial
　legislator, 1956–58 (first Nisei woman to
　so serve); U.S. Reprsentative, 1965–77, D-

Hawaii; first Japanese-American woman elected to Congress; co-founder of Women USA

Miriam (fl. c.1250–1230 B.C.)   9
Hebr. prophet, poet; d. Jochebed, s. Moses and Aaron, w. Hur

Mirrielees, Edith Ronald (1878–1962)   1265
Am. writer, educator, editor

Mistral, Gabriela (1889–1957)   1401
Chilean poet, educator, diplomat; née Lucila Godoy y Alcayaga; Nobel Prize, 1945

Mitchell, Helen Porter (see Melba, Dame Nellie)

Mitchell, Joni (1943–)   2375
Am. songwriter, singer; Grammy Award, 1969

Mitchell, Juliet (1940–)   2302
New Zeal./Eng. writer, lecturer, editor

Mitchell, Margaret (1900–1949)   1560
Am. writer; h. Marsh; Pulitzer Prize, 1937

Mitchell, Maria (1818–1889)   830
Am. astronomer, educator; first woman astronomer in U.S.; first woman member of American Academy of Arts and Sciences, Hall of Fame, 1905; discovered new comet, 1847

Mitchell, Martha (1918–1976)   1849
Am. public figure; née Jennings; w. John M- (1913– , lawyer, attorney general of the U.S., 1968–72)

Mitford, Jessica [Lucy] (1917–)   1830
Eng./Am. writer, social critic; h. Treuhaft

Mitford, Mary Russell (1787–1855)   701
Eng. poet, author, playwright; aka Sancho Panza in Petticoats

Mitford, Nancy (1904–1973)   1626
Eng. writer, biographer

Modjeska, Helena (1840–1910)   951
Pol. actor; née Opid

Modotti, Tina (1896–1942)   1491
Ital./Am./Mex. photographer, actor, revolutionist; companion to Edward Weston (1; 1850–1936, Eng./Am. photographer), Julio Antonio Mella (2; Cuban revolutionary; assassinated, 1928)

Moffat, Mary Jane (1938?–)   2245
Am. educator, writer, actor

Moirai, Catherine Risingflame (195?–)   2482
Am. poet

Moïse, Penina (1797–1880)   746
Am. poet, Jewish hymnist

Monk, Mary (?–1715)   488
Ir. poet, noble; née Molesworth, asa Monck, pseud. Marinda

Monroe, Anne Shannon (1877–1942)   1255
Am. writer, lecturer

Monroe, Harriet (1860–1936)   1079
Am. editor, poet

Monroe, Marilyn (1926–1962)   1981
Am. actor; née Norma Jean Baker; ex-w.

Joe DiMaggio (2, baseball hero), Arthur Miller (3, playwright)

Montagu, Elizabeth (1720–1800)   496
Eng. essayist, letter writer; née Robinson; first bluestocking

Montagu, Mary Wortley, Lady (1689–1762)   458
Eng. poet, letter writer, essayist; d. Evelyn Pierrepont (marquess of Dorchester and 1st duke of Kingston), w. Edward W- M- I, m. Edward W- M- II (writer and traveler)

Montansier, La (see Brunet, Marguerite)

Montessori, Maria (1870–1952)   1171
Ital. educator, physician, writer; originator of Montessori Method of education; first Italian woman to receive M.D. from University of Rome

Montgomery, countess of (see Wroth, Mary Sidney)

Montgomery, Lucy [Maud] (1874–1942)   1216
Can. writer

Montgomery, Roselle Mercier (1874–1933)   1217
Am. poet

Montolieu, Jeanne Isabelle [de Bottens], baronne, (1751–1832)   574
Swiss novelist

Montpensier, duchess de (see Orleans, Anne-Marie-Louise d')

Moodie, Susanna (1803–1885)   771
Can. writer, poet

Moody, Anne (1940–)   2303
Am. writer, activist

Moore, Grace (1901–1947)   1577
Am. opera singer, actor

Moore, Honor (1945–)   2415
Am. playwright, poet

Moore, Julia A. (1847–1920)   996
Am. poet

Moore, Marianne [Craig] (1887–1972)   1378
Am. poet; Pulitzer Prize, 1952, Bollingen Prize in Poetry, 1951, Natl. Book Award, 1952

Moore, Virginia [E.] (1903–1988)   1605
Am. poet, biographer

Moorhead, Sarah Parsons (fl. 1741/1742)   542
Am. poet

Morata, Olimpia (1526–1555)   270
Ital. scholar, poet

More, Hannah (1745–1833)   557
Eng. author, reformer, philanthropist; aka The Laureate of the Bluestockings, Stella, pseud. Will Chip

Moreau, Jeanne (1929–)   2030
Fr. actor

Morgan, Angela (1874?–1957)   1218
Am. poet, writer, lecturer

Morgan, Barbara [Brooks] (1900–)   1561
Am. photographer

Morgan, Elaine [Neville] (1920–)   1883
Welsh writer, educator

O

Oakley, Ann (1944–)   2396
Eng. sociologist, author; née Titmuss
Oakley, Annie (1860–1926)   1081
Am. markswoman, entertainer; née Phoebe
Ann Mozee; w. Frank Butler
Oates, Joyce Carol (1938–)   2246
Am. writer; Natl. Book Award, 1970
O'Brien, Edna (1932–)   2113
Ir./Eng. writer, pacifist
Ocampo, Victoria (1891–1979)   1427
Argen. writer, publisher; aka Queen of Letters; founder of *Sur* (avant-garde literary magazine)
O'Casey, Eileen (1905?–)   1644
Ir./Eng. actor, writer; née Carey; w. Sean O-(1880–1964, playwright)
Occident, Maria del (*see* Brooks, Maria)
O'Connor, Flannery (1925–1964)   1958
Am. writer; Natl. Book Award, 1972
O'Connor, Sandra Day (1930–)   2071
Am. judge, lawyer; U.S. Supreme Court Justice, 1981– ; first woman to serve on Supreme Court
O'Keeffe, Adelaide (1776–1855?)   672
Eng. poet, novelist
O'Keeffe, Georgia (1887–1986)   1379
Am. painter; widow of Alfred Stieglitz (1864–1946, "father of modern photography"); Presidential Medal of Freedom, 1977
Olesnicka, Zofia (fl. 1556)   295
Pol. poet; w. or s. Mikolaj Olesnicki, lord of Pinczow; first poet in the Polish tongue
Oliphant, Carolina (*see* Nairne, Carolina)
Oliphant, Margaret (1828–1897)   886
Eng. writer, historian; h. Wilson
Oliver, Ruth Law (1891?–1970)   1428
Am. aviator; set altitude and long-distance records
Olsen, Tillie (1913–)   1767
Am. writer
Onassis, Jacqueline Kennedy (1929–)   2032
Am. First Lady, book editor; née Bouvier; widow of John F. Kennedy (1; U.S. President, 1960–1963; assassinated) and Aristotle O- (2; Grk. shipping magnate); Emmy Award, 1962
O'Neill, Carlotta Monterey (1888–1970)   1392
Sp./Am. actor; w. Eugene O'Neill (1888–1953, playwright)
O'Neill, Henrietta (1758–1793)   601
Ir. poet; née Dungarvon
O'Neill, Moira (fl. early 1900s)   1539
Ir. poet; née Agnes Higginson Skrine
O'Neill, Rose [Cecil] (1874–1944)   1219
Am. writer, poet, illustrator; created the Kewpie Doll
Ono, Yoko (1933–)   2132
Jap./Eng. poet, songwriter, painter; widow

of John Lennon (1940–80, Eng. singer, songwriter; murdered)
Ono no Komachi (834–880)   120
Jap. poet; d. Yoshisada, lord of Dewa; legendary beauty of Japan
Opie, Amelia (1769–1853)   649
Eng. poet, novelist; née Alderson; second w. John O- (1761–1807, painter)
Orczy, [Emmuska], Baroness (1865–1947)   1122
Eng. writer, playwright; h. Barstow
O'Reilly, Jane (1936–)   2200
Am. writer, editor
Origo, Iris [Cutting], Marchesa (1902–1988)   1592
Eng./Ital. writer
Orinda (*see* Philips, Katherine Fowler)
Orléans, Anne-Marie-Louise d' (1627–1693)   388
Fr. author, noble; aka La Grande Mademoisselle, duchesse de Montpensier; grandd. Henry IV of France, d. Gaston d'O-, niece of Louis XIII of France
Orlova, Raisa Davydovna (1917–1964)   1831
Soviet/Ger. diplomat, editor, literary critic, author
Orred, Meta (fl. 1880s)   1285
Eng. poet, songwriter
Orsini, Isabella de Medici (1542–1576)   284
Ital. noble; aka duchess of Bracciano; d. Cosimo I and Eleanora de Toledo, w. Paolo Giordano d'O- , duke of Bracciano
Ortese, Anna Maria (1928?–)   2106
Ital. writer; Premio Viareggio Prize, 1953, Premio St. Vincent Prize, 1958
Osborne, Dorothy (1627–1695)   389
Eng. letter writer; aka Lady Temple
Osgood, Frances Sargent (1811–1850)   799
Am. poet; née Locke; pseud. Kate Florence Carol
Ossoli, Marchesa (*see* Fuller, Margaret)
Ostenso, Martha (1900–1963)   1563
Nor./Am. writer, poet, humorist
Otero, Caroline "La Belle" (1868–1965)   1145
Sp. actor, courtesan; née Augustine O. Iglesias
Ōtomo no Sakano-e no Iratsume (c.700–750)   110
Jap. poet, courtier; aka Lady Sakanoé, asa Sakanone; s. Tabito (governor and poet), aunt of Ōtomo no Yakamochi (poet)
Ouida (1839–1908)   945
Eng. writer; née Marie Louise de la Ramée
Owen, Anita (fl. 1890s)   1406
Am. poet
Owen, Jane (fl. 1610–d.1633?)   365
Eng. religious author
Owens, Rochelle (1936–)   2201
Am. playwright, poet, writer; h. Economou; Obie Award, 1967, 1981
Owens, Vilda Sauvage (1875–1950)   1233
Welsh/Am. poet

Oxford and Asquith, countess of (*see* Asquith, Margot)

Ozick, Cynthia (1931–)　　　2087
Am. writer

P

Packard, Clarissa (*see* Gilman, Caroline)

Pagels, Elaine (1943–)　　　2376
Am. historian of religion, educator, author; née Hiesey; National Book Award, 1980

Painter, Charlotte (1926–)　　　1984
Am. writer, educator

Painter, Pamela (1941–)　　　2328
Am. fiction writer, editor; founding editor, *Story Quarterly,* 1974–79

Paley, Grace (1922–)　　　1910
Am. writer

Palmer, Alice [Elvira] Freeman (1855–1902) 1037
Am. editor, poet, college administrator; president, Wellesley College; founder, American Assoc. of University Women; Hall of Fame, 1920

Palmer, Gretta Brooker (1905–1953)　　　1645
Am. journalist, writer

Pan Chao (c.45–c.115)　　　76
Chin. historian, poet

Pandit, Vijaya Lakshmi (1900–1990)　　　1564
Ind. government official, diplomat, pacifist; w. Jawaharlal Nehru (1889–1964, first Prime Minister of India), aunt of Indira Gandhi*; president, United Nations General Assembly, 1953

Pankhurst, Adela (1884?–?)　　　1339
Eng./Austral. suffragist, editor, political activist; w. Tom Walsh; d. Emmeline P-,* s. Christabel* and Sylvia* P-

Pankhurst, Christabel (1880–1958)　　　1291
Eng. suffragist, evangelist, writer; d. Emmeline P-,* s. Sylvia* and Adela* P-

Pankhurst, Emmeline [Goulden] (1858–1928) 1059
Eng. suffragist; m. Christabel,* Sylvia* and Adela* P-; founder, Women's Social and Political Union, 1905

Pankhurst, Sylvia (1882–1960)　　　1314
Eng. suffragist, editor, newspaper publisher, historian, social reformer; d. Emmeline P-,* s. Christabel* and Adela* P-

Pappas, Rita Boumy (1906–)　　　1665
Grk. poet, translator

Pardoe, Julia (1806–1862)　　　787
Eng. writer, historian

Parent, Gail (1940–)　　　2304
Am. scenarist, writer

Parker, Dorothy (1893–1967)　　　1459
Am. writer, poet, humorist; née Rothschild

Parker, Gail Thain (1943–)　　　2377
Am. educator, writer, college administrator

Parker, Suzy (1933–)　　　2133
Am. model, actor

Parks, Rosa (1913–)　　　1768
Am. civil rights activist; aka "The Mother of the Civil Rights Movement"; Spingarn Medal, 1979

Parr, Catherine (1513–1548)　　　254
Eng. queen, author; w. Edward, Lord Brough of Gainsorough (1), third w. Sir John Nevill, Lord Latimer (2), sixth w. Henry VIII of England (3), Thomas Seymour (4)

Parra, Violeta (1917–1967)　　　1832
Chilean folk singer, political activist

Parry, Blanche (fl. 1560s)　　　303
Eng. chief gentlewoman of the privy chamber, keeper of jewels of Elizabeth I of England,* astrologer; d. Henry P- of Newcourt and Herfordshire

Partnow, Susan (1947–)　　　2457
Am. speech therapist, workshop leader, peace activist; h. Peckenpaugh, s. Elaine P- (author, actor, researcher, arts-in-education specialist); co-founder, Families for Peace, Washington

Parton, Dolly [Rebecca] (1946–)　　　2436
Am. singer, songwriter; Grammy Award, 1978, 1979

Parton, Sara Payson Willis (*see* Fern, Fanny)

Parturier, Françoise (1919–)　　　1864
Fr. writer, feminist, columnist

Pascalina, Sister (1894–?)　　　1472
Bavarian/It. nun; née Josefine Lehnert; companion to Pope Pius XII

Pastan, Linda (1932–)　　　2114
Am. poet

Paston, Agnes (?–1479)　　　229
Eng. householder; w. William I, m. John I, Edmund I, Elizabeth, William II and Clement; m.-in-law of Margaret Mautby P-*: grandm. Margery Brews P-

Paston, Margaret Mautby (1441–1484)　　　214
Eng. householder; w. John I, m. John II, John III, Edmund II, Walter, William III, Margery and Anne; d.-in-law of Agnes P-*

Patterson, Eleanor [Medill] "Cissy" (1881–1948)　　　1303
Am. newspaper editor

Patterson, Martha Johnson (1828–fl. 1860s)　　　887
Am. society leader; d. Andrew Johnson

Pattison, E. F. S. or Francis (*see* Dilke, Emilia)

Paul, Alice (1885–1977)　　　1355
Am. suffragist; founder, National Woman's Party, 1913, chair through 1945; author of Equal Rights Amendment; National Women's Hall of Fame, 1980

Pavlova, Anna (1881–1931)　　　1304
Russ. ballet dancer

Peabody, Elizabeth (1750–?)　　　572
Am. householder; née Smith; first h. Shaw; s. Abigail Adams*

Peabody, Josephine Preston (1874–1922)　　　1220
Am. writer, poet, playwright; h. Marks

Peace Pilgrim (1908–1981)   1695
   Am. pacifist, philosopher, walker; pseud.
   only
Peel, Lady (see Lillie, Beatrice)
Pemberton, H. L. C. (see Childe-Pemberton,
Harriet L.)
Pembroke, countess of (see Herbert, Mary
Sidney)
Penelope (c.1214 B.C.–?)   48
   Grk. noble; aka Arnaea; w. Odysseus, m.
   Telemachus
Pennington, Mrs. (1734–1759)   527
   Eng. poet
Percy, Florence (see Akers, Elizabeth Chase)
Perera, Sylvia Brinton (1932–)   2115
   Writer, feminist
Perkins, Frances (1882–1965)   1315
   Am. government official, writer; U.S. Sec-
   retary of Labor, 1933–44; chair, U.S. Civil
   Service Commission, 1946–53; first woman
   in U.S. Cabinet
Perón, [Marie] Eva Duarte de (1919–1952)   1865
   Argen. politician, government official, lec-
   turer, actor; aka Evita; w. Juan Domingo P-
   (1895–1974, political leader)
Perovskaya, Sofia (1853–1881)   1030
   Russ. revolutionary; assassin of Emperor
   Alexander II
Perpetua, Vivia (183?–205)   81
   Carthaginian Catholic martyr
Perry, Eleanor (1915–1981)   1796
   Am. screenwriter; Emmy Award, 1967, 1973
Perry, Nora (1831–1896)   908
   Am. poet, writer
Perutz, Kathrin (1939–)   2271
   Am. novelist, nonfiction writer
Peterson, Virgilia (1904–1966)   1627
   Am. lecturer, writer, literary critic, trans-
   lator, television personality; h. Paulding
Pethick-Lawrence, Emmeline, Baroness (1867–
1954)   1137
   Eng. suffragist; w. Baron Frederick William
   P-L- (1871–1961)
Petigny, Maria-Louisa Rose (1768–?)   644
   Fr. poet; née Levesque
Pettröczi, Kata Szidónia (1662–1708)   427
   Hung. poet
Petry, Ann [Lane] (1908/12–)   1754
   Am. writer, journalist
Pfeiffer, Madame (1797–post-1852)   747
   Ger. adventurer, traveler, author, collector
Pharaoh's Daughter (fl. c.1250 B.C.)   7
   Egyptian princess; aka Thermuthis, Myr-
   rina, Mercis; d. Ramses II (?); rescued Moses
   and raised him as her son
Phelps, Almira Lincoln (1793–1884)   732
   Am. author, educator, botanist, poet; née
   Hart; s. Emma Hart Willard*
Phelps, Elizabeth (1815–1852)   809
   Am. writer; pseud. H. Trusta

Phelps, Elizabeth Stuart (1844–1911)   977
   Am. writer; h. Ward
Philenia (see Morton, Sarah Wentworth)
Philips, Joan (fl. 1679–1682)   449
   Eng. poet; aka Ephelia; grandd. Katherine
   P-*?
Philips, Katherine Fowler (1631–1664)   394
   Eng./Ir. poet, translator, playwright; née
   Fowler, aka Orinda, The English Sappho;
   grandm. Joan P-*?
Phillips, Julia (1944?–)   2397
   Am. film producer
Philomela (see 1. Rowe, Elizabeth; 2. Warren,
Mercy Otis)
Phinehas, Wife of (c.1040–970 B.C.)   19
   Hebr.; d.-in-law Eli, m. Ichabod, grandm.
   Ahijah
Phyrne (fl. 4th cen. B.C.)   59
   Grk. courtesan, model, beauty
Pickford, Mary (1893–1979)   1460
   Can/Am. actor, writer, philanthropist; née
   Gladys Marie Smith; aka ''America's
   Sweetheart''; co-founder, Motion Picture
   Relief Fund, co-founder, Academy of Mo-
   tion Picture Arts and Sciences, and co-
   founder, United Artists Corp., 1919; Acad-
   emy Award, 1929
Piercy, Marge (1936–)   2202
   Am. poet, writer, activist; founder of Move-
   ment for a Democratic Society (MDS)
Pierobon, Gigliola [Lola] (1950?–)   2485
   Ital. feminist
Pilkington, Laetitia (1712–1750/51)   485
   Ir./Eng. poet, playwright, printer; née Van
   Lewen
Pinar, Florencia del (fl. 1465–1499)   222
   Sp. poet
Pinckney, Eliza (1722?–1793)   502
   West Indian/Am. plantation manager; asa
   Elizabeth Lucas P-; d. George Lucas (lt.
   governor of Antigua), w. Charles P- (speaker
   of the South Carolina House of Assembly,
   1736–40, and chief justice, 1752), m.
   Thomas P- (b. 1750; governor of South
   Carolina, 1787); distinguished for her suc-
   cess in the cultivation of indigo
Pincus, Lily (1898–1981)   1524
   Czech./Eng. family relations counselor,
   nonfiction writer; co-founder, Institute of
   Marital Studies, London
Ping, Yang (see Yang Ping)
Piozzi, Hester Lynch (1741–1821)   543
   Welsh?/Eng., author; née Salusbury, aka
   Hester Thrale; w. Henry Thrale (1) and
   Gabriel P. (2); friend of Dr. Samuel John-
   son
Pitter, Ruth (1897–?)   1510
   Eng. poet
Pix, Mary Griffith (1666–1720?)   436
   Eng. playwright, novelist

Plath, Sylvia (1932–1963) 2116
Am. poet, writer; pseud. Victoria Lucas
Plato, Ann (fl. 1840s) 947
Am. poet; author of second volume of poetry by a Black woman published in the United States
Pless, Daisy, Princess of (1873–?) 1198
Ger. princess, actor, writer; née Cornwallis-West
Plotina, Pompeia (c.80–122) 78
Roman empress; w. Emperor Trajan, m. Emperor Adrian
Pocahontas (1595/96–1616/17) 343
Am. Indian princess, folk hero; aka Matoaka (Snowfeather), Rebecca (Christian name), the Nonpareil of Virginia; d. chief Powhatan, w. Kocoum (?; 1) and John Rolfe (2); first American Christian convert, legendary savior of Capt. John Smith of Jamestown
Pogrebin, Letty Cottin (1939–) 2272
Am. writer, editor, columnist
Poisson, Jeanne-Antoinette (see Pompadour, Jeanne P.)
Poitiers, Diane de (1499–1566) 242
Fr. royal mistress; aka comtesse de Breze, duchesse de Valentinois; w. Louis de Breze, comte de Maulevrier (grand seneschal of Normandy), mistress of Henry II of France
Polk, Sarah Childress (1803–1891) 772
Am. hostess; w. James P- (U.S. President, 1845–49)
Pollard, Josephine (1834–1892) 921
Am. poet, writer, naturalist
Polowy, Carol (fl. 1975) 2538
Am. educator
Pompadour, [Jeanne-Antoinette Poisson de], Madame (1721–1764) 498
Fr. salonist, art and literary patron; asa marquise de P-; d. François Poisson (equerry to the duke of Orleans), w. Lenormand d'Etoiles, mistress of Louis XV of France
Porcia (?–42 B.C.) 70
Roman noble; d. Marcus Porcius Cato (patriot, stoic philosopher), w. Decimus Junius Brutus (general, member of the conspiracy to assassinate Julius Caesar)
Porter, Adrian, Mrs. (see Heaton, Rose Henniker)
Porter, Eleanor H. (1868–1920) 1146
Am. writer; née Hodgman
Porter, Helen Grace (see Hibbard, Grace)
Porter, Jane (1776–1850) 673
Eng. novelist; s. Anna Maria P- (novelist) and Sir Robert Ker P- (artist and traveler)
Porter, Katherine Anne (1890–1980) 1417
Am. writer; Pulitzer Prize, 1966; Natl. Book Award, 1966
Porter, Sylvia (1913–) 1769
Am. economist, writer, columnist

Post, Emily (1873–1960) 1199
Am. society leader, writer; trendsetter of manners
Potor, Aurelia (fl. 1956) 2512
Am. physician
Potter, Beatrix (1866–1943) 1131
Eng. writer, illustrator
Poulsson, Emilie (1853–1939) 1031
Am. writer, editor, illustrator
Pounds, Jessie Brown (1861–?) 1092
Am. songwriter
Pratt, Minnie Bruce (1946–) 2437
Am. poet, essayist, teacher, author
Praxilla (fl. c.451 BC) 55
Grk. poet
Preedy, George Runnell (see Bowen, Marjorie)
Prentiss, Elizabeth [Payson] (1818–1878) 831
Am. hymnist, writer, poet
Prest, Wife of (?–1558) 299
Eng. religious martyr
Preston, Ann (1813–1872) 804
Am. physician, educator, writer
Preston, Margaret J. (1820–1897) 850
Am. poet, writer
Previn, Dory (1930–) 2072
Am. songwriter, singer; née Langan; ex-w. Andre P- (composer, conductor)
Price, Leontyne (1927–) 2002
Am. opera singer; Spingarn Medal, 1965; eleven Grammy Awards; Presidential Medal of Freedom, 1964
Priesand, Sally (1947–) 2458
Am. rabbi; first woman rabbi
Priest, Ivy Baker (1905–1975) 1646
Am. government official; Treasurer of the U.S.
Primrose, Diana, Lady (see Clifford, Ann)
Prince, Lucy Terry (see Terry, Lucy)
Procter, Adelaide [Anne] (1825–1864) 871
Eng. poet
Procter, Edna Dean (1829–1923) 889
Am. poet
Prostitute of Jerusalem, mother of the dead child (fl. c.950 B.C.) 27
Isr. (Biblical)
Prostitute of Jerusalem, mother of the living child (fl. c.950 B.C.) 26
Isr. (Biblical)
Pryor, Sarah Agnes [Rice] (1830–1912) 898
Am. author, Civil War hero
Ptaschkina, Nelly (1903–1920) 1608
Russ. diarist
Pulcheria, Saint Aelia (399–454) 89
Byzantine empress, scholar; d. Emperor Arcadius, s. Emperor Theodosius II, w. General Marcian; canonized and still recognized as a saint by the Greek Orthodox Church
Purim, Flora (1942–) 2354
Braz./Am. singer, songwriter

Putnam, Emily James (1865–1944)   1123
  Am. educator, writer, college administrator;
  first dean of Barnard College, New York
Pyper, Mary (fl. 1870s)   1161
  Scot. poet

Q

Qernertoq (fl. c.900–1400)   129
  Eskimo poet
Quick-To-See-Smith, Jaune (1940–)   2305
  Am. artist, poet
Quin Guanshu (1929–)   2033
  Chin. botanist
Quinn, Sally (1941–)   2329
  Am. journalist

R

Rabi'a bint Isma'il of Syria (?–755)   117
  Arabic poet
Rabi'a of Balkh (fl. 10th cen.)   128
  Iran. poet; d. Ka'b, king of Balkh
Rabi'a the Mystic (712–801)   114
  Basra (Iraq) poet, Sufi mystic, Muslim saint;
  aka Rabi'a al-Adawiyya ("that woman on
  fire with love")
Rachel (?–1732 B.C.)   6
  Hittite; d. Leban, s. Leah,* 2nd w. Jacob,
  m. Benjamin, niece of Abraham; mother of
  two of the twelve tribes of Israel
Rachel (1890–1931)   1418
  Isr. poet
Radcliffe, Ann (1764–1823)   628
  Eng. poet, novelist; née Ward; w. William
  R- (editor of the *English Chronicle*)
Radegunda, Saint (c.518–587)   95
  Thuringian/Merovingian nun, princess; w.
  Chlotar I (asa Clotaire)
Radner, Gilda (1946–1989)   2438
  Am. comedian, actor; w. Gene Wilder (pro-
  ducer, actor); Emmy Award, 1978
Raleigh, Elizabeth (fl. 1601)   354
  Eng. noble; d. Sir Nicholas Throckmorton
  (1515–71), w. Sir Walter R-
Rambert, Marie, Dame (1891–1982)   1429
  Pol./Eng. impresario, ballet teacher and di-
  rector; aka Dame Marie Dukes; w. Ashley
  Dukes (playwright, director of Mercury
  Theater); Dame Commander OBE, 1962;
  founder of Ballet Rambert, 1926 (later the
  Modern Dance Company)
Ramee, Louise de la (*see* Ouida)
Ramey, Estelle R. (1917–)   1833
  Am. endocrinologist, physiologist, biophy-
  sicist, educator
Ramsay, Martha Laurens (1759–1811)   607
  Am. letter writer
Rand. Ayn (1905–1982)   1647
  Russ./Am. novelist, philosopher, screen-
  writer; née Alissa Rosenbaum; h. O'Con-
  nor; devised philosophy of "objectivism"

Randal, Vera (1922–)   1911
  Am. (?) writer
Rank, Beata (1896–1967)   1492
  Am. psychologist; née Hoffman
Rankin, Jeanette (1880–1973)   1292
  Am. suffragist, pacifist, politician; U.S.
  Representative, 1917–19 and 1941–43, R-
  Montana; first woman elected to U.S. Con-
  gress; first winner of Susan B. Anthony
  Award from Natl. Organization for Women
  (NOW)
Rascoe, Judith (1941–)   2330
  Am. writer, scenarist
Raven (1955–)   2509
  Am. letter writer, prisoner (serving life term);
  née Doris Ann Foster
Raven, Arlene (1944–)   2398
  Am. art historian, feminist; co-founder of
  The Woman's Building and the Feminist
  Studio Workshop/College, Los Angeles,
  1973
Ravitch, Diane (1938–)   2247
  Am. writer, educator; née Silvers
Rawlings, Marjorie Kinnan (1896–1953)   1493
  Am. writer; Pulitzer Prize, 1939
Ray, Dixy Lee (1914–)   1779
  Am. politician, government official, marine
  biologist, educator; chair, U.S. Atomic En-
  ergy Commission, 1973–75; governor,
  1977–81, D-Washington; Freedom Foun-
  dation Award, 1978
Reagan, Nancy (1921–)   1893
  Am. First Lady, actor; née B. Anne Frances
  Robbins; aka Nancy Davis; w. Ronald R-
  (U.S. President, 1981–89)
Reddy, Helen (1941–)   2331
  Austral./Am. singer, songwriter; Grammy
  Award, 1972
Reed, Donna (1921–1986)   1894
  Am. actor, civil rights activist, pacifist; née
  Donna Belle Mullenger; co-founder, An-
  other Mother for Peace; Academy Award,
  1953
Reed, Esther De Berdt (1746–1780)   559
  Eng./Am. relief worker; w. Joseph R- (1741–
  80, Am. soldier and statesman, 1741–1785)
Reese, Lizette [Woodworth] (1856–1935)   1042
  Am. poet, writer
Reeves, Nancy (1913–)   1770
  Am. lawyer, writer, educator; née Goldha-
  ber
Reid, Willie Mac (1939–)   2273
  Am. politician, civil rights activist
Reiner, Max (*see* Caldwell, Taylor)
Reinharz, Shulamit (1946–)   2439
  Dutch/Am. feminist sociologist
Renard, Cecile (c.1774–1794)   666
  Fr. shopkeeper, royalist sympathizer
Renault, Mary (1905–1983)   1648
  Eng./So.Afr. novelist; née Challans

Runkle, Bertha (1878–1958) 1267
Am. writer; h. Bash
Russell, Anna (1911–) 1741
Eng./Am. comedian, singer
Russell, Countess (*see* Arnim, Mary A.)
Russell, Dora [Winifred], Countess (1894–
1986) 1474
Eng. writer, feminist, pacifist; née Black;
ex-w. Lord Bertrand R- (1872–1970, philosopher and mathematician); co-founder,
Beacon Hill School, West Sussex, 1927
(progressive school); pioneer of women's
rights
Russell, Elizabeth Hoby, Lady (1528–post–
1603) 273
Eng. diarist, courtier; d. Anthony Cooke
(tutor of Edward IV), s. Anne Cooke Bacon,* Lady Mildred Burleigh and Catherine
Killigrew,* w. Sir Thomas Hoby (1; author,
translator) and Lord John R. (2), m. Elizabeth, Ann and Thomas Posthumous Hoby,
m.-in-law Lady Margaret Hoby*; earliest
known English woman diarist
Russell, Lady (*see* Harington, Lucy)
Russell, Rachel, Lady (1636–1723) 403
Eng. letter writer; née Rachel Wriothesley;
h. Vaughn (1), w. Lord William R- (2)
Russell, Rosalind (1911–1976) 1742
Am. actor, philanthropist; h. Brisson; co-
founder, Independent Artists, Inc., 1947;
Antoinette Perry Award, 1953
Ruth (fl. 1100 B.C.) 17
Moabite; d.-in-law Naomi,* w. Mahlon (1)
and Boaz (2), m. Obed, great-grandm. David;
founder, with Boaz, of the House of David
Rutherford, Alison (*see* Cockburn, Alice)
Ru Zhijuan (1925–) 1959
Chin. writer, editor

S
Sabin, Florence [Rena] (1871–1953) 1181
Am. public health scientist, anatomist, ed-
ucator, writer
Sabina, Poppæa (fl. 50–60) 77
Roman courtier; mistress of Nero
Sachs, Nelly (1891–1970) 1430
Ger./Isr. poet, playwright; Nobel Prize, 1966
Sackville, Margaret, Lady (1881–1963) 1305
Eng. poet
Sackville-West, Vita (1892–1962) 1440
Eng. writer
Safiya bint Musafir (fl. 674) 103
Arabic poet
Sagan, Françoise (1935–) 2177
Fr. writer
St. Denis, Ruth (1880–1968) 1293
Am. dancer, choreographer, educator; née
Dennis; w. Ted Shawn (dancer); co-foun-
der, Denishawn Dance Company
Sainte-Marie, Buffy (1941–) 2332

Can. songwriter, singer, civil rights activist;
founder of North American Women's As-
sociation
St. James, Margo (1937–) 2226
Am. activist, prostitute; founder of Coyote
(civil rights for prostitutes), 1975
St. Johns, Adela Rogers (1894–1988) 1475
Am. writer, journalist; Presidential Medal
of Freedom, 1970
Sakanoé, Lady (*see* Ōtomo no Sakano-e Irat-
sume)
Salome (fl. c.A.D. 20) 38
Judean princess; d. Herodias* and Herod
Philip, grandm. Herod Antipas
Salusbury, Hester Lynch (*see* Piozzi, Hester
Lynch)
Samaritan Woman (fl. c.A.D. 25) 41
Biblical
Samson, First wife of (fl. c.1080 B.C.) 14
Philistine; first w. Samson (1), Samson's
best man (2)
Sanchez, Carol Lee (1934–) 2162
Am. poet, painter, educator; s. Paula Gunn
Allen*
Sand, George (1804–1876) 777
Fr. writer; née Amandine Aurore Lucie Du-
pin; h. Baronne Dudevant
Sanger, Margaret (1883–1966) 1328
Am. nurse, editor, writer, civil rights activ-
ist; née Higgins; founder, Planned Parent-
hood Federation of America
Sangster, Margaret E. (1838–1912) 942
Am. poet, writer, editor; née Munson
Sapphira (*see* Barber, Mary)
Sappho (fl. c.610–635 B.C.) 50
Grk. poet, dance and choral teacher; asa
Sappha, Psappho, aka The Poetess, The
Tenth Muse, The Pierian Bee; first lyric
poet
Saragossa, Maid of (*see* Augustin, Maria)
Sarah (c.1987–1860 B.C.) 3
Chaldean/Canaanite; asa Sarai; w. Abra-
ham, m. Isaac
Sarah (fl. c.724–722 B.C.) 32
Mede (from Media, ancient country of SW
Asia)/Assyrian; d. Raguel and Edna,* w.
Tobias (8); first seven husbands killed by a
demon on their wedding nights
Sarashina, Lady (1008–1060?) 142
Jap. diarist; d. Takasue no Musume (court
official), cousin of Michitsune (author)
Sarraute, Nathalie (1900–) 1566
Russ./Fr. novelist, essayist, playwright; née
Tcherniak; Internatl. Prize for Literature,
1964
Sarton, [Eleanor] May (1912–) 1755
Belg./Am. writer, poet, novelist, play-
wright
Sassen, Georgia (1949–) 2473
Am. psychologist, educator

Saunders, Cicely, Dame (1916/18–)   1813
  Eng. Anglican nun; w. Marian Bohusz-
  Szyszko (Pol. artist, 1901–); founder of
  St. Christopher's Hospice, London, 1967;
  Dame of the British Empire, 1980
Saunders, Margaret Baillie (1873–1949?)   1201
  Eng. writer
Sawyer, Diane (1945–)   2417
  Am. television journalist
Saxe-Coburg-Saafeld, duchess of (see Au-
  gusta)
Sayers, Dorothy L[eigh] (1893–1957)   1461
  Eng. writer; h. Fleming
Schaeffer, Susan Fromberg (1941–)   2333
  Am. poet, writer, educator
Schiaparelli, Elsa (1896–1973)   1495
  Ital. fashion designer
Schirmacher, Kathe (1865–1930)   1124
  Ger. feminist, author
Schlafly, Phyllis (1924–)   1941
  Am. writer, political activist
Schneir, Miriam (1933–)   2134
  Am. writer, editor, scholar
Schreiner, Olive [Emile Albertina] (1855–1920) 1038
  So. Afr. writer, feminist, social critic; pseud.
  Ralph Iron
Schroeder, Patricia (1940–)   2306
  Am. politician, lawyer, educator; née Scott;
  U.S. Representative, 1973– , D-Colorado
Schulder, Diane B. (1937–)   2227
  Am. lawyer, educator
Schumann-Heink, Ernestine (1861–1936)   1095
  Austr. opera singer; née Roessler
Schurman, Anna van (1607–1678)   362
  Dutch artist, theological scholar, author,
  letter writer
Schutzinn, Katharina (see Zell, Katherine)
Schwimmer, Rosika (1877–1948)   1257
  Hung./Am. pacifist, suffragist
Scott, Evelyn (1893–1963)   1462
  Am. writer
Scott, Hazel [Dorothy] (1920–1981)   1885
  Trinidad./Am. pianist, singer, actor; ex-w.
  Adam Clayton Powell, Jr. (1908–72, poli-
  tician and clergyman)
Scott-Maxwell, Florida (1884–?)   1342
  Am./Scot. writer, psychologist, playwright,
  suffragist, actor
Scudder, Janet (1873–1940)   1202
  Am. sculptor, painter, writer; née Neta
  Deweze Frazee S-
Scudéry, Madeleine de (1607–1701)   363
  Fr. novelist, poet; asa Magdeleine Scudéri,
  aka Sapho; s. George de S- (playwright and
  critic)
Sears, Vicki (1941–)   2334
  Am. feminist therapist, teacher, writer
Sedges, John (see Buck, Pearl)
Sedgwick, Catharine Maria (1789–1867)   708
  Am. educator, novelist, author; d. Theodore

S- (U.S. Representative and Senator, Mas-
  sachusetts State Supreme Court Justice)
Seidelman, Susan (1953–)   2502
  Am. film director
Seiffert, Marjorie Allen (1885–1968)   1358
  Am. poet
Sekaquaptewa, Helen (1898–?)   1525
  Am. autobiographer
Selena (see Harington, Lucy)
Semenow, Dorothy (1930–)   2073
  Am. psychoanalyst, feminist
Semiramis (fl. 8th cen. B.C.)   49
  Assyrian queen; aka Summuramat
Sempronia (see Lamb, Mary Ann)
Senesh, Hanna (1921–1944)   1895
  Hung./Pales. soldier, diarist, political activ-
  ist; executed by Nazis
Seton, Anya (1916–)   1814
  Am. writer
Seton, Cynthia Propper (1926–1982)   1985
  Am. novelist
Seton, Elizabeth (1774–1821)   667
  Am. nun; née Elizabeth Ann Bayley, aka
  Mother S-; w. William Magee S-; founded
  Society for Relief of Poor Widows with
  Small Children (first charitable organization
  of New York), founded Sisters of Charity
  of St. Joseph; National Women's Hall of
  Fame, 1980; first canonized American saint
Seton, Julia [Moss] (1889–?)   1402
  Am. writer, lecturer, historian; w. Ernest
  Thompson S-
Seton-Thompson, Grace (1872–1959)   1189
  Am. writer, feminist, designer, lecturer, poet
Sévigné, Marie de, Marquise (1626–1696)   387
  Fr. letter writer, salonist; née Marie de Ra-
  butin Chantel; w. Marquis Henri de S-, m.
  Comtesse Françoise Grignan*
Sewall, Harriet [Winslow] (1819–1889)   835
  Am. poet, suffragist, abolitionist, philan-
  thropist
Seward, Anna (1742–1809)   549
  Eng. poet; aka The Swan of Lichfield
Sewell, Anna (1820–1878)   851
  Eng. writer
Sewell, Sarah Ann (fl. 1870s)   1162
  Eng. writer, social critic
Sexton, Anne (1928–1974)   2018
  Am. poet; née Harvey; Pulitzer Prize, 1967
Sforza, Caterina (1462–1509)   218
  Ital. politician, military leader; d. Galeazzo
  Maria S- (duke of Milan), w. Girolamo
  Riario (1), Giacomo Feo (2) and Giovanni
  de Medici (3), m. Giovanni dalle Bande
  Nere
Sforza, Costanza Varano (1426–1447)   209
  Ital. scholar; granddd. Battista Montelfeltro
Shain, Merle (fl. 1973)   2536
  Can. writer, social worker, television com-
  mentator

Am. singer, songwriter; w. James Taylor (singer); Grammy Award, 1971

Simon, Kate (1912–)   1756
Am. writer

Simon, Patricia (1934–)   2163
Am. writer

Simonton, Stephanie (*see* Matthews-Simonton, Stephanie)

Simos, Miriam (1951–)   2493
Am. nonfiction writer, scriptwriter, lecturer, minister (wicca); pseud. Starhawk

Simpson, Becky (1936–)   2205
Am. social activist

Simpson, Nancy (1938–)   2248
Am. poet

Singer, June (1918–)   1851
Am. psychoanalyst, nonfiction writer

Singer, Maxine [Frank] (1931–)   2090
Am. biochemist

Singleton, Anne (*see* Benedict, Ruth Fulton)

Singleton, Mary (*see* Brooke, Frances)

Sitwell, Edith [Louisa], Dame (1887–1964)   1381
Eng. poet, editor, literary critic

Skau, Annie (1916?–)   1816
Nor. Evangelical nun, nurse

Skinner, Cornelia Otis (1901–1979)   1580
Am. writer, actor, entertainer; d. Otis S- (actor)

Skrine, Agnes Higgenson (*see* O'Neill, Moira)

Slick, Grace (1939–)   2276
Am. singer, songwriter; née Wing

Sloan, Margaret [Benston] (fl. 1975)   2539
Am. civil rights activist; co-founder of National Black Feminist Organization

Slocumb, Mary (1760–1836)   616
Am. patriot, plantation manager; née Hooks

S. M. [The Scottish Minstrel] (*see* Nairne, Caroline)

Smeal, Eleanor [Marie Cutri] (1939–)   2277
Am. organization executive, civil rights activist; president, National Organization for Women, 1977–87

Smedley, Agnes (1890–1950)   1476
Am. author, lecturer

Smith, Anna Young (1756–1780?)   595
Am. poet; pseud. Sylvia; niece of Elizabeth Graeme Ferguson*

Smith, Arabella [Eugenia] (1844–1916)   979
Am. poet

Smith, Barbara (1946–)   2442
Am. poet

Smith, Bessie (1898–1937)   1527
Am. singer, songwriter

Smith, Betty (1896–1972)   1496
Am. writer

Smith, Charlotte (1749–1806)   565
Eng. novelist, poet, translator; née Turner; s. Catherine Dorset (poet)

Smith, Dodie (1896–?)   1497

Eng. playwright; née Dorothy Gladys Beesley; pseud. C. L. Anthony

Smith, Dorothy E. (1926–)   1986
Am. feminist sociologist

Smith, Elizabeth Oakes (1806–1893)   788
Am. writer, lecturer, suffragist, social reformer; née Prince; pseud. Ernest Helfenstein

Smith, Evelyn E[lizabeth] (1937?–)   2229
Am. writer

Smith, Hazel Brannon (1914–1981)   1780
Am. newspaper publisher, journalist, editor; Pulitzer Prize, 1964

Smith, Lee (1944–)   2399
Am. writer

Smith, Lillian [Eugenia] (1897–1966)   1511
Am. writer, social critic

Smith, Margaret Bayard (1778–1844)   679
Am. journalist, author

Smith, Margaret Chase (1897–)   1512
Am. politician; U.S. Representative, 1940–49, U.S. Senate, 1949–73, R-Maine; first woman elected to both U.S. House and Senate

Smith, May Riley (1842–1927)   965
Am. poet, writer

Smith, Nora Archibald (1859–1934)   1070
Am. writer, educator, poet; s. Kate Douglas Wiggin*

Smith, Robyn [Carolyn] (1944–)   2400
Am. jockey; first woman jockey to win a major stakes horse race

Smith, Sophia (1796–1870)   741
Am. philanthropist; founded Smith College, Northampton, Massachusetts

Snow, Helen Foster (1907–)   1675
Am. writer, researcher, educator; pseud. Nym Whales; w. Edgar S-

Snow, Phoebe (1951–)   2494
Am. singer, songwriter

Solanis, Valerie (1940–)   2308
Am. actor, painter, feminist

Somerset, Duchess of (*see* Thrynne, Frances)

Somerville, Mary (1780–1872)   683
Scot. astronomer, physical geographer, mathematician, translator; née Fairfax; w. William S- (2); received government pension of £300 a year for work in science

Sontag, Susan (1933–)   2136
Am. writer, social critic, screenwriter

Soong Chin-ling (*see* Sun Yat-sen, Mme.)

Soong Mei-ling (*see* Chiang Kai-shek, Mme.)

Sophia Dorothea of Celle (1666–1726)   437
Eng. queen; aka princess of Celle, princess of Ahlden; d. George William, duke of Brunswick-Lunesburg-Celle, w. George I of England, m. George II of England and Sophia Dorothea (w. Frederick Wilhelm I of Prussia)

Sorrels, Rosalie (1933–)   2137
Am. folksinger, songwriter
Southampton, countess of (*see* Vernon, Elizabeth)
Southey, Caroline Anne (1786–1854)   698
Eng. poet, letter writer; née Bowles, aka Cowper of Our Modern Poetesses; second w. Robert S- (poet)
Sowerman, Ester (fl. 1617)   372
Eng. author; pseud. only
Spacks, Patricia [Ann] Meyer (1929–)   2036
Am. literary critic, educator, editor
Spalding, Catherine (1793–1858)   734
Am. nun; first mother superior of the Sisters of Charity of Nazareth, founder of St. Vincent's Orphan Asylum, founder of first Catholic infirmary in Kentucky (now St. Joseph's Hospital)
Spark, Muriel [Sarah] (1918–)   1852
Scot. writer, poet
Sparke, Anthony (*see* Lambrun, Margaret)
Speght, Rachel (1597–?)   344
Eng. author, poet; d. Thomas S- (?)
Spencer, Anna Garlin (1851–1931)   1019
Am. minister, social reformer, educator, feminist
Speranza (*see* Wilde, Jane Francesca)
Speyer, Leonora (1872–1956)   1190
Am. poet, violinist, educator; née Von Stosch; Pulitzer Prize, 1927
Spofford, Harriet [Elizabeth] (1835–1921)   929
Am. writer, poet; née Prescott
Spolin, Viola (1911?–)   1743
Am. director, producer, educator
Sproat, Nancy Dennis (1766–1826)   636
Am. poet
Spyri, Johanna (1827–1901)   883
Swiss writer; née Heusser
Staël, [Anne Louise] Germaine de (1766–1817)   637
Fr. novelist, literary critic, feminist; d. Suzanne Chardon* and Jacques Necker (minister of finance for Louis VI), w. Baron Eric Magnus de S- de Holstein (1), mistress and w. Lt. John Rocca (2), m., by Vicomte Louis de Narbonne-Lara, Auguste and Albert, cousin Mme Necker de Saussure*
Stafford, Jean (1915–1979)   1800
Am. writer; w. Robert Lowell (1; poet), Oliver Jensen (2; writer), and A. J. Liebling (3; writer); Pulitzer Prize, 1970
Stampa, Gaspara (1523–1554)   268
Ital. poet, courtesan, singer; s. Baldassare S- (poet, courtesan, singer), Cassandra S- (poet, singer)
Stanford, Sally (1904–1982)   1629
Am. madam, civic leader, author
Stanhope, Hester Lucy, Lady (1776–1839)   674
Eng./Syrian traveler, astrologer; aka White

Queen of the Desert; d. Charles, 3rd earl of S. (inventor)
Stannard, Una (1927–)   2004
Am. educator, writer
Stanton, Elizabeth Cady (1815–1902)   811
Am. suffragist, abolitionist, historian, writer; president, National Woman Suffrage Association, 1869–90
Stanwyck, Barbara (1907–1990)   1676
Am. actor; née Ruby McGee Stevens; Emmy Award, 1961, 1966
Starhawk (*see* Simos, Miriam)
Starr, Hattie (fl. 1890s)   1407
Am. songwriter
Stassinopoulos, Arianna (1950–)   2486
Grk. writer
Stead, Christina [Ellen] (1902–1983)   1594
Austral. writer; w. William J. Blake (Am. writer, d. 1968)
Steele, Anne (1717–1778/89)   491
Eng. poet, hymnist; pseud. Theodosia
Stein, Gertrude (1874–1946)   1221
Am./Fr. writer, art collector; Obie Award, 1962
Steinem, Gloria (1934–)   2164
Am. writer, feminist, editor; founder of *Ms.* magazine
Stella (*see* More, Hannah)
Steptoe, Lydia (*see* Barnes, Djuna)
Stern, Edith Mendel (1901–1975)   1581
Am. writer, social critic
Stewart, Eliza [Daniel] "Mother" (1816–1908)   818
Am. temperance leader
Stewart, Ella S[eass] (1871–?)   1182
Am. administrator, activist; née Phillips
Stewart, Maria [Frances] W. [Miller] (1803–1879)   773
Am. writer, abolitionist, public speaker, educator, social reformer
Stockton, Annis (1736–1801)   533
Am. poet; née Boudinot, pseud. Emilia (asa Amelia)
Stoddard, Elizabeth [Drew] (1823–1902)   862
Am. writer; née Barstow
Stone, Lucy (1818–1893)   832
Am. suffragist, abolitionist, editor, lecturer; w. Henry Brown Blackwell, s.-in-law of Emily* and Elizabeth* Blackwell; founder of National American Woman Suffrage Association and of *Woman's Journal,* 1870
Stone, Merlin (1931–)   2091
Am. educator, nonfiction writer
Stopes, Marie Carmichael (1880–1958)   1294
Eng. botanist, educator, lecturer, poet, feminist
Storace, Nancy (1765–1815)   633
Eng. singer; née Anna Selina S-
Storni, Alfonsina (1892–1938)   1441
Argen. poet

Stowe, Harriet [Elizabeth] Beecher (1811–1896) 800
Am. writer, social critic; s. Henry Ward Beecher; Hall of Fame, 1910

Straus, Genevieve (see Genevieve)

Streisand, Barbra (1942–) 2359
Am. singer, actor, film producer; ex-w. Elliott Gould (actor); Grammy Award, 1963, 1964, 1965, 1977; Emmy Award, 1965; Academy Award, 1968, 1976

Streshinsky, Naomi [Gottlieb] (1925–) 1960
Am. sociologist

Strozzi, Alessandra de' Machingi (1406–1471) 205
Ital. letter writer; m. Lorenzo, Filippo and Matteo S-

Struther, Jan (1901–1953) 1582
Eng. poet, writer; née Joyce Anstruther; w. Anthony Maxtone Graham

Stuart, Mary (see Mary, Queen of Scots)

Stubbes, Katherine (1571–1591/92) 316
Eng. householder; w. Philip S-

Suckow, Ruth (1892–1960) 1442
Am. writer; h. Nuhn

Suffolk, duchess of (see Willoughby, Catherine)

Sugimoto, Etsu Inagaki (1874?–1950) 1222
Jap. writer, educator

Sullam, Sarah Copia (1592–1641) 339
Ital. poet

Sullivan, Annie (1866–1936) 1132
Am. educator for deaf and blind; h. Macy; tutored Helen Keller*; invented manual alphabet

Sullivan, Leonor Kretzer (1903–1988) 1609
Am. politician; U.S. Congresswoman, 1953–77; w. John B. S- (U.S. Congressman, 1944–51)

Sulpicia (fl. 63 B.C.–A.D. 14) 69
Rom. poet; niece and ward of Messala

Sulpicia (fl. 80–99) 79
Rom. poet; aka the Roman Sappho

Sumangala, Mother of (c.3rd–1st cen. B.C.) 61
Ind. (Pali) poet

Summerskill, Edith [Clara], Baroness (1901–1980) 1583
Eng. politician, physician, women's rights activist, author; Member of Parliament, Cabinet Minister

Summuramat (see Semiramis)

Sumner, Helen L. (1876–1933) 1246
Am. government official, children's rights activist; h. Woodbury

Sun Yat-sen, Madame (1890/93–1981) 1463
Chin. political leader, lecturer, civil rights activist; née Soong Ch'ing-ling; w. Sun Yat-sen (1866–1925, founder the Republic of China), s. Mme. Chiang Kai-shek*

Sun Yün-fêng (1764–1814) 629
Chin. poet; w. Ch'en, the scholar

Suo, Lady (fl. 1035–1065) 143
Jap. poet, lady-in-waiting to Emperor Go-Reizei; d. Taira no Tsugunaka (governor of Suo)

Susanna (fl. c.587–538 B.C.) 37
Jewish; d. Hilkiah, w. Joakim

Sutcliffe, Ann (fl. 1600–1630) 352
Eng. religious writer; w. John S- (groom to His Majesty's Privy Chamber)

Sutherland, Joan (1926–) 1987
Austral. opera singer; Grammy Award, 1961

Suttner, Bertha von, Baroness (1843–1914) 970
Austr. writer, pacifist; née Kinsky; Nobel Peace Prize, 1905

Suu Kyii, Aung San (see Aung San Suu Kyii)

Suyin, Han (see Han Suyin)

Suzman, Helen (1916/18–) 1817
So. African professor, politician; Member of Parliament; United Nations Prize, 1978

Swallow, Ellen Henrietta (1850?–1911) 1015
Am. mineralogist; developed interdisciplinary science of ecology; first woman admitted to Massachusetts Institute of Technology (MIT) and first to receive degree; the first woman mineralogist, founder of the first Women's Science Laboratory at MIT; aka the First Lady of Science

Swanson, Gloria [May Josephine] (1899–1983) 1535
Am. actor, producer, businesswoman; née Svensson; w. Wallace Beery (1; actor), William Duffy (6; writer)

Swenson, May (1919–1989) 1866
Am. poet; Bollingen Prize, 1981

Swerda, Patricia (1916–) 1818
Am. artist, author, educator; née Fine; first Caucasian woman named as Ikenobo Ikebana master

Swit, Loretta (1939–) 2278
Am. actor; Emmy Award, 1980

Syfers, Judy (fl. 1970s) 2533
Am. writer

Sylva, Carmen (1843–1916) 971
Ger./Rum. writer, poet; née Pauline Elisabeth Ottilie Luise, princess of Wied; m. Elizabeth, queen of Rumania; w. Carol I of Rumania

Sylvia (see Smith, Anna Young)

Symonds, Caroline (1792–1803) 728
Eng. poet

T

Taft, Helen Herron (1861–1943) 1096
Am. First Lady; w. William Howard T-(U.S. President, 1909–13)

Taggard, Genevieve (1894–1948) 1477
Am. poet, educator, editor; h. Wolf and Durant

Talvi (see Robinson, Therese A. L.)

Tamar (fl. c.990 B.C.) 22

Eng. poet; aka duchess of Somerset; pseud.
Cleora, Eusebia

Thundercloud, Katherine (*see* Witt, Shirley
Hill)

Tibergeau, Marchioness de (fl. 17th cen.)   348
Fr. poet, patron of literature; née Silery;
niece of La Rochefoucauld (1613–80, moralist)

Tibors (c. 1130–1182)   158
Provençal *trobairitz;* s. Raimbaut d'Orange
(troubadour), w. Bertrand des Baux

Tighe, Mary (1772–1810)   662
Ir. poet; née Blackford

Tikaram, Tanita (196?–)   2524
Am. songwriter-singer

Tillmon, Johnnie (1926–)   1988
Am. welfare rights activist

Ting Ling (1904/06–1986)   1666
Chin. writer, feminist, Communist; née Jiang
Weizhi; asa Ding Ling, pseud. Chiang Ping-
tzu; Stalin Prize for Literature, 1951

Tipton, Jennifer (1937–)   2230
Am. lighting designer; Antoinette Perry
Award, 1977, Obie Award, 1979

Tirzah (*see* Zeloophehad)

Todd, Mabel Elsworth (fl. 1929–1937)   2037
Am. dancer, educator, writer

Toklas, Alice B. (1877–1967)   1258
Am./Fr. literary and art figure, writer;
companion and secretary to Gertrude
Stein*

Tollet, Elizabeth (1694–1754)   464
Eng. poet, playwright

Tolstoy, Sophie (1844–1919)   980
Russ. diarist; née Behrs; w. Leo T- (1828–
1910, novelist)

Tomlin, Lily (1936–)   2206
Am. actor, comedian; Grammy Award, 1971;
Emmy Award, 1974, 1976, 1978

Tonna, Charlotte Elizabeth (1790–1846)   718
Eng. poet, educator, author; née Browne,
h. Phelan (1)

Torelli, Barbara (1475–1533)   227
Ital. poet; h. Bentivoglio (1), w. Ercole
Strozzi (2); friend of Lucrezia Borgia*

Tornimparte, Alessandra (*see* Ginzburg, Natalia)

Torrella, Ippolita (*see* Castiglione, Ippolita)

Towne, Laura [Matilda] (1825–1901)   873
Am. educator

Townsend, Eliza (1789–1854)   709
Am. poet

Townsend, Sue (1946–)   2443
Eng. novelist, scriptwriter

Trachtenberg, Inge (1923?–)   1928
Ger./Am. writer

Tracy, Honor [Lilbush Wingfield] (1913–)   1772
Eng. writer, humorist

Trefusis, Elizabeth (fl. 1808)   793
Eng. poet; s. Lord Clinton

Trench, Melesina (1768–1827)   646
Eng./Ir. author, poet; née Chenevix, h. St.
George (1); aka Mrs. Richard T- (h. 2)

Trevisan, Anna F. (1905–)   1649
Ital./Am. playwright, drama critic

Trimmer, Sarah Kirby (1741–1810)   545
Eng. author, educator, editor; aka "Good
Mrs. T."; introduced use of picture books
for educating children

Tristan, Flora (1803–1844)   774
Peruv./Fr. feminist, novelist; founder of
Union ouvrière

Trollope, Frances Milton (1780–1863)   684
Eng. novelist; née Ternan; w. Thomas Anthony T-, m. Anthony T- (1815–52, novelist) and Thomas Adolphus T- (1810–92,
author)

Trotter, Catherine (*see* Cockburn, Catherine)

Troubridge, [Laura Gurney], Lady (fl. early
1900s–1946)   1540
Eng. writer

Truman, Bess (1885–1982)   1360
Am. First Lady; née Elizabeth Virginia
Wallace; w. Harry S. T- (U.S. President,
1945–53); m. Margaret T-*

Truman, Margaret (1924–)   1942
Am. writer, concert singer; d. Harry T-
(1884–1972, 33rd U.S. President) and Bess
T-*

Trusta, H. (*see* Phelps, Elizabeth Stuart)

Truth, Sojourner (c.1797–1883)   750
Am. slave, abolitionist, mystic, reformer,
lecturer, author; aka Isabella van Wagener
(her slave name)

Ts'ai-t'ien Chang (1862–1945)   1102
Chin. political activist, Communist

Ts'ai Yen (162?–239?)   80
Chin. poet, scholar; d. Ts'ai I (scholar,
poet); first great Chinese woman poet

Tsvetaeva, Marina (1892–1941)   1443
Russ. poet, essayist

Tubman, Harriet (1815?–1913)   812
Am. slave, abolitionist, emancipator; née
Araminta Ross; aka "Moses," "The Con-
ductor of the Underground Railroad"

Tuchman, Barbara [W.] (1912–1989)   1757
Am. historian, author; née Wertheim; m.
Jessica T- Mathews*; Pulitzer Prize, 1963,
1972; Natl. Book Award, 1980; first woman
president of American Academy of Arts and
Letters, 1979

Tucker, Anne (1945–)   2420
Am. editor, photographic critic and historian

Tucker, Sophie (1884–1966)   1344
Am. singer; aka "The Last of the Red Hot
Mamas"

Tudor, Mary (*see* 1. Mary of England; 2.
Mary of France)

Tuite, Marjorie (193?–1986)   2054

Eng. author, feminist; w. William Godwin (1756–1836, political philosopher), m. Mary Shelley*

Woo, Merle (195?–)   2483
Am. poet

Wood, Ellen (1813–1887)   805
Eng. playwright, writer, journalist; née Price

Wood, J. R., Mrs. (*see* Chambers, Jessie)

Wood, Natalie (1938–1981)   2251
Am. actor; w. Robert Wagner (actor)

Wood, Sally Sayward (1759–1855)   610
Am. novelist; née Barrell, aka Sarah Sayward Keating

Woodhull, Victoria Claflin (1838–1927)   943
Am. feminist, politial activist, writer, editor; s. Tennessee Claflin*; founder of *Woodhull & Claflin's Weekly*, 1870

Woodman, Marion (1928–)   2020
Can. Jungian analyst, author

Woodruff, Julia Louise Matilda (1833–1909)   917
Am. writer; pseud. W. M. L. Jay

Woodville-Grey, Elizabeth (*see* Grey, Lady Elizabeth W.)

Woolf, Virginia (1882–1941)   1319
Eng. writer, literary critic; née Stephen; w. Leonard W-; co-founder of Hogarth Press, London

Woolley, Hannah (1623–c.1675)   381
Eng. pioneer educator, governess

Woolsey, Mary (1832–1864)   913
Am. social worker, poet; h. Howland

Woolsey, Sarah Chauncey (*see* Coolidge, Susan)

Wordsworth, Dorothy (1771–1855)   661
Eng. diarist, naturalist; s. William W- (1770–1850, poet), s.-in-law of Mary W-*, aunt of Elizabeth W-*

Wordsworth, Elizabeth (1840–1932)   954
Am. poet; great-niece of William W- (1770–1850, Eng. poet) and Mary W-*, niece of Dorothy W-*

Wordsworth, Mary (1770–1859)   656
Eng. letter writer; née Hutchinson; w. William W- (1770–1850, poet), s.-in-law of Dorothy W-*, great aunt of Elizabrth W-*

Wortham, Anne (1941–)   2238
Am. sociologist, scholar

Worthington, Robin (1932–)   2122
Am. writer

Wright, Frances (1795–1852)   740
Scot./Am. feminist, philanthropist, social reformer, lecturer, poet, author; asa Fanny W., w. William D'Arusmont

Wright, Susanna (1697–1784)   469
Eng./Am. poet, frontierswoman, scholar, letter writer, painter

Wroth, Mary Sidney (1586?–1640?)   329
Eng. poet, patron of poets; asa Wroath, aka countess of Montgomery; d. Robert, earl of Leicester, niece of Mary Sidney Herbert*

and Sir Philip Sidney (poets), cousin of Elizabeth Manners (poet, d. Sir Philip Sidney)

Wyatt, Edith Franklin (1873–1958)   1203
Am. writer

Wylie, Elinor [Morton] (1885–1928)   1361
Am. poet, writer; née Hoyt; w. William Rose Benet

Y

Yamatohime (fl. 671)   102
Jap. poet, empress; w. Emperor Tenji

Yang, Gladys (c.1930–fl. 1950–80s)   2076
Chin. editor, translator

Yang Ping (1908–)   1698
Chin. writer, political activist, editor, journalist; pseud. Shih Ming

Yard, Molly (1914–)   1782
Chin./Am. feminist, political activist; president of National Organization of Women, 1987–90

Yearsley, Anne (1760–1806)   617
Eng. poet, novelist; aka Lactilla, Bristol Milkwoman

Yezierska, Anzia (1886–1970)   1372
Russ./Am. writer

Yglesias, Helen (1915–)   1802
Am. writer, editor; née Bassine

York, Eva Rose (1858–1925?)   1062
Can. poet, philanthropist; founder of Redemption Home and Bible School, Toronto

Young, Elizabeth (fl. 1558)   300
Eng. Protestant reformer

Younger, Maud (1870–1936)   1174
Am. union activist, writer, suffragist; aka "The Mother of the Eight-Hour Law"

Yourcenar, Marguerite (1903–1987)   1612
Belg./Am. writer; née Marguerite de Crayencour; companion of Grace Frick (translator); Grand Prix national des Lettres, Grand Prix de la Litterature de l'Académie Française; first woman elected to French Academy of Letters, 1980

Yü Hsüan-chi (c.843–868)   123
Chin. poet, Taoist priestess, courtesan

Z

Zaharias, [Mildred Ella] Babe Didrikson (1914–1956)   1783
Am. athlete; Olympic champion, 1932, Women's Sports Hall of Fame, 1980; first American to win the British Women's Championship, 1947

Zane, Betty (1766?–1831?)   638
Am. frontier hero; asa Elizabeth Z-

Zassenhaus, Hiltgunt (1916–)   1819
Ger./Am. physician, political activist; leader in underground resistance, World War II

Zaturenska, Marya (1902–1982)   1596
Russ./Am. poet, biographer; w. Horace

Subject Index

Notes to Subject Index

The numbers preceding the colons are contributor numbers; guides to these numbers are found at the top of each page in the Quotations sections. The numbers following the colons refer to the specific quotations.

Entries are in the form of nouns, present participles, or proper names. Because of the amorphous nature of the English language, however, where the use of a noun might be confusing, "the" has been added for clarification (e.g., the obvious), or a noun is given in its plural form to clarify the author's use of the word (e.g, appearance has a different connotation than appearances, speech than speeches).

In subclassifications the symbol ~ is used to replace the main word; it is placed either before or after the subentry, whichever makes a whole phrase. For example, overpopulation is listed under population as over~, while marriage laws is listed under marriage as ~ laws.

Where there are two words in a main entry with a slash between them, the broader term appears first (e.g., barbarism/barbarian; nursing/nurse). This has been done when there were too few quotations under one or the other of such related subjects to warrant a separate listing, or where the connotation is so close, as in age/aging as to make separation confusing. Where the two words have the same stem, the slash is simply used to divide the terms (e.g., child/ren). In all instances, letter by letter alphabetization applies only to the word in front of the slash.

For a statement on the purpose and style of the Subject Index, please see the Introduction.

acting (performance; *also see* actor), 590:5, 6;
951:1; 1067:1, 2; 1117:3; 1676:2; 2187:1; lack of
respect for ~ , 1859:1; 2299:5; teaching of ~ ,
1743:4

action, 21:1; 637:1, 28; 850:2; 1017:1; 1809:1;
2028:1; 2259:2; arena of ~ , 1008:1; collective
~ , 1810:5; 2183:2; men and ~ , 2189:4; need
for ~ , 301:1; 550:3; 813:3; 1147:2; 1321:3;
source of ~ , 2061:4; take ~ , 577:8; women
and ~ , 2131:1

activeness, 307:9; 1095:21; 2084:4

activism (*see* reform; woman, activist)

activity (*also see* movement [physical]), daily ~ ,
1743:2; lack of ~ , 658:4; 2281:1

actor (*also see* acting; performer; theater), 483:2;
590:9; 1000:1; 1117:3; 1118:1; 1192:2; 1459:11;
1488:6; 1551:1, 3; 2120:2; 2288:1; child ~ ,
1903:1; clothing for ~ , 1671:1; employment for
~ , 590:1; film ~ , 1623:1; ~ in relation to
audience (*also see* audience), 2288:4; masterful
~ , 2326:2; out of work ~ , 2217:6; woman ~,
1269:2

Adam & Eve (*also see* Eve), 312:1; 344:2; 920:1;
1268:3; 1378:2; 1538:1; 1735:1; 2189:1

adaptability (*also see* flexibility), 669:13; 1171:6;
1192:20; 1305:4

addiction (*see* drugs)

address, form of ~ , 1845:5; 2515:3

admiration (*also see* adoration), 496:1; 565:20; need
for ~ , 618:10; 639:30; price of ~ , 1850:2

adolescence/adolescent (*also see* teenager; years of
age; youth), 1296:1; 1437:1; 1734:2; 1921:2;
1979:3; 2007:4; 2036:3; 2389:1; dichotomies of
~ , 1480:2; 2028:28; female ~ , 1684:1; 2022:2;
food and ~ , 2262:5; friendships and ~ , 2484:2;
pre~ , 1866:2; sexuality of ~ (*also see* sex,
youth and), 2443:1

adoration (*also see* admiration), 777:23; 790:1; 1119:2

adult/hood, 1439:29; 1567:3; 1752:1; 2341:4; 2494:1;
~ in relation to child, 1679:4; threshold of ~ ,
578:3; young ~ , 1503:3

adultery (*also see* faithlessness; infidelity), 63:1;
152:1; 504:2; 1245:7; 1762:8; 2390:1

advantage, 363:4; 406:30

adventure, 327:2; 1032:7; 1088:2; 1375:5; 1428:1;
1689:1; 1915:3; 2116:3; 2168:1; 2504:1

adversity (*also see* hardship; life, struggle of; obstacle; trouble), 79:1; 261:2; 293:3; 366:13; 703:9;
805:3; 829:2; 881:1; 1120:2; 1558:4; 2060:5;
mastery of ~ , 910:13; overcoming ~ , 618:15;
1564:4

advertisement/advertising (*also see* commercialism;
marketing; publicity), 1128:2; 1341:7; 1352:2;
1565:2; 2341:3; 2523:1; 2531:3; ~ aimed at
women, 2349:16; deception in ~ (*also see* deception ~ in advertising), 1757:17; ~ in United
States, 1548:5; men and ~ , 2518:1; simplifica-
tion of ~ , 2456:6; television ~ (*also see* television, commercials), 1676:1;

advice, 458:12; 2349:15; ~ to child, 35:2; 547:2;
1434:1; woman's ~ , 910:12

advisor, 285:6; 1117:2

affectation (*also see* fop; pretension), 508:2

affection, 704:20; 1592:4; lack of ~ , 1528:3;
physical ~ , 1040:3; words of ~ , 618:40

affirmative action, 1719:1; 2023:5; 2258:2

afflicted, the, 1706:2

affliction, 239:3; 277:20; 548:2; 667:1; bearing ~ ,
495:5

affluence/affluent, the (*also see* prosperity, rich,
wealth), effects of ~ , 2451:3; tastes of ~ ,
2136:6

Africa/African (*also see specific nations;* Afro-
Americans; blacks), 520:3; 550:11; 583:3; 606:5;
703:29; 800:5, 9; 2110:4; 2159:3; depredation of
~ , 665:1; 2220:1; egotism of ~ , 2402:10; image
of ~ , 2110:5; injustice against ~ blacks, 1522:14;
oppression of ~ , 2110:2; war among ~ nations,
2402:18; ~ women, 773:2; 2407:4

Afro-American (*also see* blacks), 1103:1; ~ women
2403:3

afterlife (*also see* reincarnation), 234:2; 775:2; 829:1;
901:4; 939:5; 2304:3

afternoon, 1381:8

Age (*also see* century; era; times), Golden ~ ,
392:3; Modern ~ , 678:1; ~ of Enlightenment,
2042:1; ~ of Reason, 565:24; Space ~ , 1561:2;
Victorian ~ , 703:8

age/aging (*also see* elderly; old age; people, old),
137:1; 242:2; 308:1; 386:4; 577:7; 686:1; 703:33;
733:2; 893:14; 982:2; 1002:3; 1010:1; 1028:1;
1192:19, 24; 1238:2; 1245:10; 1300:1; 1620:2;
1641:4; 1685:4; 1690:3; 1921:1; 2079:6; advantages of ~ , 1580:1; effects of ~ , 1921:3; fear
of ~ , 1576:15; 1602:1; 1621:1; 1635:3; honoring
~ , 825:6; ~ in relation to work, 1659:2; ~ in
relation to youth, 438:12; 1576:16; men and ~
(*also see* men, aging; men, older), 2136:12; middle
~ (*also see* middle age), 2465:5; perversity of ~,
163:1; physical aspects of ~ , 1823:3; realization
of ~ , 1786:1; wisdom of ~ , 2110:3; women
and ~ (*also see* women, aging; women, old;
women, older), 1173:1; 2136:12; 2232:1

aged, the, 1975:2

ageism (*also see* prejudice), 1447:2

aggression, 1833:5

agitation, 873:2

agitator, political ~ , 750:10; 873:1; 895:1, 4;
1029:1; 1059:8, 10; 1182:1; 1875:2

agreeableness, 458:10; 618:14

aid, giving ~ , 1695:6

aimlessness, 1667:2

air, fresh ~ , 2509:1; good ~ , 346:1; polluted
~ , 576:5; ~ territories, 277:2

airplane (*also see* flying), 1515:1; woman ~ pilot,
1578:1

Aladdin's lamp, 703:16

alchemy, 253:3

alcoholic/alcoholism, 1600:5; 1682:6; 1841:1, 2;
1926:3; 2203:4; 2334:3; ~ among Native Americans, 1729:1; dangers of ~ , 818:1; ~ husband,
991:2

color, 138:11; 178:1; 701:7

Columbus, Christopher, 723:3; 2504:6

comedian (*also see* humorist), 1589:2; woman ~ , 1741:1; 2274:2

comedy (*also see* humor), 1194:2; 2274:4; performance of ~ , 2187:1; reason for ~ , 2487:5

comfort, 762:5; 909:2; 979:1; 1104:5; 1192:5; 1207:1; 1439:31; 2506:1; throw off ~ , 618:25

comfortableness, 225:5

command, 46:1

commerce (*also see* business; marketing), loathsomeness of ~ , 971:5

commercialism, 878:2; 1128:2; 1864:2; 1905:1; 1948:2; ~ in creative works, 2413:3; 2455:2; ~ in United States, 1476:4

commitment, 1291:1

commoner (*also see* people, ordinary), 1719:2; life of ~ , 2156:3

common good (*also see* public welfare), 637:2

commonplace, the (*also see* ordinariness), 984:1

common sense, 1221:26; 1268:4; 1327:1

communal society/commune, 2234:1; 2370:1; 2537:4

communication, 256:3; 551:4; 994:2; 1192:47; 1341:21; 1346:5; 2274:3; 2491:1; difficulties of ~ , 1926:1; family ~ , 1679:9; future ~ , 2499:3; lack of ~ , 1445:6; 1658:19; 1669:4; 1731:1; 2124:1; tools of ~ , 309:5; 1220:2; withholding ~ , 2327:4; ~ with women, 1648:2

communism/communist, 777:25; 1187:1; 1352:1; 1376:5; 1545:2; 1565:5; 2136:16; 2313:3; argument against ~ , 1341:16; combating ~ , 1478:1

community, ~ in relation to children, 1435:20; 2084:18; lack of ~ , 2000:4; 2456:2

companion (*also see* friend), 2375:2; identification with ~ , 1921:7

companionship (*also see* friendship), 669:40; 892:11; 966:1; 1013:2; 1050:1; 1192:50; 1390:5; need for ~ , 1682:8; 1884:1; seeking ~ , 124:1

compassion (*also see* humaneness; pity), 602:2; 777:21; 1244:4; 1268:4; 1396:1; 1758:1; 1777:3; 1867:2; lack of ~ , 27:1; 1766:2; 2456:3; need for ~ , 2378:1

compatibility, 387:8

competition, 1061:1; 1081:1; 1783:2; 1806:2; 2495:1; 2510:1; ~ between nations, 2306:1; children and ~ , 1908:5; cutthroat ~ , 2147:1; emotional cost of ~ , 2473:1; refrain from ~ , 580:1; women and ~ , 1900:2; 2337:1; worthy ~ , 736:7

complaint/complainer, 239:3; 249:5; 333:2; 506:1; 2178:4

complex/ity (*also see* neurosis; Oedipus), 1993:1; Cinderella ~ , 2239:2

compliance, 321:1

comportment (*also see* behavior; conduct), 216:1; proper ~ , 441:3

composure, 1322:3; 1881:3

compromise, 577:16; 676:3; 762:6; 1341:3; 1399:2; 1439:26; 1548:1; 1643:2; 2344:5; 2522:3; need for ~ , 1779:2

compulsion (*also see* obsession), 1311:1

computer, 2283:4; writer and ~ , 2455:4

concealment, 577:3

conceit/edness (*also see* egotism; self-centeredness), 565:16; 695:2; 833:9, 12

concentration, 2084:13

concentration camp, ~ brands, 1553:1

concept, carrying out of ~ , 642:3; global ~ , 2283:4

conception (*see* birth; fertility)

concern, practical ~ , 346:5

conciliation, 623:2

conclusion, drawing ~ , 1440:11

concreteness, 2028:15

condemnation, 577:28

conditioning (*also see* child, conditioning of; woman, conditioning of; socialization), behavioral ~ , 1767:7

conduct (*also see* behavior; comportment; manners), 224:1; 292:1; 937:2; 1302:3; 1434:1; control of ~ , 523:1; mis~ , 669:31; 704:14; ~ of women, 1420:1; poor ~ , 577:15; upright ~ , 401:1; 636:1

confession, 1024:2; 1087:3; Catholic ~ , 718:6; 1852:6; forced ~ , 318:3

confidence (*also see* self-confidence), 639:28; 673:4; 1341:23; 2367:3; lack of ~ , 627:26; sharing a ~ , 2320:3

confinement (*also see* imprisonment), 183:1; 438:21

conflict (*also see* strife; struggle), 1279:4; 1789:3; ~ and resolution (*also see* reconciliation; showdown), 2195:1; inner-~ , 622:2; 901:1; 1351:4; 1446:2; 1532:3; 1607:12; 1850:4; 1972:1; 2125:5; 2246:7; national ~ , 559:1; ~ resolution, 2457:1

conformist/conformity (*also see* propriety), 504:9; 749:8; 755:3; 1503:2; 1515:5; 1623:1; 1647:18; 1974:6; demand for ~ , 2169:1

Confucianism, 76:1; 2295:3

confusion (*also see* bewilderment), 760:2; 1378:7; 1582:1; emotional ~ , 159:1

Congress, U.S. (*also see* United States, government; legislator), 1752:2; 1873:3, 4; members of ~ (*also see* lawmakers), 1718:1; sexism in ~ , 2277:2; ~ women (*see* government, women in)

connectedness/connection, 858:1; 2311:1, 2; 2355:1; ~ among women, 2315:1; hidden ~ , 1427:3; ~ of humanity, 782:4

conscience, 285:5; 406:13; 433:1; 627:2; 800:1; 875:2; 892:21; 1030:1; 1152:4; 1330:1; 1607:2; 1976:3; awakened ~ , 192:4; clear ~ , 285:3; 292:1; 742:2; 1658:14; guilty ~ (*also see* guilt), 300:1; 1644:1; 1759:1; 1842:1; 2408:3; search one's ~ , 580:3; 637:13

conscientiousness, 1398:2; 2139:2

conscientious objector (*also see* war, opposition to), 1439:30; 2223:1

consciousness (*also see* life, inner; self-consciousness; unconscious), 1175:2; 1395:2; 1485:3; 1789:1; 2406:1; awakening of ~ , 694:4; expanding one's ~ , 2169:2; ~ raising, 1812:1;

1882:5; 2164:1; 2388:1; stream of ∼ , 1553:2; 1566:3; 2325:2

conscription, 859:5; 1244:1; 1442:1

consecration (*see* sacredness)

consensus, 2344:2

conservation (*also see* ecology), 1668:11

conservatism/conservative (*also see* moral majority; reactionary), 811:21; 1264:2

consistency, 1075:6; 1595:5

consolation, 185:1

constancy (*also see* loyalty), 277:24; 285:10; 406:14

Constitution, U.S. (*also see* United States, government), 1702:5; 1968:2; representation of women in ∼ , 1875:1; 2187:2; 2277:1; sexism in ∼ , 832:6

consumer/ism (*also see* shopping), 1075:7; 1912:2; 2470:1; ∼ in relation to art, 2028:24; power of ∼ , 2503:3

container, 1157:3

contemplation (*also see* meditation), 270:3; life of ∼ , 1140:2

contempt (*also see* scorn), ∼ for men, 584:3; object of ∼ , 363:15; 2284:4

contents, 795:17; 1032:9; 1450:2

contentiousness, 138:19; 677:4

contentment, 298:1; 489:1; 494:2; 704:14; 708:2; 893:4; 910:21; 1287:3; 2436:2; ∼ of spirit, 704:13

continuity, ∼ of life, 2435:1

contraception (*see* birth control)

contradiction (*also see* paradox), 980:3; ∼ in terms, 2079:4

contrariness, 1855:1

control (*also see* self-control), 910:3; 1083:6; 1192:51; 1307:2; lack of ∼ , 1592:2; 2303:2; letting go of ∼ , 1445:8; loss of ∼ , 448:4; 1369:5; ∼ of circumstance, 755:1

convenience, 590:11

convent, 327:1; 973:1; ∼ education, 1417:10; motivation to enter ∼ , 417:13

conventionality, 813:1; 1003:10; 1144:2; 1970:4; sticking with ∼ , 1147:2

conversation (*also see* intercourse, social), 513:23; 683:4; 749:7; 878:2; 933:2; 1221:13; 1440:6; 1445:6; 1579:4; 1775:2; art of ∼ , 557:15; 2093:1; cautious ∼ , 2175:5; decline of good ∼ , 724:2; idle ∼ , 192:3; 800:11; 2198:1; 2451:1; ∼ of friends, 403:4; ∼ of women, 674:3; religious ∼ , 438:5; repetitive ∼ , 2250:1; spiritual ∼ , 722:1; stimulating ∼ , 703:35; subject of ∼ , 517:2; 736:3; 1800:1

conversion, religious ∼ , 542:1; 671:15; 768:1

convictions (*also see* belief; principle), 1831:1; courage of ∼ , 1590:2; one's own ∼ , 868:2

cook/ing (*also see* book, cook-; recipe), 366:3; 417:19; 822:1; 1048:1; 1116:2; 1199:1; 1495:2; 1744:3; 1745:2; 1836:2; 1887:1; 1922:1, 2; men and ∼ , 798:1; 2178:3; ∼ sauces, 1258:1; ∼ with liquor, 822:1

cookie, 1439:6

Coolidge, Calvin, 1337:1

cooperation (*also see* conflict, resolution; harmony), 580:1; 910:11; 1341:3, 21, 36; 1624:5; 2195:1; 2262:6; global ∼ (*also see* peace, world; unity, of human race), 763:9; 2433:3; ∼ in business world, 1647:11

Copley, John Singleton, 647:1

corn, 1590:3

corporation, 2531:1, 2, 4; effects of ∼ competition, 2147:1; ∼ executive, 1948:3; 2363:1; multi-national ∼ , 1376:4

correspondence (*see* letters)

corruption (*also see* bribery; debauchery; graft), 408:2; 609:12; 723:24; 1393:7; 1505:1; 1542:3; 1552:3; 1938:1; ∼ among the elite, 138:4; ∼ in government, 981:2; 1835:3; 2046:3; ∼ of white race, 703:29; ∼ of women, 371:2; political ∼ , 1061:2; 1152:2; 1941:2

corset (*also see* underwear), 2046:2; 2115:2

cosmetics, 1067:2; 2004:1; 2218:7; 2349:16

cost, ∼ of living, 1924:1; ∼ of things, 1259:1

cotton, picking ∼ , 1324:1

counting, 1221:22

country (*also see* nation), leaving a ∼ , 1349:6

country life (*also see* rusticity; woman, country; countryside), 282:1; 576:4; 899:7; 1149:1; 1153:1; 1658:15; 1762:3

countryside (*also see* country life; landscape; outdoors; rusticity), 576:4; 756:10; 1486:1; 2028:9; visiting the ∼ , 627:9

couple (*also see* relationship), 763:2; 2349:10; attitudes toward ∼ , 1979:5; confines of ∼ , 1261:2; splitting up of ∼ , 2218:5; 2471:1

courage (*also see* bravery; valor), 85:1; 167:2; 462:8; 833:1; 1152:22; 1517:1; 1663:6; 2261:2; lack of ∼ , 166:1; moral ∼ , 1449:6; ∼ of convictions, 1798:3; ∼ tried, 513:18; 588:2

court (judicial), 2184:2; integrity of ∼ system, 1064:2

court (royal), ∼ life, 336:1; 458:3; 568:2; French ∼ , 400:2

courtesan (*see* prostitute)

courtesy (*also see* manners; politeness; tact), 458:17; 976:34; 1501:2; 1580:3; 1926:5; lack of ∼ , 800:21

courtiers (*also see* court [royal], life) marriage among ∼ , 303:1

courting (*also see* love), words of ∼ , 582:2

courtship (*also see* love, game of), 48:1; 474:1; 551:16; 1245:11; rules of ∼ (*also see* love, game of), 277:15

covetousness, 428:5; 462:7

cow, 1586:1

coward/cowardice, 256:5; 462:3; 703:28; 842:8; physical ∼ , 1449:6

coyness, 910:9

crack (drug), 2138:1

craftsmanship, 833:30; 1191:12; 1682:4

Craven, Earl of, 710:1

creation, 576:1; 1306:1; controlling ∼ , 1462:3; ∼ of humankind, 723:16; understanding ∼ , 2020:2

diamond, ~ bracelet, 1390:1

diaper, disposable ~ , 2336:1

diary (*also see* journal), 859:2; 1000:2; 1608:1; musing over ~ , 1213:10; reasons to keep ~ , 2022:1, 2; revelations of ~ , 980:3, 4; woman's ~ , 2245:1

dichotomy, ~ of human beings (*also see* people, dichotomy of), 1752:1; ~ of life, 387:20; 481:1; 1072:1

Dickinson, Emily, 1213:13

dictator/ship, 2013:1; 2349:2; 2501:1

Diderot, Denis, 499:1

diet (*also see* nutrition), American ~ , 1618:2, 4; obsession with ~ , 1837:1; people and ~ , 1015:3; weight loss ~ , 1192:11; 1989:2; 2484:7; women and ~ , 2292:1

differences (*also see* sexes, differences between), 1258:1; 1396:13; ~ among individuals, 1523:1; intolerance of ~ , 1445:11

digestion (*also see* eating), good ~ , 526:8

dilettante, 1722:2

diligence (*also see* effort; industriousness), 489:3; 550:1; 604:3; 1208:2; 2288:2; 2514:1; rewards of ~ , 647:1; 761:1

dining (*also see* specific meals; eating), ~ alone, 735:7; 1192:25

dinner, ~ announcement, 2287:2

Diogenes, 467:3

diplomacy/diplomat, 1328:4; 2042:1; restraints of ~ , 2083:1

direction, best ~ , 2111:1; finding ~ , 1548:4; headed in wrong ~ , 448:4

directness, 2206:2

director (*also see* theater), stage ~ , 2061:1

dirt (*also see* soil), 670:12

disability (*also see* handicap, physical), 1342:6; children with ~ , 1983:2; physical ~ , 1592:3

disabled, the (*also see* handicap, physical), 1484:3; physically ~ , 1918:2

disagreement, 704:2

disappearance, 138:13; 1192:31

disappointment, 832:3; 883:2; 967:1; little ~ , 603:1; sundry ~ , 277:14

disapproval, 577:28; 1743:1; expressing ~ , 505:1

disaster, 1422:7; 1870:2; environmental ~ , 2145:2

discipline (*also see* self-discipline), 823:6; 1702:2 2254:2

disclosure, 1191:18; effects of ~ , 2204:2; public ~ , 2246:18

discontent, 326:4; ~ of citizenry, 225:2

discord, 800:22

discourse, 2036:5

discovery, 1812:1; 2090:3; 2229:2; 2402:4; fear of ~ , 975:1

discretion, lack of ~ , 138:10

discrimination, eliminating ~ , 1341:34; 2096:1

disease (*also see* specific disorders; illness), 855:11; 1785:1; attitudes toward ~ , 2376:3; study of ~ , 1618:3

disembodiment, 184:2

disfavor, 394:2

disillusionment, 1566:5; 2435:2; fear of ~ , 1332:2

disloyalty, 448:3; 513:9

disorder, 1612:7; 1896:2

displacement, 131:1

disposition (*also see* human nature; personality; temperament), 589:2; good-natured ~ , 582:12; importance of ~ , 522:1

dissatisfaction, 241:4; 253:2; 627:15, 16; 811:5; impetus of ~ , 1039:11

dissembling, 1192:38; difficulty of ~ , 547:1; power of ~ , 1658:21

dissent, 1799:1

dissident, political ~ , 1916:1

dissipation, 1445:10

distinction (*also see* individuality), 688:14; desire for ~ , 387:10; 513:4; 577:18; woman of ~ , 448:1

distribution, 1647:2

distrust (*also see* mistrust; trust, lack of), 833:19

diversion (*also see* amusement; pleasure), 489:5; 684:1; incessant ~ , 385:3; 639:11; indifference to ~ , 373:2

diversity (*also see* variety), appreciation of ~ , 1576:4; cut off from ~ , 1376:2; elimination of ~ , 1576:3

divinity, ~ in humans, 2413:1

divorce (*also see* alimony; marriage, dissolution of), 1087:2; 1245:3; 1346:2; 1456:3; 1604:3; 2161:6; impermissible ~ , 1456:7; New York ~ , 1104:1; ~ rate, 1889:9; women and ~ , 1604:2

doctor (*see* medical profession, physician)

Dodge, Mabel, 1320:1

dog, 344:1; 781:1; 1104:8; 1220:1; 1224:2; 1393:8; 1401:9; 1425:1; 1499:1; 1965:1; admiration of ~ , 584:3; 1506:2; eyes of ~ , 550:7; ~ in relation to people, 856:1; love for ~ , 526:2; 565:9; 856:2; 1073:2

doll, 986:1

Doll's House, A, Nora of ~ , 1807:3

domesticity (*also see* tameness), 557:16; 766:14; 1200:6; women and ~ , 682:9; 811:25; 2131:1

domination, 1612:5; dissolution of male ~ , 2099:3; ~ over others, 2197:1; power of ~ , 1647:5

donkey, 1090:2

Don Quixote, 733:1

doom, 737:13

door, ~bell, 1467:2

Dostoevsky, Feodor, 988:2

double standard (*also see* sexism), 983:1; 1456:6; 2161:4; 2374:1; ~ in manners, 1747:2

double talk, 582:8

doubt (*also see* uncertainty), 216:3; 932:1; 1511:1; unfounded ~ , 794:3

Douglas, Helen Gahagan, 1341:17

dove, 714:2

Dover, White Cliffs of ~ , 1215:3

dowry, 249:2; 513:5

dragon, 1378:8

dragonfly, 1051:1

drawing, 2283:2, 3; skill at ~ , 2052:2

dread (also see fear), 790:3; 2039:9

dream (also see daydream), 618:38; 723:30; 730:5, 14; 742:6; 749:1; 890:1; 1038:23; 1192.34; 1274.3, 1450:1; 1596:1; 2168:13; 2257:3; 2347:2; ~ come true, 1281:1; conscious of ~ , 1669:1; controlling one's ~ , 1307:2; desolate ~ , 1439:27; destroying ~ , 1435:6; faded ~ , 125:1; following a ~ , 2290:3; function of ~ , 2169:2; holding a ~ , 1296:4; in search of a ~ , 1518:2; interpretation of ~ , 2136:2; meaning of ~ , 2217:5; realizing one's ~ , 1992:2; 2060:11; shared ~ , 2440:1; understanding ~ , 2169:3

dreamer (also see visionary), 910:19

dress (also see clothing; fashion), shopping for ~ , 1473:1; unadmired ~ , 990:2

drinking, 1275:1; ~ habits, 1390:4; social ~ , 1841:1

drought, 2261:3

drowning, 364:1

drug addict/ion, 1841:2; 1995:1; 2143:2; ~ among Native Americans, 1729:1; women and ~ , 2138:1

drugs (also see specific drugs), addictive ~ , 800:7; balm of ~ , 601:1; 1022:1; effect of ~ , 2333:3; 2419:2; hallucinogenic ~ , 1607:18; prescription ~ , 1841:2; social ~ , 2250:3; speed, 2228:4; steroids, 2525:1

drunkard/drunkenness, 108:1; 237:11; 310:2; 435:2

drunk driving, 2432:1; victims of ~ , 2432:2

duality, 1393:2; ~ , of the sexes, 795:7; wish for ~ , 1680:14

dullness, 599:5; advantages of ~ , 1465:1; ~ of life, 1954:2

Duncan, Isadora, 2471:4

duplicity (also see deception), 277:17; 697:39; 777:24; 1697:3; 1848:2; 1863:6; 1905:1; 2010:2; 2261:1; 2289:2; ~ of life, 2039:6

Duse, Eleonora, 1568:1

dust, 1760:2; 2116:2

duty (also see obligation; responsibility), 682:14; 745:1; 780:2; 817:1; 875:7; 926:2; 1075:23; keeping to one's ~ , 688:22; ~ of friendship, 800:18; path of ~ , 989:1; rewards of ~ , 797:1

dying (also see dead; death; death sentence), 234:1; 307:5; 513:21; 2114:2; ~ at home, 1974:4; experience of ~ , 2178:6; fear of ~ , 1136:4; renounce ~ , 1192:53; romantic notion of ~ , 237:3; solitude of ~ , 998:5; words of the ~ , 55:2; ~ young, 704:11

E

eagle, 2436:1

Earhart, Amelia, 1578:1

earliness, 210:1

earth (also see world), 2018:7; 2248:1; abundance of ~ , 1405:2; caring for ~ , 2237:1; 2306:5; connectedness to ~ , 1761:4; 2482:1; 2490:3; 2509:1; damage to ~ , 2367:1; desecration of ~ , 550:29; 617:1; enduring ~ , 367:4; interac-

tion with ~ , 2393:2; love of ~ , 1147:1; rescuing ~ , 2167:5; story of ~ , 1668:5; 2451:2; unfriendly ~ , 264:1

East Bengal, India, 1824:6

eating (also see specific meals; digestion; food), 1495:3; 2393:2; communion of ~ together, 1685:5; ~ habits, 456:1; ~ habits of youth, 2262:5; over~ , 703:20

eccentricity, 1881:4; 2106:1

echo, 639:12

ecology (also see conservation; environment; pollution), 1015:2; 1563:4; 1834:1; balance of ~ , 1781:4; management of ~ , 2258:1; principles of ~ , 2418:1; unbalanced ~ , 1576:12

economics, 1583:1; cooperative ~ , 1376:5; ~ in relation to art, 1191:21; ~ of scarcity, 2199:2; ~ of world trade, 1236:5

economy (also see inflation), backbone of American ~ , 1856:3; city ~ , 1808:5; depressed ~ , 697:18; 1315:2; false ~ , 496:10; growth of (also see development, economic) ~ , 1651:11; 1779:3; national ~ , 2433:2; unstable ~ , 578:4; 1341:11; women and ~ , 2209:1

ecstasy (see rapture)

Eden, Garden of (also see heaven; paradise), finding ~ , 697:4

editor, woman ~ , 1303:1

education (also see college; instruction; school; study), 550:4; 614:2; 703:21; 1511:6; 2394:4; American ~ (also see United States, education in), 2283:4; arts in ~ , 2048:1, 2; 2450:4; bureaucracy in ~ , 1634:1; children and ~ , 367:9; 1192:29; 1307:1; 1417:10; 1901:3; 1908:5; 2164:7; Christian ~ , 670:9; concept of ~ , 1171:3; cost of ~ , 731:3; danger of traditional ~ , 1661:5; financial assistance for ~ , 830:2; ~ for disadvantaged women, 2256:3; good ~ , 947:1; government influence on ~ , 1252:2; lack of ~ , 720:2; 1206:3; liberal ~ , 1200:1; 2084:8; 2452:3; ~ of girls, 2070:3; physical ~ , 2097:1; pleasure of ~ , 1135:9; power of ~ , 639:31; practical ~ , 569:1; public ~ , 1003:5; 1341:2; 1377:4; purpose of ~ , 609:14; 670:1; 736:5; 800:19; 2430:2; religious ~ , 439:2; 442:2; reverence for ~ , 1800:4; self-~ , 895:2; sex ~ (also see sex, education), 1615:1, 3; sexism in ~ , 138:1; 196:1; 575:2; 2031:1; 2272:2; 2538:1, 2; systems of ~ , 1132:3; wholistic ~ , 1515:4; women and ~ (also see woman, education and), 309:1; 367:5; 380:16; 434:1; 703:6; 723:7; 741:1; 762:10; 766:3; 777:27; 937:1; 1661:1; 1964:1; 2031:2

educator (see teacher)

Edward VI, king of England, 280:1

efficiency, ~ of people, 2069:1

effort (also see diligence; endeavor), 1862:7; 2123:2; futility of ~ , 309:6

Eisenhower, Dwight D., 1341:29, 35

egalitarianism, 1376:3

egg, boiled ~ , 669:22

ego (also see identity; self; self-image), 417:18;

ego (*continued*)
998:2; 1647:10; building one's ~ , 1643:3; competitive ~ , 1097:2; differentiated ~ , 2020:7; feeding the ~ , 1686:2; male ~ , 1682:2; submission of ~ , 2121:4

egocentricity/egotism (*also see* self-centeredness; self-interest; selfishness), 387:9; 417:28; 748:1; 755:2; 777:24; 833:9, 12; 910:12; 1266:2; 1390:6; 1431:4; 1433:2; 1573:1; 1926:1; 2267:2; 2446:2

Egypt, 1365:1; polygamy in ~ , 766:11

Eichmann, Adolf, 1651:8

elderly, the/elders (*also see* man, age and; old age; woman, old), 1596:2; compassion for ~ , 2165:1; death of ~ , 550:16; 2146:1; 2444:2; disregard for ~ , 1641:6; ~ in society, 1641:1; isolation of ~ , 1641:2; neighborhoods of ~ , 2139:1; responsibility of ~ , 1641:5

election, political ~ , 1341:17; 2229:1

electricity, 1932:2

elegance, 609:2; 910:8; 1536:1

elephant, 1014:5; 1349:4; 1821:7

elitism (*also see* clique; snob), 1236:2; 1456:2; 2342:4; 2515:3; weapons of ~ , 2080:1

Elizabeth, queen of Bohemia, 826:1

Elizabeth I, queen of England, 277:1, 26; 391:2; 392:1, 2

elk, 1089:1

Ellis, Sir William and Lady, 719:2

eloquence, influence of ~ , 994:1

elusiveness, 1112:4; 1752:4

emancipation (*see* liberation)

Emancipation Proclamation, U.S., 1223:2

emigrant (*also see* immigrant; refugee), haven for ~ , 1005:1; Irish ~ , 789:2

emotion (*also see* feelings; passion), 2536:1; expression of ~ , 2037:2; 2375:3; ~ in relation to social condition, 2232:4; range of ~ , 1459:20

empathy (*also see* identification), 496:3; 790:2

employee (*also see* worker), 1827:2; ~ benefits (*see* work force, benefits for); devoted ~ , 1317:2

employer, ~ attitude toward women, 2238:4; tyrannical ~ , 1034:2

employment (*also see* job; livelihood; work, finding), ~ for all, 1341:11

empowerment (*also see* power), ~ of others, 2124:2; ~ of women, 2147:2

emptiness (*also see* void), 1927:5; 1991:2; 2098:1; 2328:1; 2347:5; filling ~ , 1958:8

empty-headedness, 639:21

encouragement, benefits of ~ , 1146:3

encyclopedia, 1200:1

ending, 1082:1; 1269:1; 1706:11; ~ relationships, 2161:6

endurance (*also see* strength), 163:3; 560:3; 909:3; 1435:15; 2263:3

enemy, 386:2; confronting the ~ , 705:2; ~ to one's self, 237:10; 2371:6; treatment of ~ , 560:2; 673:5

energy, 1206:2; ~ crisis, 1779:2

England (*see* English; Great Britain), 496:12; 550:19;

669:1; attitude toward money in ~ , 1720:5; economics of ~ , 1137:1; fame of ~ , 756:2; grass in ~ , 1835:1; homes of ~ , 730:2; ~ in relation to U.S.A., 616:1; 1108:5; 1457:1; leadership in ~ , 656:2; mores in ~ , 438:23; 504:2; security of ~ , 1215:3; taxes in ~ , 1772:1; weather in ~ , 2262:2; women in ~ , 762:7

English, the (*also see* British; England; Great Britain), 438:37; 1060:11; 1747:3; 1814:1; ~ character, 704:16; 736:2; 1198:4; 1473:2; ~ language, 406:24; ~ values, 1626:3; well-bred ~ , 1461:10; ~ women, 1765:1

enigma, 401:6; 630:1

enjoyment (*also see* pleasure), 992:1; 1239:2; 1997:2

enlightenment (*also see* illumination), 235:4; 263:3; 694:8; 709:1; 1018:3; 2103:2; Age of ~ , 2042:1; ~ of nation, 1052:5; results of ~ , 811:5; spreading ~ , 1104:9; sudden ~ , 2325:2; values of ~ , 2057:3

enslavement (*also see* slavery), 1562:1; 1705:9; personal ~ , 269:8

entanglement, 1993:1

enterprise, 761:1; 811:41; 813:3; 843:2; 2099:4

entertainer (*also see* performer), 2159:8

entertainment (*also see* amusement; diversion; show business; theater), 1901:2; 2000:3; night of ~ , 2369:3

enthusiasm, 1350:1; 1825:3; 2415:3

entrepreneur, 2417:3

environment (*also see* ecology; pollution), activist for ~ , 2258:4; beauty of ~ , 1749:3; cleaning up ~ , 1695:8; controlling the ~ , 1647:16; destruction of ~ , 2258:1; natural ~ , 181:2; politics and ~ , 2434:1; pollution of ~ , 1624:3; preserving the ~ , 1779:2; product of ~ , 833:5; protecting the ~ , 2237:1; 2433:2, 3; threats to ~ , 1576:12; work ~ (*also see* workplace), 1905:3

envy (*also see* jealousy), 60:1; 123:1; 326:4; creating ~ , 1948:2; ~ of splendor, 623:1; woman's ~ , 743:1

epitaph, 277:26; 488:1; 723:1; 875:6; 894:7; 1459:22; 1535:1

equality, 811:15; 993:2; 2060:9; 2194:4; ~ at workplace (*also see* workplace), 1912:4; ~ for all, 1463:3; 1885:2; 1968:1; ~ for women (*also see* woman, equality of), 312:2; 811:9; 1218:2; 1247:7; 1576:3; 1604:11; 1680:13; 2232:5; ~ in sexist society, 2014:1; ~ of the sexes, 344:2; 362:1; 380:16; 579:1; 763:7; 780:6; 840:4, 5; 868:1, 8; 896:1; 907:1; 938:1; 1038:8; 1053:1; 1256:1; 2071:1; racial ~ , 520:2; sexual ~ , 165:1, 2; universal ~ , 2196:3

ERA (Equal Rights Amendment: *also see* feminism), 1355:2; 1604:11; 1748:1; effects of ~ , 1875:2; 1968:2; 2187:2; 2194:1; 2225:4

era (*also see* Age; century; decade; times), end of ~ , 1436:11

Eros, 50:5

eroticism, 1253:1; 2164:8; ~ in literature, 2161:3

error (*also see* mistake), 263:2; 855:8; 1757:13; conquering ~ , 855:4; excusing ~ , 462:4; human ~ , 577:15; response to ~ , 2365:4; results of ~ , 425:8; 871:2

Esalen, California, 1494.1

escape, 53:1; 2085:2; ~ from self, 1636:2; 1662:3; 1680:15

escapism, 204:1; 417:13; 1440:4

Eskimo, 2406:8; ~ child, 2321:1

ESP (*see* extrasensory perception)

espionage (*also see* spy; FBI; KGB), usefulness of ~ , 2336:1

esprit de corps (also see brotherhood; sisterhood; unity, of human race), 1463:1, 3; ~ of races, 703:34: 718:14

essence, loss of ~ , 2452:2

Establishment, the, anti~ , 1651:14; dropping out of ~ , 2308:2; philosophy of ~ , 1647:18; threat to ~ , 2408:2

Esther, 285:8; 773:1

estrangement, 2311:1

eternity (*also see* forever; infinity), 550:15; 688:25; 858:1; 1075:19

ethics (*also see* morality; principle), 309:4; 1075:21; 2189:5; changing ~ , 2013:2; grasp of ~ , 2456:6; principles of ~ , 2189:2

ethnicity (*also see* race), sensitivity of one's ~ , 1370:5

etiquette (*see* manners)

euphemism, 2079:4; ~ of war, 1752:9

Europe/an, 657:1; 2243:1; ~ character, 771:1; ~ in relation to U.S.A, 1457:1; 2060:4; post-war ~ , 1594:7; ~ women, 740:1; 2240:2

euthanasia, 1075:20; 1435:17

evasion/evasiveness, 893:3; polite ~ , 582:8

Eve (*also see* Adam and Eve), 317:1; 740:2; 750:8; 1473:1

eve/ning (*also see* night; sunset; twilight), 1375:2; New Year's ~ , 742:8

eventfulness, 1927:8

evidence, 2279:3, 5; lack of ~ , 277:1

evil (*also see* badness; evildoing; good and evil; wickedness), 174:2; 190:6; 387:4; 737:17; 1057:7; 1705:16; 2402:9; avoiding ~ , 237:15; choosing ~ , 1444:3; fighting against ~ , 1086:1; great ~ , 748:1; imaginary ~ , 893:7; portraying ~ , 363:16; suppress ~ , 583:1; tools of ~ , 2090:4

evolution, 1579:5; lessons of ~ , 868:9

exactness, 1190:7; 1926:4

exaggeration, 387:2; 1302:4; ~ in America, 951:3

examination, 2275:1

excellence (*also see* merit), 394:74; 420:1; 434:5; 637:41; 1755:2; 1944:1; desire for ~ , 590:5; 676:2

excitement, 1706:1; 1760:1

excuse (*also see* rationalization), 2349:18; weak ~ , 195:1

execution (*also see* death; lynching), ~ by decapitation, 249:4; 1476:3; facing ~ , 249:1; 584:2; 588:2; 697:36; mass ~ , 276:1

executive (*also see* businessperson), woman ~ , 2102:4

exemplar (*also see* role model), 723:31

exercise, physical ~ , 550:24; 718:3; 2262:6

exhaustion (*also see* fatigue; weariness), 243:1; 1357:1

exigency, demands of ~ , 671:13

exile, 848:2; 2347:2

existence (*also see* life), 2116:4; 2347:1; justification for ~ , 1680:6; reason for ~ , 1521:1; truth of ~ , 855:7

existentialism, 2150:1

exodus, ~ from Egypt, 9:1

expectation (*also see* anticipation), 266:3; 700:12; 998:1; 1002:6; 1270:1; disappointed ~ , 603:1; 2168:4; false ~ , 1214:1; moment of ~ , 662:1; no ~ , 1549:1; romantic ~ , 704:29

expediency, 1787:4

experience (*also see* practice), 216:5; 428:7; 1310:3; 1396:14; 2079:6; daily ~ , 1440:9; first-hand ~ , 138:2; 1083:3; gaining ~ , 1174:1; inner ~ , 1789:2; ~ is best teacher, 1712:1; lack of ~ , 1258:2; lessons of ~ , 720:2; repetition of ~ , 1862:13; understanding ~ , 2439:1

expertise (*also see* proficiency), 949:2

explanation, lack of ~ , 639:21

exploitation, 1287:8; 1835:8; ~ by the rich, 2387:6; ~ by ruling class, 2518:3; ~ in the arts, 1901:4; ~ of individual, 1522:9; ~ of sex (*see* sex, exploitation of); ~ of slaves, 800:10; ~ of the weak, 463:2; ~ of women (*also see* woman, exploitation of), 1473:1

exploration (*also see* search), 576:1; 1497:1; 2406:3; 2420:2

explorer, 723:3

expose, 218:1

extinction, ~ of bird life, 1668:10; ~ of human species, 683:1; 2413:4; threat of ~ , 2145:2

extra sensory perception, 1746:2

extravagance, 577:26; 1032:7; 1370:4; 1488:3

extremism, 1932:3; 2028:23

extroversion/extrovert, 269:5; 1398:4

eye (*also see* sight), 277:18; 411:1; 813:8; 1085:3; 2208:1; 2524:1; beauty of ~ , 777:15; bright ~ , 2402:16; loving ~ , 1407:2; lying ~ , 1406:1; use of ~ , 777:12; 1687:1

eyeglasses, 1459:4

eye witness, 438:4

F

face (human; *also see various parts of face*), 131:2; 277:7; 458:8; 808:2; 2231:2; 2493:2; beautiful ~ , 737:9; 922:1; examination of ~ , 1222:2; expression of ~ , 1073:1; features of ~ , 674:1; ~ of loved one, 688:2

fact, 1060:2; 1075:28; 1180:2; 2087:4; facing ~ , 1461:9; gathering ~ , 2344:3; ignoring ~ , 1595:6; perception of ~ , 1962:1; telling the ~ , 639:39

factionalism, 306:2; 1902:3

factory, 718:9; 1377:1

fad/dism, 2000:3; 2005:2; opposition to ~ , 1910:8

failings (also see fault; shortcoming), 2201:7

failure (also see defeat), 777:14; 840:7; 1316:1; 1375:12; 1455:1; 1669:3; 1745:2; 2089:3; handling ~ , 1391:8; reasons for ~ , 894:9; women and ~ , 2502:1

faint, 130:1

fairness (also see justice), 2256:2; lack of ~ , 2407:3

fairy, 875:1; 1070:1; 1084:1; 1250:1

faith (also see belief; conviction; religion), 261:4; 315:1; 467:7; 557:17; 777:18; 788:1; 875:8; 892:4; 1135:8; 1148:1; 1511:1; act of ~ , 550:9; ~ in humankind, 163:10; 561:3; 1435:5; ~ in nature, 1955:7; ~ in oneself, 1927:6; 2158:1; loss of ~ , 748:2; 1566:2; 2065:4; maintaining ~ , 1727:3; ~ tried, 239:2; world of ~ , 1761:1

faithfulness (also see loyalty), 81:1

faithlessness (also see adultery; infidelity), 138:18

Fall, the (biblical), 1883:2; 1958:1

fall, the (season), 894:8

falsehood (see lie/lying)

falseness (also see deception; duplicity; pretense), 495:3; 513:7

fame (also see celebrity; famous; public life; stardom), 380:13; 417:11; 424:3, 4; 458:21; 618:1; 973:2; 1121:2; 1323:1; bearing ~ , 2060:3; ephemerality of ~ , 248:2; 697:11; 1702:3; fraud of ~ , 2203:1; immortal ~ , 533:1; loneliness of ~ , 1382:1; ~ of loved one, 637:23; price of ~ , 590:7; pursuit of ~ , 639:19; value of ~ , 723:21; women and ~ , 448:8

familiarity, 307:10; 1192:8; 1631:2; 1796:1; disadvantages of ~ , 800:21

family (also see love, familial), American ~ , 2155:2, 4; ~ as training ground, 2164:10; black sheep of ~ , 565:19; changing ~ , 1989:1; 2255:1; 2330:2; 2396:3; commitment to ~ , 2012:2; ~ communication, 1679:9; death in ~ , 730:10; decline of ~ , 2264:3; 2300:2; definition of ~ , 2164:9; difficulties of ~ life, 419:3; 669:27; 697:32; 704:69; 800:17; 1497:3; discussing ~ members, 1436:2; divisiveness in ~ , 1902:3; forgiveness in ~ , 237:1; ideal of ~ , 1302:5; insensitivity of ~ members, 894:2; ~ interaction, 2457:1; ~ jokes, 1434:2; large ~ , 777:9; 1910:2; 2078:2; 2121:2; lessons of ~ life, 1075:11; 1939:2; 2159:9; nuclear ~ , 2084:18; ~ partiality, 669:36; patriarchal ~ , 2348:1; ~ planning, 1328:9; 2504:5; pro-~ , 2306:4; protection of ~ , 2240:2; ~ resemblance, 2034:17; 2451:4; role of ~ members, 1591:3; ~ size, 1328:1; two-career ~ , 1076:1; unity of ~ , 1075:10; ; women and ~ , 2293:3

famous, the (also see celebrity), 1863:1; insulting ~ , 1366:1

fantasy, 1092:1; 1373:7; 1981:2; 2028:14, 21; ~ creatures, 1563:5; criticism of ~ , 2461:2; living out ~ , 950:1; 1233:1; sexual ~ , 2461:1

farm/er, 504:7; 550:18; 820:1; 1057:5; 1208:3;

1774:2; American ~ , 1856:3; dairy ~ , 1736:1; French ~ , 2163:1; Kansas ~ , 1029:1; misery of ~ , 777:7; woman ~ , 1195:1; Yankee ~ , 703:5

farming (also see crop; land, cultivating), effect of ~ on soil, 1563:4

farm worker (also see migrant worker), ~ union, 2066:3

farsightedness, ~ of nation, 795:12

fascination, 1702:1

fascism, 1482:2; fight against ~ , 1739:1; women and ~ , 2040:1

fashion (also see clothing), 682:13; 822:2; 1322:1, 5; 1495:1; 1599:2; 1803:3; capriciousness of ~ , 550:27; ~ industry, 1948:2; ~ of different peoples, 1120:1; passing ~ , 577:27; women and ~ , 1139:1; 1314:7

fashionableness, 885:2

fastidiousness, 743:6; 1319:18

fat (see obesity; plumpness)

fatalism, 778:1; 1039:13; 1974:9

fate (also see chance; destiny; fortune; luck), 249:5; 388:2; 446:1; 457:3; 513:12; 1648:4, 5; conquering ~ , 957:1; foretelling ~ , 677:3; ironies of ~ , 269:1; 1217:3; 1336:1; persecution by ~ , 637:18; shared ~ , 249:6; winds of ~ , 1279:2

father (also see parent), 763:3; 1643:8; 1649:2; 1862:6; 1870:1; 2026:6; 2478:2; dying ~ , 2114:2; good ~ , 1552:4; homecoming of ~ , 939:2; ~ in relation to child (also see child, in relation to parent), 1072:2; 1329:2; 1658:23; 2471:2; ~ in relation to son (also see son, in relation to father), 1391:4; love for ~ , 1607:6; loving ~ , 1751:2; memory of ~ , 2018:6; obligation to ~ , 32:1; role of ~ , 2164:17; sexual relations with ~ , 4:1; symbolic ~ , 343:1; unwed ~ , 1792:3

fatherlessness (also see orphan), 1792:2

fatigue (see exhaustion; weariness)

fault (also see shortcoming), accepting one's ~ , 698:4; overcoming ~ , 256:8; revealing ~ , 417:11

faultfinding (also see critic/ism), 372:3; 609:17; 690:2

favor, conditional ~ , 332:2; political ~ , 513:2; receiving a ~ , 307:7

favoritism, 286:1; 639:34: 1719:1

FBI (see Federal Bureau of Investigation)

fear (also see dread; panic; paranoia), 213:2; 225:4; 235:5; 365:1; 1010:2; 1345:1; 1713:2; 2412:1; disguising ~ , 747:2; facing ~ , 1341:23; influence of ~ , 639:14; lack of ~ , 851:3; 2261:2; lessons of ~ , 2255:3; living in ~ , 1616:1; object of ~ , 1192:12; ~ of future, 2020:5; ~ of life, 971:4; unfounded ~ , 647:3

fearlessness (also see bravery), 1152:22

feast, 618:7; continual ~ , 232:2

fecundity, 101:1; 1896:1; 2406:9

Federal Bureau of Investigation, 1963:4

feeding (also see nutrition), forced ~ , 1059:5

feeling (also see emotion; heart; love; passion; sen-

forgetfulness (*continued*)
723:18; 875:9; 1679:8; 1771:6; balm of ~ ,
730:6; 899:8; 1539:2; 2217:1; defenses of ~ ,
1244:5; ~ of history, 1558:6

forgiveness (*also see* mercy), 239:4; 326:3; 441:1;
813:13; 870:2; 1100:1; 1595:2; conditional ~ ,
669:14; divine ~ (*also see* absolution), 384:1; ~
of self, 598:3; 2066:1; prompt ~ , 138:7; ~
withheld, 720:4

forgotten (*also see* forgetfulness), 588:4; not ~
(*also see* unforgettable), 102:1

form, ~ and function, 1494:2; ~ revolutionized,
1502:6

fortitude, 191:3; 652:2; weakening ~ , 480:1

fortune (*also see* chance; destiny; fate; luck), 163:5;
196:7; 231:3; 277:21; 309:6; 404:3; bad ~ ,
394:17; changes of ~ , 427:1; 486:1; 639:33;
677:5; 704:31; fickleness of ~ , 1488:7; good
~ , 307:2; 551:2; reverses of ~ , 603:1; ~telling
(*also see* prediction; prophecy), 2452:3; wheel of
~ , 1372:2

foundation, strong ~ , 1436:4

foundling, 1232:2

fragrance, sweet ~ , 425:6

France (*also see* Francophile; French), 285:1; 1534:1;
government of ~ , 637:37: government upheaval
in ~ , 588:7; ~ in relation to Germany, 2044:1;
mores in ~ , 504:2

Francis of Assisi, St., 1038:26

Francophile, 489:8; 700:8

Franklin, Benjamin, 510:2; 1390:5

frankness (*also see* candor), 401:3

fraud, pious ~ , 406:27

freak, 1915:2

freedom (*also see* liberation; liberty; rights), 315:2;
513:14; 718:15; 769:1; 812:1, 3; 834:2; 868:11;
890:2; 1038:23; 1189:2; 1564:5; 1628:2; 1734:5;
2028:10; 2038:1; 2159:4; 2232:6; 2362:2; 2365:6;
2537:2; demand for ~ , 2327:2; escape to ~ ,
1346:2; ~ fighters, 1410:2; fight for ~ , 1059:12;
1291:3; ~ for women, 1562:1; global ~ , 1435:11;
illusion of ~ , 513:19; lack of ~ , 1376:6; legal
~ , 1223:2; limitations of ~ , 1478:2; love of
~ , 583:5; momentary ~ , 1391:5; need for ~ ,
971:4; ~ of innocence, 404:2; ~ of press, 531:1;
1341:7; 1871:2; 2184:1; ~ of thought, 1675:1;
political ~ , 1651:11; 1961:3; poverty and ~ ,
2250:2; religious ~ , 583:5; 894:5; road to ~ ,
1885:3; sacrifice for ~ , 510:1; social ~ , 1757:18;
song of ~ , 786:2; struggle for ~ , 1059:1;
suppression of ~ , 1169:6; ~ vs. tyranny, 1651:9

free enterprise (*also see* capitalism), 1651:11

freeway, 2168:14

free will, 777:2; 1760:4; 2456:3; loss of ~ , 893:5

French, the (*also see* France), ~ character, 704:16;
~ culture, 1757:12; ~ law, 1685:2; ~ men,
1333:1; 1653:1; sex and ~ , 1390:9; ~ women,
591:2; 624:1

Freud, Sigmund, 1013:5; 1351:1; 1604:10; 1607:14;
2004:4; 2148:1; 2211:1; 2302:2; 2349:6; 2374:1

friction, 910:11; 946:2

friend (*also see* companion), 121:1; 380:8; 386:2;
394:20; 704:31; 974:1; 1075:30; 1098:2; 1322:2;
1869:1; animal ~ (*also see* pet), 833:2; best ~ ,
833:15; childhood ~ , 2484:3; choosing ~ ,
1568:1; criticism of ~ , 508:2; dear ~ , 305:1;
994:2; death of ~ , 899:2; dependable ~ , 682:23;
2324:4; faithful ~ , 201:1; 406:36; 513:24; 550:31;
feelings between ~ , 2415:4; 2419:2; loss of ~ ,
153:1; obligation to ~ , 550:30; 800:18; 802:1;
old ~ , 50:4; 1002:5; supportive ~ , 1912:3;
2349:10; true ~ , 1192:26; trusting ~ , 2034:9;
unreliable ~ , 463:1; 513:9

friendship (*also see* companionship), 387:16; 394:19;
438:8; 612:4; 737:3; 823:2; 875:12; 1093:1; 1757:6;
1904:1; basis for ~ , 627:14; ~ between men,
1045:2; ~ between men and women (*also see*
relationship, between men and women), 1476:2;
~ between women (*also see* woman, in relation
to women), 195:2; 275:1; 697:15; 2142:1; 2254:1;
breach in ~ , 201:1; 1197:1; close ~ , 811:27;
equality of ~ , 165:1; ~ grown apart, 441:2;
669:3; 1221:7; joys of ~ , 605:1; limits of ~ ,
160:2; single men and ~ , 1191:15; spark of ~ ,
557:9

frigidity, 1192:35

frivolity, 367:5; 393:4

frontier, child of ~ , 1298:1

frost, 706:1

fruit, overripe ~ , 458:24; ripe ~ , 151:1; 632:1

fulfillment, 837:3; wish ~ , 88:1

function, ~ and form, 1494:2

fundraising, 1643:11; 1898:1

funeral (*also see* burial), 639:6; cost of ~ , 1830:2;
food at ~ , 2284:5; ~ parlor, 2153:2

fur, fox ~ , 1378:9

furniture, 1375:6

futility, 1130:1; 1823:1

future, the (*also see* tomorrow), 637:31; 1218:2;
1300:1; 1659:1; 1680:6; 1705:14; 1876:5; attitude
toward the past, 777:21; better ~ , 1862:20;
dedicated to ~ , 1574:2; foretelling ~ (*also see*
foreknowledge; prophecy), 677:3; 700:15; looking to ~ , 1147:4; 1573:3; personal ~ , 777:28;
planning for ~ , 2091:3; prospects of ~ , 639:1;
959:1; responsibility to ~ , 2320:2; survival in
~ , 1561:2; women of ~ , 811:65, 66

G

galaxy, 1688:2

gambling (*also see* card playing), 1800:2

game (*also see* playing; toy), constructive ~ ,
2457:3; rules of the ~ , 1078:2

Gandhi, Mohandas Karamchand ("Mahatma"),
2189:2

garden/ing, 553:5; 875:14; 1056:1; 1439:12; 1979:1;
2287:1; lessons of ~ , 795:12; poor man's ~ ,
756:3; rose ~ , 2103:3

Garland, Judy, 1995:1

gay liberation movement (*see* homosexuality; lesbianism; rights, gay)

geese, wild ~ , 1563:1

gender (*also see* sex roles), 1982:1, 2; prison of ~ , 1970:2

generation, new ~ , 756:14

generation gap, 618:16; 1013:1; 1175:3; 1191:9; 1398:1; 1994:1; 2092:2

generosity (*also see* largess), 441:1; 462:14; 637:16; 1192:42; 2102:3; ~ toward the poor, 1081:2

genes, male ~ , 1717:2

genitalia (*also see* clitoris; penis; vagina), female ~ , 854:4

genius (*also see* greatness), 417:18; 550:1; 637:34; 763:10; 782:16; 795:11; 910:10; 934:1; 951:3; 1183:2; 1221:18; 1680:24; admiration of ~ , 795:14; cultivation of ~ , 795:19; offspring of ~ , 512:2; woman ~ , 803:1; 938:2

genocide, 34:5; 443:6; ~ of Native American, 2332:3; ~ of people of color, 2314:3

gentility, 1123:2

gentleman (*also see* man), 406:15; 1408:1; honor of ~ , 1199:2; pseudo-~ , 825:7

gentleness (*also see* tenderness), 256:12; 1111:1; 2034:18

genuineness, deceptive ~ , 1018:5

geologist, 2263:6

George III, king of England, 619:1

George IV, king of England, 641:1

German/y, ~ occupation of France, 1438:2

ghetto, 1924:2; ~ life, 2139:1

ghost, 899:2

Gibson, Althea, 1996:1

gift (*also see* present; talent), ~ as sales tool, 1557:1; ~ giving, 1178:1; 1960:1

gifted, the (*also see* exceptional), demands of ~ , 720:4

giraffe, 1349:5

girl (*also see* child; daughter), 1393:9; 2057:2; conditioning of ~ (*also see* woman, conditioning of), 501:1; 575:2; 745:3; 1138:2; 1214:1; 1503:2; 1852:3; 1950:1; 2013:4; 2070:3; 2202:3; 2225:3; 2388:2; 2412:2; dreams of ~ , 1754:3; ~ growing up, 2389:1; ~ in relation to mother (*also see* mother, in relation to daughter), 910:14; physical development of ~ , 718:3; prayers of ~ , 1756:2; respectable ~ , 1658:17; role of ~ , 1055:1; school~ , 830:2; teenaged ~ (*also see* adolescence), 1296:1

Girl Scouts of America, 1078:1, 2

giving, 307:7

gladness, 203:2

Gladstone, William E., 836:4

glamour, 1580:2; 1617:2; 2331:2

glance, 428:8

gloom, 2263:5

glory, 256:13; 527:1; finding ~ , 363:12

glowworm, 697:19; 899:11

goal (*also see* purpose; pursuit), achieving ~ , 1376:1; 2449:1; determined ~ , 1026:2; differing ~ , 2440:1; distant ~ , 458:21; idealistic ~ , 697:17; imposition of ~ , 1743:2; individual ~ , 1341:22; life ~ , 1156:1; pursuit of ~ , 1095:2; 1307:3; setting a ~ , 2028:5

God (*also see* absolution; forgiveness, divine; Holy Ghost; Christ, Jesus; religion; theology), 31:2; 145:2; 173:2; 246:1; 252:1; 256:15, 16; 260:4; 270:4; 305:2; 346:4; 353:1; 386:9; 444:3; 467:9; 511:1; 585:1; 670:7; 778.1, 2, 782.17, 792.1; 820:1; 821:2; 888:1; 939:5; 1071:1; 1098:1; 1439:3; 1579:2 1643:12; 1758:2; 1844:1; 1975:7; 2010:2, 3; 2402:12; 2406:10; alone with ~ , 380:9; awareness of ~ , 2406:8; belief in ~ , 233;1; betrayal by ~ , 1544:7; capriciousness of ~ , 1391:5; closeness to ~ , 12:1; 686:3; communing with ~ , 697:17; conception of ~ , 1789:1, 4; death and ~ , 229:2; demands of ~ , 721:1; denial of ~ , 190:8; devotion to ~ , 215:1; 257:2; diversity of ~ , 1470:1; enemies of ~ , 11:2; 192:8; existence of ~ , 366:1; 367:7; 1224:2; 2005:1; 2087:1; faith in ~ , 11:2; 948:1; 1229:1; 1911:4; fear of ~ , 739:3; forgetting ~ , 350:2; forgiveness of ~ , 1658:7; gender of ~ , 2164:4; 2402:11, 13; gifts of ~ , 131:1, 12; 295:1; 688:14; 737:1; 782:7; 833:30; glory of ~ , 834:1; 1727:2; grace of ~ , 325:2; gratitude to ~ , 297:1; 315:2; 1399:1; guidance from ~ , 181:5; 285:3; 739:1; ~ in heaven, 2018:7; inheritance of ~ , 24:1; ~ in relation to beauty, 1910:3; ~ in relation to nature, 1151:1; 1224:1; 1248:1; 1439:2; 2261:3; ~ in relation to the poor, 2099:4; ~ in relation to world, 378:1; knowledge of ~ , 245:2; lessons of ~ , 93:2; love of ~ , 105:1; 191:1; 200:1; 237:6; 254:1; 256:2; 360:1; mercy of ~ , 1803:2; messenger of ~ , 206:3; missionary of ~ , 2290:1; mystery of ~ , 192:9; omnipotence of ~ , 18:1; 31:4; 216:3; 377:2; 925:5; ominpresence of ~ , 1658:20; omniscience of ~ , 2:1; 152:2; 260:2; 344:7; 439:3; opposing ~ , 256:5; pleasing ~ , 179:1; 401:4; praise of ~ , 9:1; 145:4; 444:1; praying to ~ , 782:2, 13; providence of ~ (*also see* providence, of God), 237:11; 324:1; 341:1; 358:1; 780:2; punishment by ~ , 16:2; 360:2; questioning ~ , 1003:6; revelation from ~ , 181:6; searching for ~ , 1678:2; separated from ~ , 1554:2; serving ~ , 126:2; 837:5; snare set by ~ , 1705:7; solace of ~ , 760:2; submission to ~ , 413:2; trust in ~ , 235:9; 237:14; 289:1; 300:2; understanding ~ , 31:1; 152:3; 184:2; 293:4; 1057:6; 1153:2; 1802:2; united with ~ , 117:1; 251:2; 273:1; 548:2; ~ vs. Goddess, 1717:3; will of ~ , 230:2; 238:1; 398:1; 963:1; 965:2; ~ within, 91:1; 215:2; 240:2; 305:1; 413:4; 1431:3; 2290:1; 2474:3; women in relation to ~ (*also see* woman, in relation to God), 196:2; 367:6; 773:1; 1038:7; 2194:2; word of ~ , 191:3; 236:2, 3; 261:3; 277:23; 718:2; work of ~ , 732:4; 1727:5; worship of ~ , 114:1; 458:3

goddess, 43:1, 2; 1385:1; 1717:3; 2091:1; return of ~ , 2115:3

gods, the, 57:2; 576:2; belief in ~ , 1435:14; will of ~ , 78:1

Godwin, William, 715:1

gold (*also see* money; wealth), 311:1; 438:13; 496:4;

gold (*continued*)
lust for ~ , 756:11; ~ obtained via slavery, 800:10; spinning ~ from straw, 1436:1
goldenrod, 944:1
Golden Rule, the, 886:8; 2195:3
goldfish, 1835:10
good/ness (*also see* good and evil), 126:2; 146:3; 163:1; 317:2; 370:1; 495:10; 580:4; 623:2; 627:10; 682:6; 885:2; 954:1; 1138:1; 1444:7; 1794:2; 1910:3; 2456:1; acquired ~ , 1608:2; 2249:1; admiration for ~ , 1302:3; doing ~ , 639:24; 660:1; 688:5; 703:23; 722:3; gather ~ , 369:1; 688:8; hidden ~ , 1540:1; overdoing ~ , 1192:46; power of ~ , 1039:9; temporary ~ , 309:3; understanding ~ , 886:9; ~ works, 722:1; 825:5
good and evil (*also see* bad; evil; evildoing; good; wickedness), 783:3; 1705:6
good will, 307:7
gorilla, 2100:1
gospel (*also see* Bible; Ten Commandments), 190:9; 541:3; living the ~ , 2077:1
gossip (*also see* rumor), 138:10; 161:3; 344:1; 833:21; 1192:37, 47; 1465:1; 2036:5, 6; 2349:8; fear of ~ , 386:8; gruesome ~ , 1476:1; lewd ~ , 408:2; malicious ~ (*also see* slander), 406:8; 945:4; object of ~ , 143:1; women's ~ , 443:7
governess (*also see* teacher), 536:2
government (*also see specific forms;* heads of state; nation), 496:11; 782:18; 1152:20, 24; 1208:5; 1260:1; ~ authority, 2164:13; ~ censorship, 452:1; city ~ , 1808:4; corruption in ~ , 138:4; 639:34; democratic ~ (*also see* democracy), 1478:2; education and ~ , 2164:7; elimination of racism in ~ , 811:17; elimination of sexism in ~ , 811:17; elitism in ~ , 1515:5; 1555:1; 2080:2; faults of ~ , 2223:2; function of ~ , 1072:7; ~ growth, 1779:3; ~ in relation to art/ist, 1409:4; 1675:1; ~ in relation to environment, 2258:4; ~ in relation to property, 1059:6; ~ interests, 2223:3; ~ interference, 1442:1; men in ~ , 2028:12; militant ~ , 2501:3; oppressive ~ , 1376:6; ~ policies, 671:9; 1591:2; ~ promises, 2504:4; ~ resources or ~ , 89:1; responsibility of ~ , 1680:5; 1824:1; ~ responsibility to family, 2306:4; secrecy in ~ , 2145:1; self-determined ~ , 1052:5; training for ~ , 1757:16; undermining system of ~ , 2080:1; unprincipled ~ , 1456:8; useless ~ , 1339:4; war and ~ , 1705:8; welfare ~ , 2007:2; 2290:4; women and ~ , 1152:12; women in ~ , 703:17; 840:4, 5; 1072:3; 1341:13; 1873:4; 2112:1; world ~ , 1268:1; 1376:5; 1652:2
gown, satin ~ , 1459:8
grace, 131:12; 401:2; state of ~ , 206:5
gradualness, 1061:3
graft, 639:34; 1393:7; 2193:3
Graham, Billy, 2026:10
grandeur, 240:4; 269:7
grandparents, 1457:12; 1985:1; grandfather, 763:11; grandmother, 2172:1
grass, 801:1; 869:1; 1439:2; ~ in England, 1835:1

Grasse, France, 2163:1
grasshopper, 396:1
gratitude (*also see* appreciation), 304:2; 459:1; 685:1; sense of ~ , 1588:1; ~ to parents, 1329:2
grave (*also see* burial; cemetery; tombstone), 394:15; 698:3; 701:3; 723:20, 21; 869:1; 1430:4
Great Britain (*also see* England; Scotland; Wales), 665:2; government in ~ , 452:1; ~ in relation to Africa, 665:1; ~ in relation to Roman Empire, 74:1; ~ in relation in United States, 510:1; victories of ~ , 74:1
greatness (*also see* genius), 167:1; 328:1; 833:29; 1891:6; 1913:2; characteristics of ~ , 777:20; 1108:3; 1192:48; 1605:1; 1647:4; courage of ~ , 1449:7; demands of ~ , 720:4; enemy to ~ , 673:8; fruit of ~ , 1927:1; hazards of ~ , 609:1; true ~ , 513:20
greed (*also see* avarice), 253:1; 1488:2; 1958:2; excuses for ~ , 2099:5
greenery, 504:11
grief (*also see* mourning; sorrow), 185:1; 305:5; 552:1; 730:12; 1207:1; 1348:1; 1524:2; 1612:4; 2114:1; hopeless ~ , 782:3
Griffith, D. W., 1412:1
grooming, 1319:18; ~ of women, 551:8; 1580:2; 1599:2
group, effectiveness of ~ , 1355:1; ~ encounter, 2171:1
growing up, 800:6; 1386:1; 1565:1; 1695:1; 1791:3; 1829:6; 1845:4; 2092:9; 2113:11; 2335:1; 2346:2
growth, 1072:1; 1389:2; 1440:3; 2000:3; 2217:9; 2254:4; 2453:1; aiding ~ of others, 2000:2; artistic ~ , 1191:5; economic ~ , 2433:2; lack of ~ , 2058:1; 2217:8; need for ~ , 795:2; personal ~ (*also see* maturity), 777:22, 28; 811:45; 1171:3; 1175:2; 1436:10; 1961:3; 2435:6; spiritual ~ (*also see* spirit, development of), 138:20
guardian, ~ of child, 1447:6
guest (*also see* visitor), 1192:7; perfect ~ , 1334:1; 1378:3; welcome ~ , 703:35; woman ~ , 1325:2
guidance/guide, need for ~ , 2150:1; spiritual ~ , 2183:1
guilt (*also see* conscience, guilty), 864:3; 875:2; 1013:4; 1332:1; 1378:4; 1759:1; 2006:5; 2092:6; 2376:4
gullibility, 200:3; 253:1; 526:6; 1075:28; 2193:1; ~ of citizenry, 211:1
gun (*also see* weapon), 2277:1; fascination with ~ , 2179:2; power of ~ , 2501:3; shooting ~ , 1068:4
gynecologist (*also see* medical profession; physician), 1607:3

H

habit (*also see* custom), 1422:1; 2530:1; breaking ~ , 1207:2; evil ~ , 723:2; simple ~ , 670:4
Hagen, Uta, 2326:2
hair, grey ~ , 1602:1; ~ style, 1139:1; 1876:3
half breed (*also see* mulatto; race, mixed), 2490:2

naturalness, 1773:1

nature (*see* human nature)

nature (environment), 266:2; 458:4; 617:2; 770:1; 877:3; 1023:1; 1151:1; 1171:1; 1189:3; 1405:2; 1520:1; 1571:5; 1668:5; 1834:1; 2163:2; 2406:9; back to ~ , 1167:1; beauty of ~ , 1063:1; connectedness to ~ , 1423:2; 1493:7; 2490:3; control of ~ , 1668:11; 1717:5; 2197:1, 2; 2264:1; decay in ~ , 703:12; joy of ~ , 723:27; 1134:1; 1548:8; in harmony with ~ , 2470:1; intrusion on ~ , 2253:1; laws of ~ , 495:7; 830:5; lessons of ~ , 670:1; man and ~ , 2039:8; mystery of ~ , 1594:5; part of ~ , 1189:4; provisions of ~ , 674:4; recollection of ~ , 628:3; reverence for ~ , 811:40; rules of ~ , 795:8; splendor of ~ , 1740:1; study of ~ , 777:12; 1818:1; understanding ~ , 777:13; wonders of ~ , 732:2

Navajo Indian, 1561:1; ~ youth, 1729:1

navy, Greek ~ , 54:1

Nazi, 1352:1; 1642:1; ~ Germany, 2338:2

neatness (*also see* orderliness; tidiness), 689:2

necessity, 1060:9; 1439:6; 1705:19; benefits of ~ , 809:1; limitations of ~ , 777:1

need, 438:20; ~ for another person, 2218:8; fulfilled ~ , 2452:2; increasing ~ , 1680:18; individual ~ , 2453:1; object of ~ , 1038:15

needlecraft (*also see* knitting; sewing), 270:2; 2250:3

neglect (*see* child, neglect of),

Negro (*see* Afro-American; blacks)

neighbor, 762:3

neighborhood, mixed ~ (*also see* integration), 2263:2

nervous breakdown (*also see* mental illness), 1446:2

nervousness (*see* tension)

Netherlands, women in ~ , 1703:2

neurosis (*also see* complex), 1842:1; 1852:8

never, 2181:2

new age (*also see* civilization, new; world, new), 2169:1

New England (*also see* America; United States of America), ~ attitude, 1447:3; autumn in ~ , 1002:1

newness, 682:19

news, 743:4; ~ of the day, 550:22; 1802:3; 1902:8; 1927:9; 2442:1; unexpected ~ , 800:11

newspaper (*also see* freedom, of press); 669:5; 944:3; exaggeration in ~ , 1578:1; impartiality of ~ , 540:1; politics of ~ , 1871:1; ~ printing, 531:2; reading the ~ , 565:10; ~ reporter (*also see* journalist), 1780:1; sensationalism in ~ , 1108:4; ~ staff, 1871:2; working on a ~ , 1417:5

New Year (*also see* eve, New Year's), 916:1

New York City, 1075:26; 1163:4; 1340:2; 1764:2; 1852:9; 2060:4; 2168:1; 2241:4; people of ~ , 2121:5; poverty in ~ , 1807:2; young women in ~ , 1533:2

Niagara Falls, 723:5

Nicaragua, art education in ~ , 2450:4

nickname, 249:7

night (*also see* evening; midnight), 111:1; 248:1; 628:4; 737:10; 775:1; 928:1; 2028:9; awake at ~ , 137:4; fear of ~ , 435:1; ~ on the town, 2369:3; secrets of ~ , 141:1; shelter of ~ , 699:1

nightingale, 50:12; 504:12; 565:2

Nigeria, 2407:4

Nixon, Richard M., 1341:17, 35, 37; 1545:2; 1848:1, 2; 2317:2

Nobel Prize, ~ Committee, 1301:1

nobility (*also see* aristocracy; rank), 2029:1

nobleness, 1305:4

noise (*also see* sound), 637:29

nomad (*also see* wanderer), 686:2

nonconformity (*also see* individuality), 2136:11; 2384:3; hostility toward ~ , 1302:2

nonsense, 192:3

noviolence (*also see* pacifism; resistance, passive), 2145:3; 2313:5

normalcy, 1221:9; 2448:3; ~ in children, 2035:2

North, the/Northerners (U.S.A.; *also see* America; United States of America), ~ in relation to South, 770:2

North America, ~ in relation to South America, 2170:3

Norway, women in government of ~ , 2258:2; 2540:1

nose (*also see* smell), 587:1; 771:2

nosiness (*also see* meddlesomeness), 254:2; 1024:2; 1068:2; 1560:6; 1714:1; 2201:2; 2479:1

nostalgia (*also see* sentimentalism), 561:2; 1876:5; 2085:2; 2263:4

nothingness, 413:3; 467:5; 639:7; 1417:4; 1436:8; 1569:2; 1658:16; 2102:2; 2113:3; 2523:2; achieving ~ , 2281:1; fear of ~ , 1528:2

nourishment (*also see* nutrition), self~ , 1548:7

novel (*also see* book; fiction; literature; reading), art of ~ , 138:14; birth of a ~ , 2233:23; ending of ~ , 704:28; romantic ~ , 508:4

novelist (*see* author; writer)

novelty (*also see* originality), 577:27

November, 248:1

NOW (*see* National Organization for Women)

nuclear power (*also see* atomic bomb), use of ~ , 1894:1; ~ weapons, 2145:2

nudity, 458:8; 883:1; 1368:4; 1497:5; 2030:4

nuisance, 1567:1

numbers, knowledge of ~ , 458:14

nun, 121:5; 386:7; 698:2; 1432:1; black ~ , 2402:1

Nuremberg, ~ Trials, 1651:8

nurse (*also see* medical profession), 682:24; 849:1; 1449:2; training of ~ , 1369:1

nursemaid, 317:3

nurturing (*also see* caring), men and ~ , 2167:4; women and ~ , 2189:4

nutrition (*also see* diet; food; nourishment), 1048:2; 1979:1; 2062:4; effect of ~ on state of mind, 1618:2; good ~ , 1618:1; science of ~ , 1015:3

O

oath (*also see* promise; swearing), 277:8; 337:1; 718:8; false ~ , 448:3; keeping to one's ~ , 704:1; legal, 1595:7

poet (*continued*)
457:2; 488:2; 637:18; 884:1; 964:1; 1242:1; 1443:4;
1470:1; 1605:2; 1762:2; 2474:4, abilities of ~ ,
2283:23; according recognition to ~ , 1079:1;
boy ~ , 2484:2, 3; compulsion of ~ , 1479:1;
death of ~ , 762:1; 1381:3; function of ~ ,
857:3; ~ in relation to poems, 795:13; ~ laureate, 1502:3; message of ~ , 1401:10; styles of
~ , 1213:13; task of ~ , 1479:1; tools of ~ ,
1395:5; woman ~ , 366:2; 380:14; 397:1; 406:24;
423:1; workplace of ~ , 723:26
pogrom, 2141:2
poison, 68:3
polarization, ~ of economic classes, 2199:2
police, 2528:2; ~ mentality, 1963:4
politeness (*also see* courtesy; manners; tact), 704:6;
lack of ~ , 558:4
political convention, television and ~ , 1341:30
political party (*also see* specific parties), 1001:1;
1779:1; 1874:2; 2046:4; women in ~ , 1718:3
politician, 406:19; 1339:3; 1613:1; 2028:6; 2089:6;
2107:1; 2229:1; 2258:3; American ~ , 1931:1;
attitude toward women ~ , 811:20; Christianity
and ~ , 190:9; foolish ~ , 650:5; morals of ~ ,
1152:2; qualifications for ~ , 1757:16; sex and
~ , 2226:1; unqualified ~ , 1968:1
politics, 637:11; 697:25; 726:1; 1001:1; 1152:3;
1208:5; 1275:3; 1449:8; 1545:1; 1564:5; 2456:4;
ethics of ~ , 1752:10; election rules of ~ ,
2277:2; evils of ~ , 1607:14; leftist ~ , 1941:3;
middle-of-the-road ~ , 2344:5; money and ~ ,
1626:3; personal ~ , 811:35; pursuit of ~ ,
637:32; rules of ~ , 1291:4; sexism in ~ (*also
see* sexism, in government), 1604:13; sexual ~
(*see also* relationship, between men and women),
1075:2; 2209:1; 2343:2; 2371:4; success in ~ ,
1413:1; traditional ~ , 1651:5; weary of ~ ,
1167:1; women and ~ , 758:2; 1268:2; women
in ~ , 1375:10; 2027:4; youth in ~ , 1931:4
pollution (*also see* ecology; environment), 1565;4;
1624:3; 2434:1; air ~ , 904:1; chemical ~ ,
1668:6, 7; insidiousness of ~ , 2253:34; noise
~ , 918:1; water ~ , 1015:6; 1804:1
polygamy (*also see* marriage), 766:11; 2207:3; 2218:2
pomp (*also see* ostentation), 334:1; 444:2; 513:13
pompousness (*see* pretension)
pond, 742:2
pony express, 1024:1
poor, the (*also see* class [social], lower; poverty),
266:1; 369:2; 693:1; 697:21; 789:1; 1496:3; 1527:2;
1807:2; 1926:2; 2427:1; attitude toward ~ , 256:4;
2456:3; birth control for ~ , 1328:9; caring for
~ , 1072:5; education of ~ , 451:1 2247:1;
feeding ~ , 1856:2; ignoring ~ , 298:2; manners
of ~ , 1658:11; needs of ~ , 2205:1; 2206:3;
sympathy towards ~ , 765:1
Pope (*also see* Catholicism; Catholic Church, Roman), 383:1; 951:2; 2238:3
Pope, Alexander, 453:1
popular, 1248:1

poppy, opium ~ , 601:1; 1022:1
population, ~ control, 2349:11; ~ explosion (*also
see* overpopulation), 755:3
pornography, 1965:5; 2136:10; 2164:8; 2425:2, 4;
2461:1; response to ~ , 1635:1
portrait (*also see* art; painting), 668:1
possession (ownership; *also see* belongings), 179:2;
462:5; 1417:4; 1705:17; 1767:5; 1902:1; accu-
mulating ~ , 1135:7; holding onto ~ , 2113:2;
loss of ~ , 394:17; relinquishing ~ , 1505:4;
2334:5; trap of ~ , 1727:6
possessiveness (*also see* jealousy), 1343:2; 1443:3;
1629:2; 1752:4; 1917:3; 2113:3
possibility (*also see* impossibility; potential), 2263:9
posterity, 2034:4; fighting for ~ , 618:29; legacy
to ~ , 811:43; 1576:12; praise of ~ , 723:21
post office (*also see* mail), efficiency of ~ , 743:7
potato, 1567:2
potential (*also see* possibility), 183:1; 877:2; 1399:1;
2366:3; human ~ , 1576:4; realizing one's ~ ,
56:2; 800:20; 899:12; 1725:2; 2137:1; 2440:3;
unfulfilled ~ , 892:32
Potomac River, 880:1
poverty (*also see* poor), 121:2; 406:9; 756:5; 762:8;
906:1; 935:9; 1263:1; 1381:11; 1669:3; 1686:1;
1791:3; 1874:1; 2081:2; 2099:4; 2250:2; aid for
~ , 1314:3; disgrace of ~ , 609:9; effects of
~ , 697:32; 1706:15; 1733:5; freedom of ~ ,
1727:6; mass ~ , 697:18; trial of ~ , 721:1; wipe
out ~ , 1341:16; women and ~ , 1963:2
power (*also see* authority; empowerment; omnipotence; man, power of; women, power of), 146:3;
1396:7; 1445:9; 2503:2; abuse of ~ , 637:9;
682:12; ~ among men, 2023:6; blind obedience
to ~ , 609:4; concentration of ~ , 1641:3; desire
for ~ , 2216:4; display of ~ , 2153:1; exercising
~ , 1705:17; fear of ~ , 637:37; feeling of ~
(*see* omnipotence); fight for ~ , 258:5; 513:13;
history of ~ , 2153:4; loss of ~ , 2063:3; measure
of ~ , 2189:4; ~ of individual, 1695:11; ~ of
women (*also see* woman, power of), 811:2; 982:1;
2057:5; political ~ , 213:1; 231:2; 1040:4; political super~ (*also see* superpowers), 1652:1; redefining ~ , 2360:1; relinquish ~ , 750:11;
resisting ~ , 637:36; source of ~ , 2034:14;
threats to ~ structure, 2408:2; uses of ~ , 766:1;
1086:4; world ~ , 1236:5
Powhatan, Chief, 343:1
practice (*also see* experience), 637:1
praise, 391:1; 514:7; 1396:8; 1564:4; false ~ ,
168:1; inability to ~ , 43:4; inadequate ~ , 209:1;
posthumous ~ , 1835:5; sexist ~ , 558:4
prayer (*also see* contemplation; meditation; worship), 200:2; 550:8; 632:2; 780:1; 885:1; 1695:7;
answer to ~ , 1216:3; incapable of ~ , 181:3;
meaninglessness of ~ , 251:2
preacher (*also see* clergy), 863:1; 1612:6; 2089:6;
language of ~ , 825:5
preaching (*also see* sermon), ineffectiveness of ~ ,
256:2

reaction, faulty ~ , 673:7
reactionary (also see conservatism), 1040:4
readiness, 557:4; 1547:2
reading (also see book; fiction; literature; novel),
123:4; 523:5; 599:4; 603:2; 760:3; 766:8; 1031:1;
1319:19; 1947:1; children and ~ , 2474:2; ~
comprehension, 780:1; ~ in relation to business,
1948:3; reason for ~ , 849:3
Reagan, Nancy, 1856:2
Reagan, Ronald, 1856:2; ~ administration, 2306:4
reality (also see unreality), 700:12; 1878:1; 2089:6;
awakening to ~ , 1705:2; facing ~ , 1018:7;
1573:4; fierce with ~ , 1342:7; ~ in literature,
1508:2; ~ of life, 800:8; psychic ~ , 1980:1;
questioning ~ , 730:14
realization (also see self-realization), 1789:2
reason (also see intelligence; mind; rationality;
thinking), 417:18; 419:4; 433:1; 493:2; 565:5;
577:5; 796:3; 1039:8; 2279:57; impotence of ~
to persuade, 758:3; ~ in relation to passion,
813:5; lack of ~ , 410:1; listen to ~ , 401:10;
world of ~ , 1761:1
reasonableness/reasoning (also see logic), 2051:1
rebel/liousness, 652:1
rebellion (also see revolt; revolution), 466:1
rebirth (also see renaissance; renewal), 1137:1;
1208:1; 1829:5; 1841:3; 1958:9; 2018:3; 2349:12
recipe (also see book, cook; cook/ing), 712:1; trading ~ , 2320:4; writing a ~ , 1745:1
recognition, 2027:1; lack of ~ , 2537:3; ~ of truth,
2200:1
recollection (also see memory; remembrance), 875:9;
~ of early life, 1191:16; sweet ~ , 838:1
reconciliation (also see conflict, and resolution),
158:1; 935:3; 2085:4
recovery (also see cure; healing; rehabilitation),
1841:3; 2307:2; ~ from downfall, 346:2
red-baiting (also see McCarthyism), 1545:2
redemption (also see salvation), 285:9; 1958:1; 2089:1
Red Sea, 1129:1
Reed, John, 1273:2
refinement, 708:3; 743:5; 998:3
reflection (also see deliberation; thought), 589:3;
612:1
reform (also see specific movements; activism), 904:4;
method of ~ , 771:5
reformer (also see agitator; woman, activist), 478:2;
884:1; 1489:1; compromise of ~ , 811:23; strategies of ~ , 1059:7
refuge, 1005:1; 1972:3
refugee (also see immigrant), 1824:6; 2255:5
regret (also see remorse; sorrow), 1805:3
rehabilitation (also see recovery), 771:5; 2422:2
reincarnation, 138:3; 697:8; 900:6; 1828:3; 2304:3
rejection, 1727:1; 1777:1
rejoicing (also see joy), 1310:4
relationship (also see friendship; love; marriage;
sexes, relationship between), 763:2; 1771:7;
2527:1; age difference in ~ , 627:20; bad ~ ,
2168:11; balance of ~ , 795:4; ~ between dom-

inants and subordinates, 2286:1; ~ between men
and women (also see man, in relation to women;
politics, sexual; sexes; woman, in relation to
men), 145:3; 146:7; 165:1, 2; 1459:15; 1680:13;
1902:5; 1962:2; 2167:3; changing ~ , 1145:1;
communication in ~ , 2289:6; complexity of
~ , 1661:3; difficulties of ~ , 1104:7; 1910:1;
2320:5; 2421:3; 2499:2; dynamics of ~ , 1767:7;
fictions of ~ , 2347:3; importance of ~ with
others, 2476:2; improving ~ , 697:26; multiple
~ , 2207:3; symbiotic ~ , 627:18; temporary
~ , 2332:2
relatives (see specific relation)
relaxation (also see leisure; pleasure; rest), 496:8;
1824:7; need for ~ , 618:6
relevance, 1427:3
reliability (also see unreliability), lack of ~ in men,
867:1
religion (also see specific denominations; belief;
Christianity; church; clergy; faith; freedom, religious; God; religious life; life, spiritual), 458:13;
537:1; 670:7; 750:4; 766:2; 777:26; 800:3; 925:2;
1061:4; 1120:3; 1226:2; 1393:3; 1440:13; 1582:2;
1678:1; 1680:16; 1844:2; 1852:5; 1853:3; 2020:2;
2351:3; 2406:6; 2422:3; ancient ~ , 2091:1; art
and ~ , 1013:6; 1191:21; benefit of ~ , 704:32;
conscience and ~ , 380:9; controversies in ~ ,
542:1; cooperation among different ~ , 2376:2;
corrupting influence of ~ , 406:32; differences
between ~ , 1426:2; divisiveness of ~ , 271:3;
504:3; 704:4; fervor of ~ , 688:9; function of
~ , 2376:4; hypocrisy of ~ , 406:33; ~ in public
schools, 2513:1; ~ in relation to government,
2351:4; martyr to ~ , 257:3; personal ~ , 575:5;
politics of ~ , 2501:1; principle of ~ , 258:4;
quarrel with ~ , 855:12; respect for ~ , 1958:6;
sacrifice to ~ , 811:37; sexism in ~ (see sexism,
in religion); war and ~ , 394:4; 443:6; 2042:1;
women and ~ , 725:1; 811:19; 935:4; 1019:3;
1200:4; 2327:1; 2377:1
religious life (also see clergy; nun), 707:12; petty
ills of ~ , 754:1
religiousness, 1682:7
relocating, 2063:2
remark, stifle a ~ (also see words, unspoken),
1114:2
remedy (also see cure; healing), search for ~ ,
419:5
remembrance (also see memory; recollection), 561:4;
649:1; 697:24; ~ of loved one, 51:1; sad ~ ,
899:8
remorse (also see regret), 131:9; 813:4
renaissance (also see rebirth), global ~ , 1435:11
rendezvous, 458:2
renewal (also see reborn), 985:1; 1139:2; 1612:9;
1679:8; 2171:3
Reno, Nevada, 1604:2; 1627:1
renunciation, 413:3; 900:7; 1573:3; 1919:3; 1997:2
repentance (also see penitence), 458:1; 1128:4; enjoyment of ~ , 707:2

superficiality (*also see* trivia), 670:3; 2003:1; drawn to ~ , 639:5

superiority, 2081:3; 2250:3; feeling of ~ , 939:1; 1104:6

superpower (*also see* power, super), ~ in relation to underdeveloped nations, 2402:18

superstition, 253:3; 383:2; 657:1; defense of ~ , 87:2

supportiveness, 800:20; 893:11; 1146:3; 1451:2; 1867:2; ~ of lovers, 795:3

suppression (*also see* repression; woman, suppressed), 1310:1; 1346:2; 2289:2

Supreme Court, U.S. (*also see* judiciary), 1748:1, 2; 2071:1

surgeon/surgery, 892:2; 2178:5; permission for ~ , 1802:1

surliness, ~ of daily life, 1961:5

surprise, 387:2; 1221:14; unable to feel ~ , 639:41

surrender, ~ arms, 271:1; 528:1

surveillance (*also see* spy), object of ~ , 1916:2; ~ of private citizen, 1963:4

survival (*also see* self-protection), 1522:12; 2349:12; 2402:8; ~ of humankind, 1647:16; 1862:21

survivor, 232:3; 2065:3; 2406:2

suspicion, 277:22; 393:1; 1605:3; unfounded ~ , 1393:1

swearing (*also see* oath; vituperation), 718:8; 998:3

sweat, 2489:2

Sweden, children of ~ , 2240:3

sweetness, duality of ~ , 871:5; vulnerability of ~ , 737:6

sweets, 1270:2

Swift, Jonathan, 458:13; 595:3

sycophancy (*also see* flattery; parasite; servility), 513:9; 582:7

symbolism, understanding ~ , 2183:1

symmetry, ~ in nature, 1740:1

sympathy (*also see* compassion; understanding), 977:1; gift of ~ , 800:13

T

taboo, dichotomy of ~ , 1594:6; social ~ , 1502:6

tact (*also see* politeness), 1002:4; 1032:8; 1199:3

tailor, 438:6

talent (*also see* gifted), 424:1; 886:7; 910:10; 934:1; 1122:2; 1431:1; appreciating ~ , 680:1; artistic ~ , 1687:3; bogusness of ~ , 1503:1; delicacy of ~ , 1431:4; developing ~ , 1190:5; exceptional ~ , 935:5; ingredients of ~ , 1859:2; ~ in relation to success, 2030:2; lack of ~ , 489:3; perusing one's ~ , 2349:1; suppression of ~ , 2159:2; 2168:5; use of ~ , 131:1; 1624:4

talk/ing (*also see* speaking; speech, verbosity), 309:5; 406:5; 428:8; 1192:37; 1720:2; 1775:2; 1910:9; inability to ~ (*also see* speechlessness), 388:4; ~ to oneself, 2497:1; ~ with restraint (*also see* reticence), 408:3; 482:1

tallness, 1381:6; ~ in females, 1829:6

tameness (*also see* domesticity), price of ~ , 1955:4

Tanglewood, Massachusetts, 1930:3

Tarzan, 2110:5

task (*also see* deed), unfinished ~ , 942:1; 1134:4

taste (*also see* judgment; opinion; preference), 550:27; 693:2; 1742:1; decline of good ~ , 724:2; differences in ~ , 1927:10

tax, 205:1; 555:1; 1560:4; 2193:3; avoiding ~ , 1772:1; ~ dodge, 2053:1; federal income ~ (*see* IRS)

Taylor, Elizabeth, 2402:16

tea, 1060:11; preparation of ~ , 1026:1

teacher (*also see* governess; professor), 279:2; 292:2; 548:1; 766:9; 830:4; 981:5; 1171:5; efficient ~ , 1221:2; goal of ~ , 1401:1, 2; good ~ , 702:3; 1003:11; influence of ~ , 703:7; motivation of ~ , 2538:1; physical education ~ , 2496:2; pride of ~ , 2183:3; salary of ~ , 703:36; training of ~ , 703:36; wages of woman ~ , 731:3; woman ~ , 723:34

teaching (*also see* training), 451:1; 564:1; 735:6; 1096:2; 1743:5; 2217:3; 2394:1; 2464:2; difficulty of ~ , 1788:5; ~ language, 1132:6; method of ~ , 683:3; 702:2; 800:19; 1634:1; 1879:1; rewards of ~ , 1132:2

team, ~ spirit, 2262:6; ~ work, 811:27

tears (*also see* cry), 258:3; 285:4; 405:2; 454:1; 1445:10; 2034:2; 2339:2; idleness of ~ , 1042:4

technology, 723:16; 1680:2; 2531:4; alienation of ~ , 1680:18; disasters of ~ , 1944:2; domination of ~ , 1400:2; ill purpose of ~ , 1515:3; ~ in America, 2531:1; uses of ~ , 1287:8; 1647:16; 2090:4

teeth, false ~ , 1814:1

telegraph, 1220:2

telepathy (*also see* ESP), mental ~ , 1828:2

telephone, 1014:5; 1192:22, 39; 2113:4; ~ dial-a-prayer service, 2168:10

television, 1767:6; 2065:2; 2344:3; 2446:2; children's ~ , 2457:2; ~ commercials, 1676:1; 2155:1; ~ news personality, 2378:2; politics and ~ , 1341:31; ~ production deadline, 1846:1; racism and sexism in ~ , 2104:2

temperament (*also see* disposition), bad ~ , 502:1

temperance (*also see* prohibition), 822:1; 824:3; 1113:1

temptation, 1:1; 352:2; 514:1; 515:1; 756:1; 1232:1; 1437:1; resisting ~ , 315:1; 813:7; 1444:4

tenacity (*also see* perseverance), 1546:1; 1709:1; 1835:2

Ten Commandments (*also see* Bible; gospel), 319:1; 324:2

tenderness (*also see* gentleness), 557:2; 669:22; 1424:1; fear of ~ , 2506:2

Tennessee, 640:1; 887:1; 1983:3

tennis, 1747:1

tension (*also see* nervousness; stress), 1529:1

territorialism, 277:2

terrorism, response to ~ , 1651:7; victims of ~ , 1576:17

Texas, 1375:13
textbook, lack of reality in ~ , 2538:2
Thanksgiving, 1282:2
Thatcher, Margaret, 2238:2
theater (also see actor; stage play; playwright), 483:3; 516:2; 1068:9; 1194:3; 1198:3;1232:1; 1532:1; 1743:3; 1763:2, 3, 4; 2061:1; 2121:3; 2230:2; 2256:2; 2282:2; business of ~ , 648:1; control of ~ , 2238:1; ~ design, 1957:2; ~ director, 483:5; Federal ~ of W.P.A., 1409:1, 3; flourishing ~ , 539:1; function of ~ , 520:1; ~goer, 577:1; good ~ , 2450:3; impact of ~ , 2230:1; ~ in relation to audience, 2013:3; 2288:4; ~ in relation to government, 1409:3; life in the ~ , 1304:1; lifelessness in ~ , 2018:1; ~ lighting, 1957:1; love for ~ , 2095:3; need for ~ , 1551:2; philosophy of ~ , 1763:1; progress of ~ , 1409:2; public ~ , 1409:4; purpose of ~ , 2413:1; realism in ~ , 598:4; ruin of ~ , 406:19; women in ~ , 751:1; 2256:5
theft (see thievery)
theology, 726:1; bound by ~ , 824:1; feminist ~ , 2204:1
theory (also see hypothesis), 1135:6; 1461:2; 1934:1; 2028:15; ~ about women, 2036:1
theosophy, 901:4
therapy (also see psychotherapy), group ~ , 2171:1; ~ of life, 1351:4; shock ~ , 1932:1; social ~ , 2138:2
thievery, 983:4; 1612:6
things, evanescence of ~ , 1077:2; little ~ , 858:1
thinker, neutrality of ~ , 782:22
thinking (also see mind; thought), 200:2; 459:1; 570:1; 692:1; 766:8; 1013:2; 1057:5; 1658:2; 2191:2; ~ for oneself, 749:8; futility of ~ , 1221:17; individual ~ , 504:9; learning the process of ~ , 609:14; ~ on schedule, 1683:5; ~ person, 893:12
thinness, 1500:1; obsession with ~ , 1837:1; 2292:1, 2
Thomas, Dylan, 1381:3
thoroughness, 1393:4; 2195:2
thought (also see deliberation; reflection; thinking), 561:4; 723:17; 971:6; 995:4; 1547:3; 1695:2; analyzing ~ , 277:10; 387:13; avoiding ~ , 2451:1; controlling ~ , 575:5; difficulty of ~ , 1651:2; immoral ~ , 449:1; independent ~ , 1319:22; manipulation of ~ , 618:41: power of ~ , 871:2; ~ process, 1761:2; 2124:1; schools of ~ , 1060:3; source of ~ , 995:3; understanding ~ , 438:24
thoughtfulness, 1078:1
threat, 498:2
threesome, 843:1
thrift (also see money, saving), 202:3; 1032:7
thrush, 1330:2
thumb, opposable ~ , 1965:2
tide, ~-book, 1571:1
tidiness (also see neatness; orderliness), demands of ~ , 2010:9
tiger, 1097:1; fighting ~ , 1097:2

time (also see minute), 549:1; 688:25; 704:26; 742:8; 1279:3; 1631:4; 1767:11; 1862:4; 1911:1; 2066:6; balm of ~ , 589:3; 662:4; 762:5; 871:4; 2435:3; division of ~ , 1172:2; fixation on ~ , 2168:3; flight of ~ , 909:1; gift of ~ , 900:3; lost ~ , 1663:3; 1911:2; ~ management, 581:1; 823:6; 1522:17; misspent ~ , 225:5; passage of ~ , 248:2; 377:5; 469:2; 497:1; 543:4; 577:7; 618:27; 833:27; 869:4; 871:3; 1038:17; 1361:1; 1459:14; 1829:9; 1928:2; ~piece, 669:21; relativity of ~ , 730:8; 1375:2; 1396:14; 1426:1; 1488:1; 2024:1; 2263:6; slave of ~ , 1705:20; telling ~ , 2084:16; ~ to oneself, 277:25; use of ~ , 394:23; 491:1; 603:3; 702:2; 1599:2; 1680:2; 2421:1; ~ wasted, 2033:1; ~ well-spent, 692:2
timeliness, 1396:2; 1970:1
times, the (also see age; century; era), bad ~ , 697:27
timidity, 448:5
today (also see here and now; present), 869:3; living for ~ , 425:5
togetherness, 782:6; 899:10; 1862:11; 2405:3
tokenism, 2002:2; ~ at the workplace, 2104:2
tolerance, 363:3; 2506:1; ~ of differing opinions, 976:3; virtue of ~ , 609:5
Tolstoy, Leonid, 980:4
Toluca, Mexico, 1722:2
tombstone, 1153:3
tomorrow (also see future), 425:5; 875:16; 1230:1; 2120:1
tongue, holding one's ~ , 408:3; sharp ~ , 2018:8
tool, 1439:38
torture, 1745:4; ~ of women, 274:1; physical ~ , 2055:1
Tory, 528:1
totalitarianism, 1651:7; 1745:3
toughness (also see resilience), 1208:8; 1435:16
tourism, effect of ~ on historical preservation, 1720:4
town, small ~ , 1976:1
toy (also see game; playing), war ~ , 2179:2; 2321:1; 2457:2, 3
trade (also see occupation), 1737:2
tradition (also see custom; habit; rite), 1389:2; 1456:1; 2062:1; breaking with ~ , 1183:1; loss of ~ , 777:10; 1651:3; questioning ~ , 1762:7
tragedy, 1135:4; 1445:8
trail, carving out ~ , 1089:2
train, 2191:2; freight ~ , 1451:1
training, physical ~ , 1140:1; spiritual ~ , 1140:1
traitor (also see betrayal; treason), 277:19; 723:23
tranquility (also see peace, inner), 146:6; 406:36; foe of ~ , 577:3; satisfied with ~ , 813:3
tranquilizer (also see drugs), effects of ~ , 1529:2
transience (also see life, transience of), 844:1; 1191:22; 1383:1; 1517:2; 1829:9; 2324:3; 2369:2; ~ of life (also see life, transience of), ~ of time, 1440:3
transition, age of ~ , 1740:4
translator, 729:1

United States of America (*continued*)
637:39; 703:10; 1376:4; 1651;11; 1703:1; 1798:1
~ economy, 650:6; education in ~ (*also see*
education, American), 1252:2; egocentricity of
~ , 2136:14; 2159:7; elderly in ~ , 1641:6;
equality in ~ , 1826:1; family life in ~ , 703:37;
flag of ~ , 634:1; freedom in ~ , 1108:5; ~
government, 1456:8; 1720:68; 1803:1; 1931:4;
1941:1, 2; 2338:4; history of ~ , 763:1; 1558:6;
image of ~ , 2001:1; ~ in relation to Asian
nations, 857:1; 2295:4; ~ in relation to England,
616:1; ~ in relation to Europe, 1457:1; ~ in
relation to South America, 2149:1; ~ in relation
to U.S.S.R., 1652:1; 2306:1; ~ in relation to
Vietnam, 2055:1; 2295:1, 5; internal problems of
~ , 2001:1; law in ~ , 1685:2; life in ~ , 1264:3;
literature in ~ , 795:10; men in ~ , 1152:8;
1390:1; ~ military, 2379:1; newspapers in ~ ,
1108:4; oppression in ~ , 1810:1; politics in
~ , 1375:10; potential of ~ , 1377:1; 1931:3;
poverty in ~ , 1341:16; 1963:2; priorities of ~
government, 2155:4; prosperity of ~ , 2136:9;
racism in ~ , 2224:1; ~ responsibility to world,
1254:1; sex in ~ , 1390:9; 1394:1; space in ~ ,
1221:10; starvation in ~ , 703:20; status quo in
~ , 2136:11; ~ superiority, 2344:1; technology
in ~ , 2531:1, 4; twentieth century ~ , 1757:9;
women in ~ , 740:1; 2277:1
unity (*also see* oneness; solidarity), 1647:8; ~ , of
human race (*also see* cooperation, global), 2255:4
universe (*also see* world), 565:13; 1771:9; 2406:12;
laws of ~ , 683:1; 2246:16; understanding the
~ , 695:1; vastness of ~ , 732:3
university (*see* college)
unkindness (*also see* meanness), 419:4
unlikable, 135:3
unspoken, the (*also see* words, unspoken), 1206:5;
1731:1
unusual, the, love of ~ , 1396:5
upper class (*see* aristocracy; class [social], upper;
rich)
usefulness, 763:8; ~ is over, 1075:20
USSR (*see* Union of Soviet Socialist Republics)
utopia (*also see* Eden; paradise), 1221:19; 2121:4

V

vacation (*also see* holiday), 1881:6; family ~ ,
1881:5; festivity of ~ , 1669:5; lakeside ~ ,
994:5
vagina (*also see* genitalia; clitoris), 241:1, 2; 1331:4;
2087:5
valet (*also see* servant), 361:2
valor (*also see* bravery; courage), 271:5; 380:15
values (*also see* mores; principle; standard), authoritarian vs. humanistic ~ , 1717:3; changing
~ , 1762:11; 2343:3; cultural ~ , 2376:3; declining American ~ , 1757:9; development of
~ , 2164:10; feminist ~ , 2350:1; Judeo-Christian ~ , 1781:1; loss of ~ , 1606:1; male ~ ,
2014:1; materialistic ~ , 76:3; modern day ~ ,

2211:1, 2; ~ of good life, 1616:1; ~ of things,
2089:1; prioritizing ~ , 2196:2; questioning ~ ,
1302:5; shifting ~ of wartime, 1442:2
Vanderbilt, family, the, 943:2
vanity (*also see* pride), 271:4; 366:5; 489:2; 551:9;
618:20; 669:24; 682:8; 723:13; 893:9; 980:4;
1126:4; 1386:2; 2084:7; 2419:1; lack of ~ ,
1814:1; man's ~ , 400:5; 582:3; overcoming
one's ~ , 417:6; pampered ~ , 618:31; woman's
~ , 467:10; 1211:1
variety (*also see* diversity), 406:10
vendor, street ~ , 1263:1
vengeance (*also see* retribution; revenge; vindictiveness), 285:4; 400:4; 813:2; 889:1; renounce
~ , 285:8; 326:3; woman's ~ , 332:1
Venice, Italy, 445:2; walking in ~ , 1669:6
verbosity (*also see* talk), 482:2; ~ of women, 582:2;
vacuous ~ , 474:1
verse (*also see* poetry), rhymed ~ , 576:6
veteran (*also see* soldier), war ~ , 1461:1
vicariousness, 704:15; 872:1; 951:1; 1889:7; 2275:1
vice (*also see* sin), 309:2; 447:2; 462:9; 639:26;
720:3; 945:2; 1445:7; 1600:2
victim, 1705:12; 1863:4; 2005:2; 2257:1; indifference to ~ , 2063:3
victimization, 461:1; 1665:1; ~ of women, 2239:4;
2478:4
Victoria, queen of England, 703:8; 1340:1
Victorian, 1340:1; productivity of ~ , 1807:5; sexual repression of ~ , 2374:1
victory (*also see* winning), 363:17; 477:1; 1791:5;
1824:11; 2034:6; ~ of war, 696:1
video, 2094:4
Vietnam, ~ in relation to U.S.A., 2295:1; opposition to ~ War, 1971:1; ~ War, 1752:9; war in
~ , 2055:1
viewpoint (*also see* opinion), 682:1; 1379:2; cultural
~ , 1373:1; denying one's ~ , 2089:2; differing
~ , 199:1; sympathetic with others' ~ , 2487:2
vigil/ance, 1955:5
vigor (*also see* vitality), 2289:1; renewal of ~ ,
2037:1
villain (*also see* scoundrel) 1060:7
vindication, ~ of heroes, 1410:2
vindictiveness (*also see* vengeance), 1853:1
violence, 725:6; 2457:3; cultural ~ , 2054:1; glor-
ification of ~ , 1971:1; ~ in America, 2351:6;
~ in the media, 2162:1; ~ in the news, 1108:4;
~ in the world, 2145:3; male ~ , 2143:1; 2425:1;
~ perpetrated by government, 2145:1; reasons
for ~ , 2079:8; response of ~ , 2117:1; sanctity
of ~ , 1969:3
violet, 387:6
virgin/ity, 13:1; 55:1; 436:1; 449:1; 457:1; 1385:1;
1612:1; 1806:1; 2342:3; committed ~ , 392:2;
loss of ~ , 2257:4
Virginia, State of, 643:4
Virgin Mary (*see* Mary, Virgin)
virility (*also see* masculinity), symbols of ~ , 2405:1
virtue, 62:1; 146:2; 167:1; 184:1; 235:1; 249:2;

wealth (*continued*)
izing ~ , 1153:3; personal ~ , 2029:2; value of ~ , 1108:1
weapon/ry (*also see specific types;* arms), atomic ~ , 1624:5; development of ~ , 1169:5; outdated ~ , 2402:18
weariness (*also see* exhaustion; fatigue), 782:24; 1192:2
weather (*also see specific weather conditions*), 866:1
weed, 1186:1
weeping (*see* crying; tears)
welcome, 1040:2
well-being (*also see* health), lack of ~ , 2009:2, 3
West, the (U.S.), settling ~ , 1164:1
West, Benjamin, 703:1
Western world (*also see* Occidental), 2028:10, attitude of ~ , 1862:19; women in ~ , 2062:2; 2115:2
wetness, exposed to ~ , 1131:2
Whig, 528:1
whiskey, 2402:14
White House, Washington, D.C., 1487:1; 2032:1; ~ hospitality, 643:4
whiteness, 920:1
white race, conditioning of ~ , 1667:1; egocentricity of ~ , 2402:10; ~ in relation to blacks (*also see* blacks, in relation to whites), 2160:1; 2174:1; ~ in relation to Native American (*also see* Native American, in relation to white man), 1338:2; ~ in relation to other races, 2220:1; 2314:3
white supremacy (*also see* colonialism; racism), 993:1; 1862:19; 1885:1; 1921:4; 1962:3; 2068:1; 2110:2; 2164:15; 2264:2; 2285:2; 2332:6; 2484:1; ~ among women, 2520:2
Whittier, John Greenleaf, 857:3
whole, the, part of ~ , 858:1
wholeness, 2028:7; 2129:3; 2281:7; 2476:1; ~ of self, 1529:5; ~ of the sexes, 1770:1
wholesomeness, 2171:4
wickedness (*also see* bad; evil; evildoing; good and evil), 316:1; ~ of women, 406:8
widow/er, 537:2; 546:1; 1482:5; 1991:1, 2, 3; 2032:1; 2116:10; 2218:5
wife (*also see* housewife, spouse; woman, role of), 314:1; 369:4; 422:3; 436:1; 438:2; 551:10; 725:5; 1075:14; 1122:5; 1449:3; 1482:5; 1502:7; 1912:3; 2004:3; 2142:1; 2487:3; 2533:1; 2536:3; bad ~ , 639:5; ~ beating, 513:6; 725:6; death of ~ , 488:3; dependent ~ , 1985:4; devoted ~ , 1522:1; ~ in relation to husband (*also see* husband, in relation to wife), 236:2; 258:2; 321:1; 639:23; 643:2; 649:5; 1041:2; 1210:1; 1390:7; 1392:2; 1753:1; 2222:1; 2286:4; ~ in relation to in-laws, 17:1; loving ~ , 366:9; minister's ~ , 1019:3; obedient ~ , 426:1; 610:1; obligations of ~ , 326:1; ~ of public figure, 2160:3; philandering ~ , 326:2; 438:23; praise of ~ , 900:2; role of ~ , 147:1; 202:2; 1591:3; sex and ~ , 57:1; unhappy ~ , 551:16; 566:1; working ~ , 1595:10; wronged ~ , 513:8; 714:2

wilderness, 346:3; 2364:1; 2459:1; alone in ~ , 185:3; cherish ~ , 1955:3
wildlife (*also see* animal), connection with ~ , 1189:5; glory of ~ , 1189:1; ~ in relation to humankind, 1490:2
wildness, 1264:1
will, the, 892:30; 1648:5
willfulness, 192:7; suppression of ~ , 254:1; 439:2
willow, 629:2
Wilson, Woodrow, 1044:2
wind (*also see* breeze), 142:2; 169:2; 514:3; 628:4; 899:15; 1356:1; ~ direction, 1563:2; voice of ~ , 1279:2
windfall, 939:3
wine, 204:1; 344:4; 671:14; 688:13; 991:1; 1682:6
winning (*also see* victory), 2508:1
winter, 178:1; 663:3; 703:12; 892:6; 1290:5; 2262:2; end of ~ , 472:2
wisdom (*also see* knowledge; wise), 237:7, 10; 260:1; 309:2; 385:1; 489:2; 496:8; 855:2; 1038:4; 1119:1; 1213:9; 1348:1; 1400:1; 1767:2; 1829:1; disregard for ~ , 1680:18; ~ of women (*also see* woman, wisdom of), 717:2; search for ~ , 723:7; strive for ~ , 604:2
wise, the (*also see* knowledge; sage; wisdom), 551:14
wish, 782:13
wisteria, 2346:1
wit, 277:13; 394:8; 453:1; 514:6; 639:35; ~ in women, 496:13
witch, 1750:2; 2289:4; ~ hunt, 2211:3
witchcraft, belief in ~ , 703:30; protection from ~ , 1070:1
withdrawal, 2308:2; ; 2333:2
wizard, 1750:2
woe (*also see* misery), remembered ~ , 697:7
wolf, 498:2; afraid of ~ , 1696:1
Wollstonecraft, Mary, 610:1
woman/women (*also see* girl; lady; sexes; sex roles; womanhood; womanliness), 237:2; 428:8; 432:1; 550:23; 551:6; 723:9; 724:1; 800:23; 811:10; 840:6; 935:10; 945:1; 1038:3, 12; 1039:4; 1043:1; 1055:2; 1133:1; 1142:1; 1209:2; 1223:5; 1245:1; 1331:1; 1349:2, 3; 1385:1; 1387:1; 1396:14; 1468:1; 1471:1; 1502:11; 1607:9; 1643:3; 1648:2; 1672:1; 1767:9; 1873:1, 2; 1891:3, 7; 2095:1; 2185:1; 2252:2; 2281:7; 2284:2; 2285:1; 2293:1; 2297:3; 2366:2; 2371:5; 2474:5; 2498:1; ~ activists, 1182:1; aging ~ (*also see* age; old age, women and; people, old; woman, old; woman, older), 242:2; 375:1; 833:26; 1175:5; 1192:4, 14; 1396:6; alternatives for ~ , 1834:3; angry ~ , 618:17; ~ as upholders of morality, 777:27; attractive ~ (*also see* attractiveness, in women), 1173:2; 1765:1; bad ~ , 1540:1; beautiful ~ (*also see* beauty, women and), 307:11; books about ~ , 1680:3; capabilities of ~ , 277:3; 366:6; 449:2; 795:6; 1497:4; 1498:1; 1608:3; 1824:8; 2279:1; 2331:1; 2519:1; career ~ (*also see* business, woman; career, woman; woman, working), 1019:1; 1163:3; 1787:2; 1973:1; changing role of ~ ,

Career and Occupation Index

Notes to Career & Occupation Index

Contributors have been indexed according to the major career paths their lives have taken. They are listed alphabetically, within each category, without reference to contributor or page numbers. Contributor numbers may be quickly ascertained in the Biographical Index.

A. Academia & Criticism

Art Patrons and Collectors

Herbert, Mary Sidney
Jeanne of Navarre
Li Ch'ing-chao
Makhfi
Marguerite of Navarre
Medici, Lucrezia de'
Pfeiffer, Madame
Pompadour, Madame de
Renée de France
Stein, Gertrude
Tibergeau, Marchioness de
Wroth, Mary Sidney

Biographers, Historians, Scholars and Social Critics

Aiken, Lucy
Albery, Nobuko
Arendt, Hannah

Baudonivia
Baynard, Anne
Beard, Mary Ritter
Belenky, Mary Field
Benedict, Ruth
Benet, Laura
Beruriah
Blind, Mathilde
Bowen, Catherine Drinker
Bowen, Marjorie
Brett, Dorothy
Brodie, Fawn M.

Cam, Helen M.
Cartland, Barbara
Caulkins, Frances Manwaring
Cereta, Laura
Christine de Pisan
Coleridge, Mary
Cook, Blanche Weisen
Cooper, Anna Julia
Corday, Charlotte
Cornelia
Cruz, Juana Inés de la

Dacier, Anne
Dauenhauer, Nora
Davis, Rebecca Harding
Decter, Midge
Durant, Ariel

Edwards, Amelia
Elstob, Elizabeth
Emerson, Mary Moody
Epstein, Cynthia Fuchs

Fedele, Cassandra
Fee, Elizabeth
Fields, Annie Adams
Fraiberg, Selma
Franz, Marie-Louise von
Fraser, Antonia
Fuller, Margaret

Gelfant, Barbara H.
Gilchrist, Marie
Gilman, Charlotte Perkins
Ginzburg, Eugenia
Green, Mary A. E.
Green, Rayna
Grote, Harriet

Hamilton, Edith
Hammond, Eleanor Prescott
Han Suyin
Harrison, Jane
Hazan, Marcella
Hebard, Gracy
Higginson, Ella
Hill, Ruth Beebe
Himmelfarb, Gertrude
Huang Zongying

Jacobs, Jane
Jung, Emma

Kaplan, Temma E.
King, Georgianna

Leech, Margaret
Lerner, Gerda
Le Sueur, Meridel
Lewis, Edith
Le Ch'ing-chao
Luce, Gay Gaer

Makin, Bathsua
Malpede, Karen
Marguerite of Navarre
Martineau, Harriet
Miner, Dorothy Eugenia
Mitford, Jessica
Mitford, Nancy
Moore, Virginia
Morata, Olimpia
Morgan, Sydney Owenson
Mountain Wolf Woman

Nogarola, Isotta
Nussbaum, Martha

Oliphant, Margaret

Pagels, Elaine
Pan Chao
Pardoe, Julia
Pulcheria, St. Aelia

Raven, Arlene
Repplier, Agnes
Richter, Gisela
Ripley, Sarah Alden
Robinson, Therese
Rose, Phyllis
Rosen, Marjorie
Rossi, Alice
Rukeyser, Muriel

Schneir, Miriam
Schreiner, Olive
Sekaquaptewa, Helen
Seton, Julia
Sewell, Sarah Ann
Sforza, Costanza Varano
Sheehy, Gail
Sigea, Luisa
Smith, Lillian
Snow, Helen Foster
Sontag, Susan
Stanton, Elizabeth Cady
Stern, Edith Mendel
Stowe, Harriet Beecher

Tappan, Eva March
Tarbell, Ida
Ts'ai Yen
Tuchman, Barbara
Tucker, Anne

Warren, Mercy Otis
Weil, Simone
Wortham, Anne
Wright, Susanna

Zaturenska, Marya

Critics of the Arts, Media and Literature
Adler, Renata
Allen, Paula Gunn
Berenson, Mary
Bogan, Louise
Clark, Eleanor
Crist, Judith
Deutsch, Babette
Dilke, Emilia
Drew, Elizabeth
Finch, Anne
French, Marilyn
Gilliatt, Penelope
Goulianos, Joan
Hardwick, Elizabeth
Haskell, Molly
Iskin, Ruth
Jacobson, Ethel
Jameson, Anna
Janeway, Elizabeth
Kael, Pauline
King, Georgianna Goddard
Landowska, Wanda
Lejeune, Caroline
Leslie, Amy
Lowell, Any
Mamonova, Tayana
Mansfield, Katherine
Mason-Manheim, Madeline
McCarthy, Mary
Meynell, Alice
Miles, Josephine
Orlova, Raisa Davydovna

Peterson, Virgilia
Rittenhouse, Jessie
Rose, Phyllis
Sitwell, Edith
Spacks, Patricia Meyer
Staël, Germaine de
Trevisan, Anna F.
Tucker, Anne
Van Rensselaer, Mariana Griswold
Vendler, Helen
Wandor, Michelene
West, Rebecca
Winegarten, Renee
Winslow, Thyra Samter
Winwar, Frances
Woolf, Virginia

Educational and Foundation/Association Administrators
Astor, Brooke
Bethune, Mary McLeod
DeWit, Antoinette
Farenthold, Sissy
Gildersleeve, Virginia
Harris, Jean
Hooyman, Nancy R.
Horner, Matina
Kegel, Martha
Kreps, Juanita
Lape, Esther
Lord, Bette Bao
Lyon, Mary
Mathews, Jessica Tuchman
Michelman, Kate
Palmer, Alice Freeman
Parker, Gail Thain
Putnam, Emily James
Smeal, Eleanor
Stewart, Ella
Thomas, Martha
Ulrich, Mabel
Walters, Anna Lee
Wattleton, Faye
Zolde, Henrietta

Educators and Teachers
Adler, Freda
Aloni, Shulamit
Anastasi, Anna
Anthony, Katharine
Ashton-Warner, Sylvia
Aspasia

Baker, Dorothy Gillam
Bates, Katherine Lee
Bateson, Mary Catherine
Bazan, Emilia Pardo
Beecher, Catharine Esther
Belenky, Mary Field
Benston, Margaret Lowe

McCarthy, Sarah J.
McClintock, Barbara
Mercer, Margaret
Miles, Josephine
Miller, Alice
Miller, Jean Baker
Mirrielees, Edith Ronald
Mistral, Gabriela
Mitchell, Maria
Moffat, Mary Jane
Montessori, Maria
Morgan, Elaine

Noddings, Nel
Norman, Liane
Nussbaum, Martha

Pagels, Elaine
Painter, Charlotte
Parker, Gail Thain
Phelps, Almira Lincoln
Polowy, Carol
Pratt, Minnie Bruce
Preston, Ann
Putnam, Emily James

Ravitch, Diane
Ray, Dixy Lee
Reeves, Nancy
Rich, Adrienne
Riley, Janet Mary
Robinson, Mabel Louise
Robinson, Mary
Roepke, Gabriela
Rose, Phyllis
Ross, Susan C.
Rossi, Alice
Row, Amanda
Ruddick, Sara

St. Denis, Ruth
Sanchez, Carol Lee
Sappho
Sassen, Georgia
Schroeder, Patricia
Schulder, Diane B.
Sears, Vicki
Sedgwick, Catharine Maria
Shainess, Natalie
Sherfey, Mary Jane
Sherman, Susan
Sigea, Luisa
Sigourney, Lydia Howard
Smith, Nora
Snow, Helen Foster
Spacks, Patricia Meyer
Spencer, Anna Garlin
Speyer, Leonora
Spolin, Viola
Stannard, Una
Stewart, Maria W.
Stone, Merlin

Stopes, Marie Carmichael
Sugimoto, Etsu Inagaki
Sullivan, Annie
Suzman, Helen
Swerda, Patricia

Taggard, Genevieve
Tapp, June L.
Tarule, Jill
Terrell, Mary Church
Thomas, Martha
Thorne, Barrie
Todd, Mabel Elsworth
Tonna, Charlotte Elizabeth
Towne, Laura
Trimmer, Sarah Kirby

Van Duyn, Mona
Vendler, Helen

Waldo, Octavia
Walker, Margaret
Walters, Anna Lee
Wasserstein, Wendy
Weisstein, Naomi
Wells, Ida B.
Whitman, Marina vonNeumann
Wiggin, Kate Douglas
Wilcox, Margaret R.
Willard, Emma Hart
Winnemucca, Sarah
Witkovsky, Susan
Witt, Shirley Hill
Wolitzer, Hilma
Woolley, Hannah

Librarians, Curators and Preservationists
Ayscough, Florence
Dauenhauer, Nora
Davis, Elizabeth Gould
Mead, Margaret
Miner, Dorothy
Newman, Frances
Richter, Gisela
Vreeland, Diana

Philosophers
Adler, Renata
Agreda, Maria de
Arendt, Hannah
Beauvoir, Simone de
Bok, Sissela
Dunayevskaya, Raya
Hypatia
Koller, Alice
Langer, Susanne K.
Nussbaum, Martha
Rand, Ayn
Ruddick, Sara
Weil, Simone

B. Arts and Entertainment

Actors, Entertainers and Performers
Ace, Jane
Adams, Maude
Akhmadulina, Bella
Anderson, Judith
Anderson, Laurie
Angelou, Maya
Arnould, Sophie

Bacall, Lauren
Bai Fengxi
Ball, Lucille
Bankhead, Tallulah
Bardot, Brigitte
Barrymore, Ethel
Bergen, Candice
Bergman, Ingrid
Bernhardt, Sarah
Bisset, Jacqueline
Black, Shirley Temple
Bovasso, Julie Anne
Braverman, Kate
Bronaugh, Anne
Burnett, Carol

Campbell, Mrs. Patrick
Centlivre, Susannah
Charke, Charlotte
Chase, Ilka
Childress, Alice
Clive, Catherine
Cooper, Diana
Cryer, Gretchen
Cushman, Charlotte Saunders

Davis, Bette
Desbordes-Valmore, Marceline
Desjardins, Marie-Catherine
De Wolfe, Elsie
Dietrich, Marlene
Douglas, Helen Gahagan
Dressler, Marie
Duse, Eleonora

Elliott, Maxine
Evans, Edith

Field, Kate
Fields, Gracie
Fiske, Minnie
Fonda, Jane

Gabor, Zsa Zsa
Gallagher, Mary
Garbo, Greta
Garland, Judy
Garrick, Eva Maria
Gingold, Hermione
Glaspell, Susan
Gordon, Ruth

Grant, Lee
Guilbert, Yvette
Guinan, Texas
Gwyn, Nell

Hagen, Uta
Handl, Irene
Hayes, Helen
Haywood, Eliza
Henley, Beth
Hepburn, Katharine
Hoper, Mrs.
Horne, Lena
Huang Zongying

Janis, Elsie

Lanchester, Elsa
Langtry, Lily
Launay, Mme. de
Lawrence, Gertrude
Leachman, Cloris
Lee, Gypsy Rose
Le Gallienne, Eva
Leigh, Vivien
Lenya, Lotte
Leslie, Amy
Lillie, Beatrice
Lincoln, Abbey
Livingstone, Belle
Lloyd, Marie
Loren, Sophia
Lovell, Marie
Lupino, Ida

MacLaine, Shirley
Magnani, Anna
Mercouri, Melina
Merman, Ethel
Merry, Anne Brunton
Midler, Bette
Modjeska, Helena
Modotti, Tina
Moffat, Mary Jane
Monroe, Marilyn
Moore, Grace
Moreau, Jeanne
Morgan, Sydney Owenson

Neal, Patricia
Neuber, Friederika Karoline

Oakley, Annie
O'Casey, Eileen
O'Neill, Carlotta Monterey
Otero, Caroline

Parker, Suzy
Pickford, Mary
Pless, Daisy

Radner, Gilda
Reagan, Nancy
Reed, Donna

Richards, Beah
Riefenstahl, Leni
Robinson, Mary
Rowson, Susanna Haswell
Russell, Rosalind

Scott, Hazel
Scott-Maxwell, Florida
Shore, Dinah
Siddons, Sarah
Skinner, Cornelia Otis
Solanis, Valerie
Stanwyck, Barbara
Streisand, Barbra
Swanson, Gloria
Swit, Loretta

Taylor, Elizabeth
Terry, Ellen
Theodora
Tomlin, Lily
Tyler, Priscilla Cooper

Vestris, Eliza
Viva

Wagner, Jane
Webster, Margaret
West, Mae
Winters, Shelley
Woffington, Peg
Wood, Natalie

Songwriters, Arrangers, Composers and Lyricists
Adams, Sarah Flower
Alais
Alamanda
Alexander, Mrs. Cecil Frances
Anderson, Laurie
Ava, Frau
Azalais de Porcairages

Baez, Joan
Barnard, Charlotte
Beatritz de Dia
Bingen, Hildegard von
Bond, Carrie Jacobs
Booth, Evangeline
Brickell, Edie
Brown, Abbie Farwell
Brown, Anna Gordon
Brown, Mary Elizabeth

Caccini, Francesca
Carenza
Castelloza
Chapman, Tracy
Christian, Meg
Cockburn, Alicia
Collins, Judy
Cotten, Elizabeth

Crawford, Louisa Maccartney
Cryer, Gretchen
Cunningham, Agnes "Sis"

Davies, Mary Carolyn
Debree, Henrietta
Domna H.
Dufferin, Lady

Elliot, Jean
Elliott, Charlotte
Escot, Pozzi

Ferron
Fields, Dorothy
Fletcher, Bridget

Garsenda de Forcalquier
Garthwaite, Terry
Gore, Catherine
Guillelma de Rosers

Hankey, Katherine
Holiday, Billie

Ian, Janis
Isabella
Iselda

Janis, Elsie
Jones, Rickie Lee
Joplin, Janis

Kahn, Kathy
King, Carole
Kolb, Barbara
Kummer, Clare

Landowska, Wanda
Lathbury, Mary
Leigh, Carolyn
Littlebear, Naomi
Lombarda
Lynn, Loretta

McCaslin, Mary
Melanie
Mitchell, Joni
Moïse, Penina
Musgrave, Thea

Near, Holly
Nyro, Laura

Ono, Yoko
Orred, Meta

Parton, Dolly
Pounds, Jessie Brown
Prentiss, Elizabeth
Previn, Dory
Purim, Flora

Reddy, Helen
Reynolds, Malvina
Ronell, Ann

Tipton, Jennifer
Van Runkle, Theadora
Wagner, Jane

Designers—Graphic, Print and Illustration
Bradford, Cornelia
Carabillo, Toni
Goddard, Mary Katherine
Goddard, Sarah Updike
Hemans, Felicia Dorothea
Kent, Corita
Kollwitz, Käthe
Kuan Tao-shêng
Laurel, Alicia Bay
Laurencin, Marie
Li Yeh
Pilkington, Laetitia
Potter, Beatrix
Poulsson, Emilie
Rind, Clementina
Seton-Thompson, Grace

Directors—Stage, Film and Televison
Arzner, Dorothy
Bovasso, Julie Anne
Brunet, Marguerite
Farabough, Lee
Field, Connie
Fornes, Maria Irene
Gallagher, Mary
Grant, Lee
Gregory, Augusta
Jones, Margo
Jordan, June
Lupino, Ida
Riefenstahl, Leni
Rochefort, Christiane
Seidelman, Susan
Spolin, Viola
Varda, Agnes
Vestris, Eliza
Wagner, Jane
Webster, Margaret

Lecturers, Public Speakers and Workshop Leaders
Allen, Mary Wood
Anthony, Susan B.
Austin, Mary Hunter
Bethune, Mary McLeod
Bird, Caroline
Brotherton, Alice Williams
Brown, Charlotte
Burton, Elaine Frances
Cohen, Sherry Suib
Conkling, Grace
David-Neel, Alexandra
Douglas, Helen Gahagan

Dreifus, Claudia
Field, Kate
Flanner, Janet
Gage, Frances
Gawain, Shakti
Gilman, Charlotte Perkins
Godwin, Gail
Goldman, Emma
Gordimer, Nadine
Hortensia
Howe, Julia Ward
Johnson, Adelaide
Josefowitz, Natasha
Jung, Emma
Justin, Dena
Kellems, Vivien
Keller, Helen
King, Coretta Scott
Lease, Mary
Lerner, Gerda
Livermore, Mary
Mahler, Margaret
Mann, Erika
Mitchell, Juliet
Monroe, Anne Shannon
Morgan, Angela
Nin, Anaïs
Partnow, Susan
Perón, Eva
Peterson, Virgilia
Roosevelt, Eleanor
Ruckelshaus, Jill
Seton, Julia
Seton-Thompson, Grace
Simos, Miriam
Smedley, Agnes
Smith, Elizabeth Oakes
Stewart, Maria W.
Stone, Lucy
Stopes, Marie Carmichael
Sun Yat-sen, Madame
Thompson, Clara
Truth, Sojourner
Valenzuela, Luisa
Van Buren, Abigail
Ward, Barbara
Wells, Ida B.
Winnemucca, Sarah
Wright, Frances

Theater, Film & Media Producers, Specialists and Technicians
Allen, Dede
Ball, Lucille
Bovasso, Julie Anne
Elliott, Maxine
Flanagan, Hallie
Gilman, Charlotte Perkins
Gottlieb, Linda

Harrison, Barbara Grizzuti
Heldman, Gladys
Hernandez, Aileen Clarke
Hobson, Laura Z.
Jones, Margo
Lupino, Ida
Marbury, Elisabeth
Merry, Anne Brunton
Neuber, Frïederika Karoline
Phillips, Julia
Shange, Ntozake
Silver, Joan Micklin
Spolin, Viola
Streisand, Barbra
Swanson, Gloria
Walters, Barbara
West, Mae

Musicians, Singers and Conductors
Anderson, Margaret
Anderson, Marian
Arnim, Bettina von
Arnould, Sophie
Ava, Frau

Baez, Joan
Bailey, Pearl
Bond, Victoria
Booth, Evangeline
Brice, Fanny
Brickell, Edie

Caccini Francesca
Caldwell, Sarah
Catalani, Angelica
Céu, Violante de
Chapman, Tracy
Collins, Judy
Cotten, Elizabeth
Cryer, Gretchen
Cunningham, Agnes "Sis"
Curie, Éve

David-Neel, Alexandra
Dietrich, Marlene
Diller, Phyllis

Ferron
Fields, Gracie

Gabrielli, Caterina
Garden, Mary
Garland, Judy
Garthwaite, Terry
Genlis, Stephanie Félicité
Guillet, Pernette du

Holiday, Billie
Horne, Lena
Horne, Marilyn
Houdetot, Sophie de la Briche
Huseh, T'ao

Jackson, Mahalia
Jones, Rickie Lee
Joplin, Janis

Kahn, Kathy
King, Carole
King, Coretta Scott

Landowska, Wanda
Lehmann, Lotte
Lenya, Lotte
Lincoln, Abbey
Lind, Jenny
Li Yeh
Lynn, Loretta

Makeba, Miriam
Mara, Gertrude Elizabeth
McCaslin, Mary
McRae, Carmen
Melanie
Melba, Nellie
Merman, Ethel
Midler, Bette
Mitchell, Joni
Moore, Grace

Near, Holly
Nyro, Laura

Parra, Violeta
Parton, Dolly
Previn, Dory
Price, Leontyne
Purim, Flora

Reddy, Helen
Reynolds, Malvina
Ronell, Ann
Rondstadt, Linda
Russell, Anna

Sainte-Maric, Buffy
Schumann-Heink, Ernestine
Scott, Hazel
Shore, Dinah
Sill, Judee
Sills, Beverly
Simon, Carly
Slick, Grace
Smith, Bessie
Snow, Phoebe
Sorrels, Rosalie
Speyer, Leonora
Stampa, Gaspara
Storace, Nancy
Streisand, Barbra
Sutherland, Joan

Tikaram, Tanita
Truman, Margaret
Tucker, Sophie

Vega, Suzanne

(659)

Waring, Marilyn
Weisstein, Naomi

Painters, Sculptors and Craftspeople
Aldis, Mary Reynolds
Anguissola, Sofonisba
Arnim, Bettina von
Barnes, Djuna
Bashkirtseff, Marie
Bingen, Hildegard von
Brett, Dorothy
Carr, Emily
Carriera, Rosalba
Cassatt, Mary
Chicago, Judy
Delany, Mary
DeWit, Antoinette
Dilke, Emilia
Drexler, Rosalyn
Edwards, Betty
Fanshawe, Catherine Maria
Fukuzoyo Chiyo
Gentileschi, Artemisia
Guest, Barbara
Harjo, Joy
Hartigan, Grace
Hedström, Barbro
Hepworth, Barbara
Howells, Mildred
Hulme, Keri
Hunter, Clementine
Johnston, Henrietta
Kahlo, Frida
Killigrew, Anne
Kollwitz, Käthe
Kuan Tao-shêng
Laurencin, Marie
Layton, Elizabeth
Lin, Maya
Lisiewska-Therbusch, Anna Dorothea
Mamonova, Tatyana
Merian, Maria Sibylla
Miller, Alice
Millet, Kate
Moses, Grandma
Neel, Alice
Nevelson, Louise
O'Keeffe, Georgia
Ono, Yoko
Quick-To-See-Smith, Jaune
Rose, Wendy
Sanchez, Carol Lee
Schurman, Anna van
Scudder, Janet
Sheridan, Clare
Shikishi
Siddons, Sarah
Solanis, Valerie
Swerda, Patricia
Vigée-Lebrun, Elisabeth

Viva
Waldo, Octavia
Wright, Susanna

Photographers
Abbott, Berenice
Arbus, Diane
Beals, Jessie Tarbox
Bergen, Candice
Bourke-White, Margaret
Cameron, Julia Margaret
Cones, Nancy Ford
Cunningham, Imogen
Gilpin, Laura
Kasebier, Gertrude
Lange, Dorothea
Lord, Bette Bao
Miller, Lee
Modotti, Tina
Morgan, Barbara
Wells, Alisa
Welty, Eudora

Radio and Television Personalities
Ace, Jane
Barrett, Rona
Graham, Virginia
Grant, Toni
Kilgallen, Dorothy
Loud, Pat
McBride, Mary Margaret
Myerson, Bess
Peterson, Virgilia
Rivers, Joan
Rollin, Betty
Shain, Merle
Van Horne, Harriet
Walters, Barbara

C. Political, Social & Judicial Arena

Activists, Reformers and Revolutionaries
Abel of Beth-maacah, Woman of
Addams, Jane
Allen, Paula Gunn
Astell, Mary

Bachman, Moira
Baez, Joan
Baker, Dorothy Gillam
Baker, Ella
Beal, Frances M.
Besant, Annie Wood
Bloomer, Amelia Jenks
Bolton, Sarah Knowles
Bonner, Yelena
Booth, Evangline
Bowen, Louise de Koven
Brinker, Ruth

Schlafly, Phyllis
Schwimmer, Rosika
Senesh, Hanna
Sewall, Harriet
Shelley, Rebecca
Schnall, Susan
Simpson, Becky
Sloan, Margaret
Smith, Elizabeth Oakes
Spencer, Anna Garlin
Stanton, Elizabeth Cady
Stewart, Eliza "Mother"
Stewart, Ella
Stewart, Maria W.
Stone, Lucy
Sumner, Helen L.
Sun Yat-sen, Madame
Suttner, Bertha von

Thomas, Minnie
Tillmon, Johnnie
Truth, Sojourner
Ts'ai-t'ien Chang
Tubman, Harriet
Tuite, Marjorie

Verona, Virginia

Walker, Katharine
Wauneka, Annie Dodge
Webb, Beatrice Potter
Weil, Simone
Wells, Ida B.
Wilcox, Margaret R.
Willard, Frances
Winnemucca, Sarah
Witt, Shirley Hill
Woodhull, Victoria Claflin
Wright, Frances

Yang Ping
Yard, Molly

Zassenhaus, Hiltgunt
Zetkin, Clare
Zolde, Henrietta

Diplomats, Spies and Government Officials
Bailey, Pearl
Bazan, Emilia Pardo
Behn, Aphra
Black, Shirley Temple
Catherine of Siena, St.
Dunn, Lydia
Furness, Betty
Goddard, Mary Katherine
Hari, Mata
Harriman, Florence Hurst
Harrison, Patricia Roberts
Home, Grisell
Huldah

Keyserling, Mary
Kollontai, Aleksandra
Koontz, Libby
Kreps, Juanita
Luce, Clare Booth
Marcos, Imelda
Mendenhall, Dorothy Reed
Mercouri, Melina
Mistral, Gabriela
Myerson, Bess
Myrdal, Alva Reimer
Orlova, Raisa Davydovna
Pandit, Vijaya Lakshmi
Perkins, Frances
Perón, Eva
Priest, Ivy Baker
Ray, Dixy Lee
Roosevelt, Eleanor
Rosenberg, Ethel
Ruckelshaus, Jill
Stanford, Sally
Sumner, Helen L.
Sun Yat-sen, Madame
Ten Ying-ch'ao
Westergaard, Brita

Feminists and Suffragists
Adams, Abigail
Allred, Gloria
Aloni, Shulamit
Alta
Anger, Jane
Anthony, Susan B.
Atkinson, Ti-Grace
Austin, Mary Hunter

Bazan, Emilia Pardo
Beard, Miriam
Beauvoir, Simone de
Blackwell, Antoinette Brown
Blackwell, Elizabeth
Blackwell, Emily
Bradwell, Myra R.
Bricker-Jenkins, Mary
Brown, Olympia
Brown, Rita Mae
Brownmiller, Susan
Bunch, Charlotte

Carabillo, Toni
Carpenter, Liz
Catt, Carrie Chapman
Ch'iu Chin
Christine de Pisan
Claflin, Tennessee
Clarenbach, Kathryn
Cleyre, Voltairine de
Collins, Emily
Cruz, Juana Inés da la

Deming, Barbara
Deroine, Jeanne Françoise

Embree, Alice

Farnham, Eliza
Finch, Anne
Firestone, Shulamith
Fox, Muriel
Friedan, Betty
Fuller, Margaret

Gage, Mathilda
Grahn, Judy
Greer, Germaine
Grimké, Angelina
Grimké, Sarah Moore

Heide, Wilma Scott
Hooyman, Nancy R.
Howe, Julia Ward

Jars, Marie de
Johnson, Sonia
Johnston, Jill
Jones, Beverly
Joreen

Kaplan, Temma E.
Kellems, Vivien
Kempton, Sally
Kennedy, Florynce
Kenney, Annie
Key, Ellen

Labé, Louise
LaFollette, Suzanne
Lape, Esther
Le Baron, Marie
Lockwood, Belva
Luscomb, Florence
Lydon, Susan
Lyon, Phyllis

Mamonova, Tatyana
Maraini, Dacia
Martin, Del
Martineau, Harriet
McClung, Nellie
Mendenhall, Dorothy Reed
Mercer, Margaret
Mercouri, Melina
Michelman, Kate
Millet, Kate
Mott, Lucretia
Munda, Costantia
Murray, Judith Sargent

Nevelson, Louise

Pankhurst, Adela
Pankhurst, Christabel
Pankhurst, Emmeline
Pankhurst, Sylvia
Parturier, Françoise
Paul, Alice
Perera, Sylvia Brinton

Pethick-Lawrence, Emmeline
Pierobon, Gigliola

Rankin, Jeannette
Raven, Arlene
Reinharz, Shulamit
Robinson, Harriet
Roland, Pauline
Rose, Ernestine
Routsong, Alma
Russell, Dora

Schirmacher, Kathe
Schreiner, Olive
Schwimmer, Rosika
Sears, Vicki
Scott-Maxwell, Florida
Semenow, Dorothy
Seton-Thompson, Grace
Sewall, Harriet
Shulman, Alix Kates
Siebert, Muriel
Smeal, Eleanor
Smith, Dorothy E.
Smith, Elizabeth Oakes
Solanis, Valerie
Spencer, Anna Garlin
Staël, Germaine de
Stanton, Elizabeth Cady
Steinem, Gloria
Stone, Lucy
Stopes, Marie Carmichael

Terrell, Mary Church
Thomas, Martha
Tristan, Flora

Voznesenskaya, Yuliya

Walker, Mary
Weisstein, Naomi
Wenning, Judy
West, Rebecca
Willard, Emma Hart
Wollstonecraft, Mary
Woodhull, Victoria Claflin
Wright, Frances

Yard, Molly
Younger, Maud

Heads of State, Presidents, Premiers and Governors
Aquino, Corazon
Bhutto, Benazir
Brundtland, Gro Harlem
Chamorro, Violeta
Deborah
Gambara, Veronica
Gandhi, Indira
Grasso, Ella
Mankiller, Wilma Pearl

Meir, Golda
Ray, Dixy Lee
Thatcher, Margaret

Judges and Lawyers
Abzug, Bella
Allred, Gloria
Aloni, Shulamit
Bird, Rose
Bradwell, Myra R.
Coombs, Mary
Deborah
Doi, Takako
Edelman, Marian Wright
Farenthold, Sissy
Ginsberg, Ruth Bader
Glendon, Mary Ann
Griffiths, Martha Wright
Harris, Patricia Roberts
Hill, Anita
Kahn, Florence Prag
Le Sueur, Marian
Lockwood, Belva
Mink, Patsy Takemoto
Norton, Eleanor Holmes
O'Connor, Sandra Day
Reeves, Nancy
Ricker, Marilla
Riley, Janet Mary
Ross, Susan C.
Schroeder, Patricia
Schulder, Diane B.
Sheldon, Karin

Labor Leaders
De La Cruz, Jessie Lopez
Dreifus, Claudia
Huerta, Dolores
Jones, Mother
Kanin, Fay
Kennedy, Florynce
Younger, Maud

Politicians
Abzug, Bella
Aloni, Shulamit
Astor, Nancy
Aung San Suu Kyi
Binh, Nguyen Thi
Brown, Rosemary
Burton, Elaine Frances
Byron, Beverly Butcher
Chisholm, Shirley
Devlin, Bernadette
Doi, Takako
Douglas, Helen Gahagan
Farenthold, Sissy
Feinstein, Diane
Fenwick, Millicent
Giroud, Françoise

Grasso, Ella
Green, Edith Starrett
Griffiths, Martha Wright
Heckler, Margaret O'Shaughnessy
Holtzman, Elizabeth
Jeger, Lena May
Jordan, Barbara
Kahn, Florence Prag
Kaptur, Marcia Carolyn
Kassebaum, Nancy
Luce, Clare Booth
Mikulski, Barbara Ann
Mink, Patsy Takemoto
Mori, Nobuko
Perón, Eva
Rankin, Jeanette
Ray, Dixy Lee
Reid, Willie Mae
Schroeder, Patricia
Sforza, Caterina
Smith, Margaret Chase
Sullivan, Leonor Kretzer
Summerskill, Edith
Suzman, Helen
Thatcher, Margaret
Waring, Marilyn
Whitton, Charlotte
Williams, Helen Maria

Public Figures and Society Leaders
Adams, Abigail
Adams, Louisa Catherine
Aissé, Charlotte Elizabeth
Alden, Priscilla
Allende, Hortensia Bussi de
Alston, Theodosia Burr
Astor, Madeline Talmage

Bingham, Anne Willing
Botta, Anne
Bush, Barbara Pierce

Carter, Rosalynn
Cavendish, Georgiana
Churchill, Jennie Jerome
Cockburn, Alicia
Coolidge, Grace Goodhue
Cooper, Lady Diana

Deffand, Marie Anne du
Detourbey, Jeanne
De Wolfe, Elsie
Drouett, Juliette

Eisenhower, Mamie

Ferguson, Elizabeth Graeme
Ford, Betty
Franks, Rebecca

Garfield, Lucretia Rudolph
Geneviève

Geoffrin, Marie Thérèse Rodet
Gorbachev, Raisa Maximovna

Harding, Florence Kling
Hayes, Lucy Webb
Hill, Anita
Holland, Elizabeth
Hoover, Lou Henry
Howar, Barbara

Jackson, Rachel Robards
Johnson, Lady Bird

Kennedy, Rose Fitzgerald

La Fayette, Marie Madeleine de
Lespinasse, Julie-Jeanne-Eléonore de
Levin, Rahel
Lincoln, Mary Todd
Livingston, Belle
Longworth, Alice Roosevelt

Madison, Dolley
Mancini, Maria Anna
Marcos, Imelda
Mary, countess of Warwick
Maxwell, Elsa
Mitchell, Martha

Necker, Suzanne Chardon
Nevill, Dorothy
Nixon, Pat

Onassis, Jacqueline Kennedy

Patterson, Martha Johnson
Polk, Sarah Childress
Pompadour, Madame
Post, Emily

Reagan, Nancy
Roland, Jeanne-Marie
Roosevelt, Edith Carow
Roosevelt, Eleanor
Rosenberg, Ethel

Sévigné, Marie de

Taft, Helen Herron
Tencin, Claudine Alexandrine de
Ten Ying-ch'ao
Toklas, Alice B.
Truman, Bess
Tyler, Priscilla Cooper

Vanderbilt, Amy

Washington, Martha
Washington, Mary
Windsor, Wallis Simpson

D. Printed Word

Diarists and Letter Writers
Aiken, Lucy
Aissé, Charlotte Elizabeth

Arnold, Margaret Shippen
Augusta

Bache, Sarah
Barnard, Anne
Bashkirtseff, Marie
Bregy, Charlotte
Burton, Isabel

Campan, Jeanne Louise
Carlyle, Jane Welsh
Carter, Elizabeth
Chesnut, Mary Bokin
Choiseul, Louise Honorine de
Christina Leonora
Clifford, Anne
Colquhoun, Janet
Copley, Susannah Farnum
Cornelia
Corneul, A. M. Bigot de

Datini, Margherita
Deffand, Marie Anne du
Delaney, Mary
Dostoevsky, Anna

Eristi-Aya
Este, Isabella d'

Ferguson, Elizabeth Graeme
Fleming, Marjory
Frank, Anne

Gill, Sarah Prince
Godolphin, Margaret
Godwin, Hannah
Gonzaga, Lucrezia
Graham, Isabella
Griffiths, Hannah
Grignan, Françoise de

Harley, Brilliana
Héloise
Hoby, Margaret

James, Alice

Knight, Sarah Kemble
Knowles, Mary

Lamb, Mary Ann
Lisle, Honor
Luxborough, Henrietta

Maintenon, Françoise de
Marguerite of Valois
Maria Theresa
Martin, Martha
Masters, Mary
Michitsuna, Mother of
Montagu, Elizabeth
Montagu, Mary Wortley
Morris, Margaret

Nijo, Lady
Nin, Anaïs

Osborne, Dorothy

Ptaschkina, Nelly

Ramsay, Martha Laurens
Raven
Riedesel, Frederica de
Rilliet-Huber, Catherine
Russell, Elizabeth Hoby
Russell, Rachel

St. Johns, Adela Rogers
Sarashina, Lady
Schurman, Anna van
Senesh, Hanna
Sévigné, Marie de
Sherrington, Grace
Shikibu, Murasaki
Shonagon Sei
Southey, Caroline Anne
Strozzi, Alessandra de' Machingi

Thomas, Elizabeth
Tolstoy, Sophie

Varnhagen, Rachel Levin

Werfel, Alma Mahler
West, Ellen
Whiteley, Opal
Wilkinson, Eliza
Wilson, Harriette
Winslow, Anna Green
Winthrop, Margaret
Wordsworth, Dorothy
Wordsworth, Mary
Wright, Susanna

Dramatists—Librettists, Playwrights and Scriptwriters

Aguirre, Isidora
Aidoo, Ama Ata
Akins, Zoe
Aldis, Mary Reynolds
Ancelot, Virginie
Ariadne
Atlan, Liliane

Bagnold, Enid
Bai Fengxi
Baillie, Joanna
Barnes, Djuna
Baum, Vicki
Behn, Aphra
Bergen, Candice
Betsko, Kathleen
Bingham, Madeleine
Boothby, Frances
Bovasso, Julie Anne
Bowen, Marjorie
Brackley, Elizabeth
Brooke, Frances
Burrell, Sophia

Cavendish, Jane
Cavendish, Margaret
Centlivre, Susannah
Céu, Violante de
Charke, Charlotte
Childe-Pemberton, Harriet L.
Childress, Alice
Churchill, Caryl
Churchill, Jennie Jerome
Clive, Catherine
Cockburn, Alicia
Cockburn, Catherine
Commire, Anne
Cooper, Elizabeth
Cowley, Hannah
Craigie, Pearl
Cryer, Gretchen
Cumming, Patricia

Dane, Clemence
Dangarembga, Tsitsi
Davys, Mary
Delaney, Shelagh
Delmar, Viña
de Matteo, Donna
Didion, Joan
Di Prima, Diane
Drexler, Rosalyn
Duffy, Maureen
Du Maurier, Daphne
Duras, Marguerite

Edwards, Anne

Farabough, Laura
Ferber, Edna
Field, Rachel Lyman
Fields, Dorothy
Fiske, Minnie
Fleming, Joan
Fletcher, Lucille
Flexner, Anne Crawford
Fornes, Maria Ireene
Fradonnet, Catherine
Frank, Florence Kiper
Fumiko, Enchi

Gallagher, Mary
Gambaro, Griselda
Garson, Barbara
Gems, Pem
Gilliatt, Penelope
Glaspell, Susan
Gordon, Ruth
Gore, Catherine
Graham, Virginia
Gregory, Augusta

Hansberry, Lorraine
Harjo, Joy
Haywood, Eliza
Hellman, Lillian

Hemans, Felicia Dorothea
Henley, Beth
Hogan, Linda
Hoper, Mrs.
Howe, Tina
Hroswitha of Gandersheim

Inchbald, Elizabeth
Isaacs, Susan

Jacker, Corinne

Kanin, Fay
Kennedy, Adrienne
Kerr, Jean
Kummer, Clare

Leapor, Mary
Lejeune, Caroline
Lenéru, Marie
Lennart, Isobel
Lennox, Charlotte
Lessing, Doris
Loos, Anita
Lovell, Marie
Luce, Clare Booth

Malpede, Karen
Manley, Mary de la Riviere
Manner, Eeva-Liisa
Maraini, Dacia
Marbury, Elisabeth
Marion, Frances
McCullers, Carson
Millay, Edna St. Vincent
Mitford, MaryRussell
Moore, Honor
Mumford, Ethel Watts
Murray, Judith (Sargent)

Neuber, Frïederika Karoline
Nichols, Anne
Norman, Marsha

Orczy, Baroness
Owens, Rochelle

Parent, Gail
Peabody, Josephine Preston
Perry, Eleanor
Philips, Katherine Fowler
Pilkington, Laetitia
Pix, Mary Griffith

Rand, Ayn
Rascoe, Judith
Resnik, Muriel
Richards, Beah
Riefenstahl, Leni
Rinehart, Mary Roberts
Robinson, Mary
Rochefort, Christiane
Roepke, Gabriela

Sachs, Nelly
Sarraute, Nathalie

Sarton, May
Scott-Maxwell, Florida
Shange, Ntozake
Sheridan, Frances
Sherman, Susan
Simos, Miriam
Smith, Dodie
Sontag, Susan

Terry, Megan
Tollet, Elizabeth
Townsend, Sue
Trevisan, Anna F.
Turnbull, Margaret
Tuthill, Louisa Caroline

Valenzuela, Luisa
Voronel, Nina

Wagner, Jane
Wandor, Michelene
Warren, Mercy Otis
Wasserstein, Wendy
Weddell, Mrs.
Weil, Simone
Weldon, Fay
West, Jane
West, Mae
Wharton, Anne
Winslow, Thyra Samter
Wiseman, Jane
Wood, Ellen

Journalists, Columnists, Reporters and Editors

Abbott, Wenonah Stevens
Alcott, Louisa May
Alexander, Shana
Anthony, Susan B.

Ballard, Bettina
Barbauld, Anna Letitia
Barfoot, Joan
Barker, Myrtie Lillian
Barnes, Djuna
Barrett, Rona
Bender, Marilyn
Bernikow, Louise
Betsko, Kathleen
Bianchi, Martha Dickinson
Billings, Victoria
Birch, Alison Wyrley
Bolton, Sarah Knowles
Bombeck, Erma
Bourke-White, Margaret
Bradford, Cornelia
Bradwell, Myra R.
Beth, Brant
Brooke, Frances
Brothers, Joyce
Brown, Helen Gurley

(667)

Poets

Dolliver, Clara
Doolittle, Hilda
Dorr, Julia
Doten, Elizabeth
Doubiago, Sharon
Doudney, Sarah
Dow, Dorothy
Dowriche, Anne
Driscoll, Louise
Droste-Hülshoff, Annette Elisabeth von
Duff, Esther Lilian

Eifuku, Empress
Elizabeth of York
Elliot, Jean
Elmendorf, Mary
Erinna
Evans, Mari

Falconar, Harriet
Falconar, Maria
Fane, Violet
Fanshawe, Catherine Maria
Faugères, Margaretta Van Wyck
Ferguson, Elizabeth Graeme
Ferron
Field, Rachel Lyman
Fields, Annie Adams
Finch, Anne
Fishback, Margaret
Flanner, Hildegarde
Flint, Annie Johnson
Follen, Eliza Lee
Ford, Lena Guilbert
Fradonnet, Catherine
Fradonnet, Madeleine
Frame, Janet
Franco, Veronica
Frank, Florence Kiper
Franklin, Eleanor Anne
Fraser, Kathleen
Freeman, Mary
Frost, Frances
Fukuzoyo Chiyo
Fuller, Margaret
Fyleman, Rose

Gage, Frances
Gambara, Veronica
Gates, Ellen
Gibbons, Stella
Gilbert, Sandra
Gill, Sarah Prince
Gillan, Maria Mazziotti
Gilman, Caroline
Gilman, Charlotte Perkins
Giltinan, Caroline
Giovanni, Nikki
Goldberg, Leah
Goodale, Elaine
Goodenough, J. B.

Gorbanevskaya, Natalya
Gore, Catherine
Gore-Booth, Eva
Gormley
Gould, Hannah Flagg
Graham, Isabella
Graham, Janet
Grah, Judy
Grant, Anne
Gray, Agnes Kendrick
Green, Rayne
Gregoria, Francisco
Greiffenberg, Catharina Regina von
Greville, Frances Fulke
Grierson, Constantia
Griffin, Susan
Griffiths, Hannah
Guest, Barbara
Guillet, Pernette du
Guiney, Louise Imogen
Gurney, Dorothy
Guyon, Jeanne-Marie de la Motte

Hacker, Marilyn
Hadewijch
Hale, Sarah Josepha
Hall, Hazel
Hall, Radclyffe
Hall, Sharlot Mabridth
Hallack, Cecily R.
Hamilton, Anna E.
Hamilton, Elizabeth
Hanim, Leylâ
Han Ts'ui-p'in
Harima, young woman of
Harington, Lucy
Harjo, Joy
Harris, Marguerite
Hastings, Flora
Hatshepsut
Hatun, Mihri
Havergal, Frances Ridley
Hayden, Anna Tompson
Hayden, Esther
Haywood, Eliza
Heathorn, Henrietta
Heaton, Rose Henniker
Hemans, Felicia Dorothea
Herbert, Mary Sidney
Hewitt, Mary Elizabeth
Heyward, Jane Screven
Hibbard, Grace
Hickey, Emily
Higginson, Ella
Hind bint Utba
Hinkson, Katharine Tynan
Ho, Lady
Hochman, Sandra
Hodson, Margaret
Hogan, Linda

Holford, Margaret
Holland, Barbara
Holland, Norah M.
Home, Anne
Home, Grisell
Hŏ Nansŏrhŏn
Honnamma
Hooper, Ellen Sturgis
Hope, Laurence
Horikawa, Lady
Horta, Maria Teresa
Ho Suang-ch'ing
Houdetot, Sophie de la Briche
Howard, Anne Dacre
Howard, Anne Douglas
Howard, Isabella
Howarth, Ellen
Howe, Julia Ward
Howell, Margery Eldgredge
Howells, Mildred
Howitt, Mary
Ho Xuan Huong
Hroswitha of Gandersheim
Hsi-chün
Hsüeh T'ao
Huang O
Hume, Anna
Hutchinson, Ellen
Hwang Chin-i

Ibarbourou, Juana de
Ingelow, Jean
Irving, Minna
Isaure, Clemence
Ise, Lady
Ishikawa, Lady
Iwa no Hime
Izumi Shikibu

Jackson, Helen Hunt
Jacobsen, Josephine
Jahan, Nur
Janvier, Margaret
Jefimija
Jevgenija
Jewsbury, Maria Jane
Johnstone, Willhelmina
Jones, Mary
Jong, Erica
Jordan, Dorothea
Jordan, June
Joseph, Jenny
Judson, Sarah B.

Kasa no Iratsume
Kasmuneh
Kassia
Kaufman, Shirley
Kawai Chigetsu-Ni

Kazu-no-miya
Kemble, Fanny
Keppel, Caroline
Khatun, Padeshah
Kii, Lady
Killigrew, Anne
Killigrew, Catherine
Kilmer, Aline Murray
Kimball, Harriet
King, Georgianna Goddard
King, Harriet
Ki no Tsurayuki, Daughter of
Kinsolving, Sally
Kirsch, Sarah
Kizer, Carolyn
Knight, Sarah Kemble
Koghtnatsi, Khosrovidoukht
Kōka, stewardess of the Empress
Kouchak, Nahabed
Kshetrayya
Kuan Tao-shêng
Kubatum
Kumin, Maxine

Labé, Louise
La Coste, Marie de
Laing, Dilys
Lalleswari
Lamb, Mary Ann
Landon, Letitia
Lanier, Emilia
Laramore, Vivian Yeiser
Larcom, Lucy
Lasker-Schuler, Else
Lathbury, Mary
Laurencin, Marie
Lazarus, Emma
Leapor, Mary
Lee, Agnes
Lee, Mary Chudleigh
Le Gallienne, Hesper
Leitch, Mary Sinton
Lenngren, Anna Maria
Lennox, Charlotte
Le Row, Caroline Bigelow
Le Sueur, Meridel
Letts, Winnifred
Leveridge, Lilian
Levertov, Denise
Lewis, Sarah Anna
L'Héritier, Marie Jeanne
Liadan
Li Ch'ing-chao
Liddell, Catherine
Lindbergh, Anne Morrow
Li Yeh
Llewellyn-Thomas, Beatrice
Lorde, Audre
Lorraine, duchess of

Lowell, Amy
Ludwig, Paula
Luxborough, Henrietta
Lyon, Mrs.

Macatti, Okkur
MacLeod, Jean Sutherland
MacLeod, Mairi
Macuilxochitl
Madan, Judith
Mahādēviyakka
Mahodahi
Mahsati
Makhfi
Mamonova, Tatyana
Manner, Eeva-Liisa
Maraini, Dacia
Marguerite of Navarre
Maria of Hungary and Bohemia
Markham, Lucia Clark
Martin, Sarah Catherine
Marula
Maryam bint Abi Ya'qub al-Ansari
Mary, queen of Scots
Mason, Caroline
Mason-Manheim, Madeline
Masters, Mary
Matraini, Chiara Cantarini
May, Julia Harris
McCormick, Virginia Taylor
McGinley, Phyllis
McLeod, Irene Rutherford
Mechain, Gwerfyl
Medici, Lucrezia de'
Mehri
Melvill, Elizabeth
Mew, Charlotte
Meynell, Alice
Milbanke, Anne Isabella
Miles, Josephine
Millay, Edna St. Vincent
Miller, Alice Duer
Miller, Emily
Miriam
Mistral, Gabriela
Mitford, Mary Russell
Moirai, Catherine Risingflame
Moïse, Penina
Monk, Mary
Monroe, Harriet
Montagu, Mary Wortley
Montgomery, Roselle Mercier
Moodie, Susanna
Moore, Honor
Moore, Julia A.
Moore, Marianne
Moore, Virginia
Moorhead, Sarah Parsons
Morata, Olimpia

Morgan, Angela
Morgan, Robin
Morgan, Sydney Owenson
Morpeth, Mary
Morpurgo, Rahel
Morra, Isabella de
Morrow, Elizabeth Reeve
Morton, Sarah Wentworth
Motoni, Nomura
Moulton, Louise
Murray, Judith Sargent
Murry, Ann

Naidu, Sarojini
Nairne, Carolina
Nakatsukasa, Lady
Nannākaiyār, Kaccipēṭṭu
Nesbit, Edith
Ní Chonaill, Eibhlín Dhubh
Nijo, Empress of
Northern Mother, A
Norton, Caroline
Norton, Grace Fallow
Nukada

O'Keeffe, Adelaide
Olesnicka, Zofia
O'Neill, Henrietta
O'Neill, Moira
O'Neill, Rose
Ono, Yoko
Ono no Komachi
Opie, Amelia
Orred, Meta
Osgood, Frances Sargent
Ostenso, Martha
Ōtomo no Sakanō-e no Iratsume
Owen, Anita
Owens, Rochelle
Owens, Vilda Sauvage

Palmer, Alice Freeman
Pan Chao
Pappas, Rita Boumy
Parker, Dorothy
Pastan, Linda
Peabody, Josephine Preston
Pennington, Mrs.
Perry, Nora
Petigny, Maria-Louisa Rose
Petröczi, Kata Szidónia
Phelps, Almira Lincoln
Philips, Joan
Philips, Katherine Fowler
Piercy, Marge
Pilkington, Laetitia
Pinar, Florencia del
Pitter, Ruth
Plath, Sylvia
Plato, Ann

Pollard, Josephine
Pratt, Minnie Bruce
Praxilla
Prentiss, Elizabeth
Preston, Margaret
Procter, Adelaide
Procter, Edna Dean
Pyper, Mary

Qernertoq
Quick-To-See-Smith, Jaune

Rabi'a bint Isma'il of Syria
Rabi'a of Balkh
Rabi'a the Mystic
Rachel
Radcliffe, Ann
Reese, Lizette
Rice, Ruth Mason
Rich, Adrienne
Richards, Beah
Riding, Laura
Rittenhouse, Jessie
Roberts, Elizabeth Madox
Robinson, Agnes Mary
Robinson, Corinne Roosevelt
Robinson, Mary
Robinson, Therese
Rolls, Mrs. Henry
Rose, Wendy
Rossetti, Christina
Rowe, Elizabeth
Ruarowna, Margareta
Rukeyser, Muriel

Sachs, Nelly
Sackville, Margaret
Safiya bint Musafir
Sanchez, Carol Lee
Sangster, Margaret E.
Sappho
Sarton, May
Schaeffer, Susan
Scudéry, Madeleine de
Sears, Vicki
Seiffert, Marjorie Allen
Seton-Thompson, Grace
Sewall, Harriet
Seward, Anna
Sexton, Anne
Shane, Elizabeth
Shange, Ntozake
Sharp, Joane
Shepard, Alice M.
Sheridan, Frances
Sherman, Susan
Sherwood, Kate
Sherwood, Margaret P.
Shikigu, Murasaki
Shikishi
Shonagon Sei

Sibyl, The Jewish
Sigourney, Lydia Howard
Sila
Śilabhlaṭṭarikā
Simpson, Nancy
Sitwell, Edith
Smith, Anna Young
Smith, Arabella
Smith, Barbara
Smith, Charlotte
Smith, May Riley
Smith, Nora Archibald
Southey, Caroline Anne
Spark, Muriel
Speght, Rachel
Speyer, Leonora
Spofford, Harriet
Sproat, Nancy Dennis
Stampa, Gaspara
Steele, Anne
Stockton, Annis
Storni, Alfonsina
Struther, Jan
Sullam, Sarah Copia
Sulpicia
Sumangala, mother of
Sun Yün-fêng
Suo, Lady
Swenson, May
Sylva, Carmen
Symonds, Caroline

Taggard, Genevieve
T'ang Wan, Lady
Tappan, Eva March
Taylor, Ann
Taylor, Jane
Taylor, Mrs.
Teasdale, Sara
Telesilla
Teresa of Avila, St.
Terracina, Laura
Terry, Lucy
Thaxter, Celia
Thomas, Edith
Thomas, Elizabeth
Thomas, Louisa
Thrynne, Frances
Tibergeau, Marchioness de
Tighe, Mary
Tollet, Elizabeth
Tonna, Charlotte Elizabeth
Torelli, Barbara
Townsend, Eliza
Trefusis, Elizabeth
Trench, Melesina
Ts'ai Yen
Tsvetaeva, Marina
Tunnell, Sophie
Turell, Jane Colman

Williams, Anna
Williams, Helen Maria
Winnemucca, Sarah
Winwar, Frances
Yang, Gladys

Writers—Fiction & Nonfiction
Abbott, Sidney
Adamson, Joy
Adler, Freda
Adler, Margot
Adler, Renata
Aidoo, Ama Ata
Akins, Zoe
Albery, Nobuko
Alcott, Louisa May
Alexander, Mrs.
Alexander, Shana
Allen, Paula Gunn
Allende, Isabel
Allfrey, Phyllis Shand
Alliluyeva, Svetlana
Allingham, Margery
Aloni, Shulamit
Alonso, Dora
Ancelot, Virginie
Anderson, Margaret
Angelou, Maya
Anthony, Katharine
Antin, Mary
Antrim, Minna
Arnim, Bettina von
Arnim, Mary A.
Arnow, Harriette
Ashford, Daisy
Ashton-Warner, Sylvia
Asquith, Margot
Astor, Brooke
Atherton, Gertrude
Atkinson, Ti-Grace
Atwood, Margaret
Aubin, Penelope
Auel, Jean
Austen, Jane
Austin, Mary Hunter
Austin, Sarah Taylor

Babitz, Eve
Bachmann, Ingeborg
Bacon, Anne Cooke
Bacon, Josephine Dodge
Bagnold, Enid
Bailey, Urania Locke
Baker, Dorothy
Baldwin, Faith
Baldwin, Monica
Bannerman, Helen
Banning, Margaret Culkin
Barbauld, Anna Letitia
Barber, Margaret Fairless

Barfoot, Joan
Barker, Elsa
Barker, Jane
Barker, Myrtie Lillian
Barnes, Djuna
Barnes, Margaret Ayer
Barolini, Helen
Barr, Amelia
Barr, Mary A.
Barreno, Maria Isabel
Barton, Clara
Bateson, Mary Catherine
Baum, Vicki
Bazan, Emilia Pardo
Beard, Miriam
Beauvoir, Simone de
Beecher, Catharine Esther
Behn, Aphra
Bell, Christine
Bell, Helen Olcott
Bengis, Ingrid
Benson, Stella
Bergen, Candice
Bianchi, Martha Dickinson
Bibesco, Elizabeth Asquith
Billings, Victoria
Billings, Christine
Bingham, Charlotte
Bingham, Madeleine
Bingham, Sallie
Birch, Alison Wyrley
Bird, Caroline
Bishop, Elizabeth
Blackwell, Antoinette Brown
Bleecker, Ann Eliza
Blessington, Marguerite
Blume, Judy
Bogan, Louise
Bok, Sissela
Bolen, Jean Shinoda
Bonaparte, Marie
Botta, Anne
Botume, Elizabeth
Boucher, Sandy
Bowen, Catherine Drinker
Bowen, Elizabeth
Bowen, Marjorie
Braddon, Mary Elizabeth
Bradley, Marion Zimmer
Braverman, Kate
Bray, Ann Eliza
Bregy, Charlotte
Bremer, Frederika
Brennan, Maeve
Brett, Dorothy
Breuer, Bessie
Brine, Mary Dow
Brittain, Vera
Brontë, Anne
Brontë, Charlotte

Goulianos, Joan
Graham, Margaret Collier
Graham, Sheilah
Graham, Virginia
Grant, Anne
Grau, Shirley Ann
Gray, Francine Du Plessix
Gray, Madeline
Green, Anna
Green, Hannah
Green, Mary A. E.
Green, Rayna
Greer, Germaine
Gregory, Augusta
Griffin, Susan
Griffitts, Hannah
Grimké, Angelina
Grimké, Sarah Moore
Grymeston, Elizabeth
Gubar, Susan
Guest, Barbara
Guest, Judith
Guffy, Ossie
Guiney, Louise Imogen
Guitar, Mary Anne
Guyon, Jeanne-Marie de la Motte

Haggerty, Joan
Hale, Lucretia Peabody
Hale, Nancy
Hale, Sarah Josepha
Hall, Radclyffe
Hall, Sharlot Mabridth
Hallack, Cecily R.
Halsey, Margaret F.
Hamilton, Edith
Hamilton, Eleanor
Hamilton, Elizabeth
Hamilton, Gail
Hammond, Eleanor Prescott
Handl, Irene
Han Suyin
Harding, M. Esther
Hardwick, Elizabeth
Harris, Corra May
Harris, Janet
Harris, Jean
Harrison, Barbara Grizzuti
Harrison, Jane
Hart, Frances Noyes
Haskins, Minnie
Hathaway, Helen
Hayes, Helen
Hays, Elinor
Hayward, Brooke
Haywood, Eliza
Hazan, Marcella
Hazzard, Shirley
Head, Bessie
Hearne, Mary

Heathorn, Henrietta
Heaton, Rose Henniker
Heilbrun, Carolyn
Heldman, Gladys
Hellman, Lillian
Henley, Nancy
Herbert, Marie
Herman, Judith Lewis
Hewlett, Sylvia Ann
Hibbard, Grace
Higgonson, Ella
Hill, Ruth Beebe
Hinkle, Beatrice
Hinkson, Katharine Tynan
Hit-him-home, Jeane
Hobson, Laura Z.
Hochschild, Arlie
Hogan, Linda
Holford, Margaret
Holley, Mary
Holmes, Mary
Home, Grisell
Hoover, Eleanor
Horney, Karen
Horta, Maria Teresa
Howar, Barbara
Howard, Jane
Howard, Maureen
Howe, Julia Ward
Howe, Louise Kapp
Howitt, Mary
Hsiao Hung
Hsieh Ping-ying
Huang Zongying
Hubbard, Ruth
Hudson, Helen
Hulme, Kathryn
Hulme, Keri
Hungerford, Margaret Wolfe
Hungry Wolf, Beverly
Hunter, Kristin
Huntington, Helen
Hurnscot, Loran
Hurst, Fannie
Hurston, Zora Neale
Hutchinson, Ellen
Hutten, Bettina von
Hyde, Mary

Ingelow, Jean
Isaacs, Susan

Jacker, Corinne
Jackson, Helen Hunt
Jackson, Jacquelyn
Jackson, Shirley
Jacobs, Harriet Brent
Jacobs, Jane
Jacobsen, Josephine
Jacobson, Ethel
Jacoby, Susan

Sewell, Anna
Sewell, Sarah Ann
Shain, Merle
Shainess, Natalie
Shaw, Anna Moore
Shaywitz, Sally E.
Sheehy, Gail
Shelley, Mary
Shen Rong
Sherfey, Mary Jane
Sheridan, Clare
Sheridan, Frances
Sherwood, Margaret P.
Sherwood, Mary Martha
Shikibu, Murasaki
Shulman, Alix Kates
Sidney, Margaret
Sigourney, Lydia Howard
Silver, Joan Micklin
Silverberg, Frances
Simon, Kate
Simon, Patricia
Simos, Miriam
Singer, June
Skinner, Cornelia Otis
Smedley, Agnes
Smith, Betty
Smith, Charlotte
Smith, Elizabeth Oakes
Smith, Evelyn E.
Smith, Lee
Smith, Lillian
Smith, Margaret Bayard
Smith, May Riley
Smith, Nora Archibald
Snow, Helen Foster
Sontag, Susan
Sowerman, Ester
Spark, Muriel
Speght, Rachel
Spofford, Harriet
Spyri, Johanna
Staël, Germaine de
Stafford, Jean
Stanford, Sally
Stannard, Una
Stanton, Elizabeth Cady
Stassinopoulos, Arianna
Stead, Christina
Stein, Gertrude
Steinem, Gloria
Stern, Edith Mendel
Stewart, Maria W.
Stoddard, Elizabeth
Stone, Merlin
Stopes, Maria Carmichael
Stowe, Harriet Beecher
Struther, Jan
Suckow, Ruth
Sugimoto, Etsu Inagaki

Sutcliffe, Ann
Suttner, Bertha von
Swerda, Patricia
Syfers, Judy
Sylva, Carmen

Tappan, Eva March
Tarbell, Ida
Tarule, Jill
Tattlewell, Mary
Tencin, Claudine Alexandrine de
Thomas, Audrey
Thomas, Martha
Thompson, Clara
Thompson, Dorothy
Thornton, Alice
Thorpe, Rose Hartwick
Ting Ling
Todd, Mabel Elsworth
Toklas, Alice B.
Tonna, Charlotte Elizabeth
Townsend, Sue
Trachtenberg, Inge
Tracy, Honor
Trench, Melesina
Trimmer, Sarah Kirby
Tristan, Flora
Trollope, Frances Milton
Troubridge, Lady
Truman, Margaret
Tsvetaeva, Marina
Tuchman, Barbara
Turnbell, Agnes Sligh
Turnbull, Margaret
Tuthill, Louisa Caroline
Tyler, Anne

Ueland, Brenda
Uhnak, Dorothy
Ullman, Liv

Valenzuela, Luisa
Vanderbilt, Any
Vardill, Anna Jane
Vendler, Helen
Villanueva, Alma
Viorst, Judith
Viva
Vorse, Mary Heaton
Voznesenskaya, Yuliya

Waddles Charleszetta
Waldo, Octavia
Walker, Alice
Walker, Katharine
Walker, Margaret
Walters, Anna Lee
Walters, Barbara
Wang Anyi
Ward, Barbara
Ward, Mary Augusta
Warner, Anna Bartlett

Warner, Marina
Warner, Susan
Warner, Sylvia Townsend
Webb, Beatrice Potter
Webb, Mary
Webster, Margaret
Weinraub, Sally
Weisstein, Naomi
Weldon, Fay
Wells, Carolyn
Wells, Ida B.
Welty, Eudora
West, Jane
West, Jessamyn
West, Rebecca
Wharton, Anne
Wharton, Edith
Wheathill, Ann
Whitman, Marina vonNeumann
Whitman, Sarah
Whitney, Adeline Dutton
Whitson, Beth Slater
Whitton, Charlotte
Widdemer, Margaret
Wiggin, Kate Douglas
Wilder, Laura Ingalls
Willard, Emma Hart
Williams, Anna
Williams, Helen Maria
Williams, Sherley Anne
Willis, Gwendolyn
Willson, Dixie
Winegarten, Renee
Winn, Mary Day
Winslow, Anne Goodwin
Winslow, Thyra Samter
Winwar, Frances
Witt, Shirley Hill
Wittig, Monique
Woffington, Peg
Wolf, Christa
Wolff, Charlotte
Wolitzer, Hilma
Wollstonecraft, Mary
Wood, Ellen
Wood, Sally Sayward
Woodhull, Victoria Claflin
Woodman, Marion
Woodruff, Julia Louise Matilda
Woolf, Virginia
Worthington, Robin
Wright, Frances
Wyatt, Edith Franklin
Wylie, Elinor

Yang Ping
Yearsley, Anne
Yezierska, Anzia
Yglesias, Helen
Younger, Maud
Yourcenar, Marguerite

Zhang Jie
Zhang Kangkang
Zong Pu

E. Science & Medicine

Medical Practitioners—Physicians, Psychiatrists, Nurses, Midwives, etc.

Allen, Mary Wood
Anna of Saxony
Barton, Clara
Blackwell, Elizabeth
Blackwell, Emily
Bolen, Jean Shinoda
Bonner, Yelena
Bradwell, Myra R.
Breckinridge, Mary
Brown, Barbara B.
Calderone, Mary
Caldicott, Helen
Cavell, Edith Louisa
Chesler, Phyllis
Deutsch, Helene
Glasgow, Maude
Han Suyin
Heide, Wilma Scott
Hinkle, Beatrice
Horney, Karen
Johnson, Adelaide
Joshee, Anandabai
Kenny, Elizabeth
Knopf, Olga
Kübler-Ross, Elisabeth
Mahler, Margaret
Mendenhall, Dorothy Reed
Miller, Jean Baker
Montessori, Maria
Morgan, Elizabeth
Morris, Margaret
Nightingale, Florence
Potor, Aurelia
Preston, Ann
Rolf, Ida P.
Sanger, Margaret
Shainess, Natalie
Shaywitz, Sally E.
Sherfey, Mary Jane
Shnall, Susan
Skau, Annie
Summerskill, Edith
Thompson, Clara
Ulrich, Mabel
Walker, Mary
Wolff, Charlotte
Zassenhaus, Hiltgunt

Naturalists

Adamson, Joy
Galland, China

Laurel, Alicia Bay
Pollard, Josephine
Wordsworth, Dorothy

Psychoanalysts and Psychotherapists
Bonaparte, Marie
Borysenko, Joan
Deutsch, Helene
Fraiberg, Selma
Franz, Marie-Louise von
Freud, Anna
Kristeva, Julia
Mahler, Margaret
Matthews-Simonton, Stephanie
McDougall, Joyce
Miller, Jean Baker
Semenow, Dorothy
Singer, June
Woodman, Marion

Scientists—Biological
Bunting, Mary Ingraham
Fausto-Sterling, Anne
Fleming, Amalia
Hazan, Marcella
Hubbard, Ruth
McClintock, Barbara
Merian, Maria Sibylla
Michiel, Renier Giustina
Phelps, Almira Lincoln
Quin Guanshu
Ramey, Estelle R.
Ray, Dixy Lee
Sabin, Florence
Stopes, Marie Carmichael

Scientists—Earth
Carson, Rachel
Clark, Eugenie
Hazan, Marcella
Lappé, Frances Moore
Mathews, Jessica Tuchman
Sheldon, Karin
Swallow, Ellen Henrietta

Scientists—Physical
Benston, Margaret Lowe
Borysenko, Joan
Cannon, Annie Jump
Curie, Marie
Franklin, Rosaline
Herschel, Caroline Lucretia
Hypatia
Joliot-Curie, Iréne
Keller, Evelyn Fox
Mayer, Maria Goeppert
Mitchell, Maria
Rolf, Ida
Singer, Maxine
Somerville, Mary
Thatcher, Margaret

Scientists—Technological
Brown, Barbra B.
Hopper, Grace Murray

Social Science and Psychology
Adams, Grace
Axline, Virginia Mae
Bateson, Mary Catherine
Benedict, Ruth
Bernard, Jessie Shirley
Bieber, Margarete
Branch, Anna Hempstead
Bricker-Jenkins, Mary
Brothers, Joyce
Chiang Kai-shek, Madame
Clinchy, Blythe M.
Day, Dorothy
Dinnerstein, Dorothy
Douvan, Elizabeth
Dunbar-Nelson, Alice Ruth
Earhart, Amelia
Edwards, Marie
Faraday, Ann
Field, Joanna
Fossey, Dian
Gilligan, Carol
Goldberger, Nancy
Grant, Toni
Hamilton, Eleanor
Harding, M. Esther
Harrison, Jane
Hawkes, Jacquetta
Henley, Nancy
Hooyman, Nancy R.
Horner, Matina
Hurston, Zora Neale
Jackson, Jacquelyn
Kahn, Kathy
Kanter, Rosabeth Moss
Komarovsky, Mirra
Kübler-Ross, Elisabeth
Lee, Ettie
Lerner, Harriet
Le Shan, Eda J.
Liljestrom, Rita
Mead, Margaret
Millar, Susanna
Myers, Isabel Briggs
Oakley, Ann
Pincus, Lily
Rank, Beata
Reinharz, Shulamit
Roe, Anne
Sabin, Florence
Sassen, Georgia
Scott-Maxwell, Florida
Shain, Merle
Smith, Dorothy E.
Streshinsky, Naomi
Tapp, June L.
Ward, Mary Augusta

Wauneka, Annie Dodge
Webb, Beatrice Potter
Weisstein, Naomi
Wenning, Judy
Witt, Shirley Hill
Woolsey, Mary
Wortham, Anne

Nutritionists, Chefs and Cookbook Writers

Child, Julia
Davis, Adelle
DeWit, Antoinette
Farmer, Fannie
Fisher, M. F. K.
Hazan, Marcella
Leslie, Eliza

Engineers

Resnick, Judith

F. Other

Adventurers, Frontier Settlers, Heroes and Pilots

Antin, Mary
Arria, the Elder
Artemisia
Astorga, Nora
Augustin, Maria
Burke, Martha Jane
Cashman, Nellie
Cochran, Jacqueline
David-Neel, Alexandra
Earhart, Amelia
Eberhardt, Isabelle
Erauso, Catalina de
Fitzgerald, Zelda
Hamilton, Emma
Hart, Nancy
Hsiang Chin-yu
Ibarruri, Dolores
Jael
Joan of Arc, St.
Johnson, Osa
Judith
Keller, Helen
Langston, Dicey
Lindbergh, Anne Morrow
Nichols, Ruth Rowland
Oakley, Annie
Oliver, Ruth Law
Pfeiffer, Madame
Pocahontas
Pryor, Sarah Agnes
Resnick, Judith
Rowlandson, Mary
Royall, Anne Newport

Stanhope, Hester Lucy
Wright, Susanna
Zane, Betty

Athletic, Sports and Fitness Figures

Boudrot, Denise M.
Connolly, Olga
Devi, Indra
Dressel, Brigit
Fonda, Jane
Gibson, Althea
Griffith Joyner, Florence
Johnson, Shirbey
Joyner-Kersee, Jackie
King, Billie Jean
Lloyd, Chris Evert
Smith, Robyn
Zaharias, Babe Didrikson

Business Executives, Entrepeneurs and Industrialists

Arden, Elizabeth
Daché, Lily
Danieli, Cecilia
Dunn, Lydia
Fishback, Margaret
Fox, Muriel
Gabor, Zsa Zsa
Hernandez, Aileen Clarke
Holley, Mary Austin
Kellems, Vivien
Knight, Sarah Kemble
Lauder, Estée
Leek, Sybil
Lightner, Candy
Nelson, Paula
Pinckney, Eliza
Renard, Cecile
Rubinstein, Helena
Slocumb, Mary
Swanson, Gloria
Thomas, Lynn

Economists, Financial Specialists and Bankers

Hewlett, Sylvia Ann
Keyserling, Mary
Nelson, Paula
Porter, Sylvia
Siebert, Muriel
Ward, Barbara
Whitman, Marina vonNeumann

Farmers, Horticulturists and Agriculturists

Bricker-Jenkins, Mary
De La Cruz, Jessie Lopez
Hamer, Fannie Lou
Huerta, Dolores
Swerda, Patricia

Inventors
Abbott, Berenice

Military Personnel, Soldiers and Patriots
Draper, Mary
Erauso, Catalina de
Frietschie, Barbara
Bratton, Martha
Hopper, Grace Murray
Joan of Arc, St.
Labé, Louise
Martin, Elizabeth
Richardson, Dorcas
Roland, Jeanne-Marie
Senesh, Hanna
Sforza, Caterina
Schnall, Susan
Slocumb, Mary
Telesilla
Winnemucca, Sarah
Zenobia of Palmyra

Occultists and Prophets
Dixon, Jeane L.
Goodman, Linda
Huldah
Kempe, Margery
Krudener, Juliana
Leek, Sybil
Miriam
Stanhope, Hester Lucy
Truth, Sojourner

Philanthropists and Humanitarians
Colquhoun, Janet
Dix, Dorothea
Fletcher, Mary
Graham, Isabella
Jones, Mother
Kieko, Yamamuro
Lauder, Estée
Low, Juliette
Maria Theresa
Maxwell, Darcy
Mercer, Margaret
More, Hannah
Pickford, Mary
Ricker, Marilla
Roosevelt, Eleanor
Russell, Rosalind
Sewall, Harriet
Smith, Sophia
Wright, Frances
York, Eva Rose
Zell, Katherine

Religious Figures, Leaders and Theologians
Agreda, Maria de
Ambrose, Mother Mary

Askew, Anne
Audeley, Eleanor
Ava, Frau

Bai, Mira
Bailey, Urania Locke
Baudonivia
Bernadette, Saint
Bertegund
Bertken, Sister
Besant, Annie Wood
Bingen, Hildegard von
Blackwell, Antoinette Brown
Blavatsky, Elena
Brenner, Antonia
Bridget of Sweden, St.
Brigid of Kildare, St.
Brown, Olympia
Burrows, Eva

Cabrini, St. Frances Xavier
Caesaria, St.
Carpio de San Feliz, Sister Marcela de
Castillo y Guevara, Francisca Josefa del
Catherine of Genoa, St.
Catherine of Siena, St.
Céu, Violante de
Cibo, Caterina
Clare of Assisi, St.
Clitherow, Margaret
Corey, Martha
Crosby, Sarah
Crowe, Frances
Cruz, Juana Inés de la

Daly, Mary
Deborah
Day, Dorothy
Dyer, Mary

Eddy, Mary Baker
Egburg
Egeria
Elisabeth, St.
Elizabeth of Thuringia, St.
Ellis, Sarah
Enheduanna
Estaugh, Elizabeth Haddon
Eve

Fiedler, Maureen

Gertrude the Great
Gregoria, Francisca
Grumbach, Argula von
Guevara, Marina de
Guyon, Jeanne-Marie de la Motte

Harris, Barbara C.
Hastings, Selina
Héloise
Heyward, Carter
Hutchinson, Anne

Royalty and Courtiers

Jefimija
Jevgenija
Jezebel
Josephine
Juliana, Queen

Kamamalu
Kasa no Iratsume
Kazu-no-miya
Knesebeck, Eleonora von dem
Knollys, Lettice
Kōka, stewardess of the Empress

Lambrun, Margaret

Makhfi
Margaret of Anjou
Margaret of Austria
Margaret of Nassau
Marguerite of Valois
Maria of Hungary and Bohemia
Maria Theresa
Marie-Antoinette
Marie de France
Mariia, Grand Duchess of Russia
Mary I of England
Mary II of England
Mary of France
Mary, Queen of Scots
Mathilde
Medici, Catherine de'
Michal
Michiel, Renier Giustina
Monk, Mary

Nagako, Empress
Nukada

Orléans, Anne-Marie-Louise d'
Orsini, Isabella de Medici
Ōtomo no Sakano-e no Iratsume

Parr, Catherine
Parry, Blanche
Penelope
Pharaoh's Daughter
Pless, Daisy
Plotina, Pompeia
Pocahontas
Poitiers, Diane de
Porcia
Pulcheria, St. Aelia

Radegunda, St.
Raleigh, Elizabeth
Rich, Penelope Devereaux
Rieux, Renée de Chateauneuf
Russell, Elizabeth Hoby

Sabina, Poppæa
Salome
Semiramis
Sheba, Queen of
Shikibu, Murasaki

Shonagon Sei
Sophia Dorothea of Celle
Suo, Lady

Tamar
Theodora
Tyrwhit, Elizabeth

Vernon, Elizabeth
Victoria, Queen
Vidya

Wallada
Walsingham, Frances
Wheathill, Ann
Willoughby, Catherine

Yamatohime

Zenobia of Palmyra

Householders, Laborers, Slaves and Miscellaneous

Anna
Anna Marie of Braunschweig
Bowes, Elizabeth
Bradford, Mistress
Brews, Elizabeth
Burr, Theodosia De Visme
Calvin, Idelette de Bure
Cazalla, Maria
Clarkstone, Bessie
Copley, Susannah Farnum
Elliott, Anna
Greene, Catharine
Hall, Mrs. Daniel
Hannah
Jacobs, Harriet Brent
Jephthah the Gileadite, Daughter of
Larcom, Lucy
Leah
Leapor, Mary
Lot's Daughter (the elder)
Morpurgo, Rahel
Mother of the Seven Brothers
Naomi
Nisa
Paston, Agnes
Paston, Margaret Mautby
Peabody, Elizabeth
Phinehas, Wife of
Rachel
Raven
Robinson, Harriet
Ruth
Samaritan Woman
Samson, first wife of
Sarah
Shubrick, Mrs. Richard
Stubbes, Katherine
Susanna

Ethnicity and Nationality Index

Notes to Ethnicity and Nationality Index

Contributors have been arranged according to the nation of their birth, rather than the nation of their residence and/or death: these citations may be found in the Biography Index.

Women of color have, additionally, been arranged according to their race and/or ethnic background *within the context of their nation of birth*, whenever possible, to serve multicultural studies programs.

Ancient lands and nations no longer extant have been included under the present-day nations of their geographic origins: thus, Zenobia of Palmyra can be found under Syria. For more specific information, refer to the Biographical Index.

Contributors are listed alphabetically within appropriate categories without reference to contributor or page numbers. Contributor numbers may be quickly ascertained in the Biographical Index.

Magnani, Anna
Pharoah's Daughter
Sibyl, The Jewish

England
Abergavenny, Frances
Adams, Louisa Catherine
Adams, Sarah Fowler
Aiken, Lucy
Alden, Priscilla
Allingham, Margery
Amelia
Anger, Jane
Anne of England
Ariadne
Arnim, Mary A.
Ashford, Daisy
Askew, Anne
Asquith, Margot
Astell, Mary
Astor, Nancy
Aubin, Penelope
Austen, Jane
Austin, Sarah Taylor

Bacon, Anne Cooke
Bagnold, Enid
Baldwin, Monica
Barbauld, Anna Letitia
Barber, Margaret Fairless
Barker, Jane
Barnard, Charlotte
Barr, Amelia
Barrington, Judith
Baynard, Anne
Begbie, Janet
Behn, Aphra
Benet, Mother
Benson, Stella
Berners, Juliana
Berry, Dorothy
Besant, Annie Wood
Betsko, Kathleen
Bibesco, Elizabeth Asquith
Billson, Christine
Bingham, Charlotte
Bingham, Madeleine
Bisset, Jacqueline
Blamire, Susanna
Boadicea
Boleyn, Anne
Booth, Evangeline
Boothby, Frances
Bowen, Marjorie
Brackley, Elizabeth
Braddon, Mary Elizabeth
Bradford, Mistress
Bradley, Katharine
Bradstreet, Anne
Bray, Ann Eliza

Brereton, Jane
Brett, Dorothy
Brews, Elizabeth
Brittain, Vera
Brontë, Anne
Brontë, Charlotte
Brontë, Emily
Brooke, Frances
Browning, Elizabeth Barrett
Bryan, Margaret
Burney, Fanny
Burrell, Sophia
Burton, Elaine Frances
Burton, Isabel
Buxton, Bertha
Byron, Mary

Caldwell, Taylor
Cam, Helen
Cameron, Julia Margaret
Campbell, Mrs. Patrick
Carew, Elizabeth
Carter, Elizabeth
Cartland, Barbara
Cavell, Edith Louisa
Cavendish, Georgiana
Cavendish, Jane
Cavendish, Margaret
Chamber, Anna
Chandler, Mary
Chapone, Hester
Charke, Charlotte
Charles, Elizabeth
Childe-Pemberton, Harriet L.
Christie, Agatha
Churchill, Caryl
Churchill, Jennie Jerome
Clarkstone, Bessie
Clifford, Anne
Clinton, Elizabeth
Clitherow, Margaret
Clive, Catherine
Cobbe, Frances P.
Cockburn, Catherine
Coleridge, Mary
Collins, Anne
Compton, Elizabeth
Compton-Burnett, Ivy
Cook, Eliza
Cookson, Catherine
Cooper, Diana
Cooper, Edith
Cooper, Elizabeth
Corey, Martha
Cornford, Frances Darwin
Cowley, Hannah
Craik, Dinah Mulock
Craster, Mrs. Edmund
Crawford, Louisa Macartney
Crosby, Sarah

Yearsley, Anne
Young, Elizabeth

Finland
Manner, Eeva-Liisa

France (including Corsica)
Alais
Alamanda
Albret, Jeanne d'
Ancelot, Virginie
Antoine-Dariaux, Geneviève
Arnould, Sophie
Atlan, Liliane
Azalais de Porcairages

Bardot, Brigitte
Beatritz de Dia
Beauveau, Marie de
Beauvoir, Simone de
Bernadette, St.
Bernhardt, Sarah
Bonaparte, Marie
Bonaparte, Marie Letitia
Bourbon, Catherine de
Brunet, Marguerite

Caesaria, St.
Campan, Jeanne Louise
Carenza
Castelloza
Chanel, Coco
Choiseul, Louise Honorine de
Cixous, Helene
Coignard, Gabrielle de
Colette
Coligny, Henriette de
Corday, Charlotte
Cornuel, A. M. Bigot de
Cottin, Sophie
Curie, Eve
Curie, Marie

Daché, Lily
Dacier, Anne
David-Neel, Alexandra
Deffand, Marie Anne du
Deroine, Jeanne-Françoise
Desbordes-Valmore, Marceline
Deshoulières, Antoinette
Desjardin, Marie-Catherine
des Rieux, Virginie
Detourbey, Jeanne
Dilke, Emilia
Domna H.
Drouette, Juliette

Eleanor of Aquitaine

Farrar, Eliza Ware
Fradonnet, Catherine
Fradonnet, Madeleine

Garsenda de Forcalquier
Geneviève
Genlis, Stephanie Félicité
Geoffrin, Marie Thérèse Rodet
Gerardin, Delphine de
Grignan, Françoise de
Guercheville, Antoinette de Pons
Guilbert, Yvette
Guillema de Rosers
Guillet, Pernettet du
Guyon, Jeanne-Marie de la Motte

Housset, Madame du
Héloise
Henrietta Maria
Houdetot, Sophie de la Briche

Isaure, Clemence
Iselda

Jars, Marie de
Jeanne of Navarre
Joan of Arc
Joliet-Curie, Iréne
Josefowitz, Natasha
Josephine

Kristeva, Julia

Labé, Louise
La Fayette, Marie Madeleine de
Launay, Madame de
Laurencin, Marie
Leduc, Violette
Lenclos, Ninon dc
Lenéru, Marie
Lespinasse, Julie-Jeanne-Eléonore de
L'Héritier, Marie Jeanne
L'Incarnation, Marie de
Lombarda
Lorraine, duchess of

Maintenon, Françoise de
Marcelle, countess de
Marguerite of Navarre
Marguerite of Valois
Marie de France
Mathilde, Princess
Michel, Louise
Moreau, Jeanne

Necker, Suzanne Chardon
Necker de Saussure, Madame
Nin, Anaïs

Orléans, Anne-Marie-Louise d'

Parturier, Françoise
Petigny, Maria-Louisa Rose
Poitiers, Diane de
Pompadour, Jeanne-Antoinette Poisson de

Renard, Cecile
Renée de France
Rieux, Renée de Chateauneuf
Rochefort, Christiane
Roland, Jeanne-Marie
Roland, Pauline

Sagan, Françoise
Sand, George
Scudéry, Madeleine de
Sévigné, Marie de
Staël, Germaine de

Tencin, Claudine Alexandrine de
Tibergeau, marchioness de
Tibors

Varda, Agnes
Ventadorn, Marie de
Vigée-Librun, Elisabeth
Vreeland, Diana
Weil, Simone
Wittig, Monique

Germany (including Bavaria, Franconia, Merovingia, Prussia, Thuringia)
Albrecht of Johannsdorf, mistress of
Anna of Saxony
Anna Maria of Braunschweig
Arendt, Hannah
Arnim, Bettina von
Augusta
Ava, Frau

Bachmann, Ingeborg
Baudonivia
Bieber, Margarete
Bingen, Hildegard von
Bertegund
Blind, Mathilde

Campbell, Jane Montgomery
Caroline, Amelia Elizabeth
Catherine II of Russia

Diehl, Guida
Dietrich, Marlene
Dressel, Brigit
Droste-Hülshoff, Annette Elisabeth von

Elisabeth of Brandenburg
Elisabeth of Braunschweig
Elizabeth of Thuringia

Figes, Eva
Fleisser, Marie-Luise
Follen, Eliza Lee
Frank, Anne

Gertrude the Great
Gottschewski, Lydia
Greiffenberg, Catharina Regina von
Grumbach, Argula von

Hagen, Uta
Herschel, Caroline Lucretia
Horney, Karen
Hroswitha of Gandersheim

Jhabvala, Ruth Prawer

Kemnitz, Mathilda von
Kirsch, Sarah
Klopstock, Margaret
Knesebeck, Eleonora von dem
Kollwitz, Käthe

Lasker-Schuler, Else
Lawrence, Frieda
Lehmann, Lotte
Lenya, Lotte
Levin, Rahel
Lisiewska-Therbusch, Anna Dorothea

Mann, Erika
Mara, Gertrude Elizabeth
Margaret of Nassau
Mayer, Maria Goeppert
Mechtild von Magdeburg
Merian, Maria Sibylla
Miller, Alice

Neuber, Frïederika Karoline

Pascalina, Sister
Pfeiffer, Madame
Pless, Daisy

Radegunda, St.
Riedesel, Frederica de
Riefenstahl, Leni
Robinson, Therese Albertine Louise

Sachs, Nelly
Schirmacher, Kathe
Sylva, Carmen

Trachtenberg, Inge

Varnhagen, Rachel Levin

Wigman, Mary
Wolf, Christa
Wolff, Charlotte

Monk, Mary
Morgan, Sydney Owenson
Murdoch, Iris
Ní Chonaill, Eibhlín Dhubh
O'Brien, Edna
O'Casey, Eileen
O'Neill, Henrietta
O'Neill, Moira
Pilkington, Laetitia
Shane, Elizabeth
Sheridan, Frances
Tighe, Mary
West, Rebecca

Israel (including ancient Hebrews, Kenites, Jerusalem, Manassites, Midianites)
Abel of Beth-maacah, woman of
Anna
Bat-Miriam, Yocheved
Beruriah
Dayan, Yaël
Deborah
Esther
Goldberg, Leah
Hannah
Huldah
Jael
Jephthah the Gileadite, daughter of
Judith
Mary, Virgin
Michal
Miriam
Naomi
Phinehas, wife of
Prostitute of Jerusalem, mother of the dead child
Prostitute of Jerusalem, mother of the living child
Rachel
Susanna
Tamar
Zelophehad, the five daughters of
Zipporah

Italy (including Byzantine Empire, Holy Roman Empire)
Adler, Renata
Agrippina the Younger
Aldrude
Ambrose, Mother Mary
Anguissola, Sofonisba
Arria, the Elder
Borgia, Lucrezia
Caccini, Francesca
Carriera, Rosalba
Castellani, Maria
Castiglione, Ippoloita
Catalani, Angelica
Catherine of Genoa
Catherine of Siena
Cenci, Beatrice
Cereta, Laura

Christine de Pisan
Cibo, Caterina
Clare of Assisi
Colonna, Vittoria de
Compiuta Donzella, la
Cornelia
Danieli, Cecilia
Datini, Margherita
Duse, Eleonora
Este, Anne d'
Este, Beatrice d'
Este, Isabella d'
Fallaci, Oriana
Fedele, Cassandra
Franco, Veronica
Gabrielli, Caterina
Gambara, Veronica
Garrick, Eva Maria
Gentileschi, Artemisia
Ginzburg, Natalia
Gonzaga, Elisabetta
Gonzaga, Giulia
Gonzaga, Lucrezia
Hazan, Marcella
Hortensia
Isabella
Kassia
Loren, Sophia
Mancini, Maria Anna
Maraini, Dacia
Marinella, Lucrezia
Matraini, Chiara Cantarini
Medici, Catherine de'
Medici, Lucrezia de'
Michiel, Renier Giustina
Modotti, Tina
Montessori, Maria
Morata, Olimpia
Morpurgo, Rahel
Morra, Isabella de
Nogarola, Isotta
Orsini, Isabella de Medici
Ortese, Anna Maria
Pierobon, Gigliola
Plotina, Pompeia
Porcia
Pulcheria, St. Aelia
Rilliet-Huber, Catherine
Sabina, Poppæa
Schiaparelli, Elsa
Sforza, Caterina
Sforza, Costanza Varno
Stampa, Gaspara
Strozzi, Alessandra de' Machingi
Sullam, Sarah Copia
Sulpicia (1)
Sulpicia (2)
Terracina, Laura
Theodora
Torelli, Barbara

Guevara, Marina de
Ibarruri, Dolores
Isabella I
Kasmuneh
O'Neill, Carlotta Monterey
Otero, Caroline "La Belle"
Pinar, Florencia del
Teresa of Avila, St.

Sweden
Bergman, Ingrid
Bok, Sissela Ann
Bremer, Frederika
Bridget of Sweden, St.
Christina of Sweden
Garbo, Greta
Hedström, Barbro
Key, Ellen
Lagerlöf, Selma
Lenngren, Anna Maria
Liljestrom, Rita
Lind, Jenny
Myrdal, Alva Reimer

Switzerland
Burr, Theodosia
Franz, Marie-Louise von
Giroud, Françoise
Jung, Emma
Kübler-Ross, Elisabeth
Montolieu, Jeanne Isabelle
Spyri, Johanna

Syria (including ancient Palmyrene)
Rabi'a bint Isma'il of Syria
Zenobia of Palmyra

Tunisia (including ancient Carthage)
Perpetua, Vivia

Turkey (including ancient Harran, Hittites)
Hatun, Mihri
Leah
Rachel

United States of America
White Americans
Abbott, Berenice
Abbott, Sidney
Abbott, Wenonah Stevens
Abzug, Bella
Ace, Jane
Adams, Abigail
Adams, Grace
Adams, Maude
Addams, Jane
Adler, Freda
Adler, Margot
Akers, Elizabeth Chase
Akins, Zoë

Alcott, Louisa May
Alden, Ada
Aldis, Mary Reynolds
Alexander, Mrs.
Alexander, Shana
Allen, Dede
Allen, Mary Wood
Allerton, Ellen Palmer
Allred, Gloria
Alston, Theodosia Burr
Alta
Anastasi, Anna
Anderson, Laurie
Annan, Annie Rankin
Anthony, Katharine
Anthony, Susan B.
Antrim, Minna
Arbus, Diane
Arnold, Margaret Shippen
Arnow, Harriette
Arzner, Dorothy
Astor, Brooke
Astor, Madeleine
Atherton, Ellen
Atkinson, Ti-Grace
Auel, Jean M.
Austin, Mary Hunter
Axline, Virginia Mae

Babitz, Eve
Bacall, Lauren
Bache, Sarah
Bachman, Moira
Bacon, Josephine
Baez, Joan
Baldwin, Faith
Ball, Lucille
Ballard, Bettina
Bankhead, Tallulah
Bannerman, Helen
Banning, Margaret Culkin
Barker, Elsa
Barker, Myrtie Lillian
Barnes, Djuna
Barnes, Margaret Ayer
Barolini, Helen
Barrett, Rona
Barrymore, Ethel
Barton, Clara
Bates, Katherine Lee
Bateson, Mary Catherine
Beal, Frances
Beals, Jessie Tarbox
Beard, Mary Ritter
Beard, Miriam
Beecher, Catharine Esther
Belenky, Mary Field
Bell, Christine
Bell, Helen Olcott
Bender, Marilyn

Le Sueur, Meridel
Lewis, Edith
Lewitzky, Bella
Lightner, Candy
Lincoln, Mary Todd
Lindbergh, Anne
Livermore, Mary
Livingstone, Belle
Lloyd, Chris Evert
Lockwood, Belva
Longworth, Alice Roosevelt
Loos, Anita
Loud, Pat
Love, Barbara J.
Lowell, Amy
Luce, Clare Booth
Luce, Gay Gaer
Lurie, Alison
Luscomb, Florence
Lydon, Susan
Lynn, Loretta
Lyon, Mary
Lyon, Phyllis

MacDonald, Betty
MacLaine, Shirley
Madison, Dolley
Malpede, Karen
Manley, Joan
Mannes, Marya
Marbury, Elisabeth
Marion, Frances
Markham, Lucia Clark
Marshall, Catherine
Martin, Del
Martin, Elizabeth
Martin, Martha
Mason, Caroline
Mason-Manheim, Madeline
Mathews, Jessica Tuchman
Matthews-Simonton, Stephanie
Maxwell, Elsa
May, Julia Harris
McAuliffe, Christa
McBride, Mary Margaret
McCall, Dorothy
McCarthy, Abigail
McCarthy, Mary
McCarthy, Sarah J.
McCaslin, Mary
McClintock, Barbara
McCormick, Anne O'Hare
McCormick, Virginia Taylor
McCullers, Carson
McGinley, Phyllis
McGovern, Ann
McGrory, Mary
McIntosh, Maria
McKenney, Ruth
McRae, Carmen

Mead, Margaret
Melanie
Mendenhall, Dorothy Reed
Mercer, Margaret
Merman, Ethel
Meyer, Agnes
Michelman, Kate
Midler, Bette
Mikulski, Barbara Ann
Miles, Josephine
Millay, Edna St. Vincent
Miller, Alice Duer
Miller, Emily
Miller, Helen Hill
Miller, Jean Baker
Miller, Lee
Miller, Margaret
Millet, Kate
Miner, Dorothy Eugenia
Mirrielees, Edith Ronald
Mitchell, Joni
Mitchell, Margaret
Mitchell, Maria
Mitchell, Martha
Moffat, Mary Jane
Moïse, Penina
Monroe, Anne Shannon
Monroe, Harriet
Monroe, Marilyn
Montgomery, Roselle Mercier
Moody, Anne
Moore, Grace
Moore, Honor
Moore, Julia A.
Moore, Marianne
Moore, Virginia
Moorhead, Sarah Parsons
Morgan, Angela
Morgan, Barbara
Morgan, Elizabeth
Morgan, Julia
Morgan, Marabel
Morgan, Robin
Morris, Margaret
Morris, Mary
Morrow, Elizabeth Reeve
Morton, Sarah Wentworth
Moses, Grandma
Mott, Lucretia
Moulton, Louise
Mumford, Ethel Watts
Murray, Judith Sargent
Musser, Tharon
Myers, Isabel Briggs
Myerson, Bess

Nation, Carry
Neal, Patricia
Near, Holly
Neel, Alice